D0898089

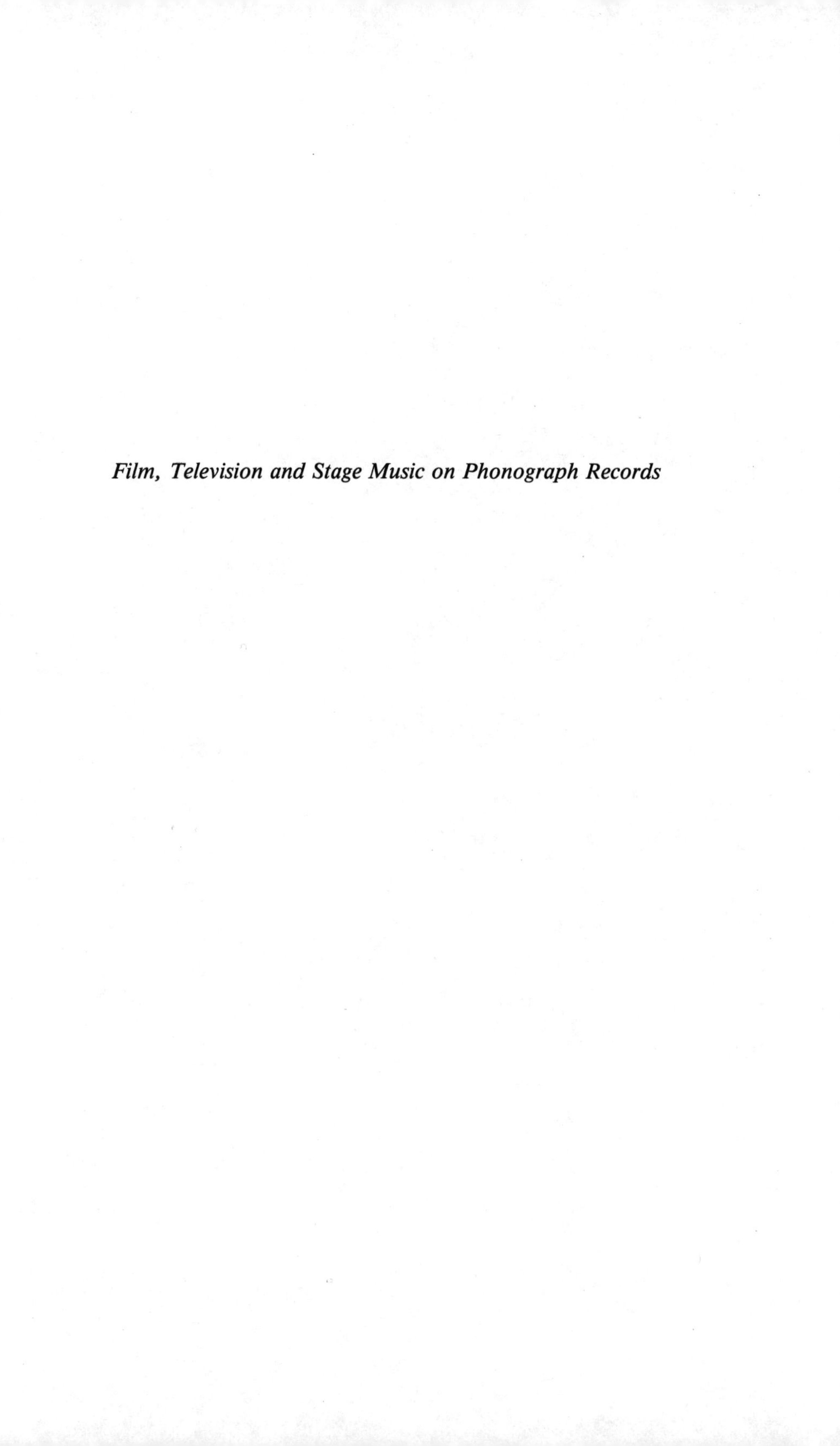

Film, Television and Stage Music on Phonograph Records

Film, Television and Stage Music on Phonograph Records

A Discography

by
Steve Harris

McFarland & Company, Inc., Publishers
Jefferson, North Carolina, and London

Library of Congress Cataloguing-in-Publication Data

Harris, Steve.
Film, television, and stage music on phonograph records.

Bibliography: p. 417.
Includes index.
1. Motion picture music—Discography. 2. Television music—Discography. 3. Musical revues, comedies, etc.—Discography. I. Title.
ML156.4.M6H3 1988 016.7899'12283 87-42509

ISBN 0-89950-251-2 (50# acid-free natural paper) ∞

Printed in the United States of America.

McFarland & Company, Inc., Publishers
Box 611, Jefferson, North Carolina 28640

for
JOAN VAN ATTA HARRIS
in loving memory

CONTENTS

PREFACE

Ten years ago, I came up with the idea of organizing the ultimate research book that would index and catalog all significant phonograph recordings of film, television and stage music from the United States and Great Britain. Records from important foreign productions would also be included. What seemed like a brilliant idea in 1978 gradually turned into a nightmare.

The project was fairly straightforward at first, but as new and previously unexplored areas of information began pouring in, the book ballooned to frightening proportions. I kept expanding the format by adding new sections and new categories. And each time I thought I was finished, something new and tantalizing would pop up.

Even now, after having spent countless hours perusing the collections of public libraries, haunting various rare record stores, plundering dozens of private record collections, and retyping the pages again and again, I fear the pages may fall short of my original lofty goals.

Still, discounting the inevitable flaws, omissions and mistakes, I believe you are holding the most comprehensive, accurate and thoroughly researched book ever published on the subject of film, television and stage music on phonograph records.

I can never regain the time and energy that I've poured into these pages, but if this book is of some value, then perhaps the last decade has not been wasted.

I gratefully acknowledge the aid and assistance of Mainerd V. Baker, Brad Bennett, Brian Burney, Bruce Kimmel, John Peterson, and the late Frank Squires. Their record collections provided valuable research material for this book.

Steve Harris

INTRODUCTION

The earliest stage music recordings date all the way back to the invention of the record player. Among the first sound recordings made on Edison's cylinder discs in the late 1800s were popular songs from stage musicals. When cylinder discs were eventually replaced by 10″ and 12″ 78-rpm single play phonograph records in the early 1900s, the practice of recording popular stage tunes was common. Indeed, the influence of these show songs on American popular music is inestimable.

In the mid-1930s, the first album appeared. These early albums featured a fold-open jacket with cover artwork and pockets for three or four individual 78-rpm discs. By this time, the 10″ disc had completely replaced the 12″ disc. In the early 1940s, complete Broadway shows were being released in this 78-rpm album format.

Serious film music recordings had a more tentative beginning. Pop songs from films were frequently recorded in the 1930s, but dramatic orchestral scores were largely ignored until "The Jungle Book" and a bootleg of "King Kong" were issued in the early 1940s. "The Song of Bernadette," "Spellbound," "The Paradine Case," and "Duel in the Sun" were also released during this period, but there was certainly no stampede to record serious film scores in the 1940s.

An important new record format was introduced in the late 1940s: the 7″ 45-rpm single play record. While the boxed 7″ 45-rpm extended play mini-album, the fold-open 7″ 45-rpm extended play album, the 10″ 33⅓-rpm single play disc, and the 7″ 33⅓-rpm extended play mini-album have all disappeared over the years, the seemingly indestructible 7″ 45-rpm single play record has endured. From the 1950s to the 1980s, the 7″ single has been a welcome haven for individual theme recordings from film, television and stage productions that did not warrant a 12″ long play album.

But even more important was the introduction of the equally enduring 12″ 33⅓-rpm long play record in the early 1950s. Finally, a full score could be presented on one disc, and the sound fidelity was vastly superior to the crudely pressed 78s and 45s. By the late 1950s, most serious film scores and stage shows were being recorded on 12″ long play albums.

As the television medium began to grow in the 1950s, recordings from mini-screen shows began to appear. After early offerings like "Danger" and "Victory at Sea," television music burst onto the pop music charts with the phenomenal success of "Peter Gunn" in 1958.

As far as the physical record formats are concerned, not much has changed since the early 1960s. Some new ideas have flourished (stereo and digital sound; cassette tapes), some new ideas have faded away (quadraphonic sound; reel-to-reel and 8-track tapes), and the future of some new ideas is still unresolved (12″ single play records; compact discs). Unfortunately, while the quality of the sound has improved, the quality of the music has declined. Most serious film, television and stage music buffs would rather listen to a good score in flat mono sound than a bad score in resplendent digital sound. Technology will never supplant artistry, so the future of film, television and stage music recordings will always be in the hands of the men and women who write the notes onto the blank paper. It is to the composers of the music that I gratefully offer homage.

It is the purpose of this book to catalog all important phonograph recordings of film, television and stage music from United States and Great Britain productions. Records from major foreign productions will also be included, but *only* if they were presented or recorded in the United States or Great Britain.

This book is divided into three major sections: film music recordings, television music recordings, and stage music recordings. Each of these categories contains a main records listing and a subsection entitled "Related Records." The composer index contains material culled from all three major sections.

The *Film Music* Section concentrates on original and adapted music composed specifically for theatrical films. A record will also qualify for inclusion if the music performance is by a soundtrack artist. This index does not include cover version recordings of traditional music used in films, nor does it include pure dialog recordings with no music. All records in this listing are verified. The "Related Records"  subsection concentrates on the oddball fringe records that are often mistaken for legitimate film music recordings. Pure dialog records, themes inspired by films, cover versions of traditional music, themes actually written for a different film or a different medium, unverified films, unfinished films, unverified records, unreleased records, and erroneous listings from other research books will be found in this subsection. Composer credits will not be supplied.

The *Television Music* section concentrates on original and adapted music composed specifically for television productions. A record will also qualify for inclusion if the music performance is by a soundtrack artist. This index does not include cover version recordings of traditional music used in television productions, nor does it include pure dialog recordings with no music. All records in this index are verified. The "Related Records" subsection concentrates on the oddball fringe records that are often mistaken for legitimate television music recordings. Pure dialog records, cover versions of traditional music, themes actually written for a different medium, unverified television shows, unverified records, and erroneous listings from other research books will be found in this listing. Composer credits will not be supplied.

The *Stage Music* section concentrates on original and adapted music composed specifically for stage musicals. A record will also qualify for inclusion if the music performance is by an original cast artist. This index does not include cover version recordings of traditional music used in stage musicals, nor does it include pure dialog or incidental music from dramatic stage plays. All records in this index are verified. The "Related Records" subsection concentrates on the fringe records that don't actually qualify as legitimate stage musical records. Cover version song medleys, record musicals, special theatrical events, and incidental music from dramatic stage plays will be found in this listing. Composer credits *will* be supplied for all incidental music recordings. This listing does not include pure dialog records from stage plays.

The *Composer Index* contains an alphabetical listing of the music composers in this book. Conductors and lyricists are not listed in this book. If a composer's full name is not known, then he or she will not be included.

While it is important to understand what material is contained in this book, it is equally important to understand what is *not*. The following items are not included (this list applies to the entire book): Individual cover versions of individual pop songs from film, stage, or television musicals; recordings from high school or college musicals; one-of-a-kind recordings such as acetate disc records, record company test pressings, and film studio master disc records; and recordings from radio and video tape productions. This book lists only conventional phonograph records. Excluded are cassette, reel-to-reel, and 8-track tapes; Edison cylinder discs; and compact discs.

Certain redundancies have been avoided. Foreign pressings are not listed if an identical United States pressing exists. A theme or excerpts recording will not be listed if a score recording containing the same material exists. An attempt has been made to limit the number of listings to three for each title.

This book concludes with December 1986 releases. The latest entry is the film soundtrack from "Three Amigos."

There are two basic types of entries for this book. Each conforms to a pattern. All are serially numbered in boldface (here represented by **000**).

Sample entry for the main listings:

000 Production Title [additional production information] (date) music quantity [additional record information] (composer credit) country of pressing: record format = record label and number [performing artists]

Sample entry for "Related Records" listings:

000 Production Title or Record Title (date) [related records code] music quantity/country of pressing: record format = record label and number [performing artists]

Some of this material is optional, and will only be supplied when it could prove to be valuable. As a general rule, composer credits will be supplied for main record listings, but not for "Related Records" listings. But there are exceptions to nearly every rule in this book. A slash mark (/) is often used for missing information, such as unknown dates or unknown composer credits.

Terminology and Codes

adapted music Traditional or previously composed music that has been rescored or recomposed. Adaptation differs substantially from arrangement and orchestration. The orchestrator is only fleshing out another composer's ideas, but the adaptor is actually recomposing the music.

additional production information Delineating alternate production titles, short subjects, cartoons, industrial films, children's shows, and industrial shows.

additional record information Delineating alternate record titles, individual track titles, different music for different releases or different productions, related record information.

alternate title Film, television and stage productions are often retitled. An alternate title may be a foreign, translation, special television, or simply changed title.

bootleg pressing Illegal and unauthorized record, usually pressed in small quantities and distributed on a limited basis.

cartoon An animated short subject usually screened before or between feature-length films. Most cartoons have a running time of 8:00.

children's show A stage musical or show written for children and performed in a very small theatre on a limited run.

classical music Used loosely in this book to include largely instrumental and vocal music of the seventeenth through nineteenth centuries.

collection album A record containing music from different productions featuring different performing artists.

composer credit The person or persons who composed the *music* on the listed record. Lyricists are not credited in this book. (The abbreviation "aka" means "also known as.")

composer credit codes

s: scores or score	as: adapted scores or score
e: excerpts or highlights	ae: adapted excerpts or highlights
t: themes or theme	at: adapted themes or theme
u: underscore	au: adapted underscore

country of pressing The country where the record was pressed and released.

country of pressing codes

AF:	Africa & South Africa	IS:	Israel
AU:	Australia	IT:	Italy
CA:	Canada	JA:	Japan
FR:	France	NZ:	New Zealand
GB:	Great Britain	RU:	Russia
GE:	Germany	SA:	South America
GR:	Greece	SW:	Switzerland
HO:	Holland & The Netherlands	US:	United States

cover version A music performance by a non-soundtrack artist or a non-original cast artist.

demo cast A special group of unidentified singers assembled to record a demonstration album of songs from a stage musical. Since privately pressed demos rarely have record numbers, an obligatory 1001 will be used. Demo albums will be listed in this book *only* if a commercial recording of the show does not exist.

dialog A spoken recording, or a recording with music and spoken words mixed.

drama A substantially verbal production. A drama may contain a few isolated songs or some orchestral background music.

erroneous listing An incorrect listing pulled from one of the works in this book's bibliography (see page 417) and corrected by the editor.

etcetera or etc. The work of additional composers is involved, but they will not be credited. This term could include both original and traditional music.

excerpts Pure music covering 3 to 5 individual tracks or a suite of themes on a long play album. The running time is 6:00 to 16:00. Excerpts are usually found on collection albums.

extended play A loose term covering 7″ and 12″ records containing about 6:00 to 10:00 playing time per side. The 12″ version is often called a mini–LP.

film music When used as a composer credit, this term denotes music originally written for a film, but reused in another medium.

highlights Pure music covering 3 to 5 individual tracks or a suite of themes on extended play or long play albums. The running time is 6:00 to 22:00. Jackets for highlights records always feature artwork from the production, and usually turn up as complete 7″ EP's, complete 10″ LP's or one complete side of a 12″ LP.

incidental music Background music from a stage drama (orchestral or vocal).

industrial short A short film produced by an industrial company as a promotional tool. Industrial shorts are quite professional, but they are rarely screened in commercial movie theatres. The running time is usually 15:00 to 30:00.

industrial show A stage musical or show created to promote an industrial company or product. These are mostly in-house productions.

inspired music A song or theme that was inspired by a film, but not actually used in the film. These inspired songs were used by the studios as promotional tools.

long play A loose term covering 10″ and 12″ records containing approximately 12:00 to 20:00 playing time per side.

medley Bits and pieces of several different songs from a stage musical or show. A medley is usually found on a 78-rpm single or an LP collection album, and usually performed by a studio cast. Composer credits will not be supplied for medleys.

multiple set A boxed or fold-open record jacket holding more than one disc.

music quantity The amount of pure music from the indexed production contained on the listed record. Music quantity terms include scores, score, highlights, excerpts, themes and theme. Letter codes are used to separate different music selections with identical music quantity terms.

musical A comedy or drama with a cohesive story line and at least ten integrated songs.

one-man show A solo artist steps out and does his or her thing. A one-man show does not really qualify as a stage musical.

original cast A music performance by one or more members of the original cast of a specific stage production.

original music Music that has been composed specifically for a film, television or stage production. Composer credits will be supplied if possible.

performing artist The person or persons performing the music on the listed record. This information is supplied for most excerpts and individual theme recordings, but rarely for film and television score recordings.

performing artist codes

AOC:	Australia original cast
LAOC:	Los Angeles original cast
LOC:	London original cast
NYOC:	New York original cast
OC:	original cast
ST:	soundtrack
@:	a collection album featuring music from several different productions performed by several different artists.

pop music Standard music that is used or played in a film, television or stage production. Pop songs, rock songs and folk tunes fall into this category. See also **traditional music.**

private pressing A non-commercial, limited edition pressing released on a private basis by the composer or an industrial company. Unlike bootleg pressings, private pressings are never sold in stores for a profit.

production date The premiere performance of the film, television show or stage production.

production title The official title for a film, television show or stage production. Foreign films will always be listed under the United States release title.

pure music A recorded piece consisting of music, no dialog.

record format The physical size, playing speed and running time of the record.

record format codes

LP:	12″ long play record; 33-rpm or 45-rpm; 30:00 to 40:00
LP-10:	10″ long play record; 33-rpm; 18:00 to 24:00
EP:	7″ extended play record; 45-rpm or 33-rpm; 10:00 to 14:00
EP-12:	12″ extended play or mini–LP record; 33-rpm or 45-rpm; 10:00 to 18:00
SP:	7″ single play record; 45-rpm or 33-rpm; 4:00 to 5:00
SP-12:	12″ single play record; 45-rpm or 33-rpm; 4:00 to 5:00
78:	10″ single play record; 78-rpm; 4:00 to 5:00
BP:	Bootleg Pressing
MS:	Multiple Set
PP:	Private Pressing

record label and number The manufacturer's name and catalog number for the record. Private and bootleg pressings often don't have this information. For theme recordings, the letter prefix that precedes the catalog number has been dropped.

record label abbreviations and codes

CSP:	Columbia Special Products	OC:	Original Cast
		UA:	United Artists
Deutsche:	Deutsche Grammophon	Varese:	Varese Sarabande
DRG:	DRG &Stet	WB:	Warner Bros.
Ducretet:	Ducretet Thomson	WRC:	World Record Club & World Records
HMV:	His Master's Voice		
MFP:	Music for Pleasure	*:	real stereo
Monmouth:	Monmouth Evergreen	e:	fake stereo

record musical A short musical written specifically for phonograph records. Composer credits will not be supplied for record musicals.

related records code This special code is used in each "Related Records" subsection to delineate the exact problem of each entry.

revival A later original cast recreation of a popular stage success.

revue A musical comedy pastiche with no specific storyline. Some are a balance of songs and comedy skits; others are all songs. The code [c] is used for continuous revues that ran for many years with the same title but rotating songs and stars.

score pure music covering two complete sides of a 12″ long play record. The playing time is usually 30:00 to 40:00.

scores Pure music covering four complete sides of two 12″ long play records. The playing time is usually 60:00 to 70:00.

sequence Incidental background music mixed with a single dialog track. The term sequence is used for collection records containing numerous dialog passages from many different productions.

short A live-action theatrical short subject, usually running 15:00 to 30:00.

show A stage comedy or drama with a cohesive storyline and at least ten integrated songs.

silent A feature film with no dialog, usually produced before 1928. Some were scored for their initial release, while many others were scored in later years. The codes:

Silent I: music written for the initial release of a silent film
Silent II: music written for a later release of a silent film

single play A loose term covering 7″, 10″ and 12″ records containing approximately 2:00 to 4:00 playing time per side.

soundtrack A music performance by a film or television soundtrack artist, or a recording taken directly from the soundtrack.

special event Unusual or spectacular stage production which overlaps into the realm of theatre. This umbrella category includes one-man dramatic recitals, one-man shows, one-night musical tributes and theatrical comedy productions.

stage music When used as a composer credit, this term denotes music originally written for the stage, but reused in another medium.

studio cast A special group of celebrity singers assembled to record a complete album of show tunes. A studio cast does not appear on stage. Studio cast albums will be listed in this book *only* if an original cast album of the show does not exist.

television music When used as a composer credit, this term denotes music originally written for television, but reused in another medium.

theme Pure music covering one side of a single play record, or one individual track on a long play record. The playing time is usually 2:00 to 3:00.

themes Pure music covering two sides of a single play record, or two individual tracks on a long play record. The playing time is usually 4:00 to 5:00.

traditional music Previously composed music, such as pop standards, rock standards, jazz standards, folk music and classical music. Composer credits will not be supplied for traditional music.

uncredited The composer credit or the performing artist credit is not listed on the phonograph record.

underscore Incidental background music mixed with multiple dialog passages. The term is used for complete LP recordings devoted to a single production.

unfinished film A film production that was started, but never completed.

unreleased soundtrack album An album that was announced by the record company, but never pressed or released.

unverified production The editor cannot confirm that this production exists.

unverified record The editor cannot confirm that this record exists.

various More than one composer wrote the music. Only significant composers are credited individually. This term includes both original and traditional music.

I. FILM MUSIC

A

1 Aakhri Khat / Theme/US:LP = Capitol 10500 [@Lata Mangeshkar:ST]

2 Aaron Loves Angela (1975) Score (Jose Feliciano) US:LP = Private Stock PS-2010* [Jose Feliciano:ST]

3 Aaron Slick from Punkin Crick (1951) Highlights (Jay Livingston & Ray Evans) US:LP-10 = RCA LPM-3006 + US:LP-BP = Motion Picture Tracks MPT-4

4 Aarti / Theme/US:LP = Capitol 10500 [@Mohd-Rafi:ST]

5 Abby (1974) Highlights (Robert O. Ragland) US:EP-PP = American International PRO-12154

6 Abdication, The (1974) Score (Nino Rota) IT:LP = Intermezzo IM-008*

7 Abdullah the Great *see* Abdullah's Harem

8 Abdullah's Harem [Abdullah the Great] [The Royal Bed] (1956) Theme (Georges Auric) US:SP = Columbia 4-40428 [Percy Faith]; Theme (Georges Auric) US:SP = Mercury 70796 [Eddie Barclay]

9 Abominable Dr. Phibes, The [Dr. Phibes] (1971) Excerpts (Basil Kirchin) US:LP = American International STA-1040* [Basil Kirchin:ST]

10 About Face (1952) Themes/US: SP = Capitol 2047 [Gordon MacRae:ST]

11 About Mrs. Leslie (1954) Theme-A (Victor Young) US:LP = Jubilee 1034* + US:LP = Citadel 6024* [Harry Sukman]; Theme-A (Victor Young) US: LP = Mercury 25192 [Richard Hayman]; Theme-B (pop music) US:LP-BP = JJA 19762 [@ Shirley Booth:ST]

12 Above Suspicion (1943) Theme/ US:LP-BP = Curtain Calls 100/23 [Joan Crawford:ST]

13 Absent-Minded Professor, The (1961) Themes + Narration (Richard & Robert Sherman) US:LP = Disneyland 1911; Themes (Richard & Robert Sherman) US:SP = Buena Vista 373 [Fred MacMurray:ST]

14 Absolute Beginners (1986) Scores (e:Gil Evans/e:various) GB:LP-MS = Virgin VD-2514*; Score (t:Gil Evans/s:various) US:LP = EMI SV-17182*

15 Accade al Penitenziario (1955) Highlights (Nino Rota) US:LP = Cerberus CST-0205

16 Accident (1967) Theme (Johnny Dankworth) US:SP = Fontana 1585 [Johnny Dankworth:ST]

17 Accused, The (1948) Theme (Victor Young) US:LP = Decca 8466 + US: LP-10 = Decca 5265 [Victor Young:ST]

18 Accused of Murder (1956) Theme (Buddy Bregman) US:SP = Era 1010 [Gogi Grant]

19 Accuser, The [L'Imprecateur] (1977) Score (Richard Rodney Bennett) FR:LP = Barclay 900.543*

20 Ace High [Revenge in El Paso] [Il Quattro dell'Ave Maria] (1969) Score (Carlo Rustichelli) IT:LP = Cinevox 33/9

21 Aces Go Places (1983) Score (Sam Hui) JA:LP = Casablanca 25-S-60*

22 Across 110'th Street (1973) Score (e:J.J. Johnson/e:Bobby Womack) US: LP = UA UAS-5225*

23 Across the Bridge (1957) Theme (James Bernard) GB:SP = Oriole 1405 [Charles McDevitt]

24 Across the Great Divide (1978) Score (Gene Kauer & Douglas Lackey) US:LP = Bella Linda BLS-1001*

25 Act of the Heart (1970) Highlights (Harry Freedman) CA:LP = Decca DL-75244*

26 Action Impossible (1983) Score (Rick Conrad & Rob Miller) JA:LP = Polydor 28-MM-0257*

27 Actualities [Short] Theme (Darius Milhaud) FR:LP = Vega 30-A-98 [@ST]; Excerpts (Darius Milhaud) RU: LP = Melodiya C10.20459.009* [Gennedy Rozhdestvensky]

28 Ada (1961) Theme (Bronislau Kaper) US:SP = MGM 13036 [Leroy Holmes]; Theme (Bronislau Kaper) US:LP = MGM 4064* [Leroy Holmes]

29 Adam and Evelyn (1949) Theme (Mischa Spoliansky) US:LP-BP = Citadel CTOFI-1 [@ST]

30 Adam's Rib (1949) Theme (Cole Porter) US:SP = RCA 54-0019 [Harry Prime]; Theme (Cole Porter) US:LP-BP = JJA 19767 [@David Wayne:ST]; Theme (Cole Porter) US:LP = RCA 1401 [Skitch Henderson]

31 Addio Giovienzza [Farewell to Youth] (1949) Theme (Blanc) US:LP = Epic 3593 [Gian Stellari]

32 Adios Amigo (1976) Excerpts (Luchi DeJesus) US:LP = London PS-666* [Infernal Blues Machine:ST]

33 Adios, Gringo (1965) Score (Benedetto Ghiglia) IT:LP = CAM CMS.33-16

34 Adios, Sabata [Indio Black] [The Bounty Killers] (1971) Themes (Bruno Nicolai) JA:SP = UA 1451* [ST]; Theme (Bruno Nicolai) GB:LP = UA 29482* [@ST]

35 Adolescente, L' (1978) Score (Philippe Sarde) FR:LP = Pathe CO66. 14731*

36 Adrift (1971) Score (Zdenek Liska) US:LP = MPO 1001*

37 Advance to the Rear [Company of Cowards] (1964) Score (Randy Sparks) US:LP = Columbia CL-2159/ CS-8959* [New Christy Minstrels:ST]

38 Adventurer, The (1921) Theme [Silent II] (Dennis Wilson) GB:LP = EMI 1075* [Band of the H.M. Royal Marines]

39 Adventurers, The (1950) *see* Great Adventure, The

40 Adventurers, The (1970) Score (s:Antonio Carlos Jobim/t:Emuir Deodato) US:LP = Paramount PAS-6001*

41 Adventures of a Young Man *see* Hemingway's Adventures of a Young Man

42 Adventures of Barry McKenzie, The (1972) Score (Peter Best) GB:LP = Bell S-228*

43 Adventures of Bullwhip Griffin, The (1967) Highlights + Dialog (t: George Bruns/etc.) US:LP = Disneyland DQ-1291

44 Adventures of Don Juan, The [The New Adventures of Don Juan] (1948) Score (Max Steiner) US:LP-BP = Tony Thomas TTMS-11; Excerpts (Max Steiner) US:LP = RCA ARL1-0912* [Charles Gerhardt]

45 Adventures of Hajji Baba, The (1954) Theme (Dimitri Tiomkin) US: SP = Capitol 2949 [Nat King Cole:ST]; Theme (Dimitri Tiomkin) US:LP = Capitol 2340 + US:LP = Capitol 11804 [Nat King Cole:ST]; Theme (Dimitri Tiomkin) US:LP = Coral 57006 [Dimitri Tiomkin:ST]

46 Adventures of Ichabod and Mr. Toad, The [The Legend of Sleepy Hollow] (1949) Themes + Narration (Gene DePaul) US:LP = Disneyland 3801 + US:LP = Disneyland 1920; Themes + Narration (Gene DePaul) US: LP-10 = Decca DL-6001 [Bing Crosby: ST]

47 Adventures of Pinocchio, The [Le Avventure di Pinocchio] (1974) Score (Fiorenzo Carpi) IT:LP = CAM SAG-9038*

48 Adventures of Robin Hood, The (1938) Score (Erich Wolfgang Korngold) US:LP = Varese 704.180* [Varujan Kojin]; Excerpts-A (Erich Wolfgang Korngold) US:LP-MS = WB 3X2736 [@ST]; Excerpts-B (Erich Wolfgang Korngold) US:LP = RCA LSC-3330* [Charles Gerhardt]; Excerpts-C (Erich Wolfgang Korngold) US:LP = RCA ARL1-0912* [Charles Gerhardt]

49 Adventures of Sherlock Holmes, The (1939) Underscore + Dialog (Cyril Mockridge) US:LP-MS = Murray Hill 55358

50 Adventures of the American Rabbit, The (1986) Score (Mark Volman

& Howard Kaylan) US:LP = Rhino RNEP-70614*

51 Adventures of the Wilderness Family, The (1976) Score (Gene Kauer & Douglas Lackey) JA:LP = Seven Seas FML-70*

52 Adventures of the Wilderness Family, Part II *see* Further Adventures of the Wilderness Family

53 Advise and Consent (1962) Score (Jerry Fielding) US:LP = RCA LOC-1068/LSO-1068*

54 Affair in Monte Carlo [24 Hours of a Woman's Life] (1952) Theme (Philip Green) GB:78 = HMV 10353 [Norrie Paramor]

55 Affair in Trinidad (1952) Themes (Lester Lee) US:LP-BP = Curtain Calls 100/23 [@Jo Ann Greer:ST]; Theme (Lester Lee) US:78 = Coral 60827 [Judy Lynn]

56 Affair to Remember, An (1957) Score (e:Hugo Friedhofer/e:Harry Warren) US:LP = Columbia CL-1013

57 Affair with a Stranger (1953) Theme (Sam Coslow) US:SP = Capitol 2543 [Vicki Young]

58 Affairs of Bel Ami, The *see* Private Affairs of Bel Ami, The

59 Affairs of Dobie Gillis, The (1953) Theme (Rinker & Huddleston) US:SP = MGM 11555 [Barbara Ruick:ST]

60 Africa Addio (1966) Score (Riz Ortolani) US:LP = UA UAL-4141/UAS-5141*

61 Africa—Texas Style (1967) Theme (Malcolm Arnold) US:SP = Liberty 55964 [Bobby Vee]

62 African Elephant, The (1971) Theme (Laurence Rosenthal) US:LP = Kapp 3665* [Roger Williams]

63 African Summer *see* Visit to a Chief's Son

64 After Midnight *see* Captain Carey, U.S.A.

65 After the Fox (1966) Score (Burt Bacharach) US:LP = UA UAL-4148/UAS-5148* + US:LP = UA LA-286*

66 Against a Crooked Sky (1975) Score (Lex DeAzevedo) US:LP = Embryo EM-1005*

67 Against All Flags (1952) Highlights (Hans J. Salter) US:LP-MS-BP = Tony Thomas TTHS-1/2

68 Against All Odds (1984) Score (e:Larry Carlton/e:Michel Colombier) US:LP = Atlantic 80152-1*

69 Agatha (1979) Score (Johnny Mandel) US:LP = Casablanca NBLP-7142*

70 Agnes of God (1985) Score (Georges Delerue) US:LP = Varese STV-81257*

71 Agony and the Ecstasy, The (1965) Score (Alex North) US:LP = Capitol MAS-2427/SMAS-2427*

72 Aguirre, The Wrath of God (1973) Score (Popol Vuh) GE:LP = KK 202.1275*

73 Air Force Dogfight (1982) Score (Keith Morrison) JA:LP = East World 90177*

74 Airplane! (1980) Underscore + Dialog (Elmer Bernstein) US:LP = Regency RY-9601*

75 Airport (1970) Score (Alfred Newman) US:LP = Decca DL-79173*

76 Airport 1975 (1975) Score (John Cacavas) US:LP = MCA 2082*

77 Airport '77 (1977) Theme (John Cacavas) US:SP = MCA 40725* [Roger Williams & John Cacavas:ST]; Theme (John Cacavas) US:LP = MCA 2279* [Roger Williams & John Cacavas:ST]

78 Airport '79 *see* Concorde—Airport '79, The

79 Al Capone (1959) Theme (David Raksin) US:SP = Columbia 4-41392 [Richard Maltby]; Themes (David Raksin) US:SP = Rakrik 100 [Bill Lee/The Jazznix:ST]

80 Al Ponerse el Sol [When the Sun Sets] (1967) Themes (Manuel Alejandro) US:LP = CBS 80321* [Raphael:ST]; Theme (Manuel Alejandro) US:LP-MS = UA 069* [@Raphael:ST]

81 Alakazam the Great (1961) Highlights + Dialog (Les Baxter) US:LP = Vee Jay LP-6000

82 Alamo, The (1960) Score-A (Dimitri Tiomkin) US:LP = Columbia CL-1558/CS8358* [Dimitri Tiomkin:ST]; Score-B (Dimitri Tiomkin) US:LP = Camden CAL-655/CAS-655* [Tex Beneke]

83 Alamo Bay (1985) Score (Ry Cooder) US:LP = Slash 25311-1*

84 Alaska Story (1978) Score

(Masaru Sato) JA:LP = King 428*

85 Albert Peckingpaw's Revenge [Jennie, Wife/Child] (1967) Score (Harley Hatcher) US:LP = Sidewalk T-5907/ST-5907*

86 Alchemist, The (1986) Highlights (Richard Band) US:LP = Varese STV-81262*

87 Alexander [Very Happy Alexander] (1970) Score (Vladimir Cosma) US:LP = Polydor 24-7001*

88 Alexander Nevsky (1938) Score (Serge Prokofiev) US:LP = RCA ARL1-1151* [Eugene Ormandy]; Score (Serge Prokofiev) US:LP = Angel S-36843* [Andre Previn]; Score (Serge Prokofiev) US:LP-MS = Vox 3-9004* [Felix Slatkin]

89 Alexander the Great (1956) Score (Mario Nascimbene) US:LP = Mercury MG-20148

90 Alexander's Ragtime Band (1938) Score (Irving Berlin) US:LP-BP = Hollywood Soundstage HS-406

91 Alf 'n' Family [Till Death Us Do Part] (1968) Highlights + Dialog (Wilfred Burns) GB:LP = Polydor 583.717*

92 Alfie (1966) Score (Sonny Rollins) US:LP = Impulse A-9111/AS-9111*; Theme (Burt Bacharach) US:SP = Imperial 66192 [Cher:ST]; Theme (Burt Bacharach) US:LP = Imperial 9320/12320* [Cher:ST]

93 Alfred the Great (1969) Score (Raymond Leppard) GB:LP = MGM CS-8112*

94 Alfredo! Alfredo! (1973) Score (Carlo Rustichelli) IT:LP = CAM SAG-9044*

95 Ali Baba Goes to Town (1937) Theme (Raymond Scott) US:78 = Brunswick 7992 [Raymond Scott:ST]

96 Alias Jesse James (1959) Theme (Burston & Altman) US:SP = RCA 47-7517 [Bob Hope:ST]

97 Alice in Wonderland (1951) Score (s:Sammy Fain/t:Gene DePaul/t:Oliver Wallace) US:LP = Disneyland DQ-1208

98 Alice's Adventures in Wonderland (1972) Score (John Barry) US:LP = WB BS-2671*

99 Alice's Restaurant (1969) Score (e:Arlo Guthrie/e:Garry Sherman) US:LP = UA UAS-5195*

100 Alien (1979) Score (Jerry Goldsmith) US:LP = 20th T-593*

101 Alien Contamination [Contamination] (1980) Score (Goblin) IT:LP = Cinevox 33/142*

102 Aliens (1986) Score (James Horner) US:LP = Varese STV-81283*

103 Aliki, My Love (1963) Score (Manos Hadjidakis) US:LP = Fontana MGF-27523/SRF-67523e

104 All About Eve (1950) Themes (Alfred Newman) US:LP = Mercury 20037 + US:LP = Citadel 6003 + US:LP = Citadel 7015 + US:LP-BP = Capricorn 1286 [Alfred Newman:ST]; Theme (Alfred Newman) US:LP = RCA 1-0183* + US:LP ± RCA 1-3706* [Charles Gerhardt]; Themes (Alfred Newman) US:SP = Mercury 1193X45 [Alfred Newman]

105 All Fall Down (1962) Theme (Alex North) US:SP = UA 473 [Nick Perito]; Theme (Alex North) US:LP = Columbia 8680* [Don Costa]

106 All Hands on Deck (1961) Highlights (Jay Livingston & Ray Evans) US:EP = Dot DEP-1098 [Pat Boone:ST]

107 All I Desire (1953) Theme (D. Lieber) US:SP = MGM 30796 [David Rose]; Theme (D. Lieber) US:SP = Decca 9-28714 [Camarata]; Theme (D. Lieber) US:LP = MGM 3134 [David Rose]

108 All Night Long (1962) Score (s:Philip Green/t:Johnny Dankworth/t:John Scott) US:LP = Epic LA-16032/BA-17032*

109 All Over Town (1949) Theme (Temple Abady) GB:78-PP = Rank FM-55 [ST]

110 All Screwed Up [Tutto a Posto e Niente in Ordine] (1974) Score (Piero Piccioni) IT:LP = Beat LPF-027*

111 All That Jazz (1979) Score (e:Ralph Burns/etc.) US:LP = Casablanca NBLP-7198*

112 All That Money Can Buy *see* Devil and Daniel Webster, The

113 All the King's Horses (1935) Themes-A-B/US:78 = Brunswick 7398 [Carl Brisson:ST]; Theme-C/US:78 = Brunswick 7397 [Carl Brisson:ST]; Theme-D/US:78 = Apollo 1051 [Carl Brisson:ST]

114 All the Loving Couples (1969)

Highlights + Dialog (Les Baxter-aka-Casanova) US:LP = GNP S-2051*

115 All the President's Men (1976) Theme (David Shire) US:SP = Elektra 45317* [David Shire:ST]; Theme (David Shire) US:LP-BP = Centurion 1600* [@David Shire:ST]

116 All the Right Moves (1983) Score (t:David Campbell/etc.) US:LP = Casablanca 814.449-1*

117 All the Right Noises (1971) Score (e:Melanie Safka/ae:John Cameron) GB:LP = Buddah 2318.034*; Excerpts (Melanie Safka) US:LP = Buddah BDS-5132* [Melanie:ST]

118 All the Way Boys [Piu Forte Ragazzi] (1972) Score (Guido & Maurizio DeAngelis) IT:LP = RCA OLS-14*; Theme (Guido & Maurizio DeAngelis) US:LP = Private Stock 7004* [Guido & Maurizio:ST]

119 All the Way Home (1963) Theme (Jule Styne) US:SP = Columbia 4-42865 [Steve Lawrence:ST]; Theme (Jule Styne) US:LP = Command 871* [Enoch Light]

120 All This and Heaven Too (1940) Excerpts (Max Steiner) US:LP = RCA ARL1-0183* + US:LP = RCA AGL1-3706* [Charles Gerhardt]

121 All This and Money Too *see* Love Is a Ball

122 All This and World War II (1976) Scores (pop music) US:LP-MS = 20th 2T-522*

123 Allegro non Troppo (1977) Score (classical music) US:LP = Deutsche 2536.400*

124 Allonsanfan (1973) Score (Ennio Morricone) IT:LP = RCA SP-8051*; Highlights (Ennio Morricone) IT:LP = RCA NL-33207*; Theme (Ennio Morricone) US:LP-BP = POO 105 [@ST]

125 Almost Perfect Affair, An (1979) Score (Georges Delerue) US:LP = Varese STV-81132*

126 Almost Summer (1978) Score (e:Mike Love & Ron Altbach/t:Charles Lloyd/etc.) US:LP = MCA 3037*

127 Along the Navajo Trail (1945) Theme/US:LP = RCA 3041 [Roy Rogers:ST]

128 Alpha City (1985) Score (e:Al Corley/e:various) GE:LP = Mercury 824-879-1*; Excerpts (Al Corley) US: LP = Mercury 822-316-1* [Al Corley:ST]

129 Alphabet Murders, The (1966) Theme-A (Ron Goodwin) US:LP = Project 5005* [Enoch Light]; Theme-B (Brian Fahey) US:LP = Epic 26323* [Norman Newell]

130 Altered States (1980) Score (John Corigliano) US:LP = RCA ABL1-3983*

131 Altrimenti ci Arrabbiamo / Theme (Guido & Maurizio DeAngelis) US:LP = Private Stock 7004* [Guido & Maurizio:ST]

132 Alvarez Kelly (1966) Theme (John Green) US:SP = Columbia 4-43811 [The Brothers Four:ST]

133 Always Leave Them Laughing (1949) Theme/US:LP-BP = JJA 19765 [@Milton Berle & Bert Lahr:ST]

134 Amadeus (1984) Scores-A (classical music) US:LP-MS = Fantasy WAM-1791*; Score-B (classical music) US:LP = Fantasy WAM-1205*

135 Amarcord (1974) Score (Nino Rota) US:LP = ARL1-0907*

136 Amazing Colossal Man, The (1957) Excerpts (Albert Glasser) US:LP = Starlog SR-1001 [Albert Glasser:ST]

137 Amazing Mr. Beecham, The [The Chiltern Hundreds] (1949) Theme (Benjamin Frankel) GB:78-PP = Rank FM-81 [ST]

138 Amazing Mrs. Holliday, The (1943) Theme (Fritz Kreisler) US:LP = Decca 75289e [Deanna Durbin:ST]

139 Amazons *see* War Goddess

140 Ambushers, The (1967) Theme (Hugo Montenegro) US:SP = A&M 893 [Boyce & Hart:ST]

141 America (1924) Excerpts [Silent II] (Lee Erwin) US:LP = Angel S-36092* [Lee Erwin:ST]

142 America, America [The Anatolian Smile] (1963) Score (Manos Hadjidakis) US:LP = WB W-1527/WS-1527*

143 America the Beautiful [Short] (1958) Highlights + Dialog (folk music) US:LP = Disneyland WDL-4020

144 American Anthem (1986) Score (t:Alan Silvestri/t:Giorgio Moroder/s: various) US:LP = Atlantic 81661-1*

145 American Autobahn (Industrial Short] Score (Douglas Bennett) US:

LP-PP = Monster DB-3

146 American Dream, An [See You in Hell, Darling] (1966) Theme (Johnny Mandel) US:SP = Columbia 4-43768 [Tony Bennett & Johnny Mandel:ST]; Theme (Johnny Mandel) US:LP = MGM 4491* [Michel Legrand]

147 American Dreamer, The (1970) Score (pop music) US:LP = Medi-Arts 4112*

148 American Flyers (1985) Score (Lee Ritenour & Greg Mathieson) US: LP = GRP A-2001*

148a American Friend, The (1977) Excerpts (Jurgen Knieper) US:LP = Enigma 73286

149 American Game, The (1980) Score (Jeffrey Kaufman) US:LP = Buddah BDS-5724*

150 American Gigolo (1980) Score (Giorgio Moroder) US:LP = Polydor PD1-6259*

151 American Graffiti (1973) Scores (pop music) US:LP-MS = MCA 2-8001*

152 American Hot Wax (1978) Scores (pop music) US:LP-MS = A&M SP-6500*

153 American in Paris, An (1951) Highlights (pop music) US:LP-10 = MGM E-93 + US:LP = MGM E-3232 + US:LP = MGM E-3767 + US:LP = Metro M-552/MS-552e

154 American Pop (1981) Score (pop music) US:LP = MCA 5201*

155 American Reunion (1974) Theme (Billy May) US:SP = MCA 40352* [Billy May:ST]

156 American Road, The [Short] (1953) Theme (Alex North) US:LP = RCA 1445* [Alex North:ST]

157 American Tail, An (1986) Score (James Horner) US:LP = MCA 39096*

158 American Werewolf in London, An (1981) Theme (Elmer Bernstein) US:LP = Casablanca 7260* [Meco]

159 Americanization of Emily, The (1964) Score (Johnny Mandel) US:LP = Reprise R-6151/RS-6151*

160 Americano, The (1955) Theme (Xavier Cugat) US:SP = Columbia 4-40377 [Xavier Cugat:ST]; Theme (Xavier Cugat) US:LP = Columbia 618 [Xavier Cugat:ST]

161 Americathon (1979) Score (t: Tom Scott/etc.) US:LP = Lorimar JS-36174*

162 Amityville Horror, The (1979) Score (Lalo Schifrin) US:LP = American International AILP-3003*

163 Amor Brujo, El (1986) Score (Antonio Gades) US:LP = EMI DS-38338*

164 Amore [Serenata d'Amore] (1956) Theme (Heino Gaze) US:SP = RCA 47-6791 [Ed Ames]; Theme (Heino Gaze) US:LP = Decca 74083* [Helmut Zacharias]

165 Amorous Adventures of Don Quixote and Sancho Panza, The (1976) Highlights (Don Great) US:EP-PP = LUV 1003*

166 Amorous Adventures of Moll Flanders (1965) Score (John Addison) US:LP = RCA LOC-1113/LSO-1113*

167 Amorous Milkman, The (1976) Theme (Roger Webb) GB:LP = EMI 1022* [Roger Webb:ST]

168 Amorous Mr. Prawn, The [The Amorous Prawn] [The Playgirl and the War Minister] (1962) Theme (John Barry) GB:SP = Columbia 4941 + GB: SP = Cherry Red 67 [John Barry:ST]

169 Amour Descend du Ciel, L' Theme (Guy Bernard) US:LP = Dot 3120 [Ray Ventura]

170 Anarkali (1956) Highlights (S. D. Burman) US:LP = Capitol T-10090

171 Anastasia (1956) Score-A (Alfred Newman) US:LP = Decca DL-8460; Score-B (Alfred Newman) US: LP = Varese STV-81125*

172 Anatolian Smile, The *see* America, America

173 Anatomy of a Marriage [La Vie Conjugal] (1963) Highlights (Louiguy) FR:EP = Barclay 70607

174 Anatomy of a Murder (1959) Score (Duke Ellington) US:LP = Columbia CL-1360/CS-8166* + US:LP = CSP JCS 8166*

175 Anche gli Angeli Mangiano Fagioli / Theme (Guido & Maurizio DeAngelis) US:LP = Private Stock 7004* [Guido & Maurizio:ST]

176 Anchors Aweigh (1945) Score (Jule Styne) US:LP-BP = Curtain Calls 100/17 + US:LP-BP = Sandy Hook SH-2024

177 And God Created Woman (1957) Highlights + Dialog (Paul Misraki) US:LP = Decca DL-8685

178 And Hope to Die [La Course du Lievre a Travers les Champs] (1972) Score (Francis Lai) FR:LP = Philips 6332.095*; Theme (Francis Lai) US:LP = UA 095* + US:LP = DRG 508* [Francis Lai:ST]

179 And Now My Love [Toute Une Vie] (1972) Scores (e:Francis Lai/etc.) FR:LP-MS = Pathe 2C0156.12967/8*; Score (Francis Lai) GB:LP = Dart ARTS-65377*; Theme (Francis Lai) US:LP = DRG 508* [Francis Lai:ST]

180 And Now Tomorrow (1944) Theme (Victor Young) US:LP = Decca 8140 [Victor Young:ST]

181 And Suddenly It's Murder! [Crimen] (1960) Theme (Pino Calvi) US:LP = Capitol 8608* [Pino Calvi:ST]

182 And the Angels Sing (1944) Highlights (James Van Heusen) US:LP-BP = Caliban 6017; Theme (Victor Young) US:78 = Capitol 10068 [Diana Lynn:ST]

183 And the Ship Sails On [E la Nave Va] (1984) Score (as:Gianfranco Plenizio) FR:LP = Milan A-228*

184 Anderson Tapes, The (1971) Theme (Quincy Jones) US:LP = A&M 3037* [Quincy Jones:ST]

185 Andrea (1969) Theme (Hammerschmid) US:SP = UA 50512* [Ferrante & Teicher]; Theme (Hammerschmid) US:LP = UA 6701* [Ferrante & Teicher]

186 Andromeda Strain, The (1971) Score (Gil Melle) US:LP = Kapp KDL-5513*

187 Andy and the Lion [Short] Sequence + Dialog (Arthur Kleiner) US:LP = Picture Book Parade 104 [@ST]

188 Andy Hardy Comes Home (1958) Theme (Hal Spina) US:SP = Capitol 4023 [The Four Preps]

189 Andy Hardy Meets Debutante (1940) Theme/US:LP = Decca 172 + US:LP = MGM 4005 [Judy Garland:ST]

190 Andy Warhol's Dracula [Blood for Dracula] (1974) Score (Claudio Gizzi) US:LP = Citadel CTV-7030*

191 Andy Warhol's Frankenstein [Flesh for Frankenstein] (1974) Score (Claudio Gizzi) US:LP = Citadel CTV-7031*

192 Angel, Angel, Down We Go [Cult of the Damned] (1969) Score (e:Fred Karger/e:Barry Mann) US:LP = Tower ST-5161*

193 Angel Baby [Jenny Angel] (1961) Theme-A (Wayne Shanklin) US:SP = Signet 280 [Heinie Beau]; Themes B/C (Wayne Shanklin/Al Sherman) US:SP = Signet 258 [Johnny Krag]; Theme-D (Rod Sherwood) US:SP = Era 45-1087 [Art & Dotty Todd]

194 Angel Unchained (1971) Score (s:Randy Sparks/t:Jim Helms) US:LP = American International STA-1037*

195 Angel Wore Red, The (1960) Theme (Bronislau Kaper) US:SP = Carlton 533 [Lew Douglas]; Theme (Bronislau Kaper) US:LP = Carlton 126* [Lew Douglas]

196 Angelique (1966) Score (Michel Magne) FR:LP = Pathe C062.14204*

197 Angels Die Hard (1970) Score (e:Bruce Cone/t:Richard Hieronymus/etc.) US:LP = UNI 73091*

198 Angels from Hell (1968) Score (Stu Phillips) US:LP = Tower ST-5128*

199 Angels of the Year 2000 [Gli Angeli Del 2000] (1969) Score (Mario Molino) IT:LP = CAM SAG-9020*

200 Angels with Dirty Faces (1938) Sequence + Dialog (Max Steiner) US:LP-MS = WB 3X2737 [@ST]

201 Angry Red Planet (1960) Theme (Paul Dunlap) US:LP = GNP 2163* [Neil Norman]

202 Animal, L' *see* Stuntwoman, The

203 Animal Crackers (1930) Theme/US:SP = Decca 9-28158 [Groucho Marx:ST]; Theme/US:LP-10 = Decca 5405 [Groucho Marx:ST]

204 Animal House *see* National Lampoon's Animal House

205 Animals, The [Les Animeaux] (1959) Highlights (Maurice Jarre) FR:EP = Phillips 434.823

206 Animals, The (1971) *see* Five Savage Men

207 Animals Film, The (1982) Score (Wyatt) GB:LP = Rough 40*

208 Animalympics (1980) Score

(Graham Gouldman) US:LP = A&M SP-4810*

209 Anna (1952) Themes (Roman Vatro/P.G. Redi) US:SP = MGM 11457 [Silvana Mangano:ST]; Themes (Roman Vatro/P.G. Redi) US:LP = MGM E-3485 [Robert Ashley]

210 Anna from Brooklyn *see* Fast and Sexy

211 Anna Karenina (1935) Highlights (Herbert Stothart) US:LP-MS-BP = Tony Thomas TTST-1/2

212 Anna Karenina (1947) Excerpts (Constant Lambert) US:LP = London SPC-21149* [Bernard Herrmann]

213 Anna Lucasta (1958) Theme (Elmer Bernstein) US:SP = Decca 9-30769 [Sammy Davis Jr.:ST]; Theme (Elmer Bernstein) US:LP = Mainstream 6094* + Choreo 11* [Elmer Bernstein:ST]

214 Anne and Muriel *see* Two English Girls

215 Anne of the Thousand Days (1969) Highlights (Georges Delerue) US: LP = Decca DL-79174*

216 Annie (1982) Score (stage songs + film songs: Charles Strouse) US:LP = Columbia/CBS JS-38000*

217 Annie Get Your Gun (1950) Highlights (stage songs: Irving Berlin) US:LP-10 = MGM E-509 + US:LP = MGM E-3227 + US:LP = MGM E-3768 + US:LP = Metro M-548/MS-548e + US:LP-MS = MGM 2SES-42e

218 Anonymous Venetian, The (1970) Score (Stelvio Cipriani) US:LP = UA UAS-5218*

219 Another Country (1984) Theme (Michael Storey) GB:LP-MS = Filmtrax 820-251-1* [@Michael Storey:ST]

220 Another Dawn (1937) Theme (Erich Wolfgang Korngold) US:LP = RCA 1-0185* [Charles Gerhardt]; Theme (Erich Wolfgang Korngold) US:LP = Decca 8060 [Victor Young]

221 Another Man, Another Chance [Un Autre Homme, une Autre Chance] (1977) Score (Francis Lai) FR:LP = UA UAP-25017*

222 Another Nice Mess (1975) Themes (Bob Emmeneger) US:SP = Capitol 3334* [Matt Moore:ST]

223 Another Shore (1948) Theme (Georges Auric) GB:78-PP = Rank FM-41

224 Another Time, Another Place (1958) Score (s:Douglas Gamley/t:Jay Livingston & Ray Evans) US:LP = Columbia CL-1180

225 Another Time, Another Place (1983) Themes (John McLeod/Corrado Sfogli) GB:SP-12 = That's Entertainment TER-12-007* [ST]

226 Antarctica [The South Pole Story] Score (Vangelis) JA:LP = Polydor 28-MM-0290*

227 Anthony Adverse (1936) Excerpts (Erich Wolfgang Korngold) US: LP = WB W-1438/WS-1438* [Lionel Newman]; Theme (Erich Wolfgang Korngold) US:LP = RCA 3330* + US: LP = RCA 1-3707* [Charles Gerhardt]

228 Antony and Cleopatra (1971) Score (John Scott) GB:LP = Polydor 2383.109*

229 Any Gun Can Play [For a Few Bullets More] [Vado, l'Ammazzo e Torno] (1967) Score (Francesco DeMasi) IT:LP = Beat CR-5*

230 Any Number Can Win [Melodie en Souse-Sol] (1963) Highlights (Michel Magne) FR:EP = Barclay 70522; Theme (Michel Magne) US:SP = Verve 135 [Jimmy Smith]; Theme (Magne) US: LP = Verve 8552* [Jimmy Smith]

231 Any Wednesday [Bachelor Girl Apartment] (1966) Score (George Duning) US:LP = WB W-1669/WS-1669*

232 Any Which Way You Can (1980) Score (e:Steve Dorff/etc.) US: LP = WB HS-3499*

233 Anyone Can Play [Le Dolci Signore] (1967) Theme (Armando Trovajoli) US:LP = Dot 25925* [The Creative Crowd]

234 Anything Goes [Tops Is the Limit] (1936) Highlights (various) US: LP-BP = Caliban 6043; Excerpts-A (various) US:LP-10 = Decca DL-6009 + US:LP = Decca DL-4251 [Bing Crosby: ST]; Excerpts-B (various) US:LP-BP = JJA 19767 [@ST]

235 Anything Goes (1956) Score (e:James Van Heusen/etc.) US:LP = Decca DL-8318

236 Anzio [Battle for Anzio] (1968) Theme (Riz Ortolani) US:SP = RCA 47-9564 [Jack Jones:ST]

237 Apache (1954) Theme (David Raksin) US:LP = Impulse 34* [Coleman Hawkins]

238 Apache Gold [Winnetou I] [Winnetou the Warrior] (1963) Highlights (Martin Bottcher) GE:LP = Polydor 46838*

239 Apache's Last Battle, The *see* Old Shatterhand

240 Apartment, The (1960) Score (Adolph Deutsch) US:LP = UA UAL-3105/UAS-6105*

241 Ape Woman, The [L'Ape Regina] (1964) Theme (Teo Usuelli) JA: LP = UA 505* [@ST]

242 Apocalypse des Animaux, L' (1970) Score (Vangelis) GB:LP = Polydor 2389.113*

243 Apocalypse Now (1979) Score + Dialog (e:Carmine Coppola/etc.) US: LP-MS = Elektra DP-90001*; Score (e:Carmine Coppola/etc.) US:LP = Elektra ELK-52-212*

244 Apollo (1983) Score (Brian Eno & Daniel Lanois) US:LP = EG ENO-5* [Brian Eno:ST]

245 Appaloosa, The (1966) Theme (Frank Skinner) US:SP = Decca 9-32020 [Trumpets Ole]; Theme (Frank Skinner) US:LP = Decca 74821* [Trumpets Ole]

246 Appassionata (1974) Score (Piero Piccioni) IT:LP = Cinevox 33/72*

247 Applause (1929) Theme/US: LP = RCA LPV-561 [@Helen Morgan: ST]

248 Apple, The (1980) Score (Coby Recht) US:LP = Cannon 1001*

249 Appleman Theme / (Bob Crewe) US:SP = Crewe 600* [The Crosstown Children]; Theme (Bob Crewe) US: SP = Crewe 601* [Lesley Gore]

250 Appointment, The (1969) Themes (John Barry) FR:SP = Polydor/ MGM 61629* [ST]; Theme (John Barry) US:LP = Columbia 1003* [J. Barry:ST]

251 Appointment with Venus *see* Island Rescue

252 April Fools, The (1969) Score (e:Marvin Hamlisch/t:Burt Bacharach/ etc.) US:LP = Columbia OS-3340*

253 April Fool's Day (1986) Score (Charles Bernstein) US:LP = Varese STV-81278*

254 April in Paris (1952) Highlights (Vernon Duke) US:LP-BP = Titania 500; Highlights (Vernon Duke) US:EP = Columbia B-1581 [Doris Day:ST]

255 April Love (1957) Score (e: Sammy Fain/ae:Alfred Newman & Cyril Mockridge) US:LP = Dot DLP-9000

256 Aquellos Tiempos del Cuple / Score (various) US:LP = Montilla FM-139 [Lilian De Celis:ST]

257 Arabesque (1966) Score (Henry Mancini) US:LP = RCA LPM-3623/ LSP-3623*

258 Arabian Fantasy / Theme (David Fanshawe) GB:LP = Philips 6558.003* [David Fanshawe:ST]

259 Arabian Nights [A Thousand and One Nights] [Il Fiore della 1001 Notte] (1974) Themes (Ennio Morricone) IT:LP = General Music 73001* [Ennio Morricone:ST]

260 Arch of Triumph (1948) Theme (Louis Gruenberg) JA:LP-MS = TAM 9001/2* [@Stanley Maxfield]

261 Aren't We All (1932) Theme/ US:LP = Audio Fidelity 709 [Gertrude Lawrence:ST]

262 Argentine Nights (1940) Theme-A/US:78 = Decca 3310 [The Andrews Sisters:ST]; Theme-B/US:78 = Decca 3328 [The Andrews Sisters:ST]; Theme-C/US:LP-MS = MCA 2-4024 [The Andrews Sisters:ST]

263 Aristocats, The (1970) Highlights + Dialog (Richard & Robert Sherman) US:LP = Disneyland ST-3995; Highlights (Richard & Robert Sherman) US:LP = Disneyland 1333

264 Arizona Colt *see* Man from Nowhere, The

265 Armed and Dangerous (1986) Score (t:Bill Meyers/s:various) US:LP = Manhattan SJ-53041*

266 Arnold's Wrecking Co. (1975) Score (Howie Solomon & Steve Blackstone) US:LP = East Coast EC-1055*

267 Around the World in 80 Days (1956) Score (Victor Young) US:LP = Decca DL-9046/DL-79046* + US:LP = MCA 2062* + US:LP = MCA 37086*

268 Around the World Under the Sea (1966) Score (Harry Sukman) US: LP = Monument 8050/18050*

269 Arrangement, The (1970) Score (David Amram) US:LP = WB WS-1824*

270 Arrivederci, Baby [Drop Dead, Darling] (1966) Score (Dennis Farnon) US:LP = RCA LOC-1132/LSO-1132*

271 Arsenic and Old Lace (1944) Excerpts (Max Steiner) US:LP-BP = Tony Thomas TTMS-17 [Max Steiner:ST]

272 Art of Killing, The *see* Budo

273 Art of Love, The (1965) Score (Cy Coleman) US:LP = Capitol T-2355/ST-2355*

274 Arthur (1981) Score (Burt Bacharach) US:LP = WB BSK-3582*

275 Artists and Models (1937) Theme/US:78 = Decca 1420 [Connie Boswell:ST]

276 Artists and Models (1955) Highlights (Harry Warren) US:EP = Capitol EAP1-702 [Dean Martin:ST]

277 Arturo's Island [L'Isola di Arturo] (1962) Highlights (Carlo Rustichelli) JA:LP = Seven Seas GHX-6051

278 As Long As They're Happy (1955) Highlights (Sam Coslow) GB:LP-10 = HMV DLPC-1

279 As Young As We Are (1959) Theme (Barlow) US:SP = MGM 12742 [Alan Dale]

280 Ascendancy (1983) Score (R. Leahy) FR:LP = WB/WEA 24.0221.4*

281 Ascenseur pour l'Echafaud, L' *see* Frantic

282 Ash Wednesday (1973) Theme (Maurice Jarre) US:SP = Paramount 0271* [Robert Goulet]; Theme (Maurice Jarre) GB:LP = EMI 1022* [Roger Webb]

283 Ashanti (1979) Score (Michael Melvoin) FR:LP = Carrere/Cobra 37022*

284 Ashes and Diamonds (1958) Theme (Zbigniew Maciejowski) GB:LP = That's Entertainment TER-1053 [@ST]

285 Ask Any Girl (1959) Themes (Jeff Alexander) US:SP = MGM 12798 [Harry James]

286 Asphalt Jungle, The (1950) Themes (Miklos Rozsa) GB:LP = Polydor 2383.384* [Miklos Rozsa:ST]

287 Assassination Bureau, The (1969) Theme (Ron Grainer) GB:LP = RCA 1020* [Ron Grainer:ST]

288 Assassination of the Duc de Guise, The [Short] (1908) Theme [Silent I] (Camille Saint-Saens) US:LP = Golden Crest 4019 [Arthur Kleiner]; Excerpts [Silent I] (Camille Saint-Saens) RU:LP = Melodiya C10.20459.009* [Gennedy Rozhdestvensky]

289 Assault on Precinct 13 (1976) Theme (John Carpenter) GB:SP = Pye 7N-4606 [ST]

290 Assoluto Naturale, L' [He and She] (1972) Score (Ennio Morricone) US:LP = Cerberus CEMS-0112*

291 Asterix and Cleopatra (1969) Score (Gerard Calvi) GE:LP = Columbia 28664

292 Astonished Heart, The (1949) Theme-A (Noel Coward) GB:78-PP = Rank FM-89 [ST]; Theme-B (Noel Coward) GB:78-PP = Rank FM-90 [ST]

293 At Close Range (1986) Theme (Pat Leonard) US:SP = Sire 7-28717* [Madonna:ST]

294 At Long Last Love (1975) Scores (pop music) US:LP-MS = RCA ABL2-0967*

295 At the Circus (1939) Themes (Bert Kalmar & Harry Ruby) US:LP-BP = JJA 19763 [@ST]; Theme (Bert Kalmar & Harry Ruby) US:SP = Decca 9-28160 [Groucho Marx:ST]

296 At the End of the Rainbow / Highlights (Billy Allen) US:EP-PP = Fantasy Films 165 [Sherry Howard:ST]

297 At War with the Army (1950) Theme-A (Jerry Livingston) US:SP = Capitol 1358 [Dean Martin:ST]; Theme-B (Jerry Livingston) US:SP = Capitol 1385 [Jerry Lewis:ST]; Theme-C (Jerry Livingston) US:SP = RCA 47-4022 [Polly Bergen:ST]

298 Athena (1954) Score (Ralph Blane & Hugh Martin) US:LP-BP = Motion Picture Tracks MPT-2; Highlights (Ralph Blane & Hugh Martin) US:LP-10 = Mercury MG-25202

299 Atlantic City (1981) Score (s:Michel Legrand/t:Paul Anka) US:LP = DRG SL-6104*

300 Atlantis *see* Forbidden Island

301a Atlantis, the Lost Continent (1960) Excerpts (Russell Garcia) US:LP = GNP GNPS-8008* [Russell Garcia:ST]

301 Atlas Against the Czar [Maciste alla Corte dello Zar] (1964) Themes (Carlo Rustichelli) IT:SP = CAM CA-2568 [ST]

302 Atomic City (1981) Score (pop music) US:LP = Rounder 1034*

303 Atomic Rulers of the World [Invaders from Space] (1964) Theme (Chumei Watanabe) JA:LP = Toho 8124 [@ST]

304 Ator (1984) Themes (Carlo M. Cordio) IT:SP = Full Time 31028* [ST]

305 Atragon (1964) Excerpts (Akira Ifukube) JA:LP = Toho 8108 [@ST]

306 Attack and Retreat [Italiani Brava Gente] (1963) Score (Armando Trovajoli) IT:LP = RCA 10382

307 Attack of the Killer Tomatoes (1979) Themes (Gordon Goodwin) US: SP = Four Square 100* [ST]

308 Attack of the Monsters (1969) Excerpts (Shunsuke Kikuchi) JA:LP = Toho 8120 [@ST]

309 Attack of the Mushroom People (1964) Themes (Betumia Sadao) JA: LP = Toho 8107 [@ST]

310 Audrey Rose (1977) Theme (Michael Small) JA:SP = Philips 2494* [Chris Carpenter]

311 August Without the Emperor (1978) Score (Masaru Sato) JA:LP = CBS/Sony 25-AH-552*

312 Aunt Sally (1933) Themes/GB: LP = WRC 113 [Cicely Courtneidge:ST]

313 Auntie Mame (1958) Highlights (Bronislau Kaper) US:LP = WB W-1242/WS-1242*

314 Author! Author! (1982) Theme (Dave Grusin) US:SP = WB 7-29951* [Michael Franks:ST]

315 Autopsy [The Victim] (1977) Themes (Ennio Morricone) JA:SP = Seven Seas FMS-9* [ST]

315a Autumn Leaves (1956) Theme (film theme from "Les Portes de la Nuit") US:LP = Capitol 16165 [Nat King Cole: ST]

316 Aviator, The (1985) Score (Dominic Frontiere) US:LP = Varese STV-81241*

317 Avanti! (1972) Theme (at:Carlo Rustichelli) US:SP = Avalanche 36018* [Gianfranco Piemizio:ST]

318 Avventura, L' (1959) Highlights (Giovanni Fusco) JA:LP = Seven Seas GHX-6051; Theme (Giovanni Fusco) US:LP = RCA FSO-4* [@ST]

319 Awakening, The (1928) Theme [Silent I] (Irving Berlin) US:SP = Decca 9-27107 [Peter Yorke]; Theme [Silent I] (Irving Berlin) US:LP = RCA 2560* [Gaylord Carter]

320 Awakening, The (1980) Score (Claude Bolling) US:LP = Entracte ERS-6520*

321 Away All Boats (1956) Theme (Frank Skinner) US:SP = Decca 9-29950 [Al Hibbler]; Theme (Frank Skinner) US:LP = Coral 57065 [George Cates]

B

322 B.S. I Love You (1971) Score (Mark Shekter) US:LP = Mercury SRM1-610*

323 Babes in Arms (1939) Score (various) US:LP-MS-BP = Curtain Calls 100/6-7

324 Babes in Toyland [March of the Wooden Soldiers] (1934) Highlights + Dialog (e:Frank Churchill/stage songs: Victor Herbert) US:LP = Mark 56 #577

325 Babes in Toyland (1961) Score (as:George Bruns) US:LP = Buena Vista BV-4022/ST-4022*

326 Babes on Broadway (1941) Score (e:Burton Lane/e:Roger Edens) US:LP-MS-BP = Curtain Calls 100/6-7

327 Babette Goes to War [Babette S'en Va-t-en Guerre] (1960) Highlights (Gilbert Becaud) FR:EP = Trianon 4365

328 Baby Doll (1956) Score (Kenyon Hopkins) US:LP = Columbia CL-958

329 Baby Face Nelson (1957) Score (Van Alexander) US:LP = Jubilee 2021

330 Baby Love (1969) Theme (G. Calabese) US:SP = Deram 45-85045 [Roberto Mann]

331 Baby Maker, The (1971) Score (Fred Karlin) US:LP = Ode SP-77002*

332 Baby Sitter, The [Un Maledetto Pasticcio] (1976) Score (Francis Lai) IT: LP = RCA TBL1-1179*

333 Baby Snakes (1979) Theme (Frank Zappa) US:SP = Zappa 10* [Frank Zappa:ST]; Theme (Frank Zappa) US:LP = Zappa 1501* [Frank Zappa:ST]

334 Baby, Take a Bow (1934) Themes/US:LP-MS = 20th 2-103 [Shirley Temple:ST]

335 Baby, the Rain Must Fall (1965) Score (Elmer Bernstein) US:LP = Mainstream 56056/S-6056* + US:LP = Ava A-53/AS-53*

336 Babylon (1981) Score (e:Dennis Bovell/etc.) US:LP = Takoma 7100*

337 Bachelor Flat (1962) Theme (John Williams) US:SP = Columbia 4-42516 [John Williams:ST]; Theme (John Williams) US:LP = RCA 3491* + US:LP = RCA 1-2805* [Andre Previn & John Williams:ST]

338 Bachelor Girl Apartment *see* Any Wednesday

339 Bachelor in Paradise (1961) Theme (Henry Mancini) US:SP = RCA 47-7964 [Gaynel Hodge]; Theme (Henry Mancini) US:LP = RCA 2604* + US:LP-MS = Camden 2-0293* [Henry Mancini:ST]

340 Bachelor Party (1957) Theme-A (Alex North) US:SP = RCA 47-6896 [Alex North:ST]; Theme-B (Alex North) US:LP = Citadel 6023* [Alex North:ST]

341 Bachelor Party (1984) Score (various) US:LP = I.R.S. SP-70047*

342 Back from Eternity (1956) Theme (Franz Waxman) US:SP = RKO Unique 359 [Tommy Reynolds]

343 Back Street (1961) Score (Frank Skinner) US:LP = Decca DL-9097/DL-79097*

344 Back to School (1986) Score (various) US:LP = MCA 6175*; Highlights (Danny Elfman) US:LP = Varese 704.370*

345 Back to the Future (1985) Score (t:Alan Silvestri/s:various) US:LP = MCA 6144*

346 Bad and the Beautiful, The (1952) Excerpts (David Raksin) US:LP = RCA ARL1-1490* [David Raksin:ST]

347 Bad Boys (1960) Excerpts (Toru Takemitsu) JA:LP = RCA/Victor 1071 [Toru Takemitsu:ST]

348 Bad Boys (1983) Score (pop music) US:LP = Capital ST-12272*

349 Bad Company (1972) Highlights (Harvey Schmidt) US:LP-PP = Chap Stk 1069*

350 Bad Guys (1986) Score (t:William Goldstein/s:various) US:LP = Casablanca 826-610-1*

351 Bad Seed, The (1956) Score (Alex North) US:LP = RCA LPM-1395 + US:LP-BP = Cinevox 33/25

352 Bahia (1978) Score (Antonio Carlos & Jocafi) FR:LP = RCA FPL1-0175*

353 Baiju Bawra / Theme/US:LP = Capitol 10500 [@Mohd-Rafi:ST]

354 Bailout at 43,000 (1957) Theme (Albert Glasser) US:SP = RKO Unique 410 [Joe Tucker]

355 Baiso / Theme (Martin Bottcher) US:SP = London 1984 [Renardo]

356 Le Bal (1983) Scores (e:Vladimir Cosma/s:pop music) FR:LP-MS = Carrere 66.073*

357 Balalaika (1939) Highlights (e:Herbert Stothart/etc.) US:LP-BP = Caliban 6004

358 Balance, La (1983) Score (Roland Bocquet) FR:LP = Milan A-188*

359 Ballad in Blue *see* Blues for Lovers

360 Ballad of a Gunfighter (1963) Theme/US:LP = Columbia 1481/8272* [Marty Robbins:ST]

361 Ballad of a Soldier (1960) Theme (Mikhail Siv) US:LP = WB 1548* [Werner Muller]; Theme (Mikhail Siv) US:LP = Kapp 1289* [Vardi]

362 Ballad of Billie Blue, The / Themes (Richard Wess) US:SP = Fresh Air 323 [Richard Wess:ST]

363 Ballad of Cable Hogue, The (1970) Themes (Jerry Goldsmith/Richard Gillis) US:SP = WB 7386 [Richard Gillis:ST]; Theme (Jerry Goldsmith) US:LP-BP = Centurion 1600 [@Richard Gillis:ST]

364 Ballad of Narayama, The (1984) Score (Shinichiro Ikebe) JA:LP = Radio City 1009*

365 Ballet Mechanique [Short] (1924) Highlights [Silent II] (George Antheil) US:LP = Columbia ML-4956 + US:LP = CSP AML-4953

366 Bambalinas / Theme (J. Velasquez) US:LP = MGM 3731* [Metropolitan Jazz Quartet]

367 Bambi (1942) Score (e:Frank Churchill/e:Ed Plumb) US:LP = Disneyland WDL-4009 + US:LP = Disneyland DQ-1203

368 Bambole! [Four Kinds of Love] [The Dolls] (1965) Score (Armando Trovajoli) IT:LP = RCA PML-10401

369 Banana Peel [Peau de Banane] (1963) Highlights (Ward Swingle) FR: EP = Fontana 27073

370 Bananas (1971) Themes (Marvin Hamlisch) US:SP = UA 50798* [Marvin Hamlisch:ST]; Theme-A (Marvin Hamlisch) US:LP-BP = Centurion 1600* [@Marvin Hamlisch:ST] Theme-B (Marvin Hamlisch) US:LP = Kapp 3650* [Roger Williams]

371 Band Concert, The [Cartoon] (1935) Theme (pop music) US:LP-MS = Ovation 5000 + US:LP = Disneyland 3805 [@ST]

372 Band of Angels (1957) Score (Max Steiner) US:LP = RCA LPM-1157 + US:LP = Entracte ERM-6003

373 Band of the Hand (1986) Score (t:Michel Rubini/s:various) US:LP = MCA 6167*

374 Band of Thieves (1962) Theme (Norrie Paramor) US:SP = Atco 45-6238 [Acker Bilk:ST]; Themes (Norrie Paramor) GB:SP = Columbia 4897 [Acker Bilk:ST]

375 Band Wagon, The (1953) Score (pop music) US:LP = MGM E-3051 + US:LP-MS = MGM 2SES-44e

376 Bandido (1956) Theme (Max Steiner) US:SP = RCA 47-6684 [Perez Prado]; Theme (Max Steiner) US:LP = RCA 1883 [Perez Prado]

377 Bandidos (1967) Score (Egisto Macchi) IT:LP = Cometa 1011/24*

378 Bandit of Sherwood Forest, The (1946) Excerpts (Hugo Friedhofer) US:LP-BP = Premiere 1201 + US:LP = AEI 3104 [uncredited]

379 Bandolero! (1968) Score (Jerry Goldsmith) US:LP = Project SD-5026*

380 Bang the Drum Slowly (1973) Score (Stephen J. Lawrence) US:LP = Paramount PAS-1014*

381 Banished (1978) Excerpts (Toru Takemitsu) JA:LP = RCA/Victor 1068 [Toru Takemitsu:ST]

382 Banjo Man (1977) Score (folk music) US:LP = Sire SA-7527*

383 Banjo on My Knee (1936) Themes/US:78 = Brunswick 7782 [Tony Martin:ST]

384 Banner in the Sky *see* Third Man on the Mountain

385 Banning (1967) Theme (Quincy Jones) US:SP = Coral 9-62527 [Pete Fountain]; Theme (Quincy Jones) US: LP = A&M 3041* [Quincy Jones:ST]; Theme (Quincy Jones) US:LP = Project 5016* [Enoch Light]

386 Barabbas (1962) Score (Mario Nascimbene) US:LP = Colpix CP-510/SCP-510* + US:LP = Varese STV-81137*

387 Barbarella (1968) Score (Charles Fox & Bob Crewe) US:LP = Dynovoice 1908/31908*

388 Barbarian, The (1933) Theme/US:LP = Stanyan 10055 [@Ramon Novarro:ST]

389 Barbarian and the Geisha, The (1958) Score (Hugo Friedhofer) US: LP = 20th 3004 + US:LP-BP = Gemini CF-3384

390 Bare Knuckles (1978) Score (Vic Caesar) US:LP = Gucci G-303*

391 Barefoot Adventure (1961) Score (Bud Shank) US:LP = Pacific Jazz PJ-35/PJS-35*

392 Barefoot Contessa, The (1954) Themes (Mario Nascimbene) US:LP = RCA 1074 [Katyna Ranieri]; Theme (Mario Nascimbene) US:SP = RCA 47-5888 [Hugo Winterhalter]; Theme (Mario Nascimbene) IT:LP-MS = Kangaroo 34209 [Mario Nascimbene:ST]

393 Barefoot Executive, The (1971) Theme (Robert F. Brunner) US:SP = Buena Vista 481 [B.D. & Company:ST]

394 Barefoot in the Park (1967) Score (Neal Hefti) US:LP = Dot DLP-3803/DLP-25803*

395 Barkleys of Broadway, The (1948) Score (e:Harry Warren/etc.) US: LP-BP = Sountrak STK-116; Highlights (e:Harry Warren/etc.) US:78-MS = MGM L-8; Highlights (e:Harry Warren/etc.) US:LP-MS = MGM 2SES-51e

396 Barocco (1977) Score (Philippe Sarde) FR:LP = Barclay 930.020*

397 Barretts of Wimpole Street, The [Forbidden Alliance] (1934) Theme (Herbert Stothart) US:LP = MGM 3694 [John Green]; Sequence + Narration (Herbert Stothart) US:LP = Coral 57125 [George Cates]

398 Barricade (1938) Theme/US: LP-BP = Scarce Rarities 5502 [Alice Faye:ST]

399 Barry Lyndon (1975) Score (ae:Leonard Rosenman/etc.) US:LP = WB BS-2903*

400 Bartleby (1971) Theme (Roger Webb) GB:LP = EMI/Columbia 349* [Roger Webb:ST]

401 I Basilischi [The Basilisks] [The Lizards] (1963) Theme (Ennio Morricone) US:LP = Capitol 8608* [Pino Calvi]

402 Bat, The (1959) Theme (Louis Forbes) US:SP = Capitol 4239 [Alvino Rey:ST]; US:LP = Dolton 8027 [The Ventures]

403 Bathing Beauty (1944) Theme/ US:78 = Columbia 36780 [Xavier Cugat: ST]; Theme/US:78 = Decca 23353 [Ethel Smith:ST]

404 Battle at Apache Pass (1952) Excerpts (Hans J. Salter) US:LP = Medallion 313 [Hans J. Salter:ST]

405 Battle Beyond the Stars (1980) Score (James Horner) US:LP = Rhino RNSP-300*

406 Battle Creek Brawl *see* Big Brawl, The

407 Battle Cry (1955) Theme (Max Steiner) US:SP = MGM 11900 [Art Mooney]; Theme (Max Steiner) US: SP = RCA 47-6025 [Sauter & Finegan]; Theme (Max Steiner) US:LP = MGM 3899* [Art Mooney]

408 Battle for Anzio *see* Anzio

409 Battle for Stalingrad, The (1944) Highlights (Aram Khatchaturian) US:LP = Classic Editions CE-9/CE-3009

410 Battle Hell [Yangtse Incident] (1957) Theme (Leighton Lucas) GB:78 = Parlophone 4342 [Leighton Lucas:ST]; Theme (Leighton Lucas) GB:LP = MFP 90075* [Band of H.M. Royal Marines]

411 Battle in Outer Space (1960) Score (Akira Ifukube) JA:LP = Toho DX-4007

412 Battle of Algiers, The (1967) Score (Ennio Morricone) US:LP = UA UAL-4171/UAS-5171* + US:LP = UA LA-293*

413 Battle of Britain (1967) Score (s:Ron Goodwin/t:William Walton) US: LP = UA UAS-5201*

414 Battle of Midway *see* Midway

415 Battle of Neretva, The (1970) Score [USA Release] (Bernard Herrmann) US:LP = Entracte ERS-6501* + US:LP = Southern Cross SCRS-5005*; Theme [European Release] (Vladimir Rajteric & Nikica Kalogjera) FR:LP = Philips 6620.025 [@ST]

416 Battle of Paris, The (1929) Themes/US:LP-BP = JJA 19767 [@Gertrude Lawrence:ST]

417 Battle of the Amazons [Karate Amazons] (1976) Score (Franco Micalizzi) JA:LP = Cine Disc 3003*

418 Battle of the Bulge (1965) Score (Benjamin Frankel) US:LP = WB W-1617/WS-1617*

419 Battle of the River Plate, The *see* Pursuit of the Graf Spee

420 Battle of the Villa Fiorita, The [Affair at the Villa Fiorita] (1965) Theme (Mischa Spoliansky) US:SP = WB 5631 [Londonderry Strings]; Theme (Mischa Spoliansky) US:SP = Regina 1327 [Jack LaForge]; Theme (Mischa Spoliansky) US:LP = Audio Fidelity 2161* [Jack LaForge]

421 Battle Squadron *see* Eagles Over London

422 Battle Stripe *see* Men, The

423 Battleship Potemkin *see* Potemkin

424 Battletruck *see* Warlords of the 21'st Century

425 Baxter (1973) Themes (Michael J. Lewis) US:SP = RCA 74-0934* [Michael J. Lewis:ST]; Theme (Michael J. Lewis) US:SP = Columbia 4-45825* [Peter Nero]; Theme (Michael J. Lewis) US:LP = MCA 324* [Roger Williams]

426 Bay of Angels [La Baie de Anges] (1963) Highlights (Michel Legrand) FR:EP = Philips 432.885

427 Bay of Naples *see* It Started in Naples

428 Bayou *see* Poor White Trash

429 Be Sick, It's Free [Il Medico della Mutua] (1968) Highlights (Piero Piccioni) IT:LP = Durium 77242*

430 Be Yourself (1930) Excerpts (various) US:LP-BP = Fanett 146 [Fanny Brice:ST]

431 Beach Blanket Bingo (1965) Score (Jerry Styner) US:LP = Capitol T-2323/ST-2323* [Donna Loren:ST]

432 Beach Girls, The (1982) Score

(s:Michael Lloyd/t:John D'Andrea) US: LP = Peter Pan TAS-12116*

433 Beach Party (1963) Highlights (e:Roger Christian & Gary Usher/t: Jerry Styner) US:LP = Buena Vista BV-3316/ST-3316* [Annette:ST]; Theme/ US:SP = Chancellor 302 [Frankie Avalon:ST]

434 Beach Party—Italian Style *see* Eighteen in the Sun

435 Beach Red (1967) Theme (E. Vid) US:SP = UA 50204 [Jean Wallace: ST]

436 Bear and the Doll, The [L'Ours et la Poupee] (1971) Highlights (t:Eddy Vartan/etc.) FR:EP = Riviera 231.364

437 Bear Country [Short] (1953) Excerpts (Paul Smith) US:LP = Disneyland WDL-4011 [Paul Smith:ST]

438 Bears, The [Peau de les Ouces] (1965) Highlights (Jean Prodromides) FR:EP = Philips 432.526

439 Beast from 20,000 Fathoms, The (1953) Sequence + Dialog (David Buttolph) IT:LP-BP = Blu 15001 [@ST]

440 Beast Within, The (1982) Themes (Les Baxter) US:SP-PP = Bax M-1* [Ronny Cox:ST]; Theme (Les Baxter) US:LP-BP = Disc 105* [@Ronny Cox:ST]

441 Beastmaster, The (1982) Score (Lee Holdridge) US:LP = Varese STV-81174*

442 Beat Generation, The (1959) Themes (Walter Kent/Louis Armstrong) US:SP = MGM 12809 [Louis Armstrong: ST]; Theme (Walter Kent) US:SP = Dot 15970 [Mamie Van Doren:ST]

443 Beat Girl [Wild for Kicks] (1960) Score (e:John Barry/etc.) GB: LP = Columbia 335-X-1125 + GB:LP = Big Beat WIK-31; Theme (John Barry) US:SP = Cub 9074 [Adam Faith:ST]

444 Beat Street (1984) Score-A (various) US:LP = Atlantic 80154-1*; Score-B (various) US:LP = Atlantic 80158-1*

445 Beau Hunks [Short] (1931) Theme/US:LP = Mark 56 #579 [Laurel & Hardy:ST]

446 Beau James (1957) Score (t:Joseph J. Lilley/etc.) US:LP = Imperial LP-9041

447 Beau Pere (1981) Score (Philippe Sarde) FR:LP = General Music 803.025*

448 Beauties of the Night [Les Belles de Nuit] (1952) Theme (Georges Van Parys) GB:78 = Philips 149 [Geraldo]

449 Beautiful Blonde from Bashful Bend, The (1949) Theme (Lionel Newman) US:SP = RCA 47-2912 [Tex Beneke]

450 Beautiful People, The (1974) Themes (Lex DeAzevedo) US:SP = Amor 102 [Peggy Clinger/Lex DeAzevedo:ST]

451 Beautiful Stranger *see* Twist of Fate

452 Beaver Valley [Short] (1950) Excerpts (Paul Smith) US:LP = Disneyland WDL-4011 [Paul Smith:ST]

453 Bebo's Girl [La Ragazza di Bube] (1964) Score (Carlo Rustichelli) US:LP = Capitol T-2316/ST-2316*

454 Because of Him (1945) Themes/US:LP = Decca 75289 [Deanna Durbin:ST]; Theme (Miklos Rozsa) US: LP = Varese 704.260* [Elmer Bernstein]

455 Because They're Young (1960) Theme-A (Dave Appell) US:SP = Cameo 175 [Bobby Rydell:ST]; Theme-B (Duane Eddy) US:SP = Jamie 1151 [Duane Eddy: ST]; Theme-C (Bert Gold) US:SP = Colpix 142 [James Darren:ST]; Themes-B-C (Bert Gold/Duane Eddy) US:LP = Jamie 3026* [Duane Eddy:ST]

456 Because You're Mine (1952) Highlights (e:Nicholas Brodszky/etc.) US:LP-10 = RCA LM-7015 [Mario Lanza:ST]

457 Becket (1964) Score (Laurence Rosenthal) US:LP = Decca DL-9117/ DL-79117*

458 Bedazzled (1967) Score (Dudley Moore) US:LP = London MS-82009*

459 Bedknobs and Broomsticks (1971) Score (Richard and Robert Sherman) US:LP = Buena Vista BV-5003*

460 Bedtime Story, A (1933) Themes/US:LP-BP = JJA 19811 [@ Maurice Chevalier:ST]

461 Bedtime Story, A (1964) Theme (Hans J. Salter) US:SP = Decca 9-31642 [Sammy Kaye]

462 Been Down So Long, It Looks Like Up to Me (1971) Theme (Garry Sherman) US:LP = Capitol 11405* [The Manhattan Transfer]

463 Before Winter Comes (1969)

Theme (Ron Grainer) GB:LP = RCA 1020* [Ron Grainer:ST]

464 Beginning of the End (1957) Theme (Albert Glasser) US:LP = Starlog 1001 [Albert Glasser:ST]

465 Behind the Great Wall (1959) Score (folk music) US:LP = Monitor 525

466 Behold a Pale Horse (1964) Score (Maurice Jarre) US:LP = Colpix CP-519/SCP-519*

467 Bel Ami *see* Private Affairs of Bel Ami, The

468 Believe in Me (1971) Theme (Fred Karlin) US:SP = MGM 14349 + US:SP = MGM 1005 [Lou Rawls:ST]; Theme (Fred Karlin) US:LP = MGM 4809* [Lou Rawls:ST]

469 Belizaire the Cajun (1985) Score (e:Howard Shore/e:Michael Doucet) US:LP = Arhoolie 5038*

470 Bell, Book and Candle (1958) Score-A (George Duning) US:LP = Colpix CP-502 + US:LP = Citadel CT-6006 + US:LP = Citadel CTV-7006; Score-B (George Duning) US:LP = Citadel CTV-7006-S*

471 Bell Jar, The (1979) Theme (Janis Ian) US:SP = Columbia 3-10979* [Janis Ian:ST]; Theme (Janis Ian) US: LP = Columbia 36139* [Janis Ian:ST]

472 Belladonna (1973) Score (Masahiko Sato) IT:LP = Cinevox 33/90*

473 Bellboy, The (1960) Themes (Walter Scharf) US:SP = Dot 16115 [Walter Scharf:ST]

474 Belle de Jour (1967) Theme (Michel Magne) FR:LP = Sonopresse 63070* (Michel Magne:ST]

475 Belle le Grand (1951) Theme (Leo Shuken) US:LP = Decca 8060 [Victor Young:ST]

476 Belle of New York, The (1952) Highlights (Harry Warren) US:LP-10 = MGM E-108 + US:LP = DRG DS-15004

477 Belle of the Nineties (1934) Themes/US:78 = RCA/Victor 24651 [Duke Ellington:ST]; Theme/US:78 = Biltmore 1014 [Mae West:ST]

478 Belle of the Yukon (1944) Theme-A/US:78 = RCA/Victor 20-1611 [Dinah Shore:ST]; Theme-B/US:78 = RCA/Victor 20-1617 [Dinah Shore:ST]; Theme-C/US:78 = RCA/Victor 20-1622 [Dinah Shore:ST]

479 Bellissima (1951) Theme (Franco Mannino) JA:LP-MS = CBS/Sony 2301 [@ST]

480 Bells Are Ringing (1960) Score (stage songs: Jule Styne) US:LP = Capitol W-1435/SW-1435* + US:LP = DRG SL-8120*

481 Bells of St. Mary's, The (1945) Excerpts (folk music) US:LP-10 = Decca DL-5052 + US:LP = Decca DL-4258 [Bing Crosby:ST]

482 Beloved Infidel (1959) Theme (Franz Waxman) US:SP = Sure 101 [Tony Faro]

483 Beloved Vagabond (1936) Excerpts (various) US:LP-BP = Caliban 6013 [@ST]

484 Belstone Fox, The [Free Spirit] (1973) Score (Laurie Johnson) GB:LP = Ronco RR-2006*

485 Ben (1972) Theme (Walter Scharf) US:SP = Motown 61234 + US: SP = Motown 1207 [Michael Jackson: ST]; Theme (Walter Scharf) US:LP = Motown 755* [Michael Jackson:ST]; Theme (Walter Scharf) US:LP = Kapp 3671* [Roger Williams]

486 Ben-Gurion (1971) Theme (Wilfred Josephs) GB:LP = Polydor 2383.294* [Marcus Dods:ST]

487 Ben-Hur (1926) Excerpts [Silent I] (William Axt & David Mendoza) US:LP = Pelican LP-2011* [Gaylord Carter]

488 Ben-Hur (1959) Score-A (Miklos Rozsa) US:LP = London SPC-21166* [Miklos Rozsa:ST]; Score-B (Miklos Rozsa) US:LP = MGM 1E-1/1SE-1* [Carlo Savina]; Score-B (Miklos Rozsa) US:LP = Lion L-70123/L-770123* [Eric Kloss]; Score-C (Miklos Rozsa) US: LP = MGM E- 3900/SE-3900* [Miklos Rozsa-aka-Eric Kloss:ST]

489 Bend of the River [Where the River Bends] (1952) Highlights (Hans J. Salter) US:LP-MS-BP = Tony Thomas TTHS-1/2; Excerpts (Hans J. Salter) US: LP = Medallion 313 [Hans J. Salter:ST]

490 Beneath the Planet of the Apes (1970) Highlights + Dialog (Leonard Rosenman) US:LP = Amos AAS-8001*

491 Beneath the 12-Mile Reef (1953) Excerpts (Bernard Herrmann) US:LP = RCA ARL1-0707* [Charles Gerhardt]

492 Benji (1974) Score (Euel Box) US:LP = Epic KSE-33010*

493 Benny Goodman Story, The (1955) Scores (pop music) US:LP-MS = Decca DL-8252/DL-78252* + US:LP-MS = MCA 4055*

494 Benvenuta (1983) Score (Frederick Devreese) FR:LP = Milan A-214*

495 Berlin Affair, The (1986) Score (Pino Donaggio) FR:LP = Milan A-286*

496 Bernadine (1957) Themes-A-B/ US:SP = Dot 15570 [Pat Boone:ST]; Themes-C-D/US:EP = Dot 1057 [Pat Boone:ST]

497 Bespoke Overcoat, The (1969) Underscore + Dialog (Les Reed) GB:LP = Golden Guinea GGS-0145*

498 Best Foot Forward (1943) Highlights (stage songs: Hugh Martin & Ralph Blane) US:LP-BP = Caliban 6039

499 Best Friends (1975) Theme (Rick Cunha) US:SP = Columbia 3-10174 [Rick Cunha:ST]

500 Best Friends (1982) Theme (Michel Legrand) US:SP = WB 7-29618* [James Ingram:ST]; Theme (Michel Legrand) US:LP = WB 23970-1* [James Ingram:ST]

501 Best Little Whorehouse in Texas, The (1982) Score (t:Dolly Parton/ stage songs:Carol Hall) US:LP = MCA 6112*

502 Best Man, The (1964) Theme (Mort Lindsey) US:SP = UA 717 [Jon Early]

503 Best of Enemies, The [I Due Nemici] (1961) Themes (Nino Rota) IT: SP = RCA 45-3032 [ST]

504 Best of Everything, The (1959) Theme (Alfred Newman) US:SP = Columbia 4-41491 [Johnny Mathis:ST]; Theme (Alfred Newman) US:LP = Columbia 1421/8218* [Johnny Mathis:ST]; Theme (Alfred Newman) US:LP = RCA 1-0184* [Charles Gerhardt]

505 Best Revenge, The (1985) Score (Keith Emerson) GB:LP = Chord 1*

506 Best Things in Life Are Free, The (1956) Score (pop music) US:LP = Capitol T-765 [Gordon MacRae:ST]

507 Best Years of Our Lives, The (1946) Score (Hugo Friedhofer) US: LP = Entracte EDP-8101* [Frank Collura]

508 Betia, La (1971) Score (Armando Trovajoli) IT:LP = RCA SP-8043*

509 Betrayal (1978) Score (s:Teo Macero/t:Janis Ian) US:LP = Inner City 4001*

510 Betrayed (1954) Theme (Walter Goehr) US:SP = MGM 30859 [Diana Coupland]

511 Betsy, The (1978) Theme (John Barry) US:LP-BP = GSF 1002 [@John Barry:ST]

512 Better Off Dead (1985) Score (Rupert Hine) US:LP = A&M SP-5071*

513 Betty Blue (1986) Score (Gabriel Yared) GB:LP = Virgin V-2396*

514 Betty Boop Scandals of 1974 (1974) Highlights + Dialog (pop music) US:LP = Mark 56 #658

515 Between Two Worlds (1944) Themes (Erich Wolfgang Korngold) US: LP = RCA 3330* + US:LP = RCA 1-3707* [Charles Gerhardt]; Theme (Erich Wolfgang Korngold) US:LP = Citadel 7010* [Albert Dominguez]

516 Beverly Hills Cop (1984) Score-A (t:Harold Faltermeyer/s:various) US: LP = MCA 5547*; Theme-B ["Shoot Out"] (Harold Faltermeyer) US:SP = MCA 52521* [Harold Faltermeyer:ST]; Theme-C ["Discovery"] (Harold Faltermeyer) US:SP = MCA 52594* [Harold Faltermeyer:ST]

517 Beware! The Blob [Son of Blob] (1972) Themes (Mort Garson) US: SP = Verve 10675 [The Blobs:ST]; Theme (Mort Garson) US:LP-BP = POO 106 [@The Blobs:ST]

518 Beyond Good and Evil [Beyond Evil] [Al Di la de Bene e del Male] (1978) Score (Daniele Paris) IT: LP = CAM SAG-9082*

519 Beyond Mombassa (1956) Themes (Monty Norman/Bill Ryder) US:SP = Capitol 3757 [Eddie Calvert]

520 Beyond the Blue Horizon (1942) Excerpts (various) US:LP-BP = Caliban 6033 [@ST]

521 Beyond the Door [Diabolica] [Chi Sei] (1975) Score (Franco Micalizzi) IT:LP = CAM SAG-9062*

522 Beyond the Door #2 [Schock] (1980) Score (Libra) IT:LP = Cinevox 33/113*

523 Beyond the Forest (1949) Score (Max Steiner) US:LP-BP = Citadel CTMS-8; Excerpts (Max Steiner) US: LP = RCA ARL1-0183* + US:LP = RCA AGL1-3706* [Charles Gerhardt]

524 Beyond the Great Wall (1964) Score (folk music) US:LP = Capitol T-10401/ST-10401e

525 Beyond the Limit [The Honorary Consul] (1984) Theme (Paul McCartney) GB:SP = Island 155* [John Williams]; Theme (Paul McCartney) GB: LP-MS = Filmtrax 820-252-1* [@John Williams]

526 Beyond the Moon *see* Gulliver's Travels Beyond the Moon

527 Beyond the Valley of the Dolls (1970) Score (Stu Phillips) US:LP = 20th S-4211*

528 Bible, The (1966) Score-A (Toshiro Mayuzumi) US:LP = 20th 4184/S-4184*; Score-B (Toshiro Mayuzumi) IT:LP = RCA PSL-10420*

529 Biches, Les (1968) Score (Pierre Jansen) IT:LP = Cinevox 33/15; Theme (Pierre Jansen) US:LP = Capitol 287* [Don Randi]

530 Bicyclettes de Belsize, Les (1969) Highlights (Les Reed) GB:LP = Polydor 583.728*; Theme (Les Reed) US:SP = Capitol 2516* [Andy Russell]; Theme (Les Reed) US:LP = Parrot 71067* [Engelbert Humperdinck]

531 Bidone, Il [The Swindle] (1955) Score (Nino Rota) IT:LP-MS = CAM 500.001; Theme (Nino Rota) US:LP = Hannibal 9301* [William Fischer]

532 Big Bad Wolf, The (1966) Highlights + Dialog (Milton DeLugg) US:LP = Camden CAL-1087/CAS-1087*

533 Big Beat, The (1958) Highlights (various) US:EP = RCA EPA-4185 [Gogi Grant:ST]

534 Big Boss, The *see* Fists of Fury

535 Big Bounce, The (1969) Score (Mike Curb) US:LP = WB WS-1781*

536 Big Boy (1930) Excerpts (various) US:LP-BP = A Jay 3749 [Al Jolson:ST]

537 Big Brawl, The [Battle Creek Brawl] (1980) Score (Lalo Schifrin) JA: LP = RCA/Victor VIP-28006*; Theme (Lalo Schifrin) US:LP = CTI 1121* [Jimmy Smith]

538 Big Broadcast, The (1932) Score (various) US:LP-BP = Soundtrak STK-101

539 Big Broadcast of 1936, The (1935) Theme-A/US:LP = Encore 101 [Ethel Merman:ST]; Theme-B/US:LP-BP = JJA 19811 [@Bing Crosby:ST]; Themes-C-D/US:78 = RCA/Victor 25105 [Ray Noble:ST]; Themes-E-F/US:78 = Melotone 351001 [Jack Oakie:ST]

540 Big Broadcast of 1937, The (1936) Theme-A/US:LP-BP = JJA 19811 [@Shirley Ross:ST]; Themes-B-C/US: 78 = RCA/Victor 25467 [Benny Good-man:ST]

541 Big Broadcast of 1938, The (1938) Excerpts (Ralph Rainger) US:LP-BP = JJA 19811 [@ST]

542 Big Business (1934) Theme-A (John Green) GB:78 = Parlophone 7135 [Gertrude Lawrence:ST]; Theme-B (John Green) GB:78 = Columbia 1379 [John Green:ST]

543 Big Chief, The (1960) Theme (Gerard Calvi) FR:SP = Vogue 8299 [ST]

544 Big Chill, The (1983) Score (pop music) US:LP = Motown 6062-ML*; Highlights (pop music) US:LP = Motown 6094-ML*

545 Big Circus, The (1959) Score (e:Paul Sawtell & Bert Shefter/e:Roy Webb/t:Sammy Fain) US:LP = Todd 5001/S-5001*

546 Big City, The (1948) Highlights (various) US:78-MS = MGM LA-23 [Betty Garrett:ST]; Highlights (various) US:78-MS = RCA/Victor MO-1226 [Lotte Lehmann:ST]

547 Big City Paper [Industrial Short] Score (uncredited) US:LP-PP = Chicago Tribune 28136

548 Big Country, The (1958) Score (Jerome Moross) US:LP = UA UAL-40004/UAS-5004e + US:LP = UA LA-270e; Highlights (Jerome Moross) US:LP-BP = Temple TLP-2001

549 Big Day, The *see* Jour de Fete

550 Big Deal at Dodge City *see* Big Hand for the Little Lady, A

551 Big Fella (1937) Theme-A/GB: 78 = HMV 8591 [Paul Robeson:ST]; Themes-B-C/GB:78 = HMV 8607 [Paul Robeson:ST]; Themes-D-E/GB:LP = WRC 328 [Elizabeth Welch:ST]

552 Big Game, The [La Macchina della Violenza] (1976) Score (Francesco DeMasi) IT:LP = Beat LPF-019*

553 Big Gundown, The (1968) Score (Ennio Morricone) US:LP = UA UAS-5190* + US:LP = UA LA-297*

554 Big Hand for the Little Lady, A [Big Deal at Dodge City] (1966) Theme (David Raksin) US:LP = Command 5005* [Enoch Light]; Theme (David Raksin) US:LP = Reprise 6219* [Don Ho]; Theme (David Raksin) US: LP = Discovery 894* [Charlie Shoemake]

555 Big Hunt, The [La Grande Caccia] [L'Ultime Grida dalle Savana] (1974) Score (Carlo Savina) IT:LP = CAM SAG-9061*; Theme (Carlo Savina) US:LP = RCA 1-5016* [Ettore Stratta]

556 Big Jake (1979) Highlights (Elmer Bernstein) US:LP = Varese 704.350* [Elmer Bernstein:ST]

557 Big Knife, The (1956) Highlights (Frank DeVol) US:SP-MS-PP = Columbia ZTST-23721/4

558 Big Land, The [Stampeded] (1957) Theme (Leonard Rosenman) US: SP = Capitol 3640 [Tex Ritter]; Theme (Leonard Rosenman) US:LP = Capitol 971 [Tex Ritter]; Theme (Leonard Rosenman) US:LP = Liberty 3050 [Myrna Fox]

559 Big Mo *see* Maurie

560 Big Night, The (1960) Theme (Randy Sparks) US:SP = Verve 10196 [Randy Sparks:ST]

561 Big Operator, The (1959) Theme (Van Alexander) US:SP = Capitol 4258 [Van Alexander:ST]; Theme (Van Alexander) US:LP-BP = Cinema 8002 [@Van Alexander:ST]

562 Big Pond, The (1930) Theme/ US:LP = MGM 3702 [Maurice Chevalier:ST]

563 Big Red (1962) Theme + Narration (Richard & Robert Sherman) US: LP = Disneyland 1916; Theme (Richard & Robert Sherman) US:SP = Buena Vista 402 [Camarata]

564 Big Show, The [Short] Sequence + Narration (Arthur Kleiner) US:LP = Picture Book Parade 108 [@ST]

565 Big Sky, The (1952) Excerpts (Dimitri Tiomkin) US:LP = RCA ARL1-1669* [Charles Gerhardt]

566 Big Sleep, The (1946) Excerpts-A (Max Steiner) US:LP-BP = Cinema 8001 [@Charles Gerhardt]; Excerpts-B (Max Steiner) US:LP = RCA ARL1-0136* [Charles Gerhardt]

567 Big Store, The (1941) Theme/ US:EP = RCA 455 [Tony Martin:ST]; Theme/GB:LP = Ace of Hearts 68 [Tony Martin:ST]

568 Big Time (1979) Score (s: Smokey Robinson/as:Sonny Burke) US: LP = Tamla T6-355*

569 Big Trouble in Little China (1986) Score (John Carpenter) US:LP = Enigma SJ-73227*

570 Big Wednesday (1978) Theme (Basil Poledouris) US:LP-BP = Disc 105* [@Film Studio Orchestra]

571 Biggest Bear, The [Short] Sequence + Narration (Arthur Kleiner) US:LP = Picture Book Parade 104 [@ST]

572 Biggest Bundle of Them All, The (1968) Score (Riz Ortolani) US:LP = MGM E-4446/SE-4446*

573 Biggles (1986) Score (Stanislas Syrewicz) GB:LP = MCA 3328*

574 Bikini Beach (1964) Highlights (Jerry Styner) US:LP = Buena Vista BV-3324/ST-3324* [Annette:ST]

575 Bilitis (1977) Score (Francis Lai) JA:LP = Seven Seas FML-78*; Theme (Francis Lai) US:LP = London 30001* [Stanley Black]; Theme (Francis Lai) US:LP = Phonogram 1-3817* [Zamfir]

576 Bill of Divorcement, A [The Right to Love] (1932) Theme (Max Steiner) US:LP = RCA 1170 [Max Steiner:ST]; Theme (Max Steiner) US: LP = Citadel 7010* [Albert Dominguez]

577 Billboard Girl [Short] (1932) Excerpts (various) US:LP = Biograph BLP-M1 [Bing Crosby:ST]

578 Billie (1965) Score (e:Dominic Frontiere/etc.) US:LP = UA UAL-4131/ UAS-5131*

579 Billion Dollar Brain (1967) Score (Richard Rodney Bennett) US: LP = UA UAL-4171/UAS-5171*

580 Billy Jack (1971) Score (e:Mundell Lowe/etc.) US:LP = WB

BS-1926* + US:LP = Billy Jack BJS-1001*

581 Billy Liar (1963) Theme (Richard Rodney Bennett) US:LP = Atco 33-170* [Acker Bilk]

582 Billy Rose's Diamond Horseshoe (1945) Highlights (Harry Warren) US:LP-BP = Caliban 6028

583 Billy Rose's Jumbo [Jumbo] (1962) Score (stage songs: Richard Rodgers) US:LP = Columbia OL-5860/OS-2260* + US:LP = CSP AOS-2260*

583a Billy the Kid Returns (1938) Theme/US:LP = Columbia 38907 [Roy Rogers:ST]

584 Bim (1977) Score (Andre Tanker) US:LP-PP = Bim 1*

585 Bingo Long Traveling All-Stars and Motor Kings, The (1976) Score (William Goldstein) US:LP = MCA 2094*

586 Bird of Paradise (1932) Highlights + Underscore + Dialog (Max Steiner) US:LP-MS = Medallion 305/6; Highlights (Max Steiner) US:LP = Medallion 309

587 Bird of Paradise, The (1951) Theme (Ken Darby) US:LP = Decca 79048* [Alfred Newman]

588 Bird with the Crystal Plumage, The (1970) Score-A (Ennio Morricone) US:LP = Capitol SW-642*; Score-B (Ennio Morricone) US:LP = Cerberus CEMS-0108*

589 Birdman of Alcatraz (1962) Score (Elmer Bernstein) US:LP-BP = BOA 101; Theme (Elmer Bernstein) US:SP = Choreo 109 [Elmer Bernstein:ST]

590 Birds and the Bees, The (1956) Theme-A (Harry Warren) US:SP = RCA 47-6483 [George Gobel:ST]; Theme-A (Harry Warren) US:SP = Coral 9-61625 [Alan Dale]; Theme-B (Walter Scharf) US:SP = Decca 9-30026 [Victor Young]

591 Birds Do It (1966) Theme (Howard Greenfield) US:SP = Epic 5-10042 [Rowan & Martin]

592 Birds of a Feather [Cartoon] (1965) Sequence + Dialog (Clarence Wheeler) US:LP = Peter Pan 1120 [@ST]

593 Birds, the Bees, and the Italians, The (1967) Score (Carlo Rustichelli) US:LP = UA UAL-4157/UAS-5157*

594 Birdy (1984) Score (Peter Gabriel) US:LP = Geffen GHS-24070*

595 Biribi (1971) Score (Mikis Theodorakis) FR:LP = Tuba 8500*

596 Birth of a Nation (1915) Scores [Silent I] (Joseph Carl Breil) US:LP-MS = X LXDR-701/2* [Clyde Allen]; Excerpts [Silent II] (Lee Erwin) US:LP = Angel S-36092* [Lee Erwin:ST]

597 Birth of the Blues (1941) Excerpts (various) US:LP = Decca DL-4255 [Bing Crosby:ST]

598 Biscuit Eater, The (1972) Theme (Shane Tatum) US:SP = Buena Vista 488 [Shane Tatum:ST]

599 Bishop's Wife, The (1947) Theme (Emil Newman) US:SP = Capitol 1627 [Nat King Cole]

600 Bite the Bullet (1975) Score (Alex North) US:LP-BP = RFO 102

601 Bitter Harvest (1963) Theme (Laurie Johnson) US:LP = Atco 33-158* [Acker Bilk]; Theme (Laurie Johnson) US:LP = Colpix 471* [Laurie Johnson: ST]

602 Bitter Harvest [Short] Underscore + Dialog (Alfred Ramirez) US:LP-PP = Orange Tree BH-101

603 Bitter Rice (1950) Excerpts (Goffredo Petrassi) US:LP = MGM E-3485 [Robert Ashley]

604 Bitter Springs [Savage Justice] (1950) Theme (Ernest Irving) GB:78-PP = Rank FM-104 [ST]; Theme (Ernest Irving) US:LP-BP = Citadel CTOFI-1 [@ST]

605 Bitter Sweet (1940) Score (stage songs: Noel Coward) US:LP-MS-BP = Sandy Hook 3SH-1

606 Bitter Victory (1950) *see* Paid in Full

607 Bizet's Carmen [Carmen] (1984) Scores (classical music) FR:LP-MS = RCA/Erato NUM-751133*; Score (classical music) US:LP = RCA/Erato HBC1-5302*

608 Black and Tan [Short] (1929) Excerpts (Duke Ellington) US:LP = Biograph BLPM-2 [@ST] + US:LP-BP = Sandy Hook 2068 [@ST]

609 Black and White in Color (1977) Score (Pierre Bachelet) US:LP = Buddah BDS-5698*

610 Black Belly of the Tarantula, The [La Tarantola dal Ventre Nero] (1972) Highlights (Ennio Morricone) US:LP = Cerberus CEMS-0116*

611 Black Belt Jones (1974) Themes (Dennis Coffey) US:SP = WB 7769 [Dennis Coffey:ST]

612 Black Caeser [The Godfather of Harlem] (1973) Score (s:James Brown/t:Barry DeVorzon) US:LP = Polydor PD-6014*

613 Black Cauldron, The (1985) Score (Elmer Bernstein) US:LP = Varese STV-81253*

614 Black Emanuelle (1977) Score (Nico Fidenco) US:LP = West End 100*

615 Black Fist (1976) Score (Warren Sams) US:LP = Happy Fox 1101*

616 Black Friday (1940) Themes (Hans J. Salter) US:LP = Citadel 6026 + US:LP = Citadel 7012 [Hans J. Salter:ST]

617 Black Girl (1972) Score (Ray Shanklin & Ed Bogas) US:LP = Fantasy 9420*

618 Black Hole, The (1979) Score (John Barry) US:LP = Buena Vista 5008*

619 Black Joy (1977) Score (pop music) GB:LP = Ronco RTL-2025

620 Black Klansman, The [I Crossed the Color Line] (1966) Themes (Tony Harris) US:SP = SSS 45-132* [Tony Harris:ST]

621 Black Knight, The (1954) Theme (J. Maguire) US:SP = Decca 9-29358 [Jana Mason]

622 Black Narcissus (1947) Theme (Brian Easdale) GB:78-PP = Rank FM-18 [ST]

623 Black Orchid, The (1959) Score (Alessandro Cicognini) US:LP = Dot DLP-3178/DLP-25178*

624 Black Orpheus (1959) Score (Luis Bonfa & Antonio Carlos Jobim) US:LP = Epic LN-3672 + US:LP = Fontana MGF-27520/SRF-67520e

625 Black Pirate, The (1926) Theme [Silent II] (Charles Hofmann) US:LP = Sounds Good 1001 [Charles Hofmann:ST]

626 Black Shield of Falworth, The (1954) Excerpts (Hans J. Salter) US:LP = Medallion ML-312 [Hans J. Salter:ST]

627 Black Sleep, The (1956) Theme (Les Baxter) US:SP = GNP 114 [Tony Martinez]

628 Black Stallion, The (1979) Score (e:Carmine Coppola/e:Shirley Walker) US:LP = UA LOO-1040*

629 Black Stallion Returns, The (1983) Score (Georges Delerue) US:LP = Liberty LO-51144*

630 Black Starlet (1974) Highlights (Joe Hinton & Dee Erwin) US:EP = Act One AOP-001

631 Black Sunday (1960) Score (Les Baxter) US:LP = Bax LB-1000 [music erroneously credited to "Black Sabbath"]

632 Black Sunday (1977) Theme (John Williams) US:SP = Caribou 8-9022* [The Sweet Inspirations]; Theme (John Williams) US:LP = Pickwick 3582* [The Birchwood Pops]; Theme (John Williams) US:LP-BP = GSF 1002 [@John Williams:ST]

633 Black Tent, The (1956) Theme (William Alwyn) GB:78-PP = Rank FM-191 [ST]

634 Black Tights (1962) Score (classical music) US:LP = RCA FOC-3/FSO-3*

635 Black Zoo, The (1963) Theme (Russ Faith) US:SP = Chancellor 1137 [Russ Faith:ST]

636 Blackboard Jungle, The (1955) Theme (Charles Wolcott) US:SP = MGM 12726 [Charles Wolcott:ST]; Theme (Charles Wolcott) US:SP = Coral 9-61396 [Gloria Wood]; Theme (Charles Wolcott) US:LP = MGM 3220 [@C. Wolcott:ST]

637 Blackmailed (1951) Theme (John Wooldridge) GB:78-PP = Rank FM-108 [ST]

638 Blacula (1972) Score (Gene Page) US:LP = RCA LSP-4806*

639 Blade Runner (1982) Score (Vangelis) US:LP = WB/Full Moon 23748-1* [The New American Orchestra]

640 Blame It on Rio (1984) Score (Ken Wannberg) US:LP = Varese STV-81210*

641 Blanche Fury (1947) Theme-A (Clifton Parker) GB:78-PP = Rank FM-5 [ST]; Theme-B (Clifton Parker) GB:78-PP = Rank FM-6 [ST]

642 Blazing Magnum *see* Strange Shadows in an Empty Room

643 Blazing Saddles (1974) Highlights (e:John Morris/t:Mel Brooks) AU:LP = WB WS-2781*; Excerpts (t:John Morris/t:Mel Brooks) US:LP = Asylum 5E-501* [ST]

644 Bless the Beasts and Children

(1971) Score (Perry Botkin, Jr. & Barry DeVorzon) US:LP = A&M SP-4322*

645 Blind Date (1959) *see* Chance Meeting

646 Blind Date (1984) Score-A (e: Stanley Myers/e:John Kongos) US: LP = Varese STV-81202*; Score-B (s:John Kongos/t:Stanley Myers) GB: LP = Audiotrax ATXLP-01*

647 Blind Goddess, The (1948) Theme (Bernard Grun) GB:78-PP = Rank FM-29 [ST]

648 Bliss of Mrs. Blossom, The (1968) Score (Riz Ortolani) US:LP = RCA LSP-4080*

649 Blithe Spirit (1945) Theme (Richard Addinsell) US:SP = Decca 9-28882 [Camarata]; Theme (Richard Addinsell) US:LP = Mercury 60238* [Clebanoff]; Theme (Richard Addinsell) US: LP = RCA 2608* [George Melachrino]

650 Blob, The (1958) Theme (Burt Bacharach) US:SP = Columbia 4-41250 [The 5 Blobs:ST]; Theme (Burt Bacharach) US:LP-BP = POO 104 [@The 5 Blobs:ST]; Theme (Burt Bacharach) US:LP = Rhino 307 [@The 5 Blobs:ST]

651 Block, The / Theme (J. DeKnight) US:SP = Crosley 341 [Joan Weber]

652 Block Busters (1944) Underscore + Dialog (Edward J. Kay) US:LP-MS = Murray Hill 57385

653 Blonde Sinner, The [Yield to the Night] (1956) Theme (Ray Martin) GB:SP = Columbia 5258 [Ray Martin]

654 Blonde Venus (1932) Themes-A-B/US:LP-BP = Wildebeest 5290 [Marlene Dietrich:ST]; Themes-B-C/ US:LP-BP = JJA 19806 [@Marlene Dietrich:ST]

655 Blondy (1974) Score (Stelvio Cipriani) FR:LP = Pathe CO66.14269*

656 Blood and Black Lace [Sei Donne per l'Assassino] (1964) Themes (Carlo Rustichelli) IT:SP = CAM CA-2559 [ST]

657 Blood and Roses [Et Mourir de Plaisir] (1960) Highlights (Jean Prodromides) FR:EP = Fontana 460.713

658 Blood and Sand (1941) Highlights (Vicente Gomez) US:LP-10 = Decca DL-5380 + US:LP = Decca DL-8279/DL-78279e + US:LP = Varese STV-81117; Excerpts (t:Alfred Newman/t:Vicente Gomez/etc.) US:LP = London 44225* [Stanley Black]

659 Blood Feast (1963) Highlights (Herschell Gordon Lewis) US:LP = Rhino RNSP-305

660 Blood Feud [Fatto di Sangue Fra Due Uomini per Causa di una Vedova] (1980) Score (Nando DeLuca & Dangio) IT:LP = RCA NL-31434*

661 Blood for Dracula *see* Andy Warhol's Dracula

662 Blood in the Streets [Revolver] (1973) Score (Ennio Morricone) IT:LP = General Music 55496*

663 Blood Money *see* Requiem for a Heavyweight

664 Blood on the Sun (1945) Score (Miklos Rozsa) US:LP = Citadel 6031

665 Blood Relatives [Les Liens de Sang] (1980) Highlights (Pierre Jansen) FR:LP = Pema 900.062*

666 Blood River [Dio Perdone, Io No] (1967) Themes (Carlo Rustichelli) IT:SP = CAM AMP-31 [ST]

666a Blood Simple (1985) Highlights (Carter Burwell) US:LP = Varese STV-81318*

667 Blood, Sweat and Fear[Mark, il Poliziotto] (1975) Score (Stelvio Cipriani) IT:LP = Cinevox 33/91*

668 Bloodline [Sidney Sheldon's Bloodline] (1979) Score (Ennio Morricone) US:LP = Varese STV-81131*

669 Bloodnight (1982) Highlights (Yan Tregger) IT:LP = Jonathan ATO-28005*

670 Bloody Judge, The *see* Night of the Blood Monster

671 Bloody Mama (1970) Score (Don Randi) US:LP = American International A-1029*

672 Bloomfield *see* Hero, The

673 Blow Out (1973) *see* La Grande Bouffe

674 Blow Out (1981) Score (Pino Donaggio) JA:LP=Polydor 25-MS-3071*

675 Blow Up (1966) Score (Herbie Hancock) US:LP = MGM E-4447/SE-4447*

676 Blowing Wild (1953) Theme (Dimitri Tiomkin) US:SP = Columbia 4-40079 [Frankie Laine:ST]

677 Blue (1968) Score (Manos Hadjidakis) US:LP = Dot DLP-25855*

678 Blue Angel, The (1931) Excerpts (Frederick Hollander) US:LP = Stanyan SR-10124 [Marlene Dietrich: ST]; Excerpts (Frederick Hollander) US:LP-BP = Caliban 6046 [@ST]

679 Blue Angel, The (1959) Theme (Jay Livingston & Ray Evans) US:SP = 20th 163 [May Britt:ST]

680 Blue Angels, The (1976) Score (Fred Myrow) JA:LP = TAM YX-5002*

681 Blue Bird, The (1940) Theme-A (Alfred Newman) US:SP = Decca 9-29567 [Alfred Newman:ST]; Theme-A (Alfred Newman) US:LP = Decca 8123 + US:LP = Vocalion 73749 + US:LP-BP = Capricorn 1286 [Alfred Newman: ST]; Theme-B/US:LP-MS = 20th 103 [Shirley Temple:ST]

682 Blue Bird, The (1976) Themes (Andre Petrov) JA:SP = Columbia 62* [ST]

683 Blue City (1986) Score (Ry Cooder) US:LP = WB 25386-1*

684 Blue Collar (1978) Score (Jack Nitzsche) US:LP = MCA 3034*

685 Blue-Eyed Bandit, The (1982) Score (Ennio Morricone) US:LP = Cerberus CEMS-0114*

686 Blue Gang, The (1973) Score (Tony Renis) IT:LP = Dischi ZSLN-55654*

687 Blue Gardenia, The (1953) Theme (Lester Lee) US:SP = Capitol 2389 [Nat King Cole:ST]; Theme (Lester Lee) US:LP = Capitol 2340 + US:LP = Capitol 11804 [Nat King Cole:ST]

688 Blue Hawaii (1961) Score (e:Sid Tepper & Roy Bennett/e:Ben Weisman/ etc.) US:LP = RCA LPM-2426/LSP-2426* + US:LP = RCA AYL1-3683* [Elvis Presley:ST]

689 Blue Lagoon, The (1949) Theme-A (Clifton Parker) GB:78-PP = Rank FM-57 [ST]; Theme-B (Clifton Parker) GB:78-PP = Rank FM-58 [ST]

690 Blue Lagoon, The (1980) Score (Basil Poledouris) US:LP = Marlin 2236*

691 Blue Max, The (1966) Score-A (Jerry Goldsmith) US:LP = Mainstream 56081/S-6081*; Score-B (Jerry Goldsmith) US:LP = Citadel CT-6008* + US:LP = Citadel CTV-7007*

692 Blue of the Night, The [Short] (1933) Excerpts (various) US:LP = Biograph BLP-M1 [Bing Crosby:ST]

693 Blue Rhythm [Cartoon] (1931) Theme (pop music) US:LP-MS = Ovation 5000 [@ST]

694 Blue Skies (1946) Score (Irving Berlin) US:LP-BP = Soundtrak STK-104; Highlights (Irving Berlin) US:LP-10 = Decca DL-5042 + US:LP = Decca DL-4259

695 Blue Thunder (1983) Score (Arthur B. Rubinstein) US:LP = MCA 6122*

696 Blue Velvet (1986) Score (Angelo Badalamenti aka Andy Badale) US:LP = Varese STV-81292*

697 Bluebeard (1972) Score (Ennio Morricone) US:LP = Cerberus CEMS-0105*

698 Blues, The (1968) Score (pop music) US:LP = Asch 101

699 Blues Brothers, The (1980) Score (pop music) US:LP = Atlantic SD-16017* [The Blues Brothers:ST]

700 Blues for Lovers [Ballad in Blue] (1966) Theme/US:SP = Atlantic 13033 + US:SP = Atlantic 1050 [Ray Charles:ST]

701 Boarding School [Passion Flower Hotel] [Deux Heures de Colle pour un Baiser] (1980) Score (Francis Lai) FR:LP = WB/WEA 56626*

702 Boat, The *see* Boot, Das

703 Bob and Carol and Ted and Alice (1969) Score (e:Quincy Jones/etc.) US:LP = Bell 1200*

704 Bob le Flambeur [Fever Heat] (1955) Theme (Eddie Barclay) US:LP = Mercury 20188 [Eddie Barclay:ST]

705 Bobbikins (1960) Theme (Max Bygraves) US:SP = London 45-1881 [Max Bygraves:ST]

706 Bobby Deerfield (1977) Score (Dave Grusin) US:LP = Casablanca NBLP-7071*

707 Bobo, The (1967) Score (Francis Lai) US:LP = WB W-1711/WS-1711*

708 Boccaccio '70 (1962) Score (e: Nino Rota/e:Armando Trovajoli) US: LP = RCA FOC-5/FSO-5*; Excerpts (Nino Rota) FR:LP = General Music 803.030* [Nino Rota:ST]

709 Body, The (1974) Score (Ron Geesin & Roger Waters) US:LP = Import IMP-1002*

710 Body Heat (1981) Score (John Barry) US:LP = X LXSE-1-002*

711 Body Love (1977) Score-A (Klaus Schulze) US:LP = Island ILPS-9510*; Score-B (Klaus Schulze) GB: LP = Metronome 60.047*

712 Body Rock (1984) Score (t:Sylvester Levay/etc.) US:LP = Capitol/EMI SO-17140*; Theme [Chilly D's Theme] (Sylvester Levay) US:SP = Capitol/EMI 8235* [Sylvester Levay:ST]; Theme [Fools Like Me] (Sylvester Levay) US:SP = Scotti Brothers 4-04686* [Lorenzo Lamas:ST]

713 Boeing Boeing (1965) Score (Neal Hefti) US:LP = RCA LOC-1121/LSO-1121*

714 Boheme, La (1926) Excerpts [Silent II] (Charles Hofmann) US:LP = Sounds Good SG-1001 [Charles Hofmann:ST]

715 Bolero (1934) Theme/US:LP-BP = JJA 19811 [@ST]

716 Bolero [Les Uns et les Autres] (1982) Scores (s:Michel Legrand/s:Francis Lai) FR:LP-MS = RCA PL-37512*; Score (e:Michel Legrand/e:Francis Lai) US:LP = Polydor PD1-6353*

717 Bolero (1984) Score (Peter Bernstein) US:LP = Varese STV-81228*

718 Bolshoi Ballet '67 (1966) Score (classical music) US:LP = Command S-11035*

719 Bon Plaisir, Le (1984) Score (Georges Delerue) FR:LP = RCA/MK 001*

720 Bon Voyage (1962) Theme (Richard & Robert Sherman) US:LP = Buena Vista 397 [Peggy King]

721 Bongo *see* Fun and Fancy Free

722 Bonjour Tristesse (1958) Score (Georges Auric) US:LP = RCA LOC-1040

723 Bonne Soupe, La (1964) Themes (Raymond Le Senechal) US: SP = 20th 483 [Les Scarabees]

724 Bonnie and Clyde (1967) Score (s:Charles Strouse/t:Earl Scruggs) US: LP = WB WS-1742*

725 Bonnie Prince Charlie (1948) Theme (Ian Whyte) GB:78 = Kalee/GB 10938 [Hubert Clifford]

726 Boogie Man, The (1980) Score (Tim Krog & Ed Christiano) US:LP-PP = SST 101*

727 Book of Numbers (1973) Score (Al Schackman) US:LP = Brut BTS-6002*

728 Boom! (1968) Score (s:John Barry/t:Johnny Dankworth) GB:LP = MCA 360*; Theme (Johnny Dankworth) US:SP = Epic 5-10546 [George Fame:ST]

729 Boot, Das [The Boat] (1982) Score (Klaus Doldinger) US:LP = Atlantic SD-19348*

730 Boot Hill [La Collina degli Stivali] (1969) Score (Carlo Rustichelli) IT:LP = Cinevox 33/28*

731 Bop Girl Goes Calypso (1957) Theme/US:SP = Decca 9-30344 [The Mary Kaye Trio:ST]

732 Bora Bora (1971) Score [USA Release] (Les Baxter) US:LP = American International A-1029*; Score [European Release] (Piero Piccioni) IT:LP = Cinevox 33/10*

733 Border, The (1981) Score (Ry Cooder) US:LP = MCA/Backstreet 6105*

734 Border Legion [Serial] Theme (William Lava) US:LP-PP = Cinemasound R-1001* [James King]

735 Borderlines *see* Caretakers, The

736 Born Again (1978) Score (Les Baxter) US:LP = Lamb & Lion LL-1041*

737 Born Free (1966) Score (John Barry) US:LP = MGM E-4368/SE-4368*

738 Born Losers (1967) Score (e: Mike Curb/t:Jerry Styner/t:Bob Summers/etc.) US:LP = Tower T-5082/ST-5082*

739 Born Reckless (1959) Theme/US:LP = Rhino 70819 [Mamie Van Doren:ST]

740 Born to Dance (1936) Score (Cole Porter) US:LP-BP = Classic International Filmusicals 3001

741 Borsalino (1970) Score (Claude Bolling) US:LP = Paramount PAS-5019* + US:LP-BP = Lumiere 1001*

742 Borsalino 2 [Borsalino and Co.] (1975) Score (Claude Bolling) FR: LP = Galloway 600.508*; Theme (Claude Bolling) US:LP = Stanyan 10113* [Rod McKuen]

743 Boss, The (1956) Theme (Albert Glasser) US:SP = Capitol 3574 [Lonnie Smith]

744 Bostonians, The (1984) Score (Richard Robbins) GB:LP = Audiotrax ATXLP-02*

745 Botany Bay (1953) Excerpts (Franz Waxman) US:LP = Varese 704.320* [Richard Mills]

746 Both Ends of the Candle *see* Helen Morgan Story, The

747 Bottom (1969) Theme (The Can) GB:LP = UA 29283* [The Can:ST]

748 Bottoms Up (1934) Theme/US: LP-BP = JJA 19806 [@John Boles:ST]

749 Boulevard Nights (1979) Score (Lalo Schifrin) US:LP = WB BSK-3328*

750 Boum, La (1980) Score (Vladimir Cosma) FR:LP = Barclay 960.030*

751 Boum II, La (1982) Score (Vladimir Cosma) FR:LP = Carrere 67953*

752 Boum sur Paris (1952) Theme (Gilbert Becaud) US:LP-MS = Atlantic 80153-1* [@Edith Piaf]

753 Bound for Glory (1976) Score (ae:Leonard Rosenman/etc.) US:LP = UA LA-695*

754 Bounty Hunters, The *see* Adios, Sabata

755 Bounty Killers, The *see* Ugly Ones, The

756 Bowery Champs (1944) Underscore + Dialog (Edward J. Kay) US:LP-MS = Murray Hill 57393

757 Boy, a Girl and a Bike, A (1949) Theme (Kenneth Pakeman) GB:78-PP = Rank FM-63 [ST]

758 Boy and the Pirates, The (1960) Excerpts (Albert Glasser) US:LP = Starlog SR-1001* [Albert Glasser:ST]

759 Boy Friend, The (1971) Score (stage songs: Sandy Wilson) US:LP = MGM 1SE-32*

760 Boy Named Charlie Brown, A (1970) Score (e:Rod McKuen/e:John Scott Trotter/etc.) US:LP = Columbia OS-3500*

761 Boy on a Dolphin (1957) Score (Hugo Friedhofer) US:LP = Decca DL-8580 + US:LP = Varese STV-81119; Theme-A (Hugo Friedhofer) US:SP = Liberty 55052 [Julie London:ST]; Theme-B (pop music) US:SP = RCA 53-0133 [Sophia Loren:ST]

762 Boy Ten Feet Tall, A [Sammy Going South] (1964) Theme (Les Baxter) US:SP = Arock 1011 [Marc Fredericks]; Theme (Les Baxter) US:SP = Prestige 45-345 [Morris Nanton]

763 Boy Who Could Fly, The (1986) Score (Bruce Broughton) US: LP = Varese STV-81299*

764 Boys, The (1962) Excerpts (The Shadows) GB:LP = MFP 50347* [The Shadows:ST]; Highlights (The Shadows) GB:EP = Columbia SEG-8193 [The Shadows:ST]

765 Boys, Boys / Themes (Fred Myrow) JA:SP = Seven Seas 49* [Fred Myrow:ST]

766 Boys from Brazil, The (1978) Score (Jerry Goldsmith) US:LP = A&M SP-4731*

767 Boys from Syracuse, The (1940) Excerpts (stage songs: Richard Rodgers) US:LP-MS-BP = Legends 1005/6 [Martha Raye:ST]

768 Boys in Brown (1950) Theme (Doreen Carwithen) GB:78-PP = Rank FM-86 [ST]

769 Boys' Night Out (1962) Theme-A (James Van Heusen) US:SP = Mercury 72013 [Patti Page:ST]; Theme-A (James Van Heusen) US:LP = Reprise 9-6079* [Les Baxter]; Theme-B (James Van Heusen) US:SP = Capitol 4799 [Vic Damone]

770 Boys of Paul Street, The (1968) Theme (Emil Petrovics) US:SP = Capitol 2618* [St. Luke's Boys Choir]

771 Brain, The [Le Cerveau] (1969) Highlights (Georges Delerue) FR:EP = Philips 370.806; Theme (Georges Delerue) US:SP = Acta 45-837* [The American Breed]

772 Brainstorm (1983) Score (James Horner) US:LP = Varese STV-81197*

773 Bramble Bush, The (1960) Theme (Leonard Rosenman) US:SP = WB 5148 [Don Ralke]

774 Brannigan (1975) Theme (Dominic Frontiere) US:SP = RCA 10255* [Danny Davis]; Theme (Dominic Frontiere) US:LP = RCA 1-1043* [Danny Davis]

775 Brass Target (1978) Score (Laurence Rosenthal) US:LP = Varese STV-81082*

776 Bravados, The (1958) Theme (Alfred Newman) US:LP = RCA 1-0184* + US:LP = RCA 1-4367* [Charles Gerhardt]

777 Brave and the Beautiful, The *see* Magnificent Matador, The

778 Brave Engineer, The [Cartoon] (1950) Theme + Dialog (Ken Darby) US:EP = RCA WY-400 [Jerry Colonna:ST]

779 Brave One, The (1956) Score (Victor Young) US:LP = Decca DL-8344 + US:LP = AEI 3107

780 Bravos II / Themes/US:SP = Parrot 3020* [Los Bravos:ST]

781 Bread and Chocolate [Pane e Cioccolata] (1978) Score (Daniele Patucchi) IT:LP = CAM SAG-9056*

782 Bread, Love And ... *see* Scandal in Sorrento

783 Bread, Love and Dreams [Pane, Amore e Fantasia] (1953) Theme (Alessandro Cicognini-aka-Icini) US:LP = UA 6360* [Riz Ortolani]

784 Bread, Love and Jealousy *see* Frisky

785 Break of Day (1976) Excerpts (George Dreyfus) AU:LP = WRC 5228* [George Dreyfus:ST]

786 Breaker Morant (1980) Score (as:Eric Cook & Jack Grimsley) US:LP = First American FA-7783*

787 Breakfast at Tiffany's (1961) Score (Henry Mancini) US:LP = RCA LPM-2362/LSP-2362*

788 Breakfast Club, The (1985) Score (Keith Forsey) US:LP = A&M SP-5045*

789 Breakfast in Hollywood (1946) Theme-A/US:78 = Capitol 234 [Andy Russell:ST]; Theme-B/US:78 = Capitol 239 [Nat King Cole:ST]

790 Breakheart Pass (1976) Score (Jerry Goldsmith) US:LP-BP = POO 101; Theme (Jerry Goldsmith) US:SP = UA 759* [Ferrante & Teicher]

791 Breakin' (1984) Score (various) US:LP = Polydor 821-919-1*

792 Breakin' 2—Electric Boogaloo (1984) Score (e:Ollie Brown/e:various) US:LP = Polydor 823-696-1*

793 Breaking Away (1979) Theme (Patrick Williams) US:LP = Columbia 36382* [Andre Kostelanetz & Patrick Williams:ST]

794 Breaking Glass (1980) Score (Hazel O'Connor) US:LP = A&M SP-4820*

795 Breaking Point, The (1950) Themes (Max Steiner) US:LP-BP = Tony Thomas TTMS-15 [Max Steiner: ST]

796 Breaking the Ice (1938) Themes-A-B/US:78 = Decca 1949 [Bobby Breen: ST]; Themes-C-D/US:78 = Decca 1950 [Bobby Breen:ST]

797 Breaking the Sound Barrier [The Sound Barrier] (1952) Excerpts (Malcolm Arnold) US:LP = Ariel CBF-13 [@Malcolm Arnold:ST]

798 Breath of Scandal, A (1960) Score (s:Alessandro Cicognini/t:Robert Stolz) US:LP = Imperial 9132/S-9132*

799 Breathless [A Bout de Souffle] (1960) Highlights (Martial Solal) FR:EP = Columbia 1306

800 Breezy (1973) Score (Michel Legrand) US:LP = MCA 384*

801 Bremen Town Musicians, The (1965) Highlights + Dialog (Milton DeLugg) US:LP = Golden LP-168

802 Brewster McCloud (1970) Score (e:Gene Page/e:John Philips/etc.) US:LP = MGM 1SE-28*

803 Brewster's Millions (1935) Themes/GB:LP = WRC 283 [Jack Buchanan:ST]

804 Bride, The (1985) Score (Maurice Jarre) US:LP = Varese STV-81254*

805 Bride of Frankenstein, The (1935) Theme (Franz Waxman) US:LP = RCA 1-0708* [Charles Gerhardt]; Theme-B (Franz Waxman) US:LP = Varese 704.320* [Richard Mills]; Underscore + Dialog (Franz Waxman) US:LP = Pelican 2006 ["Flash Gordon's Trip to Mars"]

806 Bride Wore Black, The [La Mariee Etait en Noir] (1967) Excerpts (Bernard Herrmann) US:LP-BP = Cinema LP-8006 [@ST]; Highlights (Bernard Herrmann) FR:EP = UA 36122

807 Bride Wore Red, The (1937) Theme/US:LP-BP = Curtain Calls 100/23 [Joan Crawford:ST]

808 Bride Wore Yolande, The [Industrial Short] Highlights (uncredited)

US:LP-PP = CSP/Chemstrand XTV-103047

809 Bridge at Remagen, The (1969) Theme (Elmer Bernstein) US:SP = UA 50581 [Leroy Holmes]; Theme (Elmer Bernstein) US:LP = UA 6731* [Leroy Holmes]; Theme (Elmer Bernstein) US:LP = Astro 1001* [@Elmer Bernstein:ST]

810 Bridge in the Jungle (1970) Score (Leroy Holmes) US:LP-PP = UA AH-137*

811 Bridge on the River Kwai, The (1957) Score (Malcolm Arnold) US:LP = Columbia CL-1100/CS-9426e

812 Bridge to the Sun [Pont Vers le Soleil] (1961) Theme (Georges Auric) US:SP = MGM 13036 [Leroy Holmes]; Theme (Georges Auric) US:LP = MGM 4064* + US:LP = UA 3988* [Leroy Holmes]

813 Bridge Too Far, A (1977) Score (John Addison) US:LP = UA LA-762*

814 Bridges at Toko-Ri, The (1955) Theme (Lyn Murray) US:SP = MGM 11914 [Leroy Holmes]; Theme (Lyn Murray) US:SP = Columbia 4-40455 [Liberace]; Theme (Lyn Murray) US:LP = Mercury 20156 + US:LP = Mercury 20301 [David Carroll]

815 Brief Season, A [Una Breve Stagione] (1969) Score (Ennio Morricone) IT:LP = Sagitterio 55001*

816 Brief Vacation, A [Una Breve Vacanza] (1974) Theme (Manuel DeSica) US:LP = Capitol 11657* [Joe Harnell]

817 Brigadoon (1954) Score (stage songs: Frederick Loewe) US:LP = MGM E-3135 + US:LP-MS = MGM 2SES-50e

818 Bright Eyes (1934) Theme/US:LP-MS = 20th 2-103 [Shirley Temple:ST]

819 Bright Road (1953) Theme (Millard Thomas) US:SP = RCA 47-0320 [Harry Belafonte:ST]

820 Brighton Beach Memoirs (1986) Score (Michael Small) US:LP = MCA 6193*

821 Brimstone and Treacle (1982) Score (Sting) US:LP = A&M SP-4915*

822 Bring on the Girls (1945) Theme-A/US:LP-BP = Legends 1000/2 [@ST]; Theme-B/US:78 = RCA/Victor 20-1654 [Spike Jones:ST]

823 Bring Your Smile Along (1955) Highlights (various) US:EP = Columbia B-2086 [Frankie Laine:ST]

824 Britannia of Billingsgate (1933) Theme/GB:LP = Ace of Clubs 1182 [@Violet Lorraine:ST]

825 Broadway Gondolier (1935) Excerpts (Harry Warren) US:LP-MS = Columbia C2L-44 [Dick Powell:ST]

826 Broadway Hostess (1935) Themes/US:78 = Columbia 3106 [Phil Regan:ST]

827 Broadway Melody (1929) Score + Dialog (Nacio Herb Brown) US:LP-MS = Mark 56 #847

828 Broadway Melody of 1936 (1935) Excerpts (Nacio Herb Brown) US:LP-BP = JJA 19802 [@ST]

829 Broadway Melody of 1938 (1938) Score (Nacio Herb Brown) US:LP-BP = Motion Picture Tracks MPT-3

830 Broadway Melody of 1940 (1940) Score (e:Cole Porter/etc.) US:LP-BP = Classic International Filmusicals 3002

831 Broadway Rhythm (1944) Theme-A/US:78 = Columbia 36693 [Ginny Simms:ST]; Theme-B/US:LP = Dolphin 2 [Nancy Walker:ST]

832 Broadway Serenade (1939) Highlights (Herbert Stothart & Edward Ward) US:LP-BP = Caliban 6020

833 Broadway Thru a Keyhole (1933) Excerpts (Harry Revel) US:LP-BP = Golden Legends 2000/1 [@ST]

834 Broken Arrow (1950) Theme (Hugo Friedhofer) US:LP = Dot 25097* [Elmer Bernstein]

835 Broken Blossoms (1919) Themes [Silent II] (Charles Hofmann) US:LP = Sounds Good 1001 (Charles Hofmann:ST)

836 Broken Horseshoe, The (1953) Theme (Wilfred Burns) US:EP = MGM 1197 [Wilfred Burns:ST]; Theme (Wilfred Burns) US:LP = MGM 3303 [@Wilfred Burns:ST]

837 Broken Journey, The (1948) Theme (John Greenwood) GB:78-PP = Rank FM-12 [ST]

838 Bronco Billy (1980) Score (e: Steve Dorff/etc.) US:LP = Elektra 5E-512*

839 Bronte Sisters, The [Les Soeurs Bronte] (1979) Score (as: Philippe Sarde) FR:LP = Pema 900.068*

840 Bronzes, Les (1981) Themes (Serge Gainsbourg) FR:SP = Philips 6172.187* [ST]

841 Brother from Another Planet, The (1984) Score (Mason Daring) US: LP = Daring DR-1007*

842 Brother on the Run (1974) Score (Johnny Pate) US:LP = Perception PR-45*

843 Brother Sun, Sister Moon [Fratello Sole, Sorella Luna] (1972) Score [European Release] (Riz Ortolani) IT:LP = Paramount C064.93393*; Theme [USA Release] (Donovan Leitch) US:SP = A&M 1491* [Sister Janet Mead]; Theme [USA Release] (Donovan Leitch) GB:LP = DJM 430* [Vic Lewis & Ken Thorne:ST]

844 Brotherhood, The (1968) Theme (Lalo Schifrin) US:SP = Dot 17203 [Lyn Roman]; Theme (Lalo Schifrin) US:LP = Dot 25925* [The Creative Crowd]

845 Brotherhood of the Yakuza *see* Yakuza, The

846 Brothers (1977) Score (Taj Mahal) US:LP = WB BS-3024*

847 Brothers, The (1947) Theme-A (Cedric Thorpe Davie) GB:78-PP = Rank FM-19 [ST]; Theme-B (Cedric Thorpe Davie) GB:78-PP = Rank FM-20 [ST]

848 Brothers Karamazov, The (1958) Theme (Bronislau Kaper) US: SP = MGM 12624 [Jack Hill]; Theme (Bronislau Kaper) US:SP = Coral 9-61990 [Henry Mancini]; Theme (Bronislau Kaper) US:LP = Delos 25421* [Bronislau Kaper]

849 Bruce Lee's Game of Death *see* Game of Death

850 Brussels by Night (1984) Score (Vant Groenewoud) HO:LP = EMI IA0641.19151*

851 Brute Force (1947) Highlights (Miklos Rozsa) US:LP-BP = Tony Thomas TTMR-3; Excerpts (Miklos Rozsa) US:LP = Decca DL-710015* + US:LP = Varese STV-81053* [Miklos Rozsa:ST]

852 Brutes and Savages (1980) Score (Riz Ortolani) AU:LP = Festival 36840*

853 Buccaneer, The (1959) Score (Elmer Bernstein) US:LP = Columbia CL-1278/CS-8096* + US:LP = CSP ACS-8096*

854 Buck and the Preacher (1972) Theme (Benny Carter) US:SP-PP = Buck B3KS-0516 [Benny Carter:ST]; Theme (Benny Carter) US:LP = RCA 4767* [New Birth]

855 Buck Benny Rides Again (1940) Theme (Jimmy McHugh) US:78 = Columbia 35442 [Eddie "Rochester" Anderson:ST]; Theme (Jimmy McHugh) US: LP = RCA ANL1-1050 [Tommy Dorsey & Frank Sinatra]

856 Buck Privates [Rookies] (1941) Theme-A/US:78 = Decca 3598 [The Andrews Sisters:ST]; Theme-B/US:78 = Decca 3599 [The Andrews Sisters:ST]; Theme-C/US:LP = Decca 2-4024 [The Andrews Sisters:ST]; Theme-C/US: SP = Decca 60040 [The Andrews Sisters: ST]

857 Buck Rogers in the 25th Century (1979) Score (s:Stu Phillips/t:Glen Larson) US:LP = MCA 3097* + US: LP = MCA 37087*

858 Buckskin Lady, The (1957) Theme (Albert Glasser) US:LP = Starlog 1001 [Albert Glasser:ST]

859 Bucket of Blood, A (1959) Excerpts (Fred Katz) US:LP = Rhino RNSP-304 [*see* Little Shop of Horrors, The (1960)]

860 Buddy Holly Story, The (1978) Score (pop music) US:LP = Epic/American International SE-35412*

861 Buddy System, The (1983) Theme (Patrick Williams) US:SP = Columbia 38-04333* [Gladys Knight:ST]

862 Budo (1978) Theme (Stomu Yamash'ta) JA:SP = Seven Seas 116* [ST]

863 Bugsy Malone (1976) Score (Paul Williams) US:LP = RSO RS1-3501*

864 Building a Building [Cartoon] (1933) Theme (Frank Churchill) US:LP-MS = Ovation 5000 [@ST]

865 Bullet for Pretty Boy, A (1970) Score (Harley Hatcher) US:LP = American International A-1034*

866 Bullet for Rommel, A [L'Urlo dei Giganti] (1972) Score (Armando Trovajoli) IT:LP = Beat CR-2*

867 Bullet for Sandoval, A [Quei Disperati Che Pazzano Di Sudore e di Morti] (1969) Score (Gianni Ferrio) IT: LP = Cinevox 33/19*

868 Bullet for the General, A [Quien Sabe?] (1967) Score (Luis E. Bacalov) IT:LP = Parade FPR-312

869 Bullet Is Waiting, A (1954) Theme (Dimitri Tiomkin) US:SP = MGM 11854 [Leroy Holmes]; Theme (Dimitri Tiomkin) US:LP = MGM 3172 [Leroy Holmes]; Theme (Dimitri Tiomkin) US:LP = Coral 57006 [Dimitri Tiomkin:ST]

870 Bullfighter and the Lady, The (1951) Theme (Victor Young) US:SP = Columbia 4-39851 [Mitch Miller]

871 Bullitt (1968) Score (Lalo Schifrin) US:LP = WB WS-1777*

872 Bullwhip (1958) Theme (Hal Hopper) US:SP = Kem 45-2747 [Eddie Freeman]

873 Bullwhip Griffin *see* Adventures of Bullwhip Griffin, The

874 Bundle of Blues, A [Short] (1930) Excerpts (Duke Ellington) US: LP = Biograph BLPM-2 [@ST]

875 Bundle of Joy (1956) Score (Josef Myrow) US:LP = RCA LPM-1399

876 Bunny Lake Is Missing (1965) Score (e:Paul Glass/e:The Zombies) US: LP = RCA LOC-1115/LSO-1115*

877 Bunny O'Hare (1971) Score (s:Billy Strange/t:Mike Curb) US:LP = American International A-1041*

878 Buona Sera, Mrs. Campbell (1968) Score (Riz Ortolani) US:LP = UA UAS-5192*

879 Burglars, The (1971) Score (Ennio Morricone) US:LP = Bell 1105*

880 Burke and Hare [The Horror of Burke and Hare] Theme (Roger Webb) GB:LP = EMI/Columbia 349* [Roger Webb:ST]

881 Burn! [Queimada] (1970) Score (Ennio Morricone) US:LP = UA LA-303* + US:LP-BP = FAR 101*

882 Burning, The (1981) Score (Rick Wakeman) US:LP = Varese STV-81162*

883 Bus Stop (1956) Theme-A (Ken Darby) US:SP = Columbia 4-40736 [The Four Lads]; Theme-A (Ken Darby) US: SP = Decca 9-30046 [Burl Ives]; Theme-B/US:LP-BP = Legends 1000/1 [Marilyn Monroe:ST]

884 Buster and Billie (1974) Theme (Hoyt Axton) US:SP = A&M 1497* [Hoyt Axton:ST]; Theme (Hoyt Axton) US:LP = A&M 3604* [Hoyt Axton:ST]

885 Bustin' Loose (1981) Score (e:Roberta Flack/etc.) US:LP = MCA 5141*

886 Butch and Sundance—The Early Years (1979) Score (Patrick Williams) JA:LP = Columbia SX-7012*

887 Butch Cassidy and the Sundance Kid (1969) Score (Burt Bacharach) US:LP = A&M SP-4227*

888 Butterfield 8 (1960) Theme (Bronislau Kaper) US:SP = MGM 12965 [David Rose]; Theme (Bronislau Kaper) US:LP = MGM 3894* + US:LP = MGM 3988* [David Rose]; Theme (Bronislau Kaper) US:LP = Capitol 11657* [Joe Harnell]

889 Butterfly (1981) Score (Ennio Morricone) US:LP = Applause APLP-1017*

890 Butterfly Affair, The [Popsy Pop] (1970) Score (folk music) FR:LP = Arion 30-T-106*

891 Button War, The *see* War of the Buttons

892 By Hook or By Crook *see* I Dood It

893 By Love Possessed (1961) Theme (Elmer Bernstein) US:SP = Columbia 4-42041 [Vic Damone]; Theme (Elmer Bernstein) US:SP = Mercury 71815 [Clebanoff]; Theme (Elmer Bernstein) US:LP = Mercury 60640* [Clebanoff]

894 By the Light of the Silvery Moon (1953) Highlights (pop music) US: LP-BP = Caliban 6019; Highlights (pop music) US:LP-10 = Capitol H-422 [Gordon MacRae:ST]; Highlights (pop music) US:LP-10 = Columbia CL-6248 + US:LP = CSP P-18421 [Doris Day: ST]

895 Bye Bye Birdie (1963) Score (stage songs:Charles Strouse) US:LP = RCA LOC-1081/LSO-1081*

896 Bye Bye Braverman (1968) Theme (Peter Matz) US:LP = Mercury 61149* [Derek & Ray]; Theme (Peter Matz) US:LP = Camden 2210* [The

Living Trio; Theme (Peter Matz) US: SP = Mercury 72744 [Derek & Ray]

C

897 C.C. and Company (1970) Score (Lenny Stack) US:LP = Avco AV-11003*

898 Ca Va Barder *see* There Goes Barder

899 Cab Calloway's Hi-De-Ho [Short] (1933) Excerpts (various) US: LP = Biograph BLP-M3 [@ST]

900 Cabaret (1972) Score (stage songs: John Kander) US:LP = ABC ABCD-752* + US:LP = MCA 37125*

901 Cabellera / Theme (Utrera) US:LP = MGM 3731* [Metropolitan Jazz Quartet]

902 Cabin in the Sky (1943) Score (stage songs: Vernon Duke/film songs: Harold Arlen) US:LP-BP = Hollywood Soundstage HS-5003

903 Cabinet of Caligari, The (1962) Theme (Gerald Fried) US:LP = London 3347/347* [Frank Chacksfield]

904 Cabinet of Dr. Caligari, The (1919) Themes [Silent II] (Charles Hofmann) US:LP = Sounds Good 1001 [Charles Hofmann:ST]

905 Cabiria *see* Nights of Cabiria

906 Cactus Flower (1969) Score (e: Quincy Jones/etc.) US:LP = Bell 1201*

907 Cactus in the Snow [You Can't Have Everything] (1972) Score (Joe Parnello) GB:LP = Ember 5055*; Theme (Joe Parnello) US:SP = WB 7461 [Bobby Scott:ST]

908 Caddie (1976) Score (Patrick Flynn) AU:LP = EMI 2551*; Theme (Patrick Flynn) US:LP = DRG 8202* [William Motzing]

909 Caddy, The (1953) Themes (Harry Warren) US:SP = Capitol 2589 [Dean Martin:ST]; Theme (Harry Warren) US:LP = Capitol 2601 [Dean Martin:ST]

910 Caddyshack (1980) Score (e:Johnny Mandel/e:Kenny Loggins/etc.) US:LP = Columbia JS-36737*

911 Cafe Express (1980) Theme (Giovanna Marini) IT:LP = WB/WEA 5827* [@ST]

912 Cafe Flesh (1983) Score (Mitchell Froom) US:LP = Slash 25064-1 [Mitchell Froom:ST]

913 Cage aux Folles, La (1979) Score (Ennio Morricone) US:LP = Cerberus CEMS-0102*

914 Cage aux Folles II, La (1981) Score (Ennio Morricone) US:LP = Cerberus CEMS-0107*

915 Cage aux Folles III, La (1986) Score (Ennio Morricone) FR:LP = WB 803.076*

916 Caged (1950) Excerpts (Max Steiner) US:LP-BP = Tony Thomas TTMS-15 [Max Steiner:ST]

917 Cahill—U.S. Marshal (1973) Themes (Elmer Bernstein) US:LP = Varese 704.350* [Elmer Bernstein:ST]

918 Cain and Mabel (1936) Theme/ US:LP-BP = JJA 19791 [@ST]

919 Caine Mutiny, The (1954) Highlights + Underscore + Dialog (e:Max Steiner/t:Fred Karger) US:LP = RCA LOC-1013 + US:LP-BP = CineSound CM-001; Theme-A (Max Steiner) US: LP = RCA 1-0422* + US:LP = RCA 1-3782* [Charles Gerhardt]

920 Cairo (1942) Themes-A-B/US: LP-BP = JJA 19758 [@Jeanette MacDonald:ST]; Theme-C/US:LP-BP = JJA 19763 [@Ethel Waters:ST]

921 Cajititlan [Short] (1967) Highlights (Robert Muczynski) US:LP-PP = Music Library 7119 [Robert Muczynski: ST]

922 Cal (1984) Score (Mark Knopfler) US:LP = Mercury 822-769-1*

923 Calamity Jane (1953) Highlights (Sammy Fain) US:LP-10 = Columbia CL-6273

924 Caldonia (1945) Excerpts (various) GB:LP = Krazy Kat KK-7414 [Louis Jordan:ST]; Theme/US:LP-MS = MCA 2-4079 [Louis Jordan:ST]

925 Calendar, The (1948) Theme (Arthur Wilkinson) GB:78-PP = Rank FM-25 [ST]

926 California Dreaming (1979) Score (Fred Karlin) US:LP = American International AILP-3001*

927 California Holiday *see* Spinout

928 California Suite (1978) Score (Claude Bolling) US:LP = Columbia JS-35727*

929 Caligula (1980) Score (s:Paul Clemente/t:Toni Biggs) US:LP + SP-12 = Penthouse PR-101*

930 Call Me Bwana (1963) Theme (Monty Norman) US:SP = UA 603 [Bob Hope:ST]

931 Call Me Madam (1953) Highlights (stage songs: Irving Berlin) US:LP-10 = Decca DL-5465 + US:LP = DRG DS-25001

932 Call Me Mister (1951) Highlights (stage songs: Harold Rome/film songs: Sammy Fain) US:LP-BP = Titania 510

933 Call of the Flesh (1930) Theme/US:LP = Stanyan 10055 [@Ramon Novarro:ST]

934 Calypso Heat Wave (1957) Theme/US:SP = Coral 9-61846 [Johnny Desmond:ST]

935 Camel Who Took a Walk, The [Short] Sequence + Dialog (Arthur Kleiner) US:LP-PP = Picture Book Parade 103 [@ST]

936 Camels Are Coming, The (1934) Theme/GB:LP = MFP 1236 [Jack Hulbert:ST]

937 Camelot (1967) Score (stage songs: Frederick Loewe) US:LP = WB B-1712/BS-1712*

938 Cammina Cammina (1984) Score (Bruno Nicolai) IT:LP = Edi Pan 2018*

939 Camp Followers, The [Le Soldatesse] (1964) Score (Mario Nascimbene) IT:LP = RCA SP-8010

940 Can-Can (1960) Score (stage songs + pop songs: Cole Porter) US:LP = Capitol W-1301/SW-1301* + US:LP = Capitol SM-1301*

941 Can Heironymous Merkin Ever Forget Mercy Humppe and Find True Happiness? (1969) Score (Anthony Newley) US:LP = Kapp KS-5509*

942 Candidate, The [Party Girls for the Candidate] (1964) Score (Steve Karmen) US:LP = Jubilee JCM-5029/JCMS-5029*

943 Candleshoe (1977) Theme (Ron Goodwin) GB:LP = Chandos 1014* [Ron Goodwin:ST]

944 Candy (1968) Score (e:Dave Grusin/etc.) US:LP = ABC SOC-9*

945 Cannonball Run (1981) Score (s:Al Capps/t:Chuck Mangione) JA:LP = RCA/Victor VIP-28036*; Theme (Chuck Mangione) US:SP = A&M 2354* [Chuck Mangione:ST]; Theme (Chuck Mangione) US:LP = A&M 4911* [Chuck Mangione:ST]

946 Cannonball Run II (1984) Theme (Steve Dorff) US:LP = RCA 1-4993* [Menudo:ST]; Theme (Steve Dorff) US:SP = RCA 13836* [Menudo:ST]

947 Cannonsville Story, The *see* Kinfolks

948 Can't Help Singing (1944) Highlights-A (Jerome Kern) US:LP-BP = Titania 509; Highlights-B (Jerome Kern) US:78-MS = Decca A-387 [Deanna Durbin:ST]

949 Can't Stop the Music (1980) Score (Jacques Morali) US:LP = Casablanca NBLP-7220*

950 Canta Me Buongiorno Tristezza / Theme (M. Ruccione) US:LP = Mercury 20188 [Eddie Barclay]

951 Canyon Passage (1946) Theme (Hoagy Carmichael) US:LP = Decca 8588 + US:LP = Adam 8040 [Hoagy Carmichael:ST]; Theme (Hoagy Carmichael) US:LP = RCA 1679 [Tony Perkins]

952 Caper of the Golden Bulls, The [Carnival of Thieves] (1967) Score (Vic Mizzy) US:LP = Tower T-5086/ST-5086*

953 Capricorn One (1978) Score (Jerry Goldsmith) US:LP = WB BSK-3201*

954 Caps for Sale [Short] Sequence + Dialog (Arthur Kleiner) US:LP-PP = Picture Book Parade 104 [@ST]

955 Captain Blood (1935) Theme-A (Erich Wolfgang Korngold) US:LP = RCA 3330* + US:LP = RCA 1-3707* [Charles Gerhardt]; Theme-B (Erich Wolfgang Korngold) US:LP = RCA 1-0912* [Charles Gerhardt]

956 Captain Boycott (1947) Theme (William Alwyn) GB:78-PP = Rank FM-10 [ST]

957 Captain Carey, U.S.A. [After Midnight] (1950) Theme (Jay Livingston & Ray Evans) US:SP = Capitol 6003 [Nat King Cole]; Theme (Jay Livingston & Ray Evans) US:LP = Mercury 20061 [Jack Shaindlin]

958 Captain from Castile (1947) Score (Alfred Newman) US:LP = Delos F-25411

959 Captain Horatio Hornblower (1951) Highlights (Robert Farnon) US: LP = Citadel CT-7009*

960 Captain January (1936) Excerpts (Lew Pollack) US:LP-MS = 20th 2-103 [Shirley Temple:ST]

961 Captain Kronos — Vampire Hunter (1974) Themes (Laurie Johnson) US:LP = Starlog/Varese 95002* [Laurie Johnson:ST]

962 Captain Nemo and the Underwater City (1969) Theme (Walter Stott-aka-Angela Morley) US:LP-MS = Longines 5312/6* [@Walter Stott:ST]

963 Captain Newman, M.D. (1964) Theme (Frank Skinner) US:SP = Columbia 4-42970 [Bill Pursell]; Theme (Frank Skinner) US:LP = Time 2131* [Richard Hayman]

964 Captain of the Guard (1930) Themes/US:78 = RCA/Victor 22373 [John Boles:ST]

965 Captain's Kid, The (1936) Theme/US:78-MS = Decca K-11 [Sybil Jason:ST]

966 Captain's Paradise, The (1953) Theme (Malcolm Arnold) US:SP = MGM 12525 [David Rose]; Theme (Malcolm Arnold) US:LP = MGM 4271* [David Rose]

967 Captain's Table, The (1959) Theme (Frank Cordell) US:SP = Top Rank 2043 + US:SP = Top Rank 2050 [Johnny Costa]

968 Captive (1986) Score (The Edge) GB:LP = Virgin V-2401*

969 Captive City, The *see* Conquered City, The

970 Car of Dreams (1935) Theme (Mischa Spoliansky) GB:LP = WRC 217 [@John Mills:ST]

971 Car Wash (1976) Scores (Norman Whitfield) US:LP-MS = MCA 2-6000*

972 Caravaggio (1986) Score (Simon Fisher Turner) GB:LP = Cherry Red/El ACME-6*

973 Caravan to Vaccares (1974) Theme (Stanley Myers) GB:SP = Columbia 9036* [Stanley Myers:ST]

974 Caravans (1978) Score (Mike Batt) US:LP = Columbia SE-35787*

975 Card, The *see* Promoter, The

976 Cardboard Cavalier (1949) Theme (Lambert Williamson) GB:78-PP = Rank FM-59 [ST]

977 Cardinal, The (1963) Score (Jerome Moross) US:LP = RCA LOC-1084/LSO-1084* + US:LP = Entracte ERS-6518*

978 Care Bears Movie, The (1985) Highlights + Dialog (e:John Sebastian/t:Carole King) US:LP = Kid Stuff DAR-3901*

979 Care Bears Movie II — A New Generation (1986) Highlights + Dialog (Carol & Dean Parks) US:LP = Kid Stuff DAR-3905*

980 Career (1959) Theme (James Van Heusen) US:SP = Capitol 4287 [Dean Martin:ST]; Theme (James Van Heusen) US:LP = Tower 5006 [Dean Martin:ST]

981 Carefree (1938) Highlights (Irving Berlin) US:LP-BP = Classic International Filmusicals 3004 + US:LP-BP = Sandy Hook SH-2010; Excerpts (Irving Berlin) US:LP-MS = Columbia SG2-32472 [Fred Astaire:ST]

982 Careful, He Might Hear You (1984) Score (Ray Cook) US:LP = Varese STV-81221*

983 Careless [Senilita] (1962) Score (Piero Piccioni) IT:LP = CAM CMS-30.037

984 Careless Years, The (1957) Theme (Joe Lubin) US:SP = Capitol 3745 [Sue Raney]; Theme (Joe Lubin) US:LP = RCA 1679 [Tony Perkins]

985 Caretakers, The [Borderlines] (1963) Score (Elmer Bernstein) US:LP = Ava A-31/AS-31*

986 Carey Treatment, The [Emergency Ward] (1972) Theme (Roy Budd) US:LP-BP = Eros 80544* + GB:LP = Pye 18389* [Roy Budd:ST]

987 Cargo on the Go [Industrial Short] Score (David Lee) US:LP-PP = Port of New York W4RS-1498

988 Carlos / Score (Ernst Brandner) GE:LP = Celine CL-022*

989 Carlos and de Bull / Theme (Mark Volman & Howard Kaylan) US: SP = Reprise 1142 [Flo & Eddie:ST]

990 Carmen (1984) Score (as:Paco De Lucia) US:LP = Polydor 817.247-1*

991 Carmen *see* Bizet's Carmen

992 Carmen de la Ronda [The Devil Made a Woman] [A Girl Against Napoleon] (1959) Score (various) US: LP = Columbia EX-5020 [Sarita Montiel:ST]

993 Carmen Jones (1954) Score (stage songs: Oscar Hammerstein II) US: LP = RCA LM-1881 + US:LP = RCA ARL1-0046

994 Carnal Circuit, The [The Insatiables] [Femmine Insaziabili] (1969) Score (Bruno Nicolai) IT:LP = Ariete 2006

995 Carnegie Hall [A Night at Carnegie Hall] (1947) Highlights (classical music) US:LP-10 = Columbia ML-2112

996 Carnet du Bal, Un (1937) Theme (Maurice Jaubert) US:LP = Capitol 8603* [Frank Pourcel]; Theme (Maurice Jaubert) US:LP = London 1332 [Stanley Black]

997 Carnival (1946) Theme (Nicholas Brodszky) GB:78 = Columbia 2225 [Charles Williams]

998 Carnival in Costa Rica (1947) Themes/US:LP-BP = Vedette 8701 [Dick Haymes:ST]

999 Carnival of Thieves *see* Caper of the Golden Bulls

1000 Carny (1980) Score (e:Alex North/e:Robbie Robertson) US:LP = WB HS-3455*

1001 Carolina Blues (1944) Themes/ US:78 = Columbia 36757 [Kay Kyser:ST]

1002 Carousel (1956) Score (stage songs: Richard Rodgers) US:LP = Capitol W-649/SW-649*

1003 Carpetbaggers, The (1964) Score (Elmer Bernstein) US:LP = Ava A-45/AS-45*

1004 Carrie (1952) Themes (David Raksin US:LP-MS-PP = Library of Congress LOC-RAKSIN [David Raksin: ST]

1005 Carrie (1976) Score (Pino Donaggio) US:LP = UA LA-716*

1006 Carry It On [Joan] (1971) Score (folk music) US:LP = Vanguard VDS-79313* [Joan Baez:ST]

1007 Carry Me Home Brother (1972) Theme (Harley Hatcher) US:SP = MGM 14195 [Junction:ST]

1008-9 Carthage in Flames [Cartagine in Fiamme] (1960) Score (Mario Nascimbene) IT:LP = Intermezzo IM-010*

1010 Cartouche (1964) Underscore + Dialog (Georges Auric) FR:LP-10 = Versailles 1176

1011 Casablanca (1942) Excerpts (Max Steiner) US:LP = RCA ARL1-0422* + US:LP = RCA AGL1-3782* [Charles Gerhardt]; Excerpts (pop music) US:LP-MS = WB 3X2737 [@Dooley Wilson:ST]; Themes (pop music) US:78 = Decca 40006 [Dooley Wilson:ST]; Theme (pop music) US: SP = WB 7741 [Dooley Wilson:ST]

1012 Casanova *see* Fellini's Casanova

1013 Casanova and Company *see* Sex on the Run

1014 Casanova '70 (1965) Highlights (Armando Trovajoli) US:LP = Epic LN-24195/BN-26195*

1015 Casbah (1948) Excerpts (Harold Arlen) US:LP-BP = JJA 19763 [@ST]

1016 Case Against Brooklyn, The (1958) Themes (Mort Garson/Lee Russell) US:SP = Decca 9-30619 [Bobby Helms:ST]

1017 Case Against Ferro, The [Police Python .357] (1977) Excerpts (Georges Delerue) FR:LP = Barclay 900.507* [Georges Delerue:ST]

1018 Case of the Red Monkey, The [The Little Red Monkey] (1955) Theme (Jack Jordan) US:SP = Columbia 4-39983 [Ken Griffin]; Theme (Jack Jordan) US:LP = MGM 3731* [Metropolitan Jazz Quartet]

1019 Casey at the Bat *see* Make Mine Music

1020 Casey's Shadow (1978) Score (Patrick Williams) US:LP = Columbia

PS-35344*

1021 Casino de Paree *see* Go Into Your Dance

1022 Casino Royale (1967) Score (Burt Bacharach) US:LP = Colgems COMO-5005/COSO-5005*

1023 Casper the Friendly Ghost *see* Friendly Ghost, The

1024 Cassandra Crossing, The (1977) Score-A (Jerry Goldsmith) US:LP = Citadel CT-6020*; Score-B (Jerry Goldsmith) IT:LP = RCA 31244*

1025 Cast a Giant Shadow (1966) Score (Elmer Bernstein) US:LP = UA UAL-4138/UAS-5138*

1026 Castle in the Air *see* Rainbow 'Round My Shoulder

1027 Castle on the Hudson (1940) Sequence + Dialog (Adolph Deutsch) US:LP-MS = WB 3X2737 [@ST]

1028 Cat, The *see* Chat, Le

1029 Cat and Mouse [Il Gatto, il Topo, la Paura e l'Amore] (1975) Themes (Francis Lai) IT:SP = CAM AMP-170* [ST]

1030 Cat and the Fiddle, The (1934) Highlights (Jerome Kern) US:LP-BP = Caliban 6049

1031 Cat Ballou (1965) Themes (Jerry Livingston) US:SP = Capitol 5412 [Nat King Cole & Stubby Kaye:ST]; Themes (Jerry Livingston) US:LP = Capitol 2340 + US:LP = Capitol 11804 [Nat King Cole:ST]

1032 Cat o' Nine Tails [Il Gatto a Nove Code] (1971) Theme (Ennio Morricone) IT:LP-MS = RCA 2-10599* [Ennio Morricone:ST]; Theme (Ennio Morricone) US:LP-BP = GSF 1002 [@Ennio Morricone:ST]

1033 Cat People (1982) Score (Giorgio Moroder) US:LP = MCA/Backstreet 6107*

1034 Catalepsis [La Corta Notte della Bambole di Vetro] (1972) Theme (Ennio Morricone) IT:LP-MS = RCA 2-1174* [Ennio Morricone:ST]; Theme (Ennio Morricone) IT:LP-MS-PP = General Music 33/01-04 [Ennio Morricone:ST]

1035 Catastrophe 1999 [The Last Days of Planet Earth] (1974) Score (Isao Tomita) JA:LP = Toho AX-8804*

1036 Catch My Soul (1975) Score (Jack Good & Tony Joe White) US:LP = Metromedia BML1-0176*

1037 Catch Us If You Can *see* Having a Wild Weekend

1038 Catered Affair, The (1956) Theme (Andre Previn) US:SP = MGM 12270 [David Rose]; Theme (Andre Previn) US:LP = MGM 3397 [David Rose]; Theme (Andre Previn) US:LP = Coral 57065 [Dick Jacobs & George Cates]

1039 Catherine & Co. (1974) Themes (Vladimir Cosma) FR:SP = Deesse 705* [ST]

1040 Cathy Tippel [Keetje Tippel] (1975) Themes (Rogier Van Otterloo) HO:SP = CBS 3246* [ST]

1041 Cathy's Child (1979) Theme (William Motzing) US:LP = DRG 8202* [William Motzing:ST]

1042 Catlow (1971) Highlights (Roy Budd) US:LP-BP = Eros 80544* + JA:LP = EMI/Odeon 80544*

1043 Cat's Eye (1985) Score (Alan Silvestri) US:LP = Varese STV-81241*

1044 Cattle Queen of Montana (1954) Theme (Louis Forbes) US:SP = Coral 9-61316 [Sons of the Pioneers]; Theme (Louis Forbes) US:LP = MCA 730 [Sons of the Pioneers]

1045 Caught in the Draft (1941) Theme (Louis Alter) US:78 = RCA Victor 27483 [Tommy Dorsey]

1046 Cavalcade d'Amour (1939) Excerpts (Darius Milhaud) US:LP = Westminster WGS-8348* [Leningrad State Philharmonic]

1047 Cavern, The [Sette Contro la Morte] (1964) Highlights (Carlo Rustichelli) IT:EP = CAM 45-122

1048 Ce Cher Victor *see* Cher Victor

1049 Census Taker, The (1985) Score (The Residents) US:LP = Episode ED-21*

1050 Centennial Summer (1946) Highlights (Jerome Kern) US:LP-BP = Classic International Filmusicals 3009

1051 Ceremony, The (1971) Excerpts (Toru Takemitsu) JA:LP = RCA/Victor 1064 [Toru Takemitsu:ST]

1052 Certain Fury (1985) Score (Bill Payne & Russ Kunkel) US:LP = Varese STV-81239*

1053 Certain Smile, A (1958) Score (s:Alfred Newman/t:Sammy Fain) US:LP = Columbia CL-1194/CS-8068*

1054 Cesar and Rosalie (1975) Score (Philippe Sarde) FR:LP = CAM 460.002* + JA:LP = TAM YX-5004*

1055 Cha-Cha-Cha Boom (1956) Theme/US:SP = GNP 115 [Rene Touzet: ST]

1056 Chain, The (1985) Theme (Barbara Dickson) GB:LP-MS = Filmtrax 820-252-1* [@Barbara Dickson:ST]

1057 Chain Reaction (1980) Score (Andrew Thomas Wilson) GB:LP = Seven MLF-360*

1058 Chairman, The (1969) Score (Jerry Goldsmith) US:LP = Tetragrammaton T-5007* + US:LP = AEI 3110*

1059 Chalk Garden, The (1964) Theme (Malcolm Arnold) US:SP = Columbia 4-43015 [Andy Williams]; Theme (Malcolm Arnold) US:LP = Decca 74669* [Carmen Cavallaro]; Theme (Malcolm Arnold) US:LP = Columbia 2171* [Andy Williams]

1060 Challenge, The *see* It Takes a Thief

1061 Challenge of the Salt [Industrial Short] Score (Charles Bernstein) US:LP-PP = MCV 1001*

1062 Chamade, La (1968) Themes [USA Release] (Dominic Frontiere) US: SP = UA 50575* [Dominic Frontiere: ST]; Theme [Italian Release] (Franco Cassano) IT:SP = Durium 9299* [ST]

1063 Champ, The (1979) Score (Dave Grusin) US:LP = Planet P-9001*

1064 Champagne Charlie (1944) Themes-A-B/GB:78 = Columbia 3050 [Tommy Trinder:ST]; Themes-C-D/ GB:78 = Columbia 3051 [Tommy Trinder:ST]

1065 Champagne Waltz (1937) Themes/US:78 = RCA/Victor 4324 [Gladys Swarthout:ST]

1066 Champion (1949) Theme-A (Dimitri Tiomkin) US:78 = Columbia 38511 [Herb Jeffries]; Theme-B (Dimitri Tiomkin) US:LP = Coral 57006 [Dimitri Tiomkin:ST]

1067 Champions (1984) Score (Carl Davis) US:LP = Antilles ASTA-3*

1068 Chance Meeting [Blind Date] (1959) Themes (Richard Rodney Bennett) GB:SP = Top Rank 5005 [Pinewood Studio Orchestra/Hardy Kruger:ST]

1069 Chandler (1971) Theme (George Romanis) US:SP = MGM 14346 [George Romanis:ST]

1070 Chanel Solitaire (1983) Score (Jean Musy) FR:LP = Ariola 203.337*

1071 Change for the Better, A [Industrial Short] Score (Otis Clements) US:LP-PP = Alco ADS-7765

1072 Change of Habit (1969) Excerpts (Billy Goldenberg) US:LP-BP = Centurion CLP-1601 [Billy Goldenberg: ST]; Themes-A-B/US:LP = Camden 2408* [Elvis Presley:ST]; Theme-C/US: LP = Camden 2472* [Elvis Presley:ST]

1073 Changemaker, The [Industrial Short] Score (Jac Murphy) US: LP-PP = Institution Magazine FM-300

1074 Changes (1972) Score (e:Marty Paich/etc.) US:LP = Nocturne NRS-901*

1075 Changing of the Guard (1936) Theme/GB:78-MS = Decca K-11 [Sybil Jason:ST]

1076 Chant of Jimmy Blacksmith, The (1980) Theme (Bruce Smeaton) US: LP = DRG 8202* [William Motzing]

1077 Chanticleer and the Fox [Short] Sequence + Dialog (Arthur Kleiner) US:LP-PP = Picture Book Parade 107 [@ST]

1078 Chaplin Revue, The [3 Shorts] (1960) Score (Charles Chaplin) US:LP = Decca DL-4040

1079 Chaplin's Art of Comedy (1966) Score (pop music) US:LP = Mainstream 56089/S-6089e

1080 Chapman Report, The (1962) Score (Leonard Rosenman) US:LP = WB W-1478/WS-1478*

1081 Chappaqua (1967) Score (Ravi Shankar) US:LP = Columbia OS-3230*

1082 Chapter Two (1979) Theme (Marvin Hamlisch) US:SP-PP = Raystar 111 [Marilyn McCoo:ST]; Theme (Marvin Hamlisch) US:LP-BP = Disc 105 [@Marilyn McCoo:ST]

1083 Charade (1963) Score (Henry Mancini) US:LP = RCA LPM-2755/ LSP-2755*

1084 Charade '79 *see* Somebody Killed Her Husband

1085 Charge at Feather River, The

(1953) Theme (Max Steiner) US:LP-MS-BP = Tony Thomas TTMS-9/10 [Max Steiner:ST]

1086 Charge Is Murder, The *see* Twilight of Honor

1087 Charge of the Light Brigade, The (1936) Theme-A (Max Steiner) US:LP = RCA 1287 [Max Steiner:ST]; Theme-B (Max Steiner) US:LP = RCA 1-0136* [Charles Gerhardt]

1088 Charge of the Light Brigade, The (1968) Score (John Addison) US:LP = UA UAS-5177*

1089 Chariots of Fire (1981) Score (Vangelis) US:LP = Polydor PD1-6335*

1090 Chariots of the Gods (1973) Score (Peter Thomas) US:LP = Polydor PD-6504*

1091 Charles and Lucie (1980) Themes (Pierre Perret) FR:SP = Adele 6172.907* [ST]

1092 Charles Burchfield [Short] (1967) Excerpts (Robert Muczynski) US:LP-PP = Music Library 7119 [Robert Muczynski:ST]

1093 Charles Lloyd—The Journey Within (1969) Score (Charles Lloyd) US:LP = Atlantic SD-1519* [Charles Lloyd:ST]

1094 Charleston (1979) Themes (Guido & Maurizio DeAngelis) IT:SP = RCA 6035* [ST]

1095 Charley's Aunt *see* Where's Charley?

1096 Charlie Bubbles (1968) Themes (Misha Donat) US:SP = Decca 9-32243 [Misha Donat:ST]

1097 Charlie Chan at the Opera (1936) Excerpts (Oscar Levant) US:LP = Medallion 310 [@ST]

1098 Charlotte's Web (1973) Score (Richard & Robert Sherman) US:LP = Paramount PAS-1008*

1099 Charly (1968) Score (Ravi Shankar) US:LP = World Pacific WS-21454*

1100 Charro! (1969) Theme (Billy Strange) US:SP = RCA 47-9731* + US:SP = RCA 447-0669* [Elvis Presley:ST]; Theme (Billy Strange) US:LP = Camden 2440* [Elvis Presley:ST]

1101 Chase, The (1966) Score (John Barry) US:LP = Columbia OL-6560/OS-1960*

1102 Chasing Rainbows (1930) Themes-A-B/US:78 = Brunswick 4615 [Charles King:ST]; Themes-C-D/US:78 = Brunswick 4616 [Charles King:ST]

1103 Chastity (1969) Score (s: Sonny Bono/t:Elyse Weinberg) US:LP = Atco SD-33-302*

1104 Chat, Le [The Cat] (1978) Highlights (Philippe Sarde) FR:EP = Pema 90.504*; Theme (Philippe Sarde) US:LP = DRG 9512* [@ST]

1105 Chateau in Sweden *see* Nutty, Naughty Chateau

1106 Chato's Land (1972) Highlights (Jerry Fielding) US:LP-MS-BP = Citadel CTJF-2/3*

1107 Che! (1969) Score (Lalo Schifrin) US:LP = Tetragrammaton T-5006* + US:LP = AEI 3111*

1108 Che Gioia Vivere (1960) Highlights (A.F. Lavagnino) IT:EP = RCA 30.404; Theme (A.F. Lavagnino) US:LP = RCA FSO-4 [@ST]

1109 Cheap Detective, The (1978) Theme (Patrick Williams) US:LP = RCA 1-3052* [Henry Mancini]

1110 Cheaters, The [Les Tricheurs] (1958) Highlights (t:Stan Getz/t:Coleman Hawkins/etc.) FR:EP = Barclay 74024

1111 Check and Double Check (1930) Themes-A-B/US:78 = RCA/Victor 22528 [Rhythm Boys & Cootie Williams/Duke Ellington:ST]; Theme-C/US:78 = RCA/Victor 22283 [Duke Ellington:ST]

1112 Checkpoint (1956) Theme-A (Bruce Montgomery) GB:78-PP = Rank FM-202 [ST]; Theme-B (Bruce Montgomery) GB:78-PP = Rank FM-203 [ST]

1113 Cheer Up and Smile (1930) Themes/US:78 = RCA/Victor 22443 [Whispering Jack Smith:ST]

1114 Cher Victor [Ce Cher Victor] (1977) Score (Bernard Gerard) FR:LP = Pathe CO66.96660*

1115 Cherry, Harry and Raquel (1969) Score (William Loose) US:LP = Beverly Hills BHS-23*

1116-7 Chevre, Le [The Goat] (1982) Score (Vladimir Cosma) FR:LP = WB WEA 58419*

1118 Cheyenne Autumn (1964) Score (Alex North) US:LP=X LXSE-1-003*

1119 Cheyenne Social Club, The (1970) Themes (Walter Scharf) US:SP= National General 007 [Walter Scharf/ Fonda & Stewart:ST]; Theme (Walter Scharf) US:LP-BP=Centurion 1600 [@Henry Fonda & James Stewart:ST]

1120 Chicago Chicago *see* Gaily Gaily

1121 Chicago Blues (1985) Scores (pop music) US:LP-MS=Red Lightnin' RL-0055*

1122 Chicken Chronicles, The (1977) Score (e:Ken Lauber/etc.) US: LP=UA LA-830*

1123 Chiens Perdus Sans Collier *see* Little Rebels, The

1124 Child Is Waiting, A (1963) Theme (Ernest Gold) US:LP=London 3320/320* [Ernest Gold:ST]

1125 Child Under a Leaf [Love Child] (1974) Themes (Francis Lai) FR: LP=WB/WEA 240041-1* [Francis Lai:ST]

1126 Children of a Lesser God (1986) Score (Michael Convertino) US: LP=GNP GNPS-8007*

1127 Children of Pleasure (1930) Themes/US:78=Brunswick 4775 [Lawrence Gray:ST]

1128 Children of Sanchez, The (1978) Scores (Chuck Mangione) US:LP-MS=A&M SP-6700*

1129 Children of the Corn (1984) Score (Jonathan Elias) US:LP=Varese STV-81211*

1130 Children of the Damned (1964) Theme (Ron Goodwin) US:LP-BP=POO 106 [@ST]

1131 Chilly Willy [Cartoon] (1953) Theme (Clarence Wheeler) US:SP= Cricket 7C-109 [Bobby Colt]; Theme (Clarence Wheeler) US:LP=Star Bright 101 [The Star Bright Orchestra]

1132 Chiltern Hundreds, The *see* Amazing Mr. Beecham, The

1133 Chimes at Midnight [Falstaff] (1967) Score (A.F. Lavagnino) GB:LP= Fontana 5417 + IT:LP=CAM AMG-3

1134 China Gate (1957) Theme (Victor Young) US:SP=Capitol 3702 [Nat King Cole:ST]; Theme (Victor Young) US:LP=Capitol 2340 + US: LP=Capitol 11804 [Nat King Cole:ST]

1135 China Is Near [La Cina e Vicina] (1967) Themes (Ennio Morricone) IT:SP=CAM AMP-024 [ST]

1136 China Seas (1935) Theme (Nacio Herb Brown) US:LP=World Artists 3007* [Perry Botkin, Jr.]

1137 Chinatown (1974) Score (Jerry Goldsmith) US:LP=ABC ABDP-848*

1138 Chinese Adventures in China *see* Up to His Ears

1139 Chinese Connection, The [Fist of Fury] (1973) Score (Joseph Koo) JA:LP=TAM YX-7001* + JA:LP= RCA/Victor VIP-7303*

1140 Chinmoku [Silence] (1972) Excerpts (Toru Takemitsu) JA:LP= RCA/Victor 1067 [Toru Takemitsu:ST]

1141 Chino [Valdez, the Half-breed] [The Valdez Horses] (1973) Score (Guido & Maurizio DeAngelis) JA:LP= Seven Seas FML-24*

1142 Chip 'n' Dale [Cartoon] (1948) Theme (Oliver Wallace) US:LP= Disneyland 1321 [@ST]

1143 Chisum (1970) Theme (Dominic Frontiere) US:SP=WB 7415 [January]

1144 Chitty Chitty, Bang Bang (1968) Score (Richard & Robert Sherman) US:LP=UA UAS-5188*

1145 Chivato! / Themes (Bob Ross) US:SP=Dana 4042 [Bobby Sims/Bob Ross:ST]

1146 Chocolate Soldier, The (1941) Excerpts (stage songs:Oscar Straus) US: LP-MS=RCA LOC-6005/LSO-6005* + US:LP=RCA LOC-1506/LSO-1506* [Rise Stevens:ST]; Excerpts (t:Bronislau Kaper/stage songs:Oscar Straus) US: LP=Columbia ML-4060 + US:LP= CSP P-13707 [Nelson Eddy & Rise Stevens:ST]

1147 Choice of Arms [Le Choix des Armes] (1983) Score (Philippe Sarde) US:LP=DRG SL-9510*

1148 Choirboys, The (1977) Score (Frank DeVol) US:LP=MCA 2326*

1149 Choose Me (1984) Theme (Luther Vandross) US:SP=Asylum 7-69696* [Teddy Pendergrass:ST]; Theme (Luther Vandross) US:LP=Asylum 60317* [Teddy Pendergrass:ST]

1150 Chorus Line—The Movie, A (1985) Score (stage songs:Marvin Hamlisch) US:LP = Casablanca 826-306-1*

1151 Chosen, The [Holocaust 2000] (1979) Score (Ennio Morricone) US:LP = Cerberus CEMS-0103*

1152 Christ Is Born [Short] Highlights (classical music) US:LP = Criterion CR-600

1153 Christ Is Risen [Short] Highlights (classical music) US:LP = Criterion CR-600

1154 Christa *see* Swedish Fly Girls

1155 Christiane F. (1981) Score (David Bowie & Brian Eno) US:LP = RCA ABL1-4239* [David Bowie:ST]

1156 Christine (1983) Score (t:John Carpenter/s:pop music) US:LP = Motown 6086*

1157 Christmas Holiday (1944) Themes/US:LP = Decca 8785 + US: LP = MCA 1514 [Deanna Durbin:ST]

1158 Christmas That Almost Wasn't, The (1966) Underscore + Dialog (Ray Carter) US:LP = Camden CAL-1086/CAS-1086*

1159 Christopher Columbus (1948) Excerpts (Arthur Bliss) US:LP = DRG MRS-703* [Marcus Dods]; Theme (Arthur Bliss) US:LP-BP = Citadel CTOFI-1 [@ST]

1160 Chronos (1985) Score (Mike Stearns) US:LP = Sonic Atmospheres 112*

1161 Chuck (1970) Theme (Rod McKuen) US:SP = WB 7389 [Rod McKuen:ST]

1162 Chulas Fronteras (1976) Score (various) US:LP = Arhoolie 3005*

1163 Ciao, Federico (1971) Theme (Bill Conti) US:SP-PP = Ciao C-208* [Robert Hensley:ST]

1164 Cid, El (1961) Score-A (Miklos Rozsa) US:LP = MGM E-3977/SE-3977*; Score-B (Miklos Rozsa) GB: LP = MGM 2353.046*

1165 Cimarron (1960) Theme (Franz Waxman) US:SP = ABC 10196 [Bill Snyder]; Theme (Franz Waxman) US:SP = MGM 12974 [David Rose]; Theme (Franz Waxman) US:LP = MGM 3894* + US:LP = MGM 3988* [David Rose]

1166 Cincinnati Kid, The (1965) Score (Lalo Schifrin) US:LP = MGM E-4313/SE-4313*

1167 Cinderella (1949) Score (e: Jerry Livingston/e:Oliver Wallace & Paul Smith) US:LP = Disneyland WDL-4007 + US:LP = Disneyland DQ-1207

1168 Cinderella (1966) Highlights + Dialog (Milton DeLugg) US:LP = Camden CAL-1085/CAS-1085*

1169 Cinderella—Italian Style *see* More Than a Miracle

1170 Cinderella Liberty (1973) Score (John Williams) US:LP = 20th ST-100*

1171 Cinderfella (1960) Highlights + Narration (e:Walter Scharf/e:Harry Warren) US:LP = Dot DLP-8001/DLP-38001*

1172 Cinema '76—The Continental Soldier [Industrial Short] Score (Ray Charles) US:LP-PP = Continental Insurance ILP-500

1173 Cinemiracle Adventure *see* Cinerama Holiday

1174 Cinerama Holiday [Cinemiracle Adventure] (1955) Score (e:Morton Gould/e:Jack Shaindlin) US:LP = Mercury MG-20059; Themes/US:SP = Columbia 4-48009 [Papa Celestin:ST]

1175 Cinerama's Russian Adventure [Russian Adventure] (1966) Score (t:Yuri Effimov/etc.) US:LP = Roulette R-802/RS-802*

1176 Circarama *see* America the Beautiful

1177 Circle of Deceit [Le Faussaire] (1982) Score (Maurice Jarre) FR:LP = WB/WEA 58401*

1178 Circle of Love [La Ronde] (1965) Score (Michel Magne) US:LP = Monitor 602/S-602*

1179 Circus, The (1927) Score [Silent II] (Charles Chaplin) GE:LP = UA 290571

1180 Circus Baby [Short] Sequence + Dialog (Arthur Kleiner) US:LP-PP = Picture Book Parade 103 [@ST]

1181 Circus of Horrors (1960) Score (s:Franz Reizenstein & Muir Mathieson/t:Mark Anthony) US:LP = Imperial LP-9129

1182 Circus World [The Magnificent Showman] (1964) Score Dimitri

Tiomkin) US:LP=MGM E-4252/SE-4252*

1183 Cisco Kid Returns, The (1945) Theme (Albert Glasser) US:LP=Starlog 1001 [Albert Glasser:ST]

1184 Cisco Pike (1971) Theme (Kim Fowley) US:SP=Epic 5-10901 [Rocky and the Border Kings]; Theme (Kim Fowley) US:LP=Monument 36135* [Kris Kristofferson:ST]

1185 Citizen Kane (1941) Score (Bernard Herrmann) US:LP=UA LA-372* [Leroy Holmes]; Underscore + Dialog (Bernard Herrmann) US:LP-MS=Mark 56 #810; Excerpts-A (Bernard Herrmann) US:LP=London SP-44144* [Bernard Herrmann:ST]; Excerpts-B (Bernard Herrmann) US:LP=RCA ARL1-0707* [Charles Gerhardt]

1186 Citizens Band *see* Handle With Care (1977)

1187 Cittadino si Ribella, Il / Theme (Guido & Maurizio DeAngelis) US:LP=Private Stock 7004* [Guido & Maurizio: ST]

1188 City, The [Short] (1939) Themes (Aaron Copland) US:LP=Columbia 33586* [Aaron Copland:ST]; Themes (Aaron Copland) US:LP=MGM 3334 + US:LP=MGM 3367 [Arthur Winograd]

1189 City for Conquest (1940) Theme (Max Steiner) US:LP-BP=Citadel CTMS-7 [Max Steiner:ST]

1190 City Heat (1984) Score (s:Lennie Niehaus/t:Bruce Roberts) US:LP=WB 25219-1*

1191 City Jungle, The *see* Young Philadelphians, The

1192 City Lights (1931) Theme-A (Charles Chaplin) US:LP=Paramount 6026* [Darius Brubeck]; Theme-B (Padilla & Granier) US:LP=GNP 2064* [Michel Villard]

1193 City of Women [City Without Men] (1943) Theme (Victor Young) US:SP=Decca 9-27965 [Victor Young:ST]; Theme [Victor Young] US:LP=Decca 8278 [Victor Young:ST]; Theme (Victor Young) US:LP=Jubilee 1034* + US:LP=Citadel 6024* [Harry Sukman]

1194 City's Child, A (1971) Score (Peter Pinne) GB:LP=Havoc HST-4002*

1195 Clair de Femme (1980) Score (Jean Musy) FR:LP=Riviera 900.580*

1196 Clambake (1967) Score (various) US:LP=RCA LPM-3893/LSP-3893* + US:LP=RCA APL1-2565* [Elvis Presley:ST]

1197 Clan of the Cave Bear (1986) Score (Alan Silvestri) US:LP=Varese STV-81274*

1198 Clancy Street Boys (1943) Underscore + Dialog (Edward J. Kay) US:LP-MS=Murray Hill 57385

1199 Clash of the Titans (1981) Score (Laurence Rosenthal) US:LP=Columbia JS-37386*

1200 Class of '44 (1973) Theme (David Shire) US:SP=WB 567 [David Shire:ST]; Theme (David Shire) US:LP-BP=Centurion 1600 [@David Shire:ST]

1201 Class of '74 (1972) Theme (Charles May) US:SP=Stax 0118* [Annette Thomas:ST]

1202 Class of 1984 (1981) Theme (Lalo Schifrin) US:SP=WB 7-29828* [Alice Cooper:ST]; Theme (Lalo Schifrin) US:LP=WB 23719-1* [Alice Cooper:ST]

1203 Claudine (1974) Score (s:Curtis Mayfield/as:Richard Tufo) US:LP=Buddah BDS-5602*

1204 Clean Slate *see* Coup de Torchon

1205 Cleo from 5 to 7 [Cleo de Cinq a Sept] (1961) Highlights (Michel Legrand) FR:EP=Philips 432.596; Theme (Michel Legrand) US:LP=Philips 600.071 [@ST]

1206 Cleopatra (1963) Score-A (Alex North) US:LP=20th FXG-5008/SXG-5008*; Score-B (Alex North) US:LP=RCA LPM-2766/LSP-2766* [Riz Ortolani]

1207 Cleopatra Jones (1974) Score (e:J.J. Johnson/e:Carl Brandt/t:Joe Simon) US:LP=WB WS-2719*

1208 Clockmaker, The [L'Horloger de St. Paul] (1973) Themes (Philippe Sarde) IT:SP=CAM AMP-151* [ST]

1209 Clockwork Orange, A (1971) Score (ae:Walter Carlos-aka-Wendy Carlos/etc.) US:LP=WB BS-2573*; Excerpts (Walter Carlos-aka-Wendy Carlos) US:LP=Columbia KC-31480* [Walter Carlos:ST]

1210 Close Encounters of the Third Kind (1977) Score (John Williams) US: LP = Arista AL-9500* + US:LP = Arista ABM-9500*; Excerpts-A (John Williams) US:LP = RCA ARL1-2698* [Charles Gerhardt]; Excerpts-B (John Williams) US:LP = Philips 9500.921* [John Williams:ST]

1211 Close Harmony (1929) Theme/US:LP-BP = JJA 19806 [@ Charles Buddy Rogers:ST]

1212 Clouded Yellow, The (1950) Theme (Benjamin Frankel) GB:78-PP = Rank FM-105 [ST]

1213 Clown and the Kid, The (1961) Score (Tony Velona) US:LP = Golden LP-215

1214 Clowns, The (1970) Score (Nino Rota) US:LP = Columbia S-30772*

1215 Club Paradise (1986) Score (Jimmy Cliff) US:LP = Columbia SC-40404*

1216 C'mon, Let's Live a Little (1967) Score (Don Crawford) US:LP = Liberty LRP-3430/LST-7430*

1217 Coal Miner's Daughter (1980) Score (pop music) US:LP = MCA 5107*

1218 Coast to Coast (1980) Score (pop music) US:LP = Full Moon FM-3490*

1219 Coastal Command (1942) Theme (Ralph Vaughan-Williams) GB: LP = EMI 3341* [Charles Groves]

1220 Cobra (1986) Score (e:Sylvester Levay/e:various) US:LP = Scotti Bros. SZ-40325*

1221 Cobweb, The (1955) Highlights (Leonard Rosenman) US:LP = MGM E-3501

1222 Cockleshell Heroes, The (1955) Theme (F. Vivian Dunn) US:SP = London 1636 [Frank Chacksfield]; Theme (F. Vivian Dunn) US:LP = London 1443 [Frank Chacksfield]

1223 Cocktail Molotov [Molotov Cocktail] (1980) Score (Yves Simon) FR: LP = Philips 9120.422*

1224 Cocoanut Grove (1938) Theme/US:78 = Bluebird 7528 [Harriet Hilliard:ST]

1225 Cocoanuts, The (1929) Highlights + Dialog (various) US:LP-BP = Sountrak STK-108 + US:LP-BP = Sandy Hook 2059

1226 Cocoon (1985) Score (James Horner) US:LP = Polydor 827-041-1*

1227 Code of Silence (1985) Score (David Frank) US:LP = Easy Street ESA-9900*

1228 Coffy (1973) Score (s:Roy Ayers/as:Harry Whitaker) US:LP = Polydor PD-5048*

1229 Cold Sweat (1970) Theme (Michel Magne) JA:SP = UA 1878* [Rene Clair]; Theme (Michel Magne) JA:LP = JVC 5005* [JVC Symphony Orchestra]

1230 Cold Turkey (1971) Theme (Randy Newman) US:SP = Capitol 3063* [Jimmy Helms]; Theme (Randy Newman) US:LP = Polydor 14078* [Roy Ayers]; Theme (Randy Newman) US:LP = Reprise 2064* [Randy Newman:ST]

1231 Collector, The (1965) Score (Maurice Jarre) US:LP = Mainstream 56053/S-6053*

1232 Colleen (1936) Highlights (Harry Warren) US:LP-BP = Caliban 6007

1233 College Coach (1933) Theme/ US:LP-MS = Columbia C2L-44 [Dick Powell:ST]

1234 College Confidential (1960) Score (Dean Elliot) US:LP = Chancellor 6015/S-6015*

1235 College Days *see* Freshman, The

1236 College Holiday (1936) Themes/US:LP-MS-BP = Legends 1000/5-6 [Martha Raye:ST]

1237 College Humor (1933) Excerpts (Arthur Johnston) US:LP-MS = Columbia C2L-43 [Bing Crosby:ST]

1238 College Rhythm (1934) Themes-A-B/US:LP = Columbia 2751 [@Lyda Roberti:ST]; Themes-A-B/US: 78 = Melotone 13236 [Jack Oakie:ST]; Theme-C/US:LP = Epic 6072 [@Lanny Ross:ST]; Theme-D/US:78 = Brunswick 7318 [Lanny Ross:ST]

1239 College Swing (1938) Themes/ US:LP-BP = JJA 19762 [@Gracie Allen/Martha Raye & Bob Hope:ST]

1240 Collegiate (1936) Excerpts (various) US:LP-BP = Caliban 6042 [@ST]

1241 Colonel Blimp *see* Life and Death of Colonel Blimp, The

1242 Colonel Redl (1985) Score (e: Zdenko Tamassy/e:classical music) FR: LP = Milan CH-018*

1243 Color of Money, The (1986) Score (e:Robbie Robertson/e:various) US:LP = MCA 6189*

1244 Color Purple, The (1985) Scores (e:Quincy Jones/e:Jack Hayes/t: Fred Steiner/etc.) US:LP-MS = QWEST 25389-1*

1245 Coma (1978) Score (Jerry Goldsmith) US:LP = MGM MG1-5403*

1246 Comanche! (1956) Score (Herschel Burke Gilbert) US:LP = Coral CRL-57046

1247 Comanche! (1958) *see* Tonka

1248 Comancheros, The (1961) Highlights (Elmer Bernstein) US:LP = Varese 704.280*

1249 Come Back Charleston Blue (1972) Score (Donny Hathaway) US: LP = Atco SD-7010*

1250 Come Blow Your Horn (1963) Score (s:Nelson Riddle/t:James Van Heusen) US:LP = Reprise R-6071/RS-6071*

1251 Come Dance With Me [Voulez-Vous Danser avec Moi] (1959) Highlights (Henri Crolla) FR:EP = Philips 432.454

1252 Come Impari ad Amare le Donne (1967) Score (Ennio Morricone) IT:LP = RCA SP-8020*

1253 Come Next Spring (1956) Highlights (Max Steiner) US:LP = Citadel CTV-7019

1254 Come Out Fighting (1945) Underscore + Dialog (Edward J. Kay) US:LP-MS = Murray Hill 57393

1255 Come Out of the Pantry (1935) Themes/GB:LP = Ace of Clubs 1140 [Jack Buchanan:ST]

1256 Come September (1961) Themes (Hans J. Salter/Bobby Darin) US:SP = Coral 9-62275 [Dick Jacobs]; Theme-B (Bobby Darin) US:SP = Atco 6200 [Bobby Darin:ST]; Theme-C (Bobby Darin) US:SP = Atco 6214 [Bobby Darin:ST]

1257 Come to the Stable (1949) Theme (Alfred Newman) US:SP = RCA 47-2998 [Claude Thornhill]; Theme (Alfred Newman) US:SP = Everest 2036 [Gloria Lynne]; Theme (Alfred Newman) US:LP = Decca 8123 + US:LP = Coral 20020 [Alfred Newman:ST]

1258 Comedians, The (1967) Score (Laurence Rosenthal) US:LP = MGM E-4494/SE-4494*

1259 Cometogether (1972) Score (e:Stelvio Cipriani/etc.) US:LP = Apple SW-3377*

1260 Comfort and Joy (1985) Highlights (Mark Knopfler) GB:EP-12 = Vertigo DSTR-712*

1261 Comin' Round the Mountain (1951) Theme/US:LP = Columbia 6089 [Dorothy Shay:ST]

1262 Commando [The Legion's Last Patrol] [Marcia o Crepa] (1962) Score (A.F. Lavagnino) IT:LP = RCA 430667; Theme (A.F. Lavagnino) US: SP = ABC 10477 [Ken Thorne]; Theme (A.F. Lavagnino) US:SP = London 10716 [Nino Rossi]

1263 Commando (1983) *see* Final Option, The

1264 Commandos (1968) Highlights (Mario Nascimbene) IT:LP = Cinevox 33/11

1265 Companeros! [Vamos a Matar Companeros] (1971) Excerpts (Ennio Morricone) IT:Intermezzo IMGM-009* [Ennio Morricone:ST]; Theme (Ennio Morricone) IT:LP-MS = RCA 2-10599* [Ennio Morricone:ST]

1266 Company of Cowards *see* Advance to the Rear

1267 Company of Wolves, The (1984) Score (George Fenton) US:LP = Varese STV-81242*

1268 Comperes, Les (1984) Score (Vladimir Cosma) FR:LP = Carrere 66.067*

1269 Competition, The (1980) Score (Lalo Schifrin) US:LP = MCA 5185* + US:LP-PP = COM 24986*; Highlights (classical music) US:LP = Town Hall S-31* [Lincoln Mayorga:ST]

1270 Compulsion (1959) Theme (Lionel Newman) US:SP = Decca 9-30850 [Jack Pleis]; Theme (Lionel Newman) US:SP = Mercury 71424 [Ralph Marterie]; Theme (Lionel Newman) US:LP = Edison 501 [Keith Williams]

1271 Computer Wore Tennis Shoes, The (1970) Theme (Robert F. Brunner) US:SP = Buena Vista 475 [The Electric Tennis Shoes]

1272 Conan the Barbarian (1982) Score (Basil Poledouris) US:LP = MCA 6108*

1273 Conan the Destroyer (1984) Score (Basil Poledouris) US:LP = MCA 6135*

1274 Concert for Bangla Desh, The (1972) Scores (pop music) US:LP-MS = Capitol STBK-3-12248*

1275 Concert for Kampuchea (1981) Scores (rock music) US:LP-MS = Atlantic SD2-7005*

1276 Concorde—Airport '79, The (1979) Themes (Lalo Schifrin) US:SP = MCA 41110* [Lalo Schifrin:ST]

1277 Concrete Jungle, The [The Criminal] (1960) Excerpts (Johnny Dankworth) US:LP-BP = Cinema LP-8002 [@ST]; Highlights (Johnny Dankworth) GB:EP = Columbia 8037

1278 Coney Island (1943) Highlights (Ralph Rainger) US:LP-BP = Caliban 6001

1279 Confessions of a Police Captain [Confessione di un Commissario di Polizia] (1971) Score (Riz Ortolani) IT: LP = RCA OLS-6*

1280 Confessions of a Pop Performer (1975) Score (e:Ed Welch/e:Dominic Bugatti) GB:LP = Polydor 2383.350*

1281 Confessions of a Street Walker *see* Memoirs of a French Whore

1282 Confessions of a Window Cleaner (1974) Themes (Sam Sklair/Roger Greenaway) GB:LP = Polydor 2383.350* [@ST]

1283 Confidentially Yours [Vivement Dimanche] (1983) Score (Georges Delerue) FR:LP = Milan A-213*; Highlights (Georges Delerue) US:LP = DRG SL-9519*

1284 Conflict of Wings (1954) Theme (Philip Green) GB:78 = Parlophone 3862 [Philip Green:ST]

1285 Conformist, The [Il Conformista] (1970) Score (Georges Delerue) IT:LP = Cinevox 33/43*

1286 Congiuntura, La (1965) Themes (Luis E. Bacalov) IT:SP = RCA 45-3312 [ST]; Theme (Luis E. Bacalov) US:SP = RCA 47-8635 [Luis E. Bacalov: ST]

1287 Congo Crossing (1956) Theme (Henry Mancini) US:LP = Coral 57065 [Dick Jacobs & George Cates]

1288 Congress Dances [Le Congres S'Amuse] [Der Kongress Tanzt] (1931) Theme (Werner Heymann) GB:LP = WRC 217 [@Lilian Harvey:ST]

1289 Conjugal Bed, The [Le Lit Conjugale] (1963) Highlights (Teo Usuelli) FR:EP = Festival 2340

1290 Connecticut Yankee in King Arthur's Court, A [A Yankee in King Arthur's Court] (1949) Excerpts (James Van Heusen) US:LP = Decca 4261 [Bing Crosby:ST]

1291 Conquered City [Captive City] [La Citta Prigioniera] (1962) Score (Piero Piccioni) IT:LP = CAM 30.050

1292 Conqueror, The (1956) Theme (Victor Young) US:SP = Decca 9-29855 [Frank Verna]

1293 Conquest of the Air (1940) Excerpts (Arthur Bliss) US:LP = Ariel CBF-13 [@Graham Treacher]

1294 Conspiracy of Hearts [Italy 1943] (1960) Theme (A.F. Lavagnino) US:SP = Top Rank 2043 [Johnny Costa]

1295 Constant Nymph, The (1943) Theme-A (Erich Wolfgang Korngold) US:LP = WB 1436* [Lionel Newman]; Theme-B (Erich Wolfgang Korngold) US:LP = RCA 3330* + US:LP = RCA 1-3707* [Charles Gerhardt]

1296 Contamination *see* Alien Contamination

1297 Contempt [Le Mepris] (1963) Highlights (Georges Delerue) FR:EP = Philips 434.809; Excerpts (Georges Delerue) FR:LP = Barclay 900.508 [Georges Delerue:ST]

1298 Context, The [Illustrious Corpses] [Cadaveri Eccellenti] (1976) Score (Piero Piccioni) IT:LP = General Music 10003*

1299 Continental Circus (1974) Score (Gilli Smythe) FR:LP = Philips 6332.033*

1300 Continental Divide (1981) Theme (Michael Small) US:SP = MCA 51186* [Helen Reddy:ST]

1301 Continental Twist, The [Twist

All Night] (1961) Highlights (e:Louis Prima/etc.) US:LP = Capitol T-1677/ ST-1677* [Louis Prima:ST]

1302 Contrasts in Rhythm *see* Melody Time

1303 Conversation, The (1974) Theme (David Shire) US:SP = Paramount 0305* [David Shire:ST]; Theme (David Shire) US:LP-BP = Centurion 1210* [@David Shire:ST]; Theme (David Shire) US: LP = Citadel 6021* [Ralph Gair]

1304 Conversation Piece [Il Gruppo di Famiglia] (1974) Score (Franco Mannino) IT:LP = Carosello 25052*

1305 Convicts Four [Reprieve] (1962) Theme (Leonard Rosenman) US:SP = Columbia 4-42411 [Big Miller]; Theme (Leonard Rosenman) US:LP = Verve 6-8493* [Kai Winding]

1306 Convoy (1978) Score (pop music) US:LP = UA LA-910*

1307 Coogan's Bluff (1968) Excerpts (Lalo Schifrin) US:LP-BP = Temple TLP-2001 [@Lalo Schifrin:ST]

1308 Cool Breeze (1972) Score (s: Solomon Burke/as:Gene Page) US: LP = MGM 1SE-35*

1309 Cool Hand Luke (1967) Score (Lalo Schifrin) US:LP = Dot DLP-3833/ DLP-25833*; Theme (pop music) US: LP-MS = WB 3X2737 [@Paul Newman: ST]

1310 Cool Mikado, The (1963) Score (stage songs:Gilbert & Sullivan) GB:LP = Parlophone PMC-1194

1311 Cool Ones, The (1967) Theme-A (Billy Strange) US:SP = WB 7002 [Petula Clark]; Theme-B (Lee Hazlewood) US:SP = Reprise 0636 [Nancy Sinatra]; Theme-B (Lee Hazlewood) US:LP = Reprise 6277* [Nancy Sinatra]

1312 Cool World, The (1964) Score (Mal Waldron) US:LP = Philips PHM-200-138/PHS-600-138*

1313 Coolangatta Gold, The (1985) Score (Bill Conti) AU:LP = Star Call SFL1-0116*

1314 Cooley High (1975) Scores (s:Freddie Perren/etc.) US:LP-MS = Motown M7-840*

1315 Cop or Hood *see* Flic ou Voyou

1316 Cop-Out [Stranger in the House] (1967) Themes (John Scott) US: SP = ABC 11033* [John Scott:ST]

1317 Copacabana (1947) Theme/ US:78 = Capitol 417 [Andy Russell:ST]

1318 Copacabana Palace [The Girl Game] (1962) Theme (Antonio Carlos Jobim) US:LP = Verve 6-8547* [Antonio Carlos Jobim:ST]; Theme (Antonio Carlos Jobim) US:LP = Capitol 2325* [Wanda DeSah]

1319 Copper Canyon (1950) Theme (Jay Livingston & Ray Evans) US:SP = RCA 47-3116 [Lisa Kirk]

1320 Cops and Robbers (1973) Theme (Michel Legrand) GB:LP = Philips 6382.103* [Ray Davies' Button Down Brass]

1321 Corky [Lookin' Good] (1972) Theme-A (Bill Walker) US:SP = MGM 14239 [Bill Walker:ST]; Theme-B (Pleasant) US:SP = MGM 14240 [Hank Williams, Jr.:ST]

1322 Cornbread, Earl and Me (1975) Score (Donald Byrd) US:LP = Fantasy F-9483*

1323 Coronado (1935) Theme-A/ US:78 = RCA/Victor 25178 [Eddie Duchin:ST]; Theme-B/US:LP-BP = JJA 19806 [@Johnny Downs:ST]

1324 Corrupt Ones, The [The Peking Medallion] (1967) Score (Georges Garvarentz) US:LP = UA UAL-4158/ UAS-5158*

1325 Cotton Club, The (1984) Score (t:John Barry/s:pop music) US: LP = Geffen GHS-24062*

1326 Cotton Comes to Harlem (1970) Score (Galt MacDermot) US: LP = UA UAS-5211*

1327 Cotton Pickin' Chicken Pickers, The (1967) Theme/US:SP = Decca 9-32260 [Hank Mills:ST]

1328 Cougar Country (1970) Highlights (William Loose) US:EP-PP = Rainbow 3496

1329 Counselor at Crime [Il Consigliori] (1973) Score (Riz Ortolani) IT: LP = Beat LPF-022*

1330 Counselor at Law *see* Smiling Maniacs, The

1331 Count Dracula [Il Conte Dracula] (1970) Score (Bruno Nicolai) IT:LP = Edi-Pan CS-2013*

1332 Count Three and Prey (1955) Excerpts (George Duning) US:LP = Web ST-108 [George Duning:ST]

1333 Count Your Blessings (1959) Theme (Franz Waxman) US:SP = MGM 12784 [Leroy Holmes]

1334 Count Your Bullets [Cry for Me, Billy] (1972) Themes (George Barrie/ Michael Franks) US:SP = Metromedia 257 [Jim Campbell:ST]

1335 Countdown at Kusini (1976) Score (Mau Dibango) US:LP-PP = Delta Sigma LPK-1001*

1336 Counterfeit Traitor, The (1962) Theme (Alfred Newman) US: SP = Columbia 4-42420 [Johnny Mathis]; Theme (Alfred Newman) US: LP = Columbia 8816* [Johnny Mathis]

1337 Countess from Hong Kong, A (1967) Score (Charles Chaplin) US:LP = Decca DL-1501/DL-71501*

1338 Country (1984) Score (Charles Gross) US:LP = Windham Hill WH-1039*

1339 Country Blue (1973) Themes (Abby Marable) US:SP = MGM 14612 [Abby Marable:ST]

1340 Country Fiddle, The [Short] (1960) Themes (Pete Seeger) US:LP = Folkways 3851 [Pete Seeger:ST]

1341 Country Girl, The (1954) Excerpts (Harold Arlen) US:LP-10 = Decca DL-5556 + US:LP = Decca DL-4264 [Bing Crosby:ST]

1342 Countryman (1982) Scores (e:Wally Badarou/e:various) US:LP-MS = Mango MSTDA-1*

1343 Coup de Torchon [Clean Slate] (1981) Score (Philippe Sarde) US:LP = DRG SL-9511*

1344 Coup d'Etat (1978) Themes (Pierre Bachelet) FR:SP = Deesse 737* [ST]

1345 Courage Fuyons [Courage, Let's Run] (1979) Score (Vladimir Cosma) FR:LP = WB/WEA 56756*

1346 Courage of Black Beauty, The (1957) Theme (Edward L. Alperson, Jr.) US:SP = National 105 [The Bobby Soxers]

1347 Cours du Soir [Night Class] Theme (Leo Petit) US:LP = UA 15554 [@ST]

1348 Course en Tete, La (1976) Score (e:David Munrow/etc.) US:LP = Angel S-37449* [David Munrow:ST]

1349 Court Jester, The (1956) Score (Sylvia Fine) US:LP = Decca DL-8212

1350 Court Martial of Billy Mitchell, The [One Man Mutiny] (1955) Underscore + Dialog (Dimitri Tiomkin) US:LP = Mark 56 #633

1351 Courtship of Eddie's Father, The (1963) Theme (George Stoll) US: SP = MGM 13131 [David Rose]

1352 Cousin Cousine (1976) Theme (Gerard Anfosso) FR:SP = EMI 20415* [ST]; Theme (Gerard Anfosso) FR:LP-MS = Pathe 2C150.16561* [Frank Pourcel]

1353 Cousins in Love *see* Tendres Cousines

1354 Cover Girl (1944) Highlights (Jerome Kern) US:LP-BP = Curtain Calls 100/24

1355 Covered Wagon, The (1923) Theme [Silent I] (Hugo Riesenfeld) US: LP = RCA 2560* [Gaylord Carter]

1356 Covert Action [I Was an Agent for the CIA] [Sono Statto un Agente CIA] (1978) Highlights (Stelvio Cipriani) IT:LP = Beat LPF-044*

1357 Cow and I, The (1959) Theme (Paul Durand) US:SP = Kapp 386 [Roger Williams]; Theme (Paul Durand) US:LP = Kapp 3244* [Roger Williams]

1358 Cowboy (1958) Score (George Duning) US:LP = Decca DL-8684

1359 Cowboy from Brooklyn, The (1938) Theme/US:LP = Decca 8837 [Dick Powell:ST]

1360 Cowboys, The (1972) Score (John Williams) US:LP-BP = RC 31*; Excerpts (John Williams) US:LP = Philips 6514.186* [John Williams:ST]

1361 Crack in the World (1965) Theme (Johnny Douglas) US:LP = Camden 926* [Johnny Douglas & Living Strings:ST]

1362 Crawlspace (1986) Score (Pino Donaggio) US:LP = Varese STV-81279*

1363 Crazies, The (1973) Theme (Melissa Manchester) US:SP = Scepter 12370* [Beverly Bremers:ST]

1364 Crazy Desire [La Voglia Matta] (1964) Highlights (Ennio Morricone) IT:EP = CAM 45-120

1365 Crazy Joe (1974) Themes

(Giancarlo Chiaramello) US:LP = Project 5085* [@ST]; Theme (Giancarlo Chiaramello) US:SP = Amsterdam 85031* [Alan Dale]

1366 Cream (1970) Theme (The Can) GB:LP = UA 29283* [The Can: ST]

1367 Creature from the Black Lagoon (1954) Highlights (Hans J. Salter) US:LP-BP = Tony Thomas TTHS-4; Theme (Hans J. Salter) US:LP = Coral 757240* + US:LP = Varese 81077* [Dick Jacobs]

1368 Creature with the Blue Hand [The Blue Hand] [Die Blaue Hand] (1971) Theme (Martin Bottcher) GE:LP = Celine 0011 [Martin Bottcher:ST]

1369 Creatures the World Forgot (1970) Theme (Mario Nascimbene) IT: LP-MS = Kangaroo 34209 [Mario Nascimbene:ST]

1370-71 Creepers (1985) Score (e: Goblin/e:various) US:LP = Enigma SJ-73205*

1372 Creeping Terror, The (1964) Themes (Frederick Kopp) US:LP = Rhino 307 [@Frederick Kopp:ST]

1373 Creepshow (1982) Score (John Harrison) US:LP = Varese STV-81160*

1374 Cria! [Cria Cuervos] (1976) Theme (J. Luis Perales) US:LP = Pronto 2020* [@Jeanette]

1375 Crime in the Streets (1956) Highlights (Franz Waxman) US:LP = Decca DL-8212 + US:LP = Entracte ERM-6001

1376 Crimen *see* And Suddenly It's Murder

1377 Crimes of Passion (1985) Score (Rick Wakeman) GB:LP = President TBG RW-3*

1378 Crimes of the Heart (1986) Score (Georges Delerue) US:LP = Varese STV-81298*

1379 Criminal, The *see* Concrete Jungle, The

1380 Criminal Symphony [Sette Uomini e un Cervello] Highlights (Carlo Rustichelli) IT:LP = CAM 10.017

1381 Crimson Kimono, The (1959) Theme (Harry Sukman) US:SP = Liberty 55210 [Harry Sukman:ST]; Theme (Harry Sukman) US:LP = Liberty 7135* [Harry Sukman:ST]

1382 Crisis (1950) Excerpts (Miklos Rozsa) US:LP = Citadel CT-7004* [Darryl Denning]; Themes (Miklos Rozsa) US:SP = MGM 10756 [Vicente Gomez: ST]; Themes (Miklos Rozsa) US:LP-BP = Soundstage 2308 [@Vicente Gomez:ST]

1383 Critters (1986) Score (David Newman) US:LP = Restless 72154-1*

1384 Crocodile Dundee (1986) Score (Peter Best) US:LP = Varese STV-81296*

1385 Cromwell (1970) Underscore + Dialog (Frank Cordell) US:LP = Capitol ST-640*

1386 Crook, The [Simon the Swiss] [Le Voyou] (1971) Highlights (Francis Lai) FR:EP = UA 6001; Themes (Francis Lai) US:SP = UA 50786* [Francis Lai: ST]; Theme (Francis Lai) US:LP = UA 5515* [Francis Lai:ST]

1387 Cross and the Switchblade, The (1970) Score (Ralph Carmichael) US:LP = Light LS-5550*

1388 Cross-Eyed Saint, The [Per Grazia Ricevuta] (1971) Score (Guido & Maurizio DeAngelis) IT:LP = IT 70002*

1389 Cross of Iron (1977) Score (Ernest Gold) GB:LP = EMI EMC-782*; Theme (Ernest Gold) US:LP = UA 782* [Ferrante & Teicher]

1390 Crossed Swords [The Prince and the Pauper] (1978) Score (Maurice Jarre) US:LP = WB BSK-3161*

1391 Crossover Dreams (1986) Score (e:Mauricio Smith/e:various) US: LP = Elektra 9-60470-1*

1392 Crossroads (1942) Theme (Arthur Schwartz) US:LP-BP = JJA 19758 [@Claire Trevor:ST]

1393 Crossroads (1986) Score (e:Ry Cooder/e:various) US:LP = WB 25399-1*

1394 Crowning Experience, The (1960) Highlights + Underscore + Dialog (u:Paul Dunlap/stage songs: Herbert Allen & Will Reed) US:LP-PP = Capitol/Moral Rearmament MRA-101/SMRA-101*

1395 Cruel Sea, The (1953) Theme (Alan Rawsthorne) IT:LP = RCA 43634* [@Eric Rogers]

1396 Cruel Tower, The (1957) Theme (Sherman) US:SP = Era 45-1023

[Rosalinda]; Theme (Sherman) US: LP-BP = Cinema 8001 [@Rosalinda]

1397 Cruising (1980) Score (pop music) US:LP = Columbia/Lorimar JC-36410*

1398 Cry for Happy (1961) Theme (George Duning) US:SP-PP = Cry 41743 [Miyoshi Umeki:ST]; Theme (George Duning) US:SP = Linda 666 [Mort Garson]

1399 Cry for Me, Billy *see* Count Your Bullets

1400 Cry of the Banshee (1970) Highlights (Les Baxter) US:LP = Citadel CT-7013*

1401 Crystal Eyes (1981) Score (Greg Forrest) JA:LP = Cockpit K28P-398*

1402 Cuando Tu No Estas [When You're Not There] (1966) Score (Manuel Alejandro) SA:LP = Hispana 11-112*; Excerpts (Manuel Alejandro) US:LP = CBS 80321* [Raphael:ST]; Themes (Manuel Alejandro) US:SP = UA 2805* [Raphael:ST]

1403 Cuba (1979) Theme (Patrick Williams) US:LP = Columbia 36382* [Andre Kostelanetz & Patrick Williams: ST]

1404 Cuban Love Song (1931) Themes (Herbert Stothart) US:LP-BP = Empire 804 [Lawrence Tibbett:ST]

1405 Cuban Pete (1946) Theme/ US:78 = RCA/Victor 25-1058 [Desi Arnaz:ST]

1406 Cucaracha, La (1959) Score (various) US:LP = Columbia WL-313/ WS-313* [Cuco Sanchez:ST]

1407 Cul-de-Sac (1966) Highlights (Christopher Komeda) GB:EP = Polydor 580.001; Theme (Christopher Komeda) US:LP = Impulse 9132 [Hank Jones]

1408 Cult of the Damned *see* Angel, Angel, Down We Go

1409 Cure for Love, The (1949) Theme (William Alwyn) GB:78 = HMV 9879 [Muir Mathieson:ST]

1410 Curee, La *see* Game Is Over, The

1411 Curious George Rides a Bike [Short] Sequence + Dialog (Arthur Kleiner) US:LP-PP = Picture Book Parade 105 [@ST]

1412 Curly Top (1935) Themes/US: LP-MS = 20th 2-103 [Shirley Temple:ST]

1413 Curse of Dracula, The *see* Return of Dracula, The

1414 Curse of the Hidden Vault, The [Die Gruft mit dem Ratselschlob] (1963) Theme (Peter Thomas) GE:LP = Celine 0011 [Peter Thomas:ST]

1415 Cursed Medallion, The [Night Child] [Child of the Night] [Perche] (1976) Themes (Stelvio Cirpriani) IT: SP = Cinevox MDF-074* [ST]

1416 Custer of the West (1966) Score (Bernardo Segall) US:LP = ABC SOC-5*

1417 Cycle Savages (1970) Score (Jerry Styner) US:LP = American International STA-1033*

1418 Cyclist Raiders *see* Wild One, The

1419 Cyclone (1978) Themes (Riz Ortolani) IT:SP = CAM AMP-209* [ST]

1420 Cyclops, The (1957) Theme (Albert Glasser) US:LP = Starlog 1001 [Albert Glasser:ST]

1421 Czar Wants to Sleep, The [Lieutenant Kije] [Lieutenant Kizheh] [The Czar Sleeps] (1934) Excerpts (Serge Prokofiev) US:LP = Angel S-37026* + US:LP = Angel S-32105* [Andre Previn]; Excerpts (Serge Prokofiev) US: LP = Columbia MS-6545* [Eugene Ormandy]; Excerpts (Serge Prokofiev) US: LP-MS = Vox 3-9004* [Felix Slatkin]

1422 Czarina *see* Royal Scandal, A

D

1423 D.A.R.Y.L. (1985) Theme (Marvin Hamlisch) US:SP = Asylum 7-69628* [Teddy Pendergrass:ST]

1424 D.C. Cab (1983) Score (e: Giorgio Moroder/etc.) US:LP = MCA 6128*

1425 D.I., The (1957) Theme (Herm Saunders) US:SP = Columbia 4-44092 [Monica Lewis:ST]

1426 Daddy Long Legs (1955) Highlights (Johnny Mercer) US:LP-BP = Caliban 6000; Excerpts (Johnny Mercer)

US:EP = Capitol EAP1-597 [Ray Anthony:ST]

1427 Daddy's Gone A-Hunting (1969) Theme (John Williams) US:SP = Dot 17265 [Lyn Roman]

1428 Dagmar's Hot Pants, Inc. (1971) Theme (Jimmie Haskell) US:SP = American International 171 [Mike Clifford]

1429 Dagora, The Space Monster (1964) Excerpts (Akira Ifukube) JA: LP = Toho 8107 [@ST]

1430 Dallas (1950) Theme (Max Steiner) US:LP-MS-BP = Tony Thomas TTMS-9/10 [Max Steiner:ST]

1431 Dames (1934) Highlights (Harry Warren) US:LP-BP = Caliban 6014

1432 Damien—Omen II (1978) Score (Jerry Goldsmith) US:LP = 20th T-563*

1433 Damn the Defiant [H.M.S. Defiant] (1962) Score (Clifton Parker) US:LP = Colpix CP-511/SCP-511*

1434 Damn Yankees [What Lola Wants] (1958) Score (stage songs:Richard Adler & Jerry Ross) US:LP = RCA LOC-1047

1435 Damnation Alley [Survival Run] (1977) Theme (Jerry Goldsmith) US:LP-BP = POO 104 [@Jerry Goldsmith:ST]; Theme (Jerry Goldsmith) JA:LP = Mu Land 7016* [Electoru Polyphonic Orchestra]

1436 Damned, The [La Caduta degli Dei] (1969) Score (Maurice Jarre) US:LP = WB WS-1829*

1437 Damsel in Distress, A (1937) Highlights (George Gershwin) US:LP-BP = Curtain Calls 100/19; Highlights (George Gershwin) US:LP-BP = Scarce Rarities SR-5505; Excerpts (George Gershwin) US:LP = Columbia SG-32472 + US:LP = Epic FLS-13103 [Fred Astaire:ST]

1438 Dance Craze (1981) Score (pop music) US:LP = Chrysalis 1299*

1439 Dance Girl Dance (1940) Theme/US:LP-BP = Legends 1000/2 [@Lucille Ball:ST]

1440 Dance of Life, The (1929) Excerpts (Richard A. Whiting) US:LP-BP = JJA 19806 [@ST]

1441 Dance of Love, The [Il Girotondo dell'Amore] Theme (Francis Lai) US:LP = Audio Fidelity 6301* [Francis Lai:ST]

1442 Dance With a Stranger (1985) Score (e:Richard Hartley/e:pop music) US:LP = Varese STV-81251*

1443 Dancing Co-Ed, The (1939) Highlights (various) US:LP-BP = Caliban 6023

1444 Dancing Lady (1933) Excerpts (various) US:LP-BP = Curtain Calls 100/23 [Joan Crawford:ST]

1445 Dancing on a Dime (1941) Theme/US:LP-BP = JJA [@Peter Lind Hayes:ST]

1446 Dancing Years, The (1950) Themes/GB:78 = HMV 9966 [Giselle Preville:ST]

1447 Dandy in Aspic, A (1968) Themes (Quincy Jones) US:SP = Bell 727 [Shirley Horn:ST]

1448 Danger—Diabolik [Diabolik] (1967) Theme (Ennio Morricone) US: LP-BP = POO 104 [@ST]; Theme (Ennio Morricone) IT:SP = Parade 5052 [ST]

1449 Danger—Girls at Play *see* It Happened in Rome

1450 Dangerous Love Affairs *see* Liaisons Dangereuses, Les

1451 Dangerous Moonlight *see* Suicide Squadron

1452 Dangerous Nan McGrew (1930) Themes/US:78 = RCA/Victor 22407 [Helen Kane:ST]

1453 Dangerous Youth [These Dangerous Years] (1957) Theme/US: LP = Columbia 8201* [Frankie Vaughan: ST]

1454 Dangerously Close (1986) Score (e:Michael McCarty/e:various) US:LP = Enigma SJ-73204*

1455 Daniel and the Devil *see* Devil and Daniel Webster, The

1456 Daniele and Maria (1972) Score (Nicola Piovani) IT:LP = Beat LPF-016*

1457 Dans la Poussiere du Soleil / Theme (Francis Lai) US:LP = UA 5515* [Francis Lai:ST]

1458 Danton (1983) Score (Jean Prodromides) US:LP = DRG SL-9518*

1459 Darby O'Gill and the Little People (1959) Theme + Underscore +

Dialog (Oliver Wallace) US:LP=Disneyland ST-1901

1460 Daredevil, The (1972) Themes (Robert Stringer) US:SP=Steady 99 [Lois Lee:ST]

1461 Daredevils of the Red Circle [Serial] (1939) Theme (William Lava) US:LP-PP=Cinemasound R-1001* [James King]

1462 Dark at the Top of the Stairs, The (1960) Theme-A (Max Steiner) US:SP=RCA 47-7795 [Bob Thompson]; Theme-B (Max Steiner) US:SP=Columbia 4-41796 [Percy Faith]; Theme-B (Max Steiner) US:LP=Mercury 60688* [David Carroll]

1463 Dark Corner, The (1946) Theme (Eddie Heywood) US:78=Decca 23677 [Eddie Heywood:ST]; Theme (Eddie Heywood) US:LP-10=Decca 5209 [Eddie Heywood:ST]

1464 Dark Crystal, The (1982) Score (Trevor Jones) US:LP=WB 23749-1*

1465 Dark Forces *see* Harlequin

1466 Dark Man, The (1951) Theme (Hubert Clifford) GB:78-PP=Rank FM-107 [ST]

1467 Dark of the Sun [The Mercenaries] (1968) Score (Jacques Loussier) US:LP=MGM E-4544/SE-4544*

1468 Dark Secret (1950) Theme (George Melachrino) US:LP=RCA 1000* [George Melachrino:ST]

1469 Dark Star (1974) Highlights + Dialog (John Carpenter) US:LP=Varese STV-81142*

1470 Dark Sunday / Score (Clay Smith & Arthur Smith) US:LP-PP=CMC 6074-N2*

1471 Dark Victory (1939) Excerpts-A (Max Steiner) US:LP=RCA ARL1-0183* + US:LP=RCA AGL1-3706* [Charles Gerhardt]; Excerpts-B (Max Steiner) US:LP-BP=Tony Thomas TTMS-16 [Max Steiner:ST]

1472 Dark Waters (1944) Excerpts (Miklos Rozsa) US:LP-BP=Tony Thomas TTMR-4 [Miklos Rozsa:ST]

1473 Darling (1965) Excerpts (Johnny Dankworth) US:LP=Epic LN-24195/BN-26195* [@ST]

1474 Darling Lili (1970) Score (Henry Mancini) US:LP=RCA LSPX-1000*

1475 Date with a Dream (1947) Theme (Vic Lewis) GB:LP=DJM 430* [Vic Lewis:ST]

1476 Date with a Lonely Girl, A *see* T.R. Baskin

1477 Date with Judy, A (1948) Excerpts (various) US:LP-BP=Curtain Calls 100/4 + US:LP-BP=Scarce Rarities 5503 [Jane Powell:ST]

1478 Daughter, The *see* Stay As You Are

1479 Daughters of Darkness [Les Levres Rouges] (1971) Theme (Francois DeRoubaix) US:LP-BP=POO 106 [@ST]; Theme (Francois DeRoubaix) FR:LP=Barclay 900.527 [Francois DeRoubaix:ST]; Excerpts (Francois DeRoubaix) FR:EP=Philips 4029

1480 David and Bathsheba (1951) Highlights (Alfred Newman) US:LP-BP=Temple TLP-2002 + US:LP=Sound of Hollywood 4001; Theme-A (Alfred Newman) US:LP=Decca 8123 (Alfred Newman:ST]; Theme-B (Alfred Newman) US:LP=Angel 36066* [Alfred Newman:ST]

1481 David and Lisa (1963) Highlights (Mark Lawrence) US:LP=Ava A-21/AS-21*

1482 David Copperfield (1935) Highlights (Herbert Stothart) US:LP-MS-BP=Tony Thomas TTST-1/2

1483 David's Song *see* Quest-se Qui Fait Courir David

1484 Dawn of the Dead [Zombie] (1979) Score (Goblin) US:LP=Varese VC-81106*

1485 Day After Halloween, The [Snap Shot] [One More Minute] (1981) Score (Brian May) US:LP=Citadel CTV-7020*

1486 Day and the Hour, The [Le Jour et L'Heure] (1962) Highlights (Claude Bolling) FR:EP=Barclay 70528

1487 Day at the Races, A (1937) Theme (Bronislau Kaper) US:LP=MGM 3511 [Richard Ellsasser]

1488 Day for Night [La Nuit Americaine] (1973) Themes (Georges Delerue) US:LP=DRG 9519 [@ST]; Themes (Georges Delerue) FR:SP=WB 16-274 [ST]

1489 Day of Anger (1969) Score (Riz Ortolani) US:LP = RCA LSO-1165*

1490 Day of the Animals [Something Is Out There] (1977) Theme (Lalo Schifrin) US:LP = CTI 7-5003* [Lalo Schifrin:ST]

1491 Day of the Assassins, The (1981) Score (Bebu Silvetti) US:LP = Ti-Pi 8203*

1492 Day of the Bad Man, The (1958) Theme (Hans J. Salter) US:LP = Medallion 313 [Hans J. Salter:ST]

1493 Day of the Dead (1985) Score (John Harrison) US:LP = Saturn SRLP-1701*

1494 Day of the Dolphin, The (1973) Score (Georges Delerue) US:LP = Avco AV-11014*

1495 Day of the Locust, The (1975) Score (e:John Barry/etc.) US:LP = London PS-912*

1496 Day of the Painter, The [Short] (1960) Theme (Eddy Manson) US:LP-PP = Margery 2400 [Eddy Manson:ST]; Theme (Eddy Manson) US: LP = Mercury 6005* [Richard Hayman & Eddy Manson:ST]

1497 Day Off *see* Jour de Fete

1498 Day That Shadow Mountain Died, The / Theme (Harold Beebe) US: SP = Dot 16536 [Vaughn Monroe]

1499 Day the Earth Stood Still, The (1951) Excerpts-A (Bernard Herrmann) US:LP-MS-PP = London STCO-95534* [@Bernard Herrmann:ST]; Excerpts-B (Bernard Herrmann) US:LP = London SP-44207* [Bernard Herrmann:ST]

1500 Day the Fish Came Out, The (1967) Score (Mikis Theodorakis) US: LP = 20th 4194/S-4194*

1501 Day Time Ended, The (1980) Score (Richard Band) US:LP = Varese STV-81140*

1502 Day to Remember, A (1954) Theme (Clifton Parker) GB:78-PP = Rank FM-140 [ST]

1503 Daydreamer, The (1966) Score (Maury Laws) US:LP = Columbia OL-6540/OS-1940*

1504 Daydreamer, The [Le Distrait] (1970) Themes (Vladimir Cosma) FR:SP = CBS 5349* [ST]

1505 Days of Heaven (1978) Score (Ennio Morricone) US:LP = Pacific Arts PAC8-128*

1506 Days of Wilfred Owen, The [Short] (1966) Underscore + Dialog (Richard Lewine) US:LP = WB B-1635/BS-1635*

1507 Days of Wine and Roses, The (1962) Theme (Henry Mancini) US:SP = RCA 47-8120 + US:SP = RCA 447-0708 [Henry Mancini:ST]; Theme (Henry Mancini) US:LP = RCA 2604* + US: LP = RCA 2895* [Henry Mancini:ST]

1508 De Sade (1969) Score (Billy Strange) US:LP = Tower ST-5170*

1509 Dead Image *see* Dead Ringer

1510 Dead Men Don't Wear Plaid (1982) Excerpts (Miklos Rozsa) GE:LP-MS = Colosseum CST 2-8027* [Elmer Bernstein]

1511 Dead Ringer [Dead Image] (1964) Score (Andre Previn) US:LP = WB W-1536/WS-1536*

1512 Deadfall (1968) Score (John Barry) US:LP = 20th S-4203*

1513 Deadlier Than the Male (1967) Theme (Malcolm Lockyer) US:SP = Decca 9-32084 [Malcolm Lockyer:ST]

1514 Deadline – Midnight *see* 30

1515 Deadlock (1970) Themes (The Can) GB:LP = UA 29283* [The Can:ST]

1516 Deadly Affair, The (1967) Score (Quincy Jones) US:LP = Verve V-8679/V6-8679*

1517 Deadly Friend (1986) Score (Charles Bernstein) US:LP = Varese STV-81291*

1518 Deadly Mantis, The (1957) Theme (William Lava) US:LP = Coral 757240* + US:LP = Varese 81077* [Dick Jacobs]

1519 Deadly Ray from Mars, The *see* Flash Gordon's Trip to Mars

1520 Deadly Strangers, The (1974) Theme (Ron Goodwin) GB:LP = EMI 1034* [Ron Goodwin:ST]

1521 Deadly Trap, The [The House Under the Trees] [La Maison Sous les Arbres] (1972) Score (Gilbert Becaud) FR:LP = Pathe C062.11484*

1522 Deadly Treasure of the Piranha, The *see* Killer Fish

1523 Deaf Smith and Johnny Ears [Los Amigos] (1972) Score (Daniele Patucchi) GB:LP = Columbia CO62. 94667* + IT:LP = CAM SAG-9050*

1524 Dealing: Or the Berkeley-to-Boston Forty-Brick Lost-Bag Blues (1972) Themes (Michael Small) US:SP = WB 7557 [Michael Small:ST]

1525 Dear Detective [Dear Inspector] [Tendre Poulet] (1978) Score (Georges Delerue) FR:LP = Deesse DDLX-159*

1526 Dear Heart (1965) Theme (Henry Mancini) US:SP = RCA 47-8458 + US:SP = RCA 447-0739 [Henry Mancini:ST]; Theme (Henry Mancini) US:LP = RCA 2990* + US:LP-MS = Camden 2-0293* [Henry Mancini: ST]

1527 Dear Inspector *see* Dear Detective

1528 Dear John (1966) Score (Bengt Arne Wallin) US:LP = Dunhill 55001/S-55001*

1529 Dear Louise [Louise] [Chere Louise] (1971) Themes (Georges Delerue) FR:SP = WB 16186 [ST]

1530 Dear Mr. Prohack (1948) Theme (Temple Abady) GB:78-PP = Rank FM-79 [ST]

1531 Dear Summer Sister (1972) Excerpts (Toru Takemitsu) JA:LP = RCA/Victor 1064 [Toru Takemitsu:ST]

1532 Dearest Love *see* Murmur of the Heart

1533 Death Before Dishonor (1986) Score (Brian May) US:LP = Varese STV-81310*

1534 Death Dealer [Milano Odia: La Polizia Non Puo Sparare] (1974) Theme (Ennio Morricone) IT:LP-MS = RCA 2-1174* [Ennio Morricone:ST]

1535 Death Driver (1975) Themes (Clay & Arthur Smith) US:SP = Monument 8-8676* [Clay & Arthur Smith:ST]

1536 Death Game (1977) Theme (Jimmie Haskell) JA:SP = Seven Seas 115* [Jimmie Haskell:ST]

1537 Death Has No Friends (1970) Theme (Herb Newman) US:SP = Era 111* [Herb Newman:ST]; Theme (Herb Newman) US:LP = RTV 4000* [Rare Moments Orchestra]

1538 Death in Venice (1971) Score (classical music) GB:LP = Classics for Pleasure CFP-186* + IT:LP = RCA NL-33223* [Franco Mannino:ST]

1539 Death of a Salesman (1951) Highlights (ae:Alex North) US:LP = Film Music Collection FMC-9* [Elmer Bernstein]

1540 Death of a Scoundrel (1957) Highlights (Max Steiner) US:LP = Entracte ERM-6004; Highlights (Max Steiner) US:EP = RCA EPA-919

1541 Death of Her Innocence, The *see* Our Time

1542 Death on the Nile (1978) Score (Nino Rota) US:LP = Capitol SW-11866*

1543 Death Riders (1975) Theme (Jerry Styner) US:SP = 20th 2263* [Tommy Cash:ST]

1544 Death Rides a Horse [Da Uomo a Uomo] (1968) Excerpts (Ennio Morricone) GB:LP = Sunset SLS-50248* [Ennio Morricone:ST]

1545 Death Wish (1974) Score (Herbie Hancock) US:LP = Columbia PC-33199*

1546 Death Wish II (1982) Score (Jimmy Page) US:LP = Swan Song SS-8511*

1547 Deathwatch [La Mort en Direct] (1980) Score (Antoine Duhamel) FR:LP = DJM 503.001*

1548 Decade of Decision / Theme (Hine) US:LP = Word 3164 [@Frank Boggs:ST]

1549 Deception (1946) Theme-A (Erich Wolfgang Korngold) US: LP = RCA 3330* [Charles Gerhardt]; Theme-B (Erich Wolfgang Korngold) US:LP = RCA 1-0185* [Charles Gerhardt]

1550 Decline and Fall of a Bird Watcher [Decline and Fall] (1968) Score (Ron Goodwin) GB:LP = Stateside 10259*

1551 Decline of Western Civilization, The (1980) Score (pop music) US: LP = Slash 105*

1552 Deep, The (1977) Score (John Barry) US:LP = Casablanca NBLP-7060*

1553 Deep End (1970) Theme (The Can) GB:LP = UA 29283* [The Can:ST]

1554 Deep in My Heart (1954) Score (pop music) US:LP = MGM E-3153 + US:LP-MS = MGM 2SES-54e

1555 Deep Red [The Hatchet Murders] [Susperia 2] [Profundo Rosso]

(1976) Score (s:Giorgio Gaslini/as:Goblin) IT:LP = Cinevox 33/85* + IT:LP = Cinevox 5004*

1556 Deep Throat (1973) Highlights + Dialog (uncredited) US:LP-PP = DT Music 1001 + US:LP-BP = Sandy Hook SH-2036; Theme (Hilliard) US:LP = RCA 1-0210* [Los Indios Tabajaras]; Theme (G. Damiano) US:SP = Bell 45-339 [Julius Wechter's Baja Marimba Band]

1557 Deep Throat, Part 2 (1974) Score (e:Tony Bruno/e:Michael Colicchio) US:LP = Bryan BRS-101*

1558 Deep Valley (1947) Theme (Max Steiner) US:LP-BP = Citadel CTMS-6 [Max Steiner:ST]

1559 Deer Hunter, The (1978) Score (ae:Stanley Myers/etc.) US:LP = Capitol SOO-11940*

1560 Def-Con 4 (1985) Score (Chris Young) US:LP = Cerberus CST-0212*

1561 Del Mero Corazon (1980) Score (folk music) US:LP = Arhoolie 3015*

1562 Delicate Delinquent, The (1957) Theme-A (Buddy Bregman) US: SP = Verve 10076 [Buddy Bregman:ST]; Theme-A (Buddy Bregman) US:SP = Decca 9-30382 [Sonny Burke]; Theme-B (Arthur Schwartz) US:SP = Decca 9-30370 [Jerry Lewis:ST]

1563 Delicious (1931) Excerpts (George Gershwin) US:LP-BP = JJA 19773 [@ST]

1564 Delightfully Dangerous (1944) Excerpts (Morton Gould) US:LP-BP = Curtain Calls 100/4 [Jane Powell:ST]

1565 Delinquents, The (1957) Theme (William Nolan) US:SP = Coral 9-61903 [Lew Quadling]; Theme (William Nolan) US:LP-BP = Cinema 8001 [@Lew Quadling]

1566 Deliverance (1972) Theme (at:Eric Weissberg) US:SP = WB 0309* [Eric Weissberg:ST]; Theme (at:Eric Weissberg) US:LP = WB 2683* [Eric Weissberg:ST]

1567 Delivery Boy, The [Cartoon] (1931) Theme (pop music) US:LP-MS = Ovation 5000 [@ST]

1568 Delta Factor, The (1971) Theme (Peter Thomas) US:LP = SSS 10* [The Tennessee Guitars]

1569 Delta Force, The (1985) Score (Alan Silvestri) US:LP = Enigma SJ-73201*

1570 Demon [God Told Me To] (1977) Highlights (Frank Cordell) GB: LP = Phoenix DGS-1004*; Theme (Robert O. Ragland) US:SP = Tru Luv 1119* [George Griffin:ST]

1571 Demons (1986) Score (e: Claudio Simonetti/e:various) IT:LP = RCA 34345*

1572 Depart, Le [The Departure] (1967) Highlights (Christopher Komeda) FR:EP = Philips 437.376

1573 Dernier Combat, Le [The Last Battle] (1985) Score (Eric Serra) FR: LP = RCA PL-37760*

1574 Derobade, La *see* Memoirs of a French Whore

1575 Dersu Uzala (1975) Theme (Isaac Schwartz) JA:LP-MS = TAM 9001/2* [@Stanley Maxfield]

1576 Desert of the Tartars [Il Deserto dei Tartari] (1976) Score (Ennio Morricone) IT:LP = General Music 10005*

1577 Desert Raiders [Il Dominatore del Deserto] (1963) Highlights (Carlo Rustichelli) IT:EP = CAM 45-121

1578 Desert Song, The (1943) Highlights (stage songs:Sigmund Romberg) US:LP-BP = Titania 505; Highlights (stage songs:Sigmund Romberg) US:LP-10 = RCA LPM-3105 [Kathryn Grayson: ST]; Highlights (stage songs:Sigmund Romberg) US:LP-10 = Capitol L-351 + US:LP = Capitol T-354 + US:LP = Angel 37319 [Gordon MacRae:ST]

1579 Desert Victory (1943) Theme (William Alwyn) GB:78 = Columbia 2140 [H.M. Grenadier Guards Band]

1580 Designing Woman (1957) Theme-A (Andre Previn) US:SP = Capitol 3704 [Les Baxter]; Theme-B (Tommy Edwards) US:SP = Capitol 3719 [Dolores Gray:ST]

1581 Desire (1936) Theme (Frederick Hollander) US:LP-BP = Wildebeest 5290 [Marlene Dietrich:ST]

1582 Desire Under the Elms (1958) Score (Elmer Bernstein) US:LP = Dot DLP-3095

1583 Desiree (1954) Theme-A (Alfred Newman) US:SP = Decca 9-

29357 [Bing Crosby & Alfred Newman]; Theme-A (Alfred Newman) US:LP = Decca 8123 + US:LP = Vocalion 73749 [Alfred Newman:ST]; Theme-B (Alex North) US:LP = Citadel 6023* [Alex North:ST]

1584 Desperado Trail [Winnetou III] (1965) Highlights (Martin Bottcher) GE:LP = Polydor 237.494

1585 Desperate Teenage Love Dolls (1985) Score (e:Redd Kross/e:various) US:LP = Enigma E-1140*

1586 Desperately Seeking Susan (1985) Highlights (Thomas Newman) US:LP = Varese STV-81320*; Theme (Steve Bray) US:SP = Sire 0539* [Madonna:ST]

1587 Destination Moon (1950) Score (Leith Stevens) US:LP = Omega 1003/OLS-3* + US:LP = Varese STV-81130* [Heinz Sandauer]; Highlights (Leith Stevens) US:LP-10 = Columbia CL-6151 [Leith Stevens:ST]

1588 Destroy All Monsters (1968) Themes (Akira Ifukube) JA:LP = Toho 8112 [@ST]

1589 Destroy All Planets (1968) Themes (Kenjiro Hirose) JA:LP = Toho 8120 [@ST]

1590 Destructors, The [The Marseilles Contract] (1974) Themes (Roy Budd) FR:SP = WB 16475* [Roy Budd: ST]; Theme (Roy Budd) US:LP-BP = Centurion 1600* [@Roy Budd:ST]

1591 Destry Rides Again (1939) Themes-A-B (Frederick Hollander) US: LP = Decca 5100 [Marlene Dietrich:ST]

1592 Detective, The (1968) Theme (Jerry Goldsmith) US:LP = Kapp 3588* [The Brass Hat]

1593 Devil and Daniel Mouse, The (1981) Highlights + Dialog (John Sebastian) CA:LP = Nelvana NEL-7802*

1594 Devil and Daniel Webster, The [Daniel and the Devil] [All That Money Can Buy] (1941) Highlights (Bernard Herrmann) US:LP = Unicorn UNI-72008* [Bernard Herrmann:ST]

1595 Devil and Max Devlin, The (1981) Theme (Marvin Hamlisch) US: SP = A&M 2315* [Julie Budd:ST]; Theme (Marvin Hamlisch) US:LP-BP = Disc 105* [@Julie Budd:ST]

1596 Devil and the Ten Commandments, The [Le Diable et les Dix Commandments] (1962) Highlights (Georges Garvarentz) FR:EP = Barclay 70466; Theme (Marnay & Magenta) US:SP = Mercury 72187 [Sarah Vaughan]

1597 Devil at 4 O'Clock, The (1961) Score (George Duning) US:LP = Colpix CP-509/SCP-509* + US:LP = Varese STV-81136*

1598 Devil by the Tail, The [Le Diable par le Queue] (1968) Themes (Georges Delerue) FR:SP = UA 38239 [ST]

1599 Devil in Love, The [L'Arcidiavolo] (1966) Score (Armando Trovajoli) IT:LP = Parade 314

1600 Devil in Miss Jones, The (1973) Score (Alden Shuman) US:LP = Janus JLS-3059*

1601 Devil in the Flesh (1947) Theme (Rene Cloerec) US:LP = Capitol 8603* [Frank Pourcel]

1602 Devil Is a Woman, The [The Tempter] [Il Sorriso del Grande Tentatore] (1976) Score (Ennio Morricone) IT:LP = Beat LPF-026*

1603 Devil May Care (1929) Themes/GB:78 = HMV 2778 [Ramon Novarro:ST]

1604 Devil Never Sleeps, The *see* Satan Never Sleeps

1605 Devil's Angels, The (1967) Score (s:Mike Curb/t:Jerry Styner) US: LP = Tower T-5074/ST-5074*

1606 Devil's Brigade, The (1968) Highlights (Alex North) US:LP = UA UAL-3654/UAS-6654* [Leroy Holmes]

1607 Devil's 8, The (1969) Score (s:Jerry Styner/t:Mike Curb/t:Michael Lloyd) US:LP = Tower ST-5160*

1608 Devil's Hairpin, The (1957) Themes (Nathan Van Cleave/Ross Bagdasarian) US:SP = Verve 10099 [Jean Wallace:ST]; Theme (Ross Bagdasarian) US:LP = National 106 [Kathy Linden]

1609 Devil's Hand, The (1961) Theme (Baker Knight) US:SP = Chess 1795 [Baker Knight:ST]

1610 Devotion (1946) Theme (Erich Wolfgang Korngold) US:LP = RCA 3330* + US:LP = RCA 1-3707* [Charles Gerhardt]

1611 Diabolica *see* Beyond the Door

1612 Dial M for Murder (1954) Theme (Dimitri Tiomkin) US:SP = Coral 9-61211 [Dimitri Tiomkin:ST]; Theme (Dimitri Tiomkin) US:LP = Coral 57006 [Dimitri Tiomkin:ST]; Theme (Dimitri Tiomkin) US:LP = Mercury 20156 + US:LP = Mercury 20301 [David Carroll]

1613 Diamond Head (1963) Score (s:John Williams/t:Hugo Winterhalter) US:LP = Colpix CP-440/SCP-440*

1614 Diamond Horseshoe *see* Billy Rose's Diamond Horseshoe

1615 Diamond Mercenaries *see* Killer Force

1616 Diamonds (1976) Score (Roy Budd) GB:LP = Bradley BRADS-8002*

1617 Diamonds Are Forever (1972) Score (John Barry) US:LP = UA UAS-5220* + US:LP = UA LA-301*

1618 Diane (1956) Themes (Miklos Rozsa) US:LP = Deutsche 2584.013* [Miklos Rozsa:ST]; Theme (Miklos Rozsa) US:LP = MGM 4112* [Miklos Rozsa:ST]

1619 Diaper Trouble *see* Sarilho de Fraldas

1620 Diary of a Bachelor (1964) Score (Jack Pleis) US:LP-PP = Diary DB-923/4; Theme-A (Jack Pleis) US:SP = Four Corners 4-115 [The Coronados]; Theme-B (Jack Pleis) US:LP = UA 6392* [@Jack Pleis:ST]

1621 Diary of a High School Bride (1959) Theme (Tony Casanova) US:SP = American International 45-532 [Tony Casanova:ST]

1622 Diary of a Stewardess / Theme (William Baker) US:SP = Segue 101 [Bob Grabeau:ST]

1623 Diary of Anne Frank, The (1959) Score-A (Alfred Newman) US:LP = 20th 3012; Score-B (Alfred Newman) US:LP = 20th S-3012*

1624 Dick and Jane *see* Fun with Dick and Jane

1625 Dick Deadeye [Dick Deadeye, or Duty Done] (1975) Score (as:Robin Miller & James Horowitz) GB:LP = GM GML-1018*

1626 Didn't You Hear? (1973) Score (Mort Garson) US:LP-PP = Custom Fidelity CFS-2379*

1627-8 Die Laughing (1980) Theme (Robby Benson) US:SP = WB 49211* [Robby Benson:ST]

1629 Die the Young (1970) Themes (Jay Colonna) US:SP = Simmy 101 [Johnny Bytheway:ST]

1630 Different Story, A (1978) Theme (Bob Wahler) US:SP = A&M 2060* [Cory Wells]

1631 Digital Dreams (1983) Score (Mike Batt & Bill Wyman) US:LP-PP = Ripple MRA-26264*

1632 Dil Bhi Tera Hum Bhi Tere / Theme/US:LP = Capitol 10500 [@Lata Mangeshkar:ST]

1633 Dillinger (1973) Score (e:Barry DeVorzon/etc.) US:LP = MCA 360*

1634 Dimboola (1979) Theme (George Dreyfus) US:LP = DRG 8202* [William Motzing]

1635 Dime with a Halo (1963) Theme (Ronald Stein) US:SP = GNP 199 [Rene Touzet]; Theme (Ronald Stein) US:LP = Capitol 2075* [Jimmie Haskell]; Theme (Ronald Stein) US:SP = MGM 13163 [Lalo Schifrin]

1636 Dimples (1936) Excerpts (Jimmy McHugh) US:LP-MS = 20th 2-103 [Shirley Temple:ST]

1637 Diner (1982) Scores (pop music) US:LP-MS = Elektra E1-60107*

1638 Dingaka (1965) Score (as: Bertha Egnos & Eddie Domingo) US:LP = Mercury MG-21013/SR-61013*

1639 Dinner at Eight (1933) Theme (Jimmy McHugh) US:LP = World Artists 3007* [Perry Botkin, Jr.]

1640 Dino [Killer Dino] (1957) Score (Gerald Fried) US:LP = Epic LN-3404

1641 Dion Brothers, The [The Gravy Train] (1974) Theme (Fred Karlin) US:SP-PP = Tomorrow 96640 [Marty Kaniger:ST]

1642 Dirty Angels, The [Vergogna Schifosi] (1972) Score (Ennio Morricone) IT:LP = Ariete 2003

1643 Dirty Dingus Magee (1970) Score (Jeff Alexander) US:LP = MGM 1SE-24*

1644 Dirty Dozen, The (1967) Score (Frank DeVol) US:LP = MGM E-4445/SE-4445*

1645 Dirty Feet (1966) Score (Mation Bartoo) US:LP = Fink 1007*

1646 Dirty Game, The (1966) Score

(Robert Mellin & Gian Piero Reverberi) US:LP = Laurie 2034/S-2034*

1647 Dirty Harry (1971) Themes (Lalo Schifrin) US:LP = WB/Viva 23990-1* [Lalo Schifrin:ST]

1648 Dirty Heroes, The [Dalle Ardenne all'Inferno] (1970) Excerpts (Ennio Morricone & Bruno Nicolai) IT: LP = Beat LPF-001 [@ST]; Themes (Ennio Morricone & Bruno Nicolai) IT:LP = Beat LPF-003 [@ST]

1649 Dirty Mary, Crazy Larry (1974) Theme (Danny Janssen) US:SP = Capitol 3881* [Marjorie McCoy & Jimmie Haskell:ST]; Theme (Danny Janssen) US:SP = Ember 0298* [Susan Maughan]; Theme (Danny Janssen) US:LP = Ember 1037* [Susan Maughan]

1650 Dirty Money [Un Flic] (1972) Themes (Michel Colombier) FR:SP = Barclay 1039* [ST]

1651 Dirty Outlaws, The [El Desperado] (1967) Themes (Gianni Ferrio) IT:SP = CAM AMP-029 [ST]

1652 Disappearance, The (1977) Themes (Craig Huxley) US:LP-MS = Sonic Atmospheres 101* [Craig Huxley: ST]

1653 Disc Jockey (1951) Themes-A-B/US:78 = Decca 27733 [Tommy Dorsey: ST]; Theme-C/US:78 = Decca 27332 [The Weavers:ST]; Theme-D/US: 78 = MGM 11046 [George Shearing:ST]

1654 Disc Jockey Jamboree *see* Jamboree

1655 Disco Godfather (1980) Score (Ernie Fields, Jr.) US:LP = Apple Juice AJ-152*

1656 Disco 9000 (1977) Score (Johnny Taylor & Jackie Avery) US: LP = Columbia PS-35004*

1657 Disorder [Il Disordine] (1962) Themes (Mario Nascimbene) IT:SP = Titanus 45-070 [ST]

1658 Disorderly Orderly, The (1964) Theme (Leon Carr) US:SP = Reprise 0322 [Sammy Davis, Jr.:ST]

1659 Dispatch from Reuters, A [This Man Reuter] (1940) Excerpts (Max Steiner) US:LP-BP = Tony Thomas TTMS-17 [Max Steiner:ST]

1660 Distant Trumpet, A (1964) Theme (Max Steiner) US:LP-MS-BP = Tony Thomas TTMS-9/10 [Max Steiner:ST]

1661 Diva (1982) Score (Vladimir Cosma) US:LP = DRG SL-9503*

1662 Dive Bomber (1941) Theme (film theme from "Submarine D-1") US: LP-BP = Citadel CTMS-2 [Max Steiner: ST]

1663 Divine Madness (1980) Score (pop music) US:LP = Atlantic SD-16022* [Bette Midler:ST]

1664 Divine Nymph, The (1979) Score (Cesare Bixio) US:LP = Cerberus S-0104*

1665 Divorce, American Style (1967) Score (Dave Grusin) US:LP = UA UAL-4163/UAS-5163*

1666 Divorce—Italian Style (1962) Score (Carlo Rustichelli) US:LP = UA UAL-4106/UAS-5106*

1667 Dixiana (1930) Themes/US: 78 = RCA/Victor 22471 [Everett Marshall:ST]

1668 Dixie (1943) Themes/US: LP = Decca 4257 [Bing Crosby:ST]

1669 Django (1965) Score (Luis E. Bacalov) IT:LP = Intermezzo IM-002*; Theme (Luis E. Bacalov) US:LP = UA 15549* [Jorgen Ingmann]

1670 Do Not Disturb (1965) Themes (Mort Garson/Mark Barkan) US:SP = Columbia 4-43459 [Doris Day: ST]; Theme (Mark Barkan) US:LP = Harmony 11192 [Doris Day:ST]

1671 Do You Like Women? [Aimez-vous les Femmes] (1963) Themes (Ward Swingle) FR:SP = Philips 432.902 [ST]

1672 Do You Love Me? (1946) Highlights (various) US:LP-BP = Caliban 6011

1673 Doberman Gang, The (1972) Themes (Alan Silvestri) JA:SP = Seven Seas FM-1065* [ST]

1674 Doctor Detroit (1983) Score (e:Ira Newborn/t:Lalo Schifrin/etc.) US:LP = MCA/Backstreet 6120*

1675 Doctor Dolittle (1967) Score (Leslie Bricuse) US:LP = 20th D-5101/ DS-5101*

1676 Dr. Ehrlich's Magic Bullet [The Story of Dr. Ehrlich's Magic Bullet] (1940) Excerpts (Max Steiner) US:LP-BP = Tony Thomas TTMS-17 [Max Steiner:ST]

1677 Doctor Faustus (1967) Highlights + Underscore + Dialog (Mario Nascimbene) GB:LP = CBS 63189* + CA:LP = Columbia OS-3190*

1678 Dr. Goldfoot and the Bikini Machine (1965) Theme (Jerry Styner) US:SP = Dee Gee 3010 [The Beas]; Theme (Jerry Styner) US:SP-PP = American International 59433 [The Supremes:ST]

1679 Dr. Goldfoot and the Girl Bombs (1966) Score (e:Jerry Styner/t:Les Baxter/t:Harley Hatcher/t:Bob Summers) US:LP = Tower T-5053/ST-5053*

1680 Dr. Jekyll and Mr. Hyde (1941) Excerpts (Franz Waxman) GB: LP = Decca PFS-4432* [Stanley Black]

1681 Dr. Jekyll and Sister Hyde (1971) Excerpts (David Whitaker) US: LP = Capitol ST-11340* [@ST]

1682 Dr. No (1963) Score (s:Monty Norman/t:John Barry) US:LP = UA UAL-4108/UAS-5108* + US:LP = UA LA-275*

1683 Dr. Phibes *see* Abominable Dr. Phibes, The

1684 Dr. Rhythm (1938) Excerpts (James Monaco) US:LP-10 = Decca DL-6013 + US:LP = Decca DL-4253 [Bing Crosby:ST]

1685 Dr. Strangelove: Or How I Learned to Stop Worrying and Love the Bomb (1964) Theme (Laurie Johnson) US:SP = Colpix 723 [Laurie Johnson: ST]; Theme (Laurie Johnson) US:LP = Colpix 464* [@Laurie Johnson:ST]; Theme (Laurie Johnson) US:LP = Starlog/Varese 95002* [Laurie Johnson:ST]

1686 Doctor, You've Got to Be Kidding! (1967) Theme (Lee Pockriss) US:SP = MGM 13701 [Robbie Porter]; Theme (Lee Pockriss) US:SP = RCA 47-9204 [Eddie Fisher]; Theme (Lee Pockriss) US:LP = RCA 3820* [Eddie Fisher]

1687 Doctor Zhivago (1965) Score (Maurice Jarre) US:LP = MGM 1E-6/1SE-6*

1688 Doctors' Wives (1971) Theme (Elmer Bernstein) US:SP-PP = Dunhill SPD-15* [Mama Cass Elliott:ST]

1689 Dodeskaden [Clickety-Clack] (1970) Excerpts (Toru Takemitsu) JA: LP = RCA 1066 [Toru Takemitsu:ST]

1690 Dodge City (1939) Excerpts (Max Steiner) US:LP = RCA ARL1-0912* [Charles Gerhardt]

1691 Dog of Flanders, A (1959) Score (Paul Sawtell & Bert Shefter) US: LP = 20th 3026/S-3026*

1692 Dog's Life, A (1918) *see* Chaplin Revue, The

1693 Dolce Vita, La (1961) Score (Nino Rota) US:LP = RCA FOC-1/FSO-1*

1694 Dolemite (1976) Score (Rudy Ray Moore & Arthur Wright) US:LP = Generation LP-2501*

1695 Doll Face (1945) Themes/US: 78 = RCA/Victor 20-1750 [Perry Como]

1696 Dollars [$] [The Heist] (1971) Score (Quincy Jones) US:LP = Reprise RS-2051*

1697 Dolls, The *see* Bambole!

1698 Doll's House, A (1973) Theme (John Barry) GB:LP = Polydor 2383.461* [John Barry:ST]

1699 Doll's House, A [La Maison de Poupee] (1973) Excerpts (Michel Legrand) FR:LP = Bell 2308.070* [Michel Legrand:ST]

1700 Dolly Sisters, The (1945) Score (pop music) US:LP-BP = Classic International Filmusicals 3010

1701 Domino Principal, The [The Domino Killings] (1977) Score (Billy Goldenberg) JA:LP = Seven Seas FML-84*; Theme (Billy Goldenberg) US:SP = Epic 8-50358* [Shirley Eikhard:ST]

1702 Don Giovanni (1979) Scores (classical music) US:LP-MS = Columbia M3-35192*

1703 Don Juan (1926) Theme [Silent I] (William Axt & David Mendoza) US:LP-MS = WB 3X2737 [@ST]

1704 Don Quixote (1933) Excerpts (Jacques Ibert) US:LP = Angel/Columbia H-141; Highlights (Jacques Ibert) FR:78-MS = HMV 1310

1705 Dona Flor and Her Two Husbands (1978) Score (Chico Buarque & Francis Hime) US:LP=Peters PLD-1011*

1705a Dondi (1961) Theme (Earl Shuman) US:SP = Kapp 378 [The Do-Re-Mi Children's Chorus]

1706 Donkey Skin [The Magic Donkey] [Peau d'Ane] (1972) Score (Michel Legrand) FR:LP = Paramount C062.91975*; Theme (Michel Legrand)

US:LP = Springboard 4068* [Michel Legrand:ST]

1707 Don't Cry with Your Mouth Full [Pleure Pas la Bouche Pleine] (1973) Themes (Vladimir Cosma) FR:SP = Polydor 2056.286* [ST]

1708 Don't Fence Me In (1945) Theme/US:LP = RCA 3041 [Roy Rogers:ST]

1709 Don't Get Personal (1936) Themes/US:78 = Brunswick 7653 [Pinky Tomlin:ST]

1710 Don't Go Near the Water (1957) Theme (Bronislau Kaper) US:SP = Coral 9-61899 [The Lancers:ST]

1711 Don't Just Stand There (1967) Theme (Nick Perito) US:LP = Command 936* [Ray Charles Singers:ST]

1712 Don't Knock the Twist (1957) Score (s:Kal Mann/t:Fred Karger) US:LP = Parkway P-7011/PS-7011*

1713 Don't Look Back (1967) Score (pop music) US:LP-BP = Phonygraf DLB-1 [Bob Dylan:ST]

1714 Don't Look Now (1973) Score (Pino Donaggio) GB:LP = That's Entertainment TER-1007* + GB:LP = Enterprise 3003*

1715 Don't Make Waves (1967) Score (s:Vic Mizzy/t:Jim McGuinn) US:LP = MGM E-4483/SE-4483*

1716 Don't Open the Window [Let Sleeping Corpses Lie] (1974) Score (Giuliano Sorgini) IT:LP = Beat LPF-028* + JA:LP = TAM YX-8032*

1717 Don't Turn the Other Cheek [Porgi l'Altra Guancia] (1973) Score (Guido & Maurizio DeAngelis) IT:LP = EMI 3C064.18063*

1718 Doppelganger *see* Journey to the Far Side of the Sun

1719 Dorado, El (1967) Score (Nelson Riddle) US:LP = Epic FLM-13114/FLS-15114*

1720 Dorian Gray [The Secret of Dorian Gray] [Il Dio Chimavanto Dorian] (1970) Score (Carlo Pes & Peppino DeLuca) IT:LP = CAM PRE-9*

1721 Double Dynamite (1951) Theme (Jule Styne) US:78 = Columbia 38790 [Frank Sinatra & Jane Russell:ST]

1722 Double Indemnity (1944) Themes-A (Miklos Rozsa) US:LP = RCA 1-0911* [Charles Gerhardt]; Themes-B (Miklos Rozsa) GB:LP = Polydor 2383.384* [Miklos Rozsa:ST]

1723 Double Life, A (1948) Excerpts (Miklos Rozsa) US:LP = AEI 3104 + US:LP-BP = Premiere 1201 [uncredited]; Theme (Miklos Rozsa) US:LP = Deutsche 2584.013* [Miklos Rozsa:ST]

1724 Double or Nothing (1937) Excerpts (Burton Lane) US:LP-10 = Decca DL-6011 + US:LP = Decca DL-4252 [Bing Crosby:ST]

1725 Double Trouble (1967) Score (various) US:LP = RCA LPM-3787/LSP-3787* + US:LP = RCA APL1-2564* [Elvis Presley:ST]

1726 Dougal and the Blue Cat (1972) Underscore + Dialog (Joss Baselli) GB:LP = MFP 50017*

1727 Dove, The (1974) Score (John Barry) US:LP = ABC ABDP-852*

1728 Down and Dirty [Bruti, Sporchi e Cattivi] (1979) Score (Armando Trovajoli) IT:LP = RCA TBL1-1219*

1729 Down and Out in Beverly Hills (1986) Score (e:Andy Summers/e:various) US:LP = MCA 6160*

1730 Down Argentine Way (1940) Highlights (Harry Warren) US:LP-BP = Caliban 6003 + US:LP-BP = Hollywood Soundstage 5013

1730a Down by Law (1986) Highlights (John Lurie) GB:LP = Made to Measure MTM-14*

1731 Down Liberty Road [Down Freedom Road] Theme (Jane Bowers) US:SP = Capitol 3230 [Tex Ritter]; Theme (Jane Bowers) US:LP = Capitol 971 [Tex Ritter]

1732 Down Mexico Way (1941) Theme (Alberto Colombo) US:LP-PP = Cinemasound R-1001* [James King]

1733 Down the Ancient Stairs [Per la Antiche Scale] (1978) Themes (Ennio Morricone) IT:SP = RCA 1164 [ST]

1734 Down to Earth (1947) Excerpts (Doris Fisher & Allan Roberts) US:LP-BP = Curtain Calls 100/22 [Rita Hayworth:ST]

1735 Down to the Sea in Ships (1949) Excerpts (Alfred Newman) US:LP = Entracte ERS-6506* [Fred Steiner]

1736 Downfall (1963) Theme (Mort Lindsey) US:LP = Dot 25418* [Mort Lindsey:ST]

1737 Downhill Racer (1969) Theme (Kenyon Hopkins) US:LP = Camden 2420* [The Living Strings]; Theme (Kenyon Hopkins) US:LP = Mainstream 301* [Joe Scott]

1738 Dracula (1958) *see* Horror of Dracula

1739 Dracula (1979) Score (John Williams) US:LP = MCA 3166*

1740 Dracula and Son [Dracula Pere et Fils] (1976) Themes (Vladimir Cosma) FR:SP = Vogue 140.142* [ST]

1741 Dracula Has Risen from the Grave (1968) Theme (James Bernard) US:LP-BP = POO 104 [@Geoff Love]

1742 Dragnet (1954) Theme (Herm Saunders) US:SP = Capitol 2854 [Connie Russell]

1743 Dragon Fist (1982) Score (Hikaru Hayashi) JA:LP = Columbia AF-7109*

1744 Dragon Flies, The [The Man from Hong Kong] [Sky High] (1975) Score (s:Noel Quinlan/t:Des Dyer & Clive Scott) JA:LP = Overseas SUX-1*; Theme (Des Dyer & Clive Scott) US: SP = Chelsea 3022* [Jigsaw:ST]

1745 Dragon Lord, The (1982) Score (Lei Chen Pang) JA:LP = RCA/ Victor VIP-28052*

1746 Dragonfly, The (1955) Highlights (Sulkhan Tsintsadze) US:LP = Monitor 530

1747 Dragonslayer (1981) Scores (Alex North) US:LP-MS = X LXSE-2-001*

1748 Drama of Jealousy *see* Pizza Triangle, The

1749 Drango (1957) Score (Elmer Bernstein) US:LP = Liberty LRP-3036

1750 Draughtsman's Contract, The (1983) Score (Michael Nyman) US:LP = DRG SL-9513*

1751 Dream After Dream (1981) Score (Journey) JA:LP = CBS 27-AP-1950*

1752 Dream Chaser (1984) Theme (Al Kasha & Joel Hirschhorn) US: SP = MCA 52379* [Burrito Brothers:ST]

1753 Dream Girl (1948) Theme (Jay Livingston & Ray Evans) US:78 = Capitol 494 [Freddie Stewart]

1754 Dream House [Short] (1932) Excerpts (various) US:LP = Biograph BLP-M1 [Bing Crosby:ST]

1755 Dream Maker, The [It's All Happening] (1963) Score (e:Philip Green/etc.) GB:LP = Columbia CL-1537/SCX-3486*

1756 Dream of Kings, A (1969) Score (Alex North) US:LP = National General NG-1000*

1757 Dream of Passion, A (1978) Themes (Yannis Markopoulos) FR:SP = AZ 677* [ST]

1758 Dream Walking [Cartoon] (1950) Sequence + Dialog (Philip Scheib) US:LP = RCA LBY-1031 [@ST]

1759 Dreamboat (1952) Theme/ US:LP-BP = Curtain Calls 100/21 [Ginger Rogers:ST]

1760 Dreaming Out Loud (1940) Theme/US:78 = Decca 3400 [Frances Langford:ST]

1761 Dreamland of Desire (1950) Themes (Manos Hadjidakis) US:SP = Cadence 1417 [The Chordettes]; Theme (Manos Hadjidakis) US:LP = Mercury 60688* [David Carroll]

1762 Dreamscape (1984) Score (Maurice Jarre) US:LP = Sonic Atmospheres 102*

1763 Dressed to Kill (1946) Underscore + Dialog (as:Milton Rosen) US: LP = Murray Hill 55463

1764 Dressed to Kill (1980) Score (Pino Donaggio) US:LP = Varese STV-81148*

1765 Driver's Seat, The [Identikit] (1975) Score (Franco Mannino) IT:LP = Ariete 2015*

1766 Drop Dead, Darling *see* Arrividerci, Baby

1767 Drum Crazy *see* Gene Krupa Story, The

1768 Du Beat-E-O (1985) Score (Doug Moody & Mark Wheaton) US: LP = Mystic MLP-33112*

1769 Du Mouron pour les Petites Oiseaux (1963) Theme (Georges Garvarentz) US:SP = Reprise 0438 [Charles Aznavour:ST]; Theme (Georges Garvarentz) US:SP = Decca 9-31946 [Bobby Russell]

1770 Du Rififi Chez les Hommes *see* Rififi

1771 Du Soleil Plein les Yeux (1970) Score (Francis Lai) JA:LP = UA 430*;

Theme (Francis Lai) US:LP = UA 5515* [Francis Lai:ST]

1772 Dubarry Was a Lady (1943) Highlights (e:Burton Lane/e:Roger Edens) US:LP-BP = Titania 509

1773 Dubious Patriots, The *see* You Can't Win 'Em All

1774 Duchess and the Dirtwater Fox, The (1976) Theme (Charles Fox) US:SP-PP = 20th 101611 [Bobby Vinton: ST]; Theme (Charles Fox) US:LP = ABC 957* [Bobby Vinton:ST]

1775 Duck, You Sucker [A Fistful of Dynamite] (1973) Score (Ennio Morricone) US:LP = UA UAS-5221* + US: LP = UA LA-302*

1776 Duck in Orange Sauce [L'Anatra all'Arancia] (1975) Score (Armando Trovajoli) IT:LP = Rizzoli 34001*

1777 Duel at Diablo (1966) Score (Neal Hefti) US:LP = UA UAL-4139/ UAS-5139*

1778 Duel in the Sun (1946) Score (Dimitri Tiomkin) US:LP-BP = Soundstage SS-2203; Highlights (Dimitri Tiomkin) US:78-MS = RCA 1083 [Arthur Fiedler]; Highlights (Dimitri Tiomkin) US:LP-BP = Cinema LP-8007 [Arthur Fiedler]; Excerpts (Dimitri Tiomkin) GB:LP = Unicorn DKP-9002* [Laurie Johnson]

1779 Duel of the Champions [Orazi e Curiazi] (1961) Themes (A.F. Lavagnino) IT:SP = CAM CA-2424 [ST]

1780 Duel of the Titans [Romolo e Remo] (1961) Score (Piero Piccioni) IT:LP = Phoenix PHCAM-04*

1781 Duffy (1968) Theme (Ernie Freeman) US:SP = Capitol 2252 [Lou Rawls:ST]; Theme (Ernie Freeman) US: LP = Capitol 2927* [Lou Rawls:ST]

1782 Duffy's Tavern (1945) Theme/ US:LP-BP = Vedette 8702 [Betty Hutton:ST]

1783 Duke Wore Jeans, The (1958) Highlights (various) GB:LP-10 = Decca LF-1308

1784 Dulcima (1971) Theme (Johnny Douglas) GB:LP = Contour 2870.141* [Johnny Douglas:ST]

1785 Dulcimer Street [London Belongs to Me] (1949) Theme (Benjamin Frankel) GB:78-PP = Rank FM-32 [ST]

1786 Dumbo (1941) Score (e:Frank Churchill/e:Oliver Wallace) US:LP = Disneyland WDL-4013 + US:LP = Disneyland DQ-1204

1787 Dune (1984) Score (s:Toto/t: Brian Eno) US:LP = Polydor 823-770-1*

1788 Dunwich Horror, The (1970) Score (Les Baxter) US:LP = American International A-1028* + US:LP = Varese VC-81103*

1789 Dusty and Sweets McGee (1972) Score (pop music) US:LP = WB WS-1936*

1790 Dutchman (1966) Theme (John Barry) GB:SP = CBS 63038* [John Barry:ST]; Theme (John Barry) US:LP = Columbia 9508* [John Barry: ST]

1791 Dynamic Denton [Industrial Short] Score (Jodie Lyons) US:LP-PP = Denton JLP-100

1792 Dynamite Brothers (1974) Score (Charles Earland) US:LP = Prestige 10082*

E

1793 E.T.—The Extra-Terrestrial (1982) Score (John Williams) US:LP = MCA 6109*

1794 Eadie Was a Lady (1945) Theme/US:LP-BP = Legends 1000/2 [@Ann Miller:ST]

1795 Eagle, The (1925) Theme [Silent II] (Lee Erwin) US:LP = Angel 36073* [Lee Erwin:ST]

1796 Eagle Has Landed, The (1977) Highlights (Lalo Schifrin) US:LP = Entracte ERS-6510*; Theme (Lalo Schifrin) US:SP = CTI OJ-36* [Lalo Schifrin:ST]; Theme (Lalo Schifrin) US:LP = CTI 7-5003* [Lalo Schifrin:ST]

1797 Eagles Over London [Battle Squadron] [La Battaglia d'Inghilterra] (1970) Themes (Francesco DeMasi) IT: SP = Ariete 8008 [ST]

1798 Eakins (1973) Highlights (J.K. Randall) US:LP = CRI SD-328*

1799 Early Morning (1971) Theme (Francis Lai) US:LP = UA 5630* [Francis Lai:ST]

1800 Earth Trembles, The [La Terra Trema] (1948) Theme (Willi Ferrero) JA: LP-MS = CBS/Sony 2301 [@ST]

1801 Earthling, The (1980) Theme (David Shire) US:SP = Maiden Voyage 120* [Maureen McGovern:ST]

1802 Earthquake (1974) Score (John Williams) US:LP = MCA 2081*

1803 East of Eden (1955) Excerpts-A (Leonard Rosenman) US:LP = Columbia CL-940 + US:LP = CSP ACL-940 [Ray Heindorf:ST]; Excerpts-B (Leonard Rosenman) US:LP = Imperial LP-9021 [Leonard Rosenman]

1804 East of Elephant Rock (1977) Highlights (Peter Skellern) GB:EP = Pendulum 6198-187*

1805 East Side of Heaven, The (1939) Excerpts (James Monaco) US:LP-10 = Decca DL-6014 + US:LP = Decca DL-4253 [Bing Crosby:ST]

1806 Easter Parade (1948) Highlights (pop songs:Irving Berlin) US:LP-10 = MGM E-502 + US:LP = MGM E-3227 + US:LP-MS = MGM 2SES-40e

1807 Easy Come, Easy Go (1967) Highlights (e:Gerald Nelson/etc.) US: EP = RCA EPA-4387 [Elvis Presley:ST]; Excerpts (various) US:LP = Camden CAL-2533/CAS-2533* [Elvis Presley: ST]

1808 Easy Life, The [Il Sorpasso] (1962) Theme (Riz Ortolani) US:LP = UA 6360* [Riz Ortolani:ST]

1809 Easy Money (1983) Score (e: Laurence Rosenthal/etc.) US:LP = Columbia JS-38968*

1810 Easy Money (1947) Theme/ GB:78 = Columbia 2395 [Greta Gynt: ST]

1811 Easy Rider (1969) Score (pop music) US:LP = Dunhill DXS-50063* + US:LP = MCA 2041*

1812 Easy to Love (1953) Themes (Vic Mizzy) US:SP = RCA 47-5596 [Tony Martin:ST]

1813 Eating Raoul (1982) Score (Arlon Ober) US:LP = Varese STV-81164*

1814 Eau Vive, L' (1956) Highlights (Guy Beart) FR:EP = Philips 432.511; Theme (Guy Beart) US:SP = Capitol 4242 [Frank Pourcel]; Theme (Guy Beart) US:LP = Capitol 8603* [Frank Pourcel]

1815 Eboli [Christ Stopped at Eboli] [Christo Si e Fermato a Eboli] (1979) Themes (Piero Piccioni) IT:SP = CAM 221* [ST]; Themes (Piero Piccioni) IT:LP-MS = WB/WEA 68034* [Piero Piccioni:ST]

1816 Ecco [Mondo di Notte] (1965) Score (Riz Ortolani) US:LP = WB W-1600/WS-1600*

1817 Echo Park (1986) Score (t: David Ricketts/s:various) US:LP = A&M SP-5119*

1818 Eclipse [L'Eclisse] (1962) Theme (Giovanni Fusco) IT:LP = CAM/DET 2006 [Giovanni Fusco:ST]

1819 Ecoutez Vos Murs (1982) Score (Dave Greenfield) GB:LP = Epic 25707*

1820 Eddie and the Cruisers (1983) Score (John Cafferty) US:LP = Scotti/ CBS 38929*

1821 Eddie Cantor Story, The (1954) Highlights (pop music) US:LP-10 = Capitol L-467

1822 Eddy Duchin Story, The (1954) Score (t:Morris Stoloff/s:pop music) US:LP = Decca DL-8289/DL-78289* + US:LP = Decca DL-9121/ DL-79121* + US:LP = MCA 2041* + US:LP = MCA 37088*; Excerpts (ae: George Duning) US:LP = Decca DL-8396 [@ST]

1823 Edge of the City (1957) Highlights (Leonard Rosenman) US:LP = MGM E-3501

1824 Edge of the World (1937) Theme (Lambert Williamson) GB:78 = Decca 1579 [Muir Mathieson:ST]

1825 Edith and Marcel (1984) Scores (e:Francis Lai/e:pop music) US: LP-MS = Atlantic 80153-1*

1826 Edith's Diary (1984) Score (Jurgen Knieper) US:LP = Varese STV-81255*

1827 Educating Rita (1983) Score (David Hentschel) US:LP = Mercury MERL-23*

1828 Education of Sonny Carson, The (1974) Score (Coleridge Taylor Perkinson) US:LP = Paramount PAS-1045*

1829 Eegah! (1962) Themes (Arch

Hall, Jr.) US:LP = Rhino 307 [@Arch Hall, Jr.:ST]

1830 Egyptian, The (1954) Score (e: Bernard Herrmann/e:Alfred Newman) US:LP = Decca DL-9014/DL-79014e + US:LP = MCA 2029e

1831 Eiger Sanction, The (1975) Score (John Williams) US:LP = MCA 2088*

1832 8½ (1963) Score (Nino Rota) US:LP = RCA FOC-6/FSO-6*

1833 Eight O'Clock Walk (1954) Theme (George Melachrino) US:SP = RCA 47-5579 [George Melachrino: ST]

1834 Eight on the Lam (1967) Score (George Romanis) US:LP = UA UAL-4156/UAS-5156*

1835 Eighteen and Anxious (1957) Theme (Phil Tuminello) US:SP = ABC 45-9870 [Johnny Hartman:ST]

1836 Eighteen in the Sun [Beach Party—Italian Style] [Diciottenni al Sole] (1962) Themes (Ennio Morricone) IT:SP = RCA 45-3124 [ST]

1837 80 Steps to Jonah (1969) Theme (Jason & Shayne) US:SP = Reprise 0972 [Nancy Sinatra]

1838 Eijanaika (1981) Score (Chumei Watanabe) JA:LP = RCA/Victor 1089*

1839 Electra (1962) Score (Mikis Theodorakis) GR:LP = Philips 600.508

1840 Electra Glide in Blue (1973) Score (s:James William Guercio/as:Jimmie Haskell) US:LP = UA LA-062*

1841 Electric Dreams (1984) Score (e:Giorgio Moroder/etc.) US:LP = Epic/Virgin SE-39600*

1842 Electric Horseman, The (1979) Score (e:Dave Grusin/etc.) US: LP = Columbia JS-36327*

1843 Elephant Called Slowly, An (1969) Score (Howard Blake) US:LP = Bell 1202*

1844 Elephant Man, The (1980) Score (John Morris) US:LP = Pacific Arts PAC8-143* + US:LP = 20th T-632*

1845 Elevator to the Gallows *see* Frantic

1846 Eliza Fraser (1976) Theme (Bruce Smeaton) US:LP = DRG 8202* [William Motzing]

1847 Elizabeth the Queen *see* Private Lives of Elizabeth and Essex, The

1848 Ellie (1984) Theme-A (Bill Shore) US:LP = RCA 1-5031* [Charley Pride:ST]; Theme-B (Bill Shore) US: SP = MCA 52452* [Atlanta:ST]; Theme-B (Bill Shore) US:LP = MCA 5463* [At-lanta:ST]

1849 Elmer Gantry (1960) Score (Andre Previn) US:LP = UA UAL-4069/UAS-5069*

1850 Elvis on Tour (1972) Highlights (pop music) US:LP-BP = Tiger TR 101 [Elvis Presley:ST]

1851 Elvis—That's the Way It Is (1970) Score (pop music) US:LP = RCA LSP-4445* + US:LP-BP = Amiga 1001

1852 Emanuelle in America [Emanuelle Nera in America] / Score (Nico Fidenco) IT:LP = Beat LPF-038*

1853 Emerald Forest, The (1985) Score (Brian Gascoigne) US:LP = Varese STV-81244*

1854 Emergency Exit [Sortie Secours] (1970) Score (Philippe Sarde) FR:LP = Pathe C062.11077*

1855 Emergency Ward *see* Carey Treatment, The

1856 Emily (1976) Score (Rod McKuen) US:LP = Stanyan 4025*

1857 Emmanuelle (1974) Score (Pierre Bachelet) US:LP = Arista AL-4036*

1858 Emmanuelle 2—The Joys of a Woman (1975) Score (Francis Lai) GB: LP = WB 56231*

1859 Emmanuelle 3 *see* Goodbye Emmanuelle

1860 Emmanuelle 4 (1984) Score (Michel Magne) FR:LP = Carrere 66084*

1861 Emperor of the North [Emperor of the North Pole] (1973) Theme (Frank DeVol) US:SP = MCA 40067* [Marty Robbins:ST]; Theme (Frank DeVol) US:LP = MCA 342* + US:LP = Pickwick 3742* [Marty Robbins:ST]

1862 Emperor Waltz, The (1948) Excerpts (various) US:LP-10 = Decca DL-5272 + US:LP = Decca DL-4260 [Bing Crosby:ST]

1863 Emperor's Nightingale, The

(1949) Score (Vaclav Trojan) RU:LP= Supraphon LPM-199

1864 Empire in the Sun [L'Impero del Sole] (1957) Highlights (A.F. Lavagnino) FR:EP=Philips 432.189; Theme (A.F. Lavagnino) US:LP=Columbia 107 [Michel Legrand]

1865 Empire of Passion (1976) Score (Toru Takemitsu) JA:LP=RCA/ Victor RVC-2211*

1866 Empire Strikes Back, The (1980) Scores (John Williams) US:LP-MS=RSO RS2-4201*

1867 Empty Canvas, The [La Noia] (1963) Theme (Luis E. Bacalov) IT:LP= RCA 10363 [@ST]

1868 Enchanted Cottage, The (1945) Excerpts (Roy Webb) US:LP= Entracte ERM-6515 [@Constantin Bakaleinikoff:ST]

1869 Enchanted Island, The (1958) Theme (Robert Allen) US:SP=Columbia 4-41194 [The Four Lads]; Theme (Robert Allen) US:SP=Columbia 4-41198 [Glenn Osser]; Theme (R. Allen) US:LP=Vocalion 73772* [Wayne King]

1870 Encore (1951) Theme-A (Richard Addinsell) GB:78-PP=Rank FM-124 [ST]; Theme-B (Richard Addinsell) GB:78-PP=Rank FM-125 [ST]

1871 Encounter [Incontro] (1972) Score (Ennio Morricone) IT:LP=CAM SAG-9036*; Theme (Ennio Morricone) US:LP=RCA 1-5016* [Ettore Stratta]

1872 End, The (1978) Theme (Paul Williams) US:SP=Capitol 4584* [Glen Campbell]

1873 End of the Rainbow *see* Northwest Outpost

1874 Endless Love (1981) Score (s: Jonathan Tunick/t:Lionel Richie) US: LP=Mercury/Polygram SRM1-2001*

1875 Endless Summer, The (1966) Score (John Blakeley) US:LP=World Pacific WP-1832/ST-1832*

1876 Enemy Below, The (1958) Theme (Leigh Harline) IT:LP=RCA 43634* [@Eric Rogers]

1877 Enemy Mine (1985) Score (Maurice Jarre) US:LP=Varese STV-81271*

1878 Enforcer, The [Murder, Inc.] (1951) Underscore + Dialog (David Buttolph) US:LP=Mark 56 #711

1879 Enforcer, The (1976) Excerpts (Jerry Fielding) US:LP=WB/Viva 23990-1* [@Jerry Fielding:ST]

1880 England Made Me (1973) Score (John Scott) US:LP=East Coast EC-1062*

1881 England of Elizabeth, The [Short] (1948) Excerpts (Ralph Vaughan-Williams) US:LP=RCA LSC-3280* [Andre Previn]

1882 Enigma (1983) Score (Marc Wilkinson) GB:LP=That's Entertainment TER-1027*

1883 Enter Laughing (1967) Score (Quincy Jones) US:LP=Liberty LOM-16004/LOS-17004*

1884 Enter the Dragon (1974) Score (Lalo Schifrin) US:LP=WB BS-2727*; Score + Dialog (Lalo Schifrin) JA:LP-MS=WB P-5526/7-W*

1885 Entr'acte [Entre'acte] [Short] (1924) Theme [Silent I] (Erik Satie) US: LP=Golden Crest 4019 [Arthur Kleiner]

1886 Entre Nous [Coup de Foudre] (1983) Score (Luis E. Bacalov) FR:LP= General Music 803.044*

1887 Equus (1977) Highlights + Underscore + Dialog (Richard Rodney Bennett) US:LP=UA LA-839*

1888 Eraserhead (1977) Theme + Dialog (Peter Ivers) US:LP=I.R.S. SP-70027*

1889 Eric Soya's 17 [17] (1967) Score (Ole Hoyer) US:LP=Mercury MG-21115/SR-61115*

1890 Eroe dei Nostri Tempi, Un (1955) Highlights (Nino Rota) US:LP= Cerberus CST-0205

1891 Escalation (1968) Score (Ennio Morricone) IT:LP=CAM MG-100.10

1892 Escapade [Lie Like a Gentleman] (1935) Theme (Bronislau Kaper) US:SP=MGM 10690 [Billy Eckstine]; Theme (Bronislau Kaper) US:LP-MS= DRG 2-2100 [@Billy Eckstine]; Theme (Bronislau Kaper) US:LP=MGM 3511 [Richard Ellsasser]

1893 Escapade in Japan (1957) Excerpts (Max Steiner) US:LP-BP=Tony Thomas TTMS-17 [Max Steiner:ST]

1894 Escape from Fort Bravo (1953) Theme (Jeff Alexander) US:SP= Capitol 2672 [Gordon MacRae]; Theme

(Jeff Alexander) US:SP = MGM 11620 [Bill Lee:ST]

1895 Escape from New York (1981) Score (John Carpenter) US:LP = Varese STV-81134*

1896 Escape from San Quentin (1957) Theme (Johnny Desmond) US: SP = Coral 9-61910 [Johnny Desmond: ST]

1897 Escape from the Bronx [Fuga dal Bronx] (1984) Score (Francesco De-Masi) IT:LP = Beat LPF-063*

1898 Escape from the Dark *see* Littlest Horse Thieves, The

1899 Escape Me Never (1947) Excerpts (Erich Wolfgang Korngold) US: LP = RCA LSC-3330* + US:LP = RCA AGL1-3707* [Charles Gerhardt]

1900 Escape Me Never (1935) Theme (William Walton) US:LP = London 21149* [Bernard Herrmann]

1901 Escape to Athena [Offside 7] [The Golden Raiders] (1979) Score (Lalo Schifrin) JA:LP = Seven Seas FML-124*

1902 Escape to Happiness *see* Intermezzo

1903 Escape to Montana's Glacier Park [Short] Score (Scott Warden & Don Zimmers & Jerry Lilliedahl) US:LP-PP = Tempo Two 103

1904 Escape to Witch Mountain (1975) Underscore + Dialog (Johnny Mandel) US:LP = Disneyland ST-3809*

1905 Espy (1974) Theme (Masaaki Hirao) JA:LP = Toho 8123 [@ST]

1906 Essential Oils of the Far East [Short] Score (uncredited) US:LP-PP = Fritzsche 1002

1907 Essential Oils of the Mediterranean [Short] Score (uncredited) US: LP-PP = Fritzsche CO-1213

1908 Esther Waters (1948) Theme (Gordon Jacob) GB:78-PP=Rank FM-34

1909 Eternal Sea, The (1955) Highlights (Elmer Bernstein) US:LP = Citadel CTV-7021

1910 Etoile du Nord, L' (1982) Excerpts (Philippe Sarde) US:LP = DRG SL-9512* [@ST]

1911 Etoile sans Lumiere, L' (1946) Theme (Marguerite Monnot) US:LP-MS = Atlantic 80153-1 [@Edith Piaf]

1912 Etrange Monsieur Steve, L' *see* Mr. Steve

1913 Eugenie—The Story of Her Journey into Perversion (1969) Score (Bruno Nicolai) IT:LP = Gemelli 10.024*

1914 Eureka Stockade [Massacre Hill] (1948) Theme (John Greenwood) GB:78-PP = Rank FM-49 [ST]; Theme (John Greenwood) US:LP-BP = Citadel CTOF1-1 [@ST]

1915 Europeans, The (1979) Score (classical music) US:LP = Grammavision 1010*

1916 Eva [Eve] (1962) Highlights (Michel Legrand) FR:EP = Philips 432.821

1917 Evel Knievel (1971) Themes (Patrick Williams) US:SP = Fanfare 2328 [Big Jim Sullivan]

1918 Everglade Raid [Cartoon] (1958) Sequence + Dialog (Clarence Wheeler) US:LP = Peter Pan 1120 [@ST]

1919 Evergreen (1934) Excerpts (Harry Woods) US:LP = Monmouth MES-7049 [@ST]

1920 Every Day's a Holiday (1937) Theme/US:LP-BP = Caliban 6036 [Mae West:ST]

1921 Every Day's a Holiday (1965) *see* Seaside Swingers

1922 Every Man for Himself [Sauve Qui Peut la Vie] (1980) Score (Gabriel Yared) FR:LP = WB/WEA 723.622*

1923 Every Night at Eight (1935) Highlights (e:Jimmy McHugh/etc.) US: LP-BP = Caliban 6043

1924 Every Which Way But Loose (1978) Score (e:Steve Dorff/etc.) US: LP = Elektra 5E-503*

1925 Everybody Sing (1938) Highlights (Bronislau Kaper) US:LP-BP = Pilgrim 4000

1926 Everybody's Cheering *see* Take Me Out to the Ball Game

1927 Everything I Have Is Yours (1952) Excerpts (John Green) US:LP-10 = MGM E-187 + US:LP-MS = MGM 2SES-52e [@ST]

1928 Everything Is Rhythm (1936) Highlights (Meskill & Ray) GB:LP = WRC SH-197

1929 Everything You Always Wanted to Know About Sex ... But Were Afraid to Ask (1972) Theme (Mundell Lowe) US:SP = UA 50963* [Ferrante

& Teicher]; Theme (Mundell Lowe) US: LP = UA 018* [Ferrante & Teicher]

1930 Evil Dead, The (1982) Score (Joseph Lo Duca) US:LP = Varese STV-81199*

1931 Excalibur (1981) Theme (Trevor Jones) US:SP = WB 49737* [Trevor Jones:ST]

1932 Excuse Me, Are You For or Against? [Scusi, Lei a Favorevole o Contrairio?] (1966) Themes (Piero Piccioni) IT:SP = Parade 5022 [ST]

1933 Executioner, The (1970) Theme (Ron Goodwin) GB:LP = MFP 50248* [Geoff Love]

1934 Exodus (1960) Score (Ernest Gold) US:LP = RCA LOC-1058/LSO-1058* + US:LP = RCA AYL1-3872*

1935 Exorcist, The (1973) Score (t:Jack Nitzsche/s:classical music) US:LP = WB WS-2774*

1936 Exorcist II: The Heretic (1977) Score (Ennio Morricone) US:LP = WB BS-3068*

1937 Experience (1975) Score-A (rock music) GB:LP = Bulldog BDL-4002* [Jimi Hendrix:ST]; Score-B (rock music) GB:LP = Bulldog BDL-4003* [Jimi Hendrix:ST]

1938 Experiment in Terror [The Grip of Fear] (1962) Score (Henry Mancini) US:LP = RCA LPM-2442/LSP-2442*

1939 Explorers (1985) Score (Jerry Goldsmith) US:LP = MCA 6148*

1940 Expresso Bongo (1959) Highlights (Norrie Paramor) GB:EP = Columbia SEG-7971 [Cliff Richard:ST]; Theme (Norrie Paramor) US:SP = ABC 45-10093 [Cliff Richard:ST]

1941 Exterieur Nuit (1980) Score (Karl Heinz Schafer) FR:LP = WB/WEA 883.040*

1942 Extremes (1972) Score (various) GB:LP = Deram SML-1095*

1943 Eye of the Devil [13] (1967) Theme-A (Gary McFarland) US:LP = Verve 6-8678* [Jimmy Smith]; Theme-A (Gary McFarland) US:LP = Verve 6-8682* [Gary McFarland:ST]; Themes-B-C (Gary McFarland) US:LP = Impulse 9136* [Gary McFarland:ST]

1944 Eye of the Needle (1981) Score (Miklos Rozsa) US:LP = Varese STV-81133*

1945 Eyes of a Child, The / Theme (Fred Karger) US:SP = Atherton 450* [Dick Haymes]

1946 Eyes of Laura Mars, The (1978) Score (Artie Kane) US:LP = Columbia JS-35487*

1947 Eyes Without a Face *see* Horror Chamber of Dr. Faustus, The

F

1948 F.B.I. Story, The (1959) Theme (Max Steiner) US:SP = Columbia 4-41452 [Richard Maltby]; Theme (Max Steiner) US:SP = Columbia 4-41503 [Jerry Vale]; Theme (Max Steiner) US: LP = Columbia 1421/8218* [@Richard Maltby]

1949 F for Fake [Fake] (1974) Theme (Michel Legrand) US:LP = RCA 1-0850* + US:LP = Pablo 2312.139* [Michel Legrand:ST]; Theme (Michel Legrand) US:LP = Columbia 32580* [Andre Kostelanetz]

1950 F.I.S.T. (1978) Score (Bill Conti) US:LP = UA LA-897*

1951 F.J. Holden (1977) Score (Jim Manzie) AU:LP = Festival 36222*

1952 F.M. (1978) Scores (pop music) US:LP-MS = MCA 2-12000*

1953 F.P.1 (1933) Theme / GB: LP = WRC 217 [@Conrad Veidt:ST]

1954 F/X (1986) Score (Bill Conti) US:LP = Varese STV-81276*

1955 Fabulous Dorseys, The (1947) Theme-A (at:Leo Shuken) US:78 = RCA/Victor 46-0009 [Jimmy Dorsey: ST]; Theme-B/US:78 = RCA/Victor 25523 [Tommy Dorsey:ST]; Themes-C-D/US:78=RCA/Victor 20-2064 [Tommy Dorsey:ST]

1956 Face in the Crowd, A (1957) Score (Tom Glazer) US:LP = Capitol W-872

1957 Face of Another, The (1966) Excerpts (Toru Takemitsu) JA:LP = RCA/Victor 1070 [Toru Takemitsu:ST]

1958 Face to Face [Faccia a Faccia] (1967) Score (Ennio Morricone) IT:LP = Intermezzo IMGM-004*

1959 Faces (1968) Highlights (Jack Ackerman) US:LP = Columbia OS-3290*

1960 Facing the Music (1933) Themes/GB:78 = Decca 3652 [Stanley Lupino:ST]

1961 Facts of Life, The (1960) Theme (Johnny Mercer) US:SP = UA 282 [Steve Lawrence & Eydie Gorme]

1962 Facts of Murder, The [Un Maledetto Imbroglio] (1959) Themes (Carlo Rustichelli) IT:SP = RCA PM-0943 [ST]; Theme (Carlo Rustichelli) US:LP = RCA FSO-4* [@ST]

1963 Fahrenheit 451 (1966) Excerpts (Bernard Herrmann) US:LP = London SP-44207* + US:LP = London SPC-21177* + US:LP-PP = London CSL-1001* [Bernard Herrmann:ST]

1964 Fake *see* see F for Fake

1965 Falcon and the Snowman, The (1985) Score (Pat Metheny) US: LP = EMI SV-17150*

1966 Fall of a Nation, The (1916) Theme [Silent I] (Victor Herbert) US: SP = Decca 9-29566 [Wayne King]; Theme [Silent I] (Victor Herbert) US: LP = Decca 8145 [Wayne King]

1967 Fall of Berlin, The (1949) Highlights (Dmitri Shostakovich) US: LP = Classic Editions CE-9/CE-3009

1968 Fall of the Roman Empire, The (1964) Score (Dimitri Tiomkin) US: LP = Columbia OL-6060/OS-2460*

1969 Fallen Angel (1945) Theme (David Raksin) US:78 = Decca 18920 [Dick Haymes]; Theme (David Raksin) US:LP = Impulse 19* [Manny Albam]; Theme (David Raksin) US:LP = Discovery 894* [Charlie Shoemake]

1970 Falling for You (1933) Theme/GB:LP = WRC 113 [Jack Hulbert:ST]

1971 Falling in Love Again (1980) Score (Michel Legrand) US:LP-PP = OTA 4165*

1972 False Witness *see* Zigzag

1973 Falstaff *see* Chimes at Midnight

1974 Fame (1980) Score (Michael Gore) US:LP = RSO RX1-3080*

1975 Famiglia Impossible, Una / Theme (Morbelli) US:LP = Epic 3593 [Gian Stellari]

1976 Family, The [Violent City] [Citta Violenta] (1973) Score (Ennio Morricone) IT:LP = RCA KOLS-1010*

1977 Family Plot (1976) Theme (John Williams) US:LP = Varese 704.250* [Charles Ketcham]

1978 Family Way, The (1967) Score (s:Paul McCartney/as:George Martin) US:LP = London M-76007/MS-82007*; Theme (Murray Head) US:SP = Capitol 5957 [Murray Head:ST]

1979 Fancy Pants (1950) Theme (Jay Livingston & Ray Evans) US: SP = Capitol 1042 [Bob Hope:ST]

1980 Fanfan the Tulip [Fan-Fan la Tulipe] [Soldier of Love] (1952) Highlights + Dialog (Georges Van Parys) FR:LP = Ades/Le Petit Menestrel 2913.008

1981 Fanny (1961) Score (stage music:Harold Rome/as:Harry Sukman) US:LP = WB W-1416/WS-1416*

1982 Fanny Hill (1964) Theme (Erwin Halletz) US:SP = Atco 6349 [The Gentlemen/The Girls]; Theme (Erwin Halletz) US:LP = Command 887* [Enoch Light]

1983 Fanny Hill (1971) Score (Clay Pitts) US:LP = Canyon CAY-7700*

1984 Fantasia (1940) Scores [1940 Release] (classical music) US:LP-MS = Disneyland WDX-101/SWDS-101* [Leopold Stokowski:ST]; Scores [1982 Release] (classical music) US:LP-MS = Disneyland 104* [Irwin Kostal:ST]

1985 Fantasmi a Roma *see* Ghosts of Rome

1986 Fantastic Disappearing Man, The *see* Return of Dracula

1987 Fantastic Planet [La Planete Sauvage] (1976) Score (Alain Goraguer) FR:LP = Pathe C066.12698*

1988 Fantastic Plastic Machine, The (1969) Score (Harry Betts) US:LP = Epic BN-26469*

1989 Fantastic Voyage (1966) Theme (Billy Page) US:SP = 20th 6653 [The 5'th Avenue Business:ST]

1990 Fantastica (1980) Score (Lewis Furey) FR:LP = RCA RSL-1085*

1991 Fantomes du Chapelier, Les (1982) Themes (Georges Garvarentz) FR: SP = RCA 8987* [ST]

1992 Far from the Madding Crowd

(1967) Score (Richard Rodney Bennett) US:LP = MGM 1E-11/1SE-11*

1993 Far Horizons, The (1955) Excerpts (Hans J. Salter) US:LP = Medallion ML-313 [Hans J. Salter:ST]

1994 Farewell, My Lovely (1975) Score (David Shire) US:LP = UA LA-556*

1995 Farewell Performance (1963) Theme (Joe Meek) US:SP = London 45-9614 [The Tornadoes]

1996 Farewell to Arms, A (1957) Score (Mario Nascimbene) US:LP = Capitol W-918

1997 Farewell to Youth *see* Addio Giovinezza

1998 Farewell Uncle Tom *see* Goodbye Uncle Tom

1999 Farm / Score (Doug Dragon) US:LP-PP = Dendra 2001*

2000 Farmer, The (1977) Score (e:Hugo Montenegro/e:various) US:LP-PP = HM 1001*

2001 Farmer's Daughter, The (1940) Theme-A/US:LP-MS-BP = Legends 1000/5-6 [Martha Raye:ST]; Theme-B/US:LP = Epic 3061 [Martha Raye:ST]

2002 Farmyard Symphony [Cartoon] (1938) Theme (at:Leigh Harline) GB:78 = HMV 910 [ST]

2003 Farrebique (1946) Theme (Henri Sauget) FR:LP = Vega 30-A-98 [@ST]

2004 Fascist, The (Il Federale) (1961) Theme (Ennio Morricone) IT: LP = Cinevox 35046 [Ennio Morricone: ST]

2005 Fashions of 1934 [Fashions] (1934) Theme/US:LP = UA 361 [@ Verree Teasdale:ST]

2006 Fast and Sexy [Anna from Brooklyn] (1957) Theme (Alessandro Cicognini) US:LP = Epic 3593 [Gian Stellari]

2007 Fast Break (1979) Score (David Shire) US:LP = Motown M7-915*

2008 Fast Forward (1985) Score (e: Tom Bahler/e:various) US:LP = QWEST 25263-1*

2009 Fast Times at Ridgemont High (1982) Scores (pop music) US:LP-MS = Full Moon/Asylum 60158-1*

2010 Fastest Guitar Alive, The (1967) Score (Roy Orbison) US:LP = MGM E-4475/SE-4475*

2011 Fatal Attraction (1986) Score (e:Max Hitchcock/e:various) US:LP = Fast Fire FST-7500*

2012 Fate Is the Hunter (1964) Theme (Jerry Goldsmith) US:SP = 20th 546 [Johnny Desmond]; Theme (Jerry Goldsmith) US:SP = Command 4052 [Enoch Light]; Theme (Jerry Goldsmith) US:LP = Command 871* [Enoch Light]

2013 Father Goose (1965) Themes (Cy Coleman) US:SP = Decca 9-31724 [Digby Wolfe]; Theme (Cy Coleman) US:LP = Reprise 1013* [Frank Sinatra]; Theme (Cy Coleman) US:LP = Columbia 32804* [Cy Coleman:ST]

2014 Father of the Bride (1950) Theme (Adolph Deutsch) US:LP = MGM 4144* [David Rose]

2015 Father's Doing Fine (1952) Theme (Harold Smart) GB:78 = Parlophone 3596 [ST]

2016 Fathom (1967) Score (Johnny Dankworth) US:LP = 20th 4195/S-4195*

2017 Fazil (1928) Theme (Bill Zamecnik) US:78 = RCA Victor 21633 [The Troubadours]

2018 Fear (1955) Theme (Becucci) US:LP = Audition 33-5902 [The Audition Studio Orchestra]

2019 Fear in the City *see* Night Caller, The

2020 Fear in the Night (1972) Theme (John McCabe) US:LP = Capitol 11340* [@ST]

2021 Fear Is the Key (1972) Score (Roy Budd) GB:LP = Pye NSPL-18398*

2022 Fear No Evil (1981) Score (David Spear) US:LP = Web ST-106*

2023 Federale, Il *see* Fascist, The

2024 Fedora (1979) Score (Miklos Rozsa) US:LP = Varese VC-81108*

2025 Fellini Satyricon (1969) Score (Nino Rota) US:LP = UA UAS-5208*

2026 Fellini's Casanova [Il Casanova de Fellini] (1976) Score (Nino Rota) IT:LP = CAM SAG-9075*

2027 Fellini's Roma (1972) Score (Nino Rota) US:LP = UA LA-052*

2028 Female, The [Seventy Times Seven] (1962) Theme (Perry Botkin, Sr.) US:SP = Decca 9-31120 [Chuck Connors]

2029 Female Animal, The (1970) Score (Clay Pitts) US:LP = Canyon CAY-7702*

2030 Female Bunch, The (1971) Themes (Jaime Mendoza-Nava/John Gay) US:SP = Dalia 1001 [Bruce Powers: ST]

2031 Female on the Beach (1955) Theme (Sonny Burke) US:SP = RCA 47-6194 [Leo Diamond]; Theme (Sonny Burke) US:SP = Decca 9-29563 [Victor Young]; Theme (Sonny Burke) US:LP-BP = Cinema LP-8001 [@Victor Young]

2032 Female Prisoner, The *see* Prisonniere, La

2033 Femme Publique, La (1984) Score (Alain Wisniak) FR:LP = Apache WEA 24.0393.1*

2034 Femmes Disparaissent, Des [Girls Disappear] [Women Disappear] [I Vampiri del Se So] (1958) Highlights (Art Blakey & Benny Golson) FR:LP-10 = Fontana 660.224 + FR:LP = Philips 812107; Excerpts (Art Blakey) US: LP = Fontana MGF-27532/SRF-67532* [@ST]

2035 Femmes Fatales [Calmos] (1976) Score (Georges Delerue) FR:LP = Black and Blue 33400*

2036 Ferdinand the Bull [Cartoon] (1938) Theme (Al Malotte) US:LP = ABC 194* [Bill Hayes]

2037 Ferris Bueller's Day Off (1986) Theme (General Public) US:SP = IRS 52941* [General Public:ST]

2038 Ferry Cross the Mersey (1965) Score (Gerry Marsden) US:LP = UA UAL-3387/UAS-6387*; Theme (George Martin) US:SP = UA 831 [George Martin:ST]

2039 Feudin' Rhythm (1949) Themes/US:SP = RCA 48-0136 [Eddy Arnold:ST]

2040 Fever Heat (1955) *see* Bob le Flambeur

2041 Fiddler on the Roof (1971) Scores (stage songs:Jerry Bock) US:LP-MS = UA 2-10900* + US:LP-MS = Liberty LXB-01041*

2042 Fiendish Plot of Dr. Fu Manchu, The (1980) Themes (Marc Wilkinson) US:SP-PP = WB PRO-896* [Gary Travers/Marc Wilkinson:ST]

2043 Fiesta (1947) Theme (at:John Green) US:78 = MGM 30016 [MGM Studio Orchestra]

2044 Fifi la Plume (1965) Highlights (Jean Michel Defave) FR:EP = Ducretet 460-V-680

2045 15 from Rome [Opiate '67] [I Mostri] (1963) Themes (Armando Trovajoli) IT:SP = RCA 45-3236 [ST]

2046 Fifth Day of Peace, The (1972) Theme (Ennio Morricone) FR:LP = WB/WEA 56348* [Ennio Morricone:ST]

2047 55 Days at Peking (1963) Score (Dimitri Tiomkin) US:LP = Columbia CL-2028/CS-8828*

2048 52 Pick-Up (1986) Score (Gary Chang) US:LP = Varese STV-81300*

2049 Fighter, The (1952) Highlights (Vicente Gomez) US:LP-10 = Decca DL-5415

2050 Fighter Squadron (1948) Excerpts (Max Steiner) US:LP-BP = Tony Thomas TTMS-17 [Max Steiner:ST]

2051 Fighting 7th, The *see* Little Big Horn

2052 Final Comedown, The (1972) Score (Wade Marcus) US:LP = Blue Note BST-84415*

2053 Final Conflict, The (1981) Score (Jerry Goldsmith) US:LP = Varese STV-81272*

2054 Final Countdown, The (1980) Score (John Scott) US:LP = Casablanca NBLP-7232*

2055 Final Exam (1981) Score (Gary Scott) US:LP = AEI 3105*

2056 Final Option, The [Commando] [Who Dares, Wins] (1983) Score (Roy Budd) US:LP = Varese STV-81188*

2057 Final Test, The (1953) Theme (Benjamin Frankel) GB:78-PP = Rank FM-136 [ST]

2058 Finders Keepers (1966) Score (The Shadows) GB:LP = Columbia CSX-6079*

2059 Finders Keepers [Short] Sequence + Dialog (Arthur Kleiner) US: LP-PP = Picture Book Parade 107 [@ST]

2060 Fine and Dandy *see* West Point Story

2061 Fine Mess, A (1986) Score (t:Henry Mancini/s:various) US:LP = Motown 6180-ML*

2062 Fingers (1978) Theme (George Barrie) US:SP = Buddah 591* [Jerry Vale:ST]

2063 Finian's Rainbow (1968) Score (stage songs:Burton Lane) US:LP = WB B-2550/BS-2550*

2064 Finnegans Wake [Passages from Finnegans Wake] (1968) Underscore + Dialog (Elliot Kaplan) US: LP = RCA VDS-118*

2065 Fire Down Below (1957) Score (as:Ken Jones/t:Lester Lee/t:Jack Lemmon) US:LP = Decca DL-8597

2066 Fire in the City / Themes (Krug) US:SP = Verve 10512 [Jon Hendricks]

2067 Fire on the Heather / Theme (Al Malotte) US:LP = Word 3164 [@Ralph Carmichael:ST]

2068 Fire Sale (1977) Themes (Dave Grusin) US:SP = Greedy 116* [Dave Grusin & the Greedy Band:ST]

2069 Fire with Fire (1986) Theme (Chas Sandford) US:SP = Chrysalis 4-42985* [Wild Blue:ST]

2070 Fireball Jungle (1968) Themes (Tiny Kennedy) US:SP = Americana 5969 [Tiny Kennedy:ST]

2071 Firefly, The (1937) Highlights (stage songs:Rudolf Friml) US:LP-BP = Caliban 6027; Highlights (stage songs: Rudolf Friml) US:LP-10 = RCA LM-121 [Jeanette MacDonald:ST]; Highlights (stage songs:Rudolf Friml) US:LP-10 = RCA LK-146 [Allan Jones:ST]

2072 Firepower (1979) Themes (Gato Barbieri) US:LP = A&M 4774* [Gato Barbieri:ST]; Theme (Gato Barbieri) US:SP = A&M 2141* [Gato Barbieri:ST]

2073 Fires on the Plain (1959) Excerpts (Yasushi Akutagawa) JA:LP = Toho 8083 [Yasushi Akutagawa:ST]

2074 Firestarter (1984) Score (Tangerine Dream) US:LP = MCA 6131*

2075 Firewalker (1986) Score (Gary Chang) US:LP = Varese STV-81303*

2076 First, A Girl (1935) Themes-A-B/GB:78 = Decca 5728 [Jessie Matthews:ST]; Themes-C-D/GB:78 = Decca 5729 [Jessie Matthews:ST]

2077 First Blood [Rambo] (1982) Score (Jerry Goldsmith) US:LP = Regency RI-8503*

2078 First Desire [Premiers Desirs] (1983) Score (Philippe Sarde) FR:LP = General Music 803.059*

2079 First Great Train Robbery, The *see* Great Train Robbery, The

2080 First Love (1939) Excerpts (at:Hans J. Salter/etc.) US:78-MS = Decca 75 [Deanna Durbin:ST]

2081 First Love (1958) Theme (Stanley Black) GB:LP = Ace of Hearts 60 [@ST]

2082 First Love (1970) Theme (Mark London) US:SP = Colossus 133 [Jerry Ross]

2083 First Men in the Moon (1964) Highlights (Laurie Johnson) US:LP = Varese/Starlog SV-95002*

2084 First Nudie Musical, The (1976) Score (Bruce Kimmel) US:LP-PP = First Musical 1001* + US:LP-PP = Northal 101* + US:LP = Varese VRS-81028*

2085 First of the Few *see* Spitfire, The

2086 First Time, The [You Don't Need Pajamas at Rosie's] (1969) Themes (Kenyon Hopkins) US:SP = UA 50511* [Kenyon Hopkins:ST]

2087 First Traveling Saleslady, The (1956) Theme (Irving Gertz) US:SP = Coral 9-61665 [The Lancers]; Theme (Irving Gertz) US:SP = RKO Unique 342 [Fran Warren]

2088 Firstborn (1984) Score (various) US:LP = EMI ST-17144*

2089 Fish That Saved Pittsburgh, The (1979) Score (Thom Bell) US:LP = Lorimar SZ-36303*

2090 Fisherman's Wharf (1939) Themes/US:78 = Decca 2353 [Bobby Breen:ST]

2091 Fist in His Pocket [I Pugni in Tasca] (1966) Theme (Ennio Morricone) IT:LP-MS = RCA 2-1174* + IT:LP = RCA 10486* [Ennio Morricone:ST]

2092 Fist of Fury *see* Chinese Connection, The

2093 Fistful of Dollars, A (1966) Highlights (Ennio Morricone) US:LP = RCA LOC-1135/LSO-1135*; Highlights (Ennio Morricone) US:LP = Peters PILPS-4060*

2094 Fistful of Dynamite, A *see* Duck, You Sucker

2095 Fists of Fury [The Big Boss] (1973) Score (Joseph Koo) JA:LP = TAM YX-8017* + JA:LP = RCA/Victor VIP-7304*

2096 Fitzcarraldo (1982) Score (e: Popol Vuh/etc.) US:LP = Polydor PDH1-6363*

2097 Fitzwilly [Fitzwilly Strikes Back] (1967) Score (John Williams) US: LP = UA UAL-4173/UAS-5173*

2098 Five Against the House (1955) Theme (Hal Hackady) US:SP = MGM 11915 [Billy Eckstine]

2099 Five Card Stud (1968) Theme (Maurice Jarre) US:SP = Reprise 0765 [Dean Martin:ST]; Theme (Maurice Jarre) US:SP = GNP 413* [Billy Strange]; Theme (Maurice Jarre) US: LP = GNP 2046* [Billy Strange]

2100 Five Chinese Brothers [Short] Sequence + Dialog (Arthur Kleiner) US: LP-PP = Picture Book Parade 105 [@ST]

2101 Five Days and Five Nights (1948) Highlights (Dmitri Shostakovich) US:LP-BP = Cinema LP-8003

2102 Five Days from Home (1978) Score (Bill Conti) US:LP = MCA 2362*

2103 Five Easy Pieces (1970) Score (pop music/classical music) US:LP = Epic KE-30456*

2104 Five Fingers of Death, The [King Boxer] (1971) Theme (Richard Rome) US:SP = Philadelphia 7-3532* [Bunny Sigler]

2105 Five Gates to Hell (1959) Theme (Paul Dunlap) US:SP = Capitol 4293 [Paul Dunlap:ST]

2106 Five Graves to Cairo (1943) Excerpts (Miklos Rozsa) US:LP = Deutsche 2584.021* [Miklos Rozsa:ST]

2107 Five Guns West (1955) Theme (Buddy Bregman) US:SP = Era 1006 [Buddy Bregman:ST]

2108 Five Man Army [Un Esercito di 5 Uomini] (1970) Score (Ennio Morricone) IT:LP = Ariete 2009 + IT:LP = Duse ELP-058

2109 Five Miles to Midnight (1963) Score (e:Mikis Theodorakis/e:Jacques Loussier) US:LP-PP = UA 009.014; Highlights (t:Mikis Theodorakis/e: Jacques Loussier) FR:EP = UA 36032

2110 Five Miles West [Industrial Short] Score (Richard Ralf) US:LP-PP = Volkswagen RSMC-1224

2111 Five on the Black Hand Side (1973) Theme (H.B. Barnum) US:SP = UA 338* [Keisa Brown:ST]

2112 Five Pennies, The (1959) Score (e:Sylvia Fine/t:Leith Stevens/ etc.) US:LP = Dot DLP-9500/DLP-29500*

2113 Five Savage Men [The Animals] (1971) Score (Rupert Holmes) US:LP = Vee Jay VJS-1211*

2114 Five Summer Stories (1972) Score (Richard Stekol & Steve Wood) US:LP = Granite GR-7720* [Honk:ST]

2115 5,000 Fingers of Dr. T, The (1953) Theme (Frederick Hollander) US: SP = Liberty 55633 [Jerry Lewis]; Theme (Frederick Hollander) US:LP = Capitol 878 [Carole Simpson]

2116 Five Weeks in a Baloon (1962) Theme (Jodi Desmond) US:SP = 20th 307 [Carl Lertzman]; Theme (Jodi Desmond) US:SP = Roulette 4437 [Sonny Lester]; Theme (Jodi Desmond) US: SP = Columbia 4-42507 [The Brothers Four]

2117 Flame (1975) Score (Jimmy Lea & Noddy Holder) US:LP = WB BS-2865* [Slade:ST]

2118 Flame and the Arrow, The (1950) Excerpts (Max Steiner) US:LP-BP = Citadel CTMS-2 [Max Steiner:ST]

2119 Flame and the Fire, The (1966) Theme (Michael Colicchio) US:LP = UA 6560* [Al Caiola]

2120 Flame and the Flesh, The (1954) Highlights (Nicholas Brodszky) US:EP = MGM X-1323; Themes (George Stoll) US:78 = MGM 30851 [George Stoll:ST]

2121 Flame of New Orleans, The (1941) Theme/US:LP-BP = Marsher 201 [Marlene Dietrich:ST]

2122 Flame of the Islands (1955) Theme (Sonny Burke) US:SP = Capitol 3206 [Yvonne DeCarlo:ST]; Theme (Sonny Burke) US:SP = Decca 9-27598 [Dick Haymes]

2123 Flaming Frontier [Old Surehand, L. Teil] (1965) Highlights (Martin Bottcher) GE:LP = Polydor 249.083*

2124 Flaming Star (1960) Theme (Sherman Edwards) US:LP = Camden

2304 + US:LP = Camden 2408 [Elvis Presley:ST]

2125 Flamingo Kid, The (1984) Score-A (pop music) US:LP = Varese STV-81232*; Score-B (pop music) US: LP = Motown 6131-ML*

2126 Flamingo Road (1949) Theme/US:LP-BP = Curtain Calls 100/23 [Joan Crawford:ST]

2127 Flash Gordon (1980) Score (Queen) US:LP = Elektra 5E-518*

2128 Flash Gordon's Trip to Mars [The Deadly Ray from Mars] (1938) Underscore + Dialog (stock music) US: LP = Pelican LP-2006

2129 Flashdance (1983) Score (e: Giorgio Moroder/etc.) US:LP = Casablanca/Polygram 811.492-1*

2130 Flasher, The (1977) Score (e: Rupert Holmes/e:Larry Colacino) US: LP = Greene Bottle GBS-1008*

2131 Flashpoint (1984) Score (Tangerine Dream) US:LP = EMI ST-17141*

2132 Flat Foot Fledgling [Cartoon] (1952) Sequence + Dialog (Philip Scheib) US:LP = RCA LBY-1031 [@ST]

2133 Flea in Her Ear, A (1969) Score (Bronislau Kaper) US:LP = 20th S-4200*

2134 Fleet's In, The (1942) Score (Victor Schertzinger) US:LP-BP = Hollywood Soundstage 405

2135 Flesh and Blood (1949) Theme (Charles Williams) GB:78 = Columbia 2836 [Charles Williams:ST]

2136 Flesh and Blood (1985) Score (Basil Poledoris) US:LP = Varese STV-81256*

2137 Flesh and Fantasy (1943) Theme (Alexander Tansmann) US:LP = Camden 205 + US:LP = Camden 233 [Werner Janssen]

2138 Flesh for Frankenstein *see* Andy Warhol's Frankenstein

2139 Fleur de l'Age, La / Theme (Joseph Kosma) US:LP = Columbia 569 [Juilette Greco]

2140 Fletch (1985) Score (e:Harold Faltermeyer/e:various) US:LP = MCA 6142*

2141 Flic ou Voyou [Cop or Hood] (1979) Score (Philippe Sarde) FR:LP = Carrere/Cobra 37021*; Highlights (Philippe Sarde) FR:LP = WB/WEA 58130*

2142 Flic Story [Cop Story] (1975) Theme (Claude Bolling) JA:LP-MS = TAM 9015/6* [Stanley Maxfield]

2143 Flight at Midnight (1939) Theme/US:78 = Decca 2666 [Phil Regan: ST]

2144 Flight from Ashiya (1964) Theme (Frank Cordell) US:SP = Epic 5-9686 [Adam Wade]

2145 Flight of the Doves (1971) Score (Roy Budd) US:LP = London XPS-591*

2146 Flight of the White Stallions *see* Miracle of the White Stallions

2147 Flight to Hong Kong (1956) Theme (Monty Kelly) US:SP = MGM 12359 [Rory Calhoun:ST]; Theme (Monty Kelly) US:SP = Coral 9-61717 [Hoagy Carmichael]

2148 Flipper (1963) Theme (Henry Vars) US:SP = Capitol 4996 [Jimmie Haskell]; Theme (Henry Vars) US:LP = Capitol 2075* [Jimmie Haskell]; Theme (Henry Vars) US:LP = Metro 544* [@Milton DeLugg]

2149 Flipper's New Adventure (1964) Theme (Henry Vars) US:LP = MGM 4226* [Chris Crosby]

2150 Flirtation Walk (1934) Excerpts (Allie Wrubel) US:LP-BP = Caliban 6042 [@ST]

2151 Flood Tide (1949) Theme (Robert Irving) GB : 78-PP = Rank FM-56 [ST]; Theme (Robert Irving) US:LP-BP = Citadel CTOFI-1 [@ST]

2152-3 Flower Drum Song (1961) Score (stage songs:Richard Rodgers) US:LP = Decca DL-9098/DL-79098* + US:LP = MCA 2069*

2154 Fly, The (1986) Score (Howard Shore) US:LP = Varese STV-81289*; Theme ["Help Me"] (Nile Rodgers) US:SP = WB 7-28582* [Bryan Ferry:ST]

2155 Fly-In (1975) Theme (Donald Specht) US:SP-PP = Fly-In 101 [Ralph Grierson:ST]

2156 Flying Clipper, The *see* Mediterranean Holiday

2157 Flying Down to Rio (1933) Highlights (Vincent Youmans) US:LP-

BP = Classic International Filmusicals 3004 + US:LP-BP = Sandy Hook SH-2010

2158 Flying High (1931) Theme/ US:LP-BP = JJA 19765 [@Bert Lahr: ST]

2159 Flying Mouse, The [Cartoon] (1934) Theme (Frank Churchill) US: LP = Disneyland 1283 [@uncredited]

2160 Flying Saucer, The [Il Disco Volante] (1965) Themes (Piero Piccioni) IT:SP = Style 602 [ST]

2161 Foes (1977) Score (Jeff Bruner) US:LP-PP = Foes SBSR-2978*

2162 Fog, The (1980) Score (John Carpenter) US:LP = Varese STV-81191*

2163 Folies Bergere (1935) Themes-A-B/US:LP = RCA 2076 [Maurice Chevalier:ST]; Theme-C/US:78 = RCA/ Victor 24874 [Maurice Chevalier:ST]; Theme-D/US:78 = RCA/Victor 24882 [Maurice Chevalier:ST]

2164 Folies Bergere (1958) Score (M. Philippe Gerard) US:LP = Decca DL-8571 [Roger Roger]

2165 Follow Me (1969) Score (Stu Phillips) US:LP = UNI 73056*

2166 Follow Me (1972) *see* Public Eye, The

2167 Follow Me, Boys (1966) Theme (Richard & Robert Sherman) US: LP = Disneyland 1298 [@Fred MacMurray:ST]

2168 Follow That Bird *see* Sesame Street Presents—Follow That Bird

2169 Follow That Dream (1962) Highlights (various) US:EP = RCA EPA-4368 [Elvis Presley:ST]

2170 Follow the Boys (1944) Score (e:Jule Styne/etc.) US:LP-BP = Hollywood Soundstage HS-5012

2171 Follow the Boys (1962) Highlights (Benny Davis) US:LP = MGM E-4123/SE-4123* [Connie Francis:ST]

2172 Follow the Fleet (1936) Score (Irving Berlin) US:LP-BP = Sountrak STK-118; Highlights (Irving Berlin) US: LP-BP = Scarce Rarities 5505 + US:LP-BP = Caliban 6024; Excerpts (Irving Berlin) US:LP = Columbia SG-32472 [Fred Astaire:ST]

2173 Follow the Leader (1930) Theme/US:LP = Encore 101 [Ethel Merman:ST]

2174 Follow the Leader (1944) Underscore + Dialog (Edward J. Kay) US:LP-MS = Murray Hill 57385

2175 Follow the Sun (1951) Theme (J. Magidson) US:SP = RCA 47-3941 [Tony Martin]

2176 Fool for Love (1985) Score (Sandy Rogers) US:LP = MCA 6156*

2177 Fool There Was, A (1914) Theme [Silent I] (B. Gay) US:LP = Golden Crest 4019 [Arthur Kleiner]

2178 Fool Thief [Il Ladrone] (1980) Score (Ennio Morricone) IT:LP = RCA BL-31502*

2179 Foolin' Around (1980) Theme (Charles Bernstein) US:SP-12-PP = Canon Comedy PDSC-180* [ST]

2180 Fools (1970) Score (e:Shorty Rogers/e:The First Edition) US:LP = Reprise RS-6429*

2181 Fools Rush In (1949) Theme (Wilfred Burns) GB:78-PP = Rank FM-60 [ST]

2182 Footlight Parade (1933) Excerpts (various) US:LP-MS = Columbia C2L-44 [Dick Powell:ST]

2183 Footlight Serenade (1942) Highlights (Ralph Rainger) US:LP-BP = Caliban 6002

2184 Footloose (1983) Score (various) US:LP = Columbia JS-39242*

2185 Footsteps in the Dark (1941) Theme/US:LP-BP = Legends 1000/2 [@Lee Patrick:ST]

2186 Footsteps in the Fog (1955) Theme (Benjamin Frankel) US:SP = Epic 5-9117 [Walter Stott]

2187 For a Few Bullets More *see* Any Gun Can Play

2188 For a Few Dollars More (1967) Highlights (Ennio Morricone) US:LP = Peters PILPS-4060*

2189 For Love and Gold [L'Armata Brancaleone] (1965) Themes (Carlo Rustichelli) IT:SP = Parade 5002 [ST]

2190 For Love of Ivy (1968) Score (Quincy Jones) US:LP = ABC SOC-7*

2191 For Love, One Can Die [D'Amore Si Muore] (1973) Theme (Ennio Morricone) FR:LP = Philips 9101.702* [Mireille Mathieu]

2192 For Me and My Gal (1942) Score (various) US:LP-BP = Sountrak STK-107

2193 For Pete's Sake (1966) Score (Ralph Carmichael) US:LP = Sacred LPS-74049*; Highlights (Ralph Carmichael) US:EP = Grason 6618

2194 For Singles Only (1968) Theme (Lewis & Clarke) US:SP = Colgems 66-1022 [Lewis & Clarke Expedition:ST]

2195 For the Blood of Others [Par la Sang des Autres] (1974) Theme (Francis Lai) US:LP = Audio Fidelity 6301* [Francis Lai:ST]

2196 For the First Time (1959) Score (e:George Stoll/e:classical music) US:LP = RCA LM-2338/LSC-2338* + US:LP = RCA AGL1-3977* [Mario Lanza:ST]

2197 For the Love of Benji (1977) Score (Euel Box) US:LP = Epic KSE-34867*

2198 For the Love of Mary (1948) Themes/US:LP = Decca 75289 [Deanna Durbin:ST]

2199 For the Love of Mike (1960) Theme (Rex Allen) US:SP = Buena Vista 363 [Rex Allen:ST]

2200 For Those I Loved [Au Nom de Tour les Miens] (1984) Score (Maurice Jarre) GB:LP = BBC REH-518*

2201 For Whom the Bell Tolls (1943) Score (Victor Young) US:LP = WB B-1201/BS-1201* + US:LP = Stanyan SRQ-4013* [Ray Heindorf]; Highlights (Victor Young) US:LP = Decca DL-8008 + US:LP = Decca DL-8481 [Victor Young:ST]

2202 For You Alone *see* When You're in Love

2203 For Your Eyes Only (1981) Score (Bill Conti) US:LP = Liberty LOO-1109*

2204 Forbidden Alliance *see* Barretts of Wimpole Street, The

2205 Forbidden Games [Jeux Interdits] (1951) Theme (at:Narciso Yepes) US:LP = Capitol 8603* [Frank Pourcel]

2206 Forbidden Island (1959) Score (Alexander Laszlo) US:LP = Carlton LP-106

2207 Forbidden Paradise *see* Hurricane (1979)

2208 Forbidden Planet (1956) Score (Bebe & Louis Barron) US:LP = Planet PR-001*

2209 Forbidden World [Mutant] (1982) Score (Susan Justin) US:LP = Web ST-107*

2210 Forbidden Zone (1983) Score (e:Danny Elfman/etc.) US:LP = Varese STV-81170*

2211 Force of Evil (1948) Theme-A (David Raksin) US:LP = AEI 3104 + US:LP-BP = Premiere 1201 [@uncredited]; Theme-B (David Raksin) US:LP-MS-PP = Library of Congress LOC-RAKSIN [David Raksin:ST]

2212 Force of Impulse (1961) Theme (Joseph Liebman) US:SP = Decca 9-31184 [Jack Pleis]

2213 Force 10 from Navarone (1978) Theme (Ron Goodwin) GB:LP = Chandos 1014* [Ron Goodwin:ST]

2214 Foreign Affair, A (1948) Excerpts (Frederick Hollander) US:LP-BP = Marsher 201 [Marlene Dietrich:ST]; Themes (Frederick Hollander) US: SP = Decca 9-24582 [Marlene Dietrich:ST]; Themes (Frederick Hollander) US:LP = Decca 8465 + US:LP = MCA 1501 [Marlene Dietrich: ST]

2215 Foreign Intrigue (1954) Highlights (Paul Durand) US:EP = MGM X-1080

2216 Forest Rangers, The (1942) Theme (Joseph J. Lilley) US:78 = Decca 18361 [The Merry Macs]

2217 Forever Amber (1947) Highlights (David Raksin) US:LP = RCA ARL1-1490*; Highlights (David Raksin) US:LP-BP = Cinema LP-8007 + US:78-MS = RCA 197

2218 Forever Darling (1956) Theme (Bronislau Kaper) US:SP = MGM 12144 [Desi Arnaz:ST]; Theme (Bronislau Kaper) US:SP = RCA 47-6400 [The Ames Brothers]; Theme (Bronislau Kaper) US:LP = MGM 3511 [Richard Ellsasser]

2219 Forever Female (1953) Theme (Victor Young) US:LP = Decca 8051 [Victor Young:ST]

2220 Forever Young, Forever Free (1976) Score (Lee Holdridge) US:LP = MCA 2093*

2221 Formula, The (1980) Score (Bill Conti) US:LP = Varese STV-81153*

2222 Formula for Love (1964) Excerpts (various) US:LP = Atco 33-128 [Nina & Frederick:ST]

2223 Fort Saganne (1984) Score (Philippe Sarde) FR:LP = Milan A-238*

2224 Fortuna (1966) Theme (Dov Seltzer) US:SP = Tower 4701 [Jerry Howard]; Theme (Dov Seltzer) US:LP = Columbia 9374* [Nini Rosso]

2225 Fortune Cookie, The [Meet Whiplash Willie] (1966) Score (Andre Previn) US:LP = UA UAL-4145/UAS-5145*

2226 Fortunella (1957) Score (Nino Rota) IT:LP = Cometa CMT-1017/31; Theme (Nino Rota) US:SP = Paramount 0152* [Carlo Savina]

2227 48 Hrs. (1982) Theme (Brian O'Neal) US:SP = Arista 1034* [The Busboys:ST]

2228 Forty Guns (1957) Themes (Victor Young/Harry Sukman) US:SP = RCA 47-7079 [Sons of the Pioneers:ST]; Theme (Harry Sukman) US:LP = RCA 1-4092 [Sons of the Pioneers: ST]

2229 Forty Little Mothers (1940) Theme/US:LP = Columbia 515 + US:LP = Harmony 11353 + US:LP = Epic 15105 [@Eddie Cantor: ST]

2230 49th Parallel, The *see* Invaders, The

2231 40 Pounds of Trouble (1962) Score (Mort Lindsey) US:LP = Mercury MG-20784/SR-60784*

2232 Forty-Second Street (1933) Excerpts-A (Harry Warren) US:LP = UA LA-361 [@ST]; Excerpts-B (Harry Warren) US:LP-BP = JJA 19792 [@ST]

2233 42:6 *see* Ben-Gurion

2234 Forward March (1930) Theme/US:78 = Columbia 2235 [Cliff Edwards:ST]

2235 Foul Play (1978) Score (Charles Fox) US:LP = Arista AL-9501*

2236 Fountainhead, The (1949) Highlights (Max Steiner) US:LP-MS-BP = Tony Thomas TTMS-13/14; Excerpts (Max Steiner) US:LP = RCA ARL1-0136* [Charles Gerhardt]

2237 Four Daughters (1938) Excerpts (e:Max Steiner/t:Max Rabinowitsch) US:LP-BP = Tony Thomas TTMS-15 [Max Steiner:ST]

2238 Four Days of Naples, The (1962) Theme (Carlo Rustichelli) US:LP = Capitol 8608* [Pino Calvi]; Theme (Carlo Rustichelli) US:LP = UA 6360* [Riz Ortolani]

2239 Four Feathers, The (1939) Theme (Miklos Rozsa) US:LP = RCA 1-0911* [Charles Gerhardt]

2240 Four Flies on Grey Velvet [Quattro Mosche di Velluto Grigio] (1972) Themes (Ennio Morricone) IT:SP = Cinevox MDF-031* [ST]; Themes (Ennio Morricone) IT:LP = Cinevox 33/74-75* [Ennio Morricone:ST]

2241 4 for Texas (1963) Theme (James Van Heusen) US:SP = Reprise 0246 [Dorsey Burnette:ST]

2242 Four Girls in Town (1956) Highlights (Alex North) US:LP = Decca DL-8424 + US:LP = Varese VC-81074; Theme (Henry Mancini) US:SP = Liberty 55045 [Henry Mancini:ST]

2243 Four Guns to the Border (1954) Theme (Hans J. Salter) US:LP = Medallion 313 [Hans J. Salter:ST]

2244 Four Horsemen of the Apocalypse, The (1921) Theme [Silent I] (Ernst Luz) US:LP = Golden Crest 4019 [Arthur Kleiner]

2245 Four Horsemen of the Apocalypse, The (1962) Score (Andre Previn) US:LP = MGM E-3993/SE-3993*

2246 400 Blows, The [Les 400 Coups] (1958) Highlights (Jean Constantin) FR:EP = Vogue 7631; Theme (Jean Constantin) US:SP = RCA 47-7674 [Hugo Winterhalter]; Theme (Jean Constantin) US:LP = Reprise 6009* [Leo Diamond]

2247 Four in the Morning (1966) Highlights + Dialog (John Barry) US:LP = Roulette R-805/SR-805*

2248 Four Jills in a Jeep (1944) Score (Jimmy McHugh) US:LP-BP = Hollywood Soundstage HS-407

2249 Four Kinds of Love *see* Bambole

2250 Four Musketeers, The (1975) Highlights (Lalo Schifrin) US:LP = Entracte ERS-6510*

2251 Four Poster, The (1953) Theme (Dimitri Tiomkin) US:LP = RCA 1-1669* [Charles Gerhardt]; Theme (Dimitri Tiomkin) US:LP = RCA 1007 [Al Goodman]

2252 Four Sons (1928) Theme [Silent I] (Erno Rapee) US:LP = RCA 2560* [Gaylord Carter]

2253 Four Wives (1939) Theme (at: Max Steiner) US:LP = RCA 1-0136* [Charles Gerhardt]; Theme (at:Max Steiner) US:LP = RCA 1287 [Max Steiner:ST]

2254 4th Man, The (1984) Score (Loek Dikker) US:LP = Varese STV-81222*

2255 Fox, The (1968) Score (Lalo Schifrin) US:LP = WB WS-1738*

2256 Fox and His Friends [Fox] [Faustrecht der Freiheit] (1974) Theme (Peer Raben) FR:LP = Cinedisc 88.087* [Peer Raben:ST]

2257 Fox and the Hound, The (1981) Highlights + Underscore + Dialog (e:Jim Stafford/u:Buddy Baker) US: LP = Disneyland 3106

2258 Foxes (1980) Scores (Giorgio Moroder) US:LP-MS = Casablanca NBLP2-7206*

2259 Foxfire (1955) Theme (Henry Mancini) US:SP = Decca 9-29532 [Jeff Chandler:ST]

2260 Foxy Brown (1973) Score (Willie Hutch) US:LP = Motown M6-811*

2261 Foxy Lady (1971) Score (Doug Riley) CA:LP = GRT 9230.1009*

2262 Fragment of Fear (1970) Excerpts (Johnny Harris) GB:LP = WB 46054* [Johnny Harris:ST]

2263 Frances (1982) Score (John Barry) US:LP = Southern Cross SCRS-1001*

2264 Francis of Assisi (1961) Score (Mario Nascimbene) US:LP = 20th 3053/S-3053*

2265 Frankenstein Conquers the World (1966) Excerpts (Akira Ifukube) JA:LP = Toho 8108 [@ST]

2266 Frankenstein's Daughter (1958) Theme (Page Cavanaugh) US: LP = Rhino 307 [@Harold Lloyd, Jr.: ST]

2267 Frankie and Johnny (1934) Themes/US:LP = RCA LPV-561 [Helen Morgan:ST]

2268 Frankie and Johnny (1966) Score (e:Bill Giant/e:Florence Kaye/t: Fred Karger) US:LP = RCA LPM-3553/ LSP-3553* [Elvis Presley:ST]

2269 Frantic [Lift to the Scaffold] [Ascenseur pour l'Echafaud] (1961) Score (Miles Davis) US:LP = Fontana MGF-27532/SRF-67532*; Highlights (Miles Davis) US:LP = Columbia CL-1268 + US:LP = CSP ACL-1268

2270 Fraternally Yours *see* Sons of the Desert

2271 Fraternity Row (1977) Theme (Don McLean) US:LP = Arista 4149* [Don McLean:ST]

2272 Fraulein (1958) Theme (at:Bernard Mayers) US:SP = 20th 121 [Voices of the Junior Chorale]

2273 Fraulein Doktor (1969) Themes (Ennio Morricone) IT:LP-MS-PP = General Music 33/01-02 [Ennio Morricone:ST]

2274 Freaky Friday (1976) Theme (Al Kasha & Joel Hirschhorn) US:SP = Disneyland 566* [The Osmonds]

2275 Free Ride (1986) Theme-A/ US:SP = MCA 52759* [Smile:ST]; Theme-B/US:SP-12 = Rhino 70513* [Mamie Van Doren:ST]

2276 Free Spirit *see* Belstone Fox

2277 Freebie and the Bean (1974) Theme (Dominic Frontiere) US:SP = WB 8058* [Bobby Hart:ST]

2278 Freedom (1981) Score (Don Walker) AU:LP = WB WEA 600-119*

2279 French Can-Can *see* Only the French Can

2280 French Connection, The (1971) Theme (Don Ellis) US:LP = Columbia 31766* [Don Ellis:ST]; Theme (Don Ellis) US:LP = Project 5063* [Enoch Light]; Theme (Don Ellis) US: LP = Avalanche 058* [Al Caiola]

2281 French Connection II (1975) Theme (Don Ellis) JA:LP = TAM 9001/2* + JA:LP = TAM 9015/6* [@Stanley Maxfield]

2282 French Conspiracy, The [The Plot] [L'Attentat] (1973) Score (Ennio Morricone) FR:LP = Festival 592*

2283 French Detective, The [Adieu Poulet] (1979) Themes (Philippe Sarde) FR:SP = Pathe C010.14259* [ST]

2284 French Leave [La Poudre d'Escampette] (1978) Themes (Michel Legrand) FR:SP = Bell C006.92783* [ST]

2285 French Lieutenant's Woman, The (1981) Score (Carl Davis) US:LP = DRG SL-6106*

2286 French Line, The (1954) Highlights (Josef Myrow) US:LP-10 = Mercury MG-25182

2287 French Mistress, A (1960) Theme (Roy Boulting) US:SP = London 1964 [Frank Chacksfield]; Theme (Roy Boulting) US:LP = London 3238/231* [@Frank Chacksfield]

2288 French Woman, The [Madame Claude] (1978) Score (Serge Gainsbourg) JA:LP = Philips FDX-331*

2289 Frenzy (1972) Theme (Ron Goodwin) US:LP-BP = Centurion 1210* [@Geoff Love]; Theme (Ron Goodwin) GB:LP-MS = EMI 108* [Ron Goodwin:ST]

2290 Fresh from Paris [Paris Follies of 1956] (1955) Theme/US:SP = Capitol 2913 [Margaret Whiting:ST]

2291 Freshman, The [College Days] (1925) Highlights [Silent II] (Walter Scharf) US:LP = Citadel CT-6018*

2292 Freud (1962) Score (Jerry Goldsmith) US:LP = Citadel CT-6016 + US:LP = Citadel CTV-7011

2293 Friday the 13th (1980) Score (Harry Manfredini) US:LP = Gramavision GR-1030*

2294 Friday the 13th, Part 3 (1982) Theme (Harry Manfredini) US:SP = Gramavision 4501* [Hot Ice:ST]; Theme (Harry Manfredini) US:LP = Gramavision 1030* [@Hot Ice:ST]

2295 Friday the 13th, Part VI—Jason Lives (1986) Theme (Alice Cooper) US:LP = MCA 5761* [Alice Cooper: ST]; Theme (Alice Cooper) US:SP = MCA 52904* [Alice Cooper:ST]

2296 Friendly Ghost, The [Cartoon] (1946) Theme (Jerry Livingston) US:LP = Peter Pan 8017 [collection]

2297 Friendly Persuasion (1956) Score (Dimitri Tiomkin) US:LP = RKO Unique 110 + US:LP = Venise 7026 + US:LP = Varese STV-81165; Theme (Dimitri Tiomkin) US:SP = Dot 15490 [Pat Boone:ST]; Theme (Dimitri Tiomkin) US:LP = ABC 4006* [Pat Boone:ST]

2298 Friends (1971) Score (e:Elton John/e:Paul Buckmaster) US:LP = Paramount PAS-6004*

2299 Fright Night (1985) Score (t:Brad Fiedel/s:various) US:LP = Private I SZ-40087*

2300 Frightened Bride, The [Tall Headlines] (1952) Theme (Hans May) GB:78 = Parlophone 3529 [ST]

2301 Frightened City, The (1961) Theme-A (Norrie Paramor) US:SP = Atlantic 45-2111 [The Shadows]; Theme-B (Norrie Paramor) US:SP = Capitol 4627 [Helen Shapiro]

2302 Frisky [Bread, Love and Jealousy] (1954) Theme (Alessandro Cicognini-aka-Icini) US:SP = Mercury 70669 [Richard Hayman]; Theme (Alessandro Cicognini-aka-Icini) US:LP-10 = Mercury 20123 + US:LP = Mercury 25189 [Richard Hayman]

2303 Fritz the Cat (1972) Score (s:Ray Shanklin & Ed Bogas/t: Charles Earland) US:LP = Fantasy M-89406*

2304 Frog Went A-Courtin', The [Short] Sequence + Dialog (Arthur Kleiner) US:LP-PP = Picture Book Parade 108 [@ST]

2305 From a Far Country (1982) Score (Wojciech Kilar) GB:LP = RCA 31612*

2306 From Beyond (1986) Score (Richard Band) US:LP = Enigma SJ-73240*

2307 From Hell to Victory [Contro Quattre Bandiere] (1980) Score (Riz Ortolani) IT:LP = Duse ELP-063*

2308 From Here to Eternity (1954) Excerpts (ae:George Duning) US:LP = Decca DL-8396 [@Morris Stoloff:ST]; Theme-A (Fred Karger) US:LP = Colpix 464* [@Morris Stoloff:ST]; Theme-B (Fred Karger) US:SP = Capitol 2563 [Merle Travis:ST]

2309 From Noon Till Three (1976) Theme (Elmer Bernstein) US:SP = UA 36189* [Jill Ireland:ST]; Theme (Elmer Bernstein) US:LP-BP = Centurion 1600* [@Jill Ireland:ST]

2310 From Russia with Love (1964) Score (s:John Barry/t:Lionel Bart) US: LP = UA UAL-4114/UAS-5114*

2311 From Sea to Shining Sea [Industrial Short] Score (Emanuel Vardi)

US:LP-PP = RCA/Reader's Digest RD4-1A

2312 From the Earth to the Moon (1958) Themes (Louis Forbes) US:SP = Mark 56 #803 [Louis Forbes:ST]

2313 From the Terrace (1960) Score (Elmer Bernstein) US:LP-BP = Cinema LP-8009; Themes (Elmer Bernstein) US: SP = Capitol 4426 [Elmer Bernstein:ST]; Theme (Elmer Bernstein) US:LP = 20th 3043* [The 20th Century Strings]

2314 Front Page, The (1974) Theme (Billy May) US:SP = MCA 40352* [Billy May:ST]; Theme (Billy May) US:LP = Columbia 33437* [Andre Kostelanetz]

2315 Front Page Story, The (1954) Theme (Michael Carr) GB:78 = HMV 10616 [George Melachrino]

2316 Frontier Hellcat [Among Vultures] [Unter Geiern] (1964) Score (Martin Bottcher) GE:LP = Polydor 237.422*

2317 Frontier Pony Express (1939) Theme/US:LP = Columbia 38907 [Roy Rogers:ST]

2318 Frou-Frou (1955) Theme-A (Louiguy) US:LP = Mercury 20188 [Eddie Barclay]; Theme-B (Henri Chatau) US:SP = Capitol 3579 [Frank Pourcel]

2319 Fruit Is Ripe, The (1977) Score (Gerhard Heinz) JA:LP = RCA/Victor VIP-7271*

2320 Fuehrer's Face, Der [Cartoon] (1943) Theme (Oliver Wallace) US:LP = RCA 1-1035 + US:LP = RCA 1-3748 [Spike Jones]

2321 Fugitive Kind, The (1960) Score (Kenyon Hopkins) US:LP = UA UAL-4065/UAS-5065*

2322 Full Circle [The Haunting of Julia] (1978) Score (Colin Towns) GB: LP = Virgin 2093

2323 Full Life, A (1965) Excerpts (Toru Takemitsu) JA:LP = RCA/Victor 1071 [Toru Takemitsu:ST]

2324 Full of Life (1957) Themes (George Duning) US:LP = Web 108 [George Duning:ST]; Theme (George Duning) US:SP = Decca 9-30216 [Judy Holiday:ST]; Theme (George Duning) US:LP-BP = Centurion 1210 [@Judy Holiday:ST]

2325 Fun and Fancy Free (1947) Excerpts + Dialog ["Bongo"] (Eliot Daniel) US:LP-10 = Columbia JL-8503 [Dinah Shore:ST]; Excerpts + Dialog ["Mickey and the Beanstalk"] (t:Paul Smith/etc.) US:LP = Disneyland 1248 + US:LP = Disneyland 3974; Theme ["Fun and Fancy Free"] (George David Weiss) US:78 = Capitol 466 [The Dinning Sisters:ST]

2326 Fun in Acapulco (1963) Score (e:Don Robertson/e:Sid Tepper & Roy Bennett/etc.) US:LP = RCA LPM-2756/LSP-2756* + US:LP = RCA AFL1-2756* [Elvis Presley:ST]

2327 Fun with Dick and Jane (1977) Theme (Michael Morgan) US:SP = Arista 0235* [The Movies:ST]

2328 Funeral in Berlin (1966) Score (Konrad Elfers) US:LP = RCA LOC-1136/LSO-1136*

2329 Funny Face (1957) Score (film songs:Roger Edens/stage songs:George Gershwin) US:LP = Verve 15001 + US: LP = DRG DS-15001

2330 Funny Girl (1968) Score (stage songs:Jule Styne) US:LP = Columbia OS-3220*

2331 Funny Lady (1975) Score (e: John Kander/etc.) US:LP = Arista AL-9004*

2332 Funny Thing Happened on the Way to the Forum, A (1966) Score (e: Ken Thorne/stage songs:Stephen Sondheim) US:LP = UA UAL-4144/UAS-5144* + US:LP = UA LA-284*

2332a Furies, The (1950) Excerpts (Franz Waxman) US:LP = Telarc DG-10141* [Eric Kunzel]

2333 Further Adventures of the Wilderness Family, The (1978) Score (Gene Kauer & Douglas Lackey) JA: LP = Seven Seas FML-104*

2334 Fury (1973) *see* One Russian Summer

2335 Fury, The (1978) Score (John Williams) US:LP = Arista AB-4175*

2336 Fuss Over Feathers *see* Conflict of Wings

2337 Fuzz (1972) Theme (Dave Grusin) US:LP = Blue Note 84421* [Bobbi Humphrey]; Theme (Dave Grusin) US:LP = Prestige 10070* [Gene Ammons]

2338 Fuzzy Pink Nightgown, The (1957) Score (Billy May) US:LP = Imperial LP-9042

G

2339 G.I. Blues (1960) Score (e:Sherman Edwards/e:Sid Wayne/etc.) US:LP = RCA LPM-2256/LSP-2256* + US:LP = RCA AYL1-3735* [Elvis Presley:ST]

2340 Gable and Lombard (1976) Score (Michel Legrand) US:LP = MCA 2091*

2341 Gabriela (1984) Score (Antonio Carlos Jobim) US:LP = RCA ABL1-5186*

2342 Gadfly, The (1955) Score (Dmitri Shostakovich) GB:LP = Angel/Melodiya ASD-3309*

2343 Gaily, Gaily [Chicago, Chicago] (1969) Score (Henry Mancini) US:LP = UA UAS-5202*

2344 Galaxy Express 999 (1981) Score (Nozomu Aoki) JA:LP = Columbia CQ-7025* + IT:LP = RCA 31665*

2345 Galia [I and My Love] (1967) Highlights (e:Michel Magne/at:Ward Swingle) FR:EP = Philips 437.186; Theme (at:Ward Swingle) US:LP = Philips 600.225* [The Swingle Singers: ST]

2346 Galileo (1968) Score (Ennio Morricone) IT:LP = CAM SAG-9010*

2347 Gamberge, La (1963) Highlights (Guy Beart) FR:EP = Philips 432.748; Theme (Guy Beart) US:LP = Philips 600.071 [@ST]

2348 Gambit (1966) Theme (Maurice Jarre) US:SP = Columbia 4-43993 [Roy Meriwether]; Theme (Maurice Jarre) US:SP = Decca 9-32071 [Sammy Kaye]; Theme (Maurice Jarre) US:SP = Decca 9-32084 [Malcolm Lockyer]

2349 Game Called Scruggs, A *see* Scruggs

2350 Game Is Over, The [La Curee] (1967) Score (Jean Bouchety & Jean-Pierre Bourtayre) US:LP = Atco 33-205/SD-33-205*

2351 Game of Death [Bruce Lee's Game of Death] (1978) Score (John Barry) JA:LP = TAM YX-7037*

2352 Game of Death II *see* Tower of Death

2353 Gamera the Invincible (1966) Excerpts (Tadashi Yamauchi) JA:LP = Toho 8120 [@ST]; Theme (Wes Farrell) US:SP = Date 1545 [The Moons]

2354 Gamera vs. Monster X (1970) Theme (Shunsuke Kikuchi) JA:LP = Toho 8120 [@ST]

2355 Gamera vs. Zigra (1971) Theme (Shunsuke Kikuchi) JA:LP = Toho 8120 [@ST]

2356 Games, The (1970) Score (Francis Lai) US:LP = Viking LPS-105*

2357 Games of the XXI Olympiad—Montreal 1976 (1977) Score (as: Victor Vogel) CA:LP = Polydor 2424.124*

2358 Gammera the Invincible *see* Gamera the Invincible

2359 Gandhi (1982) Score (e:Ravi Shankar/e:George Fenton) US:LP = RCA ABL1-4557*

2360 Gang's All Here, The (1943) Score (Harry Warren) US:LP-BP = Classic International Filmusicals 3003 + US:LP-BP = Sandy Hook SH-2009

2361 Gangway (1937) Themes-A-B/GB:LP = Decca 2168 [Jessie Matthews:ST]; Theme-C/GB:78 = Decca 6470 [Jessie Matthews:ST]; Theme-D/GB:78 = Decca 6471 [Jessie Matthews: ST]

2362 Garcon (1984) Highlights (Philippe Sarde) FR:LP = Milan A-222*

2363 Garde a Vue (1982) Highlights (Georges Delerue) FR:LP = RCA 37636*

2364 Garden of Allah, The (1936) Theme (Max Steiner) US:LP-BP = Citadel CTMS-6 [Max Steiner:ST]

2365 Garden of Delights, The [El Jardin de las Delicias] [Il Giardino della Delizie] (1970) Theme (Ennio Morricone) IT:LP = RCA 10481* + IT:LP = RCA 10486* [Ennio Morricone: ST]

2366 Garden of the Finzi-Continis, The (1970) Score (s:Manuel DeSica/t: Joe Brooks) US:LP = RCA LSP-4712* † Bill Conti claims to have "ghost" written this score.

2367 Gas-s-s-s! (1970) Score (Barry Melton) US:LP = American International A-1038*

2368 Gate of Hell (1953) Themes (Yasushi Akutagawa) JA:LP = Toho 8083 [Yasushi Akutagawa:ST]

2369 Gates of Hell, The [Paura nella Citta dei Morti Viventi] (1983) Score (Fabio Frizzi) IT:LP = Beat CR-11*

2370 Gates of Paris [Porte des Lilas] (1957) Themes (Georges Brassens) US:LP = Dot 3120 [Ray Ventura]

2371 Gates of the Night *see* Les Portes de la Nuit

2372 Gator (1976) Score (s:Charles Bernstein/t:Jerry Reed) US:LP = UA LA-646*

2373 Gaucho Goofy *see* Saludos Amigos

2374 Gaugin (1950) Excerpts (Darius Milhaud) GB:LP = Chandos 1012* [The Athena Ensemble]

2375 Gauntlet, The (1977) Score (Jerry Fielding) US:LP = WB BSK-3144*

2376 Gay City, The *see* Las Vegas Nights

2377 Gay Desperado, The (1936) Theme (George Posford) US:LP = Oasi 550 [Nino Martini:ST]

2378 Gay Divorcee, The (1934) Highlights (various) US:LP-BP = Sountrak STK-105

2379 Gay Lady, The [Trottie True] (1949) Theme (Benjamin Frankel) GB: 78-PP = Rank FM-72 [ST]

2380 Gay Purr-ee (1962) Score (Harold Arlen) US:LP = WB B-1479/BS-1479*

2381 Gay Senorita, The (1945) Themes/US:78 = ARA 5001 [Corrina Mura:ST]

2382 Gayarre (1964) Score (t:Salvador De Luca/s:classical music) US: LP = Angel 37852 [Alfredo Kraus:ST]

2383 Geisha Boy, The (1959) Score (Walter Scharf) US:LP = Jubilee 1096/S-1096*

2384 Gene Krupa Story, The [Drum Crazy] (1959) Score (e:Leith Stevens/etc.) US:LP = Verve 15010/V6-15010*

2385 General, The (1927) Theme [Silent II] (Lee Erwin) US:LP = Angel 36073* [Lee Erwin:ST]

2386 General with the Cock-Eyed Id, The [Industrial Short] Excerpts (Jerry Goldsmith) US:LP-BP = Temple TLP-2001 [@ST]

2387 Generation (1969) Theme (Nick Zesses) US:SP = Rare Earth 5010* [Rare Earth:ST]

2388 Generation, A [Pokolenie] (1954) Highlights (Andrzej Markowski) GB:LP = That's Entertainment TER-1053*

2389 Genesis (1986) Score (Ravi Shankar) FR:LP = Milan A-287*

2390 Genevieve (1953) Theme (Larry Adler) US:SP = Columbia 4-40124 [Percy Faith]; Theme (Larry Adler) US:LP = Columbia 577 + US: LP = London 920* [Larry Adler:ST]

2391 Genghis Khan (1965) Score (Dusan Radic) US:LP = Liberty LRP-3412/LST-7412*

2392 Genius, The [Un Genio, Due Compari, un Pollo] [A Genius, Two Friends and a Fool] (1976) Score (Ennio Morricone) IT:LP = GT 36510* + FR: LP = CBS 69231*

2393 Gentle Rain, The (1966) Score (Luis Bonfa) US:LP = Mercury MG-21016/SR-61016*

2394 Gentleman Trap, The (1975) Theme (Charles Chaplin) US:SP = MCA 40669* [Roger Williams]; Theme (Charles Chaplin) US:LP = MCA 2279* [Roger Williams]; Theme (Charles Chaplin) US:LP = Columbia 34660* [Andre Kostelanetz]

2395 Gentleman's Agreement (1947) Theme [credited to "Pinky"] (Alfred Newman) US:LP = Mercury 20037 + US:LP = Citadel 6003 + US: LP = Citadel 7015 [Alfred Newman: ST]

2396 Gentlemen Marry Brunettes (1955) Score (t:Earle Hagen / s:various) US:LP = Coral CRL-57013

2397 Gentlemen Prefer Blondes (1953) Highlights (stage songs:Jule Styne) US:LP-10 = MGM E-208 + US: LP = MGM E-3231 + US:LP = DRG DS-15005

2398 George White's Scandals (1934) Theme-A/US:LP = Columbia 3068 [Alice Faye:ST]; Themes-B-C/US: 78 = Brunswick 1727 [Cliff Edwards:ST]; Theme-D/US:78 = RCA/Victor 24581 [Rudy Vallee:ST]

2399 George White's Scandals of 1935 (1935) Themes-A-B/US:LP-BP = Totem 1032 [Alice Faye:ST]; Themes-C-

D/US:78 = Melotone 13347 [Cliff Edwards:ST]; Themes-E-F/US:78 = Melotone 13403 [Cliff Edwards: ST]

2400 Georgie [Short] Sequence + Dialog (Arthur Kleiner) US:LP-PP = Picture Book Parade 102 [@ST]

2401 Georgy Girl (1966) Theme (Tom Springfield) US:SP = Capitol 6150 [The Seekers:ST]; Theme (Tom Springfield) US:LP = Capitol 2431* [The Seekers:ST]

2402 Geraldine (1953) Theme (Victor Young) US:LP = Decca 8060 [Victor Young:ST]

2403 Germinal (1963) Highlights (Michel Magne) FR:EP = Barclay 70570

2404 Gervaise (1956) Highlights (Georges Auric) FR:EP = Versailles 90-M-133; Theme (Georges Auric) US: SP = Vik 258 [Sid Bass]; Theme (Georges Auric) US:LP = Columbia 107 [Michel Legrand]

2405 Get Carter (1971) Highlights + Underscore + Dialog (Roy Budd) JA: LP = EMI/Odeon 80424*; Theme (Roy Budd) US:LP-BP = Eros 80544* [Roy Budd:ST]

2406 Get Crazy (1983) Score (various) US:LP = Morocco 6065*

2407 Get Off My Back *see* Synanon

2408 Get Out Your Handkerchiefs [Preparez Voz Mouchoirs] (1978) Score (Georges Delerue) FR:LP = Deesse DDLX-160*

2409 Get Yourself a College Girl [The Swinging Set] [Girl Crazy] (1964) Score (stage songs:George Gershwin/ etc.) US:LP = MGM E-4273/SE-4273*

2410 Getaway, The (1972) Themes (Quincy Jones) US:SP = A&M 1404* [Quincy Jones:ST]; Theme (Quincy Jones) US:LP = A&M 3041* [Quincy Jones:ST]

2411 Getting Over (1980) Scores (e: Johnny Rogers/etc.) US:LP-MS = Maverick International MVA-1037*

2412 Getting Straight (1970) Score (e:Ronald Stein/etc.) US:LP = Colgems COMO-5010/COSO-5010*

2413 Ghidrah, The Three-Headed Monster (1965) Excerpts (Akira Ifukube) JA:LP = Toho 8112 [@ST]

2414 Ghost and Mrs. Muir, The (1947) Score (Bernard Herrmann) US: LP = Film Music Collection FMC-4* [Elmer Bernstein]; Theme (Bernard Herrmann) GB:LP-MS = Unicorn 400* [Bernard Herrmann:ST]

2415 Ghost of Dragstrip Hollow, The (1959) Theme (Nick Venet) US:SP = American International 45-537 [The Renegades:ST]

2416 Ghost of Frankenstein, The (1942) Score (Hans J. Salter) US:LP-BP = Tony Thomas TTHS-3

2417 Ghost Story (1981) Score (Philippe Sarde) US:LP = MCA 5287*

2418 Ghostbusters (1984) Score (t: Elmer Bernstein/s:various) US:LP = Arista AL8-8246*

2419 Ghosts of Rome [Fantasmi a Roma] [The Phantom Lovers] (1961) Highlights (Nino Rota) IT:EP = RCA EPA-30098; Theme (Nino Rota) US: LP = RCA FSO-4* [@ST]

2420 Giacomo Casanova—Childhood and Adolescence (1969) Score (Fiorenzo Carpi) IT:LP = RCA SP-8026*

2421 Giant (1956) Score (Dimitri Tiomkin) US:LP = Capitol W-773/DW-733e; Underscore + Dialog (Dimitri Tiomkin) US:LP = WB BS-2843 [James Dean:ST]

2422 Giddyap [Cartoon] (1950) Theme (David Raksin) US:LP-PP-MS = Library of Congress LOC-RAKSIN [David Raksin:ST]

2423 Gidget (1959) Themes (Fred Karger/Glen Larson) US:SP = Capitol 4078 [The Four Preps]; Theme (Fred Karger) US:SP = Colpix 102 [James Darren:ST]; Theme (Fred Karger) US:LP = Colpix 406* [James Darren:ST]

2424 Gidget Goes Hawaiian (1961) Themes (Fred Karger) US:SP = Colpix 189 [James Darren:ST]; Themes (Fred Karger) US:LP = Colpix 418* [James Darren:ST]; Theme (Fred Karger) US: SP = Jamie 1183 [Duane Eddy]

2425 Gidget Goes to Rome (1963) Themes (George David Weiss) US:SP = Colpix 696 [James Darren:ST]

2426 Gift of Gab, The (1934) Themes-A-B/US:78 = Columbia 2954 [Ruth Etting:ST]; Theme-C/US:78 =

Decca 348 [Ethel Waters:ST]; Theme-D/US:78 = RCA/Victor 24725 [Gene Austin:ST]

2427 Gift of Love, The (1958) Score (e:Alfred Newman/t:Sammy Fain/as: Cyril Mockridge) US:LP = Columbia CL-1113

2428 Gifts of an Eagle, The (1975) Highlights (t:Paul Bergen/t:Randy Sparks/t:Clark Gassman) US:EP = C.B. Bartell CB-110*

2429 Gigi (1948) Theme (Rachel Thoreau) US:SP = Capitol 2479 [Les Baxter]

2430 Gigi (1958) Score (Frederick Loewe) US:LP = MGM E-3641/SE-3641*

2431 Gigot (1962) Score (Jackie Gleason) US:LP = Capitol W-1754/WS-1754* [Jackie Gleason]

2432 Gilda (1946) Themes (Doris Fisher) US:LP-BP = Curtain Calls 100/22 [Anita Ellis:ST]

2433 Gimme Shelter (1971) Score (pop music) US:LP-BP = TMQ 72009 [The Rolling Stones:ST]

2434 Ginger and Fred (1986) Score (Nicola Piovani) US:LP = Varese STV-81277*

2435 Girl Can't Help It, The (1956) Highlights (various) US:EP = Capitol EAP1-823 [Gene Vincent:ST]; Theme/US:SP = Imperial 5417 [Fats Domino: ST]; Theme/US:SP = Liberty 54500 [Julie London:ST]

2436 Girl Crazy (1932) Excerpts (stage songs:George Gershwin) US:LP-BP = JJA 19773 [@ST]

2437 Girl Crazy (1943) Score (stage songs:George Gershwin/etc.) US:LP-MS = Curtain Calls 100/9-10; Highlights (stage songs:George Gershwin) US:LP-10 = Decca DL-5412

2438 Girl Crazy (1964) *see* Get Yourself a College Girl

2439 Girl from Missouri, The (1934) Excerpts (various) US:LP = World Artists WA-3007/WAS-3007* [Perry Botkin, Jr.]

2440 Girl from Petrovka, The (1974) Theme (Henry Mancini) US:LP = RCA 1-0672* [Henry Mancini:ST]

2441 Girl from San Frediano, The *see* Le Ragazze di San Frediano

2442 Girl Games *see* Copacabana Palace

2443 Girl Groups—The Story of a Sound (1983) Score (pop music) US: LP = Motown 5322-ML*

2444 Girl Happy (1965) Score (e: Bill Giant/e:Florence Kaye/etc.) US: LP = RCA LPM-3338/LSP-3338* + US:LP = RCA AFL1-3338* [Elvis Presley:ST]

2445 Girl in Gold Boots (1968) Themes (Chris Howard/Laurence Gray) US:SP = Glenolden 152 [Larry Cartell:ST]

2446 Girl in the Bikini, The [The Lighthouse Keeper's Daughter] (1952) Score (Jean Yatove) US:LP = Poplar 33-1002

2447 Girl in the Painting, The [Portrait from Life] (1948) Theme (Benjamin Frankel) GB:78-PP = Rank FM-42 [ST]

2448 Girl Most Likely, The (1958) Score (e:Hugh Martin/e:Nelson Riddle) US:LP = Capitol W-930

2449 Girl Named Tamiko, A (1963) Theme (Elmer Bernstein) US:SP = Ava 113 [Elmer Bernstein:ST]; Theme (Elmer Bernstein) US:SP = Carousel 1002 [Primo Kim]; Theme (Elmer Bernstein) US:LP=Ava 30* [@Elmer Bernstein:ST]

2450 Girl of the Golden West, The (1938) Themes-A-B/US:78 = RCA/Victor 4388 [Nelson Eddy:ST]; Themes-C-D/US:78 = RCA/Victor 4389 [Nelson Eddy:ST]

2451 Girl on a Motorcycle, The [Naked Under Leather] (1968) Score (Les Reed) US:LP=Tetragrammaton T-5000*

2452 Girl Who Couldn't Say No, The [Tenderly] [Il Suo Modo di Fare] (1968) Themes (Riz Ortolani) IT:SP = SRL 10517* [ST]

2453 Girl Who Had Everything, The (1953) Theme (Andre Previn) US:LP = MGM 4144* [David Rose]

2454 Girl with Green Eyes, The (1964) Theme (John Addison) US:SP = UA 765 [Perez Prado]; Theme (John Addison) US:LP = UA 6394* [Perez Prado]

2455 Girl with the Golden Eyes, The [La Fille aux Yeux D'Or] (1961) Highlights (Narciso Yepes) FR:EP = Philips 432.931; Theme (Narciso Yepes) US:LP = Philips 600.071 [@ST]

2456 Girls (1979) Score (Eric Stewart) JA:LP = MFP 1309*

2457 Girls, Les (1957) Highlights (Cole Porter) US:LP = MGM E-3590 + US:LP-MS = MGM 2SES-51e

2458 Girls Disappear, The *see* Des Femmes Disparaissent

2459 Girls! Girls! Girls! (1962) Score (e:Ruth Bachelor/e:Sid Tepper & Roy Bennett/etc.) US:LP = RCA LPM-2621/LSP-2621* + US:LP = RCA AFL1-2621* [Elvis Presley:ST]

2460 Girls in the Street *see* London Melody

2461 Girls Just Want to Have Fun (1985) Score (various) US:LP = Mercury 824-510-1*

2462 Girls Most Likely, The *see* Class of '74

2463 Girls of San Frediano, The *see* Le Ragazze di San Frediano

2464 Girls on the Beach (1965) Theme-A/US:LP = Capitol 16016* [The Beach Boys:ST]; Theme-B/US:SP = Capitol 4093 + US:SP = Capitol 6259 [The Beach Boys:ST]; Theme-C/US: SP = Mercury 72270 [Lesley Gore:ST]

2465 Girls' Town (1959) Theme-A (Paul Anka) US:SP = ABC 10022 + US: SP = Eric 201 [Paul Anka:ST]; Theme-B (Buck Ram) US:SP = Mercury 10018 [The Platters:ST]

2466 Giudizio Universale *see* Last Judgment, The

2467 Give a Girl a Break (1953) Highlights (Burton Lane) US:LP-PP = Mark 56 #721; Excerpts (Burton Lane) US:LP-BP = JJA 19824 [@ST]

2468 Give and Take, The [Industrial Short] Score (Richard Ralf) US:LP-PP = Volkswagen RSMC-1325

2469 Give Daddy the Knife, Cindy (1984) Score (Naz Nomad) GB:LP = Big Beat WIK-21*

2470 Give Her the Moon [Les Caprices de Marie] (1970) Highlights (Georges Delerue) FR:EP = UA C006.91100

2471 Give Me a Sailor (1938) Theme/US:LP-MS-BP = Legends 1000/5-6 [Martha Raye:ST]

2472 Give My Regards to Broadway (1948) Highlights (pop music) US: LP-BP = Caliban 6018

2473 Give Out Sisters (1942) Theme/US:LP = Decca 4919 + US:LP-MS = MCA 2-4024 [The Andrews Sisters:ST]

2474 Give Us This Day *see* Salt to the Devil

2475 Give Us This Night (1935) Excerpts (Erich Wolfgang Korngold) US: LP = Citadel CT-7005* [Maria Martino]; Highlights (Erich Wolfgang Korngold) US:LP-BP = Caliban 6049

2476 Glacier Fox, The (1978) Score (s;Narahashi Takekawa / t:Masaru Sato) JA:LP = Columbia YX-5003*

2477 Glamour Girl (1948) Theme/US:78 = Columbia 37589 [Gene Krupa: ST]

2478 Glass Bottom Boat, The (1965) Themes (Joe Lubin) US:SP = Columbia 4-43688 [Doris Day:ST]; Theme (Joe Lubin) US:SP = MGM 13517 [Arthur Godfrey:ST]; Theme (Joe Lubin) US:LP-MS = DRG 2-2100 [@Arthur Godfrey:ST]

2479 Glass Menagerie, The (1950) Excerpts (Max Steiner) US:LP-BP = Citadel CTMS-2 [Max Steiner:ST]

2480 Glass Mountain, The (1948) Themes (Nino Rota) GB:78 = HMV 9765 [George Melachrino]; Theme (Nino Rota) US:SP = RCA 47-4064 [The Three Suns]; Theme (Nino Rota) US:LP = London 1513 [Mantovani]

2481 Glass Slipper, The (1955) Theme-A (Bronislau Kaper) US:SP = MGM 30875 [David Rose]; Theme-A (Bronislau Kaper) US:LP = WB 1242* [Ray Heindorf]; Theme-B (Bronislau Kaper) US:LP = MGM 3694 [John Green:ST]

2482 Glass Sphinx, The (1967) Theme (Les Baxter) US:SP = American International 171 [Mike Clifford]

2483 Glenn Miller Story, The (1954) Score (pop music) US:LP = Decca DL-8226 + US:LP = Decca DL-9123/DL-79123 + US:LP = MCA 2036* + US:LP = MCA 37090*; Theme (Henry Mancini) US:SP = Mercury 70281 [Ralph Marterie]; Theme (Henry Mancini) US: LP = RCA 2604* + US:LP-MS = Camden 2-0293* [Henry Mancini:ST]

2484 Gli Uomini Che Mascalzoni

[What Rascals Men Are] (1932) Theme (Bixio) US:LP = Epic 3593 [Gian Stellari]

2485 Global Affair, A (1964) Theme (Dominic Frontiere) US:SP = Dolton 089 [Vic Dana:ST]

2486 Gloria (1978) Score (Bernard Gerard) FR:LP = Philips 6308.138*; Theme (Bernard Gerard) US:LP = Peters 1019* [Manuel]

2487 Glorifying the American Girl (1929) Themes-A-B/US:LP-BP = Trisklog 4 [Helen Morgan:ST]; Theme-C/US:78 = RCA/Victor 21967 [Rudy Vallee: ST]

2488 Glory Guys, The (1965) Score (Riz Ortolani) US:LP = UA UAL-4126/UAS-5126*

2489 Glory Stompers, The (1967) Score (s:Harley Hatcher/t:Jerry Styner/t:Bob Summers) US:LP = Sidewalk DT-5910*

2490 Gnome-Mobile, The (1967) Themes + Dialog (Richard & Robert Sherman) US:LP = Disneyland 1925

2491 Go-Between, The (1971) Highlights (Michel Legrand) US:LP = Columbia CBS M-35175*

2492 Go for It (1976) Score (e: Richard Henn/etc.) US:LP = Safari ST-2000*

2493 Go-Go Big Beat! (1964) Theme-A/US:SP = MGM 13242 [The Animals:ST]; Theme-B/US:SP = Imperial 66044 [The Hollies:ST]; Theme-C/US:SP = Parrot 9678 [Lulu and the Luvers:ST]; Theme-D/US:SP = Smash 1411 + US:SP = Smash 1893 [Millie Small:ST]

2494 Go, Go, Go World [Il Pelo nel Mondo] (1966) Score (Bruno Nicolai & Nino Oliviero) US:LP = Musicor MM-2059/MS-3059*

2495 Go into Your Dance [Casino de Paree] (1935) Highlights (Harry Warren) US:LP-BP = Hollywood Soundstage 402 + US:LP-BP = Golden Legends 2000/2

2496 Go, Johnny, Go! (1958) Score (various) US:LP = Reel'N'Rock JN-5705

2497 Go Naked in the World (1961) Theme (Adolph Deutsch) US:SP = Capitol 4522 [Whittemore & Lowe]

2498 Go West, Young Man (1936) Theme/US:LP-BP = Caliban 6036 [Mae West:ST]

2499 Goat, The *see* La Chevre

2500 God Forgives, I Don't [Dio Perdona, Io No] (1967) Themes (Carlo Rustichelli) IT:SP = CAM AMP-31* [ST]

2501 God Is My Co-Pilot (1945) Sequence + Dialog (Franz Waxman) US:LP-MS = WB 3X2737 [@ST]

2502 God Told Me To *see* Demon

2503 God with Us [Gott mit Uns] (1970) Themes (Ennio Morricone) IT:SP = RCA PM-3526* [ST]

2504 Godfather, The (1972) Score-A (Nino Rota) US:LP = Paramount PAS-1003*; Score-B (Carmine Coppola) US:LP = Paramount PAS-6034*

2505 Godfather, Part II, The (1974) Score (e:Nino Rota/e:Carmine Coppola) US:LP = ABC ABDP-856*

2506 God's House / Highlights (Ingram Walters) US:LP-PP = Walters W-11

2507 God's Little Acre (1958) Score (Elmer Bernstein) US:LP = UA UAL-40002

2508 Gods Must Be Crazy, The (1984) Score (Johnny Boshoff) US:LP = Varese STV-81243*

2509 Godson, The [Le Samourai] (1967) Highlights (Francois DeRoubaix) FR:EP = Philips 437.389

2510 Godson, The [Cosi di Cosa Nostra] (1971) Themes (Manuel DeSica) IT:SP = Cinevox MDF-022 [ST]

2511 Godspell (1973) Score (stage songs:Stephen Schwartz) US:LP = Bell 1118* + US:LP = Arista AL-4005*

2512 Godzilla—King of the Monsters (1955) Excerpts (Akira Ifukube) JA:LP = Toho 8112 [@ST]; Theme (Akira Ifukube) US:LP = GNP 2128* [Neil Norman]; Theme (Akira Ifukube) US:LP-BP = POO 104 [@ST]; Underscore + Dialog (Akira Ifukube) JA:LP-MS = Star Child K18G-7191/2

2513 Godzilla 1985 [Gojira] (1985) Score (Reijiro Koroku) JA:LP = Star Child K28G-7226*

2514 Godzilla on Monster Island (1971) Theme (Akira Ifukube) JA:LP = Toho 8147 [@ST]

2515 Godzilla vs. Megalon (1976)

Excerpts (Riichiro Manabe) JA:LP = Toho 8147 [@ST]

2516 Godzilla vs. the Cosmic Monster [Godzilla vs. Mecca Godzilla] (1974) Excerpts (Masaru Sato) JA:LP = Toho 8147 [@ST]

2517 Godzilla vs. the Sea Monster (1966) Theme (Masaru Sato) JA:LP = Toho 8147 [@ST]

2518 Godzilla vs. the Smog Monster (1971) Theme (Riichiro Manabe) JA: LP = Toho 8147 [@ST]

2519 Godzilla vs. the Thing (1964) Excerpts (Akira Ifukube) JA:LP = Toho 8112 [@ST]

2520 Godzilla's Revenge (1971) Theme (Kunio Miyauchi) JA:LP = Star Child K22G-7111 [@ST]

2521 Gog (1954) Theme (Harry Sukman) US:LP = Liberty 3005* [Harry Sukman:ST]; Theme (Harry Sukman) US:LP = Decca 8060 [Victor Young]

2522 Goin' All the Way (1983) Score (e:Richard Hieronymus/e:Alan Nathanson) US:LP = Regency R1-8504*

2523 Goin' Coconuts (1978) Excerpts (The Osmonds) US:LP = Polydor PD1-6169* [Donny & Marie Osmond: ST]

2524 Goin' to Town (1935) Theme/ US:LP-10 = Mezzo Tone 21 [Mae West: ST]

2525 Going Hollywood (1933) Excerpts-A (Nacio Herb Brown) US:LP-MS = Columbia C2L-43 [Bing Crosby: ST]; Excerpts-B (Nacio Herb Brown) US:LP-BP = Caliban 6039 [@ST]; Excerpts-C (Nacio Herb Brown) US:LP-BP = JJA 19802 [@ST]

2526 Going Home (1971) Themes (Red Lane) US:SP = RCA 47-0616* [Red Lane:ST]

2527 Going My Way (1944) Highlights (James Van Heusen) US:LP-10 = Decca DL-5052 + US:LP = Decca DL-4257 [Bing Crosby:ST]

2528 Going Places (1938) Highlights (Harry Warren) US:LP-BP = Caliban 6010

2529 Going Places [Les Valseuses] (1975) Highlights (Stephane Grappelli) FR:LP = Festival 629*; Theme (Stephane Grappelli) US:LP = RCA 1-5016* [Ettore Stratta]

2530 Going Steady (1958) Theme (Fred Karger) US:SP = Capitol 3865 [Molly Bee:ST]

2531 Going Steady (1980) Score (pop music) JA:LP = Sony Epic 25-3P-37*

2532 Going Surfin' (1975) Score (Richard Henn) US:LP = Cowabunga 1001*

2533 Goke—Body Snatcher from Hell (1968) Theme (Shunsuke Kikuchi) JA:LP = Toho 8124 [@ST]

2534 Gold (1974) Score (Elmer Bernstein) US:LP = ABC ABDP-855*

2535 Gold Diggers (1984) Score (Lindsay Cooper) GB:LP = Sync Pulse 0617*

2536 Gold Diggers in Paris (1938) Themes-A-B/US:78 = RCA/Victor 25835 [Rudy Vallee:ST]; Themes-C-D/ US:78 = RCA/Victor 25836 [Rudy Vallee:ST]

2537 Gold Diggers of Broadway (1929) Themes/US:78 = Brunswick 4418 [Nick Lucas:ST]

2538 Gold Diggers of 1933 (1933) Excerpts-A (Harry Warren) US:LP-MS = Columbia C2L-44 [Dick Powell: ST]; Excerpts-B (Harry Warren) US: LP = UA LA-215 [@ST]; Excerpts-C (Harry Warren) US:LP-BP = JJA 19792 [@ST]

2539 Gold Diggers of 1935 (1935) Excerpts-A (Harry Warren) US:LP-MS = Columbia C2L-44 [Dick Powell: ST]; Excerpts-B (Harry Warren) US:LP-BP = JJA 19791 [@ST]

2540 Gold Is Where You Find It (1938) Themes (Max Steiner) US:LP-BP = Citadel CTMS-6 [Max Steiner:ST]

2541 Gold of Naples, The (1955) Theme (Alessandro Cicognini) US:LP = MGM 3599 [Domenico Savino]

2542 Golden Breed, The (1967) Score (e:Jerry Styner/t:Mike Curb/t: Harley Hatcher/t:Bob Summers) US: LP = Capitol ST-2886*

2543 Golden Child, The (1986) Score (e:Michel Colombier/t:John Barry/e:various) US:LP = Capitol SJ-12544*

2544 Golden Claw's Cat Girls, The *see* Louve Solitaire, La

2545 Golden Coach, The (1954)

Score (ae:Gino Marinuzzi/etc.) US: LP = MGM E-3111

2546 Golden Dawn, The (1930) Theme/US:78 = Brunswick 4828 [Noah Beery:ST]

2547 Golden Earrings (1947) Highlights (Victor Young) US:LP = Decca DL-8008 + US:LP = Decca DL-8481 + US:LP = Varese STV-81117

2548 Golden Fish, The [Histoire d'un Poisson Rouge] (1959) Score (Henri Crolla) FR:LP = Philips 9147

2549 Golden Girl (1951) Highlights (t:Lionel Newman/etc.) US:LP-BP = Caliban 6037

2550 Golden Horde, The (1951) Highlights (Hans J. Salter) US:LP = Medallion ML-312

2551 Golden Ivory *see* White Huntress

2552 Golden Lady (1979) Score (Georges Garvarentz) GB:LP = Ariola ARL-5019*

2553 Golden Mountains, The [Les Monts d'Or] (1932) Theme (Dmitri Shostakovich) US:78 = Columbia 12881 [Efrem Kurtz]

2554 Golden Raiders, The *see* Escape to Athena

2555 Golden Rendezvous [Nuclear Terror] (1977) Themes (Jeff Wayne) JA: SP = RCA/Victor 2591* [@ST]

2556 Golden Seal, The (1983) Score (e:John Barry/e:Dana Kaproff) US: LP = Compleat CSTR-6001*

2557 Golden Voyage of Sinbad, The (1974) Score (Miklos Rozsa) US: LP = UA LA-308*

2558 Goldengirl (1979) Theme-A (Bill Conti) US:LP-PP = Jenson 800* [The Jenson Marching Band]; Theme-B (Bill Conti) US:LP-PP = Jenson 100* [The Jenson Choral Ensemble]

2559 Goldfinger (1964) Score-A (John Barry) US:LP = UA UAL-4117/UAS-5117*; Score-B (John Barry) GB: LP = UA 1076* + GB:LP = Sunset 50712*

2560 Goldwyn Follies, The (1938) Excerpts (George Gershwin) US:LP-BP = JJA 19773 [@ST]

2561 G'ole (1983) Score (Rick Wakeman) GB:LP = Charisma CAS-1162*

2562 Goliath and the Barbarians (1960) Score (Les Baxter) US:LP = American International 1001/S-1001* + US:LP = Varese VC-81078*

2563 Goliath and the Sins of Babylon [Maciste, l'Ero Piu Grande del Mondo] (1963) Score (Francesco DeMasi) IT:LP = CAM CMS-30.094

2564 Goliath II [Short] (1963) Underscore + Dialog (George Bruns) US:LP = Disneyland ST-1902 + Disneyland DQ-1278

2565 Gone Are the Days! (1963) Theme (Henry Cowen) US:SP = Golden Crest 580 [Al Gordon]

2566 Gone with the Wave (1965) Score (Lalo Schifrin) US:LP = Colpix CP-492/SCP-492*

2567 Gone with the Wind (1939) Score-A (s:Max Steiner/t:Heinz Roemheld) US:LP = MGM 1E-10/1SE-10e [ST]; Score-B (Max Steiner) US: LP = Polygram PDM1-7001 [ST]; Score-C (Max Steiner) US:LP = RCA LPM-3859/LSP-3859e [Max Steiner]; Score-D (Max Steiner) US:LP = RCA ARL1-0452* [Charles Gerhardt]

2568 Gong Show Movie, The (1980) Theme (Chuck Barris) US:SP = MCA 41245* [Chuck Barris:ST]

2569 Gonks Go Beat (1965) Score (e:Mike Leander/e:Bobby Richards/etc.) GB:LP = Decca LK-4673*

2570 Good and the Bad, The [Le Bon et les Mechants] (1977) Score (Francis Lai) FR:LP = WB/WIP 863.003*

2571 Good Companions, The (1933) Themes/GB:LP = MFP 1127 [Jessie Matthews:ST]

2572 Good Companions, The (1958) Highlights (at:Laurie Johnson/etc.) GB:EP = Parlophone 8604

2573 Good Luck, Miss Wyckoff [The Sin] (1979) Score (Ernest Gold) JA: LP = Polydor MPF-1266*

2574 Good Morning, Boys (1937) Theme/US:LP = Monmouth 7031 [@Lili Palmer:ST]

2575 Good Neighbor Sam (1964) Theme (Frank DeVol) US:SP = RCA 47-8369 [Hugo Montenegro]; Theme (Frank DeVol) US:LP = UA 6376* [@Hollywood Soundstage Orchestra]

2576 Good News (1930) Theme/

US:LP-BP = JJA 19802 [@Stanley Smith & Mary Lawlor:ST]

2577 Good News (1947) Score (film songs:various/stage songs:Ray Henderson) US:LP-BP = Sountrak STK-111; Highlights (stage songs:Ray Henderson) US:LP-10 = MGM E-504 + US:LP = MGM E-3771 + US:LP = MGM 2SES-49e

2578 Good News [Buone Notizie] (1980) Score (Ennio Morricone) IT:LP = Cometa 1013/27*

2579 Good, the Bad and the Ugly, The (1968) Score (Ennio Morricone) US: LP = UA UAL-4172/UAS-5172*

2580 Good Times (1967) Score (Sonny Bono) US:LP = Atco 33-214/SD-33-214*

2581 Good to Go (1986) Score (t:Wally Badarou/s:various) US:LP = Island 90509-1*

2582 Goodbye Again (1961) Score (as:Georges Auric) US:LP = UA UAL-4091/UAS-5091*

2583 Goodbye, Charlie (1964) Score (Andre Previn) US:LP = 20th 3165/S-4165*; Theme (Andre Previn) US:SP = Dot 16668 [Pat Boone:ST]

2584 Goodbye, Columbus (1969) Score (e:Charles Fox/e:The Association) US:LP = WB WS-1786*

2585 Goodbye, Emmanuelle [Emmanuelle 3] (1978) Score (Serge Gainsbourg) JA:LP = Philips FDX-344*

2586 Goodbye Gemini (1970) Score (Christopher Gunning) US:LP = DJM 9101*

2587 Goodbye Girl, The (1977) Theme (David Gates) US:SP = Elektra 45450* [David Gates:ST]; Theme (David Gates) US:LP = Elektra 6E-148* [David Gates:ST]; Theme (David Gates) US: LP = First American 7728* [The Brothers Four]

2588 Goodbye, Mr. Chips (1969) Score (Leslie Bricusse) US:LP = MGM 1SE-19*

2589 Goodbye Uncle Tom [Farewell Uncle Tom] [Addio Zio Tom] (1971) Score (Riz Ortolani) IT:LP = RCA OLS-8*

2590 Goodnight Vienna (1932) Themes/GB:LP = WRC 283 [Jack Buchanan:ST]

2591 Goonies, The (1985) Score (t:Dave Grusin/s:various) US:LP = Epic SE-40067*

2592 Gorath (1962) Excerpts (Ken Ishii) JA:LP = Toho 8106 [@ST]

2593 Gordon's War (1973) Score (Angelo Badalamenti aka Andy Badale) US:LP = Buddah BDS-0598*

2594 Gorgeous Bird Like Me, A *see* Such A Gorgeous Kid Like Me

2595 Gorky Park (1983) Score (James Horner) US:LP = Varese STV-81206*

2596 Gospel (1983) Score (pop music) US:LP = Savoy SL-14753*

2597 Gospel According to St. Matthew, The (1966) Score (classical music) US:LP = Mainstream 54000/S-4000*

2598 Gospel Road, The (1973) Score + Underscore + Dialog (Johnny Cash) US:LP-MS = Columbia KG2-32253*

2599 Got to Investigate Silicone *see* Love Is the Answer

2600 Gotcha! (1985) Score (t:Bill Conti/s:various) US:LP = MCA 5596*

2601 Gout de Violence, Le *see* Taste of Violence, A

2602 Goya [Short] (1959) Score (Vicente Gomez) US:LP = Decca DL-8236

2603 Grace Moore Story, The *see* So This Is Love

2604 Gracie Allen Murder Case, The (1939) Theme (Matty Malneck) US: LP-BP = JJA 19762 [@Gracie Allen: ST]; Theme (Matty Malneck) US:LP = Painted Smiles 1359* [@Blossom Dearie]

2605 Graduate, The (1967) Score (e:Dave Grusin/e:Paul Simon) US:LP = Columbia OS-3180*

2606 Grand Bluff, Le (1957) Theme (Bill Byers) US:LP = WB 1371* [Pete Rugolo]; Theme (Bill Byers) US:LP = Dot 3120 [Ray Ventura]

2607 Grand Canyon, The [Short] (1958) Score (classical music) US:LP = Disneyland WDL-4019/ST-4019*

2608 Grand Duel, The [Il Grande Duello] (1972) Theme (Luis E. Bacalov) FR:LP = General Music 803.011* [@ST]

2609 Grand Maneuver, The [Summer Manoeuvers] [Les Grandes Manoeuvres] (1955) Theme (Georges Van Parys) US:LP = Mercury 20188 [Eddie Barclay]

2610 Grand Olympics, The [La Grande Olimpiade] (1961) Theme (A.F. Lavagnino) US:LP = RCA FSO-4 [@ST]

2611 Grand Prix (1966) Score (Maurice Jarre) US:LP = MGM 1E-8/1SE-8*

2612 Grand Slam [Ad Ogni Costa] (1967) Score (Ennio Morricone) IT:LP = RCA SP-8021

2613 Grande Bouffe, La [Blow Out] (1973) Themes (Philippe Sarde) FR:SP = Barclay 61784* [ST]

2614 Grande Bourgeoise, La [Fatti di Gente per Bene] [The Murri Affair] (1977) Score (Ennio Morricone) US:LP = Cerberus CEMS-0109*

2615 Grande Olimpiade, La *see* Grand Olympics, The

2616 Grandes Manoeuvres, Les *see* Grand Maneuver, The

2617 Grandma Moses [Short] (1950) Highlights (e:Hugh Martin/ae:Alec Wilder) US:LP-10 = Columbia ML-2185

2618 Grass Is Always Greener *see* Josie's Castle

2619 Grasshopper, The (1970) Score (s:Billy Goldenberg/t:Bobby Russell) US:LP = National General NG-1001*

2620 Grasshopper and the Ants, The [Cartoon] (1934) Theme + Narration (Leigh Harline) US:LP = Disneyland 1905; Theme (Leigh Harline) US:SP = Disneyland 331 [uncredited]

2621 Gravy Train, The *see* Dion Brothers, The

2622 Grazie, Zia [Thank You, Aunt] [Come Play with Me] (1968) Highlights (Ennio Morricone) FR:EP = AZ Disc 1259

2623 Grease (1978) Scores (film songs:various/stage songs:Jim Jacobs & Warren Casey) US:LP-MS = RSO RS2-4002*

2624 Grease 2 (1982) Score (e:Dominic Bugatti & Frank Musker/e:Louis St. Louis & Howard Greenfield/etc.) US:LP = RSO RS1-3803*

2625 Great [Cartoon] (1975) Themes (Jonathan Hodge) GB:SP = Polydor 2066.699 [Jonathan Hodge:ST]

2626 Great Adventure, The [The Adventurers] (1950) Theme (Cedric Thorpe Davie) GB:78-PP = Rank FM-110 [ST]

2627 Great American Broadcast, The (1941) Excerpts (Harry Warren) US:LP = Citadel CT-6004 [Alice Faye:ST]

2628 Great Bank Robbery, The (1969) Themes (James Van Heusen/Nelson Riddle) US:LP-PP = WB PRO-329* [@Zero Mostel/Nelson Riddle:ST]

2629 Great Brain, The (1979) Score (e:Don Costa/e:Ralph Ferraro/e:The Osmonds) US:LP-PP = Kolob PRO-6778*; Theme (The Osmonds) US:SP = Mercury 74005* [Jimmy Osmond:ST]

2630 Great Caruso, The (1951) Score (classical music) US:LP = RCA LM-1127/LSC-1127e [Mario Lanza:ST]; Theme (classical music) US:LP = Lion 70108 [Ann Blyth:ST]

2631 Great Chase, The (1962) Theme (Larry Adler) US:LP = Ava 30* [@Elliot Lawrence]; Theme (Larry Adler) US:SP = World Pacific 381 [Clare Fischer]

2632 Great Dictator, The (1940) Excerpts-A (ae:Charles Chaplin) US:LP = GNP 2064* [Michel Villard]; Excerpts-B (Charles Chaplin & Meredith Willson) US:LP = London 44184* [Stanley Black]; Theme (Meredith Willson) US:LP = Paramount 6026* [Darius Brubeck]

2633 Great Escape, The (1963) Score (Elmer Bernstein) US:LP = UA UAL-4107/UAS-5107*

2634 Great Expectations (1947) Theme (Walter Goehr) GB:78 = Decca 1596 [Walter Goehr:ST]

2635 Great Gatsby, The (1974) Scores (e:Nelson Riddle/etc.) US:LP-MS = Paramount PAS-3001*

2636 Great Imposter, The (1961) Themes (Henry Mancini) US:SP = RCA 47-7830 [Henry Mancini:ST]; Themes (Henry Mancini) US:LP = Camden 928* [Henry Mancini:ST]

2637 Great John L, The (1945) Theme (James Van Heusen) US:78 = RCA Victor 20-1657 [Tommy Dorsey]

2638 Great Lie, The (1941) Theme (Max Steiner) US:LP = Citadel 7005* [Maria Martino]

2639 Great Locomotive Chase, The (1956) Themes (Paul Smith/Stan Jones) US:SP = Disneyland 37 [Camarata]

2640 Great Lover, The (1949) Theme-A (Jay Livingston & Ray Evans) US:SP = Capitol 54-783 [Bob Hope:ST]; Theme-B (Jay Livingston & Ray Evans) US:SP = RCA 47-3078 [Tony Martin]

2641 Great MacArthy, The (1975) Score (Bruce Smeaton) AU:LP = CAM WEA 600-021*

2642 Great Man, The (1956) Theme (Bobby Troup) US:SP = Liberty 55052 [Julie London:ST]

2643 Great Mouse Detective, The (1986) Theme + Dialog (Henry Mancini) US:EP = Disneyland 503 [ST]

2644 Great Muppet Caper, The (1981) Score (Joe Raposo) US:LP = Atlantic SD-16047*

2645 Great Race, The (1965) Score (Henry Mancini) US:LP = RCA LPM-3402/LSP-3402*

2646 Great Rock 'n' Roll Swindle, The (1979) Scores (pop music) US:LP-MS = Virgin VD-2510* [The Sex Pistols: ST]

2647 Great Rupert, The (1950) Theme (Jimmy Durante) US:SP = MGM 30257 [Jimmy Durante:ST]

2648 Great St. Louis Bank Robbery, The (1959) Theme (Bernardo Segall) US:SP = Dot 15793 [Jackie Cooper]

2649 Great Stone Face, The (1968) Theme (Albert Hague) US:SP = Decca 9-32350 [The Romantic Revolution]

2650 Great Train Robbery, The [The First Great Train Robbery] (1979) Score (Jerry Goldsmith) US:LP = UA LA-962*

2651 Great Unfenced, The [Short] (1964) Highlights (Robert Muczynski) US:LP-PP = Music Library MRL-7110

2652 Great Victor Herbert, The (1939) Highlights (pop music) US:LP-BP = Caliban 6033

2653 Great Waldo Pepper, The (1975) Score (Henry Mancini) US:LP = MCA 2085*

2654 Great Waltz, The (1938) Score (as:Dimitri Tiomkin) US:LP-BP = Sountrak STK-109; Highlights (ae:Dimitri Tiomkin) US:78-MS = RCA 4410 [Miliza Korjus:ST]; Excerpts (ae:Dimitri Tiomkin) US:LP = Camden CAL-279 [Miliza Korjus:ST]

2655 Great Waltz, The (1972) Score (stage songs:as:George Forrest & Robert Wright) US:LP = MGM 1SE-39*

2656 Great Ziegfeld, The (1936) Score (e:Walter Donaldson/etc.) US: LP-BP = Classic International Filmusicals 3005

2657 Greatest, The (1977) Score (Michael Masser) US:LP = Arista AL-7000*

2658 Greatest Battle, The [Il Grande Attacco] (1979) Score (Franco Micalizzi) IT:LP = Cinevox 33/118*

2659 Greatest Show on Earth, The (1952) Highlights (t:Victor Young/e: pop music) US:LP-10 = RCA LPM-3018 [Irwin Talbot]; Theme/US:LP-BP = Legends 1000/4 [Dorothy Lamour:ST]

2660 Greatest Story Ever Told, The (1965) Score (Alfred Newman) US:LP = UA UAL-4120/UAS-5120* + US:LP = UA LA-277*

2661 Greco, El (1964) Score (Ennio Morricone) IT:LP = RCA SP-8061*

2662 Greece, Land of Dreams (1966) Score (Manos Hadjidakis) FR: LP = Fontana 680.241

2663 Greed in the Sun [Cent-Mille Dollars du Soleil] (1963) Themes (Georges Delerue) JA:SP = Hit 1146 [ST]

2664 Greek Pearls, The (1968) Score (Mimis Plessas) US:LP = Lyra LYM-1008/LYS-1008e

2665 Green Berets, The (1968) Theme (Miklos Rozsa) GB:LP = MFP 5171* [Geoff Love]

2666 Green Carnation, The *see* Trials of Oscar Wilde, The

2667 Green Dolphin Street (1947) Theme (Bronislau Kaper) US:SP = ABC 11100 [Nancy Ames]; Theme (Bronislau Kaper) US:LP = WB 1242* [Ray Heindorf]; Theme (Bronislau Kaper) US: LP = Delos 25421* [Bronislau Kaper]

2668 Green Fire (1955) Theme (Miklos Rozsa) US:SP = Majar 139 [Joe Leahy]; Theme (Miklos Rozsa) US:SP =

Capitol 3020 [Connie Russell]; Theme (Miklos Rozsa) US:LP = Mercury 20156 + US:LP = Mercury 20301 [David Carroll]

2669 Green Ice (1981) Score (s:Bill Wyman/as:Ken Thorne) GB:LP = Polydor POLS-1031*

2670 Green Mansions (1959) Highlights (Heitor Villa-Lobos) US:LP = UA UAL-7007/UAS-8007* + US:LP = UA UAS-5506* [Heitor Villa-Lobos]; Theme (Bronislau Kaper) US:SP = MGM 12784 [Leroy Holmes]

2671 Green Mare, The [La Jument Verte] (1959) Highlights (Rene Cloerec) FR:EP = RCA 76.365

2672 Green Room, The [La Chambre Verte] (1978) Highlights (classical music) FR:LP = Pathe C066.14567*

2673 Green Slime, The (1969) Theme (Sherry Gaden) US:SP = MGM 14052 [The Green Slime]; Theme (Sherry Gaden) US:LP-BP = POO 104 [@The Green Slime]

2674 Green Wall, The (1969) Theme (E. Tinira) JA:LP = JVC 4B-5005* [JVC Symphony Orchestra]

2675 Greengage Summer, The *see* Loss of Innocence

2676 Greenwich Village (1944) Highlights (Nacio Herb Brown) US:LP-BP = Caliban 6026

2677 Gregory's Girl (1981) Theme (Colin Tully) GB:LP-MS = Filmtrax 820-252-1* [@Colin Tully:ST]

2678 Gremlins (1984) Score (e:Jerry Goldsmith/e:various) US:LP = Geffen GHSP-24044*

2679 Grey Fox, The (1983) Score (Martin Conway Baker) US:LP = DRG SL-9515*

2680 Greystoke—The Legend of Tarzan, Lord of the Apes (1984) Score (John Scott) US:LP = WB 25120-1*

2681 Grip of Fear, The *see* Experiment in Terror

2682 Grisbi [Touchez Pas au Grisbi] (1954) Themes (Jean Wiener) US:SP = Columbia 4-40354 [Jean Wiener:ST]; Theme (Jean Wiener) US:LP = Columbia 107 [Michel Legrand]

2683 Grizzly (1976) Score (Robert O. Ragland) US:LP = Tru Luv HWR-301* + JA:LP = Seven Seas FML-59*

2684 Ground Zero (1973) Themes (The Chosen Few) US:SP-PP = CF 001* [The Chosen Few:ST]

2685 Grounds for Marriage (1950) Highlights (t:David Raksin/e:classical music) US:LP-10 = MGM E-536

2686 Groupie Girl (1970) Score (e:John Fiddy/e:John Hawkshaw) GB:LP = Polydor 2384.021*

2687 Growing Up *see* Lemon Popsicle

2688 Guale [Short] Highlights (Max Schubel) US:LP = Opus One LP-25*

2689 Guerre Est Finie, La [The War Is Over] (1967) Score (Giovanni Fusco) US:LP = Bell 6012/S-6012*

2690 Guess Who's Coming to Dinner? (1967) Score (e:Frank DeVol/etc.) US:LP = Colgems COM-108/COS-108*

2691 Guide, The [Survival] (1965) Score (S.D. Burman) GB:LP = EMI/Odeon 1038; Theme (S.D. Burman) US:LP = Capitol 10500 [@Lata Mangeshkar:ST]

2692 Guide for the Married Man, A (1967) Theme (John Williams) US:SP = White Whale 251 [The Turtles:ST]; Theme (John Williams) US:LP = White Whale 114* [The Turtles:ST]

2693 Guitar Picks and Roach Clips Scores (various) US:LP-MS = Stoneybrook LA-101*

2694 Gulliver's Travels (1940) Highlights (Ralph Rainger) US:78-MS = Decca A-100

2695 Gulliver's Travels Beyond the Moon (1966) Score (Milton DeLugg) US:LP = Mainstream 54001/S-4001*

2696 Gumshoe (1972) Themes (Andrew Lloyd Webber) GB:SP = Polydor 2001.278 [ST]; Theme (Andrew Lloyd Webber) US:SP = Decca 9-32951 [David Axelrod]

2696a Gun Crazy [Deadly Is the Female] (1949) Theme (Victor Young) US:SP = Decca 9-27067 [Victor Young:ST]

2697 Gun Hawk, The (1963) Theme (Jimmie Haskell) US:SP = Capitol 5044 [Jimmie Haskell:ST]; Theme (Jimmie Haskell) US:LP = Capitol 2075* [Jimmie Haskell:ST]

2698 Gun Runners, The (1958) Theme (Joe Lubin) US:SP = Arwin 112 [The Pets]

2699 Gunfight at Red Sands [Gringo] [Duello nel Texas] (1965) Theme (Ennio Morricone) IT:LP = RCA 10402* + IT:LP = RCA 33155* [@ST]

2700 Gunfight at the O.K. Corral (1957) Excerpts (Dimitri Tiomkin) US: LP = Film Music Collection FMC-13* [Elmer Bernstein]; Theme (Dimitri Tiomkin) US:SP = Columbia 4-40916 [Frankie Laine:ST]

2700a Gunfight in Abilene (1967) Theme (Bobby Darin) US:SP = Atlantic 45-2376 [Bobby Darin:ST]

2701 Gung Ho! (1986) Theme (Jonathan Cain) US:SP = Geffen 7-28749* [Jimmy Barnes:ST]

2702 Gunman's Walk (1958) Theme (Fred Karger) US:SP = Dot 15767 [Tab Hunter:ST]

2703 Gunn (1967) Score (Henry Mancini) US:LP = RCA LPM-3840/LSP-3840*; Themes (Henry Mancini) US:SP = RCA 47-9256 [Laura Devon: ST]

2704 Guns at Batasi (1964) Themes (John Addison) US:SP = 20th 547 [John Addison:ST]; Theme (John Addison) US:LP = London 434* [The Band of the Grenadier]

2705 Guns Don't Argue *see* Pistole non Discutono, Le

2706 Guns for San Sebastian (1968) Score (Ennio Morricone) US:LP = MGM E-4565/SE-4565*

2707 Guns in the Afternoon *see* Ride the High Country

2708 Guns of Navarone, The (1961) Score (Dimitri Tiomkin) US:LP = Columbia CL-1655/CS-8455*; Theme ["Treu Sein"] (Dimitri Tiomkin) US:SP-PP = D.T. N80W-3008 [Elga Anderson: ST]

2709 Guns of the Pecos (1937) Theme/GB:78 = Rex 9420 [Dick Foran: ST]

2710 Guns of the Timberland (1960) Themes/US:EP = Chancellor CHLA-302 [Frankie Avalon:ST]

2711 Guru, The (1969) Score (Ustad Vilayat Khan) US:LP = RCA LSO-1158*; Theme (Mark London) US: SP = Columbia 4-44672 [The Buckinghams:ST]

2712 Guys and Dolls (1955) Score (stage songs:Frank Loesser) US:LP-BP = Motion Picture Tracks MPT-1 + US:LP-BP = JJA 19762; Highlights (stage songs:Frank Loesser) US:EP = Decca ED-2332

2713 Gwendoline *see* Perils of Gwendoline, The

2714 Gypsy (1962) Score (stage songs:Jule Styne) US:LP = WB B-1480/BS-1480*

2715 Gypsy and the Gentleman, The (1958) Theme (Hans May) GB:78 = Oriole 1418 [Hans May:ST]

2716 Gypsy Girl (1966) Themes (Milton DeLugg) US:LP = Mainstream S-6090* [@Hayley Mills/Milton DeLugg:ST]; Theme (Milton DeLugg) US: SP = Mainstream 656 [Hayley Mills:ST]

2717 Gypsy Moths, The (1969) Score (Elmer Bernstein) US:LP-BP = Cinema LP-8011

H

2718 H.M.S. Defiant *see* Damn the Defiant

2719 H-Man, The (1958) Theme (Masaru Sato) JA:LP = Toho 8107 [@ST]

2720 H2S (1968) Theme (Ennio Morricone) US:LP-BP = POO 105 [Ennio Morricone:ST]

2721 Hagbard and Signe *see* Red Mantle, The

2722 Hail to the Chief (1972) Theme (Trade Martin) US:SP = Toot MMP-1* [Trade Martin:ST]

2723 Hair (1979) Scores (stage songs:Galt MacDermot) US:LP-MS = RCA CBL2-3274*

2724 Half a Sixpence (1967) Score (stage songs:David Heneker) US:LP = RCA LOC-1146/LSO-1146*

2725 Half Moon Street (1986) Score (Richard Harvey) FR:LP = Milan A-282*

2726 Hallelujah (1929) Theme-A/US:78 = RCA/Victor 22097 [Daniel Haynes:ST]; Theme-B/US:LP-BP = JJA 19744 [@Nina Mae McKinney:ST]

2727 Hallelujah, I'm a Bum [Hallelujah, I'm a Tramp] [The Heart of New York] (1933) Highlights (Richard Rodgers) US:LP-BP = Subon 1234 + US:LP-BP = JJA 19766

2728 Hallelujah the Hills (1964) Score (Meyer Kupferman) US:LP = Fontana MGF-27524/SRF-67524*

2729 Hallelujah Trail, The (1965) Score (s:Elmer Bernstein/at:Fred Steiner) US:LP = UA UAL-4127/UAS-5127*

2730 Halloween (1978) Score (John Carpenter) US:LP = Varese STV-81176*

2731 Halloween II (1981) Score (John Carpenter) US:LP = Varese STV-81152*

2732 Halloween III (1982) Score (John Carpenter) US:LP = MCA 6115*

2733 Hambone and Hilly (1985) Score (Georges Garvarentz) JA:LP = Polydor 25MM-0517*

2734 Hamlet (1948) Excerpts (William Walton) US:LP = Angel 38088* [Charles Groves]; Theme + Underscore + Dialog (William Walton) US:LP = RCA LM-1924 + US:LP-10 = RCA LCT-5; Theme (William Walton) US:LP = Angel 36198* + US:LP = Seraphim 60205* [William Walton]

2735 Hamlet (1964) Highlights (Dmitri Shostakovich) US:LP-BP = Cinema LP-8003 + Highlights (Dmitri Shostakovich) US:LP = London SP-21132* [Bernard Herrmann]

2736 Hammerhead (1968) Score (David Whitaker) US:LP = Colgems COS-110*

2737 Hand in Hand (1960) Theme (Stanley Black) US:SP = Mercury 71790 [David Carroll]; Theme (Stanley Black) US:LP = Mercury 60688* [David Carroll]; Theme (Stanley Black) US:LP = Colpix 418* [James Darren]

2738 Handle with Care (1964) Score (Jaime Mendoza-Nava) US:LP = Preview 1001

2739 Handle with Care [Citizens Band] (1977) Theme (Bill Conti) US: LP = Casablanca 7061* [Larry Santos: ST]

2740 Hands of a Strangler, The *see* Hands of Orlac

2741 Hands of Orlac [Les Mains d'Orlac] [The Hands of a Strangler] (1961) Highlights (Claude Bolling) FR: EP = Philips 432.523

2742 Hang 'Em High (1968) Score (Dominic Frontiere) US:LP = UA UAS-5179*

2743 Hang Your Hat on the Wind (1969) Highlights + Dialog (Randy Sparks) US:LP = Disneyland DQ-1332

2744 Hanging on a Star (1978) Excerpts (Lane Caudell) US:LP = MCA 3039* [Lane Caudell:ST]

2745 Hanging Tree, The (1959) Theme (Jerry Livingston) US:SP = Columbia 4-41325 [Marty Robbins:ST]; Theme (Jerry Livingston) US:LP = Columbia 1325 [Marty Robbins:ST]; Theme (Jerry Livingston) US:LP = Columbia 1615/8415* [Frankie Laine]

2746 Hangover Square (1945) Excerpts (Bernard Herrmann) US:LP = RCA ARL1-0707* [Charles Gerhardt]; Excerpts (Bernard Herrmann) US:LP = Camden CAL-205 + US:LP-BP = Cinema LP-8006 [@Werner Janssen]

2747 Hanna K. (1983) Score (Gabriel Yared) FR:LP = RCA/Saravah SHL-1102*

2748 Hanna Mae (1973) Theme (Ala King) US:SP = Aware 034* [Deep Velvet]

2749 Hannah and Her Sisters (1986) Score (pop music) US:LP = MCA 6190*

2750 Hannah Lee *see* Outlaw Territory

2751 Hannibal Brooks (1969) Score (Francis Lai) US:LP = UA UAS-5196*

2752 Hannie Caulder (1971) Themes (Ken Thorne) GB:LP = RCA 25043* [Vic Lewis & Ken Thorne:ST]

2753 Hans Christian Andersen (1952) Highlights (Frank Loesser) US: LP-10 = Decca DL-5433 + US:LP = Decca DL-8479/DL-78479e + US:LP = MCA 148e [Danny Kaye:ST]; Excerpts (Frank Loesser) US:LP-PP = GNP 2222 [@Danny Kaye & Jeanmaire:ST]

2754 Hansel and Gretel (1954) Score (classical music) US:LP = RCA LXA-1013 + US:LP = RCA LBY-1024 + US:LP = Camden CAL-1024/CAS-1024e

2955 Hansel and Gretel (1971) Highlights + Dialog (Milton DeLugg) US: LP = Golden LP-167

2756 Ha'penny Breeze (1950) Theme (Philip Green) GB:78 = Columbia 1724 [Philip Green:ST]

2757 Happening, The (1967) Score (Frank DeVol) US:LP = Colgems COM-5006/COS-5006*

2758 Happiest Millionaire, The (1967) Score (Richard & Robert Sherman) US:LP = Buena Vista BV-5001/ST-5001*

2759 Happiness Ahead (1934) Excerpts (various) US:LP-MS = Columbia C2L-44 [Dick Powell:ST]

2760 Happiness of Us Alone, The (1962) Excerpts (Toru Takemitsu) JA: LP = RCA/Victor 1065 [Toru Takemitsu:ST]

2761 Happy (1934) Theme/GB: 78 = Decca 3974 [Stanley Lupino:ST]

2762 Happy Anniversary (1959) Themes (Robert Allen) US:SP = Laurie 3050 [Mitzi Gaynor:ST]; Theme (Robert Allen) US:SP = Columbia 4-41497 [The Four Lads]; Theme (Robert Allen) US: LP = Columbia 1421/8218* [@The Four Lads]

2763 Happy As the Grass Was Green [Hazel's People] (1973) Themes (Gino Mescoli) US:SP = Globe 101 [Lee Darin/Gino Mescoli:ST]

2764 Happy Days (1930) Themes/ US:78 = RCA/Victor 22259 [George Olsen:ST]

2765 Happy Days (1979) Score (Herb Linsey) US:LP = Funky 740601*

2766 Happy Ending, The (1969) Score (Michel Legrand) US:LP = UA UAS-5203*

2767 Happy-Go-Lovely (1950) Theme (Mischa Spoliansky) GB:78 = HMV 10166 [ST]

2768 Happy-Go-Lucky (1943) Highlights (Jimmy McHugh) US:LP-BP = Caliban 6021

2769 Happy Landing (1938) Excerpts (various) US:LP = Encore 101 [Ethel Merman:ST]

2770 Happy New Year [La Bonne Annee] (1973) Theme (Francis Lai) US: LP = AIA 90042* + US:LP = Audio Fidelity 6301* [Francis Lai:ST]; Theme (Francis Lai) FR:SP = Philips 6009.703* [Mireille Mathieu:ST]

2771 Happy Prince, The [Short] (1973) Highlights + Underscore + Dialog (Ron Goodwin) CA:LP = Capitol 6426*

2772 Happy Road, The (1957) Theme (Georges Van Parys) US:SP = MGM 12501 [Gene Kelly:ST]; Theme (Georges Van Parys) US:LP = DRG 15010 [Gene Kelly:ST]

2773 Happy Thieves, The [The Oldest Confession] (1962) Theme (Mario Nascimbene) US:LP = UA 6197* + US: LP = Unart 20001* [@Nick Perito]

2774 Happy Time, The (1952) Theme (Dimitri Tiomkin) US:LP = RCA 1007 [Al Goodman]

2775 Happy Times *see* Inspector General, The

2776 Harakiri (1962) Excerpts (Toru Takemitsu) JA:LP = RCA/Victor 1062 [Toru Takemitsu:ST]

2777 Hard Country (1981) Score (e: Michael Murphey/etc.) US:LP = Epic SE-37367*

2778 Hard Day's Night, A (1964) Score (John Lennon & Paul McCartney) US:LP = UA UAL-3366/UAS-6366* + US:LP = Capitol SW-11921* [The Beatles:ST]

2779 Hard Driver *see* Last American Hero, The

2780 Hard Part Begins, The (1973) Score (Jan Guenther) CA:LP = A&M SP-9016*

2781 Hard Ride, The (1971) Score (Harley Hatcher) US:LP = Paramount PAS-6005*

2782 Hard Times for Vampires *see* Uncle Was a Vampire

2783 Hard to Hold (1984) Score (e: Rick Springfield/t:Tom Scott/etc.) US: LP = RCA ABL1-4935*

2784 Harder They Come, The (1973) Score (Jimmy Cliff) US:LP = Mango SMAS-9202*

2785 Harder They Fall, The (1956) Theme (Hugo Friedhofer) US:LP = Verve V6-8662 [Howard Roberts]

2786 Harem, The [L'Harem] (1968) Theme (Ennio Morricone) IT:LP = RCA 31279* + FR:LP = RCA 461.011* [Ennio Morricone:ST]

2787 Harem Holiday *see* Harum-Scarum

2788 Harlequin [Dark Forces]

(1982) Score (Brian May) FR:LP = Music Movie MM-22002*

2789 Harlow (1965) Score (Al Ham & Nelson Riddle) US:LP = WB W-1599/WS-1599*

2790 Harlow (1965) Score (Neal Hefti) US:LP = Columbia OL-6390/OS-2790*

2791 Harmagedon (1982) Score (e: Keith Emerson/e:Derek Austin) GB: LP = Chord 3*

2792 Harmony Parade *see* Pigskin Parade

2793 Harold Lloyd's World of Comedy (1962) Highlights (Walter Scharf) US:LP = Citadel CT-6018*

2794 Harold Teen (1934) Themes/US:LP-MS-BP = Radiola 1215/8 [@ Chick Chandler & Rochelle Hudson: ST]

2795 Harper [Moving Target] (1966) Score (s:Johnny Mandel/t:Andre Previn) US:LP = Mainstream 56078/S-6078*

2796 Harrad Experiment, The (1972) Score (s:Artie Butler/t:Charles Fox) US:LP = Capitol ST-11182*

2797 Harrad Summer, The (1974) Score (Patrick Williams) US:LP = Capitol ST-11338*

2798 Harry and Tonto (1974) Score (Bill Conti) US:LP = Casablanca NBLP-7010*

2799 Harry and Walter Go to New York (1976) Themes (David Shire) US: SP = Shady Brook 028 [Elliott Gould & James Caan:ST]; Theme (David Shire) US:LP-BP = Centurion 1600 [@Elliott Gould & James Caan:ST]

2800 Harry in Your Pocket [Harry Never Holds] (1973) Theme (Lalo Schifrin) US:SP-PP = Unart 93430 [Lalo Schifrin:ST]

2801 Harum-Scarum [Harem Holiday] (1965) Score (e:Bill Giant/e:Florence Kaye/etc.) US:LP = RCA LPM-3468/LSP-3468* + US:LP = RCA APL1-2558* + US:LP = RCA AYL1-3734* [Elvis Presley:ST]

2802 Harvest from the Wilderness (1948) Theme (Doreen Carwithen) GB: 78-PP = Rank FM-38 [ST]

2803 Harvey Girls, The (1946) Score (Johnny Mercer) US:LP-BP = Hollywood Soundstage 5002; Highlights (Johnny Mercer) US:LP = Decca DL-8498 + US:LP = AEI 3101 [Judy Garland:ST]

2804 Hatari (1962) Score (Henry Mancini) US:LP = RCA LPM-2559/LSP-2559*

2805 Hatchet Murders, The *see* Deep Red

2806 Haunted (1977) Score (Lor Crane) US:LP = Midsong BKL1-2131*

2807 Haunting of Julia, The *see* Full Circle

2808 Have Rocket, Will Travel (1959) Themes (George Duning) US: SP = Colpix 120 [The Three Stooges:ST]

2809 Having a Wild Weekend [Catch Us If You Can] (1965) Score (Dave Clark) US:LP = Epic LN-24162/BN-26162*

2810 Hawaii (1966) Score (Elmer Bernstein) US:LP = UA UAL-4143/UAS-5143* + US:LP = UA LA-283*

2811 Hawaii Calls (1938) Theme-A/US:78 = Bluebird 7320 [Bobby Breen: ST]; Theme-B/US:78 = Bluebird 7330 [Bobby Breen:ST]

2812 Hawaiians, The [Master of the Islands] (1970) Score (Henry Mancini) US:LP = UA UAS-5210*

2813 Hawk the Slayer (1980) Score (Harry Robertson) GB:LP = Chips CHLP-1*

2814 Hawks and the Sparrows, The [Uccellacci e Uccellini] (1966) Theme (Ennio Morricone) FR:LP = RCA 10599* [Ennio Morricone:ST]

2815 Hawmps (1976) Themes (Euel Box) US:SP = Mulberry Square 3938* [Bobby Smith/Euel Box:ST]

2816 Hazel's People *see* Happy As the Grass Was Green

2817 He and She *see* Assoluto Naturale, L'

2818 He Died After the War (1971) Excerpts (Toru Takemitsu) JA:LP = RCA/Victor 1064 [Toru Takemitsu:ST]

2819 He Restoreth My Soul / Theme (Lee Pockriss) US:LP = New Life 741-10* [Merrill Womach:ST]

2820 Head (1968) Score (t:Ken Thorne/s:various) US:LP = Colgems COSO-5008*

2821 Head Over Heels (1936) Excerpts (various) GB:LP = Decca ECM-2168 [Jessie Matthews:ST]

2822 Headin' for Broadway (1980) Themes (Joe Brooks) US:SP = Columbia 1-11271* [Rex Smith:ST]

2823 Heads Up (1930) Themes-A-B/US:78 = RCA/Victor 22520 [Helen Kane:ST]; Themes-C-D/US:LP-BP = JJA 19766 [@Helen Kane:ST]

2824 Heart Beat (1980) Score (Jack Nitzsche) US:LP = Capitol SOO-12029*

2825 Heart Is a Lonely Hunter, The (1968) Score (Dave Grusin) US:LP = WB WS-1759*

2826 Heart Is a Rebel, The/Themes (Ralph Carmichael) US:LP = Word 3164 [@Georgia Lee/Ethel Waters:ST]

2827 Heart Like a Wheel (1983) Theme (Laurence Rosenthal) US:LP = Scotti Bros. 40097* [Jill Michaels:ST]

2828 Heart of a Man, The (1959) Theme/US:SP = Columbia 4-41480 [Frankie Vaughan:ST]

2829 Heart of Glass [Herz aus Glas] (1976) Score (Popol Vuh) FR:LP = Brain 60.079*

2830 Heart of New York, The *see* Hallelujah, I'm a Bum

2831 Heart of Paris, The [Griboville] (1937) Theme (Georges Auric) US:SP = ABC 45-9693 [Don Costa]; Theme (Georges Auric) US:LP = Mercury 20484 [Clebanoff]

2832 Heart of Paris, The [Le Pave de Paris] (1961) Theme (Joseph Kosma) FR:SP = Philips 432.538 [ST]

2833 Heartbreak Kid, The (1972) Highlights + Dialog (e:Garry Sherman/t:Cy Coleman) US:LP = Columbia S-32155*

2834 Heartbreakers (1984) Score (Tangerine Dream) GE:LP = Virgin 207-212-620*

2835 Heartburn (1986) Theme (Carly Simon) US:SP = Arista 1-9525* [Carly Simon:ST]

2836 Hearts Divided (1936) Theme-A/US:78 = Decca 900 [Dick Powell:ST]; Theme-B/US:LP = Decca 8837 [Dick Powell:ST]

2837 Heat and Dust (1983) Score (Richard Robbins) US:LP = Varese STV-81194*

2838 Heat's On, The [Tropicana] (1943) Theme/US:LP-BP = Caliban 6036 [Mae West:ST]

2839 Heaven Can Wait (1978) Theme (Dave Grusin) US:LP = RCA 1-3052* [Henry Mancini]; Theme (Dave Grusin) US:LP = UA 941* + US:LP = Liberty 10112* [Ferrante and Teicher]

2840 Heaven Help Us (1985) Score (pop music) US:LP = EMI SV-17154*

2841 Heaven with a Gun (1969) Theme (Johnny Mandel) US:SP = Columbia 4-44947 [Tony Bennett]; Theme (Johnny Mandel) US:LP = UA 6710* [Leroy Holmes]

2842 Heavenly Bodies (1985) Score (various) US:LP = Private I SZ-39930*

2843 Heavenly Kid, The (1985) Score (e:George Duke/e:various) US:LP = Elektra 60425-1*

2844 Heaven's Gate / Score (as:David Mansfield) US:LP = Liberty LOO-1073*

2845 Heavy Metal (1981) Score-A (Elmer Bernstein) US:LP = Full Moon/Asylum 5E-547*; Scores-B (rock music) US:LP-MS = Full Moon/Asylum DP-90004*

2846 Heavy Traffic (1973) Score (Ray Shanklin & Ed Bogas) US:LP = Fantasy FTS-9436*

2847 Hedda (1975) Excerpts (Laurie Johnson) US:LP = Starlog/Varese SV-95002* [Laurie Johnson:ST]

2848 Heidi (1937) Theme/US:LP-MS = 20th 2-103 [Shirley Temple:ST]

2849 Heidi's Song (1982) Highlights + Underscore + Dialog (e:Burton Lane/u:Hoyt Curtin) US:LP = K-Tel NU-5310*

2850 Heist, The *see* Dollars

2851 Helen Morgan Story, The [Both Ends of the Candle] (1957) Score (pop music) US:LP = RCA LOC-1030

2852 Helen of Troy (1956) Highlights (Max Steiner) US:LP = Film Music Collection FMC-1* [Elmer Bernstein]; Theme (Max Steiner) US:SP = RCA 47-6422 [Max Steiner:ST]

2853 Helga / Theme (J. Chevrier) US:LP = Mercury 20188 [Eddie Barclay]

2854 Helga and Michael *see* Michael and Helga

2855 Hell Island (1977) Score

(Shinichi Tanabe) JA:LP = Toho AX-5013*

2856 Hell on Wheels (1967) Theme/ US:SP = Columbia 4-43845 [Marty Robbins:ST]

2857 Hell Raiders of the Deep (1954) Themes (P.G. Redi) US:EP = MGM X-1108 [Nilla Pizzi/Eleonora Rossi-Drago:ST]; Theme (P.G. Redi) US:LP = MGM 3485 [Robert Ashley]

2858 Hell to Eternity (1960) Score (Leith Stevens) US:LP = Warwick 2030/ S-2030*

2859 Hell Up in Harlem (1974) Score (Freddie Perren) US:LP = Motown M5-802*

2860 Hellbenders, The [I Crudeli] (1966) Highlights (Ennio Morricone) IT: LP = Intermezzo IMGM-009*

2861 Hellcats, The (1968) Score (uncredited) US:LP = Tower ST-5124*

2862 Hello, Dolly (1969) Score (stage songs:Jerry Herman) US:LP = 20th DTCS-5103* + US:LP = 20th T-102*

2863 Hello, Everybody (1933) Theme-A/US:78 = Brunswick 6496 [Kate Smith:ST]; Theme-B/US:78 = Brunswick 6497 [Kate Smith:ST]; Theme-C/US:LP = Epic 159 [@Kate Smith:ST]

2864 Hello, Frisco, Hello (1943) Score (pop music) US:LP-BP = Hollywood Stoundstage 5005

2865 Hello, Goodbye (1970) Score (Francis Lai) US:LP = 20th S-4210*

2866 Hell's Angels on Wheels (1967) Score (Stu Phillips) US:LP = Smash 27094/67094*

2867 Hell's Angels '69 (1969) Score (Tony Bruno) US:LP = Capitol SKAO-303*

2868 Hell's Belles (1969) Score (Les Baxter) US:LP = Sidewalk ST-5919*

2869 Help! (1965) Score (e:John Lennon & Paul McCartney/e:Ken Thorne) US:LP = Capitol MAS-2386/ SMAS-2386*

2870 Help Me, My Love [Amore Mio Aiutami] (1969) Score (Piero Piccioni) IT:LP = RCA KOLS-1007*

2871 Helter Skelter (1949) Theme (Francis Chagrin) GB:78-PP = Rank FM-74 [ST]; Theme (Francis Chagrin) GB:LP = Lyrita 95*

2872 Hemingway's Adventures of a Young Man (1962) Score (Franz Waxman) US:LP = RCA LOC-1074/LSO-1074* + US:LP = Entracte ERS-6516*

2873 Hennessy (1975) Theme (John Scott) JA:LP-MS = Seven Seas FMW-31/2* [@Stanley Maxfield]

2874 Henry IV (1984) Score (Astor Piazzolla) FR:LP = Milan A-234*

2875 Henry V (1946) Highlights (William Walton) US:LP = Angel 36198/ S-36198* + US:LP = Seraphim S-60205*

2876 Henry VIII and His Six Wives (1972) Score (as:David Munrow) US: LP = Angel SFO-36895*

2877 Her Jungle Love (1938) Theme (Frederick Hollander) US:78 = Brunswick 8132 [Dorothy Lamour:ST]

2878 Her Majesty Love (1930) Theme/US:LP = Pelican 102 [@Marilyn Miller:ST]

2879 Hercules (1959) Score (Enzo Masetti) IT:LP = Phoenix PHCAM-01*; Underscore + Dialog (Enzo Masetti) US:LP = RCA LBY-1036

2880 Hercules [Short] Sequence + Dialog (Arthur Kleiner) US:LP-PP = Picture Book Parade 101 [@ST]

2881 Hercules (1983) Score (Pino Donaggio) US:LP = Varese STV-81187*

2882-3 Hercules Unchained [Ercole e la Regina di Lidia] (1959) Score (Enzo Masetti) IT:LP = Phoenix PHCAM-08*

2884 Here at the Water's Edge [Short] (1964) Highlights (ae:Leo Hurwitz) US:LP = Folkways FX-6161

2885 Here Come the Waves (1944) Excerpts (Harold Arlen) US:LP = Decca DL-4258 [Bing Crosby:ST]

2886 Here Comes the Groom (1951) Excerpts (Jay Livingston & Ray Evans) US:LP = Decca DL-4262 [Bing Crosby: ST]

2887 Here Is My Heart (1934) Excerpts-A (Ralph Rainger) US:LP-10 = Decca DL-6008 + US:LP = Decca DL-4250 [Bing Crosby:ST]; Excerpts-B (Ralph Rainger) US:LP-BP = Caliban 6042 [@ST]

2888 Here We Go 'Round the Mulberry Bush (1968) Score (Steve Winwood & Spencer Davis) US:LP = UA UAS-5175* + US:LP = UA LA-294*

2889 Here's to Romance (1935) Excerpts (Con Conrad) US:LP = Oasi 550 [Nino Martini:ST]

2890 Heretic, The *see* Exorcist II: The Heretic

2891 Hero, The [Bloomfield] (1971) Score (Johnny Harris) US:LP = Capitol SW-11098*

2892 Hero Ain't Nothin' But a Sandwich, A (1977) Score (Tom McIntosh) US:LP = Columbia PS-35046*

2893 Hero at Large (1980) Theme (Patrick Williams) US:LP-PP = Jenson 800* + US:LP-BP = Disc 105* [@The Jenson Marching Band]

2894 Heroes (1977) Score (Jack Nitzsche & Richard Hazard) US:LP = MCA 2320*

2895 Heroes at Telemark, The (1965) Score (Malcolm Arnold) US:LP = Mainstream 56064/S-6064*

2896 Heroin Gang, The *see* Sol Madrid

2897 Hers to Hold (1943) Theme/ GB:LP = Ace of Hearts 60 [Deanna Durbin:ST]

2898 Hey Boy, Hey Girl (1959) Score (various) US:LP = Capitol T-1160

2899 Hey, Let's Twist (1961) Score (Henry Glover) US:LP = Roulette R-25168/RS-25168*

2900 Hey There, It's Yogi Bear (1964) Score (e:Marty Paich/e:Doug Goodwin/t:David Gates) US:LP = Colpix CP-472/SCP-472*

2901 Hidden Room, The [Obsession] (1949) Theme (Nino Rota) GB:78 = Parlophone 3264 [Sidney Torch]

2902 Hideaway Girl (1937) Theme/ US:LP-MS-BP = Legends 1000/5-6 [Martha Raye:ST]

2903 Hiding Place, The (1975) Score (Tedd Smith) US:LP = Word WST-8697*

2904 High and Dry [The Maggie] (1954) Theme (John Addison) GB:78 = Parlophone 3827 [Sidney Torch]

2905 High and Low (1963) Highlights + Dialog (Masaru Sato) JA:LP = Toho AX-1001

2906 High and the Mighty, The (1954) Excerpts (Dimitri Tiomkin) US: LP = Film Music Collection FMC-14* [Elmer Bernstein]; Theme (Dimitri Tiomkin) US:SP = Coral 9-61211 [Dimitri Tiomkin:ST]

2907 High Anxiety (1977) Highlights (e:John Morris/t:Mel Brooks) US: LP = Asylum 5E-501*

2908 High Crime [La Polizia Incrimina la Legge Asolve] (1973) Score (Guido & Maurizio DeAngelis) IT:LP = Beat LPF-020*

2909 High Infidelity [Alta Infidelta] (1965) Theme (Armando Trovajoli) IT: LP = RCA 10388 [Armando Trovajoli: ST]

2910 High Noon (1952) Excerpts (Dimitri Tiomkin) GB:LP = Unicorn DKP-9002* [Laurie Johnson]; Theme (Dimitri Tiomkin) US:SP = Capitol 6208 [Tex Ritter:ST]; Theme (Dimitri Tiomkin) US:LP = Coral 57006 [Dimitri Tiomkin:ST]

2911 High Point (1984) Excerpts (Chris Young) US:LP = Cerberus CST-0212* [Chris Young:ST]

2912 High Road to China (1983) Score (John Barry) US:LP = Southern Cross SCRS-1003*

2913 High School Confidential (1958) Theme-A (Ron Hargrave) US: SP = Sun 296 + US:SP = Sun 110 [Jerry Lee Lewis:ST]; Themes-B-C (Mel Welles) US:SP = MGM 12661 [John Drew Barrymore:ST]

2914 High Sierra (1941) Sequence + Dialog (Adolph Deutsch) US:LP-MS = WB 3X2737 [@ST]

2915 High Society (1956) Score (Cole Porter) US:LP = Capitol W-750/ SW-750*

2916 High Time (1960) Score (s: Henry Mancini/t:James Van Heusen) US:LP = RCA LPM-2314/LSP-2314*

2917 High Treason (1951) Theme (John Addison) GB:78-PP = Rank FM-121 [ST]

2918 High, Wide and Handsome (1937) Highlights (Jerome Kern) US:LP-BP = JJA 19747 + US:LP-BP = Titania 506

2919 High, Wild and Free (1968) Theme (Jaime Mendoza-Nava) US:SP = American International 6720 [Jaime Mendoza-Nava:ST]

2920 Higher and Higher (1943) Score (Jimmy McHugh) US:LP-BP =

Hollywood Soundstage 411; Excerpts (Jimmy McHugh) US:LP = Columbia CL-2913 [Frank Sinatra:ST]

2921 Highlander, The (1986) Theme (Queen) US:SP = Capitol 5568* [Queen:ST]; Theme (Queen) US:LP = Capitol 12476* [Queen:ST]

2922 Highly Dangerous (1950) Theme (Richard Addinsell) GB:78-PP = Rank FM-106 [ST]

2923 Highway Girl *see* Return to Macon County

2924 Highway Pickup [Chair de Poule] (1963) Excerpts (Georges Delerue) FR:EP = Ducretet 460-V-594

2925 Highway Queen (1971) Score (Dov Seltzer) IS:LP = Israel 31020*

2926 Hills Run Red, The (1966) Score (Ennio Morricone-aka-Leo Nichols) US:LP-BP = POO 103; Theme (Ennio Morricone-aka-Leo Nichols) GB-LP = UA 29064 [@ST]

2927 Himiko (1974) Excerpts (Toru Takemitsu) JA:LP = RCA/Victor 1068 [Toru Takemitsu:ST]

2928 Hindenburg, The (1975) Score (David Shire) US:LP = MCA 2090*

2929 Hinotori [The Firebird] (1980) Score (s:Jun Fukamachi/t:Michel Legrand) JA:LP = Alfa 6008*

2930 Hippodrome (1959) Theme (Bert Grund) US:SP = Capitol 4557 [The Hollyridge Strings]; Theme (Bert Grund) US:SP = Columbia 4-41967 [Jerry Murad]

2931 Hips Hips Hooray (1934) Theme-A/US:78 = Brunswick 6761 [Ruth Etting:ST]; Theme-B/US:LP-BP = Take Two 203 [@Ruth Etting:ST]

2932 His Excellency (1951) Theme (Ernest Irving) GB:78-PP = Rank FM-120 [ST]

2933 His Kind of Woman (1951) Theme (Jimmy McHugh) US:78 = London 969 [Jane Russell:ST]; Theme (Jimmy McHugh) US:SP = RCA 47-4220 [Tony Martin]

2934 His Land (1971) Score (Ralph Carmichael) US:LP = Light LS-5532*

2935 His Wife's Habit (1971) Score (Jim Helms) US:LP = Capitol ST-641*

2936 History of Mr. Polly, The (1949) Theme-A (William Alwyn) US: LP-BP = Citadel CTOFI-1 [@ST]; Theme-A (William Alwyn) GB:78-PP = Rank FM-53 [ST]; Theme-B (William Alwyn) GB:78-PP = Rank FM-54 [ST]

2937 History of the World, Part I, The (1981) Highlights + Underscore + Dialog (u:John Morris/etc.) US:LP = WB HS-3579*

2938 Hit (1973) Theme (Lalo Schifrin) US:SP = Paramount 0271* [Robert Goulet]; Theme (Lalo Schifrin) US:LP = Varese 81081* [Lee Holdridge]

2939 Hit, The (1984) Score (s:Paco De Lucia/t:Eric Clapton) GB:LP = Mercury 822-668-1*

2940 Hit and Run (1957) Theme (Franz Steininger) US:SP = Capitol 3688 [Ella Mae Morse]; Theme (Franz Steininger) US:SP = RCA 47-6616 [Buddy Bregman]

2941 Hit 'Em Hard (1975) Score (Bobby Davis) US:LP = BOE 100*

2942 Hit Parade of 1937 (1936) Themes-A-B/US:78 = Brunswick 7864 [Phil Regan:ST]; Themes-B-C/US:78 = Decca 1202 [Frances Langford:ST]; Theme-D/US:78 = RCA/Victor 25514 [Eddy Duchin:ST]

2943 Hit Parade of 1941, The (1940) Themes-A-B/US:78 = RCA/Victor 26792 [Kenny Baker:ST]; Themes-A-B/US:78 = Decca 3433 [Frances Langford: ST]

2944 Hit the Deck (1955) Score (stage songs:Vincent Youmans) US: LP = MGM E-3163 + US:LP-MS = MGM 2SES-43e

2945 Hitler (1962) Score (Hans J. Salter) US:LP = Medallion ML-302

2946 Hitter, The (1979) Score (various) US:LP = Capitol SW-11920*

2947 Hochzeits Glocken / Theme (Herbert Jarczyt) US:SP = RCA 47-6015 [Eddie Fisher]

2948 Hoedown (1950) Themes/US: SP = RCA 48-0138 [Eddy Arnold:ST]

2949 Hold On! (1965) Score (e:Fred Karger/e:Phil Sloan & Steve Barri) US: LP = MGM E-4342/SE-4342*

2950 Hold That Ghost (1941) Theme-A/US:78 = Decca 3732 [The Andrews Sisters:ST]; Theme-B/US:78 = Decca 3821 [The Andrews Sisters:ST]

2951 Hold Your Man (1933) Theme (Nacio Herb Brown) US:LP = World

Artists 3007* [Perry Botkin, Jr.]

2952 Hole, The (1965) Theme (Hikaru Hayashi) JA:LP=Toho 8065 [@ST]

2953 Hole in the Head, A (1959) Themes (James Van Heusen) US:SP=Capitol 4214 [Frank Sinatra:ST]; Themes (James Van Heusen) US:LP=Capitol 2700 [Frank Sinatra:ST]

2954 Holiday Camp (1947) Theme-A (Bob Busby) GB:78-PP=Rank FM-23 [ST]; Theme-B (Jimmy Kennedy) GB:78-PP=Rank FM-24 [ST]

2955 Holiday for Henrietta (1953) Theme (Georges Auric) US:LP=Columbia 107 [Michel Legrand]

2956 Holiday for Lovers (1959) Theme (James Van Heusen) US:SP=Columbia 4-41375 [Mitch Miller]; Theme (James Van Heusen) US:LP=Columbia 1421/8218* [@Mitch Miller]

2957 Holiday in Havana (1949) Theme (Fred Karger) US:SP=MGM 12144 [Desi Arnaz:ST]; Theme (Fred Karger) US:LP=Lion 70108 + US: LP-MS=DRG 2-2100 [@Desi Arnaz:ST]

2958 Holiday in Mexico (1946) Excerpts (various) US:78-MS=Columbia X-271 [Jane Powell:ST]; Themes/US:78=Columbia 36902 [Xavier Cugat:ST]

2959 Holiday in Spain *see* Scent of Mystery

2960 Holiday Inn (1942) Score-A (Irving Berlin) US:LP-BP=Sountrak STK-112; Score-B (Irving Berlin) US:LP=Decca DL-4256 [Bing Crosby:ST]; Highlights (Irving Berlin) US:LP-10=Decca DL-5092 [Bing Crosby:ST]

2961 Hollywood Canteen (1944) Score (various) US:LP-MS-BP=Curtain Calls 100/11-12

2962 Hollywood! Hollywood! *see* That's Entertainment, Part II

2963 Hollywood Hotel (1937) Score (Richard A. Whiting) US:LP-BP=Hollywood Soundstage 5004

2964 Hollywood Knights (1980) Score (pop music) US:LP=Casablanca NBLP-7218*

2965 Hollywood on Parade (1931) Theme/US:LP-BP=Curtain Calls 100/21 [Ginger Rogers:ST]

2966 Hollywood or Bust! (1956) Highlights (Sammy Fain) US:EP=Capitol EAP1-806 [Dean Martin:ST]

2967 Hollywood Party (1934) Excerpts (Richard Rodgers) US:LP-BP=JJA 19766 [@ST]; Score (Richard Rodgers) GB:LP=Beginner's Productions BRP-2* [Studio Cast]

2968 Hollywood Revue (1929) Themes-A-B/US:LP-MS=MCA 2-11002 [@Cliff Edwards/Joan Crawford:ST]; Themes-B-C/US:LP-BP=JJA 19802 [@Cliff Edwards/Marion Davies:ST]; Theme-D/US:78=Columbia 1869 [Cliff Edwards:ST]

2969 Hollywood Vice Squad (1986) Score (Chris Spedding) US:LP=Bug/Restless 72147-1*

2970 Holocaust 2000 *see* Chosen, The

2971 Hombre (1967) Theme (David Rose) US:SP=Capitol 5837 [David Rose:ST]; Theme (David Rose) US:LP=Columbia 9527* [Robert Goulet]; Theme (David Rose) US:LP=MGM 4491* [Michel Legrand]

2972 Home Before Dark (1958) Theme (Jimmy McHugh) US:SP=WB 5020 [Mary Kaye Trio]

2973 Home from the Hill (1960) Theme (Bronislau Kaper) US:SP=Capitol 4338 [The Kingston Trio]; Theme (Bronislau Kaper) US:SP=RCA 47-7722 [Marty Gold]

2974 Home in Oklahoma (1946) Theme/US:LP=Varese STV-81212 [Roy Rogers:ST]

2975 Home Movies (1980) Score (Pino Donaggio) US:LP=Varese STV-81139*

2976 Home of the Brave (1986) Score (pop music) US:LP=WB 25400-1* [Laurie Anderson:ST]

2977 Homer (1970) Score (pop music) US:LP=Cotillion SD-9037*

2978 Hometown, U.S.A. (1979) Score (pop music) US:LP=K-Tel NU-9460*

2979 Homme du Jour, L' *see* Man of the Hour

2980 Homme et l'Enfant, L' *see* Man and Child

2981 Hondo (1953) Sequence + Dialog (Hugo Friedhofer & Emil Newman) US:LP-MS=WB 3X2737 [@ST]

2982 Honey (1930) Excerpts (W.

Franke Harling) US:LP-BP = Caliban 6018 [@ST]

2983 Honey Pot, The [It Comes Up Murder] (1967) Score (John Addison) US:LP = UA UAL-4159/UAS-5159*

2984 Honeybaby, Honeybaby (1975) Score (s:Michael Tschudin/t:Carl Maults-By) US:LP = RCA APL1-0994*

2985 Honeymoon [Luna de Miel] (1959) Score (Mikis Theodorakis) GR: LP = Sirius 5022; Theme (Mikis Theodorakis) GB:LP = EMI 2023 [@Manuel]

2986 Honeymoon Machine, The (1961) Theme (Leigh Harline) US:SP = MGM 13033 [Joe Leahy]; Theme (Leigh Harline) US:LP = MGM 3988* [Leroy Holmes & David Rose]

2987 Honeysuckle Rose (1980) Scores (Willie Nelson) US:LP-MS = Columbia S2-36752*

2988 Hong Kong Affair (1958) Theme (Louis Forbes) US:SP = Era 1066 [Ronnie Deauville]; Theme (Louis Forbes) US:LP = MGM 3753 + US: LP = Lion 70136 [Leroy Holmes]

2989 Honkers, The (1972) Theme (Bobby Russell) US:SP = UA 50888* [Bobby Russell:ST]

2990 Honky Tonk (1929) Excerpts (various) US:LP = Take Two 104 [Sophie Tucker:ST]

2991 Honky Tonk Freeway (1981) Score (t:Elmer Bernstein/t:George Martin/t:Steve Dorff/etc.) US:LP = Capitol ST-12160*

2992 Honky Tonk Man (1982) Score (t:Steve Dorff/s:various) US:LP = WB/Viva 23739-1*

2993 Honolulu (1939) Theme/US: LP-MS-BP = Radiola 1215/8 [@Gracie Allen:ST]

2994 Honorary Consul, The *see* Beyond the Limit

2995 Hooper (1978) Score (s:Bill Justis/t:Bent Myggen) US:LP = WB BSK-3234*

2996 Hoosiers (1986) Score (Jerry Goldsmith) US:LP = Polydor 831-475-1*

2997 Hootenanny Hoot (1963) Score (t:Fred Karger/s:various) US: LP = MGM E-4172/SE-4172*

2998 Horizontal Lieutenant, The (1962) Themes (George Stoll/Bennie Benjamin) US:SP = Mercury 71956 [The Diamonds]

2999 Horn Blows at Midnight, The (1945) Theme (Franz Waxman) US:LP = Varese 704.320* [Richard Mills]

3000 Hornet's Nest (1970) Highlights (Ennio Morricone) US:LP-BP = POO 105

3001 Horror Castle [Le Vergine di Norimberga] [The Virgin of Nuremberg] [Terror Castle] (1965) Score (Riz Ortolani) IT:LP = CAM CMS-30.119; Theme (Riz Ortolani) US:LP-BP = GSF 1002 [@Riz Ortolani:ST]

3002 Horror Chamber of Dr. Faustus [Les Yeux Sans Visage] [Eyes Without a Face] (1959) Highlights (Maurice Jarre) FR:EP = Vega 2043

3003 Horror Express (1976) Highlights (John Cacavas) US:LP = Citadel CT-6026* + US:LP = Citadel CTV-7012*

3004 Horror of Burke and Hare *see* Burke and Hare

3005 Horror of Dracula [Dracula] (1958) Themes (James Bernard) US: LP = Coral 757240* + US:LP = Varese 81077* [Dick Jacobs]

3006 Horror Planet *see* Inseminoid

3007 Horse Called Comanche, A *see* Tonka

3008 Horse Feathers (1932) Theme (Harry Ruby) US:LP = Decca 79168 [@Harpo Marx:ST]; Theme (Harry Ruby) US:LP = Pelican 130 [@Groucho Marx:ST]

3009 Horse Soldiers, The (1959) Score (as:David Buttolph/t:Stan Jones) US:LP = UA UAL-4035/UAS-5035*

3010 Horsemen, The (1971) Score (Georges Delerue) US:LP = Sunflower SNF-5007*

3011 Horse's Mouth, The (1959) Highlights (classical music) GB:EP = HMV 5145

3012 Hot Blood *see* Wild One, The

3013 Hot Bubble Gum (1982) Score (pop music) JA:LP = Polydor 28-MM-0045*

3014 Hot Dog—The Movie (1984) Themes (Peter Bernstein) JA:SP = RCA/Victor 1773* [Clif Magness:ST]

3015 Hot Heiress, The (1931) Excerpts (Richard Rodgers) US:LP-BP = JJA 19766 [@ST]

3016 Hot Millions (1968) Excerpts (Laurie Johnson) GB:LP = MGM CS-8104* [Laurie Johnson:ST]; Theme (Laurie Johnson) US:SP = Epic 5-10403 [Lulu:ST]

3017 Hot Parts (1972) Score (Michael Brown & Bert Sommer) US: LP = Kama Sutra KSBS-2054*

3018 Hot Rock, The [How to Steal a Diamond] (1972) Score (Quincy Jones) US:LP = Prophesy 6055*

3019 Hot Rod Gang (1958) Highlights (various) US:EP = Capitol EAP1-985 [Gene Vincent:ST]

3020 Hot Rod Rumble (1957) Score (Alexander Courage) US:LP = Liberty LRP-3048

3021 Hot Spell (1958) Theme (Alex North) US:LP = RCA 1445* [Alex North:ST]

3022 Hot Stuff (1979) Theme (Jerry Reed) US:SP = RCA 11698* [Jerry Reed: ST]; Theme (Jerry Reed) US:LP = RCA 1-3453* + US:LP = RCA 1-4167* [Jerry Reed:ST]

3023 Hotel (1967) Score (Johnny Keating) US:LP = WB W-1682/WS-1682*

3024 Hotel New Hampshire, The (1984) Score (as:Raymond Leppard) US: LP = Capitol SV-12337*

3025 Hotel Paradiso (1966) Score (Laurence Rosenthal) US:LP = MGM E-4419/SE-4419*

3026 Hotel Sahara (1951) Theme-A/US:LP = Stanyan 10055 [@Yvonne DeCarlo:ST]; Theme-B/GB:78 = Columbia 2850 [Yvonne DeCarlo:ST]

3027 Houdini (1953) Theme (Jay Livingston & Ray Evans) US:SP = RCA 47-5208 [Tony Martin]; Theme (Jay Livingston & Ray Evans) US:LP = Vocalion 73601 [Russ Morgan]

3028 Hound Dog Man (1959) Highlights (various) US:EP = Chancellor CHLA-301 [Fabian:ST]

3029 Hound of the Baskervilles, The (1939) Underscore + Dialog (Cyril Mockridge) US:LP-MS = Murray Hill 55358

3030 Hour of the Gun (1967) Score (Jerry Goldsmith) US:LP = UA UAL-4180/UAS-5180*

3031 Hours of Love, The [Le Ore dell'Amore] (1964) Highlights (Luis Bonfa) IT:EP = CAM 45-102

3032 House (1977) Score (Asei Kobayashi) JA:LP = Columbia YX-7177*

3033 House Beside the Cemetery, The [Quella Villa Accanto al Cimitero] (1981) Score (Walter Rizzati) IT:LP = Beat LPF-056*

3034 House I Live In, The [Short] (1945) Theme (Earl Robinson) US:SP = RCA 49-0554 [Lauritz Melchior]; Theme (Earl Robinson) US:LP = Columbia 2913 [Frank Sinatra:ST]

3035 House Is Not a Home, A (1964) Score (s:Joseph Weiss/t:Burt Bacharach) US:LP = Ava A-50/AS-50*

3036 House of Bamboo (1955) Theme (Leigh Harline) US:SP = Capitol 3202 [Woody Herman]; Theme (Leigh Harline) US:LP = RCA OPL1-0005 [@Woody Herman]

3037 House of Cards (1969) Theme (Francis Lai) US:LP = Decca 75070* [Wayne King]

3038 House of Darkness, The (1950) Theme (George Melachrino) GB: 78 = HMV 3570 [George Melachrino: ST]

3040 House of Fear, The (1945) Underscore + Dialog (au:Paul Sawtell) US: LP = Murray Hill 55439

3041 House of Frankenstein (1945) Theme (Hans J. Salter) US:LP = Coral 757240* + US:LP = Varese 81077* [Dick Jacobs]

3042 House of Secrets (1956) Theme (Hubert Clifford) GB:78-PP = Rank FM-200 [ST]

3043 House of Sin [La Menace] Highlights (Andre Hossein) GB:EP = Fontana 17353 + FR:EP = Fontana 460.761

3044 House of Terror (1976) Score (Ugi Ohno) JA:LP = RCA/Victor SJV-1282*

3045 House on Haunted Hill (1959) Theme (Richard Loring) US:SP = Columbia 4-41366 [Frank DeVol]; Theme (Richard Loring) US:SP = Orbit 533 [Arthur Lyman]

3046 House that Screamed, The [La Residencia] [The Boarding School] (1970) Theme (Waldo De Los Rios) SA: LP = Hispa-Vox 11-185 [Waldo De Los Rios:ST]

3047 House Under the Trees, The *see* Deadly Trap, The

3048 Houseboat (1958) Score (s:George Duning/t:Jay Livingston & Ray Evans) US:LP = Columbia CL-1222

3049 How Funny Can Sex Be [Sesso Matto] (1973) Score (Armando Trovajoli) US:LP = West End WE-101*

3050 How Green Was My Valley (1941) Highlights (Alfred Newman) US: LP-BP = Sound of Hollywood 400/1

3051 How Sweet It Is! (1968) Score (s:Patrick Williams/t:Jimmy Webb) US: LP = RCA LSP-4037*

3052 How the West Was Won (1962) Score (s:Alfred Newman/ae: Robert Emmett Dolan/t: Ken Darby) US:LP = MGM 1E-5/1SE-5*; Highlights (Alfred Newman) US:LP-BP = Lone Star LS-1983

3053 How to Be Very, Very Popular (1955) Theme (Jule Styne) US:SP = Coral 9-61448 [Teresa Brewer]

3054 How to Beat the High Cost of Living (1980) Score (Patrick Williams) US:LP = Columbia JS-36741*

3055 How to Marry a Millionaire (1953) Theme (Lionel Newman) US: SP = Crystalette 664 [Lloyd Shaffer]; Theme (Lionel Newman) US:LP-BP = Legends 1000/1 [@ST]

3056 How to Murder Your Wife (1965) Score (Neal Hefti) US:LP = UA UAL-4119/UAS-5119*

3057 How to Save a Marriage and Ruin Your Life (1968) Score (Michel Legrand) US:LP = Columbia OS-3140*

3058 How to Seduce a Woman (1974) Theme (Stu Phillips) US:SP = J.J. Records 2267 [Johnny Prophet:ST]

3059 How to Steal a Diamond *see* Hot Rock, The

3060 How to Steal a Million (1966) Score (John Williams) US:LP = 20th 4183/S-4183*

3061 How to Stuff a Wild Bikini (1965) Score (Jerry Styner) US:LP = Wand 671/S-671*

3062 How to Succeed in Business Without Really Trying (1967) Score (stage songs:Frank Loesser) US:LP = UA UAL-4151/UAS-5151*

3063 Howard the Duck (1986) Score (e:John Barry/e:Thomas Dolby) US: LP = MCA 6173*

3064 Howling, The (1981) Score (Pino Donaggio) US:LP = Varese STV-81150*

3065 How's About It? (1943) Theme-A/US:78 = Decca 18497 [The Andrews Sisters:ST]; Theme-B/US:78 = Decca 18533 [The Andrews Sisters:ST]

3066 Huckleberry Finn (1974) Score (Richard & Robert Sherman) US: LP = UA LA-229*

3067 Hucksters, The (1947) Theme (Buddy Pepper) US:78 = RCA 20-2328 [Tony Martin]

3068 Hud (1963) Theme (Elmer Bernstein) US:SP = Kapp 541 [Joe Harnell]; Theme (Elmer Bernstein) US: SP = Philips 40116 [Darrell McCall]; Theme (Elmer Bernstein) US:LP = Command 854* [Enoch Light]

3069 Hugo the Hippo (1976) Score (Robert Larimer) US:LP = UA LA-637*

3070 Huk (1956) Score (Albert Glasser) US:LP-BP = Screen Archives SAAG-10-001

3071 Human Desire (1954) Theme (Daniele Amfitheatrof) US:SP = American 109 [Mae Williams]

3072 Human Jungle, The (1954) Theme/US:LP-BP = Legends 1000/2 [@Jan Sterling:ST]

3073 Human Vapor, The (1960) Excerpts (Kunio Miyauchi) JA:LP = Toho 8107 [@ST]

3074 Humanoid, The [L'Umanoide] (1979) Score (Ennio Morricone) IT:LP = RCA 31432*

3075 Humanoids of the Deep [Monster] (1980) Score (James Horner) US:LP = Cerberus CST-0203*

3076 Humoresque (1946) Highlights (ae:Franz Waxman) US:LP-10 = Columbia ML-2103 [Franz Waxman & Isaac Stern:ST]; Excerpts (ae:Franz Waxman) US:LP = RCA LSC-3232 [Jascha Heifetz]

3077 Hunchback of Rome, The [Il Gobbo] (1960) Highlights (Piero Piccioni) IT:EP = RCA EPA-30392

3078 Hunchback of Soho, The [Der Bucklige von Soho] (1966) Theme (Peter Thomas) GE:LP = Celine 0011 [Peter Thomas:ST]

3079 Hundra (1984) Score (Ennio Morricone) US:LP = Macola MRC-0903*

3080 Hungarian Freedom Fighters *see* While I Live

3081 Hunger, The (1983) Score (Michel Rubini & Denny Jaeger) US: LP = Varese STV-81184*

3082 Hunger Canal (1964) Theme (Isao Tomita) JA:LP = King 370/1* [@ST]

3083 Hungry Hill (1947) Theme (John Greenwood) GB:78 = Decca 1579 [Muir Mathieson:ST]

3084 Hungry Minds / Score (Eldon Rathburn) CA:LP = CBC SM-119*

3085 Hunter, The (1981) Theme (Michel Legrand) JA:LP = UA K20P-4029* [The Film Studio Orchestra]

3086 Hunters, The (1958) Theme (John Gabriel) US:SP = 20th 106 [Harry Simeone]

3087 Hunting Party, The (1971) Themes (Riz Ortolani) US:SP = UA 50820* [Riz Ortolani:ST]; Theme (Riz Ortolani) US:LP-BP = Centurion 1210* [@Riz Ortolani:ST]

3088 Hurricane [Forbidden Paradise] (1979) Score (Nino Rota) US:LP = Elektra 5E-504*

3089 Hurricane, The (1937) Theme (film theme from "Mr. Robinson Crusoe") US:LP = Decca 8123 [Alfred Newman:ST]; Theme (film theme from "Mr. Robinson Crusoe") US:LP = West Coast 14002 [Dorothy Lamour:ST]

3090 Hurry Sundown (1967) Score (Hugo Montenegro) US:LP = RCA LOC-1133/LSO-1133*

3091 Hurry Up or I'll Be 30 (1973) Theme (Stephen J. Lawrence) US:SP = Avis 108* [Dennis Cooley:ST]

3092 Hush ... Hush, Sweet Charlotte (1964) Theme (Frank DeVol) US: SP = Capitol 5341 [Al Martino:ST]; Theme (Frank DeVol) US:LP = Capitol 16074* [Al Martino:ST]; Theme (Frank DeVol) US:LP = ABC 513* [Frank DeVol:ST]

3093 Hussy (1979) Theme (George Fenton) GB:SP-12 = Boyds H-1* [ST]

3094 Hustle (1975) Theme (Frank DeVol) US:SP = Ranwood 1044 [Charles Randolph Grean]

3095 Hustler, The (1961) Score (Kenyon Hopkins) US:LP = Kapp KL-1264/KS-3264*

3096 Hyde Park Cordner (1935) Themes/GB:LP = Ace of Clubs 1182 [@Binnie Hale:ST]

I

3097 I, A Lover (1966) Theme (Sven Gyldmark) US:LP = UA 6742* [Leroy Holmes]

3098 I, A Woman, Part 2 (1969) Score (Sven Gyldmark) US:LP = MGM 1SE-18*

3099 I Aim at the Stars (1960) Theme (Laurie Johnson) US:SP = Colpix 160 [Stu Phillips]; Theme (Laurie Johnson) GB:LP = MGM 8104* [Laurie Johnson:ST]

3100 I Am a Camera (1955) Theme (Joel Siegel & Carl Sigman) US:SP = Columbia 4-40493 [Mitch Miller]; Theme (Joel Siegel & Carl Sigman) US:LP = Columbia 1525 [Spencer Ross]

3101 I and My Love *see* Galia

3102 I Bury the Living (1958) Theme (Gerald Fried) US:LP-BP = POO 104 [@ST]

3103 I Confess (1953) Theme (Dimitri Tiomkin) US:LP = Coral 57006 [Dimitri Tiomkin:ST]

3104 I Could Go on Singing (1963) Score (e:Mort Lindsey/etc.) US:LP = Capitol W-1861/WS-1861*

3105 I Dood It [By Hook or By Crook] (1943) Theme (Gene DePaul) US: 78 = Decca 18571 [Jimmy Dorsey]

3106 I Dream Too Much (1935) Highlights (Jerome Kern) US:LP-BP = Grapon 15

3107 I Killed Rasputin *see* Rasputin

3108 I Live for Love (1935) Themes/ US:78 = RCA/Victor 25164 [Everett Marshall:ST]

3109 I Love All of You [Je Vous Aime] (1982) Score (Serge Gainsbourg)

FR:LP = Philips 6313.123*

3110 I Love Melvin (1953) Highlights (Josef Myrow) US:LP-10 = MGM E-190 + US:LP-MS = MGM 2SES-52e

3111 I Love You, Alice B. Toklas (1968) Score (Elmer Bernstein) US:LP-BP = Cinema LP-8010; Theme (Elmer Bernstein) US:SP = WB 7238 [Harpers Bizarre]

3112 I Love You, I Don't [Je T'Aime Moi Non Plus] (1976) Score (Serge Gainsbourg) JA:LP = Philips FDX-240*

3113 I Married an Angel (1942) Highlights (e:Herbert Stothart/etc.) US: LP-BP = Caliban 6004 + US:LP-MS-BP = Sandy Hook 3SH-1

3114 I, Mobster (1959) Themes (Edward Alperson, Jr.) US:SP = 20th 142 [Morgana King]

3115 I Never Sang for My Father (1970) Score (Al Gorgoni & Barry Mann) US:LP = Bell 1204*

3116 I Ought to Be in Pictures (1982) Theme (Marvin Hamlisch) US: SP = WB 7-29998* [Randy Crawford: ST]; Theme (Marvin Hamlisch) US:LP = WB 1-23687* [Randy Crawford:ST]

3117 I Saw What You Did (1965) Theme (Van Alexander) US:SP = Decca 9-31787 [The Tell-Tales]

3118 I Surrender Dear [Short] (1931) Excerpts (various) US:LP = Biograph BLP-M1 [Bing Crosby:ST]

3119 I, the Jury (1953) Theme (Franz Waxman) US:LP = Entracte 6001 [Franz Waxman:ST]

3120 I Walk the Line (1970) Score (Johnny Cash) US:LP = Columbia S-30397*

3121 I Want to Live (1958) Scores (Johnny Mandel) US:LP-MS = UA UXL-1/UXS-51*; Score-A (Johnny Mandel) US:LP = UA UAL-4005/UAS-5005* + US:LP = UA LA-271*; Score-B (Johnny Mandel) US:LP = UA UAL-4006/UAS-5006*

3122 I Want You (1952) Theme (Leigh Harline) US:SP = Coral 9-60625 [Horace Bailey]

3123 I Was an Agent for the CIA *see* Covert Action

3124 I Wonder Who's Kissing Her Now (1947) Highlights (pop music) US: LP-BP = Titania 502

3125 Ice (1978) Score (Tony Colton) GB:LP-PP = Bright PRO-1*

3126 Ice Castles (1979) Score (Marvin Hamlisch) US:LP = Arista AL-9502*

3127 Ice Follies of 1939 (1939) Theme/US:LP-BP = Curtain Calls 100/23 [Joan Crawford:ST]

3128 Ice Palace (1960) Theme (Max Steiner) US:LP-BP = Citadel CTMS-7 [Max Steiner:ST]

3129 Ice Station Zebra (1968) Score (Michel Legrand) US:LP = MGM 1SE-14*

3130 Iceland (1942) Themes/US: 78 = Bluebird 11574 [Joan Merrill:ST]

3131 Iceman (1984) Score (Bruce Smeaton) US:LP = Southern Cross SCRS-1006*

3132 Ichabod and Mr. Toad *see* Adventures of Ichabod and Mr. Toad

3133 Icy Breasts [Les Seins de Glace] (1975) Highlights (Philippe Sarde) IT:LP = Phoenix PHCAM-05*

3134 I'd Rather Be Rich (1964) Theme-A (David Shire) US:SP = Columbia 4-43131 [Robert Goulet:ST]; Theme-B (Gloria Shayne) US:SP = Columbia 4-43090 [Andy Williams:ST]

3135 Ideal Husband, An (1947) Themes (Arthur Benjamin) US:LP = London 21149* [Bernard Herrmann]

3136 Idiot's Delight (1939) Theme/ US:LP-MS = MCA 2-11002 [@Clark Gable:ST]

3137 Idle Class, The [Short] (1921) Theme [Silent II] (Charles Chaplin) US: LP = Camden 2581 + US:LP = RCA 1-2778* [Johnny Douglas & The Living Strings]

3138 Idle on Parade (1956) Theme (Jerry Lordan) US:SP = Decca 9-30922 [Malcolm Dodds]

3139 Idol, The (1966) Score (Johnny Dankworth) US:LP = Fontana MGF-27559/SRF-67559*

3140 Idol of Paris, The (1947) Excerpts (Mischa Spoliansky) US:LP = Columbia RL-3029 [@Sidney Torch]

3141 Idolmaker, The (1980) Score (Jeff Barry) US:LP = A&M SP-4840*

3142 If a Man Answers (1962) Themes (Bobby Darin) US:SP = Capitol 4837 [Bobby Darin:ST]

3143 If Ever I See You Again (1978) Scores (Joe Brooks) US:LP-MS = WB 2HS-3199*

3144 If He Hollers, Let Him Go (1968) Score (e:Coleridge Taylor-Perkinson/t:Sammy Fain/etc.) US:LP = Tower ST-5152*

3145 If I Had My Way (1940) Excerpts (James Monaco) US:LP-10 = Decca DL-6015 + US:LP = Decca DL-4254 [Bing Crosby:ST]

3146 If I'm Lucky (1946) Themes-A-B/US:78 = RCA/Victor 20-1945 [Perry Como:ST]; Theme-C/US:78 = Columbia 37148 [Harry James:ST]

3147 If It's Tuesday, This Must Be Belgium (1969) Score (s:Walter Scharf/t: Donovan Leitch) US:LP = UA UAS-5197*

3148 If This Be Sin [That Dangerous Age] (1950) Theme (Mischa Spoliansky) US:LP = Columbia 3029 [@Sidney Torch]

3149 If You Feel Like Singing *see* Summer Stock

3150 If You Knew Susie (1948) Theme/US:LP = Camden 870 + US: LP = Audio Fidelity 702 [Eddie Cantor: ST]

3151 I'll Be Yours (1947) Theme (Walter Schumann) US:78 = RCA 20-2095 [Vaughn Monroe]

3152 I'll Cry Tomorrow (1956) Highlights-A (t:Alex North/e:pop music) US:LP-BP = Legends 1000/3 [Susan Hayward:ST]; Highlights-B (t: Alex North/e:pop music) US:EP = MGM X-1180 [Susan Hayward:ST]; Theme (Alex North) US:LP = Citadel 6023* [Alex North:ST]

3153 I'll Get By (1950) Score (pop music) US:LP-BP = Titania 504

3154 Ill Met by Moonlight *see* Night Ambush

3155 I'll Never Forget What's 'is Name (1968) Score (Francis Lai) US: LP = Decca DL-9163/DL-79163*

3156 I'll See You in My Dreams (1951) Highlights (pop music) US:LP-10 = Columbia CL-6198 [Doris Day:ST]

3157 I'll Take Romance (1937) Theme/US:LP-BP = Empire 801 [Grace Moore:ST]

3158 I'll Take Sweden (1965) Score (e:Jimmie Haskell/t:Ken Lauber/etc.) US:LP = UA UAL-4121/UAS-5121*

3159 Illustrious Corpses *see* Context, The

3160 I'm No Angel (1933) Excerpts (Harvey Brooks) US:LP = Columbia CL-2751 [Mae West:ST]

3161 Images (1972) Score (John Williams) US:LP-BP = Classic International Film Music 1002 + US:LP-PP = JW 1*

3162 Imitation of Life (1959) Score (s:Frank Skinner/t:Sammy Fain) US: LP = Decca DL-8879/DL-78879*

3163 Immer Will Ich Dir Gehoren [I'll Belong to You Forever] Theme (Bert Reisfeld) US:SP = Epic 5-9433 [Heidi Bruhl]

3164 Immortal Bachelor, The [Histore d'Aimer] [A Mezzanotte Va Ronda del Piacere] (1980) Score (Guido & Maurizio DeAngelis) IT:LP = Cinevox 33/84* + FR:LP = Barclay 900.532*

3165 Immortal Garrison, The (1956) Score (Andre Petrov) RU:LP = MK 022043/4

3166 Imperial Venus [Venere Imperiale] (1963) Score (A.F. Lavagnino) IT:LP = CAM CMS-3-052

3167 Impossible Family, The *see* Una Famiglia Impossible

3168 Impossible Object, The [L'Impossible Objet] [The Story of a Love Story] (1974) Theme (Michel Legrand) FR:SP = Polydor 2056.248* [ST]; Theme (Michel Legrand) FR:LP = Bell 2308.070* [Michel Legrand:ST]

3169 Imprecateur, L' *see* Accuser, The

3170 In Caliente (1935) Themes-A-B/US:78 = Columbia 3035 [Phil Regan: ST]; Theme-C/US:LP = UA 361 [@Judy Canova:ST]

3171 In Cold Blood (1967) Score (Quincy Jones) US:LP = Colgems COM-107/COS-107*

3172 In Harm's Way (1965) Score (Jerry Goldsmith) US:LP = RCA LOC-1100/LSO-1100*

3173 In-Laws, The (1979) Themes (John Morris) JA:SP = Blow Up 128* [ST]; Theme (John Morris) US:LP-BP = Disc 105* [@John Morris:ST]

3174 In Like Flint (1967) Score

(Jerry Goldsmith) US:LP = 20th 4193/S-4193*

3175 In Love and War (1958) Themes (Hugo Friedhofer) US:LP = Entracte ERS-6506* [Fred Steiner]

3176 In Old Chicago (1938) Theme/US:LP-BP = Scarce Rarities 5501 [Alice Faye:ST]

3177 In Person (1935) Excerpts (Oscar Levant) US:LP-BP = Curtain Calls 100/21 [Ginger Rogers:ST]

3178 In Search of Skiing [Industrial Short] Score (stock music) US:LP-PP = Warren Miller 5167*

3179 In Search of the Castaways (1962) Highlights + Underscore + Dialog (e:Richard & Robert Sherman/u: William Alwyn) US:LP = Disneyland ST-3916

3180 In the Cool of the Day (1963) Theme (Manos Hadjidakis) US:SP = Capitol 4965 [Nat King Cole]; Theme (Manos Hadjidakis) US:LP = Capitol 2340 + US:LP = Capitol 11804 [Nat King Cole]

3181 In the Forest [Short] Sequence + Dialog (Arthur Kleiner) US:LP-PP = Picture Book Parade 105 [@ST]

3182 In the French Style (1963) Theme (Joseph Kosma) US:LP = Colpix 464* [@Norman Percival]

3183 In the Good Old Summertime (1949) Highlights (pop music) US:LP = MGM E-3232 + US:LP-MS = MGM 2SES-49e

3184 In the Heat of the Night (1967) Score (Quincy Jones) US:LP = UA UAL-4160/UAS-5160* + US:LP = UA LA-290*

3185 In the Name of the Father [Nel Nome del Padre] (1970) Score (Nicola Piovani) IT:LP = Off LP-601*

3186 In the Name of the Italian People [Nel Nome del Popolo Italiano] (1972) Highlights (Carlo Rustichelli) IT: LP = Cetra 193* + IT:LP = Beat LPF-012*

3187 In the Navy (1941) Theme/US:78 = Decca 3871 [The Andrews Sisters:ST]

3188 In the Realm of the Senses [L'Empire des Sens] (1977) Score (Minoru Miki) JA:LP = RCA/Victor VIP-6096*

3189 In the Shadow of the Sun [Short] (1980) Score (Throbbing Gristle) GB:LP = JAM 35* [Throbbing Gristle: ST]

3190 In the Year of the Lord [Nell'Anno del Signore] (1969) Score (Armando Trovajoli) IT:LP = Cinevox 33/26*

3191 In This Our Life (1942) Theme (Max Steiner) US:LP = RCA 1-0183* + US:LP = RCA 1-3706* [Charles Gerhardt]

3192 In Which We Serve (1942) Excerpts (Noel Coward) US:LP = AEI 2122 [@Mantovani]

3193 Incendiary Blonde (1945) Highlights (pop music) US:LP-BP = Athena LMIB-9

3194 Inchon (1982) Score (Jerry Goldsmith) US:LP = Regency RI-8502*

3195 Incident, The (1967) Themes (Terry Knight) US:SP = Lucky Eleven 231 [Terry Knight:ST]

3196 Incorrigible, L' (1977) Score (Georges Delerue) FR:LP = Pathe C066.14236*

3197 Incredible Journey, The (1963) Underscore + Dialog (Oliver Wallace) US:LP = Disneyland ST-1927 + US:LP-MS = Disneyland DDF-4

3198 Incredible Mr. Limpet, The (1964) Themes (Sammy Fain) US:SP = WB 5431 [Don Ralke/Don Knotts:ST]

3199 Incredible Shrinking Man, The (1957) Highlights (e:Hans J. Salter/t:Foster Carling) US:LP-BP = Tony Thomas TTHS-4; Theme (Foster Carling) US:LP = Coral 757240* + US: LP = Varese 81077* [Dick Jacobs]

3200 Incredibly Strange Creatures Who Stopped Living and Became Mixed-Up Zombies, The (1962) Themes (Libby Quinn/Danny Ware) US:SP-PP = Rel 106 [Danny Ware:ST]; Theme (Libby Quinn) US:LP = Rhino 307 [@ST]

3201 India Song (1975) Excerpts (Carlos D'Alessio) FR:LP = Chant Du Monde 74818 [@ST]

3202 Indian Fighter, The (1955) Theme (Franz Waxman) US:SP = Capitol 3355 [Big Ben Banjo Band]; Theme (Franz Waxman) US:LP = MGM 3375 [@Bernie Nee]

3203 Indian Love Call *see* Rose-Marie (1936)

3204 Indian Summer [Short] (1960) Highlights (Pete Seeger) US:LP = Folk-ways FS-3851 [Pete Seeger:ST]

3205 Indian Summer [La Prima Notte di Quiete] (1979) Score (Mario Nascimbene) IT:LP = CBS 65403*

3206 Indiana Jones and the Temple of Doom (1984) Score (John Williams) US:LP = Polydor 821.592-1*

3207 Indio Black *see* Adios Sabata

3208 Indiscreet (1931) Theme (Ray Henderson) US:78 = Brunswick 6127 [Gloria Swanson:ST]

3209 Indiscreet (1958) Theme (James Van Heusen) US:SP = Columbia 4-41181 [Percy Faith]; Theme (James Van Heusen) US:SP = Roulette 4084 [Meynard Ferguson]; Theme (James Van Heusen) US:LP = MGM 3753 + US:LP = Lion 70136 [Leroy Holmes]

3210 Indiscretion of an American Wife (1954) Highlights (Alessandro Cicognini) US:LP-10 = Columbia CL-6277 + US:LP-BP = Cinema LP-8008

3211 Inferno (1980) Score (Keith Emerson) IT:LP = Cinevox 33/138*

3212 Informer, The (1935) Excerpts (Max Steiner) US:LP-10 = Capitol T-250 + US:LP = Capitol T-387 + US:LP = Angel S-36068 [Max Steiner:ST]

3213 Ingorgo, L' *see* Traffic Jam

3214 Inherit the Wind (1960) Theme (Ernest Gold) US:SP = Columbia 4-41798 [Leslie Uggams]; Theme (Ernest Gold) US:LP = London 3320/320* [Ernest Gold:ST]

3215 Inheritance, The [Industrial Short] Highlights + Underscore + Dialog (George Kleinsinger) US:LP-PP = ACWA MS-1

3216 Inheritance, The (1962) Excerpts (Toru Takemitsu) JA:LP = RCA/Victor 1063 [Toru Takemitsu:ST]

3217 Inheritance, The [L'Erredita Ferramonti] (1976) Score (Ennio Morricone) IT:LP = CAM SAG-9067*

3218 Inheritor, The [L'Heritier] (1973) Highlights (Michel Colombier) JA:LP = A&M FML-12*

3219 Inn for Trouble (1960) Theme (Philip Green) US:SP = MGM 12914 [Leroy Holmes]

3220 Inn of the Sixth Happiness, The (1958) Score (Malcolm Arnold) US:LP = 20th 3011/S-3011*

3221 Innocent, The [L'Innocent] [The Intruder] (1979) Score (Franco Mannino) IT:LP = Cinevox 33/100 + FR:LP = Barclay 900.504*

3222 Innocent Bystanders (1973) Theme (Johnny Keating) GB:LP = DJM 430* [Vic Lewis]

3223 Innocents of Paris (1929) Excerpts (various) US:LP = RCA LPV-564 [Maurice Chevalier:ST]

3224 Inseminoid [Horror Planet] (1982) Score (John Scott) US:LP = Citadel CTV-7023*

3225 Insensiblement / Theme (Paul Misraki) US:LP = Dot 3120 [Ray Ven-tura]

3226 Inside Daisy Clover (1965) Score (Andre Previn) US:LP = WB W-1616/WS-1616*

3227 Inside Moves (1980) Score (t:John Barry/s:pop music) US:LP = Full Moon FMH-3506*

3228 Insignificance (1985) Highlights + Dialog (e:Stanley Myers/e:various) US:LP = Island Zenith ZTT-1Q4*

3229 Inspector, The *see* Lisa

3230 Inspector Clouseau (1968) Score (Ken Thorne) US:LP = UA UAS-5186*

3231 Inspector General, The (1949) Theme (Sylvia Fine) US:78 = Decca 24820 [Danny Kaye:ST]; Theme (Sylvia Fine) US:78 = Columbia 38659 [Dinah Shore]; Theme (Sylvia Fine) US:45 = Capitol 54-785 [Jo Stafford]

3232 Inspector Maigret (1958) Theme (Paul Misraki) US:SP = UA 155 [Eddie Barclay]

3233 Instruments of the Orchestra [Young Person's Guide to the Orchestra] [Short] (1947) Excerpts (Benjamin Britten) US:LP = Columbia ML-4197 [Malcolm Sargent:ST]; Excerpts (Benjamin Britten) US:LP = Angel S-36962* [Andre Previn]

3234 Interlude (1957) Highlights (ae:Frank Skinner) US:LP = Coral CRL-57159

3235 Interlude (1968) Score (e: Georges Delerue/e:classical music) US: LP = Colgems COSO-5007*

3236 Intermezzo [Escape to Happiness] (1939) Theme (Heinz Provost) US:SP = MGM 30020 [David Rose]; Theme (Heinz Provost) US:LP = RCA 3248* [Arthur Fiedler]; Theme (Heinz Provost) US:LP = London 44225* [Stanley Black]

3237 International House (1933) Theme-A/US:78 = Brunswick 6340 [Cab Calloway:ST]; Theme-B/US:78 = Brunswick 6570 [Rose Marie:ST]; Theme-C/US:78 = Bluebird 5098 [Rudy Vallee:ST]

3238 International Velvet (1978) Score (Francis Lai) US:LP = MGM MG1-5405*

3239 Interns, The (1962) Score (Leith Stevens) US:LP = Colpix CP-427/SCP-427*

3240 Interrupted Melody (1955) Score (classical music) US:LP = MGM E-3185; Score (classical music) US:LP = MGM E-3984 [Eileen Farrell:ST]

3241 Intimate Moments [Madame Claude 2] (1981) Score (Francis Lai) FR:LP = WB/WEA 2358.363*

3242 Into the Night (1985) Score (Ira Newborn) US:LP = MCA 5561*

3243 Intolerance (1916) Excerpts [Silent II] (Lee Erwin) US:LP = Angel 36092* [Lee Erwin:ST]; Excerpts [Silent I] (Joseph Carl Breil) US:LP = Angel 36092* [Lee Erwin]; Theme [Silent II] (Charles Hofmann) US:LP = Sounds Good 1001 [Charles Hofmann:ST]

3244 Intruder, The *see* Innocent, The

3245 Invaders, The [The 49th Parallel] (1941) Theme (Ralph Vaughan-Williams) US:LP = London 21149* [Bernard Herrmann:ST]; Theme (Ralph Vaughan-Williams) US:LP = Varese 1000.20* [Morton Gould]

3246 Invaders from Mars (1953) Theme (Raoul Kraushaar) JA:LP = Mu Land 7019* [Electoru Polyphonic Orchestra]

3247 Invaders from Mars (1986) Score [discarded score] (David Storrs) US:LP = Enigma SJ-73226*

3248 Invaders from Space *see* Atomic Rulers of the World

3249 Invasion of the Body Snatchers (1978) Score (Danny Zeitlin) US:LP = UA LA-940*

3250 Invasion U.S.A. (1985) Score (Jay Chattaway) US:LP = Varese STV-81263*

3251 Investigation of a Citizen Above Suspicion (1970) Score (Ennio Morricone) US:LP = Cerberus CEMS-0110

3252 Investigation of Murder, An *see* Laughing Policeman, The

3253 Invisible Boy, The (1957) Theme (Lex Baxter) US:SP = Capitol 3842 [Les Baxter:ST]

3254 Invitation (1952) Theme (film theme from "A Life of Her Own") US:LP = MGM 3694 [John Green:ST]

3255 Invitation au Voyage (1983) Score (Gabriel Yared) US:LP = Varese STV-81189*

3256 Invitation to the Dance (1956) Score (e:Andre Previn/e:Jacques Ibert) US:LP = MGM E-3207

3257 Ipcress File, The (1965) Score (John Barry) US:LP = Decca DL-9124/DL-79124*

3258 Irene (1931) Theme/US:LP-BP = Take Two 104 [@Ethel Merman:ST]

3259 Irish Eyes Are Smiling (1944) Excerpts (pop music) US:LP-BP = SRO LP-1001 [Dick Haymes:ST]

3260 Irma la Douce (1963) Score (Andre Previn) US:LP = UA UAL-4134/UAS-5134*

3261 Iron Eagle, The (1985) Score (t:Queen/s:various) US:LP = Capitol SV-12499*

3262 Iron Governor, The [Il Prefetto di Ferro] (1979) Score (Ennio Morricone) IT:LP = Beat LPF-041*

3263 Iron Maiden, The *see* Swingin' Maiden, The

3264 Irreconcilable Differences [Divorce a Hollywood] (1984) Score (Paul De Senneville) FR:LP = Delphine 824-550-1*; Themes (Paul De Senneville) US:SP = Columbia 38-04631* [Richard Clayderman:ST]; Themes (Paul De Senneville) US:LP = Columbia 39603* [Richard Clayderman: ST]

3265 Is Everybody Happy? (1943) Excerpts (various) US:LP = Decca DL-8322 + US:LP-MS = MCA 2-4101 [Ted Lewis:ST]

3266 Is Paris Burning? (1966) Score

(Maurice Jarre) US:LP = Columbia OL-6630/OS-3030*

3267 Isadora *see* Loves of Isadora, The

3268 Island, The [The Naked Island] [L'Ile Nue] (1961) Highlights (Hikaru Hayashi) FR:EP = Barclay 70420; Theme (Hikaru Hayashi) US: SP = Time 1727 [Billy May]; Theme (Hikaru Hayashi) US:LP = Time 2064* + US:LP = Time 2065* [Billy May]

3269 Island, The (1980) Score (Ennio Morricone) US:LP = Varese STV-81147*

3270 Island at the Top of the World, The (1974) Underscore + Dialog (Maurice Jarre) US:LP = Disneyland 3814*

3271 Island in the Sky (1953) Highlights (Hugo Friedhofer & Emil Newman) US:LP = Varese STV-81116; Underscore + Narration (Hugo Friedhofer & Emil Newman) US:LP-10 = Decca DL-7029 + US:LP = Varese STV-81116

3272 Island in the Sun (1957) Themes (Lord Burgess & Harry Belafonte) US:EP = RCA EPA-4084 [Harry Belafonte:ST]; Theme (Lord Burgess & Harry Belafonte) US:SP = RCA 47-6885 [Harry Belafonte:ST]

3273 Island of Dr. Moreau, The (1977) Score (Laurence Rosenthal) US: LP-BP = Wells HG-4000*; Theme (Laurence Rosenthal) JA:LP = Mu Land 7017* [Electoru Polyphonic Orchestra]

3274 Island of Love (1963) Theme (Sammy Fain) US:LP = Command 854* [Enoch Light]

3275 Island of Mutations *see* Screamers

3276 Island of the Damned [Who Can Kill a Child?] [Quien Puede Matar a un Nino?] (1976) Score (Waldo De Los Rios) SA:LP = Hispa Vox 11-326

3277 Island of the Evil Spirit (1981) Score (s:Norio Yuasa/t:Paul McCartney) JA:LP = East World 90108*

3278 Island Rescue [Appointment with Venus] (1951) Theme (Benjamin Frankel) GB:78-PP = Rank FM-123 [ST]

3279 Island Women (1957) Score-A (e:Alice Simms/etc.) US:LP = Tico LP-1043; Score-B (e:Alice Simms/etc.) US:LP = Island Artists LP-1007

3280 Islands in the Stream (1977) Score (Jerry Goldsmith) US:LP = Intrada RVF-6003*

3281 Istanbul (1957) Theme/US: EP = Capitol 824 [Nat King Cole:ST]

3282 It All Came True (1940) Theme/US:LP-BP = Marsher 201 [@ Ann Sheridan:ST]

3283 It Came from Outer Space (1953) Theme (Herman Stein) US:LP = Coral 757240* + US:LP = Varese 81077* [Dick Jacobs]

3284 It Can Be Done, Amigo! [Si Puo Fare, Amigo!] (1972) Theme (Luis E. Bacalov) IT:SP = General Music GMS-0014* [ST]; Theme (Luis E. Bacalov) FR:LP = General Music 803.011* [@ST]

3285 It Comes Up Murder *see* Honey Pot, The

3286 It Happened at the Penitentiary *see* Accade al Penitenziario

3287 It Happened at the World's Fair (1963) Score (various) US:LP = RCA LPM-2697/LSP-2697* + US: LP = RCA APL1-2568* [Elvis Presley: ST]

3288 It Happened in Athens (1962) Score (Manos Hadjidakis) GR:LP = EMI 14C062.70907; Theme (Manos Hadjidakis) US:SP = Capitol 4720 [The Hollyridge Strings]; Theme (Manos Hadjidakis) US:SP = 20th 306 [Eileen Wilson]

3289 It Happened in Brooklyn (1947) Score (Jule Styne) US:LP-BP = Hollywood Soundstage 5006; Highlights (Jule Styne) US:LP-BP = Caliban 6006; Excerpts (Jule Styne) US:LP = Columbia CL-2913 [Frank Sinatra:ST]

3290 It Happened in Rome [Danger—Girls at Play] [Girls at Play] [Souvenir d'Italie] (1957) Theme (Lelio Luttazzi) US:SP = RCA 47-7099 [Tony Martin]; Theme (Lelio Luttazzi) US:LP = Omega 10* [Pola Chapell]; Theme (Lelio Luttazzi) US:LP = Epic 3593 [Gian Stellari]

3291 It Happened One Summer *see* State Fair (1945)

3292 It Happened to Jane [Twinkle and Shine] (1959) Themes-A-B (Fred Karger/Joe Lubin) US:SP = Columbia 4-41391 [Doris Day:ST]; Theme-C (By

Dunham) US:SP = Columbia 4-41993 [Doris Day:ST]; Theme-A (Fred Karger) US:LP-PP = Columbia X-82021 [Doris Day:ST]

3293 It Happens Every Spring (1949) Theme (Josef Myrow) US:SP = Capitol 54-590 [Margaret Whiting]

3294 It Lives Again *see* It's Alive 2

3295 It Only Happens to Others (1971) Highlights [French Release] (Michel Polnareff) FR:EP = AZ Disc 337*; Themes [Italian Release] (Carlo Pes) US:SP = RCA 74-0599* [Marcello Mastroianni:ST]

3296 It Started in Naples [Bay of Naples] (1960) Score (Alessandro Cicognini & Carlo Savina) US:LP = Dot DLP-3324/DLP-25324* + US:LP = Varese STV-81122*

3297 It Started with a Kiss (1959) Theme (Charles Lederer) US:SP = MGM 12819 [Debbie Reynolds:ST]; Theme (Charles Lederer) US:LP = Metro 535 [Debbie Reynolds:ST]

3298 It Takes a Thief [The Challenge] (1960) Highlights (Bill McGuffie) GB:EP = Philips 12339

3299 It Won't Rub Off, Baby *see* Sweet Love, Bitter

3300 Italian Brigands [Il Brigante] (1961) Score (Nino Rota) US:LP = Cerberus CST-0204

3301 Italian Job, The (1969) Score (Quincy Jones) US:LP = Paramount PAS-5007*

3302 Italiani Brava Gente *see* Attack and Retreat

3303 It's a Bikini World (1967) Theme/US:SP = Era 016 [The Castaways:ST]

3304 It's a Date (1940) Excerpts (various) US:78-MS = Decca A-75 [Deanna Durbin:ST]

3305 It's a Great Feeling (1949) Highlights (Jule Styne) US:LP-BP = Caliban 6015

3306 It's a Great Life (1929) Themes-A-B/US:78 = Brunswick 4631 [Lawrence Gray:ST]; Theme-C/US:78 = RCA/Victor 22269 [The Duncan Sisters:ST]; Theme-D/US:78 = RCA/Victor 22345 [The Duncan Sisters:ST]

3307 It's a Great Life (1936) Themes/US:78 = Brunswick 7574 [Joe Morrison:ST]

3308 It's a Long Time that I've Loved You [Il y a Longtemps que Je T'Aime] (1980) Score (Gerard Anfosso) FR:LP = WB/WEA 56749*

3309 It's a Mad, Mad, Mad, Mad World (1963) Score (Ernest Gold) US:LP = UA UAL-4110/UAS-5110* + US:LP = UA LA-276*

3310 It's Alive! (1974) Excerpts (Bernard Herrmann) US:LP = Starlog SR-1002* [Laurie Johnson]

3311 It's Alive 2 [It Lives Again] (1978) Score (as:Laurie Johnson) US:LP = Starlog SR-1002*

3312 It's All Happening *see* Dream Maker, The

3313 It's All Over Town (1964) Score (various) GB:LP = Philips DL-7609 [Frankie Vaughan:ST]

3314 It's Always Fair Weather (1955) Score (Andre Previn) US:LP = MGM E-3241

3315 It's Hard to Be Good (1948) Theme (Anthony Hopkins) GB:78-PP = Rank FM-39 [ST]

3316 It's Love Again (1936) Excerpts (various) GB:LP = Decca ECM-2168 [Jessie Matthews:ST]

3317 It's Magic *see* Romance on the High Seas

3318 It's My Turn (1980) Score (e:Patrick Williams/t:Michael Masser) US:LP = Motown M8-947*

3319 It's Not Cricket (1949) Theme (Arthur Wilkinson) GB:78-PP = Rank FM-62 [ST]

3320 It's Snowing in New York Theme (Al Rubin) US:SP = Musicanza 107* [The Land of Sunshine:ST]

3321 It's Trad, Dad *see* Ring-a-Ding Rhythm

3322 Ivan the Terrible (1943) Scores (Serge Prokofiev) US:LP-MS = Vox 3-9004* [Felix Slatkin]

3323 Ivanhoe (1952) Excerpts (Miklos Rozsa) US:LP-10 = MGM E-179 + US:LP = MGM E-3507 [Miklos Rozsa:ST]

3324 I've Gotta Horse (1965) Score (various) GB:LP = Decca LK-4677

3325 Ivory Hunter, The [Where No Vultures Fly] (1951) Theme (Alan

Rawsthorne) GB:78-PP = Rank FM-119 [ST]

J

3326 Jack Ahoy (1933) Theme/ GB:LP = WRC 113 [Jack Hulbert: ST]

3327 Jack and the Beanstalk (1952) Themes (Lester Lee) US:SP = Decca 9-27980 [Dick Haymes]

3328 Jack Johnson (1971) Score (Miles Davis) US:LP = Columbia S-30455* + US:LP = Columbia PC-30455* [Miles Davis:ST]

3329 Jack of All Trades (1936) Theme-A/GB:LP = WRC 113 [Jack Hulbert:ST]; Theme-B/GB:LP = WRC 217 [Jack Hulbert:ST]; Theme-C/GB:78 = HMV 334 [Jack Hulbert:ST]

3330 Jack the Giant Killer (1962) Theme (Paul Sawtell & Bert Shefter) US: LP-BP = POO 104 [@ST]

3331 Jack the Ripper (1960) Score [USA Release] (Pete Rugolo & Jimmy McHugh) US:LP = RCA LPM-2199/ LSP-2199*; Underscore + Dialog [British Release] (Stanley Black) US: LP = Camden CAL-590

3332 Jack's the Boy (1932) Themes/GB:78 = HMV 4263 [Jack Hulbert:ST]; Theme/GB:LP = WRC 113 [Jack Hulbert:ST]

3333 Jacqueline (1956) Theme (Cedric Thorpe Davie) GB:78-PP = Rank FM-193 [ST]

3334 Jacqueline Susann's Once Is Not Enough *see* Once Is Not Enough

3335 Jagged Edge (1985) Score (John Barry) US:LP = Varese STV-81252*

3336 Jaguar Lives! (1979) Score (Robert O. Ragland) JA:LP = Seven Seas FML-116*

3337 Jail Birds *see* Pardon Us

3338 Jailhouse Rock (1957) Highlights-A (Mike Stoller) US:EP = RCA EPA-4114 [Elvis Presley:ST]; Highlights-B (Mike Stoller) US:LP-BP = Pirate PR-101 [Elvis Presley:ST]

3339 Jake Speed (1986) Score (Mark Snow) US:LP = Varese STV-81285*

3340 Jam Session (1944) Score (various) US:LP-BP = Hollywood Soundstage HS-5014

3341 Jamboree [Disc Jockey Jamboree] (1957) Score (various) US:LP-BP = JAM JLP-101; Highlights (various) US:EP = Verve 5065 [Count Basie:ST]; Themes/US:SP = Roulette 4023 [Jimmy Bowen:ST]

3342 James Dean Story, The (1957) Score (s:Leith Stevens/t:Jay Livingston & Ray Evans) US:LP = Capitol W-881

3343 Jan De Swart, Sculptor [Short] Highlights (Donald Specht) US: LP-PP = Bemus 3682

3344 Jane Eyre (1944) Excerpts (Bernard Herrmann) US:LP = London SP-44144* + US:LP = London SPC-21177*; Theme (Bernard Herrmann) GB: LP-MS = Unicorn 400* [Bernard Herrmann:ST]

3345 Janis (1975) Scores (pop music) US:LP-MS = Columbia PG-33345* [Janis Joplin:ST]

3346 Jason and the Argonauts (1963) Excerpts (Bernard Herrmann) US:LP = London SPC-21137* [Bernard Herrmann:ST]

3347 Jaws (1975) Score (John Williams) US:LP = MCA 2087* + US: LP = MCA 37171*

3348 Jaws 2 (1978) Score (John Williams) US:LP = MCA 3045*

3349 Jaws 3-D [Jaws 3] (1983) Score (Alan Parker) US:LP = MCA 6124*

3350 Jazz Dance (1956) Highlights (pop music) US:LP-10 = Jaguar 801

3351 Jazz Singer, The (1927) Score + Dialog (e:Louis Silvers/etc.) US:LP-MS = Sountrak STK-102

3352 Jazz Singer, The (1953) Highlights (e:Sammy Fain/etc.) US:LP-10 = RCA LPM-3118 [Danny Thomas:ST]; Highlights (e:Sammy Fain/etc.) US:LP-PP = RCA Custom J80P-6396 [Danny Thomas:ST]; Highlights (various) US: EP = Decca ED-2003 [Peggy Lee:ST]

3353 Jeanne Eagles (1957) Theme (George Duning) US:SP = Decca 9-30388 [Morris Stoloff:ST]; Theme (George Duning) US:SP = Liberty 55092

[Jeff Chandler]; Theme (George Duning) US:LP = Decca 8574 [Morris Stoloff:ST]

3354 Jefe, El (1957) Theme (Lalo Schifrin) US:LP = MGM 4110* [Lalo Schifrin:ST]

3355 Jeff (1969) Highlights (Francois DeRoubaix) FR:EP = Riviera 231.346*

3356 Jennie *see* Portrait of Jennie

3357 Jennie, Wife/Child *see* Albert Peckingpaw's Revenge

3358 Jennifer (1953) Theme (Matt Dennis) US:SP = Capitol 2498 [Nat King Cole]; Theme (Matt Dennis) US:LP = Kapp 1024 [Matt Dennis:ST]

3359 Jennifer on My Mind (1971) Theme (Stephen J. Lawrence) US:SP = UA 50844* [Allan Taylor:ST]; Theme (Stephen J. Lawrence) US:LP-MS = UA 089* [@Allan Taylor:ST]

3360 Jenny (1970) Theme (Bobby Scott) US:SP = Columbia 4-44016 [Diahann Carroll]

3361 Jenny Angel *see* Angel Baby

3362 Jenny's Birthday Book [Short] Sequence + Dialog (Arthur Kleiner) US:LP-PP = Picture Book Parade 105 [@ST]

3363 Jeremiah Johnson (1971) Score (John Rubinstein) US:LP = WB BS-2902*

3364 Jeremy (1974) Score (s:Lee Holdridge/t:Joe Brooks) US:LP = UA LA-145*

3365 Jericho (1937) Themes-A-B/ GB:78 = HMV 8572 [Paul Robeson:ST]; Theme-C/GB:78 = HMV 8621 [Paul Robeson:ST]

3366 Jessica (1962) Score (e:Mario Nascimbene/e:Marguerite Monnot) US: LP = UA UAL-4096/UAS-5096*

3367 Jesus (1981) Score (Riga) US: LP-PP = G.P. Records 0180*

3368 Jesus Christ Superstar (1973) Scores (stage songs:Andrew Lloyd Webber) US:LP-MS = MCA 11000*

3369 Jet Over the Atlantic (1959) Theme (Louis Forbes) US:SP = NRC 042 [Ray Stevens]

3370 Jeune Marie, Le (1983) Score (Luis E. Bacalov) FR:LP = General Music 803.045*

3371 Jeunes Loups, Les [The Young Wolves] [I Giovani Lupi] (1968) Score (Jack Arel) FR:LP = Riviera 521083; Theme (Jack Arel) US:SP = Atlantic 2516 [Nicole Croisille]

3372 Jewel of the Nile (1985) Score (t:Jack Nitzsche/s:various) US:LP = Arista JL9-8406*

3373 Jezebel (1938) Excerpts (Max Steiner) US:LP-BP = Tony Thomas TTMS-16 [Max Steiner:ST]; Theme (Max Steiner) US:LP = RCA 1-0183* + US:LP = RCA 1-3706* [Charles Gerhardt]

3374 Jig-Saw [Labyrinth] [L' Homme en Colere] (1980) Score (Claude Bolling) FR:LP = RCA 37261*

3375 Jim Thorpe—All American [Man of Bronze] (1951) Excerpts (Max Steiner) US:LP-MS-BP = Tony Thomas TTMS-9/10 [Max Steiner:ST]

3376 Jimi Hendrix (1972) Scores (pop music) US:LP-MS = Reprise RS-6481* [Jimi Hendrix:ST]

3377 Jitterbug Party [Short] (1934) Excerpts (various) US:LP = Biograph M-3 + US:LP-BP = Sandy Hook 2068 [@Cab Calloway:ST]

3378 Jo Jo Dancer, Your Life Is Calling (1986) Score (e:Herbie Hancock/ e:various) US:LP = WB 25444-1*

3379 Joan *see* Carry It On

3380 Joanna (1969) Score (Rod McKuen) US:LP = 20th S-4202*; Theme (Jack Segal) US:SP = Capitol 2390 [Matt Monro]

3381 Joe (1970) Score (Bobby Scott) US:LP = Mercury SRM1-605*

3382 Joe Louis Story, The (1953) Highlights (e:George Bassman/t:Alec Wilder) US:LP-10 = MGM E-221

3383 Joe Panther (1976) Theme (Fred Karlin) US:SP = Big Tree 16088* [England Dan & John Ford Coley:ST]

3384 John and Julie (1955) Theme (Philip Green) US:SP = Capitol 3720 [Eddie Calvert]; Theme (Philip Green) US:SP = Mercury 70720 [Ralph Marterie]; Theme (Philip Green) US:SP = X 4X0171 [The Spencer-Hagen Orchestra]

3385 John and Mary (1970) Score (s:Quincy Jones/t:Jeff Bridges) US: LP = A&M SP-4230*

3386 John F. Kennedy:Years of Lightning, Day of Drums (1966) Underscore + Dialog (u:Bruce

Herschensohn/au:William Loose) US: LP = Capitol T-2486/ST-2486*

3387 John Goldfarb, Please Come Home (1965) Theme (John Williams) US:SP = 20th 558 [Shirley MacLaine: ST]; Theme (John Williams) US:LP-BP = Centurion 1210 [@Shirley MacLaine:ST]

3388 John Paul Jones (1959) Score (Max Steiner) US:LP = WB W-1293/WS-1293* + US:LP = Varese STV-81146

3389 Johnny Angel (1945) Theme (Hoagy Carmichael) US:78 = ARA 124 [Hoagy Carmichael:ST]

3390 Johnny Apollo (1940) Theme-A (Mack Gordon) US:LP = West Coast 14002 [Dorothy Lamour:ST]; Theme-B (Lionel Newman) US:LP-BP = Legends 1000/4 [Dorothy Lamour:ST]

3391 Johnny Appleseed *see* Melody Time

3392 Johnny Belinda (1948) Highlights (Max Steiner) US:LP-MS-BP = Tony Thomas TTMS-13/14; Theme (Max Steiner) US:LP = RCA 1-0136* [Charles Gerhardt]; Theme (Max Steiner) US:LP = RCA 1170 [Max Steiner:ST]

3393 Johnny Concho (1956) Highlights (Nelson Riddle) US:EP = Capitol EAP1-754 [Nelson Riddle:ST]; Theme (Nelson Riddle) US:SP = Capitol 3469 [Frank Sinatra]

3394 Johnny Cool (1963) Score (s: Billy May/t:James Van Heusen) US: LP = UA UAL-4111/UAS-5111*

3395 Johnny Crow's Garden [Short] Sequence + Dialog (Arthur Kleiner) US:LP-PP = Picture Book Parade 106 [@ST]

3396 Johnny Dangerously (1985) Theme (Al Yankovic) US:SP = Rock'n' Roll 254-04708* [Al Yankovic:ST]; Theme (Al Yankovic) US:LP = Rock'n' Roll 40033* [Al Yankovic:ST]

3397 Johnny Fedora and Alice Blue Bonnet *see* Make Mine Music

3398 Johnny Guitar (1954) Score (Victor Young) US:LP = Citadel CTV-7026

3399 Johnny Hamlet [Dirty Story of the West] [Quella Sporca Storia Nel West] (1968) Score (Francesco DeMasi) IT:LP = CAM MAG-10.012

3400 Johnny in the Clouds *see* Way to the Stars, The

3401 Johnny Tremaine (1957) Highlights (George Bruns) US:LP = Disneyland WDL-4014

3402 Johnny Trouble (1957) Theme (Peggy Lee) US:SP = Prescott 1567 [John Carroll & Marni Nixon]

3403 Johnny Yesno (1981) Score (Cabaret Voltaire) CA:LP = Doublevision DVR-1*

3404 Johnny Yuma (1966) Themes (Nora Orlandi) IT:SP = RCA 45N-1486 [ST]

3405 Johnstown Flood, The [Cartoon] (1946) Sequence + Dialog (Philip Scheib) US:LP = Peter Pan 1118 [@ST]

3406 Joker Is Wild, The (1957) Highlights (various) US:LP-BP = Caliban 6024; Themes/US:SP = Capitol 3793 [Frank Sinatra:ST]; Themes/US: LP = Capitol 2700 [Frank Sinatra:ST]

3407 Jokers, The (1967) Theme (Mike Leander) US:SP = Capitol 5919 [Peter & Gordon:ST]; Theme (Mike Leander) US:LP = Capitol 2747* [Peter & Gordon:ST]

3408 Jolly Bad Fellow, A [They All Died Laughing] (1964) Theme (John Barry & Alan Haven) GB:SP = UA 1057 [Alan Haven]

3409 Jolson Sings Again (1949) Highlights (pop music) US:LP-10 = Decca DL-5006 [Al Jolson:ST]

3410 Jolson Story, The (1946) Score (pop music) US:LP-BP = Take Two TT-103; Excerpts-A (pop music) US:LP = Decca DL-9034 [Al Jolson: ST]; Excerpts-B (pop music) US:LP = Decca DL-9035 [Al Jolson:ST]

3411 Jonathan Livingston Seagull (1973) Score (e:Neil Diamond/ae:Lee Holdridge) US:LP = Columbia KS-32550*; Excerpts (ae:Lee Holdridge) US:LP = Varese STV-81081* [Lee Holdridge:ST]; Theme (Lee Holdridge) US:LP = Varese 704.290* [Charles Gerhardt]

3412 Josepha (1982) Highlights (Georges Delerue) FR:LP = RCA 37636*

3413 Josie's Castle [Grass Is Always Greener] (1971) Score (Jimmie Haskell) US:LP-PP = Four Star/Mascot FSAW-1

3414 Jour de Fete [The Big Day] [The Day Off] (1952) Excerpts (Jean Yatove) US:LP = UA UNS-15554 [@ST]; Highlights (Jean Yatove) FR: EP = Philips 77748

3415 Journey Back to Oz, The [The Return to Oz] (1973) Score-A (James Van Heusen) US:LP-PP = Texize T-33; Score-B (James Van Heusen) US:LP-BP = RFO 1

3416 Journey Into Fear (1975) Highlights (Alex North) US:LP = Citadel CTV-7014*

3417 Journey Through the Past (1973) Scores (Neil Young) US:LP-MS = Reprise 2XS-6480* [Neil Young:ST]

3418 Journey to Jerusalem, A [Hatikuah on Mt. Scopus] (1968) Score (classical music) US:LP = Columbia MS-7053* [Leonard Bernstein:ST]

3419 Journey to the Center of the Earth (1959) Excerpts (Bernard Herrmann) US:LP = London SP-44207* [Bernard Herrmann:ST]; Highlights (James Van Heusen) US:EP = Dot DEP-1091 [Pat Boone:ST]

3420 Journey to the Far Side of the Sun [Doppelganger] (1969) Theme (Barry Gray) GB:LP = UA 30281* [@Barry Gray:ST]

3421 Journey Within, The *see* Charles Lloyd—The Journey Within

3422 Joy (1984) Score (e:Francois Valery/e:Alain Wisniak) FR:LP = WB/WEA 240244-1*

3423 Joy House [Love Cage] (1964) Themes (Lalo Schifrin) US:LP = Verve 6-8624* [Jimmy Smith & Lalo Schifrin: ST]; Theme (Lalo Schifrin) US:SP = Verve 10503 [Jimmy Smith & Lalo Schifrin:ST]; Theme (Lalo Schifrin) US:LP = Verve 6-8587* [Lalo Schifrin:ST]

3424 Joy in the Morning (1965) Theme (Sammy Fain) US:SP = MGM 13340 [Richard Chamberlain:ST]; Theme (Sammy Fain) US:SP = Valiant 716 [Shelby Flint]

3425 Joy of Living, The (1938) Highlights (Jerome Kern) US:LP-BP = JJA 19747

3426 Joy Ride (1977) Score (e:Jimmie Haskell/e:Jeff Lynne) US:LP = UA LA-784*

3427 Juarez (1939) Theme (Erich Wolfgang Korngold) US:LP = RCA 1-0136* + US:LP = RCA 1-3706 + US: LP = RCA 3330* [Charles Gerhardt]

3428 Jubilee (1978) Score (t:Brian Eno/s:various) GB:LP = Polydor 2302.079*

3429 Jubilee Trail (1954) Theme (Victor Young) US:SP = Decca 9-29027 [Victor Young:ST]; Theme (Victor Young) US:LP = Decca 8060 [Victor Young:ST]

3430 Jud (1971) Score (Stu Phillips) US:LP = Ampex A-50101*

3431 Judge and the Assassin, The [Le Juge et l'Assassin] (1980) Score (Philippe Sarde) FR:LP = Saravah 10061*

3432 Judgment at Nuremberg (1961) Highlights + Dialog (Ernest Gold) US:LP = UA UAL-4095/UAS-5095*

3433 Judith (1966) Score (Sol Kaplan) US:LP = RCA LOC-1119/LSO-1119*

3434 Juke Box Jenny (1942) Themes/US:78 = Bluebird 11396 [Charlie Barnet:ST]

3435 Juke Box Rhythm [Juke Box Jamboree] (1959) Theme-A/US:SP = Capitol 4161 [Jack Jones:ST]; Theme-B/US:SP = Capitol 3966 [Johnny Otis:ST]

3436 Jules and Jim [Jules et Jim] (1962) Highlights (Georges Delerue) FR: EP = Philips 432.728; Theme (Georges Delerue) US:SP = Philips 40059 [Jean Defaye]; Theme (Georges Delerue) US: LP = Philips 600.071 [@Jeanne Moreau:ST]

3437 Jules Verne's Rocket to the Moon *see* Those Fantastic Flying Fools

3438 Julia (1977) Highlights (Georges Delerue) US:LP = DRG SL-9514*

3439 Julie (1956) Theme-A (Leith Stevens) US:SP = Columbia 4-40758 [Doris Day:ST]; Theme-A (Leith Stevens) US:LP = Harmony 11192 [Doris Day:ST]; Theme-B (Leonard Pennario) US:SP = Capitol 2950 [Les Baxter & Leonard Pennario:ST]; Theme-B (Leonard Pennario) US:LP = Angel 36062* [Leonard Pennario:ST]

3440 Juliet of the Spirits (1965) Score-A (Nino Rota) US:LP = Mainstream 56062/S-6062* + US:LP-BP = Lumiere 1000*; Score-B (Nino Rota) IT: LP = CAM CDR-33/2 + IT:LP-MS = CAM 500.001

3441 Juliette ou la Clef des Songes (1951) Theme (Joseph Kosma) US:LP = Columbia 569 [Juliette Greco]

3442 Julius Caesar (1953) Underscore + Dialog (Miklos Rozsa) US:LP = MGM E-3033; Excerpts-A (Miklos Rozsa) US:LP = London SPC-21132* [Bernard Herrmann]; Excerpts-B (Miklos Rozsa) US:LP = Deutsche 2584.021* [Miklos Rozsa:ST]; Theme-C (Miklos Rozsa) US:LP = Dot 25107* [Elmer Bernstein]

3443 Jumbo *see* Billy Rose's Jumbo

3444 Jumpin' Jack Flash (1986) Score (t:Thomas Newman/s:various) US:LP: = Mercury 830-545-1*

3445 Jumping for Joy (1956) Theme-A (Larry Adler) GB:78-PP = Rank FM-184 [ST]; Theme-B (Larry Adler) GB:78-PP = Rank FM-185 [ST]

3446 Jungle Book, The (1942) Highlights (Miklos Rozsa) GE:LP = Celine CL-0017* [The Nuremberg Symphony]; Highlights + Narration (Miklos Rozsa) US:LP = RCA LM-2118 [Leo Genn]; Highlights + Narration (Miklos Rozsa) US:78-MS = RCA DM-905 + US:LP = Entracte 6002 [Sabu]

3447 Jungle Book, The (1967) Score (s:Richard & Robert Sherman/t: George Bruns/t:Terry Gilkyson) US: LP = Disneyland 3105

3448 Jungle Fighters, The [The Long and the Short and the Tall] (1961) Theme (S. Simmons) US:SP = Columbia 4-42017 [Laurence Harvey:ST]

3449 Jungle Princess, The (1936) Theme (Frederick Hollander) US:SP = Coral 9-61955 [Alan Copeland]; Theme (Frederick Hollander) US:LP-BP = Legends 1000/4 [Dorothy Lamour:ST]

3450 Junior Bonner (1972) Themes (Rod Hart) US:SP-PP = ABC CIN-3815 [Rod Hart:ST]

3451 Jupiter Menace, The (1982) Score (Larry Fast) US:LP = Passport PB-6014

3452 Jupiter's Darling (1955) Excerpts (Burton Lane) US:LP-BP = JJA 19824 [@ST]

3453 Jupiter's Thigh [On a Vole la Cuisse de Jupiter] (1981) Score (Georges Hatzinassios) FR:LP = Deesse DDLX-192*

3454 Just a Gigolo (1979) Score (e:Gunther Fischer/t:David Bowie/etc.) GB:LP = Jambo JAM-1*

3455 Just Around the Corner (1938) Themes/US:LP-MS = 20th 2-103 [Shirley Temple:ST]

3456 Just for Fun (1956) Theme/ US:SP = Liberty 55521 [Bobby Vee:ST]

3457 Just for You (1952) Highlights (Harry Warren) US:LP-10 = Decca DL-5417 + US:LP = Decca DL-4263 [Bing Crosby:ST]

3458 Just One of the Guys (1985) Score (t:Tom Scott/s:various) US:LP = Elektra 60426-1*

3459 Just Tell Me You Love Me [Maui] (1980) Score (e:Richard Halligan/e:Bob Gundry) US:LP = MCA 3255*

3460 Just the Way You Are (1984) Highlights (Vladimir Cosma) US:LP = Varese STV-81247*

3461 Justine (1969) Score (Jerry Goldsmith) US:LP = Monument SLP-18123*

K

3462 Kaajal / Theme/US:LP = Capitol 10500 [@Asha Bhosle:ST]

3463 Kagemusha (1980) Score (Shinchiro Ikebe) JA:LP = Columbia YX-7238*

3464 Kaleidoscope (1966) Score (Stanley Myers) US:LP = WB W-1663/ WS-1663*

3465 Kamikaze 1989 (1982) Score (Edgar Froese) GB:LP = Virgin V-2255*

3466 Kanal (1956) Excerpts (Jan Krenz) GB:LP = That's Entertainment TER-1053 [@ST]

3467 Kapo (1960) Highlights (Carlo Rustichelli) IT:EP = RCA EPA-30389; Theme (Carlo Rustichelli) US:LP = RCA FSO-4 [@ST]

3468 Karate Kid, The (1984) Score (e:Bill Conti/etc.) US:LP = Casablanca 822-213-1*

3469 Karate Kid—Part 2, The (1986) Score (e:Bill Conti/e:various) US: LP=UA SW-40414*

3470 Kathy-O (1958) Theme (Charles Tobias) US:SP=Mercury 71330 [The Diamonds]; Theme (Charles Tobias) US:LP=Vocalion 73772 [Wayne King]; Theme (Charles Tobias) US:EP=Dot 1067 [Patty McCormack: ST]

3471 Katia *see* Magnificent Sinner

3472 Kazablan (1973) Score [English Soundtrack] (stage songs:Dov Seltzer) US:LP=MGM 1SE-48*; Score [Israeli Soundtrack] (stage songs:Dov Seltzer) IS:LP=CBS 70128*

3473 Keep 'Em Flying (1941) Themes-A-B/US:78=Columbia 36471 [Carol Bruce:ST]; Theme-C/US:78=Decca 18298 [Martha Raye:ST]

3474 Keep It Cool *see* Let's Rock!

3475 Keetje Tippel *see* Cathy Tippel

3476 Kelly and Me (1957) Theme (Henry Mancini) US:SP=Coral 9-61801 [Hal McKusick]

3477 Kelly's Heroes (1970) Score (Lalo Schifrin) US:LP=MGM 1SE-23*

3478 Kenny and Company (1978) Score (Fred Myrow) JA:LP=Seven Seas FML-88*

3479 Kentuckian, The (1955) Highlights (Bernard Herrmann) US:LP=Entracte ERS-6506* [Fred Steiner]; Theme (Irving Gordon) US:SP=MGM 12011 [James Brown]; Theme (Irving Gordon) US:LP=RCA 1679 [Tony Perkins]

3480 Key, The (1958) Score (Malcolm Arnold) US:LP=Columbia CL-1185

3481 Key Largo (1948) Excerpts (Max Steiner) US:LP=RCA ARL1-0422* + US:LP=RCA AGL1-3782* [Charles Gerhardt]

3482 Key Witness (1960) Themes (Charles Wolcott) US:SP=MGM 12944 [Charles Wolcott:ST]; Themes (Charles Wolcott) US:SP=Chief 7022 [Tobin Matthews]; Theme (Charles Wolcott) US:LP=London 3238/231* [@Ted Heath]

3483 Keys of the Kingdom (1944) Score (Alfred Newman) US:LP-BP=Cine LP-1020

3484 Khartoum (1966) Score Frank Cordell) US:LP=UA UAL-4140/UAS-5140*

3485 Kid, The (1921) Excerpts [Silent II] (Charles Chaplin) US:LP=Camden CAS-2581* + US:LP=RCA CPL1-2778* [Johnny Douglas & The Living Strings]; Theme [Silent II] (Arthur Kleiner) US:LP=Golden Crest 4019 [Arthur Kleiner:ST]

3486 Kid and the Killers, The (1959) Theme (Clarence Scott) US:SP=Jon 4219 [The Valets]

3487 Kid for Two Farthings, A [Lucky Kid] (1955) Theme (Benjamin Frankel) US:SP=Epic 5-9117 [Walter Stott]; Theme (Benjamin Frankel) US: LP=London 1443 [Frank Chacksfield]

3488 Kid from Brooklyn, The (1946) Themes (Jule Styne) US:78=RCA 20-1848 [Freddy Martin]

3489 Kid from Spain, The (1932) Theme-A/US:LP=Epic 1128 [Eddie Cantor:ST]; Theme-B/US:LP=Pelican 134 [Eddie Cantor:ST]

3490 Kid Galahad (1962) Highlights (e:Ben Weisman & Fred Wise/etc.) US: EP=RCA EPA-4380 [Elvis Presley:ST]; Excerpts (various) US:LP=Camden CAL-2533/CAS-2533* [Elvis Presley: ST]

3491 Kid Millions (1934) Highlights (e:Walter Donaldson/etc.) US:LP-BP=Classic International Filmusicals 3007 + US:LP-BP=Sandy Hook SH-2039

3492 Kidnapped (1971) Score (Roy Budd) US:LP=American International A-1042*

3493 Kidnappers, The *see* Little Kidnappers, The

3494 Kids Are Alright, The (1979) Scores (rock music) US:LP-MS=MCA 2-11005* [The Who:ST]

3495 Kill! (1972) Score (Berto Pisano) IT:LP=General Music ZSLGE-55067*

3496 Kill or Be Killed [Uccidi e Muori] (1966) Theme (Carlo Rustichelli) JA:LP-MS=Seven Seas FMW-25/26* [Carlo Rustichelli:ST]

3497 Kill or Cure (1962) Theme (Ron Goodwin) US:SP=MGM 13106 [Danny Davis]; Theme (Ron Goodwin) CA:LP=Capitol 6086 [Ron Goodwin: ST]

3498 Kill Them All and Come Back Alone [Ammazzali Tutti e Torna Solo] (1968) Highlights (Francesco DeMasi) IT:LP = Beat CR-5*

3499 Killer Dino *see* Dino

3500 Killer Fish [Agguato sul Fondo] (1980) Score (Guido & Maurizio DeAngelis) IT:LP = Ricordi 2501*

3501 Killer Force [The Diamond Mercenaries] (1976) Score (Georges Garvarentz) US:LP = Audio Fidelity AFSD-6277*

3502 Killer Spy [Pleins Feux sur Stanislas] (1965) Highlights (Georges Delerue) FR:EP = Barclay 70851

3503 Killers, The (1946) Highlights (Miklos Rozsa) US:LP-BP = Tony Thomas TTMR-4; Theme-A (Miklos Rozsa) US:LP = Decca 710015* + US:LP = Varese 81053* [Miklos Rozsa: ST]; Theme-B (Miklos Rozsa) US:LP = Deutsche 2584.021* [Miklos Rozsa:ST]

3504 Killers Three (1968) Score (s:Harley Hatcher/t:Jerry Styner) US: LP = Tower ST-5141*

3505 Killing Fields, The (1984) Score (Mike Oldfield) GB:LP = Virgin V-2328*

3506 Killing Game, The [Jeu de Massacre] (1967) Highlights (Jacques Loussier) FR:EP = Vogue 8537

3507 Killing of Sister George, The (1968) Themes (Gerald Fried) US:SP = ABC 11173* [Gerald Fried:ST]; Theme (Gerald Fried) US:SP = Columbia 4-44869 [Skitch Hen-derson]; Theme (Gerald Fried) US:LP = Command 9415* [Richard Hayman]

3508 Kimberly Jim (1963) Score (e:James Kikillus/t:Bill Walker/etc.) US:LP = RCA LPM-2780/LSP-2780e [Jim Reeves:ST]

3509 Kindred, The (1986) Score (David Newman) US:LP = Varese STV-81308*

3510 Kinfolks [The Cannonsville Story] (1958) Highlights + Dialog (folk music) US:LP = Folkways FS-3852

3511 King and I, The (1956) Score (stage songs:Richard Rodgers) US:LP = Capitol W-740/SW-740*

3512 King and the Bird, The [Le Roi et l'Oiseau (1981) Score (Wojiech Kilar) FR:LP = WB/WEA 58132*

3513 King Boxer *see* Five Fingers of Death, The

3514 King Creole (1958) Score (e: Mike Stoller/e:Ben Wiseman & Fred Wise/etc.) US:LP = RCA LPM-1884/LSP-1884e + US:LP = RCA AYL1-3733e [Elvis Presley:ST]

3515 King in New York, A (1957) Highlights (Charles Chaplin) GB:EP = Columbia 7720; Themes (Charles Chaplin) US:LP = GNP 2064* [Michel Villard]; Themes (Charles Chaplin) US: LP = Camden 2581* + US:LP = RCA 1-2778* [Johnny Douglas & The Living Strings]

3516 King Kong (1933) Score-A (Max Steiner) US:LP = Entracte ERS-6504* [Fred Steiner]; Score-B (Max Steiner) US:LP = UA LA-373* [Leroy Holmes]; Highlights (Max Steiner) US: 78-MS-PP = Allied 1001 [Max Steiner: ST]

3517 King Kong (1976) Score (John Barry) US:LP = Reprise MS-2260*

3518 King Kong Escapes (1967) Excerpts (Akira Ifukube) JA:LP = Toho 8123 [@ST]

3519 King Kong Lives (1986) Score (John Scott) US:LP = MCA 6203*

3520 King Kong vs. Godzilla (1962) Excerpts-A (Akira Ifukube) JA:LP = Toho 8100 [@ST]; Excerpts-B (Akira Ifukube) JA:LP = Toho 8112 [@ST]; Underscore + Dialog (Akira Ifukube) JA:LP-MS = StarChild K18G-7158/9

3521 King of Burlesque, The (1935) Excerpts (Jimmy McHugh) US:LP = Columbia CL-3068 [Alice Faye:ST]

3522 King of Comedy, The (1983) Score (t:Robbie Robertson/t:Bob James/s:various) US:LP = WB 23765-1*

3523 King of Hearts (1967) Score (Georges Delerue) US:LP = UA UAL-4150/UAS-5150e + US:LP = UA LA-287e

3524 King of Jazz, The (1930) Score (various) US:LP-BP = Caliban 6025; Excerpts (various) US:LP-MS = Columbia C2L-43 [Bing Crosby:ST]

3525 King of Kings (1961) Score (Miklos Rozsa) US:LP = MGM 1E-2/1SE-2*

3526 King of the Cowboys (1943)

Theme/US:LP = Varese STV-81212 [Roy Rogers:ST]

3527 King of the Khyber Rifles (1954) Theme (Bernard Herrmann) US:LP = RCA 1-2792* [Charles Gerhardt]

3528 King of the Mountain (1982) Theme (M. Kerr) US:SP-12 = Polygram 4445* [Deborah Van Valkenburgh:ST]

3529 King of the Road (1969) Themes (Harley Hatcher) US:SP = RCA 47-9661* [Don Epperson:ST]

3530 King of the Royal Mounted [Serial] Excerpts (William Lava) US:LP-PP = Cinemasound R-1001* [James King]

3531 King Rat (1965) Score (John Barry) US:LP = Mainstream 56061/S-6061*

3532 King Solomon of Broadway (1935) Theme/US:78 = Brunswick 7502 [Pinky Tomlin:ST]

3533 King Solomon's Mines (1937) Themes (Mischa Spoliansky) GB:LP = WRC 123 [Paul Robeson:ST]

3534 King Solomon's Mines (1985) Score (Jerry Goldsmith) US:LP = Restless 72106-1*

3535 King Steps Out, The (1936) Excerpts (Fritz Kreisler) US:LP = Decca DL-9593 [Grace Moore:ST]

3536 Kings Go Forth (1958) Score (Elmer Bernstein) US:LP = Capitol W-1063

3537 King's Rhapsody (1955) Highlights (stage songs:Ivor Novello) GB: EP = Parlophone GEP-8553

3538 King's Row (1941) Score (Erich Wolfgang Korngold) US:LP = Chalfont SDG-305* [Charles Gerhardt]; Excerpts (Erich Wolfgang Korngold) US:LP-MS = WB 3X2736 [@Erich Wolfgang Korngold:ST]

3539 King's Story, A (1965) Underscore + Dialog (Ivor Slaney) US:LP = DRG SL-5185*

3540 Kingsmill Suite, The [Industrial Short] (1974) Highlights (Donald Specht) US:LP-PP = Friendly Eagle BG-101*

3541 Kisenga—Man of Africa *see* Men of Two Worlds

3542 Kismet (1955) Score (stage songs:George Forrest & Robert Wright) US:LP = MGM E-3281

3543 Kiss, The (1929) Highlights [Silent I] (ae: William Axt) US:LP = Westwood LP-502

3544 Kiss and Make Up (1934) Themes/US:LP-BP = JJA 19811 [@Cary Grant/Genevieve Tobin:ST]

3545 Kiss Before Dying, A (1956) Theme (Lionel Newman) US:SP = RCA 47-6551 [Billy Regis]; Theme (Lionel Newman) US:SP = MGM 12249 [Sam Taylor]; Theme (Lionel Newman) US: LP = MGM 3380 [Sam Taylor]

3546 Kiss Kiss, Bang Bang (1966) Themes (Bruno Nicolai) IT:SP = Parade 5003 [ST]

3547 Kiss Me Deadly (1955) Theme (Frank DeVol) US:SP = Capitol 3136 [Nat King Cole:ST]

3548 Kiss Me Kate (1953) Score (stage songs:Cole Porter) US:LP = MGM E-3077 + US:LP-MS = MGM 2SES-44e

3549 Kiss Me, Stupid (1964) Theme (Andre Previn) US:SP = Columbia 4-43136 [Andre Previn:ST]; Theme (Andre Previn) US:LP = UA 6392* [@Perez Prado]; Theme (Andre Previn) US:LP = Columbia 2294/9094* [Andre Previn:ST]

3550 Kiss of Evil *see* Kiss of the Vampire

3551 Kiss of the Spider Woman (1985) Score (e:Wally Badarou/e:John Neschling) US:LP = Island 90475-1*

3552 Kiss of the Vampire [Kiss of Evil] (1963) Theme (James Bernard) US: LP-BP = POO 104 [@Geoff Love]

3553 Kiss the Boys Goodbye (1940) Themes-A-B/US:LP-BP = JJA 19762 [@Connie Boswell/Mary Martin:ST]; Theme-C/GB:LP = Ace of Hearts 67 [@Mary Martin:ST]

3554 Kiss the Girls and Make Them Die [Operazione Paradiso] (1967) Themes (Mario Nascimbene) IT:SP = Parade 5013 [ST]; Themes (Mario Nascimbene) IT:LP-MS = Kangaroo 34209 [Mario Nascimbene:ST]

3555 Kiss Them for Me (1957) Score (t:Lionel Newman/s:various) US: LP = Coral CRL-57160

3556 Kissin' Cousins (1964) Score (e:Bill Giant/e:Florence Kaye/etc.) US: LP = RCA LPM-2894/LSP-2894* [Elvis Presley:ST]

3557 Kissing Bandit, The (1948) Themes-A-B/US:LP=Columbia 2913 [Frank Sinatra:ST]; Themes-C-D/US: LP-MS=DRG 2-2100 [@Kathryn Grayson:ST/David Rose]

3558 Kitty and the Bag Man (1984) Score (Brian May) AU:LP=Festival 25380*

3559 Klondike Annie (1936) Themes/US:LP=Decca 79176 [Mae West:ST]

3560 Klute (1971) Score (Michael Small) US:LP-BP=WS 1940*; Theme (Michael Small) US:LP-MS=UA 089* [@Leroy Holmes]; Theme (Michael Small) GB:LP=WB 56089* [@Michael Small:ST]

3561 Knack ... And How to Get It, The (1965) Score (John Barry) US: LP=UA UAL-4129/UAS-5129* + US: LP=UA LA-279*

3562 Knickerbocker Holiday (1944) Excerpts (stage songs:Kurt Weill) US: LP=Mark 56 #721 + US:LP=Ariel 10 [@ST]

3563 Knight Without Armour (1937) Excerpts (Miklos Rozsa) GB:LP= Polydor 2383.384* [Miklos Rozsa:ST]

3564 Knights of the Round Table (1953) Score (Miklos Rozsa) US:LP= Varese STV-81128* [Muir Mathieson]

3565 Knock on Wood (1954) Highlights (Sylvia Fine) US:EP=Decca ED-2141 [Danny Kaye:ST]; Excerpts (Sylvia Fine) US:LP-10=Decca DL-5527 [Danny Kaye:ST]

3566 Korva Selection, The (1978) Theme (Richie Tattersall) GB:SP= Ariola 118-12* [ST]

3567 Kotch (1971) Theme (Marvin Hamlisch) US:SP-PP=ABC PRO-1 [ST]; Theme (Marvin Hamlisch) US: SP=Columbia 4-45619* [Percy Faith]; Theme (Marvin Hamlisch) US:LP= RCA 4630* [Henry Mancini]

3568 Koyaanisquatai—A Life Out of Balance (1983) Score (Philip Glass) US:LP=Antilles ASTA-1*

3569 Krakatoa, East of Java [Volcano] (1969) Score (e:Mack David/ ae:Frank DeVol) US:LP=ABC SOC-8*

3570 Kramer vs. Kramer (1979) Excerpts (classical music) US:LP=Columbia M-35873* [@ST]

3571 Kremmen—The Movie (1980) Score (Chris East & Ray Cameron) GB: LP=EMI EMC-3342*

3572 Kronos (1957) Theme (Paul Sawtell & Bert Shefter) US:LP-BP= POO 104 [@ST]

3573 Krull (1983) Score (James Horner) US:LP=Southern Cross SCRS-1004*

3574 Krush Groove (1985) Score-A (various) US:LP=WB 25295-1*; Theme-B ["Kold Krush"] (George Cooper) US:SP=WB 7-28843* [Autumn:ST]

3575 Kuni Leml in Tel Aviv (1978) Score (Dov Seltzer) IS:LP=Hed Arzi 16601*

3576 Kwaidan [Kivoidan] (1965) Excerpts (Toru Takemitsu) JA:LP= RCA/Victor 1062 [Toru Takemitsu:ST]

L

3577 Labyrinth [Short] (1967) Score (Eldon Rathburn) CA:LP=Lab S-605*

3578 Labyrinth (1980) *see* Jig-Saw

3579 Labyrinth (1986) Score (e:Trevor Jones/e:David Bowie) US:LP=EMI SV-17206*

3580 Lacemaker, The [La Dentelliere] (1977) Score (Pierre Jansen) FR:LP=Barclay 900.539*

3581 Lacombe Lucien (1974) Score (pop music) FR:LP=Pathe C064.21902*

3582 Lad: A Dog (1962) Theme (Johnny Marks) US:SP=Terrace 7503 [Paul Jeffreys]

3583 Ladies' Man (1947) Themes/ US:78=RCA/Victor 20-2092 [Spike Jones:ST]

3584 Ladies' Man, The (1961) Theme (Harry Warren) US:SP=Columbia 4-42055 [Leslie Uggams]

3585 Ladies'Man [L'Homme a Femme] (1962) Highlights (Claude Bolling) FR:EP=Philips 437.328

3586 Ladies of the Chorus (1948) Themes-A-B/US:LP-BP=Legends 1000/1 [Marilyn Monroe:ST]; Theme-C/ US:LP-BP=Legends 1000/2 [@ST]

3587 Ladies They Talk About (1933) Theme/US:LP = Epic 3206 [Lillian Roth:ST]

3588 Ladies Who Do (1963) Theme (Ron Goodwin) GB:SP = Parlophone 45-5083 [Ron Goodwin:ST]; Theme (Ron Goodwin) CA:LP = Capitol 6086 [Ron Goodwin:ST]

3589 Ladrone, La [The Thief] (1982) Score (Ennio Morricone) IT:LP = RCA 31502*

3590 Lady and the Tramp (1955) Score (s:Sonny Burke/t:Oliver Wallace) US:LP = Decca DL-8462 [Peggy Lee:ST]; Score (s:Sonny Burke/t:Oliver Wallace) US:LP = Disneyland DQ-1231

3591 Lady Be Good (1941) Score (e:Roger Edens/stage songs:George Gershwin) US:LP-BP = Hollywood Soundstage 5010; Highlights (e:Roger Edens/stage songs:George Gershwin) US:LP-BP = Caliban 6010

3592 Lady Caroline Lamb (1973) Highlights (Richard Rodney Bennett) US:LP = Angel S-36946*

3593 Lady Chatterley's Lover [L'Amant de Lady Chatterley] (1981) Score (Stanley Myers & Richard Harvey) FR: LP = Pathe C068.72416

3594 Lady Dances, The *see* Merry Widow, The (1934)

3595 Lady Hamilton *see* That Hamilton Woman

3596 Lady Ice (1973) Theme (Perry Botkin, Jr.) US:LP = A&M 4639* [Perry Botkin, Jr.:ST]

3597 Lady in Cement (1968) Score (Hugo Montenegro) US:LP = 20th S-4204*

3598 Lady in the Car with Glasses and a Gun, The (1970) Score (Michel Legrand) FR:LP = Vogue 755*

3599 Lady in the Dark (1944) Excerpts (stage songs:Kurt Weill) US:LP-BP = Curtain Calls 100/21 [Ginger Rogers:ST]; Theme (Robert Emmett Dolan) US:SP = RCA 49-1293 [Leopold Stokowski]; Theme (Robert Emmett Dolan) US:LP = Decca 8085 + US:LP = Coral 20036 [Victor Young]

3600 Lady Is a Square, The (1958) Theme/US:SP = Columbia 4-41406 [Frankie Vaughan:ST]

3601 Lady L (1965) Theme (Jean Francaix) US:SP = MGM 13529 [Allesandro]; Theme (Jean Francaix) US:LP = Command 5005* [Enoch Light]

3602 Lady of Burlesque (1943) Theme/US:LP-BP = Legends 1000/2 [@Barbara Stanwyck:ST]

3603 Lady of Monza, The [La Monaca di Monza] (1970) Highlights (Ennio Morricone) IT:LP = Intermezzo IM-002*

3604 Lady of the Pavements (1929) Theme/US:LP = RCA LPV-528 [@ Lupe Velez:ST]

3605 Lady on a Train (1945) Theme/US:LP = Decca 75289 [Deanna Durbin:ST]

3606 Lady Oscar (1979) Score (Michel Legrand) JA:LP = Kitty 1045*

3607 Lady Sings the Blues (1972) Score + Underscore + Dialog (s:pop music/u:Michel Legrand & Gil Askey) US:LP-MS = Motown M7-758* [Diana Ross:ST]; Themes (Michel Legrand/Gil Askey) US:SP = Motown 1219* [Michel Legrand/Gil Askey:ST]

3608 Lady Surrenders, A *see* Love Story (1944)

3609 Lady Takes a Sailor, The (1949) Theme (Max Steiner) US:LP-BP = Citadel CTMS-7 [Max Steiner:ST]

3610 Ladyhawke (1985) Score (Andrew Powell) US:LP = Atlantic 81248-1*

3611 Lafayette [Monsieur Lafayette] (1962) Highlights (Steve Laurent & Pierre Duclos) FR:EP = Barclay 72474; Theme (Steve Laurent & Pierre Duclos) US:SP = Colpix 689 [Stu Phillips]; Theme (Steve Laurent & Pierre Duclos) US:LP = Philips 600.071 [@ST]

3612 Lambert, The Sheepish Lion [Cartoon] (1952) Theme (George Wyle) US:LP = Disneyland 3808 [@Jeromy Stuart]; Theme (George Wyle) US:SP = Disneyland 351 [Jeromy Stuart]

3613 Lancaster Experience, The [Industrial Short] (1980) Highlights + Dialog (John Darnall) US:LP-PP = Willowbrook VFF-1012*

3614 Lancelot and Guinevere *see* Sword of Lancelot, The

3615 Land of Look Behind, The (1982) Score (K. Leimer) US:LP = Palace of Lights NMS-06.2000* [K. Leimer:ST]

3616 Land of the Book (1966) Score (Josef Marais) US:LP=Unique UM-6966/US-6966*

3617 Land of the Minotaur (1976) Excerpts (Brian Eno) US:LP=Antilles AN-7070* [Brian Eno:ST]

3618 Land of the Pharaohs (1955) Highlights (Dimitri Tiomkin) US:LP=Film Music Collection FMC-13* [Elmer Bernstein]; Theme (Dimitri Tiomkin) US:SP=Coral 9-61388 [Dimitri Tiomkin:ST]; Theme (Dimitri Tiomkin) US:LP=Coral 57006 [Dimitri Tiomkin:ST]

3619 Land Raiders, The (1969) Score (Bruno Nicolai) US:LP=Beverly Hills BHS-21*

3620 Landlord, The (1970) Score (Al Kooper) US:LP=UA UAS-5209*

3621 Landru [Bluebeard] (1963) Highlights (Pierre Jansen) FR:LP-MS=RCA 37673 [@ST]

3622 Las Vegas Nights [The Gay City] (1941) Highlights (Burton Lane & Louis Alter) US:LP-BP=Caliban 6030

3623 Las Vegas Story, The (1952) Theme (Hoagy Carmichael) US:LP=Decca 8588 [Hoagy Carmichael:ST]

3624 Lassiter (1984) Score (Ken Thorne) US:LP=Varese STV-81208*

3625 Last American Hero, The [Hard Driver] (1973) Theme (Charles Fox) US:SP=ABC 11389* [Jim Croce:ST]; Theme (Charles Fox) US:LP=ABC 797* + US:LP=ABC 835* [Jim Croce:ST]

3626 Last American Virgin, The (1982) Score (pop music) US:LP=Columbia JS-38279*

3627 Last Angry Man, The (1959) Excerpts (George Duning) US:LP=Web ST-108 [George Duning:ST]

3628 Last Command, The (1955) Highlights (Max Steiner) US:LP=Citadel CTV-7019

3629 Last Days of Mussolini, The [The Last Four Days] [Mussolini:L'Ultimo Atto] (1974) Themes (Ennio Morricone) IT:SP=Cinevox MDF-053* [ST]; Themes (Ennio Morricone) IT:LP-MS=Cinevox 33/74-75* [Ennio Morricone:ST]

3630 Last Days of Planet Earth, The *see* Catastrophe 1999

3631 Last Days of Pompeii, The [Gli Ultimi Giorni di Pompei] (1960) Score (A.F. Lavagnino) IT:LP=Phoenix PHCAM-03*

3632 Last Dragon, The [Berry Gordy's The Last Dragon] (1985) Score (t:Misha Segal/s:various) US:LP=Motown 6128-ML*

3633 Last Embrace, The (1979) Highlights (Miklos Rozsa) US:LP=Varese STV-81166*

3634 Last Fight, The (1982) Score (Jay Chattaway) US:LP=Fania 00615*

3635 Last Frontier, The (1956) Theme (Lester Lee) US:SP=Capitol 3324 [Tex Ritter]; Theme (Lester Lee) US:LP=Capitol 971 [Tex Ritter]; Theme (Lester Lee) US:SP=Columbia 4-40653 [Norman Luboff]

3636 Last Hero, The [Yogoreta Eiya] (1983) Score (Kai Yoda) JA:LP=Eastworld 90206*

3637 Last Holiday, The (1950) Theme (Francis Chagrin) GB:78=Columbia 2702 [Charles Williams]; Theme (Francis Chagrin) GB:LP=WRC 384 [@Charles Williams]

3638 Last Judgment, The [Giudizio Universale] (1961) Score (Alessandro Cicognini) IT:LP=RCA PML-10295; Theme (Alessandro Cicognini) US:LP=RCA FSO-4 [@ST]

3639 Last Married Couple in America, The (1980) Theme (Charles Fox) US:SP=WB 49177* [Maureen McGovern:ST]

3640 Last Metro, The [La Dernier Metro] (1981) Score (e:Georges Delerue/e:pop music) US:LP=DRG SL-9504*

3641 Last of the American Hoboes, The (1970) Score (Gary Revel) US:LP=Bee Gee BGS-1041*

3642 Last of the Mohicans, The *see* Last Tomahawk, The

3643 Last of the Renegades, The [Winnetou II] (1964) Highlights (Martin Bottcher) GE:LP=Polydor 237.422

3644 Last of the Secret Agents, The (1966) Score (s:Pete King/t:Neal Hefti) US:LP=Dot DLP-3714/DLP-25714*; Theme (Lee Hazlewood) US:SP=Reprise 0461 [Nancy Sinatra:ST]

3645 Last of the Ski Bums, The (1969) Score (John Blakeley) US:LP=

World Pacific WS-21884*

3646 Last Paradise, The [L'Ultimo Paradiso] (1956) Score (A.F. Lavagnino) FR:LP = Polydor 20.308 + JA:LP = Polydor 25-MM-9043

3647 Last Picture Show, The (1971) Score-A (pop music) US:LP = Columbia S-31143*; Score-B (pop music) US:LP = MGM 1SE-33* [Hank Williams:ST]

3648 Last Porno Flick, The (1975) Score (Tony Bruno) US:LP = Bryan BRS-103*

3649 Last Rebel, The (1971) Score (Jon Lord & Tony Ashton) US:LP = Capitol SW-827*

3650 Last Romantic Lover, The [Playboy] [Le Dernier Amant Romantique] Score (Pierre Bachelet) FR:LP = Pema 900.060*

3651 Last Run, The (1971) Score (Jerry Goldsmith) US:LP = MGM 1SE-30*

3652 Last Safari, The (1967) Theme (Johnny Dankworth) US:SP = Dot 17054 [Billy Vaughn]; Theme (Johnny Dankworth) US:LP-BP = Centurion 1210 [@Billy Vaughn]

3653 Last Snows of Spring, The [L'Ultima Neve di Primavera] (1974) Score (Franco Micalizzi) IT:LP = RCA TBL1-1018*

3654 Last Starfighter, The (1984) Score (Craig Safan) US:LP = Southern Cross SCRS-1007*

3655 Last Stop on the Night Train, The [L'Ultimo Treno della Notte] (1975) Themes (Ennio Morricone) IT:SP = Cinevox MDF-072* [ST]

3656 Last Summer (1969) Score (John Simon) US:LP = WB WS-1791*

3657 Last Sunset, The (1961) Theme-A (Ernest Gold) US:LP = London 3320/320* [Ernest Gold:ST]; Theme-B (Dimitri Tiomkin) US:SP = Columbia 4-42029 [Mike Clifford]

3658 Last Tango in Acapulco, The (1974) Theme (Alberto Soria) US:SP-PP = Tobalina 6756 [Alberto Soria:ST]

3659 Last Tango in Paris, The (1973) Score (Gato Barbieri) US:LP = UA LA-045*

3660 Last Time I Saw Archie, The (1961) Theme (Herm Saunders) US:SP = Columbia 4-42011 [Percy Faith]

3661 Last Time I Saw Paris, The (1954) Highlights (pop music) MGM X-1124 [Odette:ST]

3662 Last Tomahawk, The [Last of the Mohicans] [Der Letzte Mohikaner] (1965) Score (Peter Thomas) GE:LP = Telefunken 14390

3663 Last Tycoon, The (1976) Themes (Maurice Jarre) GB:SP = Decca 13703* [Johnny Dankworth & Maurice Jarre:ST]

3664 Last Unicorn, The (1984) Score (Jimmy Webb) GE:LP = Virgin 206-684*

3665 Last Valley, The (1971) Score (John Barry) US:LP = Dunhill DXS-50102*

3666 Last Wagon, The (1956) Theme (Lionel Newman) US:SP = MGM 12317 [Leroy Holmes]; Theme (Lionel Newman) US:SP = Liberty 55037 [The Hi-Fi's]; Theme (Lionel Newman) US:LP = MGM 3480 [Leroy Holmes]

3667 Last Waltz, The (1978) Scores (pop music) US:LP-MS3 = WB 3WS-3146* [The Band:ST]

3668 Last War, The [The Final War] (1960) Excerpts (Ikuma Dan) JA:LP = Toho 8123 [@ST]

3669 Last Woman, The [La Derniere Femme] (1978) Score (Philippe Sarde) FR:LP = Pathe C066.14306*

3670 Last Year at Marienbad [L'Annee Derniere a Marienbad] (1961) Highlights (Francis Seyrig) FR:EP = Philips 432.700; Theme (Francis Seyrig) US:SP = Decca 9-31370 [Henri Rene]; Theme (Francis Seyrig) US:LP = WB 1548* [Werner Muller]

3671 Late Great Planet Earth, The (1979) Underscore + Dialog (Dana Kaproff) US:LP-PP = RCR 10022*

3672 Latin Lovers (1953) Themes/US:SP = MGM 30836 [Carlos Ramirez: ST]

3673 Latitude Zero (1970) Themes (Akira Ifukube) JA:LP = Toho 8108 [@ST]

3674 Laughing Anne (1953) Themes/GB:78 = Philips 186 [Margaret Lockwood:ST]

3675 Laughing Irish Eyes (1936) Themes/US:78 = Brunswick 7623 [Phil Regan:ST]

3676 Laughing Policeman, The [An Investigation of Murder] (1973) Theme (Charles Fox) US:SP = Shady Brook 033* [New World Symphony & Charles Fox:ST]

3677 Laura (1944) Excerpts (David Raksin) US:LP = RCA ARL1-1490* [David Raksin:ST]; Excerpts (David Raksin) US:LP = Columbia CL-2113/CS-8913* [@David Raksin:ST]

3678 Laura [Laura, les Ombres Que Je T'Aime] (1980) Score (Patrick Juvet) FR:LP = Barclay 960.020*

3679 Lavender Hill Mob, The (1951) Theme (Georges Auric) GB:78-PP = Rank FM-117 [ST]

3680 Law, The *see* Where the Hot Wind Blows

3681 Lawman (1971) Highlights (Jerry Fielding) US:LP-MS = Citadel CTJF-2/3*

3682 Lawrence of Arabia (1962) Score-A (Maurice Jarre) US:LP = Colpix LE-1000/LES-1000* [Adrian Bolt: ST]; Score-B (Maurice Jarre) US:LP = Colpix CP-514/SCP-514* + US:LP = Colgems COMO-5004/COSO-5004* + US:LP = Bell 1205* [Maurice Jarre]

3683 Leadbelly (1976) Score (t:Fred Karlin/s:pop music) US:LP = ABC ABDP-939*

3684 Leap Into the Void [Salto nel Vuoto] (1982) Excerpts (Nicola Piovani) IT:LP = Beat LPF-049* [Nicola Piovani: ST]

3685 Learning Tree, The (1969) Score (s:Gordon Parks/as:Tom McIntosh) US:LP = WB WS-1812*

3686 Leather Boys, The (1963) Theme (Bill McGuffie) US:SP = Capitol 5044 [Jimmie Haskell]; Theme (Bill McGuffie) US:LP = Capitol 2075* [Jimmie Haskell]

3687 Left Hand of God, The (1955) Theme (Victor Young) US:SP = Decca 9-29695 [Victor Young:ST]; Theme (Victor Young) US:LP = Decca 8285 [Victor Young:ST]; Theme (Victor Young) US: LP = RCA 1-0422* + US:LP = RCA 1-3782* [Charles Gerhardt]

3688 Legal Eagles (1986) Score (Elmer Bernstein) US:LP = MCA 6172*; Theme (Michael Chapman) US:SP = WB 7-28668* [Rod Stewart:ST]

3689 Legend (1986) Score-A [Europe Release] (Jerry Goldsmith) GB: LP = Filmtrax 100*; Score-B [USA Release] (Tangerine Dream) US:LP = MCA 6165*

3690 Legend of Billy Jean, The (1985) Theme (Climie & Knight) US: SP = Chrysalis 4-42877* [Pat Benatar: ST]; Theme (Climie & Knight) US: LP = Chrysalis 41507* [Pat Benatar: ST]

3691 Legend of Eight Samurai, The [Satomi Hakkenden] (1984) Score (Zitto) JA:LP = East World 90258*

3692 Legend of Frank Woods, The (1978) Score (e:Bob Sisco/e:Don Norville/t:Steve Dorff) US:LP = Movie Star DH-103-77*

3693 Legend of Frenchie King, The [Les Petroleuses] (1972) Score (Francis Lai) GB:LP = MFP 50034*; Theme (Francis Lai) US:LP = AIA 90042* + US:LP = Audio Fidelity 6301* [Francis Lai:ST]

3694 Legend of Lobo, The (1962) Theme + Dialog (Richard & Robert Sherman) US:LP = Disneyland DQ-1258

3695 Legend of Lylah Clare, The (1968) Theme (Frank DeVol) US:SP = MGM 13990 [Pete Spargo]; Theme (Frank DeVol) US:LP = UA 6669* [Leroy Holmes]

3696 Legend of Nigger Charley, The (1972) Themes (John Bennings) US: SP = Paramount 0168* [Lloyd Price:ST]

3697 Legend of Rock-a-Bye Point, The [Cartoon] (1953) Sequence + Dialog (Clarence Wheeler) US:LP = Peter Pan 1120 [@ST]

3698 Legend of Sleepy Hollow, The *see* Adventures of Ichabod and Mr. Toad, The

3699 Legend of the Lone Ranger, The (1981) Score (John Barry) US:LP = MCA 5212*

3700 Legend of the Lost (1957) Theme (A.F. Lavagnino) US:SP = UA 101 [Joe Valino]

3701 Legend of the Ninja (1982) Themes (John Scott) JA:SP = Columbia 205* [ST]

3702 Legend of the Seven Golden Vampires, The [The Seven Brothers Meet Dracula] (1974) Highlights +

Underscore + Dialog (James Bernard) GB:LP = WB 56085*

3703 Legion's Last Patrol, The *see* Commando

3704 Lemon Drop Kid, The (1951) Theme (Jay Livingston & Ray Evans) US:SP = Decca 9-27229 [Bing Crosby]

3705 Lemon Grove Kids Meet the Monsters, The (1967) Theme (Don Snyder) US:LP = Rhino 307 [@ST]

3706 Lemon Popsicle [Growing Up] (1978) Score (pop music) GB:LP = Warwick WW-5050* + JA:LP = Epic/ Sony 25-3P-37*

3707 Lenny (1974) Highlights + Underscore + Dialog (Ralph Burns) US: LP = UA LA-359*

3708 Lentil [Short] Sequence + Dialog (Arthur Kleiner) US:LP-PP = Picture Book Parade 103 [@ST]

3709 Leo and Loree (1980) Theme-A (Jay Asher) US:SP = Casablanca 2248* [Donny Most:ST]; Theme-B (Jay Asher) US:SP = Casablanca 2275* [Linda Purl:ST]

3710 Leo the Last (1970) Theme (Fred Myrow) FR:LP-MS = UA 29140* [@ST]

3711 Leonor (1976) Theme (Ennio Morricone) FR:LP = General Music 803.009* [Ennio Morricone:ST]

3712 Leopard, Le (1984) Highlights (Vladimir Cosma) FR:LP = Milan A-245*

3713 Leopard, The [Il Gattopardo] (1963) Score-A (Nino Rota) US:LP = 20th FXG-5015/SXG-5015*; Score-B (Nino Rota) IT:LP = Titanus TMS-1004*; Score-C (Nino Rota) US:LP = Varese STV-81190*

3714 Leopard in the Snow (1978) Themes (Ken Jones) JA:SP = Polydor 6077* [ST]

3715 Lermontov (1943) Excerpts (Sergei Prokofiev) US:LP = Urania UX-130

3716 Let Freedom Ring (1939) Excerpts (pop music) US:LP-BP = Trisklog 4 [Nelson Eddy:ST]

3717 Let It Be (1970) Score (pop music) US:LP = Apple AR-34001* + US:LP = Capitol SW-11922* [The Beatles:ST]

3718 Let No Man Write My Epitaph (1960) Score (pop music) US:LP = Verve MGV-4043/V6-4043* [Ella Fitzgerald:ST]

3719 Let Sleeping Corpses Lie *see* Don't Open the Window

3720 Let the Balloon Go (1976) Theme (George Dreyfus) AU:LP = WRC 5228* [George Dreyfus:ST]

3721 Let the Good Times Roll (1973) Scores (pop music) US:LP-MS = Bell 9002*

3722 Let's Be Happy (1957) Highlights (Nicholas Brodszky) US:EP = RCA EPA-4060 [Tony Martin:ST]

3723 Let's Dance (1950) Highlights (Frank Loesser) US:LP-BP = Caliban 6017

3724 Let's Do It Again (1953) Themes-A-B/US:SP = Decca 9-28757 [Jane Wyman:ST]; Theme-C/US:LP-BP = Legends 1000/2 [@Jane Wyman: ST]

3725 Let's Do It Again (1975) Score (s:Curtis Mayfield/as:Gil Askey & Rich Tufo) US:LP = Curtom CU-5005*

3726 Let's Face It (1941) Theme/ US:LP-BP = JJA 19767 [@Bob Hope: ST]

3727 Let's Fall in Love Again (1934) Themes/US:LP-BP = JJA 19763 [@Ann Southern:ST]

3728 Let's Get Harry (1986) Score (Brad Fiedel) US:LP = Varese STV-81301*

3729 Let's Live Tonight (1935) Themes/US:78 = Columbia 3023 [Tullio Carminati:ST]

3730 Let's Make Love (1960) Score (James Van Heusen) US:LP = CL-1527/ CS-8327* + US:LP = CSP ACS-8327*

3731 Let's Make Music (1940) Theme-A/US:78 = Decca 3417 [Bob Crosby:ST]; Theme-B/US:78 = Decca 3611 [Bob Crosby:ST]

3732 Let's Make Up [Lilacs in the Spring] (1954) Themes/GB:78 = Philips 380 [Errol Flynn:ST]

3733 Let's Rock! [Keep It Cool] (1958) Theme-A/US:SP = ABC 45-9871 + US:SP = MCA 2411 [Danny and the Juniors:ST]; Theme-B/US:SP = ABC 45-9882 + US:SP = MCA 2402 [The Royal Teens:ST]

3734 Let's Sing Again (1936)

Theme/US:78 = Decca 798 [Bobby Breen:ST]

3735 Let's Talk About Men [Questa Volta Parliamo di Uomini] (1965) Themes (Luis E. Bacalov) IT: SP = RCA 45-3315 [ST]

3736 Letter, The (1940) Highlights (Max Steiner) US:LP-BP = Tony Thomas TTMS-12; Theme (Max Steiner) US:LP = RCA 1-0183* + US:LP = RCA 1-3706* [Charles Gerhardt]

3737 Letter to Brezhnev (1986) Score (t:Alan Gill/s:various) US:LP = MCA 6162*

3738 Letter to Three Wives, A (1949) Theme (Alfred Newman) US: SP = Mercury 1194X45 [Alfred Newman: ST]; Theme (Alfred Newman) US:LP = Mercury 20037 + US:LP = Citadel 6003 + US:LP = Citadel 7015 + US:LP-BP = Capricorn 1286 [Alfred Newman: ST]

3739 Liaisons Dangereuses, Les (1959) Score (Jack Marray) US:LP = Epic LA-16022 + US:LP = Fontana MGF-27539/SRF-67539*; Score (Duke Jordan) US:LP = Parker PLP-813/ PLPS-813*; Theme (Thelonious Monk) US:SP = Decca 9-31370 [Henri Rene]

3740 Lialeh (1974) Score (Bernard Purdie) US:LP = Bryan BRS-102*

3741 Lianna (1982) Score (Mason Daring) US:LP = Daring DR-1003*

3742 Liberation of L.B. Jones, The (1970) Highlights (Elmer Bernstein) US: LP-BP = Cinema LP-8009

3743 Liberte 1 (1963) Highlights (J. Drejac) FR:EP = Philips 424.277; Theme (J. Drejac) US:LP = Philips 600.071 [@ST]

3744 Libertine, The [La Matriarca] (1968) Theme (Armando Trovajoli) US:LP = UA 6742* [Leroy Holmes]

3745 Licensed to Kill *see* Second Best Secret Agent in the Whole Wide World, The

3746 Lie Like a Gentleman *see* Escapade

3747 Lieutenant Kije *see* Czar Wants to Sleep, The

3748 Lieutenant Wore Skirts, The (1956) Theme (Ken Darby) US:SP = Coral 9-61550 [The Lancers]

3749 Life and Death of Colonel Blimp, The [Colonel Blimp] (1943) Theme (Allan Gray) GB:78 = Decca 1724 [Jimmie Miller and the RAF Dance Band]

3750 Life and Times of Judge Roy Bean, The (1972) Score (Maurice Jarre) US:LP = Columbia S-31948*

3751 Life Begins at 8:30 [Light of Heart] (1942) Theme (Alfred Newman) US:SP = Decca 9-91566 [Alfred Newman:ST]; Theme (Alfred Newman) US: LP = Decca 8123 + US:LP = Vocalion 73749 + US:LP-BP = Capricorn 1286 [Alfred Newman:ST]

3752 Life, Love, Death [La Vie, l'Amour, la Mort] (1969) Highlights (Francis Lai) FR:EP = UA 38238; Themes (Francis Lai) US:SP = UA 50548* [Francis Lai:ST]

3753 Life of Brian *see* Monty Python's Life of Brian

3754 Life of Emile Zola, The (1937) Excerpts (Max Steiner) US:LP-BP = Citadel CTMS-7 [Max Steiner:ST]; Theme (Max Steiner) US:LP = RCA 1170 [Max Steiner:ST]

3755 Life of Her Own, A (1950) Theme [credited to "Invitation"] (Bronislau Kaper) US:SP = Decca 9-27965 [Victor Young]; Theme [credited to "Invitation"] (Bronislau Kaper) US:LP = MGM 3694 [John Green:ST]

3756 Life of the Party, The (1937) Themes/US:78 = Bluebird 7034 [Harriet Hilliard:ST]

3757 Life with Father (1947) Theme (Max Steiner) US:LP = Medallion 309 [Max Steiner:ST]

3758 Lifeforce (1985) Score (Henry Mancini) US:LP = Varese STV-81249*

3759 Lifeguard (1976) Theme (Paul Williams) US:SP = A&M 1853* [Paul Williams:ST]; Theme (Paul Williams) US:LP = A&M 4550* [Paul Williams: ST]

3760 Lifespan [Le Secret de la Vie] (1975) Score (Terry Riley) FR:LP = Stip ST-1011*

3761 Lift, The [L'Ascenseur] (1984) Score (Dick Mass) FR:LP = Milan A-242*

3762 Lift to the Scaffold *see* Frantic

3763 Light at the Edge of the

World, The [Il Faro in Capo al Mondo] (1971) Score (Piero Piccioni) IT:LP = General Music 55078*

3764 Light Fantastic, The (1963) Score (Joseph Liebman) US:LP = 20th FXG-5016/SXG-5016*

3765 Light in the Forest, The (1958) Theme (Paul Smith) US:SP = Disneyland 104 [Jerome Courtland]

3766 Light in the Piazza (1962) Theme (Mario Nascimbene) US:SP = Verve 10267 [Liane]; Theme (Mario Nascimbene) US:LP = Command 835* [Enoch Light]; Theme (Mario Nascimbene) US:LP = Columbia 1783/8583* [Percy Faith]

3767 Light of Heart *see* Life Begins at 8:30

3768 Light Touch, The [Touch and Go] (1951) Theme-A (John Addison) GB:78-PP = Rank FM-168 [ST]; Theme-B (John Addison) GB:78-PP = Rank FM-169 [ST]; Theme-A (John Addison) US:LP-BP = Citadel CTOFI-1 [@ST]

3769 Lighthouse Keeper's Daughter, The *see* Girl in the Bikini, The

3770 Li'l Abner (1959) Score (stage songs:Gene DePaul) US:LP = Columbia OL-5460/OS-2021*

3771 Lilac Time (1928) Theme [Silent I] (Nathaniel Shilkret) US:SP = Decca 9-28076 [Louis Armstrong]; Theme [Silent I] (Nathaniel Shilkret) US:LP = RCA 2560* [Gaylord Carter]; Theme [Silent I] (Nathaniel Shilkret) US:78 = RCA/Victor 21572 [Nathaniel Shilkret:ST]

3772 Lilacs in the Spring *see* Let's Make Up

3773 Lili (1952) Highlights (Bronislau Kaper) US:EP = MGM X-1025; Excerpts (Bronislau Kaper) US:LP-10 = MGM E-187 [@ST]

3774 Lili Marleen (1980) Score (Peer Raben) US:LP = DRG SL-9506*

3775 Lilies of the Field (1963) Score (Jerry Goldsmith) US:LP = Epic LN-24094/BN-26094*

3776 Lilith (1964) Score (Kenyon Hopkins) US:LP = Colpix CP-520/SCP-520*

3777 Lillian Russell (1940) Highlights (t:Alfred Newman/t:Bronislau Kaper/etc.) US:LP-BP = Caliban 6016

3778 Limbo *see* Women in Limbo

3779 Limbo Line (1968) Theme (Johnny Spence) US:LP = Fontana 67602* [Johnnie Gray]

3780 Limelight (1935) Themes- A-B/GB:78 = Decca 5880 [Arthur Tracy:ST]; Themes-C-D/GB:78 = Decca 5881 [Arthur Tracy:ST]; Themes-E-F/GB:78 = Decca 5882 [Arthur Tracy:ST]

3781 Limelight (1952) Excerpts (Charles Chaplin) IT:LP = RCA 33212* [Richard Vantellini]; Themes-A-B (Charles Chaplin) US:LP = London 1041 [Stanley Black]; Themes-A-B (Charles Chaplin) US:SP = London 45-1342 [Stanley Black]; Theme-C (Charles Chaplin) US:LP = Pelican 130 [@Charles Chaplin:ST]; Theme-D (Charles Chaplin) GB:78 = HMV 7891 [Charles Chaplin:ST]

3782 Limping Man, The (1953) Theme (Eric Spear) GB:78 = Parlophone 3645 [Eric Spear:ST]

3783 Lines Horizontal [Short] (1960) Themes (Pete Seeger) US:LP = Folkways 3851 [Pete Seeger:ST]

3784 Link (1986) Score (Jerry Goldsmith) US:LP = Varese STV-81294*

3785 Lion, The [Rage of the Lion] (1962) Score (Malcolm Arnold) US:LP = London M-76001

3786 Lion and the Horse, The (1952) Themes (Max Steiner) US:LP-MS-BP = Tony Thomas TTMS-9/10 [Max Steiner:ST]

3787 Lion in Winter, The (1968) Score (John Barry) US:LP = Columbia OS-3250*

3788 Lion of the Desert (1981) Score (Maurice Jarre) US:LP = Project PR-5107*

3789 Lions Are Loose, The [Les Lions sont Laches] (1961) Highlights (Georges Garvarentz) FR:EP = Barclay 70397

3790 Lipstick (1976) Score (Michel Polnareff) US:LP = Atlantic SD-18178*

3791 Liquid Sky (1983) Score (Slava Tsukerman & Brenda Hutchinson

& Clive Smith) US:LP-PP = Cinevista 2P-001* + US:LP = Varese STV-81181*

3792 Liquid Space (1974) Score (Phil Sorce & Dennis Noone) US:LP = Lighthouse LP1-101*

3793 Liquidator, The (1966) Score (Lalo Schifrin) US:LP = MGM E-4413/SE-4413*

3794 Lisa [The Inspector] (1962) Theme (Malcolm Arnold) US:SP = UA 470 [Ferrante & Teicher]; Theme (Malcolm Arnold) US:LP = UA 6249* [Ferrante & Teicher]; Theme (Malcolm Arnold) US:LP = Columbia 1880/8680* [Don Costa]

3795 Lisbon Story, The (1946) Themes/GB:78 = Parlophone 20545 [Richard Tauber:ST]

3796 List of Adrian Messenger, The (1963) Theme (Jerry Goldsmith) US:LP-BP = POO 104 [@ST]

3797 Listen Darling (1938) Theme-A/US:LP = Decca DEA-7-5 [Judy Garland:ST]; Theme-B/US:LP = AEI 2108 [Judy Garland:ST]

3798 Listen, Let's Make Love [Scusi, Facciamo Amore] (1968) Score (Ennio Morricone) US:LP-BP = GSF 1003

3799 Little, a Lot ... Passionately, A [Un Peu, Beaucoup ... Passionement] (1971) Score (Francois DeRoubaix) FR:LP = Pathe C062.92217*

3800 Little Ark, The (1972) Theme (Fred Karlin) US:SP = MGM 10717* [Springfield Revival:ST]; Theme (Fred Karlin) US:LP = MGM 4905* [Springfield Revival:ST]

3801 Little Big Horn [The Fighting 7th] (1951) Theme (Adams & Stock & Sigler) US:SP = RCA 47-4068 [Ralph Flanagan:ST]

3802 Little Big Man (1970) Underscore + Dialog (John Hammond) US:LP = Columbia S-30545*

3803 Little Bit of Heaven, A (1940) Themes/US:78 = Decca 3449 [Gloria Jean:ST]

3804 Little Boy Lost (1953) Excerpts (James Van Heusen) US:LP-10 = Decca DL-5556 + US:LP = Decca DL-4264 [Bing Crosby:ST]

3805 Little Colonel, The (1935) Themes / US:LP-MS = 20th 2-103 [Shirley Temple:ST]

3806 Little Damozel (1933) Theme-A/US:LP = Monmouth 7031 [Anna Neagle:ST]; Theme-B/GB:78 = HMV 4365 [Anna Neagle:ST]

3807 Little Fauss and Big Halsy (1970) Score (t:Johnny Cash/s:Carl Perkins) US:LP = Columbia S-30385*

3808 Little Fugitive, The (1953) Highlights (Eddy Manson) US:LP-10 = Folkways 35/2 + US:LP = Folkways FS-2070

3809 Little Girl Who Lives Down the Lane, The (1978) Score (Christian Gaubert) JA:LP = Polydor MPF-1087*

3810 Little House, The [Cartoon] (1952) Theme (Paul Smith) US:78 = Disneyland 88102 [ST]

3811 Little Hut, The (1957) Theme (Cochrane) US:SP = Liberty 55062 [The Jones Boys]

3812 Little Island, The [Short] Sequence + Dialog (Arthur Kleiner) US:LP-PP = Picture Book Parade 108 [@ST]

3813 Little Kidnappers, The [The Kidnappers] (1954) Theme (Bruce Montgomery) GB:78-PP = Rank FM-145 [ST]; Theme (Bruce Montgomery) US:LP-BP = Citadel CTOFI-1 [@ST]

3814 Little Laura and Big John (1973) Themes (Bill Walker) US:SP = Kodiak 711 [Mara Lynn Brown:ST]

3815 Little Lord Fauntleroy (1921) Theme [Silent II] (Arthur Kleiner) US:LP = Golden Crest 4019 [Arthur Kleiner:ST]

3816 Little Mermaid, The [Short] (1975) Highlights + Underscore + Dialog (Ron Goodwin) CA:LP = Capitol 6417*

3817 Little Minister, The (1934) Score (Max Steiner) US:LP-BP = Cinema LP-8016

3818 Little Miss Broadway (1937) Excerpts (Harold Spina) US:LP-MS = 20th 2-103 [Shirley Temple:ST]

3819 Little Miss Marker (1934) Themes / US:LP-BP = JJA 19811 [Dorothy Dell & Shirley Temple:ST]

3820 Little Nellie Kelly (1940) Highlights (e:Roger Edens/etc.) US:LP-BP = Cheerio 5000

3821 Little Night Music, A (1977) Score (stage songs:Stephen Sondheim) US:LP = Columbia JS-35333*

3822 Little Nuns, The [Le Monachine] (1965) Highlights (Ennio Morricone) US:LP = Cerberus CEMS-0115; Highlights (Ennio Morricone) IT:EP = CAM CEP-108

3823 Little Prince, The (1974) Score (Frederick Loewe) US:LP = ABC ABDP-854*

3824 Little Prince and the Eight-Headed Dragon, The (1963) Score (Akira Ifukube) JA:LP = Toho AX-8124

3825 Little Rebels, The [Chiens Perdus sans Colliers] (1955) Theme (Paul Misraki) US:SP = Mercury 12148 [Miyoshi Umeki]; Theme (Paul Misraki) US:LP = Mercury 70880 [Miyoshi Umeki]; Theme (Paul Misraki) US:LP = Mercury 20188 [Eddie Barclay]

3826 Little Red Lighthouse, The [Short] Sequence + Dialog (Arthur Kleiner) US:LP-PP = Picture Book Parade 103 [@ST]

3827 Little Red Monkey, The *see* Case of the Red Monkey, The

3828 Little Romance, A (1979) Score-A (s:Georges Delerue/t:William Goldstein) US:LP = Varese STV-81109*; Score-B (s:Georges Delerue/t:William Goldstein) JA:LP = Eastworld 81236*

3829 Little Shepherd of Kingdom Come, The (1961) Themes (Henry Vars) US:SP = Roulette 4318 [Jimmie Rodgers:ST]; Theme (Henry Vars) US:LP = London 237* [The Cambridge Strings]

3830 Little Shop of Horrors, The (1960) Score (as:Fred Katz) US:LP = Rhino RNSP-304

3831 Little Shop of Horrors (1986) Score (stage songs:Alan Menken) US:LP = Geffen GHS-24125*

3832 Little Toot *see* Melody Time

3833 Little Women (1933) Theme (Max Steiner) US:LP = RCA 1170 [Max Steiner:ST]

3834 Little Women (1949) Theme (Adolph Deutsch) JA:LP = UA MAX-32* [@Stanley Maxfield]

3835 Littlest Horse Thieves, The [Escape from the Dark] (1977) Score (Ron Goodwin) GB:LP = EMI 3148*

3836 Littlest Outlaw, The (1955) Theme + Underscore + Dialog (t:Edmund Santos/u:William Lava) US:LP = Disneyland DQ-1264 + US:LP-MS = Disneyland DDF-4

3837 Live a Little, Love a Little (1968) Excerpts (t:Billy Strange/etc.) US:LP = Camden CAS-2440* [Elvis Presley:ST]

3838 Live a Little, Steal a Lot *see* Murph the Surf

3839 Live and Let Die (1973) Score (s:George Martin/t:Paul McCartney) US:LP = UA LA-100*

3840 Live for Life (1967) Score (s:Francis Lai/t:Raymond Le Senechal) US:LP = UA UAL-4165/UAS-5165*

3841 Lively Set, The (1964) Score (Bobby Darin) US:LP = Decca DL-9119/DL-79119*

3842 Living Dead at the Manchester Morgue, The *see* Don't Open the Window

3843 Living Desert, The (1953) Highlights (Paul Smith) US:LP = Buena Vista BV-3326 + US:EP = RCA ERA-1

3844 Living End, The *see* Rock Pretty Baby

3845 Living Free (1972) Score (Sol Kaplan) US:LP = RCA LSO-1172*

3846 Living Idol, The (1957) Theme (Edward Heyman) US:LP = MGM 3480* + US:LP = MGM 4064* [Leroy Holmes]

3847 Living in a Big Way (1947) Theme/GB:LP = Decca 5265 [Gene Kelly:ST]

3848 Living It Up (1954) Highlights (Jule Styne) US:EP = Capitol EAP1-533 [Dean Martin & Jerry Lewis:ST]

3849 Living Word, The (1982) Score (Edward David Zeliff) US:LP = AEI 3112*

3850 Liza (1972) Score (Philippe Sarde) FR:LP = Epic 64.994*

3851 Lizstomania (1975) Score (as:Rick Wakeman) US:LP = A&M SP-4546*

3852 Lizzie (1957) Themes (Robert Allen/Burt Bacharach) US:SP = Columbia 4-40851 [Johnny Mathis:ST]; Themes (Robert Allen/Burt Bacharach) US:LP = Columbia 34667* [Johnny Mathis:ST]

3853 Local Hero (1983) Score

(Mark Knopfler) US:LP = WB 23827-1*

3854 Logan's Run (1976) Score (Jerry Goldsmith) US:LP = MGM MG1-5302*

3855 Lola (1982) Score (Peer Raben) FR:LP = Milan/SPI 120.123*; Highlights (Peer Raben) US:LP = DRG SL-9508*

3856 Lola Montes (1955) Themes (Georges Auric) US:SP = Columbia 4-40689 [Felicia Sanders]; Theme (Georges Auric) US:SP = RCA 47-6537 [Hugo Winterhalter]; Theme (Georges Auric) US:LP = Columbia 107 [Michel Legrand]

3857 Lolita (1962) Score (s:Nelson Riddle/t:Bob Harris) US:LP = MGM E-4050/SE-4050*

3858 Lollipop *see* Forever Young, Forever Free

3859 Lollipop Cover, The (1966) Score (Ruby Raksin) US:LP = Mainstream 56067/S-6067*

3860 London Belongs to Me *see* Dulcimer Street

3861 London Melody [Girls in the Street] (1937) Theme (Robert Farnon) GB:78 = HMV 10087 [Robert Farnon: ST]

3862 London Town (1946) Themes-A-B/GB:78 = Decca 8672 [Sid Field:ST]; Themes-C-D/GB:78 = Decca 8674 [Ann Sullivan/Beryl Davis:ST]; Theme-E/GB:78 = Decca 8675 [Beryl Davis:ST]; Theme-F/GB:78 = Decca 8676 [Beryl Davis:ST]

3863 Lone Ranger and the Lost City of Gold, The (1958) Themes (Les Baxter) US:SP = UA 129 [Bob Carroll]; Theme (Les Baxter) US:LP-BP = Disc 105 [@Bob Carroll]

3864 Lone Wolf McQuade (1983) Score (Francesco DeMasi) US:LP = Citadel CTV-7024*

3865 Lonedale Operator, The (1911) Excerpts [Silent II] (Charles Hofmann) US:LP = Sounds Good SG-1001 [Charles Hofmann:ST]

3866 Loneliness of the Long Distance Runner, The [Rebel with a Cause] (1962) Theme (John Addison) US:SP = London 9571 [Chris Barber]; Theme (John Addison) US:LP = WB 1548* [Werner Muller]

3867 Lonely Guy, The (1984) Highlights (e:Jerry Goldsmith/etc.) US:EP-12 = MCA 36010*

3868 Lonely Lady (1983) Score (e: Charles Calello/etc.) US:LP = Allegiance AV-441*

3869 Lonely Man, The (1957) Theme (Nathan Van Cleave) US:SP = Capitol 3700 [Tennessee Ernie Ford:ST]; Theme (Nathan Van Cleave) US:LP = Pickwick 3047 [Tennessee Ernie Ford: ST]

3870 Long Ago Tomorrow [The Raging Moon] (1971) Score (Stanley Myers) GB:LP = Columbia/EMI 6447*; Theme (Burt Bacharach) US:SP = Scepter 12335* [B.J. Thomas]; Theme (Burt Bacharach) US:LP = A&M 3527* [Burt Bacharach]

3871 Long and the Short and the Tall, The *see* Jungle Fighters

3872 Long Day's Dying, The (1968) Themes (Malcolm Lockyer) GB:SP = Mercury 1050 [Malcolm Lockyer:ST]

3873 Long Day's Journey into Night (1962) Theme (Andre Previn) US: SP = Columbia 4-42596 [Andre Previn: ST]; Theme (Andre Previn) US:LP-BP = Cinema 8001 [@Andre Previn:ST]; Theme (Andre Previn) US:LP = Columbia 1880/8680* [Don Costa]

3874 Long Duel, The (1967) Score (John Scott) US:LP = Atco 33-228/SD-33-228*

3875 Long Good Friday, The (1983) Score (Francis Monkman) GB: LP = Nimbus CES-1001*

3876 Long Goodbye, The (1973) Theme (John Williams) US:SP = Bluenote 189* [Lou Donaldson]; Theme (John Williams) US:LP = Bluenote 024* [Lou Donaldson] + US:LP-BP = Centurion 1600* [@Lou Donaldson]

3877 Long Hair of Death, The [I Lunghi Capelli della Morte] (1964) Themes (Carlo Rustichelli) IT:SP = CAM 45-14 [ST]

3878 Long Hot Summer, The (1958) Score (Alex North) US:LP = Roulette R-25026

3879 Long John Silver (1955) Highlights (David Buttolph) US:LP-10 = RCA LPM-3279

3880 Long Memory, The (1953)

Theme (William Alwyn) GB:78-PP = Rank FM-134 [ST]

3881 Long Ride Home, The *see* Time for Killing, A

3882 Long Riders, The (1980) Score (Ry Cooder) US:LP = WB HS-3448*

3883 Long Ships, The (1964) Score (Dusan Radic) US:LP = Colpix CP-517/SCP-517*

3884 Long Wait, The (1954) Theme (Harold Spina) US:SP = Columbia 4-39577 [Toni Arden]; Theme (Harold Spina) US:SP = MGM 11073 [Billy Eckstine]

3885 Long White Trail, The (1977) Score (s:Neil Lancaster/t:Mike Hugg) GB:LP = Philips 6308.138*

3886 Longest Day, The (1962) Highlights (e:Maurice Jarre/t:Paul Anka) FR:EP = Barclay 70474; Theme + Dialog (Paul Anka) US:LP = 20th FXG-5007/SXG-5007*; Theme (Paul Anka) US:SP = Columbia 4-42585 [Mitch Miller]

3887 Look Before You Love (1948) Theme (Bretton Byrd) GB:78-PP = Rank FM-47 [ST]

3888 Look for the Silver Lining (1949) Highlights (pop music) US:LP-BP = Titania 504

3889 Look in Any Window (1961) Theme (Paul Anka) US:SP = Columbia 4-41964 [Mike Clifford]

3890 Look Out Sister [Short] (1948) Highlights (various) GB:LP = Krazy Kat KK-7415 [Louis Jordan:ST]; Themes/US:LP = MCA 1337 [Louis Jordan:ST]

3891 Look to the Leader [Industrial Short] Score (Russ David) US:LP-PP = Budweiser U-16769

3892 Look Up and Laugh (1935) Themes-A-B/GB:78 = Regal 1793 [Gracie Fields:ST]; Theme-C/GB:78 = Regal 1794 [Gracie Fields:ST]

3893 Looker (1981) Theme (Barry DeVorzon) US:SP = WB 49851* [Sue Saad:ST]

3894 Lookin' Good *see* Corky

3895 Looking for Love (1964) Score (Stan Vincent) US:LP = MGM E-4229/SE-4229*

3896 Looking for Mr. Goodbar (1977) Score (t:Artie Kane/s:pop music) US:LP = Columbia JS-35029*

3897 Looking Glass War, The (1970) Theme (Walter Stott-aka-Angela Morley) US:LP-MS = Longines 5312/6* [@Walter Stott:ST]; Theme (Walter Stott-aka-Angela Morley) GB:LP = Philips 6308.111* [Chaquito]

3898 Looking on the Bright Side (1932) Themes-A-B/GB:78 = HMV 4258 [Gracie Fields:ST]; Themes-C-D/GB:78 = HMV 4260 [Gracie Fields:ST]; Theme-E/GB:78 = HMV 4259 [Gracie Fields:ST]

3899 Loose Connections (1983) Score (Dominic Muldowney) AU:LP = Virgin V-2306*

3900 Loot (1972) Score (Keith Mansfield & Richard Denton) GB:LP = CBS 70073*

3901 Lorca and the Outlaws (1985) Highlights (Tony Banks) US:LP = Atlantic 81680* [Tony Banks:ST]

3902 Lord Byron of Broadway (1930) Themes/US:LP-BP = JJA 19802 [@Charles Kaley:ST]

3903 Lord Jim (1965) Score (Bronislau Kaper) US:LP = Colpix CP-521/SCP-521*

3904 Lord Love a Duck (1966) Score (Neal Hefti) US:LP = UA UAL-4137/UAS-5137*

3905 Lord of the Flies (1963) Theme (Raymond Leppard) US:SP = London 9629 [Ted Heath]; Theme (Raymond Leppard) US:LP = Ava 30* [@ST]

3906 Lord of the Rings, The (1978) Score (Leonard Rosenman) US:LP-MS = Fantasy LOR-1* + US:LP-MS = Fantasy LOR-PD-2*

3907 Lord Shango (1975) Score (Howard Roberts) US:LP = Bryan BRS-104*

3908 Lords of Flatbush, The (1974) Score (Joe Brooks) US:LP = ABC ABCD-828*

3909 Loser Takes All (1956) Theme (Alessandro Cicognini) US:SP = Capitol 3503 [Cliff Townsend]

3910 Losin' It (1983) Score (pop music) US:LP = Regency RI-8507*

3911 Loss of Innocence [The Greengage Summer] (1961) Score (Richard Addinsell) US:LP = Colpix CP-508

3912 Lost Command, The (1966) Score (Franz Waxman) US:LP-BP = Cinema LP-8017

3913 Lost Continent [Continente Perduto] (1955) Score (A.F. Lavagnino) US:LP = MGM E-3635

3914 Lost Honor of Katharina Blum, The [Die Verlorene Ehre der Katharina Blum] (1975) Highlights (Hans-Werner Henze) US:LP = Varese STV-81224*

3915 Lost Horizon (1937) Highlights (Dimitri Tiomkin) US:LP = RCA ARL1-1669* [Charles Gerhardt]; Theme (Dimitri Tiomkin) US:LP = Coral 57006 [Dimitri Tiomkin:ST]

3916 Lost Horizon (1973) Score (Burt Bacharach) US:LP = Bell 1300*

3917 Lost Man, The (1969) Score (Quincy Jones) US:LP = UNI 73060*

3918 Lost Moment, The (1947) Theme (Daniele Amfitheatrof) US:LP = Decca 8060 [Victor Young]

3919 Lost Patrol, The (1934) Themes (Max Steiner) US:LP-BP = Max Steiner Music Society 25781 [Max Steiner:ST]

3920 Lost Weekend, The (1945) Score (Miklos Rozsa) US:LP-BP = Tony Thomas TTMR-2; Excerpts (Miklos Rozsa) US:LP = RCA ARL1-0911* [Charles Gerhardt]; Theme (Miklos Rozsa) US:LP = Deutsche 2584.013* [Miklos Rozsa:ST]

3921 Lost World, The (1960) Themes (pop music) US:SP = 20th 209 [Fernando Lamas:ST]

3922 Louie Bluie (1985) Score (pop music) US:LP = Arhoolie 1095*

3923 Louise *see* Dear Louise

3924 Louisiana Purchase (1941) Excerpts (stage songs:Irving Berlin) US: LP-BP = JJA 19746 [@ST]

3925 Louisiana Story (1948) Highlights-A (Virgil Thomson) US:LP = Decca DL-9616 [Thomas Scherman]; Highlights-B (Virgil Thomson) US:LP = Columbia ML-2087 [Eugene Ormandy]; Highlights-B (Virgil Thomson) US:LP = Turnabout 34534* [Siegfried Landau]

3926 Louve Solitaire, La [The Golden Claw's Cat Girls] Theme (Francis Lai) US:LP = UA 5630* [Francis Lai: ST]

3927 Love a la Carte [Hungry for Love] [A Dua e le Compagne] (1960) Theme-A (Johnny Farina) US:SP = Canadian American 182 [Santo & Johnny:ST]; Theme-B (Piero Piccioni) IT:LP = Cinevox CJO-1* [@ST]

3928 Love and Anarchy [Film d'Amore e d'Anarchia] (1972) Score (e: Nino Rota/etc.) IT:LP = Cinevox 33/67*

3929 Love and Kisses (1965) Excerpts (various) US:LP = Decca DL-4678/DL-74678* [Rick Nelson:ST]

3930 Love and Learn (1947) Theme (Ray Heindorf) US:78 = Capitol 402 [Skitch Henderson]

3931 Love and Sacrifice *see* America

3932 Love and the Frenchwoman [La Francais et l'Amour] (1960) Highlights (Paul Misraki) FR:EP = Versailles 90-M-323

3933 Love at First Bite (1979) Score (Charles Bernstein) US:LP = Parachute RRLP-9016*

3934 Love at the Top [The French Way] [Le Mouton Enrage] (1974) Themes (at:Jose Berghmans) FR:SP = RCA FPB-00019* [ST]

3935 Love Cage *see* Joy House

3936 Love Child *see* Child Under a Leaf

3937 Love Circle *see* One Night at Dinner

3938 Love Comes Along (1930) (Oscar Levant) Themes/US:78 = RCA/Victor 22283 [Bebe Daniels:ST]

3939 Love Finds Andy Hardy (1938) Theme-A/US:LP = Decca 6020 [Judy Garland:ST]; Theme-B/US:LP = MGM 4005 [Judy Garland:ST]; Theme-C/US:LP = Decca DEA-7-5 [Judy Garland:ST]; Theme-D/US:LP-BP = Out Take 3 [@Judy Garland:ST]

3940 Love Goddesses, The (1965) Highlights (Percy Faith) US:LP = Columbia CL-2209/CS-9009*

3941 Love Happy (1949) Theme (Ann Ronell) US:78 = MGM 10535 [Marion Hutton:ST]

3942 Love Has Many Faces (1965) Theme (David Raksin) US:SP = Capitol 5340 [Nancy Wilson:ST]; Theme (David Raksin) US:LP = Capitol 2321* [Nancy Wilson:ST]

3943 Love, I Think / Theme (Minucci) US: LP = RCA 1-0210* [Los Indios Tabajaras]

3944 Love in a Goldfish Bowl (1961) Theme-A (Russ Faith) US:SP = Chancellor 1079 [Fabian:ST]; Theme-B (Burt Bacharach) US:SP = Capitol 4580 [Tommy Sands:ST]; Theme-B (Burt Bacharach) US:LP = MGM 4064* [Leroy Holmes]

3945 Love in Four Dimensions (1963) Score (Franco Mannino) US: LP = Request RLP-8090/SRLP-8090*

3946 Love in Germany, A [Un Amour en Allemagne] (1984) Score (Michel Legrand) FR:LP = Milan A-218*

3947 Love in Las Vegas *see* Viva Las Vegas

3948 Love in the Afternoon (1957) Highlights (t:Matty Malneck/etc.) US: EP = Verve V-5055; Theme (Matty Malneck) US:EP = MGM 1549 [David Rose]

3949 Love in the City [L'Amore in Citta] (1953) Theme (Mario Nascimbene) IT:LP-MS = Kangaroo 34209 [Mario Nascimbene:ST]

3950 Love in the Rain [Loving in the Rain] [Un Amour de Pluie] (1974) Score (Francis Lai) FR:LP = Polydor 2393.078*; Theme (Francis Lai) US: LP = Audio Fidelity 6301* [Francis Lai: ST]

3951 Love Is a Ball [All This and Money Too] (1963) Score (Michel Legrand) US:LP = Philips PHM-200.082/PHS-600.082*

3952 Love Is a Funny Thing [Un Homme Qui Me Plait] (1969) Score (Francis Lai) US:LP = UA UAS-5207*

3953 Love Is a Many Splendored Thing (1955) Highlights (e:Alfred Newman/t:Sammy Fain) US:LP-BP = Cinema LP-8013*; Theme (Sammy Fain) US:SP = MCA 60010 [The Four Aces]; Theme (Sammy Fain) US:LP = Capitol 1652* + US:LP = Angel 36066* [Alfred Newman:ST]

3954 Love Is My Profession [En Cas de Malheur] (1958) Highlights (Rene Cloerec) US:LP = Everest LPBR-5076/ SDBR-1076*

3955 Love Is the Answer [Got to Investigate Silicone] [Industrial Short] Highlights (Harold Beebe) US:LP-PP = General Electric QP-1001*

3956 Love Letters (1945) Theme (Victor Young) US:SP = Decca 9-23468 [Victor Young:ST]; Theme (Victor Young) US:LP = Decca 8056 + US:LP = Decca 8285 + US:LP = Decca 8798 [Victor Young:ST]

3957 Love, Life and Laughter (1934) Themes-A-B/GB:78 = HMV 8140 [Gracie Fields:ST]; Themes-C-D/ GB:78 = HMV 8141 [Gracie Fields: ST]

3958 Love Lottery, The (1954) Theme (Bernard) GB:SP = Parlophone 3831 [Ron Goodwin]

3959 Love Machine, The (1971) Score (s:Artie Butler/t:Burt Bacharach) US:LP = Scepter 595*

3960 Love Mates *see* Madly

3961 Love Me Forever (1935) Theme/US:LP = Decca 9593 [Grace Moore:ST]

3962 Love Me or Leave Me (1955) Score (pop music) US:LP = Columbia CL-710/CS-8773e + US:LP = CSP ACS-8773e [Doris Day:ST]

3963 Love Me Strangely [The Lovely Monster] [Un Beau Monstre] (1970) Score (Georges Garvarentz) FR: LP = Pathe C062.11430*

3964 Love Me Tender (1956) Highlights (Vera Matson & Elvis Presley) US: EP = RCA EPA-4006 [Elvis Presley:ST]

3965 Love Me Tonight (1932) Excerpts (Richard Rodgers) US:LP-BP = JJA 19766 + US:LP-BP = Caliban 6047 [@ST]

3966 Love Melody *see* Melody

3967 Love Minus One (1972) Score (Denny Vaughan) US:LP = Margabi LM1-001*

3968 Love on a Pillow [Le Repos du Guerrier] (1962) Highlights (Michel Magne) FR:EP = Barclay 70473

3969 Love on the River (1968) Theme (J. Bradtke) US:LP = RCA 4022* [Hugo Montenegro]

3970 Love on the Run [L'Amour en Fuite] (1979) Themes (Georges Delerue) FR:SP = RCA 8300* [ST]

3971 Love Parade, The (1929) Highlights (Richard Rodgers) US:LP-BP = La Nadine 260

3972 Love Songs [Words and

Music] [Paroles et Musique] (1985) Score (Michel Legrand) US:LP = Varese STV-81258*

3973 Love Story [A Lady Surrenders] (1944) Theme (Hubert Bath) US: SP = Columbia 4-51808 [Liberace]; Theme (Hubert Bath) US:LP = Capitol 8598* + US:LP = Angel 36062* [Leonard Pennario]; Theme (Hubert Bath) US:LP-10 = Columbia 2092 [Hubert Bath:ST]

3974 Love Story (1970) Score (Francis Lai) US:LP = Paramount PAS-6002* + US:LP = MCA 27017*; Underscore + Dialog (Francis Lai) US: LP-MS = Paramount PAS-2-7000*

3975 Love with the Proper Stranger (1963) Theme (Elmer Bernstein) US: SP = Kapp 571 [Jack Jones:ST]; Theme (Elmer Bernstein) US:LP = Kapp 3365* [Jack Jones:ST]; Theme (Elmer Bernstein) US:LP = RCA 2926* [Dick Schory]

3976 Lovely Monster, The *see* Love Me Strangely

3977 Lovely to Look At [Roberta] (1952) Highlights (stage songs:Jerome Kern) US:LP-10 = MGM E-150 + US: LP = MGM E-3230 + US:LP-MS = MGM 2SES-50

3978 Lovely Way to Die, A (1968) Theme (Kenyon Hopkins) US:LP = Decca 75034* [Marge Dodson:ST]

3979 Lovemaker, The [Calle Mayor] [M'sieur la Caille] (1956) Theme (Joseph Kosma) US:SP = Columbia 4-40692 [Michel Legrand]

3980 Lover Come Back (1962) Themes (Frank DeVol/W. Landau) US: LP-PP = CSP XTV-82021 [Doris Day: ST]; Theme-A (Frank DeVol) US:SP = Columbia 4-42295 [Doris Day:ST]; Theme-B (W. Landau) US:SP = Columbia 4-42260 [Doris Day:ST]

3981 Lovers and Lollipops (1956) Themes (Eddy Manson) US:SP = MGM 12250 [Eddy Manson:ST]; Theme (Eddy Manson) US:LP = Columbia 107 [Michel Legrand]

3982 Lovers and Other Strangers (1970) Score (Fred Karlin) US:LP = ABC SOC-15*

3983 Lovers Like Us [The Savage] [Le Sauvage] (1976) Score (Michel Legrand) FR:Barclay 80590*

3984 Lovers of Teruel, The [Les Amants de Teruel] (1962) Highlights (Mikis Theodorakis) FR:EP = Philips 432.790; Theme (Mikis Theodorakis) US:LP = Philips 600.071 [@ST]

3985 Loves and Times of Scaramouche, The [Le Avventure e gli Amori de Scaramouche] (1977) Themes (Franco Bixio & Vincenzo Tempera & Fabio Frizzi) IT:SP = Cinevox MDF-088* [ST]

3986 Loves of Carmen, The (1927) Theme [Silent I] (Manuel Ponce) US: LP = RCA 2560* [Gaylord Carter]

3987 Loves of Isadora, The [Isadora] (1968) Score (e:Maurice Jarre/ae: Anthony Bowles/etc.) US:LP = Kapp KS-5511*

3988 Loves of Joanna Godden, The (1947) Excerpts (Ralph Vaughan-Williams) US:LP = Columbia RL-3029 + US:LP = Ariel CBF-13 [@Ernest Irving]

3989 Loving and Laughing (1981) Score (Paul Baillargeon) CA:LP = GAP 1052*

3990 Loving Couples (1980) Score (Fred Karlin) US:LP = Motown M8-949*

3991 Loving in the Rain *see* Love in the Rain

3992 Loving Touch, The *see* Psycho Lover

3993 Loving You (1957) Highlights-A (various) US:LP = RCA LPM-1515/ LSP-1515e + US:LP = RCA AFL1-1515e [Elvis Presley:ST]; Highlights-B (various) US:LP-BP = Pirate PR-101 [Elvis Presley:ST]

3994 Low Price of Fame, The (1970) Themes (Jim Helms) US:SP = Carvel 106* [Gary Le Mel & Jim Helms: ST]

3995 Luck of Ginger Coffey, The (1964) Theme (Bernardo Segall) US: SP = RCA 47-8424 [Ketty Lester]; Theme (Bernardo Segall) US:LP = RCA 3342* [Marty Gold]; Theme (Bernardo Segall) US:LP = WB 1575* [Joanie Sommers]

3996 Lucky Boy (1929) Theme (L. Wolfe Gilbert) US:78 = ARA 4515 [George Jessel:ST]; Theme (L. Wolfe Gilbert) US:LP = Stanyan 10096* [Rod McKuen]

3997 Lucky Duck (1928) Theme [Silent I] (H. Whitney) US:LP = Golden Crest 4019 [Arthur Kleiner]

3998 Lucky in Love (1929) Themes/US:78 = RCA/Victor 22048 [Morton Downey:ST]

3999 Lucky Kid, The *see* Kid for Two Farthings, A

4000 Lucky Lady (1975) Score (e:Ralph Burns/t:John Kander/etc.) US:LP = Arista AL-4069*

4001 Lucky Luciano (1974) Score (Piero Piccioni) IT:LP = CBS 70130*

4002 Lucky Luke (1971) Score (Claude Bolling) GB:LP = UA 29290*

4003 Lucky Luke—The Ballad of the Daltons [Lucky Luke—La Ballade des Daltons] (1978) Score (Claude Bolling) FR:LP = RCA 37195*

4004 Lucky Me (1954) Highlights (Sammy Fain) US:LP-BP = Athena LMIB-9

4005 Lucky Pierre [French Mustard] [La Moutarde Me Monte au Nez] (1974) Themes (Vladimir Cosma) FR:SP = Pathe C008.12998* [ST]

4006 Lucy Gallant (1955) Theme (Jay Livingston & Ray Evans) US:SP = Capitol 3154 [The Four Freshmen]

4007 Ludwig (1973) Score (classical music) GB:LP = Philips S1-5401* [Franco Mannino:ST]

4008 Lullaby Land [Cartoon] (1933) Theme (Frank Churchill) US:78 = RCA/Bluebird BK-6 [ST]

4009 Lullaby of Broadway, The (1951) Highlights (pop music) US:LP-10 = Columbia CL-6168 + US:LP = CSP P-18421 [Doris Day:ST]

4010 Lulu Belle (1948) Highlights (Henry Russell) US:78-MS = Coast C-10 [Dorothy Lamour:ST]

4011 Lumiere (1976) Score (Astor Piazzolla) IT:LP = Carosello 25059*

4012 Lupin III—Cagliostro Castle (1980) Score (Ugi Ohno) JA:LP = Columbia CX-7090*

4013 Lust for Life (1956) Highlights (Miklos Rozsa) US:LP = Decca DL-10015/DL-710015* + US:LP = Varese VC-81053*

4014 Luther (1974) Underscore + Dialog (John Addison) US:LP-MS = Caedmon TRS-363

4015 Luv (1967) Theme (Gerry Mulligan) US:LP = World Pacific 21864* [Bud Shank]

4016 Luxury Liner (1948) Themes-A-B/US:78 = MGM 30136 [Lauritz Melchior:ST]; Theme-C/US:78 = Columbia 38185 [Xavier Cugat:ST]; Theme-D/US:78 = Capitol 15233 [The Pied Pipers:ST]

4017 Lydia (1941) Highlights (Miklos Rozsa) US:LP = Citadel CT-7010* + US:LP = Varese STV-81166* [Albert Dominguez]; Excerpts (Miklos Rozsa) US:LP = Deutsche 2584.021* [Miklos Rozsa:ST]; Excerpts (Miklos Rozsa) US:LP = Varese 704.260* [Elmer Bernstein]

M

4018 M*A*S*H (1970) Highlights + Underscore + Dialog (Johnny Mandel) US:LP = Columbia OS-3520 + US:LP = Columbia S-32753*

4019 Macaroni (1985) Highlights (Armando Trovajoli) IT:EP-12 = General Music 30016*

4020 MacArthur (1977) Score (Jerry Goldsmith) US:LP = MCA 2287*

4021 Macbeth (1971) Score (The Third Ear Band) GB:LP = EMI/Harvest 4019*

4022 McCabe and Mrs. Miller (1971) Highlights (pop music) GB:EP = CBS 9162* [Leonard Cohen:ST]

4023 McConnell Story, The [Tiger in the Sky] (1955) Theme (film theme from "My Reputation") US:LP = RCA 1170 [Max Steiner:ST]

4024 Machine Gun Kelly (1958) Theme (Gerald Fried) US:LP-BP = GSF 1002 [@Gerald Fried:ST]

4025 Machine Gun McCain (1970) Score (Ennio Morricone) US:LP-BP = EM 1002

4026 Macho Callahan (1970) Theme (Patrick Williams) US:LP = A&R 7100.003* [Patrick Williams:ST]

4027 Mack, The (1973) Score-A [Original Release] (Willie Hutch) US:LP = Motown M6-766*; Score-B [1983 Re-Release] (Alan Silvestri) US:LP = ALA 1995*

4028 MacKenna's Gold (1969) Score (Quincy Jones) US:LP = RCA LSP-4096*

4029 Mackintosh and T.J. (1976) Score (t:Waylon Jennings/etc.) US: LP = RCA APL1-1520*

4030 Mackintosh Man, The (1973) Theme (Maurice Jarre) US:SP = WB 575* [Maurice Jarre:ST]; Theme (Maurice Jarre) US:LP-BP = Centurion 1600* [@Maurice Jarre:ST]

4031 McLintock (1963) Score (Frank DeVol) US:LP = UA UAL-4112/ UAS-5112*

4032 Macon County Line (1974) Theme (Bobbie Gentry) US:SP-PP = American International 94312 [ST]

4033 McQ (1974) Theme (Elmer Bernstein) JA:SP = TAM 1061* [Stanley Maxfield]; Theme (Elmer Bernstein) JA: LP = TAM 2007* [Stanley Maxfield]

4034 McVicar (1980) Score (s:Billy Nicholls/t:Jeff Wayne) US:LP = Polydor PD1-6284*

4035 Mad About Men (1955) Theme/GB:SP = Columbia 5149 [Glynis Johns:ST]

4036 Mad About Music (1938) Theme/US:78-MS = Decca 75 [Deanna Durbin:ST]

4037 Mad Adventures of Rabbi Jacob, The (1974) Score (Vladimir Cosma) US:LP = London PS-652*

4038 Mad Dogs and Englishmen (1970) Scores (rock music) US:LP-MS = A&M SP-6002* [Joe Cocker:ST]

4039 Mad Max (1980) Score (Brian May) US:LP = Varese STV-81144*

4040 Mad Max—Beyond Thunderdome (1985) Score (e:Maurice Jarre/ e:various) US:LP = Capitol SWAV-12429*; Theme [Fanfare/Thunderdome Music] (Maurice Jarre) US: LP = CBS 42307* [Maurice Jarre:ST]

4041 Mad Max II *see* Road Warrior, The

4042 Mad Monster Party (1967) Score (Maury Laws) US:LP-PP = Rankin/Bass RB-1001*

4043 Madame Bovary (1933) Highlights (Darius Milhaud) US:LP = Golden Crest S-4060* [Grant Johannesen]

4044 Madame Bovary (1949) Score (Miklos Rozsa) US:LP = Film Music Collection FMC-12* [Elmer Bernstein]; Excerpts (Miklos Rozsa) US:LP = MGM E-3507 [Miklos Rozsa:ST]

4045 Madame Claude *see* French Woman, The

4046 Madame Claude II *see* Intimate Moments

4047 Madame Rosa [La Vie Devant Soi] (1978) Score (Philippe Sarde) FR: LP = Polydor 2393.182*

4048 Madame X (1966) Score (e:Frank Skinner/etc.) US:LP = Decca DL-9152/DL-79152*

4049 Madchen mit Gewalt (1969) Theme (The Can) GB:LP = UA 29283* [The Can:ST]

4050 Maddalena (1971) Score (Ennio Morricone) IT:LP = General Music 55063*

4051 Made for Each Other (1971) Score (Trade Martin) US:LP = Buddah BDS-5111*

4052 Made in Italy [A l'Italienne] (1966) Score (e:Carlo Rustichelli/e:Piero Umiliani) IT:LP = RCA SP-8015*

4053 Made in Paris (1966) Theme (Burt Bacharach) US:SP = Reprise 0435 [Trini Lopez]; Theme (Burt Bacharach) US:LP = Command 894* [Enoch Light]

4054 Madeleine (1949) Theme (William Alwyn) GB:78-PP = Rank FM-100 [ST]

4055 Madeline [Cartoon] (1952) Excerpts (David Raksin) US:LP-PP-MS = Library of Congress LOC-RAKSIN [David Raksin:ST]

4056 Madeline's Rescue [Short] Sequence + Dialog (Arthur Kleiner) US: LP-PP = Picture Book Parade 108 [@ST]

4057 Madly [Love Mates] (1973) Score (Francis Lai) FR:LP = Barclay 920.283*; Theme (Francis Lai) US:LP = UA 5515* [Francis Lai:ST]

4058 Madness of the Heart (1949) Theme (Allan Gray) GB:78-PP = Rank FM-69 [ST]

4059 Mado (1977) Excerpts (Philippe Sarde) FR:LP = Festival 667* [Philippe Sarde:ST]

4060 Madron (1970) Score (Riz Ortolani) US:LP = Quad QUS-5001*

4061 Madwoman of Chaillot, The (1969) Score (Michael J. Lewis) US:LP = WB WS-1805*

4062 Mafioso (1962) Themes (Piero Piccioni) IT:SP = PMD 31316* [ST]

4063 Mag [Industrial Short] Highlights (Dick Marx) US:LP-10-PP = Time/Life U-7002

4064 Maggie, The *see* High and Dry

4065 Magic Bullet *see* Dr. Ehrlich's Magic Bullet

4066 Magic Christian, The (1970) Highlights + Underscore + Dialog (t:Paul McCartney/u:Ken Thorne/etc.) US:LP = United Commonwealth 6004*

4067 Magic Donkey, The *see* Donkey Skin

4068 Magic Fire (1956) Score (as:Erich Wolfgang Korngold) US:LP = Varese STV-81179

4069 Magic Flute, The (1976) Scores (classical music) GB:LP-MS3 = BBC REK-223*; Score (classical music) US:LP = A&M SP-4577*

4070 Magic Fountain, The (1961) Theme (Don George) US:SP = Dot 16645 [Steve Allen:ST]; Theme (Don George) US:LP = Dot 25597* [Steve Allen:ST]

4071 Magic Garden, The [Pennywhistle Blues] (1951) Theme (Willard Cele) US:SP = RCA 47-5052 [Freddy Martin]; Theme (Willard Cele) GB:78 = London 1038 [Willard Cele:ST]

4072 Magic Garden of Stanley Sweetheart, The (1970) Score (t:Michel Legrand/t:Jerry Styner/etc.) US:LP = MGM 1SE-20*

4073 Magic Michael [Short] Sequence + Dialog (Arthur Kleiner) US: LP-PP = Picture Book Parade 106 [@ST]

4074 Magic of Lassie, The (1978) Score-A (Richard & Robert Sherman) US:LP = Peter Pan 155*; Score-B (Richard & Robert Sherman) GB:LP = Pickwick SHM-992*

4075 Magic Pony, The (1979) Score (Tom Williams) US:LP = West End WE-102*

4076 Magic World, The (1957) Themes (William Van Ness) US:LP = Design DLP-21 [Pop Concert at Carnegie Hall]

4077 Magnet, The (1951) Theme (William Alwyn) GB:78-PP = Rank FM-101 [ST]

4078 Magnificent Ambersons, The (1942) Themes (Bernard Herrmann) US: LP = Unicorn 72008* [Bernard Herrmann:ST]; Theme (Bernard Herrmann) US:LP = London 44144* [Bernard Herrmann:ST]

4079 Magnificent Cuckold, The [Il Magnifico Cornuto] (1964) Theme (Armando Trovajoli) IT:LP = RCA 10388 [Armando Trovajoli:ST]

4080 Magnificent Doll, The (1946) Highlights (Hans J. Salter) US:LP-MS-BP = Tony Thomas TTHS-1/2

4081 Magnificent Matador, The [The Brave and the Beautiful] (1955) Theme (Edward L. Alperson, Jr.) US: SP = Capitol 3137 [Connie Russell]

4082 Magnificent Obsession, The (1954) Score (as:Frank Skinner) US: LP = Decca DL-8078 + US:LP = Varese STV-81118

4083 Magnificent Seven, The (1960) Score (Elmer Bernstein) US:LP = UA UAL-4146/UAS-5146* [Elmer Bernstein:ST]

4084 Magnificent Seven Deadly Sins, The (1972) Themes (Roy Budd) GB: LP = Pye 18373* [Roy Budd:ST]

4085 Magnificent Showman, The *see* Circus World

4086 Magnificent Sinner, The [Katia] (1963) Highlights (Joseph Kosma) FR:EP = Barclay 70331

4087 Magnificent Two, The *see* What Happened at Campo Grande?

4088 Magnifique, Le (1976) Score (Claude Bolling) FR:LP = Polydor 2393.075*

4089 Magnum Force (1973) Theme (Lalo Schifrin) US:LP = WB/Viva 23990-1* [Lalo Schifrin:ST]

4090 Mahler (1975) Score (classical music) GB:LP = Charisma CAS-1088* [Bernard Haitink:ST]

4091 Mahogany (1975) Score (e: Michael Masser/e:Gil Askey) US:LP = Motown M6-858*

4092 Mahoney's Last Stand (1976) Score (Ron Wood & Ronnie Lang) US: LP = Atlantic SD2-110*

4093 Mail Order Bride (1964) Theme (George Bassman) US:SP = MGM 13210 [Buddy Ebsen:ST]

4094 Main Event, The (1979) Score (various) US:LP = Columbia JS-36115*

4095 Main Street to Broadway (1953) Theme/US:LP-BP = JJA 19761 [@Mary Martin:ST]

4096 Majin [Majin, Monster of Terror] (1966) Score (Akira Ifukube) JA: LP = Columbia CX-7019

4097 Majin Strikes Again (1966) Excerpts (Akira Ifukube) JA:LP = Toho 8125 [@ST]

4098 Major Dundee (1965) Score (Daniele Amfitheatrof) US:LP = Columbia OL-6380/OS-2780*; Theme (Wood & Sullivan) US:SP = RCA 47-8516 [Eddy Arnold]

4099 Majority of One, A (1962) Theme (Max Steiner) US:SP = Mercury 71932 [Rudy & Johnny]; Theme (Max Steiner) US:LP = Decca 74274* [Carmen Cavallaro]; Theme (Max Steiner) US: LP = Impulse 19* [Manny Albam]

4100 Make a Wish (1937) Themes-A-B/US:78 = Bluebird 7158 [Bobby Breen:ST]; Theme-C/US:78 = Bluebird 7168 [Bobby Breen:ST]

4101 Make Haste to Live (1954) Highlights (Elmer Bernstein) US:LP = Citadel CTV-7021

4102 Make Mine Music (1946) Highlights [The Whale Who Wanted to Sing at the Met] (ae:Ken Darby) US:78-MS = Columbia 640 [Nelson Eddy:ST]; Highlights [Peter and the Wolf] (classical music) US:LP = Disneyland WDL-3016 + US:LP = Disneyland DQ-1242 [ST]; Theme-A [Make Mine Music] (Charles Wolcott) US:LP-MS = Ovation 5000 [@ST]; Theme-B [Two Silhouettes] (Charles Wolcott) US:78 = Columbia 37050 [Dinah Shore:ST]; Theme-C [The Martins and the Coys] (Ted Weems) US: LP-MS = Ovation 5000 [@ST]; Theme-D [All the Cats Join In] (Alec Wilder) US: 78 = Columbia 36967 [Benny Goodman: ST]; Theme-E [After You've Gone] (Creamer) US:78 = Columbia 36699 [Benny Goodman:ST]; Theme-F [Without You] (Oswald Farres) US:78 = Capitol 234 [Andy Russell:ST]; Theme-G [Johnny Fedora & Alice Blue Bonnet] (Allie Wrubel) US:78 = Decca 23474 [Andrews Sisters:ST]; Theme-H [Casey at the Bat] (Eliot Daniel) US:78 = Capitol 249 [Jerry Colonna:ST]

4103 Make Way for Ducklings [Short] Sequence + Dialog (Arthur Kleiner) US:LP-PP = Picture Book Parade 101 [@ST]

4104 Making Love (1982) Theme (Burt Bacharach) US:SP = Atlantic 4005* [Roberta Flack:ST]

4104a Making Mr. Right (1986) Highlights (Chaz Jankel) US:LP = Varese STV 81320*

4105 Making the Grade (1984) Score (Basil Poledouris) US:LP = Varese STV-81204*

4106 Malamondo (1964) Score (Ennio Morricone) US:LP = Epic LN-24126/ BN-26126*

4107 Malcolm X (1972) Highlights + Dialog (pop music) US:LP = WB BS-2619*

4108 Male Companion [Monsieur de Compagnie] (1964) Highlights (Georges Delerue) FR:EP=Barclay 70724

4109 Male Hunt [La Chasse a Homme] (1964) Highlights (Michel Magne) FR:EP = Ducretet 460-V-646

4110 Maledetto Imbroglio *see* Facts of Murder, The

4111 Malevil (1981) Score (Gabriel Yared) FR:LP = RCA RSL-1089*

4112 Malicious *see* Malizia

4113 Malizia [Malicious] (1975) Score (Fred Bongusto) IT:LP = Cinevox 33/68*

4114 Malpertuis (1979) Highlights (Georges Delerue) FR:LP = Pascal Bertrand 900.411*

4115 Malta, G.C. (1942) Highlights (Arnold Bax) GB:LP = Cloud Nine CN-7012* [Kenneth Alwyn]; Theme (Arnold Bax) US:LP = DRG 703* [Marcus Dods]

4116 Maltese Falcon, The (1941) Sequence + Dialog (Adolph Deutsch) US:LP-MS = WB 3X2737 [@ST]

4117 Mama Dracula (1981) Score (Roy Budd) FR:LP = WB/WEA 58251*

4118 Mambo (1954) Theme (Bernardo Noriega) GB:78 = HMV 3445 [Bernardo Noriega:ST]

4119 Mame (1974) Score (stage songs:Jerry Herman) US:LP = WB WS-2773*

4120 Mammy (1930) Highlights (Irving Berlin) US:LP-BP = Milloball 34031

4121 Man, a Horse and a Gun, A *see* Stranger Returns, The

4122 Man, a Woman and a Bank, A (1979) Theme (Bill Conti) US:SP = 20th 2425* [Dan Hill:ST]

4123 Man About Town (1939) Themes (Frederick Hollander) US:78 = Bluebird 10265 [Dorothy Lamour:ST]

4124 Man and a Woman, A (1966) Score-A (Francis Lai) US:LP = UA UAL-4147/UAS-5147*; Score-B (Francis Lai) US:LP = UA UAS-5184*

4125 Man and a Woman – 20 Years Later, A (1986) Score (Francis Lai) US: LP = Finnadar 90562-1*

4126 Man and Boy (1972) Score (J.J. Johnson) US:LP = Sussex 7011*

4127 Man and Child [L'Homme et l'Enfant] (1957) Theme (Jeff Davis) US: LP = WB 1371* [Pete Rugolo]; Theme (Jeff Davis) US:LP = Dot 3120 [Ray Ventura]

4128 Man Between, The (1953) Theme (John Addison) US:78 = London 1389 [Cyril Stapleton]; Theme (John Addison) US:LP = London 1487 [Cyril Stapleton]

4129 Man Called Adam, A (1966) Score (e:Benny Carter/etc.) US:LP = Reprise R-6180/RS-6180*

4130 Man Called Dagger, A (1967) Score (s:Steve Allen/as:Ronald Stein) US:LP = MGM E-4516/SE-4516*

4131 Man Called Flintstone, The (1966) Score (e:Ted Nichols/e:Doug Goodwin) US:LP = Hanna Barbera HLP-2055/HST-2055*

4132 Man Called Horse, A (1970) Score (Leonard Rosenman) US:LP = Columbia OS-3530*

4133 Man Called Noon, The [Lo Chiamavano Mezzogiorno] (1973) Score (Luis E. Bacalov) IT:LP = General Music 55493*

4134 Man Called Peter, A (1955) Theme (Alfred Newman) US:SP = Decca 9-91564 [Alfred Newman:ST]; Theme (Alfred Newman) US:LP = Decca 8123 [Alfred Newman:ST]; Theme (Alfred Newman) US:LP = Liberty 14019* [Felix Slatkin]

4135 Man Could Get Killed, A (1966) Score (Bert Kaempfert) US:LP = Decca DL-4750/DL-74750*

4136 Man for All Seasons, A (1966) Underscore + Dialog (Georges Delerue) US:LP-MS = RCA VDM-116

4137 Man from Cocody, The [Le Gentleman de Cocody] (1965) Highlights (Michel Magne) FR:EP = Barclay 70793

4138 Man from Hong Kong, The *see* Dragon Flies, The

4139 Man from Laramie, The (1955) Theme (Lester Lee) US:SP = MGM 12011 [James Brown]; Theme (Lester Lee) US:SP = Capitol 3171 [Al Martino]; Theme (Lester Lee) US:LP = MGM 3294 [@James Brown]

4140 Man from Nowhere, The [Arizona Colt] (1966) Score (Francesco DeMasi) IT:LP = RCA SP-8060*; Theme (Francesco DeMasi) US:LP = UA 6710* [Leroy Holmes]

4141 Man from Snowy River, The (1982) Score-A (Bruce Rowland) US: LP = Varese STV-81167*; Score-B (Bruce Rowland) AU:LP = Festival 37773*

4142 Man from the East, The [E Poi lo Chiamarono il Magnifico] (1972) Score (Guido & Maurizio DeAngelis) IT: LP = Smash 901*

4143 Man I Love, The (1946) Theme/US:LP-BP = JJA 19773 [@Peg La Centra:ST]

4144 Man in the Fifth Dimension, The [Short] (1968) Underscore + Dialog (Ralph Carmichael) US:LP = Camden CAL-813/CAS-813*

4145 Man in the Grey Flannel Suit, The (1956) Theme (Bernard Herrmann) US:SP = RCA 47-6528 [Henri Rene]; Theme (Bernard Herrmann) US:LP-BP = Centurion 1600 [@Henri Rene]

4146 Man in the Middle, The (1964) Score (e:John Barry/t:Lionel Bart/etc.) US:LP = 20th 3128/4128*

4147 Man in the Shadow (1957) Theme (Trevor Duncan) GB:78 = Oriole 1418 [Trevor Duncan:ST]

4148 Man in the Vault, The (1956) Theme (Henry Vars) US:SP = Capitol 3693 [Jimmy Leyden]

4149 Man in the White Suit, The (1951) Theme (Benjamin Frankel) GB: 78-PP = Rank FM-118 [ST]; Theme (Benjamin Frankel) US:LP-BP = Citadel CTOFI-1 [@ST]

4150 Man in the Wilderness (1971) Score (Johnny Harris) GB:LP = WB 46126*; Themes (Johnny Harris) US:

SP = WB 7541 [Johnny Harris:ST]

4151 Man Inside, The (1958) Theme (Charles Henderson) US:SP = London 45-1829 [Eric Rogers]; Theme (Charles Henderson) US:SP = Buena Vista 331 [Jorgen Ingmann]

4152 Man-Made Monster [The Electric Man] (1941) Excerpts (Hans J. Salter) US:LP = Citadel CT-6026 + US:LP = Citadel CTV-7012 [Hans J. Salter:ST]

4153 Man of a Thousand Faces (1957) Score (Frank Skinner) US:LP = Decca DL-8623 + US:LP = Varese STV-81121

4154 Man of Bronze *see* Jim Thorpe, All-American

4155 Man of Iron [L'Homme de Fer] (1981) Score (Andrzej Korzynski) FR:LP = General Music 803.023*

4156 Man of La Mancha (1972) Score (stage songs:Mitch Leigh) US: LP = UA UAS-9906*

4157 Man of Mayfair, A (1931) Themes/GB:LP = WRC 283 [Jack Buchanan:ST]

4158 Man of the West (1958) Theme (Bobby Troup) US:SP = Liberty 55157 [Julie London:ST]

4159 Man of the Year [Homo Eroticus] (1971) Score (Armando Trovajoli) IT:LP = RCA OLS-7*

4160 Man on Fire (1957) Theme (Sammy Fain) US:SP = Capitol 3695 [Bing Crosby:ST]; Theme (Sammy Fain) US:LP = Coral 57125 [George Cates]

4161 Man to Respect, A *see* Master Touch, The

4162 Man Who Finally Died, The (1963) Theme (Philip Green) GB:SP = Columbia 4964 [Philip Green:ST]

4163 Man Who Haunted Himself, The (1970) Theme (Michael J. Lewis) US:SP = Capitol 2869 [Allen Moorhouse]; Theme (Michael J. Lewis) US: LP-BP = GSF 1002 [@Alan Moorhouse]

4164 Man Who Knew Too Much, The (1956) Theme-A (Jay Livingston & Ray Evans) US:SP = Columbia 4-40704 [Doris Day:ST]; Theme-A (Jay Livingston & Ray Evans) US:LP = Columbia 8635* [Doris Day:ST]; Theme-B (Jay Livingston & Ray Evans) US:SP = Columbia 4-40673 [Doris Day:ST]

4165 Man Who Loved Cat Dancing, The (1973) Theme (John Williams) US:LP = A&M 3606* [Paul Williams & John Williams]; Theme (John Williams) US:LP = Reprise 2155* [Frank Sinatra]

4166 Man Who Loved Women, The [L'Homme Qui Aimait les Femmes] (1977) Theme (classical music) FR:LP = Pathe C066.14567* [@ST]

4167 Man Who Understood Women, The [The Man Who Had Power Over Women] (1959) Theme-A (Robert Emmett Dolan) US:SP = 20th 145 [Bradley Munday]; Theme-A (Robert Emmett Dolan) US:SP = WB 5074 [The Triumphs]; Theme-B (Robert Emmett Dolan) US:SP = London 1901 [Frank Chacksfield]

4168 Man Who Would Be King, The (1975) Score (Maurice Jarre) US: LP = Capitol SW-11474*

4169 Man with a Million [The Million Pound Note] (1953) Theme (William Alwyn) GB:78-PP = Rank FM-144 [ST]

4170 Man with Bogart's Face, The [Sam Marlow, Private Eye] (1980) Score (George Duning) US:LP = Web ST-105*

4171 Man with the Golden Arm, The (1955) Score (Elmer Bernstein) US: LP = Decca DL-8257/DL-78257* + US:LP = MCA 2043*

4172 Man with the Golden Gun, The (1974) Score (John Barry) US:LP = UA LA-358*

4173 Man with the Gun [The Trouble Shooter] (1955) Theme (Alex North) US:SP = Columbia 4-40624 [Merv Griffin]

4174 Man Without a Star (1955) Theme-A (Hans J. Salter) US:LP = Medallion 313 [Hans J. Salter:ST]; Theme-B (Lou Singer) US:SP = Decca 9-29355 [Kirk Douglas:ST]

4175 Manchurian Candidate, The (1962) Theme (David Amram) US:SP = Reprise 20120 [Les Baxter]; Theme (David Amram) US:LP = Liberty 3277* [Martin Denny]; Theme (David Amram) US:LP-BP = GSF 1002 [@Les Baxter]

4176 Mandragola [The Mandrake] (1965) Theme (Gino Marinuzzi, Jr.) US: SP = RCA 47-9002 [Ed Ames]

4177 Mango Tree, The (1977)

Theme (Marc Wilkinson) US:LP = DRG 8202* [William Motzing]

4178 Manhattan (1979) Score (ae:Tom Pierson/etc.) US:LP = Columbia JS-36020*

4179 Manhattan Baby [Paura Nella Citta Dei Morti Viventi] (1983) Score (Fabio Frizzi) IT:LP = Beat CR-11*

4180 Manhattan Melodrama (1934) Theme/US:LP-BP = JJA 19766 [@ Shirley Ross:ST]

4181 Manhattan Merry-Go-Round (1937) Themes-A-B/US:78 = Brunswick 7984 [Phil Regan:ST]; Theme-C/US: 78 = Variety 644 [Cab Calloway:ST]

4182 Manhattan Project, The (1986) Score (Philippe Sarde) US:LP = Varese STV-81282*

4183 Manhole (1976) Excerpts (Grace Slick) US:LP = Grunt BFL1-0347* [Grace Slick:ST]

4184 Manhunter (1986) Score (t: Michel Rubini/s:various) US:LP = MCA 6182*

4185 Maniac (1980) Score (Jay Chattaway) US:LP = Varese STV-81143*

4186 Maniacs on Wheels [Once a Jolly Swagman] (1948) Theme (Bernard Stevens) GB:78-PP = Rank FM-40 [ST]

4187 Mannequin (1938) Theme (Edward Ward) US:LP-BP = Curtain Calls 100/23 [Joan Crawford:ST]

4188 Mans, Le (1971) Score (Michel Legrand) US:LP = Columbia S-30891*

4189 Man's Castle (1933) Theme/ US:LP-BP = Legends 1000/2 [@Glenda Farrell:ST]

4190 Man's Favorite Sport (1964) Theme (Henry Mancini) US:SP = RCA 47-8295 [Ann-Margret]; Theme (Henry Mancini) US:LP = RCA 2990* [Henry Mancini:ST]

4191 Mantis in Lace (1968) Themes (Vic Lance) US:SP = Box Office 1595 [Lynn Harper:ST]

4192 Many Classic Moments (1983) Scores (e:Malani Bilyeu/e:Kirk Thompson/e:Kalapana) JA:LP-MS = Trio AW-3005/6*

4193 Many Colored Paper [Short] (1960) Themes (Pete Seeger) US:LP = Folkways 3851 [Pete Seeger:ST]

4194 Many Happy Returns (1934) Themes/US:78 = Brunswick 6874 [Guy Lombardo:ST]

4195 Many Rivers to Cross (1955) Theme (Saul Chaplin) US:SP = Cadence 1261 [Bill Hayes]

4196 Mara of the Wilderness (1965) Theme (Harry Bluestone) US:SP = Blue River 209 [Harry Bluestone:ST]

4197 Maracaibo (1958) Score (Laurindo Almeida) US:LP = Decca DL-8756

4198 Marat/Sade (1967) Highlights + Dialog (stage music:Richard Peaslee) US:LP = UA UAL-4153/UAS-5153*

4199 Marathon Man (1976) Theme (Michael Small) US:LP = Pickwick 3564* [The Birchwood Pops]

4200 March Hare, The (1956) Theme (Philip Green) US:SP = Capitol 3529 [Philip Green:ST]; Theme (Philip Green) US:SP = Decca 9-29979 [Bill Snyder]; Theme (Philip Green) US:SP = London 45-1673 [Will Glahe]

4201 March of the Wooden Soldiers *see* Babes in Toyland (1934)

4202 Marching Along *see* Stars and Stripes Forever

4203 Marcia o Crepa *see* Commando

4204 Marco Polo (1961) Themes (A.F. Lavagnino) IT:SP = CAM 2425 [ST]

4205 Marco the Magnificent (1965) Score (Georges Garvarentz) US:LP = Columbia OL-6470/OS-2870*

4206 Mardi Gras (1958) Score (Sammy Fain) US:LP = Bell 11/S-11* [Studio Cast]; Highlights (Sammy Fain) US:EP = Dot DEP-1075 [Pat Boone:ST]

4207 Marguerite de la Nuit (1956) Theme (Rene Cloerec) US:LP = Mercury 20188 [Eddie Barclay]

4208 Maria Grever Story, The / Theme (Maria Grever) US:LP = MGM 3731* [The Metropolitan Jazz Quartet]

4209 Marianne (1929) Theme-A/ US:LP = Totem 1005 [Cliff Edwards: ST]; Theme-B/US:LP-BP = JJA 19802 [@Cliff Edwards:ST]; Theme-C/US: 78 = Columbia 1907 [Cliff Edwards:ST]

4210 Maria's Lovers (1984) Score (t:Gary Remal/s:pop music) FR:LP = Milan A-262*

4211 Marie (1985) Score (Francis Lai) US:LP = Varese STV-81265*

4212 Marie Galante (1934) Theme-A/US:78 = Brunswick 7329 [Helen Morgan:ST]; Theme-B/US:LP-BP = Take Two 207 [@Helen Morgan:ST]

4213 Marie Ward (1986) Score (Elmer Bernstein) US:LP = Varese STV-81268*

4214 Marinella (1935) Themes/US: 78 = Columbia 4138 [Tino Rossi:ST]

4215 Marizinia—The Witch Beneath the Sea (1962) Themes (Enrico Simonetti) US:SP = Olympia 7006 [Johnny Star:ST]

4216 Marjoe (1972) Highlights + Dialog (t:Joe Broks/etc.) US:LP = WB BS-2667*

4217 Marjorie Morningstar (1958) Score (e:Max Steiner/e:Ray Heindorf/t: Sammy Fain) US:LP = RCA LOC-1044; Excerpts (Max Steiner) US:LP-BP = Tony Thomas TTMS-16 [Max Steiner: ST]

4218 Mark Di Suvero, Sculptor (1977) Score (Philip Glass) US:LP = Virgin VI-2085* [Philip Glass:ST]

4219 Mark of the Vampire (1957) *see* Vampire, The

4220 Mark of Zorro, The (1920) Theme [Silent I] (W. Wilowitz) US:LP = Golden Crest 4019 [Arthur Kleiner]

4221 Mark of Zorro, The (1940) Theme (Alfred Newman) US:LP-BP = Capricorn 1286 [Alfred Newman:ST]

4222 Marlowe (1969) Theme (Peter Matz) US:SP = Liberty 56107 [Johnny Mann Singers:ST]; Theme (Peter Matz) US:LP = Liberty 7620* [Johnny Mann Singers:ST]

4223 Marnie (1964) Score-A (Bernard Herrmann) US:LP-BP = Crimson CR-101; Score-B (Bernard Herrmann) US:LP-BP = Soundstage SS-2306; Excerpts (Bernard Herrmann) US:LP = London SP-44126* [Bernard Herrmann: ST]

4224 Marriage-Go-Round, The (1961) Theme (Lew Spence) US:SP = Columbia 4-41860 [Tony Bennett]

4225 Marriage Italian Style (1964) Excerpts (Armando Trovajoli) US:LP = Epic LN-24195/BN-26195* [@ST]

4226 Marriage of a Young Stockbroker, The (1971) Theme (Fred Karlin) US:SP = Capitol 3210* [Linda Ronstadt: ST]

4227 Marriage of Maria Braun, The [Die Ehe der Maria Braun] (1978) Theme (Peer Raben) FR:LP = Cine Disc 88.087* [Peer Raben:ST]

4228 Marriage on the Rocks (1965) Theme-A (Nelson Riddle) US:SP = Reprise 0412 [Nelson Riddle:ST]; Theme-B (Teddy Randazzo) US:SP = Reprise 0405 [Trini Lopez:ST]

4229 Marry Me (1932) Themes/GB: 78 = Decca 3277 [Renate Mueller:ST]

4230 Marry Me! Marry Me! (1969) Score (Emil Stern) US:LP = RCA LSO-1160*

4231 Marseille Contract, The *see* Destructors, The

4232 Marshal's Daughter, The (1953) Theme (Stan Jones) US:SP = Capitol 2475 [Tex Ritter]; Theme (Stan Jones) US:LP = Capitol 971 [Tex Ritter]

4233 Marshmallow Moon *see* Aaron Slick from Punkin Crick

4234 Martin (1978) Score (Donald Rubinstein) US:LP = Varese VC-81127*

4235 Martin and Gaston [Short] (1953) Excerpts (Temple Abady) US: LP = MGM E-3151 [@ST]

4236 Martins and the Coys, The *see* Make Mine Music

4237 Marty (1955) Theme-A (Roy Webb) US:SP = Coral 9-61425 [Les Brown]; Theme-B (Harry Warren) US: SP = Columbia 4-40513 [Jimmy Leyden]; Theme-B (Harry Warren) US: LP = MGM 3220 [@The Naturals]

4238 Marvin and Tige (1938) Score (Patrick Williams) US:LP = Capitol ST-12307*

4239 Mary Lou (1948) Theme (Arthur Lyman) US:SP = Capitol 881 [Skitch Henderson]; Theme (Arthur Lyman) US:LP = UA LA-843* [Bing Crosby]

4240 Mary Poppins (1964) Score (Richard & Robert Sherman) US:LP = Buena Vista BV-4026/ST-4026*

4241 Mary, Queen of Scots (1971) Score (John Barry) US:LP = Decca DL-79186*

4242 Maryjane (1968) Score (s: Larry Brown/t:Valjean Johns) US:LP = Sidewalk DT-5911*

4243 Mask (1985) Score (pop music) US:LP = MCA 6140*

4244 Masquerade (1965) Theme (Philip Green) US:SP = UA 860 [Danny Williams:ST]

4245 Masquerade in Mexico (1945) Theme/GB:LP = Ace of Hearts 67 [Dorothy Lamour:ST]

4246 Massacre at Fort Holman *see* Reason to Live, A Reason to Die, A

4247 Massacre Hill *see* Eureka Stockade

4248 Massacre in Grand Canyon [Massacro al Grande Canyon] (1965) Score (Gianni Ferrio) IT:LP = CAM CMS-30.097

4249 Master and Margarita, The [Il Maestro e Marherita] (1972) Themes (Ennio Morricone) IT:SP = RCA OC-27* [ST]

4250 Master Gunfighter, The (1975) Themes (Lalo Schifrin) US:SP = Billy Jack 001* [Lalo Schifrin:ST]; Theme (Lalo Schifrin) US:SP = A&M 1756* [Lalo Schifrin:ST]; Theme (Lalo Schifrin) US:LP = Centurion 1210* [@Lalo Schifrin:ST]

4251 Master of the Islands *see* Hawaiians, The

4252 Master of the World (1961) Score (Les Baxter) US:LP = Vee Jay LP-4000/SR-4000* + US:LP = Varese VC-81070*

4253 Master Touch, The [A Man to Respect] [Un Uomo da Rispettare] (1974) Score (Ennio Morricone) IT:LP = CBS 70117*

4254 Masters, The [Industrial Short] Theme (Cy Coleman) US:SP = Capitol 5086 [Cy Coleman:ST]

4255 Masters of Melody (1929) Excerpts (Richard Rodgers) US:LP-BP = JJA 19766 [@ST]

4256 Mata Hari (1984) Score (Wilfred Josephs) FR:LP = Milan CH-020*

4257 Mata Hari, Agent H-21 (1964) Highlights (Georges Delerue) FR:EP = Ducretet 460-V-665

4258 Matchless (1966) Score (Ennio Morricone) IT:LP = Cometa 1015/29*

4259 Mathias Sandorf / Highlights (Karl Hajos) FR:EP = Barclay 70501

4260 Mating Game, The (1959) Theme (Charles Strouse) US:SP = MGM 12761 [Debbie Reynolds:ST]; Theme (Charles Strouse) US:LP = Metro 535 [Debbie Reynolds:ST]

4261 Mating Season, The (1951) Theme (Marguerite Monnot) US:SP = RCA 47-4101 [Henri Rene]

4262 Mating Urge, The (1958) Score-A (Stanley Wilson) US:LP = International 7777/S-7777*; Score-B (Stanley Wilson) US:LP = Capitol T-1552/ST-1552* [Stanley Wilson:ST]

4263 Mattei Affair, The [Il Caso Mattei] (1972) Theme (Piero Piccioni) IT:LP-MS = WB/WEA 68034 + FR: LP-MS = General Music 806.029 [Piero Piccioni:ST]

4264 Matter of Honor, A [Una Questione d'Onore] (1966) Themes (Luis E. Bacalov) IT:SP = SRL 10412* [ST]

4265 Matter of Innocence, A [Pretty Polly] (1968) Score (Michel Legrand) US:LP = Decca DL-9160/DL-79160*

4266 Matter of Life and Death, A *see* Stairway to Heaven

4267 Matter of Resistance, A [La Vie de Chateau] (1966) Highlights (Michel Legrand) FR:EP = Philips 432.146*; Theme (Michel Legrand) US: LP = MGM 4491* [Michel Legrand:ST]

4268 Matter of Time, A [Nina] (1976) Score (s:Nino Oliviero/t:John Kander) IT:LP = Oceania 69301*; Theme (John Kander) US:SP-PP = American International 7615* [Liza Minnelli:ST]

4269 Matter of Who, A (1962) Theme (Bobby Russell) US:SP = Jamie 1230 [The Statesmen]

4270 Maui *see* Just Tell Me You Love Me

4271 Maurie [Big Mo] (1973) Theme (Joe Raposo) US:SP = Reprise 1190 [Frank Sinatra]; Theme (Joe Raposo) US:LP = Reprise 2155* [Frank Sinatra]; Theme (Joe Raposo) US:LP = Polydor 6034* [Arthur Fiedler]

4272 Maverick Queen, The (1956) Theme (Victor Young) US:SP = MGM 12213 [Joni James:ST]

4273 Maximum Overdrive (1986) Score (e:Malcolm Young/e:pop music) US:LP = Atlantic 81650-1* [AC/DC:ST]

4274 Maya (1966) Score (Riz Ortolani) US:LP = MGM E-4376/SE-4376*

4275 Mayerling (1968) Score (Francis Lai) GB:LP = Philips 7876*; Themes (Francis Lai) US:SP = MGM 14037 [Christian Gaubert:ST]; Theme (Francis Lai) US:LP = DRG 508* [Francis Lai: ST]

4276 Mayor of 44th Street, The (1942) Themes/US:78 = Bluebird 11437 [Freddy Martin:ST]

4277 Maytime (1937) Highlights + Dialog (stage songs:Sigmund Romberg) US:LP-BP = Pelican LP-121 + US:LP-BP = Sandy Hook SH-2008

4278 Me and the Colonel (1958) Score (George Duning) US:LP = RCA LOC-1046/LSO-1046*

4279 Me, Natalie (1969) Score (Henry Mancini) US:LP = Columbia OS-3350*

4280 Meadow, The [Il Prato] (1979) Score (Ennio Morricone) IT:LP = CAM SAG-9100*; Highlights (Ennio Morricone) US:LP = Cerberus CEMS-0115*

4281 Meaning of Life, The *see* Monty Python's The Meaning of Life

4282 Meatballs (1979) Score (Elmer Bernstein) US:LP = RSO RS1-3056*

4283 Mechanic, The (1972) Highlights (Jerry Fielding) US:LP-MS-BP = Citadel CTJF-2/3*

4284 Medicine Ball Caravan [We Have Come for Your Daughters] (1971) Score (rock music) US:LP = WB BS-2565*

4285 Mediterranean Holiday [The Flying Clipper] (1964) Score (Riz Ortolani) US:LP = London M-76003/MS-82003*

4286 Medium, The (1951) Scores (stage songs:Gian Carlo Menotti) US: LP-MS = Mercury MGL-7

4287 Medium Cool (1969) Theme (Lee & Echols) US:LP = UA 6742* [Leroy Holmes]

4288 Meet Danny Wilson (1952) Highlights (pop music) US:LP-BP = Caliban 6016

4289 Meet Me After the Show (1951) Highlights (Jule Styne) US:LP-BP = Caliban 6012

4290 Meet Me in Las Vegas [Viva Las Vegas] (1956) Highlights (at:John Green/etc.) US:EP = MGM X-1264

4291 Meet Me in St. Louis (1944) Score (Hugh Martin & Ralph Blane) US: LP-BP = Hollywood Soundstage HS-5007; Highlights (Hugh Martin & Ralph Blane) US:LP = Decca DL-8498 + US: LP = AEI 3101

4292 Meet the People (1944) Theme/US:LP-BP = JJA 19765 [@Bert Lahr:ST]

4293 Meet Whiplash Willie *see* Fortune Cookie, The

4294 Meetings with Remarkable Men (1979) Score (as:Laurence Rosenthal) US:LP = Varese STV-81129*

4295 Mefiez-Vous Filettes *see* Young Girls Beware

4296 Megaforce (1982) Theme (707) US:SP = Boardwalk 711-146* [707:ST]; Theme (707) US:LP = Boardwalk 1-33253* [707:ST]

4297 Melba (1953) Highlights (classical music) US:LP-10 = RCA LM-7012 [Patrice Munsel:ST]; Theme (Mischa Spoliansky) US:SP = Columbia 4-40032 [Marian Marlowe]; Theme (Mischa Spoliansky) US:LP = Decca 8051 [Victor Young]

4298 Melinda (1972) Score (Jerry Butler & Jerry Peters) US:LP = Pride PRD-0006*

4299 Melodiya (1977) Score (folk music) US:LP = Gateway GSLP-8501*

4300 Melody [Love, Melody] [To Love Somebody] [S.W.A.L.K.] (1971) Score (e:Richard Hewson/e:The Bee Gees) US:LP = Atco SD-33-363*

4301 Melody [Cartoon] (1953) Excerpts (Sonny Burke) US:LP = Disneyland DQ-1232 [@ST]

4302 Melody for Two (1937) Theme-A/US:78 = Decca [James Melton:ST]; Theme-B/US:LP-BP = JJA 19791 [@James Melton:ST]

4303 Melody of Life, The *see* Symphony of Six Million

4304 Melody Time (1948) Highlights + Dialog [Johnny Appleseed] (Walter Kent) US:LP = Camden CAL-1054 + US:LP = Disneyland DQ-1260 + US:LP = Disneyland ST-3996 [Dennis Day:ST]; Theme + Dialog [Pecos Bill] (Eliot Daniel) US:LP = Camden CAL-

1054 [Roy Rogers:ST]; Theme [Little Toot] (Allie Wrubel) US:LP-MS = Ovation 5000 [@The Andrews Sisters:ST]; Theme [Melody Time] (George David Weiss) US:78 = Columbia 38170 [Buddy Clarke:ST]; Theme [Blue Shadows on the Trail] (Eliot Daniel) US:78 = RCA 20-2780 [Roy Rogers:ST]; Theme [Bumble Boogie] (Jack Fina) US:78 = RCA 20-1829 [Freddy Martin:ST]; Theme [Blame It on the Samba] (Ernesto Nazareth) US: 78 = Decca 23828 [Ethel Smith:ST]

4305 Melotch / Highlights (Lazar Sarian) US:LP = Westminster XWN-18487

4306 Member of the Wedding (1952) Themes-A-B (Alex North) US: LP = RCA 1445* [Alex North:ST]; Theme-C (folk music) US:LP = Monmouth 6812 [Ethel Waters:ST]

4307 Memed, My Hawk (1984) Score (Manos Hadjidakis) GB:LP = That's Entertainment TER-1088*

4308 Memoirs of a French Whore [La Derobade] (1982) Score (Vladimir Cosma) FR:LP = AZ Disc 304*; Theme (Vladimir Cosma) US:LP = Mercury 6313.238* [Zamfir]

4309 Men, The [Battle Stripe] (1950) Theme (Dimitri Tiomkin) US: LP = Dot 25107* [Elmer Bernstein]

4310 Men in War (1957) Score (Elmer Bernstein) US:LP=Imperial LP-9032

4311 Men of the Fighting Lady (1954) Themes (Miklos Rozsa) GB:LP = Polydor 2383.384* [Miklos Rozsa:ST]

4312 Men of Two Worlds [Kisenga – Man of Africa] (1946) Theme (Arthur Bliss) GB:78 = Decca 1174 [Muir Mathieson:ST]

4313 Menage [Tenue de Soiree] (1986) Score (Serge Gainsbourg) FR: LP = Apache 240921-1*

4314 Menage all'Italiana [Menage – Italian Style] (1965) Score (Ennio Morricone) IT:LP = RCA SP-8013; Theme-A (Ennio Morricone) US:LP-BP = POO 105 [Ennio Morricone:ST]; Theme-B (Gino Paoli) US:SP = RCA 47-8728 [Anna Moffo:ST]

4315 Menschen Im Netz / Theme (Hans Martin Majewski) US:SP = 20th 285 [Bradley Mundy]

4316 Mephisto (1981) Score (Zdenko Tamassy) FR:LP = Milan/SPI 120.140*

4317 Mera Saya / Theme/US:LP = Capitol 10500 [@Asha Bhosle:ST]

4318 Mercenaries, The *see* Dark of the Sun

4319 Mercenary, The [A Professional Gun] [Il Mercenario] (1968) Score (Ennio Morricone) FR:LP = UA 29005*; Theme (Ennio Morricone) US:SP = UA 50655* [Leroy Holmes]

4320 Mermoz (1944) Theme (Arthur Honegger) GB:78 = Columbia 1059; Theme (Arthur Honegger) FR:LP = Columbia 1059

4321 Merry Andrew (1958) Highlights (Saul Chaplin) US:LP = Capitol T-1016

4322 Merry Christmas, Mr. Lawrence (1983) Score (Ryuichi Sakamoto) US:LP = MCA 6125*

4323 Merry-Go-Round [Le Baiser] (1977) Score (Francis Lai) FR:LP = Polydor 2393.068*

4324 Merry Widow, The (1934) Highlights (stage songs:Franz Lehar) US:LP-BP = La Nadine 260

4325 Merry Widow, The (1952) Highlights (stage songs:Franz Lehar) US:LP-10 = MGM E-157 + US:LP = MGM E-3228

4326 Message, The *see* Mohammed, Messenger of God

4327 Message from Space (1978) Score (Ken-Ichiro Morioka) JA:LP = Columbia CQ-7004*; Theme (Ken-Ichiro Morioka) US:LP-BP = POO 106 [@ST]

4328 Metamorphoses *see* Winds of Change, The

4329 Metello (1970) Score (Ennio Morricone) IT:LP = RCA KOLS-1009* + IT:LP = RCA CR-10020*; Theme (Ennio Morricone) US:LP = UA 095* [Francis Lai]

4330 Meteor (1979) Score (Laurence Rosenthal) JA:LP = Seven Seas FML-129*; Theme (Laurence Rosenthal) US:LP = CBS 35876* [Ettore Stratta]

4331 Meter Park [Cartoon Shorts] (1976) Score (e:Jimmy Vann/e:Richard Hieronymus) US:LP = Metric MR1-50*

4332 Metric Man [Cartoon Shorts]

(1976) Score (e:Jimmy Vann/e:Richard Hieronymus) US:LP = Metric MR1-51*

4333 Metropolis (1925) Score [Silent II] (Giorgio Moroder) US:LP = Columbia JS-39526*; Theme [Silent II] ["Obsession"] (Giorgio Moroder) US: SP = Columbia 38-04548* [Giorgio Moroder:ST]; Theme [Silent II] ["Rotwang's Party"] (Giorgio Moroder) US: SP = Columbia 38-04606* [Giorgio Moroder:ST]; Theme [Silent II] (Charles Hofmann) US:LP = Sounds Good 1001 [Charles Hofmann:ST]

4334 Metropolitan (1935) Themes/ US:78 = RCA/Victor 11877 [Lawrence Tibbett:ST]

4335 Mexican Hayride (1948) Theme (Walter Scharf) US:78 = Capitol 15343 [Andy & Della Russell]

4336 Mexican Tapes, The [Short] (1980) Highlights + Dialog (Joseph Armillas) US:LP = One Ten Records 003* [Jacki Apple:ST]

4337 Mi Ultimo Tango (1960) Score (various) US:LP = Columbia EX-5048 [Sarita Montiel:ST]

4338 Michael and Helga [Helga und Michael] (1968) Score (uncredited) US:LP-PP = Minit 83-201*

4339 Michurin (1946) Highlights (Dmitri Shostakovich) US:LP = Angel S-40181*

4340 Mickey (1948) Themes/US: 78 = Capitol 15061 [Lois Butler:ST]

4341 Mickey and the Beanstalk *see* Fun and Fancy Free

4342 Mickey One (1965) Score (Eddie Sauter) US:LP = MGM E-4312/SE-4312*

4343 Mickey's Christmas Carol [Short] (1983) Theme + Dialog (Irwin Kostal) US:LP = Disneyland 3109; Theme + Dialog (Irwin Kostal) US: EP = Disneyland 386

4344 Mickey's Follies [Cartoon] (1929) Theme (Carl Stalling) US:LP-MS = Ovation 5000 + US:LP = Disneyland 3805 [@ST]

4345 Mickey's Gala Premiere [Cartoon] (1933) Theme (Frank Churchill) US:LP-MS = Ovation 5000 [@ST]

4346 Mickey's Grand Opera [Cartoon] (1936) Theme (at:Leigh Harline) US:LP-MS = Ovation 5000 [@ST]

4347 Midas Run [A Run on Gold] (1969) Score (Elmer Bernstein) US:LP = Citadel CT-6017*

4348 Middle of the Night (1959) Theme (George Bassman) US:LP = Colpix 407* [Nina Simone]

4349 Midnight (1982) Score (e:Paul McCollough/e:Michael Mazzei) US: LP = Traq Record TR-114*

4350 Midnight Cowboy (1969) Score (e:John Barry/etc.) US:LP = UA UAS-5198*

4351 Midnight Express (1978) Score (Giorgio Moroder) US:LP = Casablanca NBLP-7114

4352 Midnight Lace (1960) Theme (Joe Lubin) US:SP = Columbia 4-41800 [Ray Conniff]; Theme (Joe Lubin) US:SP = MGM 12942 [Ray Ellis]; Theme (Joe Lubin) US:LP = Mercury 60688* [David Carroll]

4353 Midnight Man, The (1974) Theme (Dave Grusin) US:SP = MCA 40235* [Yvonne Elliman:ST]

4354 Midnight Pleasures *see* Immortal Bachelor, The

4355 Midshipmaid, The (1932) Theme/GB:LP = MFP 1127 [Jessie Matthews:ST]

4356 Midsummer Night's Dream, A (1935) Sequence + Dialog (au:Erich Wolfgang Korngold) US:LP-MS = WB 3X2737 [@ST]

4357 Midsummer Night's Sex Comedy, A (1982) Highlights (classical music) US:LP = CBS 37789*

4358 Midway [The Battle of Midway] (1976) Themes (John Williams) US: SP = MCA 40575* [John Williams:ST]; Theme (John Williams) US:LP-BP = Centurion 1600* [@John Williams:ST]; Theme (John Williams) US:LP = Philips 6302.082* [John Williams:ST]

4359 Midway, Sleep in Peace (1985) Score (e:Nelson Riddle/e:various) JA: LP = Columbia AF-7318*

4360 Mighty Khan, The *see* Terror of the Steppe

4361 Mike Mulligan and His Steam Shovel [Short] Sequence + Dialog (Arthur Kleiner) US:LP-PP = Picture Book Parade 102 [@ST]

4362 Mike's Murder (1983) Excerpts (Joe Jackson) US:LP = A&M SP-

4931* [Joe Jackson:ST]

4363 Milan / Theme/US:LP = Capitol 10500 [@Lata Mangeshkar & Mukesh:ST]

4364 Milanese Story, A (1962) Score (John Lewis) US:LP = Atlantic 1388/S-1388*

4365 Milano Calibro 9 (1974) Score (e:Luis E. Bacalov/e:Osanna) US:LP = Peters PILPS-9001*

4366 Milano Odia – La Polizia Non Puo Sparare (1975) Theme (Ennio Morricone) US:LP = Icon 9-79139-1* [John Zorn]; Theme (Ennio Morricone) IT: LP-MS = RCA 2-1174* [Ennio Morricone:ST]

4367 Milano Trema / Theme (Guido & Maurizio DeAngelis) US:LP = Private Stock 7004* [Guido & Maurizio:ST]

4368 Mildred Pierce (1945) Themes (Max Steiner) US:LP-BP = Tony Thomas TTMS-15 [Max Steiner:ST]

4369 Million, Le (1931) Theme (Georges Van Parys) GB:78 = HMV 6041 [ST]

4370 Million Pound Note, The *see* Man with a Million

4371 Millions of Cats [Short] Sequence + Dialog (Arthur Kleiner) US:LP-PP = Picture Book Parade 101 [@ST]

4372 Minaccia, La [The Menace] (1978) Score (Gerry Mulligan) US:LP = DRG MRS-506* [Gerry Mulligan:ST]

4373 Minnesota Clay (1966) Score (Piero Piccioni) IT:LP = CAM CMS-30.114

4374 Minor Miracle, A (1984) Score (Rick Patterson) US:LP = Varese STV-81193*

4375 Minute to Pray, A Second to Die, A [Un Minuto per Pregare, un Instante per Morire] (1967) Score (Carlo Rustichelli) IT:LP = RCA SP-8023

4376 Minx, The (1972) Score (Tom Dawes & Don Dannermann) US:LP = Amsterdam AMS-12007*

4377 Mio Caro Assassino [My Dear Assassin] (1982) Highlights (Ennio Morricone) US:LP = Cerberus CEMS-0116*

4378 Miracle, The (1959) Highlights (Elmer Bernstein) US:LP = Film Music Collection FMC-2* [Elmer Bernstein:ST]

4379 Miracle Can Happen, A (1948) Theme/US:78 = Coast 8036 [Dorothy Lamour:ST]

4380 Miracle Goes On, The (1977) Highlights + Underscore + Dialog (e:Ron Huff/u:John Peterson) US:LP = Paragon PR-33035*

4381 Miracle in Milan (1951) Theme (Zava) GB:78 = Philips 112 [Sam Browne]

4382 Miracle in the Rain (1956) Theme (Ray Heindorf) US:SP = Columbia 4-40584 [Jerry Vale]; Theme (Ray Heindorf) US:SP = Advance 3004 [Lorry Raine]

4383 Miracle of the Bells (1948) Theme (Jule Styne) US:LP = Columbia 2913 [Frank Sinatra:ST]

4384 Miracle of the White Stallions [The Flight of the White Stallions] (1963) Theme (Richard & Robert Sherman) US: SP = Buena Vista 421 [The Wellingtons]

4385 Miracle of Tonichi Forest, The / Highlights + Underscore + Dialog (Robert Sheets) US:LP-MS-PP = S.E. 65

4386 Miraclemaster, The *see* Beastmaster, The

4387 Miranda (1948) Theme (Temple Abady) GB:78-PP = Rank FM-9 [ST]

4388 Misadventures of Merlin Jones, The (1964) Theme (Richard & Robert Sherman) US:SP = Buena Vista 475 [Annette:ST]; Theme (Richard & Robert Sherman) US:LP = Buena Vista 3314* [Annette:ST]

4389 Miserables, Les (1952) Theme (Alex North) US:LP = Citadel 6023* [Alex North:ST]

4390 Misfits, The (1961) Highlights (Alex North) US:LP = UA UAL-4087/UAS-5087* + US:LP = UA LA-273*

4391 Mishima (1985) Score (Philip Glass) US:LP = Nonesuch 9-79113-1*

4392 Miss Don Juan *see* Ms. Don Juan

4393 Miss Sadie Thompson (1953) Highlights + Underscore + Dialog (e:Lester Lee/u:George Duning) US: LP-10 = Mercury MG-25181 + US:LP = Mercury MG-20123

4394 Missing (1982) Theme (Vangelis) GB:SP = Polydor 485* [The Shadows]; Theme (Vangelis) US:LP-BP = Disc 105* [@Zamfir] + US:LP = Mercury 6313.435* [Zamfir]

4395 Missing Link, The [Le Chainon Manquant] (1980) Score (e:Roy Budd/e:Leo Sayer) FR:LP = Arabella 202549*

4396 Mississippi (1935) Excerpts (Richard Rodgers) US:LP-10 = Decca DL-6008 + US:LP = Decca DL-4250 [Bing Crosby:ST]

4397 Mississippi Mermaid, The [La Sirene du Mississippi] (1969) Theme (Antoine Duhamel) JA:LP = UA 302* [@ST]

4398 Missouri Breaks, The (1976) Score (John Williams) US:LP = UA LA-623*

4399 Missouri Traveler, The (1958) Themes (Jack Marshall) US:SP = Disneyland 68 [Stan Jones]

4400 Mister Buddwing [Woman Without a Face] (1966) Score (Kenyon Hopkins) US:LP = Verve MG-8638/V6-8638*

4401 Mr. Bug Goes to Town [Hoppity Goes to Town] (1941) Themes (Sammy Timberg/Hoagy Carmichael) US:78 = Okeh 6565 [Frankie Masters]

4402 Mr. Hobbs Takes a Vacation (1962) Themes (Henry Mancini) US: SP = 20th 304 [Sonny Lester]; Theme (Henry Mancini) US:LP = RCA 2604* + US:LP-MS = Camden 2-0293* [Henry Mancini:ST]

4403 Mr. Hulot's Holiday [Les Vacances de Monsieur Hulot] (1953) Theme (Alain Romans) US:SP = Majar 134 [Jack Carroll]; Theme (Alain Romans) US:LP = UA 15554 [@ST]

4404 Mr. Imperium [You Belong to My Heart] (1951) Highlights (e:Harold Arlen/etc.) US:LP-10 = RCA LM-61 [Ezio Pinza:ST]

4405 Mr. Klein (1978) Score (e: Pierre Porte/e:Egisto Macchi) FR:LP = Pathe C066.14317*

4406 Mr. Majestyk (1974) Theme (Charles Bernstein) GB:LP = Philips 6382.111* [Ray Davies' Button Down Brass]

4407 Mr. Mean (1978) Score (The Ohio Players) US:LP = Mercury SRM1-3707* [The Ohio Players:ST]

4408 Mr. Music (1950) Highlights (James Van Heusen) US:LP-10 = Decca DL-5284 + US:LP = Decca DL-4262 [Bing Crosby:ST]

4409 Mr. Perrin and Mr. Traill (1948) Theme (Allan Gray) GB:78-PP = Rank FM-30 [ST]

4410 Mr. Quilp (1975) Score (Leslie Bricusse & Anthony Newley) US:LP-PP = Chap 12574* [Anthony Newley:ST]

4411 Mister Roberts (1955) Theme-A (Franz Waxman) US:LP = Varese 704.320* [Richard Mills]; Theme-B (Jay Livingston & Ray Evans) US:LP = RCA 1202 [Sauter & Finnegan]; Theme-B (Jay Livingston & Ray Evans) US:SP = Columbia 4-40542 [Mitch Miller]

4412 Mr. Robinson Crusoe (1932) Theme [credited to "The Hurricane"] (Alfred Newman) US:LP = Decca 8123 [Alfred Newman:ST]

4413 Mr. Rock and Roll (1957) Highlights-A (various) US:EP = Vik EXA-300 [Teddy Randazzo:ST]; Highlights-B (various) US:EP = Vik EXA-301 [Teddy Randazzo:ST]

4414 Mr. Skeffington (1944) Theme (Franz Waxman) US:LP = RCA 1-0183* + US:LP = RCA 1-3706* [Charles Gerhardt]

4415 Mr. Steve [L'Etrange Monsieur Steve] (1957) Theme (M. Philippe Gerard) US:LP = Dot 3120 [Ray Ventura]

4416 Mr. Sycamore (1975) Theme (Maurice Jarre) US:SP-PP = PFW 92575 [Laura Devon:ST]; Theme (Maurice Jarre) US:LP-BP = Centurion 1600 [@Laura Devon:ST]

4417 Mr. Texas / Themes (Redd Harper) US:LP = Word 3164 [@Redd Harper/Georgia Lee:ST]

4418 Mrs. Brown, You've Got a Lovely Daughter (1968) Score (Graham Gouldman) US:LP = MGM SE-4548* [Herman's Hermits:ST]

4419 Mrs. Fitzherbert (1947) Theme (Stanley Black) GB:LP = Ace of Clubs 108 [@ST]

4420 Mrs. Mike (1949) Theme (Max Steiner) US:SP = Capitol 971 [Clark Dennis]

4421 Mrs. Miniver (1942) Excerpts (t:Herbert Stothart/etc.) US:LP = London 44248* [Stanley Black]

4422 Mrs. Soffel (1984) Excerpts (Mark Isham) US:LP = Windham Hill WH-1041* [Mark Isham:ST]

4423 Mistress Don Juan *see* Ms. Don Juan

4424 Mistress for the Summer [Une Fille pour l'Ete] (1959) Highlights (Georges Delerue) FR:EP = Versailles 90-M-314

4425 Misunderstood (1984) Score (s:Michael Hoppe/as:Carlos Frazetti) US:LP = Polydor 821.238-1*

4426 Mission, The (1986) Score (Ennio Morricone) US:LP = Virgin 90567-1*

4427 Mississippi Blues (1982) Highlights (pop music) FR:LP = Milan ACH-030*

4428 Mix Me a Person (1962) Theme (Van Dyke) GB:SP = Parlophone 4930 [Adam Faith:ST]

4429 Moby Dick (1956) Score (Philip Sainton) US:LP = RCA LPM-1247 + US:LP-BP = Movie Music MM-5147

4430 Moby Dick [The Story of Moby Dick] [Short] (1957) Underscore + Dialog (Richard Mohaupt) US:LP = Dot DLP-3043

4431 Modern Girls (1986) Score (pop music) US:LP = WB 25526-1*

4432 Modern Problems (1981) Theme (Dominic Frontiere) US:SP = Capitol 5091* [The Tubes:ST]

4433 Modern Times (1936) Score [Silent I] (Charles Chaplin) US:LP = UA UAL-4049/UAS-5049e + US:LP = UA UAS-5222e

4434 Modesty Blaise (1966) Score (Johnny Dankworth) US:LP = 20th 4182/S-4182*

4435 Modification, The (1970) Themes (Francis Lai) FR:SP = UA 35228* [ST]

4436 Mohammad, Messenger of God [The Message] (1977) Score (Maurice Jarre) US:LP = Namara 79001*

4437 Mohawk (1956) Theme (Edward L. Alperson, Jr.) US:SP = Capitol 3355 [Big Ben Banjo Band]; Theme (Edward L. Alperson, Jr.) US:SP = MGM 12145 [Rush Adams]

4438 Mole People, The (1956) Theme (Hans J. Salter) US:LP = Varese 81077* + US:LP = Coral 757240* [Dick Jacobs]

4439 Moliere (1980) Score (Rene Clemencic) FR:LP = Harmonia Mundi HM-1020*

4440 Molly and Lawless John (1972) Theme (Johnny Mandel) US:SP-PP = Larry Shayne Music 8421 [Renee Armand:ST]; Theme (Johnny Mandel) US:LP = Discovery 931* [Sue Raney]

4441 Molly Maguires, The (1970) Score (Henry Mancini) US:LP = Paramount PAS-6000*

4442 Molly's Pilgrim (1986) Score (Brook Halpin) US:LP = Music Masters 20138*

4443 Moment by Moment (1978) Score (e:Lee Holdridge/etc.) US:LP = RSO RS1-3040*

4444 Moment of Truth, The (1965) Score (Piero Piccioni) US:LP = Mainstream 56057/S-6057*

4445 Moment to Moment (1966) Theme (Henry Mancini) US:SP = RCA 47-8718 [Henry Mancini:ST]; Theme (Henry Mancini) US:LP = RCA 4140* + US:LP = RCA 1-1843* [H. Mancini:ST]

4446 Moments (1974) Theme (John Cameron) GB:SP = Spark 1111* [Keith Michell]

4447 Mon Amour, Mon Amour (1967) Highlights (Francis Lai) US:EP-PP = TRO 7-03 + FR:EP = AZ Disc 1121; Theme (Francis Lai) US:SP = Columbia 4-44305 [Robert Goulet]; Theme (Francis Lai) US:LP = Kapp 3646* [Francis Lai:ST]

4448 Mon Oncle *see* My Uncle

4449 Mon Oncle d'Amerique (1981) Score (Arie Dzierlatka) US:LP = DRG SL-9505*

4450 Mona Lisa (1986) Score (Michael Kamen) GB:LP = Columbia/Filmtrax SCX-6705*

4451 Mondo Balordo (1968) Theme (Angelo Badalamenti aka Andy Badale) US:SP = Caprice 101 [ST]

4452 Mondo Cane (1963) Score (Riz Ortolani & Nino Oliviero) US:LP = UA UAL-4105/UAS-5105*

4453 Mondo Cane #2 [Mondo Pazzo] (1965) Score (Nino Oliviero) US:LP = 20th 3147/S-4147*

4454 Mondo Daytona (1968) Theme-A/US:SP = Columbia 33191 [Billy Joe Royal:ST]; Theme-B/US:SP = ABC 1226 [The Tams:ST]

4455 Mondo Hollywood (1967) Score (e:Mike Curb/e:Robert Cohen/t: Harley Hatcher) US:LP = Tower T-5083/ST-5083*

4456 Mondo Pazzo *see* Mondo Cane #2

4457 Money! Money! Money! [L'Aventure C'est l'Aventure] (1973) Score (Francis Lai) FR:LP = UA 29296*

4458 Money Pit, The (1986) Theme (Michel Colombier) US:SP = MCA 52814* [Stephen Bishop:ST]

4459 Monika [Summer with Monika] (1953) Theme (Les Baxter) US:SP = Capitol 3259 [Les Baxter:ST]; Theme (Les Baxter) US:LP = Capitol 780 + US:LP = Capitol 1252 [Les Baxter:ST]

4460 Monkey Business (1931) Theme (Sammy Fain) US:LP-10 = MGM 241 [Sammy Fain]

4461 Monkey in Winter [Un Singe en Hiver] (1962) Highlights (Michel Magne) FR:EP = Bel Air 211.067

4462 Monkeys, Go Home! (1967) Theme-A (Robert F. Brunner) US:SP = Buena Vista 456 [Robert F. Brunner: ST]; Themes-B-C (Richard & Robert Sherman) US:SP = Buena Vista 455 [Maurice Chevalier:ST]; Theme-C (Richard & Robert Sherman) US:LP = Disneyland 3940 [Maurice Chevalier:ST]

4463 Monkey's Uncle, The (1965) Theme (Richard & Robert Sherman) US:SP = Buena Vista 440 [Annette:ST]; Theme (Richard & Robert Sherman) US: LP = Buena Vista 3324* + US:LP = Silhouette 10011* [Annette:ST]

4464 Monocle, The [Le Monocle Rit Jaune] (1964) Highlights (various) FR:EP = Ducretet 460-V-647

4465 Monsieur La Caille *see* Lovemaker, The

4466 Monsieur Verdoux (1947) Theme (Charles Chaplin) US:LP = Paramount 6026* [Darius Brubeck]

4467 Monsignor (1982) Score (John Williams) US:LP = Casablanca NBLP-7277*

4468 Monster Club, The (1981) Score (t:Alan Hawkshaw/at:Douglas Gamley/etc.) GB:LP = Chips CHILP-2*

4469 Monster from a Prehistoric Planet [Gappa—Triphibian Monster] (1967) Theme (Seitaro Omori) JA:LP = Toho 8124 [@ST]

4470 Monster Zero (1970) Themes (Akira Ifukube) JA:LP = Toho 8100 [@ST]; Themes (Akira Ifukube) JA: LP = Toho 8112 [@ST]; Underscore + Dialog (Akira Ifukube) JA:LP-MS = Star Child K18G-7213/4

4471 Montana (1950) Theme (Jerry Livingston) US:SP = RCA 47-2991 [The Pied Pipers]

4472 Montana Moon (1930) Theme-A/US:78 = Columbia 2169 [Cliff Edwards:ST]; Theme-B/US:LP-BP = Curtain Calls 100/23 [Joan Crawford: ST]

4473 Monte Carlo (1930) Highlights (Richard A. Whiting) US:LP-BP = JJA 19806

4474 Monte Carlo or Bust *see* Those Daring Young Men in Their Jaunty Jalopies

4475 Monte Carlo Story, The (1956) Theme (Michel Emer) US:SP = Dot 15603 [Dino Rossi]; Theme / US:LP-BP = Marsher 201 [Marlene Dietrich:ST]

4476 Monte Walsh (1970) Theme (John Barry) US:SP = Dunhill 4253* [Mama Cass Elliot:ST]; Theme (John Barry) US:LP = Dunhill 40093* + US: LP = MCA 719* [Mama Cass Elliot:ST]; Theme (John Barry) GB:LP = Polydor 2383.300* [John Barry:ST]

4477 Monty Python and the Holy Grail (1975) Highlights + Underscore + Dialog (e:Neil Innes/u:De Wolfe) US: LP = Arista AL-4050*

4478 Monty Python's Life of Brian (1979) Themes + Underscore + Dialog (t:Eric Idle/u:Geoffrey Burgon) US: LP = WB BSK-3396*

4479 Monty Python's The Meaning of Life (1983) Highlights + Underscore + Dialog (e:Eric Idle/t:John DuPrez/u: De Wolfe) US:LP = MCA 6121*

4480 Moon Fire (1972) Themes (Norm Anderson) US:SP = Palomino 469* [Marty Robbins:ST]

4481 Moon in the Gutter, The (1983) Score (Gabriel Yared) US:LP = DRG SL-9516*

4482 Moon Is Blue, The (1953) Score (Herschel Burke Gilbert) US:LP = Crown CLP-5095/CST-130*

4483 Moon Over Burma (1940) Themes/US:LP = West Coast 14002 [Dorothy Lamour:ST]

4484 Moon Over Las Vegas (1944) Theme/US:LP = RCA 6056 [Gene Austin:ST]

4485 Moon Over Miami (1941) Highlights (Ralph Rainger) US:LP-BP = Caliban 6001

4486 Moon Pilot (1962) Theme (Richard & Robert Sherman) US:SP = Buena Vista 392 [Tom Tryon & Danny Saval:ST]

4487 Moon Spinners, The (1964) Score (s:Ron Grainer/t:Terry Gilkyson) US:LP = Buena Vista BV-3323

4488 Moonfleet (1955) Themes (Miklos Rozsa) GB:LP = Polydor 2383.384* [Miklos Rozsa:ST]

4489 Moonlight and Cactus (1944) Theme (Frank Luther) US:SP = Decca 9-27894 + US:78 = Decca 18572 [The Andrews Sisters:ST]

4490 Moonlighter, The (1953) Theme (Heinz Roemheld) US:SP = Columbia 4-40113 [Harry James]; Theme (Heinz Roemheld) US: SP = Decca 9-28947 [Victor Young]; Theme (Heinz Roemheld) US:LP = Decca 8060 [Victor Young]

4491 Moonraker (1979) Score (John Barry) US:LP = UA LA-971*

4492 Moonrise (1948) Theme (William Lava) US:78 = Metrotone 2018 [Jack Emerson]

4493 Moonshine War, The (1970) Theme-A (L. Emmerson) US:SP = MGM 14149 [The 5 Man Electrical Band]; Theme-B (Hank Williams, Jr.) US:SP = MGM 14152 [Hank Williams, Jr.:ST]

4494 More (1969) Score (Pink Floyd) US:LP = Tower ST-5163* + US: LP = Harvest/Capitol ST-11198*

4495 More American Graffiti (1979) Scores (pop music) US:LP-MS = MCA 2-11006*

4496 More Than a Miracle [Cinderella—Italian Style] [C'Era Una Volta] (1967) Score (Piero Piccioni) US:LP = MGM E-4515/SE-4515*

4497 Morgan! (1966) Theme (Johnny Dankworth) US:SP = Monument 941 [The Key Chains]; Theme (Johnny Dankworth) US:SP = Roulette 4701 [Sonny Stitt]; Theme (Johnny Dankworth) US:LP = RCA 1-5092* [Johnny Dankworth:ST]

4498 Morituri (1965) Theme (Jerry Goldsmith) US:SP = 20th 593 [Ray Ellis]; Theme (Jerry Goldsmith) US: SP = Decca 9-31839 [Robert Maxwell]; Theme (Jerry Goldsmith) US:LP = Capitol 2419* [Laurindo Almeida]

4499 Morning Glory (1933) Theme (Max Steiner) US:LP-BP = Max Steiner Music Society 25781 [Max Steiner:ST]

4500 Morning of the Earth (1973) Score (e:Brian Cadd/e:G. Wayne Thomas) JA:LP = WB P-10647*; Theme (G. Wayne Thomas) US:SP = WB 7608* [G. Wayne Thomas:ST]

4501 Morocco (1931) Themes-A-B/US:LP = Stanyan 10124 [Marlene Dietrich:ST]; Themes B-C/US:LP-BP = Marsher 201 [Marlene Dietrich: ST]

4502 Morons from Outer Space (1985) Theme (Pete Brewis) GB:SP = EMI MORON-1* [The Morons:ST]

4503 Moscow Does Not Believe in Tears (1981) Score (Sergei Nikitin) JA: LP = Columbia YX-7311*

4504 Moscow on the Hudson (1984) Score (David McHugh) US:LP = RCA ABL1-5036*

4505 Mosquito Coast, The (1986) Score (Maurice Jarre) US:LP = Fantasy FSP-21005*

4506 Most Beautiful Wife, The [La Moglie Piu Bella] (1970) Themes (Ennio Morricone) IT:SP = Cinevox MDF-017* [ST]

4507 Mother, Jugs and Speed (1976) Score (various) US:LP = A&M SP-4590*

4508 Mother Kusters Goes to Heaven [Mutter Kusters Fahrt Zum Himmel] (1975) Theme (Peer Raben) FR: LP = Cine Disc 88.087 [Peer Raben:ST]

4509 Mother Wore Tights (1947) Highlights (Josef Myrow) US:LP-BP = Classic International Filmusicals 3008

4510 Mother's Boy (1929) Themes-A-B/US:78 = RCA/Victor 21940 [Morton Downey:ST]; Themes-C-D/US:78 = RCA/Victor 21958 [Morton Downey: ST]

4511 Mothra (1961) Excerpts (Yuji Koseki) JA:LP = Toho 8123 [@ST]; Theme (Yuji Koseki) US:LP-BP = POO 104 [@ST]

4512 Mots pour le Dire, Les (1983) Score (Jean-Marie Senia) FR:LP = Milan A-224*

4513 Moulin Rouge (1934) Highlights (Harry Warren) US:LP-BP = Golden Legends 2000/1

4514 Moulin Rouge (1952) Theme (Georges Auric) US:SP = Columbia 4-39944 + US:SP = Columbia 4-33007 [Percy Faith]; Theme (Georges Auric) US:LP = Columbia 6255 [Percy Faith]

4515 Mountain, The (1956) Highlights (Daniele Amfitheatrof) US:LP = Decca DL-8449

4516 Mountain Music (1937) Theme/US:LP-MS-BP = Legends 1000/5-6 [Martha Raye:ST]

4517 Mountain of Magic [Der Zauberberg] (1979) Score (Jurgen Knieper) GE:LP = Celine 0005*

4518 Mouse and His Child, The (1977) Theme (Roger Kellaway) US:LP = Choice 6832* [Gene Lees]

4519 Move (1970) Theme (Marvin Hamlisch) US:SP = A&M 1215* [Larry Marks:ST]

4520 Move Over Darling (1963) Themes (Joe Lubin) US:SP = Columbia 4-42912 [Doris Day:ST]; Themes (Joe Lubin) US:LP = Harmony 11192 [Doris Day:ST]

4521 Movie Movie (1978) Highlights (Ralph Burns) US:LP = Film Score FS-7914* [Studio Cast]

4522 Movie Star—American Style (1970) Score (Joe Green) US:LP-PP = MSAS 1*

4523 Movin' On [Industrial Short] Score (Bonnie Dobson) US:LP-PP = United Transportation HMP-69

4524 Moving Day [Cartoon] (1936) Theme (Al Malotte) US:78 = Bluebird BK-9 [ST]

4525 Moving Violations (1985) Theme (Bruce Roberts) US:SP = RCA 14056* [Nona Hendryx:ST]

4526 Ms. Don Juan [Don Juan 1973] [Miss Don Juan] [Mistress Don Juan (1973) Score (Michel Magne) FR:LP = Barclay 80485*

4527 M'sieur la Caille *see* Lovemaker, The

4528 Mujer Perdida, La / Excerpts (various) US:LP = Pronto PHL-6015 [Sarita Montiel:ST]

4529 Mummy's Hand, The (1940) Themes (Hans J. Salter) US:LP = Citadel 6026 + US:LP = Citadel 7012 [Hans J. Salter:ST]

4530 Muppet Movie, The (1979) Score (Kenny Ascher & Paul Williams) US:LP = Atlantic SD-16001*

4531 Muppets Take Manhattan, The (1984) Score (Jeffrey Moss) US:LP = WB 25114-1*

4532 Murder at the Gallop (1963) Theme (film theme from "Murder She Said") US:LP = MGM 4185* [@Ron Goodwin:ST]

4533 Murder at the Vanities (1934) Theme-A/US:LP-MS = Epic L2N-6072 [@Carl Brisson:ST]; Theme-B/US:78 = Brunswick 6887 [Carl Brisson:ST]; Theme-C/US:78 = RCA/Victor 24622 [Duke Ellington:ST]

4534 Murder by Contract (1958) Themes (Perry Botkin) US:SP = Decca 9-30912 [Perry Botkin:ST]; Theme (Perry Botkin) US:SP = Decca 9-30936 [Tommy Dorsey Orchestra]

4535 Murder Clinic [La Lama Nel Corpo] (1966) Score (Francesco DeMasi) IT:LP = CAM CDR-33.18

4536 Murder, Inc. (1951) *see* Enforcer, The

4537 Murder, Inc. (1960) Score (e:Frank DeVol/e:George David Weiss) US:LP = Canadian American 1003

4538 Murder on the Orient Express (1974) Score (Richard Rodney Bennett) US:LP = Capitol ST-11361*

4539 Murder, She Said (1961) Theme (Ron Goodwin) US:SP = Columbia 4-42195 [Jack Pleis]; Theme (Ron Goodwin) US:LP = MGM 4185* [@Ron Goodwin:ST]

4540 Murder Without Crime (1950) Theme (Philip Green) GB:78 = Columbia 1702 [Philip Green:ST]

4541 Murderer's Row (1966) Score (Lalo Schifrin) US:LP = Colgems COMO-5003/COSO-5003* + Theme (Lalo Schifrin) US:SP = Reprise 0538 [Dean Martin:ST]

4542 Murderock (1985) Score (Keith Emerson) GB:LP = Chord 4*

4543 Murmur of the Heart [Dearest Love] (1972) Score (pop music) US:LP = Roulette RS-3006*

4544 Murph the Surf [Live a Little, Steal a Lot] [You Can't Steal Love] (1975) Score (Philip Lambro) US:LP = Motown M6-839*

4545 Murri Affair, The *see* La Grande Bourgeoise

4546 Muscle Beach Party (1964) Score (s:Roger Christian & Gary Usher/ t:Jerry Styner) US:LP = Buena Vista BV-3314/ST-3314* + US:LP = Rhino RNDF-205* [Annette:ST]

4547 Music for Millions (1944) Theme-A/US:78 = Decca 5116 [Jimmy Durante:ST]; Theme-B/US:78 = Decca 23467 [Larry Adler:ST]

4548 Music Goes Round, The (1936) Themes-A-B/US:78 = Decca 700 [Harry Richman:ST]; Themes-C-D/US: 701 [Harry Richman:ST]

4549 Music in My Heart (1940) Theme/US:78 = Decca 2932 [Tony Martin:ST]

4550 Music in the Air (1934) Highlights (stage songs:Jerome Kern) US:LP-BP = JJA 19747 [@ST]

4551 Music Is Magic (1935) Highlights (various) US:LP-BP = Caliban 6047

4552 Music Lovers, The (1971) Score (classical music) US:LP = UA UAS-5217* [Andre Previn:ST]

4553 Music Man, The (1962) Score (stage songs:Meredith Willson) US: LP = WB B-1459/BS-1459*

4554 Mussolini *see* Last Days of Mussolini

4555 Mustang Country (1976) Theme (Lee Holdridge) US:SP = MCA 40567* [Denny Brooks:ST]

4556 Mutant (1984) Score (Richard Band) US:LP = Varese STV-81209*

4557 Mutiny in the South Seas [La Morte Viene da Manila] (1965) Highlights (Francesco DeMasi) IT:EP = CAM CDR-45-18

4558 Mutiny on the Bounty (1935) Highlights (Herbert Stothart) US:LP-MS = Tony Thomas TTST-1/2

4559 Mutiny on the Bounty (1962) Score (Bronislau Kaper) US:LP = MGM 1E-4/1SE-4*

4560 My Best Friend's Girl [La Femme de Mon Pote] (1984) Score (pop music) FR:LP = Mercury 224*

4561 My Best Girl (1927) Theme [Silent II] (Lee Erwin) US:LP = Angel 36073* [Lee Erwin:ST]

4562 My Blue Heaven (1950) Highlights (Harold Arlen) US:LP-BP = Titania 503

4563 My Brilliant Career (1980) Score (as:Jack Grimsley & Nathan Waks) AU:LP = 7 Records MLF-416*

4564 My Champion (1980) Score (Jun Sato) JA:LP = Orange House ORP-8001*

4565 My Dear Assassin *see* Mio Caro Assassino

4566 My Dream Is Yours (1949) Highlights (Harry Warren) US:LP-BP = Titania 501

4567 My Fair Lady (1964) Score (stage songs:Frederick Loewe) US:LP = Columbia KOL-8000/KOS-2600*

4568 My Favorite Brunette (1947) Theme (Jay Livingston & Ray Evans) US:78 = Capitol 381 [Bob Hope & Dorothy Lamour:ST]; Theme (Jay Livingston & Ray Evans) US:SP = Capitol 1458 [Dean Martin]; Theme (Jay Livingston & Ray Evans) US:LP-BP = Legends 1000/4 [Dorothy Lamour:ST]

4569 My Favorite Spy (1942) Themes (James Van Heusen) US:78 = Columbia 36575 [Kay Kyser:ST]

4570 My Favorite Spy (1951) Theme (Jay Livingston & Ray Evans) US:SP = RCA 45-4350 [Frankie Carle]

4571 My Foolish Heart (1949) Theme (Victor Young) US:SP = Decca 9-24830 [Victor Young:ST]; Theme (Victor Young) US:LP = Decca 8364 [Victor Young:ST]; Theme (Victor Young) US: LP = Jubilee 1034* + US:LP = Citadel 6024* [Harry Sukman]

4572 My Friend Irma (1949) Themes (Jay Livingston & Ray Evans) GB:78 = Capitol 13314 + US:SP = Capitol 54-691 [Dean Martin:ST]

4573 My Friend Irma Goes West (1950) Themes (Jay Livingston & Ray Evans) US:SP = Capitol 1028 [Dean Martin:ST]; Theme (Jay Livingston &

Ray Evans) US:SP = Capitol 1682 [Dean Martin:ST]

4574 My Friends [Amici Mei] (1977) Score (Carlo Rustichelli) IT:LP = Cinevox 33/93*

4575 My Gal Sal (1942) Highlights (Ralph Rainger) US:LP-BP = Caliban 6035

4576 My Geisha (1962) Score (e:Franz Waxman/e:classical music) US:LP = RCA LOC-1070/LSO-1070*

4577 My Little Chickadee (1940) Theme (Ben Oakland) US:LP-BP = Caliban 6036 [Mae West:ST]

4578 My Little Pony—The Movie (1986) Highlights + Dialog (e:Rob Walsh/e:Tommy Goodman) US:LP = Kid Stuff DAR-3903*

4579 My Main Man from Stoney Island *see* Stoney Island

4580 My Man (1928) Excerpts (various) US:LP = Audio Fidelity 707 [Fanny Brice:ST]

4581 My Name Is Nobody (1974) Score (Ennio Morricone) US:LP = Cerberus CEMS-0101*

4582 My New Partner [Les Ripoux] (1985) Score (Francis Lai) FR:LP = WB WEA 2374.3204*

4583 My Old Kentucky Home [Cartoon] (1946) Sequence + Dialog (Philip Scheib) US:LP = Peter Pan 1118 [@ST]

4584 My Pleasure Is My Business (1975) Score (Tom Cochrane) CA:LP = Daffodil DAF-10051*

4585 My Reputation (1946) Excerpts (Max Steiner) US:LP-BP = Tony Thomas TTMS-16 [Max Steiner:ST]; Theme (Max Steiner) US:SP = MGM 12053 [The Four Joes]

4586 My Side of the Mountain (1969) Theme + Underscore + Dialog (t:Theodore Bikel/u:Wilfred Josephs) US:LP = Capitol ST-245*

4587 My Six Loves (1963) Theme-A (James Van Heusen) US:SP = Dot 16465 [Debbie Reynolds:ST]; Theme-B (James Van Heusen) US:SP = RCA 45-8161 [Peter Nero]; Theme-B (James Van Heusen) US:LP = Camden 2139* [Peter Nero]

4588 My Son, the Vampire [Old Mother Riley Meets the Vampire] [Vampire Over London] (1952) Theme (Allan Sherman) US:SP = WB 5419 [Allan Sherman:ST]

4589 My Song for You (1934) Theme (Mischa Spoliansky) GB:78 = Parlophone 8639 [ST]

4590 My Tutor (1983) Score (Webster Lewis) US:LP = Regency RI-8506*

4591 My Uncle, Mr. Hulot [Mon Oncle] (1956) Highlights (e:Frank Barcellini/t:Alain Romans) GB:EP = Fontana 17175; Themes (Frank Barcellini) US:LP = UA 15554 [@ST]

4592 My Way [The Winners] (1974) Score (Robin Netcher) JA:LP = EMI/Odeon EOS-80414*

4593 My Way—Part 2 (1977) Themes (John D'Andrea) JA:SP = WB 233* [ST]

4594 My Wild Irish Rose (1947) Highlights (pop music) US:LP-BP = Titania 505

4595 Myra Breckinridge (1970) Themes (Sammy Fain/Otis Redding) US:SP = 20th 6718* [Mae West:ST]; Themes (Sammy Fain/Otis Redding) US:LP-BP = Caliban 6036 [Mae West:ST]

4596 Mysterians, The (1957) Excerpts (Akira Ifukube) JA:LP = Toho AX-8106 [@ST]; Theme (Akira Ifukube) US:LP-BP = POO 104 [@ST]

4597 Mysteries (1979) Score (Laurens Van Rooyen) HO:LP = CBS 82869*

4598 Mysterious Island (1961) Score (Bernard Herrmann) GB:LP = Cloud Nine CN-4002; Excerpts (Bernard Herrmann) US:LP = London SPC-21137* [Bernard Herrmann:ST]

4599 Mysterious Island of Captain Nemo, The [L'Isola Misteriosa e il Capitano Nemo] (1973) Score (Gianni Ferrio) IT:LP = Cinevox 33/62*

4600 Mysterious Stranger, The [Cartoon] (1948) Sequence + Dialog (Philip Scheib) US:LP = Peter Pan 1118 [@ST]

4601 Mystery of the Sacred Shroud [Silent Witness] (1978) Score (Alan Hawkshaw) GB:LP = Gull GULP-1030*

4602 Mystifiers, The *see* Symphony for a Massacre

N

4603 Nagin (1956) Highlights (Herman Kumar) US:LP = Capitol T-10090

4604 Naked Angels, The (1969) Score (s:Jeffrey Simmons/t:Randy Steirling) US:LP = Straight STS-1056*

4605 Naked Ape, The (1974) Score (Jimmy Webb) US:LP = Playboy PB-125*

4606 Naked City, The (1948) Highlights (Miklos Rozsa) US:LP-BP = Tony Thomas TTMR-3; Themes (Miklos Rozsa) US:LP = Decca 710015* + US:LP = Varese 81053* + US:LP = Deutsche 2584.013* [Miklos Rozsa:ST]

4607 Naked Island, The *see* Island, The

4608 Naked Maja, The (1959) Score (A.F. Lavagnino) US:LP = UA UAL-4031/UAS-5031e

4609 Naked Prey, The (1966) Score (as:Moses Asch) US:LP = Folkways FS-3854

4610 Naked Runner, The (1967) Theme (Harry Sukman) US:SP = Columbia 4-44255 [Andre Kostelanetz]; Theme (Harry Sukman) US:SP = Reprise 0610 [Frank Sinatra]; Theme (Harry Sukman) US:LP = RCA 4205* [Peter Nero]

4611 Naked Sea, The (1955) Highlights (Laurindo Almeida) US:EP = Capitol EAP1-675

4612 Naked Under Leather *see* Girl on a Motorcycle

4613 Name of the Game Is Kill, The [The Female Trap] (1968) Theme (Stu Phillips) US:SP = Reprise 0287 [The Electric Prunes:ST]

4614 Name of the Rose, The (1986) Score (James Horner) GE:LP = Teldec 626-404-AS*

4615 Nameless Star, The [Mona, l'Etoile Sans Nom] (1965) Highlights (Georges Delerue) FR:EP = Barclay 71065

4616 Namu, the Killer Whale (1966) Theme (Tom Glazer) US:SP = UA 50045 [Tom Glazer:ST]; Theme (Tom Glazer) US:LP = UA 6540* [Tom Glazer:ST]

4617 Nana (1983) Score (Ennio Morricone) IT:LP = Cinevox 33/161*

4618 Nancy Goes to Rio (1950) Highlights (t:George Stoll/etc.) US:LP-10 = MGM E-508 + US:LP-MS = MGM 2SES-53

4619 Nanon / Theme (Alois Melichar) US:LP = Mercury 10001 [Erna Sack:ST]

4620 Napoleon (1927) Score [Silent II] (Carmine Coppola) US:LP = CBS 37230*; Score [Silent II] (e:Carl Davis/etc.) GB:LP = Chrysalis 1423*; Excerpts [Silent I] (Arthur Honegger) RU:LP = Melodiya C10.20459.009* [Gennedy Rozhdestvensky]

4621 Napoleon (1954) Highlights (Jean Francaix) FR:EP = Philips 432.600

4622 Napoleon and Samantha (1972) Themes (Buddy Baker) US:SP = Buena Vista 490 [Shane Tatum]

4623 Nashville (1975) Score (e:Richard Baskin/etc.) US:LP = ABC ABCD-893*

4624 Nashville Coyote, The (1974) Score (s:Buddy Baker/t:Franklyn Marks) US:LP = JMI 4005*

4625 Nashville Rebel, The (1966) Score (e:Jay Sheridan/etc.) US:LP = RCA LPM-3736/LSP-3736e

4626 Nat Gonella and His Georgians [Short] (1935) Excerpts (pop music) GB:LP = WRC SH-197 [@ST]

4627 National Lampoon's Animal House (1978) Score (t:Elmer Bernstein/t:Stephen Bishop/e:pop music) US:LP = MCA 3046*

4628 National Lampoon's Vacation (1983) Score (e:Ralph Burns/etc.) US:LP = WB 23909-1*

4629 Native Son (1986) Score (James Mtume) US:LP = MCA 6198*

4630 Natural, The (1984) Score (Randy Newman) US:LP = WB 25116-1*

4631 Nature's Half Acre [Short] (1951) Excerpts (Paul Smith) US:LP = Disneyland WDL-4011 [Paul Smith:ST]

4632 Naughty Arlette [The Romantic Age] (1949) Theme (Charles Williams) GB:78-PP = Rank FM-83 [ST]

4633 Naughty, But Nice (1939) Theme/US:78 = Decca 2387 [Dick Powell:ST]

4634 Naughty Marietta (1935) Score

(stage songs:Victor Herbert) US:LP-BP = Hollywood Soundstage HS-413; Excerpts (stage songs:Victor Herbert) US:LP = RCA LPV-526 [Jeanette MacDonald & Nelson Eddy:ST]

4635 Navajo Joe (1970) Score (Ennio Morricone-aka-Leo Nichols) US:LP = UA LA-292*

4636 Navigator, The (1924) Excerpts [Silent II] (Claude Bolling) FR:LP = Columbia XM-241 [Claude Bolling:ST]

4637 Navy Blues (1941) Excerpts (Arthur Schwartz) US:LP-BP = Marsher 201 [Ann Sheridan:ST]

4638 Necromancy (1972) Theme (Fred Karger) US:SP-PP = Zenith 101 [Fred Karger:ST]; Theme (Fred Karger) US:SP = Atherton 450 [Dick Haymes]; Theme (Fred Karger) US:LP = Ballad DHS-7* [Dick Haymes]

4639 Ned Kelly (1969) Score (Shel Silverstein) US:LP = UA UAS-5213* + US:LP = UA LA-300*

4640 Neighborhood of Angels / Score (Manos Hadjidakis) GR:LP = Odeon OMCGA-38 + GR:LP = HMV GCLP-7

4641 Nel Blu di Pinto di Blu (1959) Theme (Domenico Modugno) US:SP = Decca 9-30677 [Domenico Modugno: ST]; Theme (Domenico Modugno) US: SP = Capitol 4024 [Nelson Riddle]; Theme (Domenico Modugno) US:LP = Audio Fidelity 5915 [Jo Basile]

4642 Neptune's Daughter (1949) Themes-A-B/US:LP-BP = JJA 19762 [@ST]; Theme-C/US:78 = MGM 30197 [Ricardo Montalban:ST]

4643 Nest of Vipers [Ritratto di Borghesia in Nero] (1979) Themes (Vincenzo Tempera) IT:SP = WB 17090* [ST]

4644 Net, The *see* Project M.7

4645 Nevada Smith (1966) Score (Alfred Newman) US:LP = Dot DLP-3718/DLP-25718*

4646 Never a Dull Moment (1950) Theme (Kay Swift) US:SP = Capitol 1309 [Margaret Whiting]

4647 Never Cry Wolf (1983) Highlights (Mark Isham) US:LP = Windham Hill WH-1041* [Mark Isham:ST]

4648 Never Ending Story, The (1984) Score-A [Europe Release] (Klaus Doldinger) GE:LP = WB WEA 250-396-1*; Score-B [USA Release] (e:Giorgio Moroder/e:Klaus Doldinger) US:LP = EMI ST-17139*

4649 Never Give an Inch *see* Sometimes a Great Notion

4650 Never Let Go (1960) Themes-A-B (John Barry) GB:SP = Columbia 4665 [Adam Faith:ST]; Theme-C (John Barry) GB:SP = Columbia 4480 [John Barry:ST]; Theme-C (John Barry) GB: LP = EMI 21 [John Barry:ST]

4651 Never Love a Stranger (1958) Theme (Raymond Scott) US:LP = Wing 12136* [Ramon Duval]

4652 Never on Sunday [Les Enfants du Piree] (1960) Score (Manos Hadjidakis) US:LP = UA UAL-4070/ UAS-5070*

4653 Never Put It in Writing (1964) Theme (Pat Boone) US:SP = Dot 16576 [Pat Boone:ST]

4654 Never Say Die (1939) Theme (Ralph Rainger) US:LP-MS-BP = Legends 1000/5-6 [Martha Raye:ST]

4655 Never Say Goodbye (1946) Theme (Harry Warren) US:78 = RCA/ Victor 20-1901 [Tommy Dorsey]

4656 Never Say Never Again (1983) Score (Michel Legrand) JA:LP = Seven Seas K28P-4122*; Themes (Michel Legrand) US:SP = A&M 2596* [Lani Hall/Michel Legrand:ST]; Theme (Michel Legrand) US:LP = A&M 4988* [Lani Hall:ST]

4657 Never Too Late (1965) Theme (David Rose) US:SP = MGM 13427 [David Rose:ST]; Theme (David Rose) US:SP = WB 5668 [Vic Damone]; Theme (David Rose) US:LP = Columbia 9772* [Tony Bennett]

4658 Never Too Young to Rock (1978) Score (e:Tony Macaulay/etc.) GB:LP = GTO GTLP-004*

4659 Never Trouble Trouble (1931) Theme/GB:78 = Columbia 465 [Lupino Lane:ST]

4660 New Adventures of Don Juan, The *see* Adventures of Don Juan, The

4661 New Babylon, The (1929) Score (Dmitri Shostakovich) US:LP = Columbia M-34502*

4662 New Face in Hell, A *see* P.J.

4663 New Faces of 1937 (1937) Theme/US:78 = Bluebird 6987 [Harriet Hilliard:ST]

4664 New Interns, The (1964) Score (Earle Hagen) US:LP = Colpix CP-473/SCP-473*

4665 New Kind of Love, A (1963) Score (s:Erroll Garner/as:Leith Stevens) US:LP = Mercury MG-20859/SR-60859*; Theme (pop music) US:SP = Reprise 20-209 [Frank Sinatra:ST]

4666 New Moon (1930) Highlights (stage songs:Sigmund Romberg/t:Herbert Stothart) US:LP-BP = Pelican 2020 + US:LP-BP = Raviola BMPB-1929

4667 New Moon (1940) Highlights (stage song:Sigmund Romberg) US: LP-BP = Pelican 103; Excerpts (stage songs: Sigmund Romberg) US:LP = Columbia ML-2164 + US:LP = CSP 13878 [Nelson Eddy:ST]

4668 New Orleans (1947) Score (pop music) US:LP = Giants of Jazz GOJ-1025

4669 New World, A [Un Monde Nouveau] (1966) Highlights (Michel Colombier) FR:EP = UA 36072

4670 New World of Stainless Steel, A [Industrial Short] Score (uncredited) US:LP-PP = Republic Steel L80P-5736

4671 New Years Evil (1981) Themes (Anthony Fried) US:SP = Cannon 5001* [Made in Japan:ST]

4672 New York Eye and Ear Control (1964) Score (Albert Ayler) US:LP = ESP 1016*

4673 New York, New York (1977) Scores (e:Ralph Burns/e:John Kander/e:pop music) US:LP-MS = UA LA-750*

4674 Newsfront (1979) Score (e: William Motzing/e:pop music) AU: LP = EMI EMB-10411*; Theme (William Motzing) US:LP = DRG 8202* [William Motzing:ST]

4675 Next Man, The (1976) Score (Michael Kamen) US:LP = Buddah BDS-5685*

4676 Niagara (1953) Theme (Lionel Newman) US:SP = Columbia 4-39911 [Toni Arden]; Theme (Lionel Newman) US:SP = Capitol 2319 [Dean Martin]; Theme (Lionel Newman) US:LP = DRG 15005 + US:LP-BP = Legends 1000/1 [Marilyn Monroe:ST]

4677 Nice Girl? (1941) Excerpts (various) US:78-MS = Decca 209 [Deanna Durbin:ST]

4678 Nice Girl Like Me, A (1969) Themes (Patrick Williams) US:LP = Verve 5075* [Patrick Williams:ST]; Theme (Patrick Williams) US:SP = Verve 10640 [Patrick Williams:ST]; Theme (Patrick Williams) US:SP = Liberty 56132 [Vicki Carr:ST]

4679 Nicholas and Alexandra (1971) Score (Richard Rodney Bennett) US:LP = Bell 1103*

4680 Nicholas Nickleby (1947) Excerpts (Lord Berners) US:LP = Columbia RL-3029 + US:LP = Ariel CBF-13 [@Ernest Irving]

4681 Nickle Queen (1971) Score (Sven Libaek) AU:LP=Philips 6357.003*

4682 Night After Night (1932) Theme/US:LP-BP = Caliban 6036 [Mae West:ST]

4683 Night Ambush [Ill Met by Moonlight] (1957) Theme (Mikis Theodorakis) US:SP = MGM 12475 [Ron Hargrave]

4684 Night and Day (1946) Score (pop music) US:LP-BP = Motion Picture Tracks MPT-6

4685 Night at Carnegie Hall, A *see* Carnegie Hall

4686 Night at the Opera, A (1935) Themes + Underscore + Dialog (t: Bronislau Kaper/u:Herbert Stothart) US:LP-BP = ReSound 7051; Theme (Nacio Herb Brown) US:LP = RCA LPV-579 + US:LP = RCA ANL1-1978 [@Allan Jones:ST]

4687 Night Caller, The [Fear in the City] [Peur Sur la Ville] (1975) Score (Ennio Morricone) FR:LP = WB 56135*

4688 Night Child, The *see* Cursed Medallion, The

4689 Night Crossing (1982) Score (Jerry Goldsmith) US:LP = Intrada RVF-6004*

4690 Night Digger, The (1971) Highlights (Bernard Herrmann) US:LP-BP = Cinema LP-8015

4691 Night Evelyn Came Out of the Grave, The (1971) Theme (Bruno Nicolai) IT:LP-PP = CAM CMO-022* [Bruno Nicolai:ST]

4692 Night Flight to Moscow *see* Serpent, The

4693 Night Has Eyes, The [Terror House] (1946) Theme (Charles Williams) GB:78 = Columbia 2272 [Charles Williams:ST]; Theme (Charles Williams) GB:LP = Saga 5018* + GB:LP = Boulevard 4028* [Gilbert Vinter]

4694 Night in Casablanca, A (1946) Theme (Harry Ruby) US:SP = MGM 511 [Connie Francis]; Theme (Harry Ruby) US:LP = Capitol 903 [Nat King Cole]; Theme (Harry Ruby) US:LP = Dot 3270 [Pat Boone]

4695 Night in Heaven, A (1983) Score (t:Jan Hammer/s:various) US: LP = A&M SP-4966*

4696 Night Is Not for Sleep *see* Nude in a White Car

4697 Night Is the Phantom *see* What!

4698 Night Is Young, The (1935) Theme-A/GB:78 = HMV 2778 [Ramon Novarro:ST]; Theme-B/GB:LP = MFP 1162 [Evelyn Laye:ST]

4699 Night Moves (1975) Theme (Michael Small) US:LP = WB 2230* [Michael Franks]; Theme (Michael Small) US:LP = Elektra 119* [Dee Dee Bridgewater]

4700 Night of San Lorenzo, The *see* Night of the Shooting Stars, The

4701 Night of the Blood Monster [Bloody Jungle] [Throne of Fire] [Il Trono di Fuoco] (1972) Score (Bruno Nicolai) IT:LP = Cinevox 33/32; Theme (Bruno Nicolai) US:LP-BP = GSF-1002 [@Bruno Nicolai:ST]

4702 Night of the Comet (1984) Score (t:Bob Summers/s:various) US: LP = Macola MRC-0900*

4703 Night of the Generals, The (1966) Score (Maurice Jarre) US:LP = Colgems COMO-5002/COSO-5002*

4704 Night of the Hunter, The (1955) Highlights + Underscore + Narration (Walter Schumann) US:LP = RCA LPM-1136

4705 Night of the Iguana, The (1964) Highlights (Benjamin Frankel) US:LP = MGM E-4247/SE-4247*; Underscore + Dialog (Benjamin Frankel) US:LP-PP = MGM PR-4

4706 Night of the Living Dead (1968) Score (stock music) US:LP = Varese STV-81151

4707 Night of the Quarter Moon (1959) Themes (James Van Heusen/ Charlotte Hawkins) US:EP = Capitol EAP1-1211 [Nat King Cole:ST]; Theme (James Van Heusen) US:LP = Capitol 2340 [Nat King Cole:ST]; Theme (James Van Heusen) US:SP = Metro 20017 [Andy Ackers]

4708 Night of the Shooting Stars, The [The Night of San Lorenzo] (1983) Score (e:Nicola Piovani/e:classical music) US:LP = Varese STV-81175*

4709 Night Passage (1957) Excerpts (Dimitri Tiomkin) US:LP-BP = Cinema LP-8012 [Dimitri Tiomkin:ST]; Theme (Dimitri Tiomkin) US:SP = Coral 9-61866 [The Lancers]; Theme (Dimitri Tiomkin) GB:LP = Unicorn 9002* [Laurie Johnson]

4710 Night Porter, The [Il Portiere di Notte] (1974) Highlights (Daniele Paris) IT:LP = RCA SNL1-7271*

4711 Night Shift (1982) Score (e: Burt Bacharach/etc.) US:LP = WB 23702-1*

4712 Night Song (1947) Theme-A (Leith Stevens) US:LP = Decca 8350 [Victor Young]; Theme-B (Hoagy Carmichael) US:LP-BP = JJA 19774 [@Hoagy Carmichael:ST]

4713 Night the Lights Went Out in Georgia, The (1981) Score (e:David Shire/etc.) US:LP = Mirage WTG-16051*

4714 Night They Invented Striptease, The *see* Night They Raided Minsky's, The

4715 Night They Raided Minsky's, The (1968) Score (Charles Strouse) US: LP = UA UAS-5191*

4716 Night Visitor, The [Salem Comes to Supper] (1971) Highlights (Henry Mancini) US:LP = Citadel CT-6015*

4717 Night Walker, The (1965) Theme (Vic Mizzy) US:SP = Decca 9-31738 [Sammy Kaye]; Theme (Vic Mizzy) US:LP = Decca 74655* [Sammy Kaye]

4718 Night Watch (1973) Theme (George Barrie) US:SP = Brut 807* [John Cameron:ST]

4719 Night Without Stars (1951) Theme (William Alwyn) GB:78-PP = Rank FM-111 [ST]

4720 Nightcomers, The (1972) Score (Jerry Fielding) US:LP-BP = Citadel CTJF-1*

4721 Nightfall (1957) Theme (Peter DeRose) US:SP = Decca 9-30100 [Al Hibbler:ST]; Theme (Peter DeRose) US: SP = Decca 9-30167 [Morris Stoloff]; Theme (Peter DeRose) US:LP = Coral 57065 [Dick Jacobs & George Cates]

4722 Nighthawks (1981) Score (Keith Emerson) US:LP = MCA 5196*

4723 Nightmare (1956) Theme (Herschel Burke Gilbert) US:SP = Capitol 3486 [Billy May]; Theme (Herschel Burke Gilbert) US:LP-BP = Cinema 8002 [@Billy May]

4724 Nightmare Castle [Gli Amanti d'Oltre Tomba] (1965) Excerpts (Ennio Morricone) IT:LP-PP = RCA SP-10004 [Ennio Morricone:ST]; Theme (Ennio Morricone) US:LP-BP = GSF 1002 [@Ennio Morricone:ST]

4725 Nightmare City [City of the Walking Dead] [Incuba sulla Citta Contaminata] (1980) Score (Stelvio Cipriani) IT:LP = Cinevox 8005*

4726 Nightmare on Elm Street (1984) Score (Charles Bernstein) US: LP = Varese STV-81236*

4727 Nightmare on Elm Street, Part 2—Freddy's Revenge (1986) Score (Chris Young) US:LP = Varese STV-81275*

4728 Nights in Hollywood (1934) Theme-A/US:78 = Melotone 13220 [Alice Faye:ST]; Theme-B/US:LP = Columbia 3068 [Alice Faye:ST]

4729 Nights of Cabiria [Le Notte di Cabiria] [Cabiria] (1957) Highlights (Nino Rota) IT:EP = Pathe AQ-28; Theme (Nino Rota) US:LP = Epic 3593 [Gian Stellari]; Theme (Nino Rota) IT:LP = CAM 9053* [Nino Rota: ST]

4730 Nijinsky (1980) Score (classical music) US:LP = CBS 35861*

4731 Nikki, Wild Dog of the North (1961) Underscore + Dialog (Paul Smith) US:LP = Disneyland DQ-1913 + US:LP = Disneyland DQ-1281

4732 9½ Weeks (1986) Score (t: Jonathan Elias/s:various) US:LP = EMI SV-12470*

4733 Nine Hours to Rama (1963) Score (Malcolm Arnold) US:LP = London M-76002

4734 Nine Lives of Fritz the Cat, The (1974) Themes (Tom Scott/Max Bennett) US:SP = Ode 66048* [Tom Scott:ST]

4735 9/30/55 [September 30, 1955] [24 Hours of the Rebel] (1977) Score (as: Leonard Rosenman) US:LP = MCA 2313*

4736 9 to 5 (1980) Score (s:Charles Fox/t:Dolly Parton) US:LP = 20th T-627*

4737 1984 (1984) Score (The Eurythmics) US:LP = RCA ABL1-5349*

4738 1941 (1979) Score (John Williams) US:LP = Arista AL-9510*

4739 1900 [Novecento] (1977) Score (Ennio Morricone) IT:LP = RCA TBL1-1221*

4740 1990—The Bronx Warriors (1983) Score (Walter Rizzati) IT:LP = Beat LPF-062*

4741 99 and 44/100% Dead (1974) Theme (Henry Mancini) US:SP = RCA 0323* [Henry Mancini:ST]; Theme (Henry Mancini) US:LP = RCA 1-0672* + US:LP = RCA 1-3347* [Henry Mancini:ST]

4742 No Blade of Grass (1970) Theme (Carroll) US:SP = MGM 14214 [Casey Kasem]; Theme (Carroll) US: LP = MGM 4761* [Mike Curb Congregation]

4743 No Go! (1974) Score (folk music) US:LP = Island SMAS-9333*

4744 No Leave, No Love (1946) Highlights (t:George Stoll/etc.) US:78-MS = Cosmo DMR-102 [Pat Kirkwood: ST]

4745 No Love for Johnnie (1961) Theme (Malcolm Arnold) US:SP = London 45-10601 [Gerry Beckles]

4746 No Mercy (1986) Score (Alan Silvestri) US:LP = TVT Records TVT-3002*

4747 No, My Darling Daughter! (1961) Themes-A-B (David Lee/Norrie Paramor) GB:SP = Parlophone 4804 [Michael Redgrave & Juliet Mills/Norrie Paramor:ST]; Themes-C-D (Norrie Paramor) GB:SP = Columbia 4686 [Alex Welsh]; Theme-D (Norrie Paramor) US: SP = RCA 47-8606 [Pee Wee Spitelera];

Theme-D (Norrie Paramor) US:LP = RCA 3511* [Pee Wee Spitelera]

4748 No Nukes (1980) Scores (rock music) US:LP-MS3 = Asylum ML-801*

4749 No Orchids for Miss Blandish (1948) Theme (George Melachrino) GB: 78 = HMV 3736 [George Melachrino:ST]

4750 No Problem [Pas de Probleme] [Non C'e Problema] (1979) Themes (Philippe Sarde) FR:SP = Pathe C010. 14259* + IT:SP = CAM AMP-173* [ST]

4751 No Sad Songs for Me (1950) Highlights (George Duning) US:LP = Web ST-108

4752 No Small Affair (1984) Score (e:Rupert Holmes/e:various) US:LP = Atlantic 80189-1*

4753 No Sun in Venice [Sait-on Jamais] (1958) Score (John Lewis) US: LP = Atlantic 1284/S-1284*

4754 No Surrender (1986) Score (Daryl Runswick) GB:LP = Pact 12*

4755 No Time for Sergeants (1958) Theme (Ray Heindorf) US:LP = MGM 3753 + US:LP = Lion 70136 [Leroy Holmes]

4756 No Trees in the Street (1959) Highlights (Laurie Johnson) GB:EP = Nixa 24097

4757 No Way Out [The Big Guns] [Tony Arzenta, The Big Guns] (1973) Score (Gianni Ferrio) IT:LP = Ariete 2013*

4758 No Way to Treat a Lady (1968) Score (Stanley Myers) US:LP = Dot DLP-3846/DLP-25846*

4759 Noah's Ark [Cartoon] (1959) Excerpts (Mel Leven) US:LP = Disneyland DQ-1269 + US:LP-MS = Disneyland DDF-4 [@Jeanne Gayle]; Themes (Mel Leven) US:SP = Disneyland 126 [Jeanne Gayle]

4760 Nocturna (1979) Score (Norman Bergen) US:LP + SP-12 = MCA 2-4121*

4761 None But the Brave (1965) Theme (John Williams) US:SP = Reprise 0339 [Morris Stoloff:ST]

4762 Noose, The *see* Silk Noose, The

4763 Nora Prentiss (1947) Themes/ US:LP-BP = Marsher 201 [Ann Sheridan:ST]

4764 Norma Rae (1979) Theme (David Shire) US:SP-PP = Fox/Fanfare NR-5554 [Jennifer Warnes:ST]; Theme (David Shire) US:SP = 20th 2457* [Dusty Springfield]; Theme (David Shire) US: LP = Arista 8-8121* [Jennifer Warnes: ST]

4765 Norman ... Is That You? (1976) Theme-A (William Goldstein) US: SP = Tamla 54275* [Thelma Houston: ST]; Theme-B (William Goldstein) US: SP = Motown 54276* [Smokey Robin-son:ST]

4766 Norman Loves Rose (1982) Themes (Mike Perjanik) AU:SP = EMI 783* [ST]

4767 Norte, El (1984) Score (e:Emil Richards/e:various) US:LP = Antilles IVA-4*

4768 North by Northwest (1959) Score (Bernard Herrmann) US:LP = Starlog/Varese SV-95001* [Laurie Johnson]; Theme (Bernard Herrmann) US: LP = London 44126* [Bernard Herr-mann:ST]

4769 North to Alaska (1960) Theme (Mike Phillips) US:SP = Columbia 4-33004 [Johnny Horton:ST]; Theme (Mike Phillips) US:LP = Columbia 1569/8396* [Johnny Horton:ST]

4770 Northwest Outpost (1947) Highlights (Rudolf Friml) US:78-MS = Columbia MM-690 [Nelson Eddy:ST]

4771 Norwood (1970) Score (e:Al DeLory/e:Mac Davis) US:LP = Capitol SW-475*

4772 Nosferatu, The Vampyre (1979) Score (Popol Vuh) FR:LP = Egg 900.573*

4773 Not As a Stranger (1955) Theme (James Van Heusen) US:SP = Capitol 3130 [Frank Sinatra]; Theme (James Van Heusen) US:SP = Epic 5-9109 [Russell Arms]; Theme (James Van Heusen) US:LP = RCA 1245 [Henri Rene]

4774 Not with My Wife, You Don't! (1966) Score (John Williams) US: LP = WB W-1668/WS-1668*

4775 Nothing But a Man (1964) Score (pop music) US:LP = Motown M-630

4776 Nothing But the Best (1964) Score (Ron Grainer) US:LP = Colpix CP-477/SCP-477*

4777 Nothing But the Truth (1929) Theme / US:78 = RCA / Victor 21917 [Helen Kane:ST]

4778 Nothing in Common (1986) Score (e:Patrick Leonard/e:various) US: LP = Arista AL9-8438*

4779 Notorious (1946) Excerpts (Roy Webb) US:LP = Varese 704.250* [Charles Ketcham]

4780 Notorious Gentleman [The Rake's Progress] (1945) Theme (William Alwyn) GB:78 = Decca 1544 [Muir Mathieson:ST]; Theme (William Alwyn) US:LP = Ariel 13 [@Muir Mathieson: ST]

4781 Notte, La (1961) Highlights (Giorgio Gaslini) IT:EP = Pathe 7-EMF-274

4782 Notti Bianche, Le *see* White Nights, The

4783 Novices, The [Les Nocives] (1970) Highlights (Francois DeRoubaix) FR:EP = Barclay 71455

4784 Now and Forever (1983) Theme (Graham Russell) US:LP = Arista 8010* [Air Supply:ST]

4785 Now I'll Tell Them (1934) Theme/US:LP-BP = Scarce Rarities 5502 [Alice Faye:ST]

4786 Now, Voyager (1942) Excerpts (Max Steiner) US:LP-10 = Capitol T-250 + US:LP = Capitol T-387 + US:LP = Angel S-36068 [Max Steiner:ST]

4787 Nuclear Terror *see* Golden Rendezvous

4788 Nude Bomb, The [The Return of Maxwell Smart] (1980) Theme (Lalo Schifrin) US:SP = MCA 41266* [Merry Clayton:ST]

4789 Nude in a White Car [Night Is Not for Sleep] [Toi le Venin] (1958) Highlights (Andre Gosselain) FR:EP = Fontana 460.586; Theme (Andre Gosselain) US:SP = Waldork 10001 [Jerry Wald]

4790 Nude Odyssey [Odissea Nuda] (1960) Highlights (A.F. Lavagnino) FR: EP = RCA 75667 + IT:EP = RCA EPA-405; Theme (A.F. Lavagnino) US: LP = RCA FSO-4* [@ST]

4791 Nuit de Varennes, La (1983) Score (Armando Trovajoli) FR:LP = Polydor 2393.315*

4792 Nun and the Devil, The [Le Monache de Sant'Arcangelo] (1973) Score (Piero Piccioni) IT:LP = General Music 55492* + FR:LP = Delta/Pathe C025.40001*

4793 Nun's Story, The (1959) Score-A (Franz Waxman) US:LP = WB W-1306/WS-1306*; Score-B (Franz Waxman) US:LP = Stanyan SRO-4022*

4794 Nunzio (1978) Score (Lalo Schifrin) US:LP = MCA 2374*

4795 Nutcracker Fantasy, The (1979) Score (as:Akahito Wakatsuki & Kentaro Haneda) JA:LP = Sanrio MQF-6001*

4796 Nutcracker—The Motion Picture (1986) Scores (classical music) US: LP-MS = Telarc DG-10137*

4797 Nutty, Naughty Chateau [Chateau in Sweden] [Chateau en Suede] (1963) Highlights (Raymond Le Senechal) FR:EP = Barclay 70596; Theme US:SP = MGM 13289 [David Rose]; Theme (Raymond Le Senechal) US: LP = MGM 4271* [David Rose]

O

4798 O Lucky Man! (1973) Score (Alan Price) US:LP = WB BS-2710*

4799 OSS 117—Mission for a Killer [Furia a Bahia pour OSS 117] (1966) Highlights (Michel Magne) FR:EP = Barclay 70547

4800 Objective, Burma! (1945) Highlights (Franz Waxman) US:LP-BP = Cine LP-818; Theme (Franz Waxman) US:LP = RCA 1-0912* [Charles Gerhardt]

4801 Obsession (1949) *see* Hidden Room, The

4802 Obsession (1976) Score (Bernard Herrmann) US:LP = London SPC-21160*

4803 Occurrence at Owl Creek Bridge, An [La Riviere du Hibou] [Short] (1962) Highlights (Henri Lanoe) FR:EP = Barclay 70575

4804 Ocean's 11 (1960) Themes (James Van Heusen) US:SP = Verve 15171 [Sammy Davis, Jr.:ST]; Theme (James Van Heusen) US:SP = Capitol 4420 [Dean Martin:ST]

4805 October Man, The (1947) Theme (William Alwyn) GB:78-PP = Rank FM-15 [ST]

4806 Octopussy (1983) Score (John Barry) US:LP = A&M SP-4967*

4807 Odd Couple, The (1968) Highlights + Dialog (Neal Hefti) US:LP = Dot DLP-25862*

4808 Odd Man Out (1947) Theme (William Alwyn) US:LP = Columbia 794 [Paul Weston]

4809 Odds Against Tomorrow (1959) Score (John Lewis) US:LP = UA UAL-4061/UAS-5061*

4810 Ode to Billy Joe (1976) Score (e:Michel Legrand/etc.) US:LP = WB BS-2947*

4811 Odessa File, The (1974) Score (Andrew Lloyd Webber) US:LP = MCA 2084*

4812 Odette (1950) Theme (Anthony Collins) GB:78 = Columbia 1688 [Charles Williams]; Theme (Anthony Collins) GB:LP = WRC 384 [@Charles Williams]

4813 Odeur des Fauves, L' *see* Smell of the Savages, The

4814 Odissea Nuda *see* Nude Odyssey

4815 Oedipus Rex (1957) Underscore + Dialog (Cedric Thorpe Davie) US:LP-MS = Caedmon TC-2012

4816 O'er the Ramparts We Watched [Industrial Short] Underscore + Dialog (uncredited) US:LP-PP = U.S. Rubber 1050

4817 Oeufs de l'Autruche, Les (1957) Theme (Henri Sauget) US:LP = Dot 3120 [Ray Ventura]

4818 Of Flesh and Blood [Les Grandes Chemins] (1963) Highlights (Michel Magne) FR:EP = Barclay 70559

4819 Of Human Bondage (1934) Theme (Max Steiner) US:LP-BP = Max Steiner Music Society 25781 [Max Steiner:ST]

4820 Of Human Bondage (1946) Excerpts (Erich Wolfgang Korngold) US:LP = RCA ARL1-0185* [Charles Gerhardt]; Theme (Erich Wolfgang Korngold) US:LP = RCA 3330* + US:LP = RCA 1-3707* [Charles Ger-hardt]

4821 Of Human Bondage (1964) Themes (Ron Goodwin) US:LP = MGM 4261* [@Ron Goodwin:ST]; Theme (Ron Goodwin) US:LP = Time 2169* [The Manhattan Pops]

4822 Of Love and Desire (1963) Score (Ronald Stein) US:LP = 20th FXG-5014/SXG-5014*

4823 Of Mice and Men (1940) Underscore + Dialog (Aaron Copland) US:LP-MS = Mark 56 #602; Themes (Aaron Copland) US:LP = Columbia 33586* [Aaron Copland:ST]; Themes (Aaron Copland) US:LP = MGM 3334 + US:LP = MGM 3367 [Arthur Winograd]

4824 Office Blues (1929) Themes/ US:LP-BP = Curtain Calls 100/21 [Ginger Rogers:ST]

4825 Office Girl [Sunshine Susie] Themes/GB:78 = Columbia 687 [Renate Mueller:ST]

4826 Officer and a Gentleman, An (1982) Score (e:Jack Nitzsche/e:pop music) US:LP = Island 90017-1*

4827 Offside 7 *see* Escape to Athena

4828 Oh Dad, Poor Dad, Mama's Hung You in the Closet and I'm Feelin' So Sad (1967) Score (Neal Hefti) US: LP = RCA LPM-3750/LSP-3750*

4829 Oh, God! (1977) Theme (Jack Elliott) US:LP = UA 908* [Ferrante & Teicher]; Theme (Jack Elliott) US:LP = Columbia 35328* [Andre Kostelanetz]; Theme (Jack Elliott) US:LP = Springboard 4093* [Film Festival Orchestra]

4830 Oh, God! Book II (1980) Score (Charles Fox) US:LP-PP = Fox 1*

4831 Oh, Rosalinda! [Die Fledermaus] (1957) Score (stage music:Johann Strauss) US:LP = Mercury MG-20145

4832 Oh! Sailor Behave (1930) Themes-A-B/US:78 = Brunswick 4840 [Charles King:ST]; Theme-C/US:78 = Brunswick 4849 [Charles King:ST]

4833 Oh! What a Lovely War (1969) Score (stage songs:pop music/as: Alfred Ralston) US:LP = Paramount PAS-5008*

4834 Oh, You Beautiful Doll (1949) Highlights (pop music) US:LP-BP = Titania 502; Highlights (pop music) US: EP = RCA WP-252 [Tony Martin:ST]

4835 Oil Prince, The *see* Rampage at Apache Wells

4836 Oil Town, U.S.A. (1956) Highlights (various) US:LP-10 = International LP-10043 + US:LP-10 = RCA LPM-3000

4837 Oklahoma! (1955) Score (stage songs:Richard Rodgers) US:LP = Capitol WAO-595/SWAO-595*

4838 Oklahoma Crude (1973) Score (Henry Mancini) US:LP = RCA APL1-0271*; Theme (Henry Mancini) US:SP = Capitol 3648* [Anne Murray:ST]

4839 Oklahoma Kid, The (1939) Excerpts (Max Steiner) US:LP-MS-BP = Tony Thomas TTMS-9/10 [Max Steiner:ST]

4840 Oklahoman, The (1957) Themes (Hans J. Salter) US:LP = Medallion 313 [Hans J. Salter:ST]

4841 Old Acquaintance (1943) Theme (Franz Waxman) US:78 = Capitol 142 [Jo Stafford]; Theme (Franz Waxman) US:LP = RCA 1-0708* [Charles Gerhardt]

4842 Old Fashioned Way, The (1934) Theme/US:78 = Brunswick 6959 [Joe Morrison:ST]

4843 Old Gun, The [Le Vieux Fusil] (1975) Theme (Francois DeRoubaix) FR: LP = Barclay 900.502* [Francois DeRoubaix:ST]

4844 Old Ironsides (1926) Theme [Silent I] (Hugo Riesenfeld) US:LP = RCA 2560* [Gaylord Carter]

4845 Old Man and the Sea, The (1958) Score (Dimitri Tiomkin) US:LP = Columbia CL-1183/CS-8013* + US: LP = CSP ACS-8013*

4846 Old Mill, The [Cartoon] (1937) Theme (Leigh Harline) US:LP = Disneyland 4021 [@ST]

4847 Old Mother Riley Meets the Vampire *see* My Son, the Vampire

4848-9 Old Shatterhand [Shatterhand] [Winnetou und Old Shatterhand im Tal der Toten] (1964) Score-A [German Release] (Martin Bottcher) GE: LP = Polydor 249.288; Score-B [Italian Release] (Riz Ortolani) GE:LP = Celine CLSP-5001

4850 Old Surehand *see* Flaming Frontier

4851 Old Yeller (1957) Underscore + Dialog (Oliver Wallace) US:LP = Disneyland WDL-3024 + US:LP = Disneyland WDL-1024

4852 Oldest Confession, The *see* Happy Thieves, The

4853 Oldest Profession, The [Le Plus Vieux Metier du Monde] (1967) Highlights (Michel Legrand) FR:EP = Philips 437.336

4854 Ole Guapa / Theme (Malando) US:LP-10 = Vox 660 + US:LP = Vox 25180 [Hans Hagen]

4855 Oliver! (1968) Score (stage songs:Lionel Bart) US:LP = Colgems COSD-5501* + US:LP = RCA COSD-5501*

4856 Oliver Twist (1948) Excerpts (Arnold Bax) US:LP-10 = Columbia ML-2092 + US:LP = Ariel CBF-13 [@Muir Mathieson]; Highlights (Arnold Bax) GB:LP = Cloud Nine CN-7012* [Kenneth Alwyn]

4857 Oliver's Story (1978) Score (s: Lee Holdridge/t:Francis Lai) US:LP = ABC AA-1117*

4858 Oltre la Porta [Beyond Obsession] (1982) Score (Pino Donaggio) US: LP = Varese STV-81213*

4859 Olympic Elk [Short] (1952) Excerpts (Paul Smith) US:LP = Disneyland WDL-4011 [Paul Smith:ST]

4860 Olympic Visions *see* Visions of 8

4861 Omar Khayyam (1957) Highlights-A (Victor Young) US:LP = Decca DL-8449; Highlights-B (Victor Young) US:LP-BP = Filmusic SN-2823

4862 Omega Man, The (1971) Theme (Ron Grainer) US:LP = MMG 705* [Geoff Love]; Theme (Ron Grainer) US:LP-BP = POO 104 [@Carlo Cirino]; Theme (Ron Grainer) GB:SP = RCA 4116 [Ron Grainer:ST]

4863 Omen, The (1976) Score (Jerry Goldsmith) US:LP = Tattoo BJL1-1888*

4864 Omicron (1963) Highlights (Piero Piccioni) IT:EP = CAM 45-104

4865 Omonimo / Theme (Guido & Maurizio DeAngelis) US:LP = Private Stock 7004* [Guido & Maurizio:ST]

4866 On a Clear Day, You Can See Forever (1970) Score (stage songs:Burton Lane) US:LP = Columbia S-30086* + US:LP = CSP S-30086*

4867 On an Island with You (1948)

Theme-A/US:78 = Columbia 38194 [Xavier Cugat:ST]; Theme-B/US:LP = MGM 4207 [Jimmy Durante:ST]

4868 On Any Sunday (1971) Score (Dominic Frontiere) US:LP = Bell 1206*

4869 On Dangerous Ground (1952) Theme (Bernard Herrmann) US:LP = RCA 1-0707* [Charles Gerhardt]

4870 On Dangerous Ground (1985) Theme (Mike Rutherford) US:SP = Atlantic 7-89488* [Mike and the Mechanics:ST]

4871 On Golden Pond (1981) Highlights + Underscore + Dialog (Dave Grusin) US:LP = MCA 6106*

4872 On Her Bed of Roses (1969) Score (Joe Green) US:LP = Mira LP-3006/LPS-3006*

4873 On Her Majesty's Secret Service (1970) Score (John Barry) US:LP = UA UAS-5204* + US:LP = UA LA-299*

4874 On Moonlight Bay (1951) Highlights-A (pop music) US:LP-BP = Caliban 6006; Highlights-B (pop music) US:LP-10 = Columbia CL-6186 + US:LP = CSP P-17660 [Doris Day:ST]

4875 On My Way to the Crusades, I Met a Girl Who ... [Chastity Belt] [Cintura di Castita] (1969) Score (Riz Ortolani) IT:LP = CAM 10.006; Theme (Riz Ortolani) US:SP = Reprise 0817 [Frank Sinatra]; Theme (Riz Ortolani) US:LP = Camden 2308* [The Living Marimbas]

4876 On Stream [Industrial Short] Score (William Lava) US:LP-PP = Capitol Custom 8605

4877 On the Avenue (1937) Score (Irving Berlin) US:LP-BP = Hollywood Soundstage HS-401; Excerpts-A (Irving Berlin) US:LP = Decca DL-8837 [Dick Powell:ST]; Excerpts-B (Irving Berlin) US:LP = Columbia CL-3068 [Alice Faye: ST]

4878 On the Beach (1959) Score (Ernest Gold) US:LP = Roulette R-25098/RS-25098*

4879 On the Double (1961) Themes (Sylvia Fine) US:SP = Dot 16215 [The Lennon Sisters]

4880 On the Nickel (1980) Theme (Tom Waits) US:LP = Asylum 6E-295* [Tom Waits:ST]

4881 On the Old Spanish Trail (1947) Theme/US:LP = RCA 3041 [Roy Rogers:ST]

4882 On the Riviera (1951) Themes-A-B (Sylvia Fine) US:SP = Decca 9-27597 [Danny Kaye:ST]; Themes-C-D (Sylvia Fine) US:SP = Decca 9-27596 [Danny Kaye:ST]

4883 On the Town (1950) Score (film songs:Roger Edens/stage songs: Leonard Bernstein) US:LP-BP = Show Biz 5603

4884 On the 12th Day [Short] (1955) Underscore + Dialog (Doreen Carwithen) US:LP = MGM E-3223

4885 On the Waterfront (1954) Highlights (Leonard Bernstein) US:LP = Columbia ML-5651/MS-6251* [Leonard Bernstein:ST]

4886 On with the Show (1929) Themes/US:LP = Columbia 2792 [Ethel Waters:ST]

4887 Once (1974) Score (Aminadav Aloni) US:LP-PP = Cinema International CIR-1001*

4888 Once a Jolly Swagman *see* Maniacs on Wheels

4889 Once a Thief (1965) Excerpts (Lalo Schifrin) US:LP = Verve MG-8624/V6-8624* [Lalo Schifrin:ST]

4890 Once Before I Die (1966) Theme (Mark London) US:SP = Kapp 778 [Lenny Welch:ST]

4891 Once Bitten (1985) Score (t:John Du Prez/s:various) US:LP = MCA 6154*

4892 Once Is Not Enough (1975) Theme-A (Henry Mancini) US:SP = RCA 10355* [Henry Mancini:ST]; Theme-A (Henry Mancini) US:LP = RCA 1-3052* + US:LP = RCA 1-3347* [Henry Mancini:ST]; Theme-B (Henry Mancini) US:SP = RCA 10255* [Danny Davis]; Theme-B (Henry Mancini) US:LP = RCA 1-1043* [Danny Davis]

4893 Once Upon a Dream (1949) Theme (Arthur Wilkinson) GB:78-PP = Rank FM-51 [ST]

4894 Once Upon a Horse (1958) Theme (Jay Livingston & Ray Evans) US:SP = Decca 9-30723 [Rowan & Martin:ST]

4895 Once Upon a Time in America (1984) Score (Ennio Morricone) US:LP = Mercury 818.697-1*

4896 Once Upon a Time in the West (1968) Score (Ennio Morricone) US: LP = RCA LSP-4736* + US:LP = RCA ABL1-4736*

4897 One and Only, The (1978) Score (Patrick Williams) US:LP = ABC AA-1059*

4898 One and Only, Genuine, Original Family Band, The (1968) Score (Richard and Robert Sherman) US:LP = Buena Vista BV-5002/ST-5002*

4899 One Brief Summer (1972) Themes (Roger Webb) GB:LP = Major & Minor 5063* [Roger Webb:ST]; Theme (Roger Webb) US:LP = King 1140.498* [Manuel]

4900 One by One (1974) Score (Stomu Yamash'ta) GB:LP = Island 9269*

4901 One Deadly Summer [L'Ete Meurtrier] (1983) Score (Georges Delerue) FR:LP = Danubius 2106*

4902 One Desire (1955) Theme (Henry Mancini) US:SP = Decca 9-29584 [Gene Boyd]

4903 One-Eyed Jacks (1961) Score (Hugo Friedhofer) US:LP = Liberty LOM-16001/LOS-17001*

4904 One Flew Over the Cuckoo's Nest (1975) Score (Jack Nitzsche) US: LP = Fantasy F-9500*

4905 One Foot in Heaven (1941) Themes (Max Steiner) US:LP-BP = Citadel CTMS-2 [Max Steiner:ST]

4906 One Foot in Hell (1960) Theme (Dominic Frontiere) US:SP = Columbia 4-41734 [Dominic Frontiere:ST]

4907 One from the Heart (1981) Score (Tom Waits) US:LP = Columbia FC-37703*

4908 One Heavenly Night (1930) Theme/US:LP-BP = JJA 19802 [@John Boles:ST]

4909 One Hour Late (1935) Themes/US:78 = Brunwick 7347 [Joe Morrison:ST]

4910 One Hour with You (1932) Highlights (e:Oscar Straus/e:Richard A. Whiting) US:LP-BP = Caliban 6011

4911 100 Men and a Girl (1937) Themes-A-B/US:78-MS = Decca 35 [Deanna Durbin:ST]; Themes-B-C/US: 78 = Decca 680 [Deanna Durbin:ST]

4912 100 Rifles (1969) Theme (Jerry Goldsmith) US:SP = UA 50553* [Leroy Holmes]; Theme (Jerry Goldsmith) US: LP = UA 6710* [Leroy Holmes]; Theme (Jerry Goldsmith) US:LP = UA 6716* [Don Tweedy]

4913 101 Dalmatians (1961) Highlights + Dialog (e:Mel Leven/t:George Bruns) US:LP = Disneyland ST-4903 + US:LP = Disneyland ST-3934

4914 One in a Million (1936) Themes/US:LP = Medallion 301 [@Arline Judge/The Ritz Brothers:ST]

4915 One Is a Lonely Number (1972) Theme (Michel Legrand) US: SP = Bell 215* [Michel Legrand:ST]; Theme (Michel Legrand) US:LP = Daybreak 2015* [Nelson Riddle]

4916 One Man Mutiny *see* Court Martial of Billy Mitchell, The

4917 One Million Years B.C. (1966) Score (Mario Nascimbene) IT:LP = Intermezzo IM-005*

4918 One Minute to Zero [The Korean Story] (1952) Theme (Victor Young) US:SP = Decca 9-28224 [Jeri Southern & Victor Young]; Theme (Victor Young) US:LP = Decca 8798 [Victor Young:ST]; Theme (Victor Young) US: LP = MGM 4432* [Cyril Ornadel]

4919 One More Chance [Short] (1931) Excerpts (various) US:LP = Biograph BMPM-1 [Bing Crosby:ST]

4920 One Naked Night (1964) Score (Chet McIntyre) US:LP = Vega 2002/S-2002*

4921 One Never Knows *see* No Sun in Venice

4922 One Night at Dinner [Love Circle] [Metti una Sera a Cena] (1969) Score (Ennio Morricone) GB:LP = CBS 70067* + IT:LP = Cinevox 33/16

4923 One Night of Love (1934) Highlights (classical music) US:LP-BP = Grapon 15

4924 One Night with You (1948) Themes/GB:78 = HMV 1882 [Nino Martini:ST]

4925 One on One (1977) Score (Charles Fox) US:LP = WB BSK-3076*

4926 One on Top of the Other [Una Sull'Altra] (1971) Score (Riz Ortolani) IT:LP = Beat LPF-004*

4927 One Potato, Two Potato (1964) Theme (Kenny Bass) US:SP =

Decca 9-31664 [Kenny Bass:ST]

4928 One Russian Summer [Fury] [Il Giorno del Furore] (1973) Score (Riz Ortolani) IT:LP = CAM SAG-9047*

4929 One Silver Dollar [Un Dollaro Bucato] (1975) Score (Gianni Ferrio) IT: LP = Phoenix PHCAM-02*; Themes (Gianni Ferrio) IT:SP = Cetra 31174 [ST]

4930 One Sings, The Other Doesn't [L'Une Chante, l'Autre Pas] (1977) Score (Francois Wertheimer & Agnes Varda) FR:LP = Philips 9101.106*

4931 1000 Dollars a Touchdown (1939) Theme/US:LP-MS-BP = Legends 1000/5-6 [Martha Raye:ST]

4932 1001 Arabian Nights (1959) Score (George Duning) US:LP = Colpix CP-410/SCP-410* + US:LP = Varese STV-81138*

4933 One Trick Pony (1980) Score (Paul Simon) US:LP = WB HS-3472*

4934 One, Two, Three (1961) Theme (Andre Previn) US:LP = Kapp 3295* [Pete King]; Theme (Andre Previn) US:LP = Musicor 3002* [Roger Wayne] + US:LP = UA 6197* [@Roger Wayne]

4935 One Two Two [122 Rue de Provence] (1980) Score (Ennio Morricone) FR:LP = General Music 803.002*

4936 One Woman or Two [Une Femme ou Deux] (1986) Score (Toots Thielemans) FR:LP = WB Apache 240-787-1*

4937 One Woman's Story [Passionate Friends] (1949) Theme-A (Richard Addinsell) GB:78-PP = Rank FM-45 [ST]; Theme-B (Richard Addinsell) GB:78-PP = Rank FM-46 [ST]; Theme-A (Richard Addinsell) US:LP = Columbia 3053 [@Muir Mathieson]; Theme-A (Richard Addinsell) US:LP = Chalfont 55001* [Morton Gould]

4938 Only for Love *see* Please Not Now!

4939 Only the French Can [French Can-Can] (1954) Theme (Georges Van Parys) US:LP = Columbia 107 [Michel Legrand]

4940 Only When I Larf (1968) Theme (Ron Grainer) US:SP = Deram 85041 [Whistling Jack Smith]; Theme (Ron Grainer) GB:LP = RCA 1020 [Ron Grainer:ST]

4941 Only When I Laugh (1981) Theme (David Shire) US:SP = MCA 51195* [Brenda Lee]; Theme (David Shire) US:LP = MCA 5278* [Brenda Lee]

4942 Open City [Rome—Open City] (1945) Theme (Galdieri & D'Anzi) US:LP = Epic 3593 [Gian Stellari]

4943 Open the Door and See All the People [Peacock Feathers] (1964) Score (Alec Wilder) US:LP-PP = Fine FR-1259; Theme (Alec Wilder) US:SP = Columbia 4-43087 [Mel Torme]

4944 Operation Crossbow (1965) Theme (Ron Goodwin) GB:LP = EMI TWO-108* + GB:LP = EMI TWO-142* + GB:LP = Philips 6308.018*[Ron Goodwin:ST]

4945 Operation Kid Brother [O.K. Connery] (1967) Themes (Ennio Morricone) IT:SP = Parade 5042 [ST]

4946 Operation Mad Ball (1957) Theme (Fred Karger) US:SP = Decca 9-30441 [Sammy Davis, Jr.:ST]

4947 Operation Pacific (1951) Excerpts (Max Steiner) US:LP-BP = Citadel CTMS-7 [Max Steiner:ST]

4948 Operation Undercover *see* Report to the Commissioner

4949 Operator 13 (1934) Theme-A/ US:78 = Brunswick 6785 [The Mills Brothers:ST]; Theme-B/US:78 = Brunswick 6913 [The Mills Brothers:ST]

4950 Optimists, The (1973) Score (e:George Martin/e:Lionel Bart) US: LP = Paramount PAS-1015*

4951 Orca [Orca—The Killer Whale] (1977) Score (Ennio Morricone) JA:LP = Toho YX-7036*; Theme (Ennio Morricone) US:LP = Peter Pan 2801* [Marty Gold]

4952 Orchestra Rehearsal [Prove d'Orchestra] (1979) Highlights + Dialog (Nino Rota) IT:LP = CAM SAG-9096*

4953 Orchestra Wives (1942) Score (e:Harry Warren/etc.) US:LP-MS = 20th TCF-100/TCS-100e + US:LP-MS = 20th T-904e [Glenn Miller:ST]

4954 Ordinary People (1980) Theme (at:Marvin Hamlisch) US:SP = Planet 47922* [Marvin Hamlisch:ST]

4955 Organizer, The [I Compagni] (1964) Highlights (Carlo Rustichelli) IT: EP = CAM 45-105

4956 Orphan, The *see* Sans Famille

4957 Orphan's Benefit [Cartoon] (1934) Theme (at:Frank Churchill) US: LP-MS = Ovation 5000 + US:LP = Disneyland 3805 [@ST]

4958 Orpheus (1950) Theme (Georges Auric) FR:LP = Vega 30-A-98 [@ST]

4959 Oscar, The (1966) Score (Percy Faith) US:LP = Columbia OL-6550/OS-2950*

4960 Ossessione (1942) Excerpts (Giuseppe Rosati) JA:LP-MS = CBS/Sony 2301 [@ST]

4961 Osterman Weekend, The (1983) Score (Lalo Schifrin) US:LP = Varese STV-81198*

4962 Ostrich Has Two Eggs, The *see* Oeufs de l'Autruche, Les

4963 Otello (1986) Scores (classical music) US:LP-MS = Angel/EMI DSB-3993*

4964 Other Side of Midnight, The (1977) Score (Michel Legrand) US:LP = 20th T-542*

4965 Other Side of the Mountain, The [Window to the Sky] (1975) Score (Charles Fox) US:LP = MCA 2086*

4966 Other Side of the Mountain—Part II, The (1978) Score (Lee Holdridge) US:LP = MCA 2335*

4967 Otley (1968) Score (Stanley Myers) US:LP = Colgems COS-112*

4968 Our Latin Thing (1975) Scores (e:Johnny Pacheco/e:Ray Barretto/etc.) US:LP-MS = Fania SLP-00431*

4969 Our Little Girl (1935) Themes/US:LP-MS = 20th 2-103 [Shirley Temple:ST]

4970 Our Man Flint (1966) Score (Jerry Goldsmith) US:LP = 20th 4179/S-4179*

4971 Our Mother's House (1967) Score (Georges Delerue) US:LP-BP = E 4495 + CA:LP = MGM E-4495/SE-4495*

4972 Our Story [Notre Histoire] (1985) Score (Laurent Rossi) FR:LP = Carrere 66.135*

4973 Our Time [The Death of Her Innocence] (1974) Theme (Michel Legrand) US:SP = WB 7799 [Michel Legrand:ST]; Theme (Michel Legrand) US:LP-BP = Centurion 1600 [@ Michel Legrand:ST]

4974 Our Town (1941) Excerpts-A (Aaron Copland) US:LP = Columbia MS-7375* [Aaron Copland:ST]; Excerpts-B (Aaron Copland) US:LP = Vanguard SRV-348* [Maurice Abravanel]

4975 Our Very Own (1950) Theme (Victor Young) US:SP = Decca 9-27067 [Victor Young:ST]; Theme (Victor Young) US:SP = RCA 47-3806 [Vaughn Monroe]; Theme (Victor Young) US: LP = WB 1431* [Connie Stevens]

4976 Our Winning Season (1978) Theme (Charles Fox) US:SP = Epic 8-50578* [Dave Loggins:ST]; Themes (Charles Fox) US:SP-PP = American International 7804* [Dave Loggins:ST]

4977 Out California Way (1946) Theme (Foster Carling) US:78 = RCA Victor 20-1952 [The Sons of the Pioneers]

4978 Out of Africa (1985) Score (John Barry) US:LP = MCA 6158*

4979 Out of Bounds (1986) Score (t:Stewart Copeland/s:various) US: LP = I.R.S. 6180*

4980 Out of Sight (1966) Score (e: Al DeLory/etc.) US:LP = Decca DL-4751/DL-74751*

4981 Out of the Clouds (1955) Theme-A (Richard Addinsell) GB:78-PP = Rank FM-152 [ST]; Theme-B (Richard Addinsell) GB:78-PP = Rank FM-153 [ST]

4982 Out-of-Towners, The (1970) Theme (Quincy Jones) US:LP = Project 5051 [Enoch Light]

4983 Outback (1971) Theme (John Scott) US:SP = Capitol 6509* [Stu Phillips]

4984 Outland (1981) Score (Jerry Goldsmith) US:LP = WB HS-3551*

4985 Outlaw Blues (1977) Score (t: Charles Bernstein/s:various) US:LP = Capitol ST-11691*

4986 Outlaw Josey Wales, The (1976) Score (Jerry Fielding) US:LP = WB BS-2956*

4987 Outlaw Riders, The (1972) Score (e:Simon Stokes/e:Michael Lloyd) US:LP = MGM 1SE-26*

4988 Outlaw Territory [Hannah Lee] (1953) Theme (Stan Jones) US:SP = Columbia 4-40008 [Guy Mitchell]

4989 Outpost in Malaya [The Planter's Wife] (1952) Theme (Allan Gray) GB:78-PP = Rank FM-133 [ST]

4990 Outrage, The (1964) Theme (Alex North) US:SP = Capitol 5285 [The Vulcanes]

4991 Outrageous! (1977) Score (e: Paul Hoffert/etc.) US:LP = Polydor PD1-8902*

4992 Outside In (1972) Score (Randy Edelman) US:LP = MGM 1SE-37*

4993 Outside Man, The [Un Homme est Mort] (1973) Theme (Michel Legrand) FR:LP = Bell 2308.070* [Michel Legrand:ST]

4994 Outside of Paradise (1938) Themes/US:78 = Brunswick 8051 [Phil Regan:ST]

4995 Over the Brooklyn Bridge (1984) Score (Pino Donaggio) GB:LP = Red Bus 1200*

4996 Over the Edge (1979) Score (pop music) US:LP = WB BSK-3335*

4997 Overlanders, The (1946) Highlights (John Ireland) GB:LP = Lyrita 45* [Adrian Bolt]; Themes (John Ireland) US:LP = DRG 703* [Marcus Dods]

4998 Owl and the Pussycat, The (1970) Highlights + Underscore + Dialog (Richard Halligan) US:LP = Columbia S-30410*

P

4999 P.J. [A New Face in Hell] (1968) Theme (Neal Hefti) US:SP = Decca 9-32263 [Clebanoff]; Theme (Neal Hefti) US:LP = Decca 74956* [Clebanoff]

5000 Pacific High (1980) Themes (Robert F. Brunner) US:SP = BMC 1003* [Christa Lee McPhearson:ST]

5001 Paddy (1970) Theme (John Rubinstein) US:SP = Jubilee 5697 [Emmy Lou Harris:ST]

5002 Paddy O'Day (1935) Theme/ US:78 = Brunswick 7594 [Pinky Tomlin: ST]

5003 Padre Padrone (1977) Score (Egisto Macchi) IT:LP = Feeling FR-69403*; Highlights (Egisto Macchi) IT: LP = RCA 33207*

5004 Paesano [Paesano, A Voice in the Night] (1978) Score (Ray Sinatra) US: LP = Mediterraneo MIR-733*

5005 Pagan, The (1929) Theme/ US:LP = Stanyan 10055 [@Ramon Novarro:ST]

5006 Pagan Love Song (1950) Highlights (e:Harry Warren/etc.) US: LP-10 = MGM E-534 + US:LP = MGM 2SES-43e

5007 Pagliacci (1985) Scores (classical music) GB:LP-MS = Philips 411.484.1*

5008 Paid in Full [Bitter Victory] (1950) Theme (Victor Young) US:78 = MGM 10562 [Billy Eckstine]

5009 Paint Your Wagon (1969) Score (film songs:Andre Previn/stage songs:Frederick Loewe) US:LP = Paramount PMS-1001* + US:LP = MCA 37099*

5010 Painted Stallion, The [Serial] Theme (William Lava) US:LP-PP = Cinemasound R-1001* [James King]

5011 Painting the Clouds with Sunshine (1951) Highlights-A (pop music) US:LP-10 = Capitol L-291 [Dennis Morgan:ST]; Highlights-B (pop music) US:LP-BP = Caliban 6012

5012 Pajama Game, The (1957) Score (stage songs:Richard Adler & Jerry Ross) US:LP = Columbia OL-5210 + US:LP = CSP AOL-5210

5013 Pajama Party (1964) Score (Jerry Styner) US:LP = Buena Vista BV-3325/ST-3325* [Annette:ST]

5014 Pal Joey (1957) Score (stage songs:Richard Rodgers) US:LP = Capitol W-912/DW-912e + US:LP = Capitol SM-912e; Theme (Nelson Riddle) US:SP = Capitol 3847 [Nelson Riddle: ST]

5015 Paleface, The (1948) Excerpts (Jay Livingston & Ray Evans) US:LP-BP = Titania 511 [@ST]; Theme (Jay Livingston & Ray Evans) US:78 = Capitol 15292 [Bob Hope:ST]

5016 Palm Springs (1936) Themes-A-B/US:78 = Decca 783 [Frances Langford:ST]; Theme-C/US:78 = Decca 663 [Frances Langford:ST]

5017 Palm Springs Weekend (1963) Score (e:Frank Perkins/etc.) US:LP = WB W-1519/WS-1519*

5018 Palmy Days (1931) Theme/ US:LP = Pelican 134 [Eddie Cantor:ST]

5019 Palooka (1934) Theme/US: LP = Decca 5116 [Jimmy Durante:ST]

5020 Panama Hattie (1942) Highlights (stage songs:Cole Porter) US:LP-BP = JJA 19767 [@ST]

5021 Pancho [Short] Sequence + Dialog (Arthur Kleiner) US:LP-PP = Picture Book Parade 106 [@ST]

5022 Pandora and the Flying Dutchman (1951) Theme (Edwin Parker) US:SP = MGM 30352 [Ava Gardner: ST]; Theme (Edwin Parker) US:LP = Lion 70108 + US:LP-MS = DRG 2-2100 [@Ava Gardner:ST]

5023 Panic Button (1964) Score (Georges Garvarentz) US:LP = Musicor 2026/3026*

5024 Papa's Delicate Condition (1963) Theme (James Van Heusen) US: SP = Reprise 20151 [Frank Sinatra]; Theme (James Van Heusen) US:LP = Command 871* [Enoch Light]; Theme (James Van Heusen) US:LP = Capitol 2796* [Jackie Gleason]

5025 Paper Chase, The (1973) Theme (John Williams) US:SP = 20th 2063* [John Davidson:ST]; Theme (John Williams) US:LP = UA 195* [Ferrante & Teicher]; Theme (John Williams) US:SP = UA 367* [Ferrante & Teicher]

5026 Paper Moon (1973) Score (pop music) US:LP = Paramount PAS-1012*

5027 Paper Tiger (1975) Score (Roy Budd) US:LP = Capitol SW-11475*

5028 Papillon (1973) Score (Jerry Goldsmith) US:LP = Capitol SW-11260*

5029 Paradine Case, The (1948) Highlights (Franz Waxman) US:78-MS = Alco 10; Excerpts (Franz Waxman) US:LP = Entracte ERM-6002 + US: LP = AEI 3103 [@Franz Waxman:ST]; Excerpts (Franz Waxman) US:LP = Varese 704.320* [Richard Mills]

5030 Paradise (1982) Theme (Joel Diamond) US:SP = Columbia 18-02819* [Phoebe Cates:ST]

5031 Paradise Alley (1978) Score (Bill Conti) US:LP = MCA 5100*

5032 Paradise—Hawaiian Style (1966) Score (e:Bill Giant/e:Florence Kaye/etc.) US:LP = RCA LPM-3643/ LSP-3643* + US:LP = RCA AFL1-3643* [Elvis Presley:ST]

5033 Paradise Motel (1985) Score (various) US:LP = Gero G7-10010*

5034 Parakh / Theme/US:LP = Capitol 10500 [@Lata Mangeshkar:ST]

5035 Paramount on Parade (1930) Themes-A-B/US:LP = Monmouth 7028 [Maurice Chevalier:ST]; Theme-C/US: LP = RCA LPV-528 [Maurice Chevalier: ST]; Theme-D/US:78 = Columbia 2143 [Charles Buddy Rogers:ST]

5036 Paranoia [Orgasmo] (1969) Themes (Piero Piccioni) IT:SP = CAM CDR-60 [ST]

5037 Pardners (1956) Highlights (James Van Heusen) US:EP = Capitol EAP1-752 [Dean Martin & Jerry Lewis: ST]

5038 Pardon Mon Affaire [Un Elephant Ca Trompe Enorment] (1977) Highlights (Vladimir Cosma) FR:LP = Deesse DDLX-157*

5039 Pardon Mon Affair Too [We Will All Meet in Paradise] [Nous Irons Tous a Paradis] (1978) Highlights (Vladimir Cosma) FR:LP = Deesse DDLX-157*

5040 Pardon My Sarong (1942) Theme/US:78 = Decca 23633 [The Ink Spots:ST]

5041 Pardon Us [Gaol Birds] (1931) Theme/US:LP = Mark 56 #575 [Laurel & Hardy:ST]

5042 Parent Trap, The (1961) Highlights (Richard & Robert Sherman) US: LP = Buena Vista BV-3309/ST-3309*

5043 Pariahs of Glory [Les Parias de la Gloire] Highlights (Marc Lanjean) FR:EP = Ducretet 460-V-630

5044 Paris (1930) Themes/US:78 = Columbia 1983 [Irene Bordoni:ST]

5045 Paris Blues (1961) Score (Duke Ellington) US:LP = UA UAL-4092/ UAS-5092*

5046 Paris Does Strange Things [Elena et les Hommes] (1956) Theme (Joseph Kosma) FR:LP = Pathe 122 [@ST]

5047 Paris Holiday (1958) Score (e: Joseph J. Lilley/t:James Van Heusen/ etc.) US:LP = UA UAL-40001

5048 Paris Honeymoon (1939) Excerpts (Ralph Rainger) US:LP-10 = Decca DL-6012 + US:LP = Decca DL-4253 [Bing Crosby:ST]

5049 Paris Secret (1965) Highlights (Alain Goraguer) FR:EP = Barclay 70811

5050 Paris, Texas (1984) Score (Ry Cooder) US:LP = WB 25270-1*

5051 Paris Was Made for Lovers [Time for Loving] (1973) Score (Michel Legrand) US:LP = Audio Fidelity AFE-6300* + US:LP = ALA 1981*

5052 Paris When It Sizzles (1964) Score (Nelson Riddle) US:LP = Reprise R-6113/RS-6113*

5053 Parisian Belle *see* New Moon (1930)

5054 Parisienne, La (1958) Highlights (Andre Hodeir & Hubert Rostaing & Henri Crolla) US:EP = UA 10002

5055 Park Plaza 605 (1953) Theme (Philip Green) GB:78 = Parlophone 3797 [Philip Green:ST]

5056 Parrish (1961) Highlights (e: Max Steiner/t:John Barracuda) US: LP = WB W-1413/WS-1413*

5057 Partner (1968) Excerpts (Ennio Morricone) IT:LP = CAM SAG-9010* [@ST]

5058 Party, The (1968) Score (Henry Mancini) US:LP = RCA LPM-3997/LSP-3997*

5059 Party Crashers, The (1958) Theme (Emengger) US:SP = Wynne 105 [Mark Damon:ST]

5060 Party Girls for the Candidate *see* Candidate, The

5061 Party Party (1982) Score (rock music) US:LP = A&M SP-3212*

5062 Party's Over, The (1963) Theme (John Barry) GB:SP = Philips 7275 [Annie Ross:ST]

5063 Pas de Weekend Peur Notre Amour / Theme (R. Lucchesi) US:SP = RCA 53-0505 [Luis Mariano]

5064 Passage to India, A (1984) Score (Maurice Jarre) US:LP = Capitol SV-12389*

5065 Passage to Marseille (1944) Theme (Max Steiner) US:LP = RCA 1-0422* + US:LP = RCA 1-3782* [Charles Gerhardt]

5066 Passages from Finnegans Wake *see* Finnegans Wake

5067 Passante, La (1983) Score (Georges Delerue) FR:LP = RCA 37634*

5068 Passion (1954) Theme (Louis Forbes) US:SP = Decca 9-29311 [Victor Young]; Theme (Louis Forbes) US:LP = Decca 8060 + US:LP = Decca 8085 [Victor Young]

5069 Passion d'Amour (1981) Highlights (Armando Trovajoli) FR:EP-12 = General Music 802.010*

5070 Passion Flower Hotel *see* Boarding School

5071 Passion of Joan of Arc, The (1928) Themes [Silent II] (Charles Hofmann) US:LP = Sounds Good 1001 [Charles Hofmann:ST]

5072 Passionate Friends, The *see* One Woman's Story

5073 Passport to Pimlico (1949) Theme (Georges Auric) GB:78-PP = Rank FM-61 [ST]

5074 Passport to Shame *see* Room 43

5075 Pat Garrett and Billy the Kid (1973) Score (Bob Dylan) US:LP = Columbia S-30086*

5076 Patch of Blue, A (1965) Score-A (Jerry Goldsmith) US:LP = Mainstream 56058/S-6058*; Score-B (Jerry Goldsmith) US:LP = Citadel CT-6028 + US:LP = Citadel CTV-7008*

5077 Pather Panchali (1956) Theme (Ravi Shankar) US:SP = World Pacific 77871 + US:SP = Pacific Jazz 343 [Ravi Shankar:ST]; Theme (Ravi Shankar) US:LP = World Pacific 1416* [Ravi Shankar:ST]

5078 Patrick (1979) Score [USA Release] (Brian May) US:LP = Varese VC-81107*; Score [Italian Release] (Goblin) IT:LP = Cinevox 33/133*

5079 Patton (1970) Score (Jerry Goldsmith) US:LP = 20th S-4208* + US:LP = 20th T-902*

5080 Patty (1976) Score (e:Sammy Lowe/e:Barban & Oriolo) US:LP = Stang 1027*

5081 Paul Bunyan [Cartoon] (1958) Theme (George Bruns) US:SP = Disneyland 119 [George Bruns:ST]; Theme (George Bruns) US:SP = Cricket 118 [Dennis Day]

5082 Pawnbroker, The (1965) Score (Quincy Jones) US:LP = Mercury MG–21011/SR-61011*

5083 Payment in Blood [7 Winchester per i Massacro] (1967) Theme (Francesco DeMasi) FR:LP = General Music 803.011* [@ST]

5084 Peach Thief, The (1964) Highlights (Simeon Pironkov) US:LP = Roulette R-804/RS-804*

5085 Peacock Feathers *see* Open the Door and See All the People

5086 Pearl of Death, The (1944) Underscore + Dialog (au:Paul Sawtell) US:LP = Murray Hill 55412

5087 Pearl of the South Pacific (1955) Theme (Louis Forbes) US:SP = Coral 9-61472 [Joy Lane & George Cates]

5088 Peau de l'Ours, La (1961) Highlights (Marc Lanjean) FR:EP = Philips 432.526; Theme (Marc Lanjean) US:LP = WB 1371* [Pete Rugolo]; Theme (Marc Lanjean) US:LP = Dot 3120 [Ray Ventura]

5089 Pecado de Amor (1961) Score (various) US:LP = Columbia EX-5092 [Sarita Montiel:ST]

5090 Pee Wee's Big Adventure (1985) Highlights (Danny Elfman) US: LP = Varese 704.370*

5091 Peg o' My Heart (1933) Theme (Herbert Stothart) US:SP = RCA 47-4024 [Phil Regan]

5092 Peg of Old Drury (1935) Theme/GB:78 = Decca 5649 [Anna Neagle:ST]

5093 Peggy Sue Got Married (1986) Score (e:John Barry/e:pop music) US: LP = Varese STV-81295*

5094 Peking Medallion, The *see* Corrupt Ones, The

5095 Pele (1977) Score (s:Sergio Mendes/t:Pele) US:LP = Atlantic SD-18231*

5096 Pelle, La [The Skin] (1981) Score (Lalo Schifrin) IT:LP = Cinevox 33/147* + FR:LP = Gaumont 753.805*

5097 Pendulum (1969) Theme (Walter Scharf) US:SP = Capitol 2414 [The Lettermen]; Theme (Walter Scharf) US: LP = Evolution 3003* [Bobby Byrne]

5098 Penelope (1966) Score (John Williams) US:LP = MGM E-4426/SE-4426*

5099 Pennies from Heaven (1936) Excerpts (Arthur Johnston) US:LP-10 = Decca DL-6010 + US:LP = Decca DL-4251 [Bing Crosby:ST]

5100 Pennies from Heaven (1981) Scores (pop music) US:LP-MS = WB 2HW-3639

5101 Penny Princess (1952) Theme (Val Guest) GB:78-PP = Rank FM-126 [ST]

5102 Pennywhistle Blues *see* Magic Garden, The

5103 Penthouse, The (1967) Score (John Hawksworth) US:LP = UA UAL-4170/UAS-5170*

5104 People Next Door, The (1970) Score (e:Don Sebesky/e:English & Weiss) US:LP = Avco AVO-11002*

5105 People of the Wind (1977) Score (G.T. Moore) US:LP-PP = Carolyn CRS-1001*

5106 Pepe (1960) Score (e:Andre Previn/t:John Green/t:Hans Whitsett/ etc.) US:LP = Colpix CP-507/SCP-507*

5107 Pepe Le Moko (1937) Theme + Underscore + Dialog (Vincent Scotto) JA:LP-MS = Canyon YA-2003/4 [@ST]

5108 Peppermint Soda [Diablo Menthe] (1979) Excerpts (Yves Simon) FR:LP = RCA 37592* [Yves Simon:ST]

5109 Percy (1971) Score (s:Raymond Douglas Davies/as:Stanley Myers) GB:LP = Pye NSPL-18365*; Excerpts (Raymond Douglas Davies) US: LP-MS = Reprise RPS-2XS-6454* [The Kinks:ST]

5110 Perfect (1985) Score (various) US:LP = Arista AL9-8278*

5111 Perfect Couple, A (1979) Score (Allan Nicholls) CA:LP = Lion's Gate AQR-524*

5112 Perfect Furlough, The [Strictly for Pleasure] (1959) Theme (Frank Skinner) US:SP = Coral 9-62060 [Linda Cristal:ST]; Theme (Frank Skinner) US: SP = Decca 9-30797 [Warren Berry]

5113 Perfect Understanding (1933) Theme/US:LP = Stanyan 10055 [@ Gloria Swanson:ST]

5114 Perfect Woman, The (1949) Theme (Arthur Wilkinson) GB:78-PP = Rank FM-70 [ST]

5115 Performance (1970) Score (Jack Nitzsche) US:LP = WB BS-2554*

5116 Perilous Journey, A (1953) Theme (Victor Young) US:LP = Decca 8060 [Victor Young:ST]

5117 Perils of Gwendoline, The [Gwendoline] (1984) Score (Pierre Bachelet) FR:LP = RCA 70252*

5118 Perils of Pauline, The (1947) Excerpts (Frank Loesser) US:LP-BP = Vedette 8702 [Betty Hutton:ST]

5119 Period of Adjustment, The (1962) Theme (Lyn Murray) US:LP = Ava 14* + US:LP = Ava 30* [@Harry Betts & Bill Brown Singers]

5120 Perri (1957) Highlights + Dialog (t:Paul Smith/t:George Bruns) US:LP = Disneyland ST-3902 + US: LP = Disneyland ST-1309; Highlights (t:Paul Smith/t:George Bruns) US:EP = Disneyland DBR-31

5121 Persecution and Assassination of Jean-Paul Marat *see* Marat/ Sade

5122 Personal Property (1937) Theme (Franz Waxman) US:LP = World Artists 2007/3007* [Perry Botkin, Jr.]

5123 Pete Kelly's Blues (1955) Score-A (t:Ray Heindorf/s:pop music) US:LP = Decca DL-8166 [Peggy Lee & Ella Fitzgerald:ST]; Score-B (t:Ray Heindorf/s:pop music) US:LP = Columbia CL-690 [Ray Heindorf:ST]

5124 Pete 'n' Tillie (1972) Themes (John Williams) US:SP = Decca 33050* [Walter Matthau/Al Capps]; Theme (John Williams) US:SP = Columbia 4-45765* [Carol Burnett]; Theme (John Williams) US:LP = Capitol 11511* + US:LP-BP = Centurion 1600* [@Suzanne Stevens]

5125 Peter and the Wolf *see* Make Mine Music

5126 Peter Pan (1953) Score (s: Sammy Fain/t:Oliver Wallace/t:Frank Churchill) US:LP = Disneyland DQ-1206 + US:LP = Disneyland ST-3910

5127 Peter Rabbit and Tales of Beatrix Potter (1971) Score (John Lanchbery) US:LP = Angel S-36789*

5128 Peter the First [Peter the Great] (1937) Score (Vladimir Sherbachev) RU:LP-MS = Melodiya 11133/4

5129 Pete's Dragon (1977) Score (Al Kasha & Joel Hirschhorn) US:LP = Capitol SW-11704*

5130 Petey Wheatstraw (1978) Score (Nat Dove) US:LP = Magic Disc MD-112*

5131 Petit Con (1984) Themes (Vladimir Cosma) FR:SP = Carrere 13377* [ST]

5132 Petite Bande, La (1983) Score (Edgar Cosma) FR:LP = Milan A-202*

5133 Petrified Forest, The (1936) Sequence + Dialog (Bernhard Kaun) US:LP-MS = WB 3X-2737 [@ST]

5134 Pets [Submission] (1973) Theme (Chic Sorenson) US:SP = Seagull 741 [Terri Rinaldi:ST]

5135 Petulia (1968) Score (John Barry) US:LP = WB WS-1755*

5136 Peu de Soleil dans l'Eau Froide (1971) Score (Michel Legrand) FR:LP = Bell C062.92943*; Theme (Michel Legrand) US:LP = Bell 6017* [Michel Legrand:ST]

5137 Peyton Place (1957) Score (Franz Waxman) US:LP = RCA LOC-1042/LSO-1042* + US:LP = Entracte ERS-6515*

5138 Phaedra (1962) Score (Mikis Theodorakis) US:LP = UA UAL-4102/ UAS-5102* + US:LP = UA LA-280*

5139 Phantasm (1979) Score (Fred Myrow & Malcolm Seagrave) US:LP = Varese VC-81105*

5140 Phantom Lovers *see* Ghosts of Rome

5141 Phantom of Soho, The [Das Phantom von Soho] (1963) Theme (Martin Bottcher) GE:LP = Celine 0011 [Martin Bottcher:ST]

5142 Phantom of Terror, The *see* Bird with the Crystal Plumage

5143 Phantom of the Opera, The (1925) Theme [Silent II] (Lee Erwin) US:LP = Angel 36073* [Lee Erwin:ST]

5144 Phantom of the Opera, The (1943) Highlights + Underscore + Dialog (Edward Ward) US:LP-MS-BP = Sountrak STK-114; Theme (Edward Ward) US:78 = London 121 [Mantovani]

5145 Phantom of the Opera, The (1962) Theme (Edwin Astley) US:SP = Coral 9-62334 [Stanley Paul]

5146 Phantom of the Paradise (1974) Score (Paul Williams) US:LP = A&M SP-3653*

5147 Phantom President, The (1932) Excerpts (George M. Cohan & Richard Rodgers) US:LP-BP = JJA

19766 + US:LP-BP = Old Shep GMC-1000 + US:LP-BP = Folk RFS-604 [George M. Cohan:ST]

5148 Phar Lap (1984) Score (Bruce Rowland) US:LP = Varese STV-81230*

5149-50 Pharaoh's Curse, The (1957) Theme (Les Baxter) US:SP = GNP 121 [Tony Martinez]

5151 Philadelphia Experiment, The (1984) Score (Ken Wannberg) US:LP = Rhino RNSP-306*

5152 Philadelphia Story, The (1940) Theme (Franz Waxman) US:LP = RCA 1-0708* [Charles Gerhardt]

5153 Phynx, The (1970) Theme-A (Mike Stoller) US:SP = Spring 103 [The Boys in the Band]; Theme-B (Mike Stoller) US:LP = Capitol 429* [Nancy Wilson]

5154 Piaf [Piaf—The Early Years] (1975) Score (e:Ralph Burns/e:pop music) FR:LP = Pathe C064.15308*

5155 Picasso (1956) Score (Roman Vlad) US:LP = Folkways FS-3860

5156 Picasso Summer, The (1972) Score (Michel Legrand) US:LP = WB WS-1925* [Michel Legrand:ST]; Theme (Michel Legrand) US:SP = WB 7328 [The Jimmy Joyce Singers:ST]

5157 Piccadilly Incident (1946) Theme (Vivian Ellis) GB:78 = Decca 1559 [Louis Levy]

5158 Picnic (1955) Score (George Duning) US:LP = Decca DL-8320/DL-78320* + US:LP = MCA 2049*

5159 Picnic at Hanging Rock (1977) Themes-A-B (folk music) GB:LP = Epic 81780* [Zamfir:ST]; Theme-C (Bruce Smeaton) US:LP = DRG 8202* [William Motzing]

5160 Picture Show Man, The (1977) Themes (Peter Best) AU:LP = Festival 37789* [@Peter Best:ST]; Theme (Peter Best) US:LP = DRG 8202* [William Motzing]

5161 Piece of Action, A (1977) Score (s:Curtis Mayfield/as:Gil Askey & Richard Tufo) US:LP = Curtom CU-5019*

5162 Pieces of Dreams (1970) Theme (Michel Legrand) US:SP = Capitol 2910 [Peggy Lee:ST]; Theme (Michel Legrand) US:LP = Bell 6017* [Michel Legrand:ST]

5163 Pied Piper, The [Cartoon] (1933) Theme (Leigh Harline) GB:78 = HMV 375 [ST]

5164 Pied Piper, The (1972) Theme (Donovan Leitch) GB:LP = DJM 430* [Vic Lewis]

5165 Pied Piper of Hamelin, The (1957) Score (as:Hal Stanley & Irving Taylor) US:LP = RCA LPM-1563

5166 Pieges (1939) Themes/GB: 78 = HMV JO-13 [Maurice Chevalier: ST]

5167 Pierrot Le Fou (1965) Highlights (Antoine Duhamel) FR:LP = RCA 37673; Highlights (Antoine Duhamel) FR:EP = Barclay 70869

5168 Pigeon That Took Rome, The (1962) Theme (Alessandro Cicognini) US:SP = Capitol 4857 [Jimmie Haskell]

5169 Pigeons *see* Sidelong Glances of a Pigeon Kicker

5170 Pigpen [Porcile] (1969) Themes (Benedetto Ghiglia) IT:SP = CAM AMP-067 [ST]

5171 Pigskin Parade [Harmony Parade] (1936) Highlights (Lew Pollack) US:LP-BP = Pilgrim 4000

5172 Pilgrim, The *see* Chaplin Revue, The

5173 Pillow Talk (1959) Excerpts (t:Joe Lubin/t:Buddy Pepper/t:Sol Lake) US:LP-PP = Columbia DD-1 [Doris Day:ST]; Themes-A-B (Joe Lubin/Buddy Pepper) US:SP = Columbia 4-41463 [Doris Day:ST]; Themes-B-C (Sol Lake/Buddy Pepper) US:SP = Decca 9-30966 [Rock Hudson:ST]

5174 Pin-Up Girl (1944) Highlights (James Monaco) US:LP-BP = Caliban 6009

5175 Pink Floyd—The Wall (1982) Scores (pop music) US:LP-MS = Columbia PC2-36183* [Pink Floyd:ST]

5176 Pink Floyd at Pompeii (1971) Score (pop music) US:LP-BP = Wizardo PF-1 [Pink Floyd:ST]

5177 Pink Panther, The (1964) Score (Henry Mancini) US:LP = RCA LPM-2795/LSP-2795* + US:LP = RCA ANL1-1389*; Theme (Henry Mancini) US: LP = Painted Smiles PS-1331* [Fran Jeffries:ST]

5178 Pink Panther Strikes Again, The (1976) Score (Henry Mancini) US:

LP = UA LA-694*

5179 Pinky (1949) Theme (film theme from "Gentleman's Agreement") US:LP = Mercury 20037 + US:LP = Citadel 6003 + US:LP = Citadel 7015 + US:LP = Capitol 1652* [Alfred Newman:ST]

5180 Pinocchio (1940) Score (s: Leigh Harline/t:Paul Smith/t:Ed Plumb) US:LP = Disneyland WDL-4002 + US:LP = Disneyland DQ-1202

5181 Pipe Dreams (1976) Score (t:Dominic Frontiere/s:various) US: LP = Buddah BDS-5676*

5182 Piranha (1979) Score (Pino Donaggio) US:LP = Varese STV-81126*

5183 Piranha II [The Spawning—Piranha II] (1982) Score (Stelvio Cipriani-aka-Steve Powder) IT:LP = Polydor 2448.8133*

5184 Pirate, La [The Pirate] (1984) Highlights (Philippe Sarde) US:LP = Varese STV-81227*

5185 Pirate, The (1948) Highlights (e:Cole Porter/at:Conrad Salinger) US: LP-10 = MGM E-21 + US:LP = MGM E-3234 + US:LP-MS = MGM 2SES-43e

5186 Pirate Movie, The (1982) Scores (Terry Britten & Brian Robertson & Sue Shifrin & Kit Hain) US:LP-MS = Polydor PD2-9503*

5187 Pirates [Roman Polanski's Pirates] (1986) Score (as:Philippe Sarde) US:LP = Varese STV-81287*

5188 Pirogov (1947) Highlights (Dmitri Shostakovich) US:LP = Angel S-40160*

5189 Piscine, La *see* Swimming Pool, The

5190 Pistola per Ringo, Una [A Pistol for Ringo] (1965) Highlights (Ennio Morricone) IT:LP = RCA 33209*; Excerpts (Ennio Morricone) US:LP = Peters PILPS-4050* [Ennio Morricone:ST]

5191 Pistole Non Discutono, Le [Bullets Don't Argue] [Guns Don't Argue] (1970) Excerpts (Ennio Morricone) US:LP = Peters PILPS-4050* [Ennio Morricone:ST]

5192 Pizza Triangle, The [A Drama of Jealousy] [Drama della Geloisa] (1970) Score (Armando Trovajoli) IT: LP = RCA PSL-10457*

5193 Place for Lovers, A [Amanti] (1968) Theme (Manuel DeSica) GB:LP = Major & Minor 5063* [Roger Webb]

5194 Place in the Sun, A (1951) Excerpts (Franz Waxman) US:LP = Columbia CL-2113/CS-8913* [@Franz Waxman:ST]; Excerpts (Franz Waxman) US:LP = RCA ARL1-0708 [Charles Gerhardt]

5195 Places in the Heart (1984) Score (as:Howard Shore) US:LP = Varese STV-81229*

5196 Plague Dogs (1983) Score (Patrick Gleeson) GB:LP = CBS 70227*

5197 Plan 9 from Outer Space [Grave Robbers from Outer Space] (1959) Underscore + Dialog (au:Gordon Zahler) US:LP-BP = Pendulum EROS-009 + US:LP-BP = Hippo PLAN-9

5198 Planet of the Apes (1968) Score (Jerry Goldsmith) US:LP = Project S-5023*

5199 Planter's Wife, The *see* Outpost in Malaya

5200 Plastic Dome of Norma Jean, The [Short] (1966) Theme (Michel Legrand) US:LP = MGM 4491* [Michel Legrand:ST]

5201 Platoon (1986) Score (t: Georges Delerue/s:classical & pop music) US:LP = Atlantic 81742-1*

5202 Play Dirty (1968) Themes (Michel Legrand) US:SP = UA 50495 [Michel Legrand:ST]; Theme (Michel Legrand) US:LP = UA 6715* [Michel Legrand:ST]

5203 Play It Again, Sam (1972) Theme + Underscore + Dialog (t:Oscar Peterson/u:Billy Goldenberg) US:LP = Paramount PAS-1004*; Theme (Billy Goldenberg) US:LP = Paramount 6035* [Billy Vaughn]

5203a Play It Cool (1962) Theme (Norrie Paramor) GB:SP = Columbia 4869 [Helen Shapiro]

5204 Playboy of Paris (1930) Excerpts (Richard A. Whiting) US:LP-BP = Caliban 6013 [@ST]

5205 Playgirl (1954) Theme/US: LP-BP = Legends 1000/2 [@Shelley Winters:ST]

5206 Playgirl and the War Minister, The *see* Amorous Mr. Prawn, The

5207 Playing for Keeps (1986) Score (various) US:LP = Atlantic 81678-1*

5208 Playmates (1941) Themes-A-B/US:78 = Columbia 36441 [Kay Kyser: ST]; Themes-C-D/US:78 = Columbia 36433 [Kay Kyser:ST]

5209 Playtime (1968) Highlights (Francis Lemarque) US:LP = UA UNS-15554*

5210 Please Don't Eat the Daisies (1960) Theme-A (Joe Lubin) US:SP = Columbia 4-41630 [Doris Day: ST]; Theme-B (Joseph Hooven) US:SP = Columbia 4-41569 [Doris Day: ST]; Theme-B (Joseph Hooven) US:LP-PP = Columbia DD-1 [Doris Day:ST]

5211 Please, Not Now! [Only for Love] [Le Bride sur le Cou] (1962) Highlights (James Campbell) FR:EP = Barclay 72471

5212 Pleasure of His Company, The (1961) Theme (film theme from "The Snows of Kilimanjaro") US:LP = Angel 36066* + US:LP = Capitol 1652* [Alfred Newman:ST]

5213 Pleasure Seekers, The (1965) Score (e:Lionel Newman/e:James Van Heusen/t:Alexander Courage) US:LP = RCA LOC-1101/LSO-1101* [Ann-Margret/Lionel Newman:ST]

5214 Plot, The *see* French Conspiracy, The

5215 Plow that Broke the Plains, The [Short] (1939) Highlights (Virgil Thomson) US:LP = Angel S-37300* [Neville Marriner]; Highlights (Virgil Thomson) US:LP = Vanguard 2095* [Leopold Stokowski]; Highlights (Virgil Thomson) US:LP = Bench Mark ABM-3501 [ST]

5216 Plucked [La Morte Ha Fatto l'Uovo] (1968) Score (Bruno Maderna) IT:LP = Cinevox 33/2

5217 Plymouth Adventure (1952) Excerpts (Miklos Rozsa) US:LP-10 = MGM E-179 + US:LP = MGM E-3507 [Miklos Rozsa:ST]

5218 Pocket Money (1972) Theme (Carole King) US:SP = Ode 66022* [Carole King:ST]

5219 Pocketful of Chestnuts, A [Le Castagne Sono Bueno] (1970) Themes (Carlo Rustichelli) IT:SP = CAM AMP-081* [ST]

5220 Pocketful of Miracles, A (1961) Theme (James Van Heusen) US: SP = Reprise 20-040 [Frank Sinatra]; Theme (James Van Heusen) US:LP = Reprise 9-1010* [Frank Sinatra]

5221 Point Blank (1967) Theme (Johnny Mandel) GB:LP = Philips 6382.103* [Ray Davies' Button Down Brass]

5222 Point of Departure / Theme (Hotchkiss) GB:78 = Decca 9653 [ST]

5223 Pointed Heels (1929) Themes/ US:LP-BP = Fanett 146 [Helen Kane: ST]

5224 Police Python 357 *see* Case Against Ferro, The

5225 Pollyanna (1960) Highlights + Underscore + Dialog (Paul Smith) US:LP = Disneyland DQ-1307 + US:LP = Disneyland ST-1906; Highlights (Paul Smith) US:EP = Disneyland DBR-93

5226 Poltergeist (1982) Score (Jerry Goldsmith) US:LP = MGM MG1-5408*

5227 Poltergeist II — The Other Side (1986) Score (Jerry Goldsmith) US: LP = Intrada RVF-6002*

5228 Pom Pom Girls, The (1976) Score (Michael Lloyd) US:LP = 20th T-487* [Cotton, Lloyd & Christian:ST]

5229 Les Poneyettes / Theme (Danyel Gerard) US:SP = Prince 4087 [Bernard Ebbinghouse]

5230 Pompeii / Scores (Roger Waters/etc.) US:LP-MS-PP = Edgard Rubabande DAGO-523*

5231 Pookie *see* Sterile Cuckoo, The

5232 Pool of London (1951) Theme (John Addison) GB:78-PP = Rank FM-109 [ST]; Theme (John Addison) US:LP-BP = Citadel CTOFI-1 [@ST]

5233 Poor Cow (1967) Theme (Donovan Leitch) US:SP = Epic 5-10300 [Donovan:ST]; Theme (Donovan Leitch) US:LP = Epic 26418* [Vic Lewis]

5234 Poor Little Rich Girl (1936) Excerpts (Harry Revel) US:LP-MS = 20th TCF2-103 [Shirley Temple: ST]

5235 Poor White Trash [Bayou] (1957) Theme (Ed Fessler) US:SP = Fraternity 760 [Dick Noel:ST]

5236 Popeye (1980) Score (Harry Nilsson) US:LP = Boardwalk SW-36880*

5237 Popeye the Sailor [Cartoon] (1933) Theme (Sam Lerner) US:78 = Melotone 13402 [Billy Costello:ST]; Theme (Sam Lerner) US:EP = Wonderland 2039 [Jack Mercer]; Theme (Sam Lerner) US:LP = Golden 27 [Mitch Miller & The Sandpipers]

5238 Popi (1969) Score (Dominic Frontiere) US:LP = UA UAS-5194*

5239 Popsy Pop *see* Butterfly Affair, The

5240 Porgy and Bess (1959) Score (stage songs:George Gershwin) US:LP = Columbia OL-5410/OS:2016*

5241 Porky's (1982) Score (pop music) JA:LP = Polydor 28-MM-0228*

5242 Porky's Revenge (1985) Score (various) US:LP = Columbia JS-39983*

5243 Port of Shadows [Quai de Brumes] (1938) Theme (Maurice Jaubert) FR:LP = Vega 30-A-98 [@ST]

5244 Porte des Lilas *see* Gates of Paris, The

5245 Portes de la Nuit, Les [Gates of the Night] (1947) Theme (Joseph Kosma) US:SP = Columbia 4-50033 [Mitch Miller]; Theme (Joseph Kosma) US:LP = Columbia 555 + US:LP = Columbia 10130 [Michel Legrand]

5246 Portnoy's Complaint (1972) Theme (Michel Legrand) US:SP = WB 536* [Michel Legrand:ST]; Theme (Michel Legrand) US:LP = Polydor 5038* [Arthur Fiedler & Boston Pops]; Theme (Michel Legrand) US:LP = RCA 4669* [Doc Severinsen]

5247 Portrait from Life *see* Girl in the Painting, The

5248 Portrait of a Murder (1963) Theme (George Cates) US:SP = Liberty 55582 [Bob Florence]

5249 Portrait of Clare (1951) Theme (at:Felton Rapley) GB:78 = Columbia 2764 [Charles Williams]; Theme (at:Felton Rapley) GB:LP = WRC 384 [@ Charles Williams]

5250 Portrait of Jennie, The [Jennie] (1948) Theme (Bernard Herrmann) US:LP-10 = Columbia 612 + US:LP = Columbia 6281 [Paul Weston]; Theme (Bernard Herrmann) US:SP = Columbia 4- [J.J. Johnson]

5251 Poseidon Adventure, The (1972) Highlights (John Williams) JA: EP = Toho AX-1003; Theme-A (John Willliams) US:LP-BP = Centurion 1600 [@John Williams:ST]; Theme-A (John Williams) JA:LP = RCA/Victor 7321* [The Film Studio Orchestra]; Theme-B (Al Kasha & Joel Hirschhorn) US:SP = 20th 2010* [Maureen McGovern:ST]

5252 Possessed (1931) Theme/US: LP-BP = Curtain Calls 100/23 [@Joan Crawford:ST]

5253 Postman's Knock, The (1962) Theme (Ron Goodwin) GB:LP-MS = EMI/Studio Two 108 [Ron Goodwin:ST]

5254 Pot o' Gold (1940) Themes-A-B/US:78 = Columbia 36006 [Horace Heidt:ST]; Themes-C-D/US:78 = Columbia 36070 [Horace Heidt:ST]; Themes-E-F/US:78 = Columbia 36053 [Horace Heidt:ST]

5255 Potemkin [Battleship Potemkin] (1925) Themes [Silent II] (Charles Hofmann) US:LP = Sounds Good 1001 [Charles Hofmann:ST]; Theme [Silent II] (Arthur Kleiner) US:LP = Golden Crest 4019 [Arthur Kleiner:ST]

5256 Pound (1970) Score (Charlie Cuva) US:LP-PP = Pound PD-1/2*

5257 Power, The (1968) Score (Miklos Rozsa) US:LP-BP = Citadel CTMR-1*

5258 Power, The (1983) Score (Chris Young) US:LP = Cerberus CST-0211*

5259 Power and the Prize, The (1956) Theme (Bronislau Kaper) US: LP = MGM 3694 [John Green]

5260 Pranks (1982) Score (Chris Young) US:LP = Citadel CT-7031*

5261 Prelude to Fame (1950) Theme (Biscardi) GB:78-PP = Rank FM-95 [ST]

5262 Presenting Lili Mars (1943) Scores (e:Walter Jumann/etc.) US:LP-MS-BP = Sountrak STK-117

5263 President's Analyst, The (1967) Theme (Barry McGuire) US:SP = Dunhill 4116 [Barry McGuire:ST]

5264 President's Country, A [Short] (1966) Excerpts (ae:Dimitri Tiomkin) GB:LP = Unicorn DKP-9047* [David Willocks]

5265 President's Lady, The (1953) Theme (Alfred Newman) US:SP = Decca 9-91564 [Alfred Newman:ST]; Theme

(Alfred Newman) US:LP = Decca 8123 + US:LP = Vocalion 73749 [Alfred Newman:ST]; Theme (Alfred Newman) US:LP = MGM 3172 [Leroy Holmes]

5266 Pressure Point (1962) Theme (Ernest Gold) US:LP = London 3320/320* [Ernest Gold:ST]

5267 Pretty Baby (1978) Score (pop music) US:LP = ABC AA-1076*

5268 Pretty Boy Floyd (1960) Score (William Sanford & Del Serino) US:LP = Audio Fidelity AFLP-1936/AFSD-5936*

5269 Pretty in Pink (1986) Score (various) US:LP = A&M SP-5113*

5270 Pretty Maids All in a Row (1971) Theme (Lalo Schifrin) US:SP = MGM 14259 [The Osmonds:ST]; Theme (Lalo Schifrin) US:LP = MGM 4770* [The Osmonds:ST]

5271 Pretty Polly *see* Matter of Innocence, A

5272 Pride and the Passion, The (1957) Score (George Antheil) US:LP = Capitol W-873 + US:LP-BP = Movie Music MM-5146

5273 Priest of Love (1981) Score-A (Joseph James) GB:LP = That's Entertainment TER-1014*; Score-B (Joseph James) GB:LP-PP = SS 001*

5274 Priest's Wife, The [La Moglie del Prete] (1970) Themes (Armando Trovajoli) US:SP = WB 7479 [Sophia Loren:ST]

5275 Prime of Miss Jean Brodie, The (1969) Score (Rod McKuen) US:LP = 20th S-4207* [Arthur Greenslade:ST]; Score (Rod McKuen) US:LP = WB WS-1853* [Rod McKuen]

5276 Prince and the Pauper, The (1937) Excerpts (Erich Wolfgang Korngold) US:LP = RCA ARL1-0185* [Charles Gerhardt]

5277 Prince and the Pauper, The (1973) Score (stage songs:George Fischoff) US:LP = Pickwick SPC-3204*

5278 Prince and the Pauper, The (1977) *see* Crossed Swords

5279 Prince and the Showgirl, The (1957) Theme/US:LP-BP = Legends 1000/1 [Marilyn Monroe:ST]

5280 Prince Bayaya (1954) Score (Vaclav Trojan) RU:LP = Supraphon LPM-168

5281 Prince for Cynthia, A [Short] (1954) Excerpts (Bruce Montgomery) US:LP = MGM E-3151 [@ST]

5282 Prince of Arcadia (1933) Theme/GB:78 = Decca 3759 [Carl Bris-son:ST]

5283 Prince of the City (1981) Score (Paul Chihara) US:LP = Varese STV-81137*

5284 Prince Valiant (1954) Excerpts (Franz Waxman) US:LP = RCA ARL1-0708* [Charles Gerhardt]

5285 Prince Who Was a Thief, The (1951) Excerpts (Hans J. Salter) US:LP = Medallion ML-312 [Hans J. Salter:ST]

5286 Princes, Les (1984) Score (as:Tony Gatlif) FR:LP = Milan A-217*

5287 Princess Charming (1935) Excerpts (Ray Noble) GB:LP = MFP 1160 [Evelyn Lane:ST]

5288 Princess Tam-Tam (1935) Theme / US:LP-BP = Totem 1026 [Josephine Baker:ST]

5289 Prisoner in the Street (1980) Score (The Third World) US:LP = Island ILPS-9616* [The Third World:ST]

5290 Prisoner of Second Avenue, The (1975) Theme (Marvin Hamlisch) US:LP = Polydor 6040* [James Last]

5291 Prisoner of Zenda, The (1937) Score (Alfred Newman) US:LP = UA LA-374* [Leroy Holmes]

5292 Prisonniere, La (1968) Score (classical music) US:LP = Columbia OS-3320*

5293 Private Affairs of Bel Ami, The [Bel Ami] (1947) Theme (Jack Lawrence) US:78 = Columbia 37213 [Dinah Shore]

5294 Private Buckeroo (1942) Theme-A/US:LP = Decca 4919 [The Andrews Sisters:ST]; Theme-B/US:78 = Decca 18319 [The Andrews Sisters:ST]; Theme-C/US:78 = Decca 18398 [The Andrews Sisters:ST]

5295 Private Eyes, The (1977) Score (Sam Hui) JA:LP = Polydor MP-1219*

5296 Private Hell 36 (1954) Highlights (Leith Stevens) US:LP-10 = Coral CRL-56122 + US:LP = Coral CRL-57283/CRL-757283* [Leith Stevens:ST]

5297 Private Lessons (1981) Score (pop music) US:LP = MCA 5275*

5298 Private Life of Sherlock Holmes, The (1970) Excerpts (Miklos Rozsa) US:LP = Deutsche 2584.021* [Miklos Rozsa:ST]

5299 Private Lives of Adam and Eve, The (1960) Theme (Paul Anka) US: SP = ABC 10082 [Paul Anka:ST]; Theme (Paul Anka) US:LP = ABC 323* [Paul Anka:ST]

5300 Private Lives of Elizabeth and Essex, The [Elizabeth the Queen] (1939) Excerpts (Erich Wolfgang Korngold) US:LP = RCA ARL1-0185* [Charles Gerhardt]

5301 Private Parts (1974) Highlights (Hugo Friedhofer) US:LP = Delos F-25420

5302 Private School (1983) Highlights (e:Bill Wray/etc.) US:EP-12 = MCA 36005*

5303 Private Vices, Public Virtues [Vizi Privat, Pubbliche Virtu] (1977) Score (Francesco DeMasi) IT:LP = Beat LPF-034*

5304 Private War of Major Benson, The (1955) Theme (Henry Mancini & Herman Stein) US:SP = Decca 9-29653 [Victor Young]; Theme (Henry Mancini & Herman Stein) US:SP = Capitol 3195 [Les Baxter]; Theme (Henry Mancini & Herman Stein) US:SP = RCA 47-6221 [Henri Rene]

5305 Privilege (1967) Score (e:Mike Leander/e:Mark London) US:LP = UNI 73005*

5306 Prize, The (1963) Excerpts (Jerry Goldsmith) US:LP = MGM E-4192/SE-4192* [@Jerry Goldsmith:ST]; Highlights (Jerry Goldsmith) FR:EP = MGM 63615

5307 Prize of Gold, A (1954) Theme (Lester Lee) US:SP = London 45-1542 [Joan Regan]

5308 Prodigal, The (1931) Themes/ US:LP-BP = Empire 804 [Lawrence Tibbett:ST]

5309 Prodigal, The (1955) Theme (Bronislau Kaper) US:SP = MGM 11992 [Leroy Holmes]; Theme (Bronislau Kaper) US:LP = Liberty 14019* [Felix Slatkin]; Theme (Bronislau Kaper) US: LP = London 3257/246* [Frank Chacksfield]

5310 Producers, The (1968) Highlights + Underscore + Dialog (e:John Morris/t:Mel Brooks) US:LP = RCA LSP-4008* + US:LP = RCA ANL1-1132*

5311 Professional Gun, A *see* Mercenary, The

5312 Professionals, The (1966) Score (Maurice Jarre) US:LP = Colgems COMO-5001/COSO-5001*

5313 Project M-7 [The Net] (1953) Theme (Benjamin Frankel) GB:78-PP = Rank FM-135 [ST]

5314 Prom Night (1980) Score (Carl Zittrer & Paul Zaza) JA:LP = RCA/ Victor RPL-8089*

5315 Promise, The (1979) Score (David Shire) US:LP = MCA 3082*

5316 Promise at Dawn (1970) Score (Georges Delerue) US:LP = Polydor 24-5502*

5317 Promise Her Anything (1966) Score (s:Lyn Murray/t:Burt Bacharach) US:LP = Kapp KL-1476/KS-3476*

5318 Promises, Promises (1964) Theme (Roberta Day) US:SP = Astra 7100 [Roberta Day:ST]

5319 Promoter, The [The Card] (1952) Theme (William Alwyn) GB:78-PP = Rank FM-129 [ST]; Theme (William Alwyn) US:LP-BP = Citadel CTOFI-1 [@ST]; Theme (William Alwyn) GB:LP = UA 30281* [@Ed Welch]

5320 Proper Time, The (1960) Score (Shelly Manne) US:LP = Contemporary 3587/7587*

5321 Proud and the Beautiful, The [The Proud Ones] [Les Orgueilleux] (1953) Themes (Paul Misraki) US:SP = Columbia 4-40727 [Henry Leca]

5322 Proud and the Profane, The (1956) Theme (Victor Young) US:SP = Coral 9-61655 [George Cates]; Theme (Victor Young) US:LP = Coral 57065 [George Cates]; Theme (Victor Young) US:SP = Decca 9-29968 [Victor Young: ST]

5323 Proud Ones, The (1953) *see* Proud and the Beautiful, The

5324 Proud Ones, The (1956) Theme (Lionel Newman) US:SP = Columbia 4-40717 [Lionel Newman:ST]; Theme (Lionel Newman) US:SP = Coral 9-61663 [George Cates]; Theme (Lionel

Newman) US:LP = MGM 3480 [Leroy Holmes]

5325 Proud Rebel, The (1958) Score (Jerome Moross) US:LP-BP = Classic International Filmusic 1001; Theme (Jerome Moross) US:SP = MGM 12656 [Leroy Holmes]; Theme (Jerome Moross) US:LP = MGM 3753 + US: LP = Lion 70136 [Leroy Holmes]

5326 Proud Valley, The (1940) Themes-A-B/GB:78 = HMV 9020 [Paul Robeson:ST]; Theme-C/GB:78 = HMV 8668 [Paul Robeson:ST]; Theme-D/US: 78 = RCA/Victor 20793 [Paul Robeson: ST]

5327 Providence (1977) Score (Miklos Rozsa) US:LP = DRG SL-9502*

5328 Prowlers of the Everglades [Short] (1954) Excerpts (Paul Smith) US: LP = Disneyland WDL-4011 [Paul Smith:ST]

5329 Prudence and the Pill (1968) Score (Bernard Ebbinghouse) US:LP = 20th S-4199*

5330 Psych-Out (1968) Score (e:Ronald Stein/etc.) US:LP = Sidewalk ST-5913*

5331 Psyche 59 (1964) Theme (Ken Jones) US:LP = Colpix 464* [@Ken Jones:ST]

5332 Psycho (1960) Score (Bernard Herrmann) US:LP = Unicorn UNI-75001*

5333 Psycho Lover [Psycho Killer] [The Loving Touch] (1970) Themes (Jim Helms) US:SP = Co-Burt 107* [Gary Le Mel:ST]

5334 Psycho II (1983) Score (Jerry Goldsmith) US:LP = MCA 6119*

5335 Psycho III (1986) Score (Carter Burwell) US:LP = MCA 6174*

5336 Psychout for Murder [Salvare la Faccia] (1969) Themes (Benedetto Ghiglia) IT:SP = CAM AMP-056* [ST]

5337 Public Enemy [Enemies of the Public] (1931) Sequence + Dialog (Harry Barris) US:LP-MS = WB 3X-2737 [@ST]

5338 Public Eye, The [Follow Me] (1972) Score (John Barry) JA:LP = MCA 5137*

5339 Public Nuisance #1 (1936) Theme/GB:LP = WRC 217 [@Frances Day:ST]

5340 Public Pigeon No. 1 (1957) Theme (David Rose) US:LP = MGM 3397 [David Rose:ST]

5341 Pueblo del Sol, El (1982) Score (Lee Holdridge) SA:LP = Fonapas CCFT-100*

5342 Pufnstuf (1970) Score (Charles Fox) US:LP = Capitol SW-542*

5343 Pull My Daisy [Short] (1958) Theme (David Amram) US:LP = RCA 7089* + US:LP = Flying Fish 752* [David Amram:ST]

5344 Pulp (1972) Themes (George Martin) GB:SP = UA 35423 [George Martin:ST]

5345 Pump Trouble [Hollywood Carnival] [Cartoon] (1954) Excerpts (Carlos Surinach) US:LP = MGM E-3419 [Carlos Surinach:ST]

5346 Pumping Iron II—The Women (1985) Score (various) US:LP = Island 90273-1*

5347 Pumpkin Eater, The (1964) Theme (Georges Delerue) US:SP = Colpix 755 [Charles Albertine]

5348 Puppet on a Chain (1971) Theme (Piero Piccioni) IT:LP = General Music 55068* [Piero Piccioni:ST]

5349 Purple Noon [Plein Soleil] (1963) Highlights (Nino Rota) FR:EP = Fontana 460.800

5350 Purple Rain (1984) Score (Prince) US:LP = WB 25110-1* [Prince: ST]; Theme (Apollonia 6) US:LP = WB 25108-1* [Apollonia 6:ST]; Theme (Morris Day) US:LP = WB 25109-1* [The Time:ST]

5351 Purple Rose of Cairo, The (1985) Score (Dick Hyman) US:LP = MCA 6139*

5352 Purple Taxi Cab, The [Le Taxi Mauve] (1979) Score (Philippe Sarde) FR:LP = Vogue 20288*

5353 Pursued (1947) Highlights (Max Steiner) US:LP-BP = Citadel CTMS-5

5354 Pursuit of D.B. Cooper, The (1981) Score (t:James Horner/s:various) US:LP = Polygram/Polydor PD1-6344*

5355 Pursuit of the Graf Spee [Battle of the River Plate] (1956) Theme-A (Brian Easdale) GB:LP = MFP 90075* [Band of the Royal Marines]; Theme-A (Brian Easdale) GB:78-PP = Rank

FM-181 [ST]; Theme-B (Brian Easdale) GB:78-PP = Rank FM-182 [ST]; Theme-C (Brian Easdale) GB:78-PP = Rank FM-183 [ST]

5356 Pursuit to Algiers (1945) Underscore + Dialog (au:Mark Levant) US:LP = Murray Hill 55447

5357 Pussycat, Pussycat, I Love You (1970) Theme-A (Lalo Schifrin) US: SP = UA 50649* [Lalo Schifrin:ST]; Theme-B (Lalo Schifrin) US:SP = Liberty 56154 [Henry Shed:ST]

5358 Putney Swope (1969) Theme (Charlie Cuva) US:LP = Dunhill 50083* [The Bully Boys Band]

5359 Puttin' on the Ritz (1930) Highlights (various) US:LP-BP = Meet Patti 1930

5360 Pyassa / Theme/US:LP = Capitol 10500 [@Hemant Kumar:ST]

5361 Pyramid of the Sun Gods (1965) Highlights (Erwin Halletz) GE: LP = Telefunken 14367

Q

5362 Q [The Winged Serpent] (1982) Score (Robert O. Ragland) US: LP = Cerberus CST-0206*

5363 Quadrophenia (1979) Scores (pop music) US:LP-MS = Polydor PD2-6235* [The Who:ST]

5364 Quai des Brumes *see* Port of Shadows

5365 Quando la Preda e l'Uomo [When Man Is the Prey] Score (Ennio Morricone) US:LP = Cerberus CEM-SP-0118*

5366 Quando l'Amore e Sensualita (1973) Score (Ennio Morricone) US: LP = Cerberus CEMS-0118*

5367 Quartet (1981) Score (Richard Robbins) US:LP = Gramavision GR-1020*

5368 Quatorze Juillet [14 Juillet] (1933) Theme (Maurice Jaubert) GB: LP = WRC 248 [@ST]

5369 Queen Bee (1978) Score (Shinichi Tanabe) JA:LP = Toho AX-5018*

5370 Queen Kelly (1927) Theme [Silent II] (Lee Erwin) US:LP = Angel 36073* [Lee Erwin:ST]

5371 Queen Kong (1976) Theme (Pepper) IT:SP = CAM AMP-189* [ST]

5372 Queen Millennia (1983) Score (Kitaro) JA:LP = Canyon 28-G-0124*

5373 Queen of Hearts (1936) Themes-A-B/GB:78 = Regal 8818 [Gracie Fields:ST]; Themes-C-D/GB:78 = Regal 8819 [Gracie Fields:ST]

5374 Queens, The [Le Fate] [Les Ogresses] (1966) Themes (Armando Trovajoli) FR:SP = RCA 49.511 [ST]; Theme (Armando Trovajoli) US:LP = RCA 4038* [Rouvaun]

5375 Queen's Affair, The (1934) Themes/GB:78 = Columbia 1316 [Anna Neagle/Trefor Jones:ST]

5376 Queens of Evil [Le Regine] (1971) Highlights (A.F. Lavagnino) JA: LP = Seven Seas 6032*

5377 Queimada! *see* Burn!

5378 Querelle (1982) Score (Peer Raben) US:LP = DRG SL-9509*

5379 Qu'est ce Qui Fait Covrir David? [What Makes David Run?] (1983) Score (Michel Legrand) FR:LP = Milan 120.171*

5380 Quest for Fire (1981) Score (Philippe Sarde) US:LP = RCA ABL1-4274*

5381 Question of Adultery, A [The Case of Mrs. Loring] (1958) Theme (Bobby Troup) US:SP = Liberty 55175 [Julie London:ST]

5382 Quick, Before It Melts (1964) Excerpts (David Rose) US:LP = MGM E-4285/SE-4285* [David Rose:ST]

5383 Quicksilver (1985) Score (e:Tony Banks/e:various) US:LP = Atlantic 81631-1*; Excerpts (Tony Banks) US:LP = Atlantic 81680-1* [Tony Banks: ST]

5384 Quiet American, The (1958) Theme (Mario Nascimbene) US:SP = UA 103 [Ray Martin]

5385 Quiet Days in Clichy (1972) Score (Country Joe MacDonald) US: LP = Vanguard 79303*

5386 Quiet Man, The (1952) Highlights (Victor Young) US:LP-10 = Decca DL-5411 + US:LP = Decca DL-8566 + US:LP = Varese VC-81073

5387 Quiet Day in the Country, A [Un Tranquillo Posto di Campagna] (1968) Themes (Ennio Morricone) IT: LP-PP = General Music 33-01/02 [Ennio Morricone:ST]

5388 Quiller Memorandum, The (1966) Score (John Barry) US:LP = Columbia OL-6660/OS-3060*

5389 Quo Vadis (1951) Score (Miklos Rozsa) US:LP = London SPC-21180* [Miklos Rozsa:ST]; Highlights (Miklos Rozsa) US:LP-10 = MGM E-103 [Miklos Rozsa:ST]

R

5390 R.P.M. (1970) Score (Barry DeVorzon & Perry Botkin, Jr.) US:LP = Bell 1203*

5391 Rabbit, Run (1970) Themes (Ray Burton) US:SP = Capitol 2982 [The Frank Day Habit:ST]

5392 Race for the Wire [Industrial Short] Score (Marion Evans) US:LP-PP = Maximum XB-491

5393 Racers, The [Such Men Are Dangerous] (1955) Themes-A-B (Alex North) US:LP = RCA 1445* [Alex North:ST]; Theme-C (Alex North) US: LP = Citadel 6023* [Alex North:ST]; Theme-C (Alex North) US:SP = Coral 9-61475 [Jimmy Wakely]; Theme-C (Alex North) US:SP = Decca 9-29429 [Peggy Lee:ST]

5394 Rachel and the Stranger (1948) Highlights (Roy Webb) US:78-MS = Decca A-695 [Robert Mitchum: ST]

5395 Racing Fever (1965) Theme (Al Jacobs) US:SP = World Artists 1037 [Johnny Cool]; Theme (Al Jacobs) US: LP = Regina 319* [Jack La Forge]

5396 Racing Scene, The (1970) Theme (Don Randi) US:SP = Capitol 2916* [Joe South:ST]

5397 Racing with the Moon (1984) Theme (Dave Grusin) US:LP = GRP 1006* [Dave Grusin:ST]

5398 Rad (1986) Score (t:James Di Pasquale/s:various) US:LP = MCA 6166*

5399 Radio World (1985) Score (Io Xavier) US:LP = Do Speak DO-2*

5400 Raga (1971) Score (Ravi Shankar) US:LP = Apple SWAO-3384*

5401 Ragazze di San Frediano, Le (1954) Theme (Mascheroni) US:LP = Epic 3593 [Gian Stellari]

5402 Rage of the Lion *see* Lion, The

5403 Rage to Live, A (1965) Score (s:Nelson Riddle/t:Ferrante & Teicher) US:LP = UA UAL-4130/UAS-5130*

5404 Raggedy Ann and Andy (1977) Score (Joe Raposo) US:LP = Columbia AL-34686*

5405 Raging Moon, The *see* Long Ago Tomorrow

5406 Ragtime (1981) Score (Randy Newman) US:LP = Elektra 5E-565*

5407 Raiders, The *see* Western Approaches

5408 Raiders of the Lost Ark (1981) Score (John Williams) US:LP = Columbia JS-37373*

5409 Railroad Man, The [Man of Iron] [Il Ferroviere] (1955) Themes (Carlo Rustichelli) IT:SP = RCA 1104 [ST]

5410 Railway Children, The (1970) Score (Johnny Douglas) US:LP = Capitol ST-871*

5411 Rain (1932) Highlights + Underscore + Dialog (u:Alfred Newman/e:various) US:LP-BP = Caliban 6048

5412 Rain People, The (1969) Themes (Ronald Stein) US:LP-PP = WB PRO-329* [@Ronald Stein:ST]

5413 Rainbow Bridge (1972) Score (pop music) US:LP = Reprise RS-2040* [Jimi Hendrix:ST]

5414 Rainbow Jacket, The (1954) Theme (William Alwyn) GB:78-PP = Rank FM-150 [ST]

5415 Rainbow on the River (1936) Themes/US:78 = Decca 1053 [Bobby Breen:ST]

5416 Rainbow 'Round My Shoulder [Castle in the Air] (1952) Highlights (various) US:EP = Columbia B-1512 [Frankie Laine:ST]

5417 Rainmaker, The (1956) Score (Alex North) US:LP = RCA LPM-1434 + US:LP-BP = Cinevox 33/24

5418 Rains of Ranchipur, The

(1955) Theme (Hugo Friedhofer) US: LP = Forum 9080* + US:LP = Roulette 25023* [Jack Shaindlin]

5419 Raintree County (1957) Scores (John Green) US:LP-MS = RCA LOC-6000 + US:LP-MS = Entracte ERS-6503*; Theme (John Green) US:SP = Capitol 3782 [Nat King Cole:ST]; Scores (John Green) US:LP-MS-BP = Soundstage SS-2304

5420 Raise the Titanic (1980) Theme (John Barry) JA:SP = Seven Seas K07S-9003* [Larry Nelson]; Theme (John Barry) US:LP-BP = Disc 105* [@Larry Nelson]

5421 Rake's Progress, The *see* Notorious Gentleman, The

5422 Rambo—First Blood, Part 2 (1985) Score (Jerry Goldsmith) US:LP = Varese STV-81246*

5423 Ramona (1928) Theme [Silent I] (L. Wolfe Gilbert) US:SP = RCA 47-3802 [Tony Martin]; Theme [Silent I] (L. Wolfe Gilbert) US:LP = RCA LPV-528 [@Dolores Del Rio:ST]; Theme [Silent I] (L. Wolfe Gilbert) US:LP = RCA 2560* [Gaylord Carter]

5424 Rampage at Apache Wells [The Oil Prince] [Der Olprinz] (1965) Score (Martin Bottcher) GE:LP = Polydor 237.494*

5425 Ran (1985) Score (Toru Takemitsu) US:LP = Fantasy FSP-21004*

5426 Rancho Deluxe (1975) Score (Jimmy Buffett) US:LP = UA LA-466*

5427 Ransom *see* Terrorists, The

5428 Rape of Innocence, The [Dupont-Lajoie] (1974) Themes (Vladimir Cosma) FR:SP = Deesse 696* [ST]

5429 Rappin' (1985) Score (e:Larry Smith/e:various) US:LP = Atlantic 81252-1*

5430 Rare Breed, The (1966) Theme (John Williams) US:LP = Decca 74754* [Sammy Kaye]

5431 Rascal (1969) Theme (Bobby Russell) US:SP = Buena Vista 474 [Soundtrack Chorus:ST]; Theme (Bobby Russell) US:SP = Elf 90031 [Bobby Russell]

5432 Rashomon (1950) Highlights (Fumio Hayazaka) US:LP = Varese STV-81142*

5433 Rasputin [I Killed Rasputin] [J'ai Tue Raspoutine] (1967) Score (Andre Hossein) FR:LP = Philips 70.426

5434 Rat Fink a Boo Boo (1964) Theme (Ron Haydock) US:LP = Rhino 307 [@ST]

5435 Rat Race, The (1960) Theme (Elmer Bernstein) US:SP = Choreo 107 [Elmer Bernstein:ST]; Theme (Elmer Bernstein) US:LP = Mainstream 6094* + US:LP = Choreo 11* [Elmer Bernstein:ST]; Theme (Elmer Bernstein) US: LP = Dot 25306* [Sam Butera]; Theme (Elmer Bernstein) US:SP = Roulette 4270* [Richard Maltby]

5436 Rataplan (1979) Score (Detto Mariano) IT:LP = CAM SAG-9101*

5437 Raton Pass (1951) Excerpts (Max Steiner) US:LP-MS-BP = Tony Thomas TTMS-9/10 [Max Steiner:ST]

5438 Ravine, The [La Cattura] (1969) Themes (Riz Ortolani) IT:SP = CAM AMP-070* [ST]

5439 Raw Deal (1986) Score (Tom Bahler & Chris Boardman) US:LP = Varese STV-81286*

5440 Raw Wind in Eden (1958) Theme (Jay Livingston & Ray Evans) US:SP = Decca 9-30614 [Beverly Kennedy]

5441 Rawhide Years, The (1956) Theme (Frederick Herbert) US:SP = Decca 9-29584 [Karel Wagner]

5442 Rayo de Luz, Un / Score (Segura) US:LP = Montilla FMS-2067 [Marisol:ST]

5443 Razorback (1985) Score (Iva Davies) AU:LP = EMI 430-006*

5444 Razor's Edge, The (1946) Theme (film theme from "These Three") US:LP = Mercury 20037 + US:LP = Citadel 6003 + US:LP = Citadel 7015 [Alfred Newman:ST]

5445 Razor's Edge, The (1984) Score (Jack Nitzsche) US:LP = Southern Cross SCRS-1009*

5446 Razzle-Dazzle on the Bouzouki / Score (Stavros Xarchakos) US: LP = Capitol DT-10532* [Stavros Xarchakos:ST]

5447 Reach for the Sky (1956) Theme (John Addison) GB:78-PP = Rank FM-197 [ST]; Theme (John Addison) GB:LP = MFP 5171* [Geoff Love]

5448 Reaching for the Moon (1931) Theme/US:LP = Biograph BLPM-1 [Bing Crosby:ST]

5449 Ready, Willing and Able (1937) Theme/US:LP-BP = JJA 19806 [@Ruby Keeler & Winifred Shaw:ST]

5450 Re-Animator, The (1985) Score (Richard Band) US:LP = Varese STV-81261*

5451 Reap the Wild Wind (1942) Theme (Victor Young) US:LP-BP = JJA 19762 [@Paulette Goddard:ST]

5452 Rear Window (1954) Theme (Franz Waxman) US:SP = X 4X-0059 [Eddy Manson]; Theme (Franz Waxman) US:LP = Decca 8085 [Victor Young]; Theme (Franz Waxman) US:LP = MGM 3172 [Leroy Holmes]

5453 Reason to Live, A Reason to Die, A [Massacre at Fort Holman] [Una Ragione per Vivere una per Morire] (1974) Score (Riz Ortolani) IT:LP = Intermezzo IM-012*

5454 Rebecca (1940) Highlights (Franz Waxman) US:LP-BP = Cine 818; Excerpts (Franz Waxman) US:LP = RCA ARL1-0708* [Charles Gerhardt]

5455 Rebecca of Sunnybrook Farm (1938) Excerpts (various) US:LP-MS = 20th TCF-2-103 [Shirley Temple:ST]

5456 Rebel (1986) Score (e:Peter Best/e:pop music) AU:LP = EMI EMX-240439*

5457 Rebel in Town (1956) Theme (Les Baxter) US:SP = Mercury 70890 [The Crew Cuts]; Theme (Les Baxter) US:SP = Epic 5-9173 [Eddy Manson]; Theme (Les Baxter) US:SP = RCA 47-6576 [Diahann Carroll]

5458 Rebel Rouser (1958) Theme (Duane Eddy) US:SP = Jamie 1104 [Duane Eddy:ST]

5459 Rebel with a Cause *see* Loneliness of the Long Distance Runner

5460 Rebel Without a Cause (1955) Excerpts-A (Leonard Rosenman) US:LP = Columbia CL-940 + US:LP = CSP ACL-940 [Ray Heindorf:ST]; Excerpts-B (Leonard Rosenman) US:LP = Imperial LP-9021 [Leonard Rosenman]

5461 Rebellion [Samurai Rebellion] (1967) Excerpts (Toru Takemitsu) JA:LP = RCA/Victor 1062 [Toru Takemitsu:ST]

5462 Reckless (1935) Theme/US:LP-MS = MCA 2-11002 [@Jean Harlow:ST]

5463 Recommendation for Mercy (1975) Theme (Scott Fagan) US:SP = RCA 10678* [Scott Fagan:ST]

5464 Record City (1977) Score (Freddie Perren) US:LP = Polydor PD1-8002*

5465 Red and Blue (1967) Highlights (Cyrus Bassiak) GB:LP = UA SULP-1184* [Vanessa Redgrave:ST]

5466 Red Arrows, The [The Royal Air Force Aerobatic Team—The Red Arrows] (1981) Themes (stock music) GB:SP = BBC 95* [ST]

5467 Red Balloon, The [Le Ballon Rouge] [Short] (1956) Theme (Maurice Le Roux) FR:LP = Vega 30-A-98 [@ST]

5468 Red Baron, The *see* Von Richthofen and Brown

5469 Red Beard (1965) Highlights (Masaru Sato) JA:LP = Toho AX-1001

5470 Red Carpet, The [Short] Sequence + Dialog (Arthur Kleiner) US:LP-PP = Picture Book Parade 102

5471 Red Dance, The (1928) Theme (Erno Rapee) US:78 = RCA Victor 21633 [The Troubadours]

5472 Red Danube, The (1949) Excerpts (Miklos Rozsa) US:LP = Deutsche 2584.021* [Miklos Rozsa:ST]

5473 Red Dawn (1984) Score (Basil Poledouris) US:LP = Intrada RVF-6001*

5474 Red Desert [Deserto Rosso] (1965) Score (Giovanni Fusco) IT:LP = CAM CMS-30.124

5475 Red Garters (1954) Highlights (Jay Livingston & Ray Evans) US:LP-10 = Columbia CL-6282

5476 Red, Hot and Blue (1949) Excerpts (Frank Loesser) US:LP-BP = Vedette 8702 [Betty Hutton:ST]

5477 Red House, The (1947) Excerpts-A (Miklos Rozsa) US:LP-10 = Capitol L-453 + US:LP = Capitol L-456 [Miklos Rozsa:ST]; Excerpts-B (Miklos Rozsa) US:LP = RCA ARL1-0911* [Charles Gerhardt]

5478 Red Mantle, The [Hagbard and Signe] (1973) Score (Marc Fredricks) US:LP = RCA LSP-5815*

5479 Red Pony, The (1948) Highlights (Aaron Copland) US:LP = Columbia M-33586* [Aaron Copland:ST]; Score (Aaron Copland) US:LP = Varese STV-81259

5480 Red River (1948) Excerpts (Dimitri Tiomkin) GB:LP = Unicorn DKP-9002* [Laurie Johnson]

5481 Red Runs the River / Score (Dwight Gustafson) US:LP-PP = Unusual 1553

5482 Red Shoes, The (1949) Theme-A (Brian Easdale) US:LP-10 = Columbia ML-2083 [Muir Mathieson:ST]; Theme-A (Brian Easdale) US:LP = Odyssey 32160.338* [Vladimir Golschmann]; Theme-B (Brian Easdale) GB:78-PP = Rank FM-13 + GB:78 = Columbia 328 [Muir Mathieson:ST]

5483 Red Sky at Morning (1971) Score (e:Billy Goldenberg/etc.) US:LP = Decca DL-79180*

5484 Red Sonja (1985) Score (Ennio Morricone) US:LP = Varese STV-81248*

5485 Red Sun [Soleil Rouge] (1971) Score (Maurice Jarre) US:LP-BP = MJ 501* + FR:LP = Motors 44008*

5486 Red Tent, The (1971) Score (Ennio Morricone) US:LP = Paramount PAS-6019*

5487 Redeemer, The (1966) Highlights (David Raksin) US:LP-MS-PP = Library of Congress LOC-RAKSIN [David Raksin:ST]

5488 Reds (1981) Score (e:Dave Grusin/t:Stephen Sondheim/etc.) US:LP = Columbia BJS-37690*

5489 Reet Petite and Gone [Short] (1947) Highlights (various) GB:LP = Krazy Kat KK-7414 [Louis Jordan:ST]; Theme/US:LP = MCA 1337 [Louis Jordan:ST]

5490 Reform School Girls (1986) Score (various) US:LP = Rhino RNLP-70310*

5491 Reggae Sunsplash '81 (1982) Scores (pop music) US:LP-MS = Elektra E1-60035*

5492 Reina del Chantecler, La / Score (various) US:LP = Columbia EX-5108 [Sarita Montiel:ST]

5493 Reincarnation of Peter Proud, The (1975) Highlights (Jerry Goldsmith) US:LP-BP = Monogram 7711

5494 Reivers, The (1969) Score (John Williams) US:LP = Columbia OS-3510*

5495 Reluctant Dragon, The (1941) Theme + Narration (Charles Wolcott) US:LP = Disneyland ST-3817; Theme (Charles Wolcott) US:SP = Golden 753 [The Sandpipers]

5495a Reluctant Saint, The (1962) Themes (Nino Rota) IT:LP = CAM CMT-0010 [@ST]

5496 Reluctant Widow, The (1950) Theme (Allan Gray) GB:78-PP = Rank FM-94 [ST]

5497 Remember My Name (1978) Score (pop music) US:LP = Columbia JS-35553*

5498 Remo Williams—The Adventure Begins (1985) Theme (Tommy Shaw) US:SP = A&M 2773* [Tommy Shaw:ST]

5499 Removalists, The (1975) Score (Galapagos Duck) AU:LP = Philips 6357.020*

5500 Renaldo and Clara (1978) Highlights (pop music) US:EP-12-PP = Columbia AS-422* [Bob Dylan:ST]; Theme/US:SP = Columbia 38-04425* [Bob Dylan:ST]

5501 Repo Man (1984) Score (various) US:LP = San Andreas SAR-39019*

5502 Report to the Commissioner [Operation Undercover] (1975) Excerpts (Vernon Burch) US:LP = UA LA-342* [Vernon Burch:ST]

5503 Reprieve *see* Convicts 4

5504 Repulsion (1965) Excerpts (Chico Hamilton) IT:LP = CAM AMG-1 [@ST]

5505 Requiem for a Heavyweight [Blood Money] (1962) Theme (Laurence Rosenthal) US:SP = Colpix 659 [Manny Albam]; Theme (Laurence Rosenthal) US:LP = Colpix 458* [@Manny Albam]

5506 Rescuers, The (1977) Highlights + Underscore + Dialog (e:Carol Connors & Ann Robbins/u:Artie Butler) US:LP = Disneyland ST-1369*

5507 Restless Breed, The (1957) Score (e:Raoul Kraushaar/e:Edward L. Alperson, Jr.) US:LP = Chevron CH-3; Themes (Edward L. Alperson, Jr.) US:SP = Chevron CH-006 [ST]; Theme (Edward L. Alperson) US:SP = Atco 45-

6091 [Frank Bianco]

5508 Restless Ones, The (1965) Highlights (Ralph Carmichael) US:EP = Grason BG-6515 [Ralph Carmichael: ST]; Excerpts (Ralph Carmichael) US: LP = Supreme M-110/MS-210* [Johnny Crawford:ST]

5509 Return from the Ashes (1965) Theme (Johnny Dankworth) US:SP = UA 949 [Arnold Goland]; Theme (Johnny Dankworth) US:LP = RCA 1-5092* [Johnny Dankworth:ST]

5510 Return of a Man Called Horse (1976) Score (Laurence Rosenthal) US: LP = UA LA-692*

5511 Return of Dracula, The [The Curse of Dracula] [The Fantastic Disappearing Man] (1958) Theme (Gerald Fried) US:LP-BP = POO 104 [@ST]

5512 Return of Giant Majin, The (1966) Excerpts (Akira Ifukube) JA: LP = Toho 8125 [@ST]

5513 Return of Martin Guerre, The (1983) Highlights (Michel Portal) US: LP = DRG SL-9514*

5514 Return of Maxwell Smart, The *see* Nude Bomb, The

5515 Return of Ringo, The [Il Ritorno di Ringo] (1965) Highlights + Underscore + Dialog (Ennio Morricone) JA:LP = RCA/ARC SA-7; Highlights (Ennio Morricone) IT:LP = RCA 33209*

5516 Return of the Dragon [Way of the Dragon] (1974) Score (Joseph Koo) JA:LP = TAM 7011* + JA:LP = RCA/ Victor 7305*; Theme (Mike Nise) US: SP = Bryan 1008 [The Ninchuks]

5517 Return of the Giant Monsters (1967) Excerpts (Tadashi Yamauchi) JA: LP = Toho 8120 [@ST]

5518 Return of the Jedi (1983) Score (John Williams) US:LP = RSO 811-767-1* [John Williams:ST]; Highlights (John Williams) US:LP = Varese 704.210* [Varujan Kojin]

5519 Return of the Living Dead (1985) Score (various) US:LP = Enigma 72004-1*

5520 Return of the Pink Panther, The (1975) Score (Henry Mancini) US: LP = RCA ABL1-0968*

5521 Return of the Seven (1966) Score (film score from "The Magnificent Seven") US:LP = UA UAL-4146/UAS-5146* [Elmer Bernstein:ST]

5522 Return of the Soldier (1983) Score (Richard Rodney Bennett) GB: LP = That's Entertainment TER-1036*

5523 Return of the Tall Blond [Le Retour du Grand Blond] (1975) Score (Vladimir Cosma) FR:LP = Philips 6325.179*

5524 Return to Macon County [Highway Girl] (1975) Score (pop music) US:LP = UA LA-491*

5525 Return to Oz (1973) *see* Journey Back to Oz

5526 Return to Oz (1985) Score (David Shire) US:LP = Sonic Atmospheres 113*

5527 Return to Paradise (1953) Highlights + Underscore + Dialog (Dimitri Tiomkin) US:LP-10 = Decca DL-5489

5528 Return to Peyton Place (1961) Theme (film theme from "Peyton Place") US:SP = RCA 47-7887 [Rosemary Clooney:ST]

5529 Return to Waterloo (1985) Score (Ray Davies) US:LP = Arista AL6-8386*

5530 Reveille with Beverly (1943) Highlights (various) US:LP-BP = Hollywood Soundstage HS-5014

5531 Revenge in El Paso *see* Ace High

5532 Revenge of the Creature (1955) Theme (Herman Stein) US:LP = Coral 757240* + US:LP = Varese 81077* [Dick Jacobs]

5533 Revenge of the Gladiators [La Vendetta di Spartacus] (1964) Highlights (Francesco De Masi) IT:LP = Beat CR-13*

5534 Revenge of the Nerds (1984) Scores (t:Thomas Newman/s:various) US:LP = Scotti Bros. BFZ-39599*

5535 Revenge of the Ninja (1983) Score (Rob Walsh) US:LP = Varese STV-81195*

5536 Revenge of the Pink Panther (1978) Score (Henry Mancini) US:LP = UA LA-913*

5537 Revenge of the Vampire *see* Black Sunday (1960)

5538 Revengers, The [La Feccia] (1972) Score (Pino Calvi) IT:LP = CBS 70120*

5539 Revolt of Mamie Stover, The (1956) Theme (Sammy Fain) US:SP = Capitol 3399 [Jane Russell:ST]

5540 Revolution (1968) Score (pop music) US:LP = UA UAS-5185* + US: LP = UA LA-296*

5541 Revolver *see* Blood in the Streets

5542 Reward, The (1965) Theme (Elmer Bernstein) US:LP = Capitol 2419* [Laurindo Almeida]

5543 Rhapsody in Black and Blue (1932) Themes/US:LP = Biograph BLPM-3 [@Louis Armstrong:ST]

5544 Rhapsody in Blue (1945) Score (pop music) US:LP-BP = Titania 512

5545 Rhapsody of Steel [Industrial Short] (1958) Highlights (Dimitri Tiomkin) US:LP-PP = U.S. Steel 502; Highlights (Dimitri Tiomkin) GB:LP = Unicorn DKP-9047* [David Willcocks]

5546 Rhinestone (1984) Score (s:Dolly Parton/t:Mike Post) US:LP = RCA ABL1-5032*

5547 Rhino! (1964) Themes (Lalo Schifrin) US:SP = MGM 13251 [Lalo Schifrin:ST]

5548 Rhinoceros (1974) Underscore + Dialog (Galt MacDermot) US:LP-MS = Caedmon TRS-364

5549 Rhodes [Rhodes of Africa] (1936) Theme (Hubert Bath) GB:78 = Columbia 1607 [Louis Levy]

5550 Rhythm and Greens (1964) Excerpts (The Shadows) GB:LP = MFP 50347 [The Shadows:ST]

5551 Rhythm on the Range (1936) Excerpts (various) US:LP-10 = Decca DL-6010 + US:LP = Decca DL-4255 [Bing Crosby:ST]; Theme/US:LP = Epic 3061 + US:LP-MS-BP = Legends 1000/5-6 [Martha Raye:ST]

5552 Rhythm on the River (1940) Excerpts (Jimmy Monaco) US:LP-10 = Decca DL-6014 + US:LP = Decca DL-4255 [Bing Crosby:ST]; Themes/US: 78 = Decca 23164 [Mary Martin:ST]

5553 Rich, Young and Pretty (1951) Highlights (Nicholas Brodszky) US:LP-10 = MGM E-86 + US:LP = MGM E-3236 + US:LP = MGM 2SES-53e

5554 Richard (1972) Themes (Galt MacDermot) FR:SP = Barclay 61739* [ST]

5555 Richard III (1956) Highlights (William Walton) US:LP = Angel 36198/ S-36198* + US:LP = Seraphim S-60205* [William Walton:ST]; Underscore + Dialog (William Walton) US:LP-MS = RCA LM-6126

5556 Richer than the Earth *see* Whistle at Eaton Falls, The

5557 Ride Back, The (1957) Theme (Frank DeVol) US:SP = RCA 47-6895 [Vaughn Monroe:ST]

5558 Ride Beyond Vengeance (1966) Theme (Richard Markowitz) US: SP = RCA 47-8745 [Glenn Yarbrough: ST]; Theme (Richard Markowitz) US: LP = RCA 3983* [Glenn Yarbrough:ST]

5559 Ride the High Country [Guns in the Afternoon] (1962) Themes (George Bassman) US:SP = MGM 13078 [Robert Holliday]; Theme (George Bassman) US:LP = MGM 4185* [@Robert Holliday]; Theme (George Bassman) US: LP = WB 1476* [George Greeley]

5560 Ride the Wild Surf (1964) Theme-A (Stu Phillips) US:SP = RCA 47-8419 [The Astronauts]; Theme-B (Roger Christian) US:SP = Liberty 55724 [Jan & Dean:ST]; Theme-B (Roger Christian) US:LP = Liberty 7368* [Jan & Dean:ST]

5561 Rider on the Rain (1970) Score (Francis Lai) US:LP = Capitol ST-584*

5562 Riding High (1943) Highlights (t:Joseph J. Lilley/e:Ralph Rainger) US: LP-BP = Caliban 6034; Excerpts (t:Joseph J. Lilley/e:Ralph Rainger) US: LP-BP = Legends 1000/4 [Dorothy Lamour:ST]

5563 Riding High (1950) Excerpts (James Van Heusen) US:LP = Decca DL-4261 [Bing Crosby:ST]

5564 Riding High (1979) Score (various) GB:LP = Jambo JAM-2*

5565 Rififi [Du Rififi Chez les Hommes] (1955) Theme (M. Philippe Gerard) US:SP = RCA 47-6600 [Leo Diamond]; Theme (M. Philippe Gerard) US:LP = Audio Fidelity 6124* [Jo Basile]; Theme (M. Philippe Gerard) US: LP = Capitol 8603* [Frank Pourcel]

5566 Rififi in Paris *see* Upper Hand, The

5567 Rififi in Tokyo *see* Up to His Ears

5568 Right Approach, The (1961) Theme (Alan Bergman) US:SP = Columbia 4-41945 [The Kirby Stone Four]

5569 Right Cross (1950) Theme (David Raksin) US:LP-BP = Centurion 1210 [@David Raksin:ST]

5570 Right Stuff, The (1984) Highlights (Bill Conti) US:LP = Varese 704.310*

5571 Right to Love, The *see* Bill of Divorcement, A (1932)

5572 Right to Love, The [Le Droit d'Aimer] (1972) Highlights (Philippe Sarde) FR:EP = RCA 87500*

5573 Ring-a-Ding Rhythm [It's Trad, Dad] (1962) Score (e:Norrie Paramor/etc.) GB:LP = Columbia 5X-1412; Theme (Mort Shuman) US:SP = Legend 1019 [Gary U.S. Bonds:ST]

5574 Ring of Bright Water (1969) Highlights (Frank Cordell) GB:LP = Phoenix DGS-1004*; Theme (Frank Cordell) US:SP = Mercury 72940 [Dee Dee Warwick:ST]

5575 Ring of Fire (1961) Themes (Duane Eddy/Edward L. Alperson, Jr.) US:SP = Jamie 1187 [Duane Eddy:ST]; Theme (Duane Eddy) US:SP = UA 855 [Al Caiola]

5576 Rio Bravo (1959) Excerpts (Dimitri Tiomkin) GB:LP = Unicorn DKP-9002* [Laurie Johnson]; Excerpts (Dimitri Tiomkin) US:EP-PP = Capitol PRO-1063 [Dean Martin:ST/Nelson Riddle]; Themes (Dimitri Tiomkin) US:SP = Capitol 4175 [Dean Martin:ST]; Theme (Dave Guard) US:SP = Capitol 4167 [The Kingston Trio]

5577 Rio Conchos (1964) Highlights (Jerry Goldsmith) FR:EP-PP = 20th 730.001; Themes (Jerry Goldsmith) US:LP-BP = Centurion 1600 [@Jerry Goldsmith:ST]; Theme (Jerry Goldsmith) US:SP = 20th 546 [Johnny Desmond]

5578 Rio Grande (1950) Score (s: Victor Young/e:Stan Jones) US:LP = Varese STV-81124*

5579 Rio Rita (1929) Themes/US: 78 = RCA/Victor 22132 [Bebe Daniels: ST]

5580 Riot (1969) Theme (Christopher Komeda) US:SP = AGP 125 [Roy Hamilton]; Theme (Christopher Komeda) US:LP = Dot 25943* [Ike Cole]

5581 Riot in Cell Block 11 (1954) Theme (Herschel Burke Gilbert) GB: 78 = HMV 1323 [Ken MacKintosh]

5582 Riot on Sunset Strip (1967) Score (t:Fred Karger/s:various) US: LP = Tower T-5065/ST-5065*

5583 Rise and Rise of Casanova, The *see* Sex on the Run

5584 Rise and Shine (1941) Theme/ US:LP-BP = JJA 19811 [@Jack Oakie:ST]

5585 Risky Business (1983) Score (e:Tangerine Dream/etc.) GB:LP = Virgin V-2302*

5586 Rituals (1978) Theme (Hagood Hardy) CA:LP = Attic 1034* [Hagood Hardy:ST]

5587 Ritz, The (1976) Themes + Dialog + Narration (pop music) US:LP-PP = Suski Fallick SF-103 [Rita Moreno: ST]

5588 Rivals [Deadly Rivals] (1972) Theme (Peter Matz) US:SP = SSS 742 [Carol Hall]

5589 River, The [Short] (1936) Highlights (Virgil Thomson) US:LP = Angel S-37300* [Neville Marriner]; Highlights (Virgil Thomson) US:LP = Vanguard 2095* [Leopold Stokowski]

5590 River, The (1951) Score (as: K.N. Dandayuhapaim & M.A. Partha Sarathy) US:LP = Polymusic PR-5003

5591 River, The (1984) Score (John Williams) US:LP = MCA 6138*

5592 River Niger, The (1976) Theme (War) US:LP = Bluenote 690* [War:ST]

5593 River of No Return (1954) Excerpts (Lionel Newman) US:LP = 20th FXG-5000 + US:LP = 20th T-901 [Marilyn Monroe:ST]; Theme (Lionel Newman) US:SP = Capitol 2810 [Tennessee Ernie Ford:ST]

5594 River Rat, The (1984) Score (Mike Post) US:LP = RCA CBL1-5310*

5595 River's Edge, The (1957) Theme (Louis Forbes) US:SP = Imperial 7004 [Bob Winn]

5596 Ro-Go-Pag [Laviamoci il Cervello] (1962) Highlights (Carlo Rustichelli) IT:EP = CAM CEP-45-90

5597 Road House (1948) Theme (Lionel Newman) US:SP = Mercury

30052 [Vic Damone]; Theme (Lionel Newman) US:SP = RCA 47-3028 [Tommy Dorsey]; Theme (Lionel Newman) US:SP = Decca 8109 [Victor Young]

5598 Road Is Open Again, The (1933) Theme/US:LP-MS = Columbia C2L-44 [Dick Powell:ST]

5599 Road to Bali, The (1952) Highlights (James Van Heusen) US:LP-10 = Decca DL-5444 + US:LP = Decca DL-4263 [Bing Crosby:ST]

5600 Road to Hong Kong, The (1962) Score (e:Robert Farnon/e:James Van Heusen) US:LP = Liberty LOM-16002/LOS-17002*

5601 Road to Morocco, The (1942) Excerpts (James Van Heusen) US:LP = Decca DL-4257 [Bing Crosby:ST]

5602 Road to Rio, The (1947) Excerpts (James Van Heusen) US:LP = Decca DL-4260 [Bing Crosby:ST]

5603 Road to Salina, The [Sur la Route de Salina] [Quando il Sole Scotta] (1969) Score (e:Clinic/e:Christophe/t:Bernard Gerard) FR:LP = Motors 44001*

5604 Road to Singapore, The (1940) Excerpts (Jimmy Monaco) US:LP = Decca DL-4254 + US:LP-10 = Decca DL-6015 [Bing Crosby:ST]; Excerpts (Jimmy Monaco) US:LP = West Coast 14002 [Dorothy Lamour:ST]

5605 Road to Utopia, The (1945) Excerpts (James Van Heusen) US:LP = Decca DL-4258 [Bing Crosby:ST]; Theme (James Van Heusen) US:LP = Landmark 101 [@Dorothy Lamour:ST]

5606 Road to Zanzibar, The (1941) Excerpts (James Van Heusen) US:LP = Decca DL-4255 [Bing Crosby:ST]

5607 Road Warrior, The [Mad Max II] (1982) Score (Brian May) US:LP = Varese STV-81155*

5608 Roadhouse (1934) Theme/GB:LP = Ace of Clubs 1182 [@Violet Lorraine:ST]

5609 Roadhouse Nights (1930) Theme/US:LP-BP = Trisklog 4 [Helen Morgan:ST]

5610 Roadie (1980) Scores (various) US:LP-MS = WB 2HS-3441*

5611 Roar (1982) Score (Terence Monogue) GB:LP = G.T. 1600*

5612 Robber's Roost (1955) Theme (Tony Romano) US:SP = RCA 47-6118 [Vaughn Monroe]

5613 Robbery (1967) Score (Johnny Keating) US:LP = London M-76008/MS-82008*

5614 Robe, The (1953) Score (Alfred Newman) US:LP = Decca DL-9012/DL-79012e + US:LP = MCA 2052e

5615 Robert et Robert (1979) Score (e:Francis Lai/e:Jean Claude Nachon) FR:LP = WB/WEA 56507*

5616 Roberta (1935) Score (stage songs:Jerome Kern) US:LP-BP = Classic International Filmusicals 3011

5617 Robin and Marian (1976) Score-A (John Barry) US:LP-BP = Sherwood SH-1500; Score-B (John Barry) US:LP-BP = PRO 4345

5618 Robin and the Seven Hoods (1964) Score (James Van Heusen) US:LP = Reprise R-2021/RS-2021*

5619 Robin Hood (1952) *see* Story of Robin Hood, The

5620 Robin Hood (1973) Highlights + Dialog (e:Roger Miller/t:George Bruns) US:LP = Disneyland ST-3810 + US:LP = Disneyland ST-1352

5621 Robot Rabbit [Cartoon] (1953) Sequence + Dialog (Carl Stalling) US:LP-MS = WB 3X-2737 [@ST]

5622 Rocco and His Brothers (1961) Score (Nino Rota) US:LP = RCA FOC-2/FSO-2*

5623 Rock-a-Bye Baby (1958) Themes (Harry Warren) US:SP = Decca 9-30664 [Jerry Lewis:ST]; Theme (Harry Warren) US:LP = MGM 3753 [Leroy Holmes]

5624 Rock All Night (1957) Score (e:Buck Ram/etc.) US:LP = Mercury MG-20293

5625 Rock Around the Clock (1956) Score (pop music) US:LP = Decca Decca DL-8225 + US:LP = AEI 3106 [Bill Haley and the Comets:ST]

5626 Rock Around the World [The Tommy Steele Story] (1957) Score (Lionel Bart) US:LP = London LL-1770 [Tommy Steele:ST]

5627 Rock Baby, Rock It (1957) Score (pop music) US:LP = Rhino RNSP-309

5628 Rock 'n' Roll High School

(1979) Score (pop music) US:LP = Sire 6070*

5629 Rock, Pretty Baby (1956) Score (s:Henry Mancini/t:Sonny Burke/t:Rod McKuen) US:LP = Decca DL-8429

5630 Rock, Rock, Rock! (1956) Highlights (pop music) US:LP = Chess LP-1425

5631 Rockers (1979) Score (pop music) US:LP = Mango MLPS-9587*

5632 Rocket to the Moon *see* Those Fantastic Flying Fools

5633 Rocketship X-M (1950) Score (s:Ferde Grofe/as:Albert Glasser) US:LP = Starlog SR-1000

5634 Rockin' the Blues (1955) Score (various) US:LP = U.G.H.A. 001

5635 Rocking Horse Winner, The (1949) Theme-A (William Alwyn) GB:78-PP = Rank FM-87 [ST]; Theme-B (William Alwyn) GB:78-PP = Rank FM-88 [ST]; Theme-B (William Alwyn) US:LP-BP = Citadel CTOFI-1 [@ST]

5636 Rocky (1976) Score (Bill Conti) US:LP = UA LA-693*

5637 Rocky II (1979) Score (Bill Conti) US:LP = UA LA-972*

5638 Rocky III (1982) Score (Bill Conti) US:LP = Liberty LO-51130*

5639 Rocky IV (1985) Score-A (e:Vince Di Cola/e:various) US:LP = Scotti Bros. SZ-40203*; Theme-B ["Farewell"] (Vince Di Cola) US:SP = Scotti Bros. 4-05682* [Vince Di Cola:ST]

5640 Rocky Horror Picture Show, The (1975) Score (stage songs:Richard O'Brien) US:LP = Ode OSV-21653*; Score + Dialog + Audience (stage songs:Richard O'Brien) US:LP-MS = Ode 1032*

5641 Rocky Mountain (1950) Theme (Max Steiner) US:LP-BP = Citadel CTMS-6 [Max Steiner:ST]

5642 Rodan (1956) Excerpts (Akira Ifukube) JA:LP = Toho 8107 [@ST]

5643 Rogue Song (1930) Highlights + Dialog (e:Herbert Stothart/t:Dimitri Tiomkin) US:LP = Pelican 2019

5644 Rogues' Gallery (1968) Theme (Jimmie Haskell) US:SP = Dot 17133 [Christopher Sunday:ST]; Theme (Jimmie Haskell) US:LP = Dot 25860* [Jim mie Haskell:ST]

5645 Rogue's Regiment (1948) Theme (Jack Brooks) US:SP = RCA 47-3944 [Mindy Carson]

5646 Roi, Le *see* Royal Affair, A

5647 Roll On Texas Moon (1946) Theme/US:LP = RCA 3041 [Roy Rogers:ST]

5648 Roller Boggie (1979) Scores (Bob Esty) US:LP-MS = Casablanca NBLP2-7194*

5649 Rollerball (1975) Score (t:Andre Previn/s:classical music) US:LP = UA LA-470*

5650 Rollercoaster (1977) Score (Lalo Schifrin) US:LP = MCA 2284*

5651 Rolling Thunder (1977) Theme (Barry DeVorzon) US:SP = Buddah 585* [Denny Brooks:ST]

5652 Roma *see* Fellini's Roma

5653 Roma Come Chicago [Bandits in Rome] (1968) Themes (Ennio Morricone) US:LP-BP = POO 105 [Ennio Morricone:ST]

5654 Roman Holiday (1953) Theme (Georges Auric) JA:LP = Seven Seas 118* [The Screenland Orchestra]

5655 Roman Polanski's Forbidden Dreams *see* What? (1972)

5656 Roman Scandals (1933) Score (Harry Warren) US:LP-BP = Classic International Filmusicals 3007 + US:LP-BP = Sandy Hook SH-2039

5657 Roman Spring of Mrs. Stone, The (1961) Theme (Richard Addinsell) US:SP = London 45-9510 [The Wayfarers]

5658 Romance in the Dark (1938) Theme/US:LP = JJA 19811 [@John Boles & Gladys Swarthout:ST]

5659 Romance of a Horsethief (1971) Score (Mort Shuman) US:LP = Allied Artists 110.100*

5660 Romance on the High Seas [It's Magic] (1948) Highlights (Jule Styne) US:LP-BP = Caliban 6015

5661 Romancing the Stone (1984) Theme (Eddy Grant) US:SP = Portrait 37-04433* [Eddy Grant:ST]; Theme (Eddy Grant) US:LP = Portrait 39261* [Eddy Grant:ST]

5662 Romanoff and Juliet (1961) Theme (Mario Nascimbene) US:SP = Decca 9-31242 [Jorge Morel]; Theme (Mario Nascimbene) US:SP = King 5509

[Ron Goodwin]; Theme (Mario Nascimbene) US:LP = UA 6464* [Ron Goodwin]

5663 Romantic Age, The *see* Naughty Arlette

5664 Romantic Comedy (1983) Theme (Marvin Hamlisch) US:SP = Capitol 5283* [Roberta Flack & Peabo Bryson:ST]; Theme (Marvin Hamlisch) US:LP = Capitol 12284* [Roberta Flack & Peabo Bryson:ST]

5665 Rome Adventure (1962) Highlights (Max Steiner) US:LP = WB W-1458/WS-1458*

5666 Rome 11 O'Clock [Roma Ore 11] (1952) Theme (Mario Nascimbene) IT:LP-MS = Kangaroo 34209 [Mario Nascimbene:ST]

5667 Rome—Open City *see* Open City

5668 Romeo and Juliet (1954) Underscore + Dialog (Roman Vlad) US:LP = Epic LC-3126 + US:LP = Epic FLM-13104/FLS-15104e

5669 Romeo and Juliet (1968) Score (Nino Rota) US:LP = Capitol ST-400*; Underscore + Dialog (Nino Rota) US:LP-MS = Capitol SWDR-289*

5670 Ronde, La (1950) Theme (Oscar Straus) US:SP = Columbia 4-39617 [Mitch Miller]; Theme (Oscar Straus) GB:78 = Parlophone 6002 [Anton Walbrook:ST]; Theme (Oscar Straus) US:LP = London 1332 [Stanley Black]

5671-2 Ronde, La (1965) *see* Circle of Love

5673 Rookie, The (1960) Theme (Paul Dunlap) US:SP = Capitol 4293 [Paul Dunlap:ST]

5674 Rookies, The *see* Buck Privates

5675 Room at the Top (1958) Theme (Mario Nascimbene) US:LP = WB 1548* [Werner Muller]; Theme (Mario Nascimbene) US:LP = Reprise 6009* [Leo Diamond]; Theme (Mario Nascimbene) IT:LP-MS = Kangaroo 34209 [Mario Nascimbene:ST]

5676 Room 43 [Passport to Shame] (1958) Themes (Ken Jones) US:SP = WB 5078 [Ken Jones:ST]; Themes (Ken Jones) US:LP-BP = Cinema 8002 [@Ken Jones:ST]

5677 Room with a View (1986) Score (Richard Robbins) US:LP = DRG SBL-12588*

5678 Roots of Heaven, The (1958) Score (s:Malcolm Arnold/t:Henri Patterson) US:LP = 20th 3005

5679 Rosalie (1937) Highlights (Cole Porter) US:LP-BP = JJA 19767 [@ST]

5680 Rose, The (1979) Score (various) US:LP = Atlantic SD-16010*

5681 Rose Marie [Indian Love Call] (1936) Score (stage songs:Rudolf Friml) US:LP-BP = Hollywood Soundstage HS-414; Excerpts (stage songs: Rudolf Friml) US:LP = RCA LPV-526 [Jeanette MacDonald:ST]; Excerpts (stage songs:Rudolf Friml) US:LP = Columbia GB-3 [Nelson Eddy:ST]

5682 Rose Marie (1954) Highlights (t:George Stoll/stage songs:Rudolf Friml) US:LP-10 = MGM E-229 + US:LP = MGM E-3228 + US:LP = MGM E-3769 + US:LP = Metro M-616/MS-616e + US:LP-MS = MGM 2SES-41e

5683 Rose of Washington Square (1939) Highlights (pop music) US:LP-BP = Caliban 6002 + US:LP-BP = Sandy Hook SH-2074

5684 Rose Tattoo, The (1955) Score (Alex North) US:LP = Columbia CL-727

5685 Roseanna McCoy (1949) Theme (Frank Loesser) US:SP = RCA 47-2943 [Freddy Carson]

5686 Rosebud (1975) Excerpts (Laurent Petitgirard) FR:LP = Milan A-288*

5687 Roseland (1930) Themes/US:LP-BP = Fanett 146 [Ruth Etting:ST]

5688 Rosemary (1958) Theme (Norbert Schultze) US:SP = Epic 5-9391 [Chuck Sagle]; Theme (Norbert Schultze) US:LP = Decca 74083* [Helmut Zacharias]; Theme (Norbert Schultze) US:LP = Reprise 6009* [Leo Diamond]

5689 Rosemary's Baby (1968) Score (Christopher Komeda) US:LP = Dot DLP-25875*

5690 Rosie (1967) Theme (Harry Warren) US:SP = Brunswick 9-78024 [Louis Armstrong]; Theme (Harry Warren) US:LP = Decca 74909* [Jan Garber]

5691 Rotten to the Core (1965) Score (Michael Dress) GB:LP = Parlophone 1262

5691a Roue, La (1922) Excerpts [Silent I] (Arthur Honegger) US:LP = Vanguard VDS-274 [Maurice Abravanel]

5692 Rough Night in Jericho (1967) Themes (Don Costa) US:SP = Decca 9-32157 [The Kids Next Door]; Theme-A (Don Costa) US:LP = Decca 74909* [Jan Garber]; Theme-B (Don Costa) US: LP = Verve 6-8702* [Don Costa:ST]

5693 Round Midnight (1986) Score (e:Herbie Hancock/e:pop music) US: LP = Columbia SC-40464*

5694 Roustabout (1964) Score (e: Bill Giant/e:Florence Kaye/etc.) US: LP = RCA LPM-2999/LSP-2999* + US:LP = RCA AFL1-2999* [Elvis Presley:ST]

5695 Routes de le Sud, Les (1978) Highlights (Michel Legrand) US:LP = Gryphon G-786* [Michel Legrand:ST]

5696 Rover, The [L'Avventuriero] (1967) Score (Ennio Morricone) IT:LP = RCA SP-8022

5697 Royal Affair, A [Le Roi] (1950) Excerpts (various) US:78-MS = Decca DU-758 [Maurice Chevalier:ST]

5698 Royal Affairs in Versailles [Versailles] (1957) Highlights (Jean Francaix) FR:EP = Pathe 1036

5699 Royal Bed, The *see* Abdullah's Harem

5700 Royal Scandal, A [Czarina] (1945) Theme (Alfred Newman) US:LP = Mercury 20036 + US:LP-BP = Capricorn 1286 + US:LP = Citadel 6003 + US:LP = Citadel 7015 [Alfred Newman:ST]

5701 Royal Wedding [Wedding Bells] (1951) Highlights (Burton Lane) US:LP-10 = MGM E-543 + US:LP = MGM E-3235 + US:LP-MS = MGM 2SES-53e

5702 Ruby (1977) Theme (Don Ellis) US:SP = Prodigal 634 [Don Dunn:ST]

5703 Ruby Gentry (1953) Theme (Heinz Roemheld) US:SP = Mercury 70115 + US:SP = Mercury 70146 [Richard Hayman]; Theme (Heinz Roemheld) US:LP = Decca 8051 [Victor Young]; Theme (Heinz Roemheld) US: LP = Mercury 60238* [Clebanoff]

5704 Rud (1978) Score (John Mathews) US:LP-PP = DS 57976*

5705 Ruling Class, The (1972) Highlights + Dialog (e:John Cameron/etc.) US:LP = Avco AV-11008*

5706 Rum Runners, The [Boulevard du Rhum] (1970) Score (Francois DeRoubaix) FR:LP = Barclay 900.527*

5707 Rumble Fish (1983) Score (Stewart Copeland) US:LP = A&M SP6-4983*

5708 Run, Angel, Run! (1969) Score (Stu Phillips) US:LP = Epic BN-26474*

5709 Run for Cover (1955) Theme (Howard Jackson) US:SP = Capitol 3037 [Bob Graham & Nelson Riddle]

5710 Run for the Sun (1956) Theme-A (Fred Steiner) US:SP = Coral 9-61729 [Johnny Desmond & Lawrence Welk]; Theme-B (Fred Steiner) US:LP = Coral 57107 [Johnny Desmond & Lawrence Welk]

5711 Run for Your Wife (1966) Score (Nino Oliviero) US:SP = RCA LOC-1129/LSO-1129*

5712 Run of the Arrow (1957) Score (Victor Young) US:LP = Decca DL-8620 + US:LP = AEI 3102

5713-14 Run on Gold, A *see* Midas Run, The

5715 Run Silent, Run Deep (1958) Theme (Kenny Jacobson) US:SP = Decca 9-30641 [Jack Pleis]

5716 Run Wild, Run Free (1969) Score (David Whitaker) US:LP = SGC SD-5003*

5717 Runaway (1985) Score (Jerry Goldsmith) US:LP = Varese STV-81234*

5718 Runaway Train (1985) Score (Trevor Jones) US:LP = Enigma SJ-73200*

5719 Runner Stumbles, The (1979) Score (Ernest Gold) US:LP-PP = VC 5205* + US:LP-BP = EG 1001*

5720 Running (1979) Themes (Andre Gagnon) JA:SP = RCA/Victor 1506* [ST]

5721 Running Scared (1986) Score (e:Rod Temperton/e:various) US:LP = MCA 6169*

5722 Russ Meyer's Vixen *see* Vixen

5723 Russian Adventure *see* Cinerama's Russian Adventure

5724 Russians Are Coming, The Russians Are Coming, The (1966) Score (Johnny Mandel) US:LP = UA UAL-4142/UAS-5142*

5725 Rust Never Sleeps (1979) Score (pop music) US:LP = Reprise HS-2295* [Neil Young]

5726 Rustler's Rhapsody (1985) Score (Steve Dorff) US:LP = WB 25284-1*

5727 Ruthless Four, The [Orgunno Per Se] (1968) Score (Carlo Rustichelli) IT:LP = Intermezzo IM-011*

5728 Ruthless People (1986) Score (t:Michel Colombier/s:various) US:LP = Epic SE-40398*

5729 Ryan's Daughter (1970) Score (Maurice Jarre) US:LP = MGM 1SE-27*

S

5730 S.W.A.L.K. *see* Melody

5731 Saadia (1953) Theme (Robert Inglez) GB:78 = Parlophone 3876 [ST]

5732 Sabata (1970) Score (Marcello Giombini) JA:LP = UA NSR-455*

5733 Saboteur, Code Name—Morituri, The *see* Morituri

5734 Sabrina (1954) Themes (Frederick Hollander) US:LP = RCA 1-0422* [Charles Gerhardt]

5735 Sacco and Vanzetti (1971) Score (Ennio Morricone) US:LP = RCA LSP-4612*

5736 Sacred Idol, The *see* La Ciudad Sagrada

5737 Sad Horse, The (1959) Theme (Walter Kent) US:SP = Dot 15913 [David Ladd:ST]

5738 Sad Sack, The (1957) Theme (Burt Bacharach) US:SP = Decca 9-30503 [Jerry Lewis:ST]

5739 Saddle Pals (1947) Theme (Ernest Gold) US:LP = London 3320/320* [Ernest Gold:ST]

5740 Saddle the Wind (1958) Theme (Jay Livingston & Ray Evans) US:SP = Liberty 55108 [Julie London:ST]; Theme (Jay Livingston & Ray Evans) US:LP = RCA 1679 [Tony Perkins]

5741 Sadie McKee (1934) Themes/US:LP = RCA 6056 [Gene Austin:ST]

5742 Safety in Numbers (1930) Themes-A-B/US:78 = Columbia 2183 [Charles Buddy Rogers:ST]; Theme-C/US:LP-BP = JJA 19806 [@Carole Lombard:ST]

5743 Sag Es mit Musik / Themes/US:SP = Capitol 71112 [Bibi Johns:ST]

5744 Sahara (1984) Score (Ennio Morricone) US:LP = Varese STV-81211*

5745 Sahara (1943) Theme (Miklos Rozsa) US:LP = RCA 1-0422* + US:LP = RCA 1-3782* [Charles Gerhardt]

5746 Sail a Crooked Ship (1961) Themes (Russ Faith) US:LP = Chancellor 5022 [Frankie Avalon:ST]

5747 Sailing Along (1938) Themes-A-B/GB:78 = Decca 6672 [Jessie Matthews:ST]; Themes-C-D/GB:78 = Decca 6673 [Jessie Matthews:ST]

5748 Sailor Beware! (1952) Themes (Jerry Livingston) US:SP = Capitol 1901 [Dean Martin:ST]

5749 Sailor from Gibraltar, The (1967) Theme (Cyrus Bassiak) US:SP = UA 50159 [Al Caiola]; Theme (Cyrus Bassiak) GB:LP = UA 1184* [Vanessa Redgrave:ST]

5750 Sailor Who Fell from Grace with the Sea, The (1976) Score (s:Johnny Mandel/t:Kris Kristofferson) JA:LP = Polydor MP-1025*; Theme (Kris Kristofferson) US:SP = Monument 8-8699* [Bill Justis]; Theme (Kris Kristoffersson) US:LP = Monument 36135* [Kris Kristofferson:ST]

5751 Sailors Three (1940) Themes/GB:78 = Columbia 2531 [Tommy Trinder:ST]

5752 St. Benny, The Dip (1951) Theme/US:SP = Decca 9-27682 [Dick Haymes:ST]

5753 St. Elmo's Fire (1985) Score (David Foster) US:LP = Atlantic 81261-1*

5754 St. Francis of Assisi [Short] Score (uncredited) US:LP-PP = S.F. PR4M-0582

5755 St. Ives (1976) Theme (Lalo Schifrin) JA:LP-MS = TAM 9015/6* [@The Screenland Orchestra]

5756 Saint Joan (1957) Score

(Mischa Spoliansky) US:LP = Capitol W-865

5757 St. Louis Bank Robbery, The *see* Great St. Louis Bank Robbery, The

5758 St. Louis Blues [Short] (1929) Themes/US:LP = Biograph BLPM-3 + US:LP = Storyville 702 + US:LP-BP = Sandy Hook 2068 [@Bessie Smith:ST]

5759 St. Louis Blues (1939) Highlights (various) US:LP-BP = Caliban 6014

5760 St. Louis Blues (1958) Highlights (pop music) US:LP = Capitol W-993/SW-993 + US:LP = Capitol SN-12059* [Nat King Cole:ST]; Highlights (pop music) US:LP = RCA LPM-1661/LSP-1661* [Eartha Kitt:ST]; Highlights (pop music) US:LP = Roulette R-25037 [Pearl Bailey:ST]; Theme (Nelson Riddle) US:SP = Capitol 3980 [Nelson Riddle:ST]

5761 St. Valentine's Day Massacre, The (1967) Theme (Lionel Newman) US:LP = Decca 74909* [Jan Garber]; Theme (Lionel Newman) US:SP = Project 45-1320 [The Guitar Underground]

5762 Saints and Sinners (1949) Theme (Philip Green) US:LP = MGM 3119 [Philip Green:ST]

5763 Sait-On Jamais *see* No Sun in Venice

5764 Saladin and the Great Crusades [Saladino] (1966) Score (A.F. Lavagnino) IT:LP = Campi Editori CLP-100.007

5765 Salem Comes to Supper *see* Night Visitor, The

5766 Sallah (1965) Score (Yohanan Zarai) US:LP = Philips PHM-200.177/PHS-600.177*

5767 Sally (1929) Themes/US:LP-BP = Take Two 104 [@Marilyn Miller & Alexander Gray:ST]

5768 Sally in Our Alley (1931) Themes/GB:LP = WRC SH-170 [Gracie Fields:ST]

5769 Sally, Irene and Mary (1938) Highlights (e:Harold Spina/etc.) US:LP-BP = Caliban 6031

5770 Salo – The 120 Days of Sodom [Salo, e le 120 Giornate di Sodoma] (1975) Theme (Ennio Morricone) IT:LP = General Music 73001*

5771 Salome (1953) Highlights (e:George Duning/t:Daniele Amfitheatrof) US:LP-10 = Decca DL-6026

5772 Salt and Pepper (1968) Score (s:Johnny Dankworth/t:Leslie Bricusse) US:LP = UA UAS-5187*

5773 Salt to the Devil [Give Us This Day] (1949) Theme (Benjamin Frankel) GB:78-PP = Rank FM-82 [ST]

5774 Saludos Amigos (1943) Highlights (e:Charles Wolcott/t:Ed Plumb/t:Paul Smith/etc.) US:78-MS = Decca A-369; Excerpts (various) US:LP = Disneyland WDL-1039 + US:LP = Disneyland WDL-3039 [@ST]

5775 Salut l'Artiste [The Bit Player] (1974) Highlights (Vladimir Cosma) FR:LP = Deesse DDLX-77*

5776 Saluti e Baci (1952) Theme (G. Fanciulli) US:LP = MGM 3485 [Robert Ashley]

5777 Salvador (1985) Highlights (Georges Delerue) US:LP = Varese 704.400*

5778 Same Time, Next Year (1978) Theme (Marvin Hamlisch) US:SP = Columbia 3-10902* [Johnny Mathis & Jane Oliver:ST]; Theme (Marvin Hamlisch) US:LP = Columbia 35649* [Johnny Mathis & Jane Oliver:ST]; Theme (Marvin Hamlisch) US:LP = UA 941 + US:LP = Liberty 10112* [Ferrante & Teicher]

5779 Sammy Going South *see* Boy Ten Feet Tall, A

5780 Samoa [Short] (1956) Highlights (Oliver Wallace) US:LP = Disneyland WDL-4003

5781 Samson and Delilah (1949) Highlights (Victor Young) US:LP-10 = Decca DL-6007 + US:LP = Decca DL-8566 + US:LP = Varese VC-81073

5782 Samson in King Solomon's Mines [Maciste Nelle Miniere de re Salomone] (1963) Highlights (Francesco De Masi) IT:LP = Beat CR-13*

5783 Samson vs. the Giant King [Maciste alla Corte dello Zar] (1963) Themes (Carlo Rustichelli) IT:SP = CAM 2562 [ST]

5784 Samurai Assassin [The Assassin] (1965) Excerpts (Toru Takemitsu) JA:LP = RCA/Victor 1067 [Toru Takemitsu:ST]

5785 San Antonio (1945) Theme (Max Steiner) US:LP-MS-BP = Tony Thomas TTMS-9/10 [Max Steiner:ST]

5786 San Fernando Valley (1944) Theme/US:LP = RCA 3041 [Roy Rogers:ST]

5787 San Francisco (1936) Highlights (t:Bronislau Kaper/etc.) US:LP-BP = Caliban 6026; Theme (Bronislau Kaper) US:LP = RCA/Victrola 1515 [Jeanette MacDonald:ST]

5788 Sanctuary (1961) Theme (Alex North) US:SP = Liberty 55309 [Julie London]; Theme (Alex North) US:LP = Capitol 1626* [Don Baker]

5789 Sand Castle, The (1961) Score (Alec Wilder) US:LP = Columbia CL-1455/CS-8249*

5790 Sand Pebbles, The (1966) Score (Jerry Goldsmith) US:LP = 20th 4189/S-4189*

5791 Sanders of the River (1935) Highlights (Mischa Spoliansky) GB: EP = HMV 8185 [Paul Robeson:ST]

5792 Sandpiper, The (1965) Score (Johnny Mandel) US:LP = Mercury MG-21032/SR-61032*

5793 Sandra [Vaghe Stelle dell' Orsa] (1965) Highlights (classical music) JA:LP-MS = CBS/Sony 2305 [@ST]

5794 Sands of Iwo Jima, The (1949) Highlights (Victor Young) US:LP = Citadel CTV-7029

5795 Sands of the Kalahari (1965) Theme (Johnny Dankworth) GB:SP = Fontana 643 [Johnny Dankworth:ST]

5796 Sandya—The Music Maker Themes/US:SP = Music of India 22466 [Lata Mangeshkar:ST]

5797 Sangam / Theme/US:LP = Capitol 10500 [@Mukesh:ST]

5798 Sans Familie [The Orphan] (1958) Highlights (Paul Misraki) FR:LP-10 = Philips 76.193; Theme (Paul Misraki) US:LP = WB 1371* [Pete Rugolo]; Theme (Paul Misraki) US: LP = Dot 3120 [Ray Ventura]

5799 Santa and the Three Bears (1972) Highlights + Dialog (Joe Leahy) US:LP = Pickwick SPC-1501*

5800 Santa Claus Conquers the Martians (1964) Theme + Narration (Milton DeLugg) US:LP = Golden SLP-170; Theme (Milton DeLugg) US:SP = RCA 47-8478 [Al Hirt]; Theme (Milton DeLugg) US:LP = Rhino 307 [@Milton DeLugg:ST]

5801 Santa Claus—The Movie (1985) Score (Henry Mancini) US:LP = EMI SJ-17177*

5802 Santa Fe Satan *see* Catch My Soul

5803 Santa Fe Trail (1940) Theme (Max Steiner) US:LP-BP = Citadel CTMS-2 [Max Steiner:ST]

5804 Sapho [Sappho] (1970) Score (Georges Garvarentz) FR:LP = Barclay 920.322*

5805 Sapphire (1959) Theme (Philip Green) GB:SP = Top Rank 112 [ST]; Theme (Philip Green) US:LP = Riverside 97519* [Ernest Maxim]

5806 Sapporo Winter Olympics, The (1972) Score (Masaru Sato) JA: LP = King SKD-124*

5807 Saraband [Saraband for Dead Lovers] (1949) Theme (Alan Rawsthorne) GB:78-PP = Rank FM-31 [ST]

5808 Saratoga (1937) Theme (Walter Donaldson) US:LP = World Artists 3007* [Perry Botkin, Jr.]

5809 Saratoga Trunk (1945) Theme-A (Max Steiner) US:LP = RCA 1170 [Max Steiner:ST]; Theme-A (Max Steiner) US:LP = RCA 1-0136* [Charles Gerhardt]; Theme-B (Max Steiner) US: LP-BP = Citadel CTMS-6 [Max Steiner: ST]

5810 Sarilho de Fraldas [Diaper Trouble] (1967) Score (Jorge Pinto) US: LP = Request RLP-8062/SRLP-8062*

5811 Satan in High Heels (1962) Score (Mundell Lowe) US:LP = Parker PLP-406/PLPS-406*

5812 Satan Never Sleeps [The Devil Never Sleeps] (1962) Theme (Harry Warren) US:SP = Liberty 55410 [Timi Yuro]; Theme (Harry Warren) US:LP = Command 835* [Enoch LIght]

5813 Satan's Brew [Satansbraten] (1976) Theme (Peer Raben) FR:LP = Cine Disc 88.087* [Peer Raben:ST]

5814 Satan's Sadists (1969) Score (Harley Hatcher) US:LP = Smash 67127*

5815 Saturday Night and Sunday Morning (1960) Theme (Johnny Dankworth) US:SP = London 45-1985 [The Cambridge Strings]; Theme (Johnny Dankworth) US:LP = WB 1548* [Werner

Muller]; Theme (Johnny Dankworth) US:LP = London 44020* [International Jazz All-Stars]

5816 Saturday Night Fever (1977) Scores (e:David Shire/e:The Bee Gees/ etc.) US:LP-MS = RSO RS2-4001*

5817 Satyricon *see* Fellini Satyricon

5818 Sauvage, Le *see* Lovers Like Us

5819 Savage (1974) Score (Don Julian) US:LP = Money MS-1109*

5820 Savage Gringo [Ringo nel Nebraska] (1965) Theme (Nino Oliviero) JA:LP-MS = Seven Seas 167/8* [@ST]

5821 Savage Is Beautiful [La Fete Sauvage] (1978) Score (Vangelis) FR: LP = Pathe C066.14276*

5822 Savage Justice *see* Bitter Springs

5823 Savage Pampas (1966) Score (Waldo De Los Rios) SA:LP = Hispa Vox 11-065

5824 Savage Sam (1963) Theme + Narration (Terry Gilkyson) US:LP = Disneyland ST-1925; Theme (Terry Gilkyson) US:SP = Buena Vista 421 [The Wellingtons]

5825 Savage Seven, The (1968) Score (Jerry Styner) US:LP = Atco 33-245/SD-33-245*

5826 Savage Streets (1984) Score (various) US:LP = MCA 6134*

5827 Savage Wild, The (1970) Score (Jaime Mendoza-Nava) US:LP = American International A-1032*

5828 Save the Children (1974) Scores (pop music) US:LP-MS = Motown M-800-R2*

5829 Say Amen, Somebody (1983) Scores (pop music) US:LP-MS = DRG SB2L-12584*

5830 Say Hello to Yesterday (1970) Theme (Riz Ortolani) US:SP = WB 7453 [Tommy Oliver]; Theme (Riz Ortolani) US:LP = King 1141.498* [Manuel]

5831 Say It with Songs (1929) Highlights (Ray Henderson) US:LP-BP = Subon 1234

5832 Say One for Me (1959) Score (e:James Van Heusen/ae:Lionel Newman) US:LP = Columbia CL-1337/CS-8147*

5833 Sayonara (1957) Score (s:Franz Waxman/t:Irving Berlin) US:LP = RCA LOC-1041/LSO-1041* + US:LP = Entracte ERS-6513*

5834 Scalawag (1973) Theme (John Cameron) US:SP = Motown 1279* [Frankie Valli]

5835 Scalphunters, The (1968) Score (Elmer Bernstein) US:LP = UA UAS-5176*

5836 Scandal in Sorrento [Bread, Love and ...] (1955) Theme (Alessandro Cicognini-aka-Icini) US:SP = Prep 114 [Renaldo Loren]

5837 Scandale aux Champs Elysees Theme (Paul Durand) US:LP = Columbia 4780 [Jacqueline Francois]

5838 Scandalous John (1971) Score (Rod McKuen) US:LP = Buena Vista BV-5004*

5839 Scapegoat, The (1959) Theme (Bronislau Kaper) US:SP = Cub 9038 [Russ Conway]; Theme (Bronislau Kaper) US:LP = Columbia 8586* [Andre Previn]

5840 Scaramouche (1952) Theme (Victor Young) US:SP = MGM 30596 [Victor Marchese]

5841 Scarecrow (1973) Theme (Fred Myrow) JA:LP-MS = TAM 31/2* [@The Screenland Orchestra]

5842 Scared Stiff (1953) Theme (Jerry Livingston) US:78 = Coral 61007 [Peggy Mann]

5843 Scarface (1983) Score (Giorgio Moroder) US:LP = MCA 6126*

5844 Scarlatine, La (1984) Score (Gabriel Yared) FR:LP = Milan A-219*

5845 Scarlet Buccaneer, The *see* Swashbuckler

5846 Scarlet Claw, The (1944) Underscore + Dialog (au:Paul Sawtell) US:LP = Murray Hill 55420 + US:LP-BP = Pample 1943

5847 Scarlet Hour, The (1956) Theme (Jay Livingston & Ray Evans) US:SP = Capitol 3390 [Nat King Cole: ST]; Theme (Jay Livingston & Ray Evans) US:LP = Capitol 2340 + US: LP = Capitol 11804 [Nat King Cole:ST]

5848 Scarlet Street (1946) Score (Hans J. Salter) US:LP = Medallion ML-303

5849 Scars of Dracula, The (1970) Theme (James Bernard) US:LP-BP =

POO 106* [@Geoff Love]; Sequence + Narration (James Bernard) US:LP = Capitol 11340* [@ST]

5850 Scavenger Hunt (1979) Theme (Billy Goldenberg) US:SP-PP = VC 5204 [Scatman Crothers:ST]; Theme (Billy Goldenberg) US:LP-BP = Disc 105 [@Scatman Crothers:ST]

5851 Scent of a Woman [Parfum de Femme] (1976) Score (Armando Trovajoli) FR:LP = Pathe C066.13077*

5852 Scent of Mystery [Holiday in Spain] (1960) Score (Mario Nascimbene) US:LP = Ramrod T-6001/ST-6001*

5853 Schizoid [Una Lucertola con la Pelle di Donna] (1972) Theme (Ennio Morricone) IT:LP = General Music 55064* [Ennio Morricone:ST]

5854 Schwarze Schaf, Das / Theme (Martin Bottcher) US:SP = London 1984 [Renardo]

5855 Scorpio (1972) Score (Jerry Fielding) US:LP = Film Music Collection FMC-11*

5856 Scott Joplin (1977) Score (t: Dick Hyman/s:pop music) US:LP = MCA 2098*

5857 Scott of the Antarctic (1949) Highlights (Ralph Vaughan-Williams) GB:78-MS = HMV 3834 [Ernest Irving]; Themes (Ralph Vaughan-Williams) GB: 78-PP = Rank FM-43/44 [ST]; Excerpts (Ralph Vaughan-Williams) US:LP = Angel S-36469* [Adrian Bolt]; Excerpts (Ralph Vaughan-Williams) US:LP = RCA LSC-3066* [Andre Previn]

5858 Scream for Help (1985) Score (John Paul Jones) US:LP = Atlantic 780-190-1*

5859 Screamers [The Island of Mutations] [L'Isola degli Uomini Pesce] (1981) Score-A (Luciano Michelini) US: LP = Web ST-101*; Score-B (Luciano Michelini) IT:LP = Cometa 1009*

5860 Scrooge (1970) Score (Leslie Bricusse) US:LP = Columbia S-30258*

5861 Scruggs [A Game Called Scruggs] (1965) Theme (Johnny Dankworth) US:SP = Monument 941 [The Key Chains]

5862 Sea for Yourself / Scores (e: Doug Dragon/e:Richard Henn/etc.) US:LP-MS = Rural 002*

5863 Sea Hawk, The (1940) Excerpts-A (Erich Wolfgang Korngold) US:LP-MS = WB 3X-2736 [@Erich Wolfgang Korngold:ST]; Excerpts-A (Erich Wolfgang Korngold) US:LP = RCA LSC-3330* [Charles Gerhardt]; Score (Erich Wolfgang Korngold) US: LP = Varese 704.380* [Varujan Kojin]

5864 Sea Legs (1930) Theme/US: LP-BP = JJA 19811 [@Lillian Roth:ST]

5865 Sea Wife, The (1957) Theme (Tolchard Evans) US:SP = Capitol 3748 [Ron Goodwin]; Theme (Tolchard Evans) US:SP = London 45-1740 [David Whitfield]

5866 Sea Wolf, The (1941) Excerpts (Erich Wolfgang Korngold) US:LP = RCA ARL1-0185* [Charles Gerhardt]

5867 Sea Wolves, The (1980) Score (e:Roy Budd/etc.) GB:LP = EMI EMC-3340*

5868 Seance on a Wet Afternoon (1964) Theme (John Barry) US:SP = Ascot 2187 [Sir Julian]; Theme (John Barry) GB:SP = UA 1060 [John Barry: ST]; Theme (John Barry) US:LP = Columbia 9293* [John Barry:ST]

5869 Search for Paradise (1957) Score (Dimitri Tiomkin) US:LP = RCA LOC-1034

5870 Searchers, The (1956) Highlights (Max Steiner) US:LP-BP = Citadel CTMS-5; Theme (Stan Jones) US:SP = Capitol 3430 [Tex Ritter]; Theme (Stan Jones) US:LP = RCA 1-4092 [The Sons of the Pioneers:ST]

5871 Searching Wind, The (1946) Theme (Victor Young) US:SP = Decca 9-27455 [Tommy Dorsey & Victor Young:ST]; Theme (Victor Young) US: 78 = Decca 18920 [Dick Haymes]; Theme (Victor Young) US:LP-10 = Decca 5370 [Tommy Dorsey & Victor Young:ST]

5872 Seaside Swingers [Every Day's a Holiday] (1965) Score (Westlake & Lynch) US:LP = Mercury MG-21031/ SR-61031*

5873 Season in Hell, A [Saison en Enfer] (1970) Score (Maurice Jarre) IT: LP = General Music 55061*

5874 Sebastian (1968) Score (s: Jerry Goldsmith/t:Tristram Cary) US: LP = Dot DLP-3845/DLP-25845*

5875 Second Best Secret Agent in the Whole Wide World, The [Licensed to Kill] (1965) Theme-A (Herbert Chappell) JA:LP-MS = UA 6063/4* [@ST]; Theme-B (James Van Heusen) US:SP = Reprise 0425 [Sammy Davis, Jr.:ST]

5876 Second Chance [Si C'etait a Refaire] (1979) Themes (Francis Lai) JA: SP = WB 166* [ST]; Theme (Francis Lai) FR:LP = WB/WEA 56556* [Francis Lai:ST]

5877 Second Chorus (1940) Score (various) US:LP-BP = Hollywood Soundstage HS-404

5878 Second Fiddle (1939) Excerpts (Irving Berlin) US:LP-BP = JJA 19744 [@ST]

5879 Second Greatest Sex, The (1956) Theme-A/US:SP = Decca 9-29708 [Kitty Kallen:ST]; Theme-B/US:LP-BP = JJA 19765 [@Bert Lahr:ST]

5880 Second Wind (1976) Theme (Hagood Hardy) US:LP = Capitol 11552* [Hagood Hardy:ST]

5881 Secret, Le [The Secret] (1974) Themes (Ennio Morricone) FR:SP = WB 16471* [ST]

5882 Secret Admirer (1985) Score (t:Jan Hammer/s:various) US:LP = MCA 5611*

5883 Secret Agent Super Dragon [New York Chiama Superdrago] [Super Dragon] (1966) Score (Benedetto Ghiglia) IT:LP = CAM CDR-33.16

5884 Secret Interlude *see* View from Pompey's Head, The

5885 Secret Life of Plants, The (1978) Scores (Stevie Wonder) US:LP-MS = Tamla TI3-371-C2*

5886 Secret Life of Walter Mitty, The (1947) Theme/US:SP = Decca 9-28562 [Danny Kaye:ST]

5887 Secret of Dorian Gray, The *see* Dorian Gray

5888 Secret of NIMH, The (1982) Score (Jerry Goldsmith) US:LP = Varese STV-81169*

5889 Secret of Santa Vittoria, The (1969) Score (Ernest Gold) US:LP = UA UAS-5200*

5890 Secret of the Sword, The (1985) Theme + Underscore + Dialog (Shuki Levy) US:LP = Kid Stuff DAR-3900*

5891 Secret of the Telegian, The (1960) Themes (Sei Ikeno) JA:LP = Toho 8107 [@ST]

5892 Secret People, The (1952) Theme-A (Roberto Gerhard) GB:78-PP = Rank FM-115 [ST]; Theme-B (Roberto Gerhard) GB:78-PP = Rank FM-116 [ST]

5893 Secret Places (1984) Score (Michel Legrand) US:LP = Shanachie 82005*

5894 Secret Policeman's Ball, The (1981) Score-A (pop music) US:LP = Island ILPS-9698*; Score-B (pop music) US:LP = Island 7-90091-1*

5895 Secrets of Life, The (1956) Score (Paul Smith) US:LP = Disneyland WDL-4006

5896 Seduced and Abandoned (1964) Score (Carlo Rustichelli) US: LP = CAM 100.001

5897 Seducer, The [L'Uomo di Paglia] (1957) Highlights (Carlo Rustichelli) IT:EP = RCA 30265; Theme (Carlo Rustichelli) US:LP = RCA FSO-4* [@ST]

5898 Seduction of Mimi, The [Mimi Metallurgico] (1974) Score (Piero Piccioni) IT:LP = Cinevox 33/53*

5899 See Here, Private Hargrove (1943) Theme (Ted Grouya) US:78 = Columbia 38964 [Frank Loesser]

5900 See You in Hell, Darling *see* American Dream, An

5901 See You Monday [Au Revoir a Lundi] (1981) Score (s:Jean Daniel Mercier/t:Lewis Furey) FR:LP = RCA RSL-1077*

5902 Seekers, The (1954) Theme (William Alwyn) GB:78-PP = Rank FM-149 [ST]

5903 Selfish Giant, The [Short] (1971) Highlights + Underscore + Dialog (Ron Goodwin) CA:LP = Capitol 6410*

5904 Semi-Tough (1978) Score (pop music) JA:LP = London FML-93 [Gene Autry:ST]

5905 Send Me No Flowers (1964) Theme (Burt Bacharach) US:SP = Columbia 4-43153 [Doris Day:ST]; Theme (Burt Bacharach) US:LP = Harmony 11192 [Doris Day:ST]

5906 Senior Prom (1959) Highlights

(various) US:EP = Columbia B-2148 [Jill Corey & Paul Hampton:ST]

5907 Senso [The Wanton Contessa] (1955) Highlights (classical music) JA: LP-MS = CBS/Sony 2302 [@Franco Ferrara:ST]

5908 Separate Beds *see* Wheeler Dealers, The

5909 Separate Tables (1958) Highlights (David Raksin) US:LP-MS-PP = Library of Congress LOC-RAKSIN [David Raksin:ST]; Theme (Harry Warren) US:SP = ABC 9971 [Eydie Gorme]

5910 September 30, 1955 *see* 9/30/55

5911 Serafino (1968) Highlights (Carlo Rustichelli) IT:EP = Clan 5001*

5912 Serenade (1956) Score (e: Nicholas Brodszky/s:classical music) US:LP = RCA LM-1996 [Mario Lanza: ST]; Highlights (e:Nicholas Brodszky/t: Ray Heindorf) US:EP = Columbia 2110 [Ray Heindorf:ST]

5913 Serenade for Two Spies *see* Symphony for Two Spies

5914 Serenata d'Amore *see* Amore

5915 Sgt. Pepper's Lonely Hearts Club Band (1978) Scores (pop music) US: LP-MS = RSO RS2-4100*

5916 Sergeant York (1941) Sequence + Dialog (Max Steiner) US:LP-MS = WB 3X-2737 [@ST]

5917 Sergeants Three (1962) Score (Billy May) US:LP = Reprise R-2013/RS-2013*

5918 Serious Charge (1959) Theme (Lionel Bart) GB:SP = Columbia 4306 [Cliff Richard:ST]

5919 Serpent, The [Il Serpente] [Night Flight to Moscow] (1973) Score (Ennio Morricone) FR:LP = RCA 440.758*

5920 Serpent God, The [Il Dio Serpente] (1970) Score (Augusto Martelli) IT:LP = Cinevox 33/40* + IT: LP = Cinevox 5002*

5921 Serpent's Egg, The [Das Schlangenei] (1977) Score (Rolf Wilhelm) GE:LP = Tarantula FIC-SP-8001*

5922 Serpico (1973) Score (Mikis Theodorakis) US:LP = Paramount PAS-1016*

5923 Servant, The (1963) Theme (Johnny Dankworth) US:LP = RCA 1-5092* [Johnny Dankworth:ST]

5924 Sesame Street Presents—Follow That Bird (1985) Score (e:Lennie Niehaus & Van Dyke Parks/e:various) US:LP = RCA CBL1-5475*

5925 Seven Alone (1975) Score (Robert O. Ragland) US:LP = Seval LP-101*

5926 Seven Beauties [Pasqualino Sette Bellezze] (1976) Themes (Enzo Jannicci) IT:SP = ZUS 50570* [ST]

5927 Seven Brides for Seven Brothers (1954) Highlights (Gene DePaul) US:LP-10 = MGM E-224 + US:LP = MGM E-3235 + US:LP = MGM E-3769 + US:LP-MS = MGM 2SES-41e

5928 Seven Capital Sins, The [Les Sept Peches Capitaux] (1962) Highlights (e:Michel Legrand/t:Pierre Jansen) FR: EP = Philips 432.756; Theme-A (Sacha Distel) US:LP = Capitol 8603* [Frank Pourcel]; Theme-B (Michel Legrand) US:LP = Philips 600.071* [@Michel Legrand:ST]

5929 Seven Chances (1925) Excerpts [Silent II] (Claude Bolling) FR: LP = Columbia XM-241 [Claude Bolling:ST]

5930 Seven Cities to Atlantis *see* Warlords of Atlantis

5931 Seven Days' Leave (1942) Themes-A-B/US:78 = RCA/Victor 20-1504 [Freddy Martin:ST]; Themes-C-D/US:78 = RCA/Victor 20-1515 [Freddy Martin:ST]

5932 Seven Faces of Dr. Lao, The (1964) Theme (Leigh Harline) US:SP = Capitol 5165 [The Hollyridge Strings]; Theme (Leigh Harline) US:SP = MGM 13224 [Lalo Schifrin]; Theme (Leigh Harline) US:LP-BP = Centurion 1210 + US:LP-BP = POO 106 [@Lalo Schifrin]

5933 Seven Golden Men, The (1965) Score (Armando Trovajoli) US:LP = UA UAS-5193e

5934 Seven Golden Men Strike Again, The [Il Grande Colpo di 7 Uomini d'Oro] (1966) Score (Armando Trovajoli) IT:LP = CAM AMG-4

5935 Seven Graves for Rogan *see* Time to Die, A

5936 Seven Guns for the MacGregors [7 Pistole per i MacGregor] (1966) Themes (Ennio Morricone) US: LP = Peters 4050* [Ennio Morricone:ST]

5937 Seven Guys and a Gal [Sept Hommes et un Garce] (1967) Theme (Paul Misraki) FR:LP = Barclay 71135 [@ST]

5938 Seven Hills of Rome, The (1958) Highlights (t:Victor Young/t: George Stoll/s:various) US:LP = RCA LM-2211 [Mario Lanza:ST]

5939 Seven Little Foys, The (1955) Highlights (t:Joseph Lilley/e:various) US:LP-10 = RCA LPM-3275

5940 Seven Per-Cent Solution, The (1977) Score-A (John Addison) US:LP-BP = Citadel CTJA-1*; Theme-B (Stephen Sondheim) US:LP-MS = RCA 2-1851* [@Millicent Martin]

5941 Seven Samurai [The Magnificent Seven] (1956) Highlights (Fumio Hayazaka) US:LP = Varese STV-81142*

5942 Seven Sinners (1940) Theme-A (Frederick Hollander) US:LP = Decca 5033 [Marlene Dietrich:ST]; Theme-B (Frank Loesser) US:LP-BP = JJA 19762 [@Marlene Dietrich:ST]; Theme-C/US: LP = Columbia 6430 [Marlene Dietrich: ST]

5943 Seven Slaves Against the World [7 Slaves Against Rome] [Gli Schiavi Piu Forti] (1964) Score (Francesco DeMasi) IT:LP = CAM CDR-33.9

5944 Seven Sweethearts (1942) Theme/US:LP-BP = Azel 101 [Kathryn Grayson:ST]

5945 Seven Wonders of the World, The (1956) Highlights (pop music) US: LP-10-PP = Admiral AX-1; Theme (Emil Newman & Lionel Newman) US:SP = Coral 9-61692 [George Cates]; Theme (Emil Newman & Lionel Newman) US: LP = Coral 57065 [George Cates]

5946 Seven Year Itch, The (1955) Theme (film theme from "A Letter to Three Wives") US:LP = Decca 8123 [Alfred Newman:ST]

5947 Seventeen (1940) Theme (Frank Loesser) US:LP = RCA 1487 [The Ames Brothers]

5948 17 (1967) *see* Eric Soya's 17

5949 1776 (1973) Score (stage songs: Sherman Edwards) US:LP = Columbia S-31741*

5950 Seventh Dawn, The (1964) Score (Riz Ortolani) US:LP = UA UAL-4115/UAS-5115*

5951 Seventh Heaven (1927) Theme [Silent I] (Erno Rapee) US:SP = Mercury 1009 [Glenn Osser]; Theme [Silent I] (Erno Rapee) US:LP = RCA 2560* [Gaylord Carter]

5952 Seventh Victim, The (1943) Excerpts (Roy Webb) GB:LP = Decca PFS-4432* [Stanley Black]

5953 Seventh Voyage of Sinbad, The (1958) Score (Bernard Herrmann) US:LP = Colpix CP-504 + US:LP-BP = Request LP-1300 + US:LP = Varese STV-81135* [Kurt Graunke:ST]; Excerpts (Bernard Herrmann) US:LP = London SPC-44207* [Bernard Herrmann]

5954 Seventy Times Seven *see* Female, The

5955 Sex and the Single Girl (1964) Score (s:Neal Hefti/t:Richard Quine) US:LP = WB W-1572/WS-1572*

5956 Sex on the Run [Some Like It Cool] [Casanova & Co.] [Rise and Rise of Casanova] (1977) Score (Riz Ortolani) IT:LP = CAM SAG-9078*

5957 Sex Shop, Le [Sex Shop] (1973) Theme (Serge Gainsbourg) FR: LP = Philips 6620.025* [Serge Gainsbourg:ST]

5958 Sex with a Smile (1976) Score (Guido & Maurizio DeAngelis) IT:LP = Cometa 1008/20*

5959 Shack Out on 101 (1955) Theme (Louis Prima) US:SP = Perfect 50019 [Fran Warren]

5960 Shadow Man [Street of Shadows] (1953) Theme (Eric Spear) GB: SP = Parlophone 3645 [Eric Spear:ST]; Theme (Eric Spear) US:SP = RCA 47-5264 [Henri Rene]; Theme (Eric Spear) US:LP = Camden 312 [Henri Rene]

5961 Shadow of a Man (1955) Theme (Michael Carr) GB:SP = Columbia 5156 [Jackie Brown]

5962 Shadow of Evil [Banco a Bangkok pour OSS 117] (1964) Highlights (Michel Magne) FR:EP = Ducretet 460-V-635

5963 Shadow of the Boomerang Theme (Ralph Carmichael) US:LP = Word 3164 [@Georgia Lee:ST]

5964 Shaft (1971) Scores (Isaac Hayes) US:LP-MS = Enterprise ENS-5002* + US:LP-MS = Stax STX-88002*

5965 Shaft in America (1973) Score

(s:Johnny Pate/t:Brian Potter) US: LP = ABC 793*

5966 Shaft's Big Score (1972) Score (s:Gordon Parks/as:Richard Hazard) US:LP = MGM 1SE-36*

5967 Shaggy Dog, The (1959) Theme + Narration (Paul Smith) US: LP = Disneyland WDL-1044 + US: LP = Disneyland WDL-3044

5968 Shake Hands with the Devil (1959) Score (William Alwyn) US:LP = UA UAL-4043/UAS-5043*

5969 Shake, Rattle and Rock! (1956) Theme/US:SP = Imperial 5407 [Fats Domino:ST]

5970 Shakespeare Wallah (1966) Score (s:Satyajit Ray/as:Alok Dey) US: LP = Epic FLM-13110/FLS-15110e

5971 Shakiest Gun in the West, The (1968) Theme (Dave Blume) US:SP = Decca 9-32292 [The Wilburn Brothers: ST]

5972 Shalako (1968) Score (Robert Farnon) US:LP = Philips PHS-600.286*

5973 Shall We Dance (1937) Highlights (George Gershwin) US:LP-BP = Sountrak STK-106 + US:LP-BP = Sandy Hook SH-2028; Excerpts (George Gershwin) US:LP = Columbia SG-32472 [Fred Astaire:ST]

5974 Shame of the Jungle [Tarzoon, la Vergogna della Giungla] (1979) Themes (Teddy Lasry) IT:SP = CAM AMP-168* [ST]

5975 Shane (1953) Theme-A (Victor Young) US:SP = Decca 9-28703 [Victor Young:ST]; Theme-A (Victor Young) US:LP = Decca 8051 [Victor Young:ST]; Theme-B (Victor Young) US:SP = Mercury 70168 [Richard Hayman]; Theme-B (Victor Young) US:LP = Mercury 25189 [Richard Hayman]

5976 Shanghai Joe [My Name Is Shanghai Joe] [Il Mio Nome E Shanghai Joe] (1974) Score (Bruno Nicolai) JA: LP = TAM YX-8010*

5977 Shaolin Temple (1982) Score (Keith Morrison) JA:LP = RCA/Victor VIP-28062*

5978 Shaolin 36th Chamber (1983) Score (Jim Montgomery) JA:LP = RCA/Victor VIPX-1702*

5979 Shark Reef *see* She-Gods of Shark Reef

5980 Shark's Treasure (1975) Theme (Jefferson Pascal) US:SP = UA 710 [Josh Perez]

5981 Sharky's Machine (1981) Score (various) US:LP = WB BSK-3653*

5982 Shattered *see* Something to Hide

5983 Shatterhand *see* Old Shatterhand

5984 She (1935) Score (Max Steiner) US:LP-BP = Cinema LP-8004

5985 She (1965) Theme (James Bernard) US:LP = Capitol 11340* [@ST]

5986 She Came to the Valley (1979) Theme (Tommy Leonetti) US:LP = MCA 37109* [Freddie Fender:ST]

5987 She Done Him Wrong (1933) Themes-A-B/US:LP = Columbia 2751 [Mae West:ST]; Themes-B-C/US:LP = Decca 9016 [Mae West:ST]

5988 She-Gods of Shark Reef [Shark Reef] (1958) Theme (Jack Lawrence) US:SP = Decca 9-30218 [Sylvia Syms:ST]

5989 She Got What She Asked For [La Bellezza d'Ippolita] (1962) Highlights (Carlo Rustichelli) IT:EP = CAM CEP-45-79

5990 She Learned About Sailors (1934) Theme/US:LP = Columbia 3068 [Alice Faye:ST]

5991 She Loves Me Not (1934) Excerpts-A (various) US:LP-MS = Columbia C2L-43 [Bing Crosby:ST]; Excerpts-B (various) US:LP-BP = Caliban 6042 [@ST]

5992 She Married a Cop (1939) Theme/US:78 = Decca 2666 [Phil Regan: ST]

5993 Sheba Baby (1975) Score (Monk Higgins & Alex Brown) US:LP = Buddah BDS-5634*

5994 Sheena (1984) Score (Richard Hartley) US:LP = Varese STV-81225*

5995 Sheffey / Score (Dwight Gustafson) US:LP-PP = Unusual 8034-N5*

5996 Sheila Levine Is Dead and Living in New York (1975) Theme (Michel Legrand) US:SP = RCA 50060* [Ettore Stratta]; Theme (Michel Legrand) US:LP = RCA 1-5016* [Ettore Stratta]; Theme (Michel Legrand) US: LP = RCA 1-1028* [Michel Legrand:ST]

5997 Shenandoah (1965) Score

(Frank Skinner) US:LP = Decca DL-9125/DL-79125*

5998 Shepherd of the Hills (1962) Score (Marlin Skiles) US:LP-PP = Ode 29522

5999 Sheriff and the Satellite Kid, The (1980) Score (Guido & Maurizio De Angelis) GE:LP = Polydor 2374-152*

6000 Sheriff of Fractured Jaw, The (1958) Theme (Harry Harris) US:SP = 20th 130 [Harry Simeone]

6001 Sherlock Holmes and the Secret Weapon (1942) Underscore + Dialog (Frank Skinner) US:LP = Murray Hill 55374

6002 Sherlock Holmes and the Voice of Terror (1942) Underscore + Dialog (Frank Skinner) US:LP = Murray Hill 55366

6003 Sherlock Holmes Faces Death (1943) Underscore + Dialog (au:Hans J. Salter) US:LP = Murray Hill 55390

6004 Sherlock Holmes in Washington (1943) Underscore + Dialog (Frank Skinner) US:LP = Murray Hill 55382

6005 She's Back on Broadway (1953) Highlights (Carl Sigman) US:LP-BP = Caliban 6032

6006 She's Gotta Have It (1986) Score (Bill Lee) US:LP = Island 90528-1*

6007 She's Working Her Way Through College (1952) Highlights (Vernon Duke) US:LP-BP = Caliban 6032

6008 Shinbone Alley [Archy and Mehitabel] (1971) Highlights (stage songs: George Kleinsinger) US:LP = Columbia ML-4963 [Eddie Bracken & Carol Channing:ST]

6009 Shining, The (1980) Score (t:Wendy Carlos-aka-Walter Carlos/s: classical music) US:LP = WB HS-3449*

6010 Shining Star *see* That's the Way of the World

6011 Ship Ahoy (1942) Highlights (Burton Lane) US:LP-BP = Caliban 6035 + US:LP-BP = Hollywood Soundstage 5011

6012 Ship Cafe (1935) Themes/GB: 78 = Decca 5839 [Carl Brisson:ST]

6013 Ship of Fools (1965) Score (Ernest Gold) US:LP = RCA LM-2817/LSC-2817* [Arthur Fiedler & The Boston Pops]

6014 Shipmates Forever (1935) Theme/US:78 = Decca 613 [Dick Powell: ST]

6015 Shipyard Sally (1939) Excerpts (various) US:LP = Monmouth MES-7079 [Gracie Fields:ST]

6016 Shock [Traitement de Choc] (1973) Score (Rene Koering & Alain Jessua) JA:LP = Cine Disc 5008*

6017 Shock (1980) *see* Beyond the Door

6018 Shock Treatment (1981) Score (Richard Hartley) US:LP = Ode/WB LLA-3615*

6019 Shocking Miss Pilgrim, The (1947) Highlights (pop music) US:LP-BP = Classic International Filmusicals 3008

6020 Shoes of the Fisherman (1968) Score (Alex North) US:LP = MGM 1SE-15*

6021 Shogun Assassin (1980) Score (W. Michael Lewis & Mark Lindsay) US: LP-PP = Baby Cart 1001*

6022 Shoot, The [Der Schut] (1964) Highlights (Martin Bottcher) GE:LP = Condor 8303

6023 Shoot Loud, Louder ... I Don't Understand [Spara Forte, Piu Forte ... Non Capisco] (1966) Excerpts (Nino Rota) FR:LP = General Music 803.030* [Nino Rota:ST]; Themes (Nino Rota) IT:SP = Parade 5014 [ST]

6024 Shoot the Piano Player [Tirez Sur le Pianiste] (1962) Highlights (Georges Delerue) US:EP = GMS ST-1 + FR:EP = Philips 432.510; Theme (Georges Delerue) US:SP = Philips 40059 [Georges Delerue:ST]

6025 Shooting Party, The (1985) Score (John Scott) US:LP = Varese STV-81235*

6026 Shootist, The (1976) Excerpts (Elmer Bernstein) US:LP = Varese 704.350* [Elmer Bernstein:ST]

6027 Shop on Main Street, The (1966) Score (Zdenek Liska) US:LP = Mainstream 56082/S-6082*

6028 Shopworn Angel, The (1929) Theme (J. Fred Coots) US:LP = Coral 57084 [J. Fred Coots]

6029 Short Circuit (1986) Theme-A (David Shire) US:SP = MCA 52842* [Max Carl:ST]; Theme-B (Peter Wolf) US:SP = Gordy 1842* [El De Barge:ST]

6030 Short Eyes (1977) Score (s:Curtis Mayfield/as:Rich Tufo) US: LP = Curtom CU-5017*

6031 Shot in the Dark, A (1964) Themes (Henry Mancini) US:SP = RCA 47-8381 [Henry Mancini:ST]; Themes (Henry Mancini) US:LP = Camden 2158* [Henry Mancini:ST]

6032 Shout at the Devil [Parole d'Homme] (1976) Score (Maurice Jarre) FR:LP = Barclay 900.534*

6033 Show Boat (1929) Theme (Nathaniel Shilkret) US:SP = Coral 9-61781 [Alan Dale]; Theme (Nathaniel Shilkret) GB:78 = Decca 631 [Jules Bledsoe:ST]

6034 Show Boat (1936) Score (stage songs:Jerome Kern) US:LP-BP = Xeno 251

6035 Show Boat (1951) Highlights (stage songs:Jerome Kern) US:LP-10 = MGM E-559 + US:LP = MGM E-3230 + US:LP = MGM E-3767 + US:LP = Metro M-527/MS-527e + US: LP-MS = MGM 2SES-42e

6036 Show Business (1944) Highlights (various) US:LP-BP = Caliban 6034

6037 Show Goes On, The (1937) Themes-A-B/GB:78 = Rex 9095 [Gracie Fields:ST]; Themes-C-D/GB:78 = Rex 9096 [Gracie Fields:ST]; Themes-E-F/GB:78 = Rex 9097 [Gracie Fields:ST]

6038 Show of Shows, The (1929) Theme-A/US:78 = Columbia 2027 [Irene Bordoni:ST]; Theme-B/US:78 = Columbia 1999 [Ted Lewis:ST]; Theme-C/US:78 = Brunswick 4378 [Nick Lucas: ST]

6039 Shrike, The (1955) Theme (Jose Ferrer) US:SP = Capitol 3195 [Les Baxter]; Theme (Jose Ferrer) US:SP = Columbia 4-40546 [Pete Rugolo]; Theme (Jose Ferrer) US:LP = Harmony 7003 [Pete Rugolo]

6040 Shut Down (1978) Score (stock music) GB:LP = EMI CAPS-1018*

6041 Siberiade (1983) Score (Eduard Artemiev) GE:LP = Chant du Monde 74719*

6042 Sicilian Clan, The (1970) Score (Ennio Morricone) US:LP = 20th TFS-4209*

6043 Sid and Nancy (1986) Score (various) US:LP = MCA 6181*

6044 Siddhartha (1973) Highlights + Narration (folk music) US:LP-10-PP = Siddhartha 1

6045 Sidehackers, The [Five the Hard Way] (1969) Score (Jerry Styner) US:LP = Amaret ST-5004*

6046 Sidelong Glances of a Pigeon Kicker [Pigeons] (1971) Score (Patrick Williams) US:LP-PP = SPS 8*; Theme (Patrick Williams) US:SP = A&R 7100.504* [Patrick Williams:ST]; Theme (Patrick Williams) US:LP = A&R 7100.003* [Patrick Williams:ST]

6047 Sidewinder 1 (1977) Theme (Mundell Lowe) US:SP = Studio Seven 4501* [Michael Parks:ST]

6048 Sidney Sheldon's Bloodline *see* Bloodline

6049 Siegfried [Whom the Gods Wish to Destroy] [Die Nibelungen] (1967) Score (Rolf Wilhelm) GE:LP = Limelight 0001

6050 Sign of Aquarius, The (1969) Score (e:Tom Baker/e:Al Zbacnic) US: LP = Adell LP-216/ASLP-216*

6051 Silencers, The (1966) Score (Elmer Bernstein) US:LP = RCA LOC-1120/LSO-1120* [Elmer Bernstein:ST]; Highlights (pop music) US:LP = Reprise R-6211/RS-6211* [Dean Martin:ST]; Themes (Elmer Bernstein) US:SP = Liberty 55857 [Vikki Carr:ST]

6052 Silent Movie (1976) Score (John Morris) US:LP = UA LA-672*

6053 Silent One, The (1984) Score (Jenny McLeod) AU:LP = Jayrem 321*

6054 Silent Partner, The (1979) Score (Oscar Peterson) US:LP = Pablo 2312.103* [Oscar Peterson]

6055 Silent Running (1973) Score (Peter Schickele) US:LP = Decca DL-79188* + US:LP = Varese VC-81072*

6056 Silent Witness, The *see* Mystery of the Sacred Shroud

6057 Silent World, The (1956) Underscore + Narration (Yves Baudrier) US:LP = Colpix CP-701

6058 Silk Noose, The [The Noose] (1948) Theme (Charles Williams) GB: 78 = Columbia 1518 [Charles Williams: ST]

6059 Silk Stockings (1957) Score

(stage songs:Cole Porter) US:LP = MGM E-3542 + US:LP-MS = MGM 2SES-51e

6060 Silken Affair, A (1957) Theme (Peggy Stewart) US:SP = RKO Unique 414 [Tommy Reynolds]

6061 Silkwood (1983) Score (Georges Delerue) US:LP = DRG SL-6107*

6062 Silver Bullet (1985) Score (Jay Chattaway) US:LP = Varese STV-81264*

6063 Silver Chalice, The (1954) Score (Franz Waxman) US:LP = Film Music Collection FMC-3* [Elmer Bernstein]

6064 Silver Dream Racer (1980) Score (s:David Essex/as:John Cameron) GB:LP = Mercury MERB-7*

6065 Silver River (1948) Theme (Max Steiner) US:LP-MS-BP = Tony Thomas TTMS-9/10 [Max Steiner:ST]

6066 Silver Streak (1976) Themes (Henry Mancini) JA:SP = RCA/Victor 2523* [uncredited]; Theme (Henry Mancini) US:LP = RCA 1-2290* [Henry Mancini:ST]; Theme (Henry Mancini) US:SP = RCA 11054* [Henry Mancini: ST]

6067 Silverado (1985) Score (Bruce Broughton) US:LP = Geffen GHS-24080*

6068 Simon and Laura (1955) Theme (Benjamin Frankel) GB:78-PP = Rank FM-178 [ST]

6069 Simon Bolivar (1969) Theme (Aldemaro Romero) GB:LP = DJM 430* [Vic Lewis]

6070 Simon the Swiss *see* Crook, The

6071 Simple Story, A [Une Histoire Simple] (1979) Score (Philippe Sarde) FR:LP = Carrere/Cobra 37020*

6072 Sin, The *see* Good Luck, Miss Wyckoff

6073 Sin un Adios / Theme (Jesus Gluck) US:SP = UA 353 [Raphael:ST]; Theme (Jesus Gluck) US:LP = UA 61061* [Raphael:ST]

6074 Sinbad and the Eye of the Tiger (1977) Excerpts (Roy Budd) GB: LP-MS = BBC REF-547* [Roy Budd: ST]

6075 Since Life Began [Industrial Short] Highlights (Alec Wilder) US:LP-10-PP = Time Life U-7001

6076 Since You Went Away (1944) Scores (Max Steiner) US:LP-MS-BP = Citadel CTMS-3/4; Excerpts (Max Steiner) US:LP-10 = Capitol L-250 + US:LP = Capitol T-387 + US:LP = Angel S-36068 [Max Steiner:ST]

6077 Sincerely Yours (1955) Score (t:Liberace/s:pop music) US:LP = Columbia CL-800

6078 Sinful Davey (1969) Themes (Ken Thorne) US:SP = UA 50509 [Ken Thorne/Ester Ofarim:ST]

6079 Sing As We Go (1934) Themes-A-B/GB:78 = HMV 8208 [Gracie Fields: ST]; Themes-C-D/GB:78 = HMV 8209 [Gracie Fields:ST]

6080 Sing, Baby, Sing (1936) Highlights (various) US:LP-BP = Caliban 6029

6081 Sing Boy Sing (1958) Score (t: Lionel Newman/s:various) US:LP = Capitol T-929 [Tommy Sands:ST]

6082 Sing Me a Love Song (1936) Themes-A-B/US:78 = Decca 1093 [James Melton:ST]; Theme-C/US:78 = Brunswick 15225 [James Melton:ST]

6083 Sing You Sinners (1938) Excerpts (Jimmy Monaco) US:LP-10 = Decca DL-6012 + US:LP = Decca DL-4252 [Bing Crosby:ST]

6084 Singer Not the Song, The (1961) Theme (Philip Green) US:LP = Decca 74274* [Carmen Cavallaro]; Theme (Philip Green) US:LP = London 3238/231* [@Ronnie Aldrich]

6085 Singin' in the Rain (1952) Highlights (Nacio Herb Brown) US:LP-10 = MGM E-113 + US:LP = MGM E-3236 + US:LP = MGM E-3770 + US: LP = Metro M-599/MS-599e + US:LP-MS = MGM 2SES-40e

6086 Singing Fool, The (1928) Score (Ray Henderson) US:LP-BP = Take Two 106

6087 Singing Guns (1950) Themes/ US:SP = RCA 47-3106 [Vaughn Monroe:ST]

6088 Singing Kid, The (1936) Excerpts (Harold Arlen) US:LP-BP = Caliban 6013 [@ST]

6089 Singing Marine, The (1937) Themes-A-B/US:78 = Decca 1310 [Dick

Powell:ST]; Themes-C-D/US:78 = Decca 1311 [Dick Powell:ST]

6090 Singing Nun, The (1966) Score (s:Soeur Sourire/as:Randy Sparks) US: LP = MGM 1E-7/1SE-7*

6091 Single Room Furnished (1968) Score (Jimmy Sheldon) US:LP = Sidewalk ST-5917*

6092 Single Standard, The (1929) Highlights [Silent I] (ae: William Axt) US:LP = Westwood LP-502

6093 Sink the Bismarck (1960) Theme (Clifton Parker) GB:LP = MFP 90075* [Band of the Royal Marines]; Theme (Clifton Parker) IT:LP = RCA 43634* [@Eric Rogers]

6094 Sis Hopkins (1941) Themes/ US:LP-BP = JJA 19762 [@Judy Canova:ST]

6095 Sisters (1973) Score (Bernard Herrmann) US:LP = Entracte ERQ-7001* + US:LP = Southern Cross SCRS-5004*

6096 Sisters, The [Le Sorelle] (1971) Score (Giorgio Gaslini) IT:LP = Cinevox 33/22*

6097 Sitting Pretty (1933) Themes-A-B/US:78 = RCA/Victor 24471 [The Pickens Sisters:ST]; Theme-C/US:78 = RCA/Victor 24468 [The Pickens Sisters: ST]; Theme-D/GB:LP = EMI 1002 [Ginger Rogers:ST]

6098 Six Bridges to Cross (1955) Theme (Henry Mancini) US:SP = Decca 9-29402 [Sammy Davis, Jr.:ST]

6099 Six Days a Week [La Bugiarda] (1965) Score (Benedetto Ghiglia) IT:LP = Campi Editore 100.003

6100 Six Pack (1982) Score (Charles Fox) US:LP = Allegiance AV-430*; Theme (Kenny Rogers) US:SP = Liberty 1471* [Kenny Rogers:ST]

6101 Six Pack Annie (1975) Theme (Raoul Kraushaar) US:SP-PP = American International 7514 [ST]

6102 633 Squadron (1964) Score (Ron Goodwin) US:LP = UA LA-305*

6103 Six Thousand Dollar Nigger, The (1979) Score (Saxton Kari) US:LP = Weird World 2033*

6104 Sixteen Candles (1984) Highlights (t:Ira Newborn/etc.) US:EP-12 = MCA 36012*

6105 16 Days of Glory (1986) Score (Lee Holdridge) US:LP = Deutsche 419386-1*

6106 Skateboard (1978) Score (Mark Snow) US:LP = RCA ABL1-2769*

6107 Skaterdater [Short] (1965) Score (Mike Curb) US:LP = Mira LP-3004/LPS-3004*

6108 Skatetown, U.S.A. (1979) Score (pop music) US:LP = Columbia JC-36292*

6109 Skeleton Dance, The [Cartoon] (1929) Theme (folk music) US: LP = Disneyland 4021 [@ST]

6110 Ski Crazy (1958) Score (Henry Vars) US:LP = Electro Vox EV-2081/ EVS-2081*

6111 Ski on the Wild Side (1967) Themes (Billy Allen) US:SP = MGM 13808 [Billy Allen:ST]

6112 Ski Party (1965) Theme-A/ US:SP = Mercury 72433 [Lesley Gore: ST]; Theme-B/US:SP = Polydor 506 [James Brown:ST]

6113 Skidoo (1968) Score (s:Harry Nilsson/as:George Tipton) US:LP = RCA LSO-1152*

6114 Skirts Ahoy (1952) Theme-A/ US:LP = Metro 535 [Debbie Reynolds: ST]; Theme-B/US:78 = MGM 501 [Billy Eckstine:ST]

6114a Sklavenkarawane, Die / Theme (Bert Reisfeld) US:SP = 20th 285 [Bradley Mundy]

6115 Sky Above Heaven, The [Ciel sur la Tete, Le] (1964) Highlights (Jacques Loussier) FR:EP = Barclay 70760

6116 Sky Bandits (1986) Score (Alfi Kabiljo) US:LP = Varese STV-81297*

6117 Sky High *see* Dragon Flies

6118 Sky Terror *see* Skyjacked

6119 Sky West and Crooked *see* Gypsy Girl

6120 Skydivers, The (1963) Themes (Jimmy Bryant) US:SP = Big J Records 162 [Jimmy Bryant:ST]

6121 Skyjacked [Sky Terror] (1972) Theme (Perry Botkin, Jr.) US:SP = Marina 603 [The Marina Strings]; Theme (Perry Botkin, Jr.) US:LP = Marina 2502* [The Marina Strings]; Theme (Perry Botkin, Jr.) US:LP = Kapp 3671* [Roger Williams]

6122 Skyrocket, The (1927) Theme [Silent I] (Ferde Grofe) US:SP = MGM

30279 [David Rose]; Theme [Silent I] (Ferde Grofe) US:LP=RCA 2560* [Gaylord Carter]

6123 Sky's the Limit, The (1943) Highlights (Harold Arlen) US:LP-BP= Curtain Calls 100/19

6124 Slade in Flame *see* Flame

6125 Slap, The [La Gifle] (1974) Themes (Georges Delerue) FR:SP= Deesse 693* [ST]

6126 Slap Shot (1977) Theme (Elmer Bernstein) IT:LP=Phase 6 VPAS-954* [Peter Hamilton]

6127 Slapstick [Slapstick of Another Kind] (1984) Highlights [USA Release] (Morton Stevens) US:LP= Varese STV-61163*; Highlights [Europe Release] (Michel Legrand) US:LP= Varese STV-81163* + GE:LP=Celine CL-0019*

6128 Slaughter (1972) Theme (Billy Preston) US:SP=A&M 1380* [Billy Preston:ST]; Theme (Billy Preston) US: LP=Buddah 5129* [Cecil Holmes]

6129 Slaughter on 10th Avenue (1957) Score (as:Herschel Burke Gilbert) US:LP=Decca DL-8657/DL-78657*

6130 Slaughter Trail (1951) Theme-A (Lyn Murray) US:SP=MGM 11025 [Art Lund]; Theme-A (Lyn Murray) US: SP=Decca 9-27741 [Gloria DeHaven]; Theme-B (Lyn Murray) US:SP=Decca 9-27586 [Terry Gilkyson:ST]

6131 Slaughterhouse Five (1972) Score (as:Glenn Gould) US:LP=Columbia S-31333*

6132 Slaughter's Big Rip-Off (1973) Score (s:James Brown & Fred Wesley/ t:David Matthews) US:LP=Polydor PD-6015*

6133 Slave of Love, A (1978) Score (Eduard Artemiev) JA:LP=Columbia YX-7318*

6134 Slave of the Cannibal God [La Montagna del Dio Cannibale] (1979) Highlights (Guido & Maurizio DeAngelis) IT:LP=Cometa 1007/19*

6135 Slave Trade in the World Today (1964) Score (Teo Usuelli) US:LP= London M-76006

6136 Slaves (1969) Score (Bobby Scott) US:LP=Skye SK-11*; Theme (Bobby Scott) US:SP=Specter 12249* [Dionne Warwick:ST]

6137 Sleeping Beauty (1959) Score (as:George Bruns) US:LP=Disneyland WDL-4005/ST-4005* + US:LP=Disneyland ST-1201 + US:LP=Buena Vista STER-4036*

6138 Sleeping Beauty (1965) Highlights + Dialog (Milton DeLugg) US: LP=Golden LP-166

6139 Sleeping Beauty (1966) Score (classical music) US:LP=Roulette OS-803/OSS-803*

6140 Sleeping Car Murder, The [Compartiment Tuers] (1965) Highlights (Michel Magne) FR:EP=Barclay 70886

6141 Sleeping Car to Trieste (1948) Theme (Benjamin Frankel) GB:78-PP= Rank FM-35 [ST]

6142 Sleepless Nights (1932) Themes/GB:78=Decca 3319 [Stanley Lupino:ST]

6143 Slender Thread, The (1965) Score (Quincy Jones) US:LP=Mercury MG-21070/SR-61070*

6144 Sleuth (1972) Score (John Addison) US:LP=Columbia S-32154*

6145 Slightly Pregnant Man, A [L'Envenement le Plus Important Depuis Que l'Homme] (1973) Score (Michel Legrand) FR:LP=Philips 6325.403*

6146 Slim Carter (1957) Theme-A (Arnold Hughes) US:SP=Decca 9-30437 [Jock Mahoney:ST]; Theme-B (Beasley Smith) US:SP=Decca 9-30465 [The Four Mints]

6147 Slipper and the Rose, The (1976) Score-A (Richard & Robert Sherman) US:LP=MCA 2097*; Score-B (Richard & Robert Sherman) GB:LP= EMI EMC-3116*

6148 Slippery When Wet (1959) Score (Bud Shank) US:LP=World Pacific W-1265/WS-1265*

6149 Slither (1972) Themes (Tom McIntosh) US:SP=MGM 14526 [Tom McIntosh:ST]

6150 Slogan (1969) Theme (Serge Gainsbourg) FR:LP=Philips 6620.025* [@ST]

6151 Slow Dancing in the Big City (1978) Score (Bill Conti) US:LP=UA LA-939*

6152 Slugger's Wife, The (1985) Score (various) US:LP=MCA 5578*

6153 Slumber Party '57 (1976) Score (pop music) US:LP = Mercury SRM1-1097*

6154 Slumber Party Massacre (1982) Score (Ralph Jones) US:LP = Web ST-109*

6155 Small Change [L'Argent de Poche] (1976) Theme-A (classical music) FR:LP = Pathe C066.14567* [@ST]; Theme-B (pop music) JA:SP = Odeon 20101* [ST]

6156 Small One, The [Short] (1978) Highlights + Underscore + Dialog (t:Richard Rich/t:Don Bluth/u:Robert F. Brunner) US:LP = Disneyland 3820*

6157 Small Town Girl (1953) Themes-A-B/US:LP-BP = Scarce Rarities 5503 [Jane Powell:ST]; Theme-C/US:LP = Take Home Tunes 777* [Bobby Van:ST]; Theme-D/US:SP = Capitol 2459 [Nat King Cole:ST]

6158 Smartest Girl in Town, The (1936) Theme/US:78 = Brunswick 7796 [Gene Raymond:ST]

6159 Smash Palace (1982) Score (Sharon O'Neill) AU:LP = CBS 237751*

6160 Smash Up—The Story of a Woman (1947) Themes/US:LP-BP = Legends 1000/3 [@ST]

6161 Smashing Bird I Used to Know, The (1969) Score (Bobby Richards) GB:LP = NEMS 6-70059*

6162 Smashing Time (1967) Score (John Addison) US:LP = ABC OC-6/SOC-6*

6163 Smell of the Savages, The [L'Odeur des Fauves] Theme (Francis Lai) US:LP = UA 5630* [Francis Lai:ST]

6164 Smic, Smac, Smoc (1971) Theme (Francis Lai) US:LP = UA 5630* [Francis Lai:ST]

6165 Smilin' Through (1941) Highlights (various) US:78-MS-12 = RCA M-847 [Jeanette MacDonald:ST]

6166 Smiling Maniacs, The [Corruzione al Palazzo di Giustizia] (1974) Score (Pino Donaggio) IT:LP = Carosello 25055*

6167 Smith! (1969) Theme (Bobby Russell) US:SP = Buena Vista 473 [Bobby Russell:ST]; Theme (Bobby Russell) US:SP = Buena Vista 474 [Camarata]

6168 Smokey and the Bandit (1977) Score (s:Bill Justis/t:Jerry Reed) US:LP = MCA 2099*

6169 Smokey and the Bandit II (1980) Score (t:Al Capps/s:various) US:LP = MCA 6101*

6170 Smokey and the Bandit III (1983) Highlights (t:Larry Cansler/etc.) US:EP-12 = MCA 36006*

6171 Smurfs and the Magic Flute, The [La Flute a Six Schtroumpfs] (1983) Score (Michel Legrand) FR:LP = Polydor 2417.317*

6172 Snoopy Come Home (1972) Score (Richard & Robert Sherman) US:LP = Columbia S-31541*

6173 Snow Demons [Snow Devils] (1965) Theme (A.F. Lavagnino) US:LP-BP = POO 106 [@ST]

6174 Snow Queen, The (1959) Themes + Underscore + Dialog (t:Richard Loring/u:Frank Skinner) US:LP = Decca DL-8977/DL-78977*

6175 Snow White and Rose Red (1966) Highlights + Underscore + Dialog (Milton DeLugg) US:LP = Camden CAL-1084/CAS-1084*

6176 Snow White and the Seven Dwarfs (1937) Score-A (s:Frank Churchill/t:Leigh Harline/t:Paul Smith) US:LP = Disneyland WDL-4005; Score-B (Frank Churchill) US:LP = Disneyland ST-1201; Highlights + Underscore + Dialog (e:Frank Churchill/u:Leigh Harline & Paul Smith) US:LP-MS = Disneyland WDX-102

6177 Snow White and the Seven Dwarfs (1966) Highlights + Underscore + Dialog (Milton DeLugg) US:LP = Golden LP-165

6178 Snow White and the Three Stooges (1961) Highlights + Dialog (Harry Harris) US:LP = Columbia CL-1650/CS-8450*

6179 Snowbound (1948) Theme (Cedric Thorpe Davie) GB:78-PP = Rank FM-11 [ST]

6180 Snows of Kilimanjaro, The (1953) Excerpts-A (Bernard Herrmann) US:LP = London SP-44144* [Bernard Herrmann:ST]; Excerpts-B (Bernard Herrmann) US:LP = RCA LK-1007 [Al Goodman]; Theme (Alfred Newman) US:LP = Decca 8123 [Alfred Newman:ST]

6181 So Big (1953) Theme (Max Steiner) US:SP = Decca 9-28947 [Victor Young]; Theme (Max Steiner) US:LP = Citadel 7005* [Maria Martino]; Theme (Max Steiner) US:LP-BP = Citadel CTMS-7 [Max Steiner:ST]

6182 So Dear to My Heart (1949) Score (e:Eliot Daniel/etc.) US:LP = Disneyland DQ-1255 [Studio Cast]; Highlights (e:Eliot Daniel/etc.) US:78-MS = Capitol DD-109 [Ken Carson & John Beal:ST]; Themes (Eliot Daniel) US:SP = Decca 9-24547 [Burl Ives:ST]

6183 So Long at the Fair (1950) Themes (Benjamin Frankel) GB:LP = WRC 384 [Charles Williams]; Theme (Benjamin Frankel) US:SP = London 45-919 [Mantovani]; Theme (B. Frankel) US:LP-BP = Citadel CTOFI-1 [@ST]

6184 So Long, Joey (1974) Score (t: Ron Huff/s:various) US:LP = Word WST-8594*

6185 So This Is College (1929) Theme/US:78 = Columbia 1980 [Cliff Edwards:ST]

6186 So This Is Love [The Grace Moore Story] (1953) Highlights (classical music) US:LP-10 = RCA LOC-3000 [Kathryn Grayson:ST]

6187 So This Is Paris (1954) Highlights (Phil Moody & Pony Sherell) US: LP-10 = Decca DL-5553

6188 Sodom and Gomorrah (1963) Score (Miklos Rozsa) US:LP = RCA LOC-1076/LSO-1076*; Scores (Miklos Rozsa) IT:LP-MS = Legend DLD 1/2*

6189 Soft Skin, The [La Peau Douce] (1964) Highlights (Georges Delerue) FR:EP = Philips 434.887

6190 Sol Madrid [The Heroin Gang] (1968) Score (Lalo Schifrin) US: LP = MGM E-4541/SE-4541*

6190a Solarbabies (1986) Theme (Smokey Robinson) US:SP = Motown 1897* [Smokey Robinson:ST]

6191 Solaris (1972) Score (Eduard Artemiev) US:LP-BP = Solaris YX-7212*

6192 Soldier Arms *see* Chaplin Revue, The

6193 Soldier Blue (1970) Highlights (e:Roy Budd/t:Buffy Sainte-Marie) US: LP-BP = Eros 80544*; Highlights (e:Roy Budd/t:Buffy Sainte-Marie) GB:LP = Pye NSPL-18348*; Theme (Buffy Sainte-Marie) US:SP = Vanguard 222617 [Buffy Sainte-Marie:ST]

6194 Soldier in the Rain (1963) Themes (Henry Mancini) US:SP = Capitol 5131 [Jackie Gleason]; Theme-A (Henry Mancini) US:LP = RCA 2990* + US:LP = RCA 3557* [Henry Mancini:ST]; Theme-B (Henry Mancini) US: LP = Mercury 60863* [Quincy Jones]

6195 Soldier of Fortune (1955) Theme (Hugo Friedhofer) US:SP = MGM 12023 [The Elliott Brothers]; Theme (Hugo Friedhofer) US:LP = MGM 3220 [@The Elliott Brothers]

6196 Soldier of Orange [Soldaat van Oranje] (1979) Score (Rogier Van Otterloo) HO:LP = Polydor 2925.059*

6197 Soldiers of the King (1933) Theme/GB:LP = WRC 113 [Cicely Courtneidge:ST]; Theme/GB:LP = MFP 1236 [Cicely Courtneidge:ST]

6198 Soldier's Story, A (1985) Themes (pop music) FR:LP = Milan ACH-030* [@Patti Labelle:ST]

6199 Solid Gold Cadillac, The (1956) Theme (George Duning) US:SP = Decca 9-30030 [Morris Stoloff:ST]

6200 Solomon and Sheba (1959) Score (Mario Nascimbene) US:LP = UA UAL-4051/UAS-5051*

6201 Solomon King (1975) Score (s:Jimmy Steiger/t:Jimmy Lewis) US: LP = Sippa SP-1001*

6202 Some Came Running (1958) Score (s:Elmer Bernstein/t:James Van Heusen) US:LP = Capitol W-1109/SW-1109*

6203 Some Like It Cool *see* Sex on the Run

6204 Some Like It Hot (1939) Theme-A/US:78 = Decca 2568 [Bob Hope & Shirley Ross:ST]; Theme-B/US: LP-BP = JJA 19762 [@Shirley Ross:ST]

6205 Some Like It Hot (1959) Score (e:Adolph Deutsch/t:Matty Malneck/etc.) US:LP = UA UAL-4030/UAS-5030* + US:LP = UA LA-272*

6206 Some People (1968) Highlights (Ron Grainer) GB:EP = Pye 24158; Theme (Ron Grainer) US:SP = Atco 45-6235 [Jorgen Ingmann]

6207 Somebody Killed Her Husband [Charade '79] (1978) Score (Alex North) JA:LP = Seven Seas FML-108*

6208 Somebody Loves Me (1952) Highlights (e:Jay Livingston & Ray Evans/etc.) US:LP-10 = RCA LPM-3097

6209 Somebody Up There Likes Me (1956) Theme (Bronislau Kaper) US: SP = RCA 47-6590 [Perry Como:ST]; Theme (Bronislau Kaper) US:SP = MGM 12303 [The Crossroads Quartet]; Theme (Bronislau Kaper) US:LP = MGM 3511 [Richard Ellsasser]

6210 Something Big (1972) Theme (Burt Bacharach) US:SP = Columbia 4-45506 [Mark Lindsay:ST]; Theme (Burt Bacharach) US:SP = A&M 1489* [Burt Bacharach]; Theme (Burt Bacharach) US:LP = A&M 3527* [Burt Bacharach]

6211 Something for the Boys (1944) Highlights (Jimmy McHugh) US:LP-BP = Caliban 6030

6212 Something in the Wind (1947) Highlights (John Green) US:78-MS = Decca A-601 [Deanna Durbin:ST]

6213 Something Is Out There *see* Day of the Animals

6214 Something Money Can't Buy (1952) Theme (Nino Rota) GB:78-PP = Rank FM-128 [ST]; Theme (Nino Rota) US:SP = Mercury 70196 [Richard Hayman]; Theme (Nino Rota) US:LP-10 = Mercury 25189 [Richard Hayman]

6215 Something to Hide [Shattered] (1973) Excerpts (Roy Budd) GB: LP = Pye NSPL-18389* [Roy Budd:ST]; Theme (Roy Budd) US:SP = RCA 74-0683* [Jack Jones]; Theme (Roy Budd) US:LP-BP = Eros 80544* [Roy Budd:ST]

6216 Something to Live For (1952) Theme (Victor Young) US:SP = Columbia 4-41127 [Tony Bennett]; Theme (Victor Young) US:LP = Mercury 60369* [Richard Hayman]; Theme (Victor Young) US:LP = Decca 8051 [Victor Young:ST]

6217 Something to Shout About (1943) Excerpts (Cole Porter) US:LP-BP = JJA 19767 [@ST]

6218 Something Wild (1961) Highlights (Aaron Copland) US:LP = Columbia MS-30374* [Aaron Copland:ST]

6219 Something Wild (1986) Score (various) US:LP = MCA 6194*

6220 Sometimes a Great Notion [Never Give an Inch] (1971) Score (Henry Mancini) US:LP = Decca DL-79185*

6221 Somewhere in Time (1980) Score (John Barry) US:LP = MCA 5154*

6222 Son of Blob *see* Beware! The Blob

6223 Son of Dracula (1943) Theme (Hans J. Salter) US:LP = Coral 757240* + US:LP = Varese 81077* [Dick Jacobs]

6224 Son of Dracula (1974) Score + Underscore + Dialog (s:Harry Nilsson/u:Paul Buckmaster) US:LP = Rapple ABL1-0220*

6225 Son of Frankenstein (1939) Themes (Frank Skinner) US:LP = Citadel 6026 + US:LP = Citadel 7012 [Hans J. Salter]; Sequence + Dialog (Frank Skinner) US:LP = Decca 74833 [@ST]

6226 Son of Fury (1942) Theme (Alfred Newman) US:78 = Decca 18277 [Alfred Newman:ST]; Theme (Alfred Newman) US:LP = Capitol 1447* [Alfred Newman:ST]

6227 Son of Godzilla (1969) Themes (Masaru Sato) JA:LP = Toho 8112 [@ST]

6228 Son of Paleface (1952) Excerpts (Jay Livingston & Ray Evans) US: LP-BP = Titania 511 [@ST]; Themes-A-B (Jay Livingston & Ray Evans) US: SP = Capitol 2161 [Bob Hope:ST]; Themes-C-D (Jay Livingston & Ray Evans) US:78 = Capitol 13781 [Jane Russell:ST]; Theme-E (Jay Livingston & Ray Evans) US:SP = RCA 47-4709 [Roy Rogers:ST]

6229 Son of Robin Hood, The (1958) Theme (Sid Tepper & Roy Bennett) US:SP = 20th 147 [The Merry Men]

6230 Song Is Born, A (1948) Highlights (various) US:78-MS = Capitol CC-106; Themes/US:78 = Decca 24505 [Lionel Hampton:ST]

6231 Song o' My Heart (1930) Score (pop music) US:LP-PP = McCormack S-2707/8 [John McCormack:ST]

6232 Song of Bernadette, The (1943) Highlights (Alfred Newman) US: LP-10 = Decca DL-5358 + US:LP-BP = Cinema LP-8008 + US:LP = Varese STV-81116

6233 Song of Christmas, The [Short] Highlights (Roy Ringwald) US: LP-PP = Portafilms 8065-6220

6234 Song of Freedom (1936) Highlights (Eric Ansell) GB:EP = HMV 7EG-8431 [Paul Robeson:ST]

6235 Song of Love, The (1929) Themes-A-B/US:78 = Brunswick 4558 [Belle Baker:ST]; Theme-C/US:78 = Brunswick 4624 [Belle Baker:ST]

6236 Song of Love, The (1947) Highlights (classical music) US:78-MS = MGM L-6

6237 Song of Norway (1970) Score (stage songs:George Forrest & Robert Wright) US:LP = ABC SOC-14*

6238 Song of Scheherazade (1947) Highlights (ae:Miklos Rozsa) US:78-MS = Columbia MX-272 [Charles Kullman:ST]

6239 Song of Soho, A (1930) Theme/US:LP = Monmouth 7030 [@ Carl Brisson:ST]

6240 Song of Songs (1933) Theme (Frederick Hollander) US:LP = Columbia 4975 + US:LP = Columbia 6430 [Marlene Dietrich:ST]

6241 Song of Surrender (1949) Theme (Victor Young) US:SP = RCA 47-2980 [Mindy Carson]; Theme (Victor Young) US:78 = Columbia 38546 [Buddy Clark]; Theme (Victor Young) US:LP = MGM 3935 [Joni James]

6242 Song of the Flame, The (1930) Theme/US:78 = Brunswick 4828 [Noah Berry:ST]

6243 Song of the Islands (1942) Highlights (Harry Warren) US:LP-BP = Caliban 6009

6244 Song of the Land (1953) Theme (Serge Dupree) US:SP = MGM 30838 [George Tzipine]

6245 Song of the Open Road (1944) Excerpts (Walter Kent) US:LP-BP = Curtain Calls 100/4 [Jane Powell:ST]

6246 Song of the South [Uncle Remus] (1946) Score-A (t:Daniele Amfitheatrof/t:Charles Wolcott/etc.) US:LP = Disneyland WDL-4001; Score-B (t:Charles Wolcott/etc.) US:LP = Disneyland ST-1205

6247 Song of the West [Rainbow] (1930) Themes/US:78 = RCA/Victor 22229 [John Boles:ST]

6248 Song Remains the Same, The (1976) Scores (rock music) US:LP-MS = Swan Song SS-2-201* [Led Zeppelin:ST]

6249 Song Without End (1960) Score (classical music) US:LP = Colpix CP-506/SCP-506*; Theme (at:George Duning) US:SP = Colpix 162 [Stu Phillips]

6250 Song Writer (1984) Score (e:Kris Kristofferson/e:Willie Nelson) US:LP = Columbia FC-39531*

6251 Sonny and Jed [La Banda J&S] (1973) Highlights (Ennio Morricone) US:LP = Cerberus CEMS-0111*

6252 Sonora [Sartana Does Not Forgive] [Sartana Non Perdona] (1968) Score (Francesco DeMasi) IT:LP = Beat CR-4*

6253 Sons and Lovers (1960) Theme (Mario Nascimbene) US:SP = Columbia 4-41731 [Percy Faith]; Theme (Mario Nascimbene) US:LP = 20th 3043* [The 20th Century Strings]; Theme (Mario Nascimbene) US:LP = Carlton 126* [Lew Douglas]

6254 Sons of Katie Elder, The (1965) Score (Elmer Bernstein) US:LP = Columbia OL-6420/OS-2820*

6255 Sons of the Desert [Fraternally Yours] (1934) Highlights + Underscore + Dialog (Marvin Hatley) US:LP = Mark 56 #689

6256 Sophie's Choice (1982) Score (Marvin Hamlisch) US:LP = Southern Cross SCRS-1002*

6257 Sorcerer [Wages of Fear] (1977) Score (Tangerine Dream) US:LP = MCA 2277*

6258 Soul Hustler, The (1973) Score (Harley Hatcher) US:LP = MGM SE-4943*

6259 Soul Man (1986) Score (t:Tom Scott/s:various) US:LP = A&M SP-3903*

6260 Soul of Nigger Charley, The (1973) Score (Don Costa) US:LP = MGM 1SE-46*

6261 Soul to Soul (1972) Score (rock music) US:LP = Atlantic SD-7207*

6262 Souls in Conflict / Themes (Ralph Carmichael) US:LP = Word 3164 [@Frank Boggs/Georgia Lee:ST]

6263 Sound and the Fury, The (1959) Score (Alex North) US:LP = Decca DL-8885/DL-78885*

6264 Sound Barrier, The *see* Breaking the Sound Barrier

6265 Sound of Music, The (1965) Score (stage songs:Richard Rodgers) US:LP = RCA LOCD-2005/LSOD-2005*

6266 Sound Off (1952) Theme (Lester Lee) US:SP = RCA 47-4611 [Vaughn Monroe]

6267 Sounder (1972) Score (Taj Mahal) US:LP = Columbia S-31944*

6268 Soup for One (1982) Score (Bernard Edwards & Nile Rodgers) US: LP = Mirage/Atlantic WTG-19353*

6269 South Pacific (1958) Score (stage songs:Richard Rodgers) US:LP = RCA LOCD-2000/LSOD-2000* + US: LP = RCA AYL1-3684*

6270 South Pole Story *see* Antarctica

6271 South Seas Adventure (1958) Score (e:Alex North/e:folk music) US: LP = Audio Fidelity AFLP-1899/AFSD-5899*; Highlights (Alex North) US: LP = Citadel CTV-7014*

6272 Southern Star, The (1969) Score (Georges Garvarentz) US:LP = Colgems COSO-5009*

6273 Southward Ho (1939) Theme/ US:LP = Columbia 38907 [Roy Rogers: ST]

6274 Southwest to Sonora *see* Appaloosa, The

6275 Souvenir d'Italie *see* It Happened in Rome

6276 Space Camp (1986) Score (John Williams) US:LP = RCA ABL1-5856*

6277 Spaceman and King Arthur, The *see* Unidentified Flying Oddball

6278 Spanish Affair (1957) Score (Daniele Amfitheatrof) US:LP = Dot DLP-3078

6279 Spanish Gardener, The (1956) Theme (John Veale) GB:78-PP = Rank FM-204 [ST]

6280 Sparkle (1976) Score (s:Curtis Mayfield/as:Rich Tufo) US:LP = Atlantic SD-18176* [Aretha Franklin]

6281 Spartacus (1960) Score (Alex North) US:LP = Decca DL-9092/DL-79092* + US:LP = MCA 2068*

6282 Spartan X (1985) Themes (Keith Morrison) JA:SP = RCA Victor 1787* [ST]

6283 Spasm [Spasmo] (1974) Themes (Ennio Morricone) IT:SP = RCA 1018* [ST]

6284 Spawning, The *see* Piranha II

6285 Special Section [Section Speciale] (1976) Score (Eric Demarsan) FR: LP = RCA TBL1-0072*

6286 Specter of the Rose (1946) Theme (George Antheil) US:LP-MS = Readers Digest RD4-141* [@Charles Gerhardt]

6287 Spectre of Edgar Allan Poe, The (1974) Themes (Allen D. Allen) US: SP-PP = CR 2747 [Tom Bahler/Allen D. Allen:ST]

6288 Speed Fever [Formula One] (1978) Score (Guido & Maurizio DeAngelis) IT:LP = KTRL 13900*

6289 Speedtrap (1978) Themes (Johnny Harris) JA:SP = Seven Seas FMS-47* [ST]

6290 Speedway (1968) Score (e:Sid Tepper & Roy Bennett/e:Joy Byers/etc.) US:LP = RCA LPM-3989/LSP-3989* [Elvis Presley:ST]

6291 Spellbound (1945) Score (Miklos Rozsa) US:LP = WB W-1213/ WS-1213* + US:LP = Stanyan SRQ-4021* [Ray Heindorf]; Highlights (Miklos Rozsa) US:LP-10 = Rem LP-1 + US: LP = AEI 3103 [Miklos Rozsa:ST]

6292 Spencer's Mountain (1963) Theme (Max Steiner) US:LP-BP = Citadel CTMS-7 [Max Steiner:ST]; Theme (Max Steiner) US:LP = Command 854* [Enoch Light]

6293 Spermula (1977) Score (Jose Bartel) FR:LP = WB/WEA 56275*

6294 Spetters (1981) Themes (Scherpenzeel) HO:SP = Philips 601.7032* [ST]

6295 Spider and the Fly, The (1949) Theme (Georges Auric) GB:78-PP = Rank FM-85 [ST]

6296 Spider Woman, The (1944) Underscore + Dialog (au:Hans J. Salter) US:LP = Murray Hill 55404

6297 Spider's Web, The (1960) Theme (Tony Crombie) US:LP = Roulette 804* [@ST]

6298 Spies Like Us (1985) Score-A (Elmer Bernstein) US:LP = Varese STV-81270*; Theme-B (Paul McCartney) US: SP = Capitol 5537* [Paul McCartney: ST]

6299 Spinal Tap *see* This Is Spinal Tap

6300 Spinout (1966) Score (e:Sid Tepper & Roy Bennett/etc.) US:LP = RCA LPM-3702/LSP-3702* + US: LP = RCA APL1-2560* + US:LP = RCA AYL1-3684* [Elvis Presley:ST]

6301 Spinster, The *see* Two Loves

6302 Spirit of St. Louis, The (1957) Score-A (Franz Waxman) US:LP = RCA LPM-1472 + US:LP-BP = Film Archives F-4761; Score-B (Franz Waxman) US:LP = Entracte ERS-6507

6303 Spirit of the Tattoo (1982) Themes (Ugaki) JA:SP = Atlantic 1514* [ST]

6304 Spirits of the Dead [Tales of Mystery] [Histories Extraordinaires] (1968) Theme (Nino Rota) IT:LP = CAM 9053* [Nino Rota & Carlo Savina]

6305 Spitfire, The [The First of the Few] (1942) Excerpts (William Walton) US:LP = Varese 1000.20* [Morton Gould]; Excerpts (William Walton) US: LP = London SP-44248* [Stanley Black]; Excerpts (William Walton) GB:LP = EMI SXLP-30139* [William Walton:ST]

6306 Spivs *see* Vitelloni

6307 Splash (1984) Score (Lee Holdridge) US:LP = Cherry Lane 00301*

6308 Splendor in the Grass (1961) Theme (David Amram) US:SP = Capitol 4629 [Stan Kenton]; Theme (David Amram) US:LP = Columbia 1783/8583* [Percy Faith]; Theme (David Amram) US:LP = Flying Fish 094* [David Amram:ST]

6309 Split, The (1968) Themes (Quincy Jones) US:SP = MGM 14001 [Billy Preston]; Themes (Quincy Jones) US:LP = World Pacific 20152* [Wilton Felder]; Theme-A (Quincy Jones) US: SP = Capitol 2317 [H.B. Barnum]; Theme-B (Quincy Jones) US:SP = Capitol 2348 [Lou Rawls]

6310 Spoiled Children [Des Enfants Gates] (1979) Score (Philippe Sarde) FR:LP = Vogue 20295*

6311 Spoilers, The (1956) Theme (Hans J. Salter) US:LP = Medallion 313 [Hans J. Salter:ST]

6312 Spooks Run Wild (1942) Underscore + Dialog (Johnny Lange) US:LP-MS = Murray Hill 57393

6313 Sporting Club, The (1971) Score (Michael Small) US:LP = Buddah BDS-95002*

6314 Spring Break (1983) Score (t:Harry Manfredini/s:various) US: LP = WB 23826-1*

6315 Spring Is Here (1930) Excerpts (Richard Rodgers) US:LP-BP = JJA 19766 [@ST]

6316 Spring Parade (1940) Highlights (t:Robert Stolz/t:Charles Previn/ etc.) US:LP-BP = Caliban 6005; Excerpts (various) US:78-MS = Decca 209 [Deanna Durbin:ST]

6317 Spring Reunion (1957) Theme (Harry Warren) US:SP = Decca 9-30241 [The Mary Kaye Trio]

6318 Spring Symphony (1986) Score (classical music) US:LP = Delirium DLM-2911*

6319 Springtime in the Rockies (1943) Highlights (Harry Warren) US: LP-BP = Titania 507 + US:LP-BP = Hollywood Soundstage 5013

6320 Spy Who Came In from the Cold, The (1965) Score (Sol Kaplan) US: LP = RCA LOC-1118/LSO-1118*

6321 Spy Who Loved Me, The (1977) Score (e:Marvin Hamlisch/e:Paul Buckmaster) US:LP = UA LA-774*

6322 Spy with a Cold Nose, The (1965) Score (Riz Ortolani) US:LP = Columbia OL-6670/OS-3070*

6323 Square Jungle, The (1956) Theme (Sonny Burke) US:SP = Decca 9-29793 [Carmen McRae]

6324 Square Root of Zero, The (1966) Score (Elliot Kaplan) US:LP = Mainstream 56070/S-6070*

6325 Squeaker, The [Der Zinker] (1964) Theme (Peter Thomas) GE:LP = Celine 0011 [Peter Thomas:ST]

6326 Squeeze Play (1979) Score (s: Gary Vacca/t:Don Zimmers) US:LP = Registry 777-1*

6327 Squizzy Taylor (1983) Score (Bruce Smeaton) AU:LP = Astor 1073*

6328 Stage Fright (1950) Theme/ US:LP = Columbia 6430 + US:LP = Columbia 4975 [Marlene Dietrich:ST]

6329 Stage Struck (1936) Theme-A/ US:LP = Decca 8837 [Dick Powell:ST]; Theme-B/US:LP-BP = JJA 19763 [@Dick Powell:ST]

6330 Stage Struck (1958) Theme (Alex North) US:LP = Citadel 6023* [Alex North:ST]

6331 Stagecoach (1939) Underscore + Dialog (Leo Shuken & John Leipold) US:LP-MS = Mark 56 #783

6332 Stagecoach (1966) Score (s: Jerry Goldsmith/t:Lee Pockriss) US: LP = Mainstream 56077/S-6077* [Alexander Courage]; Theme (Lee Pockriss) US:SP = Capitol 5643 [Wayne Newton:ST]

6333 Stagedoor Canteen (1963) Score (James Monaco) US:LP-MS-BP = Curtain Calls 100/11-12

6334 Staircase (1969) Theme (Dudley Moore) US:LP = UA 6731* [Leroy Holmes]

6335 Stairway to Heaven [A Matter of Life and Death] (1946) Theme (Allan Gray) US:LP = Columbia 3029 [@Charles Williams]

6336 Stakeout on Dope Street (1958) Highlights (Richard Markowitz) US:EP = RCA EPA-4199

6337 Stalking Moon, The (1969) Theme (Fred Karlin) US:LP = UA 6710* [Leroy Holmes]

6338 Stand Up and Be Counted (1972) Theme (Ray Burton) US:SP = Capitol 3350* [Helen Reddy:ST]; Theme (Ray Burton) US:LP = Capitol 11467* [Helen Reddy:ST]

6339 Stand Up and Cheer (1934) Theme/US:LP-MS = 20th 2-103 [Shirley Temple:ST]

6340 Star! [Those Were the Happy Times] (1968) Score (t:James Van Heusen/s:pop music) US:LP = 20th DS-5102*

6341 Star, The (1952) Theme (Victor Young) US:LP = Decca 8051 [Victor Young:ST]; Theme (Victor Young) US: LP = Jubilee 1034* + US:LP = Citadel 6024* [Harry Sukman]

6342 Star Is Born, A (1937) Score (Max Steiner) US:LP = UA LA-375* [Leroy Holmes]; Theme (Max Steiner) US:SP = RCA 47-6422 [Max Steiner:ST]

6343 Star Is Born, A (1954) Score (s:Harold Arlen/t:Roger Edens) US: LP = Columbia BL-1201 + US:LP = Columbia CL-1101 + US:LP = Harmony HS-11366 + US:LP = CSP ACS-8740e

6344 Star Is Born, A (1976) Score (e:Kenny Ascher & Paul Williams/t: Rupert Holmes/etc.) US:LP = Columbia JS-34403*

6345 Star Maker, The (1939) Excerpts (James Monaco) US:LP-10 = Decca DL-6013 + US:LP = Decca DL-4254 [Bing Crosby:ST]

6346 Star of India (1953) Theme (Harry Harris) US:SP = Columbia 4-40314 [Liberace]

6347 Star Spangled Girl (1971) Theme (Charles Fox) US:SP = Bell 159 [Davy Jones:ST]

6348 Star Spangled Rhythm (1942) Score (Harold Arlen) US:LP-BP = Curtain Calls 100/20 + US:LP-BP = Sandy Hook SH-2045

6349 Star Struck (1983) Score (Phil Judd) US:LP = A&M/OZ SP-4938*

6350 Star Trek—The Motion Picture (1979) Score (Jerry Goldsmith) US:LP = Columbia JS-36334*

6351 Star Trek II—The Wrath of Khan (1982) Score (James Horner) US: LP = Atlantic SD-19363*; Theme (Craig Huxley) US:LP-MS = Sonic Atmospheres 101* [Craig Huxley:ST]

6352 Star Trek III—The Search for Spock (1984) Score (James Horner) US:LP + SP-12 = Capitol SKBK-12360*

6353 Star Trek IV—The Voyage Home (1986) Score (Leonard Rosenman) US:LP = MCA 6195*

6354 Star Wars (1977) Score (John Williams) US:LP-MS = 20th T-541

6355 Starcrash (1979) Score (John Barry) IT:LP = Durium 30314* + GE: LP = Polydor 2374.138*

6356 Stardust (1975) Scores (pop music) US:LP-MS = Arista AL-5000*

6357 Stardust Memories (1980) Score (pop music) IT:LP = Bella Musica 3014*

6358 Starlift (1951) Highlights (pop music) US:LP-BP = Titania 510; Theme (Percy Faith) US:LP = Columbia 577 [Percy Faith:ST]

6359 Starman (1984) Score (Jack Nitzsche) US:LP = Varese STV-81233*

6360 Stars and Stripes Forever [Marching Along] (1952) Highlights (pop music) US:LP-10 = MGM E-176 + US: LP = MGM E-3508

6361 Stars Are Singing, The (1952) Highlights (Jay Livingston & Ray Evans) US:EP = Columbia B-1618 [Rosemary Clooney:ST]

6362 Stars Over Broadway (1935) Themes-A-B/US:78 = RCA/Victor 25185 [James Melton:ST]; Theme-C/ US:LP = Decca DEA-7-1 [@James Melton:ST]; Theme-D/US:LP = Epic 159 [@Kay Thompson:ST]

6363 Start Cheering (1938) Theme/ US:LP = MGM 4207 [Jimmy Durante: ST]

6364 Starting Over (1979) Theme (Marvin Hamlisch) US:SP = 20th 2427* [Stephanie Mills]

6365 State Fair [It Happened One Summer] (1945) Highlights-A (Richard Rodgers) US:LP-BP = Classic International Filmusicals 3009; Highlights-B (Richard Rodgers) US:78-MS = Decca 412 [Dick Haymes:ST]

6366 State Fair (1962) Score (film songs:Richard Rodgers) US:LP = Dot DLP-9011/DLP-29011*

6367 State of Siege (1973) Score (Mikis Theodorakis) US:LP = Columbia S-32352*

6368 Statue, The (1971) Theme (Riz Ortolani) US:SP = RCA 74-0433* [The Copperfield Brass]

6369 Stavinsky (1974) Score (s:Stephen Sondheim/as:Jonathan Tunick) US:LP = RCA ARL1-0952*

6370 Stay As You Are [The Daughter] [Cosi Come Sei] (1979) Score (Ennio Morricone) IT:LP = Cinevox 33/122*

6371 Stay Away Joe (1968) Highlights (various) AU:EP = RCA 20652 [Elvis Presley:ST]; Theme (Sid Tepper & Roy Bennett) US:LP = Camden 2408* + US:LP = Camden 2440* [Elvis Presley:ST]

6372 Staying Alive (1983) Score (e:Vince DiCola/e:The Bee Gees/e:various) US:LP = RSO 813-269-1*

6373 Steamboat Bill, Jr. (1928) Excerpts [Silent II] (Claude Bolling) FR: LP = Columbia XM-241 [Claude Bolling:ST]

6374 Steamboat 'Round the Bend (1960) Score (Eddy Manson) US:LP = Folkways FP-74

6375 Steamboat Willie [Cartoon] (1928) Theme (pop music) US:LP = Disneyland 4021 + US:LP-MS = Ovation 5000 [@ST]

6376 Steel Arena, The (1973) Themes (Don Tweedy) US:SP = River 3873* [Sam Durrence/Don Tweedy:ST]

6377 Steelyard Blues [Final Crash] (1972) Score (Mike Bloomfield) US:LP = WB BS-2662*

6378 Step Lively (1944) Score (Jule Styne) US:LP-BP = Hollywood Soundstage HS-412

6379 Sterile Cuckoo, The [Pookie] (1969) Score (Fred Karlin) US:LP = Paramount PAS-5009*

6380 Stevie (1978) Highlights + Underscore + Dialog (Patrick Gowers) US:LP = Epic SE-37726*

6381 Stick (1985) Theme (Steve Dorff) US:SP = Capitol 5472* [Anne Murray:ST]

6382 Stiletto (1969) Score (Sid Ramin) US:LP = Columbia OS-3360*

6383 Sting, The (1973) Score (e: Marvin Hamlisch/e:pop music) US: LP = MCA 390* + US:LP = MCA 37091*

6384 Sting of the West [Te Deum] (1973) Themes (Guido & Maurizio De-Angelis) IT:SP = RCA OC-30* [ST]

6385 Sting II, The (1982) Score (as: Lalo Schifrin) US:LP = MCA 6116*

6386 Stir Crazy (1980) Score (e: Tom Scott/e:Michael Masser) US:LP = Posse POS-10001*

6387 Stolen Hours, The (1963) Theme (Mort Lindsey) US:SP = UA 653 [The Four Lads]; Theme (Mort Lindsey) US:LP = Capitol 2063* [Ray Anthony]; Theme (Mort Lindsey) US:LP = Dot 25765* [Mort Lindsey:ST]

6388 Stolen Life, A (1946) Theme-A (Max Steiner) US:LP = RCA 1170 [Max Steiner:ST]; Theme-B (Max Steiner) US:LP = RCA 1287 + US: LP = Entracte 6004 [Max Steiner:ST]; Theme-B (Max Steiner) US:LP = RCA 1-0183* + US:LP = RCA 1-3706* [Charles Gerhardt]

6389 Stone (1974) Score (Billy Green) JA:LP = Polydor 28-MM-0017*

6390 Stone Killer, The [L'Assassino di Pietra] (1973) Score (Roy Budd) IT:

LP = International 9032*; Highlights (Roy Budd) US:LP = Project PR-5085*

6391 Stone Soup [Short] Sequence + Dialog (Arthur Kleiner) US:LP-PP = Picture Book Parade 102 [@ST]

6392 Stony Island [My Main Man from Stony Island] (1978) Score (David Matthews) US:LP = Glades 7516*

6393 Stooge, The (1953) Highlights (pop music) US:LP-10 = Capitol L-401 [Dean Martin:ST]

6394 Stop Making Sense (1984) Score (pop music) US:LP = Sire 25186-1* [The Talking Heads:ST]

6395 Stop Press Girl (1949) Theme (Walter Goehr) GB:78-PP = Rank FM-66 [ST]

6396 Stop the World—I Want to Get Off (1966) Score (stage songs:Leslie Bricusse & Anthony Newley) US:LP = WB W-1643/WS-1643*

6397 Stop, You're Killing Me (1953) Theme (Carl Sigman) US:SP = MGM 11384 [Bill Hayes:ST]

6398 Stork Club, The (1945) Highlights (various) US:LP-BP = Caliban 6020

6399 Storm Riders (1982) Score (pop music) US:LP = PKA 1001*

6400 Stormy Weather (1943) Score (t:Cyril Mockridge/s:various) US:LP-BP = Sandy Hook SH-2037 + US:LP-BP = Sountrak STK-103

6401 Story About Ping, The [Short] Sequence + Dialog (Arthur Kleiner) US:LP-PP = Picture Book Parade 102 [@ST]

6402 Story of a Love Story, The *see* Impossible Object, The

6403 Story of a Woman, The (1969) Themes (John Williams) JA:SP = Seven Seas HIT-1957* [ST]

6404 Story of Adele H., The [L'Histoire d'Adele H.] (1976) Score (classical music) FR:LP = Pathe C066.14216*

6405 Story of Dr. Ehrlich's Magic Bullet, The *see* Dr. Ehrlich's Magic Bullet

6406 Story of G.I. Joe, The (1945) Theme (Ann Ronell) US:LP-MS = Adam 8040 [@Buddy Clark]

6407 Story of Moby Dick, The *see* Moby Dick (1957)

6408 Story of Naomi Uemura, The (1986) Score (s:Philip Aaberg/t:William Ackerman) US:LP = Windham Hill WH-1055*

6409 Story of O, The [L'Histoire d'O] (1975) Score (Pierre Bachelet) FR: LP = Barclay 80571*

6410 Story of O—Part 2, The [L'Histoire d'O, #2] (1984) Score (Stanley Myers) FR:LP = Polydor 823-524-1*

6411 Story of Robin Hood, The (1952) Highlights + Dialog (t:George Wyle/etc.) US:78-MS = Capitol 3138; Highlights + Dialog (t:George Wyle/ etc.) US:LP = Disneyland DQ-1249

6412 Story of Shirley Yorke, The (1950) Theme (George Melachrino) GB: 78 = HMV 9678 [George Melachrino:ST]

6413 Story of Three Loves, The (1953) Theme (Miklos Rozsa) US:LP = Deutsche 2584.013* [Miklos Rozsa:ST]; Theme (Miklos Rozsa) GE:LP = Antares MR-01* [Rainer Padberg]

6414 Story of Vernon and Irene Castle, The (1939) Highlights (pop music) US:LP-BP = Caliban 6000

6415 Stowaway (1936) Themes/ US:LP-MS = 20th 2-103 [Shirley Temple:ST]

6416 Stowaway in the Sky *see* Le Voyage en Ballon

6417 Strada, La (1956) Themes (Nino Rota) US:SP = Mercury 70909 [Eddie Barclay]; Themes (Nino Rota) US:LP = London 44225* [Stanley Black]; Theme (Nino Rota) US:LP = Columbia 107 [Michel Legrand]

6418 Straight on Till Morning (1972) Theme (Annie Ross) GB:SP = Columbia 8912 [Annie Ross:ST]

6419 Straight, Place and Show (1938) Excerpts (various) US:LP-BP = Vertinge 2000 [@ST]

6420 Strange Bedfellows (1965) Theme (Leigh Harline) US:SP = Decca 9-31766 [Carmen Cavallaro]

6421 Strange Brew (1983) Theme + Underscore + Dialog (t:Ian Thomas/ u:Charles Fox) US:LP = Mercury 814-104-1*

6422 Strange Countess, The [Die Seltsame Grafin] (1961) Theme (Peter Thomas) GE:LP = Celine 0011 [Peter Thomas:ST]

6423 Strange Lady in Town (1955) Theme (Dimitri Tiomkin) US:SP = Columbia 4-40457 [Frankie Laine:ST]; Theme (Dimitri Tiomkin) US:SP = Coral 9-61388 [Dimitri Tiomkin:ST]; Theme (Dimitri Tiomkin) US:LP = Coral 57006 [Dimitri Tiomkin:ST]

6424 Strange Love of Martha Ivers, The (1946) Underscore + Dialog (Miklos Rozsa) US:LP = Medallion ML-314; Theme (Miklos Rozsa) US:SP = Combo 113 [Marie Greene]; Theme (Miklos Rozsa) US:LP-BP = Sound Stage 2308 [@Marie Greene]

6425 Strange One, The [End as a Man] (1957) Score (Kenyon Hopkins) US:LP = Coral CRL-57132

6426 Strange Shadows in an Empty Room [Blazing Magnum] (1976) Score (Armando Trovajoli) IT:LP = Beat LPF-033*

6427 Stranger, The *see* Thief, The

6428 Stranger, The [Lo Straniero] (1967) Excerpts (Piero Piccioni) JA:LP-MS = CBS/Sony 2305 [@ST]; Themes (Piero Piccioni) IT:SP = Parade 5046 [ST]

6429 Stranger in the House *see* Cop-Out

6430 Stranger in Town, A [Un Dollaro Fra i Denti] (1968) Themes (Benedetto Ghiglia) JA:SP = Seven Seas HIT-1446 [ST]

6431 Stranger Left No Card, The [Short] (1954) Highlights (e:Doreen Carwithen/t:Hugo Alfven) US:LP = MGM E-3151 [@ST]

6432 Stranger Returns, The [A Man, A Horse and a Gun] [Un Uomo, un Cavallo, una Pistola] (1967) Highlights (Stelvio Cipriani) IT:LP = CAM SAG-9004*; Theme (Stelvio Cipriani) US:SP = RCA 47-9654 [Henry Mancini]; Theme (Stelvio Cipriani) US:LP = UA 6710* [Leroy Holmes]

6433 Stranger Than Paradise (1985) Highlights (John Lurie) US:LP = Enigma SJ-73213*

6434 Strangers *see* Trip to Italy, A

6435 Strangers on a Train (1951) Excerpts (Dimitri Tiomkin) US:LP = Varese 704.250* [Charles Ketcham]

6436 Strangers When We Meet (1960) Theme (George Duning) US:SP = Colpix 152 [Stu Phillips]; Theme (George Duning) US:SP = Decca 9-31106 [The Sabres]; Theme (George Duning) US:LP = Columbia 8586* [Andre Previn]

6437 Strategic Air Command (1955) Theme (Victor Young) US:SP = Decca 9-29523 [Victor Young:ST]; Theme (Victor Young) US:LP = Decca 8364 [Victor Young:ST]; Theme (Victor Young) US:LP = Roulette 25023* + US:LP = Forum 9080* [Jack Shaindlin]

6438 Straw Dogs (1972) Highlights (Jerry Fielding) US:LP-MS = Citadel CTJF-2/3*

6439 Strawberry Statement, The (1969) Scores (pop music) US:LP-MS = MGM 2SES-14*

6440 Street Angel (1928) Theme [Silent I] (Erno Rapee) US:LP = RCA 2560* [Gaylord Carter]

6441 Street City (1976) Scores (Chris Reed Pruett) US:LP-MS = Creed CD-76-4901*

6442 Street Hero (1984) Score (various) AU:LP = Festival 53133*

6443 Street Music (1982) Score (Ed Bogas) US:LP = Regency RY-9505*

6444 Street of Shadows *see* Shadow Man

6445 Street People [Gli Esecutori] (1976) Theme (Luis E. Bacalov) IT:SP = General Music 353* [ST]

6446 Street Scene (1931) Theme (Alfred Newman) US:SP = Mercury 4013 [Alfred Newman:ST]; Theme (Alfred Newman) US:LP = Mercury 25093 [Alfred Newman:ST]; Theme (Alfred Newman) US:LP = RCA 1-0184* [Charles Gerhardt]

6447 Streetcar Named Desire, A (1951) Highlights (Alex North) US:LP-10 = Capitol L-289 + US:LP = Capitol T-387 + US:LP = Angel S-36068e; Excerpts (Alex North) US:LP = RCA LPM-1445/LSP-1445* [Alex North:ST]

6448 Streets of Fire (1984) Score (t:Ry Cooder/s:various) US:LP = MCA 5492*

6449 Streets of Laredo, The (1949) Theme (Jay Livingston & Ray Evans) US:78 = RCA/Victor 20-3323 [Dennis Day]

6450 Strictly Dishonorable (1951) Themes/US:SP = RCA 49-3395 [Ezio Pinza:ST]

6451 Strictly Dynamite (1934) Excerpts (various) US:LP-BP = Caliban 6013 [@ST]

6452 Strictly for Pleasure *see* Perfect Furlough, The

6453 Strictly in the Groove (1942) Theme/US:78 = Bluebird 11180 [Ozzie Nelson:ST]

6454 Strike Me Pink (1936) Excerpts (Harold Arlen) US:LP-BP = JJA 19763 [@ST]

6455 Strike Up the Band (1940) Score (e:Roger Edens/etc.) US:LP-MS-BP = Curtain Calls 100/9-10

6456 Strip, The (1951) Theme-A (Charles Wolcott) US:SP = MGM 11061 [Monica Lewis:ST]; Theme-B (Jimmy McHugh) US:SP = Mercury 5744 [Vic Damone:ST]; Theme-C (Harry Ruby) US:SP = Mercury 5710 [Kay Brown:ST]; Theme-C (Harry Ruby) US:SP = Kapp KJB-31 [Louis Armstrong:ST]

6457 Stripper, The (1963) Theme (Jerry Goldsmith) US:SP = Capitol 4921 [George Shearing]; Theme (Jerry Goldsmith) US:LP = Verve 6-8508* [Oliver Nelson]

6458 Stroker Ace (1983) Highlights (t:Al Capps/etc.) US:EP-12 = MCA 36003*; Theme (Charlie Daniels) US:SP = Epic 34-03918* [Charlie Daniels:ST]

6459 Stud, The (1978) Score (e: Biddu/etc.) GB:LP = Ronco RTD-2029*

6460 Student Prince, The (1954) Score (film songs:Nicholas Brodszky/ stage songs:Sigmund Romberg) US: LP = RCA LM-2339/LSC-2339* [Mario Lanza:ST]; Themes/US:SP = MGM 30853 [Ann Blyth:ST]

6461 Student Tour (1934) Themes-A-B/US:LP-BP = JJA 19802 [@Phil Regan:ST]; Theme-C/US:LP-BP = Star Tone 219 [Betty Grable:ST]

6462 Study in Terror, A (1966) Score-A (John Scott) US:LP = Roulette R-801/RS-801*; Score-B (John Scott) IT:LP = CAM AMG-1

6463 Stunt Man, The (1980) Score (Dominic Frontiere) US:LP = 20th T-626*

6464 Stunt Rock (1978) Score (Sorcery) GB:LP = Groovy 19-GRL-25087*

6465 Stuntman (1969) Score (Carlo Rustichelli) IT:LP = CAM 10.020

6466 Stunts [Who Is Killing the Stunt Men?] (1977) Score (Michael Kamen) US:LP = Amerama ST-251*

6467 Stuntwoman [The Animal] [L'Animal] (1977) Score (Vladimir Cosma) FR:LP = AZ Disc 75501*

6468 Submarine D-1 (1937) Theme (Max Steiner) US:LP-BP = Citadel CTMS-2 [Max Steiner:ST]

6469 Submarine X-1 (1968) Theme (Ron Goodwin) GB:LP = Philips 6308.018* [Ron Goodwin:ST]

6470 Submersion of Japan, The *see* Tidal Wave

6471 Submission [Lo Scandalo] (1979) Score (Riz Ortolani) JA:LP = Polydor MPF-1059*

6472 Subterfuge (1968) Theme (Cyril Ornadel) US:LP = Kapp 3588* [The Brass Hat]; Theme (Cyril Ornadel) US:LP = Camden 2364* [The Living Strings]

6473 Subterraneans, The (1960) Score (Andre Previn) US:LP = MGM E-3812/SE-3812*

6474 Suburbia (1984) Score (e:Alex Gibson/etc.) US:LP = Enigma E-1093*

6475 Subway (1985) Score (Eric Serra) US:LP = Varese STV-81269*

6476 Such a Gorgeous Kid Like Me [A Gorgeous Bird Like Me] [Un Belle Fille comme Moi] (1972) Themes (Georges Delerue) US:LP = DRG 9519* [Georges Delerue:ST]

6477 Such Good Friends (1971) Score (Thomas Z Shepard) US:LP-PP = TS 79820*; Theme (Thomas Z. Shepard) US:SP = Columbia 1042* [O.C. Smith: ST]; Theme (Thomas Z. Shepard) US: LP = Columbia 31455* [@O.C. Smith: ST]

6478 Such Men Are Dangerous *see* Racers, The

6479 Sucker, The [Le Corniaud] (1965) Highlights (Georges Delerue) FR: EP = Barclay 70773

6480 Sucre, Le [Sugar] (1980) Score (Philippe Sarde) FR:LP = Pathe C066. 14705*

6481 Sudden Fear (1952) Theme (Elmer Bernstein) US:LP = Mainstream 6094 + US:LP = Ava 11* [Elmer Bernstein:ST]

6482 Sudden Impact (1983) Excerpts

(Lalo Schifrin) US:LP = Viva/WB 23990-1* [Lalo Schifrin:ST]

6483 Sugar Cane Alley [Rue Casas Negres] (1984) Score (e:Euzhan Palcy/etc.) FR:LP = Saravah 1104*

6484 Sugar Colt (1970) Themes (Luis E. Bacalov) IT:SP = Parade 5007 [ST]

6485 Sugar Hill [Voodoo Girl] [The Zombies of Sugar Hill] (1974) Theme (Nick Zesses) US:SP = Soul 35112* [The Originals:ST]

6486 Sugarfoot (1951) Theme (Max Steiner) US:LP = Coral 757267* [Lawrence Welk]; Theme (Max Steiner) US:LP = Columbia 8400* [Johnny Gregory]

6487 Suicide Squadron [Dangerous Moonlight] (1941) Theme (Richard Addinsell) US:LP-10 = Columbia ML-2092 [@Muir Mathieson:ST]; Theme (Richard Addinsell) US:LP = Capitol 8598* + US:LP = Angel 36062* [Leonard Pennario]; Theme (Richard Addinsell) US:SP = Kapp 246 [Roger Williams]

6488 Suitor, The [Le Soupirant] (1963) Highlights (Jean Paillaud) FR:EP = Philips 27036

6489 Suleiman the Conqueror [Solimano il Conquistatore] (1962) Scores (Francesco DeMasi) IT:LP-MS = Beat CR-6-7

6490 Summer and Smoke (1961) Score (Elmer Bernstein) US:LP = RCA LOC-1067/LSO-1067* + US:LP = Entracte ERS-6519*

6491 Summer Holiday (1963) Score-A (Peter Myers & Ronald Cass) US:LP = Epic LN-24063/BN-26063*; Score-B (s:Peter Myers & Ronald Cass/t:Stanley Black) GB:LP = Columbia CX-1052

6492 Summer Love (1958) Score (s:Henry Mancini/t:Rod McKuen) US:LP = Decca DL-8714

6493 Summer Lovers (1982) Score (t:Basil Poledouris/s:various) US:LP = WB 23695-1*

6494 Summer Madness *see* Summertime

6495 Summer Magic (1963) Score (Richard & Robert Sherman) US:LP = Buena Vista BV-4025/ST-4025*

6496 Summer Manoeuvres *see* Grand Maneuver, The

6497 Summer of '42 (1971) Themes (Michel Legrand) US:LP = WB 1925* [Michel Legrand:ST]; Theme (Michel Legrand) US:SP = WB 7486* [Michel Legrand:ST]

6498 Summer Place, A (1959) Highlights (Max Steiner) US:LP = Film Music Collection FMC-1* [Elmer Bernstein]

6499 Summer Run (1974) Theme (Patrick Farrell) US:SP = Far-Out 101* [Patrick Farrell:ST]

6500 Summer Soldiers (1972) Excerpts (Toru Takemitsu) JA:LP = RCA/Victor 1070 [Toru Takemitsu:ST]

6501 Summer Stock [If You Feel Like Singing] (1950) Highlights (Harry Warren) US:LP-10 = MGM E-519 + US:LP = MGM E-3234 + US:LP-MS = MGM 2SES-52

6502 Summer Wishes, Winter Dreams (1973) Theme (Johnny Mandel) US:LP = CTI 6045* [George Benson]

6503 Summer with Monika *see* Monika

6504 Summerdog (1977) Score (Jim Lamont) US:LP-PP = JM 1177*

6505 Summertime [Summer Madness] (1956) Themes (Alessandro Cicognini-aka-Icini) US:SP = RCA 47-6201 [Rossano Brazzi:ST]; Theme (Alessandro Cicognini-aka-Icini) US:SP = Coral 9-61864 [Dick Jacobs]; Theme (Alessandro Cicognini-aka-Icini) US:LP = MGM 3397* [David Rose]

6506 Summertime Killer, The (1972) Score (Luis E. Bacalov) JA:LP = Seven Seas FML-6*

6507 Summit (1968) Themes (Mario Nascimbene) IT:SP = Parade 5065 [ST]

6508 Sun Also Rises, The (1957) Score (e:Hugo Friedhofer/t:Lionel Newman/t:Alexander Courage/etc.) US:LP = Kapp KDL-7001

6509 Sun Comes Up, The (1949) Theme (Andre Previn) US:SP = RCA 49-0773 [Jeanette MacDonald:ST]

6510 Sun Shines Bright, The (1953) Excerpts (Victor Young) US:LP = Citadel CTV-7029 [@ST]

6511 Sun Valley Serenade (1941) Score (e:Harry Warren/etc.) US:LP-MS = 20th TCF-100/TCS-100e + US:LP-MS = 20th 2T-904e

6512 Sunbonnet Sue (1945) Themes/US:78 = Majestic 7161 [Phil Regan:ST]

6513 Sunburn (1979) Score (e:John Cameron/etc.) US:LP = Arrival NU-9540*

6514 Sunday in New York (1963) Score (Peter Nero) US:LP = RCA LPM-2827/LSP-2827*

6515 Sunday in the Country, A [Un Dimanche a la Campagne] (1984) Highlights (t:Philippe Sarde/e:classical music) US:LP = Varese STV-81227*

6516 Sunday on the Range / Highlights (Tim Spencer) US:LP-10 = Sacred LP-7023

6517 Sunday Woman, The [La Donna della Domeneca] (1975) Themes (Ennio Morricone) IT:SP = Cinevox MDF-087* [ST]

6518 Sundays and Cybele (1962) Theme (Maurice Jarre) US:LP = WB 1548* [Werner Muller]

6519 Sundowners, The (1961) Score (Dimitri Tiomkin) US:LP-BP = Cinema LP-8014; Theme (Dimitri Tiomkin) US: SP = Liberty 55282 [Felix Slatkin]; Theme (Dimitri Tiomkin) US:LP = Dot 25349* [Billy Vaughn]

6520 Sunflower, The (1970) Score (Henry Mancini) US:LP = Avco AV-11001*

6521 Sunny Side of the Street, The (1951) Highlights (various) US:LP-10 = Mercury MG-25100 [Frankie Laine/Billy Daniels:ST]

6522 Sunny Skies (1930) Theme/ US:78 = Brunswick 4798 [Benny Rubin: ST]

6523 Sunnyside (1979) Score (e: Stephen Longfellow Fiske/etc.) US: LP = American International AILP-3002* [The New York City Band: ST]

6524 Sunrise at Campobello (1960) Excerpts (Franz Waxman) US:LP = Entracte ERS-6506* [Fred Steiner]

6525 Sunset Boulevard (1950) Excerpts (Franx Waxman) US:LP = RCA ARL1-0708* [Charles Gerhardt]

6526 Sunset, Sunrise (1974) Score (Nino Rota) JA:LP = Cine Disc 3001*

6527 Sunshine Susie *see* Office Girl

6528 Sunstruck (1972) Highlights (t:Peter Knight/e:various) AU:EP = Philips 6205.022

6529 Super Fuzz [Poliziotto Superpiu] (1981) Score (La Bionda) IT:LP = Durium 30.365*

6530 Super Spook / Themes (Rheet Taylor) US:SP-PP = Superspook 3540 [Sonny Smith:ST]

6531 Superdad (1974) Theme (Shane Tatum) US:SP = Buena Vista 561 [Bobby Goldsboro:ST]

6532 Superfly (1972) Score (s:Curtis Mayfield/as:Johnny Pate) US:LP = Curtom CU-8014* + US:LP = RSO RS1-3046*

6533 Superfly T.N.T. (1973) Score (Osibisa) US:LP = Buddah BDS-5136*

6534 Supergirl (1984) Score (Jerry Goldsmith) US:LP = Varese STV-81231*

6535 Superman (1978) Scores (John Williams) US:LP-MS = WB 2BSK-3257*

6536 Superman II (1981) Score (as: Ken Thorne) US:LP = WB HS-3505*

6537 Superman III (1983) Score (e: Giorgio Moroder/ae:Ken Thorne) US: LP = WB 23879-1*

6538 Surf Party (1964) Score (e: Jimmie Haskell/etc.) US:LP = 20th 3131

6539 Surfer Girls (1978) Score (Michael Gabbert) US:LP = Oakwood SUS-1001*

6540 Surprise Package (1960) Theme (James Van Heusen) US:SP = Dot 16192 [Louis Prima & Keely Smith]

6541 Surprise Party (1984) Score (Michel Magne) FR:LP = WEA Flarenasch 723-658*

6542 Survival Run (1977) *see* Damnation Alley

6543 Survival Run (1979) Highlights (Gary William Friedman) US:LP-PP = OC 8020*

6544 Survivor, The (1980) Score (Brian May) FR:LP = Disco Shop DS-1*

6545 Susan Slept Here (1954) Theme (Richard Myers) US:SP = Coral 9-61206 [Don Cornell:ST]; Theme (Richard Myers) US:LP = Richmond 20060 [Cyril Stapleton]

6546 Susie, The Little Blue Coup [Cartoon] (1952) Theme (Buddy Ebsen) US:LP = Disneyland 1335 [@ST]

6547 Suspects, The [Les Suspects]

(1974) Themes (Francois De Roubaix) FR:SP = Philips 2232* [ST]

6548 Susperia (1977) Score (Goblin) GB:LP = EMI EMC-3222* + IT:LP = Cinevox 33/108*

6549 Susperia II *see* Deep Red

6550 Suspicion (1941) Excerpts (Franz Waxman) US:LP = Varese 704.250* [Charles Ketcham]

6551 Suzy (1936) Theme/US:LP-MS = MCA 2-11002 [@Cary Grant:ST]

6552 Swallows and Amazons (1974) Underscore + Dialog (Wilfred Josephs) GB:LP = MFP 50155*

6553 Swamp Thing (1982) Score (Harry Manfredini) US:LP = Varese STV-81154*

6554 Swan, The (1956) Score (Bronislau Kaper) US:LP = MGM E-3300

6555 Swan Lake (1957) Score (classical music) US:LP = Melodiya M-27018/MS-27018*

6556 Swan Lake / Scores (classical music) US:LP-MS = Angel B-3706/SB-3706* [John Lanchbery:ST]

6557 Swanee River (1939) Highlights (pop music) US:LP-10 = Decca DL-5303 [Al Jolson:ST]; Highlights + Dialog (pop music) US:LP-BP = Totem 1028 [Al Jolson:ST]

6558 Swann in Love [Un Amour de Swann] (1984) Highlights (Hans-Werner Henze) US:LP = Varese STV-81224*

6559 Swarm, The (1978) Score (Jerry Goldsmith) US:LP = WB BSK-3208*

6560 Swashbuckler [The Scarlet Buccaneer] (1976) Score (John Addison) US:LP = MCA 2096*

6561 Sweater Girl (1942) Themes/ US:LP-BP = JJA 19767 [@Betty Jane Rhodes:ST]

6562 Sweden, Heaven and Hell (1969) Score (Piero Umiliani) US:LP = Ariel LP-216/ASLP-216*

6563 Swedish Fly Girls [Christa] (1972) Score (Mose Henry) US:LP = Juno S-1003*

6564 Sweeney (1978) Theme (Denis King) GB:SP = EMI 2578* [Denis King: ST]

6565 Sweeney II (1979) Theme (Tony Hatch) GB:SP = EMI 2780* [Tony Hatch:ST]

6566 Sweet Adeline (1935) Highlights-A (Jerome Kern) US:LP-BP = JJA 19747 [@ST]; Highlights-B (Jerome Kern) US:LP-BP = Titania 506

6567 Sweet and Sour [Dragees au Poivre] (1962) Highlights (Ward Swingle) FR:EP = Philips 432.962

6568 Sweet Body of Deborah, The [Il Dolce Corpo di Deborah] (1969) Score (Nora Orlandi) IT:LP = CAM 10.011

6569 Sweet Charity (1969) Score (stage songs:Cy Coleman) US:LP = Decca DL-71502*

6570 Sweet Dreams (1985) Score (pop music) US:LP = MCA 6149*

6571 Sweet Ecstasy [Douce Violence] (1963) Highlights (Georges Garvarentz) FR:EP = Philips 460.815; Theme (Georges Garvarentz) US:LP = Philips 600.071* [@ST]

6572 Sweet Jesus, Preacher Man (1973) Theme (Landy McNeal) US:SP = Lion 148* [We the People:ST]

6573 Sweet Love, Bitter [It Won't Rub Off, Baby] (1967) Score (Mal Waldron) US:LP = Impulse A-9142/AS-9142*

6574 Sweet Movie (1975) Score (Manos Hadjidakis) FR:LP = Spot 69624*

6575 Sweet Music (1935) Themes-A-B/US:LP = Audio Rarities 2330 [Helen Morgan:ST]; Themes-C-D/US: 78 = RCA/Victor 24827 [Rudy Vallee: ST]; Themes-E-F/US:78 = RCA/Victor 24833 [Rudy Vallee:ST]

6576 Sweet November (1968) Themes (Michel Legrand/Leslie Bricusse & Anthony Newley) US:SP = WB 7174 [Michel Legrand/Anthony Newley:ST]; Theme (Leslie Bricusse & Anthony Newley) US:LP = Reprise 6324* [Sammy Davis, Jr.]

6577 Sweet Ride, The (1968) Score (s:Pete Rugolo/t:Lee Hazlewood) US: LP = 20th S-4198*

6578 Sweet Rosie O'Grady (1943) Highlights (e:Harry Warren/etc.) US: LP-BP = Titania 507

6579 Sweet Sixteen (1983) Score (Mark Wertman & Joel Wertman) US: LP = Regency RI-8505*

6580 Sweet Smell of Success, The

(1957) Score-A (Elmer Bernstein) US: LP = Decca DL-8610; Score-B (Fred Katz & Chico Hamilton) US:LP = Decca DL-8614

6581 Sweet Sweetback's Baadasssss Song (1971) Score (Melvin Van Peebles) US:LP = Stax STS-3001*

6582 Sweetheart of the Campus (1941) Theme/US:78 = Bluebird 11155 [Harriet Hilliard:ST]

6583 Sweethearts (1938) Highlights + Dialog (stage songs:Victor Herbert) US:LP-BP = Pelican LP-143 + US:LP-BP = Sandy Hook SH-2025

6584 Sweetie (1929) Excerpts (Richard A. Whiting) US:LP-BP = Caliban 6018 [@ST]

6585 Swept Away . . . (1974) Score (Piero Piccioni) US:LP = Peters PLD-1005*

6586 Swimmer, The (1968) Score (s: Marvin Hamlisch/as:Leo Shuken & Jack Hayes) US:LP = Columbia OS-3210*

6587 Swimming Pool, The [La Piscine] (1968) Excerpts (Michel Legrand) US:LP = UA UAS-6715* [Michel Legrand:ST]; Theme (Michel Legrand) US:SP = Columbia 4-45250* [Robert Goulet]

6588 Swindle, The *see* Il Bidone

6589 Swing Fever (1944) Highlights (various) US:LP-BP = Caliban 6038

6590 Swing High, Swing Low (1937) Themes-A-B/US:LP-BP = Legends 1000/4 [Dorothy Lamour:ST]; Theme-C/US:LP = Epic 159 [@Dorothy Lamour:ST]; Theme-D/US:LP-BP = Star Tone 205 [@Carole Lombard:ST]

6591 Swing Time (1936) Highlights (Jerome Kern) US:LP-BP = Sountrak STK-106 + US:LP-BP = Sandy Hook SH-2028; Excerpts (Jerome Kern) US: LP = Columbia SG-32472 [Fred Astaire: ST]

6592 Swing While You're Able (1937) Theme/US:78 = Brunswick 7849 [Pinky Tomlin:ST]

6593 Swinger, The (1966) Excerpts (t:Marty Paich/t:Andre Previn/etc.) US:LP = RCA LPM-3710/LSP-3710* [Ann-Margret:ST]

6594 Swingers' Paradise [Wonderful Life] (1964) Score (e:Ronald Cass & Peter Myers/etc.) US:LP = Epic LN-24145/BN-26145* [Cliff Richard:ST]

6595 Swingin' Maiden, The [The Iron Maiden] (1962) Theme (Eric Rogers) GB:SP = Decca 11585 [Eric Rogers:ST]

6596 Swingin' Summer, A (1966) Score (uncredited) US:LP = Hanna Barbera HLP-8500/HST-9500*

6597 Swinging Set, The *see* Get Yourself a College Girl

6598 Swirl of Glory *see* Sugarfoot

6599 Swiss Cheese Family Robinson [Cartoon] (1947) Sequence + Dialog (Philip Scheib) US:LP = Peter Pan 1118 [@ST]

6600 Swiss Family Robinson, The (1960) Theme + Narration (Terry Gilkyson) US:LP = Disneyland DQ-1280 + US:LP = Disneyland ST-1907; Theme (Terry Gilkyson) US:SP = Buena Vista 365 [Camarata]

6601 Swiss Miss (1938) Theme/US: LP = Mark 56 #575 [Laurel & Hardy:ST]

6602 Swiss Miss [Cartoon] (1951) Sequence + Dialog (Philip Scheib) US: LP = Peter Pan 1118 [@ST]

6603 Switzerland [Short] (1955) Highlights (Paul Smith) US:LP = Disneyland WDL-4003

6604 Sword and the Sorcerer, The (1982) Score (David Whitaker) US:LP = Varese STV-81158*

6605 Sword in the Stone, The (1963) Highlights + Narration (Richard & Robert Sherman) US:LP = Disneyland DQ-1236 + US:LP = Disneyland ST-4901 + US:LP-MS = Disneyland DDF-3 [Studio Cast]

6606 Sword of Lancelot, The [Lancelot and Guinevere] (1963) Theme (Ron Goodwin) GB:LP-MS = EMI TWO-108* + GB:LP = EMI TWO-339* [Ron Goodwin:ST]

6607 Sylvester (1985) Highlights (various) US:EP-12 = MCA 39026*

6608 Sylvia (1965) Score (David Raksin) US:LP = Mercury MG-21004/SR-61004*

6609 Symphony for a Massacre [The Mystifiers] [Symphonie pour un Massacre] (1965) Themes (Michel Magne) US:SP = Audio Fidelity 108 [Michel Magne:ST]; Theme (Michel

Magne) US:LP = Camden 2161* [The Living Strings]

6610 Symphony for Two Spies [Serenade for Two Spies] [Sinfonia per Due Spie] (1966) Score (Francesco DeMasi) IT:LP = CAM CDR.33-5

6611 Symphony Hour [Cartoon] (1941) Theme (at:Charles Wolcott) US: LP-MS = Ovation 5000 [@ST]

6612 Symphony in Black [Short] (1935) Excerpts (pop music) US:LP = Biograph BLPM-2 [Duke Ellington: ST]

6613 Symphony of Six Million [The Melody of Life] (1932) Theme (Max Steiner) US:LP-BP = Max Steiner Music Society 25781 [Max Steiner:ST]

6614 Symposium on Popular Songs, A [Cartoon] (1962) Theme (Richard & Robert Sherman) US:LP = Glendale 6032* ["Dawgs" Stage Cast]

6615 Synanon [Get Off My Back] (1965) Score (Neal Hefti) US:LP = Liberty LRP-3413/LST-7413*

6616 Syncopation (1929) Themes-A-B/US:78 = RCA/Victor 21860 [Morton Downey:ST]; Themes-B-C/US:78 = RCA/Victor 21870 [Fred Waring:ST]

T

6617 T.A.M.I. Show, The (1964) Theme-A/US:SP = Mercury 30124 [Lesley Gore:ST]; Theme-B/US:SP = Motown 405 [Marvin Gaye:ST]; Theme-C/US:SP = Motown 427 [The Supremes: ST]; Theme-D/US:SP = Liberty 55766 [Jan and Dean:ST]; Theme-E/US:SP = King 5853 [James Brown:ST]; Theme-F/ US:SP = London 9708 [The Rolling Stones:ST]

6618 T.R. Baskin [A Date with a Lonely Girl] (1972) Score (Jack Elliott) US:LP = Paramount PAS-6018*

6619 Taboos of the World [Tabu] [I Tabu] (1965) Score (e:A.F. Lavagnino/e:Armando Trovajoli) IT:LP = CAM 30-079

6620 Tabu *see* Taboos of the World

6621 Tahiti, My Island [Short] (1954) Theme (Victor Young) US:SP = Decca 9-27598 [Dick Haymes & Victor Young:ST]; Theme (Victor Young) US:78 = MGM 30369 [Macklin Marrow]

6622 Tail Spin (1939) Theme-A/ US:LP-BP = Scarce Rarities 5502 [Alice Faye:ST]; Theme-B/US:LP-BP = Choice Cuts 500/1 [@Alice Faye:ST]

6623 Tai-Pan (1986) Score (Maurice Jarre) US:LP = Varese STV-81293*

6624 Take a Chance (1933) Theme-A/US:LP = Epic 15105 [@Cliff Edwards: ST]; Theme-B/US:LP = Epic B2N-164 [@Cliff Edwards:ST]; Theme-C/US: LP-BP = JJA 19802 [@Lillian Roth:ST]

6625 Take a Giant Step (1959) Theme (Jay Livingston & Ray Evans) US:SP = ABC 10046 [Johnny Nash:ST]

6626 Take Her, She's Mine (1963) Theme (Jerry Goldsmith) GB:EP = 20th/Stateside 1021 [Bill Ramal]

6627 Take Me High (1973) Score (Tony Cole) GB:LP = EMI EMC-3016* [Cliff Richard:ST]

6628 Take Me Out to the Ball Game (1949) Score (e:Roger Edens/etc.) US: LP-BP = Curtain Calls 100/18

6629 Take My Life (1947) Theme (William Alwyn) GB:78-PP = Rank FM-21 [ST]

6630 Take My Tip (1937) Theme/ GB:LP = WRC 113 [Jack Hulbert:ST]

6631 Take the High Ground (1953) Theme-A (Dimitri Tiomkin) US:SP = MGM 30778 [John Green]; Theme-B (Dimitri Tiomkin) US:SP = Capitol 2568 [Les Baxter]; Theme-B (Dimitri Tiomkin) US:LP = Capitol 594 [Les Baxter]

6632 Take the Money and Run (1969) Theme (Marvin Hamlisch) US: LP = Command 941* [Richard Hayman]

6633 Take This Job and Shove It (1981) Score (t:Michael Lloyd/s:various) US:LP = Epic SE-37177*

6634 Taking Off (1971) Score (various) US:LP = Decca DL-79181*

6635 Tale of the Priest and His Hired Man Balda, The (1933) Excerpts (Dmitri Shostakovich) GB:LP = EMI Melodiya ASD-1650331* [Gennady Rozhdestvensky]

6636 Tale of Two Cities, A (1958) Theme (Richard Addinsell) US:LP-BP = Citadel CTOFI-1 [@ST]; Theme

(Richard Addinsell) US:LP = Rondolette 160 [Russ Case]; Theme (Richard Addinsell) GB:LP = Saga 5018* + GB: LP = Boulevard 4028* [Gilbert Vintner]

6637 Tales of Hoffmann, The (1951) Scores (classical music) US:LP-MS = London LLPA-4

6638 Tales of Mystery *see* Spirits of the Dead

6639 Tales of Paris [Les Parisiennes] (1962) Highlights (Georges Garvarentz) FR:EP = Fontana 460.820

6640 Tall Blond Man with One Black Shoe, The [Le Grand Blond avec Une Chaussure Noire] (1972) Highlights (Vladimir Cosma) FR:LP = Deesse DDLX-77*

6641 Tall Headlines *see* Frightened Bride, The

6642 Tall Men, The (1955) Theme (at:Ken Darby) US:SP = Decca 9-29659 [Victor Young:ST]; Theme (at:Ken-Darby) US:LP = Decca 8364 [Victor Young:ST]; Theme (at:Ken Darby) US: SP = Columbia 4-42147 [Johnny Cash]

6643 Tall Story (1960) Theme (Andre Previn & Shelly Manne) US:SP = Atco 6161 [Bobby Darin:ST]

6644 Tall Stranger, The (1957) Themes (Hans J. Salter) US:LP = Medallion 313 [Hans J. Salter:ST]

6645 Tall Timbers (1937) Theme (Evans & Rasbach) US:LP = DRG 8202* [William Motzing]

6646 Tamarind Seed, The (1974) Theme (John Barry) GB:LP = Polydor 2383.300* [John Barry:ST]

6647 Taming of the Shrew, The [La Bisbetica Domata] (1967) Excerpts (Nino Rota) IT:LP = CAM SAG-9054* [Nino Rota & Carlo Savina:ST]; Underscore + Dialog (Nino Rota) US:LP = RCA VDM-117

6648 Tammy and the Bachelor (1957) Highlights (e:Frank Skinner/t:Jay Livingston & Ray Evans) US:LP = Coral CRL-57159

6649 Tammy Tell Me True (1961) Theme (Dorothy Squires) US:SP = Decca 9-31265 [Sandra Dee:ST]; Theme (Dorothy Squires) US:SP = Columbia 4-42011 [Percy Faith:ST]; Theme (Dorothy Squires) US:LP = Columbia 8427* [Percy Faith:ST]

6650 Tanga Tiki (1953) Theme (E. Lund) US:SP = Columbia 4-40100 [Mitch Miller]; Theme (E. Lund) US: LP = Capitol 1447* [Alfred Newman]

6651 Tarantula (1955) Theme (Henry Mancini) US:LP = Coral 757240* + US:LP = Varese 81077* [Dick Jacobs]

6652 Taras Bulba (1962) Score (Franz Waxman) US:LP = UA UAL-4100/UAS-5100*

6653 Target for Tonight (1941) Theme (Leighton Lucas) GB:78 = EMI EPX-21 [Leighton Lucas:ST]; Theme (Leighton Lucas) GB:78 = HMV RAF-11 [The Central Band of the Royal Air Force]

6654 Tarka the Otter (1979) Highlights + Underscore + Dialog (David Fanshawe) GB:LP = Argo ZSW-613*

6655 Tarot (1973) Highlights (Michel Colombier) JA:LP = A&M 12*

6656 Tarzan, The Ape Man (1960) Score (Shorty Rogers) US:LP = MGM E-3798/SE-3798* [Shorty Rogers:ST]

6657 Taste of Violence, A [Le Gout de Violence] (1964) Highlights (Andre Hossein) FR:EP = Fontana 460.783; Theme (Andre Hossein) US:LP = Philips 600-071 [@ST]

6658 Taste the Blood of Dracula (1970) Sequence + Narration (James Bernard) US:LP = Capitol 11340* [@ST]

6659 Taxi Driver (1976) Score (Bernard Herrmann) US:LP = Arista AL-4079* + US:LP = Sweet Thunder 2* + US:LP = Arista ALS-8179* [Bernard Herrmann:ST/Dave Blume]

6660 Taxi for Tobruk [Un Taxi pour Tobbrouk] (1965) Highlights (Georges Garvarentz) FR:EP = Bel Air 211.035; Theme (Georges Garvarentz) US:LP = Mercury 60741* [Charles Aznavour]

6661 Tchaikovsky (1970) Highlights + Underscore + Narration (u: Dimitri Tiomkin/e:classical music) GB: LP-MS = Philips 6641.048*

6662 Tchao Pantin (1985) Score (Charlelie Couture) GE:LP = Island 205-985-320*

6663 Tea for Two (1950) Highlights-A (pop music) US:LP-10 = Columbia CL-6149 + US:LP = CSP P-17660

[Doris Day:ST]; Highlights-B (pop music) US:LP-BP = Caliban 6031

6664 Teachers (1984) Score (various) US:LP = Capitol SV-12371*

6665 Teacher's Pet (1958) Theme-A (Joe Lubin) US:SP = Columbia 4-41123 [Doris Day:ST]; Theme-A (Joe Lubin) US:LP = Columbia 8635* [Doris Day: ST]; Theme-B/US:LP = Rhino 70819 [Mamie Van Doren:ST]

6666 Teahouse of the August Moon (1956) Theme (Saul Chaplin) US: SP = MGM 12392 [Leroy Holmes]; Theme (Saul Chaplin) US:LP = Dot 25364* [Elmer Bernstein]

6667 Teen Wolf (1985) Score (Miles Goodman) US:LP = Southern Cross SCRS-1010*

6668 Teenage Cruisers (1980) Score (pop music) US:LP = Rhino RNLP-016*

6669 Teenage Millionaire (1961) Score (uncredited) US:LP = Ace LP-1014 [Jimmy Clanton:ST]

6670 Teenage Rebel (1956) Theme (Lionel Newman) US:SP = Coral 9-61711 [Dorothy Collins]; Theme (Lionel Newman) US:SP = Decca 9-30042 [Eddie Fontaine]

6671 Teenage Rebellion (1967) Score (e:Bob Summers/t:Mike Curb/t: Harley Hatcher/etc.) US:LP = Sidewalk 5903/ST-5903*

6672 Tell Me Lies [U.S.] (1967) Score (stage songs:Richard Peaslee) US: LP = Gre Gar 5000/S-5000*

6673 Tell Me That You Love Me, Junie Moon (1970) Score (Philip Springer) US:LP = Columbia OS-3540*

6674 Tell Me Tonight / Theme (Mischa Spoliansky) US:SP = RCA 47-3987 [Tony Martin]; Theme (Mischa Spoliansky) GB:SP = Parlophone 8639 [ST]

6675 Tempest, The (1980) Theme/ GB:SP = Industrial 0012* [Elisabeth Welch:ST]

6676 Tempest (1982) Score (Stomu Yamashta) US:LP = Casablanca NBLP-7269*

6677 Tempi Duri per i Vampire *see* Uncle Was a Vampire

6678 Tempter, The (1974) *see* Devil Is a Woman, The

6679 Tempter, The [L'Anticristo] (1979) Themes (Ennio Morricone) IT: SP = Beat BTF-089* [ST]

6680 Temptress, The (1926) Excerpts (Ernst Luz) US:LP = Pelican LP-2011* [Gaylord Carter]

6681 10 (1979) Score (Henry Mancini) US:LP = WB BSK-3399*

6682 Ten Commandments, The (1956) Scores-A (Elmer Bernstein) US: LP-MS = Dot DLP-3054; Scores-B (Elmer Bernstein) US:LP-MS = Dot DLP-25054* + US:LP-MS = Paramount PAS-1006*

6683 Ten Days' Wonder [La Decade Prodigieuse] (1971) Highlights (Pierre Jansen) FR:LP = RCA 37653*

6684 Ten Thousand Bedrooms (1957) Highlights (Nicholas Brodszky) US:EP = Capitol EAP1-840 [Dean Martin:ST]; Theme/US:SP = Capitol 3648 [Dean Martin:ST]

6685 10 to Midnight (1983) Score (Robert O. Ragland) US:LP = Varese STV-81172*

6686 Ten to Survive (1983) Score (t:Luis E. Bacalov/t:Ennio Morricone/ t:Nino Rota/t:Egisto Macchi/etc.) IT: LP = WB/WEA 58442*

6687 Ten Who Dared (1960) Themes (Stan Jones) US:SP = Buena Vista 364 [The Ranger Chorus]

6688 Tender Dracula [La Grande Trouille] (1975) Score (Karl Heinz Schafer) FR:LP = Eden Roc 62503*; Theme (Karl Heinz Schafer) US:LP-BP = GSF 1002 [@Karl Heinz Schafer: ST]

6689 Tender Is the Night (1962) Score (t:Sammy Fain/s:pop music) US: LP = 20th FXG-3054/FXS-3054*

6690 Tender Mercies (1983) Score (e:Charlie Craig/etc.) US:LP = Liberty LO-51147*

6691 Tender Moment, The [Le Lecon Particuliere] (1968) Score (Francis Lai) FR:LP = AZ Disc 7231*; Theme (Francis Lai) US:SP = Quad 110* [Neely Plumb]

6692 Tender Trap, The (1955) Theme (James Van Heusen) US:SP = MGM 12086 [Debbie Reynolds:ST]; Theme (James Van Heusen) US:SP = Capitol 3290 [Frank Sinatra:ST]; Theme (James Van Heusen) US:LP = MGM

3294 [@Debbie Reynolds:ST]; Theme (James Van Heusen) US:LP = Capitol 2700 [Frank Sinatra:ST]

6693 Tendres Cousines [Tender Cousins] [Cousins in Love] (1981) Themes (Jean-Marie Senia) FR:SP = Riviera 620.602* [ST]

6694 Tenebrae (1983) Score (Claudio Simonetti & Fabio Pignatelli & Massimo Morante) GB:LP = That's Entertainment TER-1064*

6695 Tension at Table Rock (1956) Themes (Dimitri Tiomkin/Josef Myrow) US:EP-PP = RCA DJ-14 [Vaughn Monroe/Eddy Arnold:ST]; Theme-A (Dimitri Tiomkin) US:SP = RCA 47-6703 [Vaughn Monroe]; Theme-B (Josef Myrow) US:SP = RCA 47-6699 [Eddy Arnold:ST]

6696 Tentacles (1977) Score (Stelvio Cipriani) IT:LP = CAM SAG-9079*

6697 Tenth Victim, The [La Decima Vittima] (1965) Score (Piero Piccioni) US:LP = Mainstream 56071/S-6071*

6698 Teorema [Theoreme] (1968) Score (e:Ennio Morricone/e:classical music) IT:LP = Ariete 2002 + FR:LP = Barclay 80128*

6699 Tepepa (1968) Score (Ennio Morricone) US:LP = Cerberus CEMS-0106*

6700 Teresa the Thief [Teresa la Ladra] (1979) Theme (Riz Ortolani) FR:LP = EMI C054.17961* [@Riz Ortolani:ST]

6701 Terminator, The (1984) Score (e:Brad Fiedel/e:various) US:LP = Enigma 72000-1*

6702 Terms of Endearment (1983) Highlights + Underscore + Dialog (Michael Gore) US:LP = Capitol SV-12329*

6703 Terra Sancta [Short] (1967) Excerpts (Robert Muczynski) US:LP-PP = Music Library 7119 [Robert Muczynski:ST]

6704 Terror After Midnight [Minuten Nach Mitternach] (1962) Score (Bert Kaempfert) GE:LP = Polydor 46581

6705 Terror by Night (1946) Underscore + Dialog (au:Milton Rosen) US:LP = Murray Hill 55455

6706 Terror House *see* Night Has Eyes, The

6707 Terror in the Woods [Whatever Happened to Solange?] [Cosa Avete Fatto a Solange?] (1973) Score (Ennio Morricone) IT:LP = RCA SP-8062*

6708 Terror of Mecha-Godzilla, The (1978) Themes (Akira Ifukube) JA:LP = Toho 8100 [@ST]

6709 Terror of the Steppe [The Mighty Khan] [I Predoni della Steppa] (1963) Highlights (Carlo Rustichelli) IT:EP = CAM 45-115

6710 Terror of Tiny Town, The (1938) Theme (Lew Porter) US:LP = Rhino 307 [@ST]

6711 Terror Vision (1986) Score (e:Richard Band/e:various) US:LP = Restless 72120-1*

6712 Terrorists, The [Ransom] [Un Homme Voit Rouge] (1975) Score (Jerry Goldsmith) GB:LP = Dart 65376* + FR:LP = Pathe C066.96525*

6713 Tess (1980) Score-A (Philippe Sarde) US:LP = MCA 5193*; Score-B (Philippe Sarde) FR:LP = Philips 9101.279*

6714 Texans, The (1938) Theme (Ralph Rainger) US:78 = Decca 2001 [Bing Crosby]

6715 Texas Across the River (1966) Theme (James Van Heusen) US:SP = Decca 9-32040 [The Kingston Trio:ST]

6716 Texas Carnival (1951) Themes/ US:78 = MGM 444 [Howard Keel:ST]

6717 Texas Chainsaw Massacre, Part 2 (1986) Score (various) US:LP = IRS 6184*

6718 Texas Lady (1955) Theme (Paul Sawtell) US:SP = Capitol 3301 [Les Paul and Mary Ford]

6719 Texas Romance—1909, A (1964) Highlights (Harvey Schmidt) US:LP-PP = Chap Stk 1069*

6720 Texican, The [Ringo il Texano] (1966) Score (Nico Fidenco) IT:LP = RCA SP-8014

6721 Thank God It's Friday (1978) Scores (t:Alec R. Costandinos/t:Giorgio Moroder/etc.) US:LP-MS = Casablanca NBLP-7099*

6722 Thank You, Aunt *see* Grazie, Zia

6723 Thank Your Lucky Stars (1943) Score (Arthur Schwartz) US:LP-BP = Curtain Calls 100/8 + US:LP-

BP = Sandy Hook SH-2012 + US:LP-BP = Show Biz 5606

6724 Thanks a Million (1935) Highlights (Arthur Johnston) US:LP-BP = Caliban 6021

6725 Thanks for the Memory (1938) Theme/US:LP-BP = JJA 19762 [@Bob Hope & Shirley Ross:ST]

6726 That Certain Age (1938) Theme-A/US:78-MS = Decca 35 [Deanna Durbin]; Theme-B/US:LP = Decca 8785 [Deanna Durbin:ST]

6727 That Certain Feeling (1956) Themes (Winton Freedley) US:SP = RCA 47-6577 [Bob Hope:ST]

6728 That Cold Day in the Park (1969) Theme (Johnny Mandel) US:LP = A&M 3023* [Quincy Jones]

6729 That Dangerous Age *see* If This Be Sin

6730 That Darn Cat (1965) Score (s:Robert Brunner/t:Richard & Robert Sherman) US:LP = Buena Vista BV-3334/ST-3334*

6731 That Funny Feeling (1965) Theme (Bobby Darin) US:SP = Capitol 5481 [Bobby Darin:ST]

6732 That Goes Double [Short] (1933) Excerpts (Russ Columbo) US:LP-BP = Golden Legends 2000/1 [@ST]

6733 That Hamilton Woman [Lady Hamilton] (1941) Theme (Miklos Rozsa) US:LP = Deutsche 2584.021* [Miklos Rozsa:ST]; Theme (Miklos Rozsa) US:LP = Varese 1000.20* [Morton Gould]

6734 That Lady in Ermine (1948) Theme (Frederick Hollander) US:LP-BP = Out Take 3 [@Betty Grable:ST]

6735 That Lucky Touch (1975) Theme (John Scott) GB:SP = Motivation 405* [Brian Bennett:ST]

6736 That Man from Rio [L'Homme de Rio] (1964) Highlights-A (Georges Delerue) GB:EP = UA 1007; Highlights-B (Georges Delerue) FR:EP = UA 36045

6737 That Man in Istanbul (1966) Score (Georges Garvarentz) US:LP = Mainstream 56072/S-6072*

6738 That Midnight Kiss (1949) Highlights (t:Bronislau Kaper/e:classical music) US:LP-10 = RCA LM-86 + US:LP = RCA LM-2422 [Mario Lanza:ST]

6739 That Most Important Thing—Love [L'Important C'est d'Aimer] (1974) Excerpts (Georges Delerue) FR:LP = Barclay 900.508* [Georges Delerue:ST]

6740 That Night (1957) Theme (Mario Nascimbene) US:SP = Decca 9-30385 [Bill Snyder]; Theme (Mario Nascimbene) US:LP = Decca 8629 [Bill Snyder]

6741 That Night in Rio (1941) Highlights (Harry Warren) US:LP-BP = Curtain Calls 100/14

6742 That Splendid November [Un Bellissimo Novembre] (1969) Highlights (Ennio Morricone) IT:LP = Intermezzo IMGM-002*

6743 That Summer (1979) Score (pop music) GB:LP = Arista SPART-1088*

6744 That Was Then, This Is Now (1985) Score (Keith Olsen & Bill Cuomo) US:LP = Easy Street ESA-9903*

6745 That'll Be the Day (1974) Scores (pop music) GB:LP-MS = Ronco MR-2002/3*

6746 That's a Good Girl (1934) Excerpts (stage songs:Phil Charig & Joseph Meyer) GB:LP = WRC SH-283 [Jack Buchanan:ST]

6747 That's Dancing! (1985) Score (t:Henry Mancini/s:pop music) US:LP = EMI SJ-17149*

6748 That's Entertainment (1974) Scores (film songs:various) US:LP-MS = MCA 11002e

6749 That's Entertainment, Part 2 [Hollywood! Hollywood!] (1976) Score (film songs:various) US:LP = MGM MG1-5301e

6750 That's Right, You're Wrong (1939) Themes-A-B/US:78 = Columbia 35238 [Kay Kyser:ST]; Themes-C-D/US:78 = Columbia 35295 [Kay Kyser:ST]

6751 That's the Way of the World [Shining Star] (1974) Score (Earth, Wind, & Fire) US:LP = Columbia PC-33280* [Earth, Wind & Fire:ST]

6752 Theater of Blood (1973) Theme (Michael J. Lewis) US:LP-BP = POO 104 + FR:LP = MFP 2M046.96966* [Geoff Love]

6753 Theirs Is the Glory [Short] (1946) Theme (Guy Warrack) GB:78 = Decca 1571 [Muir Mathieson]

6754 Them! (1954) Sequence + Dialog (Bronislau Kaper) IT:LP-BP = BLU 15001 [@ST]

6755 There Goes Barder [Ca Va Barder] [Give 'Em Hell] (1955) Theme (Jeff Davis) US:SP = MGM 12433 [Leroy Holmes]

6756 There Goes the Bride (1932) Theme/GB:LP = MFP 1127 [Jessie Matthews:ST]

6757 There Is No 13 (1974) Themes (Riz Ortolani) IT:SP = CAM AMP-142* [ST]

6758 There Was a Crooked Man (1970) Theme (Charles Strouse) US:SP = Reprise 0975 [Trini Lopez:ST]

6759 There Was a Young Lady (1952) Theme (Wilfred Burns) US:EP = MGM 1197 [Wilfred Burns:ST]; Theme (Wilfred Burns) US:LP = MGM 3303 [@Wilfred Burns:ST]

6760 There's a Girl in My Soup (1970) Theme (Mike D'Abo) US:SP = Bell 956 [Mike D'Abo:ST]

6761 There's No Business Like Show Business (1954) Score (Irving Berlin) US:LP = Decca DL-8091; Excerpts (Irving Berlin) US:LP = 20th FXG-5000 + US:LP = 20th T-901 [Marilyn Monroe:ST]

6762 Therese Desqueyroux (1962) Highlights (Maurice Jarre) FR:EP = Ducretet 450-V-453

6763 These Dangerous Years *see* Dangerous Youth

6764 These Thousand Hills (1959) Theme (Harry Warren) US:SP = Verve 10167 [Randy Sparks:ST]

6765 These Three (1936) Theme [credited to "The Razor's Edge"] (Alfred Newman) US:LP = Mercury 20037 + US:LP = Citadel 6003 + US:LP = Citadel 7015 [Alfred Newman:ST]

6766 These Wilder Years (1956) Theme (Jeff Alexander) US:LP = MGM 3480 [Leroy Holmes]

6767 They All Died Laughing *see* Jolly Bad Fellow, A

6768 They All Laughed (1981) Themes (Charlie Craig/Earl Poole Ball) US:SP-PP = Moon Pictures 0001* [Colleen Camp:ST]

6769 They Call It an Accident (1983) Score (e:Steve Winwood/t:Wally Badarou/etc.) US:LP = Island ILPS-9757*

6770 They Call Me Mister Tibbs! (1970) Score (Quincy Jones) US:LP = UA UAS-5214*

6771 They Call Me Trinity [Lo Chiamavano Trinita] (1971) Score (Franco Micalizzi) IT:LP = Ariete 2011*

6772 They Came to Cordura (1959) Theme (James Van Heusen) US:SP = Capitol 4284 [Frank Sinatra]; Theme (James Van Heusen) US:LP = Capitol 2700 [Frank Sinatra]

6773 They Came to Rob Las Vegas (1968) Score (Georges Garvarentz) GB: LP = Philips 7898*

6774 They Died with Their Boots On (1942) Excerpts-A (Max Steiner) US: LP-BP = Citadel CTMS-6 [Max Steiner: ST]; Excerpts-B (Max Steiner) US:LP = RCA ARL1-0912* [Charles Gerhardt]

6775 They Got Me Covered (1943) Theme/US:LP-BP = Legends 1000/2 [@Nan Wynn:ST]

6776 They Learned About Women (1930) Themes/US:78 = RCA/Victor 22352 [Gus Van & Joe Schenck:ST]

6777 They Met in Argentina (1941) Theme/US:78 = Columbia 36213 [Alberto Vila:ST]

6778 They Might Be Giants (1971) Theme (John Barry) US:LP-BP = Disc 105 [@ST]

6779 They Shoot Horses, Don't They? (1969) Score (as:John Green) US: LP = ABC SOC-10*

6780 They Were Not Divided (1950) Theme (Lambert Williamson) GB:78-PP = Rank FM-93 [ST]; Theme (Lambert Williamson) US:LP-BP = Citadel CTOFI-1 [@ST]

6781 They're Coming to Get You [Tutti i Colori del Buio] (1973) Score (Bruno Nicolai) IT:LP = Gemelli 10.014*

6782 Thief (1981) Score (Tangerine Dream) US:LP = Elektra 5E-521*

6783 Thief, The (1952) Theme (Herschel Burke Gilbert) US:SP = RCA 47-6056 [Tony Martinez]

6784 Thief, The *see* La Ladrone

6785 Thief of Bagdad, The (1924) Highlights [Silent I] (James Bradford) US:LP = Pelican LP-2011* [Gaylord Carter]

6786 Thief of Bagdad, The (1940) Score (Miklos Rozsa) US:LP = Film Music Collection FMC-8* + US:LP = WB BSK-3183* [Elmer Bernstein]; Highlights (Miklos Rozsa) GB:LP = UA UAS-29725* [Miklos Rozsa:ST]; Highlights + Narration (Miklos Rozsa) US:LP = RCA LM-2118 [Miklos Rozsa & Leo Genn]

6787 Thief of Bagdad, The (1961) Score (Carlo Rustichelli) IT:LP = Phoenix PHCAM-10

6788 Thief of Hearts (1984) Score (s:Harold Faltermeyer/t:Giorgio Moroder) US:LP = Casablanca 822-942-1*

6789 Thief Who Came to Dinner, The (1973) Score (Henry Mancini) US:LP = WB WS-2700*

6790 Thieves After Dark [Les Voleurs de la Nuit] (1985) Score (Ennio Morricone) FR:LP = General Music 803-054*

6791 Thin Ice (1937) Theme/US: LP-BP = Pelican 130 [@Joan Davis:ST]

6792 Thing, The [The Thing from Another World] (1951) Excerpts (Dimitri Tiomkin) US:LP = RCA ARL1-2792* [Charles Gerhardt]

6793 Thing, The (1982) Score (Ennio Morricone) US:LP = MCA 6111*

6794 Thing with Two Heads, The (1972) Themes/US:LP = Pride 0005* [Jerry Butler/The Mike Curb Congregation:ST]

6795 Things Are Looking Up (1935) Theme/GB:LP = WRC 113 [Cicely Courtneidge:ST]

6796 Things of Life, The [Les Choses de la Vie] (1970) Score (Philippe Sarde) FR:LP = Philips 6311.021*; Theme (Philippe Sarde) US:SP = RCA 74-0395* [Jane Morgan]; Theme (Philippe Sarde) US:LP = Paramount 6047* [Frank Pourcel]

6797 Things to Come (1936) Highlights (Arthur Bliss) GB:LP = EMI ASD-3416* [Charles Groves]; Excerpts-A (Arthur Bliss) US:LP = RCA LM-2257/LSC-2257* + US:LP = London STS-15112* [Arthur Bliss:ST]; Excerpts-B (Arthur Bliss) US:LP = London SPC-21149* [Bernard Herrmann]

6798 Third Day, The (1965) Theme (Percy Faith) US:SP = Columbia 4-43326 [Percy Faith:ST]; Theme (Percy Faith) US:LP = Command 887* [Enoch Light]

6799 Third Man, The (1949) Excerpts (Anton Karas) IT:LP = RCA 43890* [@Anton Karas:ST]; Themes (Anton Karas) US:SP = London 5N-59045 [Anton Karas:ST]; Themes (Anton Karas) US:LP = London 1560 [Anton Karas:ST]

6800 Third Man on the Mountain [Banner in the Sky] (1959) Theme (Franklyn Marks) US:SP = Buena Vista 352 [Camarata]

6801 13 *see* Eye of the Devil

6802 13 Days in France [13 Jours en France] (1968) Score (Francis Lai) GB: LP = Sonet 605* + FR:LP = Saravah 12193*; Theme (Francis Lai) US:LP = UA 5515* [Francis Lai:ST]

6803 13th Letter, The (1951) Theme (Alex North) US:LP = Citadel 6023* [Alex North:ST]

6804 30 [Deadline—Midnight] (1959) Theme (Don Ralke) US:SP = WB 5115 [The Nortones]

6805 30 Is a Dangerous Age, Cynthia (1968) Score (Dudley Moore) US: LP = London MS-82010*

6806 39 Steps, The (1935) Underscore + Dialog (Louis Levy) US:LP-BP = Spybusters 3939

6807 39 Steps, The (1959) Theme (Clifton Parker) US:LP-BP = Citadel CTOFI-1 [@ST]

6808 39 Steps, The (1979) Score (Ed Welch) GB:LP = UA UAS-30208*

6809 36 Hours (1964) Score (Dimitri Tiomkin) US:LP = Vee Jay 1131/S-1131e + US:LP = Varese VC-81071e

6810 This Could Be the Night (1957) Score (e:Ray Anthony/t:George Stoll/t:Pete Rugolo/etc.) US:LP = MGM E-3530

6811 This Earth Is Mine (1959) Score (s:Hugo Friedhofer/t:James Van Heusen) US:LP = Decca DL-8915/DL-78915* + US:LP = Varese VC-81076*

6812 This Gun for Hire (1942) Theme (Jacques Press) US:LP-BP = Wallysrite 42 [@ST]

6813 This Happy Feeling (1958) Theme (Jay Livingston & Ray Evans) US:SP = Coral 9-61986 [Debbie Reynolds:ST]

6814 This Is Cinerama (1953) Score (t:Howard Jackson/t:Paul Sawtell/t: Max Steiner/t:Roy Webb) US:LP = Peter Pan 152*

6815 This Is Elvis (1981) Scores (pop music) US:LP-MS = RCA CPL2-4031* [Elvis Presley:ST]

6816 This Is Kung Fu (1983) Score (Kojan Saito) JA:LP = Columbia AF-7230*

6817 This Is My Love (1954) Theme (Franz Waxman) US:SP = Capitol 2981 [Connie Russell:ST]; Theme (Franz Waxman) US:SP = Mercury 70510 [Gary Mann]

6818 This Is Spinal Tap (1984) Score (Guest & Reiner & McKean & Shearer) US:LP = Polydor 817-846-1*

6819 This Is the Army (1943) Score (stage songs:Irving Berlin) US:LP-BP = Hollywood Soundstage HS-408 + US: LP-BP = Sandy Hook SH-2035

6820 This Is the Moment *see* That Lady in Ermine

6821 This Island Earth (1955) Themes (Herman Stein) US:LP = Coral 757240* + US:LP = Varese 81077* [Dick Jacobs]

6822 This Man Is Mine (1946) Theme (Allan Gray) US:LP = Columbia 3029 [@Charles Williams]

6823 This Man Reuter *see* Dispatch from Reuters

6824 This Property Is Condemned (1966) Score (s:Kenyon Hopkins/t:Jay Livingston & Ray Evans) US:LP = Verve MG-8664/V6-8664*

6825 This Rebel Age *see* Beat Generation, The

6826 This Special Friendship [Les Amities Particulieres] (1964) Highlights (Jean Prodromides) FR:EP = Philips 434.943

6827 This Time for Keeps (1947) Theme-A/US:78 = MGM 30035 [Jimmy Durante:ST]; Theme-B/US:LP = MGM 4207 [Jimmy Durante:ST]; Theme-C/ US:78 = Columbia 37829 [Xavier Cugat: ST]

6828 This Way Please (1937) Themes/US:LP-BP = Star Tone 219 [Betty Grable:ST]

6829 This Week of Grace (1933) Excerpts (various) GB:LP = WRC 170 [Gracie Fields:ST]

6830 This'll Make You Whistle (1937) Excerpts (various) GB:LP = Ace of Clubs 1140 [Jack Buchanan:ST]

6831 Thomas Crown Affair, The (1968) Score (Michel Legrand) US:LP = UA UAS-5182* + US:LP = UA LA-295*

6831a Thoroughly Modern Millie (1967) Score (t:James Van Heusen/s: pop music) US:LP = Decca DL-1500/ DL-75100*

6832 Those Calloways (1964) Theme (Max Steiner) US:SP = MGM 13316 [Johnny Tillotson:ST]; Theme (Max Steiner) US:LP = MGM 4328* [Johnny Tillotson:ST]

6833 Those Daring Young Men in Their Jaunty Jalopies [Monte Carlo or Bust] (1969) Score (Ron Goodwin) US: LP = Paramount PAS-5006*

6834 Those Dirty Dogs [Campa Carogna la Taglia Cresce) (1973) Themes (Nico Fidenco) IT:SP = CAM AMP-111* [Nico Fidenco/Stephen Boyd:ST]

6835 Those Fantastic Flying Fools [Rocket to the Moon] (1967) Score (John Scott) GB:LP = Polydor 583.013*; Themes (John Scott) US:SP = Sidewalk 923 [John Scott:ST/Mike Clifford]

6836 Those Magnificent Men in Their Flying Machines (1965) Score (Ron Goodwin) US:LP = 20th 3174/S-4174*

6837 Those Redheads from Seattle (1953) Themes-A-B/US:SP = Coral 9-61067 [Teresa Brewer:ST]; Theme-C/ US:SP = Columbia 4-40035 [Guy Mitchell:ST]; Theme-D/US:SP = RCA 47-5433 [The Bell Sisters:ST]

6838 Those Were the Happy Times *see* Star!

6839 Thousand Clowns, A (1965) Theme (Gerry Mulligan) US:SP = UA 974 [Rita Gardner:ST]; Theme (Gerry Mulligan) US:SP = Ascot 2203 [Ray Ellis]

6840 Thousands Cheer (1943) Score (various) US:LP-BP = Hollywood Soundstage HS-409

6841 Three (1969) Themes (Laurence Rosenthal) US:SP = UA 50632* [Laurence Rosenthal:ST]

6842 Three Amigos (1986) Score (e:Elmer Bernstein/e:Randy Newman) US:LP = WB 25558-1*

6843 Three Bites of the Apple (1967) Score (s:Eddy Manson/t:David McCallum) US:LP = MGM E-4444/SE-4444*

6844 Three Brothers [Tre Fratelli] (1980) Theme (Piero Piccioni) IT:LP-MS = WB/WEA 68034* + FR:LP-MS = General Music 806.029* [Piero Piccioni:ST]

6845 Three Caballeros, The (1944) Highlights (t:Charles Wolcott/t:Ed Plumb/t:Ary Barroso/etc.) US:78-MS = Decca A-373; Excerpts (various) US:LP = Disneyland WDL-3039 [@ST]

6846 Three Cheers for Love (1936) Theme/US:LP-BP = JJA 19811 [@Robert Cummings:ST]

6847 Three Coins in the Fountain (1954) Theme-A (Jule Styne) US:SP = Capitol 2816 [Frank Sinatra:ST]; Theme-A (Jule Styne) US:LP = Capitol 1011 [Frank Sinatra:ST]; Theme-B (Manlio & D'Esposito) US:LP = Omega 1010/10* [Pola Chapell]

6848 Three Daring Daughters [The Birds and the Bees] (1948) Themes-A-B/US:SP = RCA 49-1023 [Jeanette MacDonald:ST]; Theme-C/US:LP-BP = Scarce Rarities 5503 [Jane Powell:ST]

6849 Three Days of the Condor (1975) Score (Dave Grusin) US:LP = Capitol SW-11469*

6850 Three for All (1975) Score (various) GB:LP = DJM 448*

6851 Three for the Show (1955) Highlights (t:George Duning/e:various) US:LP-10 = Mercury MG-25204

6852 Three in the Attic (1968) Score (Chad Stuart) US:LP = Sidewalk ST-5918*

6853 Three in the Cellar *see* Up in the Cellar

6854 Three Little Girls in Blue (1946) Score (Josef Myrow) US:LP-BP = Hollywood Soundstage HS-410

6855 Three Little Pigs, The [Cartoon] (1933) Theme + Narration (Frank Churchill) US:LP = Disneyland ST-1910 + US:LP = Disneyland 3963; Theme (Frank Churchill) US:SP = Disneyland 303 [uncredited]; Theme (Frank Churchill) US:78 = Bluebird/Victor BK-10 [ST]

6856 Three Little Wolves, The [Cartoon] (1936) Theme (Frank Churchill) US:78 = Bluebird/Victor BK-10 [ST]

6857 Three Little Words (1950) Highlights (pop music) US:LP-10 = MGM E-516 + US:LP = MGM E-3229 + US:LP = MGM E-3768 + US:LP = Metro M-615/MS-615e + US:LP-MS = MGM 2SES-45e

6858 Three Lives of Thomasina, The (1963) Theme (Terry Gilkyson) US:LP = Disneyland 1333 [@The Wellingtons]

6859 Three Mesquiteers, The [Serial] Highlights (e:William Lava/t:Cy Feuer) US:LP-PP = Cinemasound R-1001* [James King]

6860 Three Musketeers, The (1935) Excerpts (Max Steiner) US:LP-BP = Max Steiner Music Society 25781 [Max Steiner:ST]

6861 Three Musketeers, The (1974) Score (Michel Legrand) Bell 1310*

6862 Three Penny Opera, The (1964) Score [USA Release] (stage songs: Kurt Weill) US:LP = RCA LOC-1086/LSO-1086*; Score [German Release] (stage songs:Kurt Weill) US:LP = London M-76004

6863 Three Rooms in Manhattan [Trois Chambre a Manhattan] (1965) Theme (Mal Waldron) JA:LP = Columbia 5090 [@ST]

6864 Three Sailors and a Girl (1953) Highlights (Sammy Fain) US:LP-10 = Capitol L-485

6865 Three Smart Girls (1937) Highlights (t:Bronislau Kaper/e:various) US:LP-BP = Caliban 6006

6866 Three Smart Girls Grow Up (1939) Themes/US:78-MS = Decca 75 [Deanna Durbin:ST]

6867 3:10 to Yuma, The (1957) Score (George Duning) US:LP-BP = Tony Thomas TTGD-2; Theme (George Duning) US:SP = Columbia 4-40962 [Frankie Laine:ST]; Theme (George Duning) US:LP = Columbia 8415* [Frankie Laine:ST]

6868 Three the Hard Way (1974) Score (Rich Tufo) US:LP = Curtom CU-8602*

6869 Three Tough Guys (1974) Score (Isaac Hayes) US:LP = Enterprise ENS-7504*

6870 Three Treasures, The (1958)

Excerpts (Akira Ifukube) JA:LP = Toho 8106 [@ST]

6871 Three Violent People (1957) Theme-A (Walter Scharf) US:SP = RKO Unique 383 [Joe Leahy]; Theme-B (Mack David) US:SP = Fraternity 57 [Cathy Carr]

6872 Three Worlds of Gulliver, The (1960) Score (Bernard Herrmann) GB:LP = Cloud Nine CN-4003; Highlights (Bernard Herrmann) US:LP = London SPC-21137* [Bernard Herrmann:ST]; Theme + Underscore + Dialog (t:George Duning/u:Bernard Herrmann) US:LP = Colpix CP-414 + US:LP = Citadel CTV-7018

6873 Thrill of a Lifetime (1937) Highlights (various) US:LP-BP = Caliban 6046

6874 Thrill of a Romance (1945) Excerpts (t:George Stoll/etc.) US:LP = Camden CAL-424 [Lauritz Melchior: ST]; Themes/US:78 = RCA/Victor 20-1625 [Tommy Dorsey:ST]

6875 Thrilling (1965) Themes (Ennio Morricone) IT:SP = ARC 4068 [ST]

6876-7 Throne of Fire *see* Night of the Blood Monster

6878 Thumb Tripping (1972) Themes (Bob Thompson) US:SP = Bell 233 [Jerry Fuller:ST]

6879 Thunder Alley (1967) Score (e:Jerry Styner/e:Mike Curb/etc.) US: LP = Sidewalk T-5902/ST-5902*

6880 Thunder at the Border [Mein Freund Winnetou] (1966) Score (Peter Thomas) GE:LP = Europa 1156926

6881 Thunder in the East (1953) Theme (Jay Livingston & Ray Evans) US:SP = Columbia 4-39862 [Frankie Laine]; Theme (Jay Livingston & Ray Evans) US:SP = MGM 11331 [Leroy Holmes]; Theme (Jay Livingston & Ray Evans) US:LP = Capitol 1891 [Nat King Cole]

6882 Thunder of Drums, A (1961) Theme (Harry Sukman) US:SP = Capitol 4600 [The Hollyridge Strings]

6883 Thunder Road (1958) Theme-A (Jack Marshall) US:SP = Capitol 3978 [Jack Marshall:ST]; Theme-B (Don Raye & Robert Mitchum) US:SP = Capitol 3986 [Robert Mitchum:ST]; Theme-C (Don Raye & Robert Mitchum) US:SP = Capitol 3975 [Keely Smith:ST]

6884 Thunderball (1965) Score (John Barry) US:LP = UA UAL-4132/UAS-5132*

6885 Thunderbirds (1952) Theme (Victor Young) US:LP = Decca 8051 [Victor Young:ST]; Theme (Victor Young) US:LP = Mercury 60369* [Richard Hayman]

6886 Thunderbirds Are Go (1966) Excerpts (t:Barry Gray/t:The Shadows) GB:LP = EMI NUT-2* [The Shadows: ST]; Theme (The Shadows) GB:SP = Columbia 8510 [Cliff Richard:ST]

6887 Thunderbirds Six (1968) Themes (Barry Gray) GB:LP = UA 30281* [@Barry Gray:ST]

6888 Tiara Tahiti (1962) Theme (Philip Green) US:LP = London 3347/347* [Frank Chacksfield]

6889 Tick ... Tick ... Tick ... (1970) Score (Tompall Glaser) US:LP = MGM SE-4667*

6890 Tickle Me (1965) Highlights (various) US:EP = RCA EPA-4383 [Elvis Presley:ST]

6891 Ticklish Affair, A (1963) Theme (George Stoll) US:SP = Kapp 534 [Jack Jones]; Theme (George Stoll) US: LP = Capitol 2075* [Jimmie Haskell]

6892 Tidal Wave [Submersion of Japan] (1973) Highlights (Masaru Sato) JA:EP = Toho 1051

6893 Tiger Bay (1959) Theme (Laurie Johnson) GB:SP = Top Rank 112 [ST]; Theme (Laurie Johnson) GB:LP = MGM 8104* [Laurie Johnson:ST]

6894 Tiger Tamer, The (1955) Highlights (Moisei Vainberg) US:LP = Monitor M-530

6895 Tight Little Island [Whiskey Galore] (1949) Theme (Ernest Irving) GB:78-PP = Rank FM-64 [ST]; Theme (Ernest Irving) US:LP-BP = Citadel CTOFI-1 [@ST]

6896 Tight Spot (1955) Theme (George Duning) US:SP = X 4X0161 [The Spencer/Hagen Orchestra]; Theme (George Duning) US:SP = MGM 12030 [Leroy Holmes]; Theme (George Duning) US:LP = MGM 3172 [Leroy Holmes]

6897 Tiko and the Shark [Ti-Koyo il suo Pescecane] (1962) Score (Francesco DeMasi) IT:LP = CAM CMS-30.112

6898 Till Death Us Do Part *see* Alf 'n' Family

6899 Till Marriage Do Us Part [Mio Dio Come Sono Caduta in Basso] (1979) Themes (Fiorenzo Carpi) IT:SP = CAM AMP-141* [ST]

6900 Till the Clouds Roll By (1946) Scores (pop music) US:LP-MS-BP = Sountrak STK-115; Highlights (pop music) US:LP-10 = MGM E-501 + US: LP = MGM E-3231 + US:LP = MGM E-3770 + US:LP = Metro M-578/MS-578e + US:LP-MS = MGM 2SES-45e

6901 Tilt (1979) Score (s:Bill Wray/ t:Lee Holdridge) US:LP = ABC AA-1114*

6902 Timber Tramps, The (1975) Theme (Dave Williamson) US:SP-PP = AP 001* [Claude Akins:ST]

6903 Timberjack (1955) Theme (Victor Young) US:SP = Coral 9-61343 [The Lancers:ST]

6904 Time After Time (1979) Score (Miklos Rozsa) US:LP = Entracte ERS-6517*

6905 Time for Killing, A [The Long Ride Home] (1967) Theme (Van Alexander) US:SP = RCA 47-9265 [Eddy Arnold:ST]

6906 Time for Loving *see* Paris Was Made for Lovers

6907 Time Machine, The (1960) Score (Russell Garcia) US:LP = GNP GNPS-8008*

6908 Time Masters [Les Maitres du Temps] (1982) Themes (Jean Pierre Bourtayre) FR:SP = Philips 6010.506* [ST]

6909 Time of Indifference, A [Gil Indifferenti] (1964) Score (Giovanni Fusco) IT:LP = Campi Editore CLP-100.002

6910 Time of Wonder, A [Short] Sequence + Dialog (Arthur Kleiner) US: LP-PP = Picture Book Parade 107 [@ST]

6911 Time Out for Rhythm (1941) Themes/US:78 = Bluebird 11149 [Joan Merrill:ST]

6912 Time Out of Mind (1947) Theme (at:Mario Castelnuevo-Tedesco) US:LP = AEI 3104 + US:LP-BP = Premiere 1201 + US:LP-BP = Tony Thomas TTMR-4 [@uncredited]

6913 Time, the Place and the Girl, The (1946) Highlights (Arthur Schwartz) US:LP-BP = Titania 511

6914 Time to Die, A (1984) Score (Ennio Morricone) US:LP = Cerberus CEMS-0119*

6915 Time to Love and a Time to Die, A (1958) Score (Miklos Rozsa) US: LP = Decca DL-8778 + US:LP = Varese VC-81077

6916 Time to Run (1975) Score (Tedd Smith) US:LP = Creative Sound CSS-1575* + US:LP = World Wide WWR-1001*

6917 Time to Sing, A (1968) Score (pop music) US:LP = MGM E-4540/ SE-4540*

6918 Time Within Memory [Longing] (1972) Excerpts (Toru Takemitsu) JA:LP = RCA/Victor 1065 [Toru Takemitsu:ST]

6919 Times of Harvey Milk, The (1984) Excerpts (Mark Isham) US:LP = Windham Hill WH-1041* [Mark Isham: ST]

6920 Times Square (1980) Scores (pop music) US:LP-MS = RSO RS2-4203*

6921 Tin Drum, The [Le Tambour] (1979) Score (Maurice Jarre) GE:LP = Dominion 6041* + FR:LP = RCA 37337*

6922 Tin Pan Alley (1940) Score (pop music) US:LP-BP = Sountrak STK-110

6923 Tin Star, The (1957) Theme (Elmer Bernstein) US:SP = MGM 12547 [Dean Jones]

6924 Tis Pity She's a Whore [Addio Fratello Crudele] (1972) Score (Ennio Morricone) FR:LP-MS = CAM 500. 002*

6925 Titfield Thunderbolt, The (1953) Theme (Georges Auric) GB:78-PP = Rank FM-137 [ST]; Theme (Georges Auric) US:LP-BP = Citadel CTOFI-1 [@ST]

6926 To Be or Not to Be (1983) Themes + Underscore + Dialog (t:Mel Brooks/u:John Morris) US:LP = Antilles 8-ASTA-2*

6927 To Bed or Not to Bed [Il Diavolo] (1963) Score (Piero Piccioni) US:LP = London M-76005

6928 To Catch a Cop [Retenez-

Moi, ou Je Fais un Malheur] (1984) Themes (Vladimir Cosma) FR:SP = Carrere 13376* [ST]

6929 To Catch a Thief (1955) Highlights (e:Lyn Murray/t:George Auld) US:EP = Coral EC-81083; Excerpts (e:Lyn Murray/t:George Auld) US:LP = Coral CRL-57032 [George Auld & Lyn Murray:ST]

6930 To Die in Madrid [Mourir a Madrid] (1963) Highlights (t:Maurice Jarre/etc.) FR:EP = Philips 432.881

6931 To Die of Love (1970) Theme (Charles Aznavour) US:SP = MGM 14369 [Charles Aznavour:ST]

6932 To Fill a Need / Score (Jim Bredouw & Martin Lund) US:LP-PP = TFAN 71378*

6933 To Forget Venice [Dimenticare Venezia] (1980) Score (Benedetto Ghiglia) IT:LP = Duse LPF-045*

6934 To Have and Have Not (1944) Themes-A-B (Franz Waxman) US:LP = RCA 1-0422* + US:LP = RCA 1-3782* [Charles Gerhardt]; Themes-C-D (Hoagy Carmichael) US:SP = WB 5222 [Hoagy Carmichael:ST]

6935 To Hell and Back (1955) Theme (Bert Gold) US:SP = Decca 9-29703 [Russ Morgan]; Theme (Bert Gold) US:LP = MGM 3294 [@Joe Lipman]

6936 To Kill a Mockingbird (1962) Score-A (Elmer Bernstein) US:LP = Ava A-20/AS-20* + US:LP = Citadel CTV-7024*; Score-B (Elmer Bernstein) US:LP = Film Music Collection FMC-7* + US:LP = WB BSK-3184*

6937 To Kill in Silence [Uccidere in Silenzio] (1972) Themes (Stelvio Cipriani) IT:SP = CAM AMP-097* [ST]

6938 To Live and Die in L.A. (1985) Score (Wang Chung) US:LP = Geffen GHS-24081*

6939 To Love Somebody *see* Melody

6940 To Ride a White Horse (1975) Score (Sven Libaek) AU:LP = Festival 1932627*

6941 To Sir with Love (1967) Score (s:Ron Grainer/t:Mark London) US:LP = Fontana SRF-18030*

6942 Toast of New Orleans, The (1950) Highlights (e:Nicholas Brodszky/e:classical music) US:LP-10 = RCA LM-75 + US:LP = RCA LM-2422 [Mario Lanza:ST]; Highlights (Nicholas Brodszky) US:SP-MS = RCA WDM-1417 [Mario Lanza:ST]; Themes (Nicholas Brodszky) US:LP-BP = Azel 104 [Kathryn Grayson & Mario Lanza:ST]

6943 Toby Damit *see* Spirits of the Dead

6944 Toby Tyler (1960) Theme + Dialog (Richard Loring) US:LP = Disneyland ST-1904 + US:LP-MS = Disneyland DDF-5; Theme (Richard Loring) US:EP = Disneyland 49 [Mr. Stubbs]

6945 Toccata for Toy Trains [Short] (1958) Highlights (Elmer Bernstein) US:LP = Film Music Collection FMC-2*

6946 Todo es Posible en Granada / Theme (Halffter) US:LP = Mercury 20188 [Eddie Barclay]

6947 Todos los Dias, un Dia (1979) Score (Rafael Ferro) US:LP = CBS DML-50316* [Julio Iglesias:ST]

6948 Together [Amo non Amo] (1979) Score-A [USA Release] (Burt Bacharach) US:LP = RCA ABL1-3541*; Score-B [Italian Release] (Goblin) IT:LP = Cinevox 33/126*

6949 Together Brothers (1974) Score (s:Barry White/t:Gene Page) US:LP = 20th S-101*

6949a Tokyo File 212 (1951) Score (Albert Glasser) US:LP = Screen Archives 10.002

6950 Tokyo Olympiad (1966) Score (Toshiro Mayuzumi) US:LP = Monument LP-8046/SLP-18046*

6951 Tom Jones (1963) Score (John Addison) US:LP = UA UAL-4113/UAS-5113*

6952 Tom Sawyer (1973) Score (Richard & Robert Sherman) US:LP = UA LA-057*

6953 Tom Thumb (1958) Highlights + Underscore + Dialog (e:Fred Spielman/t:Peggy Lee/u:Ken Jones & Douglas Gamley) US:LP = Lion L-70084 + US:LP = MGM CH-104 + US:LP = MCA 25006

6954 Tom Thumb [Le Petit Poucet] (1976) Score (Francis Lai) CA:LP = Gama LP-165*

6955 Tomb of Dracula (1980) Score

(Seiji Yokoyama) JA:LP = Columbia CQ-7057*

6956 Tombola / Score (A. Alguero) US:LP = Montilla FMS-2079

6957 Tommy Steele Story, The *see* Rock Around the World

6958 Tommy the Toreador (1959) Highlights (Lionel Bart) GB:EP = Decca DFE-6607 [Tommy Steele:ST]

6959 Tomorrow (1970) Score (e: Hugo Montenegro/etc.) GB:LP = RCA CSA-3008*; Theme (Mark Barkan) US: SP = RCA/Kirshner 63-5005* [Don Kirshner Singers]

6960 Tomorrow Is Forever (1946) Highlights (Max Steiner) US:LP-MS-BP = Tony Thomas TTMS-13/14; Theme (Max Steiner) US:LP = MCA 1546 [Dick Haymes]

6961 Tongue (1977) Score (Roger Hamilton Spotts) US:LP = Chocolate Cities CCS-1000*

6962 Tonka (1958) Theme (George Bruns) US:SP = Disneyland 119 [George Bruns:ST]; Theme (George Bruns) US: 78 = Golden 531 [Wayne Sherwood]

6963 Tonight and Every Night (1945) Themes/US:LP-BP = Curtain Calls 100/22 [Martha Mears-for-Rita Hayworth:ST]

6964 Tonight We Sing (1952) Highlights (pop music/classical music) US: LP-10 = RCA LM-7016

6965 Tonnerre de Dieu, Le / Theme (Georges Garvarentz) US:SP = Columbia 4-44019 [Robert Goulet]

6966 Tony Draws a Horse (1950) Theme (Bretton Byrd) GB:78-PP = Rank FM-96 [ST]

6967 Tony Fontane Story, The (1962) Score (pop music) US:LP = RCA LPM-2526/LSP-2526* [Tony Fontane: ST]

6968 Tony Rome (1967) Theme (Lee Hazlewood) US:SP = Reprise 0636 [Nancy Sinatra:ST]

6969 Too Late Blues (1962) Highlights (David Raksin) US:LP = Dot DLP-25844* [David Raksin:ST]

6970 Too Many Chefs? *see* Who Is Killing the Great Chefs of Europe?

6971 Too Many Girls (1940) Theme/US:LP-BP = JJA 19734 [@ Frances Langford:ST]

6972 Too Much Harmony (1933) Excerpts-A (Arthur Johnston) US:LP-MS = Columbia C2L-43 [Bing Crosby: ST]; Excerpts-B (Arthur Johnston) US: LP-BP = Caliban 6039 [@ST]

6973 Too Much Soft Living (1980) Score (Special Affect) US:LP-PP = Special Affect 008028*

6974 Too Much, Too Soon (1958) Score (Ernest Gold) US:LP = Mercury MG-20381/SR-60019*

6975 Too Young for Love [L'Eta dell'Amore] (1953) Theme (Mario Nascimbene) IT:LP-MS = Kangaroo 34209 [Mario Nascimbene:ST]

6976 Toot, Whistle, Plunk and Boom [Cartoon] (1953) Highlights + Dialog (Sonny Burke) US:LP = Disneyland DQ-1232 + US:LP = Disneyland DQ-1287

6977 Tootsie (1982) Score (Dave Grusin) US:LP = WB 23781-1*

6978 Top Gun (1986) Score-A (e: Giorgio Moroder/t:Harold Faltermeyer/ e:various) US:LP = Columbia JS-40323*; Theme-B [Dog Fight] (Harold Faltermeyer) US:SP = Columbia 38-06137* [Harold Faltermeyer:ST]; Theme-C [Memories] (Harold Faltermeyer) US: SP = Columbia 38-06282* [Harold Faltermeyer:ST]

6979 Top Hat (1935) Highlights (Irving Berlin) US:LP-BP = Sountrak STK-105; Excerpts (Irving Berlin) US: LP = Columbia SG-32472 [Fred Astaire: ST]

6980 Top o' the Morning (1949) Excerpts (various) US:LP-10 = Decca DL-4261 + US:LP = Decca DL-5272 [Bing Crosby:ST]

6981 Top of the Heap (1972) Themes (J.J. Johnson) US:SP = CAS/ Fanfare 9000* [J.J. Johnson:ST]

6982 Top of the Town (1937) Themes-A-B/US:78 = Brunswick 7818 [Gertrude Niesen:ST]; Themes-C-D/ US:78 = Brunswick 7837 [Gertrude Niesen:ST]

6983 Top of the World (1955) Excerpts (Albert Glasser) US:LP = Starlog SR-1001 [Albert Glasser:ST]

6984 Top Secret (1984) Score (Maurice Jarre) US:LP = Varese STV-81219*; Highlights (pop music) US:EP-12 = Passport PB-3603* [Val Kilmer:ST]

6985 Topaz (1969) Themes (Maurice Jarre) US:SP = Kapp 2073 [Stanley Wilson]; Theme (Maurice Jarre) US:SP = Decca 732624* [Sammy Kaye]; Theme (Maurice Jarre) US:LP = Decca 75176* [Sammy Kaye]

6986 Topkapi (1964) Score (Manos Hadjidakis) US:LP = UA UAL-4118/UAS-5118*

6987 Topo, El (1972) Score (Alexandro Jodorowsky) US:LP = Apple SW-3388*

6988 Tops Is the Limit *see* Anything Goes (1936)

6989 Tora! Tora! Tora! (1970) Theme (Jerry Goldsmith) US:LP = Springboard 4088* [The Film Festival Orchestra]; Theme (Jerry Goldsmith) JA: LP-MS = UA 6063/4* [@The Ventures]

6990 Torch Singer (1933) Theme/ US:LP-BP = Pelican 130 [@Claudette Colbert:ST]

6991 Torch Song (1953) Highlights (t:Adolph Deutsch/e:various) US:LP-10 = MGM E-214

6992 Toriton in the Sea (1978) Score (Kohsetsu Minami) JA:LP = Columbia CS-7044*

6993 Torn Curtain (1966) Score-A (John Addison) US:LP = Decca DL-9155/DL-79155*; Score-B [discarded score] (Bernard Herrmann) US:LP = WB BSK-3185* + US:LP = FMC 10* [Elmer Bernstein]

6994 Torpedo Bay [Finche Dura la Tempesta] (1963) Highlights (Carlo Rustichelli) IT:EP = CAM 45-99

6995 Torso [I Corpi Presentano Tracce di Violenza Carnale] (1973) Theme (Guido & Maurizio DeAngelis) IT:LP = RCA 33006* [Guido & Maurizio:ST]

6996 Touch and Go *see* Light Touch, The

6997 Touch of Class, A (1973) Score (e:John Cameron/e:George Barrie) US:LP = Brut 6004*

6998 Touch of Evil (1958) Score-A (Henry Mancini) US:LP = Citadel CTV-7016; Score-B (Henry Mancini) US:LP = Challenge CHL-602; Score-C (Henry Mancini) US:LP = Challenge CHL-615

6999 Touchables, The (1969) Score (e:Ken Thorne/etc.) US:LP = 20th S-4206*

7000 Touched (1983) Theme (David Shire) US:LP = Atlantic 80052-1* [Laura Branigan:ST]

7001 Touchez Pas au Grisbi *see* Grisbi

7002 Tough Enough (1983) Score (s:Michael Lloyd/t:John D'Andrea) US: LP = Liberty LT-51141*

7003 Tough Guys (1986) Theme (Burt Bacharach) US:LP = RCA 5633-1* [Kenny Rogers:ST]; Theme (Burt Bacharach) US:SP = RCA 5016-7* [Kenny Rogers:ST]

7004 Toughest Man in Arizona, The (1952) Themes-A-B (Smith/Schram) US:SP = RCA 47-4941 [Vaughn Monroe:ST]; Theme-C (Joe Lubin) US:SP = RCA 47-4942 [Vaughn Monroe:ST]

7005 Tourist Trap (1979) Score (Pino Donaggio)US:LP = Varese VC-81102*

7006 Tovarich (1937) Theme (Max Steiner) US:LP-BP = Citadel CTMS-6 [Max Steiner:ST]

7007 Toward the Terra (1980) Score (Masaru Sato) JA:LP = Columbia CQ-7041*

7008 Tower of Death [Game of Death II] (1984) Score (Keith Morrison) JA:LP = RCA Victor VIP-28022*

7009 Towering Inferno, The (1974) Score (s:John Williams/t:Al Kasha & Joel Hirschhorn) US:LP = WB BS-2840*

7010 Town Without Pity (1961) Highlights (Dimitri Tiomkin) US:LP-BP = Cinema LP-8012; Theme (Dimitri Tiomkin) US:SP = Musicor 1009 [Gene Pitney:ST]; Theme (Dimitri Tiomkin) US:LP = UA 6197* [@Gene Pitney: ST]

7011 Toy, The [Le Jouet] (1979) Themes (Vladimir Cosma) FR:SP = Deesse 721* [ST]

7012 Toys in the Attic (1963) Score (George Duning) US:LP-BP = Citadel CTGD-1; Theme (George Duning) US: SP = Kapp 551 [Jack Jones]; Theme (George Duning) US:LP = WB 1535* [Ray Heindorf]

7013 Trackdown (1976) Theme (Larry Butler) US:LP = UA 607* [Kenny Rogers:ST]

7014 Trade Winds (1938) Theme (Alfred Newman) US:LP = Decca 79048*

+ US:LP-BP = Centurion 1286* [Alfred Newman:ST]

7015 Traffic (1972) Score (Charles Dumont) CA:LP = London 20082*

7016 Traffic Jam [L'Ingorgo] (1980) Score (Fiorenzo Carpi) IT:LP = Edi Pan 2008*

7017 Tragedy of a Ridiculous Man, The [La Tragedie d'un Homme Ridicule] (1982) Score (Ennio Morricone) FR: LP = General Music 803.027*

7018 Tragedy of Carmen, The (1984) Scores (classical music) FR:LP-MS = EMI 1654403*

7019 Trail of the Pink Panther, The (1982) Themes (Henry Mancini) US: LP = Liberty 51139* [Henry Mancini:ST]; Theme (Henry Mancini) US:SP = Liberty 1489* [Henry Mancini:ST]

7020 Trail of the Lonesome Pine (1936) Theme (Louis Alter) US:LP = MCA 1563 [The Sons of the Pioneers]

7021 Trailin' West (1936) Theme/ US:78 = Decca 1039 [Dick Foran:ST]

7022 Train, The (1965) Score (Maurice Jarre) US:LP = UA UAL-4122/ UAS-5122*

7023 Train, Le [The Train] (1973) Score (Philippe Sarde) FR:LP = Polydor 2393.072*; Excerpts (Philippe Sarde) US:LP = DRG SL-9512* [@ST]

7024 Train of Events (1949) Theme (Leslie Bridgewater) GB:78-PP = Rank FM-77 [ST]

7025 Train Ride to Hollywood (1976) Score (Bloodstone) US:LP = London PS-665*

7026 Traitor's Gate [Das Verratertor] (1964) Themes (Peter Thomas) GE: LP = Celine 0011 [Peter Thomas:ST]

7027 Transatlantic Merry-Go-Round (1934) Excerpts (Richard A. Whiting) US:LP-BP = JJA 19806 [@ST]

7028 Transformers – The Movie (1986) Score (e:Vince Di Cola/e:various) US:LP = Scotti Bros. SZ-40430*

7029 Transylvania 6-5000 (1985) Score (Lee Holdridge) US:LP = Varese STV-81267*

7030 Trap, The (1966) Score (Ron Goodwin) US:LP = Atco SD-33-204*

7031 Trapeze (1956) Score (e:Malcolm Arnold/etc.) US:LP = Columbia CL-870

7032 Trapp Family, The (1961) Score (Franz Grothe) US:LP = 20th 3044/S-3044*

7033 Trauma (1962) Themes (Buddy Collette) US:SP = Chattahoochee 721 [Buddy Collette:ST]

7034 Traveling Saleswoman, The (1950) Theme/US:LP-BP = Legends 1000/2 [@Adele Jergens:ST]

7035 Travels with My Aunt (1972) Theme (Tony Hatch) US:LP-BP = Centurion 1210* [@Tony Hatch:ST]; Theme (Tony Hatch) GB:LP = Pye 41029* [Tony Hatch:ST]

7036 Traviata, La (1983) Scores (classical music) US:LP-MS = Elektra 9-60267*

7037 Treasure Island (1950) Underscore + Dialog (Clifton Parker) US: LP = Disneyland ST-1251 + US:LP = Disneyland DQ-3997

7038 Treasure of San Gennaro, The (1968) Score (Armando Trovajoli) US:LP = Buddah BDS-5011*

7039 Treasure of Silver Lake, The [Der Schatz im Silbersee] (1962) Highlights (Martin Bottcher) GE:LP = Polydor 46838*

7040 Treasure of the Aztecs, The (1965) Highlights (Erwin Halletz) GE: LP = Telefunken 14367

7041 Treasure of the Four Crowns, The [Le Tresor des 4 Couronnes] (1983) Score (Ennio Morricone) FR:LP = General Music 803.053*

7042 Treasure of the Sierra Madre, The (1948) Highlights (Max Steiner) US: LP-MS-BP = Tony Thomas TTMS-13/ 14; Excerpts (Max Steiner) US:LP = RCA ARL1-0422* + US:LP = RCA AGL1-3782* [Charles Gerhardt]

7043 Tree Is Nice, A [Short] Sequence + Dialog (Arthur Kleiner) US: LP-PP = Picture Book Parade 107 [@ST]

7044 Trespasser, The (1929) Themes/US:78 = RCA/Victor 22079 [Gloria Swanson:ST]

7045 Trial, The [Le Proces] (1962) Score (e:Jean Ledrut/e:classical music) FR:LP = Philips 77908; Theme (at:Jean Ledrut) US:LP = Philips 600-071 [@ST]

7046 Trial of Billy Jack, The (1974) Score (e:Elmer Bernstein/etc.) US:LP = ABC ABCD-853*

7047 Trials of Oscar Wilde, The [The Green Carnation] (1960) Theme (Ron Goodwin) GB:SP = RCA 4892 [Ron Goodwin:ST]; Theme (Ron Goodwin) CA:LP = Capitol 6086* [Ron Goodwin:ST]

7048 Tribute (1980) Theme (Barry Manilow) US:LP = Arista 9537* [Barry Manilow:ST]

7049 Tribute to a Bad Man (1956) Theme (Miklos Rozsa) GB:LP = Polydor 2383.384* [Miklos Rozsa:ST]; Theme (Miklos Rozsa) US:LP = Varese 1000.20* + US:LP = Varese 1008* [Morton Gould]

7050 Tricheurs [Cheaters] (1984) Score (Peer Raben) FR:LP = Milan A-240*

7051 Tricheurs, Les *see* Cheaters, The (1958)

7052 Trick or Treat [Cartoon] (1952) Theme + Underscore + Dialog (t:Jerry Livingston/u:Oliver Wallace) US:LP = Disneyland DQ-1358

7053 Trick or Treat (1986) Score (Fastway) US:LP = Columbia SC-40549*

7054 Trinity Is Still My Name [Continuvvano a Chiamarlo Trinita] (1972) Score (Guido & Maurizio DeAngelis) IT:LP = RCA OLS-9*

7055 Trio (1950) Theme (John Greenwood) GB:78-PP = Rank FM-99 [ST]

7056 Trio Infernal, Le [The Infernal Trio] (1974) Score (Ennio Morricone) FR:LP = Yuki 873.001*

7057 Trip, The (1967) Score (Mike Bloomfield) US:LP = Sidewalk T-5908/ST-5908*

7058 Trip to Italy, A [Strangers] [A Trip in Italy] (1954) Highlights (Renzo Rossellini) US:EP = Mercury EP1-3273

7059 Triple Cross (1967) Score (Georges Garvarentz) US:LP = UA UAL-4162/UAS-5162*

7060 Triumph of Michael Strogoff, The [Le Triomphe de Michel Strogoff] (1964) Highlights (Hubert Giraud) FR:EP = Fontana 460.817

7061 Triumph of the Will (1934) Underscore + Dialog (Herbert Windt) US:LP-MS-PP = Communications 271477

7062 Trocadero Lemon Blue (1979) Score (Alec Costandinos) US:LP = Casablanca NBLP-7117*

7063 Troll (1986) Score (Richard Band) US:LP = Restless 72119-1*

7064 Tron (1982) Score (s:Wendy Carlos-aka-Walter Carlos/t:Journey) US:LP = CBS SM-37782*

7065 Trooper Hook (1957) Themes (Gerald Fried) US:SP = Capitol 3754 [Tex Ritter & Gerald Fried:ST]; Theme (Gerald Fried) US:LP = Capitol 971 [Tex Ritter:ST]

7066 Tropic Holiday, A (1938) Themes-A-B/US:LP-BP = Legends 1000/4 [Dorothy Lamour:ST]; Theme-C/US:78 = Brunswick 8154 [Dorothy Lamour:ST]; Theme-D/US:LP-BP = Choice Cuts 500/1 [@Martha Raye:ST]

7067 Tropico de Notte / Themes (H. Tical) US:SP = KC 101 [Armando Sciascia:ST]

7068 Trottie True *see* Gay Lady

7069 Trouble in Mind (1986) Score (Mark Isham) US:LP = Island 90501-1*

7070 Trouble Man (1973) Score (s: Marvin Gaye/as:Leo Shuken & Jack Hayes) US:LP = Tamla T-322*

7071 Trouble Shooter *see* Man with the Gun

7072 Trouble with Angels, The (1966) Score (Jerry Goldsmith) US:LP = Mainstream 56073/S-6073*

7073 Trouble with Girls, The (1969) Theme (Billy Strange) US:SP = RCA 47-9747 [Elvis Presley:ST]; Theme (Billy Strange) US:LP = Camden 2440* [Elvis Presley:ST]

7074 Trouble with Harry, The (1955) Excerpts (Bernard Herrmann) US:LP = London SP-44126* + US:LP = London SPC-21177* [Bernard Herrmann:ST]; Theme (Raymond Scott) US:SP = Decca 9-29770 [Ray McKinley]

7075 Trouble with Women, The (1947) Theme/US:LP-BP = Legends 1000/2 [@Iris Adrian:ST]

7076 Troublemaker, The (1964) Highlights (Cy Coleman) US:LP = Ava A-49/AS-49*

7077 Trout, The *see* La Truite

7078 Truck Turner (1974) Scores (Isaac Hayes) US:LP-MS = Enterprise ENS-7507*

7079 True Confessions (1981) Score (e:Georges Delerue/e:classical music) US:LP = Varese STV-81141*

7080 True Grit (1969) Score (Elmer Bernstein) US:LP = Capitol ST-263* [Artie Butler & Elmer Bernstein]; Highlights (Elmer Bernstein) US:LP = Varese 704.280* [Elmer Bernstein:ST]

7081 True Stories (1986) Score-A (David Byrne) US:LP = Sire 25512-1*; Score-B (David Byrne) US:LP = Sire 25515-1*

7082 True Story of Eskimo Nell, The (1977) Score (Brian May) AU:LP = Festival 35506*

7083 True Story of the Civil War, The [Short] (1958) Underscore + Dialog (Ernest Gold) US:LP = Coral CRL-59100 + US:LP = MCA 34778

7084 True to Life (1943) Theme (Hoagy Carmichael) US:LP = Decca 8588 [Hoagy Carmichael:ST]

7085 Truite, La [The Trout] (1982) Score (Richard Hartley) FR:LP = Gaumont 753.812*

7086 Truth, The [La Verite] (1960) Highlights (various) IT:EP = Ricordi 45-M-120

7087 Tuesday in November, A [Short] (1944) Highlights (Virgil Thomson) US:LP = Bench Mark ABM-3501

7088 Tuff Turf (1985) Score (e: Jonathan Elias/e:various) US:LP = Rhino RNSP-308*

7089 Tumbleweeds (1925) Theme [Silent II] (Charles Hofmann) US:LP = Sounds Good 1001 [Charles Hofmann: ST]

7090 Tunes of Glory (1960) Score (as:Malcolm Arnold) US:LP = UA UAL-4086/UAS-5086*

7091 Tunnel of Love (1958) Theme (Patty Fisher) US:SP = Columbia 4-41252 [Doris Day:ST]; Theme (Patty Fisher) US:LP = Harmony 11192 [Doris Day:ST]

7092 Tunnelvision (1976) Themes (Brian Potter) US:SP-PP = ABC R-374* [ST]; Theme (Brian Potter) US:SP = Haven 805* [The Space Cadets]

7093 Turkish Delight [Turks Fruit] (1973) Score (Rogier Van Otterloo) HO: LP = CBS 65451*

7094 Turn Off the Moon (1937) Themes/US:78 = Vocalion 3533 [Phil Harris:ST]

7095 Turn On, Tune In, Drop Out (1967) Score (e:Lars Eric/e:Richard Bond) US:LP = Mercury SR-61131*

7096 Turn the Key Softly (1953) Theme (Mischa Spoliansky) GB:78-PP = Rank FM-139 [ST]

7097 Turning Point, The (1977) Score (classical music) US:LP = 20th T-549*

7098 Twelve Angry Men (1957) Theme (Kenyon Hopkins) US:SP = Cadence 1322 [Kenyon Hopkins:ST]

7099 Twelve Chairs, The (1970) Score (John Morris) US:LP = Varese STV-81159*

7100 Twelve O'Clock High (1949) Theme (Alfred Newman) US:LP-BP = Capricorn 1286 [Alfred Newman:ST]

7101 20th Century Oz [Oz] (1978) Score (Ross Wilson) US:LP = Celestial OZ-4001*

7102 25th Hour, The (1967) Score (Georges Delerue) US:LP = MGM E-4185/SE-4185*

7103 24 Hours of a Woman's Life *see* Affair in Monte Carlo

7104 24 Hours of the Rebel *see* 9/30/55

7105 24 Hours to Kill (1965) Theme (Wilfred Josephs) GB:LP = Polydor 2383.294* [Marcus Dods]

7106 20 Million Sweethearts (1934) Highlights (Harry Warren) US:LP-BP = Milloball 34031

7107 20,000 Leagues Under the Sea (1954) Theme-A (Sonny Burke) US:LP = Coral 57065 [Dick Jacobs & George Cates]; Theme-B (Al Hoffman) US:SP = Decca 9-29355 [Kirk Douglas:ST]; Theme-B + Narration (Al Hoffman) US:LP = Disneyland DQ-1314 + US: LP = Disneyland ST-1924

7108 Twice a Woman [Twee Vrouwen] (1980) Score (Willem Breuker) GE:LP = BVHAAST 024*

7109 Twilight of Honor [The Charge Is Murder] (1963) Excerpts (John Green) US:LP = MGM E-4185/SE-4185* [@John Green:ST]

7110 Twilight Zone—The Movie (1983) Score (Jerry Goldsmith) US:LP = WB 23887-1*

7111 Twinkle and Shine *see* It Happened to Jane

7112 Twinkle, Twinkle, Little Star *see* Move Over, Darling

7113 Twins of Evil (1971) Theme (Harry Robinson) GB:SP = DJM DJS-254* [Essjay]; Theme (Harry Robinson) US:LP-BP = GSF 1002 [@Essjay]

7114 Twist, The [Pazzi Borghesi] (1976) Score (Manuel DeSica) IT:LP = Produttori 71*

7115 Twist All Night *see* Continental Twist, The

7116 Twist Around the Clock (1961) Theme-A/US:SP = Laurie 3110 [Dion:ST]; Theme-B/US:SP = Laurie 3115 [Dion:ST]

7117 Twist of Fate [Beautiful Stranger] (1954) Theme (Jose Ferrer) US:SP = London 45-1488 [Lita Roza]; Theme (Jose Ferrer) US:EP = Columbia 1932 [Rosemary Clooney]

7118 Twisted Nerve (1969) Highlights (Bernard Herrmann) US:LP-BP = Cinema LP-8006 + GB:LP = Polydor 583.728*

7119 Twister (1973) Score (Steve Eastin) US:LP-PP = Fortune BR-1000*

7120 Two a Penny (1968) Score (e: Mike Leander/etc.) US:LP = Light LS-5530* [Cliff Richard:ST]

7121 Two English Girls [Anne and Muriel] [Les Deux Anglaises et le Continent] (1971) Score (Georges Delerue) FR: LP = AZ Disc 117*

7122 Two for the Road (1967) Score (Henry Mancini) US:LP = RCA LPM-3802/LSP-3802*

7123 Two for the Seesaw (1962) Score (Andre Previn) US:LP = UA UAL-4103/UAS-5103*

7124 Two for Tonight (1935) Excerpts (Harry Revel) US:LP-10 = Decca DL-6009 + US:LP = Decca DL-4250 [Bing Crosby:ST]

7125 Two Girls and a Sailor (1943) Score (t:George Stoll/s:various) US:LP-BP = Soundstage SS-2307

7126 Two Guys from Texas (1948) Theme/GB:LP = UA 311 [@Dennis Morgan & Jack Carson:ST]

7127 Two Hearts in Waltz Time (1930) Themes-A-B/GB:78 = Decca 3968 [Carl Brisson:ST]; Themes-C-D/GB: 78 = Decca 3969 [Carl Brisson:ST]

7128 200 Motels (1971) Scores (Frank Zappa) US:LP-MS = UA UAS-9956*

7129 Two Kennedys, The [I Due Kennedy] (1969) Score (Carlo Savina) IT:LP = Cinevox 33/19*

7130 Two Loves [The Spinster] (1961) Themes (Bronislau Kaper) US: SP = RPC 505 [The Teen Starlets]

7131 Two Men of Karamoja [The Wild and the Brave] (1974) Theme (Charles Randolph Grean) US:SP = Ranwood 972 [Charles Grean:ST]

7132 Two Minute Warning (1976) Theme (Charles Fox) US:LP-BP = Centurion 1210* [@Stanley Maxfield]

7133 Two Mrs. Carrolls, The (1947) Excerpts (Franz Waxman) US:LP = RCA ARL1-0422* + US:LP = RCA AGL1-3782* [Charles Gerhardt]

7134 Two Mules for Sister Sara (1970) Score (Ennio Morricone) US: LP = Kapp KRS-5512*

7135 Two of a Kind (1983) Score (various) US:LP = MCA 6127*

7135a Two of Us, The [Le Vieil Homme l'Enfant] (1967) Theme (Georges Delerue) FR:SP = Philips 1139* [ST]

7136 Two on a Guillotine (1965) Theme (Max Steiner) US:SP = Decca 9-31734 [Robert Maxwell]; Theme (Max Steiner) US:LP = RCA 4205* [Peter Nero]

7137 Two Seasons of Life, The [Le Due Stagione de la Vita] (1972) Score (Ennio Morricone) IT:LP = General Music 55079*

7138 Two Texas Knights *see* Two Guys from Texas

7139 2001: A Space Odyssey (1968) Score-A (classical music) US:LP = MGM 1SE-13*; Score-B (classical music) US:LP = MGM SE-4722*

7140 2010 (1984) Score (David Shire) US:LP = A&M SP-5038*

7141 Two Thousand Maniacs (1964) Highlights (Herschell Gordon Lewis) US:LP = Rhino RNSP-305

7142 2000 Years Later (1969) Themes (Stu Phillips) US:SP = WB 7266 [Stu Phillips:ST]

7143 Two Tickets to Broadway (1951) Highlights (e:Jule Styne/etc.) US:

LP-10=RCA LPM-39 [Tony Bennett:ST]

7144 Two Tickets to Paris (1962) Score (Henry Glover) US:LP = Roulette R-25182/SR-25182*

7145 Two-Way Stretch (1960) Theme (Ken Jones) US:SP = Mercury 71790 [David Carroll]; Theme (Ken Jones) US:LP = Mercury 60688* [David Carroll]

7146 Two Weeks in Another Town (1962) Theme (David Raksin) US:SP = Choreo 109 [Elmer Bernstein]; Theme (David Raksin) US:LP = Ava 30* [@Elmer Bernstein]

7147 Two Weeks in September [A Coeur Joie] (1967) Theme-A (Kaye & Lake) US:LP = World Pacific 21864* [Bud Shank]; Theme-B (Michel Magne) FR:LP = Sonopresse 63070* [Michel Magne:ST]

7148 Two Weeks with Love (1950) Highlights (pop music) US:LP-10 = MGM E-530 + US:LP = MGM E-3233 + US:LP-MS = MGM 2SES-49e

7149 Two White Arms (1932) Theme/US:LP = Monmouth 7031 [@Adolphe Menjou:ST]

7150 Two Women [La Ciociara] (1960) Highlights (Armando Trovajoli) IT:EP = RCA EPA-30.394

7151 Typhoon (1940) Theme (Frederick Hollander) US:LP = West Coast 14002 [Dorothy Lamour:ST]

U

7152 Uccidete il Vitello Grasso el Arrositelo (1969) Highlights (Ennio Morricone) US:LP = Cerberus CEMSP-0117*

7153 Uei Paesano / Theme (Nicola Paone) US:SP = Capitol 2737 [Al Martino]

7154 Ugly Dachshund, The (1966) Theme + Narration (Richard & Robert Sherman) US:LP = Disneyland DQ-1290

7155 Ugly Ones, The [The Bounty Killer] (1966) Score (Stelvio Cipriani) IT: LP = Phoenix PHCAM-11*

7156 Ultimo Cuple, El / Score (various) US:LP = London LL-5409 [Sarita Montiel:ST]

7157 Ulysses (1953) Score (Alessandro Cicognini) IT:LP = Intermezzo IM-007

7158 Ulysses (1967) Score (Stanley Myers) US:LP = RCA LOC-1138/LSO-1138*

7159 Umbrellas of Cherbourg, The [Les Parapluies de Cherbourg] (1964) Scores (Michel Legrand) FR:LP-MS = Philips B2L-0054*; Score (M. Legrand) US:LP = Philips PCC-216/PCC-616*

7160 Unchained (1955) Theme-A (Alex North) US:SP = Columbia 4-40455 [Liberace]; Theme-A (Alex North) US: LP = Citadel 6023* [Alex North:ST]; Theme-B (Alex North) US:LP = RCA 1445* [Alex North:ST]

7161 Uncle Joe Shannon (1978) Score (Bill Conti) US:LP = UA LA-935*

7162 Uncle Remus *see* Song of the South

7163 Uncle Tom's Cabin (1968) Score (Peter Thomas) US:LP = Philips PHS-600.272*

7164 Uncle Was a Vampire [Hard Times for Vampires] [Tempi Duri per i Vampiri] (1959) Theme (Martini Brighetti) US:LP = RCA FSO-4* [@ST]

7165 Undefeated, The (1969) Highlights (Hugo Montenegro) US:LP-BP = Lone Star LS-1983; Theme (Hugo Montenegro) US:SP = UNI 55173 [The Marketts]

7166 Under Capricorn (1949) Theme (Richard Addinsell) GB:78 = Decca 9291 [Richard Addinsell:ST]

7167 Under Fire (1983) Score (Jerry Goldsmith) US:LP = WB 23965-1*

7168 Under Paris Skies *see* Under the Paris Sky

7169 Under the Cherry Moon (1986) Excerpts (Prince) US:LP = WB 25395-1* [Prince:ST]

7170 Under the Counter Spy [Cartoon] (1954) Sequence + Dialog (Clarence Wheeler) US:LP = Peter Pan 1120 [@ST]

7171 Under the Paris Sky [Under Paris Skies] (1951) Theme (Hubert Giraud) US:SP = Columbia 4-40661 [Michel Legrand]; Theme (Hubert Giraud) US: SP = Columbia 4-40100 [Mitch Miller]; Theme (Hubert Giraud) US:LP = MGM 3731* [The Metropolitan Jazz Quartet]

7172 Under the Roofs of Paris (1930) Theme (Raoul Moretti) US:LP = Capitol 8603* [Frank Pourcel]

7173 Under the Yum-Yum Tree (1963) Theme (James Van Heusen) US: SP = Colpix 708 [James Darren]; Theme (James Van Heusen) US:SP = Columbia 4-42885 [Robert Goulet]

7174 Under Western Stars (1938) Theme/US:LP = Columbia 38907 [Roy Rogers:ST]

7175 Under Your Spell (1936) Theme/US:LP-BP = JJA 19757 [@Lawrence Tibbett:ST]

7176 Undercover (1984) Score (e: Bruce Smeaton/e:Dorothy Dodds) AU: LP = WB WEA 250346-1*

7177 Underpup, The (1939) Excerpts (various) US:78-MS = Decca A-125 [Gloria Jean:ST]

7178 Underwater! (1955) Themes (Perez Prado/Louiguy) US:SP = RCA 47-5965 [Perez Prado:ST]; Theme (Louiguy) US:LP = RCA 6066 [Perez Prado: ST]

7179 Unfaithfully Yours (1984) Theme (Stephen Bishop) US:SP = WB 7-29345* [Stephen Bishop:ST]

7180 Unfinished Dance, The (1947) Highlights (t:Sammy Fain/ae:Herbert Stothart) US:78-MS = MGM 412; Excerpts (ae:Herbert Stothart) US:LP = MGM E-3148 [@Herbert Stothart:ST]

7181 Unforgettable Year—1919, The (1951) Theme (Dmitri Shostakovich) US:LP = EMI Angel 34489 [Jerzy Maksymiuk]

7182 Unforgiven, The (1960) Score (Dimitri Tiomkin) US:LP = UA UAL-4068/UAS-5068*

7183 Unholy Matrimony (1962) Theme (Warren Schatz) US:SP = Parkway 990 [The Warmest Spring:ST]

7184 Unicorn in the Garden, The [Cartoon] (1954) Theme (David Raksin) US:LP = Classic Editions 1055 [The Manhattan Recorder Consort]

7185 Unidentified Flying Oddball, The [The Spaceman and King Arthur] (1980) Theme (Ron Goodwin) GB:LP = Chandos 1014* [Ron Goodwin:ST]

7186 Uninhibited, The [Les Pianos Mechaniques] (1965) Highlights (Georges Delerue) FR:EP = Riviera 231.088

7187 Uninvited, The (1944) Theme (Victor Young) US:SP = Decca 9-23468 [Victor Young:ST]; Theme (Victor Young) US:LP = Decca 8025 + US: LP = Decca 8798 [Victor Young:ST]; Theme (Victor Young) US:LP = MGM 4432* [Cyril Ornadel]

7188 Unmarried Woman, An (1978) Score (Bill Conti) US:LP = 20th T-557*

7189 Unsinkable Molly Brown, The (1964) Score (stage songs:Meredith Willson) US:LP = MGM E-4232/SE-4232*

7190 Untamed (1929) Themes/US: LP-BP = Curtain Calls 100/23 [Joan Crawford:ST]

7191 Untamed Frontier (1952) Excerpts (Hans J. Salter) US:LP = Medallion ML-313 [Hans J. Salter:ST]

7192 Untamed Youth (1957) Highlights (Les Baxter) US:EP = Prep M1-1 [Mamie Van Doren:ST]; Excerpts (Les Baxter) US:LP = Rhino 70819 [Mamie Van Doren:ST]; Theme (Eddie Cochran) GB:LP = Charly 30168 [Eddie Cochran: ST]

7193 Until They Sail (1957) Theme (David Raksin) US:SP = ABC 9852 [Eydie Gorme & David Raksin:ST]

7194 Unwed Mother (1958) Theme (Ron Hargrave) US:SP = MGM 12644 [Ron Hargrave:ST]

7195 Uomo di Paglia, L' *see* Seducer, The

7196 Up from the Beach [Le Jour d'Apres] (1965) Highlights (Edgar Cosma) FR:EP = 20th 730.005; Themes (Edgar Cosma) US:SP = 20th 592 [Richard DeBenedictis & Ray Ellis]

7197 Up in Arms (1944) Score (e: Harold Arlen/t:Sylvia Fine/etc.) US: LP-BP = Sountrak STK-113

7198 Up in Smoke (1978) Highlights + Dialog (e:Danny Kortchmar/e: pop music) US:LP = WB BSK-3249*

7199 Up in the Cellar [Three in the Cellar] (1970) Score (s:Don Randi/t: Dory Previn) US:LP = American International STA-1036*

7200 Up the Academy (1980) Score (pop music) US:LP = Capitol S00-12091*

7201 Up the Creek (1984) Score (e:

Randy Bishop/etc.) US:LP = Pasha SZ-39333*

7202 Up the Down Staircase (1967) Score (Fred Karlin) US:LP = UA UAL-4169/UAS-5169*

7203 Up the Junction (1968) Score (Mike Hugg) US:LP = Mercury SR-61159*

7204 Up the MacGregors [Sette Donne per i MacGregor] (1966) Theme (Ennio Morricone) IT:LP-MS = RCA 31543* [Ennio Morricone:ST]

7205 Up the Sandbox (1972) Themes (Billy Goldenberg) US:SP = Columbia 4-45780* [Barbra Streisand/Billy Goldenberg:ST]; Theme (Billy Goldenberg) US:LP-BP = Centurion 1600 [@Barbra Streisand:ST]; Theme [discarded score] (Dave Grusin) US:LP = Columbia 33815* [Barbra Streisand]

7206 Up Tight (1971) Score (Booker T. Jones) US:LP = Stax STS-2006*

7207 Up to His Ears [Chinese Adventures in China] (1965) Score (Georges Delerue) AU:LP = UA AUSLP-1003 + NZ:LP = UA UAL-4136 + US:LP-BP = POO 108

7208 Up to His Neck (1954) Theme (Benjamin Frankel) GB:78-PP = Rank FM-151 [ST]; Theme (Benjamin Frankel) US:LP-BP = Citadel CTOFI-1 [@ST]

7209 Upper World (1934) Theme/US:LP-BP = Curtain Calls 100/21 [Ginger Rogers:ST]

7210 Upstairs and Downstairs (1959) Highlights (Philip Green) GB:EP = Top Rank 8053

7210a Uptown Saturday Night (1974) Themes (Tom Scott) US:SP = WB 8021 [Bill Harris:ST]

7211 Upturned Glass, The (1947) Theme (Bernard Stevens) GB:78-PP = Rank RM-17 [ST]

7212 Urban Cowboy (1980) Scores (pop music/various composers) US:LP-MS = Asylum DP-90002*; Score (pop music/various composers) US:LP = Full Moon/Epic SE-36921*

7213 Urgh! A Music War (1982) Scores (pop music) US:LP-MS = A&M SP-6019*

7214 Used Cars (1980) Theme (Patrick Williams) US:SP = Columbia 1-11365* [Bobby Bare:ST]; Theme (Patrick Williams) US:LP-BP = Disc 105* [@Bobby Bare:ST]

7215 Utamaro's World / Score (Ryohei Hirose) JA:LP = RCA/Victor VIP-7233*

7216 Utu (1983) Score (John Charles) US:LP = Southern Cross SCRS-1008*

7217 VIP—My Brother Superman [VIP—Vio Fratello Superuomo] [The Super VIPs] (1968) Score (Franco Godi) IT:LP = CAM SAG-9009*

7218 V.I.P.s, The (1963) Score (Miklos Rozsa) US:LP = MGM E-4152/SE-4152*

7219 Vagabond King, The (1930) Highlights (stage songs:Rudolf Friml) US:LP-BP = Vertigo 2002

7220 Vagabond King, The (1956) Score (t:Victor Young/stage songs:Rudolf Friml) US:LP = RCA LM-2004 [Oreste:ST]

7221 Vagabond Lover, The (1929) Themes-A-B/US:78 = RCA/Victor 22193 [Rudy Vallee:ST]; Themes-C-D/US:78 = RCA/Victor 22227 [Rudy Vallee:ST]; Theme-E/US:LP = RCA 2507 + US:LP = RCA 3816 [Rudy Vallee:ST]

7222 Valachi Papers, The (1972) Score (Riz Ortolani) GB:LP = Philips 6303.075*; Excerpts (Riz Ortolani) US:LP = Project PR-5085* [@ST]

7223 Valdez Horses, The *see* Chino

7224 Valentino (1951) Themes (Heinz Roemheld) US:LP = Decca DL-5347 [The Castillians]; Theme (Heinz Roemheld) US:SP = Decca 9-27511 [The Castillians]; Theme (Heinz Roemheld) US:LP = MCA 530 [The Castillians]

7225 Valentino (1977) Score (e:Stanley Black/e:pop music) US:LP = UA LA-810*

7226 Valley, The (1972) Score (Pink Floyd) US:LP = Harvest ST-11078* [Pink Floyd:ST]

7227 Valley Girl (1983) Highlights (pop music) US:EP-12 = Roadshow RS-101*

7228 Valley of the Dolls (1967) Score (e:Andre Previn/ae:John Williams) US:LP = 20th 4196/S-4196*; Excerpts (Andre Previn) US:LP = UA UAL-3623/UAS-6623* [Patty Duke: ST]; Theme (Andre Previn) US:SP = Scepter 12203* [Dionne Warwick:ST]; Theme (Andre Previn) US:LP = Liberty 7544* [Tony Scotti:ST]

7229 Valley of the Eagles (1951) Theme (Nino Rota) GB:78-PP = Rank FM-122 [ST]

7230 Vamp (1986) Score (Jonathan Elias) US:LP = Varese STV-81288*

7231 Vampire, The [Mark of the Vampire] (1957) Theme (Gerald Fried) US:SP = RKO Unique 410 [Joe Tucker]

7232 Vampire Lovers, The (1970) Theme [Harry Robinson] US:LP = Capitol 11340* [@ST]

7233 Vampire of Dusseldorf, The (1965) Highlights (Andre Hossein) FR: EP = Festival 1445

7234 Van, The (1977) Score (Sammy Johns) US:LP = WB BS-3063*

7235 Van Nuys Blvd. (1979) Score (Ron Wright & Ken Mansfield) US:LP = Mercury SRM1-3794*

7236 Vanina Vanini (1961) Score (Renzo Rossellini) IT:LP = CAM CMS-30.032

7237 Vanishing Point (1971) Score (e:Jimmy Bowen/e:Mike Settle) US: LP = Amos AAS-8002*

7238 Vanishing Prairie, The (1954) Highlights (Paul Smith) US:LP-10 = Columbia CL-6332 + US:LP = Buena Vista BV-3326

7239 Varan the Unbelievable (1958) Excerpts (Akira Ifukube) JA:LP = Toho 8107 [@ST]; Theme (Akira Ifukube) US:LP-BP = POO 106 [@ST]

7239a Variety (1983) Highlights (John Lurie) GB:LP = Made to Measure MTM-14*

7240 Variety Girl (1947) Highlights (Frank Loesser) US:LP-BP = Caliban 6007

7241 Varsity Show, The (1937) Excerpts (Richard A. Whiting) US:LP = MCA 1511 [Dick Powell:ST]; Highlights (Richard A. Whiting) US:LP-BP = Vertinge 2001

7242 Venetian Affair, The (1967) Themes (Lalo Schifrin) US:SP = MGM 13670 [Lalo Schifrin:ST]; Theme (Lalo Schifrin) US:LP = MGM 4742* [Lalo Schifrin:ST]; Theme (Lalo Schifrin) US: LP = World Pacific 21864* [Bud Shank]

7243 Vengeance of Kali, The [Kali-Yug, La Dea della Vendetta] (1965) Score (A.F. Lavagnino) IT:LP = CAM CMS-30.093

7244 Vengeance of She, The (1967) Theme (Mario Nascimbene) IT:LP-MS = Kangaroo 34209 [Mario Nascimbene:ST]

7245 Vera Cruz (1954) Theme (Hugo Friedhofer) US:SP = Capitol 2997 [Nelson Riddle]; Theme (Hugo Friedhofer) US:SP = RCA 47-5946 [Tony Martin]; Theme (Hugo Friedhofer) US:LP = Mercury 70514 [Richard Hayman]

7246 Verboten! (1959) Theme (Harry Sukman) US:SP = ABC 9937 [Paul Anka]; Theme (Harry Sukman) US:LP = Liberty [Harry Sukman:ST]

7247 Veronika Voss (1982) Score (Peer Raben) GE:LP = Teldec Jupiter 625-120*; Highlights (Peer Raben) US: LP = DRG SL-9508*

7248-9 Vertigo (1958) Score (Bernard Herrmann) US:LP = Mercury MG-20384 + US:LP-BP = Sound Stage SS-2301 + US:LP = Mercury SRI-75117* [Muir Mathieson:ST]; Excerpts (Bernard Herrmann) US:LP = London SP-44126* [Bernard Herrmann]

7250 Very Happy Alexander *see* Alexander

7251 Very Private Affair, A [La Vie Privee] (1962) Highlights (Fiorenzo Carpi) FR:EP = Barclay 70436; Themes (Fiorenzo Carpi) US:SP = MGM 13099 [Brigitte Bardot:ST]

7252 Veuve Couderc, La (1971) Excerpts (Philippe Sarde) US:LP = DRG SL-9512* [@ST]

7253 Vice and Virtue [Le Vice et la Vertu] (1965) Highlights (Michel Magne) FR:EP = Barclay 70509

7254 Vice Squad [Brigade Mondaine] (1978) Score (Carrone) FR:LP = WB/Malligator 772-811*

7255 Vice Versa (1945) Theme-A (Anthony Hopkins) GB:78-PP = Rank FM-7 [ST]; Theme-B (Anthony Hopkins) GB:78-PP = Rank FM-8 [ST]; Theme-B (Anthony Hopkins) US:LP-BP = Citadel CTOFI-1 [@ST]

7256 Vicious Breed, The (1955) Theme (Charles Norman & Les Baxter) US:SP=Capitol 3728 [Les Baxter:ST]

7257 Vicki (1953) Theme (Ken Darby) US:SP=Coral 9-28877 [Hamlish Menzies]

7258 Victim, The *see* Autopsy

7259 Victor/Victoria (1982) Score (Henry Mancini) US:LP=MGM/Polygram MG1-5407*

7260 Victors, The (1963) Score (Sol Kaplan) US:LP=Colpix CP-516/SCP-516*

7261 Victory March [Marcia Trionfale] (1976) Score (Nicola Piovani) IT: LP=Beat LPF-032*

7262 Vida Sigue Igual, La / Score (Julio Iglesias) US:LP=CBS DIL-50314* [Julio Iglesias:ST]

7263 Videodrome (1983) Score (Howard Shore) US:LP=Varese STV-81173*

7264 Vie de Chateau, La *see* Matter of Resistance, A

7265 Vie Est un Roman, La [Life Is a Book] (1983) Score (M. Philippe Gerard) FR:LP=RCA 310.143*

7266 View from Pompey's Head, The (1955) Theme (Elmer Bernstein) US: LP=Dot 25097* [Elmer Bernstein:ST]

7267 View to a Kill, A (1985) Score (John Barry) US:LP=Capitol SJ-12413*

7268 Vigilante (1984) Theme (Willie Colon) US:LP=Fania 610* [Willie Colon:ST]

7269 Vikings, The (1958) Score (Mario Nascimbene) UA UAL-40003/ UAS-5003e

7270 Viktor und Viktoria [Victor and Victoria] (1933) Theme (Heino Gaze) GE:LP=Polydor 45151 [@ST]

7271 Villa Rides (1968) Score (Maurice Jarre) US:LP=Dot DLP-25870*

7272 Village Harvest (1945) Theme (Benjamin Britten) GB:78=Decca 874 [Charles Brill]

7273 Village of 8 Gravestones, The (1978) Score (Yasushi Akutagawa) US: LP=Varese VC-81084*

7274 Village of the Damned (1960) Sequence + Dialog (Ron Goodwin) IT:LP-BP=Blu 15001 [@ST]

7275 Vincent, Francois, Paul and the Others [Vincent, Francois, Paul et les Autres] (1976) Score (Philippe Sarde) FR:LP=Polydor 2393.098*

7276 Viola (1973) Score (Ravi Shankar) US:LP=Spark SPA-06* [Ravi Shankar:ST]

7277 Violated (1953) Theme (Tony Mottola) US:LP-10=MGM 300 [Tony Mottola:ST]

7278 Violent City *see* Family, The

7279 Violent Men, The (1955) Theme (Max Steiner) US:LP-MS-BP= Tony Thomas TTMS-9/10 [Max Steiner: ST]

7280 Violent Summer [L'Estate Violenta] (1959) Highlights (Mario Nascimbene) IT:EP=RCA EPA-30.353

7281 Violetera, La (1958) Score (e: Martinez Abades/e:various) US:LP= Columbia EX-5056 [Sarita Montiel:ST]

7282 Violette (1978) Highlights (Pierre Jansen) FR:LP=Pema 900.062*

7283 Violettes Imperiales (1952) Theme (Francis Lopez) US:SP=Capitol 2579 [Les Baxter]

7284 Violin, The / Highlights (Maurice Solway) CA:LP=RCA KXL1-0029*

7285 Virgin and the Gypsy, The (1970) Score (Patrick Gowers) US:LP= Steady S-122*

7286 Virgin of Nuremberg, The *see* Horror Castle

7287 Virgin Soldiers, The (1969) Theme (Raymond Davies) US:SP= RCA 74-0322* [Leon Bibb]

7288 Virginia City (1940) Theme-A (Max Steiner) US:LP-MS-BP=Tony Thomas TTMS-9/10 [Max Steiner:ST]; Theme-B (Max Steiner) US:LP=RCA 1-0422* + US:LP=RCA 1-3782* [Charles Gerhardt]

7289 Virus (1981) Score-A (Teo Macero) JA:LP=Columbia YX-5027*; Score-B (Teo Macero) JA:LP=Columbia YX-7274*

7290 Vision Quest (1985) Score (various) US:LP=Geffen GHS-24063*

7291 Visions of 8 [Olympic Visions] (1973) Score (Henry Mancini) US: LP=RCA ABL1-0231*

7292 Visit to a Chief's Son [African Summer] (1974) Theme (Francis Lai) US: LP=Audio Fidelity 6301 [Francis Lai: ST]

7293 Visit to a Small Planet (1960) Theme (Mort Shuman) US:LP = ABC 333* [Francis Panama]

7294 Visiteurs du Soir, Les (1942) Highlights (Maurice Thiriet) FR:EP = Decca 460.780; Theme (Maurice Thiriet) US:LP = Columbia 1178 [Michel Legrand]

7295 Visitor, The [Stridulum] (1979) Score (Franco Micalizzi) IT:LP = RCA 31433*

7296 Vitelloni [I Vitelloni] [Spivs] [The Drifters] [The Wastrels] [Young and Passionate] (1953) Theme (Nino Rota) US:LP = Hannibal 9301* [William Fischer]; Theme (Nino Rota) IT:LP = CAM 9053* [Nino Rota & Carlo Savina: ST]

7297 Viva Knievel (1977) Theme (Charles Bernstein) US:SP = WB 682* [Charles Bernstein:ST]

7298 Viva la Vie (1984) Score (Didier Barbelivien) FR:LP = Talar Pathe 240-1341*

7299 Viva Las Vegas (1956) *see* Meet Me in Las Vegas

7300 Viva Las Vegas [Love in Las Vegas] (1964) Score (various) US:LP-BP = Lucky LR-711 [Elvis Presley:ST]; Highlights (various) US:EP = RCA EPA-4382 [Elvis Presley:ST]; Theme (Mort Shuman) US:SP = RCA 447-0646 [Elvis Presley:ST]

7301 Viva Maria (1965) Score-A (Georges Delerue) US:LP = UA UAL-4135/UAS-5135*; Score-B (Georges Delerue) FR:LP = Philips 70.321*

7302 Viva Max! (1970) Score (e: Hugo Montenegro/e:Ralph Dino & John Sembello) US:LP = RCA LSP-4275*

7303 Viva Villa! (1934) Highlights (Herbert Stothart) US:LP-MS-BP = Tony Thomas TTST-1/2

7304 Viva Zapata (1952) Highlights (Alex North) US:LP = Film Music Collection FMC-9* [Elmer Bernstein]; Theme (Alex North) US:LP = Citadel 6023* [Alex North:ST]

7305 Vivacious Lady (1938) Theme/ US:LP-BP = Curtain Calls 100/21 [Ginger Rogers:ST]

7306 Vive Les Femmes (1984) Themes (Nicholas Errera) FR:SP = Carrere 13411* [ST]

7307 Vixen [Russ Meyer's Vixen] (1968) Score (William Loose) US:LP = Beverly Hills BHS-22*

7308 Voice in the Mirror (1958) Theme (Bobby Troup) US:SP = Liberty 55139 [Julie London:ST]

7309 Voices (1979) Score (Jimmy Webb) US:LP = Planet P-9002*

7310 Volcano *see* Krakatoa, East of Java

7311 Von Richthofen and Brown [The Red Baron] (1971) Highlights (Hugo Friedhofer) US:LP = Delos F-25420

7312 Von Ryan's Express (1965) Theme (Jerry Goldsmith) US:SP = 20th 593 [Ray Ellis]; Theme (Jerry Goldsmith) US:SP = Capitol 5451 [The Gallants]; Theme (Jerry Goldsmith) US:LP = Command 887* [Enoch Light]

7313 Voodoo Girl *see* Sugar Hill

7314 Vortex (1983) Score (Adele Bertei) US:LP = Neutral N-6*

7315 Vote for Huggett (1949) Theme (Anthony Hopkins) GB:78-PP = Rank FM-50 [ST]

7316 Voyage, The [Il Viaggio] (1973) Score (Manuel DeSica) IT:LP = CAM SAG-9057*

7317 Voyage en Ballon [Stowaway in the Sky] (1960) Score (Jean Prodromides) US:LP = Philips PHM-200-029/PHS-600-029*

7318 Voyage of the Damned (1976) Score-A (Lalo Schifrin) US:LP = Entracte ERS-6508* + US:LP-PP = Voyage 1001*; Score-B (Lalo Schifrin) JA: LP = Seven Seas FML-77*

7319 Voyage of the Rock Aliens *see* When the Rain Begins to Fall

7320 Voyage to Italy, A *see* Trip to Italy, A

7321 Voyage to the Bottom of the Sea (1961) Theme (Russ Faith) US:SP = Chancellor 1081 [Frankie Avalon:ST]; Theme (Russ Faith) US:LP-BP = GSF 1002 [@Frankie Avalon:ST]

7322 W.C. Fields and Me (1976) Score (Henry Mancini) US:LP = MCA 2092*

7323 W.W. and the Dixie Dancekings (1975) Score (t:Dave Grusin/s: various) US:LP = 20th ST-103*

7324 Wabash Avenue (1950) Highlights (Josef Myrow) US:LP-BP = Caliban 6029

7325 Wackey World of Mother Goose, The (1967) Score (George Wilkins) US:LP = Epic LN-24230/BN-26230*

7326 Waco (1966) Themes (Jimmie Haskell) US:SP = RCA 47-8901 [Lorne Greene:ST]

7327 Wages of Fear, The (1977) *see* Sorcerer

7328 Wagon Master, The (1929) Theme/US:SP = Columbia 2310 [Ken Maynard:ST]

7329 Wagonmaster, The (1950) Themes (Stan Jones) US:SP = RCA 48-0315 [The Sons of the Pioneers:ST]; Themes (Stan Jones) US:LP = RCA 1-4092 [The Sons of the Pioneers:ST]

7330 Waikiki Wedding (1937) Excerpts (Ralph Rainger) US:LP-10 = Decca DL-6011 + US:LP = Decca DL-4252 [Bing Crosby:ST]

7331 Wait Until Dark (1967) Themes (Henry Mancini) US:SP = RCA 47-9340 [Henry Mancini:ST]; Theme-A (Henry Mancini) US:LP = RCA 4022* [Henry Mancini:ST]; Theme-B (Henry Mancini) US:LP = RCA 4466* [Henry Mancini:ST]

7332 Wake Me When It's Over (1960) Theme (James Van Heusen) US: SP = Cadence 1378 [Andy Williams:ST]

7333 Wake Up and Dream [Short] (1934) Excerpts (Russ Columbo) US:LP-BP = Golden Legends 2000/1 [@ST]

7334 Wake Up and Kill [Svegliati e Uccidi] (1966) Score (Ennio Morricone) IT:LP = RCA SP-8018

7335 Wake Up and Live (1937) Score (Harry Revel) US:LP-BP = Hollywood Soundstage HS-403

7336 Walk, Don't Run (1966) Score (Quincy Jones) US:LP = Mainstream 56080/S-6080*

7337 Walk in the Spring Rain, A (1970) Highlights (Elmer Bernstein) US: LP-BP = Cinema LP-8013*; Theme (Elmer Bernstein) US:SP = Columbia 4-45137* [Ray Conniff]

7338 Walk in the Sun, A (1946) Highlights (Earl Robinson) US:LP = Folkways FS-2324 [Earl Robinson:ST]

7339 Walk Like a Dragon (1960) Theme (Mel Torme) US:SP = Verve 10211 [Mel Torme:ST]

7340 Walk on the Wild Side (1962) Score (Elmer Bernstein) US:LP = Mainstream 56083/S-6083* + US:LP = Choreo A-4/AS-4* + US:LP = Citadel CTV-7028*

7341 Walk Proud (1980) Theme (Robby Benson) US:SP = MCA 41027* [Robby Benson:ST]

7342 Walk the Proud Land (1956) Themes (Hans J. Salter) US:LP = Medallion 313 [Hans J. Salter:ST]

7343 Walk with Love and Death, A (1969) Score (Georges Delerue) US: LP = Citadel CT-6025

7344 Walkabout (1971) Score (John Barry) US:LP-BP = POO 102 + US:LP-BP = GSF 1005; Theme (John Barry) US: LP = Columbia 31219* [Tony Bennett]; Theme (John Barry) GB:LP = Polydor 2383.300* [John Barry:ST]

7345 Walking Tall (1973) Theme (Walter Scharf) US:SP = Columbia 4-45777* [Johnny Mathis:ST]

7346 Wall, The *see* Pink Floyd—The Wall

7347 Waltz Across Texas (1982) Theme/US:LP = RCA 1-3602* [Waylon Jennings:ST]

7348 Waltz of the Toreadors (1962) Theme (Richard Addinsell) GB:SP = Parlophone 4906 [ST]

7349 Wanderer, The [Le Grand Meaulnes] (1967) Theme (Jean-Pierre Bourtayre) JA:SP = Philips 2087* [ST]; Theme (Jean-Pierre Bourtayre) FR: LP = Philips 6620.025* [@ST]

7350 Wanderers, The (1979) Score (pop music) US:LP = WB BSK-3359*

7351 Wandering Wind, The (1961) Theme (T. Hudgings) US:SP = Orange Empire 9164 [Mickey Rooney, Jr.:ST]

7352 Wanted—Babysitter *see* Babysitter, The

7353 Wanted for Murder (1946) Theme (Mischa Spoliansky) US:LP = Columbia 3029 [@Charles Williams]

7354 Wanton Contessa *see* Senso

7355 War and Peace (1956) Score

(Nino Rota) US:LP = Columbia CL-930 + US:LP = CSP ACL-930

7356 War and Peace (1968) Score (Vyacheslav Ovchinnikov) US:LP = Capitol SWAO-2918*

7357 War Games (1983) Highlights + Underscore + Dialog (Arthur B. Rubinstein) US:LP = Polydor 815-005-1*

7358 War Goddess [The Amazons] [Les Amazones] (1973) Score (Riz Ortolani) JA:LP = Cine Disc 5010*

7359 War Is Over, The *see* La Guerre Est Finie

7360 War Lord, The (1965) Score (s:Jerome Moross/t:Hans J. Salter) US: LP = Decca DL-9149/DL-79149*

7361 War Lover, The (1962) Theme (Richard Addinsell) US:SP = Colpix 658 [Bernie Leighton]; Theme (Richard Addinsell) US:LP = Colpix 458* + US: LP = Colpix 512* [@Shiro Hirosaki]; Theme (Richard Addinsell) US:LP = Capitol 1836* [Semprini]

7362 War of the Buttons [The Button War] [La Guerre des Boutons] (1962) Score (Jose Berghmans) FR:LP = Philips 76.233; Theme (Jose Berghmans) US: LP = Philips 600-071* [@ST]

7363 War of the Gargantuas (1966) Excerpts (Akira Ifukube) JA:LP = Toho 8120 [@ST]

7364 War of the Monsters (1966) Excerpts (Chuji Kinoshita) JA:LP = Toho 8120 [@ST]

7365 War of the Worlds (1953) Highlights (Leith Stevens) US:LP-BP = Quasi PAL-1951/1953; Theme (Leith Stevens) US:LP = GNP 2163* [Neil Norman]

7366 War Wagon, The (1967) Theme (Dimitri Tiomkin) US:SP = RCA 47-9249 [Ed Ames:ST]; Theme (Dimitri Tiomkin) US:SP = Decca 9-32151 [Mike Callahan]; Theme (Dimitri Tiomkin) US:LP-BP = Centurion 1210 [@Mike Callahan]

7367 Warlords of Atlantis [Seven Cities to Atlantis] (1978) Theme (Mike Vickers) JA:LP = Mu Land 7017* [The Electoru Polyphonic Orchestra]

7368 Warlords of the 21st Century [Battletruck] (1982) Score (Kevin Peek) JA:LP = Nexus K28P-4099* + FR:LP = Dynasty/Ades 2105*

7369 Warm Life, The [La Calda Vita] (1964) Score (Carlo Rustichelli) IT: LP = CAM CMS-30.089

7370 Warning Shot (1967) Highlights (Jerry Goldsmith) US:LP = Liberty LRP-3498/LST-7498* [Si Zentner]

7371 Warning Sign (1985) Score (Craig Safan) US:LP = Southern Cross SCRS-1012*

7372 Warning to Wantons (1949) Theme (Hans May) GB:78-PP = Rank FM-48 [ST]

7373 Warriors, The (1979) Score (e: Barry DeVorzon/e:various) US:LP = A&M SP-4761*

7374 Wasn't That a Time [The Weavers—Wasn't That a Time] (1983) Highlights (pop music) US:LP = Loom 1681* [The Weavers:ST]

7375 Wastrel, The [Il Relitto] (1960) Highlights (A.F. Lavagnino) IT: EP = RCA EPA-396

7376 Water (1985) Score (e:Mike Moran/e:Eddy Grant/e:various) GB: LP = Filmtrax 820-263-1*

7377 Water Babies (1979) Score (Phil Coulter) GB:LP = Ariola/MFP 50503*

7378 Waterhole #3 (1967) Highlights + Underscore + Narration (Dave Grusin) US:LP = Smash SRM-27096/SRS-67096*

7379 Waterloo (1970) Score (Nino Rota) US:LP = Paramount PAS-6003*

7380 Watermelon Man (1970) Score (Melvin Van Peebles) US:LP = Beverly Hills BHS-26*

7381 Watership Down (1978) Score (s:Angela Morley-aka-Walter Stott/t: Mike Batt/t:Malcolm Williamson) US: LP = Columbia JS-35707*

7382 Watts [Short] Theme (Gil Melle) US:LP = Jazz Chronicles 702* [Gil Melle:ST]

7383 Wattstax (1972) Scores-A (pop music) US:LP-MS = Stax STS-3010*; Scores-B (pop music) US:LP-MS = Stax STS-3018*

7384 Wave, The (1935) Highlights (Silvestre Revueltas) US:LP = RCA ARL1-2320* [Silvestre Revueltas:ST]

7385 Wavelength (1983) Score (Tangerine Dream) US:LP = Varese STV-81207*

7386 Way of the Dragon, The *see* Return of the Dragon

7387 Way Out West (1930) Theme/ US:LP-BP = Take Two 205 [Cliff Edwards:ST]

7388 Way Out West (1936) Highlights + Underscore + Dialog (Marvin Hatley) US:LP = Mark 56 #688 + US: LP-MS = Murray Hill 60165

7389 Way to Love, The (1933) Excerpts (Ralph Rainger) US:LP-BP = Caliban 6013 [@ST]

7390 Way to the Gold, The (1957) Theme (Lionel Newman) US:LP-MS = Reader's Digest RD4-39* [@Charles Gerhardt]

7391 Way to the Stars, The [Johnny in the Clouds] (1945) Themes (Nicholas Brodszky) GB:78 = Columbia 2180 [Charles Williams]; Themes (Nicholas Brodszky) GB:LP = WRC 384 [@Charles Williams]; Theme (Nicholas Brodszky) US:LP = Capitol 1836* [Semprini]

7392 Way ... Way Out (1966) Theme (Lalo Schifrin) US:SP = 20th 6651 [The Girls]; Theme (Lalo Schifrin) US:LP = 20th 3192* [Harry Betts]

7393 Way We Were, The (1973) Score (e:Marvin Hamlisch/e:pop music) US:LP = Columbia KS-32830*

7394 Way West, The (1967) Score (Bronislau Kaper) US:LP = UA UAL-4149/UAS-5149*

7395 We All Loved Each Other So Much [C'Eravamo Tanto Amati] (1977) Score (Armando Trovajoli) IT:LP = Duse ELP-54*

7396 We Are the Lambeth Boys (1959) Themes (Johnny Dankworth) GB: SP = Top Rank 209 [Johnny Dankworth:ST]

7397 We Have Come for Your Daughters *see* Medicine Ball Caravan

7398 We of the Never Never (1982) Score (Peter Best) AU:LP = Festival 37932*

7399 We Still Kill the Old Way (1968) Score (Luis E. Bacalov) US:LP = UA UAS-5183*

7400 We, the Women [Siamo Donne] (1953) Theme (Alessandro Cicognini) JA:LP-MS = CBS/Sony 2301 [@ST]

7401 Weaker Sex, The (1948) Theme (Arthur Wilkinson) GB:78-PP = Rank FM-33 [ST]

7402 Web of Fear [Constance aux Enfer] (1964) Highlights (Claude Bolling) FR:EP = Philips 434.829

7403 Web of the Spider [Nella Stretta Mors a del Ragno] (1972) Score (Riz Ortolani) IT:LP = RCA SP-8037*

7404 Wedding Bells *see* Royal Wedding

7405 Wedding Breakfast *see* Catered Affair, The

7406 Wedding in Blood [Les Noces Rouges] (1973) Themes (Pierre Jansen) FR:SP = RCA FPA1-0001* [ST]

7407 Weekend at Dunkirk, A [Weekend a Zuydcoote] (1965) Highlights (Maurice Jarre) FR:EP = Barclay 70737

7408 Weekend at the Waldorf (1945) Theme/US:78 = Columbia 36694 [Xavier Cugat:ST]

7409 Weekend in Havana (1941) Highlights (e:Harry Warren/etc.) US: LP-BP = Curtain Calls 100/14; Excerpts (various) US:78-MS = Decca A-295 [Carmen Miranda:ST]

7410 Weekend Murders, The [Concerto per Pistola Solista] (1970) Score (Francesco DeMasi) IT:LP = CAM SAG-9034*

7411 Week's Vacation, A [Une Semaine de Vacances] (1982) Score (Pierre Papadiamandis) FR:LP = Barclay 900.587*

7412 Weird Science (1985) Score (t: Ira Newborn/s:various) US:LP = MCA 6146*

7413 Welcome Stranger (1947) Excerpts (James Van Heusen) US:LP = Decca DL-4260 [Bing Crosby:ST]

7414 Welcome to L.A. (1977) Score (Richard Baskin) US:LP = UA LA-703*

7415 Welcome to My Nightmare (1976) Score (pop music) US:LP = Atco SD-19157* [Alice Cooper:ST]

7416 We're Not Dressing (1934) Excerpts (Harry Revel) US:LP-MS = Columbia C2L-43 [Bing Crosby:ST]

7417 Werewolf in a Girls' Dormitory (1962) Theme (Jim Stewart) US: SP = Cub 9123 [The Fortunes:ST]

7418 West of Zanzibar (1954) Theme (Georges Sigara) US:SP = Columbia 4-40318 [The Mariners]; Theme (Georges Sigara) US:SP = London 45-1485 [The Johnston Brothers]

7419 West Point Story, The [Fine and Dandy] (1950) Highlights (Jule Styne) US:LP-BP = Titania 501

7420 West Side Story (1961) Score (stage songs:Leonard Bernstein) US:LP = Columbia OL-5670/OS-2070*

7421 Western Approaches [The Raiders] (1944) Theme (Clifton Parker) GB:78 = Decca 1544 [Muir Mathieson]; Theme (Clifton Parker) US:LP = London 44248* [Stanley Black]

7422 Westward Ho (1935) Theme (Tim Spencer) US:LP = MCA 1563 [The Sons of the Pioneers]

7423 Westward Ho the Wagons! (1956) Highlights (e:George Bruns/t:Paul Smith) US:LP = Disneyland WDL-3041 + US:LP = Disneyland WDL-4008

7424 Westworld (1973) Score (Fred Karlin) US:LP = MGM 1SE-47*

7425 Wet Blanket Policy [Cartoon] (1948) Theme (George Tibbles) US:SP = Columbia 13-33315 [Kay Kyser]; Theme (George Tibbles) US:LP = MCA 13300 [Clarence Wheeler]; Theme (George Tibbles) US:LP = Star Bright 101 [uncredited]

7426 Wetherby (1985) Highlights (Nick Bicat) US:LP = Varese STV-81247*

7427 Whale Who Wanted to Sing at the Met, The *see* Make Mine Music

7428 Whaler Out of New Bedford [Short] (1962) Highlights (Ewan MacColl) US:LP = Folkways FS-3850

7429 What! [La Frusta e il Corpo] (1964) Score (Carlo Rustichelli-aka-Jim Murphy) IT:LP = CAM CMS-30.132

7430 What? [Che?] [Forbidden Dreams] [Roman Polanski's Forbidden Dreams] (1972) Score (t:Claudio Gizzi/s:classical music) IT:LP = Cinevox 33/63*

7431 What a Way to Go! (1964) Score (e:Nelson Riddle/etc.) US:LP = 20th 3143/S-4143*

7432 What a Whopper! (1961) Theme (Van Dyke) GB:SP = Parlophone 4837 [Adam Faith]

7433 What Am I Bid? (1967) Score (e:Gene Nash/etc.) US:LP = MGM E-4506/SE-4506*

7434 What Comes Around (1986) Score (s:Jerry Reed/t:Al De Lory) US:LP = Capitol ST-12444*

7435 What Did You Do in the War, Daddy? (1966) Score (Henry Mancini) US:LP = RCA LPM-3648/LSP-3648*

7436 What Do You Say to a Naked Lady? (1970) Score (Steve Karmen) US:LP = UA UAS-5206*

7437 What Ever Happened to Baby Jane? (1962) Themes (Frank DeVol) US:SP = Columbia 4-42620 [Frank DeVol:ST]; Themes (Frank DeVol) US:SP = MGM 13107 [Debbie Burton & Bette Davis:ST]; Theme (Frank DeVol) US:LP = Citadel 7030* [Bette Davis:ST]

7438 What Ever Happened to Solange? *see* Terror in the Woods

7439 What Ever Happened to the Human Race? (1979) Score (Tim Simonec) US:LP = Word WSB-8832*

7440 What Happened at Campo Grade? [The Magnificent Two] (1967) Theme (Ron Goodwin) GB:SP = Parlophone 5618 [Ron Goodwin:ST]

7441 What Lola Wants *see* Damn Yankees

7442 What Makes David Run? [Qu'est ce Qui Fait Courir David?] (1985) Score (Michel Legrand) FR:LP = Milan 120.171*

7443 What Price Glory (1927) Theme [Silent I] (Erno Rapee) US:SP = Mercury 71989 [Richard Hayman]; Theme [Silent I] (Erno Rapee) US:LP = MGM 4033* [Cyril Ornadel]; Theme [Silent I] (Erno Rapee) US:LP = RCA 2560* [Gaylord Carter]

7444 What Price Glory (1952) Theme (Jay Livingston & Ray Evans) US:SP = Capitol 2219 [Jane Froman]

7445 What Rascals Men Are *see* Gli Uomini Che Mascalzoni

7446 What's Cookin'? (1942) Theme-A/US:78 = Decca 4182 [The Andrews Sisters:ST]; Theme-B/US:78 = Decca 4188 [Woody Herman:ST]; Theme-C/US:78 = Decca 18346 [Woody Herman:ST]

7447 What's New Pussycat? (1965) Score (Burt Bacharach) US:LP = UA UAL-4128/UAS-5128* + US:LP = UA LA-278*

7448 What's So Bad About Feeling Good? (1968) Theme (Dave Blume) US: SP = Decca 9-32335 [Dick Jacobs]

7449 What's the Matter with Helen? (1971) Score (David Raksin) US: LP-BP = Dynamation DY-1200

7450 What's Up, Tiger Lily? (1966) Score (John Sebastian) US:LP = Kama Sutra 8053/S-8053*

7451 Wheeler Dealers, The [Separate Beds] (1963) Theme (Randy Sparks) US:SP = Columbia 4-42887 [The New Christy Minstrels:ST]

7452 When Eight Bells Toll (1971) Theme (Walter Stott-aka-Angela Morley) GB:LP = Philips 6308.111* [John Gregory and Chaquito]

7453 When Knights Were Bold (1935) Themes/GB:78 = Brunswick 2153 [Jack Buchanan:ST]

7454 When Ladies Meet (1941) Theme/US:LP-BP = Curtain Calls 100/23 [@Joan Crawford & Greer Garson:ST]

7455 When Love Becomes Lust *see* Quando l'Amore e Sensualita

7456 When My Baby Smiles at Me (1948) Theme/US:LP-BP = Star Tone 219 [Betty Grable:ST]

7457 When Sex Was a Knightly Affair *see* Amorous Adventures of Don Quixote and Sancho Panza, The

7458 When the Boys Meet the Girls [Girl Crazy] (1965) Score (t:Fred Karger/stage songs:George Gershwin) US:LP = MGM E-4334/SE-4334*

7459 When the Rain Begins to Fall [Voyage of the Rock Aliens] (1985) Excerpts-A (Jack White) US:LP = MCA 5557* [Pia Zadora:ST]; Theme-B (Richard Friedman) US:SP = MCA 52429* [Three Speed:ST]

7460 When the Sun Sets *see* Al Ponerse el Sol

7461 When the Wind Blows (1986) Score (e:Roger Waters/t:David Bowie/etc.) GB: LP = Virgin VL-2406*

7462 When Women Had Tails [Quando le Donne Avevando la Coda] (1970) Score (Ennio Morricone) US:LP-BP = EM 1001* + IT:LP = CAM SAG-9032*

7463 When Worlds Collide (1951) Highlights (Leith Stevens) US:LP-BP = Quasi PAL-1951/1953; Theme (Leith Stevens) US:LP = MMG 702* [Geoff Love]

7464 When You're in Love [For You Alone] (1937) Highlights (e:Jerome Kern/etc.) US:LP-BP = Caliban 6044

7465 Where Angels Go, Trouble Follows! (1968) Theme (Lalo Schifrin) US:SP = A&M 919 [Boyce & Hart:ST]

7466 Where Do We Go from Here? (1945) Highlights (Kurt Weill) US:LP = Mark 56 #721 + US:LP = Ariel AWH-10 [Studio Cast]

7467 Where Eagles Dare (1969) Score (Ron Goodwin) US:LP = MGM 1SE-16*

7468 Where It's At! (1969) Theme (Jeff Barry) US:SP = UA 50529 [Jeff Barry:ST]

7469 Where Love Has Gone (1964) Theme (James Van Heusen) US:SP = Kapp 608 [Jack Jones:ST]; Theme (James Van Heusen) US:LP = Kapp 3396 [Jack Jones:ST]

7470 Where No Vultures Fly *see* Ivory Hunter

7471 Where the Boys Are (1960) Theme (Howard Greenfield) US:SP = MGM 12971 [Connie Francis:ST]; Theme (Howard Greenfield) US:LP = MGM 3942* [Connie Francis:ST]

7472 Where the Boys Are (1984) Score (t:Sylvester Levay/s:various) US: LP = RCA ABL1-5039*

7473 Where the Buffalo Roam (1980) Score (e:Neil Young/etc.) US: LP = MCA/Backstreet 5126*

7474 Where the Hot Wind Blows [The Law] [La Loi] (1960) Highlights (e: Roman Vlad/t:Jimmy McHugh) US: LP = Everest LPBR-5076/SDBR-1076*

7475 Where the Lilies Bloom (1974) Score (e:Earl Scruggs/etc.) US:LP = Columbia KC-32806*

7476 Where the River Bends *see* Bend of the River

7477 Where the River Runs Black (1986) Score (James Horner) US:LP = Varese STV-81290*

7478 Where the Spies Are (1966) Themes (Mario Nascimbene) US:SP = Verve 132 + US:SP = Verve 10382 [Jimmy Smith:ST]; Theme (Mario Nascimbene) US:LP = Metro 565* [The Revengers]; Theme (Mario Nascimbene)

IT:LP-MS = Kangaroo 34209 [Mario Nascimbene:ST]

7479 Where the Truth Lies [Witchcraft] [Les Malefices] (1962) Highlights (Pierre Henry) FR:EP = Philips 432.762

7480 Where Were You When the Lights Went Out? (1968) Theme (Dave Grusin) US:SP = Capitol 2218 [The Lettermen:ST]

7481 Where's Charley? [Charley's Aunt] (1952) Score (stage songs:Frank Loesser) US:LP-BP = Ecnad 216

7482 Where's Jack? (1969) Score (Elmer Bernstein) US:LP = Paramount PAS-5005*

7483 Where's Poppa? [Going Ape] (1970) Score (Jack Elliott) US:LP = UA UAS-5216*

7484 Which Way Is Up? (1977) Theme (Norman Whitfield) US:SP = MCA 40825* [Stargard:ST]; Theme (Norman Whitfield) US:LP = MCA 2321* [Stargard:ST]

7485 Whiffs [C.A.S.H.] (1975) Theme (George Barrie) US:SP = 20th 2246* [Steve Lawrence:ST]; Theme (George Barrie) US:LP = Columbia 34157 [Andre Kostelanetz]

7486 While I Live [Dream of Olwen] (1948) Themes (Charles Williams) GB:78 = Columbia 72688 [Charles Williams:ST]; Themes (Charles Williams) GB:LP = WRC 384 [@Charles Williams:ST]; Theme (Charles Williams) US:LP = Columbia 3029 [@Charles Williams:ST]

7487 While the City Sleeps (1956) Theme (Herschel Burke Gilbert) US:SP = Columbia 4-40716 [Les Elgert]; Theme (Herschel Burke Gilbert) US:LP = Coral 57065 [George Cates]

7488 While There's War, There's Hope [Finche C'e Guerra, C'e Sperazza] (1975) Score (Piero Piccioni) IT:LP = General Music 10001*

7489 Whirlpool (1959) Highlights (Ron Goodwin) GB:EP = Odeon/EMI SOE-3571

7490 Whiskey Galore *see* Tight Little Island

7491 Whisper in the Night, A [Un Sussurro Buio] (1977) Themes (Pino Donaggio) IT:SP = Produttori 3265* [ST]

7492 Whisperers, The (1967) Score (John Barry) US:LP = UA UAL-4161/UAS-5161*

7493 Whispering City (1947) Theme (Andre Mathieu) GB:78 = Columbia 2526 [Charles Williams]

7494 Whistle at Eaton Falls, The (1951) Theme (Carleton Carpenter) US:SP = MGM 30424 [Carleton Carpenter:ST]

7495 Whistle Down the Wind (1961) Theme (Malcolm Arnold) US:SP = London 45-9510 [The Wayfarers]; Theme (Malcolm Arnold) US:SP = London 45-9520 [Mantovani]; Theme (Malcolm Arnold) GB:LP = UA 30281* [@Ed Welch]

7496 White Christmas (1954) Score (Irving Berlin) US:LP = Decca DL-8083 [Bing Crosby & Danny Kaye:ST]; Highlights (Irving Berlin) US:LP-10 = Columbia CL-6338 [Rosemary Clooney:ST]

7497 White Dawn, The (1974) Excerpts (Henry Mancini) US:LP = RCA APL1-1379* [Henry Mancini:ST]

7498 White Heat (1949) Sequence + Dialog (Max Steiner) US:LP-MS = WB 3X-2737 [@ST]

7499 White Huntress [Golden Ivory] (1954) Theme (Philip Green) GB:78 = Parlophone 3941 [Philip Green:ST]

7500 White Nights, The [Le Notti Bianche] (1957) Theme-A (M. Malgoni) US:LP = Epic 3593 [Gian Stellari]; Theme-B (Nino Rota) IT:LP = CAM SAG-9054* [Nino Rota & Carlo Savina:ST]; Theme-C (Nino Rota) JA:LP-MS = CBS/Sony 2302 [@ST]

7501 White Nights (1985) Score (t: Michel Colombier/s:various) US:LP = Atlantic 81275-1*

7502 White Orchid, The (1954) Theme (Chuy Hernandez) US:SP = RCA 47-6032 [Henri Rene]

7503 White Rock (1977) Score (Rick Wakeman) US:LP = A&M SP-4614*

7504 White Rose of Athens, The *see* Dreamland of Desire

7505 White Sheik, The [Lo Sceicco Bianco] Theme (Nino Rota) IT:LP = CAM SAG-9053* [Nino Rota & Carlo Savina:ST]; Theme (Nino Rota) US:LP = Hannibal 9301* [William Fischer]

7506 White Snow, Bright Snow

[Short] Sequence + Dialog (Arthur Kleiner) US:LP-PP = Picture Book Parade 106 [@ST]

7507 White Voices [Le Voci Bianche] (1964) Score (Gino Marinuzzi, Jr.) IT:LP = CAM CMS-30.110

7508 White Witch Doctor (1953) Excerpts (Bernard Herrmann) US:LP = RCA ARL1-0707* [Charles Gerhardt]

7509 Who Are the Debolts, and Where Did They Get 19 Kids? (1977) Highlights (Ed Bogas) JA:EP = Toho AT-6004

7510 Who Dares, Wins *see* Final Option, The

7511 Who Done It? (1956) Excerpts (Philip Green) GB:78-MS = Rank FM-187/190 [ST]

7512 Who Is Harry Kellerman, and Why Is He Saying Those Terrible Things About Me? (1971) Score (Shel Silverstein) US:LP = Columbia S-30791*

7513 Who Is Killing the Great Chefs of Europe? [Too Many Chefs] (1978) Score (Henry Mancini) US:LP = Epic SE-35692*

7514 Who Is Killing the Stuntmen? *see* Stunts

7515 Who Killed Cock Robin? [Cartoon] (1935) Theme (Frank Churchill) US:78 = Bluebird BK-5 [ST]

7516 Who Killed Teddy Bear? (1965) Theme (Bob Gaudio) US:SP = Atlantic 40716 [Leslie Uggams]

7517 Who Was That Lady? (1960) Theme-A (Andre Previn) US:SP = Columbia 4-41577 [Vic Damone]; Theme-A (Andre Previn) US:LP = Colpix 418* [James Darren]; Theme-B (James Van Heusen) US:SP = Capitol 4328 [Dean Martin:ST]; Theme-B (James Van Heusen) US:LP = Tower 5018 [Dean Martin:ST]

7518 Whom the Gods Wish to Destroy *see* Siegfried

7519 Whoopee (1930) Highlights (stage songs:Walter Donaldson) US:LP-BP = Meet Patti PRW-1930

7520 Whoopee Party [Cartoon] (1932) Theme (pop music) US:LP-MS = Ovation 5000 [@ST]

7521 Who's Afraid of Virginia Woolf? (1966) Score (s:Alex North/t:Sonny Burke) US:LP = WB B-1656/BS-1656*

7522 Who's Got the Action? (1962) Theme (George Duning) US:SP = Reprise 20116 [Dean Martin:ST]

7523 Wichita (1955) Theme (Hans J. Salter) US:SP = Capitol 3179 [Tex Ritter:ST]; Theme (Hans J. Salter) US:LP = Capitol 971 [Tex Ritter:ST]

7524 Wicked Dreams of Paula Schultz, The (1968) Themes (Jimmie Haskell) US:SP = UA 50250 [Jimmie Haskell:ST]; Theme (Jimmie Haskell) US:LP = Dot 25860* [Jimmie Haskell:ST]

7525 Wicked Lady, The (1983) Score (Tony Banks) US:LP = Atlantic 80073-1*

7526 Wicked Woman (1954) Themes (Buddy Baker) US:SP = Trend 45-67 [Herb Jeffries & Buddy Baker:ST]

7527 Wife Child *see* Albert Peckingpaw's Revenge

7528 Wifemistress [Mogliamente] (1977) Themes (Armando Trovajoli) IT:SP = WB 17047* [ST]

7529 Wild and the Innocent, The (1959) Theme (Richard Loring) US:SP = Decca 9-30834 [Ray Charles]; Theme (Richard Loring) US:SP = Dot 15910 [Brian Davis]

7530 Wild and the Willing, The *see* Young and Willing

7531 Wild Angels, The (1966) Score-A (s:Mike Curb/t:Larry Brown/t:Harley Hatcher) US:LP = Tower T-5043/ST-5043*; Score-B (s:Mike Curb/t:Davie Allan) US:LP = Tower T-5056/ST-5056*

7532 Wild Blue Yonder, The (1951) Theme/US:78 = RCA/Victor 20-3968 [Phil Harris:ST]

7533 Wild Bunch, The (1969) Score (Jerry Fielding) US:LP = WB WS-1814* + US:LP = Varese STV-81145*

7534 Wild Child, The [L'Enfant Sauvage] (1970) Excerpts (ae:Antoine Duhamel) FR:LP-MS = UA 29140/1* [@ST]

7535 Wild Eye, The [L'Occhio Selvaggio] (1968) Score (Gianni Marchetti) US:LP = RCA LPM-4003/LSP-4003*

7536 Wild for Kicks *see* Beat Girl

7537 Wild Geese, The (1978) Score (Roy Budd) US:LP = A&M SP-4730*

7538 Wild Geese II (1985) Score (Roy Budd) GB:LP = CBS 26462*

7539 Wild Goose Chase, The [La Course a l'e Chalote] (1975) Themes (Vladimir Cosma) FR:SP = Deesse 704* [ST]

7540 Wild Guitar (1962) Themes (Alan O'Day) US:SP = Fairway 45-102 [Arch Hall, Jr.:ST]; Themes (Alan O'Day) US:LP = Rhino 307 [@Arch Hall, Jr.:ST]

7541 Wild in the Country (1961) Theme-A/US:SP = RCA 47-7850 [Elvis Presley:ST]; Theme-B/US:LP = RCA 2370* [Elvis Presley:ST]; Theme-C/ US:LP = RCA 3450* [Elvis Presley:ST]

7542 Wild in the Streets (1968) Score (e:Les Baxter/e:Barry Mann) US: LP = Tower SKAO-5099*; Themes (Harley Hatcher) US:LP = Tower 5139* [Davie Allan and the Arrows:ST]

7543 Wild Is the Wind (1957) Score (Dimitri Tiomkin) US:LP = Columbia CL-1090; Theme (F.Albano) US:SP = Verve 10113 [Anna Magnani:ST]

7544 Wild Life, The (1984) Score (various) US:LP = MCA 5523*

7545 Wild on the Beach (1965) Score (s:By Dunham & Bobby Beverly/ t:Jimmie Haskell) US:LP = RCA LPM-3441/LSP-3441*

7546 Wild One, The [Hot Blood] [Cyclist Raiders] (1954) Score (Leith Stevens) US:LP = Decca DL-8349

7547 Wild Party, The (1956) Score (Buddy Bregman) US:LP = Verve MGV-2042 [Buddy Bregman:ST]

7548 Wild Party, The (1975) Theme (Walter Marks) US:SP = Flying Dutchman 10295* [Bob Thiele]; Theme (Walter Marks) US:LP = Flying Dutchman 1-0964* [Bob Thiele]

7549 Wild Racers, The (1968) Score (Mike Curb & Bob Summers) US:LP = Sidewalk ST-5914*

7550 Wild Rebels, The (1967) Theme (Al Jacobs) US:SP = ABC 45-10917 [Steve Alaimo:ST]

7551 Wild River (1960) Theme (Kenyon Hopkins) US:SP = Capitol 4385 [Kenyon Hopkins:ST]

7552 Wild Rovers (1971) Score-A (Jerry Goldsmith) US:LP = MGM 1SE-30*; Score-B (Jerry Goldsmith) US: LP = MCA 25141*

7553 Wild Style (1983) Score (various) US:LP = Animal APE-6005*

7554 Wild Westerners, The (1963) Theme (Duane Eddy) US:SP = RCA 47-8047 [Duane Eddy:ST]

7555 Wild Wheels (1969) Score (Harley Hatcher) US:LP = RCA LSO-1156*

7556 Wild, Wild Winter (1966) Score (e:Jerry Long/etc.) US:LP = Decca DL-4699/DL-74699*

7557 Wildcats (1986) Score-A (James Newton Howard) US:LP = WB 25388-1*; Theme-B [Half Time] (James Newton Howard) US:SP = WB 7-28765* [James Newton Howard:ST]

7558 Wilderness Family, Part 2, The *see* Further Adventures of the Wilderness Family, The

7559 Will Penny (1968) Highlights (David Raksin) US:LP = Dot DLP-25844*

7560 Willie Dynamite (1973) Score (J.J. Johnson) US:LP = MCA 393*

7561 Willie the Operatic Whale *see* Make Mine Music

7562 Willy Wonka and the Chocolate Factory (1971) Score (e:Leslie Bricusse & Anthony Newley/ae:Walter Scharf) US:LP = Paramount PAS-6012* + US:LP = MCA 37124*

7563 Wind and the Lion, The (1975) Score (Jerry Goldsmith) US:LP = Arista AL-4048*

7564 Windjammer, The (1958) Score (e:Morton Gould/e:Terry Gilkyson/etc.) US:LP = Columbia CL-1158/ CS-8651* + US:LP = CSP ACS-8651*

7565 Window in the Sky *see* Other Side of the Mountain, The

7566 Winds of Change, The [Metamorphoses] (1978) Score (Alec Costandinos) US:LP = Casablanca NBLP-7167*

7567 Windsplitter, The (1971) Theme (Joyce Taylor) US:SP = RCA 74-0556* [Michael Dees:ST]

7568 Windwalker, The (1980) Score (Merrill Jenson) US:LP = Cerberus CST-0202*

7569 Wings (1927) Theme [Silent II] (Lee Erwin) US:LP = Angel 36073* [Lee Erwin:ST]

7570 Wings of Eagles, The (1957)

Theme (Jeff Alexander) US:SP = MGM 12430 [David Rose]

7571 Winners, The *see* My Way

7572 Winnie the Pooh and the Blustery Day [Short] (1967) Highlights + Dialog (Richard & Robert Sherman) US:LP = Disneyland ST-3953

7573 Winnie the Pooh and the Honey Tree [Short] (1965) Highlights + Dialog (Richard & Robert Sherman) US: LP = Disneyland ST-3928

7574 Winning (1969) Score (Dave Grusin) US:LP = Decca DL-79169*

7575 Winter Equinox (1977) Score (e:Richard Henn/e:Chris Darrow/etc.) US:LP = Festival LP-1007*

7576 Winter Rose (1984) Themes (Michael Hoppe) JA:SP = Seven Seas 75.9015* [ST]

7577 Wintertime of Love *see* Thunderbirds (1952)

7578 Witch Crafty [Cartoon] (1955) Sequence + Dialog (Clarence Wheeler) US:LP = Peter Pan 1120 [@ST]

7579 Witch Doctor *see* Men of Two Worlds

7580 Witchcraft *see* Where the Truth Lies

7581 Witches, The [Le Strege] (1967) Themes (Ennio Morricone/Piero Piccioni) IT:SP = UA 3113 [ST]; Themes (Piero Piccioni) JA:LP-MS = CBS/Sony 2305 [@ST]; Theme (Ennio Morricone) US:LP-BP = POO 106 [@ST]

7582 With a Song in My Heart (1952) Score (pop music) US:LP = Capitol L-309 + US:LP = Capitol M-11891 [Jane Froman:ST]; Highlights (pop music) US:LP-BP = Legends 1000/3 [@ST]

7583 With Love and Kisses (1936) Themes-A-B/US:78 = Brunswick 7897 [Pinky Tomlin:ST]; Theme-C/US:78 = Brunswick 7502 [Pinky Tomlin:ST]; Theme-D/US:78 = Brunswick 7525 [Pinky Tomlin:ST]

7584 With Six You Get Eggroll (1968) Theme (Robert Mersey) US:SP = Columbia 4-44637 [Johnny Mathis:ST]

7585 Without a Stitch (1971) Theme (Ole Hoyer) HO:LP = EMI E052.38017 [Ole Hoyer:ST]

7586 Without Apparent Motive [Senza Movente] [Sans Mobile Apparent] (1971) Themes (Ennio Morricone) IT:SP = General Music 50242* [ST]

7587 Without Honor (1949) Themes (Max Steiner) US:LP-BP = Tony Thomas TTMS-15 [Max Steiner: ST]

7588 Witness (1985) Score (Maurice Jarre) US:LP = Varese STV-81237*

7589 Witness for the Prosecution (1957) Theme (Ralph Roberts) US:SP = Dot 15723 [Marlene Dietrich:ST]

7590 Wives and Lovers (1963) Theme (Lyn Murray) US:LP = UA 6376* [@ST]

7591 Wiz, The (1978) Scores (film songs:Quincy Jones/stage songs:Charlie Smalls) US:LP = MCA 2-14000*

7592 Wizard of Baghdad, The (1960) Themes (Fuller & Saxon) US:SP = 20th 234 [Dick Shawn:ST]

7593 Wizard of Oz, The (1939) Highlights + Underscore + Dialog (e: Harold Arlen/u:Herbert Stothart) US: LP = MGM E-3464 + US:LP = MGM E-3996/SE-3996e; Highlights (Harold Arlen) US:LP = Decca DL-8387 [Judy Garland:ST/Victor Young]

7594 Wizards of the Water (1981) Score (various) AU:LP = Polydor WOW-001*

7595 Wolf Song, The (1929) Theme/US:78 = RCA/Victor 21932 [Lupe Velez:ST]

7596 Wolfman, The (1941) Sequence + Dialog (Frank Skinner & Hans J. Salter) US:LP = Decca DL-74833e [@ST]; Excerpts (Hans J. Salter) US: LP-BP = Tony Thomas TT-HS-3 ["Ghost of Frankenstein":ST]

7597 Woman at Her Window, A [La Donna alla Finestra] (1978) Score (Carlo Rustichelli) IT:LP = Cidias 38.001*

7598 Woman Commands, A (1932) Theme/US:LP = Pelican 130 [@Pola Negri:ST]

7599 Woman Hater (1948) Theme (Lambert Williamson) GB:78-PP = Rank FM-36 [ST]

7600 Woman in Flames, A [La Femme Flambee] (1983) Score (Peer Raben) FR:LP = RCA 70266*

7601 Woman in Green, The (1945) Underscore + Dialog (au:Mark Levant) US:LP = Murray Hill 55471

7602 Woman in Question, The (1950) Theme (John Wooldridge) GB:78-PP = Rank FM-98 [ST]

7603 Woman in Red, The (1984) Score (Stevie Wonder) US:LP = Motown 6108-ML*

7604 Woman in the Dunes (1964) Excerpts (Toru Takemitsu) JA:LP = RCA/Victor 1070 [Toru Takemitsu:ST]

7605 Woman in the Hall (1947) Theme (Temple Abady) GB:78-PP = Rank FM-22 [ST]

7606 Woman in the Moon [Frau im Mond] (1929) Highlights (Willy Schmidt-Gentner) GE:78-MS = Polyphone UTA-504

7607 Woman in White, The (1948) Theme (Max Steiner) US:LP-BP = Citadel CTMS-6 [Max Steiner:ST]

7608 Woman Is a Woman, A [Un Femme Est un Femme] (1964) Highlights (Michel Legrand) FR:EP = Philips 432.595

7609 Woman Is Sweeter (1971) Score (Galt MacDermot) US:LP = Kilmarnock 70003*

7610 Woman Next Door, The (1981) Score (Georges Delerue) US:LP = DRG SL-9507*

7611 Woman of Straw (1964) Theme (Norman Percival) US:SP = Veep 1202 [The Windsor Strings]; Theme (Norman Percival) US:SP = UA 765 [Perez Prado]; Theme (Norman Percival) US:LP = UA 6392* [@Perez Prado]

7612 Woman of Summer, The *see* Stripper, The

7613 Woman of the River (1954) Themes (Roman Vatro) US:SP = MGM 12518 [Robert Ashley]; Themes (Roman Vatro) US:LP = MGM 3485 [Robert Ashley]; Theme (Roman Vatro) US: SP = RCA 47-6385 [Sophia Loren:ST]

7614 Woman Times Seven (1967) Score (Riz Ortolani) US:LP = Capitol T-2800/ST-2800*

7615 Woman to Woman (1947) Theme (George Melachrino) GB:78 = HMV 9535 [George Melachrino:ST]

7616 Woman Without a Face *see* Mister Buddwing

7617 Woman's Angle, The (1952) Theme (Kenneth Leslie-Smith) GB:78 = HMV 1829 [Charles Williams]; Theme (Kenneth Leslie-Smith) GB:LP = WRC 384 [@Charles Williams]

7618 Woman's Devotion, A (1956) Theme (Les Baxter) US:SP = Capitol 3624 [Les Baxter:ST]

7619 Woman's World, A (1954) Theme (Cyril Mockridge) US:SP = MGM 11846 [Bob Stewart]; Theme (Cyril Mockridge) US:SP = Decca 9-29269 [The Four Aces]; Theme (Cyril Mockridge) US:LP = Decca 4013 [The Four Aces]

7620 Wombling Free (1978) Score (Mike Batt) GB:LP = CBS 70155*

7621 Women Disappear, The *see* Des Femmes Disparaissent

7622 Women Everywhere (1930) Themes/US:78 = Brunswick 4836 [J. Harold Murray:ST]

7623 Women in Limbo [Limbo] (1972) Theme (Anita Kerr) US:SP = Decca 9-33032 [Anita Kerr:ST]

7624 Women in Love (1969) Theme (Georges Delerue) US:SP = UA 50655* [Leroy Holmes]; Theme (Georges Delerue) US:LP = UA 6742* [Leroy Holmes]; Theme (Georges Delerue) US:LP = King 1140.498* [Manuel]

7625 Women of Our Time (1949) Theme (Malcolm Arnold) GB:78-PP = Rank FM-37 [ST]

7626 Women of Pitcairn Island, The (1956) Theme (Walter Jurman) US:SP = RCA 47-6721 [Carole Richards]

7627 Women of the World (1963) Score (s:Riz Ortolani/t:Nino Oliviero) US:LP = Decca DL-9112/DL-79112*

7628 Won Ton Ton, The Dog Who Saved Hollywood (1976) Theme (Neal Hefti) JA:SP = RSO 6019* [The Silver Screen Orchestra]

7629 Wonder Bar (1934) Highlights (Harry Warren) US:LP-BP = Hollywood Soundstage HS-402 + US:LP-BP = Golden Legends 2000/2

7630 Wonder Man (1945) Theme (David Rose) US:78 = RCA/Victor 20-1674 [Vaughn Monroe]

7631 Wonder of Women, The (1929) Theme/GB:78 = HMV 3282 [Peggy Wood:ST]

7632 Wonderful Country, The (1959) Score-A (Alex North) US:LP =

UA UAL-4050/UAS-5050*; Score-B (Alex North) FR:LP = UA/Sonopresse UAS-5050*

7633 Wonderful Life *see* Swinger's Paradise

7634 Wonderful to Be Young [The Young Ones] (1962) Score (s:Ronald Cass & Peter Myers/t:Stanley Black/t: Norrie Paramor) US:LP = Dot DLP-3474/DLP-25474*

7635-6 Wonderful World of the Brothers Grimm, The (1962) Highlights + Dialog + Narration (Bob Merrill) US:LP = MGM 1E-3/1SE-3*; Highlights (Bob Merrill) US:LP = MGM E-4077/SE-4077* [David Rose]

7637 Woodpecker in the Moon [Cartoon] (1952) Sequence + Dialog (Clarence Wheeler) US:LP = Peter Pan 1120 [@ST]

7638 Woodstock (1970) Scores-A (pop music) US:LP-MS = Cotillion 3-500*; Scores-B (pop music) US:LP-MS = Cotillion 2-400*

7639 Woody Guthrie (1984) Score (pop music) US:LP = Arloco ARL-284*

7640 Words and Music (1948) Highlights (pop music) US:LP-10 = MGM E-505 + US:LP = MGM E-3233 + US:LP = MGM E-3771 + US:LP = Metro M-580/MS-580e + US:LP-MS = MGM 2SES-54e

7641 Working Class Goes to Heaven, The [La Classe Operaia Vi in Paradiso] (1970) Score (Ennio Morricone) IT:LP = RCA SP-8038* + IT: LP = RCA 37644*

7642 World By Night, The [Il Mondo di Notte] (1960) Score (Piero Piccioni) IT:LP = RCA 10078

7643 World in My Corner, The (1956) Theme (Henry Mancini) US:SP = Decca 9-29847 [Victor Young]; Theme (Henry Mancini) US:SP = Decca 9-29903 [Sylvia Syms]

7644 World Is Full of Married Men, The (1979) Scores (e:Dominic Bugatti/e:various) GB:LP-MS = Ronco RTD-2038*

7645 World of Georgie Best, The (1970) Theme (Johnny Harris) US:SP = Decca 9-32696 [Don Fardon]

7646 World of Suzie Wong, The (1960) Score (s:George Duning/t:James Van Heusen) US:LP = RCA LOC-1059/LSO-1059*

7647 World Safari II (1985) Score (Mario Millo) AU:LP = Powder Works POW-6095*

7648 World, the Flesh and the Devil, The (1959) Theme-A (Robert Nemeroff) US:SP = RCA 47-7550 [Harry Belafonte:ST]; Theme-B (Miklos Rozsa) US:LP = Varese 704.260* [Elmer Bernstein]

7649 Worlds Apart / Score (John Peterson) US:LP-PP = Youth Films U3RS-0367*

7650 World's Greatest Athlete, The (1973) Themes (Marvin Hamlisch) US: SP = Buena Vista 491 [Marvin Hamlisch: ST]; Theme (Marvin Hamlisch) US:LP-BP = Centurion 1210 [@Marvin Hamlisch:ST]

7651 World's Greatest Lover, The (1977) Highlights + Underscore + Dialog (e:John Morris/t:Gene Wilder/etc.) US:LP = RCA ABL1-2709*

7652 Wraith, The (1986) Score (various) US:LP = Scotti Brothers SZ-40429*

7653 Written on the Wind (1956) Highlights-A (e:Frank Skinner/t:Victor Young) US:LP = Decca DL-8424; Highlights-B (e:Frank Skinner/t:Victor Young) US:LP = Varese VC-81074

7654 Wrong Box, The (1966) Score (John Barry) US:LP = Mainstream 56088/S-6088*

7655 Wrong Kind of Girl, The *see* Bus Stop

7656 Wrong Man, The (1957) Theme (Bernard Herrmann) US:LP-BP = Centurion 1210 [@Bernard Herrmann:ST]

7657 Wuthering Heights (1939) Score (Alfred Newman) US:LP = Film Music Collection FMC-6* [Elmer Bernstein]; Theme (Alfred Newman) US: LP = Decca 8123 [Alfred Newman:ST]

7658 Wuthering Heights (1970) Score (Michel Legrand) US:LP = American International ST-1039*

X

7659 X-15 (1961) Theme (Nathan Scott) US:SP = Reprise 20039 [Neal Hefti]

7660 X from Outer Space, The (1967) Theme (Taku Izumi) JA:LP = Toho 8124 [@ST]

7661 X, Y and Zee (1972) Theme (Ted Meyers) US:SP = Dunhill 4306 [Three Dog Night:ST]

7662 Xtro (1983) Score (Harry Davenport) GB:LP = That's Entertainment TER-1052*

Y

7663 Yakuza, The (1975) Theme (Dave Grusin) US:LP-BP = Centurion 1210* [@Stanley Maxfield]

7664 Yangtse Incident *see* Battle Hell

7665 Yank in the R.A.F., A (1941) Themes/US:LP-BP = JJA 19811 [@Betty Grable:ST]

7666 Yankee at King Arthur's Court, A *see* Connecticut Yankee in King Arthur's Court, A

7667 Yankee Doodle Dandy (1942) Score (pop music) US:LP-BP = Curtain Calls 100/13; Excerpts (pop music) US: LP-MS = WB 3X-2736 [@ST]

7668 Yankee Painter [Short] (1964) Highlights (Robert Muczynski) US:LP-PP = Music Library MRL-7110*

7669 Yanks (1979) Score (Richard Rodney Bennett) US:LP = MCA 3181*

7670 Ye Raat Phir Na Aayegi Theme/US:LP = Capitol 10500 [@Mahinder Kapoor:ST]

7671 Year Is Worth a Lifetime, A (1939) Highlights (Dmitri Shostakovich) US:LP = Angel S-40181*

7672 Year of Living Dangerously, The (1983) Score (Maurice Jarre) US: LP = Varese STV-81182*

7673 Year of the Cannibals, The [The Cannibals] [I Cannibali] (1971) Highlights (Ennio Morricone) US:LP = Cerberus CEMS-0111*

7674 Year of the Dragon (1985) Score (David Mansfield) US:LP = Varese STV-81266*

7675 Years of Lightning, Day of Drums *see* John F. Kennedy, Years of Lightning, Day of Drums

7676 Years Without Days *see* Castle on the Hudson

7677 Yellow Canary, The (1963) Score (Kenyon Hopkins) US:LP = Verve MG-8548/V6-8548*

7678 Yellow Rolls Royce, The (1965) Score (Riz Ortolani) US:LP = MGM E-4292/SE-4292*

7679 Yellow Rose of Texas, The (1944) Theme/US:LP = RCA 3041 [Roy Rogers:ST]

7680 Yellow Submarine (1968) Score (e:George Martin/e:John Lennon & Paul McCartney) US:LP = Apple SW-153*

7681 Yellowneck (1955) Theme (Laurence Rosenthal) US:SP = Decca 9-29356 [Jack Pleis]; Theme (Laurence Rosenthal) US:LP = Decca 8422 [Jack Pleis]

7682 Yentl (1983) Score (Michel Legrand) US:LP = Columbia JS-39152*

7683 Yes, Giorgio (1982) Score (t: Michael J. Lewis/t:John Williams/at: Alexander Courage/etc.) US:LP = London PDV-9001*

7684 Yes! Mr. Brown (1933) Themes/GB:LP = WRC 283 [Jack Buchanan:ST]

7685 Yes Sir, That's My Baby (1949) Highlights (Walter Scharf) US: LP-BP = Caliban 6019

7686 Yesterday (1980) Score (Paul Baillargeon) JA:LP = RCA/Victor RPL-8014*

7687 Yesterday, Today and Tomorrow [Ieri, Oggi e Domani] (1964) Score (Armando Trovajoli) US:LP = WB W-1552/WS-1552*

7688 Yeti [Yeti, il Gigante del Secolo] (1977) Score (Santa Maria Romitelli) IT:LP = Aris LM-10*

7689 Yield to the Night *see* Blonde Sinner, The

7690 Yog—The Monster from Space (1971) Themes (Akira Ifukube) JA:LP = Toho 8108 [@ST]

7691 Yojimbo (1962) Score (Masaru Sato) US:LP = MGM E-4096/SE-4096*

7692 Yol (1982) Score (Sebastian Argol) US:LP = WB 23816-1*

7693 Yolanda and the Thief (1945) Highlights (Harry Warren) US:LP-BP = Hollywood Soundstage HS-5001

7694 Yor, the Hunter from the Future (1983) Score (e:John Scott/e: Guido & Maurizio DeAngelis) US:LP = Southern Cross SCRS-1005*

7695 Yosemite Is My Home (1964) Score (Gene Kauer & Douglas Lackey) US:LP-PP = Ruthsan R-1935

7696 You Are What You Eat (1968) Score (John Simon) US:LP = Columbia OS-3240*

7697 You Belong to Me (1934) Theme/US:LP = Audio Rarities 2330 [Helen Morgan:ST]

7698 You Belong to My Heart *see* Mr. Imperium

7699 You Can't Have Everything (1937) Highlights (Harry Revel) US:LP-BP = Titania 508

7700 You Can't Have Everything (1972) *see* Cactus in the Snow

7701 You Can't Run Away from It (1956) Highlights (Gene DePaul) US: LP = Decca DL-8396

7702 You Can't Steal Love *see* Murph the Surf

7703 You Can't Win 'Em All [The Dubious Patriots] (1970) Themes (Bert Kaempfert) US:SP = Decca 9-32715* [Bert Kaempfert:ST]; Themes (Bert Kaempfert) US:LP = Decca 75234* [Bert Kaempfert:ST]

7704 You Don't Need Pajamas at Rosie's *see* The First Time

7705 You Light Up My Life (1977) Score (Joe Brooks) US:LP = Arista AB-4159*

7706 You Only Live Twice (1967) Score (John Barry) US:LP = UA UAL-4155/UAS-5155* + US:LP = UA LA-289*

7707 You Only Love Once [Tu Seras Terriblement Gentille] (1969) Score (Jacques Loussier) US:LP = London PS- 561*

7708 You Were Meant for Me (1948) Highlights (pop music) US:LP-BP = Titania 503

7709 You Were Never Lovelier (1942) Highlights (Jerome Kern) US:LP-BP = Curtain Calls 100/24

7710 You'll Find Out (1940) Themes-A-B/US:78 = Columbia 35762 [Kay Kyser:ST]; Themes-C-D/US:78 = Columbia 35761 [Kay Kyser:ST]

7711 You'll Never Get Rich (1941) Highlights (Cole Porter) US:LP-BP = Hollywood Soundstage HS-5001

7712 Young Americans, The (1967) Theme/US:SP = ABC 10998 [The Young Americans:ST]

7713 Young and Dangerous (1957) Theme (Paul Dunlap) US:SP = Capitol 3846 [Billy May]

7714 Young and the Cool, The *see* Continental Twist, The

7715 Young and Willing [The Wild and the Willing] (1962) Theme (Norrie Paramor) GB:SP = Columbia 8190 [ST]

7716 Young at Heart (1954) Highlights-A (t:Ray Heindorf/e:pop music) US:LP-10 = Columbia CL-6339 [Doris Day & Frank Sinatra:ST]; Highlights-B (t:Ray Heindorf/e:pop music) US:LP-BP = Titania 500

7717 Young Bess (1953) Score (Miklos Rozsa) US:LP = Film Music Collection FMC-5* [Elmer Bernstein]; Excerpts (Miklos Rozsa) US:LP = Deutsche 2584.013* [Miklos Rozsa:ST]

7718 Young Billy Young (1969) Score (Shelly Manne) US:LP = UA UAS-5199*

7719 Young Cassidy (1965) Theme (Sean O'Riada) US:SP = Columbia 4-43269 [The Clancy Brothers]

7720 Young Doctors in Love (1982) Underscore + Dialog (Maurice Jarre) US:LP = Regency RI-8501*

7721 Young Dracula *see* Son of Dracula (1974)

7722 Young Frankenstein (1975) Theme + Underscore + Dialog (John Morris) US:LP = ABC ABDP-870*

7723 Young Girls Beware [Mefiez-Vous Fillettes] (1957) Theme (Paul Misraki) US:LP = Dot 3120 [Ray Ventura]

7724 Young Girls of Rochefort, The (1968) Scores (Michel Legrand) US: LP-MS = Philips PCC-226/PCC-626*; Score (Michel Legrand) US:LP = Philips PCC-227/PCC-627*

7725 Young Guns of Texas, The (1962) Theme (Paul Sawtell & Bert Shefter) US:SP = 20th 315 [Kenny Miller:ST]

7726 Young Land, The (1959) Theme (Dimitri Tiomkin) US:SP = Verve 10147 [Randy Sparks & Dimitri Tiomkin:ST]; Theme (Dimitri Tiomkin) US:SP = RCA 47-7294 [Gogi Grant]

7727 Young Lions, The (1958) Score (Hugo Friedhofer) US:LP = Decca DL-8719/DL-78719* + US:LP-PP = Star/MCA DL-78719* + US:LP = Varese STV-81115*

7728 Young Lovers, The (1964) Score (Sol Kaplan) US:LP = Columbia OL-7010/OS-2510*

7729 Young Man of Music *see* Young Man with a Horn

7730 Young Man with a Horn [Young Man of Music] (1950) Score (t: Ray Heindorf/s:pop music) US:LP = Columbia CL-582 + US:LP = CSP ACL-582; Excerpts (Max Steiner) US: LP-BP = Citadel CTMS-6 [Max Steiner: ST]

7731 Young Master, The (1981) Score (Akira Inoue & Ryudo Uzaki) JA: LP = RCA/Victor VIP-28016*

7732 Young Ones, The (1961) *see* Wonderful to Be Young

7733 Young People (1940) Excerpts (Harry Warren) US:LP-MS = 20th TCF-2-103 [Shirley Temple:ST]

7734 Young Philadelphians, The [The City Jungle] (1959) Theme (Ernest Gold) US:LP = London 3320/320* [Ernest Gold:ST]

7735 Young Rebel, The [Les Aventures Extraordinaires de Cervantes] (1968) Highlights (Jean Ledrut) FR: EP = Barclay 71261

7736 Young Runaways, The (1968) Theme (Fred Karger) US:SP = Verve 10620 [Arthur Prysock:ST]

7737 Young Savages, The (1961) Score (David Amram) US:LP = Columbia CL-1672/CS-8472*

7738 Young Sherlock Holmes (1985) Score (Bruce Broughton) US: LP = MCA 6159*

7739 Young Warriors, The (1983) Score (Rob Walsh) US:LP = Varese STV-81186*

7740 Young Winston (1972) Score (e:Alfred Ralston/e:classical music) US: LP = Angel SFO-36901*

7741 Young Wolves, The *see* Les Jeunes Loups

7742 Youngblood (1978) Score (War) US:LP = UA LA-904*

7743 Youngblood (1985) Score (t: William Orbit/s:various) US:LP = RCA ABL1-7172*

7744 Youngblood Hawke (1964) Theme (Max Steiner) US:SP = Columbia 4-43149 [Mitch Miller]; Theme (Max Steiner) US:SP = Groove 58-0051 [Mike Daniels]; Theme (Max Steiner) US:LP = RCA 3342* [Marty Gold]

7745 Your Cheatin' Heart (1964) Score (pop music) US:LP = MGM E-4260/SE-4260*

7746 You're a Big Boy Now (1966) Score (John Sebastian) US:LP = Kama Sutra 8058/S-8058*

7747 You're a Sweetheart (1937) Theme-A/US:LP-BP = Scarce Rarities 5502 [Alice Faye:ST]; Theme-B/US: LP = Valiant 122 [Alice Faye:ST]

7748 You're Never Too Young (1955) Themes (Arthur Schwartz) US: SP = Capitol 3153 [Dean Martin:ST]

7749 You're the One (1941) Themes-A-B/US:78 = Columbia 35848 [Orrin Tucker:ST]; Themes-C-D/US:78 = Columbia 35858 [Orrin Tucker:ST]; Theme-E/US:78 = Columbia 35866 [Jerry Colonna:ST]

7750 Yours, Mine and Ours (1968) Score (Fred Karlin) US:LP = UA UAS-5181*

7751 You've Got to Walk It Like You Talk It or You'll Lose That Beat (1971) Score (Scott Fagan) US:LP = Spark SPA-02* + US:LP = Visa IMP-7005* [Becker & Fagan:ST]

Z

7752 Z (1969) Score (Mikis Theodorakis) US:LP = Columbia OS-3370* + US:LP = CSP AOS-3370*

7753 Z.P.G. [Zero Population Growth] (1972) Theme (Jonathan Hodge) JA:LP = Seven Seas GXC-45* [@ST]; Theme (Jonathan Hodge) JA: LP = Mu Land 7016* [The Electoru Polyphonic Orchestra]

7754 Zabriskie Point (1971) Score

(e:Pink Floyd/e:various) US:LP = MGM SE-4468*

7755 Zachariah (1971) Score (e:Jimmie Haskell/t:John Rubinstein/etc.) US:LP = ABC SOC-13*

7756 Zapped (1982) Score (e: Charles Fox/e:various) US:LP = Regency RY-38-152*

7757 Zarak (1956) Theme (Auyar Hosseini) US:SP = Coral 9-61760 [Eydie Gorme]

7758 Zardoz (1974) Theme (David Munrow) JA:LP = Mu Land 7017* [The Electoru Polyphonic Orchestra]

7759 Zebra in the Kitchen (1965) Theme (Hal Hopper) US:SP = MGM 13350 [The Standells]

7760 Zed and Two Noughts, A (1986) Score (Michael Nyman) GB:LP = That's Entertainment TER-1106*

7761 Zee and Company *see* X, Y and Zee

7762 Zelig (1983) Theme (Dick Hyman) US:LP = RCA 1-4850* + US:LP-BP = Disc 105* [Larry Elgart]

7763 Zenabel (1969) Score (Bruno Nicolai) IT:LP = Gemelli 10-002*

7764 Zeppelin (1971) Themes (Roy Budd) GB:LP = Pye 18373* [Roy Budd: ST]; Theme (Roy Budd) US:LP-BP = Eros 80544* [Roy Budd:ST]

7765 Zero Hour (1957) Theme (Arthur Hamilton) US:SP = Columbia 4-41054 [Peggy King]

7766 Zero Population Growth *see* Z.P.G.

7767 Ziegfeld Follies (1946) Scores (e:Roger Edens/e:various) US:LP-MS-BP = Curtain Calls 100/15-16

7768 Ziegfeld Girl (1941) Score (e:Roger Edens/e:various) US:LP-BP = Classic International Filmusicals 3006

7769 Zig Zig (1976) Score (Karl Heinz Schafer) FR:LP = Eden Roc 62504*

7770 Ziggy Stardust and the Spiders from Mars (1983) Scores (pop music) US:LP-MS = RCA CPL2-4862* [David Bowie:ST]

7771 Zigzag [False Witness] (1970) Score (s:Oliver Nelson/t:Mike Curb) US:LP = MGM 1SE-21*

7772 Zita (1969) Score (Francois DeRoubaix) US:LP = Philips PHS-600-287e

7773 Zombie [Island of the Living Dead] [Zombie II] [Sanguelia] (1980) Theme (Fabio Frizzi) JA:LP = East World 80146* [@ST]

7774 Zombie (1979) *see* Dawn of the Dead

7775 Zombies of Sugar Hill, The *see* Sugar Hill

7776 Zone Troopers (1986) Highlights (Richard Band) US:LP = Varese STV-81262*

7777 Zoo Story (1984) Score (Steven Brown) FR:LP = Soundworks ZS-1001*

7778 Zoot Suit (1981) Score (e: Daniel Valdez/e:Lalo Guerrero/etc.) US:LP = MCA 5267*

7779 Zorba the Greek (1964) Score-A (Mikis Theodorakis) US:LP = 20th 3167/S-4167* + US:LP = 20th T-903*; Score-B (Mikis Theodorakis) GR:LP = HMV GCLP-1002

7780 Zorro (1975) Score (Guido & Maurizio DeAngelis) FR:LP = Pathe C066-13058*

7781 Zoya (1942) Highlights (Dmitri Shostakovich) US:LP = Angel SR-40160*

7782 Zulu (1964) Highlights (John Barry) US:LP = UA UAL-4116/UAS-5116*

7783 Zulu Dawn (1979) Score (Elmer Bernstein) US:LP = Cerberus CST-0201*

Related Records

A

7784 Above the Stars [erroneous listing—this is a song title from the film "The Wonderful World of the Brothers Grimm"] US:LP = Columbia 8680* [Don Costa]

7785 African Safari (1969) [inspired music] Theme = US:SP = Philips 40618 [Harley Hatcher]

7786 Aftermath, The (1982) [unreleased soundtrack album] SBR Records

7787 All in a Night's Work (1961) [inspired music] Theme = US:SP = Capitol 4551 [Dean Martin]

7788 Amorous Adventures of Don Quixote and Sancho Panza, The (1976) [unreleased soundtrack album] LUV Records

7789 Annie Get Your Gun [unfinished film—1950 Judy Garland production] Excerpts = US:LP-BP = Sandy Hook 2053 + Soundstage 2302 + Star Screen 100

7790 Annie Hall (1977) [pop music] Theme = US:LP = Pickwick 3582* [The Birchwood Pops]

7791 Anniversary, The (1968) [pop music] Theme = US:SP = Fontana 1612 [The New Vaudeville Band]

7792 Anti-Climax [unverified production] Score = US:LP = G.N. 1*

7793 Ator (1984) [unreleased soundtrack album] Citadel CTV-7032

7794 Autumn Sonata (1978) [classical music] Theme = GB:LP = Proprius 7829* [Kabi Laretei]

B

7795 Badlands (1973) [classical music] Theme = US:SP = BASF 15354* [Carl Orff]

7796 Barracuda (1978) [unreleased soundtrack album] Island Records

7797 Battleground (1949) [pop music] Theme = US:LP = Springboard 4088* [The Film Festival Orchestra]

7798 Bear, The (1984) [unreleased soundtrack album] RCA Records

7799 Bedevilled (1955) [pop music]Theme = US:SP = Columbia 4-40085 [Felicia Sanders]

7800 Beginning and End of the World, The [erroneous listing—music for a museum exhibit] CA:LP = Omni 1001*

7801 Best of Enemies, The (1961) [inspired music] Theme = US:SP = Colpix 659 [Manny Albam]

7802 Beyond Our Ken [unverified production] Score = GB:LP = Parlophone PMC-1238

7803 Beyond the Moon [erroneous listing—correct film title is "Gulliver's Travels Beyond the Moon"] US:LP = Cinema 8005

7804 Bill Cosby—Himself (1982) [dialog] US:LP = Motown 6026-ML*

7805 Billy Sunday [dialog] US: LP = Word W-3267

7806 Bird of Paradise (1951) [inspired music] Theme = US:SP = MGM 30360 [Macklin Marrow]

7807 Birds, The (1963) [inspired music—plus soundtrack sound effects] Theme = US:SP = Decca 9-31477 [The Surf Riders]

7808 Birobidzhan [pop music] Theme = US:LP = Monitor 713 [The Andreyev Balalaika Ensemble]

7809 Black Sabbath (1964) [erroneous listing—this record contains the complete score from "Black Sunday" (1960), not "Black Sabbath"] US:LP = Bax LB-1000

7810 Blackbeard's Ghost (1968) [dialog] US:LP = Disneyland DQ-1305 + Disneyland ST 3978

7811 Blackboard Jungle, The (1955) [pop music] Theme = US:SP = Decca 9-29124 [Bill Haley]

7812 Blade Runner (1982) [unreleased soundtrack album] Polygram Records

7813 Blue Veil, The (1951) [pop music] Theme = US:SP = Columbia 4-50010 [Sammy Kaye]

7814 Bluegrass Country [unverified production] Theme = US:SP = BOO

6018* [Denis Lepage]

7815 Boatniks, The (1970) [dialog] US:LP = Disneyland ST-3999

7816 Body and Soul (1947) [pop music] Theme = US:78 = Decca 23902 [John Green]

7817 Body Double (1984) [pop music] Theme = US:SP = Island 7-99805* [Frankie Goes to Hollywood]

7818 Booby Trap [unverified production] Theme/US:LP = MCA 5752* [The Yellowjackets]

7819 Born Yesterday (1950) [pop music] Theme = US:EP = RCA EPB-1097 [Eddie Fisher]

7820 Boum, La (1982) [unreleased soundtrack album] MCA Records

7821 Boy with Green Hair, The (1948) [pop music] Theme = US:SP = Capitol 6068 [Nat King Cole]; [pop music] Theme = US:LP = Capitol 16165 [Nat King Cole]

7822 Brain Leeches, The [unverified production] Theme = US:SP = SPI 86-41 [Paul Jones]

7823 Bravados, The (1958) [inspired music] Theme = US:SP = 20th 106 [Harry Simeone]

7824 Brave Bulls, The (1951) [pop music] Theme = US:SP = Columbia 4-39678 [Harry James]

7825 Brave Little Tailor, The [Cartoon] (1938) [dialog] US:EP = Disneyland 334

7826 Breakthrough [unverified production] Theme = US:LP = Limelight 86069

7827 Breathless (1983) [pop music] Theme = US:SP = Elektra 7-69825* [X]

7828 Brides of Dracula (1960) [inspired music] Theme = GB:SP = Coral Q72-378 [Bob McFadden]

7829 Brink's Job, The (1978) [pop music] Themes = JA:SP = 20th FMS-87 [Glenn Miller]

7830 But Not for Me (1959) [pop music] Theme = US:LP-MS = Verve 2-2525 [Ella Fitzgerald:ST]

7831 Butley (1974) [dialog] US:LP-MS = Caedmon TRS-362*

7832 Butterflies Are Free (1972) [stage music—from "Butterflies Are Free"] Theme = US:SP = Project 45-1370* [The Free Design]

C

7833 Cactus in the Snow (1972) [unreleased soundtrack album] Capitol SW-822

7834 Cannery Row (1982) [classical music] Theme = US:LP = RCA XRL1-4316* [collection]

7835 Cannonball Run (1981) [unreleased soundtrack album] WB HS-3580

7836 Captain Lockheed and the Star Fighters [erroneous listing—this is a rock album] US:LP = Import IMP-1011*

7837 Carnal Knowledge (1971) [pop music] Theme = GB:LP = Capitol 1038 [Frank Sinatra]

7838 Cat on a Hot Tin Roof (1958) [film music—from "The Blackboard Jungle"] Theme = US:SP = MGM 12726 [Morty Craft]; [film music—from "The Blackboard Jungle"] Theme = US:LP = MGM 4144* [David Rose]

7839 Chain Lightning (1950) [pop music] Theme = US:LP = MGM 4359* [The MGM Strings]

7840 Chase a Crooked Shadow (1958) [unverified record] Phonolog Listing

7841 Cheaper by the Dozen (1950) [pop music] Theme = US:78 = MGM 10685 [Leroy Holmes]

7842 Children of Babylon, The [unconfirmed production] Score = GB: LP = Rainbow RLP-1020*

7843 China Syndrome, The (1979) [pop music] Theme = JA:LP = RCA Victor 8301* [collection]

7844 Clarence, the Cross-Eyed Lion (1965) [inspired music] Theme = US:SP = MGM 13333 [Glenn Sutton]

7845 Clash by Night (1952) [pop music] Theme = US:SP = RCA 47-4560 [Dennis Day]

7846 Comancheros, The (1961) [inspired music] Theme = US:SP = Capitol 4664 [The Hollyridge Strings]; [inspired music] Theme = US:SP = Columbia 4-42196 [Claude King]; [inspired music] Theme = US:LP = Liberty 14031* [Tommy Garrett]

7847 Condemned of Altona, The

(1963) [classical music] Excerpts = US: LP = London CS-7160* [Bernard Haitink]

7848 Condor, El (1970) [unreleased soundtrack album] National General Records

7849 Conquista (1971) [unverified record] Excerpts = GB:LP = JSD 100* [John Scott]

7850 Cop and the Hooker, The [unverified production] Theme = US:LP = ABC 11348 [Dave Crawford]

7851 Corn Is Green, The (1945) [pop music] Themes = US:SP = Decca 9-30770 [Russ Morgan]

7852 Country Cousin, The [Cartoon] (1936) [dialog] US:LP = Disneyland DQ-1306 + Disneyland ST-1903

7853 Courtship of Eddie's Father, The (1963) [pop music] Theme = US: SP = Decca 9-25597 [Wayne King]

7854 Cover Me Babe [Run, Shadow, Run] (1970) [unverified record] Theme=US:SP=Zig Zag 1001 [Macabre]

7855 Cries and Whispers (1973) [classical music] Theme = GB:LP = Proprius 7829* [Kabi Laretei]

D

7856 Dam Busters, The (1955) [pop music] Theme = US:LP = Odyssey 3216-0318* [Adrian Bolt]

7857 Damaged Goods [unverified production] Theme = US:SP = Dolton 078 [The Ventures]

7858 Damn the Defiant (1962) [inspired music] Theme = US:SP = Colpix 653 [Ernie Royal]

7859 Dark Passage (1947) [pop music] Theme = US:78 = RCA Victor 20-2293 [Tony Martin]

7860 Darling, How Could You? (1951) [inspired music] Theme = US: SP = Decca 9-27756 [Jerry Gray]

7861 David and Goliath (1960) [inspired music] Theme = US:SP = Columbia 4-41987 [Frank DeVol]

7862 Davy Crockett—King of the Wild Frontier (1955) [erroneous listing—this is television music] US: LP = Columbia CL-666

7863 Dawn of the Mummy (1981) [unreleased soundtrack album] Saban Records

7864 Dead Men Don't Wear Plaid (1982) [unreleased soundtrack album] X LXSE-1-005

7865 Deadly Passion (1984) [unreleased soundtrack album] Teal Records

7866 Death Race 2000 (1975) [unreleased soundtrack album] Citadel CTV-7024

7867 Delicate Balance, A (1973) [dialog] US:LP-MS = Caedmon TRS-360*

7868 Deliver Us from Evil [unverified production] Theme = US:SP = Polydor 14287* [Enchantment]

7869 Devil's Bride, The [The Devil Rides Out] (1968) [inspired music] Theme = GB:SP = Spark 1012 [Icarus]

7870 Devil's Commandment, The [erroneous listing—the correct film title is "Uncle Was a Vampire"] US:LP = RCA FSO-4*

7871 Devil's Eye, The (1960) [classical music] Excerpts = GB:LP = Proprius 7829* [Kabi Laretei]

7872 Discovery of Brazil, The (1937) [classical music] Excerpts = FR: LP = Pathe 602/3

7873 Drowning of Lucy Hamilton, The [unverified production] Score = GB: LP = Widowspeak WSP-2*

E

7874 Earrings of Madame De, The (1953) [unverified record] Theme = US: LP = Riviera 6580

7875 Elmer Elephant [Cartoon] (1936) [dialog] US:LP = Disneyland DQ-1283

7876 Elvira Madigan (1967) [classical music] Excerpts = US:LP = Deutsche 138783* [Geza Anda]; [classical music] Theme = US:SP = MGM 13953 [James Last]

7877 Emil and the Detectives (1964) [dialog] US:LP = Disneyland DQ-1262

7878 Ensign Pulver (1964) [pop music] Theme = US:LP = Command 871* [Enoch Light]

7879 Evil Under the Sun (1982) [pop music] Highlights = US:LP = RCA AYL1-4309* [Various Artists]

7880 Excalibur (1981) [unreleased soundtrack album] WB BSK-3574; [classical music] Highlights = US:LP = Island ILPS-9682*; [classical music] Highlights = US:LP = Angel S-37841*

F

7881-2 Face to Face (1976) [classical music] Theme = GB:LP = Proprius 7829* [Kabi Laretei]

7883 Female Fugitives [unverified production] Theme = US:SP-PP = NH 113 [Dyanna Whitman]

7884 Feminine Touch, The [The Gentle Touch] (1941) [pop music] Theme = US:SP = RCA 47-5463 [The Three Suns]

7885 Festival [unverified production] Theme = US:LP = London 127 [Mantovani]

7886 Fighting Kentuckian, The [erroneous listing—the correct film title is "The Kentuckian"] US:LP = MGM 3220 [@James Brown]

7887 First Man Into Space, The (1959) [inspired music] Theme = US:SP = MGM 12768 [Ray Ellis]

7888 Flesh Gordon (1973) [unverified record] Score = US:LP-PP = Mammoth 1001*

7889 Flight of the Phoenix, The (1965) [pop music] Theme = US:SP = Liberty 55874 [Trombones Unlimited]; [pop music] Theme = US:LP = Dunhill 50008* [The Brass Ring]

7890 Flim-Flam Man, The (1967) [inspired music] Theme = US:SP = 20th 6687 [Mother Love]

7891 Fool Killer, The (1965) [inspired music] Theme = US:SP = Epic 5-9782 [David Houston]

7892 Forbidden Planet (1956) [inspired music] Theme = US:SP = MGM 12243 [David Rose]; [inspired music] Theme = US:LP = MGM 3397 [David Rose]

7893 Forever My Love (1962) [inspired music] Theme = US:SP = Kapp 450 [Jane Morgan]

7894 Fort Apache (1948) [pop music] Theme = IT:LP = RCA 43493* [@Robert Shaw]

7895 Fortune and Men's Eyes (1971) [unreleased soundtrack album] MGM Records

7896 Fountains of Rome, The [Short] (1959) [classical music] Excerpts = US:LP = Columbia MS-6587* [Eugene Ormandy]

7897 Four Seasons, The (1981) [classical music] Excerpts = US:LP = RCA XRL1-4316* [collection]

7898 Freedom's Finest Hour (1966) [dialog] US:LP = Decca DL-74943* + US:LP = MCA 37122*

7899 From Mao to Mozart—Isaac Stern in China (1980) [classical music] Highlights = FR:LP = CBS 60030* [Isaac Stern]

G

7900 Gaby (1956) [pop song] Theme = US:SP = MGM 12253 [Jimmie Haskell]; [inspired music] Theme = US:SP = RKO Unique 337 [Jack Carroll]

7901 Gallipoli (1981) [classical music] Themes = US:LP = RCA XRL1-4316* [collection]; [pop music] Themes = US:LP = DRG 8202* [William Motzing]

7902 Games [erroneous listing—this Mercury album contains no music from the 1967 film "Games"] US:LP = Mercury 61149* [Derek & Ray]

7903 Geneva Convention, The [unverified production] Score = US:LP-PP = Geneva STGS-101

7904 Ghetto Man [unverified production] Theme = US:SP = UA 50867 [War]; [unverified production] Theme = US:LP = UA 5546* [War]

7905 Give 'Em Hell, Harry! (1975) [dialog] US:LP-MS = UA LA-504*

7906 Go Tell the Spartans (1978) [unverified record] Phonolog Listing

7907 Godzilla's Revenge (1971) [unverified record] Theme = US:SP = Crown Records

7908 Goliath and the Barbarians (1959) [inspired music] Theme = US: SP = American International 545 [Judy Harriet]

7909 Good King Bad [unverified production] Theme = US:LP = CTI 6062* [George Benson]

7910 Good Life, The [erroneous listing—this is a song title from the film "The Seven Capital Sins"] US:LP = Capitol 8603* [Frank Pourcel]

7911 Grass Is Greener, The (1960) [pop music] Theme = US:SP = Medallion 603 [Errol Victor]

7912 Great Adventure, The (1954) [inspired music] Theme = US:SP = RKO Unique 319 [Joe Leahy]

7913 Great Divide, The [unverified production] Theme = US:SP = Elektra 45067* [Harry Chapin]

7914 Green Berets, The (1968) [pop music] Theme = US:SP = RCA 47-8739 [Barry Sadler]

7915 Guns of the Magnificent Seven, The (1969) [film music—from "The Magnificent Seven"] Theme = JA: LP = UA SR-281*

H

7916 Hangman, The (1959) [inspired music] Theme = US:SP = Dot 45-15942 [John Ashley]

7917 Happy [television music—the correct television title is "Happy Days"] Theme = US:LP = Elektra 209* [Pink Lady]

7918 Harold and Maude (1971) [pop music] Excerpts = US:LP = A&M SP-4260* [Cat Stevens]

7919 Hatchet Man, The (1932) [dialog] US:LP-BP = Caliban 6041

7920 Hate Kills [erroneous listing—this is a rock album] US:LP = Paramount PAS-5031*

7921 Haunting, The (1963) [inspired music] Theme = US:SP = MGM 13163 [Lalo Schifrin]; [inspired music] Theme = US:LP = MGM 4192* [Lalo Schifrin]

7922 Heartbeeps (1981) [unreleased soundtrack album] MCA Records + X LXSE-1-006

7923 Heiress, The (1949) [inspired music] Theme = US:SP = RCA 47-3086 [Fran Warren]; [inspired music] Theme = US:SP = Everest 19403 [Bernie Wayne]

7924 Hi, Mom (1970) [unreleased soundtrack album] Skye Records

7925 Homecoming, The (1973) [dialog] US:LP-MS = Caedmon TRS-361*

7926 Hopscotch (1980) [classical music] Themes = US:LP = Deutsche 2535-469-10* [collection]

7927 Hot Spell (1958) [inspired music] Theme = US:SP = RCA 47-7236 [Ernie Felice]

7928 House of Usher, The (1960) [unreleased soundtrack album] American International Records

7929 Huey [dialog] US:LP = Folkways FD-5402

I

7930 I Wake Up Screaming (1941) [film music—from "Street Scene"] Theme = US:LP-BP = Cinema 8002 [@Lionel Newman]

7931 I Was an American Spy (1951) [pop music] Theme = US:SP = Capitol 1760 [Les Baxter]

7932 Iceman Cometh, The (1973) [dialog] US:LP-MS = Caedmon TRS-359*

7933 In a Lonely Place (1950) [pop music] Theme = US:78 = MGM 10686 [Ziggy Elman]

7934 In Paris Parks [unverified production] Theme = US:LP = Classic Editions 1043

7935 In the Dark [unverified production] Theme = US:SP = London 45-90009* [Ronnie Aldrich]

7936 Island of Dr. Moreau, The (1977) [unreleased soundtrack album] Varese VC-81086

7937 It Happened One Bite [unfinished film] Score = US:LP = WB BSK-3158* [Dan Hicks]

7938 It's a Pleasure (1945) [pop music] Theme = US:SP = Columbia 13-33317 [Xavier Cugat]

7939 I've Always Loved You (1946) [classical music] Theme = US:LP = Diplomat 2298 [Nicholas Adriano]

J

7940 Jerusalem File, The (1971) [unverified record] Excerpts = GB:LP = JSD 100* [John Scott]

7941 John and Mary (1969) [inspired music] Theme = US:SP = Decca 9-32622 [John and Mary]

7942 Journey to the Center of the Earth (1959) [inspired music] Theme = US:EP = Dot DEP-1091 [Pat Boone]

7943 Julia Misbehaves (1948) [pop music] Theme = US:LP = MGM 4144* [David Rose]

7944 Just Another Hobo [unverified production] Theme = US:SP = Madison 122 [Dick Woods]

7945 Just for Fun (1963) [unconfirmed record] Decca Records

K

7946 King Heroin [unverified production] Theme = US:SP = Polydor 14116 [James Brown]

7947 King of the Mountain (1981) [unreleased soundtrack album] Polygram Records

7948 Kingdom of the Spiders (1977) [television music—from "The Twilight Zone"] Theme = US:LP-BP = POO 106 [collection]

7949 Kiss of Death (1947) [film music—from "Street Scene"] Theme = US:78 = RCA Victor 20-2665 [Tommy Dorsey]

7950 Klute (1971) [unreleased soundtrack album] WB WS-1940

L

7951 L-Shaped Room, The (1963) [pop music] Theme = US:LP = Pacific Jazz 76* [The Jazz Crusaders]; [pop music] Themes = GB:SP = Parlophone 4977 [Phil Woods]

7952 Lady from Shanghai, The (1948) [pop music] Theme = US:LP-MS = Reader's Digest RDA-39* [@ Charles Gerhardt]

7953 Last of Sheila, The (1973) [pop music] Theme = US:SP = Atlantic 45-2980 [Bette Midler]

7954 Lazarus [unverified production] Theme = US:SP = M&B 100 [Bob Grabeau]

7955 Legend of Nigger Charley, The (1972) [unreleased soundtrack album] National General Records

7956 Legend of the Living Sea, The [erroneous listing—music for a museum exhibit] US:LP = Ocean OR-7111*

7957 Life of Albeniz, The (1946) [classical music] Highlights = US:LP = RCA LOP-1092

7958 Lifehouse [unfinished film] Theme = US:SP = Decca 9-32846 [The Who]; [unfinished film] Themes = US: LP = Decca 79189* [The Who]

7959 Lili Marlene (1950) [pop music] Theme = US:SP = Coral 9-60559 [Martha Tilton]

7960 Lilly Lilly [unverified production] Theme = US:SP = Rust 5076 [Ernie Maresca]

7961 Lisa and the Devil [The House of Exorcism] (1975) [classical music] Highlights = IT:LP = Philips 644.505*

7962 Lisbon (1956) [pop music] Theme = US:SP = Capitol 3287 [Nelson Riddle]

7963 Listen Whitey [dialog] US: LP = Folkways FD-5402

7964 Little Hiawatha [Cartoon] (1936) [dialog] US:LP = Disneyland DQ-1283

7965 Little Sex, A (1982) [pop music] Theme = US:LP = Arista 9574* [Melissa Manchester]

7966 Little Women (1949) [pop music] Theme = US:LP = MGM 4144* [David Rose]

7967 Lost Hour, The [unverified production] Theme = US:LP = Coral 57016 [Alfredo Antonini]

7968 Love and Death (1975) [classical music] Excerpts = US:LP = Columbia MS-6545* [Eugene Ormandy]

7969 Love Bug, The (1969) [dialog] US:LP = Disneyland ST-3986

7970 Love in the Country [erroneous listing—this is a song title from the film "McLintock"] US:LP = Mercury 60887* [Clebanoff]

7971 Lovelines (1984) [unreleased soundtrack album] EMI America Records

7972 Lovers, The (1958) [classical music] Theme = US:LP = Turn On 1002 [collection]

7973 Lust for a Vampire (1971) [unverified record] Phonolog Listing

M

7974 Mad Monster Party (1967) [unreleased soundtrack album] RCA Records

7975 Magnificent Seven Ride, The (1973) [film music—from "The Magnificent Seven"] Theme = US:LP = Avalanche 058* [Al Caiola]

7976 Mahu and the Monkey [unverified production] Theme = US:LP-10 = MGM 513 [Philip Green]

7977 Mambo (1954) [inspired music] Theme = US:SP = MGM 11981 [Dave Robbins]; [unverified record] Highlights = IT:LP-10 = RCA 10V0003

7978 Man Alone, A [erroneous listing—this is a song title from the film "The Ipcress File"] US:LP = Camden 927* [Ray Martin]

7979-80 Man in the White Suit, The (1951) [inspired music] Theme = US: SP = Coral 9-60588 [Jack Parnell]

7981 Man Who Shot Liberty Valance, The (1962) [inspired music] Theme = US:SP = Musicor 1020/Musicor 1901 [Gene Pitney]; [inspired music Theme = US:LP = Musicor 3161* [Gene Pitney]

7982 Martin Luther [dialog] US: LP-PP = Lutheran Church 11528

7983 Mary, Mary, Bloody Mary (1975) [unverified record] Phonolog Listing

7984 Masters of the Congo Jungle (1959) [unreleased soundtrack album] 20th 4001

7985 Mephisto Waltz, The (1971) [classical music] Excerpts = US:LP = Columbia MS-6241* [Eugene Ormandy]

7986 Millionaire for Christy, A (1951) [pop music] Theme = US:SP = International 4053 [Bud Herrmann]

7987 Miracle Worker, The (1962) [pop music] Theme = US:SP = UA 466 [June Valli]; [pop music] Theme = US: LP = Columbia 8680* [Don Costa]

7988 Mirror Cracked, The (1980) [pop music] Theme = JA:SP = Towa 17144* [The Film Studio Orchestra]

7989 Mission Mars (1968) [unverified recording] Phonolog Listing

7990 Mr. Moses (1965) [inspired music] Theme = US:SP = UA 874 [Jim Lowe]

7991 Mr. Potts Goes to Moscow *see* Top Secret (1952)

7992 Mogambo (1953) [inspired music] Theme = US:LP = Mercury 20156/Mercury 20301 [Richard Hayman]

7993 Mouse on the Moon, The (1963) [inspired music] Theme = US: SP = UA 610 [The Grand Fenwick Orchestra]

7994 Movie Star—American Style (1969) [unreleased soundtrack album] Mira MS-3007

7995 Mummy, The (1959) [inspired song] Theme = GB:SP = Coral Q72-378 [Bob McFadden]

7996 My Darling Clementine (1946) [pop music] Theme = US:LP = RCA OPL1-0001* [@Heine Beau]

7997 My Father's House (1947) [pop music] Theme = US:78 = Disc 932 [The Folk Band]

7998 Myra Breckinridge (1970) [unreleased soundtrack album] 20th S-4210

N

7998a Neon Maniacs (1985) [unreleased soundtrack album] Easy Street Records

7999 Night Crossing (1981) [unreleased soundtrack album] X LXSE-1-004

8000 Night Has a Thousand Eyes, The (1948) [inspired music] Theme = US: LP = Atlantic 80108-1* [Freddie Hubbard]

8001 Night Heaven Fell, The [Heaven Fell That Night] (1957) [inspired music] Theme = US:SP = Columbia 4-41237 [Tony Bennett]; [inspired music] Theme = US:LP = WB 1371* [Pete Rugolo]

8002 Nine Lives of Fritz the Cat, The (1974) [unreleased soundtrack album] Ode Records

8003 Nine Men (1943) [pop music] Theme = US:LP = Odyssey 3216-0318* [Adrian Bolt]

8004 No Down Payment (1957) [pop music] Theme = US:LP = Audition 33-5911 [The Audition Orchestra]

8005 Nobody Waved Goodbye (1964) [inspired music] Theme = US: SP = Kapp 675 [The Greenwood Country Singers]

8006 None But the Lonely Heart (1944) [classical music] Theme = US: LP = Metro 585* [David Rose]

8007 Not of This Earth [erroneous listing – this is a pop song] US:LP = GNP 2111* [Neil Norman]

8008 Notorious Landlady, The (1962) [inspired music] Theme = US: SP = Choreo 104 [Fred Astaire]; [inspired music] Theme = US:LP = DRG 15004 [Fred Astaire]

8009 November Children, The [unverified production] Score = US:LP-PP = Kare KLP-101

O

8010 O Cangaceiro – The Story of a Bandit [The Bandit] (1953) [pop music] Theme = US:SP = Columbia 4-40323 [Percy Faith]

8011 Off Beat [unverified production] Theme = US:SP = Arvee 5017 [Steve Stevens]

8012 Oh, Heavenly Dog (1980) [pop music] Theme = US:LP = MCA 37068* [Elton John]

8013 Old Boyfriends (1979) [unreleased soundtrack album] Columbia Records

8014 One More Train to Rob [erroneous listing – no such record number exists] US:SP = Kapp 001

8015 Our Man in Havana (1959) [pop music] Themes = US:SP = Dot 45-16069 [George Hernandez]

8016 Outlaw, The (1943) [classical music] Theme = US:LP = Diplomat 2298 [Nicholas Adriano]

8017 Outsider, The (1962) [pop music] Theme = US:SP = UA 421 [Shirley Bassey]

8018 Owd Bob *see* To the Victor

P

8019 Pacific 231 [Short] (1931) [film music – from "La Roue"] Excerpts = US: LP = Vanguard VDS-274* [Maurice Abravanel]

8020 Pancho Villa (1972) [unverified record] Phonolog Listing

8021 Pandora and the Flying Dutchman (1951) [inspired music] Theme = US:SP = MGM 10996 [Billy Eckstine]

8022 Parbola (1937) [classical music] Excerpts = US:LP = Angel S-37442* [Leonard Bernstein]

8023 Persuader, The [erroneous listing – this is music from the television series "The Persuaders"] US:SP = Epic 5-10865 [John Barry]

8024 Phantom Planet [erroneous listing – this is a pop song] US:LP = GNP 2128* [Neil Norman]

8024a Phffft (1954) [inspired music] Theme = US:SP = Decca 9-29318 [Sonny Burke]

8025 Philanderer, The [erroneous listing – this is not a film theme] US: LP = Golden Crest 4019 [Arthur Kleiner]

8026 Picasso Summer, The (1972)

[unreleased soundtrack album] WB WS-1811

8027 Pickup on South Street (1953) [pop music] Theme = US:SP = Mercury 71003 [Dick Contino]

8028 Pit and the Pendulum, The [erroneous listing—this record is a radio spot ad, not a film theme] US:SP = AIR 609

8029 Play Misty for Me (1971) [pop music] Theme = US:LP = Kirshner 116* [James Darren]

8030 Point of Order (1964) [dialog] US:LP = Columbia OS-2470*

8031 Portrait of Jennie (1948) [inspired music] Theme = US:SP = RCA 47-2906 [Freddy Martin]

8032 Premature Burial (1962) [pop music] Theme = US:LP = Verve V6-8493* [Kai Winding]

8033 Principle Edwards Magic Theatre [erroneous listing—this is a rock album] US:LP = Dandelion D9-103*

8034 Proud and the Profane, The (1956) [inspired music] Theme = US:SP = RKO Unique 338 [Jack Smith]

Q

8035 Quarter Horse (1977) [dialog] US:LP = Western American SR-100*

8036 Quest for the Best [unverified production] Theme/US:LP = Riza 85-105* [Afterglow]

R

8037 Raggedy Man, The (1981) [unreleased soundtrack album] MCA Records

8038 Raging Bull (1980) [classical music] Excerpts = US:LP = Deutsche 2353-469-5* [collection]; [classical music] Theme = US:SP = Motown 1504* [Joel Diamond]

8039 Razor's Edge, The (1946) [pop music] Theme = US:SP = Mercury 71003 [Dick Contino]; [pop music] Theme = US:LP = WB 1335* [Sonny Moon]

8040 Recko the Robot [Cartoon] [unverified production] Theme = US:SP = S.A. 1989 [Cathy Carter]

8040a Recruits (1986) [unreleased soundtrack album] Filmtrax Records

8041 Red Balloon, The [Short] (1956) [dialog + record music] US:LP = Nonesuch 2001/72001*

8042 Redwoods [Short] (1967) [classical music] Excerpts = US:LP = Columbia MS-6843* [Leonard Bernstein]

8043 Regina Maris [unverified production] Score = US:LP-PP = Metronome KMLP-306

8044 Return of the Islander [unverified production] Score = US:LP-PP = Talisman 1003

8045 Return to Peyton Place (1961) [film music—from "Peyton Place"] Theme = US:LP = Kapp 1289* [Vardi]

8046 Richard Pryor—Here and Now (1983) [dialog] US:LP = WB 23981-1*

8047 Richard Pryor—Live on the Sunset Strip (1982) [dialog] US:LP = WB BSK-3660*

8048 Richard's Things (1981) [unreleased soundtrack album] DRG Records

8049 Right On! (1970) [dialog] US:LP = First Poets 1001*

8050 Right Stuff, The (1983) [unreleased soundtrack album] Geffen GHS-4024

8051 Rising of the Moon, The (1957) [pop music] Theme = US:LP = London 44020* [The Jazz All-Stars]

8052 Roaring Twenties, The (1939) [pop music] Excerpts = US:LP = MGM SE-4359* [The MGM Strings]

8053 Rook, The [unverified production] Theme = US:LP = Metromedia 1023* [Merv Griffin]

8054 Rose Tattoo, The (1955) [inspired music] Theme = US:SP = Columbia 4-40588 [Percy Faith]

8055 Run, Shadow, Run *see* Cover Me Babe

8056 Rush to Judgment [dialog] US:LP = Vanguard VDS-9242*

8057 Ruthless Four, The (1968) [pop music] Theme = US:SP = Decca 9-32622 [John and Mary]

S

8058 Sabrina (1954) [pop music] Excerpts = US:LP = WB WS-1247* [Matty Malneck]; [inspired music] Theme = US:SP = Columbia 4-40588 [Mitch Miller]

8059 Say Goodbye [unverified production] Theme = US:SP = Mediarts 107* [Dory Previn]

8060 Secret of My Success, The (1965) [pop music] Theme = US:SP = MGM 13407 [Bill McElhiney]

8061 Seems Like Old Times (1980) [unreleased soundtrack album] Audio Fidelity Records

8062 September Affair (1950) [pop music] Theme = US:EP = EPB-1000 [George Melachrino]

8063 Seven Beauties (1975) [classical music] Theme = US:LP = Turn On 1002* [collection]

8064 Seven Days in May (1964) [inspired music] Theme = US:SP = Columbia 4-42995 [Jerry Murad]; [inspired music] Theme = US:LP = Columbia 2166/8966* [Jerry Murad]

8065 Seventh Voyage of Sinbad, The (1958) [inspired music] Theme = US: SP = Capitol 3980 [Nelson Riddle]

8066 She Wore a Yellow Ribbon (1949) [pop music] Theme = US:LP = Vocalion 73611 [The Andrews Sisters]

8067 Sign of the Gladiator (1958) [unreleased soundtrack album] American International AILP-501

8068 Silver Metere [erroneous listing—this is a rock album] US:LP = National General NG-2000*

8069 Sink the Bismarck! (1960) [inspired music] Theme = US:SP = Columbia 4-41568 [Johnny Horton]

8070 Sitting Pretty (1948) [pop music] Theme = US:LP = Audition 33-5926 [The Audition Orchestra]

8071 Situation Hopeless, But Not Serious (1965) [inspired music] Theme = US:SP = Kapp 704 [Harry Simeone]

8072 Ski on the Wild Side (1967) [unreleased soundtrack album] MGM SE-4439

8073 Sleeper (1973) [pop music] Theme = US:LP = Pickwick 3375* [The Birchwood Pops]

8074 Smile (1975) [unreleased soundtrack album] UA LA-467

8075 Son of Flubber (1963) [film music—from "The Absent-Minded Professor"] Themes = US:SP = Buena Vista 555 [Fred MacMurray]

8076 Song of the Thin Man (1947) [pop music] Theme = US:78 = RCA Victor 20-2328 [Tony Martin]

8077 Soylent Green (1973) [classical music] Excerpts = JA:LP = Seven Seas GXC-45* [@Leon Pops]

8078 Sphinx (1981) [unreleased soundtrack album] WB HS-3545

8079 Spook Who Sat by the Door, The (1973) [unreleased soundtrack album] Skye Records

8080 Stalag 17 (1953) [pop music] Theme = US:LP = WB 1247* [Matty Malneck]

8081 Stay Hungry (1977) [unverified record] Theme = US:SP = UA 709* [Larry Butler]

8082 Story of Three Loves, The (1953) [pop music] Theme = US:SP = Columbia 4-40099 [Liberace]; [pop music] Theme = US:LP = London 1513 [Mantovani]

8083 Street of Dreams [pop music] Theme = US:LP = Capitol 8608* [Pino Calvi]

8084 Streets of Laredo, The (1949) [pop music] Theme = US:LP-MS = UA LA-082* [@Felix Slatkin]

8085 Strong Together [unverified production] Score = US:LP-PP = Big Tree 76016

8086 Subject Was Roses, The (1968) [pop music] Theme = US:SP = Elektra 45639 [Judy Collins]

8087 Successful Side of Summerhill, The [unverified production] US:LP-MS = Atsum 13434*

8088 Surf II (1983) [unreleased soundtrack album] Capitol Records

8089 Sunday, Bloody Sunday (1971) [classical music] Excerpts = US: LP = RCA LSC-3245* [collection]

8090 Sweet Bird of Youth (1962) [pop music] Theme = US:SP = London 45-9519 [Frank Chacksfield]; [pop music] Theme = US:LP = MGM 4271 [David Rose]

T

8091 Take the High Road [unverified production] Score = US:LP-PP = Highway 101

8092 Task Force (1949) [pop music] Theme = US:SP = RCA 47-2906 [Freddy Martin]

8093 Taste of Honey, A (1961) [stage music—from "A Taste of Honey"] US: LP = UA 14018 [Lloyd G. Mayers]

8094 Taxi for Tobruk (1961) [inspired music] Theme = US:SP = Epic 5-9745 [Garry Sherman]

8095 Ten North Frederick (1958) [pop music] Theme = US:SP = Seeco 45-6001 [Jose Melis]; [pop music] Theme = US:LP = Audition 33-5928 [The Audition Orchestra]

8096 Teresa (1951) [inspired music] Theme = US:SP = MGM 30360 [Macklin Marrow]

8097 Testament of Orpheus, The (1960) [dialog] FR:LP = Columbia 1075

8098 That Kind of Woman (1959) [inspired music] Theme = US:SP = Roulette 4185 [Joe Williams]; [inspired music] Theme = US:LP = Roulette 52039 [Joe Williams]

8099 Thank You, Masked Man [Cartoon] [dialog] US:LP = Fantasy 7017 [Lenny Bruce]

8100 They Shall Have Music [Melody of Youth] (1939) [classical music] Theme = US:LP-PP = GNP 2222 [collection]

8101 Thirst (1980) [unreleased soundtrack album] Varese STV-81141

8102 This Angry Age (1958) [inspired music] Theme = US:SP = Dot 45-15761 [Alvy West]

8103 This Man Is Dangerous (1941) [unverified record] Theme = US:LP = Riviera 6580

8104 Three Ring Circus (1955) [pop music] Theme = US:SP = MGM 11914 [Leroy Holmes]

8105 Till the End of Time (1946) [classical music] Theme = US:LP = London 1526 [Cyril Stapleton]

8106 Time Out of Mind (1947) [film music—from "Lydia"] Excerpts = US: LP = Varese 704.260* [Elmer Bernstein]

8107 To Each His Own (1946) [pop music] Theme = US:SP = Kapp 264 [Jane Morgan]; [pop music] Theme = US:LP = Design 215 [The Sound Stage Orchestra]

8108 To Please a Lady (1950) [pop music] Theme = US:SP = MGM 30279 [David Rose]

8109 To the Victor [Owd Bob] (1948) [pop music] Theme = US:78 = RCA Victor 20-2666 [Freddy Martin]; [pop music] Theme = US:LP = WB 1368* [John Scott Trotter]

8110 Tomboy (1985) [unreleased soundtrack album] MCA Records

8111 Tonite, Let's All Make Love in London (1967) [dialog] GB:LP = Instant 002*

8112 Top Secret [Mr. Potts Goes to Moscow] (1952) [pop music] Theme = US:SP = London 45-9503 [Ted Heath]

8113 Topper Takes a Trip (1939) [unverified record] Theme = US:LP = Music Box TMH-4305

8114 Touched by Love (1983) [pop music] Theme = JA:SP = RCA RPS-38* [Elvis Presley]

8115 Town Without a Face, The (1963) [unverified record] Theme = US: SP = Qualiton 7095

8116 Toy Tiger (1956) [film music—from "The Private War of Major Benson"] Theme = US:SP = Coral 9-61648 [The Lennon Sisters]

8117 Trancers (1985) [unreleased soundtrack album] Radioactive Records

8118 Trouble with Harry, The (1956) [inspired music] Theme = US: SP = Columbia 4-40617 [Les Elgart]

8119 Twilight's Last Gleaming (1977) [pop music] Theme = JA:LP = Columbia SW-7075* [The Movie Sounds Orchestra]

U

8120 Ugly Duckling, The [Cartoon] (1931) [dialog] US:LP = Disneyland DQ-1283

8121 Uncle Meat [unfinished film]

Scores = US:LP-MS = Reprise RS-2024* [Frank Zappa]

8122 Undercurrent (1946) [classical music] Theme = US:LP = RCA 1008 [Al Goodman]

8123 Underground (1976) [dialog] US:LP = Folkways FD-5752

8124 Unfaithfully Yours (1984) [classical music] Themes = US:LP = RCA XRL1-4867* [collection]

8125 Unknown, The (1946) [unverified record] Theme = US:LP = Sonodor 105 [Orchestra Del Oro]

V

8126 Valley Girl (1983) [unreleased soundtrack album] Epic FE-23816

8127 Vertigo (1958) [inspired music] Theme = US:SP = Mercury 71325 [Billy Eckstine]

8128 Waltz Across Texas (1982) [pop music] Theme = US:LP = RCA 1-3602* [Waylon Jennings]

8129 War of the Satellites [erroneous listing—this is a pop song, not a film theme] US:LP = GNP 2133* [Neil Norman]

8130 Warrior Empress [erroneous listing—the correct film title is the 1970 production "Sapho"] FR:LP = Barclay 920.322*

8131-2 Welcome to the Queen [Short] (1954) [classical music] Excerpts = US:LP = RCA LSC-2257* [Arthur Bliss]

8133 White Rose of Athens, The [erroneous listing—this is a song title from the film "Dreamland of Desire"] US:LP = Mercury 60688* [David Carroll]

8134 Who's Been Sleeping in My Bed? (1963) [inspired music] Theme = US:SP = Congress 204 [Linda Scott]

8135 Wilderness Trail, The [erroneous listing—this is record music, not film or television music] US:LP = National Geographic 07708*

8136 Windsong [unverified production] Excerpts = US:LP = Composers Recordings 193

8137 Winnie the Pooh and Tigger Too [Short] (1974) [film music—from "Winnie the Pooh and the Honey Tree"] Themes = US:LP = Disneyland 3813

8138 Wives and Lovers (1963) [inspired music] Theme = US:SP = Kapp 551 [Jack Jones]; [inspired music] Theme = US:LP = Columbia 2166/8966* [Jerry Murad]

8138a Wonderwall [unverified production] Score = US:LP = Apple SW-3350* [George Harrison]

8139 World's Fair Encounter [unverified production] Theme = US:LP = Light 5544* [Clare Fischer]

8140 Yesterday's Hero (1979) [unverified record] Score = GB:LP = Warwick W-7726*

8141 You Came Along (1945) [pop music] Theme = US:SP = MGM 11743 [Dick Hayman]

II. TELEVISION MUSIC

A

8142 A for Andromeda (1961) Theme (Trevor Duncan) GB:LP = BBC 324* [@Patrick Michael]

8143 A-Team, The (1983) Score (Mike Post & Pete Carpenter) GB:LP = Indiana AT-4444*; Theme (Mike Post & Pete Carpenter) US:SP = RCA 13859* [Mike Post:ST]; Theme (Mike Post & Pete Carpenter) US:LP = RCA 1-5415* [Mike Post:ST]

8144 ABC Monday Night Football (1971) Theme (Charles Fox) US:SP = Atco 6876* [Bob's Band]

8145 ABC 1980 Winter Olympics (1980) Theme (Chuck Mangione) US: SP = A&M 2211* [Chuck Mangione:ST]; Theme (Chuck Mangione) US:LP = A&M 3715* [Chuck Mangione:ST]

8146 ABC's Wide World of Sports Theme (Charles Fox) US:LP-PP = Jenson 3-001* [The Jenson Marching Band]

8147 A.D. Anno Domini (1985) Score (Lalo Schifrin) GB:LP = BBC REB-561*

8148 Adam-12 (1968) Theme (Frank Comstock) US:LP = MCA 5380* [Warren Schatz]; Theme (Frank Comstock) US:LP-MS = Tee Vee Toons 1100 [@ST]

8149 Addams Family, The (1964) Score (Vic Mizzy) US:LP = RCA LPM-3421/LSP-3421*

8150 Adventure in Color, An [Walt Disney Presents] (1961) Themes (Richard & Robert Sherman) US:SP = Disneyland 729 [Ludwig Von Drake:ST]

8151 Adventurer, The (1972) Theme (John Barry) GB:SP = Polydor 2058.275* [John Barry:ST]; Theme (John Barry) GB:LP = Polydor 2383.156* [John Barry:ST]; Theme (John Barry) GB:LP = Polydor 2383.461* [John Barry: ST]

8152 Adventures in Paradise (1959) Theme (Lionel Newman) US:SP = Medallion 606 [Vardi]; Theme (Lionel Newman) US:LP = 20th 3043* [20th Century Strings]; Theme (Lionel Newman) US:LP = Choreo 6* [Harry Betts]

8153 Adventures of Black Beauty, The (1972) Underscore + Dialog (Denis King) GB:LP = Contour 2870.309*; Theme (Denis King) GB:LP = Polydor 2482.240* [@John Schroeder]

8154 Adventures of Champion, The [Champion, The Wonder Horse] (1956) Theme (Norman Luboff) GB: LP = Contour 2870.185* [Cy Payne]

8155 Adventures of Huckleberry Finn, The (1986) Excerpts (William Perry) US:LP-PP = Trobriand TRO-1001* [William Perry:ST]

8156 Adventures of Jim Bowie, The (1956) Theme (Ken Darby) US:LP = RCA 1004 [@The Prairie Chiefs]; Theme (Ken Darby) US:SP = RCA WBY-73 [The Prairie Chiefs]

8157 Adventures of Jonny Quest, The (1964) Theme + Narration (Hoyt Curtin) US:LP = Hanna Barbera HLP-2030; Theme (Hoyt Curtin) US:LP-BP = Cinema 8001 [@uncredited]; Theme (Hoyt Curtin) US:EP = Hanna Barbera 7043 [uncredited]

8158 Adventures of Marco Polo, The (1956) Score (as:Clay Warnick & Mel Pahl) US:LP = Columbia ML-5111

8159 Adventures of Rin Tin Tin, The (1954) Theme-A (Hal Hopper) US: SP = MGM 12350 [James Brown:ST]; Theme-B (Hal Hopper) US:SP = MGM 12384 [James Brown:ST]

8160 Adventures of Robin Hood, The (1955) Theme (Carl Sigman) US:

SP = Capitol 3287 [Nelson Riddle]; Theme (Carl Sigman) US:SP = RCA 47-6308 [Joe Reisman]; Theme (Carl Sigman) US:LP-MS = Tee Vee Toons 1200 [@ST]

8161 Adventures of Sir Prancelot, The / Underscore + Dialog (Alan Parker) GB:LP = BBC/Roundabout 12*

8162 Adventures of Superman, The (1951) Theme (Leon Klatzkin) US:SP = Churchill 7730* [Chase]; Theme (Leon Klatzkin) US:LP = GNP 2133* [Neil Norman]; Theme (Leon Klatzkin) US: LP-MS = Tee Vee Toons 1100 [@ST]

8163-4 Adventures of Zorro, The *see* Zorro

8165 Africa (1967) Score-A (Alex North) US:LP = MGM E-4462/SE-4462*; Score-B (folk music) US:LP = Verve 3021/S-3021*

8166 Africans, The (1986) Score (t:Peter Howell/s:folk music) US:LP = Antilles AN-7085*

8167 Against the Wind (1979) Score (Mario Millo) AU:LP = Polydor 2907.048*

8168 Agatha Christie Hour, The (1983) Theme (Harry Rabinowitz) GB: LP = Red Bus 1004* [@The Olympic Orchestra:ST]

8169 Air Power (1956) Score (Norman Dello Joio) US:LP = Columbia ML-5214/MS-6029*

8170 Airline (1982) Theme (Tony Hatch) GB:SP = Tube 003* [Tony Hatch: ST]

8171 Airwolf (1985) Theme (Sylvester Levay) GB:LP = Indiana ATVP-5555* [@ST]

8172 Aladd (1976) Highlights (Jo Adler) US:LP = Bag-A-Tale BAT-1000*

8173 Aladdin (1958) Score (Cole Porter) US:LP = Columbia CL-1117 + US:LP = DRG DS-15027*

8174 Alan Freed's Big Beat Rock 'n' Roll Dance Party (1957) Excerpts + Dialog (pop music) US:LP = Silhouette SM-10016 [Alan Freed:ST]

8175 Alcoa Premiere [Premiere] [Fred Astaire Presents Premiere Theatre] (1961) Theme-A [Main Title] (John Williams) US:LP = Decca 74481* [Stanley Wilson]; Theme-A [Main Title] (John Williams) US:LP = Carlton 143* [Valjean]; Themes-B-C ["Blues for a Hanging"] (John Williams) US:SP = Ava 115 [Herb Stewart]

8176 Alcoa Theatre (1955) Theme ["A Small Bouquet"] (George Duning) US:SP = Capitol 4305 [Kenny Loran]

8177 Alexander / Highlights (Gary William Friedman) US:LP-PP = OC 8020*

8178 Alexander the Great (1964) Score (Leonard Rosenman) US:LP-PP = ABC Promo ATG-1

8179 Alfred Hitchcock Hour, The (1962) Theme ["Annabel"] (Lyn Murray) US:LP = Decca 74481* [Stanley Wilson]

8180 Alias Smith and Jones (1971) Theme (Billy Goldenberg) US:LP = MCA 5380* [Warren Schatz]; Theme (Billy Goldenberg) GB:SP = MCA 5090* [Universal Sounds Orchestra]; Theme (Billy Goldenberg) GB:LP = MFP 50091* [Geoff Love]

8181 Alice (1976) Theme (David Shire) US:LP = Pickwick 3566* [The Birchwood Pops]

8182 Alice in Wonderland *see* New Alice in Wonderland, The

8183 Alice Through the Looking Glass (1966) Score (Moose Charlap) US: LP = RCA LOC-1130/LSO-1130*

8184 All Creatures Great and Small (1978) Highlights (Johnny Pearson) GB: LP = Rampage RAMP-1*; Theme (Johnny Pearson) US:LP-MS = BBC 2-22000* [@Johnny Pearson:ST]

8185 All in the Family (1971) Themes + Dialog (Roger Kellaway/pop song) US:LP = Atlantic SD-7210; Theme-A (Roger Kellaway) US:SP = A&M 1321* [Roger Kellaway:ST]; Theme-B (pop song) US:SP = Atlantic 45-2847 [Carroll O'Connor & Jean Stapleton:ST]

8186 All My Children (1970) Theme (Dina Paul) US:LP = Capitol Custom SL-8076* [The New Christy Minstrels]

8187 All You Need Is Cash *see* Rutles, The

8188 Aloha Paradise (1981) Theme (Charles Fox) US:LP = Applause 1001* [Steve Lawrence:ST]

8189 Alvin and the Chipmunks

(1983) Score (e:Janice Karman/etc.) US:LP = I.J.E. LP-3300*

8190 Alvin Show, The (1961) Score (Ross Bagdasarian) US:LP = Liberty LRP-3209/LST-7209*

8191 Amahl and the Night Visitors (1951) Score (Gian Carlo Menotti) US: LP = RCA LM-1701 + US:LP = RCA VIC-1512

8192 Amahl and the Night Visitors (1963) Score (Gian Carlo Menotti) US: LP = RCA LM-2762/LSC-2762*

8193 American Bandstand (1957) Theme-A (Charles Albertine) US:SP = Columbia 4-40625 [Les Elgart:ST]; Theme-A (Charles Albertine) US:LP = RCA 1-4850* [Larry Elgart]; Theme-B (Jerry Styner & Mike Curb) US:SP = Forward 124 [Mike Curb:ST]

8194 American Idea, The (1973) Highlights (Richard Rodgers) US:LP-PP = Ford AI-1

8195 American Scene Magazine, The *see* Jackie Gleason's American Scene Magazine

8196 American Song Festival, The (1976) Score (pop music) US:LP-PP = ASF 101

8197 Anatomy of a Seduction (1979) Theme (Hagood Hardy) CA: LP = Attic 1097* [Hagood Hardy:ST]

8198 Anastasia—The Story of Anna (1986) Score (Laurence Rosenthal) US: LP = Southern Cross SCRS-1015*

8199 Andre Previn's Music Night *see* Music Night

8200 Androcles and the Lion (1967) Score (Richard Rodgers) US:LP = RCA LOC-1141/LSO-1141*

8201 Andy Griffith Show, The (1960) Highlights (Earle Hagen) US: LP = Capitol T-1611/ST-1611*

8202 Andy Panda (1953) Theme (Maria Bird) GB:LP = Golden Hour 547* [uncredited]

8203 Andy Williams Show, The (1962) Score-A (t:George Wyle/s:pop music) US:LP = Columbia CL-2015/CS-8815* [Andy Williams & George Wyle: ST]; Score-B (pop music) US:LP = MGM E-4146/SE-4146* [The Osmond Brothers & George Wyle:ST]

8204 Andy Williams Show, The (1969) Score (pop music) US:LP = Columbia KC-30105* [Andy Williams & Mike Post:ST]

8205 Angel (1980) Underscore + Dialog (Mark Gibbons) US:LP-PP = ZIV 1004*

8206 Angels, The (1976) Theme (Alan Parker) GB:LP = BBC 236* + GB:LP = BBC 310* [@Alan Parker:ST]; Theme (Alan Parker) GB:LP-MS = Pickwick 50-DA-315* [Bruce Baxter]

8207 Angie (1979) Theme (Charles Fox) US:SP = WB 8835* [Maureen McGovern:ST]; Theme (Charles Fox) US:LP = WB 3327* [Maureen McGovern:ST]; Theme (Dan Foliart & Howard Pearl) US:LP = Riza 85-105* [Afterglow:ST]

8208 Animal Kwackers (1972) Scores (various) GB:LP-MS = Handkerchief KYD-201*

8209 Animal Magic (1983) Theme (Laurie Johnson) GB:LP = BBC 486* [@Laurie Johnson:ST]

8210 Anna and the King (1972) Theme (Jerry Goldsmith) GB:SP = GM 013* [Silver Star Orchestra]

8211 Annabel *see* Alfred Hitchcock Hour

8212 Anne of Avonlea / Theme (Ed Welch) GB:LP = BBC 214* [@James M. Hughes]

8213 Annette *see* Mickey Mouse Club, The

8214 Annie Get Your Gun (1957) Score (stage songs:Irving Berlin) US: LP = Capitol W-913

8215 Annie Oakley (1953) Theme (Ben Weisman) US:SP = RCA WBY-88 [Gail Davis:ST]; Theme (Ben Weisman) US:LP = RCA 1027 [@Gail Davis:ST]; Theme (Ben Weisman) US:LP = Golden 27 [The Sandpipers & Mitch Miller]

8216 Another Evening with Fred Astaire (1959) Score (pop music) US:LP-PP = Chrysler K80P-1088; Score (pop music) US:LP-MS = DRG S3L-5181

8217 Another World (1964) Theme (Arthur Rubenstein) US:LP = Capitol Custom SL-8076* [The New Christy Minstrels]

8218 Anything Goes (1954) Highlights (stage songs:Cole Porter) US:LP-BP = Larynx 567 + US:LP-BP = Sandy Hook 2043

8219 Anzacs (1985) Score (Bruce Rowland) AU:LP = Wheatley WRLP-1015*

8220 Aphrodite Inheritance, The (1979) Score (George Kotsonis) GB: LP = BBC REB-356*; Themes (George Kotsonis) US:LP-MS = BBC 2-22000* [@George Kotsonis:ST]

8221 Apology (1986) Score (Maurice Jarre) US:LP = Varese STV-81284*

8222 Appointment with Adventure (1955) Theme (Vic Mizzy) US:SP = Mercury 70675 [Denise Lor:ST]

8223 Archie Show, The (1968) Score (Jeff Barry) US:LP = Calendar KES-101*

8224 Archy and Mehitabel *see* Shinbone Alley

8225 Armstrong Circle Theatre (1950) Theme ["The Son"] (Ross Bagdasarian) US:SP = Columbia 4-39467 [Rosemary Clooney]

8226 Arrest and Trial (1963) Theme (Bronislau Kaper) US:LP = WB 1529* [Carl Brandt]

8227 Art Linkletter's House Party (1952) Score (pop music) US:LP = Capitol T-1284/ST-1284* [Muzzy Marcellino:ST]

8228 Arthur Godfrey Show, The (1953) Score ["The Calendar Show"] (Joan Edwards) US:LP = Columbia GL-521 [Arthur Godfrey:ST]

8229 Arthur Hailey's The Moneychangers *see* Moneychangers, The

8230 As the World Turns (1956) Theme (Jack Cortner) US:LP = Capitol Custom SL-8076* [The New Christy Minstrels]

8231 Asphalt Jungle, The (1961) Themes (Duke Ellington) US:SP = Columbia 4-42144 [Duke Ellington:ST]; Theme (Duke Ellington) US:LP-MS = Atco 2-304* [Duke Ellington:ST]; Theme (Duke Ellington) US: LP = Choreo 6* [Harry Betts]

8232 Assignment – Munich (1972) Theme (George Romanis) US:LP = Avalanche 058* [Al Caiola]

8233 Astaire Time (1960) Score (pop music) US:LP-PP = Chrysler M80P-1003; Score (pop music) US:LP-MS = DRG S3L-5181

8234 Attack of the Killer Bees *see* Savage Bees, The

8235 Auf Wiedersehen, Pet (1983) Score (Andy MacKay) GB:LP = Towerbell AUF-1*

8236 Avengers, The (1961) Theme-A [Main Title #1] (Johnny Dankworth) US:LP = Roulette 25096* [Johnny Dankworth:ST]; Theme-A [Main Title #1] (Johnny Dankworth) US:LP = Philips 600-027* [Johnny Gregory]; Theme-B [Main Title #2] (Laurie Johnson) US:SP = Hanna Barbera 470 [Laurie Johnson:ST]; Theme-B [Main Title #2] (Laurie Johnson) US:LP = Hanna Barbera 8506* [Laurie Johnson: ST]; Theme-C ["Tag Scene"] (Laurie Johnson) GB:LP = MGM 8104* [Laurie Johnson:ST]; Excerpts-B-D-E (Laurie Johnson) US:LP = Varese/Starlog 95003* [Laurie Johnson:ST]

8237 Autobiography of Miss Jane Pittman, The (1973) Theme (Fred Karlin) US:LP = UA 200* [Tina Turner]

B

8238 B.A.D. Cats (1979) Theme (Barry DeVorzon) US:LP-PP = Jenson 0800* [The Jenson Marching Band]

8239 Baa Baa Black Sheep [Black Sheep Squadron] (1976) Theme (Mike Post & Pete Carpenter) US:SP = Epic 8-50324* [Mike Post:ST]

8240 Baby I'm Back (1978) Theme (Jeff Barry) US:LP = Motown 905* [Prime Time]

8241 Bachelor Father (1957) Theme (John Williams) US:LP = MCA 5380* [Warren Schatz]

8242 Ballad of Hector the Stowaway Pup, The *see* Hector the Stowaway Pup

8243 Ballad of Smokey the Bear, The (1966) Themes (Johnny Marks) US: SP = Columbia 4-43926 [Harry Simeone]; Theme (Johnny Marks) US:LP = UA 6666* [Al Caiola]

8244 Ballad of the Irish Horse, The (1985) (Paddy Moloney) US:LP = Shanachie 79051*

8245 Ballad of Yermo Red, The *see* Studio One

8246 Banacek [Detour to Nowhere] (1972) Theme (Billy Goldenberg) US: LP = Mercury 1-1089* [Johnny Gregory]

8247 Banana Splits, The (1972) Score-A (e:Ritchie Adams/e:Jimmy Radcliffe/etc.) US:LP = Decca DL-75075*; Highlights-B (t:Hoyt Curtin/ etc.) US:EP-PP = Kelloggs 34579*; Highlights-C (t:Ritchie Adams/etc.) US: EP-PP = Kelloggs 34578*

8248 Baquine de Angelitos Negros, El (1977) Score (Willie Colon) US:LP = Fania JM-00506*

8249 Barbara Stanwyck Show, The (1960) Theme (Earle Hagen) US:LP = Mercury 60706* [Pete Rugolo]

8250 Barbara Woodhouse's World of Horses and Ponies (1981) Theme (Steve Jolly) GB:LP = Red Bus 1004* [@The New Horizon Orchestra]

8251 Barbra Streisand and Other Musical Instruments (1972) Score (pop music) US:LP = Columbia KC-32655* [Barbra Streisand:ST]

8252 Baretta (1975) Theme (Dave Grusin) US:SP = 20th 2282* [Sammy Davis, Jr. & Dave Grusin:ST]; Theme (Dave Grusin) US:LP = Sheffield 500* [Dave Grusin:ST]; Theme (Dave Grusin) US:LP = Columbia 34312* [Ray Conniff]

8253 Barlow / Theme (Anthony Isaac) GB:LP = Contour 2870.439* [Malcolm Lockyer]

8254 Barnaby Jones (1973) Theme (Jerry Goldsmith) US:LP-MS = Tee Vee Toons 1300 [@ST]

8255 Barney Miller (1975) Theme (Jack Elliott & Allyn Ferguson) US:SP = Feel 8700* [Elliott & Ferguson:ST]; Theme (Jack Elliott & Allyn Ferguson) US:LP-MS = Tee Vee Toons 1300 [@ST]

8256 Baron, The (1966) Theme (Edwin Astley) US:SP = Parrot 10816 [Edwin Astley:ST]; Theme (Edwin Astley) US:LP = Metro 565* [The Revengers]; Theme (Edwin Astley) GB:LP = EMI TWO-175* [Brian Fahey]

8257 Basil Brush Show, The (1962) Highlights + Dialog (George Martin) GB:LP = EMI/Starline SRS-5051*

8258 Bat Masterson (1959) Theme (M. Wray) US:LP = Chancellor/Sea Horse 7002 [Gene Barry]; Theme (M. Wray) US:LP = UA 6161* [Al Caiola]; Theme (M. Wray) US:LP = Roulette 25073* [Bud Wattles]

8259 Batman (1966) Score (s:Nelson Riddle/t:Neal Hefti) US:LP = 20th 3180/S-3180*

8260 Battle of the Planets [Gatchaman] (1977) Score (Koichi Sygiyama) JA:LP = Columbia CQ-7009*

8261 Battlestar Galactica (1978) Score (s:Stu Phillips/t:John Andrew Tartaglia) US:LP = MCA 3051 + US: LP = MCA 37079*

8262 Beacon Hill (1975) Theme (Marvin Hamlisch) US:SP = A&M 1775* [Marvin Hamlisch:ST]

8263 Beagles, The (1966) Themes (W. Biggers) US:SP = Columbia 4-43789 [The Beagles:ST]

8264 Bear Who Slept Through Christmas, The (1983) Highlights + Dialog (Larry Mayfield) US:LP = Starland S-1034*

8265 Beatles, The (1965) Highlights (pop music) US:LP = Capitol T-2309/ ST-2309* [The Beatles:ST]

8266 Beatles' Magical Mystery Tour, The *see* Magical Mystery Tour

8267 Beauty and the Beast (1958) *see* Shirley Temple's Storybook

8268 Beauty and the Beast (1976) Theme (Ron Goodwin) GB:LP = Chandos 1014* [Ron Goodwin: ST]

8269 Befrienders, The / Theme (Anthony Isaac) GB:LP = Decca 2163* [Ike Isaacs]

8270 Bell Telephone Hour, The (1959) Scores (pop music) US:LP-MS = Longines 5-STS-5112/6*; Theme (Hershy Kay) US:LP = Carlton 143* [Valjean]

8271 Ben Casey (1961) Theme (David Raksin) US:SP = Carlton 573 [Valjean]; Theme (David Raksin) US: LP = Mercury 60706* [Pete Rugolo]; Theme (David Raksin) US:LP = Capitol 1771* [Nelson Riddle]

8272 Benny Hill Show, The / Highlights + Dialog (Benny Hill) US:LP = Capitol SN-12049* [Benny Hill:ST]

8273 Benson (1979) Theme (George Tipton) US:LP-PP = Jenson 0800* [The Jenson Marching Band]

8274 Bergerac (1985) Theme (George Fenton) GB:SP = BBC 508* [@ST]

8275 Berlin Alexanderplatz (1980) Score (Peer Raben) US:LP = Varese STV-81217 + GE:LP = RCA 28393*

8276 Best in Football, The / Theme (Tony Hatch) GB:LP = Pye 41029* [Tony Hatch:ST]

8277 Best of Steinbeck, The / Theme (Eddy Manson) US:LP = Vik 1134 [Eddy Manson:ST]

8278 Best Sellers *see* NBC's Best Sellers

8279 Beverly Hillbillies, The (1962) Themes (Paul Henning) US:LP = Columbia 2570/9370* [Flatt & Scruggs: ST]; Theme-A (Paul Henning) US:SP = MGM 13210 [Buddy Ebsen]; Theme-A (Paul Henning) US:SP = Columbia 13-33074 [Flatt & Scruggs:ST]; Theme-B (Paul Henning) US:SP = Columbia 4-42755 [Flatt & Scruggs:ST]

8280 Bewitched (1964) Theme (Howard Greenfield) US:SP = Columbia 4-43192 [Steve Lawrence]; Theme (Howard Greenfield) US:LP = ABC 513* [Frank DeVol]; Theme (H. Greenfield) US:LP = Audio Fidelity 6146* [Dick Dia]

8281 Big Apple City *see* Strawberry Shortcake in Big Apple City

8282 Big Blue Marble, The (1975) Score-A (e:Carol Hall/etc.) US:LP = A&M SP-3401*; Highlights-B (Paul Baillargeon) US:LP-PP = Blue Marble Company BMC-1001*

8283 Big Deal (1985) Theme (Bobby G.) GB:LP = BBC 508* [@ST]

8284 Big Foot and Wild Boy *see* Krofft Supershow, The

8285 Big Match, The / Theme (M. Harper) GB:LP = Polydor 2460.188* [@Harry Robinson]; Theme (M. Harper) GB:LP = EMI 5143* [The Pandora Orchestra]

8286 Big Town (1951) Excerpts (Albert Glasser) US:LP = Starlog SR-1001 [Albert Glasser:ST]

8287 Big Valley, The (1965) Score (George Duning) US:LP = ABC 527/S-527*; Theme ["Hell Hath No Fury"] (Lalo Schifrin) US:LP = RCA 4104* [Hugo Montenegro]

8288 Bill Anderson Show, The (1966) Theme (Weldon Myrick) US:SP = RCA 47-8750 [Weldon Myrick:ST]

8289 Bill Cosby Show, The (1969) Theme (Quincy Jones) US:SP = UNI 55184* [Bill Cosby & Quincy Jones:ST]; Theme (Quincy Jones) US:LP = A&M 3037* [Quincy Jones & Bill Cosby:ST]

8290 Bill Dana Show, The (1963) Theme (Earle Hagen) US:SP = 20th 427 [Lionel Newman]; Theme (Earle Hagen) US:LP = 20th 4105* [Lionel Newman]; Theme (Earle Hagen) US:LP = WB 1529* [Carl Brandt]

8291 Bionic Woman, The (1976) Theme-A (Jerry Fielding) US:LP = Pickwood 3566* [The Birchwood Pops]; Theme-A (Jerry Fielding) US:LP = Peter Pan 8197* [The Peter Pan Orchestra]; Theme-B (Joe Harnell) US:LP = Capitol 11657* [Joe Harnell:ST]

8292 Bird's Eye View (1969) Theme (Johnny Dankworth) US:LP = RCA 1-5092* [Johnny Dankworth:ST]

8293 Biskitts, The (1983) Theme + Dialog (Hoyt Curtin) US:EP = Parachute 814-937-7 + US:EP = Parachute 814-938-7

8294 Black and White Minstrel Show, The (1958) Score (pop music) GB: LP = HMV CSD-1327* [The George Mitchell Singers:ST]

8295 Black Beauty *see* Adventures of Black Beauty, The

8296 Black Saddle (1959) Theme (Jerry Goldsmith & Arthur Morton) US: LP=Dot 25421* [Herschel Burke Gilbert: ST]; Theme (Goldsmith & Morton) US: LP = RCA 2163* [Marty Gold]; Theme (Goldsmith & Morton) US:LP = RCA 2042* [Buddy Morrow]; † *composer credit is incorrect on RCA recordings*

8297 Black Sheep Squadron *see* Baa Baa Black Sheep

8298 Blake's 7 (1978) Themes (Dudley Simpson) GB:SP = BBC 58* [Dudley Simpson:ST]; Theme (Dudley Simpson) GB:LP = BBC 365 + GB:LP = BBC 442* [@Dudley Simpson:ST]; Theme (Dudley Simpson) US:LP = MMG 705* [Geoff Love]

8299 Bless This House (1973) Theme (Geoff Love) GB:LP = MFP 5272* [Geoff Love:ST]

8300 Blood and Honor (1983) Score

(Ernst Brandner) GE:LP = Celine CL-0018*

8301 Blood of the Tiger *see* Maya

8302 Blue Knight, The (1975) Theme (Henry Mancini) US:SP = RCA 10888* [Henry Mancini:ST]; Theme (Henry Mancini) US:LP = RCA 1-1896* [Henry Mancini:ST]

8303 Blue Light (1966) Theme (Lalo Schifrin) US:LP = Metro 565* [The Revengers]

8304 Blue Peter (1955) Theme-A (Ashworth Hope) GB:LP = BBC 214 + GB:LP = BBC 454 + GB:LP = BBC 486 [@Sidney Torch]; Theme-A (Ashworth Hope) GB:LP = Contour 2870.185* [Cy Payne]; Theme-B (Mike Oldfield) GB: SP = Virgin 317* [Mike Oldfield:ST]

8305 Blues for a Hanging *see* Alcoa Premiere

8306 Bob Crosby Show, The (1953) Score (pop music) US:LP = Columbia CL-766 [Bob Crosby:ST]

8307 Bob Cummings Show, The [Love That Bob!] (1955) Theme (Frank Stanton) US:LP = MGM 3729* [The Metropolitan Jazz Quartet]; Theme (Frank Stanton) US:LP = World Pacific 411 [Bud Shank]

8308 Bob Newhart Show, The (1972) Theme (Lorenzo Music) US:SP = Bareback 530* [The Inner City Jam Band]; Theme (Lorenzo Music) US:LP = PAUSA 7060* [Patrick Williams:ST]

8309 Bobby Jo and the Big Apple Goodtime Band (1972) Theme (Jerry Fuller) US:SP = MGM/Lion 14476* [The Boone Family]; Theme (Jerry Fuller) US:LP = MGM/Lion 1008* [The Boone Family]

8310 Bobby Vinton Show, The (1975) Score (pop music) US:LP = ABC ABCD-924* [Bobby Vinton:ST]

8311 Boca Raton (1976) Themes (Paul Baillargeon) US:LP-PP = Blue Marble Company 1001* [Paul Baillargeon:ST]

8312 Body in Question, The (1980) Theme (Peter Howell) GB:SP = BBC 98* [BBC Radiophonic Workshop:ST]; Theme (Peter Howell) GB:LP=BBC 391* [@BBC Radiophonic Workshop:ST]

8313 Bold Ones, The (1969) Theme (Dave Grusin) US:LP = MCA 5380* [Warren Schatz] † *composer credit is incorrect on record label.*

8314 Bonanza (1959) Score-A (s: David Rose/t:Jay Livingston & Ray Evans) US:LP = MGM E-3960/SE-3960* [David Rose:ST]; Score-B (e: David Rose/e:Harry Sukman/t:Jay Livingston & Ray Evans) US:LP-MS = Capitol STBB-626* [Xanadu Pleasure Dome]

8315 Boney (1978) Score (Sven Libaek) AU:LP = Festival 34660*

8316 Bonjour la Vie *see* Climax

8317 Boon (1980) Theme (Jim Diamond) GB:SP = A&M 296* [Jim Diamond:ST]

8318 Borgia Stick, The (1967) Themes (George Benson) US:SP = Columbia 4-43998 [George Benson:ST]

8319 Borgias, The (1982) Score (Georges Delerue) GB:LP = BBC REP-428*

8320 Born and Bred (1978) Theme (Ron Grainer) US:LP = DRG 15018* [Ron Grainer:ST]

8321 Born Yesterday (1956) Theme (Joe Bushkin) US:SP = RCA 47-6694 [Mary Martin]

8322 Borrowers, The (1973) Score (Rod McKuen) US:LP = Stanyan SRQ-4014*

8323 Bosom Buddies (1980) Theme (Dan Foliart & Howard Pearl) US:LP = Riza 85-105* [Afterglow:ST]

8324 Both Ends Meet / Theme (Max Harris) GB:LP = EMI 5143* [The Pandora Orchestra]

8325 Bouquet of Barbed Wire, A (1976) Theme (Dennis Farnon) GB:LP = DJM 20522* + GB:LP = DJM 22081* [@Harry Rabinowitz]; Theme (Dennis Farnon) GB:LP = Red Bus 1004* [@The South Bank Orchestra]

8326 Bourbon Street Beat (1959) Score (e:Don Ralke/t:Jerry Livingston/ etc.) US:LP = WB W-1321/WS-1321*

8327 Bowling Stars [Bowling Time] Theme (Charles Tobias) US:SP = RCA EDVW-3910 [Dick Liebert:ST]

8328 Boy in the Plastic Bubble, The (1976) Theme (Paul Williams) US:SP = Midsong 11206* [John Travolta:ST]; Theme (Paul Williams) US:LP = Midsong 1-2211* [John Travolta:ST]

8329 Boy Meets Girl / Theme (Ron Grainer) GB:LP = RCA 1020* [Ron Grainer:ST]

8330 Boy Named Charlie Brown, A (1969) Score (Vince Guaraldi) US:LP = Fantasy 8430*

8331 Boys of the Western Sea *see* Mickey Mouse Club, The

8332 Bracken's World (1969) Theme (David Rose) US:SP = Capitol 2938* [The Lettermen]; Theme (David Rose) US:LP = Capitol 634* [The Lettermen]; Theme (David Rose) US:LP = Capitol 393* [David Rose:ST]

8333 Brady Bunch, The (1969) Score (various) US:LP = Paramount PAS-6032* [The Brady Bunch:ST]; Theme (Frank DeVol) US:LP-MS = Tee Vee Toons 1200 [@ST]

8334 Branded (1965) Theme (Dominic Frontiere) US:SP = UA 859 [Art Lund:ST]; Theme (Dominic Frontiere) US:LP-MS = Tee Vee Toons 1100 [@ST]

8335 Brave Stallion *see* Fury

8336 Breakaway (1980) Theme (Joe Griffiths) GB:SP = BBC 74* [Joe Griffiths:ST]; Theme (Joe Griffiths) GB: LP = BBC 391* [Joe Griffiths:ST]

8337 Breaking Point, The (1963) Theme (David Raksin) US:LP = 20th 4105* [Lionel Newman]; Theme (David Raksin) US:LP = WB 1529* [Carl Brandt]

8338 Brendan Chase (1981) Theme (Michael J. Lewis) GB:SP = RCA 318* [Michael J. Lewis:ST]

8339 Bret Maverick (1981) Theme (Glenn Ray) US:SP = MCA 52109* [Ed Bruce:ST]; Theme (Glenn Ray) US: LP = MCA 5323* [Ed Bruce:ST]

8340 Brian's Song (1971) Theme (Michel Legrand) US:SP = Bell 45-171* [Michel Legrand:ST]; Theme (Michel Legrand) US:LP = Bell 6071* [Michel Legrand:ST]; Theme (Michel Legrand) US:LP = RCA 4629* [Henry Mancini]

8341 Brideshead Revisited (1981) Score (Geoffrey Burgon) US:LP = Chrysalis CHR-1367*

8342 Bridge Builders, The (1962) Theme (Bill Mendelson) US:SP-PP = BFM 1001 [The Californians]

8343 Brigadoon (1968) Score (stage songs:Frederick Loewe) US:LP-PP = CSP CMM-385/CSM-385*

8344 Brigitte Bardot Special, The *see* Special Bardot

8345 Bristleface [Walt Disney Presents] (1964) Theme (Richard & Robert Sherman) US:LP = Glendale 6032* ["Dawgs" Stage Cast]

8346 British Empire, The (1972) Theme (Wilfred Josephs) GB:LP = Polydor 2383.294* [Marcus Dods:ST]

8347 Broadway Goes Latin (1962) Score (pop music) US:LP = London LL-3277/PS-277* [Edmundo Ros:ST]

8348 Broadway Rose *see* Rose on Broadway

8349 Broken Arrow (1956) Theme (Paul Sawtell) US:SP = RCA WBY-69 [The Prairie Chiefs]; Theme (Paul Sawtell) US:LP = RCA 1004 [@The Prairie Chiefs]; Theme (Paul Sawtell) US:LP = Coral 757267* [Lawrence Welk]

8350 Bronco (1958) Theme (Jerry Livingston) US:LP = Columbia 8400* [Johnny Gregory]

8351 Brothers, The (1973) Theme (Dudley Simpson) GB:SP = BBC 12* [The Band of H.M. Welsh Guards]; Theme (Dudley Simpson) GB:LP = MFP 50091* [Geoff Love]; Theme (Dudley Simpson) GB:LP-MS = Pickwick 50-DA-315* [Bruce Baxter]

8352 Buckskin (1958) Theme (Stanley Wilson) US:SP = RCA WBY-102 [The Sons of the Pioneers]; Theme (Stanley Wilson) US:LP = Tops 1661* [Richard Gleason]; Theme (Stanley Wilson) US:LP = Coral 757267* [Lawrence Welk]

8353 Bugaloos, The (1970) Score (s: Hal Yoergler/t:Charles Fox) US:LP = Capitol SW-621* [The Bugaloos:ST]

8354 Bugs Bunny Show, The (1960) Theme (Jerry Livingston) US:LP-MS = Tee Vee Toons 1100 [@ST]

8355 Bullwinkle Show, The *see* Rocky and His Friends

8356 Burke's Law (1963) Score (e: Herschel Burke Gilbert/e:Joseph Mullendore/t:Jimmie Haskell) US:LP = Liberty LRP-3374/LST-7374*

8357 Bus Stop (1961) Theme (Arthur Morton) US:LP = Choreo 6* [Harry Betts]; Theme (Arthur Morton) US:LP = Capitol 1830* [Jackie Gleason]

8358 By the Sword Divided (1983) Themes (Alan Blakley & Ken Howard) GB:SP = BBC 137* [ST]; Theme (Alan Blakley & Ken Howard) US:LP-MS = SQN 5057-1* [@ST]

C

8359 CBS Thursday Night Movie, The [Thursday Night at the Movies] (1965) Sequence + Narration (Morton Stevens) US:LP = Epic 26224* [Bob Crane]

8360 Cade's County (1971) Theme (Henry Mancini) US:SP = RCA 0575* [Henry Mancini:ST]; Theme (Henry Mancini) US:LP = RCA 4630* [Henry Mancini:ST]

8361 Caesar's Hour (1954) Theme-A (Bernard Green) US:SP = Coral 9-61794 [Dick Jacobs]; Theme-A (Bernard Green) US:LP = Coral 57127 [Dick Jacobs]; Theme-B (Bernard Green) US: LP = Barbary Coast 33015* [Bernard Green:ST]

8362 Cage Without a Key (1975) Themes (Michel Legrand) US:LP = RCA 1-1028* [Michel Legrand:ST]

8363 Cagney and Lacey (1983) Theme (Bill Conti) US:LP = Mirage 90456-1* [The Spinners]; Theme (Bill Conti) GB:LP = BBC 508 [@Bill Conti: ST]

8364 Calendar Show, The *see* Arthur Godfrey Show, The

8365 Cain's Hundred (1961) Theme (Jerry Goldsmith) US:LP = Choreo 6* [Harry Betts]

8366 Californians, The (1957) Theme (Harry Warren) US:SP = RCA WBY-100 [The Sons of the Pioneers]; Theme (Harry Warren) US:LP = RCA 1027 [@The Sons of the Pioneers]

8367 Call My Bluff (1965) Theme (Russell Garcia) GB:LP = BBC 238* [Norrie Paramor]

8368 Callan (1967) Theme (Jack Trombey) GB:LP = Philips 6308.087* [Johnny Gregory]; Theme (Jack Trombey) GB:LP = Decca 2163* [Ike Isaacs]

8369 Calling Dr. Gannon *see* Medical Center

8370 Cal's Corral / Score (pop music) US:LP-PP = Cal's Corral CCLP-100

8371 Camberwick Green (1972) Highlights + Dialog (Freddie Phillips) GB:LP = BBC REC-263*

8372 Camp Runamuck (1965) Theme (Hugo Montenegro) US:SP = RCA 47-8707 [Hugo Montenegro:ST]

8373 Candid Camera (1948) Theme (Alex Textor) US:LP = Epic 26224* [Bob Crane]

8374 Candy Candy (1980) Underscore + Dialog (Mark Gibbons) US: LP-PP = ZIV 1002*

8375 Cannon (1971) Theme (John Parker) US:SP = Philips 40805* [Johnny Gregory]; Theme (John Parker) US: LP = Mercury 1-1089* [Johnny Gregory]

8376 Captain Future (1980) Underscore + Dialog (Mark Gibbons) US:LP-PP = Ziv 1003*

8377 Captain Kangaroo (1955) Scores-A (e:Rick Segal/etc.) US:LP-MS = Chelsea CHS-701/2*; Score-B (Clark Gesner) US:LP = Peter Pan 8007; Score-C (Jeffrey Moss) US:LP = Peter Pan 8067

8378 Captain Scarlet and the Mysterons (1967) Underscore + Dialog (Barry Gray) GB:LP = Hallmark HMA-227; Themes (Barry Gray) GB:LP-10 = PRT DOW-3 [Barry Gray:ST]

8379 Captain Zep (1983) Theme (David Aitken) GB:LP = BBC 486* [@The Spacewalkers]

8380 Captains and the Kings (1976) Theme (Elmer Bernstein) GB:LP = DJM 20522* [@Denis King]

8381 Car 54, Where Are You? (1961) Theme (John Strauss) US:LP-MS = Tee Vee Toons 1200 [@ST]

8382 Caravan of Courage—An Ewok Adventure (1984) Highlights (Peter Bernstein) US:LP = Varese STV-81281*

8383 Carousel (1969) Score (stage songs:Richard Rodgers) US:LP-PP = CSP CMM-479/CSM-479*

8384 Carter Country (1977) Theme (Pete Rugolo) US:LP = Motown 905* [Prime Time]; Theme (Pete Rugolo) US: SP = Motown 1444* [Prime Time]

8385 Case of the Ancient Astronauts, The / Theme (Peter Howell) GB: LP = BBC 324* [@BBC Radiophonic Workshop:ST]

8386 Case of the Dangerous Robin, The (1960) Theme (David Rose) US: LP = Mercury 60706* [Pete Rugolo]

8387 Cassie and Co. (1982) Theme (Grover Washington, Jr.) US:LP = Elektra 9-60215-1* [Grover Washington, Jr.: ST]

8388 Catweasle (1970) Theme (M. Dicks) GB:LP = EMI 5143* [@The London Symphony]

8389 Cattanooga Cats, The (1971) Score (Mike Curb & Michael Lloyd) US: LP = Forward STF-1018*

8390 Champion, The Wonder Horse *see* Adventures of Champion, The

8391 Champions, The (1967) Theme (Tony Hatch) GB:LP = Pye 41029* [Tony Hatch:ST]; Theme (Tony Hatch) GB:LP = Marble Arch 1179* [@Tony Hatch:ST]

8392 Chance at Love, A *see* Studio One

8393 Changes, The / Theme (Paddy Kingsland) GB:LP = BBC 214* [BBC Radiophonic Workshop:ST]

8394 Charlie (1984) Theme (Harry South) GB:SP = Towerbell 49* [ST]

8395 Charlie Brown Christmas, A (1965) Score (Vince Guaraldi) US:LP = Fantasy 5019/85019*

8396 Charlie Brown's All-Stars (1966) Underscore + Dialog (Vince Guaraldi) US:LP = Charlie Brown 2602

8397 Charlie's Angels (1976) Theme (Jack Elliott & Allyn Ferguson) US:SP = RCA 10888* [Henry Mancini]; Theme (Jack Elliott & Allyn Ferguson) US: LP = RCA 1-2290* [Henry Mancini]; Theme (Jack Elliott & Allyn Ferguson) US:LP = Liberty 10224* [The Ventures]

8398 Cheaters, The (1960) Theme (Bill Le Sage) US:LP = Roulette 804* [@uncredited]

8399 Checkmate (1960) Score (John Williams) US:LP = Columbia CL-1591/CS-8391*

8400 Cheers (1982) Theme (Gary Portnoy) US:SP = Applause 106* + US: SP = Earthtone 7004* [Gary Portnoy:ST]

8401 Chesterfield Supper Club, The (1948) Theme (Ed Klenner) US:LP = RCA 1020 [Hugo Winterhalter]

8402 Cheyenne (1955) Theme (William Lava) US:SP = RCA WBY-46 [The Sons of the Pioneers]; Theme (William Lava) US:LP = Columbia 8400* [Johnny Gregory]; Theme (William Lava) US:LP = RCA 2163* [Marty Gold]

8403 Chico and the Man (1974) Themes (Jose Feliciano) US:SP = RCA 10145* [Jose Feliciano:ST]; Themes (Jose Feliciano) US:LP = RCA 1-0407* [Jose Feliciano:ST]

8404 Chigley (1976) Highlights (Freddie Phillips) GB:LP = BBC REC-234*

8405 Child Is Born, A (1956) Highlights (Bernard Herrmann) US:LP-10-PP = General Electric C-55; Highlights (Bernard Herrmann) US:LP-BP = Temple TLP-2002

8406 Chinese Detective, The (1981) Theme (Harry South) GB:SP = BBC 91* [Harry South:ST]; Theme (Harry South) GB:LP = BBC 424* [@Harry South:ST]

8407 Chinese Nightingale, A *see* Shirley Temple's Storybook

8408 Chips (1977) Theme (John Parker) US:SP = Midsong 11552* [Corniche]

8409 Christmas Carol, A (1954) Score (Bernard Herrmann) US:LP-MS-PP = Chrysler RR-23070; Score (Bernard Herrmann) US:LP-BP = Unicorn RHS-850

8410 Christmas in Hawaii with Jim Nabors (1981) Score (pop music) US: LP = Bluewater SLP-725*

8411 Christmas Raccoons, The (1983) Highlights + Dialog (Kevin Gillis) US:LP = Starland ARI-1031*

8412 Christmas Story, The *see* Dragnet

8413 Christmas with Bing Crosby (1972) Score (pop music) US:LP-BP = Ho Ho 1088 [The Crosby Family & Frank Sinatra:ST]

8414 Christopher Columbus (1985) Score-A [USA Version] (Riz Ortolani) US:LP = Varese STV-81245*; Score-B [German Version] (Ernst Brandner) GE: LP = Condor 831105*

8415 Cider with Rosie (1971) Theme (Wilfred Josephs) GB:LP = Polydor 2383.294* [Marcus Dods:ST]

8416 Cimarron City (1958) Theme (Stanley Wilson) US:LP = RCA 2163* [Marty Gold]; Theme (Stanley Wilson) US:LP = Tops 1661* [Richard Gleason]; Theme (Stanley Wilson) US:LP = RCA 1027 [@The Hollywood Soundstage Orchestra]

8417 Cinderella (1957) Score (Richard Rodgers) US:LP = Columbia OL-5190/OS-2005*

8418 Cinderella (1965) Score (Richard Rodgers) US:LP = Columbia OL-6330/OS-2730*

8419 Cinema (1964) Theme (Reg Tilsley) GB:LP = Polydor 2460.188* [@Harry Robinson]

8420 Circuit Eleven—Miami (1979) Theme (Richard Denton & Martin Cook) GB:SP = BBC 70* [Richard Denton & Martin Cook:ST]; Theme (Richard Denton & Martin Cook) GB:LP = BBC 385* [Richard Denton & Martin Cook:ST]

8421 Citadel, The (1983) Theme (Michael Stuckey) US:LP-MS = SQN 5057-1 [@ST]

8422 Cities for People / Themes (John Lewis) US:LP = Columbia 33534* [John Lewis:ST]

8423 Clancy [Looking for Clancy] Theme (M. Wade) GB:LP = BBC 236* [@Leonard Hunter]; Theme (M. Wade) GB:LP-MS = Reader's Digest 9414* [@Leonard Hunter]

8424 Clayhanger (1976) Score (t: Richard Hill/s:pop music) GB:LP = Bradleys 8001*

8425 Cleopatras, The (1983) Theme (Nick Bicat) GB:SP = BBC 128* [Nick Bicat:ST]

8426 Climax (1954) Theme-A ["The Sands of Time"] (J. Leshay) US:SP = Roulette 4053 [Lennie Hayton]; Theme-B ["Bonjour La Vie"] (J. Leshay) US:SP = Disneyland 48 [Viveca Lindfors]; Theme-C ["When You Love"] (J. Leshay) US:SP = MGM 12629 [Michael Hale]; Theme-D ["Let It Be Me"] (Mann Curtis) US:SP = Columbia 4-40878 [Jill Corey]; Theme-E ["Keep Me in Mind"] (Tom August) US:SP = Coral 9-61910 [Johnny Desmond]

8427 Clochemerle (1973) Highlights (ae:Alan Roper) GB:EP = BBC RESL-8*; Themes (at:Alan Roper) GB:LP = BBC 188* [@Raymond Jarniat:ST]

8428 Clouds of Witness [Lord Peter Wimsey] (1972) Theme (Herbert Chappell) GB:SP = BBC 7* [The Boyfriends:ST]; Theme (Herbert Chappell) GB:LP = BBC 188* [@The Boyfriends: ST]; Theme (Herbert Chappell) US:LP-PP = WGBH 10* + US:LP-MS = BBC 22000* [@The Boyfriends:ST]

8429 Clown Alley / Sequence + Dialog (David Rose) US:SP = Columbia 4-44798 [Red Skelton:ST]

8430 Club Durant *see* Jimmy Durante Show, The

8431 Colbys, The (1985) Theme (Bill Conti) GB:LP = MFP 5759* [The Power Pack Orchestra]

8432 Cold Warrior, The (1984) Theme (Brian Osborne) GB:SP = BBC 149* [ST]

8433 Colditz (1974) Theme (Robert Farnon) GB:LP = Philips 6436.021* [Robert Farnon:ST]; Theme (Robert Farnon) US:LP = DRG 703* [Marcus Dods]; Theme (Robert Farnon) GB: LP = Sunset 50339* [The London Concert Orchestra]

8434 Cole Porter—A Remembrance (1965) Score (pop music) US:LP-PP = Pontiac ST3TP-1 [William Walker:ST]

8435 Cole Porter in Paris (1973) Score (pop music) US:LP-PP = Bell System PH-36508

8436 Collector's Item / Excerpts [pilot] (Bernard Herrmann) US:LP = Cerberus CST-0210 [Bernard Herrmann:ST]

8437 Color Me Barbra (1966) Score (pop music) US:LP = Columbia CL-2478/CS-9278* [Barbra Streisand:ST]

8438 Colt .45 (1957) Theme (Hal Hopper) US:LP = Roulette 25073* [Bud Wattles]

8439 Columbo *see* Ransom for a Dead Man

8440 Combat (1962) Theme (Leonard Rosenman) US:SP = ABC 10628 [Frank DeVol]; Theme (Leonard Rosenman) US:LP-MS = Tee Vee Toons 1100 [@ST]; Theme (Leonard Rosenman) US:LP = Capitol 10480* [The Japanese Defense Force Band]

8441 Come to Me *see* Kraft Television Theatre

8442 Comet Is Coming, The (1982) Theme (Malcolm Clarke) GB:LP = BBC 442* [@Malcolm Clarke:ST]

8443 Coming of Christ, The [Project 20] (1960) Underscore + Dialog (Robert Russell Bennett) US:LP = Decca DL-9093/DL-79093*

8444 Commanding Sea, The (1981) Excerpts (Carl Davis) GB:LP = EMI EMC-3361* [Carl Davis:ST]

8445 Conflict [Warner Brothers Presents] (1957) Theme ["Girl on the Run," pilot for "77 Sunset Strip"] (Howard Jackson) US:LP = WB 1289* [Warren Barker]

8446 Conquest of Space, The Theme (Eddy Manson) US:LP-PP = Margery 2400 [Eddy Manson:ST]

8447 Copacabana (1985) Score (Barry Manilow) US:LP-PP = RCA SML1-7178*; Theme (Barry Manilow) US:LP = RCA 1-7044* [Barry Manilow:ST]

8448 Corky and White Shadow *see* Mickey Mouse Club, The

8449 Coronation Street (1960) Theme (Eric Spear) GB:LP = EMI 168* [Geoff Love]; Theme (Eric Spear) GB: LP = DJM 22081* [@Laurie Holloway]; Theme (Eric Spear) GB:LP-MS = Pickwick 50-DA-315* [Bruce Baxter]

8450 Coronet Blue (1967) Theme (Laurence Rosenthal) US:SP = Kapp 712 [Lenny Welch:ST]; Theme (Laurence Rosenthal) US:LP = Kapp 1457* [Lenny Welch:ST]

8451 Cosby Show, The (1985) Score (Stu Gardner) US:LP = Columbia JS-40270*

8452 Cosmos (1980) Score (pop music & classical music) US:LP = RCA ABL1-4003*

8453 Country Diary of an Edwardian Lady, The (1984) Score (e:Jon Lord/e:Alfred Ralston) GB:LP = Safari 1*

8454 Country Matters (1974) Theme (Derek Hilton) US:LP-PP = WGBH 10* + US:LP-MS = SQN 5057-1* [@Derek Hilton:ST]; Theme (Derek Hilton) GB:LP = EMI 2069* [Reginald Dixon]

8455 Courageous Cat and Minute Mouse (1961) Theme (Johnny Holiday) US:LP-MS = Tee Vee Toons 1200 [@ST]

8456 Courtship of Eddie's Father, The (1969) Theme (Harry Nilsson) US: SP = MGM 14198 [Bill Bixby & Brandon Cruz]; Theme (Harry Nilsson) US:LP-MS = Tee Vee Toons 1200 [@Harry Nilsson:ST]

8457 Cousteau Amazon (1984) Score (John Scott) US:LP = Varese STV-81220*

8458 Cover (1981) Theme (Roger Webb) GB:SP = Chips 104* [Roger Webb:ST]

8459 Crackerjack / Score (Bert Hayes) GB:LP = BBC REC-185*

8460 Crane (1965) Theme (T.H. Sakelaridis) US:SP = Coral 9-62365 [Pete Fountain]

8461 Crazy Like a Fox (1985) Theme (Mark Snow) GB:LP = MFP 5768* [The Power Pack Orchestra]

8462 Cricket on the Hearth (1967) Score (Maury Laws) US:LP = RCA LOC-1140/LSO-1140*

8463 Crossroads (1964) Theme (Tony Hatch) US:SP = Reprise 0356 [Tony Hatch:ST]; Theme (Tony Hatch) GB:LP = Pye 41029* [Tony Hatch:ST]

8464 Crown Court (1972) Theme (Reno) US:SP = Vanguard 35175 [Simon Park]; Theme (Reno) GB:LP = EMI 2069* [Reginald Dixon]

8464a Curt Massey Time (1950) Score (pop music) US:LP = Capitol T-1313 [Curt Massey:ST]

D

8465 D.A.'s Man, The (1959) Theme (Frank Comstock) US:SP = WB 5060 [Frank Comstock:ST]; Theme (Frank Comstock) US:LP = WB 1290* [Frank Comstock:ST]

8466 D.H. Lawrence (1966) Theme (Wilfred Josephs) GB:LP = Polydor 2383.294* [Marcus Dods:ST]

8467 Dad's Army (1967) Theme (M. Perry) GB:SP = Pye 7N17854 [Bud Flanagan]; Theme (M. Perry) GB:LP = BBC 236 + GB:LP = BBC 387 + GB:LP = BBC 454 [@Bud Flanagan]

8468 Daktari (1966) Score (Shelly

Manne) US:LP = Atlantic 8157/SD-8157*; Underscore + Dialog ["House of Lions"] (Shelly Manne) US:LP = Leo CH-1043

8469 Dallas (1979) Score (s:John Parker/t:Jerrold Immel) US:LP = First American FA-7780*

8470 Dames at Sea (1970) Score (stage songs:Jim Wise) US:LP-PP = Bell System K-4900

8471 Dan August (1970) Theme (Dave Grusin) GB:LP = DJM 22076* [Ray Davies and the Button Down Brass]

8472 Danger (1950) Highlights (Tony Mottola) US:LP-10 = MGM E-111

8473 Danger Grows Wild *see* Poppy Is Also a Flower, The

8474 Danger Man (1961) Theme (Edwin Astley) US:SP = London 45-1975 [Ted Heath]

8475 Danger UXB (1980) Highlights (Simon Park) GB:LP = Decca SKL-5304*

8476 Dangerous Christmas of Red Riding Hood, The (1965) Score (Jule Styne) US:LP = ABC 536/S-536*

8477 Dangerous Days of Kiowa Jones, The (1966) Theme (Steve Karliski) US:LP = MGM 4428* [Hank Williams, Jr.:ST]

8478 Daniel Boone [Walt Disney Presents] (1960) Theme (Stan Jones) US:SP=Disneyland DBR-97 [Stan Jones:ST]

8479 Daniel Boone (1964) Theme (Lionel Newman) US:SP = Mercury 75 [The Young Americans]; Theme (Lionel Newman) US:LP = RCA 2973* [Fess Parker]; Theme (Lionel Newman) US:LP = RCA 3460* [Ed Ames]

8480 Danny Kaye Show, The (1963) Score (pop music) US:LP-PP = Rambler/Dena XTV-92557 [Danny Kaye:ST]

8481 Danny Thomas Show, The *see* Make Room for Daddy

8482 Dark Shadows (1969) Score (Robert Cobert) US:LP = Philips PHS-600-314*

8483 Dark Side of the Sun, The (1983) Score (Stavros Xarchakos) GB:LP = BBC REB-487*

8483a Dastardly and Muttley in Their Flying Machines (1969) Theme (Hoyt Curtin) US:LP-MS = Tee Vee Toons 1300 [@ST]

8484 Database (1985) Theme (Rick Wakeman) GB:SP = President 2* [ST]

8485 Dateline—London (1962) Theme (John Barry) GB:SP = Columbia 4806 + GB:SP = Cherry Red 67 [John Barry:ST]

8486 Dating Game, The (1966) Theme (Chuck Barris) US:LP = World Pacific 21859* [The Mariachi Brass]; Theme (Chuck Barris) US:LP = Friends 1001* [Chuck Barris Orchestra:ST]

8487 David Copperfield (1972) Score (Malcolm Arnold) US:LP = GRT 10008*

8488 David Frost Show, The *see* Frost Over England

8489 Davy Crockett [Walt Disney Presents] Underscore + Dialog (George Bruns) US:LP = Columbia CL-666 + US:LP = Disneyland 1926; Themes-A-B (George Bruns) US:SP = Columbia 4-40449 [Fess Parker:ST]; Themes-C-D (George Bruns) US:SP = Columbia 4-40568 [Fess Parker:ST]; Theme-E (George Bruns) US:78 = Columbia 254 [Fess Parker:ST]

8490 Days of Our Lives, The (1965) Theme (Tommy Boyce & Bobby Hart) US:LP = Capitol Custom SL-8076* [The New Christy Minstrels]; Theme (Tommy Boyce & Bobby Hart) US:LP = Pickwick 3566* [The Birchwood Pops]

8491 Dean Martin Show, The (1966) Score (pop music) US:LP = Reprise R-6233/RS-6233* [Dean Martin: ST]; Theme (Van Alexander) US:LP = BBP 1001* [Van Alexander:ST]

8492 Dear Doctor *see* Fireside Theatre

8493 Dear Heart (1982) Theme (Andy Wilson) GB:SP = BBC 111* [The Lonelyhearts:ST]

8494 Death Dance at Banner *see* Stranger on the Run

8495 Death Valley Days (1952) Theme (H. Taylor) US:LP = Coral 757267* [Lawrence Welk]

8496 Dedicato a Una Coppia / Theme (Guido & Maurizio DeAngelis) US:LP = Private Stock 7004* [Guido & Maurizio:ST]

8497 Defenders, The (1961) Theme (Leonard Rosenman) US:SP = Capitol 4843 [Nelson Riddle]; Theme (Leonard Rosenman) US:LP = Capitol 1771* [Nelson Riddle]; Theme (Leonard Rosenman) US:LP = 20th 4109* [Bill Ramal]

8498 Delitto di Regime / Theme (Guido & Maurizio DeAngelis) US:LP = Private Stock 7004* [Guido & Maurizio:ST]

8499 Delta House (1979) Theme (Jim Steinman) US:SP = MCA 41010* [Michael Simmons:ST]

8500 Demolition Man (1973) Score (Bill Livsey) GB:LP = UA UAG-29901*

8501 Dempsey and Makepeace (1985) Theme (Alan Parker) GB:SP = Sierra FED-9* [ST]

8502 Dennis the Menace (1959) Underscore + Dialog (Irving Friedman) US:LP = Colpix CP-204; Theme (William Loose) US:LP-MS = Tee Vee Toons 1100 [@ST]

8503 Department S (1971) Theme (Edwin Astley) GB:LP = Marble Arch 1179* [@Cyril Stapleton]; Theme (Edwin Astley) GB:LP-MS = Pickwick 50-DA-315* [Bruce Baxter]

8504 Deputy, The (1959) Theme (Jack Marshall) US:LP = UA 6161* [Al Caiola]; Theme (Jack Marshall) US: LP = RCA 2180* [Buddy Morrow]

8505 Deputy Dawg (1960) Underscore + Dialog (Philip Scheib) US: LP = Camden CAL-1048

8506 Desperate People (1963) Theme (Roger Roger) GB:SP = Fontana 267268 [Roger Roger:ST]

8507 Detective, The / Theme (Ron Grainer) GB:LP = RCA 1020* [Ron Grainer:ST]

8508 Detectives, The [Robert Taylor's The Detectives] (1959) Theme (Herschel Burke Gilbert) US:LP = Dot 25421* [Herschel Burke Gilbert:ST]; Theme (Herschel Burke Gilbert) US: LP = Camden 627* [Mundell Lowe]

8509 Detour to Nowhere *see* Banacek

8510 Devlin Connection, The (1982) Theme (Patrick Williams) US: LP = PCM 1001* [Patrick Williams:ST]

8511 Diagnosis: Unknown (1960) Theme (Irwin Kostal) US:SP = Decca 9-31146 [Warren Covington]; Theme (Irwin Kostal) US:LP = Decca 74448* [Warren Covington]

8512 Dial Hot Line (1970) Theme [pilot for "Matt Lincoln"] (Oliver Nelson) US:SP = UNI 55266* [God's Children]

8513 Diamonds in the Sky (1980) Theme (Richard Denton & Martin Cook) GB:SP = BBC 72* [Richard Denton & Martin Cook:ST]; Theme (Richard Denton & Martin Cook) GB:LP = BBC 385* [Richard Denton & Martin Cook:ST]

8514 Diana (1971) Score (pop music) US:LP = Motown MS-719* + US: LP = Motown M5-155* [Diana Ross:ST]

8515 Diana (1983) Themes (Stanley Myers) GB:SP = BBC 141* [Stanley Myers:ST]

8516 Dick Powell Show, The (1961) Themes (Herschel Burke Gilbert/Richard Shores) US:LP = Dot 25421* [Herschel Burke Gilbert:ST]; Theme-A (Herschel Burke Gilbert) US:SP = London 45-10524 [Tony Hatch]; Theme-B (Richard Shores) US:LP = Mercury 60706* [Pete Rugolo]

8517 Dick Powell's Zane Grey Theatre *see* Zane Grey Theatre

8518 Dick Turpin (1979) Themes (Denis King) GB:SP = EMI 9061* [Denis King:ST]

8519 Dick Van Dyke Show, The (1961) Theme (Earle Hagen) US:SP = 20th 427 [Lionel Newman]; Theme (Earle Hagen) US:LP = 20th 4105* [Lionel Newman]; Theme (Earle Hagen) US:LP = Mercury 60706* [Pete Rugolo]

8520 Dickens of London (1978) Score (Monty Norman) GB:LP = Transatlantic TRA-330*

8520a Diff'rent Strokes [Arnold et Willy] (1978) Theme (Alan Thicke) FR:SP = Polydor 2056.997* [ST]

8521 Dinah Shore Show, The (1951) Score (pop music) US:LP-PP = Dinah SH-1 [Dinah Shore:ST]

8522 Ding Dong School (1952) Score (various) US:LP = Golden GLP-49 [Miss Frances:ST]

8523 Directions (1972) Score ["Saint Patrick's Mass"] (Philip Green) US:LP = RCA LSC-3276* [Philip Green:ST]

8524 Disco Magic (1978) Theme (Steve Wittmack) US:SP = Good Sounds 9505* [Laura Taylor:ST]

8525 Disneyland [Walt Disney Presents] [Walt Disney's Wonderful World of Color] (1954) Score (film songs) US: LP = Disneyland DQ-1245

8526 Disraeli (1979) Theme (Wilfred Josephs) US:LP-PP = WGBH 10* + US:LP-MS = SQN 5057-1* [@Marcus Dods:ST]

8527 District Nurse (1984) Theme (David Mindel) GB:LP = BBC 524* [@David Mindel:ST]

8528 Diver Dan (1961) Highlights + Dialog (Tony Piano) US:LP = Harmony HL-9544

8529 Divorce His/Divorce Hers (1972) Theme (Stanley Myers) US:LP = London 44203* [Ronnie Aldrich]

8530 Dixon of Dock Green (1955) Theme (Jack Warner) GB:SP = Oriole 1426 [Jack Warner:ST]; Theme (Jack Warner) GB:LP = BBC 454 [@Jack Warner:ST]; Theme (Jack Warner) GB: LP-MS = Pickwick 50-DA-315* [Bruce Baxter]

8531 Dobie Gillis *see* Many Loves of Dobie Gillis, The

8532 Doctor at Large *see* Doctor in the House

8533 Doctor Dolittle (1970) Score (Doug Goodwin) US:LP = Carousel CAR-3504*

8534 Dr. Finlay's Casebook (1959) Theme (Trevor Duncan) GB:SP = Boosey 2359 [The New Concert Orchestra]; Theme (Trevor Duncan) GB:LP = BBC 454 [@The New Concert Orchestra]; Theme (Trevor Duncan) GB:LP-MS = Pickwick 50-DA-315* [Bruce Baxter]

8535 Doctor in the House [Doctor at Large] (1971) Theme (Alan Tew) GB: LP = EMI 5143* [@The London Symphony]

8536 Dr. Kildare (1961) Theme-A (Jerry Goldsmith) US:SP = MGM 13075 [Richard Chamberlain]; Theme-A (Jerry Goldsmith) US:LP = Mercury 60706* [Pete Rugolo]; Theme-B (M. Kaye) US: SP = MGM 13191 [Chris Crosby]; Theme-C (Burt Bacharach) US:SP = MGM 13285 [Richard Chamberlain]

8537 Doctor Simon Locke (1971) Theme (Victor Roberts) US:SP = Atco 6876* [Bob's Band]

8538 Dr. Syn, Alias the Scarecrow *see* Scarecrow of Romney Marsh, The

8539 Dr. Who (1963) Score (e:Malcolm Clarke/e:Peter Howell/e:Roger Limb/t:Ron Grainer) US:LP = BBC 22462*; Underscore + Dialog ["Genesis of the Daleks"] (Dudley Simpson) US: LP = BBC 22364*; Themes (Ron Grainer/Dudley Simpson) GB:LP = BBC 214* [@BBC Radiophonic Workshop:ST]

8540 Doctors, The (1963) Theme (John Geller) US:LP = Capitol Custom SL-8076* [The New Christy Minstrels]

8541 Don Ho Show, The (1976) Score (pop music) US:LP = Reprise RS-6367*

8542 Donna Reed Show, The (1958) Theme (Howard Greenfield) US:LP-MS = Tee Vee Toons 1100 [@ST]

8543 Donny and Marie Show, The (1976) Score (t:The Osmonds/s:pop music) US:LP = Polydor PD-6068* [Donny and Marie:ST]

8544 Don't Do Me Any Favors *see* Robert Montgomery Presents

8545 Don't Forget to Write (1977) Theme (Anthony Isaac) GB:SP = BBC 57* [Anthony Isaac:ST]; Theme (Anthony Isaac) GB:LP = BBC 365* [@Anthony Isaac:ST]

8546 Doonesbury (1977) Excerpts (Jimmy Thudpucker) US:LP = Windsong BXL1-2589* [Jimmy Thudpucker:ST]

8547 Dora's World (1974) Score (pop music) US:LP-PP = Cozy ST-102* [Dora Hall:ST]

8548 Double Deckers, The [Here Come the Double Deckers] (1970) Score (Ivor Slaney) US:LP = Capitol ST-672*

8549 Down in the Valley (1950) Highlights (stage songs:Kurt Weill) US: LP-10 = RCA LM-16 [Marion Bell:ST]

8550 Dragnet (1955) Highlights + Underscore + Dialog (e:Walter Schumann/u:Nathan Scott) US:LP-10 = RCA LPM-3199; Theme-A (Walter Schumann) US:SP = RCA 47-5398 [Buddy Morrow]; Theme-A (Walter Schumann) US:LP = London 44077* [Frank Chacksfield]; Theme-B (Arthur Hamilton) US:SP = Columbia 4-40437 [Peggy King:ST]

8551 Dreams (1984) Score (various) US:LP = Columbia BFC-39886*; Theme [Main Title—"One Night Band"] (Trevor Veitch) US:SP = Columbia 38-04644* [Dreams:ST]

8552 Drum Is a Woman, A (1955) Score (Duke Ellington) US:LP = Columbia CL-951 [Duke Ellington]

8553 Drumbeat (1959) Score (pop music) GB:LP = Parlophone PMC-1101

8554 Drummer Man *see* Kraft Television Theatre

8555 Duchess of Duke Street, The (1979) Themes (Alexander Faris) US: LP-MS = BBC 2-22000* + US:LP-MS = SQN 5057-1* [@Alexander Faris: ST]; Themes (Alexander Faris) GB: SP = BBC 45* [Alexander Faris:ST]

8556 Dukes of Hazzard, The (1979) Theme (Waylon Jennings) US:SP = RCA 12067* [Waylon Jennings:ST]; Theme (Waylon Jennings) US:LP = RCA 1-3602* [Waylon Jennings:ST]

8557 Dynasty (1981) Theme (Bill Conti) US:SP = Arista 1021* [Bill Conti: ST]; Theme (Bill Conti) US:LP = RCA 1-1043* [Danny Davis]

E

8558 Earl Scruggs with Family and Friends (1968) Score (folk music) US: LP = Columbia PC-30584* [Earl Scruggs:ST]

8559 East of Eden (1981) Score (Lee Holdridge) US:LP = Elektra 5E-520*

8560 East Side, West Side (1963) Score (Kenyon Hopkins) US:LP = Columbia CL-2123/CS-8923*

8561 Eastenders (1985) Theme (Simon May) GB:SP = BBC 160* [ST]; Theme (Simon May) GB:LP = BBC 508* [@ST]

8562 Echo Four-Two (1960) Theme (Laurie Johnson) US:LP = Philips 600-027* [Johnny Gregory]; Theme (Laurie Johnson) GB:SP = Pye 7N-15383 [Laurie Johnson:ST]

8563 Ed Sullivan Show, The (1955) Scores (pop music) US:LP-MS-PP = CSP 1056/1060 [Various Artists:ST]; Score (pop music) US:LP-MS = RCA CPM6-5172 [Elvis Presley:ST]; Highlights (pop music) GB:EP = CBS SP-910 [The Beatles:ST]

8564 Edge of Darkness, The (1985) Highlights (Michael Kamen) GB:EP-12 = BBC 12RSL-178*

8565 Edge of Night, The (1956) Theme (Jack Cortner) US:LP = Capitol Custom SL-8076* [The New Christy Minstrels]

8566 Edward and Mrs. Simpson (1980) Score (e:Ron Grainer/etc.) US: LP = DRG-15019*

8567 Edward VII *see* Edward the King

8568 Edward the King [Edward VII] (1979) Scores (e:Cyril Ornadel/etc.) US:LP-MS = DRG DARC2-1104*

8569 Eight Is Enough (1977) Theme-A (Fred Werner) US:LP = Motown 905* [Prime Time]; Theme-B (Lee Holdridge) US:LP-PP = Jenson 3011* [The Jenson Marching Band]

8570 87th Precinct (1961) Theme (Morton Stevens) US:LP = Decca 74481* [Stanley Wilson]; Theme (Morton Stevens) US:LP = Mercury 60706* [Pete Rugolo]

8571 Eleanor and Franklin [Eleanor and Franklin—The White House Years] (1976) Theme (John Barry) US:SP = Casablanca 887* [John Barry: ST]; Theme (John Barry) US:LP = Citadel 6021* [Ralph Gair]

8572 Electric Company, The (1972) Score (Joe Raposo) US:LP = WB BS-2636*

8573 Elephant Boy, The / Underscore + Dialog (Charles Marawood) GB:LP = Windmill WMD-223

8574 Eleven Against the Ice (1958) Score (Kenyon Hopkins) US:LP = RCA LPM-1618

8575 Eleventh Hour, The (1962) Theme (Harry Sukman) US:SP = RCA 47-8104 [Al Hirt]; Theme (Harry Sukman) US:LP = UA 6315* [Ferrante & Teicher]; Theme (Harry Sukman) US: LP = 20th 4109* [Bill Ramal]

8576 Elizabeth R (1971) Highlights (ae:David Munrow) GB:EP = BBC RELS-1; Themes (at:David Munrow) GB:LP = BBC 188 [@David Munrow: ST]; Theme (at:David Munrow) US: LP-MS = BBC 2-22000 + US:LP-MS = SQN 5057-1* [@David Munrow: ST]

8577 Elizabeth Taylor in London

(1963) Highlights + Dialog (John Barry) US:LP = Colpix CP-459/SCP-459* [Johnnie Spence:ST]; Excerpts (John Barry) US:LP = Capitol T-2527/ST-2527* [John Barry]

8578 Elvira's Movie Macabre *see* Movie Macabre

8579 Elvis (1968) Score (pop music) US:LP = RCA LPM-4088 [Elvis Presley: ST]

8580 Elvis (1978) Score (pop music) US:LP-PP = Precision TVLP-79* [Ronnie McDowell:ST]

8581 Elvis—Aloha from Hawaii (1973) Scores (pop music) US:LP-MS = RCA VPSX-6089* [Elvis Presley:ST]

8582 Elvis in Concert (1977) Scores (pop music) US:LP-MS = RCA APL2-2587* [Elvis Presley:ST]

8583 Elvis Presley's Graceland (1985) Theme (Bill Medley) US:LP = RCA 1-5352* [Bill Medley:ST]

8584 Emergency (1972) Theme (Nelson Riddle) US:LP = MCA 5380* [Warren Schatz]

8585 Emergency Ward 10 (1957) Theme (S. Yorke) GB:LP-MS = Pickwick 50-DA-315* [Bruce Baxter]

8586 Emmerdale Farm (1972) Theme (Tony Hatch) GB:LP = Pye 41029* [Tony Hatch:ST]

8587 Emperor's New Clothes, The Highlights (Maury Laws) US:LP-10-PP = Rankin/Bass 72-6304 [Danny Kaye:ST]

8588 Empire Road (1978) Theme (Matumbi) GB:LP= BBC 365* [@Matumbi:ST]

8589 End of the Trail [Project 20] Score (Robert Russell Bennett) US:LP-PP = RCA Custom L80P-1609

8590 Enemy at the Door (1978) Themes (Wilfred Josephs) GB:SP = DJM 10837* [The Mansell Chorale/Max Harris]; Theme (Wilfred Josephs) GB: LP = DJM 22081* [@Max Harris]

8591 Engineer Bill Show, The Theme (Del Porter) US:SP = Mark 56 #832 [The Gandy Dancers]

8592 Enigma Files, The (1980) Theme (Anthony Isaac) GB:SP = BBC 68* [Anthony Isaac:ST]; Theme (Anthony Isaac) GB:LP = BBC 391* [@Anthony Isaac:ST]

8593 Ennal's Point (1982) Theme (Mike Townsend) GB:SP = BBC 109*

8594 Enola Gay (1980) Score (Maurice Jarre) US:LP = Varese STV-81149*

8595 Entertainer, The (1976) Theme (Marvin Hamlisch) US:LP = BBC 22398* [Bing Crosby]

8595a Entertainment Tonight (1981) Theme (Michael Mark) US:LP-MS = Tee Vee Toons 1300 [@ST]

8596 Eric (1975) Score (s:Dave Grusin/t:John Savage) JA:LP = Seven Seas FML-57*

8597 Ernie Kovacs Show, The (1955) Theme + Underscore + Dialog (t:Newlon/etc.) US:LP = Columbia BL-34250 [Ernie Kovacs:ST]; Theme-A [Main Title] (Newlon) US:SP = MGM 12408 [Leroy Holmes]; Theme-B ["Song of the Nairobi Trio"] (Robert Maxwell) US:SP = Decca 9-31839 [Robert Maxwell]

8598 Escapade in Florence [Walt Disney Presents] (1962) Themes (Richard & Robert Sherman) US:SP = Buena Vista 407 [Annette:ST]

8599 Ethan Allen / Excerpts [pilot] (Bernard Herrmann) US:LP = Cerberus CST-2029 [Bernard Herrmann:ST]

8600 Euro-Fashions '68 (1968) Theme (Tony Hatch) GB:LP = Marble Arch 853* [@Tony Hatch:ST]

8601 Evening Primrose (1966) Themes (Stephen Sondheim) US:LP-MS = WB 2-2705* [@Marti Ralph & Victoria Mallory]

8602 Evening with Edgar Allan Poe, An (1970) Highlights (Les Baxter) US:LP = Citadel CTV-7013*

8603 Evening with Fred Astaire, An (1958) Score (e:David Rose/e:pop music) US:LP-PP = Chrysler CC-1; Score (e:David Rose/e:pop music) US: LP-MS = DRG S3L-5181

8604 Ewoks—The Battle for Endor (1985) Highlights (Peter Bernstein) US: LP = Varese STV-81281*

8605 Expert, The (1970) Theme (Dudley Simpson) GB:LP = Decca 2163* [Ike Isaacs]

8606 Explorers, The (1975) Theme (Robert Sharples) GB:LP = BBC 236* [@Robert Sharples:ST]

8607 Exploring (1962) Score (Paul Ritts) US:LP = Harmony HL-9547

8608 Eyes of the Lion, The *see* Tarzan

F

8609 F.B.I., The (1965) Theme (Bronislau Kaper) US:LP = RCA 3540* [Hugo Montenegro]; Theme (Bronislau Kaper) US:LP = Camden 927* [Ray Martin]

8610 F Troop (1965) Theme (William Lava) US:LP = Epic 26224* [Bob Crane]; Theme (William Lava) US: LP-MS = Tee Vee Toons 1100 [@ST]

8610a Facts of Life, The (1979) Theme (Alan Thicke) US:LP-MS = Tee Vee Toons 1300 [@ST]

8611 Fair Stood the Wind for France (1981) Excerpts (Carl Davis) GB: LP = EMI EMC-3361* [Carl Davis:ST]

8612 Falcon Crest (1981) Theme (Bill Conti) US:SP = Arista 1021* [Bill Conti:ST]

8613 Fall and Rise of Reginald Perrin, The (1978) Theme (Ronnie Hazlehurst) GB:LP = Polydor 2384.107* [Ronnie Hazlehurst:ST]

8614 Fall Guy, The (1981) Theme (Glen Larson) US:SP = Scotti Brothers 5-03170* [Lee Majors:ST]

8615 Fame (1981) Score-A (various) US:LP = RCA AFL1-4259*; Score-B (various) US:LP = RCA AFL1-4525*

8616 Family Affair (1966) Theme (Frank DeVol) US:SP = Dot 17044 [Mike Minor]; Theme (Frank DeVol) US:LP = Dot 25774* [Lawrence Welk]

8617 Family Game, The (1967) Theme (Chuck Barris) US:LP = Friends 1001 [Chuck Barris Orchestra]

8618 Family Ties (1982) Theme (Tom Scott) US:LP = Special Music Co. 4004* [Meadlowbrook Pops]

8619 Fantasy Island (1978) Theme (Laurence Rosenthal) US:LP = RCA 1-3052* [Henry Mancini]

8620 Far Pavilions, The (1984) Score (Carl Davis) US:LP = Chrysalis FV-41464*

8621 Farmer Al Falfa (1962) Underscore + Dialog ["The Mechanical Cow"] (Philip Scheib) US:LP = RCA LBY-1031 [@ST]

8622 Fat Albert and the Cosby Kids (1972) Theme (Ed Fournier) US:LP-MS = Tee Vee Toons 1300 [@ST]

8623 Father Brown (1974) Theme (Jack Parnell) GB:LP = MFP 90061* [Jack Parnell:ST]

8624 Fawlty Towers (1977) Theme + Dialog (Dennis Wilson) US:LP = BBC 454; Theme (Dennis Wilson) US: LP-MS = BBC 2-22000* [@Dennis Wilson:ST]

8624a Fawn Story [ABC After School Special] (1975) Theme (W. Michael Lewis & Laurin Rinder) US:SP = AVI 170* [W. Michael Lewis:ST]

8625 Feathertop (1961) Score (Mary Rodgers) US:LP-PP = Mars Candy LB-2931

8626 Felix the Cat (1960) Underscore + Dialog (Winston Sharples) US: LP = Playhour CR-28; Theme (Pete Wendling) US:LP-MS = Tee Vee Toons TVT-1100 [@ST]

8627 Fenn Street Gang, The (1970) Theme (Denis King) GB:LP = EMI 5143* [The Pandora Orchestra]

8628 Fenwick (1966) Score (Jack Boring) US:LP-PP = Motorola FLP-621

8629 Film Night [Film '72] Theme (Billy Taylor) US:LP = K-Tel 4780* [Sounds Orchestral]; Theme (Billy Taylor) GB:LP = Polydor 2460.188* [@Harry Robinson]

8630 Finder of Lost Loves (1984) Theme (Burt Bacharach) US:SP = Arista 1-9281* [Dionne Warwick:ST]; Theme (Burt Bacharach) US:LP = Arista 8-8262* [Dionne Warwick:ST]

8631 Fire and Ice (1986) Score (Carl Davis) GB:LP = First Night CAST-7*

8632 Fireball XL-5 (1963) Themes (Barry Gray) US:SP = 20th 440 [Don Spencer]; Theme (Barry Gray) US:LP-MS = Tee Vee Toons 1100 [@ST]

8633 Firedog / Theme (Ray Davies) GB:LP = DJM 2023* [Ray Davies and the Button Down Brass Band:ST]

8634 Fireside Theatre (1949) Theme ["Dear Doctor"] (Harry Lubin) US: LP = Decca 74151* [Harry Lubin:ST]

8635-6 First Easter Rabbit, The / Score (Maury Laws) US:LP-PP = Rankin/Bass F4RM-0019

8637 Flambards (1980) Score (David Fanshawe) GB:LP = Philips 9109.226*

8638 Flame Trees of Thika, The (1981) Score (Alan Blakley & Ken Howard) GB:LP = EMI EMC-3385*; Themes (Alan Blakley & Ken Howard) US:LP-MS = SQN 5057-1* [@ST]

8639 Flashbeagle *see* It's Flashbeagle, Charlie Brown

8640 Flickers (1982) Theme (Ron Grainer) US:LP-MS = SQN 5057-1* [@ST]

8641 Flight of the Condor (1982) Score (Inti Illimani) US:LP = BBC 22440*

8642 Flintstones, The (1960) Theme (Hoyt Curtin) US:LP = Reprise 9-6018* [Neal Hefti]; Theme (Hoyt Curtin) US: LP-MS = Tee Vee Toons 1100 [@ST]

8643 Flip Wilson Show, The (1970) Underscore + Dialog (George Wyle) US:LP = Little David LD-1001* [Flip Wilson:ST]

8644 Flood, The [Noah and the Flood] (1962) Score (classical music) US: LP = Columbia ML-5757/MS-6357* [Laurence Harvey & Orchestra:ST]

8645 Flumps, The / Underscore + Dialog (Paul Reade) GB:LP = BBC REC-309*

8646 Flying Nun, The (1967) Theme (Dominic Frontiere) US:LP = Colgems 106* [Sally Field:ST]; Theme (Dominic Frontiere) US:LP = Camden 2210* [The Living Trio]

8647 Follow the Sun (1961) Theme (Sonny Burke) US:LP = Choreo 6* [Harry Betts]

8648 Follyfoot (1972) Score (e: Dennis Farnon/e:Robert Sharples/t: Stephen Francis) GB:LP = York 715*

8649 Ford 50th Anniversary Show, The (1953) Excerpts (pop music) US:LP-10 = Decca DL-7027 [Mary Martin & Ethel Merman:ST]

8650 Foreign Intrigue (1951) Theme (Charles Norman) US:SP = Capitol 3478 [Les Baxter]; Theme (Charles Norman) US:SP = MGM 12281 [Paul Durand]

8651 Fortunate Life, A (1986) Score (Mario Millo) AU:LP = Polydor 829-085-1*

8652 Forty-five Minutes from Broadway (1959) Highlights (stage songs:George M. Cohan) US:LP = AEI 1159

8653 Fosters, The (1976) Theme (Denis King) GB:LP = DJM 20522* [@Laurie Holloway]

8654 Four Feathers, The (1978) Themes (Allyn Ferguson) GB:SP = EMI 2818* [J.J. Williams]

8655 Fourth Dimension, The / Theme (Paddy Kingsland) GB:LP = BBC 214* [BBC Radiophonic Workshop:ST]

8656 Fox (1980) Score (George Fenton) GB:LP = EMI EMC-3325*

8657 Fraggle Rock (1982) Score (Philip Balsam) US:LP = Muppet Music MLP-1200*

8658 Frances Langford Show, The (1951) Score (pop music) US:LP-PP = KB 2157 [Frances Langford:ST]

8659 Frank Sinatra Show, The (1957) Score (pop music) US:LP-BP = Sinatra S-4 [Frank Sinatra & Elvis Presley:ST]

8660 Frank Sinatra—The Man and His Music (1965) Scores (pop music) US: LP-MS = Reprise R-1016/RS-1016* [Frank Sinatra:ST]

8661 Fred Astaire Presents Premiere *see* Alcoa Premiere

8662 Fred Astaire Show, The (1968) Theme (Neal Hefti) US:SP = Capitol 2261 [Howard Roberts]; Theme (Neal Hefti] US:LP = Capitol 2901* [Howard Roberts]; Theme (Neal Hefti) US:LP = Monument 7627* [Boots Randolph]

8663 Free to Be . . . You and Me (1974) Score (e:Mary Rodgers/e:Stephen J. Lawrence/e:Carol Hall) US:LP = Arista AL-4003* [Marlo Thomas & Cast:ST]

8664 French Chef, The (1963) Theme (John Morris) US:LP = Polydor 5032* [Arthur Fiedler & the Boston Pops]; Theme (John Morris) US:LP-MS = Deutsche 2721.215* [Arthur Fiedler & The Boston Pops]

8665 Frog Prince, The (1972) Highlights + Dialog (Joe Raposo) US:LP = Columbia CC-23530*

8666 From Sea to Shining Sea (1974) Theme (Michel Legrand) US: SP = Dot 17533 [Tommy Overstreet]

8667 Front Line, The (1985) Theme (Black Roots) GB:LP = BBC 508* [@ST]

8668 Frontier (1955) Theme (Cadby) US:SP = MGM 12252 [Danny Knight]

8669 Frost Over London [The David Frost Show] (1966) Theme (George Martin) US:LP = UA 6647* [George Martin:ST]; Theme (George Martin) US:LP = Bell 6049* [Billy Taylor]

8670 Frosty the Snowman (1970) Highlights + Underscore + Dialog (Maury Laws) US:LP = MGM SE-4733*

8671 Frosty's Winter Wonderland (1976) Highlights + Underscore + Dialog (Maury Laws) US:LP = Disneyland 1368

8672 Fugitive, The (1963) Theme (Pete Rugolo) US:SP = Cameo 366 [John Schroeder]; Theme (Pete Rugolo) US:LP = 20th 4109* [Bill Ramal]; Theme (Pete Rugolo) US:LP = Liberty 7353* [Si Zentner]

8673 Fun Brigade, The *see* Sheriff John's Fun Brigade

8674 Funny Face (1971) Theme (Dave Grusin) US:SP = RCA 74-0573* [Jack Jones]

8675 Funny Man (1980) Score (pop music) GB:LP = WRC SH-396

8676 Fury (1955) Theme (Davie & Csida) US:LP = RCA 1027 [@The Prairie Chiefs]

8677 Future Cop (1977) Theme (J.J. Johnson) GB:LP = DJM 22076* [Ray Davies and the Button Down Brass]

G

8678 Gallant Men, The (1962) Theme (Sy Miller) US:SP = WB 5313 [Eddie Fontaine]

8679 Games of the 23rd Olympiad, The (1984) Score (t:John Williams/t:Bill Conti/t:Philip Glass/t:Quincy Jones/t:Burt Bacharach/t:Toto/t:Bob James/t:Herbie Hancock/t:Giorgio Moroder) US:LP = Columbia JS-39322*

8680 Gangsters (1976) Theme (Dave Greenslade) GB:LP = BBC 310* [@Dave Greenslade:ST]

8681 Garry Moore Show, The (1958) Theme (Joe Hamilton) US:LP = Liberty 7321* [Dave Pell]

8682 Gene Austin Story, The (1958) Highlights (pop music) US:EP = RCA EPA-4057 [Gene Austin:ST]

8683 General Electric Theatre (1953) Score (Elmer Bernstein) US:LP = Columbia CL-1395/CS-8190* + US:LP = CSP ACS-8190*; Theme (Stanley Wilson) US:LP = Mercury 60706* [Pete Rugolo]; Theme (Stanley Wilson) US:LP = Carlton 143* [Valjean]

8684 General Electric Theatre Presents Sammy! *see* Sammy!

8685 General Hospital (1963) Theme [USA Series] (Kip Walton) US:LP = ABC 513* [Frank Devol]; Theme [USA Series] (Jack Urbont) US:LP = Capitol Custom SL-8076* [New Christy Minstrels]; Theme [USA Series] (Kip Walton) US:SP = ABC 10628 [Frank DeVol]

8686 General Hospital / Theme [British Series] (Derek Scott) GB:LP = Decca 333* [Ray Martin]

8687 General Motors 50th Anniversary Show (1957) Score (t:Sammy Fain/s:pop music) US:LP = RCA LOC-1037

8688 Generation Game, The (1970) Theme-A (Ronnie Hazlehurst) GB:LP = BBC 236* [@Ronnie Hazlehurst:ST]; Theme-B (Bruce Forsythe) US:LP = K-Tel 4780* [Sounds Orchestra]

8689 Genesis of the Daleks *see* Dr. Who

8690 Gentle Ben (1967) Theme (Harry Sukman) US:LP = Century City 70101* [The Good Time People:ST]

8691 Gentle Touch, The (1979) Theme (Roger Webb) GB:LP = Chandos 1050* [Roger Webb:ST]

8692 Geoffrey Smith's World of Flowers (1984) Theme (H. Conzelmann) GB:SP = Brull 9057* [Mayfair Orchestra]; Theme (H. Conzelmann) GB:LP = BBC 524* [@Mayfair Orchestra]

8693 George Gobel Show, The (1954) Theme (John Scott Trotter) US:SP = Mercury 70616 [Richard Hayman]; Theme (John Scott Trotter) US:LP = WB 1333* [John Scott Trotter:ST]

8694 George of the Jungle (1967)

Theme (Stan Worth) US:LP-MS = Tee Vee Toons 1200 [@ST]

8695 Gertrude Berg Show, The [Mrs. G Goes to College] (1961) Themes (Herschel Burke Gilbert) US:LP = Dot 25421* [Herschel Burke Gilbert:ST]

8696 Get Smart (1965) Underscore + Dialog (Irving Szathmary) US:LP = UA UAL-3533/UAS-6533* [Don Adams:ST]; Theme (Irving Szathmary) US:SP = Epic S-10038 [Bob Crane]

8697 Ghost Squad (1960) Theme (Philip Green) US:SP = London 45-10505 [Tony Hatch]; Theme (Philip Green) US:LP = Mercury 600-027* [Johnny Gregory]

8698 Gidget (1965) Theme (Howard Greenfield) US:SP = MGM 13408 [Johnny Tillotson:ST]; Theme (Howard Greenfield) US:LP-MS = Tee Vee Toons 1200 [@ST]

8699 Gift of the Magi (1959) Score (Richard Adler) US:LP = UA UAL-4013/UAS-5013*

8700 Gilligan's Island (1964) Theme (George Wyle) US:LP-MS = Tee Vee Toons 1100 [@ST]

8700a Gimme a Break (1983) Theme (R. Page) US:LP-MS = Tee Vee Toons 1300 [@Nell Carter:ST]

8701 Girl from U.N.C.L.E., The (1966) Score (s:Dave Grusin/t:Richard Shores) US:LP = MGM E-4410/SE-4410* [Teddy Randazzo]

8702 Girl on the Run *see* Conflict

8703 Glass House, The (1965) Highlights (Priscilla Paris) US:LP-PP = Unifilms ULP-505 [The Paris Sisters]

8704 Glass Menagerie, The (1973) Theme (John Barry) GB:SP = WB 27337* [John Barry:ST]; Theme (John Barry) GB:LP = Polydor 2383.300* [John Barry:ST]

8705 Globetrotters, The *see* Harlem Globetrotters, The

8706 Godfather Saga, The (1978) Excerpts (Carmine Coppola & Francesco Pennino) US:LP = Sunnyvale SSP-2000* [Carmine Coppola:ST]

8707 Goggles *see* Looking Through Super Elastic Goggles

8708 Goin' Back to Indiana (1972) Score (t:Dick DeBenedictis/s:pop music) US:LP = Motown M-742* + US:LP = Motown M5-5261* [The Jackson 5:ST]

8709 Going Places (1973) Theme [pilot] (Charles Fox) US:SP = Verve 10673 [Kacher's Late Show]

8710 Going Straight (1978) Theme (Tony Macaulay) GB:SP = EMI 2768* [Ronnie Barker:ST]; Theme (Tony Macaulay) GB:LP = BBC 387* [@Ronnie Barker:ST]

8711 Golddiggers, The [Dean Martin Presents the Golddiggers] (1968) Score (t:Lee Hale/s:pop music) US:LP = Metromedia MD-1009* [The Golddiggers:ST]

8712 Golden Circle, The (1959) Score (pop music) US:LP-PP = ABC PRO-311* [Steven Lawrence & Eydie Gorme:ST]

8713 Goldilocks (1970) Highlights + Dialog (Richard & Robert Sherman) US:LP = Disneyland ST-3998 + US:LP-PP = Armstrong ALP-3511 [Bing Crosby:ST]

8714 Goldorak [UFO Robot Grandizer] (1975) Underscore + Dialog (various) CA:LP = CBS 90561*

8715 Golf for Swingers [Lee Trevino's Golf for Swingers] (1972) Themes (Denny Vaughan) US:SP = Mouse 1001 [Denny Vaughan:ST]

8716 Gomer Pyle, U.S.M.C. (1964) Theme (Earle Hagen) US:LP-MS = Tee Vee Toons 1200 [@ST]

8717 Good Companions, The (1980) Score (David Fanshawe) GB:LP = Tritel TL-1201*

8718 Good Soldier, The (1982) Theme (at:John McCabe) US:LP-MS = SQN 5057-1* [@ST]

8719 Good Times (1974) Theme (Dave Grusin) US:SP = Motown 1444* [Prime Time]; Theme (Dave Grusin) US:LP = Motown 905* [Prime Time]

8720 Goodbye, Darling (1980) Theme (M. Canwell) GB:SP = BBC 75* [Leon Young:ST]; Theme (M. Canwell) GB:LP = BBC 424* [@Leon Young:ST]

8721 Goodies, The (1970) Score-A (Bill Oddie) GB:LP = Bradleys 1010* [The Goodies:ST]; Themes (Bill Oddie) US:SP = 20th 2189* [The Goodies:ST]

8722 Goodwill Games—Moscow '86 (1986) Score (Michel Camilo) US:

LP-PP = Turner Broadcasting System TBS-002*

8723 Grand Jury (1958) Theme (Ray Ellis) US:SP = MGM 12942 [Ray Ellis:ST]

8724 Grand Tour—This Is Your World / Score (t:Ray Heindorf/t:Joseph J. Lilley/s:pop music) US:LP-PP = Co-Co LP-1001

8725 Grandstand / Theme-A (James Stevens) GB:LP = BBC 454 [@Symphonia Orchestra]; Theme-B (Keith Mansfield) GB:LP = BBC 236* [Keith Mansfield:ST]

8726 Grange Hill (1978) Theme (Alan Hawkshaw) GB:SP = BBC 64* [Alan Hawkshaw:ST]; Theme (Alan Hawkshaw) GB:LP = BBC 486* [@Alan Hawkshaw:ST]

8727 Grasshopper Island / Theme (Wilfred Josephs) GB:LP = Polydor 2383.294* [Marcus Dods:ST]

8728 Great Dinosaur Discovery, The (1973) Score (Dennis Lisonbee & Steve Amundsen) US:LP-PP = KBYU 12913*

8729 Great Egg Race, The (1979) Themes (Richard Denton & Martin Cook) GB:SP = BBC 65* [Richard Denton & Martin Cook:ST]; Theme (Richard Denton & Martin Cook) GB:LP = BBC 385* [Richard Denton & Martin Cook:ST]

8730 Great Expectations (1974) Score (Maurice Jarre) GB:LP = Pye NSPL-18452*

8731 Great Space Coaster, The (1980) Score (e:Tommy Goodman/etc.) US:LP = Columbia PC-37704*

8732 Great War, The [Project 20] Score (Robert Russell Bennett) US:LP-PP = RCA Custom 680P-8961

8733 Great War, The (1964) Excerpts (Wilfred Josephs) GB:LP = Polydor 2383.294* [Marcus Dods:ST]

8734 Great Whales, The (1977) Theme (Lee Holdridge) US:LP = Varese 704.290* [Charles Gerhardt]

8735 Greatest American Hero, The (1981) Theme (Mike Post) US:SP = Elektra 47147* [Joey Scarbury & Mike Post: ST]; Theme (Mike Post) US:LP = Elektra 1-60028* [Mike Post & Joey Scarbury:ST]

8736 Green Acres (1965) Theme (Vic Mizzy) US:SP = Columbia 4-43757 [Eddie Albert:ST]; Theme (Vic Mizzy) US:LP-MS = Tee Vee Toons 1100 [@ST]

8737 Green Hornet, The (1966) Score (Billy May) US:LP = 20th 3186/S-3186*

8738 Griff (1973) Theme (Elliot Kaplan) GB:LP = Philips 6308.255* [Johnny Gregory]

8739 Groovie Goolies, The (1971) Score (Martin & Gayden) US:LP = RCA LPM-4420/LSP-4420* [The Groovie Goolies:ST]

8740 Guiding Light, The (1952) Theme (Rob Mounsey) US:LP = MMR 2200* [Bartholomew & Joyce]

8741 Gunslinger, The (1961) Theme (Dimitri Tiomkin) US:LP = UA 6161* [Al Caiola]; Theme (Dimitri Tiomkin) US:SP = Columbia 4-41974 [Frankie Laine:ST]

8742 Gunsmoke (1955) Theme (Rex Koury) US:SP = Capitol 3230 [Tex Ritter & Rex Koury]; Theme (Rex Koury) US:LP = UA 6161* [Al Caiola]; Theme (Rex Koury) US:LP = Coral 757267* [Lawrence Welk]

H

8743 H.R. Pufnstuf (1969) Highlights (Les Szarvas) US:EP-PP = Capitol Custom CP-57* [Jack Wild & Billie Hayes:ST]

8744 Hadleigh (1972) Theme (Tony Hatch) GB:LP = Pye 41029* [Tony Hatch:ST]

8745 Hadley (1968) Theme (Alan Moorhouse) GB:LP = DJM 018* [@Alan Moorhouse:ST]

8746 Hallelujah / Score (pop music) GB:LP = Fontana TL-5356/TS-5356*

8747 Hamlet (1970) Underscore + Dialog (John Addison) US:LP-MS = RCA VDM2-119

8748 Hammer House of Horror (1981) Theme (Roger Webb) GB:SP = Chips 104* [Roger Webb:ST]

8749 Hancock's Half Hour (1963) Underscore + Dialog (Walter Stott-aka-Angela Morley) US:LP = BBC 22260

[Tony Hancock:ST]; Theme (Derek Scott) GB:SP = Pye 7N-15500 [Derek Scott:ST]

8750 Hanged Man, The (1965) Theme (pop music) US:SP = MGM 530 [Stan Getz & Astrud Gilberto:ST]

8751 Hanged Man, The (1975) Score (Alan Tew) GB:LP = Contour 2870.437*

8752 Hans Brinker (1958) Score (Hugh Martin) US:LP = Dot DLP-9001

8753 Hansel and Gretel (1958) Highlights (Alec Wilder) US:LP = MGM E-3690

8754 Happening in Central Park, A (1967) Score (pop music) US:LP = Columbia CS-9710* [Barbra Streisand:ST]

8755 Happy Days (1974) Theme (Charles Fox) US:SP = Reprise 0117* [Pratt & McClain]; Theme (Charles Fox) US:LP = Columbia 34312* [Ray Conniff]; Theme-B (Charles Fox) US:SP = Chelsea 3061* [Anson Williams:ST]

8756 Happy Endings (1982) Score (Peter Skellern) GB:LP = BBC REB-430*

8757 Happy Ever After (1975) Theme (Ronnie Hazlehurst) GB:LP = Polydor 2384.107* [Ronnie Hazlehurst: ST]

8758 Happy Goodman Family Hour, The / Score (pop music) US:LP-PP = Canaan CAS-8755* [Happy Goodman:ST]

8759 Hard to Get *see* Justice

8760 Hardy Boys, The (1955) *see* Mickey Mouse Club, The

8761 Hardy Boys, The (1969) Score-A (e:Ed Fournier/etc.) US:LP = RCA LPM-4217/LSP-4217* [The Hardy Boys:ST]; Score-B (e:Ed Fournier/etc.) US:LP = RCA LPM-4315/LSP-4315* [The Hardy Boys:ST]

8762 Harlem Globetrotters, The (1970) Score (e:Jeff Barry/etc.) US:LP = Kirshner KES-108* [The Globetrotters: ST]

8763 Harness, The (1971) Excerpts (Billy Goldenberg) US:LP-BP = Centurion CLP-1601 [Billy Goldenberg:ST]

8764 Harris and Company *see* Love Is Not Enough

8765 Harry and Lena (1970) Score (pop music) US:LP-PP = RCA Custom PRS-295* [Harry Belafonte & Lena Horne:ST]

8766 Harry O (1974) Theme (Billy Goldenberg) US:LP = Mercury 1-1089* [Johnny Gregory] † *the composer credit is incorrect on the record*

8767 Harry's Game (1982) Themes (Paul Brennan) GB:SP = RCA 292* [Clannad:ST]

8768 Hart to Hart (1979) Theme (Mark Snow) US:LP-PP = Jenson 0800* [The Jenson Marching Band]

8769 Hatty Town / Theme (Johnny Pearson) GB:LP = Golden Hour 547* [uncredited]

8770 Have Gun—Will Travel (1957) Excerpts (Bernard Herrmann) US:LP = Cerberus CST-0209* [Bernard Herrmann:ST]; Theme (Johnny Western) US:SP = Columbia 4-41260 [Johnny Western:ST]

8771 Hawaii Five-O (1968) Score (Morton Stevens) US:LP = Capitol ST-410*

8772 Hawaiian Eye (1959) Score-A (t:Jerry Livingston/t:Charles Henderson/t:Maurice DePackh/etc.) US:LP = WB W-1355/WS-1355*; Score-B (pop music) US:LP = WB W-1382/WS-1382* [Connie Stevens:ST]

8773 Heads and Tails (1980) Theme (Derek Griffiths) GB:LP = BBC 486* [@Derek Griffiths:ST]

8773a Heart to Call My Own, A (1956) Themes (Alec Wilder) US:SP = Columbia 4-40688 [Lisa Kirk:ST]

8774 Heaven Can Wait (1961) Theme (Robert Cobert) US:SP = Columbia 4-41877 [Spencer Ross]

8775 Hec Ramsey (1972) Theme (Joe Johnson) US:SP = Decca 9-33036* [Jerry Wallace]; Theme ["Mystery of the Yellow Rose"] (Lee Holdridge) US:LP = Varese 81081* [Lee Holdridge:ST]

8776 Hector Heathcote Show, The (1963) Underscore + Dialog (Philip Scheib) US:LP = Camden CAL-1031/CAS-1031*

8777 Hector, The Stowaway Pup [The Ballad of Hector, the Stowaway Pup] [Walt Disney Presents] (1964) Theme + Dialog (Richard & Robert Sherman) US:LP = Disneyland ST-1921

8778 Hee Haw (1969) Score (pop music) US:LP = Capitol ST-437* [Buck

Owens & Roy Clark & Cast:ST]

8779 Heidi (1968) Theme + Underscore + Dialog (John Williams) US:LP = Capitol SKAO-2995*

8780 Heifetz on Television (1971) Score (classical music) US:LP = RCA LSC-3205* [Jascha Heifetz:ST]

8781 Helen Morgan Story, The (1957) Score (pop music) US:LP = Columbia CL-994 [Polly Bergen:ST]

8782 Hell Hath No Fury *see* Big Valley, The

8783 Hello World *see* Let's Take a Trip

8784 Hemingway Play, The (1971) Theme (Lee Holdridge) US:LP = Varese 704.290* [Charles Gerhardt]

8785 Hennesey (1959) Score (Sonny Burke) US:LP = Signature 1049/S-1049*

8786 Here and Now (1962) Theme (Heino Gaze) GB:SP = Columbia 4765 [Eddie Calvert]

8787 Here Come the Brides (1968) Theme-A (Hugo Montenegro) US:SP = RCA 47-9722 [Perry Como]; Theme-A (Hugo Montenegro) US:LP = Metromedia 1014* [Bobby Sherman:ST]; Themes-B-C (Hugo Montenegro) US:LP = RCA 4022* [Hugo Montenegro:ST]

8788 Here Come the Double Deckers *see* Double Deckers, The

8789 Here Comes Garfield (1982) Highlights (Ed Bogas) US:LP = Epic FE-38136* [Lou Rawls:ST]

8790 Here's Pat O'Brien (1964) Themes + Dialog (pop music) US:LP = RIC M-1003 [Pat O'Brien:ST]

8791 He's Your Dog, Charlie Brown (1968) Underscore + Dialog (Vince Guaraldi) US:LP = Charlie Brown 2603

8792 Hey, Hey, Hey—It's Fat Albert! (1967) Themes (Jack Elliott) US:SP = Tetragrammaton 1500 [Fat Albert:ST]

8793 Hi-Di-Hi (1980) Theme (M. Perry) GB:SP = EMI 5180* [Paul Shane: ST]; Theme (M. Perry) GB:LP = BBC 424* [@Paul Shane:ST]

8794 Hi Summer / Theme (Lynsey DePaul) GB:LP = DJM 20522* [@Joan Brown]

8795 High Adventure with Lowell Thomas (1957) Theme ["Tibet"] (Harry Lubin) US:LP = Decca 74151* [Harry Lubin:ST]

8796 High Chaparral, The (1967) Score (e:David Rose/e:Harry Sukman) US:LP-MS = Capitol STBB-626* [Xanadu Pleasure Dome]; Theme (David Rose) US:SP = Capitol 2094 [David Rose:ST]

8797 High Tor (1956) Score (Arthur Schwartz) US:LP = Decca DL-8272

8798 Highway Patrol (1956) Theme (Richard Llewelyn) US:SP = London 45-1697 [Cyril Stapleton]; Theme (Richard Llewelyn) US:LP = RCA 2042* [Buddy Morrow]

8799 Highway to Heaven (1985) Theme (David Rose) US:LP = Klavier 5025* [Rex Koury]

8800 Hill Street Blues (1980) Score (Mike Post) GB:LP = Indiana HSBP-2222*; Theme (Mike Post) US:SP = Elektra 47186* [Mike Post:ST]; Theme (Mike Post) US:LP = Elektra 1-60028* [Mike Post:ST]

8801 History Man, The (1984) Theme (George Fenton) GB:LP = BBC 524* [@George Fenton:ST]

8802 History of the Motor Car, The / Theme (Ron Geesin) GB:LP = Ron 28* [Ron Geesin:ST]

8803 Hoagy Carmichael's Music Shop *see* Stark Reality, The

8804 Hobbit, The (1977) Highlights + Underscore + Dialog (Maury Laws) US:LP-MS = Buena Vista 103*

8805 Hogan's Heroes (1965) Theme (Jerry Fielding) US:SP = Sunset 61001 [Hogan's Heroes & Jerry Fielding]; Theme (Jerry Fielding) US:LP = Sunset 5137* [Hogan's Heroes & Jerry Fielding]; Theme (Jerry Fielding) US:LP = Epic 26224* [Bob Crane]

8806 Holiday 80 (1980) Theme (Gordon Giltrap) GB:SP = Electric Records 19* [Gordon Giltrap:ST]; Theme (Gordon Giltrap) GB:LP = BBC 391* [@Gordon Giltrap:ST]

8807 Hollywood (1979) Score (Carl Davis) US:LP = DRG DS-15006*

8808 Hollywood A-Go-Go [Let's Go-Go] (1965) Theme (Barry Young) US:SP = A&M 747 [Barry Young:ST]

8809 Hollywood and the Stars (1963) Theme (Elmer Bernstein) US: SP = UA 774 [Jon Early]

8810 Hollywood Palace, The (1964) Score (pop music) US:LP = Command S-902* [Mitchell Ayres:ST]

8811 Hollywood Squares, The (1966) Theme (Jimmie Haskell) US: LP = Dot 25930* [Peter Marshall]

8812 Hollywood Wives (1985) Theme (unknown) GB:LP = Indiana ATVP-5555* [@ST]

8813 Holocaust (1978) Score (Morton Gould) US:LP = RCA ARL1-2785*

8814 Home Tonight (1962) Theme (H. Cochrane) GB:SP = Columbia 4765 [Eddie Calvert]

8815 Hondo (1967) Theme (Richard Markowitz) GB:LP = MFP 1405* [Geoff Love]

8816 Honey West (1965) Score (Joseph Mullendore) US:LP = ABC 532/S-532*

8817 Honeymooners, The (1955) Theme (Jackie Gleason) US:SP = Capitol 3337 [Jackie Gleason:ST]; Themes (Jackie Gleason) US:LP = Murray Hill 000237 [@Jackie Gleason:ST]

8818 Hong Kong (1960) Score (e: Lionel Newman/t:Marty Paich/t:Billy May/t:Frank Comstock) US:LP = ABC 367/S-367*

8819 Hong Kong Beat (1978) Themes (Richard Denton & Martin Cook) GB:SP = BBC 52* [Richard Denton & Martin Cook:ST]; Themes (Richard Denton & Martin Cook) GB:LP = BBC 385* [Richard Denton & Martin Cook:ST]

8820 Horseman Riding By, A (1977) Themes (John Hankinson/Max Harris) GB:SP = BBC 55* [Max Harris: ST]; Theme (John Hankinson) GB:LP = BBC 365* [@Max Harris:ST]

8821 Horsemasters, The [Walt Disney Presents] (1961) Theme (Richard & Robert Sherman) US:SP = Buena Vista 388 [Annette]

8822 Hot Fudge (1976) Score-A (Larry Santos & Barry Hurd) US:LP = Parachute 810.317*; Score-B (Larry Santos & Barry Hurd) US:LP = Parachute 810.318*; Score-C (Larry Santos & Barry Hurd) US:LP = Parachute 810.319*; Score-D (Larry Santos & Barry Hurd) US:LP = Parachute 810.320*

8823 Hot Wheels (1969) Score (Mike Curb) US:LP = Forward ST-1023*

8824 Hotel (1983) Theme (Henry Mancini) GB:LP = MFP 5759* [The Power Pack Orchestra]

8825 Hotel de Paree (1959) Theme (Dimitri Tiomkin) US:LP-BP = Cinema LP-8012 [Dimitri Tiomkin:ST]

8826 House Calls (1979) Theme (Jack Elliott & Allyn Ferguson) US: LP = MCA 5380* [Warren Schatz]

8827 House of Caradus, The (1978) Theme (Johnny Pearson) GB:LP = Rampage 7* [Johnny Pearson:ST]

8828 House of Lions, The *see* Daktari

8829 House Party *see* Art Linkletter's House Party

8830 How the Grinch Stole Christmas (1966) Highlights + Dialog (Albert Hague) US:LP = Leo LE-901/ LES-901*

8831 How the West Was Won *see* MacAhans, The

8832 Howard's Way (1985) Theme (Simon May) GB:SP = BBC 174* [ST]; Theme (Simon May) GB:LP = BBC 508* [@ST]

8833 Howdy Doody (1950) Highlights + Dialog (Edward Kean) US: LP = RCA LPM-4546/LSP-4546e

8834 Huckleberry Hound (1958) Theme (Hoyt Curtin) US:SP = Golden 550 [The Golden Orchestra & Chorus]; Theme (Hoyt Curtin) US:LP = Golden 285 [The Golden Orchestra & Chorus]

8835 Hullabaloo (1965) Theme (John Aylesworth) US:LP = Columbia 9210* [The Hullabaloo Singers:ST]

8836 Human Jungle, The (1964) Theme (Bernard Ebbinghouse) GB:SP = Columbia 7003 [John Barry]; Theme (Bernard Ebbinghouse) GB:LP = EMI 21 [John Barry]

8837 Hunter (1986) Theme (Mike Post & Pete Carpenter) US:LP = Polydor 422-833-985-1* [Mike Post:ST]

I

8838 I Claudius (1977) Theme (Wilfred Josephs) US:LP-PP = WGBH 10* + US:LP-MS = SQN 5057-1*; [@

Marcus Dods:ST]; Theme (Wilfred Josephs) GB:LP=BBC 424* [@Marcus Dods:ST]; Theme (Wilfred Josephs) GB:LP=Polydor 2384.107* [Ronnie Hazlehurst]

8839 I Didn't Know You Cared (1975) Theme (Ronnie Hazlehurst) GB: LP=Polydor 2384.107* [Ronnie Hazlehurst:ST]

8840 I Dream of Jeannie (1965) Theme (Hugo Montenegro) US:SP=RCA 47-9050 [Hugo Montenegro:ST]; Theme (Hugo Montenegro) US:LP-MS=Tee Vee Toons 1100 [@ST]

8841 I Love Lucy (1951) Theme (Eliot Daniel) US:SP=Columbia 4-39937 [Desi Arnaz:ST]; Theme (Eliot Daniel) US:LP-MS=Tee Vee Toons 1100 [@ST]; Score (t:Eliot Daniel/s:pop music) US:LP-PP=Star Merchants SM-1951 [Desi Arnaz:ST]

8842 I Remember Mama *see* Mama

8843 I Married Joan (1952) Theme (Richard Mack) US:LP-MS=Tee Vee Toons 1200 [@ST]

8844 I Spy (1965) Score-A (s:Earle Hagen/t:Hugo Friedhofer) US:LP=WB W-1637/WS-1637*; Score-B (s:Earle Hagen/t:Hugo Friedhofer) US:LP=Capitol T-2839/ST-2839*

8845 Ichabod and Me (1961) Theme (at:Pete Rugolo) US:LP=Mercury 60706* [Pete Rugolo:ST]

8846 Idol, The (1961) Score (Ernie Freeman) US:LP-PP=Irwin & O'Donnell LP-1

8847 I'm a Fan (1972) Score (Leroy Holmes) US:LP-PP=UA UAS-5574*

8848 I'm Dickens, He's Fenster (1962) Theme (Irving Szathmary) US: LP=Capitol 1869* [Nelson Riddle]

8849 Imagine That! / Score (s:Sy Miller/t:H.B. Barnum) US:LP-PP=Premore PL-280*

8850 In for a Penny (1971) Theme (J. Hunter) GB:LP=EMI 5143* [The Pandora Orchestra]

8851 In Love with an Older Woman (1984) Theme (Lee Holdridge) US:LP=Atlantic 80052-1* [Laura Branigan:ST]

8852 In Search Of . . . (1977) Score (W. Michael Lewis & Laurin Rinder) US:LP=AVI AVL-6008*

8853 In Search of the Trojan War (1985) Score (Terry Oldfield) GB:LP=BBC REB-553*

8854 Incredible Hulk, The (1978) Themes (Joe Harnell) US:SP=MCA 40953* [Joe Harnell:ST]; Theme (Joe Harnell) US:LP=RCA 1-3613* [Floyd Cramer]

8855 Inner Space (1975) Score (Sven Libaek) AU:LP=Festival 34520*

8856 Innocents Abroad (1983) Excerpts (William Perry) US:LP-PP=Trobriand TRO-1001* [William Perry:ST]

8857 Inspector Gadget (1983) Theme (Shuki Levy) US:LP-MS=Tee Vee Toons 1300 [@ST]

8858 International Detective (1959) Theme (Leroy Holmes) US:LP=RCA 2180* [Buddy Morrow]; Theme (Leroy Holmes) US:LP=Roulette 804* [uncredited]

8859 Interneige / Theme (Michel Magne) US:LP=Monument 18070* [Eddie Barclay]

8860 Invaders, The (1967) Theme (Dominic Frontiere) US:LP=GNP 2163* [Neil Norman]

8861 Irish R.M., The (1983) Score (Nick Bicat) US:LP=Release RRL-8012* + GB:LP=Ritz LP-0011*

8862 Irish Rovers, The (1976) Score (pop music) US:LP=Sandcastle SCR-1032* [The Irish Rovers:ST]

8863 Ironside (1967) Theme-A (Quincy Jones) US:SP=A&M 1323* [Quincy Jones:ST]; Theme-A (Quincy Jones) US:LP=A&M 3037* [Quincy Jones:ST]; Themes-B-C (Billy Goldenberg) US:SP=Decca 9-32487* [B.J. Baker:ST]

8864 Ishi—The Last of His Tribe (1978) Underscore + Dialog (Maurice Jarre) US:LP-PP=Ishi LP-1*

8865 It Ain't Half Hot Mum (1973) Theme (M. Perry) GB:LP=BBC 387* [@ST]

8866 It Takes a Thief (1968) Theme (Dave Grusin) US:SP=Decca 9-32413 [Dave Grusin:ST]; Theme (Dave Grusin) US:SP=Capitol 2672* [The Little Big Horns]; Theme (Dave Grusin) GB:LP=Philips 6308.087* [Chaquito & Johnny Gregory]

8867 It Was a Short Summer,

Charlie Brown (1969) Underscore + Dialog (Vince Guaraldi) US:EP = Charlie Brown 410

8868 It's a Brand New World (1976) Score (Angelo Badalamenti-aka-Andy Badale) US:LP-PP = Redbird 1001*

8869 It's a Mystery, Charlie Brown (1974) Underscore + Dialog (Vince Guaraldi) US:EP = Charlie Brown 409

8870 It's About Time (1966) Theme (Gerald Fried) US:LP = Leo 1023* [@Wade Denning]

8871 It's Flashbeagle, Charlie Brown (1984) Highlights (Ed Bogas) US: LP = Charlie Brown 2518*

8872 It's Good to Be Alive (1974) Theme (Michel Legrand) US:SP = Bell 447* [Michel Legrand:ST]; Theme (Michel Legrand) US:LP = UA 316* [Ferrante & Teicher]

8873 It's the Great Pumpkin, Charlie Brown (1966) Underscore + Dialog (Vince Guaraldi) US:LP = Charlie Brown 2604

8874 It's Your First Kiss, Charlie Brown (1977) Underscore + Dialog (Ed Bogas) US:EP = Charlie Brown 407

J

8875 Jack and Phyllis Show, The Score (Jack Spear) US:LP-PP = Darosa JP-1 [Jack and Phyllis Spear:ST]

8876 Jack and the Beanstalk (1956) Score (Jerry Livingston) US:LP = RKO Unique 111 [Studio Cast]

8877 Jack and the Beanstalk (1967) Score (James Van Heusen) US:LP = Hanna Barbera HLP-8511/HLPS-8511* + US:LP = 51 West 16101* [Gene Kelly: ST]

8878 Jack Benny Special, The (1968) Highlights + Dialog (pop music) US:LP-PP = Garrison 1116 [Jack Benny & Cast:ST]

8879 Jack Lemmon in 'S Wonderful, 'S Marvelous, 'S Gershwin *see* 'S Wonderful, 'S Marvelous, 'S Gershwin

8880 Jack Paar Show, The (1954) Theme (Jose Melis) US:LP = Seeco 462* [Jose Melis:ST]; Theme (Jose Melis) US: LP = MGM 3729* [The Metropolitan Jazz Quartet]

8881 Jackanory (1976) Theme (Richard Fiske) GB:LP = Golden Hour 547* [uncredited]

8882 Jackie Gleason Show, The (1952) Theme-A [Main Title] (Jackie Gleason) US:SP = RCA 47-6299 [Hugo Winterhalter]; Theme-A [Main Title] (Jackie Gleason) US:LP = Capitol 2796* [Jackie Gleason:ST]; Theme-B ["Where Is She Now?"] (Jackie Gleason) US: SP = Capitol 4062 [Jackie Gleason:ST]; Highlights ["Tawny"] (Jackie Gleason) US:EP = Capitol EAP1-471 [Jackie Gleason:ST]; Excerpts ["Tawny"] (Jackie Gleason) US:LP-10 = Capitol H-471 [Jackie Gleason:ST]

8883 Jackie Gleason's American Scene Magazine (1962) Themes (Jackie Gleason) US:SP = Capitol 4933 [Jackie Gleason:ST]; Theme (Jackie Gleason) US:LP = Capitol 2796* [Jackie Gleason: ST]; Score (pop music) US:LP = ABC 442/S-442* [Frank Fontaine:ST]

8884 James at 15 (1977) Theme (John F. Coley) US:LP = Motown 905* [Prime Time]

8885 James Paul McCartney (1973) Score (pop music) US:LP-BP = TMQ 72008 [Paul McCartney:ST]

8886 Jane Eyre (1970) Score (John Williams) US:LP = Capitol SW-749*

8887 Jason King (1971) Theme (Laurie Johnson) GB:LP = MFP 5272* [Geoff Love]

8888 Jazz Age, The / Theme (Ron Grainer) GB:LP = RCA 1020* [Ron Grainer:ST]

8889 Jazz on Stage (1977) Score (pop music) US:LP = JAS 4005* [Various Artists:ST]

8890 Jean Arthur Show, The (1966) Theme (Johnny Keating) US:LP = WB 1666* [Johnny Keating:ST]

8891 Jeffersons, The (1975) Theme (Jeff Barry) US:SP = Monument 45-263* [Boots Randolph]; Theme (Jeff Barry) US:LP = Monument 7627* [Boots Randolph]; Theme (Jeff Barry) US:LP = Motown 905* [Prime Time]

8892 Jennie — Lady Randolph Churchill (1975) Theme (Andre Previn) GB:LP = Red Bus 1004* [@The London

Symphony Orchestra:ST]; Theme (Andre Previn) GB:LP=EMI 2069* [Reginald Dixon]

8893 Jeopardy (1964) Theme (Merv Griffin) US:LP=TAV 4004* [Merv Griffin & Mort Lindsey:ST]

8894 Jesus of Nazareth (1977) Score (Maurice Jarre) GB:LP=Pye NSPL-28504*; Underscore + Dialog (Maurice Jarre) US:LP=RCA ABL1-4284*

8895 Jetsons, The (1962) Theme (Hoyt Curtin) US:LP-MS=Tee Vee Toons 1100 [@ST]

8896 Jewel in the Crown, The (1984) Score (George Fenton) US:LP=Chrysalis FV-41465*

8897 Jim Bowie *see* Adventures of Jim Bowie, The

8898 Jim Nabors Hour, The (1969) Score (pop music) US:LP=Columbia C-30449* [Jim Nabors:ST]

8899 Jim'll Fix It (1975) Theme (David Mindel) GB:LP=BBC 236* [@David Mindel:ST]

8900 Jimmie Rodgers Show, The (1959) Score (pop music) US:LP=Roulette R-25071/RS-25071* [Jimmie Rodgers:ST]

8901 Jimmy Durante Show, The (1954) Highlights (pop music) US:LP=Decca DL-9049/DL-79049e [Jimmy Durante:ST]

8902 Joe 90 (1968) Themes (Barry Gray) GB:LP-10=PRT DOW-3* [Barry Gray:ST]; Theme (Barry Gray) GB:SP=PRT 7P-216* [Barry Gray:ST]

8903 Joey (1956) Theme (Sammy Fain) US:78=Epic 9165 [Tony Perkins:ST]; Theme (Sammy Fain) US:SP=Decca 9-29905 [The Dream Weavers]

8904 John Brown's Body (1962) Underscore + Dialog (George Kleinsinger) US:LP-PP=B'nai B'rith XTV-87288

8905 John Denver and The Muppets—A Christmas Together (1979) Score (pop music) US:LP=RCA AFL1-3451* [John Denver & The Muppets:ST]

8906 John Denver and The Muppets—A Rocky Mountain Holiday (1983) Score (pop music) US:LP=RCA AFL1-4721* [John Denver and The Muppets:ST]

8907 Johnny Cash Show, The (1969) Score (t:Bill Walker/s:pop music) US:LP=Columbia KC-30100* [Johnny Cash:ST]

8908 Johnny Jarvis (1984) Theme (M. Shail) GB:LP=BBC 524* [@Mitch Dalton:ST]

8909 Johnny Mann's Stand Up and Cheer (1971) Score (pop music) US:LP=Epic KE-31954* [The Johnny Mann Singers:ST]

8910 Johnny Ringo (1959) Theme (Don Durant) US:SP=RCA 47-7760 [Don Durant:ST]

8911 Johnny Shiloh [Walt Disney Presents] (1963) Theme (Richard & Robert Sherman) US:SP=Buena Vista 417 [Billy Strange]; Theme (Richard & Robert Sherman) US:LP=Disneyland 3921 [@The Wellingtons]

8912 Johnny Staccato *see* Staccato

8913 Jonny Quest *see* Adventures of Jonny Quest, The

8914 Josie and the Pussycats (1970) Score (Danny Janssen) US:LP=Capitol ST-665*; Theme (Hoyt Curtin) US: LP-MS=Tee Vee Toons 1300 [@ST]

8915 Journey into Space / Theme (Van Phillips) GB:LP=BBC 324* [@Frank Weir]

8916 Judy Garland Show, The (1963) Score-A (pop music) US:LP=Capitol W-2062/DW-2062* [Judy Garland:ST]; Score-B (pop music) US:LP=Radiant 711-0101* [Judy Garland:ST]; Score-C (pop music) US:LP=Radiant 711-0102* [Judy Garland:ST]; Score-D (pop music) US:LP=Radiant 711-0103* [Judy Garland:ST]; Score-E (pop music) US:LP=Radiant 711-0105* [Judy Garland:ST]; Score-F (pop music) US: LP=Radiant 711-0106* [Judy Garland:ST]

8917 Juhyo (1984) Theme (Sadao Watanabe) US:LP=Inner City 6015* [Sadao Watanabe:ST]

8918 Juke Box Jury (1960) Theme (John Barry) GB:SP=Columbia 4414 [John Barry:ST]; Theme (John Barry) GB:LP=EMI 21 [John Barry:ST]; Theme (John Barry) GB:LP=BBC 454 [@John Barry:ST]

8919 Julia (1968) Theme (Elmer

Bernstein) US:SP = Fantasy 620 [Merl Saunders]

8920 Juliet Bravo (1980) Theme (at: Derek Goom) GB:SP = BBC 84* [Derek Goom:ST]; Theme (at:Derek Goom) GB:LP = BBC 424* [@Derek Goom:ST]

8921 June Allyson Show, The (1959) Theme (Herschel Burke Gilbert) US:LP = Dot 25421* [Herschel Burke Gilbert:ST]

8922 Junior Miss (1958) Highlights (Burton Lane) US:EP = Columbia B-2142 [Studio Cast]

8923 Just Good Friends (1983) Theme (J. Sullivan) GB:SP = Fly 1095* [Paul Nicholas:ST]; Theme (J. Sullivan) GB:LP = BBC 524* [@Paul Nicholas: ST]

8924 Just Love / Theme (Paddy Kingsland) GB:LP = BBC 93* [The BBC Radiophonic Workshop:ST]

8925 Just William (1976) Theme (Denis King) GB:LP = DJM 20522* + GB:LP = DJM 22081* [@Denis King: ST]

8926 Justice (1954) Theme ["Hard to Get"] (Jack Segal) US:SP = X 0137 [Gisele MacKenzie:ST]

K

8927 K-9 and Co. (1982) Theme (Ian Levine) GB:LP = BBC 442* [@BBC Radiophonic Workshop:ST]

8928 Kaptain Kool and the Kongs *see* Krofft Supershow, The

8929 Kaz (1978) Theme (Fred Karlin) US:LP-PP = Jenson 3011* [The Jenson Marching Band]

8930 Keep Me in Mind *see* Climax

8931 Ken Murray Show, The (1948) Theme (Ken Murray) US:SP = Capitol 1534 [Jimmy Wakely]

8932 Kenny and Dolly—A Christmas to Remember (1984) Score (e:Dolly Parton/e:pop music) US:LP = RCA ASL1-5307* [Kenny Rogers & Dolly Parton:ST]

8933 Kent State (1981) Score (Ken Lauber) US:LP = RCA ABL1-3928*

8934 Kentucky Jones (1964) Theme (Vic Mizzy) US:SP = RCA 47-8477 [Vic Mizzy:ST]

8935 Kid Power (1972) Score (Bob Summers & Perry Botkin, Jr.) US: LP = Pride PRD-0010*

8936 Kidnapped [David Balfour] (1978) Score (Vladimir Cosma) GB:LP = Decca MOR-525*

8937 Kids from C.A.P.E.R., The (1976) Score (Hegel & George) US:LP = Kirshner KS-34347* [The Kids from C.A.P.E.R.:ST]

8938 Kids from Fame, The (1982) Score (pop music) US:LP = RCA AFL1-4674* [The Kids from Fame:ST]

8939 King and Mrs. Candle, The (1955) Themes (Moose Charlap) US: SP = RCA 47-6209 [Tony Martin]

8940 King Family Show, The (1965) Score (pop music) US:LP = WB W-1601/WS-1601* [The King Family:ST]

8941 King Kong (1966) Score (Maury Laws) US:LP = Epic LN-24231/ BN-26231*

8942 Kinky (1964) Theme (John Scott) US:LP = Capitol 2527* [John Barry]

8943 Kiss Me Kate (1970) Score (stage songs:Cole Porter) US:LP-PP = CSP CMM-645/CSM-645*

8944 Kiss of Blood, The / Theme (Ray Davies) GB:LP = DJM 2023* [Ray Davies and the Button Down Brass:ST]

8945 Klondike (1960) Theme (Vic Mizzy) US:SP = 20th 222 [Hugo Montenegro & Vic Mizzy:ST]; Theme (Vic Mizzy) US:LP = Choreo 6* [Harry Betts]; Theme (Vic Mizzy) US:LP = 20th 3043* [The 20th Century Strings]

8946 Knight Rider (1983) Theme (Stu Phillips) US:LP = Bainbridge 6261* [Sounds of the Screen Orchestra]

8947 Knots Landing (1980) Theme (Jerrold Immel) US:LP = RCA 1-3613* [Floyd Cramer]; Theme (Jerrold Immel) GB:SP = BBC 87* [Frank Barber]

8948 Kojak (1973) Theme-A (Billy Goldenberg) US:SP = Bluenote 977* [Willie Bobo]; Theme-A (Billy Goldenberg) US:LP = Mercury 1-1089* [Johnny Gregory]; Theme-B (John Cacavas) US:SP = SAM 78-5009* [John Davis]; Theme-B (John Cacavas) US: LP = MCA 5380* [Warren Schatz]

8949 Kraft Television Theatre (1947) Score (Wladimir Selinsky) US: LP = RKO Unique 127 + US:LP = Golden Tone 4065/S-4065*; Theme-A [Main Title] (Norman Clautier) US: LP = RCA 1020 [Hugo Winterhalter]; Theme-B ["The Singing Idol"] (Joe Allison) US:SP = Capitol 3639 [Tommy Sands:ST]; Theme-C ["Come to Me"] (Robert Allen) US:SP = Vik 4X-0312 [Julie Wilson:ST]; Theme-D ["The Sound of Trouble"] (Robert Allen) US: SP = Columbia 4-41068 [Jill Corey]; Theme-E ["Flesh and Blood"] (Frank DeHaven) US:SP = Capitol 3723 [Tommy Sands:ST]; Theme-F ["Drummer Man"] (Joe Allison) US:SP = Epic 5-9216 [Sal Mineo:ST]

8950 Krofft Supershow, The (1976) Score ["Kaptain Kool and the Kongs"] (e:Gino Cunico/etc.) US:LP = Epic JE-35447* [Kaptain Kool and the Kongs: ST]; Underscore + Dialog ["Big Foot and Wild Boy"/"Magic Mongo"/"Wonderbug"] (Michael Melvoin/Jimmie Haskell) US:LP = Peter Pan 8221

8951 Kukla, Fran and Ollie (1950) Highlights + Dialog (Jack Fascinato) US:LP = Camden CAL-207/CAS-207e [Burr Tillstrom & Fran Allison:ST]

8952 Kung Fu (1972) Highlights + Underscore + Dialog (Jim Helms) US: LP = WB BS-2726*

L

8953 L.A. Law (1986) Highlights (Mike Post) US:LP = Polydor 422-833-985-1* [Mike Post:ST]

8954 Lads, The (1963) Theme (Trevor Peacock) US:SP = MGM 13341 [Herman's Hermits]; Theme (Trevor Peacock) US:LP = MGM 4282* + US:LP = MGM 4548* [Herman's Hermits]

8955 Lady from Philadelphia, The [See It Now] (1957) Highlights + Dialog (pop music) US:LP = RCA LM-2212 [Marian Anderson/Edward R. Murrow: ST]

8956 Lady in the Dark (1954) Score (stage songs:Kurt Weill) US:LP = RCA LM-1882

8957 Land of the Giants (1968) Theme (John Williams) US:LP = GNP 2163* [Neil Norman]

8958 Landmark / Theme [pilot] (Bernard Herrmann) US:LP = Cerberus CST-0210 [Bernard Herrmann]

8959 Laramie (1959) Theme (Cyril Mockridge) US:LP = UA 6161* [Al Caiola]; Theme (Cyril Mockridge) US: LP = Columbia 8400* [Johnny Gregory]; Theme (Cyril Mockridge) US:LP = MCA 5380* [Warren Schatz]

8960 Laredo (1965) Theme (Russell Garcia) US:LP = MCA 5380* [Warren Schatz]

8961 Larry King Show, The (1982) Theme (Chuck Mangione) US:LP = Columbia 38686* [Chuck Mangione:ST]

8962 Lassie (1954) Theme (unknown) US:LP = Golden 27 [Mitch Miller & the Sandpipers]; Theme (unknown) US:SP = 20th 181 [Roger Massenet]

8963 Last Dinosaur, The (1977) Theme (Maury Laws) JA:SP = Capitol 20311* [Nancy Wilson:ST]

8964 Last Grave at Socorro Creek, The *see* Virginian, The

8965 Last of the Summer Wine, The (1974) Theme (Ronnie Hazlehurst) GB:LP = Polydor 2384.107* + GB: LP = BBC 387* [Ronnie Hazlehurst:ST]

8966 Last Place on Earth, The (1986) Score (Trevor Jones) GB:LP = Island ISTA-8*

8966a Late Night America (1983) Theme (Joseph Lo Duca) US:SP = Volley VR-1* [Joseph Lo Duca:ST]

8967 Laugh-in *see* Rowan and Martin's Laugh-in

8968 Laverne and Shirley (1976) Theme (Charles Fox) US:SP = Private Stock 086* [Cindy Greco:ST]; Theme (Charles Fox) US:LP = Private Stock 2014* [Cindy Greco:ST]; Theme (Charles Fox) US:LP = Columbia 34312* [Ray Conniff]

8969 Law and Mr. Jones, The (1960) Theme (at:Hans J. Salter) US: LP = Dot 25421* [Herschel Burke Gilbert:ST]

8970 Law of the Plainsman (1959) Theme (Leonard Rosenman) US:LP = Dot 25421* [Herschel Burke Gilbert:ST]

8971 Lawman (1958) Theme (Jerry Livingston) US:LP = UA 6161* + US: LP = Sunset 4027* [Al Caiola]; Theme (Jerry Livingston) US:LP = Roulette 25073* [Bud Wattles]

8972 Lawrence Welk Show, The (1955) Score (pop music) US:LP = Coral CRL-57025 [Lawrence Welk & Cast: ST]; Theme (Jack Elliott) US:SP = Ranwood 915 [Lawrence Welk:ST]

8973 Leave It to Beaver (1957) Theme (Dave Kahn & Melvyn Lenard) US:LP = Tops 1661* [Richard Gleason]; Theme (Dave Kahn & Melvyn Lenard) US:LP-MS = Tee Vee Toons 1100 [@ST]

8974 Leaving (1984) Theme (Ronnie Hazlehurst) GB:SP = BBC 147* [ST]

8975 Lee Trevino's Golf for Swingers *see* Golf for Swingers

8976 Legacy for the Future (1978) Score (Toru Takemitsu) JA:LP = NHK 6001*; Theme (Toru Takemitsu) US: LP = RCA 1-4003* ["Cosmos" ST]

8977 Legend of Jesse James, The (1965) Theme (Irving Gertz) GB:LP = MFP 1405* [Geoff Love]

8978 Legend of the Black Hand, The [Alle Origini della Mafia] (1979) Score (s:Nino Rota/as:Gino Marinuzzi, Jr.) IT:LP = Dischi 6198*

8979 Lend an Ear (1956) Score (stage songs:Charles Gaynor) US:LP-MS-PP = Chrysler RR-23071

8980 Let It Be Me *see* Climax

8981 Let Me Go Lover *see* Studio One

8982 Let's Face It (1954) Excerpts (stage songs:Cole Porter) US:LP-BP = JJA 19767 [Gene Nelson & Vivian Blaine:ST]

8983 Let's Take a Trip (1955) Highlights + Dialog ["Hello World"] (William Mayer) US:LP = RCA LM-2332 [Eleanor Roosevelt:ST]

8984 Liars, The (1966) Theme (Armando Sciasscia) US:LP = Roulette 804* [uncredited]

8985 Liberace Show, The (1969) Score (pop music) US:LP = Forward STF-1017* [Liberace:ST]

8986 Liberty (1986) Score (William Goldstein) US:LP = Citadel CTD-8100*

8987 Lidsville (1971) Theme (Les Szarvas) GB:LP = Golden Hour 547* [uncredited]

8988 Lieutenant, The (1963) Theme (Jeff Alexander) US:LP = WB 1529* [Carl Brandt]; Theme (Jeff Alexander) US:LP = 20th 4105* [Lionel Newman]; Theme (Jeff Alexander) US:LP = 20th 4109* [Bill Ramal]

8989 Life and Adventures of Nicholas Nickleby, The (1982) Score (stage songs:Stephen Oliver) US:LP = DRG SBL-12583*

8990 Life and Legend of Wyatt Earp, The (1955) Theme (Harry Warren) US:SP = Cadence 1275 [Bill Hayes]; Theme (Harry Warren) US:LP = Coral 757267* [Lawrence Welk]; Theme (Harry Warren) US:LP = ABC 203* [Hugh O'Brien:ST]

8991 Life and Times of Grizzly Adams, The (1977) Score (s:Bob Summers/t:Thom Pace) GE:LP = Polydor 2374.162*; Theme (Thom Pace) US: SP = Capitol 4842* [Thom Pace:ST]

8992 Life in the Thirties [Project 20] Score (Robert Russell Bennett) US: LP-PP = RCA Custom K80P-1040

8993 Life of Leonardo da Vinci, The (1972) Score (Roman Vlad) IT:LP = Ariston 12069*

8994 Life on the Mississippi (1980) Excerpts (William Perry) US:LP-PP = Trobriand TRO-1001* [W. Perry:ST]

8995 Likely Lads, The (1973) Theme (Mike Hugg) GB:SP = BBC 10* [Highly Likely:ST]; Theme (Mike Hugg) GB:LP = BBC 188* + GB:LP = BBC 387* [@Highly Likely:ST]; Theme (Mike Hugg) GB:LP = Pickwick 50-DA-315* [Bruce Baxter]

8996 Lillie (1978) Score (as:Joseph Horowitz) GB:LP = Decca MOR-516*; Theme (Joseph Horowitz) US:LP-PP = WGBH 10* + US:LP-MS = SQN 5057-1* [@Laurie Holloway:ST]

8997 Line-Up, The [San Francisco Beat] (1960) Theme (Jerry Goldsmith) US:LP = RCA 2180* [Buddy Morrow]

8998 Lisa, Bright and Dark (1973) Score (Rod McKuen) US:LP = Stanyan 10094*

8999 Little House on the Prairie, The (1974) Theme (David Rose) US: LP = RCA 1-3052* [Henry Mancini]; Theme (David Rose) US:LP = RCA 1-

3613* [Floyd Cramer]; Theme (David Rose) US:LP = Peter Pan 8197* [The Peter Pan Orchestra & Chorus]

9000 Little Lulu (1980) Underscore + Dialog (Mark Gibbons) US:LP-PP = ZIV 1001*

9001 Little Women (1957) Score (Richard Adler) US:LP = Kapp KL-1104

9002 Lively Ones, The [The Vic Damone Show] (1962) Theme (Jack Wohl) US:LP = Liberty 7321* [Dave Pell]

9003 Liver Birds, The (1969) Theme (M. Gorman) GB:SP = Parlophone 5812 [The Scaffold:ST]; Theme (M. Gorman) GB:LP = BBC 387 [@The Scaffold:ST]

9004 Living Planet, The (1984) Score (Elizabeth Parker) GB:LP = BBC REB-496*

9005 Liza with a Z (1973) Score (pop music) US:LP = Columbia KC-31762* [Liza Minnelli:ST]

9006 Locke the Superman (1983) Score (Fukio Tsuchikata) JA:LP = Columbia CX-7084*

9007 Logan's Run (1977) Theme (Laurence Rosenthal) US:LP = MMG 705* [Geoff Love]

9008 London and Davis in New York (1985) Theme (Chuck Mangione) US:LP = Columbia 39067* [Chuck Mangione:ST]

9009 Long Search, The (1979) Theme (Carl Davis) US:LP = DRG 704* [Carl Davis:ST]

9010 Long Way Home, A (1981) Score (Ray Evans) JA:LP = Seven Seas K28P-4110*

9011 Look at Monaco, A (1963) Score (Percy Faith) US:LP = Columbia CL-2019/CS-8819e

9012 Look Stranger / Theme (Johnny Dankworth) US:LP = RCA 1-5092* [Johnny Dankworth:ST]

9013 Looking for Clancy *see* Clancy

9014 Looking Through Super Plastic Elastic Goggles at Color (1971) Score (Eddie Newmark) US:LP = Audio Fidelity AFSD-6244* [The Goggles:ST]

9015 Lord Don't Play Favorites, The (1956) Highlights (Hal Stanley & Irving Taylor) US:EP = RCA EPA-960 [Kay Starr:ST]; Themes (Hal Stanley & Irving Taylor) US:SP = RCA 47-6330 [Louis Armstrong:ST]

9016 Lord Peter Wimsey *see* Clouds of Witness

9017 Loretta Young Show, The (1953) Score (Harry Lubin) US:LP = Decca DL-4124/DL-74124*; Theme ["Reminiscing"] (Harry Lubin) US:LP = Decca 74151* [Harry Lubin:ST]

9018 Lost Empires (1986) Score (t: Derek Hilton/s:pop music) GB:LP = That's Entertainment TER-1119*

9019 Lost in Space (1965) Themes (John Williams) US:LP = GNP 2163* [Neil Norman]; Theme (John Williams) US:LP-MS = Tee Vee Toons 1100 [@ST]

9020 Lotus Eaters, The (1974) Theme (Stavros Xarchakos) GB:LP = BBC 171* [Norrie Paramor]; Theme (Stavros Xarchakos) GB:LP = EMI 2069* [Reginald Dixon]

9021 Lou Grant (1977) Themes (Patrick Williams) US:LP = PAUSA 7060* [Patrick Williams:ST]; Theme (Patrick Williams) US:SP = PCM 201* [Patrick Williams:ST]; Theme (Patrick Williams) US:LP = PCM 1001* [Patrick Williams:ST]

9022 Louisiana (1984) Score (Claude Bolling) US:LP = CBS 39353*

9023 Louisiana Purchase (1951) Excerpts (stage songs:Irving Berlin) US:LP-BP = JJA 19746 [Irene Bordoni & Victor Moore:ST]

9024 Love American Style (1969) Score (Charles Fox) US:LP = Capitol SM-11250*

9025 Love Among the Ruins (1975) Theme (John Barry) GB:LP = Polydor 2383.300* [John Barry:ST]

9026 Love Boat, The (1977) Theme (Charles Fox) US:SP = Applause 101* [Jack Jones:ST]; Theme (Charles Fox) US:LP = MGM 1-5023* [Jack Jones:ST]; Theme (Charles Fox) US:LP = Salsoul 8515* [Charo]

9027 Love for Lydia (1979) Score (as:Max Harris/t:Harry Rabinowitz) GB:LP = DJM 20514*; Theme (Harry Rabinowitz) US:LP-PP = WGBH 10* + US:LP-MS = SQN 5057-1* [@Harry Rabinowitz:ST]

9028 Love Is Not Enough (1978) Theme [pilot for "Harris and Company"] (Coleridge-Taylor Perkinson) US:LP = WB 3189* [David Sanborn & Coleridge-Taylor Perkinson:ST]

9029 Love Me to Pieces *see* Studio One

9030 Love of Life (1951) Theme (Hagood Hardy) US:LP = Capitol Custom SL-8076* [The New Christy Minstrels]; Theme (Hagood Hardy) CA: LP = Attic 1073* [Hagood Hardy:ST]

9031 Love Song of Barney Kempinski, The (1966) Theme (Murray Schisgal) US:SP = Columbia 4-43787 [Alan Arkin:ST]

9032 Love Special, The / Score (pop music) US:LP-PP = NH Records LS-100* [Nancy Harmon:ST]

9033 Love Story (1965) Theme-A (Jack Parnell) GB:LP = MFP 5272* [Geoff Love]; Theme-B (Tony Hatch) GB:LP = Pye 41029* [Tony Hatch:ST]; Theme-C (Johnny Pearson) GB:LP = Marble Arch MALP-1179* [@Sounds Orchestral]

9034 Love that Bob! *see* Bob Cummings Show, The

9035 Love Thy Neighbor (1973) Theme (Pete Rugolo) US:SP = MGM 14571 [Solomon Burke:ST]

9035a Loving (1982) Theme (Michael Karp) US:LP = MMR 2200* [Bartholomew & Joyce]

9036 Lucy Show, The (1962) Theme (Wilbur Hatch) US:LP = Capitol 1869* [Nelson Riddle]

9037 Lyndon Johnson's Texas [LBJ's Texas] (1966) Theme (Glenn Paxton) US:LP = RCA 3008* [Arthur Fiedler and the Boston Pops]; Theme (Glenn Paxton) US:SP = UA 50070 [Al Caiola]

9038 Lytton's Diary (1985) Theme (Rick Wakeman) GB:SP = President 2*

M

9039 M Squad (1957) Score (e: Benny Carter/e:John Williams/e:Stanley Wilson/t:Count Basie) US:LP = RCA LPM-2062/LSP-2062*

9040 MacAhans, The (1976) Theme [pilot for "How the West Was Won"] (Jerrold Immel) US:LP-PP = Jenson 3010* [The Jenson Concert Band]

9041 McCloud (1970) Theme-A [pilot "Who Killed Miss U.S.A." aka "Portrait of a Dead Girl"] (David Shire) US:LP = Impress 1614* [Dennis Weaver: ST]; Theme-A [pilot "Who Killed Miss U.S.A." aka "Portrait of a Dead Girl"] (David Shire) US:LP = Mercury 1-1089* [Johnny Gregory]; Theme-B [Main Title #2] (Glen Larson) GB:LP-MS = Pickwick 50-DA-315* [Bruce Baxter]; Theme-C ["Ain't That Just the Way"] (Stu Phillips) US:SP = Playboy 6056* [Barbi Benton & Stu Phillips:ST]; Theme-D ["All It Would Have Taken"] (Stu Phillips) US:LP = MCA 5380* [Warren Schatz]

9042 McHale's Navy (1962) Theme (Axel Stordhal) US:LP = Capitol 1869* [Nelson Riddle]; Theme (Axel Stordhal) US:LP = MCA 5380* [Warren Schatz]; Theme (Axel Stordhal) US:LP-MS = Tee Vee Toons 1100 [@ST]

9043 MacKenzie (1980) Theme (Anthony Isaac) US:LP-MS = BBC 2-22000* [@Anthony Isaac:ST]; Theme (Anthony Isaac) GB:SP = BBC 82* [Anthony Isaac: ST]; Theme (Anthony Isaac) GB:LP = BBC 424* [@Anthony Isaac:ST]

9044 McMillan and Wife *see* Once Upon a Dead Man

9045 Magic Horn, The (1956) Score (pop music) US:LP = RCA LPM-1332 [Ruby Braff:ST]

9046 Magic Mongo *see* Krofft Supershow, The

9047 Magic of the Dance (1980) Score (classical music) US:LP = BBC 22363*

9048 Magic Roundabout, The Underscore + Dialog (Alain Legrand) GB:LP = BBC REC-243*; Theme (Alain Legrand) GB:LP = BBC 214* [@ST]

9049 Magical Mystery Tour, The (1967) Highlights (John Lennon & Paul McCartney) US:LP = Capitol MAL-2835/SMAL-2835* [The Beatles:ST]

9050 Magician, The (1973) Theme (Patrick Williams) US:SP = Capitol 3940* [Patrick Williams:ST]; Theme (Patrick Williams) US:SP = 20th 2071* [Gordon & Osborne Orchestra]; Theme (Patrick Williams) GB:LP = Philips 6382.103* [Ray Davies and the Button Down Brass]

9051 Magilla Gorilla Show, The (1964) Theme (Hoyt Curtin) US:LP-MS = Tee Vee Toons 1100 [@ST]

9052 Magnavox Presents Frank Sinatra (1973) Score (pop music) US:LP-PP = Reprise PRO-578* [Frank Sinatra & Cast:ST]

9053 Magnum P.I. (1980) Theme (Mike Post & Pete Carpenter) US:SP = Elektra 47400* [Mike Post:ST]; Theme (Mike Post & Pete Carpenter) US:LP = Elektra 1-60028* [Mike Post:ST]; Theme (Mike Post & Pete Carpenter) US:LP = MCA 5380* [Warren Schatz]

9054 Magpie / Theme (Spencer Davis) GB:LP = Decca 217* [@The Murgatroyd Band]

9055 Maigret [Inspector Maigret] (1958) Score (Ron Grainer) GB:LP = Ace of Clubs 1135; Excerpts (Ron Grainer) GB:LP = RCA CAS-1020* [Ron Grainer:ST]; Themes (Ron Grainer) US:SP = WB 5176 [Ron Grainer:ST]

9056 Main Event, The (1974) Score (pop music) US:LP = Reprise RS-2207* [Frank Sinatra:ST]

9057 Major Adams—Trailmaster (1963) Theme [syndicated "Wagon Train"] (Stanley Wilson) US:LP = Decca 74481* [Stanley Wilson:ST]

9058 Make Me Laugh (1979) Theme (Artie Butler) US:SP = Lukehil 45793* [Artie Butler:ST]

9059 Make Room for Daddy [The Danny Thomas Show] (1953) Score (pop music) US:LP-PP = Columbia 60818/9 [Danny Thomas & Earle Hagen:ST]

9060 Makin' It (1978) Scores (Freddie Perren) US:LP-MS = RSO PRO-1007*; Themes (Freddie Perren) US:SP = RSO 916* [David Naughton:ST]

9061 Making of the President 1960, The (1963) Underscore + Dialog (Elmer Bernstein) US:LP-MS = UA UX-9/UXS-9*

9062 Malice Aforethought (1981) Theme (Ron Grainer) US:LP = DRG 15018* [Ron Grainer:ST]

9063 Mama [I Remember Mama] (1949) Theme (Joe Darion) US:LP = RCA 1020 [Hugo Winterhalter]

9064 Man Alive (1978) Theme (Tony Hatch) GB:SP = Pye 628* [Tony Hatch:ST]; Theme (Tony Hatch) GB:LP = Pye 41029* [Tony Hatch:ST]; Theme (Tony Hatch) GB:LP = BBC 391* [@Tony Hatch:ST]

9065 Man and the Challenge, The (1959) Theme (Warren Barker) US:SP = WB 5113 [Warren Barker:ST]

9066 Man Called Ironside,The *see* Ironside

9067 Man from Interpol, The (1960) Score (Tony Crombie) US:LP = Top Rank TR-327/RS-327*

9068 Man from U.N.C.L.E., The (1964) Score-A (e:Jerry Goldsmith/e:Walter Scharf/e:Lalo Schifrin/e:Morton Stevens) US:LP = RCA LPM-3475/LSP-3475* [Hugo Montenegro]; Score-B (e:Robert Drasnin/e:Gerald Fried) US:LP = RCA LPM-3574/LSP-3574* [Hugo Montenegro]; Themes (Lalo Schifrin) US:LP = Verve 6-8624* [Lalo Schifrin:ST]

9069 Man in a Suitcase (1968) Theme (Ron Grainer) GB:LP = EMI TWO-391* [Alan Hawkshaw]

9070 Man in the Iron Mask (1977) Theme (Allyn Ferguson) GB:LP = RCA 25043* [Vic Lewis]

9071 Man in the News / Theme (Ron Grainer) GB:LP = EMI 5143* [@The London Symphony]

9072 Man of Mystery (1960) Theme (Michael Carr) US:LP = UA 6435* [Al Caiola]; Theme (Michael Carr) GB:SP = Columbia 10213 [The Shadows]

9073 Man of Our Times, A (1968) Theme (James Clarke) GB:LP = Fontana 966* [James Clarke:ST]

9074 Man Outside, The / Theme (Dudley Simpson) GB:LP = Decca 2163* [Ike Isaacs]

9075 Mancini Generation, The (1974) Score (t:Henry Mancini/s:pop music) US:LP = RCA LSP-4689* [Henry Mancini:ST]

9076 Manhunt (1951) Theme (Robert Cobert) US:SP = Roulette 4328 [Richard Maltby]

9077 Mannix (1967) Score (s:Lalo Schifrin/t:Richard Hazard/t:Shorty Rogers) US:LP = Paramount PAS-5004*

9078 Man's World, A *see* Studio One

9079 Many Loves of Dobie Gillis,

The (1959) Themes (Lionel Newman/ Earle Hagen) US:SP = Decca 9-31066 [Lionel Newman:ST]; Theme (Lionel Newman) US:LP = Mercury 60706* [Pete Rugolo]

9080 Marco Polo (1982) Score (Ennio Morricone) US:LP = Arista AL-8304*

9081 Marcus Welby, M.D. (1969) Theme (Leonard Rosenman) US:SP = Ranwood 872 [Charles Randolph Grean]; Theme (Leonard Rosenman) US:LP = Ranwood 8075* [Charles Randolph Grean]; Theme (Leonard Rosenman) US:LP = 5380* [Warren Schatz]

9082 Marie Curie (1977) Excerpts (Carl Davis) US:LP = DRG MRS-704* [Carl Davis:ST]

9083 Mark Twain's America [Project 20] Score (Robert Russell Bennett) US:LP-PP = RCA Custom LBOP-4404

9084 Markham (1959) Theme (Stanley Wilson) US:SP = Capitol 4244 [Nelson Riddle]; Theme (Stanley Wilson) US:LP = RCA 2180* [Buddy Morrow]; Theme (Stanley Wilson) US:LP = Decca 74481* [Stanley Wilson:ST]

9085 Marlo Thomas and Friends In ... Free to Be You and Me *see* Free to Be You and Me

9086 Marshal Dillon *see* Gunsmoke

9087 Martin Kane—Private Eye (1950) Theme (Charles Paul) US:78 = Capitol 2609 [Nelson Riddle]; Theme (Charles Paul) US:EP = RCA 555 [Al Caiola]

9088 Mary Hartman, Mary Hartman (1976) Highlights (Mary Kay Place) US:LP = Columbia PC-34353* [Mary Kay Place:ST]; Theme (B. White) US:SP = Phantom 10709* [The Deadly Nightshade]; Theme (B. White) US:LP = Pickwick 3566* [The Birchwood Pops]

9089 Mary, Mungo and Midge (1973) Underscore + Dialog (Johnny Pearson) GB:LP = BBC REC-265*

9090 Mary Tyler Moore Show, The (1970) Theme (Sonny Curtis) US:SP = Ovation 1006* [Sonny Curtis:ST]; Theme (Sonny Curtis) US:LP = Elektra 283* [Sonny Curtis:ST]; Theme (Sonny Curtis) US:LP = Columbia 34312* [Ray Conniff]

9091 Masada (1980) Score (Jerry Goldsmith) US:LP = MCA 5168*

9092 Master of the Game (1984) Score (Allyn Ferguson) GB:LP = BBC REB-521*

9093 Mastermind (1970) Theme (Neil Richardson) GB:LP = BBC 365* [@Neil Richardson:ST]

9094 Match of the Day (1964) Theme (Mike Stoller) GB:SP = Pye 7N-25534 [Mike Vickers]; Theme (Mike Stoller) GB:LP = BBC 454* [@Mike Vickers]; Theme (Mike Stoller) GB: LP = Decca 333* [Ray Martin]

9095 Matinee Theatre (1955) Theme (E. Truman) US:SP = Capitol 3717 [Nelson Riddle]

9096 Matt Lincoln *see* Dial Hot Line

9097 Maude (1972) Theme (Dave Grusin) US:LP = Motown 905* [Prime Time]

9098 Maverick (1957) Theme (David Buttolph) US:SP = WB 5011 [Tommy Oliver]; Theme (David Buttolph) US:LP = Coral 757267* [Lawrence Welk]; Theme (David Buttolph) US:LP = UA 6161* + US:LP = Sunset 4027* [Al Caiola]

9099 Maya (1967) Score (Hans J. Salter) US:LP = Citadel CT-6017; Underscore + Dialog ["Blood of the Tiger"] (Hans J. Salter) US:LP = Leo CH-1044

9100 Maybury (1981) Theme (Daryl Runswick) GB:SP = BBC 89* [Daryl Runswick:ST]; Theme (Daryl Runswick) GB:LP = BBC 424* [@Daryl Runswick: ST]

9101 Mayor of Casterbridge, The (1979) Themes (Carl Davis) US:LP = DRG 704* [Carl Davis:ST]

9102 Medic (1954) Theme-A [Main Title] (Victor Young) US:SP = Decca 9-29433 [Victor Young:ST]; Theme-A [Main Title] (Victor Young) US:LP = Decca 8285 + US:LP = Decca 8798 [Victor Young:ST]; Theme-B ["Never Come Sunday"] (Victor Young) US:SP = Decca 9-29968 [Victor Young:ST]; Theme-B ["Never Come Sunday"] (Victor Young) US:LP = Decca 8350 [Victor Young:ST]

9103 Medical Center (1969) Theme (Lalo Schifrin) US:SP = MGM 14180

[Lalo Schifrin:ST]; Theme (Lalo Schifrin) US:LP = MGM 4742* [Lalo Schifrin:ST]

9104 Meet Mr. Callaghan (1956) Theme (Eric Spear) US:SP = Columbia 4-39851 [Mitch Miller]; Theme (Eric Spear) US:SP = London 45-1248 [Harry Grove]; Theme (Eric Spear) US:LP = MGM 3731* [The Metropolitan Jazz Quartet]

9105 Meet Mr. Lincoln [Project 20] Score (Robert Russell Bennett) US:LP-PP = RCA Custom K80P-7409

9106 Melina's Greece / Score (Stavros Xarchakos) GR:LP = Columbia 33-X-14

9107 Melody Ranch (1964) Score (pop music) US:LP-PP = Melody Ranch MR-101 [Gene Autry & Cast:ST]

9108 Men, The (1972) Theme (Isaac Hayes) US:SP = Enterprise 9058* [Isaac Hayes:ST]; Theme (Isaac Hayes) US: LP = Stax 8515* [Isaac Hayes:ST]

9109 Men from Shiloh, The (1970) Theme (David Shire) US:SP = Kapp 2116 [Tim Morgon]; Theme (David Shire) US: LP = Decca 75240* [The Midas Touch]

9110 Men into Space (1959) Theme (David Rose) US:LP = RCA 2180* [Buddy Morrow]

9111 Merv Griffin Show, The (1962) Theme [Main Title] (Merv Griffin) US: LP = MGM 4326* [Merv Griffin:ST]; Score ["The 1965 Christmas Show"] (pop music) US:LP = MGM E-4401/SE-4401* [Merv Griffin & David Soul & Cast:ST]

9112 Metro News, Metro News (1976) Theme (Rod McKuen) US:SP = Stanyan 250* [Rod McKuen:ST]

9113 Miami Vice (1984) Score (e: Jan Hammer/e:various) US:LP = MCA 6150*

9114 Michael Shayne (1960) Theme (Leith Stevens) US:LP = Dot 25421* [Herschel Burke Gilbert:ST]

9115 Michael Strogoff (1975) Score (Vladimir Cosma) GB:LP = Cube 30*; Theme (Vladimir Cosma) US:LP = Peters 1023* [Roberto Delgado]

9116 Mickey Mouse Club, The (1955) Score-A [Clubhouse Songs] (Jimmie Dodd) US:LP = Disneyland 1362 + US:LP = Mickey Mouse 12; Score-B [Clubhouse Songs] (e:Jimmie Dodd/e: George Bruns/e:Franklyn Marks/etc.) US:LP = Disneyland 3815 + US:LP = Mickey Mouse 14; Score-C ["Annette"/"Boys of the Western Sea"/ "Corky and White Shadow"/"The Hardy Boys"/"Spin and Marty"/"What I Want to Be"] (e:Paul Smith/t:George Bruns/t: William Lava/t:Stan Jones/t:Buddy Baker) US:LP = Disneyland 1229 + US:LP = Mickey Mouse 24

9117 Mickie Finn's (1966) Score (t:Fred Finn/s:pop music) US:LP = Dunhill 50013/S-50013* [Mickie & Fred Finn:ST]

9118 Midweek / Theme (John Scott) GB:LP = Polydor 2460.188* [@ John Scott:ST]; Theme (John Scott) GB: LP = MFP 50091 [Geoff Love]; Theme (John Scott) GB:LP = Pye 41029* [Tony Hatch]

9119 Mighty Continent, The (1975) Theme (Herbert Chappell) GB:SP = BBC 21* [Band of H.M. Welsh Guards]; Theme (Herbert Chappell) GB:LP = BBC 188* [@Band of H.M. Welsh Guards]

9120 Mighty Hercules, The (1960) Highlights + Underscore + Dialog (Winston Sharples) US:LP = Golden LP-108

9121 Mikado, The (1960) Score (stage songs:Gilbert & Sullivan) US: LP = Columbia OL-5480/OS-2022* + US:LP = CSP AOL-5480

9122 Mike Douglas Show, The (1965) Score (pop music) US:LP = Epic LN-24205/BN-26205* [Mike Douglas: ST]

9123 Mike Hammer (1958) Score (Dave Kahn & Melvyn Lenard) US: LP = RCA LPM-2140/LSP-2140* [Skip Martin]

9124 Milton Berle Show, The (1955) Excerpts (pop music) US:LP-MS = RCA CPM6-5172 [Elvis Presley: ST]

9125 Miracle, The / Score (as: David Rose) US:LP = Dino DP-3001 [Dino & David Rose:ST]

9126 Miracle on 34th Street, The (1959) Theme-A (Robert Ascher) US: SP = Columbia 4-41532 [Spencer Ross]; Theme-B (Robert Ascher) US:LP = Columbia 1525 [Spencer Ross]

9127 Misadventures of Sheriff Lobo, The (1979) Theme (Glen Larson) US:LP = MCA 5380* [Warren Schatz]

9128 Miss Marple (1985) Theme (Ken Howard & Alan Blakley) GB: LP = BBC 508* [@ST]

9129 Mission: Impossible (1966) Score-A (Lalo Schifrin) US:LP = Dot DLP-3831/DLP-25831*; Score-B (s:Lalo Schifrin/t:Richard Hazard/t:Shorty Rogers) US:LP = Paramount PAS-5002*

9130 Mister Broadway (1957) Score (pop songs:George M. Cohan) US:LP = RCA LPM-1520 [Mickey Rooney:ST]

9131 Mr. Broadway (1964) Score (Dave Brubeck) US:LP = Columbia CL-2275/CS-9075* [Dave Brubeck:ST]; Theme ["Toki's Theme"] (Dave Brubeck) US:SP = Columbia 4-43091 [Dave Brubeck:ST]

9132 Mr. Ed (1961) Theme + Underscore + Dialog (t:Jay Livingston & Ray Evans/u:Dave Kahn & Raoul Kraushaar) US:LP = Colpix CP-209; Theme (Jay Livingston & Ray Evans) US:LP-MS = Tee Vee Toons 1100 [@ST]

9133 Mr. I. Magination (1950) Highlights + Dialog (Ray Carter) US: LP = Musicor MM-5002 [Paul Tripp:ST]

9134 Mr. Lucky (1959) Score (Henry Mancini) US:LP = RCA LPM-2198/LSP-2198*

9135 Mr. Magoo (1963) Underscore + Dialog (Shorty Rogers) US:LP = Wonderland 318

9136 Mr. Men / Score (Joe Campbell & Roger Hargreaves) GB:LP = BBC REC-345*; Theme (Joe Campbell & Roger Hargreaves) US:SP = Vanguard 35200* [Arthur Lowe & Mr. Men]

9137 Mr. Novak (1963) Themes-A (Lyn Murray) US:LP = MGM E-4222/ SE-4222* [Nick Venet]; Themes-B ["The Faculty Follies"] (Jim Stevens) US:SP = MGM 13319 [Vince Howard]

9138 Mr. Peepers (1952) Theme (Bernard Green) US:SP = Coral 9-61058 [Tex Beneke]; Theme (Bernard Green) US:LP = Decca 8422 [Jack Pleis]; Theme (Bernard Green) US:LP = Barbary Coast 33015* [Bernard Green:ST]

9139 Mr. Rogers' Neighborhood (1967) Score-A (Fred Rogers) US:LP = Columbia CC-24516*; Score-B (Fred Rogers) US:LP = Columbia CC-24517*; Score-C (Fred Rogers) US:LP = Columbia CC-24518*; Score-D (Fred Rogers) US:LP = Columbia CC-24519*; Score-E (Fred Rogers) US:LP = Columbia CC-24520*

9140 Mr. Rose (1967) Theme (Mark Snow) GB:LP = EMI TWO-175* [Brian Fahey]

9141 Mrs. G Goes to College *see* Gertrude Berg Show, The

9142 Mistral's Daughter (1984) Score (Vladimir Cosma) US:LP = CBS/ Carrere SZ-39902*

9143 Mitzi Zings into Spring (1977) Highlights (pop music) US:LP-PP = Armstrong ICPR-3-77 [Mitzi Gaynor: ST]

9144 Mixed Blessings (1978) Theme (Peter Davidson) GB:LP = DJM 22081* [@Chris Blake]

9145 Mod Squad, The (1968) Theme-A (Shorty Rogers) US:SP = Capitol 2633* [The Modernaires]; Theme-B (Earle Hagen) US:LP = Avalanche 058* [Al Caiola]; Theme-B (Earle Hagen) US: LP-MS = Tee Vee Toons 1100 [@ST]

9146 Modern Romances (1954) Theme-A ["I Dreamed"] (Charles Randolph Grean) US:SP = Bally 7-1020 [Betty Johnson:ST]; Theme-B ["Talkin' to the Blues"] (Jim Lowe) US:SP = Dot 15569 [Jim Lowe:ST]

9147 Mole and Lollipop / Theme (M. Perry) GB:LP = Golden Hour 547* [uncredited]

9148 Moment of Fear, The (1960) Theme (Vic Mizzy) US:LP = Choreo 6* [Harry Betts]

9149 Moneychangers, The (1976) Theme (Henry Mancini) US:LP = RCA 1-2290* [Henry Mancini:ST]

9150 Monitor / Theme (Dag Wiren) GB:LP = EMI 5028* [Ron Goodwin]; Theme (Dag Wiren) GB:LP = BBC 454 [@Stig Westerberg]

9151 Monkees, The (1966) Score (t: Tommy Boyce & Bobby Hart/e:The Monkees/etc.) US:LP = Colgems COM-101/COS-101* [The Monkees:ST]

9152 Monkey (1979) Theme (Narahashi Takekawa) GB:SP = BBC 66* [Godiego:ST]; Theme (Narahashi

Takekawa) GB:LP = BBC 486* [@ Godiego:ST]

9153 Monty Nash (1972) Theme (Michael Lloyd) US:SP = Quad 112* [Good Stuff:ST]

9154 Monty Python's Flying Circus (1969) Underscore + Dialog (stock music) US:LP = Pye 12116

9155 Moonbase 3 / Theme (Dudley Simpson) GB:SP = BBC 13* [BBC Radiophonic Workshop:ST]; Theme (Dudley Simpson) GB:LP = BBC 188* + GB: LP = BBC 214* + GB:LP = BBC 324* [@BBC Radiophonic Workshop:ST]

9156 Mooncussers, The [Walt Disney Presents] (1962) Theme (Richard & Robert Sherman) US:SP = Buena Vista 406 [Billy Strange]

9157 Moonlighting (1986) Score (t: Lee Holdridge/s:pop music) US:LP = MCA 6214*

9158 Morecambe and Wise / Score (pop music) GB:LP = EMI SRS-5066* [Morecambe and Wise:ST]

9159 Mork and Mindy (1978) Theme (Perry Botkin, Jr.) US:SP = Ariola 7767* [Cake and Perry Botkin, Jr.:ST]

9160 Moses, the Lawgiver (1975) Score (Ennio Morricone) US:LP = RCA TBL1-1106*

9161 Most Wanted (1976) Theme (Lalo Schifrin) US:LP = CTI 7-5003* [Lalo Schifrin:ST]; Theme (Lalo Schifrin) GB:SP = Polydor 2015* [Lalo Schifrin:ST]

9162 Mountbatten – The Last Victory (1985) Score (John Scott) US:LP = Varese STV-81273*

9163 Mouse Factory, The (1972) Score (film songs) US:LP = Disneyland 1342

9164 Mousercise (1983) Score (various) US:LP = Disneyland 62516*

9165 Movie Macabre [Elvira's Movie Macabre] (1980) Themes (Mark Pierson) US:SP-12 = Rhino 401* [Elvira/ Mark Pierson:ST]; Theme (Mark Pierson) US:LP = Rhino 810* [Elvira & Mark Pierson:ST]

9166 Movin' On (1974) Theme (Merle Haggard) US:SP = Capitol 4085* [Merle Haggard:ST]; Theme (Merle Haggard) US:LP = Capitol 11365* [Merle Haggard:ST]

9167 Movin' with Nancy (1967) Score (pop music) US:LP = Reprise R-6277/RS-6277* [Nancy Sinatra & Cast: ST]

9168 Multiplication Rock (1973) Score (Bob Dorough) US:LP = Capitol SJA-11174*

9169 Munsters, The (1964) Theme (Jack Marshall) US:SP = Capitol 5288 [Jack Marshall:ST]; Theme (Jack Marshall) US:LP = Golden 139 [Jack Marshall & TV Cast]; Theme (Jack Marshall) US:LP-MS = Tee Vee Toons 1100 [@ST]

9169a Muppet Babies (1985) Score (s:Alan O'Day/t:Rob Walsh) US:LP = Columbia PC-40772*

9170 Muppet Musicians of Bremen, The (1975) Highlights + Underscore + Dialog (Jack Elliott) US:LP = Columbia CC-24521*

9171 Muppet Show, The (1977) Score-A (t:Sam Pottle/s:pop music) US:LP = Arista AB-4152*; Score-B (t: Sam Pottle/e:Derek Scott/e:pop music) US:LP = Arista AB-4192*

9172 Murder She Wrote (1984) Theme (John Addison) GB:LP = MFP 5768* [The Power Pack Orchestra]

9173 Music Bingo (1958) Score (pop music) US:LP = Golden Crest CR-3052 [Johnny Gilbert:ST]

9174 Music from Schubert Alley (1959) Score (pop music) US:LP-PP = Sinclair Paints OSS-2250* [Andy Williams & Cast:ST]

9175 Music Night [Andre Previn's Music Night] [Previn and the Pittsburgh] Theme (Andre Previn) GB:LP = EMI 3131* [Andre Previn:ST]

9176 My Favorite Martian (1963) Theme (George Greeley) US:LP = WB 1529* [Carl Brandt]

9177 My Little Corner of the World (1980) Highlights (pop music) US:EP-PP = ABM 1-413* [Anita Bryant:ST]

9178 My Mother the Car (1965) Theme (Paul Hampton) US:SP = Columbia 4-43585 [Jerry Van Dyke:ST]; Theme (Paul Hampton) US:LP = Reprise 6188* [Sammy Davis, Jr.]

9179 My Name Is Barbra (1965) Score-A (pop music) US:LP = Columbia CL-2336/CS-9136* [Barbra Streisand:

ST]; Score-B (pop music) US:LP = Columbia CL-2409/CS-9209* [Barbra Streisand:ST]

9180 My Partner, The Ghost [Randall and Hopkirk] (1973) Theme (Edwin Astley) FR:LP = EMI 2C126.52664* [Harry Stoneham]

9181 My Seventeenth Summer Themes (Paul Baillargeon) US:LP-PP = Blue Marble Company BMC-1001* [Paul Baillargeon:ST]

9182 My Sweet Charlie (1970) Theme (Gil Melle) US:LP = Jazz Chronicles 702* [Gil Melle:ST]

9183 My Three Sons (1960) Theme (Frank DeVol) US:SP = Dot 16198 [Lawrence Welk]; Theme (Frank DeVol) US: LP = Mercury 60706* [Pete Rugolo]; Theme (Frank DeVol) US:LP = ABC 513* [Frank DeVol:ST]

9184 Mysterious Stranger, The (1982) Excerpts (William Perry) US:LP-PP = Trobriand TRO-1001* [William Perry:ST]

9185 Mystery Movie *see* NBC Mystery Movie

N

9186 NBC Mystery Movie (1971) Theme (Henry Mancini) US:SP = RCA 74-0575* [Henry Mancini:ST]; Theme (Henry Mancini) US:LP = RCA 4630* + US:LP = RCA 1-3347* [Henry Mancini:ST]; Theme (Henry Mancini) US: LP = Columbia 34312* [Ray Conniff]

9187 NBC Nightly News / Theme-A (Henry Mancini) US:LP = RCA 1-3052* [Henry Mancini:ST]; Theme-B (John Williams) US:LP = Philips 420-178-1* [John Williams:ST]

9188 NBC's Best Sellers (1976) Theme (Elmer Bernstein) US:LP = Ranwood 8168* [The Enchanted Piano]; Theme (Elmer Bernstein) GB:LP = DJM 20522* [@Denis King]

9189 N.Y.P.D. (1967) Theme (Charles Gross) US:SP = Prestige 455 [Johnny Smith]; Theme (Charles Gross) US:LP = Prestige 7549* [Johnny Smith]

9190 Naked City (1958) Highlights + Underscore + Dialog (George Duning) US:LP = Colpix CP-505/SCP-505*; Theme [Main Title #2] (Billy May) US: SP = Cameo 261 [Maynard Ferguson]; Theme [Main Title #2] (Billy May) US: LP = Mercury 60706* [Pete Rugolo]; Theme [Main Title #3] (Nelson Riddle) US:LP = Capitol 1869* [Nelson Riddle: ST]

9191 Naked Civil Servant, The (1975) Theme (Carl Davis) GB:SP = State 85* [Carl Davis:ST]

9192 Name of the Game, The (1968) Theme (Dave Grusin) US:SP = Decca 9-32413 [Dave Grusin:ST]; Theme (Dave Grusin) US:SP = UNI 55121* [Derry O'Leary]; Theme (Dave Grusin) GB:LP = Philips 6308.087* [Chaquito & Johnny Gregory]

9193 Name That Tune (1953) Score (pop music) US:LP = RKO Unique ULP-145 [George DeWill & Harry Salter:ST]

9194 Nancy Astor (1982) Theme (Stanley Myers) GB:SP = BBC 110* [Stanley Myers:ST]

9195 Nanny (1981) Theme (Grant Hossack) GB:LP = BBC 424* [@Grant Hossack:ST]

9196 Nat King Cole Show, The (1957) Score (pop music) US:LP-BP = Sandy Hook SH-2054 [Nat King Cole & Cast:ST]

9197 National Velvet (1960) Theme (Robert Armbruster) US:SP = Dolton 56 [Hank Levine]; Theme (Robert Armbruster) US:LP = Choreo 6* [Harry Betts]

9198 Nationwide / Theme (John Scott) GB:LP = Polydor 2460.188* + GB:LP = BBC 454* [@John Scott:ST]; Theme (John Scott) GB:LP = MFP 50091* + GB:LP=EMI 168* [Geoff Love]

9199 Navy Log (1955) Theme (Fred Steiner) US:LP = Tops 1661* [Richard Gleason]

9200 New Adventures of Pinocchio, The (1961) Score (Eddie Thomas) US:LP-PP = FTP MLP-7002

9201 New Adventures of Wonder Woman, The *see* New, Original Wonder Woman, The

9202 New Alice in Wonderland, The (1966) Highlights + Dialog (Charles Strouse) US:LP = Hanna Barbera HLP-2051/HLPS-2051* [Bill Dana & Cast:ST]

9203 New Avengers, The (1978) Excerpts (Laurie Johnson) US:LP=Starlog/Varese ASV-95003* [Laurie Johnson:ST]; Underscore + Dialog ["Eagle's Nest"] (Laurie Johnson) GB:EP=EMI 2562*

9204 New Faces (1973) Theme (Tony Macaulay) GB:LP=Pye 41029* [Tony Hatch]

9205 New Mickey Mouse Club, The (1976) Score (Marc Ray & Peter Martin) US:LP=Disneyland 2501*

9206 New Odd Couple, The (1982) Themes (Dan Foliart & Howard Pearl) US:LP=Riza 85-105* [Afterglow:ST]

9207 New, Original Wonder Woman, The (1975) Theme [pilot for "Wonder Woman"] (Charles Fox) US:SP=Shady Brook 033* [New World Symphony & Charles Fox:ST]; Theme [pilot for "Wonder Woman"] (Charles Fox) US:LP=Roadshow 1-3390* [The Wonderland Band]; Theme [pilot for "Wonder Woman"] (Charles Fox) GB:LP=MFP 50439* [Geoff Love]

9208 New Scotland Yard / Theme (Max Harris) GB:LP=EMI 5143* [The Pandora Orchestra]

9209-10 New Treasure Hunt, The (1973) Theme (Chuck Barris) US:LP=Friends 1001* [The Chuck Barris Orchestra:ST]

9211 New Zoo Revue, The (1973) Score (Douglas Momary) US:LP=Disneyland STER-1344*

9212 Newcomers, The (1964) Theme (John Barry) US:LP=Capitol 2527* [John Barry:ST]

9213 Newlywed Game, The (1966) Theme (Chuck Barris) US:LP=Decca 74821* [Trumpets Ole]

9214 News at Ten / Theme (Johnny Pearson) GB:LP=Decca 333* [Ray Martin]

9215 Night Court (1984) Theme (Jack Elliott) US:LP-MS-PP=Jenson 7600* [The Jenson Marching Band]

9216 Night Gallery (1970) Theme-A [Main Title] (Gil Melle) US:LP=MCA 5380* [Warren Schatz]; Theme-B ["The Tune in Dan's Cafe"] (Hal Mooney) US:SP=Decca 9-32989* [Jerry Wallace]; Theme-B ["The Tune in Dan's Cafe"] (Hal Mooney) US:LP=Decca 75349* [Jerry Wallace]

9217 Night Stalker, The (1974) Theme (Gil Melle) US:LP=MCA 5380* [Warren Schatz]

9218 Nine Lives of Elfego Baca, The [Walt Disney Presents] (1958) Theme (Richard Dehr) US:SP=Kapp 242 [Bill Hayes]; Theme (Richard Dehr) US:LP=Disneyland 3921 [@The Wellingtons]

9219 Nine to Five (1982) Themes (Dan Foliart & Howard Pearl) US:LP=Riza 85-105* [Afterglow:ST]

9220 Ninotchka (1960) Themes (Richard Gordon) US:SP=Columbia 4-41666 [Alevanno]

9221 Ninth Day, The *see* Playhouse 90

9222 No—Honestly! (1975) Theme (Lynsey DePaul) GB:LP-MS=Pickwick 50-DA-315* [Bruce Baxter]

9223 No Hiding Place (1960) Theme (Laurie Johnson) GB:LP=EMI 2179* [The G.U.S. Military Band]; Theme (Laurie Johnson) GB:SP=HMV 45-713 [Ken Mackintosh]

9224 No Man Can Tame Me (1959) Highlights (Jay Livingston & Ray Evans) US:LP-PP=Empire EBC-597487

9225 Noah and the Flood *see* Flood, The

9226 North and South (1985) Highlights (Bill Conti) US:LP=Varese 704.310*

9227 Not So Long Ago [Project 20] Score (Robert Russell Bennett) US:LP-PP=RCA Custom L80P-0721; Underscore + Dialog (Robert Russell Bennett) US:LP=RCA LOC-1055/LSO-1055 [Bob Hope:ST]

9228 Not the Nine O'Clock News (1979) Highlights + Dialog (e:Howard Goodall & Richard Curtis/t:Nic Rowley) GB:LP=BBC REB-400*; Highlights + Dialog (e:Howard Goodall & Richard Curtis/t:Nic Rowley) GB:LP=BBC REB-421*; Theme (Nic Rowley) GB:LP=BBC 424* [@Nic Rowley:ST]

O

9229 Ocean Quest [Oceanscape] (1985) Score (William Goldstein) US:LP = CBS FM-42226*

9230 Of Thee I Sing (1973) Score (stage songs:George Gershwin) US:LP = Columbia S-31763*

9231 Oh, Boy! (1958) Score (pop music) GB:LP = Parlophone PMCL-072

9232 Oh Happy Band (1980) Theme (M. Prior) US:LP-MS = BBC 2-22000* [@ST]; Theme (M. Prior) GB:SP = BBC 79* [ST]

9233 Oh, Madeline (1983) Theme (Dan Foliart & Howard Pearl) US:LP = Riza 85-105* [Afterglow:ST]

9234 Old Curiosity Shop, The (1979) Excerpts (Carl Davis) GB:LP = EMI EMC-3361* [Carl Davis:ST]

9235 Old Pull 'n' Push, The (1961) Theme (Terry Lightfoot) GB:SP = Columbia 4567 [Terry Lightfoot:ST]

9236 Oliver in the Overworld (1973) Score (Mike Hazlewood) GB:LP = CBS 70096*

9237 Olympus 7-0000 (1966) Score (Richard Adler) US:LP = Command CS-07/SCS-07*

9238 Omnibus (1952) Highlights + Dialog ["The World of Jazz"] (pop music) US:LP = CSP 91A-02053 [Leonard Bernstein:ST]

9239 On Broadway (1971) Score (pop music) US:LP = Motown MS-699* [Diana Ross and The Supremes:ST]

9240 On the Buses (1970) Theme (M. Russell) GB:LP = EMI 5143* [@The London Symphony]

9241 On the Flip Side (1966) Score (Burt Bacharach) US:LP = Decca DL-4836/DL-74836*

9242 On the Line (1983) Theme (Steve Jolley) GB:LP = Red Bus 1004* [@The Illusion Orchestra]

9243 On the Move (1968) Score (pop music) US:LP-PP = Capitol Custom SL-6658* [Glen Campbell & Burt Bacharach & Dionne Warwick:ST]

9244 On the Move (1975) Theme (Alan Hawkshaw) GB:LP = BBC 236* [@Alan Hawkshaw:ST]; Theme (Alan Hawkshaw) GB:LP-MS = Pickwick 50-DA-315* [Bruce Baxter]

9245 Once Upon a Dead Man (1971) Theme [pilot for "McMillan and Wife"] (Jerry Fielding) US:LP = Mercury 1-1089* [Johnny Gregory]

9246 Once Upon a Tour (1971) Score (t:Jack Elliott & Allyn Ferguson/ s:pop music) US:LP-PP = Cozy 2000* [Dora Hall & Cast:ST]

9247 One Day at a Time (1975) Theme (Jeff Barry) US:LP = Peter Pan 8197* [The Peter Pan Orchestra & Chorus]

9248 One Life to Live (1968) Theme (Jack Urbont) US:LP = Capitol Custom SL-8076* [The New Christy Minstrels]

9249 One More Time (1968) Score (pop music) US:LP = MGM E-4549/SE-4549* [Wayne Newton:ST]

9250 One Step Beyond [Alcoa Presents One Step Beyond] (1959) Score (Harry Lubin) US:LP = Decca DL-8970/ DL-78970* + US:LP = Varese STV-81120*

9251 Open Golf '73 (1973) Theme (Paddy Kingsland) GB:SP = BBC 93* [BBC Radiophonic Workshop:ST]; Theme (Paddy Kingsland) GB:LP = BBC 188* [@BBC Radiophonic Workshop:ST]

9252 Opera Gala, An [Kennedy Center Tonight] (1982) Score (classical music) US:LP = RCA ARL1-4667* [Original TV Cast]

9253 Opera Sauvage (1979) Score (Vangelis) US:LP = Polydor VAN-04* + GB:LP = Polydor 2490.161*

9254 Operation: Entertainment (1968) Theme (Chuck Barris) US:LP = Friends 1001* [The Chuck Barris Orchestra:ST]

9255 Operation Petticoat (1977) Theme (Artie Butler) US:LP = MCA 5380* [Warren Schatz]

9256 Oppenheimer (1982) Excerpts (Carl Davis) GB:LP = EMI EMC-3361* [Carl Davis:ST]

9257 Oral Roberts on Country Roads (1972) Score (as:Ralph Carmichael) US:LP = Light LS-5603*

9258 Orson Welles' Great Mysteries (1973) Theme (John Barry) GB:SP = Polydor 6069* [John Barry:ST]; Theme

(John Barry) GB:LP = Polydor 2383.300* [John Barry:ST]

9259 Other One, The (1978) Theme (Ronnie Hazlehurst) GB:LP = Polydor 2384.107* [Ronnie Hazlehurst:ST]

9260 Other World of Winston Churchill, The (1965) Underscore + Dialog (Carl Davis) US:LP = Mercury MG-21033/SR-61033e

9261 Our Love Is Here to Stay—The Gershwin Years (1975) Scores (pop music) US:LP-MS = Stage Two 711* [Steve Lawrence & Eydie Gorme:ST]

9262 Our Mutual Friend (1976) Theme (Carl Davis) US:LP = DRG 704* [Carl Davis:ST]

9263 Our Town (1955) Highlights (James Van Heusen) US:EP = Capitol EPA1-673 [Frank Sinatra:ST]

9263a Out (1978) Theme (George Fenton) GB:SP = EMI 565* [ST]

9264 Outcasts, The (1968) Theme (Hugo Montenegro) US:LP = Polydor 823-323-1* [Ralph MacDonald]; Theme (Hugo Montenegro) US:LP = RCA 4104* [Hugo Montenegro:ST]

9265 Outer Limits, The (1963) Theme (Dominic Frontiere) US:LP = GNP 2128* [Neil Norman]; Theme (Dominic Frontiere) US:LP = Epic 26125* [Milton DeLugg]

9266 Owen, M.D. / Theme (Johnny Pearson) US:SP = Columbia 4-45595* [Ray Conniff]; Theme (Johnny Pearson) US:LP = K-Tel 4780* [Sounds Orchestral]; Theme (Johnny Pearson) GB: LP = BBC 171*[Norrie Paramor]

P

9267 Paddington Bear (1972) Theme (Herbert Chappell) GB:LP = BBC 486* [@The Boyfriends:ST]

9268 Paisano *see* Best of Steinbeck, The

9269 Pallisers, The (1975) Themes (Herbert Chappell/Wilfred Josephs) US:LP-MS = BBC 2-22000* [@Marcus Dods:ST]; Themes (Herbert Chappell/Wilfred Josephs) GB:SP = BBC 19* [Marcus Dods:ST]; Themes (Herbert Chappell/Wilfred Josephs) GB:LP = BBC 188* [@Marcus Dods:ST]

9270 Panama Hattie (1954) Highlights (stage songs:Cole Porter) US:LP-BP = Larynx 567 + US:LP-BP = Sandy Hook 2043

9271 Panel Beaters, The / Theme (Paddy Kingsland) GB:LP = BBC 196* [BBC Radiophonic Workshop:ST]

9272 Panorama / Theme [Main Title] (pop music) GB:LP = EMI TWO-372* [Johnny Keating]; Theme [Episode Theme] (Walter Stott-aka-Angela Morley) GB:LP = MFP 1087* [Richard Dimbleby]

9273 Paradise Postponed (1986) Score (Roger Webb) GB:LP = EMI SCX-6706*

9274 Pardon Miss Westcott (1959) Score (Peter Stannard) US:LP = Radiola RL-1501 [Studio Cast]

9275 Parent Game, The (1972) Theme (Chuck Barris) US:LP = Friends 1001* [The Chuck Barris Orchestra:ST]

9276 Parkinson (1973) Theme (Harry Stoneham) GB:LP = BBC 391* [Harry Stoneham:ST]

9277 Partridge Family, The (1970) Score (various) US:LP = Bell 1107* [The Partridge Family:ST]; Theme (Danny Janssen) US:LP-MS = Tee Vee Toons 1200 [@ST]

9278 Party (1975) Theme (Ronald Bell) US:SP = Gang 1325* [The Kay Gees:ST]

9279 Pathfinders, The (1972) Theme (Malcolm Lockyer) GB:LP = Polydor 2460.188* [@Harry Robinson]; Theme (Malcolm Lockyer) GB:LP = Sunset 50339* [The London Concert Orchestra]

9280 Patty Duke Show, The (1963) Theme (Sid Ramin) US:LP = WB 1529* [Carl Brandt]; Theme (Sid Ramin) US: LP-MS = Tee Vee Toons 1100 [@ST]

9281 Paul Temple / Theme (Ron Grainer) US:LP = DRG 15018* [Ron Grainer:ST]

9282 Penmarric (1979) Theme (Richard Hartley) US:LP-MS = BBC 2-22000* [@Richard Hartley:ST]; Theme (Richard Hartley) GB:SP = BBC 71* [Richard Hartley:ST]; Theme (Richard Hartley) GB:LP = BBC 391* [@Richard Hartley:ST]

9283 Pennies from Heaven (1977)

Scores (pop music) GB:LP-MS = Decca DDV-5007/8

9284 Perry Como Show, The (1950) Highlights (pop music) US:LP-10 = RCA LPM-3013 [Perry Como:ST]; Themes (Kenyon Hopkins) US:LP = ABC 325* [Creed Taylor & Kenyon Hopkins:ST]

9285 Perry Mason (1957) Theme (Fred Steiner) US:SP = Columbia 4-41040 [Ray Conniff]; Theme (Fred Steiner) US:LP = Philips 600-027* [Johnny Gregory]; Theme (Fred Steiner) US:LP = RCA 2042* [Buddy Morrow]

9286 Personal Cinema / Theme (Holroyd) GB:LP = Decca 217* [@Les Sans Nom]

9287 Persuaders, The (1971) Theme (John Barry) US:SP = Epic 5-10865* [John Barry:ST]; Theme (John Barry) GB:LP = CBS 64816* [John Barry:ST]

9288 Pete Kelly's Blues (1959) Score (e:Dick Cathcart/etc.) US:LP = WB W-1303/WS-1303*

9289 Peter Cottontail's Adventures (1980) Underscore + Dialog (Mark Gibbons) US:LP-PP = ZIV 1005*

9290 Peter Gunn (1958) Score-A (Henry Mancini) US:LP = RCA LPM-1956/LSP-1956* + US:LP = RCA ANL1-2143*; Score-B (Henry Mancini) US:LP = RCA LPM-2040/LSP-2040*; Score-C (Henry Mancini) US:LP = Columbia CL-1327/CS-8133* [Lola Albright & Henry Mancini:ST]; Theme ["My Cousin from Naples"] (Henry Mancini) US:LP = Camden 928* [Henry Mancini:ST]

9291 Peter Lind Hayes Show, The (1958) Highlights (pop music) US: LP = Kapp KL-1021 [Peter Lind Hayes & Mary Healy:ST]

9292 Peter the Great (1985) Score (Laurence Rosenthal) GB:LP = Silva Screen FILM-006*

9293 Petticoat Junction (1963) Theme (Curt Massey) US:SP = Capitol 5135 [Curt Massey:ST]; Theme (Curt Massey) US:SP = Columbia 4-42982 [Flatt & Scruggs]; Theme (Curt Massey) US:LP = Columbia 9370* [Flatt & Scruggs]

9294 Phil Silvers Show, The (1962) Theme (Harry Geller) US:LP = 20th 4105* [Lionel Newman]

9295 Philadelphia Story, The (1960) Theme (Robert Ascher) US:SP = Columbia 4-41532 [Spencer Ross]; Theme (Robert Ascher) US:LP = Columbia 1525 [Spencer Ross]; Theme (Robert Ascher) US:LP = Kapp 1187* [Jack Elliott]

9296 Philco Television Playhouse (1948) Theme-A [Main Title] (Morris Mamorsky) US:LP = RCA 1020 [Hugo Winterhalter]; Theme-B ["Play Me Hearts and Flowers"] (Mann Curtis) US: EP = Camden 289 [Gisele Mackenzie: ST]; Theme-C ["Watch Me Die"] (Bill Russo) US:SP = Capitol 3134 [Stan Kenton]

9297 Pick of the Pops (1960) Theme (Brian Fahey) GB:LP = BBC 454* + GB:LP = EMI TWO-175* [Brian Fahey: ST]

9298 Pictures (1983) Theme (Jim Parker) US:LP-MS = SQN 5057-1* [@ST]

9299 Pinocchio (1957) Score (Alec Wilder) US:LP = Columbia CL-1055

9300 Pinocchio (1965) Score (Jeanne Bargy) US:LP = Peter Pan 8042* + US:LP = Entertainment Media 999*

9301 Pins and Needles (1966) Highlights (stage songs:Harold Rome) US: LP-BP = JJA 19783

9302 Pit, The *see* Studio One

9303 Planet of the Apes (1974) Themes (Lalo Schifrin) US:SP = 20th 2150* [Lalo Schifrin:ST]; Theme (Lalo Schifrin) US:LP = Wonderland 301* [Jeff Wayne]

9304 Play Away / Score-A (Lionel Morton) GB:LP = BBC REC-242*; Score-B (Lionel Morton) GB:LP = BBC REC-244*; Score-C (Lionel Morton) GB:LP = BBC REC-209*

9305 Play Me Hearts and Flowers *see* Philco Television Playhouse

9306 Play School (1975) Score-A (Paul Reade) GB:LP = BBC REC-212*; Score-B (Paul Reade) GB:LP = BBC REC-332*

9307 Playboy's Penthouse (1960) Theme (Cy Coleman) US:SP = Playboy 1001 [Cy Coleman:ST]; Theme (Cy Coleman) US:LP = RCA 2258* [Henry Mancini]

9308 Playhouse 90 (1956) Theme-A [Main Title] (Alex North) US:SP = RCA 47-6896 [Alex North:ST]; Theme-A [Main Title] (Alex North) US:LP = WB 1290* [Warren Barker & Frank Comstock]; Theme-B ["The Ninth Day"] (Robert Allen) US:SP = Columbia 4-40772 [Mitch Miller]; Theme-C ["Rumors of Evening"] (Dave Guard/ Jack Segal) US:SP = Capitol 3970 [The Kingston Trio]; Theme-D ["The Time of Your Life"] (Jackie Gleason) US:SP = Capitol 4062 [Jackie Gleason:ST]

9309 Please Don't Eat the Daisies (1965) Theme (Mike Stoller) US:SP = Verve 10479 [The Righteous Brothers]

9310 Please, Sir (1968) Theme (Sam Fonteyn) GB:LP = EMI 5143* [@The London Symphony]

9311 Point, The (1970) Score (Harry Nillson) US:LP = RCA LSPX-1003*

9312 Poldark (1976) Theme (Kenyon Emrys-Roberts) US:LP-PP = WGBH 10* + US:LP-MS = SQN 5057-1* [@Kenyon Emrys-Roberts:ST]; Theme (Kenyon Emrys-Roberts) US: LP = K-Tel 4780 [Sounds Orchestral]; Theme (Kenyon Emrys-Roberts) GB: LP = BBC 424* [@Marcus Dods]

9313 Police Story (1973) Theme (Jerry Goldsmith) US:SP = Shady Brook 018* [Union City Orchestra]; Theme (Jerry Goldsmith) US:SP = Columbia 3-10416* [Ray Conniff]; Theme (Jerry Goldsmith) US:LP = Columbia 34312* [Ray Conniff]

9314 Police Surgeon *see* Doctor Simon Locke

9315 Police Woman (1974) Theme (Morton Stevens) US:SP = A&M 1840* [Tony Camillo's Bazuka]; Theme (Morton Stevens) US:LP = RCA 1-1896* [Henry Mancini]; Theme (Morton Stevens) US:LP = Mercury 1-1089* [Johnny Gregory]

9316 Poppy Is Also a Flower, The [Danger Grows Wild] (1966) Highlights (Georges Auric) IT:EP = Cinevox 33/1

9317 Portrait of a Dead Girl *see* McCloud

9318 Portrait of an Escort (1980) Theme (Hagood Hardy) CA:LP = Attic 1097* [Hagood Hardy:ST]

9319 Power Game, The (1965) Theme (W. Hill) GB:LP = Marble Arch 1179* [@Cyril Stapleton]; Theme (W. Hill) GB:LP = EMI TWO-175* [Brian Fahey]

9320 Premiere *see* Alcoa Premiere

9321 Presenting Karen Akers [PBS Special] (1981) Score (pop music) US: LP = Blackwood 81-750091* [Karen Akers:ST]

9322 Pride and Prejudice (1980) Theme (Wilfred Josephs) US:LP-PP = WGBH 10* + US:LP-MS = SQN 5057-1*; Theme (Wilfred Josephs) US:LP-MS = BBC 2-22000* [@Patrick Halling]; Theme (Wilfred Josephs) GB:SP = BBC 77* [Patrick Halling]

9323 Prince Regent (1979) Score (Carl Davis) GB:LP = Decca SKL-5313*

9324 Prisoner, The (1968) Score (s: Albert Elms/t:Ron Grainer/t:Wilfred Josephs) GB:LP = BAM CARUSO WEBA-066*; Theme (Ron Grainer) US: LP = GNP 2163* [Neil Norman]

9325 Prisoner – Cell Block H (1979) Themes (Allan Caswell) US:SP = Hilltak 7903* [Lynne Hamilton:ST]

9326 Private History of a Campaign that Failed, The (1981) Excerpts (William Perry) US:LP-PP = Trobriand TRO-1001* [William Perry:ST]

9327 Pro-Am Golf / Theme (Benson & Lewis) GB:LP = Polydor 2384. 107* [Ronnie Hazlehurst]

9328 Professionals, The (1980) Highlights (Laurie Johnson) US:LP = Varese/Starlog ASV-95003*

9329 Profile / Theme (Benson & Lewis) GB:EP = RCA 2238* [Tony King]

9330 Profiles in Courage (1964) Theme + Underscore + Dialog (Nelson Riddle) US:LP = RCA VDM-103

9331 Protectors, The (1972) Theme (Peter Callendar) GB:LP = DJM 22076* [Ray Davies and the Button Down Brass]; Theme (Peter Callendar) GB:LP = Polydor 2460.188* [@Harry Robinson]; Theme (Peter Callendar) GB:LP-MS = Pickwick 50-DA-315* [Bruce Baxter]

9332 Pudd'n Head Wilson (1984) Theme (William Perry) US:LP-PP = Trobriand TRO-1001* [William Perry: ST]

9333 Pufnstuf *see* H.R. Pufnstuf (1969)

Q

9334 QB VII (1974) Score (Jerry Goldsmith) US:LP = ABC ABCD-822*

9335 Q.8. (1979) Theme (Spike Milligan) GB:LP = BBC 387* [@Spike Milligan:ST]

9336 Quarenta Giorni di Liberta Theme (Guido & Maurizio DeAngelis) US:LP = Private Stock 7004* [Guido & Maurizio:ST]

9337 Queen of the Stardust Ballroom, The (1975) Theme (Billy Goldenberg) US:LP = UA 941* + US:LP = Liberty 10112* [Ferrante & Teicher]; Theme (Billy Goldenberg) US:LP = Audio Fidelity 6276* [Carroll O'Connor]

9338 Quiller (1975) Theme (Richard Denton & Martin Cook) US:LP-MS = BBC 2-22000* [@Richard Denton & Martin Cook:ST]; Theme (Richard Denton & Martin Cook) GB:LP = BBC 236* + GB:LP = BBC 385* [Richard Denton & Martin Cook:ST]

9339 Quillow and the Giant (1960) Score (Ralph Blane) GB:LP = Philips BBL-653/SBBL-653*

9340 Quincy, M.E. (1976) Theme (Stu Phillips & Glen Larson) US:LP = MCA 5380* [Warren Schatz] † *the composer credit is incorrect on the record*

R

9341 Raccoons on Ice (1983) Highlights + Dialog (Kevin Gillis) US: LP = Starland ARI-1030*

9342 Racket Squad (1950) Theme (Joseph Mullendore) US:LP = RCA 2042* [Buddy Morrow]

9343 Rag Trade, The (1978) Theme (Lynsey DePaul) GB:LP = DJM 20522* [@Joan Brown]

9344 Ragtime / Score (Peter Gosling) GB:LP = BBC REC-182*

9345 Rainbow / Score (Matthew Corbett) GB:LP = Tempo TMP-9003*

9346 Randall and Hopkirk *see* My Partner, the Ghost

9347 Ransom for a Dead Man (1971) Excerpts [pilot for "Columbo"] (Billy Goldenberg) US:LP-BP = Centurion CLP-1601 [Billy Goldenberg:ST]; Theme [Pilot for "Columbo"] (Billy Goldenberg) US:LP = Mercury 1-1089* [Johnny Gregory]

9348 Rat Catchers, The (1965) Theme (Johnny Pearson) US:LP = Fontana 67565 [Reg Guest]

9349 Rat Patrol, The (1966) Theme (Dominic Frontiere) US:SP = UA 50098 [Al Caiola]; Theme (Dominic Frontiere) US:LP = UA 6560* [Al Caiola]; Theme-B ["That Tiny World"] (Richard Loring) US:SP = RCA 47-9365 [Jack Jones]

9350 Rawhide (1959) Theme (Dimitri Tiomkin) US:SP = Columbia 4-41230 [Frankie Laine:ST]; Theme (Dimitri Tiomkin) US:LP = Columbia 1615/8415* + US:LP = Harmony 30406* [Frankie Laine:ST]; Theme (Dimitri Tiomkin) US:LP = UA 6161* + US: LP = Sunset 4027* [Al Caiola]

9351 Ray Anthony Show, The (1949) Theme (Ray Anthony) US:SP = Capitol 3593 [Ray Anthony:ST]; Theme (Ray Anthony) US:LP = Capitol 2043* [Ray Anthony:ST]

9352 Reading Rainbow (1981) Score (Steve Horelick) US:LP = Caedmon TC-1757*

9353 Real Ghostbusters, The (1986) Score (Ollie Brown) US:LP = Polydor 831-236-1*

9354 Real McCoys, The (1957) Theme (Harry Ruby) US:LP = WB 1290* [Warren Barker & Frank Comstock]; Theme (Harry Ruby) US:LP = Reprise 6018* [Neal Hefti]

9355 Really Rosie (1974) Score (Carole King) US:LP = Ode SP-77027* + US:LP = Epic PE-34955* [Carole King:ST]

9356 Rebecca (1980) Themes (at: Ron Grainer) US:LP = DRG 15018* [Ron Grainer:ST]

9357 Rebel, The (1959) Theme (Richard Markowitz) US:SP = Columbia 4-41995 [Johnny Cash:ST]; Theme (Richard Markowitz) US:LP = Columbia 8853* [Johnny Cash:ST]; Theme (Richard Markowitz) US:LP = UA 6161* + US:LP = Sunset 4027* [Al Caiola]

9358 Rebop (1976) Theme (Quincy Jones) US:LP = A&M SP-6507* [Quincy Jones:ST]

9359 Record Breakers, The / Theme (Roy Castle) GB:LP = BBC 214* [@Roy Castle:ST]

9360 Red Buttons Show, The (1952) Theme (Elliott Lawrence) US:SP = Columbia 4-40243 [Red Buttons:ST]; Theme (Elliott Lawrence) US:LP = MGM 3729* [The Metropolitan Jazz Quartet]

9361 Red Skelton Show, The (1951) Score (Alan Copeland) US:LP-PP = CBS Promo 6617 [The Alan Copeland Singers:ST]; Theme-A ["The Christmas Tree"] (David Rose) US:LP = MGM 3748* [David Rose:ST]; Theme-B ["Red's Red White & Blue March"] (Red Skelton) US:SP = Columbia 4-44798 [Red Skelton:ST]

9362 Reilly, Ace of Spies (1983) Theme (at:Harry Rabinowitz) US:SP = GNP 831* [The Olympic Orchestra:ST]; Theme (at:Harry Rabinowitz) US:LP = GNP 2166* [@The Olympic Orchestra: ST]; Theme (at:Harry Rabinowitz) GB: LP = Red Bus 1004* [@The Olympic Orchestra:ST]

9363 Remington Steele (1982) Theme (Henry Mancini) GB:LP = MFP 5768* [The Power Pack Orchestra]

9364 Reporter, The (1964) Score (Kenyon Hopkins) US:LP = Columbia CL-2269/CS-9069*

9365 Restless Gun, The (1957) Theme (Dave Kahn & Melvyn Lenard) US:SP = RCA WBY-71 [The Sons of the Pioneers]; Theme (Dave Kahn & Melvyn Lenard) US:LP = Coral 757267* [Lawrence Welk]; Theme (Dave Kahn & Melvyn Lenard) US:LP = Tops 1661* [Richard Gleason]

9366 Return of the King (1980) Highlights + Underscore + Dialog (Maury Laws) US:LP = Disneyland 3822*

9367 Return of the Saint (1979) Theme (Irving Martin) GB:LP = MFP 50439* [Geoff Love]

9368 Return to Eden (1985) Theme (Brian May) US:LP = Varese STV-81260*

9369 Rhoda (1974) Theme (Billy Goldenberg) US:LP = BBP 1001* [Van Alexander]

9370 Rich Little's A Christmas Carol (1981) Highlights + Dialog (Saul Ilson) CA:LP = Columbia PEC-90580* [Rich Little & Cast:ST]

9371 Rich Man, Poor Man (1976) Score (Alex North) US:LP = MCA 2095*

9372 Richard Boone Show, The (1963) Theme (Henry Mancini) US:SP = RCA 47-8458 [Henry Mancini:ST]; Theme (Henry Mancini) US:LP = RCA 2990* + US:LP = RCA 3557* [Henry Mancini:ST]

9373 Richard Diamond (1957) Score (Pete Rugolo) US:LP = Mercury MG-36162/SR-80045*

9374 Richie Brockelman, Private Eye (1977) Theme (Mike Post & Pete Carpenter) US:SP = Elektra 47477* [Mike Post:ST]; Theme (Mike Post & Pete Carpenter) US:LP = Elektra 1-60028* [Mike Post:ST]

9375 Riel (1978) Score (William McCauley) CA:LP = GRT 9230.1080*

9376 Rifleman, The (1958) Theme (Herschel Burke Gilbert) US:LP = Dot 25421* [Herschel Burke Gilbert:ST]; Theme (Herschel Burke Gilbert) US:LP-MS = Tee Vee Toons 1100 [@ST]

9377 Ring-a-Ding / Theme (Derek Griffiths) GB:LP = BBC 214* [@Derek Griffiths:ST]

9378 Riptide (1985) Theme (Mike Post & Pete Carpenter) US:LP = RCA 1-5415* [Mike Post:ST]

9379 Rise and Fall of the Third Reich, The (1968) Highlights + Narration (Lalo Schifrin) US:LP = MGM 1E-12/1SE-12*

9380 Rising the Roof (1972) Theme (Cyril Stapleton) GB:LP = Pye 82153* [Cyril Stapleton:ST]

9381 Riverboat (1959) Themes (Elmer Bernstein) US:SP = Bristol 70 [Monica Lewis]; Theme (Elmer Bernstein) US:LP = RCA 2180* [Buddy Morrow]

9382 Road Runner Show, The (1967) Theme (Barbara Cameron) US: LP = MS Tee Vee Toons 1200 [@ST]

9383 Roads to Freedom, The (1970) Themes (James Cellan Jones) GB:SP = Fly BUG-5* [Georgia Brown:ST]

9384 Roald Dahl's Tales of the Unexpected *see* Tales of the Unexpected

9385 Roaring 20's, The (1960) Score (t:Jerry Livingston/s:pop music) US: LP = WB W-1394/WS-1394* [Dorothy Provine:ST]

9386 Robert Montgomery Presents (1950) Theme-A [Main Title] (Robert Busby) US:SP = Decca 9-29507 [The Queen's Hall Orchestra]; Theme-A [Main Title] (Robert Busby) US:LP = RCA 1020 [Hugo Winterhalter]; Theme-B ["Please Don't Forget Me Dear" aka "Don't Do Me Any Favors"] (Johnny Desmond) US:SP = Coral 9-61632 [Johnny Desmond:ST]

9387 Robert Q. Lewis Show, The (1954) Score (pop music) US:LP = X LXA-1033 [Robert Q. Lewis & Cast:ST]

9388 Robin Hood *see* Adventures of Robin Hood, The

9389 Robin of Sherwood (1984) Score (Clannad) US:LP = RCA AFL1-5084* + GB:LP = RCA PL-70188* [Clannad:ST]

9390 Rocambole (1962) Highlights (Jacques Loussier) FR:EP = Philips 432.997

9391 Rock Follies (1977) Score-A (Andy MacKay) GB:LP = Island ILPS-9362*; Score-B (Andy MacKay) GB: LP = Polydor 2302.072*

9392 Rockford Files, The (1974) Theme (Mike Post & Pete Carpenter) US:SP = MGM 14772 [Mike Post:ST]; Theme (Mike Post & Pete Carpenter) US:LP = MGM 5005* + US:LP = Elektra 1-60028* [Mike Post:ST]

9393 Rocky and His Friends [The Bullwinkle Show] (1965) Underscore + Dialog (Dennis Farnon) US:LP = Golden LP-64; Theme [Main Title] (Fred Steiner) US:SP = Dore 636 [Billy Joe and the Checkmates]

9394 Rod McKuen Show, The [Rod McKuen and Friends] Score (pop music) GB:LP = WB WS-3015* [Rod McKuen: ST]

9395 Rod Serling's Night Gallery *see* Night Gallery

9396 Rogues, The (1964) Score (Nelson Riddle) US:LP = RCA LPM-2976/LSP-2976*

9397 Rolf on Saturday / Score (Rolf Harris) GB:LP = BBC REH-353* [Rolf Harris:ST]

9398 Rollin' on the River (1971) Score (pop music) US:LP = Jolly Rogers JR-5003* [Kenny Rogers and the First Edition:ST]

9399 Romper Room (1953) Score (various) US:LP = Peter Pan 8062

9400 Rona Barrett Looks At ... (1969) Themes (John D'Andrea) US: SP = Romar 702* [The R.P.M. Generation:ST]

9401 Rondo Veneziano (1983) Score (Gian Piero Reverberi) GB:LP = RON 1*

9402 Roobarb / Score (Paul Travis) GB:LP = Bell S-268*

9402a Rookies, The (1972) Theme (Elmer Bernstein) US:LP-MS = Tee Vee Toons 1300 [@ST]

9403 Room 222 (1969) Theme (Jerry Goldsmith) US:SP = Viking 1009* [The Non-Profit Organization Orchestra]; Theme (Jerry Goldsmith) US:SP = RCA 47-9841* [Floyd Cramer]; Theme (Jerry Goldsmith) US:LP = RCA 4312* [Floyd Cramer]

9404 Roots (1977) Score (e:Quincy Jones/e:Gerald Fried) US:LP = A&M SP-4626* [Quincy Jones:ST]; Underscore + Dialog (Gerald Fried) US:LP-MS = WB 3WS-3048*

9405 Roots (1981) Theme (Silva) GB:SP = Mercury 83* [Peter Skellern]

9406 Ropers, The (1979) Theme (Joe Raposo) US:LP-PP = Jenson 0800* [The Jenson Marching Band]

9407 Rose on Broadway (1973) Score (pop music) US:LP-PP = Cozy PL-9206* [Dora Hall & Cast:ST]

9408 Rosemary Clooney Show, The (1957) Themes (Nelson Riddle) US: SP = Columbia 4-40781 [Joe Seymour]

9409 Roundabout (1959) Theme (Tony Osborne) US:SP = Roulette 4189 [Tony Osborne:ST]; Theme (Tony Osborne) GB:LP = BBC 454* [@Tony Osborne:ST]

9420 Route 66 (1960) Theme (Nelson Riddle) US:SP = Capitol 6217 + US: SP = Capitol 4741 [Nelson Riddle:ST]; Theme (Nelson Riddle) US:LP = Capitol 4603* + US:LP = Capitol 11764* [Nelson Riddle:ST]; Theme (Nelson Riddle) US:LP = Philips 600-027* [Johnny Gregory]

9411 Rowan and Martin's Laugh-In (1968) Highlights + Underscore + Dialog-A (e:Billy Barnes/u:Ian Bernard) US:LP = Epic FXS-15118*; Highlights + Underscore + Dialog-B (e:Billy Barnes/ u:Ian Bernard) US:LP = Reprise RS-6335*; Theme [Main Title] (Ian Bernard) US:SP = Show Town 508* [Power Formula]

9412 Roy Rogers Show, The (1951) Theme (Dale Evans) US:SP = 20th 467* [Roy Rogers:ST]; Theme (Dale Evans) US:SP = RCA WBY-65 [Roy Rogers & Dale Evans:ST]; Theme (Dale Evans) US:LP = RCA 1004 [@Roy Rogers & Dale Evans:ST]

9413 Royal Romance of Charles and Diana, The (1982) Themes (David Palmer) US:SP-12 = Chrysalis CY-1000 [Laurie Beechman/David Palmer:ST]

9414 Rubovia / Highlights + Dialog (Freddie Phillips) GB:LP = BBC REC-282*

9415 Rudolph the Red-Nosed Reindeer (1964) Highlights (Johnny Marks) US:LP = Decca DL-4815/DL-74815* + US:LP = MCA 15003*

9416 Rugby Special / Theme (M. Bennett) GB:LP = BBC 236* [@Tony King]

9417 Ruggles of Red Gap (1957) Score (Jule Styne) US:LP = Verve MG-15000 + US:LP = DRG DL-15007

9418 Rumors of Evening *see* Playhouse 90

9419 Run, Buddy, Run (1966) Theme (Jerry Fielding) US:LP = RCA 3716* [Al Hirt]

9420 Run for Your Life (1965) Theme (Pete Rugolo) US:LP = RCA 3716* [Al Hirt]; Theme (Pete Rugolo) US:LP = MCA 5380* [Warren Schatz]

9421 Rupert the Bear / Theme (Paul Roker) GB:SP = MFP 10048* [Geoff Love]; Theme (Paul Roker) GB:LP = Contour 2870.185* [Cy Payne]

9422 Russell Harty (1984) Theme (David Mindel) GB:LP = BBC 524* [@David Mindel:ST]

9423 Rutland Weekend (1975) Score (Neil Innes) US:LP = ABC/Passport 98018* + GB:LP = BBC REC-233* [Eric Idle & Neil Innes:ST]

9424 Rutles, The [All You Need Is Cash] (1978) Score (Neil Innes) US:LP = WB HS-3151* [The Rutles:ST]

9425 Ryan's Hope (1975) Theme-A (Carey Gold) US:LP = Capitol Custom SL-8076* [The New Christy Minstrels]; Theme-B (Kathy Wakefield) US:LP = Columbia 39601* [Johnny Mathis:ST]

S

9426 'S Wonderful, 'S Marvelous, 'S Gershwin (1972) Score (pop music) US:LP = Daybreak DR-2009*

9427 S.W.A.T. (1975) Theme (Barry DeVorzon) US:SP = ABC 12135* [Rhythm Heritage]; Theme (Barry DeVorzon) US:LP = Mercury 1-1089* [Johnny Gregory]; Theme (Barry DeVorzon) US:LP = Arista 4104* [Barry DeVorzon:ST]

9428 Saga of Andy Burnett, The [Walt Disney Presents] (1957) Themes (George Bruns) US:SP = Disneyland 59 [Jerome Courtland:ST]; Themes (George Bruns) US:LP = Mickey Mouse 18 [@Jerome Courtland:ST]

9429 Saint, The (1967) Score (s:Edwin Astley/t:Ken Jones) US:LP = RCA LPM-3631/LSP-3631*

9430 St. Elsewhere (1983) Theme (Dave Grusin) US:SP = GRP 3005* [Dave Grusin:ST]; Theme (Dave Grusin) US:LP = GRP 1006* [Dave Grusin:ST]; Theme (Dave Grusin) US:LP = RCA 1-5183* [Mike Post]

9431 Saint Patrick's Mass *see* Directions

9432 Saints and Sinners (1962) Theme (Elmer Bernstein) US:SP = Choreo 107 [Elmer Bernstein:ST]; Theme (Elmer Bernstein) US:LP = Choreo 11* [Elmer Bernstein:ST]

9433 Salsa / Theme (Randy Ortiz) US:LP = Fania 00478* [Seguida:ST]

9434 Sam (1973) Theme (John McCabe) GB:LP = MFP 90035* [Jack Parnell]

9435 Sam Benedict (1962) Theme (Nelson Riddle) US:LP = Capitol 1771* [Nelson Riddle:ST]

9436 Sam Riddle Show, The *see* Hollywood A-Go-Go

9437 Sammy! (1971) Score (pop music) US:LP = MGM SE-4838* [Sammy Davis, Jr. & Cast:ST]

9438 Sammy Davis, Jr. Show, The (1966) Score (pop music) US:LP = Reprise R-6188/RS-6188* [Sammy Davis, Jr. & Cast:ST]

9439 Sammy the Way-Out Seal [Walt Disney Presents] (1962) Theme (Oliver Wallace) US:LP = Disneyland 1245 [@ST]

9440 San Francisco Beat *see* Line-Up, The

9441 Sands of Time, The *see* Climax

9442 Sandy's Hour / Theme (Red Saunders) US:SP = Okeh 4-7166 [Red Saunders & Sandy Becker:ST]

9443 Sanford and Son (1972) Theme + Dialog (Quincy Jones) US: LP = RCA LPM-4739; Theme (Quincy Jones) US:SP = A&M 1455* [Quincy Jones:ST]; Theme (Quincy Jones) US: LP = A&M 3041* [Quincy Jones:ST]

9444 Santa Claus Is Coming to Town (1971) Highlights + Underscore + Dialog (Maury Laws) US:LP = MGM SE-4732*

9445 Sara Dane (1981) Theme (Don Burrows) AU:LP = Cherry Pie 37856* [Don Burrows:ST]

9446 Satchmo the Great (1957) Score (pop music) US:LP = Columbia CL-1077 [Louis Armstrong:ST]

9447 Satin and Spurs (1954) Highlights (Jay Livingston & Ray Evans) US: LP-10 = Capitol L-547

9448 Saturday Night at Mickie Finn's *see* Mickie Finn's

9449 Saturday Night Live! (1975) Highlights + Underscore + Dialog (various) US:LP = Arista AL-4107*; Theme (Howard Shore) US:LP-MS = Tee Vee Toons 1300 [@ST]

9450 Saturday Superstore (1982) Theme (B. Robertson) GB:LP = BBC 486* [@The Assistants:ST]

9451 Savage Bees, The [Attack of the Killer Bees] (1976) Theme (Walter Murphy) US:SP = Private Stock 45-123* [Walter Murphy:ST]

9452 Saving the Wildlife (1985) Score (Chip Davis) US:LP = American Gramaphone AG-2086*

9453 Say Goodbye, Maggie Cole (1972) Theme (Hugo Montenegro) US: SP = Dunhill 4357* [Dusty Springfield: ST]; Theme (Hugo Montenegro) US: LP = RCA 1-0025* [Hugo Montenegro: ST]

9454 Scales of Justice, The (1963) Theme (Johnny Douglas) US:SP = London 45-9614 [The Tornadoes]

9455 Scarecrow and Mrs. King (1983) Theme (Arthur Rubinstein) GB: LP = MFP 5768* [The Power Pack Orchestra]

9456 Scarecrow of Romney Marsh, The [Dr. Syn, Alias the Scarecrow] [Walt Disney Presents] (1964) Theme (Terry Gilkyson) US:SP = Disneyland 774 [The Wellingtons]; Theme (Terry Gilkyson) US:LP = Disneyland 1245 [@The Wellingtons]

9457 Scarlet and the Black, The (1983) Score (Ennio Morricone) US: LP = Cerberus CEMS-0120*

9458 Scarlett Hill (1962) Theme (M. Taylor) GB:SP = Pye 7N-15472 [Peter Knight]

9459 Scooby Doo, Where Are You? (1969) Theme (Hoyt Curtin) US:LP-MS = Tee Vee Toons 1300 [@ST]

9460 Screws / Theme (Larry Adler) US:LP = London 920* [Larry Adler:ST]

9461 Sea Hunt (1958) Theme (Richard Llewelyn) US:LP = RCA 2042* [Buddy Morrow]

9462 Search for the Nile, The (1972) Theme (Joseph Horowitz) US:SP = Capitol 3284* [Joseph Horowitz:ST]; Theme (Joseph Horowitz) GB:LP = Decca 2163* [Ike Isaacs]

9463 Search for Tomorrow (1951) Theme (Jack Cortner) US:LP = Capitol Custom SL-8076* [The New Christy Minstrels]

9464 Seaside Special (1978) Score (t:Mike Batt/s:various) GB:LP = Epic PC-81432* [Sunshine Saturday:ST]

9465 Seaway (1965) Theme (Edwin Astley) GB:LP = EMI TWO-175* [Brian Fahey]

9466 Secret Agent (1965) Score (s: Edwin Astley/t:Steve Barri) US:LP = RCA LPM-3630/LSP-3630* [Edwin Astley:ST]; Theme (Steve Barri) US: SP = UA 101 [Johnny Rivers:ST]

9467 Secret Army, The (1979) Score (e:Angela Richards & Leslie Osborne/ etc.) GB:LP = BBC REC-412* [Angela Richards:ST]; Theme [Main Title] (Robert Farnon) GB:LP = Polydor 2384.107* [Ronnie Hazlehurst]

9468 See It Now *see* Lady from Philadelphia, The

9469 Sensitive, Passionate Man, A (1977) Theme (Bill Conti) US:SP = Buddah 572* [Melba Moore:ST]

9470 Sesame Street (1969) Score-A (e:Joe Raposo/e:Jeffrey Moss) US:LP = Columbia CS-1069* + US:LP = CTW 22064*; Score-B (e:Joe Raposo/e:Jeffrey Moss) US:LP = WB HS-2569* + US: LP = CTW 22074*; Score-C (e:Joe Raposo/e:Jeffrey Moss) US:LP = Columbia KC-32343* + US:LP = CTW 22091*; Score-D (e:Jeffrey Moss/etc.) US:LP = CTW 22101*; Score-E (e:Sam Pottle/etc.) US:LP = CTW 79007*

9471 Seven Faces of Woman, The (1978) Theme (Charles Aznavour) US: SP = RCA 10021* [Charles Aznavour: ST]; Theme (Charles Aznavour) US: LP = Phonogram 1-3817* [Gheorgh Zamfir]; Theme (Charles Aznavour) GB: LP = EMI 2069* [Reginald Dixon]

9472 77 Sunset Strip (1958) Score (t: Jerry Livingston/t:Warren Barker/etc.) US:LP = WB W-1289/WS-1289*; Score [Jazz Tracks] (e:Sy Oliver & Frankie Ortega/etc.) US:LP = Jubilee JLP-1106/ SD-1106*; Theme-A ["Kookie, Kookie"] (Irving Taylor) US:SP = WB 5047 [Edd Byrnes:ST]; Theme-B [Main Title #2] (Jerry Livingston) US:LP = WB 1529* [Carl Brandt]

9473 Sex Symbol, The (1975) Theme (Francis Lai) US:SP = RCA 10060* [Henry Mancini:ST]; Theme (Francis Lai) US:LP = RCA 1-0672* [Henry Mancini:ST]

9474 Sexton Blake (1978) Theme (Anthony Isaac) GB:SP = BBC 57* [Anthony Isaac:ST]; Theme (Anthony Isaac) GB:LP = BBC 365* [@Anthony Isaac:ST]

9475 Shangri-La (1960) Highlights (stage songs:Harry Warren) US:LP-BP = Sound of Broadway 300/1

9476 Shari Lewis Show, The [Shari-Land] (1957) Highlights + Dialog-A (Lan O'Kun) US:LP = Camden CAL-1006 [Shari Lewis:ST]; Highlights + Dialog-B (Lan O'Kun) US: LP = RCA LPM-2463/LSP-2463* + US:LP = Camden CAL-1052/CAS-1052* [Shari Lewis:ST]

9477 Sharon—Portrait of a Mistress (1977) Theme (Roger Kellaway) US: LP = Choice 6832* [Roger Kellaway:ST]

9478 Sheriff John's Fun Brigade / Themes (L. Penny) US:SP = Imperial 8302 [Sheriff John:ST]

9479 Sheriff Lobo *see* Misadventures of Sheriff Lobo, The

9480 Sheriff of Cochise, The (1956) Theme (Stan Jones) US:SP = Disneyland 64 [Stan Jones:ST]; Theme (Stan Jones) US:LP = RCA 1027 [@The Prairie Chiefs]

9481 Shinbone Alley [Archy and Mehitabel] (1960) Highlights (stage songs:George Kleinsinger) US:LP-BP = The Sound of Broadway 300/1

9482 Shirley Temple's Storybook (1959) Theme-A [Main Title] (Vic Mizzy) US:LP = Choreo 6* [Harry Betts]; Theme-B ["Beauty and the Beast"] (Jerry Livingston) US:SP = Columbia 4-41086 [Tony Bennett]; Theme-C ["The Chinese Nightingale"] (Jerry Livingston) US: SP = RCA 47-7146 [Gogi Grant]

9483 Shoestring (1979) Theme (George Fenton) GB:SP = BBC 67* [George Fenton:ST]; Theme (George Fenton) GB:LP = BBC 391* [@George Fenton:ST]

9484 Shogun (1980) Score (Maurice Jarre) US:LP = RSO RX1-3088*

9485 Shotgun Slade (1959) Score (Gerald Fried) US:LP = Mercury MG-20595/SR-60235*

9486 Shoulder to Shoulder (1975) Theme (at:Stanley Myers) US:LP-PP = WGBH 10* + US:LP-MS = SQN 5057-1* [@Georgia Brown:ST]

9487 Show Street (1964) Theme

(David Axlerod) US:LP = ABC 513 [Frank DeVol]

9488 Sigmund and the Sea Monsters (1973) Score (Danny Janssen) US: LP = Chelsea BCL1-0332* [Johnny Whitaker:ST]

9489 Sil the Beachcomber [Sil de Strandjutter] (1976) Score (Johnny Pearson) HO:LP = Pathe C064.25459*

9490 Silent Years, The (1971) Score (William Perry) US:LP-PP = Eastbrook SY-1001*

9491 Silk Road, The (1983) Score-A (Kitaro) US:LP = Gramavision 18-7009-1* [Kitaro:ST]; Score-B (Kitaro) US:LP = Gramavision 18-7011-1* [Kitaro:ST]

9492 Simon and Simon (1981) Themes (Barry DeVorzon) US:SP = Earthtones 7005* [Barry DeVorzon:ST]; Theme (B. DeVorzon) US:LP = MCA 5380* [Warren Schatz]; Theme (Barry DeVorzon) US:LP = Arista 8-8098* [Meco]

9493 Simon Locke *see* Doctor Simon Locke

9494 Sinatra – The Main Event *see* Main Event, The

9495 Sing Along with Mitch (1962) Score-A (pop music) US:LP = Columbia CL-1628/CS-8428* [Mitch Miller:ST]; Score-B (pop music) US:LP = Columbia CL-1705/CS-8505* [Diana Trask:ST]; Score-C (pop music) US:LP = Columbia CL-1706/CS-8506* [Leslie Uggams:ST]; Score-D (pop music) US:LP = Columbia CL-1865/CS-8665* [Leslie Uggams:ST]

9496 Sing It Again / Score-A (pop music) GB:LP = Columbia 33-SX-1124*; Score-B (pop music) GB:LP = Columbia 33-SX-1187*

9497 Singer Presents Liza with a Z *see* Liza with a Z

9498 Singing Idol, The *see* Kraft Television Theatre

9499 Six-Five Special, The (1957) Score (pop music) GB:LP = Parlophone PMC-1047

9500 Six Million Dollar Man, The (1974) Theme (Oliver Nelson) US:LP = Mercury 1-1089* [Johnny Gregory]; Theme (Oliver Nelson) US:LP = Peter Pan 8197* [Peter Pan Orchestra]; Theme (Oliver Nelson) US:LP = Flying Dutchman 1-1146* [Richard Groove Holmes]

9501 Six Proud Walkers (1954) Theme (Ray Martin) US:SP = RCA 47-5828 [George Melachrino]; Theme (Ray Martin) US:LP = RCA 1184* [George Melachrino]

9502 Six Wives of Henry VIII, The (1971) Highlights (ae:David Munrow) GB:EP = BBC RELS-4*; Theme (at: David Munrow) US:LP-MS = BBC 2-22000* [@David Munrow:ST]

9503 $64,000 Question, The (1955) Theme (Norman Leyden) US:SP = RCA 47-6476 [Tony Travis]

9504 67 Melody Lane / Score (pop music) US:LP = Columbia CL-724 [Ken Griffith:ST]

9505 Skippy, The Bush Kangaroo (1969) Highlights (Eric Jupp) AU:EP = Parlophone 70052

9506 Skorpion (1977) Theme (Simon May) GB:LP = Red Bus 1004* [@The Limelight Orchestra]

9507 Small Bouquet, A *see* Alcoa Theatre

9508 Smike (1974) Score (Simon May) GB:LP = Pye NSPL-18423*

9509 Smiley's People (1982) Score (Patrick Gowers) GB:LP = BBC REP-439*

9510 Smokey the Bear *see* Ballad of Smokey the Bear, The

9511 Smothers Brothers Comedy Hour, The (1967) Highlights + Dialog (e:Mason Williams/etc.) US:LP = Mercury SR-61193*; Theme [Main Title] (Mason Williams) US:LP = Liberty 7532* [Nelson Riddle:ST]

9512 Smugglers, The (1968) Score (Lyn Murray) US:LP-PP = Smugglers S-1001

9512a Smurfs, The (1981) Theme (Hoyt Curtin) US:LP-MS = Tee Vee Toons 1300 [@ST]

9513 Snooker (1985) Theme (Douglas Wood) GB:LP = BBC 508* [@ST]

9514 Snow Goose, The (1971) Excerpts (Carl Davis) US:LP = DRG MRS-704* [Carl Davis:ST]

9515 Snowman, The (1983) Highlights (Howard Blake) US:LP = CBS FM-39216* + GB:LP = CBS 71116*

9516 Soap (1977) Theme (George Tipton) GB:LP = EMI 168* [Geoff Love]

9516a Solid Gold (1980) Theme (Miller & Pitchford) US:LP-MS = Tee

Vee Toons 1300 [@Dionne Warwick:ST]

9517 Some Mothers Do 'Ave 'Em (1974) Theme (Ronnie Hazlehurst) GB: LP = Polydor 2384.107* [R. Hazlehurst: ST]; Theme (Ronnie Hazlehurst) GB: LP = BBC 387* [@R. Hazlehurst:ST]

9518 Somerset Maugham (1970) Theme (Wilfred Josephs) GB:LP = Polydor 2383.294* [Marcus Dods:ST]; Theme (Wilfred Josephs) GB:LP = Marble Arch 1179* [@Cyril Stapleton]

9519 Something for Joey (1977) Themes (David Shire) JA:SP = Cine Disc X-5* [David Shire:ST]

9520 Song for a Summer Night *see* Studio One

9521 Songwriters, The (1978) Score (pop music) GB:LP = BBC REB-325*

9522 Sons and Daughters (1982) Theme (Peter Pinne) GB:LP = MFP 5759* [The Power Pack Orchestra]

9523 Sooner or Later (1979) Excerpts (Stephen J. Lawrence) US:LP = Columbia JC-35813* [Rex Smith:ST]

9524 Sooty (1953) Theme (Harry Corbett) GB:LP = BBC 454 [@Harry Corbett:ST]

9525 Sophia Loren in Rome (1964) Score (John Barry) US:LP = Columbia OL-6310/OS-2710*

9526 Soul Train (1971) Theme (Don Cornelius) US:SP = Soul Train 10400* [The Soul Train Gang:ST]; Theme (Don Cornelius) US:LP = Motown 905* [Prime Time]

9527 Sound of Jazz (1957) Score (pop music) US:LP = Columbia CL-1098

9528 Sound of Trouble, The *see* Kraft Television Theatre

9529 Soupy Sales Show, The (1955) Theme (J. Mortimer) US:SP = Dolton 52 [The Miniature Men]; Theme (J. Mortimer) US:LP = Reprise 6010* [Soupy Sales Orchestra]

9530 South Riding (1974) Theme (Ron Grainer) GB:LP = MFP 90061* [Jack Parnell]

9531 Space Cruiser Yamato (1977) Score (Hiroshi Miyagawa) JA:LP = Columbia CQ-7001*; Highlights + Underscore + Dialog [13 Record Set] (Hiroshi Miyagawa) JA:LP-MS = Columbia CB-7068/7080*

9532 Space for Man / Theme (Peter Howell) GB:LP = BBC 324* [@BBC Radiophonic Workshop:ST]

9533 Space 1999 (1975) Score (Barry Gray) US:LP = RCA ABL1-1422*; Theme [Main Title #2] (Derek Wadsworth) US:LP = GNP 2163* [Neil Norman]

9534 Space Patrol / Score (Peter Thomas) GE:LP = Fontana 6434.261*

9535 Spaceflight (1985) Score (Randy Farrar) US:LP = Noran NRLP-003*

9536 Speak for Yourself (1980) Theme (George Fenton) GB:SP = BBC 85* [Roger Chapman:ST]; Theme (George Fenton) GB:LP = BBC 424* [@Roger Chapman:ST]

9537 Special Bardot (1968) Score (pop music) US:LP-PP = Burlington BC-1000 [Brigitte Bardot:ST]

9538 Special Branch (1969) Theme (Robert Earley) GB:LP = Philips 6308.255* [Johnny Gregory]

9539 Spectre Man / Theme (Jerry Winn & Bob Todd) FR:LP-MS = Pathe 2C150.16561* [Frank Pourcel]

9539a Speed Racer (1967) Theme (N. Koshibe) US:LP-MS = Tee Vee Toons 1300 [@ST]

9540 Spider Man (1967) Theme (Bob Harris) GB:LP = MFP 50439* [Geoff Love] † *the composer credit is incorrect on the record*

9541 Spies, The (1966) Theme (Max Harris) US:LP = UA 6560* [Al Caiola]

9542 Spin and Marty *see* Mickey Mouse Club, The

9543 Sports Night / Theme (Tony Hatch) GB:LP = Pye 41029* [Tony Hatch:ST]

9544 Spring and Autumn / Theme (Michael J. Lewis) GB:LP = Decca 391* [Malcolm Lockyer]

9545 Spring Thing (1969) Score (pop music) US:LP-PP = Celanese 31769 [Bobbi Gentry & Noel Harrison & Shirley Bassey:ST]

9546 Spyship (1983) Theme (Richard Harvey) GB:SP = BBC 140* [June Tabor:ST]; Theme (Richard Harvey) GB:LP = BBC 524* [@June Tabor:ST]

9547 Squadron (1982) Themes (Anthony Isaac) GB:SP = BBC 120* [Anthony Isaac:ST]

9548 Square Pegs (1982) Theme (The Waitresses) US:SP = Polydor 2225* [The Waitresses:ST]; Theme (The Waitresses) US:LP = Polydor PX1-507* [The Waitresses:ST]

9549 Staccato [Johnny Staccato] (1959) Score (Elmer Bernstein) US:LP = Capitol T-1287/ST-1287*

9550 Stage Show (1956) Highlights (pop music) US:LP-BP = Golden Archives GA-100 [Elvis Presley:ST]

9551 Stand Up and Cheer *see* Johnny Mann's Stand Up and Cheer

9552 Star Blazers *see* Space Cruiser Yamato

9553 Star Search (1985) Score (t: Joey Carbone/s:various) US:LP = MCA 5732*

9554 Star Trek (1966) Score-A (Alexander Courage) US:LP = GNP 8005*; Score-B (e:George Duning/e: Gerald Fried) US:LP = X LXDR-703* [Tony Bremner]; Score-C (e:Jerry Fielding/e:Sol Kaplan/e:Samuel Matlovsky/ e:Joseph Mullendore) US:LP = X LXDR-704* [Tony Bremner]; Score-D (e:Fred Steiner/e:Sol Kaplan) US:LP = Varese 704.270*; Score-E (e:Fred Steiner/e:George Duning/e:Jerry Fielding US:LP = Varese 704.300*; Theme-F ["Beyond Antares"] (Wilbur Hatch) US: SP = R-Way 1001* [Nichelle Nichols: ST]

9555 Stark Reality, The / Scores ["Hoagy Carmichael's Music Shop"] (pop music) US:LP-MS = AJP LPS-5166/7* [Hoagy Carmichael & Monty Stark:ST]

9556 Starsky and Hutch (1976) Theme-A (Tom Scott) US:SP = Ode 8-50433* [Tom Scott:ST]; Theme-A (Tom Scott) US:LP = Ode 34966* [Tom Scott: ST]; Theme-B (Mark Snow) GB:LP = DJM 22081* [@Laurie Holloway]

9557 Steptoe and Son (1963) Theme (Ron Grainer) GB:SP = Pye 7N-45141 [Ron Grainer:ST]; Theme (Ron Grainer) GB:LP = RCA 1020* [Ron Grainer:ST]

9558 Steve Allen Show, The (1956) Score (pop music) US:LP = Dot DLP-3480/DLP-25480* [Steve Allen:ST]; Theme [Main Title] (Steve Allen) US: LP = World Pacific 411 [Bud Shank]

9559 Steve Lawrence Show, The (1965) Score (t:Arthur Malvin/s:pop music) US:LP = Columbia CL-2419/ CS-9219* [Steve Lawrence:ST]

9560 Stingiest Man in Town, The (1956) Score (Fred Spielman) US:LP = Columbia CL-950

9561 Stingray (1965) Themes (Barry Gray) GB:LP-10 = PRT DOW-3* [Barry Gray:ST]; Theme-A (Barry Gray) GB: LP = Contour 2870.185* [Cy Payne]; Theme-B (Barry Gray) US:SP = RCA 76-2360 [Marco Muniz]

9562 Stoney Burke (1962) Themes (Dominic Frontiere) US:SP = UA 565 [Maurene Bayand]; Theme (Dominic Frontiere) US:SP = Roulette 4470 [Sonny Lester]; Theme (Dominic Frontiere) US: LP = Capitol 1869* [Nelson Riddle]

9563 Storefront Lawyers, The (1970) Theme (Morton Stevens) US: SP = Liberty 56189 [The Ventures & Morton Stevens:ST]

9564 Story of Christmas, The (1963) Score (Roger Wagner) US:LP = Capitol T-1964/ST-1964* [Roger Wagner:ST]

9565 Straightaway (1961) Score (Maynard Ferguson) US:LP = Roulette R-52076/SR-52076*

9566 Strange Report, The (1971) Theme (Roger Webb) GB:LP = MFP 5272* [Geoff Love]

9567 Strange World of Gurney Slade, The (1960) Themes (Max Harris) US:SP = Atco 6187 [Max Harris:ST]; Theme (Max Harris) US:SP = Capitol 4513 [Ray Anthony]; Theme (Max Harris) US:LP = London 3238/231* [@Ted Heath]

9568 Stranger on the Run [Death Dance at Banner] (1967) Theme (Kay Scott) US:SP = Decca 9-32215 [Bill Anderson:ST]

9569 Strauss Family, The (1973) Scores (ae:Cyril Ornadel/s:classical music) US:LP-MS = Polydor DD2-3506*

9570 Strawberry Shortcake in Big Apple City (1981) Highlights + Dialog (Mark Volman & Howard Kaylan) US: LP = Kid Stuff KS-163*

9571 Strawberry Shortcake—Pets on Parade (1982) Highlights + Dialog (Mark Volman & Howard Kaylan) US: LP = Kid Stuff KS-5024*

9572 Streetcar Named Desire, A (1984) Score (Marvin Hamlisch) US: LP = Allegiance AV-439*

9573 Streets of San Francisco, The (1972) Theme (Patrick Williams) US: SP = Capitol 4036* [Patrick Williams: ST]; Theme (Patrick Williams) US:LP = RCA 1-1896* [Henry Mancini]; Theme (Patrick Williams) US:LP = Mercury 1-1089* [Johnny Gregory]

9574 Strike Force (1981) Theme (Dominic Frontiere) US:LP-PP = Jenson 2300* [The Jenson Concert Band]

9575 Strike It Rich (1985) Theme (David Mindel) GB:SP = BBC 177* [ST]

9576 Studio One (1948) Theme-A [Main Title] (Vic Oliver) US:SP = Columbia 4-39912 [Art Lowry]; Theme-A [Main Title] (Vic Oliver) US:LP = RCA 1020 [Hugo Winterhalter]; Theme-B ["Let Me Go Lover"] (J. Carson) US: SP = Columbia 4-40366 [Joan Weber: ST]; Theme-C ["Song of a Summer Night"] (Robert Allen) US:SP = Columbia 4-40730 [Mitch Miller]; Theme-D ["A Man's World"] (Alec Wilder) US: SP = Columbia 4-40772 [Mitch Miller]; Theme-E ["Love Me to Pieces"] (Endsley) US:SP = Columbia 4-40955 [Jill Corey:ST]; Theme-F ["Ballad of Yermo Red"] (Terry Gilkyson) US:SP = Columbia 4-40742 [Terry Gilkyson:ST]; Theme-G ["The Pit"] (Jack Brooks) US: SP = Epic 9122 [Neal Hefti]; Theme-H ["A Chance at Love"] (Carl Sigman) US: SP = Columbia 4-40561 [Paul Weston]

9577 Studs Lonigan (1981) Theme (Ken Lauber) US:SP = Sandcastle 30735* [The Dukes of Dixieland]

9578 Sullivans, The (1976) Theme (Geoff Harvey) GB:LP = MFP 5759* [The Power Pack Orchestra]

9579 Sunday Cricket / Theme (Benson & Lewis) GB:EP = RCA 2238* [Tony King]

9580 Sunday Night at the Movies [The ABC Sunday Night Movie] (1963) Theme (Winston Sharples) US:LP = ABC 513* [Frank DeVol]

9581 Sunshine (1973) Highlights + Dialog (John Denver) US:LP = MCA 387*

9582 Super Circus (1949) Highlights (pop music) US:LP-10 = Mercury MG-25136 [Claude Kirchner & Mary Hartline:ST]

9583 Supercar (1962) Theme (Barry Gray) US:LP = Capitol 1869* [Nelson Riddle]

9584 Surf's Up (1965) Score (various) US:LP = Vault 109 [The Challengers:ST]

9585 Superman *see* Adventures of Superman, The

9586 Surfside 6 (1960) Theme (Jerry Livingston) US:SP = Decca 9-31194 [Alexander Courage]; Theme (Jerry Livingston) US:LP-MS = Tee Vee Toons 1100 [@ST]

9587 Suspicion / Theme (Wilfred Josephs) GB:LP = Polydor 2383.294* [Marcus Dods:ST]

9588 Sutherland's Law (1976) Theme (J. McCann) GB:LP = Contour 2870.439* [Malcolm Lockyer]

9589 Swamp Fox, The [Walt Disney Presents] (1959) Theme (Buddy Baker) US:SP = Disneyland 125 [Rex Allen:ST]; Theme (Buddy Baker) US: LP = Buena Vista 3307 [Rex Allen:ST]; Theme (Buddy Baker) US:LP = Disneyland 3921 [@Rex Allen:ST]

9590 Swap Shop (1981) Theme (B. Robertson) GB:LP = BBC 486* [@ Brown Sauce:ST]

9591 Sweeney (1974) Theme (Harry South) US:LP = K-Tel 4780* [Sounds Orchestral]; Theme (Harry South) GB: LP = Philips 6308.255* [Johnny Gregory]; Theme (Harry South) GB:LP-MS = Pickwick 50-DA-315* [Bruce Baxter]

9592 Swing into Spring [Texaco Star Theatre] (1958) Score (pop music) US:LP-BP = Sandy Hook SH-2057

9593 Switch (1975) Theme (Glen Larson) GB:LP = DJM 2023* [Ray Davies and the Button Down Brass]

T

9594 TCB (1970) Score (pop music) US:LP = Motown MS-682* + US:LP = Motown M5-171* [The Supremes and The Temptations:ST]

9595 T.H.E. Cat (1966) Theme (Lalo Schifrin) US:LP = RCA 3716* [Al Hirt]; Theme (Lalo Schifrin) US:LP = Wyncote 9184* [The Wyncote Orchestra & Chorus]

9596 TV Eye (1978) Theme (Carl Davis) GB:SP = State 85* [Carl Davis: ST]

9597 TV's Top Tunes (1954) Highlights (pop music) US:LP-10 = Capitol H-9118 [Ray Anthony:ST]

9598 Tab Hunter Show, The (1960) Theme (Pete Rugolo) US:LP = Mercury 2016* [Pete Rugolo:ST]

9599 Take Another Look (1973) Theme (Paddy Kingsland) GB:LP = BBC 188* [@BBC Radiophonic Workshop:ST]

9600 Take Five / Theme [pilot] (Elmer Bernstein) US:LP = Choreo 11* [Elmer Bernstein:ST]

9601 Take Hart (1980) Theme (Bob Morgan) GB:LP = BBC 486* [@Bob Morgan:ST]

9602 Take Three—Composers / Theme (John Cacavas) US:LP = Golden Crest 4080* [John Cacavas:ST]

9603 Tale of Beatrix Potter, The (1984) Theme (Carl Davis) US:LP-MS = SQN 5057-1* [@ST]

9604 Tales of Cri-Cri, The [Les Contes de Cri-Cri] (1984) Score (Francisco Soler) US:LP = CBS FM-41002*

9605 Tales of the Gold Monkey (1982) Theme (Mike Post & Pete Carpenter) US:LP = MCA 5380* [Warren Schatz]

9606 Tales of the Texas Rangers (1958) Theme (Irving Friedman) US: SP = RCA WBY-63 [Shorty Long]; Theme (Irving Friedman) US:LP = RCA 1004 [@Shorty Long]

9607 Tales of the Unexpected (1979) Theme (Ron Grainer) US:LP = DRG 15018* [Ron Grainer:ST]

9608 Tales of Wells Fargo (1957) Theme (Stanley Wilson) US:SP = RCA WBY-79 [The Prairie Chiefs]; Theme (Stanley Wilson) US:LP = Columbia 8400* [Johnny Gregory]; Theme (Stanley Wilson) US:LP = RCA 2158* [Dale Robertson:ST]

9609 Talkin' to the Blues *see* Modern Romances

9610 Tall Man, The (1960) Theme-A (Billy Strange) US:SP = Capitol 4524 [Clu Gulager:ST]; Theme-B (Esquivel) US:LP = UA 6161* [Al Caiola]

9611 Tamariu / Theme (Paddy Kingsland) GB:LP = BBC 93* [BBC Radiophonic Workshop:ST]

9612 Target: The Corruptors (1961) Theme (Rudy Schrager) US:LP = Dot 25421* [Herschel Burke Gilbert:ST]

9613 Tarzan (1966) Theme + Underscore + Dialog ["The Eyes of the Lion"] (t:Sydney Lee/u:Walter Greene) US:LP = Leo LE-902/LES-902*; Theme [Main Title #1] (Sydney Lee) US:SP = Columbia 4-43749 [Marty Manning]; Theme [Main Title #2] (Nelson Riddle) US:LP = Liberty 7532* [Nelson Riddle: ST]

9614 Tawny *see* Jackie Gleason Show, The

9615 Taxi (1978) Score (Bob James) US:LP = Columbia FC-38678* [Bob James:ST]

9616 Ted Mack and the Original Amateur Hour (1949) Scores (pop music) US:LP-MS = UA UXL-2

9617 Telford's Change (1979) Themes (Johnny Dankworth) GB:SP = BBC 63* [Johnny Dankworth:ST]; Theme (Johnny Dankworth) GB:LP = BBC 365* [@Johnny Dankworth:ST]

9618 Tell Me on a Sunday (1980) Score (stage songs:Andrew Lloyd Webber) US:LP = Polydor PD1-6260* [Marti Webb:ST]

9619 Tender Is the Night (1985) Score (e:Richard Rodney Bennett/e:pop music) GB:LP = BBC REB-582*

9620 Tennessee Ernie Ford Show, The (1955) Score (pop music) US:LP = Capitol T-1751/ST-1751* [Tennessee Ernie Ford:ST]

9621 Terrahawks (1984) Score (Richard Harvey) GB:LP = Anderburr HX-100*

9622 Terror in Teakwood, The *see* Thriller

9623 Texaco Star Theatre *see* Swing Into Spring (1958)

9624 Texan, The (1958) Theme (William Loose) US:LP = RCA 2163* [Marty Gold] + Theme (William Loose) US:SP = Columbia 4-41369 [Mr. Roberts]

9625 Texas John Slaughter [Walt Disney Presents] (1958) Theme (Stan Jones) US:LP = Disneyland 3921 [@Stan Jones:ST]

9626 Texas Wheelers, The (1974) Theme (John Prine) US:SP = Atlantic 3218* [John Prine:ST]

9627 That Girl (1966) Theme (Earle Hagen) US:LP-MS = Tee Vee Toons 1200 [@ST]

9628 That Was the Week That Was (1964) Highlights + Dialog [British Series] (t:Ron Grainer/e:various) GB: LP = Parlophone PMC-1197; Highlights + Dialog [USA Series] (t:Ron Grainer/ e:Tom Lehrer) US:LP-BP = Radiola MR-1123; Score [USA Series] (Tom Lehrer) US:LP = Reprise R-6179/RS-6179* [Tom Lehrer]; Theme [Main Title] (Ron Grainer) US:LP = Mio International 5006* [John Cacavas]; Theme ["A Tribute to John F. Kennedy"] (David Lee) US:SP = ABC 10514 [Millicent Martin:ST]

9629 That's Life (1975) Theme (David Lee) GB:LP = EMI 168* [Geoff Love]

9630 Then Came Bronson (1969) Excerpts (James Hendricks) US:LP = MGM E-4662/SE-4662* [Michael Parks: ST]; Theme [Main Title] (George Duning) US:SP = Capitol 2672* [The Little Big Horns]; Themes ["The Forest Primeval"] (Gil Melle) US:LP = Jazz Chronicles 702* [Gil Melle:ST]

9631 Thicke of the Night (1983) Theme (Alan Thicke) US:SP = Atlantic 7-89701* [Alan Thicke:ST]

9632 Thin Man, The (1957) Theme (Pete Rugolo) US:SP = Mercury 71447 [Pete Rugolo:ST]; Theme (Pete Rugolo) US:LP = Mercury 60109* [Pete Rugolo: ST]; Theme (Pete Rugolo) US:LP = Somerset 8800* [Skip Martin]

9633 Think Again (1983) Theme (Francis Monkman) GB:LP = BBC 486* [@Francis Monkman:ST]

9634 This Is Your Life (1952) Score (t:Alexander Laszlo/s:pop music) US: LP = Imperial LP-9051 [Von Dexter:ST]

9635 This Is Your World *see* Grand Tour

9636 Thomas and Sarah (1979) Theme (Harry Rabinowitz)GB:LP = DJM 22081* [@Max Harris]

9637 Thorn Birds, The (1983) Themes (Henry Mancini) US:SP = WB 29697-7* [Henry Mancini:ST]; Themes (Henry Mancini) US:LP = RCA 1-5315* [Henry Mancini:ST]

9638 Three Days That Changed the World, The / Score (pop music) US:LP-PP = DSEA 258*

9639 Three Men in a Boat (1980) Theme (David Fanshawe) GB:SP = BBC 35* [David Fanshawe:ST]

9640 Three's Company (1977) Theme (Joe Raposo) US:LP = RCA 1-3052* [Henry Mancini]; Theme (Joe Raposo) US:SP = Dore 947 [Rambling Willie]

9641 Thriller (1960) Score (Pete Rugolo) US:LP = Time 2034/S-2034*; Theme ["Terror in Teakwood"] (Caesar Giovannini) US:SP = Decca 9-31529 [Stanley Wilson]; Theme ["Terror in Teakwood"] (Caesar Giovannini) US: LP = Decca 74481* [Stanley Wilson]

9642 Thunderbirds (1968) Underscore + Dialog (Barry Gray) GB:LP = UA SULP-1159 + GB:LP = Hallmark SH-227; Theme-A (Barry Gray) US:LP = MMG 702* [Geoff Love]; Themes-A-B (Barry Gray) GB:LP-10 = PRT DOW-3* [Barry Gray:ST]; Themes-A-C (Barry Gray) GB:LP = UA 30281 [@Barry Gray:ST]

9643 Thursday Night at the Movies *see* CBS Thursday Night Movie, The

9644 Tibet *see* High Adventure with Lowell Thomas

9645 Tightrope (1959) Theme (George Duning) US:SP = Kapp 325 [Vic Schoen]; Theme (George Duning) US: LP = Philips 600-027* [Johnny Gregory]; Theme (George Duning) US:LP = Camden 627* [Mundell Lowe]

9646 Time of Your Life, The *see* Playhouse 90

9647 Time Tunnel, The (1966) Theme (John Williams) US:LP = GNP 2133* [Neil Norman]

9648 Tinker, Tailor, Soldier, Spy (1980) Theme (Geoffrey Burgon) US:LP-MS = BBC 2-22000* [@Paul Phoenix: ST]; Theme (Geoffrey Burgon) GB:SP = Different 20* [Paul Phoenix:ST]; Theme (Geoffrey Burgon) GB:LP = BBC 391* [@Paul Phoenix:ST]

9649 Tiny Tree, The (1978) Themes (Johnny Marks) US:SP-PP = Tiny Tree 101* [Roberta Flack:ST]

9650 Tito Rodriguez Show, The Score (pop music) US:LP = UA L-31057/LS-61057* [Tito Rodriguez:ST]

9651 To Rome with Love (1969) Theme (Jay Livingston & Ray Evans) US:SP = Ranwood 856* [The Exotic Guitars]; Theme (Jay Livingston & Ray Evans) US:LP = Ranwood 8061* [The Exotic Guitars]

9652 To Serve Them All of My Days (1982) Themes (Kenyon Emrys-Roberts) US:LP-MS = SQN 5057-1* [@ST]

9653 Today / Theme (Irving Friedman) GB:LP = Pickwick 50-DA-315* [Bruce Baxter]

9654 Today Show, The / Score ["From Ragtime to Rock"] (pop music) US:LP-PP = Mrs. Paul's 24RM-0189

9655 Together with Music (1955) Scores (pop music) US:LP-MS = DRG DARC2-1103 [Noel Coward & Mary Martin:ST]

9656 Tom Ewell Show, The (1960) Theme (Jerry Fielding) US:LP = Dot 25421* [Herschel Burke Gilbert:ST]

9657 Tom Sawyer (1957) Score (Frank Luther) US:LP = Decca DL-8432

9658 Tomorrow's World (1957) Theme-A (Johnny Dankworth) GB:LP = BBC 324* [@Johnny Dankworth:ST]; Theme-B (Richard Denton & Martin Cook) GB:SP = BBC 78* [Richard Denton & Martin Cook:ST]; Theme-B (Richard Denton & Martin Cook) GB:LP = BBC 385* + GB:LP = BBC 391* [Richard Denton & Martin Cook:ST]; Theme-C (Paul Hart) GB:LP = BBC 508* [@Paul Hart:ST]

9659 Tonight / Theme (J. Spencer) GB:LP = BBC 454 [@The Hilbersum Orchestra]

9660 Tonight Show, The (1953) Score-A (pop music) US:LP = Coral CRL-57070 [Steve Allen & Steve Lawrence & Eydie Gorme:ST]; Score-B (Steve Allen) US:LP = Coral CRL-57004 [Steve Allen:ST]

9661 Tonight Show, The (1962) Highlights + Dialog (pop music) US:LP-MS = Casablanca SPNB-1296* [Johnny Carson & Cast:ST]; Score (various) US:LP = Columbia CL-2367/CS-9167* [Skitch Henderson:ST]; Theme [Main Title] (Paul Anka) US:SP = Amherst 310* [Doc Severinsen:ST]

9662 Tony Hancock Show, The *see* Hancock's Half Hour

9663 Top Cat (1961) Theme (Hoyt Curtin) US:LP-MS = Tee Vee Toons 1100 [@ST]

9664 Top of the Form / Theme (M. Ross) GB:LP = Decca 333* + GB:LP = BBC 454* [Ray Martin]

9665 Tops in Blue (1970) Score (pop music) US:LP-PP = TIB LP-1*

9666 Town Like Alice, A (1981) Theme (Bruce Smeaton) US:LP-MS = SQN 5057-1* [@ST]

9667 Toyah (1980) Score (pop music) GB:LP = Safari LIVE-2*

9668 Trailmaster, The *see* Major Adams — Trailmaster

9669 Train Now Standing, The Theme (Ron Grainer) GB:LP = EMI 5143* [The Pandora Orchestra]

9670 Training Dogs the Woodhouse Way (1982) Theme + Dialog (Sam Fonteyn) GB:LP = BBC 455*

9671 Travels of Jamie McPheeters, The (1963) Theme (Leigh Harline) US:SP = MGM 13210 [The Osmond Brothers:ST]; Theme (Leigh Harline) US:LP = 20th 4109* [Bill Ramal]

9672 Travels with Charley (1968) Theme (Rod McKuen) US:LP = Stanyan 10045* [Arthur Greenslade]

9673 Tre Donne (1970) Highlights (Ennio Morricone) US:LP = Cerberus CEM-SP-0117*

9674 Treasure Hunt (1956) Theme (Tommy Wolf) US:LP = MGM 3729* [The Metropolitan Jazz Quartet]

9675 Treasure Island (1976) Excerpts (Paul Baillargeon) US:LP-PP = Blue Marble Company BMC-1001* [Paul Baillargeon:ST]

9676 Trials of O'Brien, The (1965) Theme (Sid Ramin) US:SP = UA 932 [Al Caiola]; Theme (Sid Ramin) US:LP = Camden 927* [Ray Martin]

9677 Tribes [The Soldier Who Declared Peace] (1970) Theme (Marty Cooper) US:SP = Happy Tiger 574 [Brooks Anderson:ST]

9678 Tribute to John F. Kennedy, A *see* That Was the Week That Was

9679 Trini Lopez Show, The (1971) Score (pop music) US:LP = Reprise R-6361/RS-6361* [Trini Lopez & Cast:ST]

9680 Tripods (1985) Theme (Ken Freeman) GB:LP = BBC 508* [@ST]

9681 Trouble in Tahiti (1952) Score (stage songs:Leonard Bernstein) US:LP = MGM E-3646 + US:LP = Helidor H-25020/HS-25020*

9682 Troubleshooters, The (1965) Theme (Tom Springfield) GB:LP = EMI TWO-175* [Brian Fahey]; Theme (Tom Springfield) GB:LP = MFP 5272* [Geoff Love]; Theme (Tom Springfield) GB: LP = Philips 6308.087* [Chaquito and Johnny Gregory]

9683 Trumpton (1976) Highlights (Freddie Phillips) GB:LP = BBC REC-234*

9684 Tukiki and His Search for a Merry Christmas (1979) Theme (Hagood Hardy) CA:LP = Attic 1097* [Hagood Hardy:ST]

9685 Tune in Dan's Cafe, The *see* Night Gallery

9686 Turn the Key Deftly (1961) Theme (Stan Zabka) US:SP = Columbia 4-41620 [Frank DeVol]; Theme (Stan Zabka) US:LP = Laurie 2025* [Stan Zabka:ST]

9687 'Twas the Night Before Christmas (1976) Highlights + Underscore + Dialog (Maury Laws) US:LP = Disneyland 1367*

9688 Twelve O'Clock High (1964) Theme (Dominic Frontiere) US:LP = Metro 544* [@Milton DeLugg]; Theme (Dominic Frontiere) US:LP = Audio Fidelity 6146* [Dick Dia]; Theme (Dominic Frontiere) US:LP = Spinorama 161 [The Spinorama Orchestra]

9689 20 Minute Workout (1983) Score (s:Andy Muson/t:Ira Newborn) US:LP = Ronco RTV-2007* [Shiva:ST]

9690 25 Years of Life (1961) Highlights + Dialog (pop music) US:LP-10-PP = Time-Life 5803 [Bob Hope & Cast: ST]

9691 26 Men (1958) Theme (Hal Hopper) US:SP = RCA 47-7201 [Lee Adrian]; Theme (Hal Hopper) US:LP = RCA 1027 [@Lee Adrian]

9692 Twilight Zone, The (1959) Score-A (e:Jerry Goldsmith/e:Bernard Herrmann/e:Nathan Van Cleave/e: Franz Waxman/t:Marius Constant) US: LP = Varese STV-81171; Score-B (e:Jerry Goldsmith/e:Bernard Herrmann/e:Nathan Scott/e:Fred Steiner) US:LP = Varese STV-81178; Score-C (e:Jerry Goldsmith/e:Bernard Herrmann/e:Leonard Rosenman/e:Nathan Van Cleave) US:LP = Varese STV-81185; Score-D (e: Jerry Goldsmith/e:Fred Steiner/e:Nathan Van Cleave/t:Bernard Herrmann) US:LP = Varese STV-81192; Score-E (e: Jerry Goldsmith/e:Nathan Van Cleave/ e:Jeff Alexander/e:Fred Steiner/t:Bernard Herrmann) US:LP = Varese STV-81205

9693 Twin Detectives (1976) Theme (The Hudson Brothers) US:SP = MCA/ Rocket 40508* [The Hudson Brothers: ST]; Theme (The Hudson Brothers) US: LP = MCA/Rocket 2169* [The Hudson Brothers:ST]

9694 Two Ronnies, The (1978) Score (Ronnie Barker) GB:LP = Spot 8518* [Ronnie Barker & Ronnie Corbett: ST]; Theme [Main Title] (Ronnie Hazlehurst) GB:LP = Polydor 2384.107* [Ronnie Hazlehurst:ST]

9695 Two Up, Two Down (1979) Theme (Dominic Bugatti) GB:LP = BBC 365* [@Paul Nicholas:ST]

9696 Tycoon, The (1978) Theme (unknown) GB:SP = BBC 56* [Bob Elgar]

U

9697 U.F.O. (1972) Theme (Barry Gray) US:LP = GNP 2163* [Neil Norman]; Theme (Barry Gray) US:LP = MMG 702* [Geoff Love]; Theme (Barry Gray) GB:LP = Contour 2870.185* [Cy Payne]

9698 U.S. Marshal (1958) Theme (Ray Ellis) US:SP = MGM 12874 [Ray Ellis:ST]

9699 Ugliest Girl in Town, The (1968) Theme (Howard Greenfield) US: SP = SGC 45-004* [The Will-O-Bees:ST]

9700 Ultraman (1967) Score (Tohru Fuyuki) JA:LP = Columbia CQ-7020*

9701 Uncle Floyd Show, The (1974) Score (e:Floyd Vivino/etc.) US:LP = Mercury 811-149-1* [Uncle Floyd & Cast: ST]

9702 Uncommon Love, An (1984) Theme (Bruce Roberts) US:SP = Atlantic 7-89636* [Laura Branigan:ST]; Theme (Bruce Roberts) US:LP = Atlantic 80147* [Laura Branigan:ST]

9703 Underdog (1964) Theme (W. Biggers) US:LP-MS = Tee Vee Toons 1200 [@ST]

9704 Unknown War, The (1978) Scores (e:Rod McKuen/e:Vitaley Gueviksman/e:Liut Guidravitchus) US:LP-MS-PP = Stanyan SRP-201*; Excerpts (Rod McKuen) US:LP = Stanyan SR-5098* [Rod McKuen:ST]

9705 Untouchables, The (1959) Score (Nelson Riddle) US:LP = Capitol T-1430/ST-1430*

9706 Up with the People (1965) Score-A (various) US:LP = Pace 1101/S-1101*; Score-B (various) US:LP = Pace 1103/S-1103*; Score (various) US:LP = Pace 1104/S-1104*

9707 Upstairs, Downstairs (1973) Themes (Alexander Faris) US:LP-PP = WGBH 10* + US:LP-MS = SQN 5057-1* [@Harry Rabinowitz:ST]; Theme (Alexander Faris) GB:LP = DJM 20522* [@Harry Rabinowitz:ST]; Theme (Alexander Faris) GB:LP = MFP 50091* [Geoff Love]

V

9708 Valiant Years, The *see* Winston Churchill—The Valiant Years

9709 Van Der Valk (1972) Theme (Jack Trombey) US:SP = Vanguard 35175 [Simon Park:ST]; Theme (Jack Trombey) US:LP = K-Tel 4780* [Sounds Orchestral]; Theme (Jack Trombey) US: LP = Peters 1024 [Manuel]

9710 VEGA$ (1978) Theme (Dominic Frontiere) US:LP-PP = Jenson 0400*[The Jenson Jazz Band]; Theme (Dominic Frontiere) US: LP-PP = Jenson 3011* [The Jenson Marching Band]

9711 Velveteen Rabbit, The (1985) Score (George Winston) US:LP = Dancing Cat DC-3007*

9712 Vendetta (1966) Themes (John Barry) GB:SP = CBS 2390 [John Barry: ST]; Themes (John Barry) GB:LP = CBS 64816 [John Barry:ST]

9713 Vic Damone Show, The *see* Lively Ones, The

9714 Victory at Entebbe (1976) Themes (Charles Fox) GB:SP = WB 7050* [Charles Fox:ST]; Theme (Charles Fox) US:LP-BP = Centurion 1600* [@Charles Fox:ST]

9715 Victory at Sea (1952) Score-A (s:Richard Rodgers/as:Robert Russell Bennett) US:LP = RCA LM-2335/LSC-2335* + US:LP = RCA ANL1-0970*; Score-B (s:Richard Rodgers/as:Robert Russell Bennett) US:LP = RCA LM-2226/LSC-2226* + US:LP = RCA ANL1-1432*; Score-C (s:Richard Rodgers/as:Robert Russell Bennett) US: LP = RCA LM-2523/LSC-2523*

9716 Villa Alegre (1976) Score-A (Moises Rodriguez) US:LP = Peter Pan 8170*; Score-B (Moises Rodriguez) US: LP = Peter Pan 8171*; Score-C (Moises Rodriguez) US:LP = Peter Pan 8172*

9717 Vincent Lopez Show, The (1956) Score (pop music) US:LP = Coral CRL-57168 [Vincent Lopez:ST]

9718 Virginian, The (1962) Highlights ["The Last Grave at Socorro Creek"] (Bernard Herrmann) US:LP-BP = Cine Sound CSR-301 [Bernard Herrmann:ST]; Themes (Percy Faith) US:LP = Columbia 9009* [Percy Faith: ST]; Theme (Percy Faith) US:SP = Columbia 4-42979 [Percy Faith:ST]

9719 Vision On (1973) Theme (Olivier Toussaint) GB:LP = BBC 214* [@Pete Winslow]

9720 Voice of Firestone, The (1949) Theme (Idabelle Firestone) US:LP = RCA 1020 [Hugo Winterhalter]

9721 Voyage Around My Father, A (1969) Theme (Wilfred Josephs) GB:LP = Polydor 2383.294 [Marcus Dods:ST]

9722 Voyage of the Heroes (1985)

Theme (Howard Davidson) GB:SP = BBC 169* [ST]; Theme (Howard Davidson) GB:LP = BBC 508* [@ST]

9723 Voyage to the Bottom of the Sea (1964) Theme (Paul Sawtell) US: LP = GNP 2133* [Neil Norman]; Theme (Paul Sawtell) US:LP = Audio Fidelity 6146* [Dick Dia]

W

9724 WKRP in Cincinnati (1979) Theme (Tom Wells) US:SP = MCA 51205* [Steve Carlisle:ST]; Theme (Tom Wells) US:LP = MCA 5304* [Steve Carlisle:ST]

9725 Wagon Train (1957) Score (e: John Williams/t:Jerome Moross/t:Laurindo Almeida/t:David Buttolph/t:Cyril Mockridge/t:David Raksin/t:Leo Shuken/t:Roy Webb/t:Stanley Wilson) US: LP = Mercury MG-20502/SR-60179* [Stanley Wilson: ST]; Theme-A [Main Title #1] (Rene & Russell) US:LP = RCA 1027 [@Shorty Rogers]; Theme-B [Main Title #2] (Sammy Fain) US:LP = RCA 1004 [@Johnny O'Neill]; Theme-B [Main Title #2] (Sammy Fain) US:SP = RCA 47-7379 [Johnny O'Neill]

9726 Walt Disney Presents *see* Disneyland

9727 Waltons, The (1972) Theme (Jerry Goldsmith) US:SP = Ranwood 947* [The Magic Organ]; Theme (Jerry Goldsmith) US:LP = RCA 1-1043* [Danny Davis]; Theme (Jerry Goldsmith) US:LP = Columbia 33193* [@Roger Kellaway]

9728 Waltz King, The [Walt Disney Presents] (1963) Score (as:Helmuth Froschauer) GB:LP = HMV CLP-1733

9729 Wanted: Dead or Alive (1958) Theme-A (Rudy Schrager) US:LP = Dot 25421* [Herschel Burke Gilbert:ST]; Theme-B (William Loose) US:LP = Roulette 25073* [Bud Wattles]

9730 Warship (1973) Theme (Anthony Isaac) US:LP = Chalfont 77.008* [Band of H.M. Royal Marines]; Theme (Anthony Isaac) GB:LP = Pickwick 50-DA-315* [Bruce Baxter]; Theme (Anthony Isaac) GB:LP = EMI 2069* [Reginald Dixon]

9731 Washington: Behind Closed Doors (1977) Score (Dominic Frontiere) US:LP = ABC AB-1044*

9732 Watch (1978) Score (Jim Parker) GB:LP = BBC REC-314*

9733 Watch Me Die *see* Philco Television Playhouse

9734 Water Margin, The (1978) Theme (Masaru Sato) GB:SP = BBC 50* [Pete MacJunior]; Theme (Masaru Sato) GB:LP = BBC 310* [@Pete MacJunior]

9735 Waterfront (1954) Theme (Alexander Laszlo) US:LP = RCA 2042* [Buddy Morrow]

9736 We the Accused (1980) Themes (Daryl Runswick) US:LP-MS = BBC 2-22000* [@Daryl Runswick:ST]; Themes (Daryl Runswick) GB:SP = BBC 83* [Daryl Runswick:ST]; Theme (Daryl Runswick) GB:LP = BBC 424* [@Daryl Runswick:ST]

9737 Weavers Green (1966) Theme (Wilfred Josephs) GB:LP = Polydor 2383.294* [Marcus Dods:ST]

9738 Welcome Back, Kotter (1975) Theme (John Sebastian) US:SP = Reprise 1349* [John Sebastian:ST]; Theme (John Sebastian) US:LP = Reprise 2249* [John Sebastian:ST]; Theme (John Sebastian) US:LP = Peter Pan 8185* [The Peter Pan Orchestra & Chorus]

9739 We'll Get By (1975) Theme (Joe Raposo) US:LP = Polydor 6034* [Arthur Fiedler & The Boston Pops]

9740 Wells Fargo *see* Tales of Wells Fargo

9741 What I Want to Be *see* Mickey Mouse Club, The

9742 What It Was Was Love (1969) Score (Gordon Jenkins) US:LP = RCA LSP-4115* [Steve Lawrence & Eydie Gorme:ST]

9743 What Really Happened to the Class of '65? (1977) Theme (Don Costa) US:SP = MCA 40876* [Venice & Don Costa:ST]

9744 What's Happening? (1976) Theme (Henry Mancini) US:LP = RCA 1-2290* + US:LP = RCA 1-3347* [Henry Mancini:ST]; Theme (Henry Mancini) US:SP = RCA 11054* [Henry Mancini:ST]

9745 Wheel of Fortune (1975) Theme (Merv Griffin) US:LP=TAV 4004* [Merv Griffin & Mort Lindsey:ST]

9746 Wheelbase (1965) Theme (David Lee) GB:LP=Decca 333* [Ray Martin]

9747 When the Boat Comes In (1975) Theme (at:David Fanshawe) GB: LP-MS=Reader's Digest 9411* [@Alex Glasgow]; Theme (at:David Fanshawe) GB:LP=BBC 236* [@Alex Glasgow]

9748 When the Kissing Had to Stop (1962) Theme (Laurie Johnson) GB: LP=MGM 8104* [Laurie Johnson:ST]

9749 When You Love *see* Climax

9750 Where the Action Is (1965) Score (t:Tommy Boyce & Bobby Hart/s: pop music) US:LP=ABC 531/S-531* [Steve Alaimo:ST]

9751 Whicker (1984) Themes (Graham DeWilde) GB:SP=BBC 143* [Graham DeWilde:ST]; Themes (Graham DeWilde) GB:LP=BBC 524* [@Graham DeWilde:ST]

9752 White House Years, The *see* Eleanor and Franklin

9753 White Shadow, The (1979) Theme (Mike Post & Pete Carpenter) US: LP=Elektra 1-60028* [Mike Post:ST]

9754 Who-Dun-It / Theme (Tony Hatch) GB:LP=Marble Arch 1179* [@Tony Hatch:ST]

9755 Who Pays the Ferryman (1978) Score (Yannis Markopoulos) GB: LP=BBC REB-315*; Theme (Yannis Markopoulos) US:LP-MS=BBC 2-22000* [@Yannis Markopoulos:ST]

9756 Whodunit / Theme (Freddie Perrin) GB:LP=DJM 22076* [Ray Davies and the Button Down Brass]

9757 Wichita Town (1959) Score (Hans J. Salter) US:LP=Citadel CT-6022

9758 Wide Country (1962) Theme (John Williams) US:LP=Decca 74481* [Stanley Wilson]

9759 Wide, Wide World (1956) Score (David Broekman) US:LP=RCA LPM-1280

9760 Wilburn Brothers Show, The (1963) Score (pop music) US:LP=Decca DL-4721/DL-74721* [The Wilburn Brothers & Loretta Lynn:ST]

9761 Wild Wild West, The (1965) Theme (Richard Markowitz) US:LP-MS=Tee Vee Toons 1100 [@ST]

9762 Will Shakespeare (1978) Score (Richard Hill) GB:LP=Pye NSPH-22*

9763 Willo the Wisp (1981) Theme + Underscore + Dialog (Tony Kinsey) GB:LP=BBC REC-427*

9764 Wimbledon / Theme (Benson & Lewis) GB:EP=RCA 2238* [Tony King]

9765 Wimbledon '74 (1974) Theme (Paddy Kingsland) GB:SP=BBC 93* [BBC Radiophonic Workshop:ST]

9765a Wind in the Willows, The (1983) Score (Keith Hopwood) GB:LP= Powderworks POW-4033*

9766 Winds of War, The (1982) Score (Robert Cobert) US:LP=Varese STV-81180*

9767 Wings (1976) Themes (Alexander Faris) GB:SP=BBC 37* [Alexander Faris:ST]; Theme (Alexander Faris) US:LP=K-Tel 4780* [Sounds Orchestral]; Theme (Alexander Faris) GB: LP=BBC 310* [@Alexander Faris:ST]

9768 Winning Streak (1985) Theme (Alan Hawkshaw) GB:SP=Ten Records 67* [ST]

9769 Winston Churchill—The Valiant Years (1960) Score (s:Richard Rodgers/as:Robert Emmett Dolan) US: LP=ABC 387/S-387*

9770 Within These Walls (1974) Theme (Denis King) GB:LP=DJM 20522* + GB:LP=DJM 22081* [@ Denis King:ST]; Theme (Denis King) GB:LP=Contour 2870.439* [Malcolm Lockyer]

9771 Wizard of Odds, The (1973) Theme (Alan Thicke) US:SP=L.A. Records 10067* [Stan Worth:ST]

9772 Wizards and Warriors (1983) Excerpts (Lee Holdridge) US:LP=Varese 704.290* [Charles Gerhardt]

9773 Woman Called Moses, A (1978) Score (s:Van McCoy/t:Coleridge-Taylor Perkinson) US:LP=MCA 3054*

9774 Woman of Substance, A (1984) Theme (Nigel Hess) GB:LP=Sierra FEDL-101* [@ST]

9775 Wombles, The (1971) Score-A (Mike Batt) US:LP=Columbia PC-33140*; Score-B (Mike Batt) GB:LP= CBS 80526*; Score-C (Mike Batt) GB: LP=CBS 80997*

9776 Wonder Woman *see* New, Original Wonder Woman, The

9777 Wonderama Score-A (Joe Raposo) US:LP = Buddah BDS-5030* [Bob McAllister:ST]; Score-B (Artie Kaplan) US:LP = Kid Stuff KS-1001* [Bob McAllister:ST]

9778 Wonderbug *see* Krofft Supershow, The

9779 Wonderful Town (1958) Score (stage songs:Leonard Bernstein) US: LP = Columbia OL-5360/OS-2008*

9780 Woody Woodpecker Show, The (1957) Highlights (Clarence Wheeler) US:EP = Wonderland 2040

9781 World at War, The (1972) Score (e:Carl Davis/e:pop music) GB: LP = Decca SPA-325*

9782 World Cup Grandstand (1982) Theme (Andrew Lloyd Webber) GB: SP = BBC 116* [ST]

9783 World Cup '74 (1974) Theme (Benson & Lewis) GB:SP = BBC 22* [Tony King]; Theme (Benson & Lewis) GB:LP = BBC 188* [@Tony King]

9784 World Cup '82 (1982) Theme (Jeff Wayne) GB:SP = CBS 2493* [Jeff Wayne:ST]

9785 World of Jazz, The *see* Omnibus

9786 World of Liberace, The (1975) Score (pop music) US:LP = American Variety AVL-1029* [Liberace:ST]

9787 World of Science, The / Theme (Paddy Kingsland) GB:LP = BBC 196* [BBC Radiophonic Workshop:ST]

9788 World of Sport, The / Theme (M. Harper) GB:LP = MFP 50091* [Geoff Love]

9789 World of Strawberry Shortcake, The (1981) Highlights + Dialog (Mark Volman & Howard Kaylan) US: LP = Kid Stuff KS-165*

9790 World Tonight, The / Theme (Armando Sciasscia) US:LP = Roulette 804* [uncredited]

9791 World War I (1964) Score (Morton Gould) US:LP = RCA LM-2791/LSC-2791 + US:LP = RCA ANL1-2334*

9792 World's End (1981) Theme (Alan Price) GB:SP = BBC 100* [Alan Price:ST]

9793 Worzel Gummidge (1978) Excerpts (Denis King) GB:LP = MMT 111* [John Pertwee & Cast:ST]

9794 Wuthering Heights (1978) Themes (Carl Davis) US:LP = DRG 704* [Carl Davis:ST]

9795 Wyatt Earp *see* Life and Legend of Wyatt Earp, The

Y

9796 Yancy Derringer (1958) Theme (Henry Russell) US:SP = Felsted 8561 [Tommy Mara:ST]

9797 Year at the Top, A (1977) Score (e:Paul Shaffer/e:Hegel & George) US:LP = Casablanca NBLP-7068* [Greg Evigan & Paul Shaffer:ST]

9798 Year of the French, The (1983) Score (Paddy Moloney) US:LP = Shanachie 79036* [The Chieftans:ST]

9799 Yellow Rose, The (1984) Theme (Johnny Lee) US:SP = WB 29375-7* [Johnny Lee & Lane Brody:ST]; Theme (Johnny Lee) US:LP = WB 25056-1* [Johnny Lee & Lane Brody:ST]

9800 Yogi Bear (1958) Theme (Hoyt Curtin) US:LP-MS = Tee Vee Toons 1100 [@ST]

9801 Young and the Restless, The (1975) Score (Jerry Winn & Bob Todd) US:LP = PIP 6812*

9802 Young Man from Boston, The (1963) Highlights + Dialog (Allan Jay Friedman) US:LP-PP = ABC Promo WR-4546

9803 Young Set, The (1965) Theme (Ray Martin) US:LP = Camden 927* [Ray Martin:ST]

9804 You're a Good Man, Charlie Brown (1973) Score (stage songs:Clark Gesner) US:LP = Atlantic SD-7252*

9805 You're a Good Sport, Charlie Brown (1975) Underscore + Dialog (Vince Guaraldi) US:EP = Charlie Brown 408

9806 You're in Love, Charlie Brown (1967) Underscore + Dialog (Vince Guaraldi) US:LP = Charlie Brown 2605

9807 You're the Greatest, Charlie Brown (1979) Underscore + Dialog (Ed Bogas) US:EP = Charlie Brown 411

Z

9808 Zane Grey Theatre [Dick Powell's Zane Grey Theatre] (1956) Theme-A (Joseph Mullendore) US:LP = Dot 25421* [Herschel Burke Gilbert:ST]; Theme-B (Harry Lubin) US:LP = Decca 74151* [Harry Lubin:ST]

9809 Zoo Gang, The (1975) Theme (Paul McCartney) GB:SP = Capitol 5997* [Paul McCartney & Wings:ST]

9810 Zoom (1974) Score (Newton Wayland) US:LP = A&M SP-3402*

9811 Zorro (1957) Theme + Underscore + Dialog (t:George Bruns/u:William Lava) US:LP = Disneyland 3601; Theme (George Bruns) US:SP = Capitol 3993 [Fred Waring]

Related Records

A

9812 ABC Movie of the Week (1969) [pop music] Theme = US:LP = A&M 3501* [Burt Bacharach]

9813 Adventures of Parsley, The [dialog] GB:LP = BBC 18*

9814 Adventures of Rin-Tin-Tin, The (1954) [dialog + record music] US: LP-10 = Columbia CL-679 + US:LP = Harmony HL-9502

9814a Affairs of the Heart [classical music] Theme = GB:LP = Contour 2870. 439 [Malcolm Lockyer]

9815 Ages of Man, The (1966) [dialog] US:LP = Columbia OL-5390

9816 Alfred Hitchcock Presents (1955) [classical music] Theme = US: SP = Sunset 2021 [Stanley Wilson]; [classical music] Theme = US:LP = London 44077* [Frank Chacksfield]

9817 Alice in Wonderland (1986) [dialog] US:LP = Kid Stuff DAR-3902*

9818 Amos and Andy Show, The (1951) [pop music] Theme/US:SP = Decca 9-25195 [Jesse Crawford]; [pop music] Theme/US:LP = Decca 8300 [Jesse Crawford]

9819 Anna Karenina (1978) [classical music] Theme = GB:LP = Decca 580* [@collection]

9820 Apollo [classical music] Theme = GB:LP = BBC 324* [@Carl Bohm]

9821 Apollo-Soyuz (1975) [classical music] Theme = GB:LP = BBC 324* [@Aaron Copland]

9822 Archers, The [radio music] Theme = GB:LP-MS = BBC 454 [@collection]

9823 Aspen (1977) [pop music] Theme = US:SP = A&M 1990* [Herb Alpert]

9824 Astro Boy (1963) [dialog] US: LP = Simon Says M-31

B

9825 Billy Budd (1963) [dialog] US: LP-PP = General Electric BB-1

9826 Billy Walker Show, The [unverified production] Score = US:LP = MGM SE-4863*

9827 Blithe Spirit [dialog] US:LP-BP = Sandpiper SP-1 + US:LP-BP = Beastly Hun 1100

9828 Bluegrass Country [unverified production] Theme = US:SP = BOO 6018* [Denis Lepage]

9829 Bob Hope Show, The (1952) [pop music] Theme = US:LP = Liberty 7321* [Dave Pell]

9830 Born Free (1974) [film music—from "Born Free"] Theme = US: SP = Columbia 4-43801 [John Barry]

9831 Buck Rogers in the 25th Century (1979) [film music—from "Buck Rogers in the 25th Century"] Score = US: LP = MCA 3097* + US:LP = MCA 37087*

C

9832 CBS Sunday Morning [classical music] Theme = US:LP = RCA 1-4574* [The Canadian Brass]

9833 Caine Mutiny Court Martial, The (1956) [dialog] US:LP-MS = Mark 56 LP-741

9834 Candid Camera (1948) [dialog] US:LP = RCA LPM-3679/LSP-3679*

9835 Captain Video and His Video Rangers (1950) [dialog] US:EP-MS = RCA VY-2009

9836 Casanova (1971) [classical music] Theme = GB:LP = MFP 5272* [Geoff Love]; [classical music] Theme = GB:LP = Decca 217* [@Karl Münchinger]

9837 Casper, the Friendly Ghost (1953) [film music from "The Friendly Ghost"] Theme = US:LP-MS = Tee Vee Toons 1100 [collection]

9838 Celebrity Bowling (1971) [dialog] US:LP-BP = Custom Fidelity CFS-3347*

9839 Cisco Kid, The (1951) [film music—from "The Cisco Kid Returns"] Theme = US:LP = Starlog 1001 [Albert Glasser]

9840 Coke Time [pop music] Theme = US:LP = RCA 1020 [Hugo Winterhalter]

9841 Cop-Out [unverified production] Theme = US:LP = Friends 1001 [Chuck Barris]

9842 Courageous Cat (1961) [dialog] US:LP = Simon Says M-32

9843 Cowboys, The (1974) [film music—from "The Cowboys"] Theme = US:LP = Philips 6514-186* [John Williams]

D

9844 Daphne's Cartoon Castle [inspired music] Theme = US:LP = Pacific Jazz 10070* [Roger Kellaway]

9845 Dave Garroway Show, The (1949) [pop music] Theme = US:LP = MGM 3729* [Metropolitan Jazz Quartet]

9846 Dawn, The [unverified production] Score = US:LP = American Recording Society SP-1052

9847 Dick Barton—Special Agent [radio music] Theme = GB:LP = MFP 50439* [Geoff Love]

9848 Disco Train [unverified production] Theme = US:SP = Tokeh 45-101* [Donnie Vann]

9849 Discomania [unverified production] Theme = US:SP-12 = Pye 12100 [Discomania Orchestra]

9850 Doris Day Show, The (1968) [pop music] Theme = US:SP = Columbia 13-33029 [Doris Day]

E

9851 Eddie Fisher Show, The (1951) [pop music] Theme = US:LP = World Pacific 411 [Bud Shank]

F

9852 Face the Music [pop music] Theme = GB:LP = Decca 580* [@collection]

9853 Family at War, A (1970) [pop music] Theme = GB:LP = Sunset 50339* [London Concert Orchestra]

9853a Famous Adventures of Mr. Magoo, The (1964) [film music] Theme = US:LP-MS = Tee Vee Toons 1300 [@ST]

9854 Fang Face (1978) [dialog] US:LP = Peter Pan 1107

9855 Fat Albert and the Cosby Kids (1972) [dialog] US:LP = Paramount PAS-6053*

9856 First Churchills, The (1971) [classical music] Theme = US:LP-PP = WGBH 10* + US:LP-MS = SQN 5057-1* [@Yehudi Menuhin]

9857 Flaxton Boys, The [classical music] Theme = GB:LP = Decca 217* [@Ernest Ansermet]

9858 Flintstones, The (1960) [dialog + record music] US:LP = Colpix CP-302

9859 Flipper (1964) [film music—from "Flipper"] Theme = US:SP = Capitol 4996 [Jimmie Haskell]; [film music—from "Flipper"] Theme = US:LP = Metro 544* [Milton DeLugg]

9860 For Johnny [radio music] Highlights = GB:LP = Philips 6382-043

9861 Forsyte Saga, The (1969) [classical music] Theme = US:LP-MS = BBC 2-22000* [@Eric Coates]

9862 Frank Sinatra Show, The (1957) [pop music] Theme = US:LP = World Pacific 411 [Bud Shank]

9863 Frost Report, The (1966) [dialog] GB:LP = Pye NSPL-18199*

9864 Funky Phantom, The (1971) [dialog] US:LP = Peter Pan 8216

G

9865 George Burns and Gracie Allen Show, The (1950) [pop music] Theme = US:LP = World Pacific 411 [Bud Shank]

9866 Ghost Story (1972) [dialog] US:LP = Peter Pan 8114

9867 Going for a Song (1986) [classical music] Theme = GB:LP = Decca 217* [@Istvan Kertesz]

9868 Good Life, The (1971) [pop music] Theme = US:LP = Kapp 3599* [Sacha Distel]

9869 Grand Hotel (1965) [classical music] Theme = GB:LP = BBC 454 [@Reginald Leopold]

9870 Great Divide, The [unverified production] Theme = US:SP = Elektra 45067 [Harry Chapin]

H

9871 Hallmark Hall of Fame (1951) [pop music] Theme = US:LP = RCA 1020 [Hugo Winterhalter]; [dialog] US:LP-MS-PP = RCA PRM-202

9872 Harper Valley P.T.A. (1981) [pop music] Theme = US:SP = Plantation 003 [Jeannie C. Riley]

9873 Hitch-hiker's Guide to the Galaxy (1982) [radio music + dialog] US:LP = Hannibal HNBL-1307 + US:LP-MS = Hannibal HNBL-2301

9874 Hollywood Squares, The (1966) [dialog] US:LP = Event EV-6903

9875 Home from the Sea [pop music] Theme = GB:LP = BBC 365* [@Band of H.M.S. Ark Royal]

9876 Horse of the Year [classical music] Theme = GB:LP = Decca 333* [Ray Martin]

9877 Huckleberry Hound (1958) [dialog + record music] US:LP = Colpix CP-202 + US:LP = Colpix CP-207

I

9878 It Ain't Half Hot, Mum (1973) [dialog] GB:LP = EMI ECC-3074*

9879 It's Time to Pray, America [dialog] US:LP = House Top HTR-702

J

9880 Jackanory [dialog] GB:LP = BBC 229*

9881 Jazz Alive [unverified production] Theme = US:LP = Antilles 1012* [Ben Sidran]

9882 Jetsons, The (1962) [dialog + record music] US:LP = Colpix CP-213

K

9883 Kennedy-Nixon Television Debates, The (1959) [dialog] US:LP-MS = Columbia D2L-372

L

9884 Lariat Sam [unverified production] US:LP = Peter Pan 8004

9885 Late Show, The [pop music] Theme = US:LP = London 44077* [Frank Chacksfield]

9886 Life and Times of David Lloyd George, The (1981) [film music – from "Maddalena"] Theme = GB:LP = BBC 424* [@Ennio Morricone]

9886a Life Styles of the Rich and Famous (1984) [film music – from "Five Days from Home"] Theme = US:LP = MCA 2362* [Bill Conti]

9887 Light of Experience, The [classical music] Theme = GB:LP = BBC 310* [@Zamfir]

9888 Linus the Lionhearted (1964) [dialog] US:LP-PP = Post/General Foods L-10

9889 Lone Ranger, The (1949) [classical music] Theme = US:LP-MS = Tee Vee Toons 1100 [collection]

9890 Loner – Rod McKuen, The [unverified production] Theme = US: LP = Stanyan 10045* [Arthur Greenslade]

9891 Long Hot Summer, The (1965) [film music – from "The Long Hot Summer"] Theme = US:SP = Roulette 4045 [Jimmie Rogers]

9892 Lost Hour, The [unverified production] Theme = US:LP = Coral 57016 [Alfredo Antonini]

9893 Love Story (1973) [film music – from "Love Story"] Theme = US:SP = Capitol 2991* [Al DeLory]

M

9894 M*A*S*H (1972) [film music – from "M*A*S*H"] Theme = US:SP = Capitol 2811* [Al DeLory]

9895 Magilla Gorilla Show, The (1964) [dialog] US:LP = Golden LP-120

9896 Mahu and the Monkey [unverified production] Theme = US:LP-10 = MGM 513 [Philip Green]

9897 Manhunt (1970) [classical music] Theme = GB:LP = EMI TWO-372* [Johnny Keating]

9898 Mark Twain Tonight (1967) [dialog] US:LP = Columbia OS-3080*

9899 Masterpiece Theatre (1971) [classical music] Theme = US:SP = Ranwood 922* [Charles Randolph Grean]; [classical music] Theme = US:LP-PP = WGBH 10* + US:LP-MS = SQN 5057-1* [@Roland Douatte]

9900 Mickey Spillane's Mike Hammer [Mike Hammer] (1983) [pop music] Theme = US:SP = Mercury M-71915 [Clebanoff]

9901 Midnight Movie, The [unverified production] Theme = US:LP = Laurie 2025* [Stan Zabka]

9902 Morecambe and Wise [dialog] GB:LP = BBC 258*

9903 Movie Four [unverified production] Theme = US:LP = Laurie 2025* [Stan Zabka]

9904 Munsters, The (1964) [dialog + record music] US:LP = Golden LP-139

9905 My Son, My Son (1981) [pop music] Theme = GB:LP = BBC 365* [@Rick Wakeman]

N

9905a New York Knickerbockers, The [unverified record and production] Theme = GB:LP-PP = JSD 100* [John Scott]

9906 Nina, the Pinta and the Santa Maria, The [unverified production] Score = US:LP = Dot DLP-9009

9907 9 to 5 (1982) [film music – from "9 to 5"] Theme = US:SP = RCA 12316* [Dolly Parton]

O

9908 Odd Couple, The (1970) [film music – from "The Odd Couple"] Theme = US:SP = Dot 45-17105 [Neal Hefti]

9909 Old Grey Whistle Test, The [pop music] Theme = GB:LP = BBC 310* [@Area Code 615]

9910 On Approval (1982) [pop music] Theme = US:LP-MS = SQN 5057-1* [@David Ralph]

9911-12 Onedin Line, The (1974) [classical music] Theme = US:LP = K-Tel 4780* [Sounds Orchestral]; [classical music] Theme = GB:LP = MFP 5272* [Geoff Love]

P

9913 Patti Page Show, The (1956) [pop music] Theme = US:LP = MGM 3729* [Metropolitan Jazz Quartet]

9914 Paul Wallach Show, The [radio music] Theme = US:SP = Orange 4050 [Ian Whitcomb]

9915 Pebble Mill at One [pop music] Theme = GB:LP = BBC 171* [Norrie Paramor]

9916 Peyton Place (1964) [film music – from "Peyton Place"] Theme = US:SP = Vee Jay 635 [Themes, Inc.]; [inspired music] Score = US:LP = Epic 26147* [Randy Newman]

9917 Popeye the Sailor (1958) [film music – from "Popeye the Sailor"] Theme = US:LP-MS = Tee Vee Toons 1100 [collection]

9918 Porridge (1974) [dialog] GB: LP = BBC 270*

9919 Prince and the Pauper, The [Walt Disney Presents] (1962) [dialog + record music] US:LP = Disneyland 1311 + US:LP-MS = Disneyland DDF-3

Q

9920 Quatermass Experiment, The (1953) [classical music] Theme = US: LP = MMG 702* [Geoff Love]; [classical music] Theme = GB:LP = BBC 324* [@Andre Previn]

9921 Quick and the Dead, The [radio dialog] US:LP = RCA LM-1130

9922 Quick Draw McGraw (1959) [dialog + record music] US:LP = Colpix CP-203 + US:LP = Colpix CP-211

R

9923 Rag Trade, The (1958) [dialog] GB:LP = EMI PMC-1188

9924 Red Skelton Show, The (1951) [pop music] Theme = US:LP = MGM 3215* + US:LP = MGM 3748* [David Rose]

9925 Robotech [Super Dimension Fortress Macross] (1984) [dialog] US: EP = Peter Pan 2041

9926 Rocky Jones, Space Ranger (1954) [dialog] US:EP = Columbia MJV-4-153

9927 Rosemary Clooney Show, The (1957) [pop music] Theme = US: LP = World Pacific 411 [Bud Shank]

9928 Royal Heritage (1977) [classical music] Theme = GB:LP = BBC 580* [@collection]

9929 Royal Windsor Horse Show, The [unverified production] Score = GB: LP = MSD 00601*

9930 Ruff and Ready (1957) [dialog + record music] US:LP = Colpix CP-201

S

9931 Sailor (1976) [pop music] Theme = US:LP = Peters 1024* [Manuel]; [pop music] Theme = GB:LP = BBC 310* [@Band of H.M.S. Ark Royal]

9932 Saturday Night at the Mill [pop music] Theme = GB:LP = BBC 310* [@Kenny Ball]

9933 Shaft (1974) [film music – from "Shaft"] Theme = US:SP = UA 50851* [The Ventures]

9934 Shakespeare Plays, The (1978) [dialog] US:LP-MS-PP = WNET TelEd-2/3; [dialog] US:LP-PP = WNET TelEd-1

9935 Shakespeare – Soul of an Age [dialog] US:LP = Caedmon 1170

9936 Shazzan! (1967) [dialog + record music] US:LP = Hanna Barbera 2061*

9937 She Lives (1973) [pop music]

Theme = US:LP = Lifesong 8007* [Jim Croce]

9938 Side Street [unverified production] Theme = US:LP = A&M 3219* [Chuck Mangione]

9939 Sir Francis Drake (1962) [unverified record] Theme = GB:LP = HMV 1565

9940 Sky at Night, The [classical music] Theme = GB:LP = BBC 324* + GB:LP = BBC 442* [@Frank Chacksfield]

9941 Softly Softly (1966) [classical music] Theme = GB:SP = BBC 35* [David Fanshawe]; [classical music] Theme = GB:LP = BBC 310* [@David Fanshawe]

9942 Soldier's Tale, A (1983) [classical music] Score = US:LP = Delos DMS-3014*

9943 Soul [unverified production] Theme = US:LP = Strata East 8003* [New York Bass Violin Choir]

9944 Space Shuttle, The (1982) [classical music] Theme = GB:SP = CBS 1688* [Donald Johanos]; [classical music] Theme = GB:LP = BBC 442* [@Donald Johanos]

9945 Stranger on the Shore (1962) [pop music] Theme = US:SP = Atco 45-6217 [Acker Bilk]

9946 Sugarfoot (1957) [film music from—"Sugarfoot"] Theme = US:LP = Coral 757267* [Lawrence Welk]; [film music—from "Sugarfoot"] Theme = US: LP = Columbia 8400* [Johnny Gregory]

9947 Sunday Showcase [unverified production] Theme = US:LP = Laurie 2025 [Stan Zabka]

T

9948 Thanks for the Memory (1961) [dialog] US:LP-10-PP = RCA Custom M80L-5803

9949 Third Man, The (1960) [film music—from "The Third Man"] Theme = US:SP = London 5N-59045 [Anton Karas]; [film music—from "The Third Man"] Theme = US:LP = London 1560 [Anton Karas]

9950 This Happy Breed [dialog] US:LP-PP = Mary 710

9951 Till Death Us Do Part (1964) [dialog] GB:LP = Golden Hour GH-550

9952 Tom Corbett, Space Cadet (1950) [dialog] US:EP-MS = RCA WY-449

9953 Tonight Show, The [unverified production] Theme = US:LP = Laurie 2025 [Stan Zabka]

9954 Top Cat (1961) [dialog + record music] US:LP = Colpix CP-212

9955 Top Secret (1961) [pop music] Theme = US:LP = Philips 600-027* [John Gregory]; [pop music] Theme = GB:SP = Pye 7N-15383 [Laurie Johnson]

V

9956 Vincent Van Gogh—A Self Portrait (1962) [dialog] US:LP = Caedmon 1180

9957 Visit to Washington with Mrs. Lyndon B. Johnson, A (1966) [dialog] US:LP = MGM SE-4353*

W

9958 War and Peace (1973) [classical music] Theme = US:LP-MS = BBC 2-22000* [@Desmond Walker]; [classical music] Theme = GB:LP = BBC 188* [@Desmond Walker]

9959 What's My Line? (1950) [dialog] US:LP = Dot DLP-3153

9960 Wild Bill Hickok (1952) [dialog + record music] US:LP = Sunset 5000

9961 Wilderness Trail, The [record music] US:LP-PP = National Geographic 07708*

Y

9962 Yanks Are Coming, The (1974) [dialog] US:LP-PP = Texaco TYAC-1001

9963 Yogi Bear (1958) [dialog + record music] US:LP = Colpix CP-205

Z

9964 Z Cars (1960) [classical music] Theme = GB:SP = Piccadily 7N-35032 [Johnny Keating]; [classical music] Theme = GB:LP = BBC 454* [@Johnny Keating]

III. STAGE MUSIC

A

9964 A to Z (1921) Theme-A/US: LP = Monmouth 7043 [Gertrude Lawrence:1921 LOC] + Theme-B/GB:LP = MFP 1160 [Jack Buchanan:1921 LOC] + Theme-C/GB:LP = Parlophone 7150 [Jack Buchanan:1921 LOC]

9965 AM Route 66 [Industrial Show] Score (Hank Beebe) US:LP-PP = American Motors 4732 [OC]

9966 Absent Minded Dragon, The [Children's Show] Score (Martha Coe) US:LP = Simon Says SS-25 [OC]

9967 Abyssinia (1906) Theme-A/ US:78 = Columbia 3410 + Theme-B/ US:78 = Columbia 3504 + Theme-C/ US:LP = Audio Rarities 2290 [Bert Williams:1906 NYOC]

9968 Ace of Clubs (1950) Highlights (Noel Coward) GB:LP-MS = WRC SH-179/180 + US:LP-MS = Monmouth MES-7062/3 [1950 LOC]

9969 Across America [Industrial Show] Score (Shirley Grossman) US:LP-PP = Westinghouse WGL-1001 [OC]

9970 Act, The (1977) Score (John Kander) US:LP = DRG SL-6101* [1977 NYOC]

9971 Adventures of a Bear Named Paddington, The [Children's Show] Score (Herbert Chappell) GB:LP = Spark SRLM-505* [OC]

9972 Afgar (1919) Excerpts-A-B-C/ GB:LP = WRC SH-164 [Alice Delysia: 1919 LOC] + Themes-D-E/GB:78 = Columbia 1027 [Alice Delysia:1919 LOC] + Themes-F-G/GB:78 = Columbia 1025 [Lupino Lane:1919 LOC] + Themes-H-I/GB:78 = Columbia 1026 [Harry Welchman:1919 LOC] + Themes-J-K/ GB:78 = Columbia 1024 [John Humphries:1919 LOC]

9973 Africana (1927) Excerpts (various) US:LP = Columbia KG-31571 [Ethel Waters:1927 NYOC]

9974 After the Ball (1954) Score (Noel Coward) GB:LP = Philips BL-7005 [1954 LOC]

9975 Ain't Misbehavin' (1978) Scores (pop music) US:LP-MS = RCA CBL2-2956* [1978 NYOC]

9976 Ain't Supposed to Die a Natural Death (1971) Scores (Melvin Van Peebles) US:LP-MS = A&M SP-3510* [1971 NYOC]

9977 Airs on a Shoestring (1953) Excerpts (Donald Swann) GB:LP = EMI EMC-3088* [Flanders & Swann: 1953 LOC]

9978 Aladd [Children's Show] Highlights (Jo Adler) US:LP = Bag-A-Tale 1000* [OC]

9979 Aladdin (1960) Score (television songs:Cole Porter) GB:LP = Columbia 33-SX-1211* [1960 LOC]

9980 Aladdin (1979) Score (Sandy Wilson) GB:LP = President PTLS-1072* [1979 LOC]

9981 Aladdin and His Wonderful Lamp (1964) Score (The Shadows) GB: LP = Columbia SCX-3522* [1964 LOC]

9982 Alec Wilder – Clues to a Life (1982) Score (stage songs) US:LP = OC 8237* [1982 NYOC]

9983 All About Life [Industrial Show] Score (Jerry Powell) US:LP-PP = Time/Life 89424 [OC]

9984 All American, The (1962) Score (Charles Strouse) US:LP = Columbia KOL-5760/KOS-2160* + CSP AKOS-2160 [1962 NYOC]

9985 All in Love (1961) Score (Jack Urbont) US:LP = Mercury OCM-2204/ OCS-6204* [1961 NYOC]

9986 All in One (1955) Score [Trouble in Tahiti] (Leonard Bernstein) US:

LP = MGM E-3646 + US:LP = Heliodor H-25020/HS-25020* [Studio Cast]

9987 All Night Strut, The (1976) Score (various) US:LP-PP = Playhouse PHS-CLE-1001* [1976 Cleveland OC]

9988 Allegro (1947) Score (Richard Rodgers) US:LP = RCA LOC-1099/LSO-1099e + US:LP = RCA CBM1-2757e [1947 NYOC]

9989 Alma, Where Do You Live? (1910) Themes/US:78 = Columbia 1092 [Truly Shattuck:1910 NYOC]

9990 Alone at Last (1914) Theme/US:78 = Columbia 1926 [Roy Atwell:1914 NYOC]

9991 Along Fifth Avenue (1949) Theme/US:LP = Dolphin 2 [Nancy Walker:1949 NYOC]

9992 Amazing Adele, The (1955) Themes/US:SP = Coral 9-61570 [Johnny Desmond:1955 NYOC]

9993 Ambassador, The (1971) Score (Don Gohman) GB:LP = RCA SER-5618* [1971 LOC]

9994 American Beauty, An (1900) Theme/GB:78 = Berliner 3191 [Edna May:1900 LOC]

9995 America's Her Name (1985) Score (Gene Bone & Howard Fenton) US:LP = Soaring Records SR-1007* [1985 Florida OC]

9996 Amy (1975) Score (Ian Butler) GB:LP-PP = Custom 006* [1975 LOC]

9997 Andy Capp (1982) Score (Alan Price) GB:LP = Key 4* [1982 LOC]

9998 Angel (1978) Score (Gary Geld & Peter Udell) US:LP-PP = Abrams GUA-001* [1978 NYOC]

9999 Angel in the Wings (1947) Theme/US:LP = Painted Smiles 1369* [Elaine Stritch:1947 NYOC]

10000 Animal Crackers (1928) Theme/US:LP-10=Decca 5405 [Groucho Marx:1928 NYOC]

10001 Ankles Aweigh (1955) Score (Sammy Fain) US:LP = Decca DL-9025 + US:LP = AEI 1104 [1955 NYOC]

10002 Ann Veronica (1969) Score (Cyril Ornadel) GB:LP = CBS 70052* [1969 LOC]

10003 Anne of Green Gables (1969) Score (television songs:Norman Campbell) GB:LP = CBS 70053* [1969 LOC]

10004 Annie (1965) Highlights-A (William Reed) GB:EP = Philips BE-12600 [1965 LOC]; Highlights-B (William Reed) GB:EP = Philips BE-12602 [1965 LOC]

10005 Annie (1977) Score-I (Charles Strouse) US:LP = Columbia PS-34712 [1977 NYOC]; Score-II (Charles Strouse) GB:LP = CBS 70160* [1978 LOC]; Score-III (Charles Strouse) AU:LP = Festival 36861* [1979 AOC]

10006 Annie Get Your Gun (1946) Score-I (Irving Berlin) US:LP = Decca DL-8001 + US:LP = Decca DL-9018/DL-79018e + US:LP = MCA 2031e + US:LP = MCA 37092e [1946 NYOC]; Highlights-II (Irving Berlin) GB:LP = WRC SH-393 + US:LP = Stanyan SR-10069 [1947 LOC]; Score-III (Irving Berlin) US:LP = RCA LOC-1124/LSO-1124* [1966 Revival NYOC]

10007 Anya (1965) Score (as:George Forrest & Robert Wright) US:LP = UA UAL-4133/UAS-5133* [1965 NYOC]

10008 Anyone Can Whistle (1964) Score (Stephen Sondheim) US:LP = Columbia KOL-6080/KOS-2480* + US:LP = CSP AS-32608* [1964 NYOC]

10009 Anything Goes (1934) Score-I (Cole Porter) US:LP-PP = Smithsonian R-007 [1934 NYOC]; Excerpts-I (Cole Porter) US:LP-MS = Decca DX-153 [Ethel Merman:1934 NYOC]; Highlights-II (Cole Porter) GB:LP = WRC SHB-26 [1935 LOC]; Score-III (Cole Porter) US:LP = Epic FLM-13100/FLS-15100* [1962 Revival NYOC]; Score-IV (Cole Porter) GB:LP = Decca SKL-5031* [1969 Revival LOC]

10010 Applause (1970) Score (Charles Strouse) US:LP = ABC OCS-11* [1970 NYOC]

10011 Apple Blossoms (1919) Theme-A/US:78 = Vocalion 20001 [John Charles Thomas:1919 NYOC]; Theme-B/US:78 = Vocalion 20002 [John Charles Thomas:1919 NYOC]; Theme-C/US:78 = RCA/Victor 64902 [Fritz Kreisler:1919 NYOC]; Themes-D-E/US:78 = RCA/Victor 956 [Fritz Kreisler 956 [Fritz Kreisler:1919 NYOC]

10012 Apple Sauce (1940) Theme/GB:LP = Parlophone 7154 [Florence Desmond:1940 LOC]

10013 Apple Tree, The (1966) Score (Jerry Bock) US:LP = Columbia KOL-6620/KOS-3020* [1966 NYOC]

10014 Arabian Nights (1954) Score (John Loeb & Carmen Lombardo) US: LP = Decca DL-9013 [1954 NYOC]

10015 Arc de Triomphe (1943) Excerpts (Ivor Novello) GB:LP = WRC SH-216 [1943 LOC]

10016 Arcadians, The (1910) Score (Lionel Monckton) GB:LP = Columbia TWO-233* [Studio Cast]

10017 Archy and Mehitabel *see* Shinbone Alley

10018 Are You with It? (1945) Themes/US:78 = Majestic 1026 [Joan Roberts:1945 NYOC]

10019 Ari (1970) Score (Walt Smith) US:LP-PP = Ari 1001 [Demo Cast]

10020 Arms and the Girl (1950) Highlights (Morton Gould) US:LP-10 = Decca DL-5200 + US:LP-BP = JJA 19752 + US:LP = CSP X-14879 [1950 NYOC]

10021 Around the World in 80 Days (1947) Excerpts (Cole Porter) US: LP-BP = JJA 19745 [1947 NYOC]

10022 Arrivederci Pittsburgh (1964) Score (Stan Freeman & Jack Lawrence) US:LP-PP = Arrivederci 1001 [Demo Cast]

10023 Artists and Models of 1927 (1927) Theme-A/US:78 = Columbia 1207 [Ted Lewis:1927 NYOC]; Theme-B/US: 78 = Columbia 1391 [Ted Lewis:1927 NYOC]

10024 Artist's Model, An (1895) Theme/GB:78 = Berliner 2125 [Maurice Farkoa:1895 NYOC]

10025 As the Girls Go (1948) Themes/US:LP-BP = JJA 19752 [@ Bobby Clark:1948 NYOC]

10026 As Thousands Cheer (1933) Excerpts (Irving Berlin) US:LP = Monmouth MES-6811* [Studio Cast]; Themes-A-B/US:LP = Columbia 2792 [Ethel Waters:1933 NYOC]; Theme-C/ US:LP = RCA LPV-565 [@Clifton Webb:1933 NYOC]; Themes-D-E/US: LP-PP = JJA 19744 [@Clifton Webb:1933 NYOC]

10027 As You Were (1918) Excerpts (various) GB:LP = WRC SH-164 [Alice Delysia:1918 LOC]

10028 At Home Abroad (1935) Excerpts (Arthur Schwartz) US:LP-BP = JJA 19757 [@1935 NYOC]

10029 At the Drop of a Hat (1957) Score-I (Donald Swann) US:LP = Angel 65042 [1957 LOC]; Highlights-I (Donald Swann) GB:EP = Parlophone GEP-8636 [1957 LOC]

10030 At the Drop of Another Hat (1963) Score (Donald Swann) GB:LP = Parlophone PMC-1216* + US:LP = Angel S-36388* [1963 LOC]; Highlights (Donald Swann) GB:EP = Parlophone GEP-8900 [1963 LOC]

10031 At the Grand (1958) Score (George Forrest & Robert Wright) US: LP-PP = Grand 1001 [Demo Cast]

10032 Athenian Touch, The (1964) Score (Willard Straight) US:LP = Broadway East 101/S-101* [1964 NYOC]

B

10033 Baal (1981) Highlights (Dominic Muldowney) GB:EP = RCA BOW-11* + US:EP-12 = RCA CPL1-4346* [David Bowie:1981 LOC]

10034 Babes in Arms (1937) Excerpts (Richard Rodgers) US:LP-BP = JJA 19771 [@1937 NYOC]

10035 Babes in the Woods (1964) Score (Rick Besoyan) US:LP-PP = Babes 1001 [Demo Cast]

10036 Babes in Toyland (1903) Highlights (Victor Herbert) US:LP-10 = Decca DL-7004 + US:LP = Decca DL-8458 [Studio Cast]; Score (e:Victor Herbert/e:Shelly Markham & Annette Leisten) US:LP-PP = Babes in Toyland 91550* [1979 Revival NYOC]

10037 Baby (1983) Score (David Shire) US:LP = Polydor 821-593-1* [1983 NYOC]

10038 Back Again (1919) Theme/ GB:LP = Parlophone 7150 [@Lee White:1919 LOC]

10039 Bajour (1964) Score (Walter Marks) US:LP = Columbia KOL-6300/ KOS-2700* [1964 NYOC]

10040 Baker Street (1965) Score (Marian Grudeff & Raymond Jessel) US:

LP = MGM E-7000/SE-7000* [1965 NYOC]

10041 Baker's Wife (1976) Score (Stephen Schwartz) US:LP = Take Home Tunes 772* [1976 LAOC]

10042 Balalaika (1936) Highlights (George Posford & Bernard Grun) GB: LP = WRC SH-794 [Studio Cast]

10043 Ballad for Bimshire (1963) Score (Irving Burgie) US:LP = London AM-48002/AMS-78002* [1963 NYOC]

10044 Ballad of Baby Doe, The (1958) Scores (Douglas Moore) US:LP-MS = MGM 3-GC-1* + US:LP-MS = Heliodor 250-35-3* [1958 NYOC]

10045 Ballroom (1979) Score (Billy Goldenberg) US:LP = Columbia JS-35762* [1979 NYOC]

10046 Band Wagon, The (1931) Highlights (Arthur Schwartz) US:LP-10 = RCA L-24003 + US:LP = RCA LVA-1001 + GB:LP = RCA RD-7756 + US:LP = Smithsonian R-021 [1931 NYOC]

10047 Banjo Eyes (1941) Theme/ US:78 = Decca 4314 [Eddie Cantor:1941 NYOC]

10048 Bar Mitzvah Boy (1978) Score (Jule Styne) GB:LP = CBS 70162* [1978 LOC]

10049 Barney 'n' Me (1956) Highlights (Robert Waldman) US:LP-10-PP = Barney G80L-4234 [1956 OC]

10050 Barnum (1980) Score-I (Cy Coleman) US:LP = Columbia JS-36576* [1980 NYOC]; Score-II (Cy Coleman) GB:LP = Air CDL-1348* [1981 LOC]; Score-III (Cy Coleman) AU:LP = RCA VPL1-0366* [1981 AOC]

10051 Barry of Ballymore (1911) Theme-A/US:78 = Columbia 1310 [Chauncey Olcott:1911 NYOC]; Theme-B/US:78 = Columbia 1337 [Chauncey Olcott 1911 NYOC]

10052 Bashville (1983) Score (Denis King) GB:LP = That's Entertainment TER-1072* [1983 LOC]

10053 Bathrooms Are Coming, The [Industrial Show] Score (Larry Siegel) US:LP-PP = GS 1115 [OC]

10054 Be Kind to People Week (1975) Highlights (Jack Bussins) US: EP-PP = Nutty For You 1001* [1975 NYOC]

10055 Be My Guest (1959) Score (various) US:LP-PP = Guest XCTV-10302 [1959 Illinois OC]

10056 Beatlemania (1978) Scores (pop music) US:LP-MS = Arista AL-8501* [1978 NYOC]

10057 Beauty and the Beast (1974) Highlights (Michael Valenti) US:LP = Take Home Tunes 775* [1974 NYOC]

10058 Beauty Shop, The (1914) Theme/US:78 = Vocalion 35010 [Raymond Hitchcock:1914 NYOC]

10059 Because of Elizabeth (1978) Score (Larry Bastian) US:LP-PP = KM 2445* [1978 Illinois OC]

10060 Beg, Borrow or Steal [Clara] (1960) Score (Leon Pober) US:LP = Contemporary CNT-02 [Betty Garrett: 1960 NYOC]

10061 Beggar's Opera, The (1751) Score (John Gay) GB:LP = CBS 70046* [1968 Revival LOC]

10062 Bei Mir Bistu Schoen (1961) Score (Shalom Secunda) US:LP = Decca DL-9115/DL-79115* [1961 NYOC]

10063 Believers, The (1968) Score (The Believers) US:LP = RCA LOC-1151/LSO-1151* [1968 NYOC]

10064 Belle (1961) Score (Monty Norman) GB:LP = Decca SKL-4136* + GB:LP = That's Entertainment TER-1048* [1961 LOC]

10065 Belle, La (1962) Score (William Roy) US:LP-PP = La Belle 1001 [Demo Cast]

10066 Belle of New York, The (1897) Excerpts (Gustave Kerker) GB: LP = Encore 178 [Studio Cast]; Themes-A-B/CA:LP = Rococo 4007 [@Edna May:1897 NYOC]; Theme-C/GB:78 = Berliner 2265 [Frank Lawton:1898 LOC]

10067 Belle Paree, La (1911) Theme/US:LP = Decca 9095 [Al Jolson: 1911 NYOC]

10068 Bells Are Ringing (1956) Score (Jule Styne) US:LP = Columbia OL-5170/OS-2006* [1956 NYOC]

10069 Below the Belt (1966) Highlights (various) US:LP-PP = Upstairs 37-W56-2 [1966 NYOC]

10070 Ben Franklin in Paris (1964) Score (Mark Sandrich, Jr.) US:LP = Capitol VAS-2191/SVAS-2191* [1964 NYOC]

10071 Beowulf (1974) Score (Victor

Davies) CA:LP = Daffodil 30050* [1974 Canadian OC]

10072 Berlin to Broadway with Kurt Weill (1974) Scores (stage songs) US:LP-MS = Paramount PAS-4000* [1974 NYOC]

10073 Best Foot Forward (1941) Excerpts-I (Hugh Martin & Ralph Blane) US:LP-BP = JJA 19743 [@1941 NYOC]; Score-II (Hugh Martin & Ralph Blane) US:LP = Cadence CE-4012/CS-24012* + US:LP = DRG DS-15003* [1963 Revival NYOC]

10074 Best Little Whorehouse in Texas, The (1978) Score (Carol Hall) US: LP = MCA 3049* [1978 NYOC]

10075 Best of Burlesque, The (1957) Score (pop music) US:LP = MGM E-3644/SE-3644* [1957 NYOC]

10076 Betjemania (1980) Score (John Gould) GB:LP = That's Entertainment TER-1002* [1980 LOC]

10077 Betsy (1926) Theme/US: 78 = Brunswick 6507 [Borrah Minnevitch:1926 NYOC]

10078 Betty (1915) Theme/US:78 = RCA/Victor 55080 [Raymond Hitchcock:1915 NYOC]

10079 Between the Devil (1938) Excerpts (Arthur Schwartz) US:LP-MS = Monmouth MES-6604/5* [Studio Cast]; Themes/US:LP-BP = JJA 19758 [@The Tune Twisters:1938 NYOC]

10080 Beyond the Rainbow (1978) Score (Armando Trovajoli) GB:LP = MCA MCF-2874* [1978 LOC]

10081 Biff, Bing, Bang (1919) Theme/CA:78 = HMV 216366 [Red Newman:1919 Canadian OC]

10082 Big Boy (1925) Excerpts (various) US:LP-BP = Pelican 111 [Al Jolson:1925 NYOC]

10083 Big River (1984) Score (Roger Miller) US:LP = MCA 6147* [1984 NYOC]

10084 Big Sun City (1978) Score (John Heather) GB:LP = Logo 1004* [1978 LOC]

10085 Billie (1928) Theme-A/US: LP-BP = JJA 19804 [@Polly Walker: 1928 NYOC]; Theme-B/US:LP-MS = RCA 4-0407 [@Polly Walker:1928 NYOC]

10086 Billy (1969) Score (Ron Dante & Gene Allen) US:LP-PP = Billy 1001 [Demo Cast]

10087 Billy (1974) Score (John Barry) GB:LP = CBS 70133* [1974 LOC]

10088 Billy Barnes – Live at Studio One (1977) Score (Billy Barnes) US:LP = Huzzah 1020* [1977 LAOC]

10089 Billy Barnes Revue, The (1959) Score (Billy Barnes) US:LP = Decca DL-9706/DL-79076* [1959 NYOC]

10090 Billy Barnes' L.A. (1963) Score (Billy Barnes) US:LP = BB 1001/S-1001* + US:LP = AEI 1134* [1963 LAOC]

10091 Billy Bishop Goes to War (1980) Score (John Gray) CA:LP = Tapestry GD-7372* [1980 Canadian OC]

10092 Billy No Name (1970) Score (Johnny Brandon) US:LP = Roulette OC-11/SROC-11* [1970 NYOC]

10093 Bing Boys Are Here, The (1916) Theme/GB:LP = Parlophone 7145 [@Violet Loraine:1916 LOC]

10094 Biograph Girl (1980) Score (David Heneker) GB:LP = That's Entertainment TER-1003* [1980 LOC]

10095 Bird of Paradise, The (1912) Themes-A-B/US:78 = RCA Victor 65344 + Themes-C-D/US:78 = RCA Victor 65340 + Themes-E-F/US:78 = RCA Victor 65346 + Themes-G-H/US: 78 = RCA Victor 65348 + Themes-I-J/US:78 = RCA Victor 65345 + Themes-K-L/US:78 = RCA Victor 65343 + Themes-M-N/US:78 = RCA Victor Victor 65338 + Themes-O-P/US:78 = RCA Victor 65341 [Hawaiian Quintette:1912 NYOC]

10096 Birthday Garland for Mr. James Cash Penny, A [Industrial Show] Score (Michael Brown) US:LP-PP = A&R 2076 [OC]

10097 Bistro Car on the C.N.R., The [Jubalay] (1979) Score (Patrick Rose) CA:LP = Berandol 9069* [1979 Canadian OC]

10098 Bitter Sweet (1929) Excerpts (Noel Coward) GB:LP-MS = WRC SH-179/180 + US:LP-MS = Monmouth MES-7062/3 [@1929 LOC]; Themes/GB:LP = MFP 1162 [Evelyn Laye:1929 NYOC]; Score (Noel Coward) US:LP = Angel S-35814* [Studio Cast]

10099 Black Mikado, The (1975) Score (stage songs:Gilbert & Sullivan/ as:Janos Bajtala) GB:LP = Transatlantic TRA-300* [1975 LOC]

10100 Black Nativity (1961) Score (as:Langston Hughes) US:LP = Vee Jay LP-5022/SR-5022* + US:LP = Vee Jay SR-8503 + US:LP = Trip 7022* [1961 NYOC]

10101 Black Vanities (1941) Themes-A-B/GB:78 = Decca 7854 [Frances Day: 1941 LOC]; Themes-C-D/GB:78 = Decca 7867 [Frances Day:1941 LOC]; Themes-E-F/GB:78 = Decca 7951 [Bud Flanagan & Frances Day:1941 LOC]

10102 Black Velvet (1939) Themes/ GB:LP = WRC 26 [@Pat Kirkwood: 1939 LOC]

10103 Blackbirds (1926) Excerpts (various) GB:LP = WRC SH-265 [@The Plantation Orchestra:1926 LOC]

10104 Blackbirds of 1928 (1928) Score (Jimmy McHugh) US:LP = Revue LP-1 + US:LP = Sutton SU-270/SSU-270e + US:LP = Columbia OL-6770 [1928 NYOC]

10105 Blackbirds of 1930 (1930) Excerpts (Eubie Blake) US:LP = Columbia CL-2792 [Ethel Waters:1930 NYOC]

10106 Blackbirds of 1936 (1936) Excerpts (Rube Brown) GB:LP = WRC SH-265 [@1936 LOC]

10107 Bless the Bride (1947) Excerpts (Vivian Ellis) GB:LP = WRC SH-228 [@1947 LOC]

10108 Bless You All (1950) Excerpts (Harold Rome) US:LP = Heritage 0063 [Studio Cast]

10109 Blitz! (1962) Score (Lionel Bart) GB:LP = HMV CSD-1441* + US:LP = AEI 1117* [1962 LOC]; Highlights (Lionel Bart) GB:EP = HMV 7EG-8788 [1962 LOC]

10110 Blondel (1983) Score (Stephen Oliver) GB:LP = MCA DBL-1* [1983 LOC]

10111 Blondes and Bombshells (1980) Score (as:Ronnie Cass) GB:LP = 58 Dean Street 100* [1980 LOC]

10112 Blood Brothers (1983) Score (Willy Russell) GB:LP = Legacy LLP-101* [1983 LOC]

10113 Bloomer Girl (1945) Score (Harold Arlen) US:LP = Decca DL-8015: + US:LP = Decca DL-9126/ DL-79126e + US:LP = MCA 2072e [1945 NYOC]

10114 Blossom Time [Lilac Time] (1916) Score (Franz Schubert) US:LP = RCA LK-1018 + US:LP = Angel S-35817* [Studio Cast]; Themes-I-A-B/ GB:78 = Vocalion 05068 [Clara Butterworth:1922 LOC] + Themes-I-C-D/GB: 78 = Vocalion 05065 [Courtice Pounds: 1922 LOC] + Themes-I-E-F/GB:78 = Vocalion 05067 [Courtice Pounds:1922 LOC] + Themes-I-G-H/GB:78 = Vocalion 05066 [Percy Hemming:LOC]; Themes-II-A/US:78 = Decca 225 [Everett Marshall:1938 NYOC] + Themes-II-B/US:78 = Decca 15002 [Everett Marshall:1938 NYOC]; Themes-III-A-B/ GB:78 = Parlophone 20256 + Themes-III-C-D/GB:78 = Parlophone 20504 + Themes-III-E-F/GB:78 = Parlophone 20506 + Themes-III-G-H/GB:78 = Parlophone 20507 [Richard Tauber:1942 LOC]

10115 Blue Eyes (1929) Excerpts (Jerome Kern) GB:LP = WRC SH-171 + US:LP = Monmouth MES-7064 [@1929 LOC]

10116 Blue Kitten, The (1925) Highlights (Rudolf Friml) GB:LP = WRC SHB-37 [1925 LOC]

10117 Blue Mazurka (1920) Theme/GB:78 = HMV 1331 [Elisabeth Pechy:1927 LOC]

10118 Blue Skies (1927) Theme/ GB:78 = HMV 2494 [Jack Smith:1927 LOC]

10119 Bobby, Get Your Gun (1938) Theme/GB:78 = Columbia 1824 [Gertrude Niesen:1938 LOC]

10120 Body Beautiful, The (1958) Score (Jerry Bock) US:LP-BP = Blue Pear BP-1006 [1958 NYOC]

10121 Bohemian Girl, The (1843) Excerpts (William Balfe) GB:LP = HMV 3651 [Studio Cast]

10122 Bombo (1921) Themes-A-B/ US:LP = Decca 9035 + Theme-C/US: LP = Decca 9036 + Theme-D/US:78 = Columbia 2940 + Theme-E/US:78 = Columbia 3513 + Theme-F/US:78 = Columbia 3540 + Theme-G/US:78 = Columbia 3626 + Theme-H/US:78 = Columbia 3779 [Al Jolson:1921 NYOC]

10123 Bonanza Bound (1947) Highlights (Saul Chaplin) US:LP-BP = JJA 19764 [1947 Philadelphia OC]

10124 Boodle (1925) Themes/GB: LP = WRC 329 [Jack Buchanan:1925 LOC]

10125 Boogie Woogie Bubble 'n' Squeak (1983) Themes/GB:SP = That's Entertainment 001-EP* [1983 LOC]

10126 Booth Is Back in Town (1971) Score (Arthur Rubinstein) US:LP-PP = Booth 1001 [Demo Cast]

10127 Bordello (1974) Score (Al Frisch) US:LP-BP = RFO 103* [1974 LOC]

10128 Bottomland (1927) Themes-A-B/US:78 = Columbia 14241 + Theme-C/US:78 = Columbia 14244 + Theme-D/ US:78 = Columbia 14314 + Theme-E/US:78 = Okeh 8672 [Clarence Williams:1927 NYOC]

10129 Bottoms Up for Swingers (1970) Score (Otto Ortwein & Bob Lees) US:LP-PP = WP 1-3650* [1970 Las Vegas OC]

10130 Boy, The [Good Morning, Judge] (1917) Themes-A-B/GB:HMV 834 [Peter Gawthorne & Nellie Taylor: 1917 LOC] + Theme-C/GB:78 = HMV 833 [Nellie Taylor:1917 LOC] + Theme-D/GB:78 = HMV 888 [Peter Gawthorne:1917 LOC] + Theme-E/GB:78 = HMV 02776 [W.H. Berry:1917 LOC]

10131 Boy Friend, The (1954) Score-I (Sandy Wilson) GB:LP = HMV DLP-1078 + US:LP = Stanyan SR-10008 [1954 LOC]; Score-II (Sandy Wilson) US:LP = RCA LOC-1018 [1954 NYOC]; Score-III (Sandy Wilson) GB: LP = Parlophone PCS-7044* [1967 Revival LOC]; Score-IV (Sandy Wilson) AU:LP = Ace of Clubs SCL-1263* [1968 Revival AOC]; Score-V (Sandy Wilson) US:LP = Decca DL-79177* + US:LP = MCA 2074* [1970 Revival NYOC]

10132 Boy Meets Boy (1975) Score-I (Bill Solly) US:LP = JO 13* + US: LP = AEI 1102* [1975 NYOC]; Score-II (Bill Solly) US:LP-PP = Private Editions 37090* [1975 Minneapolis OC]

10133 Boys from Syracuse, The (1938) Score-I (Richard Rodgers) US: LP = Capitol TAO-1933/STAO-1933* [1963 Revival NYOC]; Score-II (Richard Rodgers) GB:LP = Decca SKL-4564* + US:LP = DRG DS-15016* [1963 Revival LOC]

10134 Boy's Own Macbeth, A (1979) Score (Grahame Bond) AU:LP = Dunsinane 1641* [1979 AOC]

10135 Brainchild (1974) Score (Michel Legrand) US:LP-PP = Brainchild 1001 + US:LP-BP = POO 108 [Demo Cast]

10136 Bran Pie (1919) Theme-A/ GB:LP = WRC 275 + Theme-B/GB: LP = Parlophone 7150 [@Beatrice Lillie:1919 LOC]

10137 Bravo, Giovanni! (1962) Score (Milton Schafer) US:LP = Columbia KOL-5800/KOS-2200* [1962 NYOC]

10138 Breakfast at Tiffany's [Holly Golightly] (1966) Score (Bob Merrill) US:LP-BP = SPM 4788 [1966 NYOC]

10139 Brecht on Brecht (1961) Highlights + Dialog (stage songs) US: LP-MS = Columbia 02L-203/02S-203* [1961 NYOC]

10140 Bric-a-Brac (1915) Excerpts (various) GB:LP = WRC SH-186 [@1915 LOC]

10141 Brigadoon (1947) Score (Frederick Loewe) US:LP = RCA LOC-1001/LSO-1001e + US:LP = RCA AYL1-3091e [1947 NYOC]

10142 Brigham! (1976) Score (Newell Dayley & Arnold Sundgaard) US:LP-PP = BYU CO-176-M* [1976 Utah OC]

10143 Bring Back Birdie (1981) Score (Charles Strouse) US:LP = OC 8132* [1981 NYOC]

10144 Broadway Brevities of 1920 (1920) Themes/US:78 = Columbia 3305 [Bert Williams:1920 NYOC]

10145 Bubbling Brown Sugar (1976) Score (e:Danny Holgate/etc.) US: LP = H&H 60911* [1976 NYOC]; Scores (e:Danny Holgate/etc.) GB:LP-MS = Pye NSPD-504* [1977 LOC]

10146 Buccaneer, The (1953) Score (Sandy Wilson) GB:LP = HMV CLP-1064 + US:LP = AEI 1115 [1953 LOC]

10147 Bugsy Malone (1983) Themes (film songs:Paul Williams) GB:SP = A&M Bugsy-1* [1983 LOC]

10148 Burlesque (1927) Score (various) US:LP-BP = Star Tone ST-207 [1927 NYOC]

10149 Business as Usual (1914) Theme/GB:LP = Parlophone 7145 [@Unity More:1914 LOC]

10150 Buzz-Buzz (1918) Theme-A/ GB:LP = Parlophone 7135 + Theme-B/ GB:LP = Parlophone 7145 + Theme-C/ GB:78 = Columbia 1293 [Gertrude Lawrence:1918 LOC]

10151 By Jupiter (1942) Theme (Richard Rodgers) US:LP-PP = Friends of the Theatre 545 [@Benay Venuta:1942 NYOC]; Score (Richard Rodgers) US:LP = RCA LOC-1137/ LSO-1137* [1967 Revival NYOC]

10152 By the Beautiful Sea (1954) Score (Arthur Schwartz) US:LP = Capitol S-531 + US:Lp = Capitol T-11652

10153 By the Way (1925) Themes/ GB:78 = Brunswick 208 [Cicely Courtneidge:1925 NYOC & 1925 LOC]

10154 Bye Bye Birdie (1960) Score-I (Charles Strouse) US:LP = Columbia KOL-5510/KOS-2025* + US:LP = CSP COS-2025* [1960 NYOC]; Score-II (Charles Strouse) GB:LP = Philips SABL-205* + US:LP = Wing MGW-13000/SRW-17000* [1961 LOC]

C

10155 Cabaret (1966) Score-I (John Kander) US:LP = Columbia KOL-6640/ KOS-3040* [1966 NYOC]; Score-II (John Kander) GB:LP = CBS 70039* [1968 LOC]; Score-III (John Kander) SW-LP = Preiser 3220* [1970 Austria OC]

10156 Cabaret Girl (1922) Theme/ GB:LP = WRC 171 [@Dorothy Dickson:1922 LOC]

10157 Cabaret Tac (1938) Themes-A-B/US:78-PP = TAC 2 [June Havoc/ Beatrice Kay:1938 NYOC] + Theme-C/ US:78-PP = TAC 1 [Michael Loring: 1938 NYOC]

10158 Cabin in the Sky (1940) Highlights-I (Vernon Duke) US:LP = AEI 1107 [1940 NYOC]; Score-II (Vernon Duke) US:LP = Capitol W-2073/SW-2073* [1964 Revival NYOC]

10159 Cage aux Folles, La (1983) Score-I (Jerry Herman) US:LP = RCA HBC1-4824* [1983 NYOC]

10160 Call It Love (1960) Highlights (Sandy Wilson) GB:EP = Decca DFE-6640 [1960 LOC]

10161 Call Me Madam (1950) Highlights-I (Irving Berlin) US:LP = Decca DL-8035 + US:LP = Decca DL-9022/ DL-79022e + US:LP = MCA 2055e [Ethel Merman:1950 NYOC]; Highlights-I (Irving Berlin) US:LP = RCA LOC-1000 + US:LP = RCA CBM1-2032 [Supporting Cast:1950 NYOC]; Score-II (Irving Berlin) GB:LP = Columbia 33-X-1002 [1952 LOC]; Highlights-II (Irving Berlin) US:LP = Monmouth MES-7073 [1952 LOC]

10162 Call Me Mister (1946) Highlights (Harold Rome) US:LP-10 = Decca DL-7005 + US:LP-BP = JJA 19742 + US:LP = CSP X-14877 [1946 NYOC]

10163 Cambridge Circus (1963) Score (e:Bill Oddie/etc.) GB:LP = Parlophone PCS-1208*

10164 Camelot (1960) Score-I (Frederick Loewe) US:LP = Columbia KOL-5620/KOS-2031* + US:LP = Columbia S-32602* [1960 NYOC]; Score-II (Frederick Loewe) GB:LP = MFP 50368* [Paul Daneman:1962 AOC]; Score-III (Frederick Loewe) GB:LP = HMV CSD-1756* + US:LP = DRG DS-15022* [1964 LOC]; Score-IV (Frederick Loewe) US:LP = Varese OCV-81168* [1982 Revival LOC & 1982 NYOC]

10165 Can-Can (1953) Score-I (Cole Porter) US:LP = Capitol S-452/ DW-452e [1953 NYOC]; Highlights-II (Cole Porter) GB:LP-10 = Parlophone PMD-1017 + US:LP = Monmouth MES-7073 [1954 LOC]

10166 Canada (1977) Score (Bruce Molloy & Zachary Morfogen) US:LP = Broadway Baby 776* [1977 New Jersey OC]

10167 Candide (1956) Score-I (Leonard Bernstein) US:LP = Columbia OL-5180/OS-2350e [1956 NYOC]; Scores-II (Leonard Bernstein) US:LP-MS = Columbia 2SX-32923* [1974 Revival NYOC]; Scores-III (Leonard Bernstein) US:LP-MS = New World NW-340/1* [1982 Revival NYOC]

10168 Canterbury Tales (1968) Score-I (Richard Hill & John Hawkins) GB:LP = Decca SKL-4956* [1968 LOC]; Score-II (Richard Hill & John Hawkins) US:LP = Capitol SW-299* [1969 NYOC]

10169 Captain Crash vs. the Zzorg Women (1981) Score (Steve Hammond & Rick Jones) US:LP = Web OC-103 [1981 LAOC]

10170 Captain Jinks of the Horse Marines (1975) Scores (Jack Beeson) US: LP-MS = RCA ARL2-1727* [1975 Kansas City OC]

10171 Card, The (1973) Score (Tony Hatch) GB:LP = Pye NSPL-18408* + US:LP = AEI 1124* [1973 LOC]

10172 Carefree Heart, The (1957) Score (George Forrest & Robert Wright) US:LP-PP = Carefree 1001 [Demo Cast]

10173 Careless Rapture (1936) Highlights (Ivor Novello) GB:LP = WRC SHB-23 [1936 LOC]

10174 Carib Song (1945) Highlights (Baldwin Bergersen) US:78-MS = International B-401/6 [Studio Cast]

10175 Carmelina (1980) Score (Burton Lane) US:LP = OC 8019* [1980 NYOC]

10176 Carmen Jones (1943) Score (as:Oscar Hammerstein II) US:LP = Decca DL-8014 + US:LP = Decca DL-9021/DL-79021e + US:LP = MCA 2054e [1943 NYOC]

10177 Carmilla (1973) Score (Benjamin Johnston) US:LP = Vanguard VDS-79322* [1973 NYOC]

10178 Carminetta (1917) Excerpts (various) GB:LP = WRC SH-164 [Alice Delysia:1917 LOC]

10179 Carnival (1961) Score-I (Bob Merrill) US:LP = MGM E-3946/SE-3946* [1961 NYOC]; Score-II (Bob Merrill) GB:LP = HMV PCS-1612* [1963 LOC]

10180 Caroline (1923) Themes/US: 78 = Vocalion 14549 [J. Harold Murray: 1923 NYOC]

10181 Caroline [Australian Show] Score/AU:LP = W&G 5515 [AOC]

10182 Carousel (1945) Score-I (Richard Rodgers) US:LP = Decca DL-8003 + US:LP = Decca DL-9020/DL-79020e + US:LP = MCA 2033e + US: LP = MCA 37093e [1945 NYOC]; Excerpts-II (Richard Rodgers) GB:LP = WRC SH-393 [@1950 LOC]; Score-III (Richard Rodgers) US:LP = RCA LOC-1114/LSO-1114* [1965 Revival NYOC]

10183 Carry Nation (1968) Scores (Douglas Moore) US:LP-MS = Desto DC-6463/5 [1968 OC]

10184 Casino Girl, The (1900) Themes/GB:78 = Favorite 1-66034 [Marie George:1900 LOC]

10185 Castles in the Air (1926) Excerpts (Percy Wenrich) US:LP-BP = JJA 19796 [@1926 LOC]

10186 Cat and the Fiddle, The (1931) Themes-I-A-B (Jerome Kern) US: LP-BP = JJA 19778 [@Georges Metaxa:1931 NYOC]; Excerpts-II (Jerome Kern) GB:LP = WRC SH-171 + US:LP = Monmouth MES-7064 [@1932 LOC]

10187 Catch My Soul (1968) Score (Ray Pohlman & Emil Zoghby) GB: LP = Polydor 2383.035* [1968 LOC]

10188 Cats (1981) Scores-I (Andrew Lloyd Webber) GB:LP-MS = Polydor CATX-001* + US:LP-MS = Geffen 2GHS-2017* [1981 LOC]; Scores-II (Andrew Lloyd Webber) US:LP-MS = Geffen 2GHS-2031* [1982 NYOC]; Score-III (Andrew Lloyd Webber) GE: LP = Polydor 817-365-1* [1983 German OC]

10189 Cavalcade (1931) Excerpts (Noel Coward) US:LP-MS = Monmouth MES-7062/3 [Studio Cast]

10190 Caviar (1934) Themes/US: 78 = Liberty Music 165 [Jane Winston: 1934 NYOC]

10191 Celebration (1969) Score (Harvey Schmidt) US:LP = Capitol SW-198* [1969 NYOC]

10192 Change (1969) Score (Ed Kreslie & Drey Sheppard) US:LP-PP = Change 1001 [Demo Cast]

10193 Chaperons (1902) Theme-A/ US:LP = Monmouth 3621 [@Joseph Miron:1902 NYOC]; Theme-B/US: LP = Monmouth 3622 [@Walter Jones:1902 NYOC]

10194 Charlie Girl (1965) Score-I (David Heneker & John Taylor) GB: LP = CBS 62627* [1965 LOC]; Score-II (David Heneker & John Taylor) AU: LP = HMV OCSD-7687* [1966 AOC]

10195 Charlie Sent Me (1984) Score (Richard Sherman & Milt Larsen) US: LP = Glendale GL-6035* [1984 LAOC]

10196 Charlot Show of 1926, The (1926) Themes-A-B/GB:LP = Parlophone 7150 [@Jessie Matthews:1926 LOC] + Themes-C-D/GB:78 = Columbia 4192 [Jessie Matthews:1926 LOC] + Themes-E-F/GB:78 = Columbia 4191 [Henry Lytton/Herbert Mundin:1926 LOC] + Theme-G/GB:78 = Columbia 4190 [Dick Francis:1926 LOC] + Theme-H/GB:78 = Columbia 4189 [Jessie Matthews:1926 LOC]

10197 Charlot's Masquerade (1930) Theme/GB:LP = Parlophone 7154 [@Patrick Waddington:1930 LOC]

10198 Charlot's Revue [C] Themes-I-A-B/GB:LP = Parlophone 7135 [@Gertrude Lawrence:1924 LOC]; Theme-II/GB:LP = Parlophone 7135 [@Gertrude Lawrence:1925 LOC]; Themes-III-A-B/GB:78 = Columbia 514 [Gertrude Lawrence:1926 LOC] + Theme-III-C/GB:78 = Columbia 512 [Gertrude Lawrence:1926 LOC] + Theme-III-D/GB:LP = Parlophone 7135 [@Gertrude Lawrence:1926 LOC] + Theme-III-E/GB:78 = Columbia 513 [Beatrice Lillie:1926 LOC]

10199 Charlotte Sweet (1983) Scores (Gerald Jay Makoe) US:LP-MS = John Hammond W2X-38680* [1983 NYOC]

10200 Chee-Chee (1928) Highlights (Richard Rodgers) US:LP = Ava A-26/AS-26* [Studio Cast]

10201 Cheep (1917) Themes-A-B/GB:LP = Parlophone 7135 [@Beatrice Lillie:1917 LOC]; Theme-C/GB:LP = Parlophone 7145 [@Lee White & Clay Smith:1917 LOC]

10202 Cherry (1972) Score (Ron Miller & Tom Baird) US:LP-PP = Cherry 1001 [Demo Cast]

10203 Chevrolet Experience, The [Industrial Show] Score (pop music) US: LP-PP = Chevrolet VC-4500 [OC]

10204 Chicago (1975) Score (John Kander) US:LP = Arista AL-9005* [1975 NYOC]; Themes (John Kander) US: SP = Columbia 3-10178* [Liza Minnelli: 1975 Replacement NYOC]

10205 Chin-Chin (1914) Themes/US:78 = RCA 18149 [Six Brown Brothers: 1914 NYOC]

10206 Chinese Honeymoon, A (1901) Theme-A/GB:78 = G&T 3409 + Theme-B/GB:78 = G&T 3415 + Theme-C/GB:78 = G&T 3416 + Theme-D/GB: 78 = G&T 3417 [Marie Dainton:1901 LOC]

10207 Chocalonia (1976) Score (Glenn Houle) US:LP = Crissy CR-2034* [1976 LAOC]

10208 Chocolate Dandies, The (1924) Theme-A/US:LP = RCA LPV-560 + Theme-B/US:78 = RCA/Victor 19494 + Theme-C/US:78 = EBW 4417; Theme-D/US:LP = Eubie Blake 7 + Theme-E/US:78 = Edison 51572 + Theme-F/US:78 = Pathe 20210 [Noble Sissle & Eubie Blake:1924 NYOC]

10209 Chocolate Soldier, The (1909) Scores (Oscar Straus) US:LP-MS = RCA LOP-6005/LSO-6005* [Studio Cast]

10210 Chorus Line, A (1975) Score (Marvin Hamlisch) US:LP = Columbia PS-33581* [1975 NYOC]

10211 Christine (1960) Score (Sammy Fain) US:LP = Columbia OL-5220/OS-2026* [1960 NYOC]

10212 Christmas Rappings (1969) Score (Al Carmines) US:LP-PP = Judson JU-1002* [1969 NYOC]

10213 Christy (1979) Score (Lawrence J. Blank) US:LP = OC 7913* [1979 NYOC]

10214 Chrysanthemum (1958) Score (Robb Stewart) GB:LP = Nixa NPL-18026 + US:LP = AEI 1108 [1958 LOC]

10215 Chu-Chem (1966) Score (Mitch Leigh) US:LP-PP = Chu-Chem 1001 [Demo Cast]

10216 Chu-Chin-Chow (1916) Score (Frederic Norton & Oscar Asche) GB:LP = HMV CSD-1269* + GB:LP = MFP 1012* [Studio Cast]; Theme-A/GB:78 = Columbia 1114 [Aileen D'Orme:1916 LOC] + Theme-B/GB:78 = Columbia 1379 [Frank Cochrane:1916 LOC] + Theme-C/GB:78 = HMV 03528 [Violet Essex:1916 LOC] + Theme-D/GB:78 = HMV 04186 [Courtice Pounds:1916 LOC] + Theme-E/GB:78 = HMV 4-2812 [Courtice Pounds:

1916 LOC] + Theme-F/GB:78 = Homochord 530 [Bryn Gwyn:1916 LOC]

10217 Ciao, Rudy (1966) Score-I (Armando Trovajoli) IT:LP = RCA 10411* [1966 Italian OC]; Score-II (Armando Trovajoli) IT:LP = RCA OLS-13* [1972 Italian OC]

10218 Cinderella (1959) Score (television songs:Richard Rodgers) GB:LP = Decca SKL-4050* [1959 LOC]

10219 Cinderella (1967) Score (The Shadows) GB:LP = Columbia SX-6103* [1967 LOC]

10220 Cindy (1964) Score (Johnny Brandon) US:LP = ABC OC-2/SOC-2* [1964 NYOC]

10221 Cindy-Ella (1963) Score (Caryl Brahms) GB:LP = Decca SKL-4559* + US:LP = DRG DL-15023* [1963 LOC]

10222 Cingalee, The (1904) Theme-A/GB:78 = G&T 3-2589 + Theme-B/GB:78 = G&T 3-2244 + Theme-C/GB:78 = G&T 4372 + Theme-D/GB:78 = G&T 4373 [Louis Bradfield:1904 LOC]

10223 Circus Girl, The (1896) Theme/GB:78 = G&T 3340 [Ellaline Terriss:1896 LOC]

10224 City Chap, The (1925) Theme-A/US:LP-BP = JJA 19796 + Theme-B/US:78 = RCA 19761 [George Olsen:1925 NYOC]

10225 Clara *see* Beg, Borrow or Steal

10226 Clarksmanship [Industrial Show] Score (Norman Paris) US:LP-PP = Clark Tools SS-17674 [OC]

10227 Clownaround (1972) Score (Moose Charlap) US:LP = RCA LSP-4741* [1972 Supporting NYOC]

10228 Clowns in Clover (1927) Theme-A/US:LP-BP = JJA 19794 [@Cicely Courtneidge:1927 LOC]; Theme-B/GB:LP = Parlophone 7150 [@June Trip:1927 LOC]

10229 Clues to a Life *see* Alec Wilder—Clues to a Life

10230 Co-Optimists, The [The Optimists] (1921) Scores (Melville Gideon) GB:LP-MS = WRC SHB-25 [LOC]

10231 Coach with the Six Insides, The (1966) Score (Teiji Ito) US:LP = ESP 1019/S-1019* [1966 NYOC]

10232 Coca-Cola Grande, El [El Grande Coca-Cola] (1973) Highlights (various) US:EP-PP = Bottle Cap BC-1001 [1973 San Francisco OC]

10233 Cochran's 1930 Revue (1930) Excerpts (various) GB:LP = WRC SHB-28 [Leslie Hutchinson:1930 LOC]

10234 Cockeyed Tiger, The (1977) Highlights (Eric Blau) US:EP-PP = COGS 3121 [1977 NYOC]

10235 Coco (1970) Score (Andre Previn) US:LP = Paramount PAS-1002* [1970 NYOC]

10236 Cohan Review of 1918, The (1918) Theme/US:78 = Columbia 6038 [Nora Bayes:1918 NYOC]

10237 Cole (1975) Scores (stage & film songs) GB:LP-MS = RCA LRLZ-5054* + US:LP-MS = RCA CRL2-5054* [1975 LOC]

10238 Colette (1970) Highlights + Dialog (Harvey Schmidt) US:LP = Mio International MCS-3001* [1970 NYOC]

10239 Colette (1980) Score (Johnny Dankworth) GB:LP = Sepia RSR-1006* [1980 LOC]

10240 Colette (1982) Excerpts (Harvey Schmidt) US:LP = Painted Smiles PS-1381* [John Reardon:1982 NYOC + Studio Cast]

10241 Come of Age (1934) Themes/US:78 = Liberty Music 158 [Ralph Stuart:1934 NYOC]

10242 Come Spy with Me (1966) Score (Bryan Blackburn) GB:LP = Decca SKL-4810* [1966 LOC]

10243 Come Summer (1969) Score (David Baker) US:LP-PP = Come Summer 1001 [Demo Cast]

10244 Comedy [Smile, Smile, Smile] (1972) Score (George David Weiss) US:LP-PP = Comedy 1001 [Demo Cast]; Theme (George David Weiss) US:SP = Avco 4615 [The Hugo & Luigi Music Machine]

10245 Company (1970) Score-I (Stephen Sondheim) US:LP = Columbia OS-3550* [1970 NYOC]; Score-II (Stephen Sondheim) GB:LP = CBS 70108* [1971 LOC]

10246 Connecticut Yankee, A (1943) Highlights (Richard Rodgers) US:LP-BP = JJA 19733 + US:LP-BP = Show Biz 5601 [1943 NYOC]

10247 Conquering Hero, The (1961)

Score (Moose Charlap) US:LP-PP = Hero 1001 [Demo Cast]

10248 Consul, The (1950) Scores (Gian Carlo Menotti) US:LP-MS = Decca DX-101 [1950 NYOC]

10249 Continental Varieties (1934) Highlights (various) US:78-MS = Columbia MM-694 [Lucienne Boyer:1934 NYOC]

10250 Continental Varieties of 1936 (1936) Themes-A-B/US:78 = Columbia 3123 + Theme-C/US:78 = Columbia 3124 [Lucienne Boyer:1934 NYOC]

10251 Conversation Piece (1934) Highlights (Noel Coward) GB:LP-MS = WRC SH-179/180 + US:LP-MS = Monmouth MES-7062/3 [1934 LOC]; Highlights + Dialog (Noel Coward) US:LP-MS = Columbia 02L-163 + US:LP-MS = CSP A2L-163 [Noel Coward:1934 LOC]

10252 Cool Off (1961) Score (Jerome Weidman & Harold Blankman) US:LP-PP = Cool Off 1001 [Demo Cast]

10253 Copper and Brass (1957) Themes/US:SP = Decca 9-30476 [Dick Williams:1957 NYOC]

10254 Cotton Club Revue of 1958, The (1958) Score (Clay Boland) US:LP = Gone GLP-101 [1958 NYOC]

10255 Count of Luxembourg, The (1909) Score (Franz Lehar) GB:LP = That's Entertainment TER-1050* [Studio Cast]

10256 Countess Maritza, The [Maritza] (1926) Score (Emmerich Kalman) GB:LP = That's Entertainment TER-1051* [Studio Cast]; Theme-I-A/US:78 = Gennett 6043 [Walter Woolf:1926 NYOC]; Themes-II-A-B/GB:78 = Parlophone 1200 [Douglas Byng:1936 Revival LOC] + Themes-II-C-D/GB:78 = HMV 8787 [John Garrick:1936 Revival LOC]

10257 Country Girl, A (1894) Theme-A/GB:78 = G&T 2-2111 + Theme-B/GB:78 = G&T 2-2136 + Theme-C/GB:78 = G&T 4062 + Theme-D/GB:78 = G&T 4084 [Henry Lytton:1902 Revival LOC] + Theme-E/GB:78 = G&T 3419 [Evie Greene:1902 Revival LOC] + Theme-F/GB:78 = G&T 3530 [Isobel Jay:1902 Revival LOC]

10258 Cowardy Custard (1973) Scores (stage songs) GB:LP-MS = RCA SER-5656/7* + US:LP-MS = RCA LSO-6010* [1973 LOC]

10259 Cradle Will Rock, The (1937) Score-I (Marc Blitzstein) US:LP-PP = American Legacy T-1001 [1937 NYOC]; Scores-II (Marc Blitzstein) US:LP-MS = MGM E-4259/SE-4259* + US:LP-MS = CRI SD-266* [1964 Revival NYOC]

10260 Cranks (1956) Score (John Addison) GB:LP = HMV CLP-1082 [1956 LOC]

10261 Crest of the Wave (1937) Excerpts (Ivor Novello) GB:LP = WRC SH-216 [@1937 LOC]

10262 Crooked Mile, The (1959) Score (Peter Greenwell) GB:LP = HMV CLP-1298 + US:LP = AEI 1114 [1959 LOC]

10263 Crowning Experience, The (1958) Highlights + Underscore + Dialog (e:George Fraser/e:Herbert Allen/e:Will Reed/film underscore) US:LP-PP = Capitol Custom MRA 101* [Muriel Smith:1958 NYOC + 1960 Film]

10264 Cry for Us All (1970) Score (Mitch Leigh) US:LP = Project TS-1000* [1970 NYOC]

10265 Crystal Heart, The (1957) Score (Baldwin Bergersen) US:LP-PP = CK 1 + US:LP-BP = Blue Pear BP-1001 [1957 NYOC]

10266 Curley McDimple (1967) Themes/US:SP = Capitol 2116 [Bayn Johnson & Paul Cahill:1967 NYOC]

10267 Cyrano (1958) Score (David Shire) US:LP-PP = RCA Custom J80P-4263 [1958 NYOC]

10268 Cyrano (1973) Score + Underscore + Dialog (Michael J. Lewis) US:LP-MS = A&M SP-3702* [1973 NYOC]

10269 Cyrano [Children's Musical] Score (Judith Dvorkin) US:LP = Peter Pan 8041/58041* [OC]

D

10270 Daddy Goodness (1979) Theme/US:LP = Capitol 12003* [Freda Payne:1979 Washington OC]

10271 Dad's Army (1975) Score

(pop music) GB:LP = WB K-56186* [1975 LOC]

10272 Dames at Sea (1968) Score-I (Jim Wise) US:LP = Columbia OS-3330* [1968 NYOC]; Score-II (Jim Wise) GB: LP = CBS 70063* [1969 LOC]

10273 Damn Yankees (1955) Score (Richard Adler & Jerry Ross) US:LP = RCA LOC-1021/LSO-1021e + US:LP = RCA AYL1-3948e [1955 NYOC]

10274 Dance a Little Closer (1982) Excerpts (Jule Styne) GB:LP = RCA VIP-83004* [Liz Robertson:1982 LOC]

10275 Dance and Grow Thin (1917) Theme/US:78 = RCA/Victor 18258 [Gus Van & Joe Schenck:1917 NYOC]

10276 Dancing Around (1914) Theme/US:78 = Columbia 1671 [Al Jolson:1914 NYOC]

10277 Dancing Years, The (1939) Highlights-I (Ivor Novello) GB:LP-10 = HMV DLP-1028 [1939 LOC]; Score-II (Ivor Novello) GB:LP = RCA SF-7958* [1968 LOC]

10278 Dandelion Wine (1967) Score (Billy Goldenberg) US:LP-PP = BS 321* [1967 NYOC]

10279 Darling of the Day (1968) Score (Jule Styne) US:LP = RCA LOC-1149/LSO-1149* [1968 NYOC]

10280 Darwin's Theories (1960) Score (Darwin Venneri) US:LP-PP = Town Hall THM-1002 [1960 NYOC]

10281 Dawgs! (1983) Score (e:Richard & Robert Sherman/e:John Henry/etc.) US:LP = Glendale GLS-6032* [1983 LAOC]

10282 Day Before Spring, The (1945) Excerpts (Frederick Loewe) US: LP = Painted Smiles PS-1337* [Studio Cast]

10283 Day in Hollywood, a Night in the Ukraine, A (1980) Highlights + Dialog (various) US:LP = DRG SBL-12580* [1980 NYOC]

10284 Dear World (1969) Score (Jerry Herman) US:LP = Columbia BOS-3260* + US:LP = CSP AOS-3260* [1969 NYOC]

10285 Dearest Enemy (1925) Score (Richard Rodgers) US:LP = Beginner's Productions BRP-1* [Studio Cast]; Excerpts (Richard Rodgers) US:LP = Painted Smiles PS-1366* [@Nancy Andrews:1976 Revival NYOC]

10286 Decline and Fall of the Entire World As Seen Through the Eyes of Cole Porter, The (1965) Score (stage songs) US:LP = Columbia OL-6410/OS-2810* + US:LP = CSP AOS-2810* [1965 NYOC]

10287 Demi-Dozen (1957) Score (e: Harvey Schmidt/e:Michael Brown/etc.) US:LP = Off Beat 4015 [1957 NYOC]

10288 Desert Song, The (1926) Highlights (Sigmund Romberg) GB: LP = WRC SH-254 + US:LP = Monmouth MES-7054 [1927 LOC]

10289 Destry Rides Again (1959) Score-I (Harold Rome) US:LP = Decca DL-9075/DL-79075* [1959 NYOC]; Score-II (Harold Rome) GB:LP = That's Entertainment TER-1034* [1982 Revival LOC]

10290 Devil and Daniel Webster, The (1939) Score (Douglas Moore) US: LP = Desto DST-6450* [Studio Cast]

10291 Diamond Lil (1928) Themes/ US:LP-BP = Proscenium 22 [Mae West: 1948 Revival NYOC]

10292 Diamond Studs (1975) Highlights (Bland Simpson) US:EP-PP = Pasquotank PS-337-003* [1975 NYOC]

10293 Die Fledermaus [The Bat] (1874) Score (Johann Strauss, Jr.) GB:LP = EMI CSD-6450* [1959 Revival LOC]

10294 Diesel Dazzle [Industrial Show] Score (Hank Beebe) US:LP-PP = Detroit Diesel M-00011 [OC]

10294a Different Times (1972) Score (Michael Brown) US:LP = Painted Smiles PS-1332* [1972 NYOC]

10295 Dime a Dozen (1964) Scores (e:William Roy/e:Lesley Davison/e: Michael Brown/etc.) US:LP-MS = Cadence 3063/26063* [1964 NYOC]

10296 Dingo Girl (1982) Score (C. Harriott) AU:LP = Green LRG-119* [1982 AOC]

10297 District Leader, The (1906) Theme/US:78-MS = Deluxe 18 [Joe Howard:1906 NYOC]

10298 Divorce Me, Darling! (1965) Score (Sandy Wilson) GB:LP = Decca SKL-4675* + US:LP = DRG DS-15009* [1965 LOC]

10298a Do Black Patent Leather Shoes Really Reflect Up? (1980) Score

(James Quinn) US:LP = CBS DP-18852* [1980 Chicago OC]

10299 Do I Hear a Waltz? (1965) Score (Stephen Sondheim) US:LP = Columbia KOL-6370/KOS-2770* + US:LP = CSP AKOS-2770* [1965 NYOC]

10300 Do Re Mi (1960) Score-I (Jule Styne) US:LP = RCA LOCD-2002/LSOD-2002* + US:LP = RCA LOC-1105/LSO-1105* [1960 NYOC]; Score-II (Jule Styne) GB:LP = Decca SKL-4145* [1961 LOC]

10301 Do What You Will! (1969) Score (Alan Wasser) US:LP-PP = Do 9-348/9 [1969 Oregon OC]

10302 Dr. Jazz (1975) Excerpts (Buster Davis) US:LP = Take Home Tunes THT-777* [Studio Cast]

10303 Doctor Selavy's Magic Theatre (1974) Score (Stanley Silverman) US:LP = UA LA-196* [1974 NYOC]

10304 Doll's Life, A (1982) Score (Larry Grossman) US:LP = OC 8241* [1982 NYOC]

10305 Donnybrook (1961) Score (Johnny Burke) US:LP = Kapp KDL-8500/KDS-8500* [1961 NYOC]

10306 Don't Bother Me, I Can't Cope (1972) Score (Micki Grant) US:LP = Polydor PD-6013* [1972 NYOC]

10307 Don't Play Us Cheap (1972) Scores (Melvin Van Peebles) US:LP-MS = Stax STS-2-3006* [1972 NYOC]

10308 Doonesbury (1983) Score (Elizabeth Swados) US:LP = MCA 6129* [1983 NYOC]

10309 Down in the Valley (1948) Highlights (Kurt Weill) US:LP-10 = RCA LM-16 [Marion Bell:1948 Indiana OC + 1950 TV Cast]

10310 Downriver (1975) Score (John Braden) US:LP = Take Home Tunes THT-7811* [1975 NYOC]

10311 Dragon, The *see* Invisible Dragon, The

10312 Drake's Dream (1977) Score (Richard Riley) GB:LP = President PTLS-1068* [1977 LOC]

10313 Drat! The Cat! (1965) Score (Milton Schafer) US:LP-BP = Blue Pear BP-1005 [1965 NYOC]

10314 Dreamgirls (1982) Score (Henry Krieger) US:LP = Geffen GHSP-2007* [1982 NYOC]

10315 Dressed to the Nines (1960) Score (e:William Roy/etc.) US:LP = MGM E-3914/SE-3914* [1960 NYOC]

10316 Dubarry, The (1932) Highlights-I (Karl Millocker) GB:EP = Parlophone GEP-8623 [Anny Ahlers:1932 LOC]; Excerpts-II (Karl Millocker) US:LP-BP = JJA 19779 [@Grace Moore: 1932 NYOC]

10317 Dubarry Was a Lady (1939) Excerpts (Cole Porter) US:LP = Painted Smiles PS-1340* [Studio Cast]; Theme-I-A/US:LP = Reprise 6032* [Ethel Merman:1939 NYOC]; Theme-II-A/GB:78 = Decca 7867 + Theme-II-B/GB:78 = Decca 7951 [Frances Day:1941 LOC]

10318 Dude [The Highway Life] (1972) Score (Galt MacDermot) US:LP = Kilmarnock KIL-72007* [1972 NYOC]

10319 Duel [Pagent in Exile] (1979) Score (Randal Wilson) US:LP = OC 7916* [1979 NYOC]

10320 Dumas and Son (1968) Score (George Forrest & Robert Wright) US:LP-PP = Dumas 1001 [Demo Cast]

E

10321 Earl and the Girl, The (1903) Theme-A/GB:G&T 2-2462 + Theme-B/GB:78 = G&T 2-2463 [Henry Lytton: 1903 LOC]

10322 Earl Carroll's Sketch Book (1929) Themes/US:78 = RCA/Victor 22127 [Don Howard:1929 NYOC]

10323 Earl Carroll's Vanities [C] Themes-I-A-B/US:78 = Columbia 765 + Theme-I-C/US:78 = Columbia 881 [Don Voorhees:1926 NYOC]; Themes-II-A-B/GB:78 = Columbia 4192 + Theme-II-C/GB:78 = Columbia 4189 [Jessie Matthews:1927 NYOC] + Themes-II-D-E/GB:LP = Parlophone 7150 [@Henry Lytton/Herbert Mundin:1927 NYOC] + Theme-II-F/GB:78 = Columbia 4191 [Herbert Mundin:1927 NYOC]; Themes-III-A-B/US:78 = Brunswick 4059 [Vincent Lopez:1928 NYOC]; Themes-IV-A-B/US:78 = Brunswick 6381 [Ray Kavanaugh:1932 NYOC]

10324 Earl of Ruston, The (1970) Score (C.C. Courtney & Peter Link) US: LP = Capitol ST-465* [1970 NYOC]

10325 Early to Bed (1943) Excerpts-A (Fats Waller & George Marion) US: LP = Collector's Classics CC-19 [Studio Cast]; Excerpts-B (Fats Waller & George Marion) US:EP = RCA EPA-449 [Studio Cast]

10326 Earthquake (1973) Score (C.B. Jackson) US:LP = Inner City LRS-6075* [1973 LAOC]

10327 Eclipse, The (1919) Themes/ GB:LP = WRC 26 [@Nancy Gibbs & F. Pope Stamper:1919 LOC]

10328 Ecstasy of Rita Joe, The (1967) Score (Ann Mortifee & Willie Dunn) CA:LP = Jupiter 6.25307* [1980 Revival OC]

10329 Ed Wynn Carnival (1920) Themes-A-B/US:78 = Vocalion 14106 + Theme-C/US:78 = Gennett 9075 [Ray Miller:1920 NYOC]

10330 Education of Hyman Kaplan, The (1968) Score (Oscar Brand) US:LP-PP = Kaplan 1001 [Demo Cast]

10331 81 Proof (1982) Score (John Everest) US:LP = OC 8236* [1982 LAOC]

10332 Eileen (1917) Score (Victor Herbert) US:LP = Camden CAL-210 [Studio Cast]; Themes-A-B/US:78 = RCA/Victor 18285 [Greek Evans & Scott Welsh:1917 NYOC] + Theme-C/US: 78 = Columbia 2247 [Victor Stiles:1917 NYOC]

10333 Elephant Calf, The (1963) Score (Arnold Black) US:LP = Asch FL-9831 [1967 NYOC]

10334 Emperor's New Clothes, The [Children's Show] Highlights (Douglas Moore) US:LP = Children's Records CR-15007 [OC]

10335 Emperor's Nightingale, The (1965) Score (Philip Fleishman) US: LP = Folkways FC-7588 [1965 NYOC]

10336 Ernest in Love (1960) Score (Lee Pockriss) US:LP = Columbia OL-5530/OS-2027* [1960 NYOC]

10337 Eubie! (1978) Score (pop music) US:LP = WB HS-3267* [1978 NYOC]

10338 Evening with W.S. Gilbert, An (1980) Score (pop music) US:LP = OC 8026* [1980 NYOC]

10339 Ever Green (1930) Excerpts (Richard Rodgers) US:LP = Monmouth MES-7049* [Studio Cast]; Theme/GB: LP = WRC 183 [@Jessie Matthews:1930 LOC]

10340 Everybody, Everybody [Children's Show] Highlights (Donald Ashwander) US:LP = Paper Bag Players PBP-5* [OC]

10341 Everybody's Doing it (1912) Theme/GB:LP = Parlophone 7145 [@Robert Hale & Ida Crispi:1912 LOC]

10342 Everybody's Welcome (1931) Theme/US:LP-BP = JJA 19778 [@ Frances Williams:1931 NYOC]

10343 Evita (1978) Score-I (Andrew Lloyd Webber) GB:LP = MCA 3527* [1978 LOC]; Scores-II (Andrew Lloyd Webber) US:LP-MS = MCA 2-11007* [1979 NYOC]; Score-III (Andrew Lloyd Webber) AU:LP = MCA EV-1* [1980 AOC]; Scores-IV (Andrew Lloyd Webber) SP:LP-MS = Epic 88524* [1980 Spanish OC]

10344 Exchange [Tamalpais Exchange] (1970) Score (Mike Brandt & Michael Knight) US:LP = Atlantic SD-8263* [1970 NYOC]

10345 Expresso Bongo (1958) Score (David Heneker & Monty Norman) GB:LP = Nixa NPL-18016 + US:LP = AEI 1110 [1958 LOC]

F

10346 Face the Music (1932) Excerpts (Irving Berlin) US:LP-10 = RCA L-16008 + US:LP-BP = JJA 19744 [Studio Cast]

10347 Fade Out, Fade In (1964) Score (Jule Styne) US:LP = ABC OC-3/ SOC-3* [1964 NYOC]

10348 Faggot, The (1973) Score (Al Carmines) US:LP-BP = Blue Pear BP-1008 [1973 NYOC]

10349 Family Affair, A (1962) Score (John Kander) US:LP = UA UAL-4099/UAS-5099* [1962 NYOC]

10350 Fanny (1954) Score (Harold Rome) US:LP = RCA LOC-1015/LSO-1015e [1954 NYOC]

10351 Fantasticks, The (1960) Score (Harvey Schmidt) US:LP = MGM E-3872/SE-3872* [1960 NYOC]

10352 Festival (1979) Score (Stephen Downs) US:LP = OC 7916* [1979 NYOC]

10353 Fiddler on the Roof (1964) Score-I (Jerry Bock) US:LP = RCA LOC-1093/LSO-1093* [1964 NYOC]; Score-II (Jerry Bock) US:LP = Columbia OL-6610/OS-3010* [Herschel Bernardi:1966 Replacement NYOC]; Score-III (Jerry Bock) GB:LP = CBS 70030* + US:LP = Columbia SX-30742* [1967 LOC]; Themes-IV (Jerry Bock) US:SP = Elektra 632 [Theodore Bikel:1967 Touring OC]; Score-V (Jerry Bock) US:LP = Columbia OL-6650/OS-3050* [1967 Israel OC]; Score-VI (Jerry Bock) AF:LP = RCA 38-149* [1969 South Africa OC]; Score-VII (Jerry Bock) US:LP = London 99470* [1969 German OC]; Scores-VIII (Jerry Bock) JA:LP-MS = Canyon Records C50H-0025/6* [1982 Japanese Revival OC]

10354 Fifth of July, The (1980) Theme/US:SP = Pensteman 757* [Jonathan Hogan:1980 NYOC]

10355 Fifty Miles from Boston (1908) Theme/US:LP = Audio Rarities 2295 [George M. Cohan:1908 NYOC]

10356 Fig Leaves Are Falling (1969) Score (Albert Hague) US:LP-PP = Fig Leaves 1001 [Demo Cast]

10357 Fings Ain't Wot They Used t'Be (1960) Score (Lionel Bart) GB:LP = Decca DKL-4092* + GB:LP = That's Entertainment TER-1047* [1960 LOC]

10358 Finian's Rainbow (1947) Score-I (Burton Lane) US:LP = Columbia US:LP = Columbia OL-4062/OS-2080e [1947 NYOC]; Score-II (Burton Lane) US:LP = RCA LOC-1057/LSO-1057* [1960 Revival NYOC]

10359 Fiorello! (1959) Score (Jerry Bock) US:LP = Capitol WAO-1321/SWAO-1321* [1959 NYOC]

10360 Firebrand of Florence, The (1945) Highlights (Kurt Weill) US:LP = Mark 56 #721 [Studio Cast]

10361 Firefly, The (1912) Score (Rudolf Friml) US:LP = RCA LM-121 [Studio Cast]

10362 Fireman's Flame, The (1937) Themes/US:78 = Liberty Music 229 [Ben Cutler:1937 NYOC]

10363 First Impressions (1959) Score (George David Weiss) US:LP = Columbia OL-5400/OS-2014* + US:LP = CSP AOS-2014* [1959 NYOC]

10364 Five After Eight (1980) Score (Michael Bitterman) US:LP = OC 8207* [1980 NYOC]

10365 5-6-7-8, A (1976) Score (e: Jerry Sternbach/etc.) US:LP = Spotlight 2222* [1976 LAOC]

10366 Flahooley (1951) Score (Sammy Fain) US:LP = Capitol S-284 + US:LP = Capitol T-11649 [1951 NYOC]

10367 Fleet's Lit Up, The (1938) Theme/GB:LP = WRC 26 [@Frances Day:1938 LOC]

10368 Floodlight (1937) Theme/GB:LP = Parlophone 7154 [@Frances Day:1937 LOC]

10369 Flora the Red Menace (1965) Score (John Kander) US:LP = RCA LOC-1111/LSO-1111* + US:LP = RCA CBM1-2760* [1965 NYOC]

10370 Florodora (1899) Theme-A/GB:78 = Berliner 4521 + Theme-B/GB:78 = Berliner 4522 + Theme-C/GB:78 = Berliner 2395 [Louis Bradfield:1899 LOC] + Theme-D/GB:78 = Berliner 4119 + Theme-E/GB:78 = Berliner 3205 + Theme-F/GB:78 = Berliner 3204 [Kate Cutler:1899 LOC] + Theme-G/GB:78 = Berliner 3210 + Theme-H/GB:78 = Berliner 3209 + Theme-I/GB:78 = Berliner 3211 [Ada Reeve:1899 LOC]; Score (Leslie Stuart) GB:LP = Opal 835 [1899 LOC]

10371 Flower Drum Song (1958) Score-I (Richard Rodgers) US:LP = Columbia OL-5350/OS-2009* [1958 NYOC]; Score-II (Richard Rodgers) GB:LP = HMV CSD-1359* + US:LP = Angel 35886/S-35886* [1960 LOC]

10372 Flowers for Algernon (1980) Score (Charles Strouse) US:LP = OC 8021* [1980 NYOC]

10373 Flush Left, Stagger Right [Industrial Show] Score (Jerry Powell) US:LP-PP = Flush LP-1000 [OC]

10374 Fly Blackbird (1960) Score-I (C.B. Jackson) US:LP-PP = Korf Imaginate LK1-V13786 [1960 LAOC]; Score-II

(C.B. Jackson) US:LP = Mercury OCM-2206/OCS-6206* [1962 NYOC]

10375 Fly with Me (1920) Score (Richard Rodgers) US:LP = OC 8023* [1980 Revival NYOC]

10376 Flying Colors (1932) Excerpts (Arthur Schwartz) US:LP-10 = RCA L-16016 [@Jean Sargent:1932 NYOC & Studio Cast]

10377 Flying High (1930) Excerpts (Ray Henderson) US:LP-BP = JJA 19777 [@Al Goodman Orchestra:1930 NYOC]; Theme/US:LP-BP = JJA 19765 [Bert Lahr:1930 NYOC + 1931 Film Cast]

10378 Folies Bergere (1964) Score (Gerard & Betti) US:LP = Audio Fidelity AFLP-2135/AFSD-6135* [1964 NYOC]

10379 Follies (1971) Score (Stephen Sondheim) US:LP = Capitol SO-761* [1971 NYOC]

10380 Follow a Star (1930) Theme-A/US:LP-BP = JJA 19794 + Themes-B-C/GB:78 = Broadcast 5195 + Theme-D/GB:78 = Broadcast 5196 [Sophie Tucker: 1930 LOC]

10381 Follow Me (1916) Theme-A/US:78 = Emerson 7137 + Theme-B/US:78 = Emerson 7197 [Henry Lewis:1916 NYOC]

10382 Follow That Girl (1960) Score (Julian Slade) GB:LP = HMV CLP-1366 + US:LP = AEI 1121 [1960 LOC]

10383 Follow the Girls (1944) Themes-I-A-B/US:LP = Decca 5138 [Gertrude Niesen:1944 NYOC]; Theme-II/GB:78 = Decca 8587 [Evelyn Dall: 1944 LOC]

10384 Follow the Star (1975) Score (Jim Parker) GB:LP = Philips 6382.120* [1975 LOC]

10385 Follow Thru (1929) Themes-A-B/US:78 = Brunswick 4204 [Zelma O'Neal:1929 NYOC] + Theme-C/US:78 = Bluebird 2-5521 [Eleanor Powell: 1929 NYOC]

10386 Fools Rush In (1934) Themes-A-B/US:78 = Liberty Music 176 + Themes-C-D/US:78 = Liberty Music 177 [Teddy Lynch:1934 NYOC] + Theme-E/US:78 = Liberty Music 175 [Bill Haywood & Cliff Allen:1934 NYOC]

10387 For Goodness' Sake [Stop Flirting] (1922) Themes/GB:LP = WRC 144 [Fred and Adele Astaire:1922 NYOC + 1922 LOC]

10388 For the Love of Mike (1931) Themes/GB:LP = WRC 136 [Bobby Howes:1931 LOC]

10389 Forbidden Broadway (1983) Score (stage songs) US:LP = DRG SBL-12585* [1983 NYOC]

10390 Fortuna (1962) Score (Francis Thorne) US:LP = Owl ORLP-4 [Studio Orchestra]

10391 Fortune Teller, The (1898) Excerpts (Victor Herbert) US:LP-PP = Smithsonian R-017 [@Alice Nielsen: 1898 NYOC]

10392 Forty-five Minutes from Broadway (1906) Highlights + Dialog (George M. Cohan) US:LP = AEI 1159 [Television Cast]

10393 42nd Street (1980) Score (film songs:Harry Warren) US:LP = RCA CBL1-3891* [1980 NYOC]

10394 40 Years On (1960) Score (Carl Davis) GB:LP = Decca SKL-4987* [1969 LOC]

10395 Four Below Strikes Back, The (1960) Score (various) US:LP = Off Beat 4017 [1960 NYOC]

10396 Four Degrees Over (1966) Score (David Wood & John Gould) GB:LP = Parlophone PCS-7014* [1966 LOC]

10397 Four Musketeers, The (1967) Score (Laurie Johnson) GB:LP = Philips SAL-4987* [1967 LOC]

10398 Four Saints in Three Acts (1934) Scores (Virgil Thomson) US:LP-MS = RCA LM-2756 [OC]

10399 Four to the Bar (1962) Score (Bryan Blackburn) GB:LP = Philips SBBL-678* [1962 LOC]

10400 Fox Trot (1978) Score (Harry Bannink) GB:LP = Philips 6423.101* [1978 LOC]

10401 Foxy (1964) Score (Robert Emmett Dolan) US:LP-BP = SPM 4636 [1964 NYOC]

10402 Freddy *see* Heimweh Nach St. Pauli

10403 Frederica (1929) Themes-A-B/GB:78 = HMV 3589 + Themes-C-D/GB:78 = HMV 3590 [Joseph Hislop: 1929 LOC] + Themes-E-F/GB:78 = Columbia 131 + Themes-G-H/GB:78 = Columbia 269 [Lea Seidl:1929 LOC]

10404 Free as Air (1957) Score (Julian Slade) GB:LP = Oriole MG-20016 [1957 LOC]

10405 Free for All (1931) Theme/ US:78 = Columbia 2542 [Benny Goodman:1931 NYOC]

10406 Freedomland, U.S.A. [Industrial Show] Score (Jule Styne) US: LP = Columbia CL-1484/CS-8275* [Studio Cast]

10407 Fresh Airs (1956) Excerpts (Donald Swann) GB:LP = EMI EMCM-3088* [Flanders & Swann:1956 LOC]

10408 Front Street Gaieties (1980) Score (Jeffrey Silverman) US:LP = AEI 1133* [1980 LAOC]

10409 Fudgeripple Follies, or Nobody Likes a Smart Ass, The / Score (e:Sam Adams/e:Bill Holliday/e:Walter Perseveaux) US:LP-PP = Spade LP-102/SLP-202* [New Orleans OC]

10410 Fun of the Fayre, The (1921) Theme/GB:LP = Parlophone 7150 [@Alfred Lester:1921 LOC]

10411 Funny Face (1927) Highlights (George Gershwin) US:LP-PP = Smithsonian R-019 + GB:LP = WRC SH-144 [Fred & Adele Astaire:1927 NYOC + 1928 LOC]

10412 Funny Game, Politics (1964) Score (Peter Lewis & Peter Dobereiner) GB:LP = Parlophone PCS-1225* [1964 LOC]

10413 Funny Girl (1964) Score-I (Jule Styne) US:LP = Capitol VAS-2059/ SVAS-2059* [1964 NYOC]; Excerpts-II (Jule Styne) US:LP = Custom Fidelity CFS-2736* [Mimi Hines:1965 Replacement NYOC]; Highlights-III (Jule Styne) GB:EP = Pye 24257 [Lisa Shane: 1966 Replacement LOC]

10414 Funny Thing Happened on the Way to the Forum, A (1962) Score-I (Stephen Sondheim) US:LP = Capitol WAO-1717/SWAO-1717* [1962 NYOC]; Score-II (Stephen Sondheim) GB:LP = HMV CSD-1518* [1963 LOC]

G

10415 Gantry (1970) Score (Stan Lebowsky) US:LP-PP = Gantry 1001 [Demo Cast]

10416 Garrick Gaieties, The [C] Theme/US:78 = Liberty Music 200 [Nan Blackstone:1930 NYOC]

10417 Gay Deceivers, The (1935) Theme-A/US:LP = Stanyan 10055 + Theme-B/GB:78 = HMV 8324 [Charlotte Greenwood:1935 LOC]

10418 Gay Divorce (1932) Excerpts (Cole Porter) US:LP-BP = JJA 19779 [@Fred Astaire:1932 NYOC]

10419 Gay Life, The (1961) Score (Arthur Schwartz) US:LP = Capitol WAO-1560/SWAO-1560* [1961 NYOC]

10420 Gay's the Word (1951) Highlights (Ivor Novello) GB:LP = WRC SH-216 [1951 LOC]

10421 Geisha, The (1896) Theme-A/CA:LP = Rococo 4007 [@Marie Tempest:1896 LOC] + Theme-B/GB:78 = Zonophone 2291 [Conway Dixon:1896 LOC]

10422 Genius Farm (1965) Score (Hal Borne & Norman Retchin) US:LP-PP = Genius 1001 [Demo Cast]

10423 Gentlemen Prefer Blondes [Lorelei] (1949) Score-I (Jule Styne) US: LP = Columbia OL-4290/OS-2310e + US:LP = Columbia S-32610e [1949 NYOC]; Score-II (Jule Styne) GB:LP = HMV CSD-1464* [1962 Revival LOC]; Score-III (Jule Styne) US: LP = MGM MV-5097* + US:LP = MGM M3G-55* [1974 Revival NYOC]

10424 George M! (1968) Score (pop music) US:LP = Columbia KOS-3200* [1968 NYOC]

10425 George Washington, Jr. (1906) Theme/US:LP = Audio Rarities 2295 [George M. Cohan:1906 NYOC]

10426 George White's Music Hall Varieties (1932) Theme/US:LP = Epic 2-6072 [@Harry Richman:1932 NYOC]

10427 George White's Scandals [C] Theme-I/US:78 = Brunswick 2046 [Lester O'Keefe:1920 NYOC]; Themes-II-A-B/US:78 = RCA/Victor 18950 [Paul Whiteman:1922 NYOC] + Highlights-II

(George Gershwin) US:LP = Turnabout TUS-34638* ["Blue Monday"/Studio Cast]; Theme-III/US:78 = RCA/Victor 19151 [Charles Dornberger:1923 NYOC]; Theme-IV/US:78 = Vocalion 14866 [Tom Patriocola:1924 NYOC]; Theme-V-A/US:LP = Pelican 124 [Harry Richman: 1926 NYOC] + Theme-V-B/US:78 = Vocalion 15412 [Harry Richman:1926 NYOC]; Themes-VI-A-B/US:78 = Brunswick 3909 + Theme-VI-C/US: 78 = Brunswick 4037 [Arnold Johnson: 1928 NYOC] + Theme-VI-D/US:LP = Pelican 124 [Harry Richman:1928 NYOC]; Themes-VII/US:78 = Brunswick 4503 [Frances White:1929 NYOC]; Excerpts-VIII (various) US:LP-BP = JJA 19778 [@Rudy Vallee & Everett Marshall:1931 NYOC]; Theme-VIII/US: LP = Decca 5053 [Ethel Merman:1931 NYOC]; Themes-IX-A-B/US:78 = Columbia 35243 + Theme-IX-C/US:LP = New World 215 [Ella Logan:1939 NYOC]

10428 Georgy (1970) Score (George Fischoff) US:LP-PP = Georgy 1001 [Demo Cast]

10429 Gertrude Stein's First Reader (1969) Score (Ann Sternberg) US:LP = Polydor PD-247-002* [1969 NYOC]

10430 Gigi (1974) Score-I (film songs:Frederick Loewe) US:LP = RCA ABL1-0404* [1974 NYOC]; Score-II (film songs:Frederick Loewe) GB:LP = Safari GIGI-1* [1985 LOC]

10431 Gilbert and Sullivan Go Kosher (1971) Score (pop music) GB: LP = Pye GS-10467* [1971 LOC]

10432 Gilda Radner—Live from New York! (1979) Highlights + Dialog (e:Paul Shaffer/etc.) US:LP = WB HS-3320* [1979 NYOC]

10433 Girl Behind the Counter, The (1906) Theme-A/GB:78 = Favorite 1-65030 + Theme-B/GB:78 = Favorite 1-67001 [Fred Allandale:1906 LOC] + Theme-C/GB:78 = Favorite 1-66015 + Theme-D/GB:78 = Favorite 1-69003 [Isobel Jay:1906 LOC]

10434 Girl Crazy (1930) Excerpts-A (George Gershwin) US:LP = Reprise RS-6032* + US:LP = Stanyan 10070* [Ethel Merman:1930 NYOC] + Excerpts-B (George Gershwin) US:LP-BP = JJA 19777 [@1930 Supporting NYOC]; Score (George Gershwin) US:LP = Columbia CS-7060* [Studio Cast]

10435 Girl Friend, The (1926) Excerpts (Richard Rodgers) US:LP = Epic LN-3685 [Studio Cast]; Theme/US: LP = RCA LPV-549 [George Olsen Orchestra:1926 NYOC]

10436 Girl from Kays, The (1902) Theme-A/GB:78 = Columbia 25152 + Theme-B/GB:78 = Columbia 25157 + Theme-C/GB:78 = Columbia 25156 + Theme-D/GB:78 = G&T 2-2932 + Theme-E/GB:78 = G&T 2-2946 + Theme-F/GB:78 = G&T 2-2999 + Theme-G/GB:78 = G&T 02042 + Theme-H/GB:78 = G&T 02033 + Theme-I/GB:78 = Columbia 25160 + Theme-J/GB:78 = Columbia 25151 [Louis Bradfield:1902 LOC]

10437 Girl from Utah, The (1914) Themes/US:78-MS = Decca 245 [Julia Sanderson & Frank Crumit:1914 NYOC]

10438 Girl in Pink Tights, The (1954) Score (Sigmund Romberg) US: LP = Columbia OL-4890 [1954 NYOC]

10439 Girl in the Train, The (1908) Theme/GB:78 = HMV 03189 [Phyllis Dare:1908 LOC]

10440 Girl on the Film, The (1913) Theme/GB:78 = HMV 02500 [George Grossmith:1913 LOC]

10441 Girl Who Came to Supper, The (1963) Score (Noel Coward) US: LP = Columbia KOL-6020/KOS-2420* [1963 NYOC]

10442 Girls Against the Boys, The (1959) Highlights (Richard Lewine) US: EP-PP = Capitol PRO-1429 [Studio Cast]; Theme/US:LP-BP = JJA 19765 [Bert Lahr:1959 NYOC]

10443 Glamorous Night (1935) Score (Ivor Novello) GB:LP = Columbia TWO-243* [Studio Cast]; Excerpts (Ivor Novello) GB:LP = HMV CLP-1059 [@1935 LOC]

10444 Go Fight City Hall (1961) Score (Murray Rumshinsky) US:LP = Tikva T-72 [Studio Cast]

10445 Go Fly a Kite [Industrial Show] Scores (s:John Kander/s:Walter Marks) US:LP-MS-PP = General Electric GE-101/2 [OC]

10446 Godspell (1971) Score-I (Stephen Schwartz) US:LP = Bell 1102* + US:LP = Arista AL-4001* [1971 NYOC]; Score-II (Stephen Schwartz) GB:LP = Bell S-203* [1972 LOC]; Score-III (Stephen Schwartz) AU:LP = Festival SFL-934486* + US:LP = SFL 934486* [1972 AOC]

10447 Going Greek (1937) Themes/ GB:78 = HMV 462 [Roy Royston & Louise Browne:1937 LOC]

10448 Going Up (1918) Themes-A-B/HMV 860 [Evelyn Laye:1918 LOC] + Theme-C/GB:78 = HMV 03613 + Theme-D/GB:78 = HMV 03614 + Theme-E/GB:78 = HMV 04234 [Marjorie Gordon:1918 LOC] + Theme-F/ GB:78 = HMV 04233 [Evelyn Laye & Marjorie Gordon:1918 LOC] + Theme-G/GB:78 = HMV 04232 + Theme-H/ GB:78 = HMV 04235 [Joseph Coyne: 1918 LOC]

10449 Golden Apple, The (1954) Score (Jerome Moross) US:LP = RCA LOC-1014 + US:LP = Elektra ELK-5000 [1954 NYOC]

10450 Golden Boy (1964) Score (Charles Strouse) US:LP = Capitol VAS-2124/SVAS-2124* + US:LP = Capitol ST-11655* [1964 NYOC]

10451 Golden Dawn, The (1927) Theme/US:78 = Brunswick 3869 [Robert Chisholm:1927 NYOC]

10452 Golden Knight, The (1962) Score (Glenn Wescott) US:LP-PP = Sound Inc. SI-1205 [1962 LAOC]

10453 Golden Rainbow (1968) Score (Walter Marks) US:LP = Calendar KOM-1001/KOS-1001* [1968 NYOC]

10454 Golden Screw, The (1966) Score (Tom Sankey) US:LP = Atco 33-208/SD-33-208* [1966 NYOC]

10455 Goldilocks (1958) Score (Leroy Anderson) US:LP = Columbia OL-5340/OS-2007* + US:LP = CSP COS-2007* [1958 NYOC]

10456 Gone with the Wind [Scarlett] (1970) Score-I (Harold Rome) GB:LP = Columbia SCXA-9252* + US: LP = AEI 1113* [1972 LOC]; Scores-II (Harold Rome) JA:LP-MS = RCA SJET-9210/1* [1970 Japanese OC]

10457 Good Boy (1928) Theme/US: LP = RCA LPV-523 [@Helen Kane: 1928 NYOC]

10458 Good Companions, The (1931) Themes/GB:LP = WRC 217 [@ John Gielgud & Adele Dixon:1931 LOC]

10459 Good Companions, The (1974) Score (Andre Previn) GB:LP = EMI EMC-3042* + US:LP = DRG DS-15020* [1974 LOC]

10460 Good Morning Dearie / Excerpts (Jerome Kern) US:LP = Painted Smiles PS-1363* [Studio Cast]

10461 Good Morning Judge *see* Boy, The

10462 Good News (1927) Excerpts-I (Ray Henderson) US:LP-BP = JJA 19803 [George Olsen Orchestra:1927 NYOC] + Theme-I/US:78 = Brunswick 3864 [Zelma O'Neal:1927 NYOC]; Score-II (Ray Henderson) US:LP-PP = GN U-17889 [1963 Chicago Revival OC]; Scores-III (Ray Henderson) US:LP-MS-PP = SA 101 [1974 Revival NYOC]

10463 Good News About Olds [Industrial Show] Score (e:Lew Brown/etc.) US:LP-PP = WOR 112272 [OC]

10464 Good Old Bad Old Days, The (1973) Score (Leslie Bricusse & Anthony Newley) GB:LP = EMI EMA-751* + US:LP = AEI 1116* [1973 LOC]

10465 Goodbye Dear, I'll Be Back in a Year (1983) Score (pop music) US: LP = Glendale GLS-6026* [1983 LAOC]

10466 Goodbye, Mr. Chips (1982) Score (film songs & new songs:Leslie Bricusse) GB:LP = That's Entertainment TER-1025* [1982 LOC]

10467 Goodtime Charley (1975) Score (Larry Grossman & Hal Hackady) US:LP = RCA ARL1-1011* [1975 NYOC]

10468 Gospel at Colonus, The (1985) Score (Bob Telson) US:LP = WB 25182-1* [1985 NYOC]

10469 Got to Investigate Silicone [Industrial Show] Highlights (Hank Beebe) US:LP-PP = Quintal QP-1001* [OC]

10470 Grab Me a Gondola (1956) Score (James Gilbert) GB:LP = HMV CLP-1103 + US:LP = AEI 1119 [1956 LOC]

10471 Grand Street Follies of 1928, The (1928) Themes/US:78 = Columbia 1618 [The Von Hallberg Trio:1928 NYOC]

10472 Grand Tour (1959) Score (David Shire) US:LP-PP = Carillon K80P-6075 [1959 New Haven OC]

10473 Grand Tour (1979) Score (Jerry Herman) US:LP = Columbia JS-35761* [1979 NYOC]

10474 Grandpa [Children's Show] Highlights (Donald Ashwander) US: LP = Paper Bag Players PBP-5* [OC]

10475 Grass Harp, The (1971) Score (Claibe Richardson) US:LP = Painted Smiles PS-1354* [1971 NYOC]

10476 Grease (1972) Score-I (Jim Jacobs & Warren Casey) US:LP = MGM 1SE-34* [1972 NYOC]; Score-II (Jim Jacobs & Warren Casey) AF:LP = MFP SRSJ-8079* [1978 South Africa OC]

10477 Great American Backstage Musical, The (1976) Score (Bill Solly) US:LP = AEI 1101* [1976 LAOC]

10478 Great Day (1929) Excerpts (Vincent Youmans) US:LP-MS = Monmouth MES-6401/2* [Studio Cast]

10479 Great Waltz, The (1934) *see* Waltzes from Vienna

10480 Great Waltz, The (1965) Score-I (classical music/as:George Forrest & Robert Wright) US:LP = Capitol VAS-2426/SVAS-2426* [1965 LAOC]; Score-II (classical music/as:George Forrest & Robert Wright) GB:LP = Columbia SCX-6429* [1970 LOC]

10481 Greek Slave, A (1898) Theme-A/GB:78 = Berliner 2338 + Theme-B/GB:78 = Berliner 2984 [Scott Russell:1898 LOC]

10482 Green Grow the Lilacs (1931) Excerpts (various) US:LP = Capitol ST-213 [Tex Ritter:1931 NYOC]

10483 Greenwich Village Follies, The [C] Theme-I-A/US:78 = Columbia 2908 + Theme-I-B/US:78 = Columbia 2927 [Ted Lewis:1919 NYOC]; Theme-II-A/US:78 = Columbia 3332 + Theme-II-B/US:78 = Columbia 3415 [Frank Crumit:1920 NYOC] + Themes-II-C-D/ US:78 = RCA/Victor 18767 [Ford Hanford:1920 NYOC]; Theme-III-A/ US:78 = Columbia 2246 + Theme-III-B/US:78 = Columbia 3538 + Theme-III-C/US:78 = Columbia 3662 [Ted Lewis:1921 NYOC]; Themes-IV-A-B/ US:78 = Brunswick 3914 [Arnold Johnson:1928 NYOC]

10484 Greenwich Village, U.S.A. (1960) Scores (Jean Bargy) US:LP-MS = 20th TCP-105/TCS-105* + US:LP-MS = AEI 1129* [1960 NYOC]

10485 Greenwillow (1960) Score (Frank Loesser) US:LP = RCA LOC-2001/LSO-2001* + US:LP = CSP P-13974* [1960 NYOC]

10486 Grind (1985) Score (Larry Grossman) US:LP = Polydor 827-072-1* [1985 NYOC]

10487 Grosse Valise (1965) Score (Harold Rome) US:LP-PP = Grosse 1001 [Demo Cast]

10488 Guys and Dolls (1950) Score-I (Frank Loesser) US:LP = Decca DL-8036 + US:LP = Decca DL-9023/DL-79023e + US:LP = MCA 2034e + US: LP = MCA 37094e [1950 NYOC]; Highlights-II (Frank Loesser) GB:EP = Columbia 8593 [Edmund Hockridge:1953 LOC] + Themes-II/GB:78 = HMV 10508 [Lizbeth Webb:1953 LOC]; Score-III (Frank Loesser) US:LP = Motown M6-876-S1* [1976 Revival NYOC]; Score-IV (Frank Loesser) GB:LP = Chrysalis CSL-1388* [1982 Revival LOC]

10489 Gypsy (1959) Score-I (Jule Styne) US:LP = Columbia OL-5420/OS-2017* + US:LP = Columbia S-32607* [1959 NYOC]; Score-II (Jule Styne) GB: LP = RCA SERL-5686* + US:LP = RCA LBL1-5004* [1973 Revival LOC]; Score-III (Jule Styne) AF:LP = Philips STO-774* [1976 South Africa Revival OC]

10490 Gypsy Baron, The (1885) Highlights (Johann Strauss, Jr.) US: LP = Reader's Digest RD-40-10* [Studio Cast]

H

10491 Hair (1967) Score-I (Galt MacDermot) US:LP = RCA LOC-1143/ LSO-1143* + US:LP = RCA ANL1-0986* [1967 Off Broadway OC]; Score-II-A (Galt MacDermot) US:LP = RCA LOC-1150/LSO-1150* + Score-II-B (Galt MacDermot) US:LP = RCA LOC-1163/LSO-1163* [1968 NYOC]; Score-

III-A (Galt MacDermot) US:LP = Atco SD-7002* + Score-III-B (Galt MacDermot) US:LP = Polydor 24-5501* [1968 LOC]; Score-IV (Galt MacDermot) AU:LP = Spin SEL-933-544* [1969 AOC]; Score-V (Galt MacDermot) HO: LP = Polydor 2441-002* [1969 Holland OC]; Score-VI (Galt MacDermot) US: LP = Philips PHS-600-329* [1969 French OC]; Score-VII (Galt MacDermot) US: LP = RCA LOC-1170/LSO-1170* [1969 Japanese OC]; Score-VIII (Galt MacDermot) GE:LP = Polydor 249-266* [1969 German OC]; Score-IX (Galt MacDermot) IT:LP = RCA PSL-10479* [1969 Italian OC]

10492 Half a Sixpence (1963) Score-I (David Heneker) GB:LP = Decca SKL-4521* [1963 LOC]; Score-II (David Heneker) US:LP = RCA LOC-1110/LSO-1110* [1965 NYOC]

10493 Half Past Wednesday [Rumplestiltskin] (1962) Score (Robert Colby & Nita Jones) US:LP = Columbia KOL-6690/KOS-2050* [1962 NYOC]

10494 Hallelujah, Baby! (1967) Score (Jule Styne) US:LP = Columbia KOL-6690/KOS-3090* [1967 NYOC]

10495 Ham Tree, The (1905) Theme-A/US:78 = Columbia 3277 + Theme-B/US:78 = RCA/Victor 4592 [Harry Tally:1905 NYOC]

10496 Hand Is on the Gate, A (1966) Highlights + Dialog (folk music) US:LP-MS = Verve F-9040/FS-9040* [1966 NYOC]

10497 Hans Anderson (1974) Score-I (film songs & new songs:Frank Loesser) GB:LP = Pye NSPL-18451* [1974 LOC]; Score-II (film songs & new songs:Frank Loesser/e:Marvin Laird) GB:LP = Pye NSPL-18551* [1976 LOC]

10498 Hansel and Gretel (1893) Score (Engelbert Humperdinck) US: LP = RCA LXA-1013 [Studio Cast]

10499 Happiest Girl in the World, The (1961) Score (classical music) US:LP = Columbia KOL-5650/KOS-2050* [1961 NYOC]

10500 Happy as a Sandbag (1975) Score (pop music) GB:LP = Decca SKL-5217* [1975 LOC]

10501 Happy Day, A (1916) Theme/GB:LP = WRC 169 [Jose Collins:1916 LOC]

10502 Happy End (1929) Score (Kurt Weill) US:LP = Columbia KOL-5630/KOS-2032* [Studio Cast]

10503 Happy Hunting (1956) Score (Harold Karr) US:LP = RCA LOC-1026 [1956 NYOC]

10504 Happy Time, The (1968) Score (John Kander) US:LP = RCA LOC-1144/LSO-1144* [1968 NYOC]

10505 Hard Job Being God, A (1972) Score (Tom Martel) US:LP = GWP ST-2036* [1972 NYOC]

10506 Hark! (1972) Scores (Dan Goggin & Marvin Solley) US:LP-MS-PP = Ellison STK-1015/8* [1972 NYOC]

10507 Harmony Close (1959) Score (Ronald Cass) GB:LP = Oriole MG-20014 [1959 LOC]

10508 Havana (1908) Theme/GB: 78 = Columbia 26461 [Jessie Broughton: 1908 LOC]

10509 Have a Heart (1917) Theme/US:LP = Folkways 601 [Billy Van:1917 NYOC]

10510 Have a Holiday [Industrial Show] Score (Michael Brown) US:LP-PP = OSS 1555 [OC]

10511 Have I Got One for You (1968) Theme/US:LP-BP = Vendette 8703 [Gloria DeHaven:1968 NYOC]

10512 Hazel Flagg (1953) Score (Jule Styne) US:LP = RCA LOC-1010 + US:LP = RCA CBM1-2207 [1953 NYOC]

10513 Heads Up! (1929) Excerpts (Richard Rodgers) US:LP = Painted Smiles PS-1367* [Studio Cast]

10514 Hear! Hear! (1955) Score (as:Fred Waring) US:LP = Decca DL-9031 [1955 NYOC]

10515 Heart o' th' Heather, The (1916) Themes/US:78 = RCA/Victor 45097 [George MacFarlane:1916 Boston OC]

10516 Heathen! (1972) Score (Eaton Magoon, Jr.) US:LP-PP = Heathen 1001* [1972 Hawaii OC]; Excerpts (Eaton Magoon, Jr.) US:LP = Lehua SL-7002* [Studio Cast]

10517 Heimweh Nach St. Pauli [Freddy] (1963) Score (Lotar Olias) US: LP = MGM E-4195/SE-4195* [1963 German OC]

10518 Hell Can Be Heaven (1983) Score (Hereward K.) GB:LP = That's Entertainment TER-1068* [1983 LOC]

10519 Hello Daddy (1928) Themes-A-B/US:78 = RCA/Victor 21858 + Theme-C/US:78 = Okeh 41189 [Ben Pollack:1928 NYOC]

10520 Hello, Dolly (1964) Score-I (Jerry Herman) US:LP = RCA LOC-1087/LSO-1087* + US:LP = RCA AYL1-3814* [1964 NYOC]; Theme-II-A/US:LP-BP = Citel 2201 + Theme-II-B/US:LP-BP = Curtain Calls 100/21 [Ginger Rogers:1965 Replacement NYOC]; Score-III (Jerry Herman) GB: LP = RCA SF-7768* + US:LP = RCA LOC-2007/LSO-2007* [1965 LOC]; Score-IV (Jerry Herman) US:LP = Columbia OL-6710/OS-3110* [1966 German OC]; Theme-V/US:LP-BP = Scarce Rarities 5501 [Betty Grable:1967 Replacement NYOC]; Excerpts-VI (Jerry Herman) US:LP-MS-BP = Legends 1000/5-6 [Martha Raye:1967 Replacement NYOC]; Score-VII (Jerry Herman) US: LP = RCA LOC-1147/LSO-1147* + US: LP = RCA AYL1-3814* [1967 Replacement NYOC]; Themes-VIII/US:SP-BP = Bar Mike EM-1A-IFA [Ethel Merman:1970 Replacement NYOC]

10521 Hello Out There (1953) Score (Jack Beeson) US:LP = Desto DST-6451* [Studio Cast]

10522 Hello, Solly (1967) Score (pop music) US:LP = Capitol W-2731/SW-2731* [1967 NYOC]

10523 Hello, Yourself (1928) Themes-A-B/US:78 = RCA/Victor 21783 + Theme-C/US:78 = RCA 21870 [Fred Waring:1928 NYOC]

10524 Hellzapoppin '67 (1967) Score (Marian Grudeff & Raymond Jessell) US:LP-PP = Hellzapoppin 1001 [Demo Cast]

10525 Hellzapoppin '77 (1977) Score (e:Jule Styne/e:Cy Coleman) US: LP-PP = Hellzapoppin 1002 [Demo Cast]

10526 Hen-Pecks, The (1911) Theme-A/US:LP = Decca 5424 + Theme-B/US:LP = Mercury 20224 [Blossom Seeley:1911 NYOC]

10527 Henry, Sweet Henry (1968) Score (Bob Merrill) US:LP = ABC OC-4/SOC-4* [1968 NYOC]

10528 Her Family Tree (1920) Theme/US:78 = Columbia 3360 [Nora Bayes:1920 NYOC]

10529 Her First Roman (1970) Score (Ervin Drake) US:LP-BP = SPM 7751 [1970 NYOC]

10530 Her Soldier Boy [Soldier Boy] (1916) Themes-A-B/GB:78 = Columbia 1262 [Laurence Leonard:1916 LOC] + Themes-C-D/GB:78 = Columbia 1263 [Fred Duprez:1916 LOC] + Themes E-F/GB:78 = Columbia 1264 [Maisie Gay:1916 LOC] + Themes-G-H/GB:78 = Columbia 1265 [Dewey Gibson:1916 LOC] + Themes-I-J/GB:78 = Columbia 1266 [Winifred Barnes:1916 LOC]

10531 Here Comes the Bride (1930) Theme-A/US:LP-PP = Smithsonian 021 + Theme-B/GB:78 = Columbia 70 [Jean Colin & Clifford Mollison:1930 LOC] + Themes-C-D/US:LP-BP = JJA 19794 [@Vera Bryer & Richard Dolman:1930 LOC] + Themes-E-F/GB:78 = Columbia 72 [Maria Minetti:1930 LOC]

10532 Here's Howe (1928) Themes/US:78 = Brunswick 3913 [Ben Bernie: 1928 NYOC]

10533 Here's Love (1963) Score (Meredith Willson) US:LP = Columbia KOL-6000/KOS-2400* [1963 NYOC]

10534 Here's Where I Belong (1968) Score (Robert Waldman & Alfred Uhry) US:LP-PP = Here 1001 [Demo Cast]

10535 Hi Diddle Diddle (1934) Theme/GB:78 = Decca 5249 [Douglas Byng:1934 LOC]

10536 Hide and Seek (1937) Themes-A-B/GB:78 = HMV 8675 + Theme-C/GB:LP = WRC 136 [Bobby Howes:1937 LOC] + Themes-D-E/GB: 78 = HMV 8674 [Cicely Courtneidge: 1937 LOC]

10537 High Button Shoes (1947) Score (Jule Styne) US:LP = Camden CAL-457 + US:LP = RCA LOC-1107/LSO-1107e [1947 NYOC]

10538 High Jinks (1913) Themes-A-B/GB:78 = HMV 720 [Marie Blanche & Perry Gawthorne:1913 LOC] + Themes-C-D/GB:78 = HMV 712 + Themes-E-F/GB:78 = HMV 721 [Maisie Gay:1913 LOC] + Theme-G/GB:LP = WRC 34

+ Theme-H/GB:78=HMV 02679 + Theme-I/GB:78=HMV 04175 + Theme-J/GB:78=HMV 4-2784 [W.H. Berry:1913 LOC]

10539 High Kickers (1941) Theme/US:78=RCA 22049 [Sophie Tucker: 1941 NYOC]

10540 High Spirits (1964) Score-I (Timothy Grey & Hugh Martin) US: LP=ABC OC-1/SOC-1* [1964 NYOC]; Score-II (Timothy Grey & Hugh Martin) GB:LP=Pye NSPL-18100* [1964 LOC]

10541 Higher and Higher (1940) Excerpts (Richard Rodgers) US:LP-BP=Show Biz 5604 + US:LP-BP=JJA 19734 [@1940 NYOC]

10542 Highway Life, The *see* Dude

10543 Hip-Hip-Hooray (1915) Theme/US:78=Columbia 2057 [1915 OC Chorus + Ray Burnside]

10544 His Monkey Wife (1972) Score (Sandy Wilson) GB:LP=President PTLS-1051* [1972 LOC]

10545 Hit the Deck (1927) Theme-I (Vincent Youmans) US:LP=RCA LPV-560 [@Louise Groody & Charles King: 1927 NYOC]; Highlights-II (Vincent Youmans) GB:LP=WRC SH-176 [1927 LOC]

10546 Hitchy-Koo (1917) Themes-A-B/US:78=RCA/Victor 45137 + Theme-C/US:78=RCA/Victor 45149 [Frances White:1917 NYOC]

10547 Hokey-Pokey (1912) Theme/US:LP=Audio Rarities 2290 [Lillian Russell:1912 NYOC]

10548 Hold on to Your Hats (1940) Highlights (Burton Lane) US:LP=Painted Smiles PS-1372* [Studio Cast]

10549 Holiday in Fashion [Industrial Show] Score (Michael Brown) US:LP-PP=DC 10158 [OC]

10550 Holly Golightly *see* Breakfast at Tiffany's

10551 Home and Beauty (1937) Theme-A/GB:LP=WRC 129 [Binnie Hale:1937 LOC] + Theme-B/GB:LP=Parlophone 7154 [Gitta Alpar:1937 LOC]

10552 Honeymoon Express, The (1913) Excerpts-A (various) US:LP-BP=Olympic 7114 [Al Jolson:1913 NYOC]; Excerpts-B (various) US:LP-BP=Take Two 103 [Al Jolson:1913 NYOC]

10553 Honeymoon Lane (1926) Themes-A-B/US:78=Columbia 810 [Kate Smith:1926 NYOC] + Themes-C-D/US:78=Columbia 750; Theme-E/US:78=Okeh 40704 [Johnny Marvin: 1926 NYOC]

10554 Hooray for Daisy (1961) Score (Julian Slade) GB:LP=HMV CSD-1434* + US:LP=AEI 1118* [1961 LOC]

10555 Hoot Mon (1927) Theme/US:78=RCA/Victor 20524 [The Mask & Wig Singing Chorus:1927 NYOC]

10556 Hot-Cha! (1932) Excerpts (Ray Henderson) US:LP-10=RCA L-16008 [Studio Cast]; Theme (Ray Henderson) US:LP-BP=JJA 19779 [@Lupe Velez:1932 NYOC]

10557 Hot Chocolates (1929) Score (Fats Waller & Harry Brooks) US:LP-PP=Smithsonian R-012 [1929 NYOC]

10558 Hot Rhythm (1930) Themes-A-B/US:78=RCA/Victor 23010 + Theme-C/US:78=RCA/Victor 38624 [Edith Wilson:1930 NYOC]

10559 Hot September (1965) Score (Kenneth Jacobson) US:LP-BP=Blue Pear BP-1012 [1965 NYOC]

10560 Houp-La (1916) Excerpts (various) GB:LP=WRC SH-186 [Gertie Millar:1916 LOC]

10561 House of Flowers (1954) Score-I (Harold Arlen) US:LP=Columbia OL-4969/OS-2320e + US:LP=CSP COS-2320e [1954 NYOC]; Score-II (Harold Arlen) US:LP=UA UAS-5180* [1968 Revival NYOC]

10562 House of Leather (1970) Score (Dale Menton) US:LP=Fontana SRF-67591* [1970 NYOC]

10563 House of Love (1960) Score (e:Tommy Wolf/e:Gerald Dolin) US: LP=20th 3049 [Jayne Mansfield:1960 Las Vegas OC]

10564 House That Jack Built, The (1929) Theme/GB:LP=WRC 113 [Jack Hulbert:1929 LOC]

10565 Housewife—Superstar! (1977) Score (Barry Humphries) US: LP=Charisma CAS-1123* [1977 NYOC]

10566 Housewives Cantata (1981) Score (Mira Spektor) US:LP=OC 8133* [1981 NYOC]

10567 How Do You Do, I Love

You (1967) Score (David Shire) US: LP-PP = How 1001 [Demo Cast]; Excerpts (David Shire) US:LP = RCA ABL-2360* [Studio Cast]

10568 How Now, Dow Jones (1967) Score (Elmer Bernstein) US:LP = RCA LOC-1142/LSO-1142* [1967 NYOC]

10569 How to Steal an Election (1968) Score (Oscar Brand) US:LP = RCA LSO-1153* [1968 NYOC]

10570 How to Succeed in Business Without Really Trying (1961) Score-I (Frank Loesser) US:LP = RCA LOC-1066/LSO-1066* [1961 NYOC]; Score-II (Frank Loesser) GB:LP = RCA RDS-7564* [1963 LOC]

10571 Hullo America (1919) Theme/GB:LP = Parlophone 7145 [@ Maurice Chevalier:1919 LOC]

10572 Hullo Ragtime (1912) Theme-A/GB:LP = Parlophone 7145 + Theme-B/GB:78 = HMV 04100 + Theme-C/GB:78 = HMV 04108 [Lew Hearn & Bonita:1912 LOC] + Theme-D/ GB:78 = HMV 04097 [Shirley Kellogg:1912 LOC] + Theme-E/GB:78 = HMV 03377 [Ethel Levey:1912 LOC]

I

10573 I and Albert (1972) Score (Charles Strouse) GB:LP = That's Entertainment TER-1004* [1972 LOC]

10574 I Can Get It for You Wholesale (1962) Score (Harold Rome) US: LP = Columbia KOL-5780/KOS-2180* [1962 NYOC]

10575 I Can't Keep Running in Place (1981) Score (Barbara Schottenfeld) US:LP = Painted Smiles PS-1346* [1981 NYOC]

10576 I Do! I Do! (1966) Score-I (Harvey Schmidt) US:LP = RCA LOC-1128/LSO-1128* [1966 NYOC]; Score-II (Harvey Schmidt) GB:LP = RCA SF-7938* [1968 LOC]

10577 I Had a Ball (1965) Score (Jack Lawrence & Stan Freeman) US: LP = Mercury OCM-2210/OCS-6210* [1965 NYOC]

10578 I Like Mike (1968) Score (Dov Seltzer) IS:LP = CBS 70037* [1968 Israel OC]

10579 I Love My Wife (1977) Score-I (Cy Coleman) US:LP = Atlantic SD-19107* [1977 NYOC]; Score-II (Cy Coleman) US:LP = Atlantic SD-19107* [1977 NYOC]; Score-II (Cy Coleman) AU:LP = Festival 37934* [1978 AOC]; Score-III (Cy Coleman) AF:LP = EMI 11552* [1978 South Africa OC]

10580 I Married an Angel (1938) Excerpts-A (Richard Rodgers) US:LP = Painted Smiles PS-1367* [Studio Cast]; Themes/US:LP-BP = JJA 19734 [@Audrey Christie:1938 NYOC]

10581 I Remember Mama / Score (Richard Rodgers) US:LP = Polydor 827-336-1* [Original Cast & Studio Cast]

10582 Ice Follies [C] Themes-I-A-B/US:78-PP = Ice Follies 4008 + Themes-I-C-D/US:78-PP = Ice Follies 4007 [Jean Norman & John Woodbury: 1949 OC]; Themes-II/US:78-PP = Ice Follies FR-51 [Gil Mershon & Bill Reeve: 1951 OC]; Themes-III/US:78-PP = Ice Follies 22268 [Norma Zimmer & Bill Reeve:1956 OC]; Score-IV (e:Richard Friesen/etc.) US:LP = Dot DLP-3757/DLP-25757* [Debbie Williams:1967 OC + Studio Cast]

10583 I'd Rather Be Right (1937) Excerpts-A (Richard Rodgers) US:LP-BP = JJA 19734 [Studio Cast]; Excerpts-B (Richard Rodgers) US:LP = Painted Smiles PS-1367* [Studio Cast]

10584 Illya Darling (1967) Score (Manos Hadjidakis) US:LP = UA UAL-8901/UAS-9901* [1967 NYOC]

10585 I'm Getting My Act Together and Taking It on the Road (1978) Score-I (Nancy Ford) US:LP = CSP X-14885* [1978 NYOC]; Score-II (Nancy Ford) GB:LP = That's Entertainment TER-1006* [1980 LOC]

10586 I'm Solomon (1968) Score (Ernest Gold) US:LP-PP = Solomon 1001 [Demo Cast]

10587 In Circles (1967) Score (Al Carmines) US:LP = Avant Garde M-108/S-108* [1967 NYOC]

10588 In Trousers (1979) Score (William Finn) US:LP = OC 7915* [1979 NYOC]

10589 In White America (1964) Highlights + Dialog (folk music) US: LP = Columbia KOS-2430* [1964 OC]

10590 Inner City (1972) Score (Helen Miller) US:LP = RCA LSO-1171* [1972 NYOC]

10591 Inside U.S.A. (1948) Highlights (Arthur Schwartz) US:78-MS = RCA K-14 + US:LP-BP = JJA 19733 [1948 NYOC]

10592 Instant Marriage (1964) Score (Laurie Holloway) GB:LP = Oriole PS-40062* [1964 LOC]

10593 International Soiree (1958) Score (as:Jo Basile) US:LP = Audio Fidelity AFLP-1881/AFSD-5881* [1958 NYOC]

10594 Invisible Dragon, The [The Dragon] [Children's Musical] Highlights (Jo Adler) US:LP = Bag-A-Tale 1000* [OC]

10595 Iphigenia (1972) Score (Peter Link & C.C. Courtney) US:LP-PP = Iphigenia 1001 [Demo Cast]

10596 Ipi Tombi (1976) Scores (Bertha Egnos) GB:LP-MS = Galaxy GALD-26000* + US:LP-MS = Ash Tree ASH-26000* [1976 LOC]

10597 Irene (1919) Score-I (Harry Tierney) US:LP = Monmouth MES-7057 [Edith Day:1919 NYOC + 1920 LOC]; Score-II (e:Harry Tierney/new songs:Charles Gaynor) US:LP = Columbia KS-32266* [1973 Revival NYOC]; Score-III (e:Harry Tierney/new songs: Charles Gaynor) GB:LP = EMI EMC-3139* [1976 Revival LOC]

10598 Irma la Douce (1956) Excerpts-I (Marguerite Monnot) FR:LP = Vogue LD-395 [Colette Renard:1956 French OC]; Score-II (Marguerite Monnot) GB:LP = Philips B-10738 [1958 LOC]; Score-III (Marguerite Monnot) US:LP = Columbia OL-5560/OS-2029* + US:LP = CSP AOS-2029* [1960 NYOC]; Score-IV (Marguerite Monnot) FR:LP = Vega 16.089 [1967 Revival French OC]

10599 Is There Life After High School? (1982) Score (C. Carnelia) US: LP = OC 8240* [1982 NYOC]

10600 Isabel's a Jezebel (1971) Score (Galt MacDermot) GB:LP = UA UAG-29148* [1971 LOC]

10601 Isle o' Dreams (1913) Theme-A/US:78 = Columbia 1310 + Theme-B/ US:78 = Columbia 1337 [Chauncey Olcott:1913 NYOC]

10602 It Happened in Tanjablanca [Red, White and Boogie] (1968) Score-I (Peter Pinne) AU:LP = W&G 5502 [1968 AOC]; Highlights-II (Peter Pinne) AU: LP = Trigpoint TPR-001* [1973 Revival AOC]

10603 It's a Bird, It's a Plane, It's Superman! (1966) Score (Charles Strouse) US:LP = Columbia KOL-6570/ KOS-2970* + US:LP = CSP AKOS-2970* [1966 NYOC]

10604 It's Holiday Time [Industrial Show] Score (Michael Brown) US:LP-PP = DC 52258 [OC]

J

10605 Jack and Jill (1923) Theme/ US:78 = RCA/Victor 19051 [Brooke Johns:1923 NYOC]

10606 Jack and the Beanstalk [Children's Show] Score (Clay Boland, Jr.) US:LP = Peter Pan 8043/58043* [OC]

10607 Jacques Brel Is Alive and Well and Living in Paris (1968) Scores-I (pop music) US:LP-MS = Columbia D2S-779* [1968 NYOC]; Score-II (pop music) US:LP-PP = Synchronicity 1306* [1968 NYOC]; Scores-III (pop music) US:LP-MS-PP = Playhouse Square CLE-2S-101* [1973 Cleveland OC]; Score-IV (pop music) AF:LP = MVN 3541* [1974 South Africa OC]

10608 Jamaica (1957) Score (Harold Arlen) US:LP = RCA LOC-1036*/LSO-1036* + US:LP = RCA LOC-1103/LSO-1103* [1957 NYOC]

10609 January the Twenty-Sixth / Score/AU:LP = Control 154317 [AOC]

10610 Jean (1973) Score (Ralph Chicorel) US:LP-PP = Pleasure 103* [1973 Wisconsin OC]

10611 Jeeves (1975) Score (Andrew Lloyd Webber) GB:LP = MCA MCF-2726* [1975 LOC]

10612 Jennie (1963) Score (Arthur Schwartz) US:LP = RCA LOC-1083/ LSO-1083* [1963 NYOC]

10613 Jericho Jim Crow (1964) Scores (Langston Hughes) US:LP-MS = Folkways FL-9671 [1964 NYOC]

10614 Jerry's Girls (1984) Scores (stage songs) US:LP-MS = Polydor 820-207-2* [1984 NYOC]

10615 Jesus Christ Superstar (1971) Score-I (Andrew Lloyd Webber) US: LP = Decca DL-71503 [1971 NYOC]; Scores-II (Andrew Lloyd Webber) GB: LP-MS = MCA MDKS-8008* + US:LP-MS = Decca DXSA-7206* + US:LP-MS = MCA 2-10000* [1972 LOC]; Score-III (Andrew Lloyd Webber) AU:LP = MCA MAPS-6244* [1972 AOC]; Score-IV (Andrew Lloyd Webber) FR:LP = Philips 6325.007* [1973 French OC]

10616 Jill Darling (1934) Excerpts (Vivien Ellis) GB:LP = WRC SH-263 [@1934 LOC]

10617 Jimmy (1969) Score (Bill & Patti Jacob) US:LP = RCA LSO-1162* [1969 NYOC]

10618 Jingle Jangle (1982) Score (Geoff Morrow) GB:LP = Class JJ-001* [1982 LOC]

10619 Joan (1971) Scores (Al Carmines) US:LP-MS = Judson JU-1001* [1971 NYOC]

10620 Joan of Arkansas (1925) Theme/US:78 = RCA/Victor 19626 [The Mask & Wig Club Quartet:1925 NYOC]

10621 Joe Lives! (1971) Scores (various) GB:LP = MWM 10038* [1971 LOC]

10622 John Murray Anderson's Almanac (1953) Themes-A-B/US:LP = Dolphin 1 [Elaine Dunn:1953 NYOC] + Theme-C/US:LP = Dolphin 7 [Hermione Gingold:1953 NYOC] + Theme-D/US:SP = RCA 477-0322 + Theme-E/US:SP = RCA 47-5722 + Theme-F/US:EP = RCA EPB-1022 [Harry Belafonte:1953 NYOC]

10623 John, Paul, George, Ringo and Bert (1975) Score (Willy Russell) GB: LP = RSO 2394.141* [1975 LOC]

10624 Johnny Johnson (1936) Score (Kurt Weill) US:LP = MGM E-3447 + US:LP = Heliodor H-25024/HS-25024e [Studio Cast]

10625 Johnny the Priest (1960) Score (Anthony Hopkins) GB:LP = Decca SKL-4352* + GB:LP = That's Entertainment TER-1044* [1960 LOC]

10626 Joker of Seville, The (1974) Score (Galt MacDermot) US:LP-PP = SEMP CL-2575* [1974 Trinidad OC]

10627 Jolly Bachelors, The (1910) Theme-A/US:LP = Pelican 102 [@Nora Bayes:1910 NYOC] + Theme-B/US: 78 = RCA/Victor 60014 [Jack Norworth: 1910 NYOC] + Theme-C/US:78 = RCA/Victor 70015 + Theme-D/US: 78 = RCA/Victor 70016 + Theme-E/US:78 = Victor 70019 [Nora Bayes & Jack Norworth:1910 NYOC]

10628 Jolson Revue, The (1975) Score (pop music) GB:LP = UA UAS-29712* [1975 LOC]

10629 Jorrocks (1966) Score (David Heneker) GB:LP = HMV CSD-3591* [1966 LOC]

10630 Joseph and the Amazing Technicolor Dreamcoat (1972) Score-I (Andrew Lloyd Webber) GB:LP = RSO 2394.103* [1972 LOC]; Score-II (Andrew Lloyd Webber) AF:LP = MFP SRSJ-8008* [1975 South Africa OC]; Score-III (Andrew Lloyd Webber) GB:LP = MFP 50455* [Paul Jones:1979 LOC]; Highlights-IV (Andrew Lloyd Webber) GB: EP = Kerrysmile KSR-001* [1980 LOC]; Score-V (Andrew Lloyd Webber) US: LP = Chrysalis CHR-1387* [1982 NYOC]

10631 Joseph McCarthy Is Alive and Well and Living in Dade County (1976) Score (Ray Scantlin) US:LP = AEI 1103* [1976 LAOC]

10632 Joy (1970) Score (Oscar Brown, Jr.) US:LP = RCA LSO-1166* [1970 NYOC]

10633 Joyce Grenfell Requests the Pleasure (1954) Score (Richard Addinsell) GB:LP = Philips BBL-7004 + US:LP = DRG SL-5186 [1954 LOC]

10634 Joyful Noise, A (1966) Score (Oscar Brand) US:LP-PP = Joyful 1001 [Demo Cast]

10635 Jubalay *see* Bistro Car on the C.N.R., The

10636 Jubilee (1935) Highlights (Cole Porter) US:LP = Columbia KS-31456 [Studio Cast]

10637 Julie and Carol at Carnegie Hall (1962) Score (e:Ken Welch/etc.) US:LP = Columbia OL-5840/OS-2240* [1962 NYOC]

10638 Jumbo [Billy Rose's Jumbo] (1935) Score (Richard Rodgers) Columbia OL-5860/OS-2260* + US:LP = CSP AOS-2260* [Film Cast]; Themes-A-B/US:LP-BP = JJA 19734 [Gloria Grafton & Paul Whiteman:1935 NYOC] + Theme-C/US:LP = King 1935 [Jimmy Durante & Paul Whiteman:1935 NYOC]

10639 Jump for Joy (1941) Highlights (Duke Ellington) FR:LP = RCA FXM1-7201 [1941 LAOC]; Themes-A-B/US:78 = RCA/Victor 27639 [Ivie Anderson & Ray Nance:1941 LAOC] + Theme-C/US:78 = RCA/Victor 27380 [Duke Ellington:1941 LAOC]

10640 Juno (1959) Score (Marc Blitzstein) US:LP = Columbia OL-5380/OS-2013* [1959 NYOC]

10641 Just for Openers (1965) Score (e:Rod Warren/etc.) US:LP-PP = Upstairs at the Downstairs UD-37W56* [1965 NYOC]

K

10642 Ka-Boom! (1980) Score (Joe Ercole) US:LP = CYM 8130* [1980 NYOC]

10643 Karl Marx Play, The (1973) Score (Galt MacDermot) US:LP = Kilmarnock KIL-72010* [1973 NYOC]

10644 Katinka (1915) Theme-A/US:78 = Operaphone 1076 [May Naudain:1915 NYOC] + Theme-A/US:78 = Columbia 1952 [Sam Ash:1915 NYOC]

10645 Katja, The Dancer (1923) Themes-A-B/GB:78 = Columbia 3625 + Themes-C-D/GB:78 = Columbia 3627 [Lilian Davies & Gregory Stroud: 1923 LOC] + Themes-E-F/GB:78 = Columbia 3626 [Gregory Stroud & Ivy Tresmand:1923 LOC] + Themes-G-H/GB:78 = Columbia 3628 [Ivy Tresmand: 1923 LOC]

10646 Kazablan (1966) Score (Dov Seltzer) IS:LP = CBS 70028* [1966 Israel OC]

10647 Kean (1961) Score (George Forrest & Robert Wright) US:LP = Columbia KOL-5720/KOS-2120* [1961 NYOC]

10648 Keep Off the Grass (1940) Themes-A-B/US:78 = Columbia 35578 + Themes-C-D/US:78 = Columbia 35632 [Virginia O'Brien:1940 NYOC] + Theme-E/US:78 = MGM 151 [Jimmy Durante:1940 NYOC]

10649 Keep Shufflin' (1928) Themes/US:78 = RCA/Victor 21348 [Fats Waller:1928 NYOC]

10650 Kelly (1965) Score (Moose Charlap) US:LP-PP = Kelly 1001 + US:LP = OC 8025 [Demo Cast]

10651 Kicks and Company (1959) Excerpts (Oscar Brown, Jr.) US:LP = Columbia CL-1774/CS-8574* [Oscar Brown, Jr.:Studio Cast]

10652 Kid Boots (1923) Excerpts (Harry Tierney) US:LP = Audio Fidelity 702 [Eddie Cantor:1923 NYOC]

10653 Kill That Story (1934) Theme/ US:78 = RCA/Victor 24717 [Gloria Grafton:1934 NYOC]

10654 King and I, The (1951) Score-I (Richard Rodgers) US:LP = Decca DL-9008/DL-79008e + US:LP = MCA 2028e + US:LP = MCA 37095e [1951 NYOC]; Score-II (Richard Rodgers) GB:LP = Philips BBL-7002 + US:LP = DRG DS-15014 [1953 LOC]; Score-III (Richard Rodgers) US:LP = RCA LOC-1092/LSO-1092* [1964 Revival NYOC]; Score-IV (Richard Rodgers) US:LP = RCA ABL1-2610* [1977 Revival NYOC]; Highlights-V (Richard Rodgers) GB:EP-12 = RIM 1000* [Virginia McKenna:1979 Revival LOC]

10655 King Kong (1960) Score (Todd Matshikiza) GB:LP = Decca SKL-4132* + US:LP = London 5762* [1960 LOC]

10656 King of Hearts (1978) Score (Peter Link) US:LP = OC 8028* [1978 NYOC]

10657 King of the Entire World, The (1978) Score (Daniel Pisello) US:LP-PP = Fourth Wall 4 [1978 NYOC]

10658 King of the Whole Damn World, The (1962) Score (Robert Larimer) US:LP-PP = R.L. 101 [1962 NYOC]

10659 King's Rhapsody (1949) Highlights (Ivor Novello) GB:LP-10 = HMV DLP-1010 + GB:LP = WRC SHB-23 [1949 LOC]

10660 Kismet [Timbuktu!] (1953) Score-I (as:George Forrest & Robert Wright) US:LP=Columbia OL-4850/OS-2060e + US:LP=Columbia S-32605e [1953 NYOC]; Score-II (as: George Forrest & Robert Wright) US: LP=RCA LOC-1112/LSO-1112* [1965 Revival NYOC]; Themes-III/US:LP-PP=April/Blackwood 33782-01* [Eartha Kitt:1978 Revival NYOC]

10661 Kiss Me Kate (1948) Score-I (Cole Porter) US:LP=Columbia OL-4140/OS-2300e + US:LP=Columbia S-32609e [1948 NYOC]; Highlights-II (Cole Porter) GB:LP=WRC SHB-26 [1951 LOC]

10662 Kissing Time (1919) Themes-A-B/GB:78=Columbia 1318 + Theme-C/GB:78=Columbia MC-15 + Theme-D/GB:78=Columbia MC-16 [Yvonne Arnaud:1919 LOC] + Theme-E/GB: 78=Columbia MC-9 + Theme-F/GB: 78=Columbia MC-10 [Leslie Henson: 1919 LOC] + Theme-G/GB:78=Columbia MC-11 + Theme-H/GB:78=Columbia MC-12 + Theme-I/GB:78=Columbia MC-13 + Theme-J/GB:78=Columbia MC-14 [Phyllis Dare:1919 LOC] + Theme-K/GB:78=Columbia MC-17 [Tom Walls:1919 LOC]

10663 Kittiwake Island (1960) Score (Alec Wilder) US:LP-PP=Adelphi AD-2015 [1960 NYOC]

10664 Kitty Grey (1901) Theme/GB:78=G&T 2-2528 [Maurice Farkoa: 1901 LOC]

10665 Knickerbocker Holiday (1938) Score (Kurt Weill) US:LP-BP=Joey 7243 + US:LP=AEI 1148 [1938 NYOC]

10666 Knotty, The / Score/AU: LP=Argo ZTR-125 [AOC]

10667 Kosher Widow, The (1961) Score (Shalom Secunda) US:LP=Golden Crest 4018/S-4018* [1961 LAOC]

10668 Kurt Weill Cabaret, A (1963) Score (stage songs) US:LP=MGM E-4180/SE-4180* [1963 NYOC]

10669 Kwa Zulu (1975) Score (Victor Ntoni) GB:LP=Philips 6355.031* [1975 LOC]

10670 Kwamina (1961) Score (Richard Adler) US:LP=Capitol W-1645/SW-1645* [1961 NYOC]

L

10671 Ladies First (1918) Theme-A/US:78=Columbia 2823 + Theme-B/US:78=Columbia 6138 [Nora Bayes: 1918 NYOC]

10672 Lady Be Good (1924) Score (George Gershwin) US:LP=Monmouth MES-7036 + US:LP-PP=Smithsonian R-008 + GB:LP=WRC SH-124 [1924 NYOC & 1926 LOC]

10673 Lady in the Dark (1941) Highlights (Kurt Weill) US:LP-10=RCA LRT-7001 + US:LP=RCA LPV-503 [Gertrude Lawrence:1941 NYOC]; Highlights (Kurt Weill) US:LP=AEI 1146 [1941 NYOC]; Excerpts (Kurt Weill) US:LP=Columbia CL-6249 + US: LP=Harmony HL-7012 + US:LP=Harmony HL-7314 [Danny Kaye:1941 NYOC]

10674 Lady Luck (1927) Themes/GB:LP=WRC 183 [@Laddie Cliff & Phyllis Monkman:1927 LOC]

10675 Lady Madcap [My Lady's Maid] (1904) Theme-A/GB:78=G&T 3-2254 + Theme-B/GB:78=G&T 3-2255 + Theme-C/GB:78=G&T 4374 [Maurice Farkoa:1904 LOC]

10676 Land of Joy, The (1917) Themes/US:78=Columbia 2475 [Lacalle's Spanish Orchestra:1917 NYOC]

10677 Land of Smiles, The [Yours Is My Heart] (1929) Themes-I/GB:78=Parlophone 20500 [Richard Tauber:1931 LOC + 1946 Revival NYOC]; Score-II (Franz Lehar) GB:LP=HMV CSD-1267* [1959 Revival LOC]

10678 Last Sweet Days of Isaac, The (1970) Score (Nancy Ford) US: LP=RCA LSO-1169* [1970 NYOC]

10679 Last Waltz, The (1920) Themes-A-B/GB:78=Columbia 911 [Jose Collins:1920 LOC] + Themes-C-D/GB:78=Columbia 913 [Kingsley Lark:1920 LOC] + Themes-E-F/GB: 78=Columbia 910 + Themes-G-H/GB:78=Columbia 912 [Jose Collins & Kingsley Lark:1920 LOC]

10680 Late Joys (1964) Score (various) GB:Lp=Decca SKL-4628* [1964 LOC]

10681 Lead the Carefree Life [Industrial Show] Score (Michael Brown) US:LP-PP = OSS 1555 [OC]

10682 Leader of the Pack (1984) Scores (pop music) US:LP-MS = Elektra 9-60409-1* [1984 NYOC]

10683 Leave Him to Heaven (1976) Score (as:Ken Lee) GB:LP = Chrysalis CHR-1118* [1976 LOC]

10684 Leave It to Jane (1917) Score (Jerome Kern) US:LP = Strand 1002/S-1002* + US:LP = DRG DS-15002* [1959 Revival NYOC]

10685 Leave It to Me (1938) Themes/US:78 = Columbia 31456 [Mary Martin:1938 NYOC]

10686 Lemmings *see* National Lampoon's Lemmings

10687 Lena Horne — The Lady and Her Music (1981) Scores + Dialog (pop music) US:LP-MS = Quest/WB 2QW 3597* [1981 NYOC]

10688 Lend an Ear (1948) Score (Charles Gaynor) US:LP-MS = Chrysler RR-23071 [Television Cast]; Excerpts (Charles Gaynor) US:LP-MS = Longines 5100/4* [Carol Channing:1948 NYOC]

10688a Let 'em Eat Cake (1933) Score (George Gershwin) US:LP-MS = CBS S2M-42522* [Studio Cast]

10689 Let It Ride (1961) Score (Jay Livingston & Ray Evans) US:LP = RCA LOC-1064/LSO-1064* [1961 NYOC]

10690 Let My People Come (1974) Score (Earl Wilson, Jr.) US:LP = Libra 1069* [1974 NYOC]

10691 Let's Face It (1941) Excerpts (Cole Porter) US:LP-BP = JJA 19732 [@1941 NYOC]; Excerpts (Cole Porter) US:LP-PP = Smithsonian R-016 [@1941 NYOC]

10692 Let's Sing Yiddish (1966) Score (Murray Rumshinsky) US:LP = Roulette R-42022/SR-42022* [1966 NYOC]

10693 Lew Leslie's International Revue (1930) Themes-A-B/US:LP = Decca 8673 [Gertrude Lawrence:1930 NYOC] + Themes-C-D/US:LP-BP = JJA 19777 [@Harry Richman:1930 NYOC]

10694 Lido Lady (1926) Excerpts (Richard Rodgers) GB:LP = WRC SH-183 [@1926 LOC]

10695 Lieutenant, The (1975) Scores (Chuck Strand & Gene Curty) US:LP-MS-PP = Lieutenant 001* [1975 NYOC]

10696 Life and Adventures of Nicholas Nickleby, The (1980) Score (Stephen Oliver) GB:LP = RSC 1001* + US:LP = DRG SBL-12583* [1980 LOC + 1981 NYOC + Television Cast]

10697 Life Begins at 8:40 (1934) Excerpts-A (Harold Arlen) US:LP = Painted Smiles PS-1345* [Studio Cast]; Excerpts-B (Harold Arlen) US:LP-BP = JJA 19759 [Studio Cast]

10698 Lights Up (1940) Themes-A-B/GB:LP = MFP 1162 + Theme-C/GB:LP = MFP 1236 [Evelyn Laye:1940 LOC]

10699 Li'l Abner (1956) Score (Gene DePaul) US:LP = Columbia OL-5150 [1956 NYOC]

10700 Lilac Domino, The (1916) Highlights (Charles Cuvillier & Robert Smith) GB:EP = HMV GES-5778 [Studio Cast]; Themes-A-B/GB:78 = Columbia 1238 + Themes-C-D/GB:78 = Columbia 1239 + Themes-E-F/GB:78 = HMV 1240 [Clara Butterworth:1914 LOC] + Themes-G-H/GB:78 = Columbia 1400 + Theme-I/GB:78 = Columbia 1404 [Vincent Sullivan & Frank Lalor: 1914 LOC]

10701 Lilac Time *see* Blossom Time

10702 Lily of Killarney (1862) Excerpts (Julius Benedict) GB:LP = HMV 3651 [Studio Cast]

10703 Little Jessie James (1923) Theme/US:78 = RCA/Victor 19151 [Paul Whiteman:1923 NYOC]

10704 Little Johnny Jones (1904) Excerpts (George M. Cohan) US:LP = Audio Rarities 2295 [George M. Cohan: 1904 NYOC]

10705 Little Mary Sunshine (1959) Score-I (Rick Besoyan) US:LP = Capitol WAO-1240/SWAO-1240* [1959 NYOC]; Score-II (Rick Besoyan) GB:LP = Pye NSPL-18071* + US:LP = AEI 1105* [1962 LOC]

10706 Little Me (1962) Score-I (Cy Coleman) US:LP = RCA LOC-1078/LSO-1078* [1962 NYOC]; Score-II (Cy Coleman) GB:LP = Pye NSPL-83023* [1964 LOC]

10707 Little Michus, The (1897) Theme-A/GB:78 = G&T 2364 [Louis Bradfield:1905 Revival LOC] + Theme-B/GB:78 = Odeon 44055 [Bob Evett: 1905 Revival LOC] + Theme-C/GB: 78 = G&T 4385 [Denise Orme/Gladys Roberts:1905 Revival LOC]

10708 Little Miss Bluebird (1923) Themes/US:78 = RCA/Victor 19199 [Irene Bordoni:1923 NYOC]

10709 Little Miss Fix-It (1911) Theme-A/US:LP = RCA LPV-560 + Theme-B/CA:LP = Rococo 4009 + Theme-C/GB:78 = RCA/Victor 60041 [Nora Bayes & Jack Norworth:1911 NYOC]

10710 Little Night Music, A (1973) Score-I (Stephen Sondheim) US:LP = Columbia KS-32265* [1973 NYOC]; Score-II (Stephen Sondheim) GB:LP = RCA LRL1-5090* + US:LP = RCA LRL1-5090* [1975 LOC]

10711 Little Shop of Horrors, The (1982) Score (Alan Menken) US:LP = Geffen GHSP-2020* [1982 NYOC]

10712 Little Show, The [C] Excerpts (various) US:LP = RCA LPM-3155 [Studio Cast]; Theme-A/US:78 = Brunswick 4446 + Theme-B/US:78 = Brunswick 4506 [Libby Holman:1929 NYOC]

10713 Little Willie Jr.'s Resurrection (1977) Score (Johnny Thompson) US:LP-PP = Glory JC-1044* [1977 NYOC]

10714 Littlest Revue, The (1956) Score (e:Vernon Duke/etc.) US:LP = Epic LN-3275 + US:LP = Painted Smiles PS-1361 [1956 NYOC]

10715 Live It Up! (1964) Score (Bill Lockwood) US:LP-PP = Three Arts 101 [1964 LAOC]

10716 Living for Pleasure (1958) Score (Richard Addinsell) GB:LP = HMV CLP-1223 [1958 LOC]

10717 Liza (1922) Theme/US:78 = RCA/Victor 19159 [Gertrude Saunders: 1922 NYOC]

10718 Liza of Lambeth (1976) Score (Cliff Adams) GB:LP = Thames THA-100* [1976 LOC]

10719 Lizzie Borden (1965) Scores (Jack Beeson) US:LP-MS = Desto DST-6455/7* [1965 NYOC]

10720 Lock Up Your Daughters (1959) Score (Laurie Johnson) GB:LP = Decca LK-4320 + US:LP = London 5766 [1959 LOC]

10721 Lola (1982) Score (Claibe Richardson) US:LP = Painted Smiles PS-1335* [Studio Cast]

10722 Lola Montez (1967) Score (Peter Stannard) AU:LP = Columbia OCX-7514 + AU:LP = Columbia SCXO-8043* [1967 AOC]

10723 Lolita My Love (1971) Score (John Barry) US:LP-BP = Blue Pear BP-1009 [1971 NYOC]

10724 London Calling (1923) Excerpts (Noel Coward) GB:LP = WRC SHB-44 [@1923 LOC]

10725 Look Ma, I'm Dancin' (1948) Highlights (Hugh Martin) US:LP-10 = Decca DL-5231 + US:LP-BP = JJA 19742 + US:LP = CSP X-14879 [1948 NYOC]

10726 Look to the Lilies (1970) Score (Jule Styne) US:LP-PP = Look 1001 [Demo Cast]

10727 Look Where I'm At! (1971) Score (Jordan Ramin) US:LP-PP = LWIA 1001 [Demo Cast]

10728 Look Who's Here (1960) Score (Ted Dicks) GB:LP = HMV CLP-1357 [1960 LOC]

10729 Lord Chamberlain Regrets (1961) Score (Ronald Cass) GB:LP = Pye NSPL-18065* [1961 LOC]

10730 Lorelei *see* Gentlemen Prefer Blondes

10731 Lorna (1979) Score (Jim Thomas) GB:LP = Miller M-108-SL* [1979 LOC]

10732 Lost in the Stars (1949) Score (Kurt Weill) US:LP = Decca DL-8028 + US:LP = Decca DL-9120/DL-79120e + US:LP = MCA 2071e [1949 NYOC]

10733 Louisiana Purchase (1940) Highlights (Irving Berlin) US:LP-BP = JJA 19746 [@1940 NYOC]

10734 Love and Let Love [The Twelfth Night] (1968) Score (Stanley Gelber) US:LP-PP = Sam Fox X4RS-0371* [1968 NYOC]

10735 Love from Judy (1952) Highlights (Hugh Martin) US:LP-BP = JJA 19743 [@1952 LOC]

10736 Love Letter, The (1921)

Theme/US:LP-BP = Oasi 527 [John Charles Thomas:1921 NYOC]

10737 Love Life (1948) Excerpts-A (Kurt Weill) US:LP = Painted Smiles PS-1375* [Studio Cast]; Excerpts-B (Kurt Weill) US:LP = Heritage 0600 [Studio Cast]

10738 Love Match (1968) Score (David Shire) US:LP-PP = Love Match 1001 [Demo Cast]; Excerpts (David Shire) US:LP = RCA ABL1-2360* ["Starting Here, Starting Now" Cast]

10739 Love Song (1976) Score (Michael Valenti) US:LP = OC 8022* [1976 NYOC]

10740 Lovers (1974) Score (Steve Sterner) US:LP-PP = Gold Dust PG-723* [1974 NYOC]

10741 Love's Lottery (1904) Theme/CA:LP = Rococo RLP-5335 [@ Ernestine Schumann-Heink:1904 NYOC]

10742 Luckee Girl (1928) Theme/US:78 = Columbia 1641 [The Diplomats: 1928 NYOC]

10743 Lulu-Wena (1977) Score (Bertha Egnos) GB:LP = CBS 81806* [1977 LOC]

10744 Lute Song (1946) Highlights (Raymond Scott) US:LP = Decca DL-8030 [1946 NYOC]

M

10745 Ma Rainey's Black Bottom (1984) Highlights + Dialog (pop music) US:LP-MS = Manhattan SUBO-53001* [1984 NYOC]

10746 Mack and Mabel (1974) Score (Jerry Herman) US:LP = ABC ABCH-830* [1974 NYOC]

10747 Macushla (1912) Themes-A-B/US:78 = Columbia 2988 + Themes-C-D/US:78 = Columbia 3525 [Chauncey Olcott:1912 NYOC]

10748 Mad Show, The (1965) Score (Mary Rodgers) US:LP = Columbia OL-6530/OS-2930* [1965 NYOC]

10749 Madame Pompadour (1922) Themes-A-B/GB:78 = Columbia 966 + Themes-C-D/GB:78 = Columbia 967 + Themes-E-F/GB:78 = Columbia 3372 [Evelyn Laye & Derek Oldham:1922 LOC] + Themes-G-H/GB:78 = Columbia 3371 [Huntley Wright:1922 LOC]

10750 Mademoiselle Modiste (1905) Highlights (Victor Herbert) US:LP = Reader's Digest 40-1 [Studio Cast]; Excerpts (Victor Herbert) US:LP = RCA LPM-3153 [Studio Cast]

10751 Magdalena (1948) Score (George Forrest & Robert Wright) US:LP-PP = Magdalena 1001 [Demo Cast]; Excerpts (George Forrest & Robert Wright) US:LP = Premier 001* [Studio Cast:Judy Kaye]

10752 Maggie (1981) Score (Michael Wild) GB:LP = Overtures 1002* [1981 LOC]

10753 Maggie Flynn (1968) Score (George David Weiss) US:LP = RCA LSOD-2009* [1968 NYOC]

10754 Maggie May (1964) Score-A (Lionel Bart) GB:LP = Decca SKL-4643* + Highlights-B (Lionel Bart) GB:EP = Decca DFE-8602 + Score-C (Lionel Bart) GB:LP = That's Entertainment TER-1046 [1964 LOC]

10755 Magic Pudding (1983) Score (Larry McManus) AU:LP = Cherry Pie 25378* [1983 AOC]

10756 Magic Show, The (1974) Score (Stephen Schwartz) US:LP = Bell 9003* [1974 NYOC]

10757 Magyar Melody (1939) Themes/GB:LP = WRC 129 [Binnie Hale:1939 LOC]

10758 Maid of the Mountains (1917) Score-I (Harold Fraser-Smith) GB:LP = WRC SH-169 [1917 LOC]; Score-II (Harold Fraser-Smith) GB: LP = Columbia SCS-6504* [1972 Revival LOC]

10759 Make a Wish (1951) Score (Hugh Martin) US:LP = RCA LOC-1002 + US:LP = RCA CBM1-2033 [1951 NYOC]

10760 Make It Snappy (1922) Themes-A-B/US:78 = Columbia 3624 + Theme-C/US:78 = Columbia 3754 [Eddie Cantor:1922 NYOC]

10761 Make Me an Offer (1960) Score (David Heneker & Monty Norman) GB:LP = HMV CSD-1295* + US: LP = AEI 1112* [1960 LOC]

10762 Make Mine Manhattan (1948) Highlights (Richard Lewine) US: LP = Painted Smiles PS-1369* [Studio Cast]

10763 Mamba's Daughters (1939) Theme/US:78 = Bluebird 10022 [Ethel Waters:1939 NYOC]

10764 Mame (1966) Score (Jerry Herman) US:LP = Columbia KOL-6600/KOS-3000* [1966 NYOC]; Theme (Jerry Herman) US:LP-BP = Curtain Calls 100/21 [Ginger Rogers:1972 LOC]

10765 Man from Broadway, The (1962) Score (Lou Fortunate) US:LP-PP = Moby 0703 [1962 Detroit OC]

10766 Man from China, The (1904) Theme/US:78 = Edison 23 [Stella Mayhew:1904 NYOC]

10767 Man in the Moon, The (1963) Score (Jerry Bock) US:LP = Golden LP-104 [1963 NYOC]

10768 Man Named Brown, A [Industrial Show] Score (Raymond Scott) US:LP-PP = Forman & Brown 16071 [OC]

10769 Man of La Mancha (1965) Score-I (Mitch Leigh) US:LP = Kapp KL-4505/KS-5505* + US:LP = MCA 2018* [1965 NYOC]; Scores-II (Mitch Leigh) GB:LP-MS = MCA MUPS-334* + US:LP-MS = Decca DXS-7203* + US:LP-MS = MCA 10010* [1968 LOC]; Score-III (Mitch Leigh) FR:LP = Barclay 80381* [1968 French OC]

10770 Man of Magic [Houdini] (1966) Score (William Wylam) GB:LP = CBS 70027* [1966 LOC]

10771 Man on the Moon (1975) Excerpts (John Phillips) US:LP = Paramour PR-5088* [Genevieve Waite:1975 NYOC]

10772 Man with a Load of Mischief (1966) Score (John Clifton) US:LP = Kapp KL-4508/KS-5508* [1966 NYOC]

10773 Manchild / Score/AU:LP = M7 Records 002 [AOC]

10774 Man's a Man, A (1962) Highlights + Dialog (Joe Raposo) US:LP = Spoken Arts 870 [1962 NYOC]

10775 Marat/Sade [The Persecution and Assassination of Jean-Paul Marat] (1966) Highlights + Dialog (Richard Peaslee) US:LP-MS = Caedmon M-312/S-312* [1966 LOC]

10776 March of the Falsettos (1981) Score (Bill Finn) US:LP = DRG SBL-12581* [1981 NYOC]

10777 Mardi Gras (1965) Score (Carmen Lombardo) US:LP = Decca DL-4696/DL-74696* [Studio Orchestra]; Themes (Carmen Lombardo) US:SP = Capitol 5716 [Louis Armstrong:1966 Jones Beach OC]

10778 Mardi Gras (1976) Score (Alan Blakley & Ken Howard) GB:LP = EMI EMC-3123* [1976 LOC]

10779 Marigold (1959) Score (Charles Zwar) GB:LP = HMV CLP-1275 + US:LP = AEI 1120 [1959 LOC]

10780 Marinka (1945) Themes/US: LP-10 = Quality 71926 [Joan Roberts: 1945 NYOC]

10781 Maritana (1845) Excerpts (William Wallace) GB:LP = HMV 3651 [@Studio Cast]

10782 Maritza *see* Countess Maritza, The

10783 Marry Me a Little (1981) Score (Stephen Sondheim) US:LP = RCA ABL1-4159* [1981 NYOC]

10784 Mary C. Brown and the Hollywood Sign (1972) Score (Dory Previn) US:LP = UA UAS-5657* [Studio Cast]

10785 Mask and Gown (1957) Score (e:Ronny Graham/e:Arthur Siegel/e: various) US:LP = AEI 1178 [1957 NYOC]

10786 Mass (1971) Scores (Leonard Bernstein) US:LP-MS = Columbia M2-31008* [1971 NYOC]

10787 Mata-Hari (1967) Score (Edward Thomas) US:LP-PP = Mata-Hari 1001 [Demo Cast]

10788 Match Girls, The (1966) Score (Tony Russell) GB:LP = Pye CCS-30172* + US:LP = AEI 1109* [1966 LOC]

10789 Mavourneen (1895) Theme/ US:78 = Columbia 1309 [Chauncey Olcott:1895 NYOC]

10790 Mayfair and Montmartre (1922) Theme/GB:LP = WRC 164 [Alice Delysia:1922 LOC]

10791 Mayflower, The (1970) Score (Tommie Connor) GB:LP = Avenue International 700* [1970 LOC]

10792 Maytime (1917) Highlights

(Sigmund Romberg) US:LP-BP = Pelican LP-121 [Film Cast]; Theme/US:LP-BP = Oasi 527 [John Charles Thomas: 1918 Replacement NYOC]

10793 Me and Bessie (1976) Score (pop music) US:LP = Columbia PC-34032* [1976 NYOC]

10794 Me and Juliet (1953) Score (Richard Rodgers) US:LP = RCA LOC-1012 + US:LP = RCA LOC-1098/LSO-1098e [1953 NYOC]

10795 Me and My Girl (1937) Theme-I/ GB:LP = MFP 1236 [Lupino Lane:1937 LOC]; Score-II (Noel Gay) US:LP = MCA 6196* [1985 Revival NYOC]; Score-III (Noel Gay) US:LP = Manhattan PV-53030* [1985 Revival LOC]

10796 Me Nobody Knows, The (1970) Score (Gary William Friedman) US:LP = Atlantic S-1566* [1970 NYOC]

10797 Medium, The (1947) Score (Gian Carlo Menotti) US:LP-MS = Columbia OSL-154 [1947 NYOC]; Score (Gian Carlo Menotti) US:LP = Columbia MS-7387* [Washington OC]

10798 Megilla of Itzik Manger, The (1968) Score (Dov Seltzer) US:LP = Columbia OS-3270* [1968 NYOC]

10799 Mercenary Mary (1925) Excerpts (various) US:LP-BP = JJA 19796 [@1925 LOC] + Themes-A-B/GB:78 = Columbia 3810 [June Hale/A.W. Bascomb:1925 LOC] + Theme-C/GB: 78 = Col. 3809 [June Hale:1925 LOC]

10800 Merrie England / Scores (Edward German Taylor) GB:LP-MS = EMI DUO-121 [LOC]

10801 Merrily We Roll Along (1981) Score (Stephen Sondheim) US: LP = RCA CBL1-4197* [1981 NYOC]

10802 Merry Malones, The (1927) Themes/US:78 = Brunswick 3687 [Polly Walker:1927 NYOC]

10803 Merry-Merry (1925) Themes-A-B/US:78 = Brunswick 3003 + Themes-C-D/US:78 = Brunswick 3155 [Harry Archer:1925 NYOC]

10804 Merry Widow, The (1905) Theme-I-A/GB:78 = Odeon 122 + Theme-I-A/GB:78 = Odeon 128 + Theme-I-C/GB:78 = Odeon 140 [Robert Evett & Elizabeth Firth:1907 LOC]; Score-II (Franz Lehar) GB:LP = HMV CLP-1226 [1958 Revival LOC]; Score-III (Franz Lehar) US:LP = RCA LOC-1094/LSO-1094* [1964 Revival NYOC]; Score-IV (Franz Lehar) US:LP = Angel S-37500* [1978 Revival NYOC]

10805 Merry Widow and the Devil, The (1909) Theme/US:LP-BP = Audio Rarities 2290 [@Blanche Ring:1909 NYOC]

10806 Messenger Boy, The (1900) Themes-A-B/GB:78 = Berliner 3160/1 [Connie Ediss:1900 LOC] + Theme-C/ GB:78 = G&T 3-2039 [Fred Wright, Jr.: 1900 LOC]

10807 Messin' Around (1929) Themes-A-B/US:78 = Columbia 14417 + Theme-C/US:78 = Columbia 14247 [James P. Johnson:1929 NYOC]

10808 Mexican Hayride (1944) Highlights (Cole Porter) US:LP-10 = Decca DL-5232 + US:LP = CSP X-14878 [1944 NYOC]

10809 Midnight Girl, The (1914) Theme/US:78 = RCA 60118 [Margaret Romaine:1914 NYOC]

10810 Midnight Rounders, The [C] Theme/US:78 = Pathe 20480 [Jane Green:1920 NYOC]; Themes/US:LP = Audio Fidelity 702 [Eddie Cantor:1921 NYOC]

10811 Midnight Sons, The (1909) Themes/US:78 = RCA/Victor 5731 [Blanche Ring:1909 NYOC]

10812 Midsummer Night's Dream, A (1980) Score (R. Tallman & Steve MacKenroth) US:LP-PP = Doda LPM-7801* [1980 Chicago OC]

10813 Milk and Honey (1961) Score (Jerry Herman) US:LP = RCA LOC-1065/LSO-1065* [1961 NYOC]

10814 Mine Fair Sadie (1961) Score (Alf Fogel) GB:LP = Oriole MG-20054 [1961 LOC]

10815 Minnie's Boys (1970) Score (Hal Hackady & Larry Grossman) US: LP = Project TS-6002* [1970 NYOC]

10816 Miserables, Les (1980) Score-I (Claude-Michel Schonberg) GB:LP = First Night SCENE-2* [1980 French OC]; Score-II (Claude-Michel Schonberg) GB: LP = First Night ENCORE-1* [1985 LOC]; Scores-III (Schonberg) US:LP-MS = Geffen GHS-24151* [1986 NYOC]

10817 Miss Caprice (1912) Theme/

US:78 = RCA/Victor 60120 [George MacFarlane:1912 NYOC]

10818 Miss Julie (1979) Score (Ned Rorem) US:LP = Painted Smiles PS-1338* [1979 NYOC]

10819 Miss Gulch Returns (1984) Score (Fred Barton) US:LP-PP = MGR 5757* [Fred Barton:1984 NYOC]

10820 Miss Liberty (1949) Score (Irving Berlin) US:LP = Columbia OL-4220 + US:LP = CSP AOL-4220 [1949 NYOC]

10821 Miss Moffat (1974) Themes/ US:LP-MS-PP = Friends of the Theatre AC-1/4* [@Dorian Harewood & Avon Long:1974 Philadelphia OC]

10822 Miss Springtime (1916) Theme/US:LP = Folkways 601 [George MacFarlane:1916 NYOC]

10823 Mr. and Mrs. (1968) Score (John Taylor) GB:LP = CBS 70048* [1968 LOC]

10824 Mr. Cinders (1929) Score (1929 songs:Vivian Ellis/1982 songs: Richard Myers) GB:LP = That's Entertainment TER-1037* [1982 Revival LOC]

10825 Mr. Hamlet of Broadway (1908) Theme-A/US:78 = RCA/Victor 5671 + Theme-B/US:78 = RCA/Victor 5715 [Maude Raymond:1908 NYOC]

10826 Mr. Manhattan (1916) Theme/US:78 = Vocalion 35010 [Raymond Hitchcock:1916 LOC]

10827 Mr. President (1962) Score (Irving Berlin) US:LP = Columbia KOL-5870/KOS-2270* [1962 NYOC]

10828 Mr. Sholom Aleichem (1970) Score (Sonny Vale) US:LP-PP = Custom Fidelity CFS-2386* [1970 LAOC]

10829 Mr. Whittington (1934) Theme-A/GB:LP = WRC 283 + Theme-B/GB:LP = MFP 1160 + Theme-C/GB:78 = HMV 8109 [Jack Buchanan:1934 LOC] + Theme-D/GB: 78 = HMV 8110 [Elsie Randolph:1934 LOC]

10830 Mr. Wonderful (1956) Score (Jerry Bock & George David Weiss) US: LP = Decca DL-9032 [1956 NYOC]

10831 Mr. Woolworth Had a Notion [Industrial Show] Score (Michael Brown) US:LP-PP = Donahue 2686 [OC]

10832 Mrs. Patterson (1954) Score (James Shelton) US:LP = RCA LOC-1017 [1954 NYOC]

10833 Mrs. Wilson's Diary (1967) Score (Jeremy Taylor) GB:LP = Parlophone PCS-7043* [1967 LOC]

10834 Mitford Girls, The (1982) Score (Peter Greenwell) GB:LP = Philips 6359.088* [1982 LOC]

10835 Mixed Doubles (1966) Scores (various) US:LP-MS-PP = Upstairs UD-37-W56-2* [1966 NYOC]

10836 Mkhumbane (1962) Score (Todd Matshikiza) AF:LP = Gallotone GALP-1103 [1962 South Africa OC]

10837 Monologues and Songs (1958) Score (Richard Addinsell) US: LP = Elektra EKL-184 [1958 NYOC]

10838 Monsieur Beaucaire (1919) Theme-A/GB:78 = Columbia 1312 + Theme-B/GB:78 = Columbia 1313 + Theme-C/GB:78 = Columbia 1314 + Theme-D/GB:78 = Columbia 1315 + Theme-E/GB:78 = Columbia 1316 [Marion Green & Maggie Teyte:1919 LOC] + Themes-F-G/GB:78 = Columbia 1306 + Themes-H-I/GB:78 = Columbia 1307 [Marion Green:1919 LOC] + Themes-J-K/GB:78 = Columbia 1308 [John Clarke & Alice Moffat:1919 LOC] + Themes-L-M/GB:78 = Columbia 1309 [John Clarke:1919 LOC]

10839 Monsieur de Pourceaugnac (1978) Score (Howard Harris) US:LP = Broadway Baby BBD-789* [1978 NYOC]

10840 Monte Cristo, Jr. (1919) Theme/US:78 = RCA/Victor 18613 [Ester Walker:1919 NYOC]

10841 Moonlight Is Silver (1934) Theme/GB:LP = MFP 1245 [Gertrude Lawrence:1934 LOC]

10842 Most Happy Fella (1956) Scores-I (Frank Loesser) US:LP-MS = Columbia O3L-240 + US:LP-MS = CSP C03L-240 [1956 NYOC]; Score-II (Frank Loesser) GB:LP = HMV CLP-1365 + US:LP = Angel 35887 [1960 LOC]

10843 Mother Courage / Score (Paul Dessau) US:LP = Vanguard VRS-9022* [Studio Cast]

10844 Mother Earth (1972) Score (Ron Thornson & Toni Shearer) US:LP-PP = Environmental SP-1001* [1972 LAOC]

10845 Mother of Pearl (1933) Theme/GB:LP = WRC 164 [Alice Delysia:1933 LOC]

10846 Mother's Kiss, A (1968) Score (Richard Adler) US:LP-PP = Mother 1001 [Demo Cast]

10847 Movie Star (1983) Score (Billy Barnes) US:LP = AEI 1142* [Studio Cast]

10848 Mozart (1926) Themes/US: 78-MS = RCA C-8 [Yvonne Printemps: 1926 NYOC]

10849 Murray Anderson's Almanac (1929) Themes-A-B/US:78 = Brunswick 4500 + Theme-C/US:78 = Brunswick 4510 [Red Nichols:1929 NYOC]

10850 Music Box Revue, The [C] Theme-I-A/US:LP-BP = JJA 19744 + Theme-I-B/US:LP-BP = Famous Personality 1001 [@The Bronx Sisters:1921 NYOC]; Theme-II-A/US:LP-BP = JJA 19744 + Theme-II-B/US:78 = Victor 18990 [John Steel:1922 NYOC]; Themes-III-A-B/US:78 = Victor 19219 [John Steel:1923 NYOC] + Theme-III-C/US: LP-BP = JJA 19744 [@The Bronx Sisters:1923 NYOC]; Themes-IV-A-B/US: LP-BP = JJA 19744 [@Grace Moore: 1924 NYOC]

10851 Music in the Air (1932) Excerpts-I (Jerome Kern) GB:LP = WRC SH-171 [@Mary Ellis:1933 LOC]; Highlights-II (Jerome Kern) US:LP-10 = RCA LK-1025 [Jane Pickens:1951 Revival NYOC]

10852 Music Man, The (1957) Score-I (Meredith Willson) US:LP = Capitol WAO-990/SWAO-990* [1957 NYOC]; Score-II (Meredith Willson) GB:LP = HMV CSD-1361* + US:LP = Stanyan SR-10035* [1961 LOC]

10853 Musical Chairs (1980) Score (Tom Savage) US:LP = OC 8024* [1980 NYOC]

10854 Mutiny (1986) Score (David Essex) GB:LP = Telstar STAR-2261* [1986 LOC]

10855 My Cousin Josefa (1969) Score (Robert Austin) US:LP-PP = Harlequin H-3270* [1969 San Diego OC]

10856 My Fair Lady (1956) Score-I (Frederick Loewe) US:LP = Columbia OL-5090 + US:LP = CSP AOL-5090 [1956 NYOC]; Score-II (Frederick Loewe) GB:LP = Philips SRBL-1001* + US:LP = Columbia OS-2015* [1958 LOC]; Score-III (Frederick Loewe) US: LP = Columbia OL-8060/OS-2660* [1959 Italian OC]; Score-IV (Frederick Loewe) US:LP = Columbia PS-34197* [1976 Revival NYOC]

10857 My Fairfax Lady (1957) Score (Sid Kuller) US:LP = Jubilee JGM-2030 [1957 LAOC]

10858 My Lady Molly (1903) Theme/GB:78 = Odeon 0222 [Walter Hyde:1903 LOC]

10859 My Lady's Maid *see* Lady Madcap

10860 My Magnolia (1926) Theme/ US:78 = RCA/Victor 19359 [Eddie Hunter:1926 NYOC]

10861 My Maryland (1927) Themes/US:78 = RCA/Victor 20995 [Evelyn Herbert:1927 NYOC]

10862 My One and Only (1983) Score (stage & film songs) US:LP = Atlantic 80110-1* [1983 NYOC]

10863 My People (1966) Score (Duke Ellington) US:LP = Contact C-1/ CS-1* [1966 Chicago OC]

10864 Mystery of Edwin Drood, The (1985) Score (Rupert Holmes) US: LP = Polygram 827-969-1* [1985 NYOC]

N

10865 Name of the Game, The [Industrial Show] Score (Julian Stein) US: LP-PP = Listerine 200-809 [OC]

10866 Nancy Brown (1903) Theme/ US:78 = RCA/Victor 45125 [Marie Cahill:1903 NYOC]

10867 Nashville, New York (1979) Score (pop music) GB:LP = That's Entertainment TER-1001* [1979 LOC]

10868 National Lampoon's Lemmings (1973) Score (e:Paul Jacobs/e: Christopher Guest/etc.) US:LP = Blue Thumb BTS-6006* [1973 NYOC]

10869 Naughty Cinderella (1925) Themes/US:78 = RCA/Victor 19966 [Irene Bordoni:1925 NYOC]

10870 Naughty Marietta (1910) Highlights (Victor Herbert) US:LP-10 =

Columbia ML-2094 [Studio Cast]; Highlights (Victor Herbert) US:LP-10 = Capitol L-468 [Studio Cast]

10871 Ned Kelly / Score/AU:LP = Hamlyn HG-001 [AOC]

10872 Nefertiti (1978) Score (David Spangler) US:LP = Take Home Tunes THT-7810* [1978 NYOC]

10873 Nell (1969) Score (John Worth) US:LP-PP = Nell 1001 [Demo Cast]

10874 Nervous Set, The (1959) Score (Tommy Wolf) US:LP = Columbia OL-5430/OS-2018* [1959 NYOC]

10875 New Cranks (1960) Score (David Lee) GB:LP = HMV CSD-1375* [1960 LOC]

10876 New Faces (1934) Theme/ US:78 = NF 501 [Billie Haywood:1934 NYOC]

10877 New Faces of '52 (1952) Score (e:Ronny Graham/e:June Carroll & Arthur Siegel/etc.) US:LP = RCA LOC-1008 + US:LP = RCA CBM1-2206 [1952 NYOC]

10878 New Faces of '56 (1956) Score (e:June Carroll & Arthur Siegel/ e:Marshall Barer & Dean Fuller/etc.) US:LP = RCA LOC-1025 [1956 NYOC]

10879 New Faces of '62 (1962) Score (June Carroll & Arthur Siegel) US: LP-PP = New Faces 1001 [Demo Cast]

10880 New Faces of '68 (1968) Score (e:Clark Gesner/etc.) US:LP = WB BS-2551* [1968 NYOC]

10881 New Girl in Town (1957) Score (Bob Merrill) US:LP = RCA LOC-1027/LSO-1027* + US:LP = RCA LOC-1106/LSO-1106* [1957 NYOC]

10882 New Moon (1928) Excerpts-I (Sigmund Romberg) US:LP-BP = JJA 19804 [@1928 NYOC]; Highlights-II (Sigmund Romberg) GB:LP = WRC SH-254 + US:LP = Monmouth MES-7051 [1929 LOC]; Score-III (Sigmund Romberg) US:LP = RCA LK-1011 [Earl Wrightson:1944 Revival NYOC]

10883 New York Summer, A (1979) Themes/US:SP-PP = Radio City Music Hall J3RS-2208* [1979 NYOC]

10884 New Yorkers, The (1930) Excerpts (Cole Porter) US:LP-BP = JJA 19777 [@1930 NYOC]

10885 Nifties of 1923 (1923) Theme/ US:78 = Columbia 6 [Gus Van & Joe Schenck:1923 NYOC]

10886 Night in Spain, A (1927) Theme-A/US:78 = RCA/Victor 21116 [Marion Harris:1927 NYOC] + Theme-A/GB:78 = HMV 2688 [Grace Hayes: 1927 NYOC]

10887 Night in Venice, A (1883) Score (Johann Strauss, Jr.) US:LP = Everest LPBR-6028/SDBR-3028* [1952 Revival Jones Beach OC]

10888 Night Out, A (1920) Themes/ GB:LP = WRC 26 [Lily St. John:1920 LOC]

10889 Nightingale (1983) Score (Charles Strouse) GB:LP = That's Entertainment TER-1031* [1983 LOC]

10890 Nina Rosa (1930) Themes-A-B/GB:78 = Decca 2467 [Geoffrey Gwyther:1930 LOC] + Themes-C-D/ GB:78 = Decca 2468 [Helen Gilliland: 1930 LOC]

10891 Nine (1982) Score (Maury Yeston) US:LP = CBS JS-38325* [1982 NYOC]

10892 Nine Sharp (1938) Excerpts (various) GB:LP = Parlophone 7154 [@1938 LOC]

10893 Nite Club Confidential (1985) Score (e:Dennis Deal & Albert Evans/e:pop music) US:LP-PP = Confidential 1001* [1985 LAOC]

10894 No for an Answer (1951) Score (Marc Blitzstein) US:LP = Theme TALP-103 + US:LP-BP = JJA 19772 [1951 NYOC]

10895 No, No, Nanette (1925) Highlights-I (Vincent Youmans) GB:LP = WRC SH-176 + US:LP = Stanyan 10035 [1925 LOC]; Score-II (Vincent Youmans) US:LP = Columbia S-30563* [1971 Revival NYOC]; Score-III (Vincent Youmans) GB:LP = CBS 70126* [1973 Revival LOC]

10896 No Sky So Blue (1938) Themes/A-B/GB:78 = Columbia 1779 + Theme-C/GB:78 = Columbia 1780 [Gertrude Niesen:1938 LOC]

10897 No Strings (1962) Score-I (Richard Rodgers) US:LP = Capitol W-1695/SW-1695* [1962 NYOC]; Score-II (Richard Rodgers) GB:LP = Decca SKL-4576* + US:LP = DRG DS-15013* [1963 LOC]

10898 Now Is the Time for All Good Men (1967) Score (Nancy Ford) US:LP = Columbia OL-6730/OS-3130* [1967 NYOC]

10899 Nowhere to Go But Up (1962) Score (Sol Berkowitz & James Lipton) US:LP-PP = Nowhere 1001 [Demo Cast]

10900 Nuclear / Score/AU:LP = HMV OCSD-7700* [AOC]

10901 Nunsense (1986) Score (Dan Goggin) US:LP = DRG SBL-12589* [1986 NYOC]

10902 Nymph Errant (1933) Highlights (Cole Porter) GB:LP = WRC SHB-26 + US:LP = Monmouth MES-7043 + US:LP-10 = RCA LRT-7001 [1933 LOC]

O

10903 O Mistress Mine (1936) Theme-A/GB:LP = HMV 1539 + Theme-B/GB:LP = WRC 26 [Yvonne Printemps:1936 LOC]

10904 O Say Can You See! (1962) Score (Jack Holmes) US:LP-PP = Columbia XTV-87195/6* [1962 NYOC]

10905 Odds and Ends (1917) Themes/US:78 = Pathe 29210 [Jack Norworth:1917 NYOC]

10906 Of Thee I Sing (1931) Score (George Gershwin) US:LP = Capitol S-350 + US:LP = Capitol T-11650 [1952 Revival NYOC]

10907 Oh, Boy [Oh, Joy] (1917) Highlights (Jerome Kern) GB:LP = WRC SHB-32 [1919 LOC]

10908 Oh, Brother! (1983) Score (Michael Valenti) US:LP = OC 8342* [1983 NYOC]

10909 Oh! Calcutta (1969) Score-I (Peter Schickele & Stanley Waldman) US:LP = Aidart AID-9903* [1969 NYOC]; Score-II (Peter Schickele & Stanley Waldman) AU:LP = RCA INTS-1178* [1970 AOC]

10910 Oh, Captain! (1958) Score (Jay Livingston & Ray Evans) US:LP = Columbia OL-5280 + US:LP = CSP AOS-2002* [1958 NYOC] + Themes/US:SP = RCA 47-7169 [Abbe Lane:1958 NYOC]

10911 Oh, Coward! (1972) Scores (stage & pop songs) US:LP-MS = Bell 2-9001* [1972 NYOC]

10912 Oh, Kay! / Score-I (George Gershwin) US:LP-PP = Smithsonian R-011 [1926 NYOC + 1927 LOC + Studio Cast]; Excerpts-II (George Gershwin) GB:LP = WRC SH-185 + US:LP = Monmouth MES-7043 [1927 LOC]; Score-III (George Gershwin) US:LP = 20th 4003/S-4003* + US:LP = DRG DS-15017* [1960 Revival NYOC]

10913 Oh, Lady! Lady!! (1918) Excerpts (Jerome Kern) US:LP = Painted Smiles PS-1378* [Studio Cast]

10914 Oh, Look! (1918) Theme/US:78 = Columbia 2557 [Harry Fox:1918 NYOC]

10915 Oh! Oh! Delphine (1912) Theme/GB:78 = HMV 03326 [Dorothy Jardon:1912 LOC]

10916 Oh, Please (1926) Themes/US:78 = RCA/Victor 20361 [Beatrice Lillie:1926 NYOC]

10917 Oh What a Lovely War! (1964) Score (pop music/as:Charles Chilton) GB:LP = Decca SKL-4542* + US:LP = London 5906/25906* [1964 LOC]

10918 Oklahoma! (1943) Score-I (Richard Rodgers) US:LP = Decca DL-8000 + US:LP = Decca DL-9017/DL-79017e + US:LP = MCA 2030e [1943 NYOC] + Highlights/US:78-MS = Decca A-383 + Highlights/US:LP-BP = JJA 19761 [1943 NYOC]; Highlights-II (Richard Rodgers) GB:LP = WRC SH-393 + US:LP = Stanyan SR-10069 [1947 LOC]; Score-III (Richard Rodgers) US:LP = RCA CBL1-3572* [1979 Revival NYOC]; Score-IV (Richard Rodgers) GB:LP = Stiff OAK-1* [1980 Revival LOC]; Score-V (Richard Rodgers) AU:LP = RCA VPL1-0376* [1982 Revival AOC]

10919 Old Botany Bay / Score/AU:LP = MFP 8120 [AOC]

10920 Old Chelsea (1943) Score (Richard Tauber) US:LP-BP = Sounds Rare SR-5007 [1943 LOC]

10921 Old Town, The (1910) Theme-A/US:LP = Audio Rarities 2290

+ Theme-B/CA:LP = Rococo 4006 [David Montgomery & Fred Stone:1910 NYOC]

10922 Oliver! (1960) Score-I (Lionel Bart) GB:LP = Decca SKL-4105* + GB:LP = That's Entertainment TER-1042* [1960 LOC]; Score-II (Lionel Bart) US:LP = RCA LOCD-2004/LSOD-2004* + US:LP = RCA AYL1-4113* [1963 NYOC]

10923 On a Clear Day You Can See Forever (1965) Score (Burton Lane) US:LP = RCA LOCD-2006/LSOD-2006* [1965 NYOC]

10924 On the Brighter Side (1963) Score (e:Ian Fraser/etc.) GB:LP = London 5767 + US:LP = London 5767 [1963 LOC]

10925 On the Level (1966) Score (Ron Grainer) GB:LP = CBS 70021* [1966 LOC]

10926 On the Town (1944) Score-I (Leonard Bernstein) US:LP = Columbia OL-5540/OS-2028* + US:LP = Columbia S-31005* [1944 NYOC]; Score-II (Leonard Bernstein) GB:LP = CBS 60005* [1963 Revival LOC]

10927 On the Twentieth Century (1978) Score (Cy Coleman) US:LP = Columbia JS-35330* [1978 NYOC]

10928 On with the Dance (1925) Themes/GB:LP = WRC 164 [Alice Delysia:1925 LOC]

10929 On Your Toes (1936) Excerpts-I (Richard Rodgers) US:LP-BP = JJA 19771 [@1936 NYOC]; Excerpts-II (Richard Rodgers) GB:LP = WRC SH-183 + US:LP = Monmouth MES-7049 [Jack Whiting:1937 LOC]; Score-III (Richard Rodgers) US:LP = Decca DL-9015 + US:LP = DRG DS-15024 [1954 Revival NYOC]; Scores-IV (Richard Rodgers) GB:LP-MS = That's Entertainment TER-2-1063* + Score-IV (Richard Rodgers) US:LP = Polydor 813-667-1* [1983 Revival NYOC]

10930 Once Upon a Mattress (1959) Score-I (Mary Rodgers) US:LP = Kapp KDL-7004/KDS-7004* + US:LP = Kapp KL-4507/KS-5507* + US:LP = MCA 2079* + US:LP = MCA 37097* [1959 NYOC]; Score-II (Mary Rodgers) GB:LP = HMV CSD-1410* [1960 LOC]

10931 Once Upon a Time [Children's Show] Score (Roger Webb) GB: LP = EMI/Starline SRS-5152* [Studio Cast]

10932 One Dam' Thing After Another (1927) Theme-A/GB:WRC 183 [Edythe Baker:1927 LOC] + Theme-A/GB:LP = Decca 2168 [Jessie Matthews:1927 LOC]

10933 110 in the Shade (1964) Score (Tom Jones) US:LP = RCA LOC-1085/LSO-1085* [1964 NYOC]

10934 One Little Girl [Industrial Show] Score (Kay Swift) US:LP-PP = Campfire Girls/RCA Custom LOP-2300 [OC]

10935 One Mo' Time (1980) Score (pop music) US:LP = WB HS-3454* [1980 NYOC]

10936 One Night Stand (1981) Score (Jule Styne) US:LP = OC 8134* [1981 NYOC]

10937 One Over the Eight (1961) Score (Lance Mulcahy) GB:LP = London 5760 [1961 LOC]

10938 One Star Rising (1976) Score (Robert Moore) US:LP-PP = Rising RS-0001* [1976 New Orleans OC]

10939 One Touch of Venus (1943) Score (Kurt Weill) US:LP = Decca DL-9122/DL-79122* + US:LP = AEI 1136* [1943 NYOC]

10940 One-Way Ticket to Broadway (1979) Score (Dan Goggin) US:LP-PP = Theatre Arts TA-8001* [1979 NYOC]

10941 Onward Victoria (1982) Score (Keith Herrmann) US:LP = OC 8135* [1982 NYOC]

10942 Operette (1938) Excerpts (Noel Coward) GB:LP-MS = WRC SH-179/180 [@1938 LOC] + US:LP-MS = Monmouth MES-7062/3 [@1938 LOC]

10943 Opportunity Unlimited [Industrial Show] Score (Rob Haymes) US: LP-PP = RCA Custom SR4M-5380 [OC]

10944 Optimists, The *see* Co-Optimists, The

10945 Orchid, The (1903) Theme-A/GB:78 = G&T 3-2022 + Theme-B/GB:78 = G&T 3-2023 + Theme-C/GB:78 = G&T 3-2038 + Theme-D/GB:78 = G&T 3-2044 [Fred Wright, Jr.:1903 LOC]

10946 Our Man Crichton (1965) Score (David Lee) GB:LP = Parlophone PCS-3066* [1965 LOC]

10947 Our Miss Gibbs (1946) Excerpts (Lionel Monckton) GB:LP = WRC SH-186 [@1946 LOC]

10948 Out of the Bottle (1932) Theme/US:LP-BP = JJA 19794 [@ Frances Day:1932 LOC]

10949 Out of This World (1950) Score (Cole Porter) US:LP = Columbia ML-4390 + US:LP = CSP CML-4390 [1950 NYOC]

10950 Over Here (1974) Score (Richard & Robert Sherman) US:LP = Columbia KS-32961* [1974 NYOC]

P

10951 Pacific 1860 (1946) Highlights (Noel Coward) US:LP-PP = AMR 300 + US:LP-BP = Show Biz 5601 + US:LP = DRG DS-15006 [1946 LOC]

10952 Pacific Overtures (1976) Score (Stephen Sondheim) US:LP = RCA ARL1-1367* [1976 NYOC]

10953 Paddington / Excerpts (Shirlie Roden) GB:LP = Audio Trax ATXLP-07* [Studio Cast]

10954 Paganini (1925) Theme/GB: LP = MFP 1162 [Evelyn Laye:1937 Revival LOC]

10955 Pagent in Exile *see* Duel

10956 Paint Your Wagon (1951) Score (Frederick Loewe) US:LP = RCA LOC-1006/LSO-1006e [1951 NYOC]

10957 Pajama Game, The (1954) Score-I (Richard Adler & Jerry Ross) US:LP = Columbia OL-4840 + US: LP = Columbia S-32606 [1954 NYOC]; Score-II (Richard Adler & Jerry Ross) GB:LP = HMV CLP-1062 [1955 LOC]

10958 Pal Joey (1940) Score-I & II (Richard Rodgers) US:LP = Columbia OL-4364 + US:LP = CSP COL-4364 [1940 NYOC & 1952 Revival NYOC] + Theme-I/GB:LP = Decca 5265* [Gene Kelly:1940 NYOC]; Score-II (Richard Rodgers) US:LP = Capitol S-310 [1952 Revival Supporting OC]; Excerpts-III (Richard Rodgers) GB:LP = Philips 27980 [@1954 Revival LOC]; Score-IV (Richard Rodgers) GB:LP = That's Entertainment TERX-1005* [1980 Revival LOC]

10959 Panama Hattie (1940) Highlights (Cole Porter) US:LP-BP = JJA 19745 [@1940 NYOC]

10960 Parade (1960) Score (Jerry Herman) US:LP = Kapp KDL-7005/ KDS-7005* [1960 NYOC]

10961 Pardon My English (1933) Theme/US:LP = Epic 2-6072 [@Lyda Roberti:1933 NYOC]

10962 Paris (1928) Themes-A-B/US:78 = RCA/Victor 21742 [Irene Bordoni:1928 NYOC] + Theme-C/US: 78 = RCA/Victor 21745 [Irving Aaronson's Commanders:1928 NYOC]

10963 Paris '90 (1952) Score (Kay Swift) US:LP = Columbia ML-4619 [1952 NYOC]

10964 Parisian Model, The (1906) Theme/US:78 = RCA/Victor 5201 [Henri Leoni:1906 NYOC]

10965 Party Time with Mr. Men (1985) Score (Malcolm Sircom) GB: LP = Stylus SMR-8510* [1985 LOC]

10966 Party with Betty Comden and Adolph Green, A (1958) Score-I (stage songs) US:LP = Capitol WAO-1197/SWAO-1197* [1958 NYOC]; Scores-II (pop music) US:LP-MS = DRG S2L-5177* [1977 Revival NYOC]

10967 Passing Show, The [C] Theme-I-A/GB:LP = Parlophone 7145 [@Elsie Janis:1914 LOC] + Theme-I-B/ GB:LP = WRC 130 [@Gwendoline Brogden:1914 LOC]; Theme-II/US:78 = Columbia 2084 [Dolly Donnolly:1917 NYOC]

10968 Passion Flower Hotel (1965) Score (John Barry) GB:LP = CBS 62598* [1965 LOC]

10969 Paul Sills' Story Theatre (1970) Highlights + Dialog (e:Hamid Hamilton Camp/etc.) US:LP = Columbia SG-30415* [1970 NYOC]

10970 Peace (1969) Score (Al Carmines) US:LP = Metromedia MP-33001* [1969 NYOC]

10971 Pee Wee Herman Show, The (1981) Highlights + Dialog (Jay Condom) US:LP-PP = Fatima 1981 [1981 LAOC]

10972 Peg (1967) Score (Johnny Brandon) US:LP-PP = Peg 1001 [Demo Cast]

10973 Peg (1983) Score (David Heneker) GB:LP = That's Entertainment TER-1024* [1983 LOC]

10974 Peggy (1911) Theme-A/GB: 78 = HMV 04083 + Theme-B/GB:78 = HMV 02316 + Theme-C/GB:78 = HMV 04082 [George Grossmith:1911 LOC] + Theme-D/GB:78 = HMV 03251 + Theme-E/GB:78 = HMV 03252 [Connie Ediss:1911 LOC] + Theme-F/GB:78 = HMV 03230 [Phyllis Dare:1911 LOC] + Theme-G/GB:78 = HMV 02344 [Robert Hale:1911 LOC] + Theme-H/GB:78 = HMV 03231 [Olive May:1911 LOC]

10975 Peggy-Ann (1926) Theme/ GB:LP = WRC 183 [@Dorothy Dickson:1926 LOC]

10976 Pell-Mell (1916) Theme-A/ GB:LP = WRC 164 [Alice Delysia:1916 LOC] + Theme-B/GB:LP = Parlophone 7145 [@Nat D. Ayer:1916 LOC]

10977 Penny Proud [Industrial Show] Score (Michael Brown) US:LP-PP = A&R 2195 [OC]

10978 People to People [Industrial Show] Score (William Roy) US:LP-PP = ABC TV PTP-1 [OC]

10979 Perchance to Dream (1944) Highlights (Ivor Novello) GB:LP = Decca ACL-1112 [1944 LOC]

10980 Persecution and Assassination of Jean-Paul Marat, The *see* Marat/Sade

10981 Perspective for the '70s [Industrial Show] Score (Stanley Lebowsky) US:LP-PP = Westinghouse/RCA Custom X4RS-0747 [OC]

10982 Peter Pan (1950) Score (Leonard Bernstein) US:LP = Columbia OL-4312 + US:LP = CSP AOL-4312 [1950 NYOC]

10983 Peter Pan (1954) Score (e: Moose Charlap/e:Jule Styne) US:LP = RCA LOC-1019/LSO-1019e + US:LP = RCA AYL1-3762e [1954 NYOC]

10984 Petticoats and Pettifoggers (1969) Score (James Prigmore) US:LP-PP = Creative Sound CSS-1525* [1969 Wyoming OC]

10985 Phantom of the Opera, The (1986) Scores (Andrew Lloyd Webber) US:LP-MS = Polydor 831-273-1-Y2* [1986 LOC]

10986 Phil the Fluter (1969) Score (David Heneker) GB:LP = Philips SBL-7916* [1969 LOC]

10987 Philemon (1975) Score (Harvey Schmidt) US:LP-PP = Gallery OC-1* [1975 NYOC]

10988 Phoenix '55 (1955) Excerpts (David Baker) US:LP = Dolphin 2 + US:LP = DRG SL-2002 [Nancy Walker: 1955 NYOC]

10989 Piano Bar (1978) Score (Rob Fremont) US:LP = OC 7812* [1978 NYOC]

10990 Pickwick (1963) Score (Cyril Ornadel) GB:LP = Philips SBL-3431* + GB:LP = Philips 6382.070* [1963 LOC]

10991 Pieces of Eight (1957) Score (e:Laurie Johnson/etc.) GB:LP = Decca SKL-4084 + US:LP = London 5761 [1957 LOC]

10992 Pieces of Eight (1959) Score (e:William Roy/e:Bud McCreery/etc.) US:LP = Off Beat 4016 [1959 NYOC]

10993 Pied Piper, The (1908) Theme/US:78 = Edison 10265 [Grace Cameron:1908 NYOC]

10994 Pinocchio [Children's Show] Score (Jeanne Bargy) US:LP = Peter Pan 8042/58042* + US:LP = Entertainment Media 999* [OC]

10995 Pins and Needles [Industrial Show] Score (Harold Rome) US:LP-BP = JJA 19783 [OC]; Score (Harold Rome) US:LP = Columbia OS-2210* [Studio Cast]

10996 Pipe Dream (1955) Score (Richard Rodgers) US:LP = LOC-1023 + US:LP = RCA LOC-1097/LSO-1097e [1955 NYOC]

10997 Pippin (1972) Score-I (Stephen Schwartz) US:LP = Motown M-760* [1972 NYOC]; Score-II (Stephen Schwartz) AU:LP = EMI EMC-2510* [1973 AOC]; Score-III (Stephen Schwartz) AF:LP = Satbel 23008* [1975 South Africa OC]

10998 Pirates of Penzance, The (1879) Scores (Gilbert & Sullivan) US: LP-MS = Elektra VE-601* [1980 Broadway Revival OC]

10999 Plain and Fancy (1955) Score-

I (Albert Hague) US:LP = Capitol W-603/DW-603e [1955 NYOC]; Highlights-II (Albert Hague) GB:LP-10 = Oriole MG-10009 + US:LP = Dot DLP-3048 [1956 LOC]

11000 Plantation Revue (1922) Theme/US:78 = Columbia 3653 [Edith Wilson:1922 NYOC]

11001 Platinum (1978) Score (Gary William Friedman) US:LP-PP = Platinum 1001 [Demo Cast]

11002 Playgirls, The (1964) Score (Jackie Barnett) US:LP = WB W-1530/WS-1530* [1964 Las Vegas OC]

11003 Please (1933) Theme-A/GB:LP = Parlophone 7135 + Theme-B/GB:LP = London 5471 [Beatrice Lillie:1933 LOC]

11004 Please Teacher (1935) Theme/GB:LP = WRC 136 [Bobby Howes:1935 LOC]

11005 Pleasures and Palaces (1965) Score (Frank Loesser) US:LP-PP = Pleasures 1001 [Demo Cast]

11006 Point, The (1978) Score (television songs:Harry Nilsson) GB:LP = MCA MCF-2826* [1978 LOC]

11007 Policy Players, The (1900) Theme/US:78 = RCA/Victor 998 [Bert Williams:1900 NYOC]

11008 Polonaise (1945) Score (Bronislau Kaper) US:LP = Camden CAL-210 [Studio Cast]

11009 Pom-Pom (1916) Themes/US:78 = RCA/Victor 45091 [Mizzi Hajos:1916 NYOC]

11010 Pomegranada (1966) Score (Al Carmines) US:LP = Patsan PS-1101* [1966 NYOC]

11011 Poppy (1924) Themes/US:78 = Columbia 9009 [W.H. Berry:1924 NYOC]

11012 Poppy (1982) Score (Monty Norman) GB:LP = WEA/RSC 25000-1* [1982 LOC]

11013 Porgy and Bess (1935) Score-I & II (George Gershwin) US:LP = Decca DL-7006 + US:LP = Decca DL-8042 + US:LP = Decca DL-9024/DL-79024e + US:LP = MCA 2035e [1935 NYOC & 1942 Revival NYOC]; Highlights-I & II (George Gershwin) US:78-MS = Decca A-351 + US:LP = AEI 1107 [1935 NYOC & 1942 Revival NYOC]; Score-III (George Gershwin) US:LP = RCA LM-2679 + US:LP = RCA LPM-3156 [1953 Revival NYOC]; Scores-IV (George Gershwin) US:LP-MS = RCA ARL3-2109* [1976 Revival NYOC]

11014 Portofino (1957) Theme/US:LP = Painted Smiles 1381* [@Helen Gallagher:1957 NYOC]

11015 Postcard from Morocco (1972) Scores (Dominick Argento) US:LP-MS = Desto DC-7137/8* [1972 NYOC]

11016 Poupees de Paris, Les (1964) Score (James Van Heusen) US:LP = RCA LOC-1090/LSO-1090* [1964 Las Vegas OC]

11017 Preppies (1984) Score (Gary Portnoy) US:LP = Alchemy AL-1001* [1984 NYOC]

11018 Pretty Belle (1971) Score (Jule Styne) US:LP = OC 8238* [1971 NYOC]

11019 Primrose (1924) Score (George Gershwin) GB:LP = WRC SH-214 + US:LP = Monmouth MES-7071 [1924 LOC]

11020 Prince and the Pauper, The (1963) Score (George Fischoff) US:LP = London 28001/98001* [1963 NYOC]

11021 Prince of Grand Street, The (1978) Score (Bob Merrill) US:LP-PP = Prince 1001 [Demo Cast]

11022 Princess Charming (1926) Themes-A-B/GB:78 = Columbia 4188 [W.H. Berry:1926 LOC] + Themes-C-D/GB:78 = Columbia 4186 [Winnie Melville:1926 LOC] + Themes-E-F/US:LP-BP = JJA 19794 [@John Clarke:1926 LOC]

11023 Princess Pat, The (1915) Theme/US:78 = Columbia 1937 [Eleanor Painter:1915 NYOC]

11024 Private Lives (1930) Excerpts (various) US:LP = Monmouth MES-7042 + US:LP = RCA LCT-1156 [Noel Coward & Gertrude Lawrence:1930 LOC]

11025 Privates on Parade (1978) Score (Denis King) GB:LP = EMI EMC-3233* [1978 LOC]

11026 Promenade (1969) Score (Al Carmines) US:LP = RCA LSO-1161* [1969 NYOC]

11027 Promises, Promises (1968)

Score-I (Burt Bacharach) US:LP = UA UAS-9902* [1968 NYOC]; Score-II (Burt Bacharach) GB:LP = UA UAS-29075* [1969 LOC]; Score-III (Burt Bacharach) IT:LP = CGD 5063* [1970 Italian OC]

11028 Pull Both Ends (1982) Score (John Schroeder & Tony King) GB:LP = That's Entertainment TER-1028* [1982 LOC]

11029 Pump Boys and Dinettes (1982) Score (Jim Wann) US:LP = CBS FM-37790* [1982 NYOC]

11030 Purlie (1970) Score (Gary Geld & Peter Udell) US:LP = Ampex A-401* [1970 NYOC]

11031 Put and Take (1921) Themes-A-B/US:78 = Columbia 3479 [Edith Wilson:1921 NYOC] + Theme-C/US:78 = Okeh 4296 + Theme-D/US:78 = Okeh 4471 [Mamie Smith:1921 NYOC]

Q

11032 Quaker Girl (1946) Excerpts (Lionel Monckton) GB:LP = WRC SH-186 [@1946 LOC]

11033 Queen High (1926) Theme-I-A/US:LP-BP = JJA 19796 + Theme-I-B/GB:78 = Columbia 4204 [Joyce Barbour:1926 LOC]; Theme-II/US:78 = RCA/Victor 20486 [Frank Crumit:1927 NYOC]

11034 Queen o' Hearts (1922) Themes/US:78 = Columbia 3742 [Nora Bayes:1922 NYOC]

R

11035 R.S.V.P. (1926) Theme/GB: LP = Parlophone 7150 [@Joyce Barbour: 1926 LOC]

11036 R.S.V.P.—The Cole Porters (1973) Score (stage & film songs) US:LP-PP = Respond PMS-299* [1973 Las Vegas OC]

11037 Rachael Lily Rosenbloom (1973) Excerpts (various) US:LP = Casablanca NBLP-7163* + Theme/US:SP = A&M 1741* [Paul Jabara:1973 NYOC]

11038 Ragged Robin (1910) Theme/US:78 = Columbia 1308 [Chauncey Olcott:1910 NYOC]

11039 Rainbow (1928) Theme/US: LP = Monmouth 6501 [Libby Holman: 1928 NYOC]

11040 Raisin (1974) Score (Judd Woldin) US:LP = Columbia KS-32754* [1974 NYOC]

11041 Rap Master Ronnie (1985) Score (Elizabeth Swados) US:LP = AEI 1177* [1985 LAOC]

11042 Really Rosie (1980) Score (television songs:Carole King) US:LP = Caedmon TRS-368* [1980 NYOC]

11043 Red, Hot and Blue (1936) Highlights (Cole Porter) US:LP = AEI 1147 [1936 NYOC]

11044 Red Mill, The (1906) Score (Victor Herbert) US:LP = Decca DL-8016 + US:LP = Decca DL-8458 [Studio Cast]; Score (Victor Herbert) US:LP = Turnabout 34766* [Studio Cast]

11045 Red, White and Boogie *see* It Happened in Tanjablanca

11046 Redhead (1959) Score (Albert Hague) US:LP = RCA LOC-1048/LSO-1048* + US:LP = RCA LOC-1104/LSO-1104* [1959 NYOC]

11047 Reedy River / Score/AU: LP = W&G 25-5147 [AOC]

11048 Regina / Scores (Marc Blitzstein) US:LP-MS = Columbia 03L-260/03S-202* + US:LP-MS = Odyssey Y3-35236* [1958 Revival NYOC]

11049 Revenge with Music (1934) Excerpts (Arthur Schwartz) US:LP = Monmouth MES-6604* [Studio Cast]; Themes/US:LP-BP = JJA 19756 [@ Libby Holman:1934 NYOC]

11050 Rex (1976) Score (Richard Rodgers) US:LP = RCA ABL1-1683* [1976 NYOC]

11051 Rhapsody in Black (1931) Theme/US:LP = Columbia 2792 [Ethel Waters:1931 NYOC]

11052 Ride! Ride! (1976) Score (Penelope Thwaites) GB:LP = Grapevine 101 [1976 LOC]

11053 Rikky (1978) Score (Steve Birch) GB:LP = Rikky LP-001* [1978 LOC]

11054 Rink, The (1983) Score (John

Kander) US:LP = Polydor 823-125-1* [1983 NYOC]

11055 Rio Rita (1927) Excerpts-I (Harry Tierney) US:LP-BP = JJA 19803 [@J. Harold Murray:1927 NYOC]; Highlights-II (Harry Tierney) US:LP = Monmouth MES-7058 [1930 LOC] + Excerpts-II (Harry Tierney) GB:LP = WRC SH-138 [1930 LOC]

11056 Rise and Fall of the City of Mahagonny, The (1931) Scores (Kurt Weill) US:LP-MS = Columbia K3L-243 [Lotte Lenya:1931 German OC + Studio Cast]

11057 Riverside Nights (1926) Theme/US:LP = Stanyan 10055 [@Elsa Lanchester:1926 LOC]

11058 Riverwind (1962) Score (John Jennings) US:LP = London 48001/78001* [1962 NYOC]

11059 Roar of the Greasepaint, The Smell of the Crowd, The (1964) Score (Leslie Bricusse & Anthony Newley) US:LP = RCA LOC-1109/LSO-1109* [1964 NYOC]

11060 Robber Bridegroom, The (1977) Score (Robert Waldman & Alfred Uhry) US:LP = CSP P-14589* [1977 NYOC]

11061 Robert and Elizabeth (1964) Score (Ron Grainer) GB:LP = HMV CSD-1575* + US:LP = AEI 1111* + US:LP = DRG DS-15021* [1964 LOC]

11062 Roberta (1933) Score (Jerome Kern) US:LP = Columbia CL-841 [Studio Cast]; Score (Jerome Kern) US:LP = Decca DL-8007 [Studio Cast]

11063 Robin Hood (1891) Highlights (Reginald DeKoven) US:LP-10 = REM LP-9 [Studio Cast]; Theme-I-A/US:LP = Mark 56 #828 [@Jessie Bartlett Davis:1891 NYOC] + Theme-I-B/US:78 = Columbia 963 [W.H. MacDonald:1891 NYOC]; Themes-II-A-B/US:78 = Pathe 50007 [Herbert Waterous:1919 Revival NYOC] + Themes-II-C-D/Pathe 50005 [James Stevens:1919 Revival NYOC] + Themes-II-E-F/US:78 = Pathe 50010 [Cora Tracey & Herbert Waterous:1919 Revival NYOC] + Themes-II-G-H/US:78 = Pathe 50009 [Cora Tracey & Ivy Scott:1919 Revival NYOC]; Score (Reginald DeKoven) US:LP = AEI 1179 [Studio Cast]

11064 Robinson Crusoe, Jr. (1916) Theme-A/US:78 = Columbia 2007 + Theme-B/US:78 = Columbia 2041 + Theme-C/US:LP = Decca 9063; Theme-D/US:LP = Decca 9035 + Themes-E-F/US:LP = Totem 1010 [Al Jolson:1916 NYOC]

11065 Rock Justice (1980) Score (Mark Varney) US:LP = EMI SWAK-17036* [1980 NYOC]

11066 Rockabye Hamlet [Kronborg: 1582] (1974) Score (Cliff Jones) CA:LP = Rising RILP-103* [1974 Canadian OC + 1976 NYOC]

11067 Rockafella (1979) Score (Ken Bolam & Les Scott) GB:LP = Stage Two JBLP-301* [1979 LOC]

11068 Rocky Horror Show, The (1973) Score-I (Richard O'Brien) GB:LP = UK 1006* [1973 LOC]; Score-II (Richard O'Brien) US:LP = Ode SP-77026* [1974 LAOC & 1975 NYOC]; Score-III (Richard O'Brien) AU:LP = Elephant ELA-7000* [1975 AOC]

11069 Romance of Athlone, A (1899) Theme/CA:LP = Rococo 4009 [@Chauncey Olcott:1899 NYOC]

11070 Rose-Marie (1924) Highlights (Rudolf Friml) GB:LP = WRC SHB-37 [1925 LOC] + Excerpts (Rudolf Friml) US:LP = Monmouth MES-7058 [Edith Day:1925 LOC]

11071 Rose of Persia, The (1899) Theme/GB:78 = Odeon 0851 [C.H. Workman:1899 LOC]

11072 Rosy Rapture, The Pride of the Beauty Chorus (1915) Themes-A-B/GB:78 = Columbia 524 + Themes-C-D/GB:78 = Columbia 525 + Themes-E-F/GB:78 = Columbia 526 [Jack Norworth & Gertrude Lang:1915 LOC]

11073 Rothchilds, The (1970) Score (Jerry Bock) US:LP = Columbia S-30337* [1970 NYOC]

11074 Round the Map (1917) Theme/GB:LP = WRC 130 [@Alfred Lester:1917 LOC]

11075 Rufus LeMaire's Affairs (1927) Themes-A-B/US:78 = Columbia 895 + Themes-C-D/US:78 = Columbia 1017 [Ted Lewis:1927 NYOC]

11076 Rugantino (1962) Score-I (Armando Trovajoli) IT:LP = CAM CMS-30-051 [1962 Italian OC]; Score-II

(Armando Trovajoli) US:LP=WB H-1528/HS-1528* [1964 NYOC]; Score-III (Armando Trovajoli) IT:LP=CAM SAG-9092* [1978 Revival Italian OC]

11077 Rumple (1957) Score (Ernest G. Schweikert) US:LP-PP=Rumple 1001 [Demo Cast]

11078 Rumplestiltskin [Children's Show] Score (Jack Urbont) US:LP= Peter Pan 8047/58047* [OC]

11079 Rumplestiltskin (1962) *see* Half Past Wednesday

11080 Run, Little Chillun! (1933) Theme/US:78=RCA/Victor 4547 [Hall Johnson:1933 NYOC]

11081 Runaway Girl (1898) Themes-A-B/GB:78=G&T 3457 [Ellaline Terriss:1898 LOC] + Theme-C/CA:LP=Rococo 4007 [@Connie Ediss: 1898 LOC]

11082 Runaways (1978) Score (Elizabeth Swados) US:LP=Columbia JS-35410* [1978 NYOC]

11083 Runnin' Wild (1923) Theme/US:LP=Monmouth 7080 [@Adelaide Hall:1923 NYOC]

11084 Rupert Show, The [Children's Show] Score (Martyne & Cullen) GB:LP=Philips 6414.311* [OC]

S

11085 Sacred Cow / Score/AU: LP=Festival 36831* [AOC]

11086 Saga of the Dingbat [Industrial Show] Score (Julian Stein) US: LP-PP=New York Herald Tribune 105844 [OC]

11087 Sail Away (1961) Score-I (Noel Coward) US:LP=Capitol WAO-1643/SWAO-1643* [1961 NYOC]; Score-II (Noel Coward) GB:LP=HMV CSD-1445* + US:LP=Stanyan SR-10027* [1962 LOC]

11088 St. Louis Woman (1946) Highlights (Harold Arlen) US:LP-10= Capitol L-355 + Score (Harold Arlen) US:LP=Capitol W-2742/DW-2742e [1946 NYOC]

11089 Saint of Bleecker Street, The (1954) Scores (Gian Carlo Menotti) US: LP-MS=RCA LM-6032 + US:LP-MS=RCA CBM2-2714 [1954 NYOC]

11090 Salad Days (1955) Score-I (Julian Slade) GB:LP=Oriole MG-20004 + US:LP=London 5474 [1955 LOC]; Score-II (Julian Slade) GB:LP= That's Entertainment TER-1018* [1982 Revival LOC]

11091 Sale and a Sailor, A (1926) Theme/US:78=RCA/Victor 19982 [The Mask & Wig Club:1926 NYOC]

11092 Sally (1921) Score (Jerome Kern) GB:LP=WRC SHB-34 + US: LP=Monmouth MES-7053 [1921 LOC]

11093 Sally in Our Alley (1902) Theme/US:78=RCA/Victor 45125 [Marie Cahill:1902 NYOC]

11094 Salvation (1969) Score (Peter Link & C.C. Courtney) US:LP=Capitol SO-337* [1969 NYOC]

11095 San Francisco Mime Troupe, The (1981) Score (e:Bruce Barthol/e: Eduardo Robledo) US:LP=Flying Fish FF-316* [1981 San Francisco OC]

11096 San Toy (1899) Theme-A/GB:78=Berliner 2960 + Theme-B/GB:78=Berliner 2985 + Theme-C/GB: 78=Berliner 4078 + Theme-D/GB:78= Berliner 4082 [Scott Russell:1899 LOC] + Theme-E/GB:78=Zonophone [Conway Dixon:1899 LOC]

11097 Sandhog (1954) Score (Earl Robinson) US:LP=Vanguard VRS-9001 [Studio Cast]

11098 Sandy Wilson Thanks the Ladies [Sandy Wilson at the Players] (1971) Score (stage & pop songs) GB: LP=Overtures 1001* [1971 LOC]

11099 Sap of Life (1961) Score (David Shire) US:LP-BP=Blue Pear 1002 [1961 NYOC]

11100 Saratoga (1959) Score (Harold Arlen) US:LP=RCA LOC-1051/LSO-1051* [1959 NYOC]

11101 Saturday Night (1954) Excerpts (Stephen Sondheim) US:LP-MS=RCA CBL2-4745* ["A Stephen Sondheim Evening" Cast]

11102 Savage (1981) Score (e:Sonny Kamahele/etc.) US:LP-PP=Don Over 1001* [1981 Hawaiian OC]

11103 Say, Darling (1958) Score (Jule Styne) US:LP=RCA LOC-1045/LSO-1045* [1958 NYOC]

11104 Say When (1928) Themes/ US:78 = RCA/Victor 21674 [Henry Busse:1928 NYOC]

11105 Say When (1934) Themes/ US:78 = Columbia 2965 [Harry Richman: 1934 NYOC]

11106 Scrambled Feet (1980) Highlights + Dialog (John Driver & Jeff Haddow) US:LP = DRG SL-6105* [1980 NYOC]

11107 Second Shepherd's Play, The (1976) Score (Steve Kitsakos) US:LP = Broadway Baby BBD-774* [1976 NYOC]

11108 Secret Diary of Adrian Mole, The (1984) Score (Ken Howard & Alan Blakley) GB:LP = EMI UKADE-1* [1984 LOC]

11109 Secret Life of Walter Mitty, The (1964) Score (Leon Carr) US:LP = Columbia KOL-6320/KOS-2720* + US:LP = CSP AOS-2720* [1964 NYOC]

11110 See Saw (1973) Score (Cy Coleman) US:LP = Buddah BDS-950061* + US:LP = CSP 15563* [1973 NYOC]

11111 See You Later (1951) Excerpts (Sandy Wilson) GB:LP = Overtures 1001* [Sandy Wilson:Studio Cast]

11112 Selling of the President, The (1971) Score (Bob James) US:LP-PP = Selling 1001 [Demo Cast]

11113 Selma (1976) Scores (Tommy Butler) US:LP-MS = Cotillion SD2-110* [1976 NYOC]

11114 Sensations (1970) Score (Wally Harper & Paul Zakrzewski) US: LP-PP = Sensations 1001 [Demo Cast]

11115 Sentimental Bloke / Score/ AU:LP = Talent City TC-003* [AOC]

11116 Serenade, The (1897) Theme/US:78 = Berliner 3020 [W.H. MacDonald & Jessie Davis:1897 NYOC]

11117 Sergeant Brue (1904) Theme-A/GB:78 = Pathe 50220 + Theme-B/ GB:78 = Pathe 50221 [Olive Morrell: 1904 LOC]

11118 Set to Music (1939) Excerpts (Noel Coward) US:LP = JJC M-3003/ ST-3003e [Beatrice Lillie:1939 NYOC]

11119 Seven Brides for Seven Brothers (1986) Score (film songs:Gene De Paul/e:Al Kasha & Joel Hirschhorn) GB:LP = First Night Cast-2* [1986 LOC]

11120 Seven Come Eleven (1961) Score (e:Michael Brown/etc.) US:LP-PP = Columbia XLP-55477 [1961 NYOC]

11121 Seven Deadly Sins [Little Mahagonny] (1933) Score (Kurt Weill) US:LP = Columbia KL-5175 + US: LP = CSP CKL-5175 [Studio Cast]

11122 Seven Lively Arts, The (1944) Themes-A-B/US:LP-BP = Sound Stage 2305 [@Benny Goodman:1944 NYOC] + Themes-B-C/US:LP-BP = JJA 19732 [@Benny Goodman & Teddy Wilson:1944 NYOC] + Theme-D/US: LP = Painted Smiles 1371* [Dolores Gray:1944 NYOC]

11123 Seventh Heaven (1955) Score (Victor Young) US:LP = Decca DL-9001 [1955 NYOC]

11124 Seventeen (1951) Score (Walter Kent) US:LP = RCA LOC-1003 + US:LP = RCA CBM1-2034 [1951 NYOC]

11125 1776 (1969) Score (Sherman Edwards) US:LP = Columbia BOS-3310* [1969 NYOC]; Score-II (Sherman Edwards) GB:LP = Columbia SCX-6424* [1970 LOC]

11126 70 Girls, 70 (1971) Score (John Kander) US:LP = Columbia S-30589* [1971 NYOC]

11127 Shameen Dhu (1914) Theme/ US:78 = Columbia 1410 [Chauncey Olcott:1914 NYOC]

11128 Shamus O'Brien (1896) Theme/US:78 = G&T 2-2567 [Joseph O'Mara:1896 NYOC]

11129 Shangri-La (1956) Highlights (Harry Warren) US:LP-BP = Sound of Broadway 300/1 [Television Cast]

11130 Share My Lettuce (1957) Score (Patrick Gowers) GB:LP = Nixa NPL-18001 + US:LP = AEI 1106 [1957 LOC]

11131 She Loves Me (1963) Scores-I (Jerry Bock) US:LP-MS = MGM E-4118/SE-4118* + US:LP-MS = DRG DS-15008* [1963 NYOC]; Score-II (Jerry Bock) GB:LP = HMV CSD-1745* [1964 LOC]

11132 She Loves Me Not (1933) Themes/US:LP-BP = JJA 19757 [@ John Beal:1933 NYOC]

11133 She Shall Have Music (1959)

Score (Deed Meyer) US:LP-PP = Denison FR-6205 [1959 Ohio OC]

11134 Shelter (1973) Score (Nancy Ford) US:LP-PP = F&C 101* [1973 NYOC] + Themes/US:SP = Columbia 4-45812 [Tony Wells & Marcia Rodd: 1973 NYOC]

11135 Shenandoah (1975) Score (Gary Geld) US:LP = RCA ARL1-1019* [1975 NYOC]

11136 Shephard's Pie (1939) Theme/ GB:LP = Parlophone 7154 [@Arthur Riscoe:1939 LOC]

11137 Sherry (1967) Score (Laurence Rosenthal) US:LP-PP = Sherry 1001 [Demo Cast]

11138 She's a Good Fellow (1919) Theme/US:78 = RCA/Victor 19352 [The Duncan Sisters:1919 NYOC]

11139 She's My Baby (1928) Excerpts (Richard Rodgers) GB:LP = WRC SH-183 [Studio Cast]; Theme/GB:LP = Parlophone 7135 + US:LP-BP = JJA 19804 [@Beatrice Lillie:1928 NYOC]

11140 Shinbone Alley [Archy and Mehitabel] (1957) Score (George Kleinsinger) US:LP-BP = Mastertone 1251 [1957 NYOC]; Score (George Kleinsinger) US:LP = Columbia OL-4963 + US: LP = CSP AOL-4963 [Eddie Bracken: 1957 NYOC + Studio Cast]

11141 Shipstad & Johnson Ice Follies *see* Ice Follies

11142 Shoestring '57 (1957) Score (e:Shelly Mowell/e:Claibe Richardson/ e:G. Wood/etc.) US:LP = Off Beat 4012 + US:LP = Painted Smiles PS-1362 [1957 NYOC]

11143 Shoestring Revue, The (1955) Score (various) US:LP = Off Beat 4011 + US:LP = Painted Smiles PS-1360 [1955 NYOC]

11144 Shop Girl (1894) Theme/GB: 78 = HMV 2432 [Seymour Hicks:1894 LOC & 1895 NYOC]

11145 Show Boat (1927) Score-I & II (Jerome Kern) US:LP = CSP C-55 [Helen Morgan:1927 & 1932 NYOC + Paul Robeson:1932 NYOC]; Highlights-III (Jerome Kern) GB:LP = WRC SH-240 [1928 LOC] + Excerpts-III (Jerome Kern) US:LP = Monmouth MES-7058 [Edith Day:1928 LOC]; Score-IV (Jerome Kern) US:LP = Columbia OL-4058 [1946 Revival NYOC]; Score-V (Jerome Kern) US:LP = RCA LOC-1126/LSO-1126* [1966 Revival NYOC]; Scores-VI (Jerome Kern) GB:LP-MS = Columbia SCX-6480* + US:LP-MS = Stanyan SR-10048* [1971 Revival LOC]

11146 Show Girl (1929) Excerpts (George Gershwin) US:LP = Decca DL-9049 [Jimmy Durante:1929 NYOC]

11147 Show Girl (1961) Score (Charles Gaynor) US:LP = Roulette R-80001/SR-80001* + US:LP = Forum F-9054/SR-9054* [1961 NYOC]

11148 Show Is On, The (1936) Theme-A/US:LP-MS = DRG 2-1101 [@Beatrice Lillie:1936 NYOC] + Theme-B/US:LP-BP = JJA 19765 [Bert Lahr:1936 NYOC]

11149 Shuffle Along (1921) Excerpts-A (Eubie Blake) US:LP = Eubie Blake Music LP-4 + Excerpts-B (Eubie Blake) US:LP-MS = Columbia C2S-3154 [@1921 NYOC]; Excerpts-II (Eubie Blake) US:LP = RCA LPM-3154 [1952 Revival NYOC]

11150 Side by Side by Sondheim (1976) Scores-I (stage songs) US:LP-MS = RCA CBL2-1851* [1976 LOC]; Scores-II (stage songs) AU:LP-MS = RCA VRL2-0156* [1977 AOC]; Scores-III (stage songs) GB:LP-MS = RAM RMLP-1026* [1977 Ireland OC]

11151 Sigh No More (1945) Highlights (Noel Coward) GB:LP = WRC SHB-44 + US:LP = DRG DS-15006 [Noel Coward:Studio Cast]; Themes-A-B/GB:78 = Decca 8562 [Graham Payn: 1945 NYOC] + Themes-C-D/GB:78 = Decca 8561 [Joyce Grenfell:1945 NYOC]

11152 Silk Stockings (1955) Score (Cole Porter) US:LP = RCA LOC-1016 + US:LP = RCA LOC-1102/LSO-1102e + US:LP = RCA CBM1-2208e [1955 NYOC]

11153 Silks and Satins (1920) Theme/US:78 = RCA/Victor 18691 [Aileen Stanley:1920 NYOC]

11154 Silver Slipper, The (1901) Theme-A/GB:78 = G&T 2433 + Theme-B/GB:78 = G&T 2414 + Theme-C/GB: 78 = Columbia 25155 [Louis Bradfield: 1901 LOC] + Theme-D/GB:78 = G&T 3266 + Theme-E/GB:78 = G&T 3267 [Connie Ediss:1901 LOC]

11155 Silverlake / Scores (Kurt Weill) US:LP-MS = Nonesuch 79003* [1980 Revival NYOC]

11156 Simple Simon (1930) Excerpts (Richard Rodgers) US:LP = Painted Smiles PS-1341* [Studio Cast]; Themes/US:78 = Columbia 5050 [Ruth Etting:1930 NYOC]

11157 Simply Heavenly (1957) Score (David Martin) US:LP = Columbia OL-5240 [1957 NYOC]

11158 Sinbad (1918) Excerpts (e: Sigmund Romberg/etc.) US:LP = Decca DL-9035 + Excerpts (e:Sigmund Romberg/etc.) US:LP-BP = Audio Rarities 2285 [Al Jolson:1918 NYOC]

11159 Sing a Rude Song (1970) Score (Ron Grainer) GB:LP = Polydor 2383.018* [1970 LOC]

11160 Sing a Song of Sewing [Industrial Show] Score (Michael Brown) US:LP-PP = A&R 1095 [OC]

11161 Sing for Your Supper (1939) Highlights (Earl Robinson) US:LP = Decca DL-8020 [Bing Crosby:Studio Cast]; Highlights (Earl Robinson) US: LP = RCA AVM1-1736 [Paul Robeson: Studio Cast]

11162 Sing Muse! (1961) Score (Joe Raposo) US:LP-PP = C.H. 1093 [1961 NYOC]

11163 Sing Out, Sweet Land! (1944) Score (as:Elie Siegmeister) US: LP = Decca DL-8023 + US:LP = Decca DL-9019/DL-79019e + US:LP = AEI 1137 [1944 NYOC]

11164 Sing Out the News (1938) Excerpts (Harold Rome) US:LP = Coral CRL-57082 [Harold Rome:Studio Cast]

11165 Singin' in the Rain (1984) Score (film songs:Nacio Herb Brown) GB:LP = Safari RAIN-1* [1984 LOC]

11166 1600 Pennsylvania Avenue (1976) Excerpts (Leonard Bernstein) US: LP = Painted Smiles PS-1377* [Studio Cast]

11167 Sky High (1925) Themes/ US:78 = Columbia 370 [Willie Howard: 1925 NYOC]

11168 Skyscraper (1965) Score (James Van Heusen) US:LP = Capitol VAS-2422/SVAS-2422* [1965 NYOC]

11169 Sleeping Beauty [Children's Show] Score (Ann Sternberg) US:LP = Peter Pan 8046/58046* [OC]

11170 Slim Goodbody's Galactic Health Adventure [Industrial Show] Score (John Burstein) US:LP = Caedmon TC-1729* [OC]

11171 Slim Princess, The (1911) Themes-A-B/US:78 = RCA/Victor 60093 [Elsie Janis:1911 NYOC] + Theme-C/US:78 = RCA/Victor 5843* + Theme-D/US:78 = RCA/Victor 5847 [Charles King & Elizabeth Brice:1911 NYOC]

11172 Smike! (1983) Score (television songs:Simon May) GB:LP = Smike 1* [1983 LOC]

11173 Smile, Smile, Smile *see* Comedy

11174 Smiles / Excerpts (Vincent Youmans) US:LP-MS = Monmouth MES-6401/2* [Studio Cast]

11175 Smiling, the Boy Fell Dead (1961) Score (David Baker) US:LP-BP = Sunbeam LB-549 [1961 NYOC]

11176 Snapshots of 1921 (1921) Theme/US:78 = Columbia 3471 [Nora Bayes:1921 NYOC]

11177 Snoopy (1975) Score-I (Larry Grossman & Hal Hackady) US:LP-PP = Power Exchange P-015* [1975 San Francisco OC]; Score-II (Larry Grossman & Hal Hackady) US:LP = DRG DS-6103* [1977 LAOC]; Score-III (Larry Grossman & Hal Hackady) GB:LP = That's Entertainment TER-1073* [1979 LOC]

11178 Snow White and the Seven Dwarfs [Children's Show] Highlights (Michael Valenti) US:LP = Take Home Tunes THT-775* [Studio Cast]

11179 Snow White and the Seven Dwarfs (1979) Score (film songs:Frank Churchill/new stage songs:Jay Blackton) US:LP-PP = Buena Vista 5009* [1979 NYOC]

11180 So Long 174th Street (1976) Score (Stan Daniels) US:LP = OC 8131* [1976 NYOC]

11181 Soldier Boy *see* Her Soldier Boy

11182 Something for Everybody's Mother *see* Hark!

11183 Something for the Boys (1943) Score-I (Cole Porter) US:LP = AEI 1157 [1943 NYOC]; Themes-II/GB:

78 = Decca 8429 [Evelyn Dall:1944 LOC]

11184 Something in the Air (1943) Theme/GB:LP = WRC 113 [Cicely Courtneidge:1943 LOC]

11185 Something More (1964) Score (Sammy Fain) US:LP-PP = Something More 1001 [Demo Cast]

11186 Sondheim – A Musical Tribute (1973) Scores (stage songs) US: LP-MS = WB WS-2705* [1973 NYOC]

11187 Song and Dance (1982) Scores ["Tell Me on a Sunday" + "Variations"] (stage songs:Andrew Lloyd Webber) GB:LP-MS = Polydor POVD-4* [1982 LOC]

11188 Song of Norway (1944) Highlights-I (as:Robert Wright & George Forrest) US:78-MS = Columbia M-562 + US:LP-BP = JJA 19782 [Irra Petina:1944 NYOC] + Score-I (as: Robert Wright & George Forrest) US: LP = Decca DL-8002 + US:LP = Decca DL-9019/DL-79019e + US:LP = MCA 2032e [1944 Supporting NYOC]; Score-II (as:Robert Wright & George Forrest) US:LP = Columbia CL-1328/CS-8135* [1959 Revival NYOC]

11189 Songbook (1979) Score (Monty Norman) GB:LP = Pye NSPL-18609* [1979 LOC]

11190 Sons o' Fun (1941) Themes/ US:78 = Decca 23226 [Carmen Miranda: 1941 NYOC]

11191 Sons of Ham (1902) Theme-A/US:78 = RCA/Victor 992 + Theme-B/US:78 = RCA/Victor 994 + Theme-C/US:78 = RCA/Victor 1084 + Theme-D/US:78 = RCA/Victor 1086 [Bert Williams:1902 NYOC]

11192 Sophie (1963) Score (Steve Allen) US:LP-PP = Sophie 1001 + US: LP = AEI 1130 [Libi Staiger:1963 NYOC + Demo Cast]

11193 Sophisticated Ladies (1980) Scores (pop music) US:LP-MS = RCA CBL2-4053* [1980 NYOC]

11194 Soul Kiss, The (1908) Theme-A/US:78 = RCA/Victor 5654 + Theme-B/US:78 = RCA/Victor 5661 [Ralph Herz:1908 NYOC]

11195 Sound of Music, The (1959) Score-I (Richard Rodgers) US:LP = Columbia KOL-5450/KOS-2020* + US: LP = Columbia S-32601* [1959 NYOC]; Score-II (Richard Rodgers) GB:LP = HMV CSD-1365* + GB:LP = Royal SRS-5003* [1961 LOC]; Highlights-III (Richard Rodgers) US:LP = Camden CAL-599/CAS-599* [Florence Henderson:1961 Touring OC]; Score-IV (Richard Rodgers) AU:LP = HMV OCSD-7580* [1961 AOC]; Score-V (Richard Rodgers) GB:LP = Epic 70212* [1980 Revival LOC]

11196 South Pacific (1949) Score-I (Richard Rodgers) US:LP = Columbia OL-4180/OS-2040e + US:LP = Columbia S-32604e [1949 NYOC]; Highlights-II-A (Richard Rodgers) GB:EP = Columbia SEG-7668 + US:EP = Columbia DB-2954 + Highlights-II-B (Richard Rodgers) GB:EP = Columbia SEG-7688 + US:EP = Columbia DB-2958 [1951 LOC]; Highlights-III (Richard Rodgers) US:EP = RCA EPA-4063 [Giorgio Tozzi:1957 Revival LAOC]; Score-IV (Richard Rodgers) US:LP = Columbia OL-6700/ OS-3100* [1967 Revival NYOC]

11197 Southern Maid, A (1920) Themes/GB:LP = WRC 169 [Jose Collins:1920 LOC]

11198 Space Is So Startling (1963) Score (Herbert Allen & Cecil Broadhurst) GB:LP = Philips 6308.095* [1963 LOC]

11199 Sparkles (1980) Score (Jim Murdock) US:LP = Web OC-105* [LAOC]

11200 Spirit of Achievement, The [Industrial Show] Score (Claibe Richardson) US:LP-PP = Exxon 1886 [OC]

11201 Spoon River Anthology (1963) Highlights + Dialog (Naomi Hirshhorn) US:LP = Columbia OL-6010/OS-2410* [1963 NYOC]

11202 Spring Is Here (1929) Excerpts (Richard Rodgers) US:LP-BP = JJA 19766 [@1930 Film Cast]

11203 Spring Maid, The (1909) Theme-A/US:78 = RCA/Victor 60060 + Theme-B/US:78 = RCA/Victor 60061 [Christie MacDonald: 1909 NYOC] + Theme-C/CA:LP = Rococo 4006 [@ Tom McNaughton:1909 NYOC]

11204 Stages (1978) Score (Bruce Kimmel) US:LP = Varese VC-81083* [1978 LAOC]

11205 Stand Up and Sing (1931) Excerpts (Phil Charig) US:LP-BP = JJA 19794 [@1931 LOC] + Themes/GB: 78 = Columbia 486 [Jack Buchanan:1931 LOC]

11206 Star Gazer, The (1917) Theme/US:78 = Vocalion 60053 [John Charles Thomas:1917 NYOC]

11207 Star Is Torn, A (1982) Highlights (various) GB:EP-12 = Cube HBUG-92* [Robyn Archer:1982 LOC]

11208 Starlight Roof (1947) Themes/GB:78 = Columbia 2400/1 [Julie Andrews & Pat Kirkwood:1947 NYOC]

11209 Stars in Your Eyes (1939) Highlights (Arthur Schwartz) US:LP = AEI 1147 [1939 NYOC] + Excerpts (Arthur Schwartz) US:LP = JJC M-3004/ ST-3004e [Ethel Merman:1939 NYOC]

11210 Starting Here, Starting Now (1977) Score (stage songs) US:LP = RCA ABL1-2360* [1977 NYOC]; Score-II (stage songs) AF:LP = EMI EMCJ-11539* [1978 South Africa OC]

11211 Steel Town (1984) Score (e: Bruce Barthol/etc.) US:LP = Flying Fish FF-347* [1984 San Francisco OC]

11212 Step This Way (1916) Themes/US:78 = RCA/Victor 18105 [Marguerite Farrell:1916 NYOC]

11213 Stephen Foster Story, The / Score (pop music) US:LP-PP = S.F. XSBV-11387 [Kentucky OC]

11214 Stephen Sondheim Evening, A (1983) Scores (stage songs) US:LP-MS = RCA CBL2- 4745* [1983 NYOC]

11215 Stirrings in Sheffield on a Saturday Night (1973) Score (Horn) GB: LP = EMI SLCW-1019* [1973 LOC]

11216 Stop Flirting *see* For Goodness' Sake

11217 Stop! Look! Listen! [Follow the Crowd] (1915) Theme-I/US:LP = Mercury 20224 [Blossom Seeley:1915 NYOC]; Themes-A-B/GB:LP = Parlophone 7145 [@Fay Compton & Ethel Levey:1916 LOC] + Theme-C/GB:78 = HMV 04157 [Fay Compton:1916 LOC] + Theme-D/GB:78 = HMV 664 [Blanche Tomlin:1916 LOC] + Theme-E/GB:78 = HMV 02647 + Theme-F/ GB:78 = HMV 02648 [Joseph Coyne: 1916 LOC] + Theme-G/GB:78 = HMV 03476 + Theme-H/GB:78 = HMV 03477 [Ethel Levey:1916 LOC] + Theme-I/GB:78 = HMV 01132 + Theme-J/GB:78 = HMV 01133 + Theme-K/ GB:78 = HMV 02646 [Robert Hale:1916 LOC] + Theme-L/GB:78 = HMV 02647 [Joseph Coyne:1916 LOC] + Theme-M/ GB:78 = HMV 665 [Tom Walls:1916 LOC]

11218 Stop the World, I Want to Get Off (1961) Score (Leslie Bricusse & Anthony Newley) GB:LP = Decca SKL-4408* [1961 LOC]; Score-II (Leslie Bricusse & Anthony Newley) US:LP = London 58001/88001* [1962 NYOC]; Score-III (Leslie Bricusse & Anthony Newley) US:LP = WB HS-3214* [1978 Revival NYOC]

11219 Strada, La (1969) Score (Lionel Bart) US:LP = UA UAS-6688* [Studio Orchestra]

11220 Straw Hat Revue, The (1939) Themes-A-B/US:78 = Royale 1782 [James Shelton:1939 NYOC] + Theme-C/US:LP = Columbia 6023 [Danny Kaye:1939 NYOC]

11221 Streamline (1933) Highlights (Vivien Ellis) GB:LP = WRC SH-263 [1933 LOC]

11222 Street Scene (1947) Score (Kurt Weill) US:LP = Columbia OL-4139 + US:LP = CSP COL-4139 [1947 NYOC]

11223 Streets of New York, The (1963) Score (Richard Chodosh) US:LP-PP = Capitol SRB-450/1* [1963 NYOC]

11224 Streets of Paris, The (1939) Excerpts-A (various) US:78-MS = Decca A-109 + Excerpts-B (various) US:LP = Coral/MCA 8029 [Carmen Miranda: 1939 NYOC]

11225 Strike Up the Band (1930) Excerpts (George Gershwin) US:LP-BP = JJA 19777 [@1930 NYOC]

11226 Strip for Action (1956) Highlights (Jimmy McHugh) US:EP = Capitol EAP1-709 [Nat King Cole:Studio Cast]

11227 Stripper, The (1983) Score (Richard Hartley) AU:LP = RCA VPL1-0401* [1983 AOC]

11228 Student Gypsy, The (1963) Score (Rick Besoyan) US:LP-PP = Student 1001 [Demo Cast]

11229 Student Prince, The (1924)

Highlights (Sigmund Romberg) US: LP = Monmouth MES-7054 + GB: LP = WRC SH-279 [Paul Clemon:1924 NYOC + 1926 LOC]; Score-II (Sigmund Romberg) GB:LP = Philips SBL-7850* [1968 Revival LOC]; Score-III (Sigmund Romberg) GE:LP = Kanon KL-01132* [1980 Revival German OC]

11230 Subways Are for Sleeping (1961) Score (Jule Styne) US:LP = Columbia KOL-5730/KOS-2130* + US: LP = CSP AKOS-2130* [1961 NYOC]

11231 Sugar (1972) Score (Jule Styne) US:LP = UA UAS-9905* [1972 NYOC]

11232 Sugar Babies (1979) Score (e: Arthur Malvin/etc.) US:LP = Broadway Entertainment BE-8302* [1979 NYOC]

11233 Summer Song (1956) Score (Bernard Grun) GB:LP = Philips 7070 [1956 LOC]

11234 Summer Widowers, The (1910) Theme/US:78 = Emerson 7165 [Irene Franklin:1910 NYOC]

11235 Sun Never Sets, The (1938) Themes/GB:78 = Columbia 1778 [Todd Duncan:1938 LOC]

11236 Sunday in the Park with George (1983) Score (Stephen Sondheim) US:LP = RCA HBC1-5042* [1983 NYOC]

11237 Sunny (1925) Themes-I-A-B/ US:LP = RCA LPV-549 + Theme-I-C/ US:78 = RCA/Victor 19834 [George Olsen:1925 NYOC] + Theme-D/US: 78 = Pathe 10904 [Cliff Edwards:1925 NYOC]; Highlights-II (Jerome Kern) GB:LP = WRC SH-240 + US:LP = Stanyan 10035 [1926 LOC]

11238 Sunshine Girl, The (1912) Theme-A/GB:78 = HMV 02404 + Theme-B/GB:78 = HMV 02406 [George Grossmith, Jr.:1912 LOC] + Theme-C/ GB:78 = Polyphon 5628 [Violet Essex: 1912 LOC]

11239 Survival of St. Joan, The (1971) Scores (Hank & Gary Ruffin) US: LP-MS = Paramount PAS-9000* [1971 NYOC]

11240 Swan Down Gloves (1982) Score (Nigel Hess) GB:LP = That's Entertainment TER-1017* [1982 LOC]

11241 Swan Ester (1983) Score (N. Munns) GB:LP = MCA 3166* [1983 LOC]

11242 Sweeney Todd (1979) Scores (Stephen Sondheim) US:LP-MS = RCA CBL2-3379* [1979 NYOC]

11243 Sweet Adeline (1929) Highlights (Jerome Kern) US:LP-BP = JJA 19747 [Film Cast]; Themes/US:LP = Audio Rarities 2330 [Helen Morgan: 1929 NYOC]

11244 Sweet Bye and Bye, The (1974) Scores (Jack Beeson) US:LP-MS = Desto 7179* [1974 Kansas City OC]

11245 Sweet Charity (1966) Score-I (Cy Coleman) US:LP = Columbia KOL-6500/KOS-2900* [1966 NYOC]; Score-II (Cy Coleman) GB:LP = CBS 70035* [1968 LOC]; Score-III (Cy Coleman) US: LP = EMI America SV-17196* [1985 Revival NYOC]

11246 Sweet Fanny Adams (1974) Highlights (Peter Pinne) AU:LP = Trigpoint TPR-001* [1974 AOC]

11247 Sweethearts (1913) Score (Victor Herbert) US:LP = RCA LK-1015 [Studio Cast]; Score (Victor Herbert) US:LP = MMG 1129* [Studio Cast]

11248 Sweeties (1929) Excerpts (various) US:LP-BP = Fanett 146 [Helen Kane:1929 NYOC]

11249 Swingin' the Dream (1939) Theme-A/US:78 = Columbia 35210 + Theme-B/US:78 = Columbia 35254 + Theme-C/US:78 = Columbia 35319 + Theme-D/US:78 = Columbia 35331 [Benny Goodman:1939 NYOC]

11250 Sybil (1916) Theme/US:78 = RCA/Victor 35529 [Joseph Cawthorn: 1916 NYOC]; Theme-II-A/GB:78 = Columbia 1068 + Theme-II-B/GB:78 = Columbia 1069 + Theme-II-C/GB: LP = WRC 169 [Jose Collins:1921 LOC]

T

11251 Tabs (1918) Themes-A-B/ GB:78 = Columbia 1256 + Themes-C-D/GB:78 = Columbia 1257 + Themes-E-F/GB:78 = Columbia 1258 [Beatrice Lillie:1918 LOC] + Themes-G-H/GB: 78 = Columbia 1259 [Alfred Austin &

Margaret Campbell:1918 LOC] + Themes-I-J/GB:78 = Columbia 1260 [Harry Glen & Guy Lefeuvre:1918 LOC]

11252 Take a Chance (1932) Excerpts (Vincent Youmans) US:LP-MS = Monmouth MES-6401/2* [Studio Cast]; Themes/US:LP-MS = Decca DX-153 [Ethel Merman:1932 NYOC]

11253 Take Five (1958) Score (e: Steven Vinaver/etc.) US:LP = Off Beat 4013 [1958 NYOC]

11254 Take It from Here [Industrial Show] Score (Wilson Stone) US:LP-PP = Xerox LP-701 [OC]

11255 Take Me Along (1959) Score (Bob Merrill) US:LP = RCA LOC-1050/LSO-1050* [1959 NYOC]

11256 Take Over (1964) Score (Alf Fogel) GB:LP = Oriole MG-20095 [1964 LOC]

11257 Take the Air (1927) Themes-A-B/US:78 = Columbia 1293 [1927 NYOC] + Theme-C/US:78 = Columbia 1226 [Max Fisher:1927 NYOC]

11258 Taking My Turn (1984) Score (Gary William Friedman) US:LP = Broadway Limited BLR-1001* [1984 NYOC]

11259 Tamalpais Exchange *see* Exchange

11260 Tambourines to Glory (1958) Score (Langston Hughes) US:LP = Folkways FL-3538 [Studio Cast]

11261 Tangerine (1921) Themes/US:78-MS = Decca A-245 [Julia Sanderson & Frank Crumit:1921 NYOC]

11262 Tango Argentino (1985) Scores (pop music) US:LP-MS = Atlantic 81636-1* [1985 NYOC]

11263 Tap Dance Kid, The (1984) Score (Henry Krieger) US:LP = Polydor 820-210-1* [1984 NYOC]

11264 Telephone, The (1947) Scores (Gian Carlo Menotti) US:LP-MS = Columbia SL-154 [1947 NYOC]

11265 Tell Her the Truth (1932) Themes-A-B/US:LP-BP = JJA 19779 [@Bobby Howes & Carlyle Cousins: 1932 LOC] + Theme-C/GB:LP = WRC 136 [Bobby Howes:1932 LOC]

11266 Tell Me Lies *see* U.S.

11267 Tell Me More (1925) Themes-A-B/US:78 = Columbia 368 [Alexander Gray:1925 NYOC] + Theme-C/US:78 = RCA/Victor 19079 [Lou Moltez: 1925 NYOC]

11268 Tell Me on a Sunday *see* Song and Dance

11269 Tenderloin (1960) Score (Jerry Bock) US:LP = Capitol WAO-1492/SWAO-1492* [1960 NYOC]

11270 Texas, Li'l Darlin' (1949) Highlights (Robert Emmett Dolan) US:LP-10 = Decca DL-5188 + US:LP-BP = JJA 19752 + US:LP = CSP X-14878 [1949 NYOC]

11271 Thank Heaven for the Heathen *see* Heathen!

11272 That 5 A.M. Jazz (1964) Score (Will Holt) US:LP-PP = Jazz 1001 [Demo Cast]

11273 That Other Woman's Child (1982) Score (Sherry Landrum & George Clinton) US:LP = Web OC-110* [1982 NYOC]

11274 That's a Good Girl (1928) Highlights (Phil Charig & Joseph Meyer) GB:LP = WRC SH-329 [1928 LOC]

11275 That's the Ticket (1947) Excerpts (Harold Rome) US:LP = Heritage 0063 [Harold Rome:Studio Cast]

11276 Theodore and Co. (1916) Excerpts (Jerome Kern) GB:LP = WRC SHB-34 [@1916 LOC]

11277 They're Playing Our Song (1978) Score-I (Marvin Hamlisch) US:LP = Casablanca NBLP-7141* [1978 NYOC]; Score-II (Marvin Hamlisch) GB:LP = Chopper CHOP-6* [1979 LOC]; Score-III (Marvin Hamlisch) AU:LP = Festival 37356* [1980 AOC]

11278 Thing-Fish (1986) Scores (Frank Zappa) US:LP-MS = Barking Pumpkin SKO-74201* [1986 NYOC]

11279 Third Little Show, The (1931) Theme/GB:LP = London 5471 [Beatrice Lillie:1931 NYOC]

11280 13 Daughters (1961) Score (Eaton Magoon, Jr.) US:LP = Mahalo M-3003/MS-3003* [1961 Hawaiian OC]

11281 This Is Oldsmobility [Industrial Show] Score (pop music) US:LP-PP = Oldsmobile HR-118 [OC]

11282 This Is the Army (1942) Highlights (Irving Berlin) US:LP-10 = Decca DL-5108 + US:LP-BP = JJA 19742 + US:LP = CSP X-14877 [1942 NYOC]

11283 This Was Burlesque (1962) Highlights + Dialog (Sonny Lester & Bill Grundy) US:LP = Roulette R-25185/SR-25185* [1962 NYOC]

11284 This Year of Grace (1928) Excerpts (Noel Coward) GB:LP = WRC SHB-44 [@1928 NYOC]

11285 Thomas and the King (1977) Score (John Williams) GB:LP = That's Entertainment TER-1009* [1977 LOC]

11286 Thousand Miles of Mountains, A [Industrial Show] Score (Norman Richards) US:LP-PP = Northern Pacific Railroad KB-4368 [Studio Cast]

11287 Three for Tonight (1955) Excerpts (various) US:LP = RCA LPM-1150/LSP-1150e [Harry Belafonte:1955 NYOC]

11288 Three Little Maids (1902) Theme-A/GB:78 = G&T 3425 + Theme-B/GB:78 = G&T 3426 + Theme-C/GB:78 = G&T 3427 [Madge Crichton:1902 LOC & 1903 NYOC] + Theme-D/GB:78 = G&T 2-2762 [G.P. Huntley:1902 LOC]

11289 Three Musketeers, The (1930) Highlights (Rudolf Friml) GB: LP = WRC SHB-37 + US:LP = Monmouth MES-7050 [1930 LOC]

11290 Three Sisters, The (1934) Excerpts (Jerome Kern) US:LP-BP = JJA 19794 [@1934 LOC]

11291 Three to Make Music (1958) Highlights (Linda Rodgers & Mary Rodgers) US:LP = RCA LPM-2012/LSP-2012* [Mary Martin:1958 NYOC]

11292 Three Waltzes, The *see* Les Trois Valses

11293 Three Wishes for Jamie (1952) Score (Ralph Blane) US:LP = Capitol S-317 + US:LP = DRG DS-15012 [1952 NYOC]

11294 Threepenny Opera, The (1928) Score-I (Kurt Weill) GE:LP = Telefunken NT-529 [1928 German OC]; Scores-I (Kurt Weill) US:LP-MS = Columbia 02L-257/02S-201* [Lotte Lenya & Willy Trenk-Trebitsch:1928 German OC + Studio Cast]; Score-II (Kurt Weill) US:LP = MGM E-3121/SE-3121e [1954 Revival NYOC]; Theme-III/US: LP = MGM 4056* [Jerry Orbach:1959 Revival NYOC]; Score-IV (Kurt Weill) US:LP = Columbia PS-34326* [1976 Revival NYOC]

11295 Three's a Crowd (1930) Excerpts (Arthur Schwartz) US:LP = Monmouth MES-6604* [Studio Cast]; Themes/US:LP-BP = JJA 19777 [@ Libby Holman:1930 NYOC]

11296 Through the Years (1932) Excerpts (Vincent Youmans) US:LP-MS = Monmouth MES-6401/2* [Studio Cast]

11297 Timbuktu! *see* Kismet

11298 Time Changes (1969) Score (Harry Palmer) US:LP = ABC S-681* [1969 NYOC]

11299 Time for Singing, A (1966) Score (John Morris) US:LP = WB W-1639/WS-1639* [1966 NYOC]

11300 Time, the Place and the Girl, The (1907) Themes/US:78 = Brunswick 4340 [Joe Howard:1942 Revival NYOC]

11301 Tinseltown (1980) Score (Mark Miller) US:LP = Web OC-102* [1980 LAOC]

11302 Tintypes (1981) Scores (pop music) US:LP-MS = DRG 2SL-5196* [1981 NYOC]

11303 Tip Toes (1925) Highlights (George Gershwin) GB:LP = WRC SH-185 + US:LP = Monmouth MES-7052 [1926 LOC + Allen Kearns:1925 NYOC]

11304 Tip Top (1920) Theme-A/US:78 = RCA/Victor 18714 [Six Brown Brothers:1920 NYOC] + Theme-B/US: 78 = RCA/Victor 19050 [The Duncan Sisters:1920 NYOC]

11305 To Broadway with Love (1964) Score (e:Jerry Bock/etc.) US: LP = Columbia OL-8030/OS-2630* [1964 World's Fair NYOC]

11306 To Live Another Summer—To Pass Another Winter (1972) Scores (Dov Seltzer) US:LP-MS = Buddah BDS-95004* [1972 NYOC]

11307 Together Again (1982) Score (Bruce Kimmel) US:LP = Cerberus COC-0301* [1982 LAOC]

11308 Tom Brown's Schooldays (1972) Score (Chris Andrews) GB:LP = Decca SKL-5137* [1972 LOC]

11309 Tom Foolery (1980) Score (pop songs) GB:LP = Multi-Media MMT-001* [1980 LOC]

11310 Tom Jones (1907) Score (Edward German) GB:LP = EMI CSD-3628* [Studio Cast]

11311 Tom Jones (1960) Score (Robert Archer) US:LP-PP = Carillon L80P-5436/7 [1960 New Haven OC]

11312 Tom Jones (1968) Score (Paul Holden) US:LP-PP = T.J. 101* [1968 Las Vegas OC]

11313 Tommy (1969) Scores (Pete Townshend) US:LP-MS = Decca DXSW-7205* + US:LP-MS = MCA 10005* [The Who:OC]

11314 Toni (1924) Highlights (Stephen Jones & Hugo Hirsch) GB: LP = WRC SH-329 [1924 LOC]

11315 Tonight at 8:30 (1936) Excerpts ["Shadow Play" & "Family Affair"] (Noel Coward) US:LP = Monmouth MES-7042 + US:LP = RCA LCT-1156 [@1936 NYOC]

11316 Tonight's the Night (1914) Themes-A-B/GB:78 = HMV 574 + Theme-C/GB:78 = HMV 577 + Theme-D/GB:78 = HMV 584 + Theme-E/GB: LP = WRC SHB-34 [George Grossmith: 1914 NYOC & 1915 LOC] + Themes-H-I/GB:78 = HMV 657 [Henri Leoni:1915 LOC]

11317 Too Many Girls (1939) Highlights (Richard Rodgers) US:LP = Painted Smiles PS-1368* [Studio Cast]; Excerpts (Richard Rodgers) US:LP-BP = JJA 19734 [@1939 NYOC]

11318 Top Banana (1951) Score (Johnny Mercer) US:LP = Capitol S-308 + US:LP = Capitol T-11650 [1951 NYOC]

11319 Topsy and Eva (1924) Themes-A-B/US:78 = RCA/Victor 19206 + Theme-C/US:78 = RCA/Victor 19050 + Theme-D/GB:78 = RCA/Victor 19311 [The Duncan Sisters:1924 NYOC]

11320 Toreador, The (1901) Theme-A/GB:78 = G&T 3447 [Connie Ediss: 1901 LOC] + Theme-B/CA:LP = Rococo 4007 [Gertie Millar:1901 LOC]

11321 Touch (1970) Score (Kenn Long) US:LP = Ampex A-50102* [1970 NYOC]

11322 Touch and Go (1949) Themes/US:LP = Painted Smiles PS-1369* [@Nancy Andrews:1949 NYOC]

11323 Tovarich (1963) Score (Lee Pockriss) US:LP = Capitol TAO-1940/STAO-1940* + US:LP = Capitol STAO-11653* [1963 NYOC]

11324 Transatlantic Rhythm (1936) Themes-A-B/GB:78 = Rex 8881 [Ruth Etting:1936 LOC] + Theme-C/GB: LP = WRC 265 [John W. Bubbles:1936 LOC]

11325 Travelling Music Show, The (1978) Score (pop music) GB:LP = CBS 70156* [1978 LOC]

11326 Treasure Girl (1928) Theme-A/US:LP = Decca 8673 [Gertrude Lawrence:1928 NYOC] + Themes-B-C/US:LP-BP = JJA 19741 [@Victor Arden & Phil Ohman:1928 NYOC]

11327 Treasure Island (1974) Score (Cyril Ornadel) GB:LP = EMI/Starline SRS-5191* [1974 LOC]

11328 Tree Grows in Brooklyn, A (1951) Score (Arthur Schwartz) US:LP = Columbia OL-4405 + US:LP = CSP AML-4405 [1951 NYOC]

11329 Treemonisha (1915) Scores (Scott Joplin) US:LP-MS = Deutsche 2707.083* [1975 Revival NYOC]

11330 Trelawny (1972) Score (Julian Slade) GB:LP = Decca SKL-5144* [1972 LOC]

11331 Tricks (1973) Score (Lonnie Burnstein & Jerry Blatt) US:LP-PP = Tricks 1001 [Demo Cast]

11332 Trilby (1895) Theme/US: 78 = RCA/Victor 45068 [George MacFarlane:1915 Revival NYOC]

11333 Trois Valses, Les [The Three Waltzes] (1937) Score-I (Oscar Straus) FR:LP = Pathe OP-3320 [1937 French OC]; Themes-II/GB:78 = HMV 9414 [Evelyn Laye:1945 Revival LOC]

11334 Tropicana Holiday (1957) Score (Gordon Jenkins) US:LP = Capitol T-1048/ST-1048* [1957 Las Vegas OC]

11335 Troubadour (1980) Score (Ray Holder) GB:LP = Lyntone LYN-6299* [1980 LOC]

11336 Trouble in Tahiti *see* All in One

11337 Tuppence Coloured (1947) Theme/GB:LP = WRC 415 [Elisabeth Welch:1947 LOC]

11338 Turnabout (1941) Score (Forman Brown) US:LP = Pelican LP-142* [1941 LAOC]

11339 Tuscaloosa's Calling Me, But I'm Not Going! (1975) Score (Hank

Beebe) US:LP = Vanguard VSD-79376* [1975 NYOC]

11340 Twang! (1966) Score (Lionel Bart) GB:LP = UA SULP-1116* [1966 LOC]

11341 Twelfth Night, The *see* Love and Let Love

11342 Twenties and All that Jazz, The / Score/AU:LP = Festival 36341* [AOC]

11343 Twenty Minutes South (1954) Score (Peter Greenwell) GB:LP = Oriole MG-20007 [1954 LOC]

11344 Twirly Whirly (1902) Theme/US:LP = Audio Rarities 2290 [Lillian Russell:1902 NYOC]

11345 2 (1978) Score (Julie Mandel) US:LP = Take Home Tunes THT-788* [1978 NYOC]

11346 Two by Two (1970) Score (Richard Rodgers) US:LP = Columbia S-30338* [1970 NYOC]

11347 Two Cities (1969) Score (Jeff Wayne) GB:LP = Columbia SCX-6330* [1969 LOC]

11348 Two Gentlemen of Verona (1972) Scores (Galt MacDermot) US:LP-MS = ABC BCSY-1001* [1972 NYOC]; Score-II (Galt MacDermot) GB:LP = RSO 2394.110* [1973 LOC]

11349 Two on the Aisle (1951) Score (Jule Styne) US:LP = Decca DL-8040 [1951 NYOC]

11350 Two's Company (1952) Score (Vernon Duke) US:LP = RCA LOC-1009 + US:LP = RCA CBM1-2757 [1952 NYOC]

U

11351 U.S. [Tell Me Lies] (1966) Score (Richard Peaslee) US:LP = Gre-Gar 5000/S-5000* [1966 LOC & Film Cast]

11352 Underneath the Arches (1982) Score (Patrick Garland) GB: LP = That's Entertainment TER-1015* [1982 LOC]

11353 Unsinkable Molly Brown, The (1961) Score (Meredith Willson) US: LP = Capitol WAO-1509/SWAO-1509* + US:LP = Capitol W-2152/SW-2152* [1961 NYOC]

11354 Up and Doing (1940) Theme-A/GB:LP = Parlophone 7154 [@Cyril Ritchard:1940 LOC] + Theme-B/GB: LP = WRC 183 [@Patricia Burke:1940 LOC]

11355 Up in Central Park (1945) Highlights (Sigmund Romberg) US: LP = Decca DL-8016 + US:78-MS = Decca A-395 + US:LP-BP = JJA 19782 [Wilbur Evans & Betty Bruce:1945 NYOC + Studio Cast]

11356 Up in the Air, Boys (1974) Score (Robert Dahdah & Mary Boylan) US:LP-PP = Up 1001 [Demo Cast]

11357 Up with the People (1972) Scores (e:Frank Fields/etc.) US:LP-MS = Up with the People 1110* [1972 Washington OC]

11358 Ups-a-Daisy (1928) Themes/ US:78 = Columbia 1633 [Constance Mering & Muriel Pollock:1928 NYOC]

11359 Upstairs at O'Neal's (1983) Score (various) US:LP = Painted Smiles PS-1344* [1983 NYOC]

11360 Utter Glory of Morrissey Hall, The (1979) Score (Clark Gesner) US:LP = OC 7918* [1979 NYOC]

V

11361 Vagabond King, The (1925) Score (Rudolf Friml) US:LP = RCA LK-1010 [Studio Cast] + Score (Rudolf Friml) US:LP = RCA LM-2509/LSC-2509* [Studio Cast]; Themes-I/US:LP-BP = JJA 19796 [@Dennis King & Carolyn Thompson:1925 NYOC]; Excerpts-II (Rudolf Friml) GB:LP = WRC SHB-37 [@1927 LOC]

11362 Valmouth (1959) Score-I (Sandy Wilson) GB:LP = Pye NSPL-19029* + US:LP = AEI 1123* [1959 LOC]; Score-II (Sandy Wilson) GB: LP = That's Entertainment TER-1019* [1982 Revival LOC]

11363 Vanessa (1958) Scores (Gian Carlo Menotti & Samuel Barber) US:LP-MS = RCA LM-6138/LSC-6138* + US: LP-MS = RCA ARL2-2094* [1958 NYOC]

11364 Vanishing Island, The (1958) Scores (Cecil Broadhurst & George Fraser & Will Reed) GB:LP-MS = Philips 99538/9 [1958 LOC]

11365 Vanity Fair (1916) Themes-A-B/GB:LP = Parlophone 7145 [@Teddie Gerard & Nelson Keys:1916 LOC] + Theme-C/GB:LP = WRC 34 [@Regine Flory:1916 LOC]

11366 Venetian Twins, The (1982) Score (Terence Clarke) AU:LP = Larkin LRN-086* [1982 AOC]

11367 Vera Violetta (1911) Themes/US:LP = Audio Rarities 2285 [Al Jolson: 1911 NYOC]

11368 Very Good Eddie (1915) Score (Jerome Kern) US:LP = DRG SL-6100* [1975 Revival NYOC]

11369 Very Warm for May (1939) Score (Jerome Kern) US:LP = AEI 1156 [1939 NYOC]

11370 Via Galactica (1972) Score (Galt MacDermot) US:LP-PP = Via Galactica 1001 [Demo Cast]; Score (Galt MacDermot) US:LP = Kilmarnock 72009* [OC Orchestra]

11371 Vintage '60 (1960) Theme/US:LP = Epic 596 [Fay DeWitt:1960 NYOC]

11372 Virgin (1972) Scores (John O'Reilly) US:LP-MS = Paramount PAS-8000* [1972 NYOC]

11373 Virginia (1937) Excerpts (Arthur Schwartz) US:LP-BP = JJA 19757 [@Studio Cast]

11374 Virtue in Danger (1963) Score (James Bernard) GB:LP = Decca SKL-4536* [1963 LOC]

W

11375 W.T. Grant's 50th Anniversary Show [Industrial Show] Score (Michael Brown) US:LP-PP = Fine Sound 935 [OC]

11376 Wait a Minim! (1962) Score-I (e:Jeremy Taylor/etc.) AF:LP = Gallotone GALP-1221* [1962 South Africa OC]; Score-II (e:Jeremy Taylor/etc.) GB:LP = Decca SKL-4610* [1964 LOC]; Score-III (e:Jeremy Taylor/etc.) US:LP = London 58002/88002* [1966 NYOC]

11377 Wake Up and Dream (1929) Excerpts-I (Cole Porter) GB:LP = WRC SHB-28 [@Leslie Hutchinson:1929 LOC] + Theme-I-A/GB:LP = WRC SHB-26 [@George Metaxa:1929 LOC] + Theme-I-B/GB:78 = Dominion 125 [Elsie Carlisle:1929 LOC]; Theme-II/GB:78 = Columbia 9462 [Jack Buchanan: 1929 NYOC]

11378 Walking Happy (1966) Score (James Van Heusen) US:LP = Capitol VAS-2631/SVAS-2631* [1966 NYOC]

11379 Wall, The (1960) Score (pop music) US:LP = Folkways FG-3558 [1960 NYOC]

11380 Waltz Dream (1908) Score (Oscar Straus) GB:LP = HMV CSD-1321* [Studio Cast]; Highlights (Oscar Straus) US:LP = Reader's Digest 40-2 [Studio Cast]; Themes/GB:78 = Odeon 0413 [Robert Evett:1908 LOC]

11381 Waltzes from Vienna [The Great Waltz] (1931) Themes/GB:78 = Columbia 620 [Marie Burke:1931 LOC & 1934 NYOC]

11382 Watch Your Step (1914) Theme/US:78 = Columbia 1944 [Charles King & Elizabeth Brice:1914 NYOC]; Themes-II-A-B/GB:78 = HMV 611 + Themes-II-C-D/GB:78 = HMV 612 [Ethel Levey:1915 LOC] + Themes-II-E-F/GB:78 = HMV 536 [Joseph Coyne: 1915 LOC] + Theme-II-G/GB:78 = HMV 622 + Theme-II-H/GB:78 = HMV 624 [George Graves:1915 LOC]

11383 Water Gipsies, The (1955) Highlights (Vivien Ellis) GB:LP-10 = HMV DLP-1097 + GB:LP = WRC SH-228 [1955 LOC]; Highlights (Vivien Ellis) US:LP = Dot DLP-3048 [Studio Cast]

11384 Wayward Way, The (1953) Score (Lorne Huycke) GB:LP = HMV CSD-1587* [1965 Revival LOC]

11385 We Take the Town (1962) Score (Harold Karr) US:LP-PP = We Take 1001 [Demo Cast]

11386 We'd Rather Switch (1969) Score (Larry Crane) US:LP-PP = Varieties 100 [1969 NYOC]

11387 Wedding in Paris (1965) Score (Hans May) GB:LP = Parlophone PCS-1011* [1965 LOC]

11388 West Side Story (1957) Score-I (Leonard Bernstein) US:LP= Columbia OL-5230/OS-2001* + US: LP=Columbia S-32603* [1957 NYOC]; Highlights-II (Leonard Bernstein) GB: EP=HMV 7EG-8429 [Don McKay & Marlys Watters:1958 LOC] + Excerpts (Leonard Bernstein) GB:LP=Saga 8106* + US:LP=Forum 9045* [George Chakiris:1958 LOC + Studio Cast]; Scores-III (Leonard Bernstein) JA:LP-MS= Express ETP-60262/3* [Japanese OC]

11389 What a Crazy World! (1965) Score (Alan Klein) GB:LP=Piccadilly SNLP-38011* [1965 LOC]

11390 What a Way to Run a Revolution! (1971) Score (Guy Woolfenden) GB:LP=Grosvenor GRS-1010* [1971 LOC]

11391 What Makes Sammy Run? (1964) Score (Ervin Drake) US:LP= Columbia KOL-6040/KOS-2440* + US:LP=CSP COS-2440* [1964 NYOC]

11392 What's a Nice Country Like You Doing in a State Like This? (1973) Highlights-I (Cary Hoffman) CA:EP= RMSC 747003* [1973 Canadian OC]; Score-II (Cary Hoffman) GB:LP=Galaxy GAL-6004* [1976 LOC]

11393 What's the Meaning of This? (1966) Score (Richard Wilson) US:LP-PP=Lutheron S7-7956* [1966 Dallas OC]

11394 When in Rome (1965) Highlights (Kramer) GB:EP=Oriole 7026 [1965 LOC]

11395 When You're Young (1966) Score (John Hanson) GB:LP=Philips SBL-7701* [1966 LOC]

11396 Where's Charley? (1948) Score-I (Frank Loesser) US:LP-BP= Ecnad 216 [1948 NYOC & Film Cast]; Score-II (Frank Loesser) GB:LP=Columbia 33-SX-1085* + US:LP=Monmouth MES-7029* [1958 Revival LOC]

11397 Whirl of Society, The (1912) Theme/US:LP-10=Decca 5424 [Blossom Seeley:1912 NYOC]

11398 Whispers on the Wind (1970) Score (Lor Crane) US:LP-PP=Friends of Lincoln Center SS-492* [1970 NYOC]

11399 White Hen, The (1907) Theme/US:78=RCA/Victor 5661 [Ralph Herz:1907 NYOC]

11400 White Horse Inn (1930) Score (Robert Stolz) US:LP=Angel 35815/S-35815* [Studio Cast]

11401 Whoop-Up (1958) Score (Moose Charlap) US:LP=MGM E-3745/SE-3745* [1958 NYOC]

11402 Whoopee! (1928) Score (Walter Donaldson) US:LP-PP=Smithsonian R-012 [1928 NYOC]

11403 Widow Jones, The (1895) Theme/US:78=RCA/Victor 31642 [May Irwin:1895 NYOC]

11404 Wilberforce (1983) Score (Laurence Rugg) GB:LP=Northern Theatre Company FMR-075* [1983 LOC]

11405 Wild Grows the Heather (1957) Highlights (Robert Lindon) GB: LP-10=HMV DLP-1125 [1957 LOC]

11406 Wildcat! (1960) Score (Cy Coleman) US:LP=RCA LOC-1060/ LSO-1060* [1960 NYOC]

11407 Wildest Dreams (1961) Score (Julian Slade) GB:LP=HMV CSD-1377* + US:LP=AEI 1122* [1961 LOC]

11408 Wildflower (1923) Excerpts (Vincent Youmans) GB:LP=WRC SH-279 + US:LP=Monmouth MES-7052 [@1923 LOC]

11409 Will o' the Whispers (1928) Themes-A-B/GB:78=HMV 2665 + Themes-C-D/GB:78=HMV 2706 + Theme-E/GB:78=HMV 2666 + Theme-F/GB:78=HMV 2718 + Theme-G/GB:LP=Parlophone 7150 [Jack Smith:1928 LOC]

11410 Windy City (1982) Score (Tony Macaulay) GB:LP=EMI EMC-3420* [1982 LOC]

11411 Winged Victory (1943) Highlights (David Rose) US:78-MS=Decca A-363 + US:LP-BP=JJA 19783 [1943 NYOC]

11412 Winter's Tale, The (1971) Highlights (Guy Woolfenden) GB:EP= Grosvenor 1000* [1971 LOC]

11413 Wish You Were Here (1952) Score (Harold Rome) US:LP=RCA LOC-1007 + US:LP=Camden CAL-621 + US:LP=RCA LOC-1108/LSO-1108e [1952 NYOC]; Score-II (Harold Rome) US:LP=DRG DS-15015 [1953 LOC]

11414 Wiz, The (1975) Score (Charlie Smalls) US:LP = Atlantic SD-18137* [1975 NYOC]

11415 Wizard of the Nile, The (1895) Score (Victor Herbert) US:LP-PP = Schenectady Light Opera Company 101* [Studio Cast]

11416 Woman of the Year (1980) Score (John Kander) US:LP = Arista AL-8303* [1980 NYOC]

11417 Wonder Bar, The (1930) Themes-I-A-B/GB:78 = Decca 2127 + Themes-I-C-D/GB:78 = Decca 2128 [Carl Brisson:1930 LOC] + Themes-E-F/GB:78 = Columbia 394 [Elsie Randolph:1930 LOC] + Theme-I-G/GB:78 = Columbia 393 [Gwen Farrar: 1930 LOC]; Theme-II/US:LP = Decca 9038 [Al Jolson:1931 NYOC]

11418 Wonder Woman / Score/ AU:LP = Festival 45711* [AOC]

11419 Wonderful Town (1953) Score-I (Leonard Bernstein) US:LP = Decca DL-9010/DL-79010e + US:LP = MCA 2050e [1953 NYOC]; Score-II (Leonard Bernstein) US:LP-PP = Location 1261-368 [1961 Revival LAOC]; Score-III (Leonard Bernstein) GB:LP = First Night CAST-6* [1986 Revival LOC]

11420 Wonderful World of Chemistry, The [Industrial Show] Highlights-A (Michael Brown) US:EP-PP = Dupont R-4LM-4826 [OC]; Highlights-B (Michael Brown) US:EP-PP = Dupont R-4LM-5970 [OC]

11421 Words and Music (1932) Excerpts-A (Noel Coward) GB:LP = WRC SHB-44 [Noel Coward:Studio Cast] + Excerpts-B (Noel Coward) US:LP = Columbia MG-30088 [Noel Coward: Studio Cast]; Theme/GB:LP = Parlophone 7154 [@Doris Hare:1932 LOC]

11422 Words and Music (1974) Score (pop music) US:LP = RCA LRL1-5079* [1974 LOC]

11423 Working (1978) Score (e: Stephen Schwartz/e:Micki Grant/e: Craig Carnelia) US:LP = Columbia JS-35411* [1978 NYOC]

11424 Worzel Gummidge (1982) Score (Denis King) GB:LP = MMT LP-111* [1982 LOC]

11425 Wotcher Mates [Live at Danny La Rue's] (1969) Score (e:Bill Solly/etc.) GB:LP = Page One POLS-018* [1969 LOC]

11426 Yankee Consul, The (1904) Theme-A/US:78 = Columbia 5231 + Theme-B/US:78 = Columbia 5257 [Raymond Hitchcock:1904 NYOC]

11427 Yankee Girl, The (1910) Theme-A/US:LP = RCA LPV-560 + Theme-B/US:78 = RCA/Victor 60024 + Theme-C/US:78 = RCA/Victor 60025 [Blanche Ring:1910 NYOC]

11428 Yankee Tourist, A (1907) Theme/US:78 = Columbia 5165 [Raymond Hitchcock:1907 NYOC]

11429 Yearling, The (1965) Score (Michael Leonard) US:LP-BP = Yearling CA-300 [1965 NYOC]

11430 Yes, Madam (1934) Excerpts (Joseph Tunbridge & Jack Waller) GB: LP = WRC SH-136 [Bobby Howes:1934 LOC]

11431 Yip Yip Yaphank (1918) Theme/US:LP = Decca 5108 [Irving Berlin:1918 NYOC]

11432 Yokel Boy (1939) Theme/ US:78 = Varsity 8094 [Judy Canova:1939 NYOC]

11433 Young Abe Lincoln [Children's Show] Score (Victor Ziskin) US: LP = Golden LP-76 + US:LP = Wonderland WLP-76 [OC]

11434 Young Visitors, The (1969) Score (Ian Kellam) GB:LP = RCA SB-6792* [1969 LOC]

11435 Your Arms Too Short to Box with God (1977) Score (e:Micki Grant/e: Alex Bradford) US:LP = ABC AB-1004* [1977 NYOC]

11436 Your Own Thing (1967) Score (Danny Apolinar & Hal Hester) US:LP = RCA LOC-1148/LSO-1148* [1967 NYOC]

11437 You're a Good Man, Charlie Brown (1967) Score (Clark Gesner) US: LP = MGM 1E-9/1SE-9* [1967 NYOC]

11438 Yours Is My Heart *see* Land of Smiles, The

11439 Yvonne (1926) Excerpts (Vernon Duke) US:LP-BP = JJA 19794 [@1926 LOC]

Z

11440 Zenda (1963) Score (Vernon Duke) US:LP-BP = Blue Pear BP-1007 [1963 NYOC]

11441 Ziegfeld Follies, The [C] [1909 NYOC] Theme-A/CA:LP = Rococo 4006 [@Eve Tanguay]; [1910 NYOC] Themes-A-B/US:LP = Sunbeam 506 [Bert Williams] + Themes-C-D/US:78 = Columbia 929 [Bert Williams]; [1911 NYOC] Theme/US:LP = Sunbeam 506 [Bert Williams]; [1912 NYOC] Theme-A/US:78 = Columbia 1289 + Theme-B/US:78 = Columbia 1354 [Bert Williams]; [1913 NYOC] Themes-A-B/US:LP-BP = Veritas 107 [Jose Collins & Nat Wills] + Theme-C/US:78 = RCA/Victor 17461 [Nat Wills]; [1914 NYOC] Theme/US:78 = Columbia 1504 [Bert Williams]; [1915 NYOC] Theme/US:78 = Columbia 1817 [Bert Williams]; [1917 NYOC] Theme-A/US:78 = Columbia 2438 [Bert Williams] + Themes-B-C/US:LP = Vocalion 1220 [Eddie Cantor]; [1919 NYOC] Score (various) US:LP-PP = Smithsonian R-009 [Eddie Cantor & John Steel & Gus Van & Joe Schenck] + Themes/US:78 = Columbia C-25 [Bert Williams]; [1920 NYOC] Theme-A/US:78 = Columbia 3319 + Theme-B/US:78 = Columbia 3336 [Gus Van & Joe Schenck] + Theme-C/US:LP-BP = Veritas 107 [@Fanny Brice] + Theme-D/US:78 = Columbia 2899 [Art Hickman] + Theme-E/US:78 = RCA/Victor 18687 + Theme-F/US:LP-BP = JJA 19744 + Theme-G/US:LP-BP = JJA 19805 [John Steel]; [1921 NYOC] Themes-A-B/US:78 = RCA/Victor 18813 [John Steel] + Themes-C-D/US:LP = Audio Fidelity 707 [Fanny Brice] + Themes-E-F/US:78 = Columbia 3461 + Theme-G/US:78 = Columbia 3427 + Theme-H/US:78 = Columbia 3490 [Gus Van & Joe Schenck]; [1922 NYOC] Theme/US:78 = RCA/Victor 18941 [Ed Gallagher & Al Shean]; [1923 NYOC] Theme-A/US:78 = RCA/Victor 19145 + Theme-B/US:78 = RCA/Victor 19185 + Theme-C/US:78 = RCA/Victor 19204 [Paul Whiteman] + Theme-D/US:78 = RCA/Victor 19204 [Brooke Johns] + Theme-E/US:78 = Okeh 40017 [Olga Steck] + Themes-F-G/US:78 = Columbia 3934 [Eddie Cantor]; [1924 NYOC] Theme/US:78 = RCA/Victor 19429 [George Olsen]; [1927 NYOC] Themes-A-B/US:LP = New World 238 [@Ruth Etting] + Theme-C/US:78 = RCA/Victor 20900 + Theme-D/US:78 = Brunswick 3639 [Franklyn Baur]; [1931 NYOC] Excerpts (various) US:LP-BP = JJA 19778 [@Ruth Etting]; [1934 NYOC] Theme/US:LP = Capitol 354 [Jane Froman]

11442 Ziegfeld Follies of 1958, The (1958) Theme/US:SP = Epic 5-9248 [Kaye Ballard:1958 NYOC]

11443 Ziegfeld's Midnight Frolic [C] Theme-I/US:78 = RCA/Victor 45149 [Frances White:1916 NYOC]; Theme-II/US:LP-BP = Pelican 102 [@Helen Morgan:1928 NYOC]

11444 Zig-Zag (1917) Themes-A-B/GB:78 = Columbia 1144 [Shirley Kellogg:1917 LOC] + Themes-C-D/GB:78 = Columbia 1145 + Themes-E-F/GB:78 = Columbia 1146 + Themes-G-H/GB:78 = Columbia 1223 [George Robey:1917 LOC] + Themes-I-J/GB:78 = Columbia 1139 + Themes-K-L/GB:78 = Columbia 1141 + Themes-M-N/GB:78 = Columbia 1222 [Daphne Pollard:1917 LOC] + Themes-O-P/US:LP-BP = JJA 19794 [@Cicely Debenham:1917 LOC]

11445 Zorba (1968) Score-I (John Kander) US:LP = Capitol SO-118* [1968 NYOC]; Score-II (John Kander) US:LP = RCA ABL1-4732* [1983 Revival NYOC]

11446 Zulu and the Zayda, The (1965) Score (Harold Rome) US:LP = Columbia KOL-6480/KOS-2880* [1965 NYOC]

Related Records

A

11447 Adele (1913) [medley] Themes = US:78 = RCA Victor 35339

11448 After the Fall (1964) [incidental music] Theme (David Amram) US:LP = RCA LSP-7089* [David Amram]

11449 Aladdin [record musical] Highlights + Dialog = GB:LP = EMI SRS-5147*

11450 Algeria (1908) [medley] Themes = US:78 = RCA Victor 31766

11451 Ali Baba and the 40 Thieves [record musical] Highlights + Dialog = US:LP = Golden 29820

11452 Alice in Wonderland [record musical] Highlights + Dialog = US:78-MS = Decca A-376

11453 Alice in Wonderland [record musical] Highlights + Dialog = GB: LP = MFP 1267

11454 America Is 200 Years Old . . . And There's Still Hope [record musical] Highlights + Dialog = US: LP = Capitol ST-11538*

11455 Andorra [incidental music] Theme (Ron Grainer) GB:LP = RCA 1020* [Ron Grainer]

11456 Anna Russell's Little Show [special event] Score = US:LP = Columbia CL-4594

11457 Any Wednesday (1964) [incidental music] Theme (Albert Hague) US:SP = Sunset 54-6500 [Barbara Cook]

11458 Appearing Nightly — Lily Tomlin (1977) [special event] Dialog = US:LP = Arista AB-4142*

11459 Arthur [record musical] Score = US:LP = Reprise RS-6366*

11460 As You Like It (1967) [incidental music] Excerpts (Marc Wilkinson) US:LP = London AMS-88003*

11461 Auction, The [record musical] Score = US:LP = Decca DL-75355*

11462 Axe, an Apple and a Buckskin Jacket, An [record musical] Highlights + Dialog = US:LP = Columbia CC-24508

B

11463 Babette (1903) [medley] Themes = US:LP-BP = JJA 19805

11464 Balkan Princess, The (1910) [medley] Themes = US:78 = RCA Victor 31821

11465 Ballad of Fanny Hill, The [record musical] Score = US:LP = Fax LPS-5201*

11466 Barbara Cook at Carnegie Hall (1975) [special event] Score = US: LP = Columbia M-33438*

11467 Beau Brummel (1928) [incidental music] Theme (Edward Elgar) GB:LP = HMV/EMI ESD-7068* [Lawrence Collingwood]

11468 Beauty and the Beast (1982) [incidental music] Highlights (Bill Nelson) GB:LP-MS = Mercury WHIRL-3*

11469 Beauty Spot, The (1909) [medley] Themes = US:78 = RCA Victor 31745

11470 Belle of Brittany, The (1908) [medley] Themes = US:78 = RCA Victor 31765

11471 Bells of Santa Ynez, The [record musical] Score = US:LP = Capitol ST-1849*

11472 Benito Cereno (1964) [incidental music] Underscore + Dialog (Yehudi Wyner) US:LP-MS = Columbia DOL-319/DOS-719*

11473 Beyond the Fringe (1962) [incidental music] Underscore + Dialog (Dudley Moore) US:LP = Capitol W-1792/SW-1792*

11474 Beyond the Fringe '64 (1964) [incidental music] Underscore + Dialog (Dudley Moore) US:LP = Capitol W-2702/SW-2072*

11475 Big Man — The Story of John Henry [record musical] Highlights + Dialog = US:LP-MS = Fantasy 79006*

11476 Billy the Kid [record musical] Score = US:LP = Caedmon TC-1552*

11477 Black Eagle, The [record musical] Scores = US:LP-MS = Stanyan 2SR-5087*

11478 Blues, Ballads and Sin Songs (1954) [special event] Score = US:LP = Monmouth MES-6501 [Libby Holman]

11479 Bob and Ray—The Two and Only (1970) [special event] US:LP = Columbia S-30412*

11480 Broken Idol, The (1909) [medley] Themes = US:78 = RCA Victor 31757

11481 Buddies (1919) [medley] Themes = US:78 = Columbia 6142

11482 Butterflies Are Free (1969) [incidental music] Theme (Stephen Schwartz) US:SP = Platypus 9100* [Keir Dullea]

11483 Butterfly Ball, The [record musical] Score = US:LP = UK 56000*

C

11484 Cabinet of Dr. Caligari, The (1981) [incidental music] Score (Bill Nelson) GB:LP = Cocteau JC-2*

11485 California [record musical] Score = US:LP = Decca DL-78011*

11486 Call It Love [record musical] Highlights = GB:EP = Decca DEP-6640

11487 Captain Beaky and His Band [record musical] Score = GB:LP = Polydor 2383-462*

11488 Carol Channing Show, The (1956) [special event] Score = US:LP = Vanguard VDS-2041

11489 Casino de Paris (1965) [special event] Score = US:LP = London SW-99338*

11490 Catherine Wheel, The (1981) [incidental music] Score (David Byrne) US:LP = Sire SRK-3645*

11491 Celebration of Richard Rodgers, A (1972) [special event] Score = US:LP-PP = Friends of the Theatre 545*

11492 Chango on Safari [record musical] Highlights + Dialog = GB: LP = Philips 6308-081*

11493 Chimes of Normandy, The (1877) [medley] Themes = US:78 = RCA Victor 31788

11494 Christmas Story, A [record musical] Score = US:LP = Ampex 10142*

11495 Chu-Chin-Chow (1916) [medley] Themes = US:78 = RCA Victor 36138

11496 Clams on the Half Shell (1975) [special event] Scores = US:LP-MS = Atlantic SD2-9000* [Bette Midler]

11497 Cleo Lane at Carnegie Hall (1973) [special event] Score = US:LP = RCA LPL1-5015*

11498 Cocoanuts, The (1925) [medley] Themes = US:LP-BP = JJA 19744

11499 Comedy in Music (1953) [special event] Highlights + Dialog = US:LP = Columbia CL-554 [Victor Borge]

11500 Committee, The (1964) [special event] Underscore + Dialog = US:LP = Reprise RS-2023*

11501 Company (1983) [incidental music] Excerpts (Philip Glass) US:LP = Nonesuch 9-79111-1* [The Kronos Quartet]

11502 Connection, The (1959) [incidental music] Score (Freddie Redd) US:LP = Blue Note BN-84027*

11503 Connection, The (1961) [incidental music] Score (Cecil Payne) US: LP = Parker PLPS-806*

11504 Cryer and Ford (1975) [special event] Score = US:LP = RCA APL1-1235* [Gretchen Cryer & Nancy Ford]

11505 Cue Magazine's Salute to ASCAP (1966) [special event] Score = US:LP-PP = Dick Charles 52666

11506 Curious Evening with Gypsy Rose Lee, A (1961) [special event] Score = US:LP = Stereo Oddities CG-1

11507 Cyrano de Bergerac (1946) [incidental music] Underscore + Dialog (Paul Bowles) US:LP = Capitol S-283 + US:LP = Angel 37342

D

11508 Dear Anyone [record musical] Score = GB:LP = DJM 20541*

11509 Death of a Salesman (1949) [incidental music] Underscore + Dialog (Alex North) US:LP-MS = MCA 2-4182

11510 Dick Tracy in B-Flat [record musical] Highlights + Dialog = US:LP-BP = Curtain Calls CC-100/1

11511 Dr. Faustus (1972) [incidental music] Themes (Guy Woolfenden) GB:LP = Abbey LPB-657*

11512 Doll Girl, The (1913) [medley] Themes = US:LP-BP = JJA 19781

11513 Dollar Princess, The (1909) [medley] Themes = US:78 = RCA Victor 31751

11514 Duffer (1971) [incidental music] Highlights (Galt MacDermot) US:LP = Kilmarnock 72001*

11515 Dylan (1964) [incidental music] Underscore + Dialog (Laurence Rosenthal) US:LP-MS = Columbia DOS-701*

E

11516 Eddie Cantor at Carnegie Hall (1950) [special event] Score = US:LP = Audio Fidelity AFLP-702

11517 Elsa Lanchester—Herself! (1961) [special event] Score = US:LP = Verve MGVS-15024*

11518 Erminie (1885) [medley] Themes = US:78 = RCA Victor 31818

11519 Evening with Alan Jay Lerner, An (1971) [special event] Score = US:LP-PP = Laureate 602*

11520 Evening with Beatrice Lillie, An (1952) [special event] Score = US:LP = London LL-1373

11521 Evening with Diana Ross, An (1976) [special event] Scores = US:LP-MS = Motown M7-877*

11522 Evening with Fred Ebb and John Kander, An (1973) [special event] Score = US:LP-PP = Laureate 605*

11523 Evening with George Burns, An (1974) [special event] Highlights + Dialog = US:LP-MS = Pride PD-00011*

11524 Evening with Groucho Marx, An (1972) [special event] Highlights + Dialog = US:LP-MS = A&M SP-3515*

11525 Evening with Johnny Mercer, An (1971) [special event] Score = US:LP-PP = Laureate 601*

11526 Evening with Michael Brown and His Friends, An (1966) [special event] Score = US:LP-PP = A&R 2758*

11527 Evening with Mike Nichols and Elaine May, An (1960) [special event] US:LP = Mercury SR-60865*

11528 Evening with Quentin Crisp, An (1980) [special event] US:LP-MS = DRG S2L-5188*

11529 Evening with Richard Nixon, An (1972) [special event] US:LP = Ode SP-77015*

11530 Evening with Sammy Cahn, An (1972) [special event] Score = US:LP-PP = Laureate 604*

11531 Evening with Sheldon Harnick, An (1971) [special event] Score = US:LP-PP = Laureate 603*

11531a Every Good Boy Deserves Favour [incidental music] Underscore + Dialog (Andre Previn) US:LP = RCA ABL1-2855*

F

11532 Finnerty Flynn and the Singing City [record musical] Highlights + Dialog = US:LP = Columbia 21524*

11533 Flora Bella (1916) [medley] Themes = US:78 = RCA Victor 35592

11534 Flowering Peach, The (1954) [incidental music] Highlights (Alan Hovhaness) US:LP = MGM E-3164

11535 For Colored Girls Who Have Considered Suicide When the Rainbow Is Enuf (1976) [incidental music] Theme + Dialog (Diana Wharton) US:LP = Buddah BDS-95007*

11536 Forbidden Melody (1936) [medley] Themes = US:78 = RCA Victor 36189

11537 Frankie and Johnny [record musical] Score US:LP = MGM SE-3499*

11538 From the Second City *see* Second City

G

11539 Gala Tribute to Joshua Logan, A (1975) [special event] Scores = US:LP-MS-PP = Friends of the Theatre AC-1*

11540 Gertrude Stein! Gertrude Stein! Gertrude Stein! (1979) [special event] US:LP-MS = Caedmon TRS-367*

11541 Girofle Girofla (1874) [medley] Themes = US:78 = RCA Victor 31827

11542 Give 'Em Hell, Harry (1974) [special event] US:LP-MS = UA LA-504*

11543 Glass Menagerie, The (1945) [incidental music] Themes (Paul Bowles) US:SP-PP = Major SR4M-3085

11544 Golden Girl, The (1909) [medley] Themes = US:78 = RCA Victor 31758

11545 Good Evening [Behind the Fridge] (1973) [special event] US:LP = Island ILS-9298*

11546 Great White Hope, The (1968) [incidental music] Underscore + Dialog (Charles Gross) US:LP-MS = Tetragrammaton TDL-5200*

11547 Grownups [record musical] Highlights + Dialog US:LP = Golden LP-128

H

11548 Hail Mary [record musical] Score US:LP = Everest SDBR-5113*

11549 Half Horse, Half Alligator (1966) [special event] US:LP = RCA VDS-113*

11550 Hamlet (1932) [incidental music] Highlights (Dmitri Shostakovich) US:LP = Louisville S-683*

11551 Henry the Fourth, Part One (1964) [incidental music] Underscore + Dialog (Wilfred Josephs) US:LP-MS = Caedmon SRS-217*

11552 Henry the Fourth, Part Two (1964) [incidental music] Underscore + Dialog (Wilfred Josephs) US:LP-MS = Caedmon SRS-218*

11553 Henry V (1968) [incidental music] Underscore + Dialog (Marc Wilkinson) US:LP-MS = Caedmon SRS-219*

11554 Hiawatha (1980) [incidental music] Highlights + Underscore + Dialog (Jeff Teare) GB:LP = MMT 104*

11555 Hold Everything (1928) [medley] Themes US:78 = RCA Victor 35970

11556 Hollow Crown, The [incidental music] Highlights + Dialog (folk music) US:LP-MS = London A-4253

11557 Honey Girl, The (1920) [medley] Themes = US:78 = RCA Victor 35705

11558 How Lovely Is Christmas [record musical] Highlights + Dialog = US:LP = Golden LP-121

I

11559 Idol's Eye, The (1897) [medley] Themes = US:LP = Mark 56 LP-795

11560 Incident at Vichy (1964) [incidental music] Underscore + Dialog (David Amram) US:LP-MS = Mercury OCS2-6211*

11561 Iole (1913) [medley] Themes US:78 = RCA Victor 35385

11562 Isn't This Where We Came In? [record musical] Score = US:LP = Deram SML-1028*

11563 It Happened in Nordland (1904) [medley] Themes = US:78 = RCA Victor 31851

J

11564 J.B. (1959) [incidental music] Undrscore + Dialog (David Amram) US:LP-MS = RCA LDS-6075*

11565 Jack O'Lantern (1917) [medley] Themes = US:78 = RCA Victor 35666

11566 Jimmie (1920) [medley] Themes = US:78 = RCA Victor 35705

11567 Jimmy Shine (1968) [incidental music] Theme (John Sebastian) US: SP = Kama Sutra 254 [John Sebastian]

11568 John Brown's Body (1953) [incidental music] Underscore + Dialog (Walter Schumann) US:LP-MS = Columbia O2L-181

11569 Josephine Baker Show, The (1964) [special event] Score = US:LP = RCA LSC-2427*

11570 Journey to the Center of the Earth [record musical] Score = US:LP = A&M SP-3621*

11571 Judy Garland and Liza Minnelli – Live at the London Palladium (1964) [special event] Scores = US:LP-MS = Capitol ST-11191*

11572 Judy Garland at Carnegie Hall (1961) [special event] Score = US: LP-MS = Capitol SWBO-1569*

11573 Judy Garland – At Home at the Palace (1967) [special event] Score = US:LP = ABC S-620*

11574 Julie Andrews and Carol Burnett at Lincoln Center (1971) [special event] Score = Columbia S-31153*

11575 Julius Caesar [incidental music] Underscore + Dialog (Marc Blitzstein) US:LP = Ariel SHO-9

K

11576 King Arthur (1923) [incidental music] Highlights (Edward Elgar) GB:LP = Chandos 1001* [George Hurst]

11577 King Dodo (1902) [medley] Themes = US:78 = RCA Victor 31884

11578 King Lear (1972) [incidental music] Themes (Guy Woolfenden) GB: LP = Abbey LPB-657*

11579 King of Elflan's Daughter, The [record musical] Highlights + Dialog = US:LP = Chrysalis 1137*

11580 King Solomon and the Bee [record musical] Highlights = US:EP = La Noar 45-1 [Marni Nixon]

L

11581 Lady in Red, The (1919) [medley] Themes = US:78 = RCA Victor 35491

11582 Lady Mary (1928) [medley] Themes = US:LP-BP = JJA 19794

11583 Lady of the Slipper, The (1912) [medley] Themes = US:LP-BP = JJA 19805

11584 Laughing Husband, The (1913) [medley] Themes = US:LP-BP = JJA 19781

11585 Laughs and Other Events with Stanley Holloway (1960) [special event] Highlights + Dialog = US:LP = Columbia CL-5162

11586 Legend (1976) [incidental music] Score (Dan Goggin) US:LP-PP = Theatre Archives TA-101*

11587 Lenny (1969) [incidental music] Underscore + Dialog (Tom O'Horgan) US:LP-MS = Blue Thumb BTS-9001*

11588 Leonardo (1983) [incidental music] Theme (Chuck Mangione) US: LP = Columbia MS-39479* [Chuck Mangione]

11589 Let 'Em Eat Cake (1933) [medley] Themes = US:LP-BP = JJA 19766

11590 Let's Have Fun [record musical] Score = US:LP-BP = Mar Bren 744

11591 Letter, The [record musical] Score = US:LP = Capitol STAO-1188* [Judy Garland]

11592 Libation Bearers, The [Les Choephores] (1935) [incidental music] Score (Darius Milhaud) US:LP = Columbia MS-6396*

11593 Lie of the Mind, A (1985) [incidental music] Score (Mike Craver & Jack Herrick) US:LP = Sugar Hill SH-8501*

11594 Listen Lester (1918) [medley] Themes = US:78 = RCA Victor 35691

11595 Little Cafe, The (1913) [medley] Themes = US:78 = RCA Victor 35349

11596 Little Mouse That Roared,

The [record musical] Score = US:LP = Arrow 3004*

11597 Little Star of Bethlehem, The [record musical] Highlights + Dialog = US:LP = Cricket CRX-1

11598 Littlest Clown, The [record musical] Highlights + Dialog = US: LP = Golden GRS-4003

11599 Liza at the Wintergarden (1974) [special event] Score = US:LP = Columbia PC-32854*

11600 Lonesome Train, The [record musical] Highlights + Dialog = US:LP-10 = Decca DL-5054

11601 Love for Love (1966) [incidental music] Underscore + Dialog (Marc Wilkinson) US:LP-MS = RCA VDS-112*

11602 Love o' Mike, The (1917) [medley] Themes = US:LP-BP = JJA 19781

11603 Love Song, The (1925) [medley] Themes = US:78 = Columbia 50015

11604 Lucky (1927) [medley] Themes = US:78 = Columbia 50039

M

11605 Macbird (1966) [incidental music] Underscore + Dialog (John Duffy) US:LP-MS = Evergreen EVR-004

11606 Madame Sherry (1903) [medley] Themes = US:78 = RCA Victor 31824

11607 Madcap Duchess, The (1913) [medley] Themes = US:LP-BP = JJA 19805

11608 Maid in America (1915) [medley] Themes = US:78 = RCA Victor 35404

11609 Man from the East, The (1972) [incidental music] Score (Stomu Yamash'ta) US:LP = Capitol SMAS-9334*

11610 Man with Three Wives, The (1908) [medley] Themes = US:78 = RCA Victor 31883

11611 Manhattan Tower [record musical] Score = US:LP = Decca DL-8011 + US:LP = MCA 166

11612 Mark Twain Tonight (1959) [special event] US:LP = Columbia OS-2019* + US:LP = Columbia OS-2030*

11613 Marlene Dietrich in London (1964) [special event] Score = US:LP = Columbia OL-6430

11614 Marriage Market, The (1913) [medley] Themes = US:LP-BP = JJA 19781

11615 Mary (1920) [medley] Themes = US:78 = RCA Victor 35702

11616 Mascotte (1880) [medley] Themes = US:78 = RCA Victor 31813

11617 Master Builder, The (1965) [incidental music] Underscore + Dialog (Norman Stenfalt) US:LP-MS = Caedmon TRS-307*

11618 Max Morath at the Turn of the Century (1969) [special event] Score = US:LP = RCA LSO-1159*

11619 Medicin Volant, Le (1937) [incidental music] Excerpts (Darius Milhaud) US:LP = Crystal S-353* [The Westwood Winds]

11620 Midsummer Night's Dream, A [incidental music] Highlights (Felix Mendelssohn) US:LP = Columbia Columbia MS-6628* [Eugene Ormandy]; [incidental music] Underscore + Dialog (Felix Mendelssohn) US:LP-MS = RCA LM-6115

11621 Miss Daisy (1914) [medley] Themes = US:78 = RCA Victor 35404

11622 Misty, the Mischievous Mermaid [record musical] Highlights + Dialog = US:LP = Disneyland ST-3982

11623 Mocking Bird, The (1902) [medley] Themes = US:78 = RCA Victor 35473

11624 Modern Eve, A (1915) [medley] Themes = US:LP-BP = JJA 19781

11625 Mommy, Gimme a Drinka Water [record musical] Score = US:LP = Capitol SM-937

11626 Monty Python – Live at City Center (1979) [special event] Highlights + Dialog = US:LP = Arista AB-4073*

11627 Moses and the Impossible Ten [record musical] Score = US:LP = BASF B1-25120*

11628 Much Ado About Nothing (1919) [incidental music] Highlights

(Erich Wolfgang Korngold) US:LP = Angel S-36999* [Willy Mattes]

11629 Much Ado About Nothing (1965) [incidental music] Underscore + Dialog (Nino Rota) US:LP-MS = RCA VDS-104*

11630 My Square Laddie [record musical] Score = US:LP = Formost FML-1

11631 My Turn on Earth [record musical] Score = US:LP = Embryo ER-2003*

N

11632 Nagshead [record musical] Score = US:LP = O'Barton OBS-1114

11633 Naked Carmen, The [record musical] Score = US:LP = Mercury SRM1-604*

11634 Nathaniel, The Grublet [record musical] Score = US:LP = Birdwing/MCA 9917*

11635 Natural Affection (1963) [incidental music] Theme (John Lewis) US:LP = Atlantic SD-1414* [John Lewis]

11636 Never Too Late (1962) [incidental music] Theme (Jerry Bock) US:SP = Decca 9-31452 [Warren Covington]; [incidental music] Theme (Jerry Bock) US:SP = Columbia 4-42636 [Joe Quijano]

11637 Night Boat (1920) [medley] Themes = US:LP-BP = JJA 19781

11638 Nina, the Pinta and the Santa Maria, The [record musical] Score = US:LP = Dot DLP-9009 + US:LP = Jelly Bean 1492

11639 No Time for Sergeants (1955) [incidental music] Theme (Frank Rutheford) US:SP = Capitol 3498 [Andy Griffith]

11640 Nobody Home (1915) [medley] Themes = US:LP-BP = JJA 19781

11641 Noteworthy Occasion, A (1971) [special event] Score = US:LP-PP = Noteworthy 1001*

O

11642 Oba Kaso—The King Did Not Hang (1975) [incidental music] Score (Duro Ladipo) US:LP = Kaleidophone KS-2201*

11643 Of Love Remembered (1968) [incidental music] Theme (Michel Legrand) US:LP-PP = UA UAMG-102* [Michel Legrand]

11644 Oh, I Say! (1913) [medley] Themes = US:LP-BP = JJA 19781

11645 Old Dutch (1909) [medley] Themes = US:LP = Mark 56 LP-795

11646 Old Fool Back on Earth [record musical] Score = US:LP-MS = Columbia C2X-38211*

11647 Olivette (1879) [medley] Themes = US:78 = RCA Victor 31801

11648 One Flew Over the Cuckoo's Nest (1963) [incidental music] Theme (John Jacob Niles) US:LP = RCA 3460* [Ed Ames]

11649 Only Girl, The (1914) [medley] Themes = US:78 = Columbia 5639

11650 Orange Bird, The [record musical] Highlights + Dialog = US: LP = Disneyland ST-3991

11651 Order Is Love, The [record musical] Score = US:LP = Trilogy T-1001*

11652 Oregon! Oregon! [record musical] Score = US:LP-PP = JB 2177

11653 Othello (1964) [incidental music] Underscore + Dialog (Richard Hampton) US:LP-MS = RCA VDS-108*

11654 Our Country 'Tis of Thee [record musical] Highlights + Dialog = US:LP = Camden CAS-1082*

11655 Owl and the Pussycat Went to See, The [record musical] Highlights + Dialog = GB:LP = Philips 6382-068*

P

11656 Passing Fair [record musical] Score = US:LP = Proscenium PR-25

11657 Paul Bunyan [record musical] Score = US:LP = Folkways FL-4050

11658 Pericles (1968) [incidental music] Underscore + Dialog (Marc Wilkinson) US:LP-MS = Caedmon SRS-237*

11659 Pied Piper, The [record musical] Highlights + Dialog = US: LP = Simon Says SS-23

11660 Pink Lady, The (1911) [medley] Themes = US:78 = RCA Victor 31823

11661 Pinocchio [record musical] Score = US:LP = Decca DL-8463

11662 Play It Again, Sam (1969) [incidental music] Theme (Larry Grossman) US:SP = Columbia 4-44855 [Tony Bennett]

11663 Playback [record musical] Score = US:LP = Verve/Foremost FTS-3042*

11664 Plymouth Rock to Moon Rock [record musical] Score = US:LP = Educord EDU-1620

11665 President, The [record musical] Highlights + Dialog = US: LP = Liberty LST-7241*

11666 Prince of Pilsen, The (1903) [medley] Themes = US:78 = RCA Victor 31795

11667 Prince of Tonight, The (1909) [medley] Themes = US:78 = RCA Victor 31748

11668 Princess Flavia (1925) [medley] Themes = US:LP-BP = JJA 19796

11669 Purple Road, The (1913) [medley] Themes = US:78 = RCA Victor 35349

11670 Puss in Boots [record musical] Score = US:LP = Golden GRS-4001

Q

11671 Queen of the Movies (1914) [medley] Themes = US:78 = RCA Victor 35365

11672 Queen's Lace Handkerchief, The (1880) [medley] Themes = US:78 = RCA Victor 31880

11673 Quiet City, The (1939) [incidental music] Highlights (Aaron Copland) US:LP = Columbia MS-7375* [Aaron Copland]

R

11674 Raggedy Ann [record musical] Score = US:LP = Vocalion VL-73665

11675 Ragtime Years, The (1978) [special event] Score = US:LP = Vanguard VSD-79346*

11676 Rainbow Girl, The (1918) [medley] Themes = US:78 = RCA Victor 35677

11677 Raising a Family for Fun and Profit [record musical] Highlights + Dialog = US:LP = Scarsdale 209

11678 Rashomon (1962) [incidental music] Score (Laurence Rosenthal) US: LP = Carlton S-5000*

11679 Real Ambassadors, The [record musical] Score = US:LP = Columbia OS-2250*

11680 Reign or Shine [record musical] Score = US:LP = Kilmarnock MRS-LPM-9*

11681 Revenger's Tragedy, The (1972) [incidental music] Themes (Guy Woolfenden) GB:LP = Abbey LPB-657*

11682 Reverend Johnson's Dream [record musical] Highlights = US:78-MS = Decca A-170

11683 Revolt of Emily Young, The [record musical] Score = US:LP = Decca DL-75193*

11684 Revolution [record musical] Score = US:LP = Aladdin LP-2348

11685 Revuers, The (1938) [medley] Themes = US:LP-BP = JJA 19764

11686 Rob Roy (1884) [medley] Themes = US:78 = RCA Victor 81858

11687 Rock-a-Bye Baby (1918) [medley] Themes = US:78 = RCA Victor 35677

11688 Rolito [record musical] Score = US:LP = Decca DL-8021

11689 Romeo and Juliet (1937) [incidental music] Excerpts (Darius Milhaud) GB:LP = Chandos 1012* [The Atlanta Ensemble]

11690 Romeo and Juliet (1972) [incidental music] Themes (Guy Woolfenden) GB:LP = Abbey LPB-657*

11691 Rose of Algeria, The (1909) [medley] Themes = US:LP-BP = JJA 19805

11692 Rosencrantz and Gildenstern Are Dead (1967) [incidental music] Excerpts (Marc Wilkinson) US:LP = London AMS-88003* [Marc Wilkinson]

11693 Royal Hunt of the Sun, The (1966) [incidental music] Excerpts (Marc Wilkinson) US:LP = London AMS-88003* [Marc Wilkinson]

11694 Rumplestiltskin [record musical] Highlights + Dialog = GB: LP = EMI Starline SRS-5174*

S

11695-6 Sari (1912) [medley] Themes = US:78 = RCA Victor 35365

11697 Saturday's Warrior [record musical] Score = US:LP = Embryo EM-1001*

11698 Second City [From the Second City] (1961) [special event] Underscore + Dialog = US:LP = Mercury OCS-6201*

11699 Send Me No Flowers (1960) [incidental music] Theme = US:SP = Gulf 45-029 [David Wayne]

11700 Seven Dreams [record musical] Score = US:LP = Decca DL-79011* + US:LP = MCA 2051*

11701 Seven Year Itch, The [incidental music] Theme (Olsen & Suesse) US:SP = Mercury 70332 [Jerry Murad]

11702 Shirley MacLaine—Live at the Palace (1976) [special event] Score = US:LP = Columbia PC-34223*

11703 Singing Girl, The (1899) Themes = US:78 = Columbia 5423

11704 Sir Oliver's Song [record musical] Score = US:LP = Birdwing 2017*

11705 Sixth Finger in a Five Finger Glove, The [incidental music] Theme (Charles Strouse) US:SP = RCA 47-6710 [Leo Diamond]

11706 Somebody's Sweetheart (1918) [medley] Themes = US:78 = RCA Victor 35691

11707 Sometime (1918) [medley] Themes = US:78 = RCA Victor 35694

11708 Songs of Couch and Consultation [record musical] Score = US: LP = Commentary CNT-01

11709 Starlight Express (1915) [incidental music] Scores (Edward Elgar) GB:LP-MS = HMV/EMI ESDW-711* [Vernon Handley]

11710 Story of Celeste, The [record musical] Highlights + Dialog = US: LP = Leo CH-1034

11711 Strike Me Pink (1933) [medley] Themes = US:LP-BP = JJA 19776

11712 Suburbia [record musical] Highlights + Dialog = US:LP = Seeco 2101

11713 Sultan of Sulu, The (1902) [medley] Themes = US:78 = RCA Victor 31850

11714 Supper Club Revue, The [special event] Score = US:LP = AEI 1135

11715 Susie Heartbreaker [record musical] Score = US:LP = RCA APL1-1046*

T

11716 Take This Bread [record musical] Score = US:LP = Kilmarnock KIL-72011*

11717 Tale of Jemima Puddle Duck, The [record musical] Highlights + Dialog = US:LP = Golden LP-224

11718 Tale of Mrs. Piggy Winkle, The [record musical] Highlights + Dialog = US:LP = Golden LP-224

11719 Tall Story (1959) [incidental music] Theme (Hornsby & Hansen) US: SP = Decca 9-62088 [Mickey Moon]

11720 Tall Tom Jefferson [record musical] Highlights + Dialog = US: LP = Golden LP-270

11721 Taming of the Shrew, The

(1972) [incidental music] Themes (Guy Woolfenden) GB:LP = Abbey LPB-657*

11722 Tarot (1970) [incidental music] Score (Tom Constanten) US:LP = UA UAS-5563*

11723 Tartuffe (1968) [incidental music] Underscore + Dialog (Gabriel Charpentier) US:LP-MS = Caedmon TRS-332*

11724 Taste of Honey, A (1960) [incidental music] Score (Bobby Scott) US:LP = Atlantic SD-1355*

11725 Tattooed Man, The (1907) [medley] Themes = US:LP = Mark 56 LP-795

11726 Tempest, The (1951) [incidental music] Underscore + Dialog (Paul Bowles) US:LP-MS = Polymusic PR-5001

11727 Tempest, The (1964) [incidental music] Underscore + Dialog (Wilfred Josephs) US:LP-MS = Caedmon TRS-201*

11728 Tevya and His Daughters (1957) [incidental music] Underscore + Dialog (Serge Hovey) US:LP = Columbia OL-5225

11729 Thief of Bagdad, The [record musical] Score = US:LP = Golden GRS-4002*

11730 Threads of Glory [record musical] Score = US:LP = Deseret 4741*

11731 Three Billion Millionaires [record musical] Score = US:LP = UA UXS-4*

11732 Three Twins (1908) [medley] Themes = US:78 = RCA Victor 31809

11733 Thurber Carnival, A (1960) [incidental music] Underscore + Dialog (Don Elliott) US:LP = Columbia KOS-2024*

11733a Time [record musical] Scores = US:LP-MS = Capitol SWBK-12447*

11734 Time Remembered (1957) [incidental music] Score (Vernon Duke) US:LP = Mercury SR-60380*

11735 Tom Jones [record musical] Score = US:LP = Theatre S-9000*

11736 Too Late the Phalarope (1956) [incidental music] Highlights (Josef Marais) US:LP = Decca DL-9047

11737 Toy Box, The [record musical] Highlights + Dialog = US:LP = Cricket CRX-1

11738 Truth of Truths [record musical] Scores = US:LP-MS = Oak OR-1001*

11739 Tubby the Tuba [record musical] Highlights + Dialog = US:LP = Decca DL-8479 + US:LP = MCA 148

11740 Tyger (1971) [incidental music] Score (Mike Westbrook) GB:LP = RCA SER-5612*

U

11741 Ulysses [record musical] Scores = US:LP-MS = 20th 2T-1101*

11742 United States of America, The [record musical] Score = US:LP = Capitol SW-1573*

W

11743 War of the Worlds [record musical] Scores = US:LP-MS = Columbia PC2-35290*

11744 Wasps, The (1909) [incidental music] Highlights (Ralph Vaughan-Williams) US:LP = Angel S-37276*

11745 Way of the World, The (1968) [incidental music] Underscore + Dialog (Marc Wilkinson) US:LP-MS = Caedmon TRS-339*

11746 We Were Happy There [record musical] Score = US:LP = Decca DL-75145*

11747 What So Proudly We Hail [record musical] Highlights + Dialog = US:LP = Decca DL-8020

11748 When Dreams Come True (1913) [medley] Themes = US:78 = RCA Victor 35336

11749 White Mansions [record musical] Scores = US:LP-MS = A&M SP-6004*

11750 Will Rogers' U.S.A. (1971) [special event] US:LP-MS = Columbia SG-30546*

11751 William Shatner – Live (1981) [special event] US:LP = K-Tel NC-494*

11752 Wings [record musical] Score = US:LP = A&M SP-3503*

11753 Wonderful O, The [record musical] Score = US:LP = Colpix CP-6000

11754 Wonderful World of Wynken, Blynken and Nod, The [record musical] Highlights + Dialog = US: LP = Camden CAS-1202*

11755 World of Miracles, A [record musical] Highlights + Dialog = US:LP = Liberty LST-7244*

11756 World of Sholom Aleichem, The (1953) [incidental music] Underscore + Dialog (Serge Hovey) US:LP-10 = Rachel R-1

11757 World of Suzie Wong, The (1958) [incidental music] Theme = US: SP = B.G. Records 45-1 [Benny Goodman]

11758 Wry and Ginger [record musical] Highlights = US:LP = Kilmarnock MRS-LPM-9*

11759 Yankee Princess, The (1922) [medley] Themes = US:78 = RCA Victor 35722

11760 You're in Love (1917) [medley] Themes = US:LP = Camden CAL-252

11761 Zizi Jeanmarie (1964) [special event] Score = US:LP = Philips PHS-600-161*

BIBLIOGRAPHY

Baer, D. Richard. *The Film Buff's Checklist of Motion Pictures, 1912–1979.* Hollywood, CA: Hollywood Film Archive, 1979.

Halliwell, Leslie. *Halliwell's Film Guide.* New York: Granada, 1980.

________. *Halliwell's Television Companion.* New York: Granada, 1982.

Hammonds, G. Roger. *Recorded Music for the Science Fiction, Fantasy and Horror Film.* STAR, 1982.

________. *Recorded Music for the Western Film.* STAR, 1983.

Hummel, David. *The Collector's Guide to the American Musical Theatre.* Hummel, 1977.

Katz, Ephraim. *The Film Encyclopedia.* New York: Perigee, 1979.

Lenburg, Jeff. *The Encyclopedia of Animated Cartoon Series.* New York: Da Capo, 1981.

Limbacher, James L. *Film Music.* Metuchen, NJ: Scarecrow, 1974.

________. *Keeping Score.* Metuchen, NJ: Scarecrow, 1981.

Maltin, Leonard. *Of Mice and Magic.* New York: New American Library, Plume, 1980.

________. *TV Movies.* New York: New American Library, Plume, 1983.

Raymond, Jack. *Show Music on Record.* New York: Ungar, 1982.

Scheuer, Steven H. *Movies on TV.* New York: Bantam, 1981.

Smolian, Steven. *A Handbook of Film, Theater, and Television Music on Record, 1948–1969.* The Record Undertaker, 1970.

Terrace, Vincent. *Complete Encyclopedia of Television Programs, 1947–1979.* San Diego, CA: Barnes, 1979.

________. *Television, 1970–1980.* San Diego, CA: Barnes, 1981.

Van De Ven, Luc. "Soundtrack!—The Collector's Quarterly." Mechelen, Belgium: quarterly magazine.

Weldon, Michael. *The Psychotronic Encyclopedia of Film.* New York: Ballantine, 1983.

COMPOSER INDEX

A

B

C

D

E

F

G

H

I

J

K

L

M

N

O

P

Q

R

S

W

Z